CASES AND ... MINAL LAW

ELLIOTT AND WOOD'S CASES AND MATERIALS ON CRIMINAL LAW

TWELFTH EDITION

By

MICHAEL J. ALLEN LL.M., BARRISTER-AT-LAW
Formerly Commissioner, Criminal Cases Review Commission

and

SIMON COOPER MA, LLB
Lecturer, Manchester Law School, Manchester Metropolitan University

SWEET & MAXWELL

D. W. Elliott & J. C. Wood, First Edition 1963
Second Impression 1967
D. W. Elliott & J. C. Wood, Second Edition 1969
Second Impression 1971
D. W. Elliott & J. C. Wood, Third Edition 1974
D. W. Elliott & Celia Wells, Fourth Edition 1982
D. W. Elliott & Michael J. Allen, Fifth Edition 1989
D. W. Elliott & Michael J. Allen, Sixth Edition 1993
Michael J. Allen, Seventh Edition 1997
Second Impression 1999
Michael J. Allen, Eighth Edition 2001
Reprinted 2001, 2002 (twice), 2003
Michael J. Allen & Simon Cooper, Ninth Edition 2006
Michael J. Allen & Simon Cooper, Tenth Edition 2010
Michael J. Allen & Simon Cooper, Eleventh Edition 2013
Michael J. Allen & Simon Cooper, Twelfth Edition 2016

Published in 2016 by Thomson Reuters (Professional) UK, trading as Sweet & Maxwell,
Friars House, 160 Blackfriars Road, London, SE1 8EZ
(Registered in England & Wales, Company No 1679046.
Registered Office and address for service:
2nd Floor, 1 Mark Square, Leonard Street, London, EC2A 4EG

Typeset by Servis Filmsetting Ltd, Stockport, Cheshire
Printed in Great Britain by CPI Group (UK) Ltd, Croydon, CR0 4YY

No natural forests were destroyed to make this product;
only farmed timber was used and replanted

British Library Cataloguing in Publication Data
A CIP catalogue record for this book
is available from the British Library

ISBN 9780414055698

©
Thomson Reuters (Professional) UK Limited
2016

PREFACE

In the three years since the last edition there has been some significant judicial decisions in various areas of the criminal law helping to clarify some issues and occasionally leaving new uncertainties in their wake. In this edition, the chapter on homicide receives further revision to take account of the case law consequent upon the changes made by the Coroners and Justice Act 2009 which replaced the law of provocation with the new defence of loss of control as well as reforming the law of diminished responsibility. Some of the more notable case law new to this edition is *Jogee* clarifying the mens rea of secondary parties and overruling the decision in *Chan Wing-Siu*, *Adebolajo* on the meaning of the "Queen's Peace" in homicide, *Dawes* on the loss of self-control, *Robinson v The State (Trinidad and Tobago)* and *Brennan* on the practice of accepting guilty pleas to manslaughter by reason of diminished responsibility, *Golds* on the meaning of "substantially impaired" in relation to diminished responsibility, *Pace and Rogers* on the mental element for attempt, *Robinson-Pierre* on "state of affairs" offences and *Batchelor* on duress.

As well as being comprehensively updated, the text contains extracts from numerous Law Commission papers and reports that should assist the reader in understanding the complex nature of criminal law and the problems that it poses for the lawmakers.

We would like to express our gratitude to the team at Sweet & Maxwell for their support.

The law is stated as at February 2016.

Mike Allen and Simon Cooper
February 2016

CONTENTS

ACKNOWLEDGMENTS

Grateful acknowledgment is made to the following authors and publishers for permission to quote from their works:

Copyright Permissions

Alldridge, P. "The Coherence of Defences" [1983] Criminal Law Review 665.

Andrews, J. "Robbery" [1966] Criminal Law Review 524.

Ashworth, A. "Belief, Intent and Criminal Liability". In J. Eekelaar and J. Bell (eds), *Oxford Essays in Jurisprudence*, 3rd edn (Oxford: Clarendon Press, 1987), p.1.

Ashworth, A., *Principles of Criminal Law*, 3rd edn (Oxford: Oxford University Press, 1999), pp.24-27, 132, 141-144, 460.

Ashworth, A., *Principles of Criminal Law*, 6th edn (Oxford: Oxford University Press, 2009), pp.439-440, 442-443.

Ashworth, A. "Taking the Consequences". In S. Shute, J. Gardner and J. Horder (eds), *Action and Value in Criminal Law* (Oxford: Clarendon Press, 1993), p.107.

Brett, P., and Waller, L., *Criminal Law Text and Cases*, 4th edn (Melbourne: Butterworths, 1978), p.145.

Cross, R. "Murder under Duress" (1978) 28 University of Toronto Law Journal 369. Reprinted with permission from University of Toronto Press (*www.utpjournals.com*).

Fitzgerald, P.J. "A Concept of Crime" [1960] Criminal Law Review 257.

Fletcher, G.P., *Rethinking Criminal Law* (Boston: Little, Brown, 1978), pp.362, 368, 396-397, 421, 798-800, 810-812. © 2000 by George Fletcher. By Permission of Oxford University Press.

Galligan, D.J. "The Return to Retribution in Criminal Theory". In C. Tapper (ed), *Crime, Proof and Punishment: Essays in Memory of Sir Rupert Cross* (London: Butterworths, 1981), pp.144, 146 and following.

Glazebrook, P.R. "Criminal Omissions: The Duty Requirement in Offences Against the Person" (1960) 76 Law Quarterly Review 386.

Gobert, J. "The Fortuity of Consequence" (1993) 4 Criminal Law Forum 1. With kind permission from Springer Science+Business Media.

Griew, E. "Consistency, Communication and Codification: Reflections on Two Mens Rea Words". In P. Glazebrook (ed), *Reshaping the Criminal Law* (Stevens & Sons, 1978), pp.57-59.

Gross, H., *A Theory of Criminal Justice* (New York: Oxford University Press, 1979), pp.13-14. Reprinted with permission of the author.

Hart, H.L.A. "Act of Will and Responsibility". In *Punishment and Responsibility*, 2nd edn (Oxford: Oxford University Press, 2008), p.90.

Hogan, B. "Omissions and the Duty Myth". In P. Smith (ed), *Criminal Law: Essays in Honour of J.C. Smith* (London: Butterworths, 1987).

Horder, J. "Pleading Involuntary Lack of Capacity" (1993) 52 Cambridge Law Journal 298.

Hutchinson, A.C. "Note on *Sault Ste Marie*" (1979) 17 Osgoode Hall Law Journal 415.

Kenny, A.P., *Freewill and Responsibility* (Routledge & Kegan Paul, 1978), pp.36-38. By kind permission of Taylor and Francis Books UK.

Lacey, N. "Contingency and Criminalisation". In I. Loveland (ed), *Frontiers of Criminality* (London: Sweet & Maxwell, 1995), pp.4, 14-15.

Leigh, L.H., *Strict and Vicarious Liability* (London: Sweet & Maxwell, 1982), pp.58-61.

Lindgren, J. "Unravelling the Paradox of Blackmail" (1984) 84 Columbia Law Review 670.

Mackay, R.D., and Kearns, G. "More Fact(s) about the Insanity Defence" [1999] Criminal Law Review 714.

MacKenna, Sir B. "Blackmail: A Criticism" [1966] Criminal Law Review 466.

Norrie, A. "Oblique Intention and Legal Politics" [1989] Criminal Law Review 793.

Packer, H.L., *The Limits of the Criminal Sanction* (Stanford University Press, 1969), pp.261 and following. Copyright © 1968 Herbert L. Packer. All rights reserved. Used with the permission of Stanford University Press, *www.sup.org*.

Patient, I.H.E. "Transferred Malice – A Misleading Misnomer" (1990) 54 Journal of Criminal Law 116.

Paulus, I. "Strict Liability: Its Place in Public Welfare Offences" (1978) 20 Criminal Law Quarterly 445.

Sayre "Public Welfare Offences" (1933) 33 Columbia Law Review 55.

Smith, A.T.H. "On Actus Reus and Mens Rea". In P. Glazebrook (ed), *Reshaping the Criminal Law* (Stevens & Sons, 1978), pp.97-101.

Smith, J.C. "Responsibility in Criminal Law". In Bean and Whynes (eds), *Barbara Wootton, Essays in Her Honour* (Tavistock Publications, 1986), pp.141 and 153. By kind permission of Taylor and Francis Books UK.

Smith, J.C., *Smith's Law of Theft*, 9th edn (Oxford: Oxford University Press, 2007), pp.279-280. By permission of Oxford University Press.

Smith, K.J.M. "Proximity in Attempt: Lord Lane's Midway Course" [1991] Criminal Law Review 576.

Smith, K.J.M. "Duress and Steadfastness: In Pursuit of the Unintelligible" [1999] Criminal Law Review 363.

Spencer, J.R. "The Metamorphosis of Section 6 of the Theft Act" [1977] Criminal Law Review 653.

Spencer, J., and Virgo, G. "Encouraging and Assisting Crime: Legislate in Haste, Repent in Leisure" [2008] 9 Archbold News 7.

Temkin and Ashworth "The Sexual Offences Act 2003: Rape, Sexual Assaults and the Problems of Consent" [2004] Criminal Law Review 328.

Thomas, D.A. "Form and Function in Criminal Law". In P. Glazebook (ed), *Reshaping the Criminal Law* (Stevens & Sons, 1978), p.30.

Walker, N., *Crime and Criminology: A Critical Introduction* (Oxford: Oxford University Press, 1987), pp.140-141.

Wasik, M. "Duress and Criminal Responsibility" [1977] Criminal Law Review 453.

Wells, C. "Whither Insanity?" [1983] Criminal Law Review 787.

Williams, G. "The Definition of Crime" (1955) Current Legal Problems 107.

Williams, G., *Criminal Law: The General Part* (Stevens & Sons, 1961), p.30.

Williams, G. "Finis for Novus Actus" (1989) Cambridge Law Journal 391.

Williams, G. "Oblique Intention" (1987) 46 Cambridge Law Journal 417.

Williams, G., *Textbook of Criminal Law*, 1st edn (London: Stevens & Sons, 1978), p.726.

Williams, G., *Textbook of Criminal Law*, 2nd edn (Stevens & Sons, 1983), pp.75, 138.

Williams, G. "The Theory of Excuses" [1982] Criminal Law Review 732.

Williams, G. "Temporary Appropriation Should Be Theft" [1981] Criminal Law Review 129.

Wootton, B., *Crime and the Criminal Law*, 2nd edn (Stevens, 1981), pp.46-48.

TABLE OF CASES

TABLE OF STATUTES

Foreign statutes

France

Hong Kong

New Zealand

Singapore

USA

TABLE OF REPORTS AND OFFICIAL PROPOSALS

1 INTRODUCTORY

The subject matter of this book is the substantive criminal law of England and Wales. In some Commonwealth jurisdictions, e.g. Queensland, the criminal law is in the form of a code. In England and Wales, despite an attempt in that direction in the nineteenth century, no general code has reached the statute book. The criminal law is, accordingly, derived from a mixture of common law and statute. Most of the general principles of liability are to be found in the common law and some offences, such as murder, manslaughter and incitement are offences at common law. Parliament has intervened with increasing frequency throughout the past 150 years to place more offences and defences on a statutory footing. The various statutes which have been enacted, however, largely represent ad hoc responses to particular problems and do not add up to form a coherent code. The criminal law is replete with inconsistencies and incongruities with the result that discovering what the law is on any point (rather than where it is to be found) can be an immensely difficult task with an uncertain outcome. While this makes the study of criminal law both challenging and interesting, it leaves the practice of law fraught with difficulty and the risk of injustice all the greater as prosecutors, defence advocates, trial judges and juries grapple to discover and apply elusive and even ephemeral principles.

In Law Commission, *A Criminal Code for England and Wales* (TSO, 1989), Law Com. No.177, the Law Commission recommended to Parliament a Draft Criminal Code Bill, extracts from which appear throughout this book. This generally was a restatement of the law where the law was clear but where reports of the Law Commission or other public bodies (e.g. the Criminal Law Revision Committee) have recommended changes these have been incorporated into the Draft Code. Where the law contained indefensible inconsistency the Draft Code sought to eliminate it.

Since publication of the Draft Code the Law Commission has come to the view that there is little likelihood of Parliament giving up the time necessary to enact the Code in its entirety. It considers that the best hope for implementation is through a series of Bills each dealing with a discrete area of the criminal law (see Law Commission, *Legislating the Criminal Code: Offences Against the Person and General Principles* (TSO 1993), Law Com. No.218 para.1.3). As there has been no sign of Parliament enacting the proposed Criminal Law Bill appended to this report, the prospect of a Criminal Code for England and Wales is becoming fainter with the passage of time.

In the remainder of this chapter we will consider some preliminary questions before moving on to look at the substantive criminal law in the chapters which follow. These are: What is a crime? What functions does the criminal law serve? Why is particular conduct classified as criminal? This chapter concludes with a consideration of the impact of the Human Rights Act 1998.

1. The Concept of Crime

G. WILLIAMS, "THE DEFINITION OF CRIME" (1955) C.L.P. 107

Is the effort [to define crime] worth making? The answer is that lawyers must try to clarify the notion of 'crime', because it suffuses a large part of the law. For example: there is generally no time limit for criminal proceedings, whereas civil proceedings are commenced differently, and often in different courts. A criminal prosecutor generally need not be the victim of the wrong, and a private criminal prosecutor is for many purposes not regarded as a party to the proceedings; he is certainly not 'master' of the proceedings in the sense that he can drop them at will; these rules are different in civil cases. The law of procedure may generally be waived in civil but not in criminal cases. There are many differences in the law of evidence, and several in respect of appeal . . .

. . . The common-sense approach is to consider whether there are any intrinsic differences between the acts constituting crimes and civil wrongs respectively. It is perhaps natural to suppose that since 'a crime' differs from 'a civil wrong', there must be something *in* a crime to make it different from a civil wrong.

As everybody knows, there is one serious hindrance to a solution of this kind. This is the overlap between crime and tort. Since the same act can be both a crime and a tort, as in murder and assault, it is impossible to divide the two branches of the law by reference to the type of act. So also it is impossible to divide them by reference to the physical consequences of the act, for if the act is the same the physical consequences must be the same.

It has occurred to some that there is a possible escape from this difficulty. Although the act, and its consequences, are the same, the act and consequences have a number of different characteristics or aspects; and it may be possible to identify some of these characteristics as criminal and some as civil. Pursuing this line of thought, two separate aspects have been seized upon as identifying crime: the aspect of moral wrong and the aspect of damage to the public . . .

The proposition that crime is a moral wrong may have this measure of truth: that the average crime is more shocking, and has graver social consequences, than the average tort. Yet crimes of strict responsibility can be committed without moral wrong, while torts and breaches of trust may be, and often are, gross moral wrongs.

Even where a forbidden act is committed intentionally, a court deciding that it is a crime is not committed to the proposition that it is a moral wrong. Thus in holding that a summary proceeding for an offence under the Game Act was criminal in character, Lord Campbell C.J. said: 'It is our business, not to estimate the degree of moral guilt in the act of the appellant, but to see how such act is treated by the legislature . . . I cannot be bound by any opinion that I may form of the morality of that act: but I must see what it is that the legislature has chosen to punish: *Cattell v Ireson* (1858) E.B. & E. at pp.97–98.'

There are crimes of great gravity in the legal calendar, such as mercy-killing and eugenic abortion, which are disputably moral wrongs, though they are indisputably crimes. The same is true of numerous summary offences. Lord Atkin put the situation pungently. The criminal quality of an act cannot be discerned by intuition; nor can it be discovered by reference to any standard but one: is the act prohibited with penal consequences? Morality and criminality are far from coextensive; nor is the sphere of criminality necessarily part of a more extensive field covered by morality—unless the moral code necessarily disapproves of all acts prohibited by the state, in which case the argument moves in a circle: *Proprietary Articles Trade Association v Att-Gen for Canada* [1931] A.C. 324 (P.C.) . . .

The second intrinsic difference between crimes and civil wrongs found by some writers is in respect of the damage done. In tort there is almost invariably actual damage to some person, whereas in crime such damage is not essential, the threat being to the community as a whole . . . Again there are formidable objections. Some torts do not require damage (such as trespass and libel), while many crimes do involve private damage. Some crimes are punished as an affront to the moral feelings of the community although they cause no damage to the community as a whole. This is true of the group of crimes having in differing degrees a religious aspect: blasphemy, attempted suicide, abortion, bigamy. It is also largely true of obscenity and adult homosexuality. Even murder need not cause public damage: for example, when a mother kills her infant child. This creates no general sense of insecurity; the only material loss to society is the loss of the child, and whether that is economically a real loss or a gain depends on whether the country is under- or over-populated at the time. Evidently, the social condemnation of infant-killing rests on non-utilitarian ethics. Some forms of public nuisance, too, are crimes although they positively benefit the community: *Ward* (1836) 4 Ad. & El. 384.

Even where an act injures the community, it need not be exclusively a crime. Thus some crimes, as has already been pointed out, may be made the occasion either of a criminal prosecution or of a civil action (generally a relator action) for an injunction by the Attorney-General; in the latter event the crime is treated not as a crime but as a civil wrong to the public. There are civil public wrongs that are not crimes, for which there is no remedy, but a relator action as where statutory powers are being exceeded. Indeed, an ordinary tort to property may be committed against public property and so become a public wrong . . .

We have rejected all definitions purporting to distinguish between crimes and other wrongs by reference to the sort of thing that is done or the sort of physical, economic or social consequences that follow from it. Only one possibility now remains. A crime must be defined by reference to the *legal* consequences of the act. We must distinguish, primarily, not between crimes and civil wrongs but between criminal and civil proceedings. A crime then becomes an act that is capable of being followed by criminal proceedings, having one of the types of outcome (punishment, etc.) known to follow these proceedings . . .

As stated at the outset, there are many differences of procedure between crimes and civil wrongs. Often these differences are of no help in distinguishing between the two, because they are consequential differences—it is only when you know that the act is a crime or a civil wrong respectively that you know which procedure to select. However, some elements in procedure do assist in making the classification. When Parliament passes a statute forbidding certain conduct, it may refer in terms to certain procedural matters—such as trial on indictment, or summary conviction—which indicate that the act is to be a crime. Again, when it is disputed whether a given proceeding, such as a proceeding for a penalty, is criminal or civil, a point can be scored by showing that this proceeding has been held in the past to be governed by some procedural rule which is regarded as indicative of a criminal or civil proceeding, as the case may be. For example, the fact that a precedent decides that a new trial may be granted in a particular proceeding indicates that the proceeding is civil, since new trials are not granted in criminal cases. [But see now Criminal Appeal Act 1968 s.7.] On the other hand a precedent deciding that evidence of character is admissible in a certain proceeding indicates that it is criminal, since evidence of character is not admissible in civil cases, apart from certain quite definite exceptions.

Since the courts thus make use of the whole law of procedure in aid of their task of classification, an attempt to define crime in terms of one item of procedure only is mistaken. This remark applies to the test of crime adopted by Kenny, following Austin and Clark, which links crime with the ability of the Crown to remit the sanction. This test tells you whether an act is a crime only if you already know whether the sanction is remissible by the Crown. Almost always, however, the latter has to be deduced from the former, instead of vice versa. Thus Kenny defines *ignotum per ignotius*. This objection would not be open if Kenny's chosen procedural test were made available *along with all the others*. The procedural test does not give full assistance unless one is allowed to use the whole law of procedure.

. . . In short, a crime is an act capable of being followed by criminal proceedings having a criminal outcome, and a proceeding or its outcome is criminal if it has certain characteristics which mark it as criminal. In a marginal case the court may have to balance one feature, which may suggest that the proceeding is criminal, against another feature, which may suggest the contrary.

P.J. FITZGERALD, "A CONCEPT OF CRIME" [1960] CRIM. L.R. 257, 259

In the question what is a crime there seems to be entangled three different though related questions.

1. The question may be simply the request of the non-lawyer as to how he is to tell whether an act is a crime or not. Here we may give an imperative definition by saying that a crime is a breach of the criminal law. Though dismissed by Glanville Williams as circular, such a definition is useful firstly in emphasising that a crime is not necessarily a moral wrong and vice versa. Secondly, its value is that it directs attention away from abstract speculation on the nature of the act and focuses it on the need to study the provisions of the criminal law itself . . .

2. The request for a definition of crime may be the request of the non-lawyer to be told what it means for the law to lay down that certain conduct shall be criminal. In other words he may want to know the effect of the law providing that an act is a crime. Here lies the usefulness of the definition proposed by Glanville Williams which distinguishes criminal wrongs from other legal wrongs . . .

3. The quest for a definition of crime may be a more sophisticated question, of a lawyer reflecting on the criminal law, namely, what have all crimes in common other than the fact that they are breaches of the criminal law? In so far as the motive behind such a question is the desire for a simple test to decide whether conduct is criminal or not without reference to the provisions of the law, Glanville Williams' discussion is helpful and illuminating in demonstrating that this is a search for the unattainable. But what may lie

behind the question 'What is a crime?' may be the idea that Parliament and still more the courts have not created crimes arbitrarily or irrationally. Given that the aim of the criminal law is to announce that certain acts are not to be done, and to bring about that fewer of these acts are done, what is the principle or principles that have led the criminal law to prohibit the acts it has prohibited?

Question

When Parliament legislates making particular conduct criminal (or abolishing criminal liability for particular conduct) does the nature or morality of that conduct change or is it simply the (potential) consequences of the conduct which change?

----

2. THE FUNCTION OF THE CRIMINAL LAW

A. ASHWORTH, "BELIEF, INTENT, AND CRIMINAL LIABILITY" IN EEKELAAR AND BELL (EDS), OXFORD ESSAYS IN JURISPRUDENCE, 3RD EDN (CLARENDON PRESS, 1987), P.1

The fundamental reason for having a system of criminal law is to provide a framework for the state punishment of wrongdoers, and thereby to preserve an acceptable degree of social order. Without criminal laws and their enforcement, each individual's person, property, and family would be substantially less safe from deliberate violation by others. It would hardly be sufficient to declare that individual members of society have certain rights, to physical integrity, security of property, and so on. It is also necessary inter alia to take steps to see that rights are not violated, a first step to which is to declare that individuals have duties not to violate the rights of others. Various branches of the civil law require those who negligently breach a duty to pay compensation to those whose rights were thus violated, and other parts of the civil law provide remedies for some deliberate breaches of duty. The specific technique of the criminal law is to provide for the conviction and punishment of those who culpably breach the more serious duties. Typically, the criminal law will declare which forms of conduct and omissions constitute such a serious breach of duty that they call for prosecution, conviction, and sentence under a special 'criminal' procedure and separately from private disputes among citizens. Attached to that declaration will be a system of enforcement and sentencing which operates, by and large, to influence people not to violate these laws. Even those who adopt a retributivist or rights-based approach to criminal liability and punishment surely cannot maintain a general indifference towards the frequency with which these more serious rights and duties are breached. A major part of the reason for having a system of criminal law and punishment is surely to reduce the frequency of those violations.

Note

In the extract which follows Walker, a criminologist, identifies objectives which may be pursued through the use of the criminal law.

N. WALKER, CRIME AND CRIMINOLOGY: A CRITICAL INTRODUCTION (OXFORD: OXFORD UNIVERSITY PRESS, 1987), PP.140–141

i. Objectives of the criminal law

Is it possible to discuss the proper content of the criminal law in general terms? If the contents of criminal codes are examined with a sociological eye, no fewer than fourteen different objectives can be discerned:

(a) the protection of human persons (and to some extent animals also) against intentional violence, cruelty, or unwelcome sexual approaches;

(b) the protection of people against some forms of unintended harm (for example from traffic, poisons, infections, radiation);

(c) the protection of easily persuadable classes of people (that is, the young or the weak-minded) against the abuse of their persons or property (for example by sexual intercourse or hire-purchase);

(d) the prevention of acts which, even if the participants are adult and willing, are regarded as 'unnatural' (for example incest, . . . bestiality, drug 'trips');

(e) the prevention of acts which, though not included under any of the previous headings, are performed so publicly as to shock other people (for example public nakedness, obscene language, or . . . copulation between consenting adults);

(f) the discouragement of behaviour which might provoke disorder (such as insulting words at a public meeting);

(g) the protection of property against theft, fraud, or damage;

(h) the prevention of inconvenience (for example the obstruction of roads by vehicles);

(i) the collection of revenue (for example keeping a motor car or television set without a licence);

(j) the defence of the State (for example espionage or—in some countries—political criticism);

(k) the enforcement of compulsory benevolence (for example the offence of failing to send one's children to school);

(l) the protection of social institutions, such as marriage or religious worship (for example by prohibiting bigamy or blasphemy);

(m) the prevention of unreasonable discrimination (for example against ethnic groups, religions, the female sex);

(n) the enforcement of the processes regarded as essential to these other purposes (for example offences connected with arrest, assisting offenders to escape conviction, and testimony at trials).

Note

Prominent in the objectives outlined above by Walker are those of protection of individuals and the prevention of offending. How these objectives are achieved also depends on the consequences which flow from conviction. Criminalisation cannot be divorced from the purposes which punishment may serve. This, however, is a matter of continuing controversy.

D.J. GALLIGAN, "THE RETURN TO RETRIBUTION IN CRIMINAL THEORY" IN *CRIME, PROOF AND PUNISHMENT: ESSAYS IN MEMORY OF SIR RUPERT CROSS* (LONDON: BUTTERWORTHS, 1981), PP.144, 146 AND FOLLOWING

If one were to attempt to explain the principal functions of that complex amalgam of institutions, persons, rules, and practices which we loosely refer to as the system of criminal justice, then two particular things would seem to call out for special attention. First, criminal justice is concerned centrally with trying, convicting and punishing those who are guilty of breaking the criminal law. Secondly, such systems are concerned to punish those who are convicted with a view to upholding the authority and effectiveness of the criminal law by sanctions that seek to deter, to prevent, to reform, or to incapacitate. These two tasks will often, but not necessarily, be compatible with each other. One view of criminal justice is to emphasise the forward-looking or utilitarian functions while another view sees the backward-looking or retributive aspect as primary. How one perceives the system will largely determine how one explains it and the kind of justifications that one finds acceptable . . .

Utilitarian accounts usually begin with the assumption that the central purpose of criminal of justice is to reduce crime. This purpose is achieved by taking coercive action against selected individuals, usually those who have broken the law and who can be held personally responsible for so doing. There is an increasing body of offences which do not require responsibility in the usual legal sense, but nevertheless, with respect to the main corpus of criminal laws there is still a meticulous concern to be sure that before a person is punished he is guilty in the sense that he is responsible. But why should this be so? It is an important aspect of forward-looking explanations of criminal justice that the punishment of wrong-doers is not itself part of the general aim or purpose. Rather, confinement of impositions to the guilty law-breaker is a costly constraint on pursuit of the general reductivist aim. One approach faces this problem by suggesting that these constraints are misguided, in that inquiries into matters of personal responsibility are inevitably very crude, and unfairly selective in that there are large areas where action is taken without the requirement of responsibility. According to this view criminal justice should not be thought of as significantly different from other methods of social protection, such as confining dangerous mental defectives. Society has an interest in protecting itself from the person who has or is likely to commit serious crime and may legitimately take whatever preventive action is necessary. Although such an understanding of criminal justice has been anathema to most, a few modifications show it in a much better light. A modified approach might see considerable advantages such as economy, humanitarianism and the reduction of suffering in retaining the basic constraints of the aim of reducing crime, but since these would be conditional they could be departed from if to do so would provide better service to the general aim. It is worth noting that much of the practice of criminal justice is indeed compatible with this position for while coercion is normally based on responsibility, it is also often departed from if we bear in mind the preventive powers of the police and courts, the areas of strict and vicarious liability and the means available for confining mental defectives.

Views of this kind, however, have never dominated explanations of criminal justice. Most forward-looking accounts of criminal justice, no matter how different in other respects, seek to show that while the general purpose of criminal justice is forward looking, the responsibility constraints on that purpose are explicable, justifiable and necessary. Since Bentham's famous but flawed defence of punishing only those responsible for their actions, a range of increasingly subtle and sophisticated explanations have been advanced. There is, for example, the pragmatist argument that as a matter of practicalities it would be virtually impossible to design an efficacious system of criminal justice that did not limit the distribution of sanctions to the responsible offender. Alternatively there is the suggestion that the purpose of criminal justice is not only reduction through-deterrence, but also reduction-through-respect for the law. Unless the administration of criminal justice is in accordance with values esteemed in the community then respect for law is hardly to be earned and naturally most people think that a man should only be punished if he is guilty.

There is much to be said for this view; notice however that it puts forward the responsibility constraint not as an independent value in itself, but of value because it maximises the efficacy of law . . .

Finally, it is a frequently heard criticism of utilitarian accounts that since the aim is crime control, there are difficulties in finding principles that limit the amount of punishment that may be inflicted on any offender. To the practical reformer this is the central issue, for recent penal history has shown the difficulty of controlling punishment distributed according to forward-looking goals. Retributive accounts, with their emphasis on punishment according to deserts, is naturally an attractive alternative to the unruly policies of rehabilitation and deterrence . . .

Retributive explanations emphasise the concern of the criminal justice system to punish those who break the law. The core of the idea of retribution is the moral notion that the wrongdoer ought to be punished.

Thus a system that is centrally concerned with punishing offenders is retributive. In explaining the practice of criminal justice in this way, the retributive approach avoids the difficulties in explanation that beset forward-looking accounts. There is no need to distinguish between aim and distribution since the aim provides the criterion of distribution. The person who has not broken the law, or who could not help breaking it, or who can offer some other acceptable excuse is not a wrongdoer and is not liable for punishment. In other words within the context of criminal justice as we know it, punishment means inflicting sanctions on wrongdoers. This does not imply that coercion is never used against people in other ways; all it claims is that the reasons for coercing wrongdoers are different from the reasons that would explain other areas of coercion.

Put in this bald way, retribution includes both a description of criminal justice and a justification. Just as the utilitarian sees criminal justice as primarily concerned with reducing crime, so the retributivist sees the punishment of offenders as the dominant purpose. The logic of punishment consists in singling out an offender, condemning him for his offence and imposing punitive treatment upon him. The retributivist sees these three elements as part of one unified and justifiable social process: the offender has done wrong which, by punishment, is somehow righted. In short, the distinctive feature of retribution as a justifying principle, is that it provides a basis not just for singling out and condemning the offender, but also for inflicting punitive treatment.

3. CLASSIFYING CONDUCT AS CRIMINAL

Note

Decisions whether to criminalise or decriminalise certain behaviour do not occur in a vacuum. The criminal law is not a "given" in any society. Choices are made as to where the boundaries of criminal liability are to be drawn and the drawing of these boundaries can be a highly political process. R. Quinney, *The Social Reality of Crime* (Transaction Publishers, 1970) states:

> "First, my perspective is based on a special conception of society. Society is characterized by diversity, conflict, coercion and change, rather than by consensus and stability. Second, law is a result of the operation of interests, rather than an instrument that functions outside of particular interests. Though law may control interests, it is in the first place created by interests. Third, law incorporates the interests of specific persons and groups; it is seldom the product of the whole society. Law is made by [people], representing special interests, who have the power to translate their interests into public policy."

LACEY, "CONTINGENCY AND CRIMINALISATION" IN I. LOVELAND (ED), *FRONTIERS OF CRIMINALITY* (LONDON: SWEET & MAXWELL, 1995) PP.4, 14–15

To speak . . . of 'criminalisation' or of the 'frontiers of criminality' appears to presuppose that something or someone is, or has, been 'doing' the criminalising or 'constructing' the frontiers. Here we confront an ambiguity which is central to the idea of 'crime' in contemporary Britain. One culturally endorsed way of looking at crime is as something which is not primarily a legal, but rather a moral, category and hence, on one influential view, as outside the ambit of deliberate legislative change. Hence the role of criminal law is basically to reflect and articulate a pre-existing conception of wrongdoing. Yet from another culturally endorsed point of view, criminal law-making actually creates rather than reproduces categories of 'crime'. The relevance of both perspectives have sometimes been expressed in terms of the ideas of *mala in se* and *mala prohibita*, and reconciled, somewhat uncomfortably, on the basis that they refer to different areas of criminal law . . .

[It is important to look] beyond the material or instrumental to attend to what are sometimes called the symbolic aspects of criminalisation or decriminalisation policies. Indeed, the recognition of what we might call the 'materiality of discourse' shows that we must be careful not to draw a strong dichotomy between the instrumental and the symbolic. For broader cultural understandings of crime affect particular policies, and are capable of subverting the intended meaning of legal or executive change, or indeed of supplying an astute decision-maker with possibilities of pursuing more than one political end by means of any one reform strategy. For example, observe how government decisions to criminalise or decriminalise by legislation can score political points by exploiting the ambiguity in the notion of crime identified above. On the one hand, government is constructing law and order problems as *political* issues, to which it is responding; formal legislation thus offers government the opportunity to represent itself as instrumentally effective. At the same time, it can draw on a prevailing discourse of crime as in some sense *pre-political*—that is, as wickedness or mere lawlessness or even pathology—as something from which we—that is, any 'good citizen'—would distance him or herself. In this sense, formal criminalisation is exploited as an occasion for the evocation of an underlying, symbolic consensus, appeal to which may be a significant mode of governmental self-legitimation. In such instances, government's legislative shifting of the boundaries of liability itself depends upon and expresses the contingency of crime, yet simultaneously deploys a powerful social discourse which constructs crime as 'given'. The purpose of the legislation is to make criminal that which is not already criminal, yet its rationale is that that behaviour is in another sense already criminal. Conversely, a decision to decriminalise can enjoy a similar dual legitimation; government's liberal credentials are fostered in that it gets credit for actually drawing back the boundaries of 'criminality'; yet its action is justified in part by the implication that the conduct in question was never really criminal in the first place.

It is also important to recognise that deliberate legislative or judicial shifts (perhaps we should say 'attempted shifts') in the frontiers of criminal liability often have symbolic effects which are less obviously envisaged or welcome. For example, the formal criminalisation of a kind of conduct, the practical proscription of which proves for one reason or another to be impossible or very difficult to enforce, may be counterproductive. This counter-productiveness may consist in the proscription's being seen as implicitly legitimating that form of behaviour. Incitement to racial hatred would be a good example here; its virtual non-enforcement is seen by many as implying covert approval of the behaviour formally proscribed. It may also consist in undermining the images of instrumental effectiveness, universality and evenhandedness, which persist even in the face of the general selec-tiveness and patterning of enforcement practices, and which are central to criminal law's perceived legitimacy (examples here might include those of gaming laws and a variety of offences concerning sexual 'morality').

Note

What conduct should be criminalised? Undoubtedly there will be general agreement on some matters but varying opinions on others. The issue which arises is the extent to which the criminal law should legislate for morality, particularly where views on morality differ and where the conduct involved does not involve harm to others.

H. GROSS, *A THEORY OF CRIMINAL JUSTICE* (NEW YORK: OXFORD UNIVERSITY PRESS, 1979), PP.13–14

It seems obvious that those crimes of violence, theft, and destruction that stand as paradigms of crime and com-prise the core of any penal code are also moral wrongs. Everyone has a right to be free of such harm inflicted by others, and when murder, rape, arson, assault, or larceny is committed there is also a moral wrong since a moral duty to refrain from doing harm to others has been breached. The right to be free of such harm does not have its origin in law but in a general consensus on the rights enjoyed by any member of society, or even by any person, no matter how he lives. This consensus is a more fundamental element of society even than the law, and for that reason the violation of such a right is a moral wrong and not simply a legal wrong.

Question

To what extent does the criminal law, particularly in areas of morality, create criminals? H.S. Becker, *Outsiders: Studies in the Sociology of Deviance* (Free Press, 1963) states (p.9):

> "[T]he central fact about deviance [is that] it is created by society. I do not mean this in the way it is ordinarily understood, in which the causes of deviance are located in the social situation of the deviant or in 'social factors' which prompt his action. I mean, rather, that *social groups create deviance by making rules whose infraction constitutes deviance*, and by applying those rules to particular people and labelling them as outsiders. From this point of view, deviance is *not* a quality of the act the person commits, but rather a consequence of the application by others of rules and sanctions to an 'offender'. The deviant is one to whom that label has successfully been applied; deviant behaviour is behaviour that people so label."

Do you agree in whole or in part with this statement? If the latter, to which offences do you think it more accurately applies?

H.L. PACKER, *THE LIMITS OF THE CRIMINAL SANCTION* (STANFORD UNIVERSITY PRESS, 1969), PP.261 AND FOLLOWING

IMMORALITY: A NECESSARY CONDITION

The debate over the relationship between law and morals is perennial. It has rarely taken specific enough account, however, of what kind of law is at issue. The criminal sanction represents a very special kind of law, itself morally hazardous. As we have seen, the rationale of criminal punishment requires that no one should be treated as a criminal unless his conduct can be regarded as culpable. The flouting of this requirement that takes place when offenses are interpreted as being of 'strict liability' contributes to the dilution of the criminal law's moral impact. The ends of the criminal sanction are disserved if the notion becomes widespread that being convicted of a crime is no worse than coming down with a bad cold. The question we now have to face is what role, if any, the moral force of the criminal sanction should have in determining what conduct should be treated as criminal . . .

Can we then assert that there is any kind of connection between the immorality of a category of conduct and the appropriate use of the criminal sanction? I think we can, but only on a prudential basis. Leaving aside for the moment the question of what we mean by immoral, we may discern an analogy between the requirement of culpability in the individual case and a limiting criterion for the legislative invocation of the criminal sanction: only conduct generally considered 'immoral' should be treated as criminal. Several reasons support this prudential limitation. To begin with, the principles of selection we use in determining what kinds of undesirable conduct to treat as criminal should surely include at least one that is responsive to the basic character of the criminal sanction, i.e. its quality of moral condemnation. To put it another way, we should use the strengths of the sanction rather than ignore or undermine them. If the conduct with which the original sanction deals is already regarded as being morally wrong, the processes of the criminal law have, so to speak, a 'leg up' on the job. This is a matter partly of public attitude and partly of the morale maintained by those who operate the criminal processes. The way to keep those processes running at peak efficiency is to ensure that those who operate them are convinced that what they are doing is right. The surest way to persuade them that what they are doing is right is to have them act only against what they think is wrong. If the criminal sanction is widely used to deal with morally neutral behavior, law enforcement officials are likely to be at least subconsciously defensive about their work, and the public will find the criminal law a confusing guide to moral, or even acceptable, behavior.

[Packer dismisses the argument that the criminal sanction can condition people's view of what is moral, and continues:]

The question remains: whose morality are we talking about? It is easy to slide into the assumption that somewhere in society there is an authoritative body of moral sentiment to which the law should look. That assumption becomes particularly dangerous, as we shall see, when it is used to buttress the assertion that the immorality of a given form of conduct is a *sufficient* condition for declaring that conduct to be criminal. But when one is talking about immorality as a *necessary* condition for invocation of the criminal sanction, the inquiry should simply be whether there exists any significant body dissent from the proposition that the conduct in question is immoral. Is there any social group that will be alienated or offended by making (or keeping) the conduct in question criminal? If there is, then prudence dictates caution in employing the criminal sanction.

We can sum up this prudential limitation as follows: the criminal sanction should ordinarily be limited to conduct that is viewed, without significant social dissent, as immoral. The calendar of crimes should not be enlarged beyond that point and, as views about morality shift, should be contracted.

IMMORALITY: AN INSUFFICIENT CONDITION

If the immorality of conduct is a generally necessary condition for invocation of the criminal sanction, is it a generally sufficient one? That is the gist of the 'law and morals' debate. Conventional morality, it is asserted, is what holds society together. It must be not only taught but enforced. The enforcement of morals needs no other justification. The usual lines of attack upon this argument are, first, that there is no easy way to determine what should count as immoral and, second, that other considerations (primarily of enforceability) should also be taken into account in determining whether immoral conduct should be made criminal. To these may be added a third: it simply is not true that we use the criminal law to deal with all conduct that we consider immoral; even the most extreme of legal moralists have never pressed for that. Therefore, unless the choice of proscribed conduct is to be purely whimsical, we must take other factors into consideration . . .

The extent of disagreement about moral judgments is an obvious reason for hesitancy about an automatic enforcement of morals . . .

In a society that neither has nor wants a unitary set of moral norms, the enforcement of morals carries a heavy cost in repression. We don't begin to agree about the 'morality' of smoking, drinking, gambling, fornicating, or drug-taking, for example, quite apart from the gap between what we say and what we do. The more heterogeneous the society, the more repressive the enforcement of morals must be. And the more heterogeneous the society, the more foreign to its ethos that kind of repression is likely to be . . .

Immorality clearly should not be viewed as a sufficient or even a principal reason for proscribing conduct as criminal. Morals belong to the home, the school, and the church; and we have many homes, many schools, many churches. Our moral universe is polycentric. The state, especially when the most coercive of sanctions is at issue, should not seek to impose a spurious unity upon it . . .

If a legislator can think of no better reason to proscribe conduct than that he (or his constituency) abhors it, he had better think twice about doing it.

HARM TO OTHERS

[Packer goes on to consider "harm to others" as a limiting principle on the use of the criminal sanction.]

'Harm to others' does not, of course, mean identifiable others. It has become fashionable to talk about 'victimless crimes', meaning those in which there is no immediately identifiable victim to lodge a complaint. The absence of an identifiable victim can make enforcement difficult, and can encourage undesirable enforcement practices. But the prospect of these difficulties should not end the inquiry into the wisdom of any given use of the criminal sanction. Many offenses against the administration of government are 'victimless crimes' in the sense that there is nobody to complain. Consensual transactions like bribery and espionage are admittedly difficult to detect because of the absence of an identifiable victim; yet they do not necessarily cause so little 'harm to others' that we can forget about subjecting them to the criminal sanction.

The 'harm to others' formula seems to me to have two uses that justify its inclusion in a list of limiting criteria for invocation of the criminal sanction. First, it is a way to make sure that a given form of conduct is not being subjected to the criminal sanction purely or even primarily because it is thought to be immoral. It forces an inquiry into precisely what bad effects are feared if the conduct in question is not suppressed by the criminal law. Second, it immediately brings into play a host of secular inquiries about the effects of subjecting the conduct in question to the criminal sanction. One cannot meaningfully deal with the question of 'harm to others' without weighing benefits against detriments. In that sense, it is a kind of threshold question, important not so much in itself as in focusing attention on further considerations relevant to the ultimate decision. It is for these two instrumental reasons rather than for either its intrinsic rightness or its ease of application that it deserves inclusion.

[Packer summarises as follows the "limiting criteria" he regards as useful for the purpose of establishing a benchmark for the optimal use of the criminal sanction:]

(1) The conduct is prominent in most people's view of socially threatening behavior, and is not condoned by any significant segment of society.

(2) Subjecting it to the criminal sanction is not inconsistent with the goals of punishment.

(3) Suppressing it will not inhibit socially desirable conduct.

(4) It may be dealt with through even-handed and non-discriminatory enforcement.

(5) Controlling it through the criminal process will not expose that process to severe qualitative or quantitative strains.

(6) There are no reasonable alternatives to the criminal sanction for dealing with it.

Note

Walker in *Crime and Criminology: A Critical Introduction* (Oxford: Oxford University Press, 1987), pp.142–150 outlines the following "limiting principles" which if applied would improve the decision-making process on where the boundaries of the criminal law are to be drawn.

Moral limits

(A) Prohibitions should not be included in the criminal law for the sole purpose of ensuring that breaches of them are visited with retributive punishment. (See Beccaria, *Of Crimes and Punishments* (1764).)

(B) The criminal law should not be used to penalise behaviour which does no harm. (See Bentham, *An Introduction to the Principles of Morals and Legislation* (1789).)

(C) The criminal law should not be used where measures involving less suffering are as effective or almost as effective in reducing the frequency of the conduct in question. (Cf. Bentham, above.)

(D) The criminal law should not include prohibitions whose by products are more harmful than the conduct which they are intended to discourage. (Cf. Bentham, above.)

(E) The criminal law should not be used for the purpose of compelling people to act in their own best interests. (Cf. J.S. Mill, *On Liberty* (1859).)

Pragmatic limits

(F) The criminal law should not include prohibitions which do not have strong public support. (Cf. James Fitzjames Stephen, *Liberty, Equality, Fraternity* (1873).)

(G) A prohibition should not be included in the criminal code if only a small percentage of infringements of it could be proved against infringers.

Questions

1. Can you think of conduct which is criminal which does not involve causing harm to non-consenting persons and/or which seeks to compel people to act in their own best interests?

2. What alternative measures are available to reduce the frequency of conduct which currently is criminalised, for example, the taking of proscribed drugs or illicit sexual relationships?

3. Can you identify any by-products of criminalising the above examples of conduct? Do you consider these to be more harmful than the conduct? What criteria would you adopt in making this assessment?

4. Can you identify laws which are virtually unenforceable? Does this undermine respect for the law or do laws, despite their unenforceability, still perform a symbolic function and affirm a common core of morality in society?

5. Around two-thirds of male prisoners and four-fifths of female prisoners admit to heavy drinking before committing their offence. The cost of alcohol-related admissions to hospitals currently exceeds £3 billion per year. Is this sufficient reason to criminalise drinking alcohol?

Note

Dealing specifically with private consensual sexual behaviour between adults Becker identified the following reasons why the criminal sanction was an inappropriate response:

(1) Rarity of enforcement creates a problem of arbitrary police and prosecutorial discretion.

(2)   The extreme difficulty of detecting such conduct leads to undesirable police practices.

(3)   The existence of the proscription tends to create a deviant subculture.

(4)   Widespread knowledge that the law is violated with impunity by thousands every day creates disrespect for law generally.

(5)   No secular harm can be shown to result from such conduct.

(6)   The theoretical availability of criminal sanctions creates a situation in which extortion and, on occasion, police corruption may take place.

(7)   There is substantial evidence that the moral sense of the community no longer exerts strong pressure for the use of criminal sanctions.

(8)   No utilitarian goal of criminal punishment is substantially advanced by proscribing private adult consensual sexual conduct.

The only countervailing argument is that relaxation of the criminal proscription will be taken to express social approval of the conduct at issue.

Note

The above debate on where the boundaries of the criminal law should be drawn is a continuing one. It features in the speeches of their Lordships in *R. v Brown*, below p.542 and also featured in debates in Parliament preceding the passage of the Criminal Justice and Public Order Act 1994 which by s.145 reduced the age of consent to homosexual acts to 18 and which also criminalised trespass in wide-ranging provisions in Pt V. It also features in the debate over the decriminalisation of proscribed drugs.

A. ASHWORTH, *PRINCIPLES OF CRIMINAL LAW*, 3RD EDN (OXFORD: OXFORD UNIVERSITY PRESS, 1999), PP.24–27

THE POLITICS OF LAWMAKING

Creating a new criminal offence may often be regarded as an instantly satisfying political response to public worries about a form of conduct that has been given publicity by the newspapers and television. The pressure on politicians to be seen to be doing something may be great, and considered responses such as consultation and commissioning research may invite criticisms of indecision and procrastination. Thus, in many countries, the growth of the criminal law may reflect particular phases in contemporary social history, as written by the mass media and politicians.

We may consider two examples of recent legislative extension of the range of the criminal law: the offences in Part V of the Criminal Justice and Public Order Act 1994 and, first, the offence of causing harassment, alarm or distress in the Public Order Act 1986. In its reform of public order law in the 1980s, the government added to the offences recommended by the Law Commission a further offence, consisting of disorderly behaviour or threatening, abusive or insulting behaviour, likely to cause 'harassment, alarm or distress': Public Order Act 1986, section 5. The reason for adding this offence was to give the police the power to intervene at the early stages of disorder, and also to deal with minor acts of hooliganism. Much could be said about the origins and import of this provision. For present purposes, it is sufficient to note that the new offence is additional to that created by section 4 of the Act, of using threatening, abusive or insulting words or behaviour with intent to cause others to fear violence or with intent to provoke others to use violence. This raises the question whether there was a satisfactory justification for the further police powers and wider offence in section 5: the requirements of section 5 are so modest and broadly-stated that it could be used to cast the net of criminality very wide. Research into the use of section 5 shows just this: although the reliance of the police on section 5 varies considerably from area to area, one feature is that it has been much used to criminalize people who swear at police officers. This demonstrates at once the use by the police of public order offences as 'resources' to use when people show disrespect, and also the way in which criminalization ostensibly aimed at one set of situations (e.g. disturbing residents by kicking over dustbins) can then be adapted to deal with situations for which its use was not envisaged (i.e. swearing at the police).

The Criminal Justice and Public Order Act 1994 contains various new crimes aimed at penalizing trespassers on land. For many years the general principle has been that trespass to land is not appropriate for criminalization—there are civil remedies, disputes are better decided in the civil courts, and accelerated orders for possession are available to landowners. A few exceptional offences did exist before, but the 1994 Act goes much further by criminalizing aggravated trespass on land with intent to disrupt lawful activities thereon (section 68), by extending the police power to order trespassers off land, with associated offences for non-compliance (section 61), by permitting house owners to take stronger action against squatters (section 72), and by creating a new offence of unauthorized camping (section 77). There may be more political symbolism in these new offences than a real prospect of large-scale police action, but the offences are now on the statute book and several questions arise. Is such conduct so serious that the criminal law ought to be invoked rather than the civil process? Is there not a danger that, as with the Public Order Act 1986, section 5, the wide drafting of these offences will permit their use by the police against other forms of conduct? Aggravated trespass is an offence supposedly aimed at hunt saboteurs, but its wording could encompass many other forms of protest. Unauthorized camping is an offence supposedly aimed at New Age travellers, but its wording is clearly apt to criminalize gypsies for following their long-established way of life. Much will therefore turn on patterns of enforcement. If the experience of the 1986 Act, section 5, is a fair indicator, there will be local variations, with some police forces using the powers fully and others declining to do so, and with much depending on the dynamics of particular situations. Senior police officers have already expressed discomfort about enforcing the new offence of unauthorized camping against gypsies, but perhaps the politicians are content that an offence has been created and thus 'something has been done about it'.

These two examples serve to illustrate the complexity of the issues that arise in the criminalization debate. Even on a theoretical plane, fixing the proper boundaries of the criminal law is likely to involve not sharp distinctions and clearly defined categories, but rather judgments of degree relating to such matters as how proximate the harm should be to justify criminalization, and how relevant the availability of alternative mechanisms for enforcement should be. Although in practice examples of political pressures overcoming principled arguments are abundant, they do not account for all instances of criminalization. In some spheres such as financial regulation there is constant debate about the proper boundaries of criminal and regulatory or civil controls. In others, such as bail offences, law enforcement agents themselves may be the main force behind criminalization. In others it may be a report of the Law Commission or other committee, after due consultation, that results in new criminal law. And in still others, the political argument may be won by a pressure group which has campaigned for expanding the criminal law in areas such as domestic violence, drinking and driving, and so forth. Sheer vote winning, or preserving the position of the powerful over the powerless, accounts for some, but certainly not all, decisions to create new crimes.

Note

While most of the offences considered in the remainder of this book do not fall within the area of morality on which debate as to the location of the boundaries of the criminal law centres, it is, nonetheless, an important debate in which criminal lawyers must engage. This is particularly so in the case of proposals for new criminal offences which may be supported by a section of the populace and where legislation may benefit the popularity of the political party promoting it. It is at such times that the principles suggested by writers such as Packer and Walker must be fed into the debate if all hopes of achieving a rational and principled criminal code are not to be abandoned.

----

4. THE HUMAN RIGHTS ACT 1998

The Human Rights Act 1998 (HRA) enshrines in statute the protection afforded to individuals under the European Convention on Human Rights (ECHR). The HRA requires the courts to interpret legislation so as to be consistent with the ECHR and outlaws a public authority from acting in a way which is incompatible with a Convention Right. (Both the courts and the Crown Prosecution Service are public authorities for the purposes of the HRA.)

It was always anticipated that the HRA and the ECHR would have a significant impact on the criminal justice system. Since the Act came fully into force in October 2001 it has had a much greater impact on criminal evidence and procedure than on the substantive criminal law but the latter, even though there have been few successful challenges, has been affected in numerous ways.

THE CONVENTION RIGHTS

Article 2

1. Everyone's right to life shall be protected by law. No one shall be deprived of his life intentionally save in the execution of a sentence of a court following his conviction of a crime for which this penalty is provided by law.

2. Deprivation of life shall not be regarded as inflicted in contravention of this Article when it results from the use of force which is no more than absolutely necessary:

   (a) in defence of any person from unlawful violence;
   (b) in order to effect a lawful arrest or to prevent the escape of a person lawfully detained;
   (c) in action lawfully taken for the purpose of quelling a riot or insurrection.

This article provides that the Government and public authorities must protect the right to life. This may require, for example, that the police have to protect a person whose life is under immediate threat. It could also be used to argue that a patient should be able to get treatment that would save their life. It has direct relevance to the defence of self-defence and the defence of necessity to a charge of murder.

Article 3

No one shall be subjected to torture or inhuman or degrading treatment or punishment.

The European Court has made it clear that inhuman or degrading treatment or punishment has to be very serious to be in breach of art.3.

Article 5

1. Everyone has the right to liberty and security of person. No one shall be deprived of his liberty save in the following cases and in accordance with a procedure prescribed by law—

   (a) the lawful detention of a person after conviction by a competent court;
   (b) the lawful arrest or detention of a person for non-compliance with the lawful order of a court or in order to secure the fulfilment of any obligation prescribed by law;
   (c) the lawful arrest or detention of a person effected for the purpose of bringing him before the competent legal authority on reasonable suspicion of having committed an offence or when it is reasonably considered necessary to prevent his committing an offence or fleeing after having done so;
   (d) the detention of a minor by lawful order for the purpose of educational supervision or his lawful detention for the purpose of bringing him before the competent legal authority;
   (e) the lawful detention of persons for the prevention of the spreading of infectious diseases, of persons of unsound mind, alcoholics or drug addicts or vagrants;
   (f) the lawful arrest or detention of a person to prevent his effecting an unauthorised entry into the country or of a person against whom action is being taken with a view to deportation or extradition.

2. Everyone who is arrested shall be informed promptly, in a language which he understands, of the reason for his arrest and of any charge against him.

3. Everyone arrested or detained in accordance with the provisions of paragraph 1(c) of this Article shall be brought promptly before a judge or other officer authorised by law to exercise judicial power and shall be entitled to trial within a reasonable time or to release pending trial. Release may be conditioned by guarantees to appear for trial.

4. Everyone who is deprived of his liberty by arrest or detention shall be entitled to take proceedings by which the lawfulness of his detention shall be decided speedily by a court and his release ordered if the detention is not lawful.

5. Everyone who has been the victim of arrest or detention in contravention of the provisions of this Article shall have an enforceable right to compensation.

Article 5 limits the circumstances in which someone can be detained. In the context of substantive criminal law it will be relevant, for example, in the way defendants found to be insane are treated.

Article 6

1. In the determination of his civil rights and obligations or of any criminal charge against him, everyone is entitled to a fair and public hearing within a reasonable time by an independent and impartial tribunal established by law. Judgment shall be pronounced publicly, but the press and public may be excluded from all or part of the trial in the interests of morals, public order or national security in a democratic society, where the interests of juveniles or the protection of the private life of the parties so require, or to the extent strictly necessary in the opinion of the court in special circumstances where publicity would prejudice the interests of justice.

2. Everyone charged with a criminal offence shall be presumed innocent until proved guilty according to law.

3. Everyone charged with a criminal offence has the following minimum rights—

    (a) to be informed promptly, in a language which he or she understands and in detail, of the nature and cause of the accusation against him;
    (b) to have adequate time and facilities for the preparation of his defence;
    (c) to defend himself in person or through legal assistance of his own choosing or, if he has not sufficient means to pay for legal assistance, to be given it free when the interests of justice so require;
    (d) to examine or have examined witnesses against him and to obtain the attendance and examination of witnesses on his behalf under the same conditions as witnesses against him;
    (e) to have the free assistance of an interpreter if he cannot understand or speak the language used in court.

This article is especially relevant to the law on evidence and criminal procedure but could be interpreted as affecting the legitimacy of offences of strict liability. It also has real significance for the law on burdens of proof.

Article 7

1. No one shall be held guilty of any criminal offence on account of any act or omission which did not constitute a criminal offence under national or international law at the time when it was committed. Nor shall a heavier penalty be imposed than the one that was applicable at the time the criminal offence was committed.

2. This Article shall not prejudice the trial and punishment of any person for any act or omission which, at the time it was committed, was criminal according to the general principles of law recognised by civilised nations.

This article makes it clear that no one can be found guilty of a criminal offence if what they did was not a criminal offence at the time that they did it. It prevents Parliament passing criminal statutes retrospectively, although this was already an established principle of common law. It also has the effect of requiring that the law must is clear so that people have the opportunity of knowing whether or not what they are doing is unlawful.

Article 8

1. Everyone has the right to respect for his private and family life, his home and his correspondence.

2. There shall be no interference by a public authority with the exercise of this right except such as is in

accordance with the law and is necessary in a democratic society in the interests of national security, public safety or the economic well-being of the country, for the prevention of disorder or crime, for the protection of health or morals, or for the protection of the rights and freedoms of others.

This article has a clear relevance in criminal law when dealing with sexual offences. There have been a number of cases in which the European Court has made it clear that laws which prohibit gay men having sex breach art.8.

Article 9

1.   Everyone has the right to freedom of thought, conscience and religion; this right includes freedom to change his religion or belief, and freedom, either alone or in community with others and in public or private, to manifest his religion or belief, in worship, teaching, practice and observance.

2.   Freedom to manifest one's religion or beliefs shall be subject only to such limitations as are prescribed by law and are necessary in a democratic society in the interests of public safety, for the protection of public order, health or morals, or for the protection of the rights and freedoms of others.

Article 10

Article 10 of the ECHR protects the right to freedom of expression. Prior to the HRA coming into force, the right to freedom of expression was a negative one: you were free to express yourself, unless the law otherwise prevented you from doing so. Following the incorporation of the ECHR into English law, the right to freedom of expression is now expressly guaranteed.

However, the right to freedom of expression may, in certain circumstances, be interfered with. Interferences with the right to freedom of expression may be permitted if they are prescribed by law, pursue a legitimate aim and are necessary in a democratic society. The legitimate purposes for which freedom of expression can be limited are:

- National security, territorial integrity or public safety.

- The prevention of disorder or crime.

- The protection of health or morals.

- The protection of the reputation or rights of others.

- The prevention of the disclosure of information received in confidence.

- For maintaining the authority and impartiality of the judiciary.

Article 11

1.   Everyone has the right to freedom of peaceful assembly and to freedom of association with others, includ-ing the right to form and to join trade unions for the protection of his interests.

2.   No restrictions shall be placed on the exercise of these rights other than such as are prescribed by law and are necessary in a democratic society in the interests of national security or public safety, for the prevention of disorder or crime, for the protection of health or morals or for the protection of the rights and freedoms of others. This Article shall not prevent the imposition of lawful restrictions on the exercise of these rights by members of the armed forces, of the police or of the administration of the state.

Article 14

The enjoyment of the rights and freedoms set forth in this convention shall be secured without discrimination on any ground such as sex, race, colour, language, religion, political or other opinion, national or social origin, association with a national minority, property, birth or other status.

R. V RIMMINGTON

[2005] 3 W.L.R. 982 HL

The House of Lords was asked to consider whether the common law offence of public nuisance violated the principles of certainty in art.7 of the ECHR.

LORD BINGHAM OF CORNHILL

32. The appellants submitted that the crime of causing a public nuisance, as currently interpreted and applied, lacks the precision and clarity of definition, the certainty and the predictability necessary to meet the requirements of either the common law itself or article 7 of the European Convention. This submission calls for some consideration of principle.

33. In his famous polemic Truth versus Ashurst, written in 1792 and published in 1823, Jeremy Bentham made a searing criticism of judge-made criminal law, which he called 'dog-law'.

> 'It is the judges (as we have seen) that make the common law. Do you know how they make it? Just as a man makes laws for his dog. When your dog does anything you want to break him of, you wait till he does it, and then beat him for it. This is the way you make laws for your dog: and this is the way the judges make law for you and me. They won't tell a man beforehand what it is he should not do-they won't so much as allow of his being told: they lie by till he has done something which they say he should not have done, and then they hang him for it.'

The domestic law of England and Wales has set its face firmly against 'dog-law'. In *R. v Withers* [1975] A.C. 842 the House of Lords ruled that the judges have no power to create new offences: see Lord Reid, at p.854g; Viscount Dilhorne, at p.860e; Lord Simon of Glaisdale, at pp.863d, 867e; Lord Kilbrandon, at p.877c. Nor (per Lord Simon, at p.863d) may the courts nowadays widen existing offences so as to make punishable conduct of a type hitherto not subject to punishment. The relevant principles are admirably summarised by Judge LJ for the Court of Appeal (Criminal Division) in *R. v Misra* [2005] 1 Cr.App.R. 328, paras 29–34, in a passage which I would respectfully adopt.

29. To develop his argument on uncertainty, Mr Gledhill [for Dr Misra] focused our attention on art.7 of the Convention, entitled 'No punishment without law' which provides: '7(1) No one shall be held guilty of any criminal offence on account of any act or omission which did not constitute a criminal offence under national or international law at the time when it was committed nor shall a heavier penalty be imposed than the one that was applicable at the time the criminal offence was committed.' In our view the essential thrust of this article is to prohibit the creation of offences, whether by legislation or the incremental development of the common law, which have retrospective application. It reflects a well-understood principle of domestic law, that conduct which did not contravene the criminal law at the time when it took place should not retrospectively be stigmatised as criminal, or expose the perpetrator to punishment. As Lord Reid explained in *Waddington v Miah* (1974) 59 Cr.App.R. 149, 151 and 152: 'There has for a very long time been a strong feeling against making legislation, and particularly criminal legislation, retrospective . . . I use retrospective in the sense of authorising people being punished for what they did before the Act came into force.'

30. Mr Gledhill demonstrated that the Convention contained repeated references to expressions in English such as 'prescribed by law': in French, the same phrase reads 'prévue par la loi'. We shall assume that the concepts are identical. Article 7 therefore sustains his contention that a criminal offence must be clearly defined in law, and represents the operation of 'the principle of legal certainty' (see, for example, *Brumarescu v Romania* (2001) 33 E.H.R.R. 35, para.61 and *Kokkinakis v Greece* (1993) 17 E.H.R.R. 397, para.52). The principle enables each community to regulate itself: 'with reference to the norms prevailing in the society in which they live. That generally entails that the law must be adequately accessible-an individual must have an indication of the legal rules applicable in a given case-and he must be able to foresee the consequences of his actions, in particular to be able to avoid incurring the sanction of the criminal law.' (*S.W. v United Kingdom: C.R. v United Kingdom* (1995) 21 E.H.R.R. 363).

31. Mr Gledhill further emphasised that in *Grayned v City of Rockford* (1972) 408 U.S. 104 the United States Supreme Court identified 'a basic principle of due process that an enactment is void for vagueness if its prohibitions are not clearly defined. Vagueness offends several important values . . . A vague law impermissibly delegates basic policy matters to policemen, judges and juries for resolution on an ad hoc and subjective basis,

with the attendant dangers of arbitrary and discriminatory application.' He pointed out that Lord Phillips MR had approved these dicta in *R. (L.) v Secretary of State for the Home Department* [2003] 1 W.L.R. 1230, para.25.

32. We acknowledge the force of these submissions, but simultaneously emphasise that there is nothing novel about them in our jurisprudence. Historic as well as modern examples abound. In the 17th century Bacon proclaimed the essential link between justice and legal certainty: 'For if the trumpet give an uncertain sound, who shall prepare himself to the battle? So if the law give an uncertain sound, who shall prepare to obey it? It ought therefore to warn before it strikes . . . Let there be no authority to shed blood; nor let sentence be pronounced in any court upon cases, except according to a known and certain law . . . Nor should a man be deprived of his life, who did not first know that he was risking it.' (Quoted in *Coquillette*, Francis Bacon pp.244 and 248, from *Aphorism 8* and Aphorism 39-A Treatise on Universal Justice). The judgment of the Supreme Court of the United States in *Grayned* effectively mirrored Blackstone: 'Law, without equity, though hard and disagreeable, is much more desirable for the public good than equity without law: which would make every judge a legislator, and introduce most infinite confusion; as there would then be almost as many rules of action laid down in our courts, as there are differences of capacity and sentiment in the human mind.' (*Commentaries*, 3rd ed., 1769, vol. 1 p.62).

33. Recent judicial observations are to the same effect. Lord Diplock commented in *Black-Clawson International Ltd v Papierwerke Waldhof-Aschaffenberg AG* [1975] A.C. 591, 638: 'The acceptance of the rule of law as a constitutional principle requires that a citizen, before committing himself to any course of action, should be able to know in advance what are the legal consequences that will flow from it.' In *Fothergill v Monarch Airlines Ltd* [1981] A.C. 251, 279 he repeated the same point: 'Elementary justice or, to use the concept often cited by the European court, the need for legal certainty demands that the rules by which the citizen is to be bound should be ascertainable by him (or more realistically by a competent lawyer advising him) by reference to identifiable sources that are publicly accessible.' More tersely, in *Warner v Metropolitan Police Commissioner* (1968) 52 Cr.App.R. 373, 414, [1969] 2 A.C. 256, 296, Lord Morris of Borth-y-Gest explained in terms that: 'In criminal matters it is important to have clarity and certainty.' The approach of the common law is perhaps best encapsulated in the statement relating to judicial precedent issued by Lord Gardiner LC on behalf of himself and the Lords of Appeal in Ordinary on July 26, 1966 Practice Statement (Judicial Precedent) (1986) 83 Cr.App.R. 191, [1966] 1 W.L.R. 1234. 'Their Lordships regard the use of precedent as an indispensable foundation upon which to decide what is the law and its application to individual cases. It provides at least some degree of certainty upon which individuals can rely in the conduct of their affairs, as well as a basis for orderly development of legal rules.' In allowing themselves (but not courts at any other level) to depart from the absolute obligation to follow earlier decisions of the House of Lords, their Lordships expressly bore in mind: 'the danger of disturbing retrospectively the basis on which contracts, settlements of property and fiscal arrangements have been entered into and also the especial need for certainty as to the criminal law.'

34. No further citation is required. In summary, it is not to be supposed that prior to the implementation of the Human Rights Act 1998, either this court, or the House of Lords, would have been indifferent to or unaware of the need for the criminal law in particular to be predictable and certain. Vague laws which purport to create criminal liability are undesirable, and in extreme cases, where it occurs, their very vagueness may make it impossible to identify the conduct which is prohibited by a criminal sanction. If the court is forced to guess at the ingredients of a purported crime any conviction for it would be unsafe. That said, however, the requirement is for sufficient rather than 'absolute certainty'. There are two guiding principles: no one should be punished under a law unless it is sufficiently clear and certain to enable him to know what conduct is forbidden before he does it; and no one should be punished for any act which was not clearly and ascertainably punishable when the act was done. If the ambit of a common law offence is to be enlarged, it 'must be done step by step on a case by case basis and not with one large leap': *R. v Clark (Mark)* [2003] 2 Cr.App.R. 363, para.13.

34. These common law principles are entirely consistent with article 7(1) of the European Convention, which provides:

'No punishment without law
1. No one shall be held guilty of any criminal offence on account of any act or omission which did not constitute a criminal offence under national or international law at the time when it was committed. Nor shall a heavier penalty be imposed than the one that was applicable at the time the criminal offence was committed.'

The European court has repeatedly considered the effect of this article, as also the reference in art.8(2) to 'in accordance with the law' and that in art.10(2) to 'prescribed by law'.

35. The effect of the Strasbourg jurisprudence on this topic has been clear and consistent. The starting point is the old rule nullum crimen, nulla poena sine lege (*Kokkinakis v Greece* (1993) 17 E.H.R.R. 397, para.52; *S.W. v*

United Kingdom (1995) 21 E.H.R.R. 363, para.35/33): only the law can define a crime and prescribe a penalty. An offence must be clearly defined in law (*S.W. v United Kingdom* 21 E.H.R.R. 363), and a norm cannot be regarded as a law unless it is formulated with sufficient precision to enable the citizen to foresee, if need be with appropriate advice, the consequences which a given course of conduct may entail (*Sunday Times v United Kingdom* (1979) 2 E.H.R.R. 245, para.49; *G. v Federal Republic of Germany* (1989) 60 DR 256, 261, para.1; *S.W. v United Kingdom* 21 E.H.R.R. 363, para.34/32). It is accepted that absolute certainty is unattainable, and might entail excessive rigidity since the law must be able to keep pace with changing circumstances, some degree of vagueness is inevitable and development of the law is a recognised feature of common law courts (*Sunday Times v United Kingdom* 2 E.H.R.R. 245 para.49; *X Ltd and Y v United Kingdom* (1982) 28 DR 77, 81, para.9; *S.W. v United Kingdom* 21 E.H.R.R. 363, para.36/34). But the law-making function of the courts must remain within reasonable limits (*X Ltd and Y v United Kingdom* 28 D.R. 77, para.9). Article 7 precludes the punishment of acts not previously punishable, and existing offences may not be extended to cover facts which did not previously constitute a criminal offence (ibid). The law may be clarified and adapted to new circumstances which can reasonably be brought under the original concept of the offence (*X Ltd and Y v United Kingdom* 28 D.R. 77, para.9; *G. v Federal Republic of Germany* 60 DR 256, 261–262). But any development must be consistent with the essence of the offence and be reasonably foreseeable (*S.W. v United Kingdom* 21 E.H.R.R. 363, para.36/34), and the criminal law must not be extensively construed to the detriment of an accused, for instance by analogy (*Kokkinakis v Greece* 17 E.H.R.R. 397, para.52).

36. How, then, does the crime of causing a public nuisance, as currently interpreted and applied, measure up to these standards? Mr Perry, for the Crown, pointed out, quite correctly, that offences such as blasphemous libel (*X Ltd and Y v United Kingdom* 28 D.R. 77), outraging public decency (*S. and G. v United Kingdom* (Application No.17634/91) (unreported) 2 September 1991) and blasphemy (*Wingrove v United Kingdom* (1996) 24 E.H.R.R. 1) had withstood scrutiny at Strasbourg. Only in *Hashman and Harrup v United Kingdom* (1999) 30 E.H.R.R. 241 had a finding that the applicants had acted contra bonos mores been held to lack the quality of being 'prescribed by law'. It was suggested, as put by Emmerson & Ashworth, *Human Rights and Criminal Justice* (2001), para.10–23, that: 'the standard of certainty required under the Convention, and under comparable constitutional principles, is not a particularly exacting one.' I would for my part accept that the offence as defined by Stephen, as defined in *Archbold* (save for the reference to morals), as enacted in the Commonwealth codes quoted above and as applied in the cases (other than *R. v Soul* 70 Cr.App.R. 295) referred to in paras 13 to 22 above is clear, precise, adequately defined and based on a discernible rational principle. A legal adviser asked to give his opinion in advance would ascertain whether the act or omission contemplated was likely to inflict significant injury on a substantial section of the public exercising their ordinary rights as such: if so, an obvious risk of causing a public nuisance would be apparent; if not, not.

37. I cannot, however, accept that *R. v Norbury* [1978] Crim.L.R. 435 and *R. v Johnson (Anthony)* [1997] 1 W.L.R. 367 were correctly decided or that the convictions discussed in paras 23 to 27 above were soundly based (which is not, of course, to say that the defendants' conduct was other than highly reprehensible or that there were not other charges to which the defendants would have had no answer). To permit a conviction of causing a public nuisance to rest on an injury caused to separate individuals rather than on an injury suffered by the community or a significant section of it as a whole was to contradict the rationale of the offence and pervert its nature, in Convention terms to change the essential constituent elements of the offence to the detriment of the accused. The offence was cut adrift from its intellectual moorings. It is in my judgment very significant that when, in 1985, the Law Commission addressed the problem of poison-pen letters, and recommended the creation of a new offence, it did not conceive that the existing offence of public nuisance might be applicable. It is hard to resist the conclusion that the courts have, in effect, re-invented public mischief under another name.

It is also hard to resist the conclusion expressed by Spencer in his article cited above [1989] C.L.J. 55, 77:

'almost all the prosecutions for public nuisance in recent years seem to have taken place in one of two situations: first, where the defendant's behaviour amounted to a statutory offence, typically punishable with a small penalty, and the prosecutor wanted a bigger or extra stick to beat him with, and secondly, where the defendant's behaviour was not obviously criminal at all and the prosecutor could think of nothing else to charge him with.'

As interpreted and applied in the cases referred to in paras 23 to 27 above, the offence of public nuisance lacked the clarity and precision which both the law and the Convention require, as correctly suggested by the commentators in [1978] Crim.L.R. 435, 436 and [1980] Crim.L.R. 234, *Spencer* [1989] C.L.J. 55, 77–79, and Professor Ashworth in his commentary on the present cases at [2004] Crim.L.R. 303, 304–306. See also *McMahon & Binchy*, Law of Torts, 3rd ed. (2000), p.676, fn 6.

38. It seems to me clear that the facts alleged against Mr Rimmington, assuming them to be true, did not cause common injury to a section of the public and so lacked the essential ingredient of common nuisance, whatever other offence they may have constituted. The Crown contended that, if persistent and vexatious telephone calls were a public nuisance, it was a small and foreseeable step to embrace persistent and vexatious postal communications within that crime also. I would agree that if the telephone calls were properly covered it would be a small and foreseeable development, involving no change in the essential constituent elements of the offence, to embrace postal communications also. But, for reasons already given, the crime of public nuisance does not extend to separate and individual telephone calls, however persistent and vexatious, and the extension of the crime to cover postal communications would be a further illegitimate extension. The judge and the Court of Appeal, bound by *R. v Johnson* [1997] 1 W.L.R. 367, reached a different conclusion. I am of opinion that for all the reasons given above, and those given by my noble and learned friends, this appeal must be allowed.

Appeal allowed

2   ACTUS REUS

1. ELEMENTS OF CRIME ACTUS REUS

Traditionally, lawyers refer to the elements of a crime as the actus reus and mens rea. The terms actus reus and mens rea when used to describe the elements of a criminal offence are deceptively simple. Not only is there a host of conceptual pitfalls concealed within each, but there is also no agreement amongst lawyers as to the precise divide between them. Liability for a criminal offence always requires an actus reus and, generally, requires mens rea. Mens rea refers to the mental element of the crime; the blameworthy state of mind that accompanies the act (or conduct) and this concept will be dealt with in Ch.3.

The actus reus of an offence is often explained as being the "conduct" element of the crime. In this context though, the word "conduct" frequently embraces much more than the positive performance of a single physical act. Conduct in this context may, for example, include an omission. Numerous crimes can be committed by an "omission" or a failure to act (see further p.27 below). For example, the driver of a motor vehicle who is suspected of being intoxicated and who, without reasonable excuse, *fails* to provide a specimen of breath for analysis when required to do so commits an offence (see Road Traffic Act 1988 s.7(6)). The central feature of the refusing driver's "conduct" lies in a failure to act. There are other crimes that are described as "state of affairs" offences and which are committed by a defendant who is responsible for that state of affairs. For example, the defendant who is found to be in charge of a motor vehicle while unfit through drink or drugs commits an offence (see Road Traffic Act 1988 s.5(1)(b)) and the offence continues for as long as this state of affairs lasts. The offending conduct lies in the defendant's permitting the state of affairs to exist and continue rather than the performance of a single positive act.

Another aspect of actus reus can be found in the requirement that certain crimes demand that a particular *consequence* (or result) ensues from the conduct. A simple and obvious example would be the crime of murder which requires the defendant's conduct to cause the *consequence* of the victim's death. And there are other crimes that require the presence of particular *circumstances* to accompany the defendant's conduct. An example of this can be seen in the offence of theft which requires the accompanying circumstance that the property *belongs to another* at the time the defendant appropriates it (see further Ch.10, p.599 below). Already, it can be seen that the term actus reus may involve far more than just a simple act.

A.T.H. SMITH, "ON ACTUS REUS AND MENS REA" IN P. GLAZEBROOK (ED), *RESHAPING THE CRIMINAL LAW* (LONDON: SWEET & MAXWELL, 1978), PP.95–98

As the elliptic statements of the basic ingredients of criminal liability that they are frequently taken to be, both expressions [*actus reus* and *mens rea*] are incomplete and misleading. While the term *mens rea* is used in at least three distinct senses, so that failure to distinguish clearly between them leads inevitably to confusion, the terminology of *actus reus* tends to conceal the important principles that are at stake when the courts are deciding what sorts of conduct deserve condemnation as criminal. I do not mean to suggest that the traditional terminology should be abandoned; rather I would argue that a sharper awareness of its limitations might help us to see more clearly what the preconditions to criminal liability really are, and how far they really reflect the principles they are commonly supposed to encapsulate . . .

This division of crime into its constituent parts is an exercise of analytical convenience: the concepts of *actus reus* and *mens rea* are simply tools, useful in the exposition of the criminal law. Great care should, therefore, be taken to avoid determining questions of policy by reference to definition and terminology. Such observations as that the maxim *actus non facit reum nisi mens sit rea* serves the 'important purpose of stressing two basic requirements of criminal liability', make *actus reus* and *mens rea* seem rather more than analytical tools. They have been converted from the descriptive to the normative: to propositions that criminal liability *should* be based on harmful conduct, and *should* require a mental element . . .

The raw material of any crime is the particular social mischief that the legislator is seeking to suppress. But for ascertaining the *actus reus* of any given offence, the starting point for the courts is the statute, or, as it may still be, the common law definition. Questions of statutory interpretation must be solved before the exact scope of the proscribed activity can be known. Where the defendant's conduct can fairly be described as coming within the terms of the proscribed activity, an offence has, prima facie, been committed: liability will ensue unless he advances some explanation of his conduct which shows that it was justified, in which case there is no *actus reus*. As one writer puts it, 'the *actus reus* is a defeasible concept'. But some lawyers are content to say that the requirements of *actus reus* are satisfied whenever the terms of the definition are fulfilled. The danger of taking such a very limited view of what is entailed in the *actus reus*, is that it may too readily be concluded that the harm that the law seeks to prevent has occurred. Much depends on the view taken of the role of defences . . .

Glanville Williams [C.L.G.P., p.20] inclines to the view that all the elements of a crime are divisible into either *actus reus* or *metis rea* and holds that the *actus reus* includes absence of defence. By implication, therefore, all defences are a denial that the prosecution has proved a requisite part of its case. Although they nowhere clearly articulate the point, Professors Smith and Hogan seem to prefer the view that the constituent ingredients of crime are threefold, and include defences which are themselves composites of physical (or external) and mental elements. This mode of analysis is becoming increasingly widespread amongst academic writers, and has been carried furthest by Professor Lanham [[1976] Crim.L.R. 276]. He says that:

> 'as a matter of analysis we can think of a crime as being made up of three ingredients, *actus reus*, *mens rea* and (a negative element) absence of a valid defence. Some defences (e.g. alibi) negative the *actus reus*. Some defences (e.g. I did not mean to do it) negative the *mens rea*. A third group of defences e.g. self-defence) operate without negativing either positive element, in effect as a confession and avoidance. But there is a fourth kind of defence (sic) which is perfectly capable of standing as a confession and avoidance but which normally will negative one or other (or both) of the *actus reus* and *mens rea*.'

According to this view, then *actus reus* and *mens rea* do not encapsulate all the ingredients of a crime.

Notes

1. The use of Latin terminology is not without its critics; Lord Diplock stated in *Miller* [1983] 2 A.C. 161 at 174:

    > "My Lords, it would I think be conducive to clarity of analysis of the ingredients of a crime that is created by statute, as are the great majority of offences today, if we were to avoid bad Latin and instead to think and speak . . . about the conduct of the accused and his state of mind at the time of that conduct, instead of speaking of *actus reus* and *mens rea*."

    This counsel has been adopted by the Law Commission's *Draft Criminal Code Bill* which uses the term "act" to describe the external elements of offences in preference to "actus reus" in the narrow sense as used by Lanham. For "mens rea" the phrase "fault element" is used.

2. Most writers seem agreed that the "act" implied in the phrase "actus reus" does not stop at bodily movements or overt acts:

> "Some acts can only be engaged in, some can only be performed, some only are done, and there are even some that can only take place; and this suggests the richness and variety of those bits of the world that we may choose to regard as acts." (H. Gross, *A Theory of Criminal Justice* (New York: Oxford University Press, 1979), p.133).

Williams takes the view that:

> "the proposition that an offence requires an act requires to be so qualified by exceptions that its utility comes to seem doubtful . . . It is therefore less misleading to say that a crime requires some *external state of affairs* that can be categorised as criminal." (G. Williams, *The Textbook of Criminal Law*, 2nd edn (Stevens & Sons, 1983), p.31).

(The normal mode of definition of offences is *result-oriented* requiring proof of an act or omission and usually proof that the conduct caused a specified result. This mode of definition is backed up with the law of attempts to cover cases where the intended result does not occur. An alternative mode of definition is that which concentrates on conduct, the *inchoate mode*, making it an offence to do certain acts in order to produce a certain outcome; the offence is committed whether or not the outcome results. An example of a result crime is murder where it must be proved that the deceased died as a result of the accused's conduct. An example of a conduct offence is perjury where the relevant conduct is the making of a statement on oath which the maker does not believe to be true; it is not a requirement of the offence that anyone else should believe the statement. For further discussion of result and conduct crimes see: Smith and Hogan, *Criminal Law*, 12th edn (Oxford: Oxford University Press, 2008), pp.46–47; Smith, "The Element of Chance in Criminal Liability" [1971] Crim. L.R. 63; Ashworth, "Defining Criminal Offences Without Harm" in P. Smith (ed), *Criminal Law: Essays in Honour of J.C. Smith* (1987).)

----

2. VOLUNTARINESS

Criminal liability is founded on the notion of individual autonomy. A person should only be criminally liable where he or she is responsible for his or her conduct. Responsibility presumes that the conduct was voluntarily engaged on by that person. If the conduct is involuntary there should be no criminal liability. This raises the question, however, of what does "voluntary" or "involuntary" mean?

H.L.A. HART, "ACT OF WILL AND RESPONSIBILITY" IN *PUNISHMENT AND RESPONSIBILITY*, 2ND EDN (OXFORD: OXFORD UNIVERSITY PRESS, 2008), P.90

The General Doctrine
In this lecture I propose to air some doubts which I have long felt about a doctrine, concerning criminal responsibility, which has descended from the philosophy of conduct of the eighteenth century, through Austin, to modern English writers on the criminal law. This is the doctrine that, besides the elements of knowledge of circumstances and foresight of consequences, in terms of which many writers define *mens rea*, there is another 'mental' or at least psychological element which is required for responsibility: the accused's 'conduct' (including his omissions where these are criminally punishable) must, so it is said, be voluntary and not involuntary. This element in responsibility is more fundamental than *mens rea* in the sense of knowledge of circumstances or foresight of consequences; for even where *mens rea* in that sense is not required, and responsibility is 'strict' or 'absolute' . . ., this element, according to some modern writers, is still required . . .

In many textbooks there are general assertions that for *all* criminal responsibility conduct must be 'voluntary', 'conduct [must be] the result of the exercise of his will' there must be an 'act with its element of will', 'an act due to the deliberate exercise of the will'. Yet, surely, even if there is any such general doctrine, these phrases are very dark. What does doctrine mean? What after all is the will? . . .

We know now what the general doctrine means: it defines an act in terms of the simplest thing we can do: this is the minimum feat of contracting our muscles. Conduct is 'voluntary' or 'the expression of an act of will' if the muscular contraction which, on the physical side, is the initiating element in what are loosely thought of as simple actions, is caused by a desire for the same contractions. This is all the mysterious element of the 'will' amounts to: it is this which is the minimum indispensable link between mind and body required for responsibility even where responsibility is strict . . .

The . . . theory that has got into our law books through Austin is first, nonsensical when applied to omissions, and secondly cannot characterise what is amiss even in involuntary interventions; for the desire to move our muscles, which it says is missing there, is not present in normal voluntary action either.

Consider Hart's alternative definition under which he seeks to classify those acts generally regarded as not voluntary:

"... We could characterise involuntary movements such as those made in epilepsy, or in a stroke, or mere reflex actions to blows or stings, as movements of the body which occurred although they were not appropriate, i.e. required for any action (in the ordinary sense of action) which the agent believed himself to be doing."

G. WILLIAMS, *TEXTBOOK OF CRIMINAL LAW*, 2ND EDN (STEVENS & SONS, 1983), P.148

Lawyers sometimes speak of a voluntary act meaning only that it was willed. Since every act is by definition willed, there is no need to call it voluntary.

The element of volition in an act has greatly exercised the philosophers. I can look at my hand, say to myself 'Hand, move to the left', and then cause it to move to the left. But that is not the way in which I usually live and move. I do not consciously direct orders to my muscles. Two philosophers, Ryle and Melden, have attempted to argue away the notion of will. They build their case upon the difficulty of identifying conscious volitions accompanying bodily movement. Certainly it would be false to assume that every act is the result of deliberation: I may scratch my nose while thinking, without knowing I am doing it or recollecting I have done it. Even when the act is conscious, introspection does not show a conscious exercise of will preceding conduct. When I move my arms, say in writing a letter, I do not consciously decide to move them before moving them. It is true that electrical impulses run from the motor nerve cells in the spinal cord through the nerve fibres to the muscles; and these muscles are under the control of my brain. But the mental functioning that controls movement is not conscious determination, and it takes place at practically the same time as the movement. Will is the mental activity accompanying the type of bodily movement that we call an act. It is, of course, possible to will the absence of an act, as when we sit still.

A bodily movement is said to be willed, generally speaking, when the person in question could have refrained from it if he had so willed, that is, he could have kept still. Movements that are the result of epilepsy, for example, are involuntary or unwilled because the person concerned cannot by any mental effort avoid them. Whatever the difficulties in explaining what we mean by volition, everyone realises the important difference between doing something and having something happen to one; and this distinction is a basic postulate of a moral view of human behaviour.

Note

Voluntariness and consciousness

Where a person performs an act in a state of unconsciousness or impaired consciousness this is referred to as automatism. Automatism may arise from a variety of causes. Where it arises from illness or disease it may amount to insanity. Automatism and insanity are dealt with in Ch.4. It is not *necessary* for a person to be unconscious before his or her acts are said to be involuntary. A person suffering from St Vitus Dance, or having a muscle spasm, is acting involuntarily under either the Hart "inappropriateness" formula, or the Williams "inability to refrain" test. Nor is unconsciousness in itself *sufficient* to avoid liability. As Lord Denning said in *Bratty v Attorney General for Northern Ireland* [1963] A.C. 386 at 410: "It is not every involuntary act which leads to a complete acquittal." This dictum applies in particular where the defendant is responsible for his or her own incapacity, for example, where he or she is voluntarily intoxicated. In this situation *moral* voluntariness, arising from the prior voluntary act of getting drunk (for which the defendant is responsible), suffices to establish criminal liability for the unconsciously committed subsequent act (see further Ch.4).

Is voluntariness a purely physical concept or does the law recognise moral involuntariness in the sense that while a person may will an action, other factors may be operating which suggest that the exercise of will in this situation was not free, for example due to a threat emanating from a human agent or to dangers or threats emanating from the situation in which he or she is placed? The law does not recognise moral involuntariness as a denial of the actus reus but confines voluntariness to a consideration of the purely physical. Allowances may be made for moral involuntariness through the defences of necessity, duress and duress of circumstances but these are limited by policy considerations which would not be possible if moral involuntariness operated to deny the existence of an actus reus, i.e. no actus reus no crime (see further Ch.6).

The case which follows has also been criticised for ignoring the requirement of voluntariness.

R. V LARSONNEUR

(1933) 97 J.P. 206

The defendant, a French subject, landed in the UK with a French passport. This was indorsed with conditions prohibiting her employment here. On March 22 these conditions were varied by a condition requiring her to leave the UK that day. This she did, going to the Irish Free State. The Irish authorities ordered her deportation and she was brought to Holyhead in the custody of the Irish police and she was there handed over to the English police. She was charged that "she being an alien to whom leave to land in the United Kingdom has been refused, was found in the United Kingdom contrary to arts 1(3)(g) and 18(1)(b) of the Aliens Order, 1920, as amended by S.R. & O. No.326 of 1923 and 715 of 1931." She was convicted at London Sessions and appealed.

LORD HEWART CJ

The fact is, as the evidence shows, that the appellant is an alien. She has a French passport, which bears this statement under the date March 14, 1933. 'Leave to land granted at Folkestone this day on condition that the holder does not enter any employment, paid or unpaid, whilst in the United Kingdom', but on March 22 that condition was varied and one finds these words: 'The condition attached to the grant of leave to land is hereby varied so as to require departure from the United Kingdom not later than March 22, 1933.' Then follows the signature of an Under-Secretary of State. In fact, the appellant went to the Irish Free State and afterwards, in circumstances which are perfectly immaterial, so far as this appeal is concerned, came back to England. She was at Holyhead on April 21, 1933, practically a month after the day limited by the condition of her passport . . .

Appeal dismissed

Notes

Part of the problem with this case is that the prohibition related to a state of affairs rather than a physical act. One way of solving the apparent injustice is by the implication of mens rea into the offence:

as in *Lim Chin Aik v R.*, below, p.162. But it may still be possible to reconcile the case with the doctrine of a voluntary act. Lanham defends the decision, though not the reasoning, in "Larsonneur Revisited" [1976] Crim. L.R. 276. He suggests that Miss Larsonneur was herself responsible for her seemingly unfortunate fate, and no more deserved acquittal than a person who becomes an automaton through drink or drugs. It appears from a confession which she made to the police that Miss Larsonneur had gone to Ireland to arrange a marriage between herself and an Englishman, and had been told by the Irish police to leave by 17 April:

> "Miss Larsonneur's story . . . reveals that the defendant brought upon herself the act of compulsion which led to her being charged . . . No-one could claim that *Larsonneur* stood as a shining example of jurisprudence. But it can hardly be regarded as the last word in judicial depravity. If Miss Larsonneur had been dragged kicking and screaming from France into the United Kingdom by kidnappers and the same judgment had been given by the Court of Criminal Appeal, the defence of unforeseeable compulsion would truly have been excluded and the case would be the worst blot on the pages of the modern criminal law. But she wasn't and it wasn't and it isn't."

See also *Winzar v Chief Constable of Kent*, *The Times*, March 28, 1983. The appellant had been brought to hospital on a stretcher. He was diagnosed as being drunk and was asked to leave. When he was later found slumped on a seat in the corridor the police were called. They removed him to the highway and then placed him in the police car charging him with being drunk on the highway contrary to s.12 of the Licensing Act 1872. The Queen's Bench Divisional Court upheld his conviction on the basis that as the purpose of the offence was to deal with the nuisance of public drunkenness, it was sufficient to establish guilt to prove that the person was drunk while in a public place; how he came to be there was considered to be irrelevant.

In *Robinson-Pierre* [2013] EWCA Crim 2396, the defendant was tried for an offence of being the owner of a dog that caused injury while dangerously out of control in a public place (see ss.3(1) and (4) of the Dangerous Dogs Act 1991). The Court of Appeal considered the question of liability should the dog have been unleashed by a third party and not by any act of the defendant. The Court stated that Parliament *did* have the power to create a "state of affairs" offence for which the defendant would be liable even though that state of affairs may not have been brought about by any act of the defendant, provided that clear statutory wording made it clear that this was Parliament's intention. In this case, the statute was not clear as to whether this was Parliament's intention and thus the defendant would not be liable for the act of the third party.

It seems that "voluntariness" is a slippery concept which raises, but does not answer, all sorts of questions about responsibility.

For further exploration of the utility of strict liability, see Ch.3, p.145.

Questions

1. In both *Larsonneur* and *Winzar* it is possible to identify a prior moral fault on the part of each defendant which preceded the commission of the situational offence. Is it appropriate for a court to delve into history to find such a prior moral fault? If so, how far back should a court be permitted to delve?

2. In *Winzar* could the police officers have been charged with procuring his offence?

3.   Is it ever justifiable to hold a defendant liable for the act of a third party which is performed without his knowledge?

----

3. OMISSIONS

P.R. GLAZEBROOK, "CRIMINAL OMISSIONS: THE DUTY REQUIREMENT IN OFFENCES AGAINST THE PERSON" (1960) 76 L.Q.R. 386 AT 387

Although a failure to act may have as serious consequences as an act, and although any difference between acts and omissions is often denied, the distinction is deeply embedded in the law. This fact is no less inescapable because there is no precise test for distinguishing an act from an omission. Human conduct may often be described in either positive or negative terms, though usually one way rather than the other will appear more natural . . . But difficult cases there will be, and their very existence leads to the imposition of liability for omissions. A man is in his spring cart; the reins are not in his hands, but lying on the horse's back. While the horse trots down a hill a young child runs across the road in front of the cart, is knocked down and killed. Had the man held the reins he could have pulled the horse up. Did he kill the child by driving the cart recklessly, or by recklessly failing to drive the cart?

The facts of the case cited in the last sentence are those of *R. v Dalloway* (below, p.48).
   One distinction which is important is that between offences whose essence is an omission and those which, though usually committed by a positive act, can also be committed by omission. The former are *conduct* crimes while the latter are *result* crimes.

G.P. FLETCHER, *RETHINKING CRIMINAL LAW* (BOSTON: LITTLE, BROWN, 1978), P.421

Both 'acts' and 'omissions' can be brought under the general rubric of 'conduct' . . . If there is a special problem in punishing omissions, we can learn what it is only by examining the contexts in which lawyers conventionally talk about 'omissions' or 'failing to act'. In fact, there is a radical cleavage between two forms of liability for 'omissions'. According to one type, the focus of liability is a breach of statutory obligation to act [appropriate English examples would be failure to display a vehicle tax disc, failure to report an accident] . . . We shall call this the field of liability for 'breach of duty to act'. The contrasting field is the imposition of liability for failing to intervene, when necessary, to prevent the occurrence of a serious harm such as death or the destruction of property we shall refer to this second type of liability as 'commission by omission'. The substantive difference [between the two] is that liability for breach of a statutory duty does not presuppose the occurrence of harm . . . In contrast, the death of the victim is essential for committing homicide by omission. The gravamen of liability for 'breach of duty' is the breach itself; for commission by omission, the occurrence of a particular result.

B. HOGAN, "OMISSIONS AND THE DUTY MYTH" IN P. SMITH (ED), *CRIMINAL LAW: ESSAYS IN HONOUR OF J.C. SMITH* (LONDON: BUTTERWORTHS, 1987)

[T]here is no way you can *cause* an event by doing nothing (or is it, more precisely, by not doing anything?) to prevent it . . .
   But we immediately encounter the problem of what is meant by doing nothing, or, rather, not doing anything. The vexing problem of the distinction between act and omission. And 'although any difference between act and omission is often denied', wrote Mr. Peter Glazebrook, 'the distinction is deeply embedded in the law'. True enough, but my own view is that the distinction is at best unhelpful and at worst misleading. It is, however, well entrenched, has found its way into the Draft Criminal Code Bill and, whatever I say, is likely to stay entrenched for some time yet. But that does not deter me from putting another view which I believe to be more logically attractive and even to express more accurately the common law . . .

[I]t would be much more conducive to clarity of thought if we spoke of conduct and causation. If any proposition is self-evident (and, arguably, none is) it is that a person cannot be held to have caused an event which he did not cause . . .

This is not to say that I am against liability for omissions . . . There are of course numerous instances where Parliament (and a handful where the common law) has penalised omissions but what is noteworthy is that the defendant is penalised for the omission but not visited with liability for the consequences of that omission. Thus it is an offence under s.6(l) of the Maritime Conventions Act 1911, punishable with two years' imprisonment on indictment, for the master of a vessel to fail to render assistance to anyone in danger of being lost at sea. Fair enough, but it is to be noted that the master is made liable in respect of the omission; he is not, rightly enough, made liable in respect of any death or injury for any such death or injury is not of his doing. Exceptionally a statute may punish an omission as severely as the completed offence. A well-known example arises under the Road Traffic Act 1972, as amended, under which the punishment for a failure to provide a specimen is the same as for driving with an excessive blood-alcohol concentration. The driver is, however, convicted and punished in respect of the omission; he is not convicted and punished for the separate offence of driving etc. Since this has not been proved. In these circumstances it is entirely acceptable to punish the motorist for his omission as severely as for the driving offence but it would be wrong to convict him for the driving offence and unnecessarily to deem him to have driven over the prescribed limit . . .

'[I]n no sense am I against liability for omissions. I would ask only two conditions of a law punishing omissions. One is that it be clearly articulated and the other is that it seeks to punish the defendant for his dereliction and does not artificially treat him as a cause of the event he has not brought about by his conduct.'

While Hogan's arguments are persuasive they do not yet represent the law which still speaks in terms of duties. Accordingly, Fletcher's two-fold classification will be used as a framework for considering the cases in this area.

i. Breach of Duty to Act

Note

Williams' *Textbook of Criminal Law*, 2nd edn (1983), p.148 states:

> "a crime can be committed by omission, but there can be no omission in law in the absence of a duty to act. The reason is obvious. If there is an act, someone acts; but if there is an omission, everyone (in a sense) omits. We omit to do everything in the world that is not done. Only those of us omit in law who are under a duty to act.
>
> When a statute expressly or impliedly creates an offence of omission, it points out the person under the duty by the wording of the offence."

The common law rarely imposed liability purely for omissions; an example was misprison of felony. Occasionally an indictment has been found to lie at common law for neglect of a duty imposed by common law or statute; see the following case.

R V DYTHAM

[1979] 3 All E.R. 641

The defendant, a police constable, was on duty in uniform near a club when a man was ejected from the club and kicked to death by a "bouncer". D took no steps to intervene and drove off. He appealed against conviction for misconduct whilst acting as an officer of justice.

LORD WIDGERY CJ

[T]he argument . . . ran deep into constitutional and jurisprudential history. The effect of it was that not every failure to discharge a duty which devolved on a person as the holder of a public office gave rise to the common law offence of misconduct in that office. As counsel for the appellant put it, non-feasance was not enough. There must be a malfeasance or at least a misfeasance involving an element of corruption. In support of this contention a number of cases were cited from 18th and 19th century reports. It is the fact that in nearly all of them the misconduct asserted involved some corrupt taint; but this appears to have been an accident of circumstances and not a necessary incident of the offence. Misconduct in a public office is more vividly exhibited where dishonesty is revealed as part of the dereliction of duty. Indeed in some cases the conduct impugned cannot be shown to have been misconduct unless it was done with a corrupt or oblique motive . . .

[I]n Stephen's Digest of the Criminal Law are to be found these words:

'Every public officer commits a misdemeanour who wilfully neglects to perform any duty which he is bound either by common law or by statute to perform provided that the discharge of such duty is not attended with greater danger than a man of ordinary firmness and activity may be expected to encounter.'

In support of this proposition *R. v Wyat* (1705) 1 Salk. 380 is cited as well as *R. v Bembridge* (1783) 3 Doug.K.B. 327, a judgment of Lord Mansfield. The neglect must be wilful and not merely inadvertent; and it must be culpable in the sense that it is without reasonable excuse or justification.

In the present case it was not suggested that the appellant could not have summoned or sought assistance to help the victim or to arrest his assailants. The charge as framed left this answer open to him. Not surprisingly he did not seek to avail himself of it, for the facts spoke strongly against any such answer. The allegation made was not of mere non-feasance but of deliberate failure and wilful neglect. This involves an element of culpability which is not restricted to corruption or dishonesty but which must be of such a degree that the misconduct impugned is calculated to injure the public interest so as to call for condemnation and punishment. Whether such a situation is revealed by the evidence is a matter that a jury has to decide.

Appeal dismissed

Question

Did the officer's failure to act cause the death of the victim of the bouncer's assault?

Note

In *Attorney General's Reference (No.3 of 2003)* [2005] Q.B. 73, the Court of Appeal confirmed the elements of the offence of misconduct in a public office are: (1) a public officer acting as such; (2) who wilfully neglects to perform his duty and/or wilfully misconducts himself; (3) to such a degree as to amount to an abuse of the public's trust in the office holder; (4) without reasonable excuse or justification. As with other criminal charges, it will be for the jury to decide whether the offence is proved. As to the meaning of "wilfully" see Ch.3, p.155.

----

ii. Commission by Omission

Note

An alternative heading would be *"liability for failing to intervene"*. Offences are usually worded in terms requiring active conduct; can liability arise from causing the prohibited result by omitting to act? It is generally recognised that the attitude adopted by the common law is well summarised in the passage below.

LORD MACAULAY'S WORKS, EDITED BY LADY TREVELYAN (1866), VOL.VII, P.497

It is, indeed, most highly desirable that men should not merely abstain from doing harm to their neighbours, but should render active services to their neighbours. In general, however, the penal law must content itself with keeping men from doing positive harm, and must leave to public opinion, and to the teachers of morality and religion, the office of furnishing men with motives for doing positive good. It is evident that to attempt to punish men by law for not rendering to others all the service which it is their duty to render to others would be preposterous.

We must grant impunity to the vast majority of those omissions which a benevolent morality would pronounce reprehensible, and must content ourselves with punishing such omissions only when they are distinguished from the rest by some circumstance which marks them out as peculiarly fit objects of penal legislation.

Not all offences are susceptible of commission by omission. Most of the cases concern murder or manslaughter although liability could arise in a similar way for causing grievous bodily harm under section 20 of the Offences Against the Person Act 1861.

Not all omissions give rise to liability; liability depends on there being a duty, recognised by the law, to act or intervene in the circumstances. There are four situations in which such duties have been recognised: duties arising out of contract, duties arising out of relationship, duties arising from care of the helpless and infirm, duty arising from creation of a dangerous situation.

(a) Duty arising out of contract

R. V PITTWOOD

(1902) 19 T.L.R. 37

The defendant was a gatekeeper on the Somerset and Dorset Railway. He had to keep the gate shut whenever a train was passing during the period 07.00 to 19.00. One afternoon the gate was open and a hay cart which was crossing the line was hit by a train. One man was killed and another was seriously injured. Witnesses testified that the road was an accommodation road and not a public road. The accused was charged with manslaughter.

Wright J, without calling upon the prosecution, gave judgment. He said he was clearly of opinion that in this case there was gross and criminal negligence, as the man was paid to keep the gate shut and protect the public. In his opinion there were three grounds on which the verdict could be supported: (1) There might be cases of misfeasance and cases of mere nonfeasance. Here it was quite clear there was evidence of misfeasance as the prisoner directly contributed to the accident. (2) A man might incur criminal liability from a duty arising out of contract. The learned judge quoted in support of this *R. v Nicholls* (1875) 13 Cox 75; *R. v Elliott* (1889) 16 Cox 710; *R. v Benge* (1865) 4 F. & F. 594; *R. v Hughes* (1857) Dears. & B. 248. The strongest case of all was, perhaps, *R. v Instan*, [below, p.31] and that case clearly governed the present charge. (3) With regard to the point that this was only an occupation road, he clearly held that it was not, as the company had assumed the liability of protecting the public whenever they crossed the road . . .

Verdict: Guilty

(b) Duty arising out of relationship

Note

The existence of close relationships can give rise to a duty to act, such as that owed by parents to their children or spouses to each other. There is little common law authority on the point although it is generally accepted that there is such a duty. In *Gibbins and Proctor* (1918) 13 Cr. App. R. 134 the father of a child and his partner were convicted of murdering the child who had died as a result of their withholding food from it. The father had breached the duty owed by parents to care for their children while Proctor, by taking money to buy food, had assumed a duty towards the child. Statute has largely intervened in the case of parents' duty to their children. For a case on wilful neglect under the Children and Young Persons Act 1933 see *Sheppard*, below, p.118.

(c) Duty arising from the assumption of care for the helpless and infirm

R. V INSTAN

[1893] 1 Q.B. 450

The defendant lived with her aunt who was 73 years old. The aunt was healthy until shortly before her death. During the last 12 days of her life she had gangrene in her leg and could not fend for herself, move about nor summon help. Only the defendant knew of this condition. She appeared not to have given her aunt any food nor did she seek medical or nursing aid. She was charged with manslaughter and convicted.

LORD COLERIDGE CJ

We are all of opinion that this conviction must be affirmed. It would not be correct to say that every moral obligation involves a legal duty; but every legal duty is founded on a moral obligation. A legal common law duty is nothing else than the enforcing by law of that which is a moral obligation without legal enforcement. There can be no question in this case that it was the clear duty of the prisoner to impart to the deceased so much as was necessary to sustain life of the food which she from time to time took in, and which was paid for by the deceased's own money for the purpose of the maintenance of herself and the prisoner; it was only through the instrumentality of the prisoner that the deceased could get the food. There was, therefore, a common law duty imposed upon the prisoner which she did not discharge.

   Nor can there be any question that the failure of the prisoner to discharge her legal duty at least accelerated the death of the deceased, if it did not actually cause it. There is no case directly in point; but it would be a slur upon and a discredit to the administration of justice in this country if there were any doubt as to the legal principle, or as to the present case being within it. The prisoner was under a moral obligation to the deceased from which arose a legal duty towards her; that legal duty the prisoner has wilfully and deliberately left unperformed, with the consequence that there has been an acceleration of the death of the deceased owing to the non-performance of that legal duty. It is unnecessary to say more than that upon the evidence this conviction was most properly arrived at.

Conviction affirmed

Note

Consider the two following cases in light of the following extract from the judgment of Erie CJ in *R. v Charlotte Smith* (1865) 10 Cox 82, where a master was charged with the homicide of his servant by, amongst other things, neglecting to give her sufficient food or wholesome lodgings:

> "The law is undisputed that, if a person having the care or custody of another who is helpless, neglects to supply him with the necessaries of life and thereby causes or accelerates his death, it is a criminal offence. But the law is clear, that if a person having the exercise of free will, chooses to stay in a service where bad food and lodging is provided, and death is thereby caused, the master is not criminally liable".

R. V WILLIAM SMITH

(1826) 2 C. & P. 449; 172 E.R. 203

The defendants were two brothers and a sister. They had lived with their mother and with a helpless idiot brother. The mother died and it was alleged that the idiot brother was neglected and suffered in health. The defendants were charged with assault and false imprisonment.

BURROUGH J

I am clearly of opinion that on the facts proved there is no assault and no imprisonment in the eye of the law, and all the rest of the charge is nonfeasance. In the case of *Squires* and his wife for starving the apprentice, the husband was convicted, because it was his duty to maintain the apprentice, and the wife was acquitted, because there was no such obligation on her. I expected to have found in the will of the father that the defendants were bound, if they took the father's property, to maintain his brother; but, under the will, they are only bound to pay him £50 a year, and not bound to maintain him. William Smith appears to have been the owner of the house, and Thomas and Sarah were mere inmates of it, as their idiot brother might be; as to these latter, there could clearly be no legal obligation on them: and how can I tell the jury that either of the defendants had such a care of this unfortunate man as to make them criminally liable for omitting to attend to him. There is strong proof that there was some negligence; but my point is, that omission, without a duty, will not create an indictable offence. There is a deficiency of proof of the allegation of care, custody and control, which must be taken to be legal care, custody and control. Whether an indictment might be so framed, as to suit this case, I do not know; but on this indictment I am clearly of opinion that the defendants must be acquitted.

Verdict: Not guilty

R. V STONE AND DOBINSON

[1977] 1 Q.B. 354

S, who was 67, partially deaf, nearly blind and of low intelligence, cohabited with D, aged 43, who was described as ineffectual and inadequate. Also living with them was S's mentally subnormal son. S's younger sister, F, came to live there in 1972, suffering from anorexia nervosa. She stayed in her room most of the time though she was known to creep down and cook herself something to eat when S and D went to the pub. S and D attempted to find her doctor in spring 1975 though she refused to tell them his name. In July, D and a neighbour washed F who, by this time, was confined to bed and lying amidst her own excrement. The defendants were unable to use the telephone and a neighbour was unsuccessful in getting a local doctor to visit F. No one was informed of F's condition, even though a social worker came to the house from time to time to visit S's son. F died in August. The pathologist's report suggested that she had been in need of urgent medical attention for days, if not weeks. S and D appealed against their convictions for manslaughter.

GEOFFREY LANE LJ

There is no dispute, broadly speaking, as to the matters on which the jury must be satisfied before they can convict of manslaughter in circumstances such as the present. They are (1) that the defendant undertook the care of a person who by reason of age or infirmity was unable to care for himself; (2) that the defendant was grossly negligent in regard to his duty of care; (3) that by reason of such negligence the person died . . .

[Counsel for the appellants] submitted that the evidence which the judge had suggested to the jury might support the assumption of a duty by the appellants does not, when examined, succeed in doing so. He suggests that the situation here is unlike any reported case. Fanny came to this house as a lodger. Largely, if not entirely due to her own eccentricity and failure to look after herself or feed herself properly, she became increasingly infirm and immobile and eventually unable to look after herself. Is it to be said, asks Mr. Coles rhetorically, that by the mere fact of becoming infirm and helpless in these circumstances she casts a duty on her brother and the appellant Dobinson . . .? The suggestion is that, heartless though it may seem, this is one of those situations where the appellants were entitled to do nothing; where no duty was cast upon them to help, any more than it is cast upon a man to rescue a stranger from drowning, however easy such a rescue might be.

. . . Whether Fanny was a lodger or not she was a blood relation of the appellant Stone; she was occupying a room in his house; the appellant Dobinson had undertaken the duty of trying to wash her, of taking such food to her as she required. There was ample evidence that each appellant was aware of the poor condition she was in by mid-July. It was not disputed that no effort was made to summon an ambulance or the social services or the police . . .

This was not a situation analogous to the drowning stranger. They did make efforts to care. They tried to get a doctor; they tried to discover the previous doctor. The appellant Dobinson helped with the washing and the provision of food. All these matters were put before the jury in terms which we find it impossible to fault. The jury were entitled to find that the duty had been assumed. They were entitled to conclude that once Fanny became helplessly infirm, as she had by July 19, the appellants were, in the circumstances, obliged either to summon help or else to care for Fanny themselves . . .

Appeal dismissed

Questions

1.   Can this case be distinguished from *R. v William Smith*, p.32 above? Does the following statement of principle by Brett J in *R. v Nicholls* (1875) 13 Cox 75 help?

"If a grown up person chooses to undertake the charge of a human creature helpless either from infancy, simplicity, lunacy or other infirmity, he is bound to execute that charge without (at all events) *wicked* negligence."

2.   Would Stone and Dobinson have been liable if F was Stone's sister-in-law (i.e. his brother's wife)? What was crucial in giving rise to the duty on Stone: the fact that Fanny was his sister; that he allowed her to live in his house; or both?

3.   Would they have been liable if they had made no efforts to help at all?

4.   Did Stone and Dobinson *cause* F's death? Farrier's Note at (1978) 41 M.L.R. 211, n.6 raises the question whether the restrictive policy adopted in *Blaue*, below, p.51 should apply where the causal conduct consists of an omission.

Note

The situations in which a duty may arise, however, are not closed: new situations may give rise to the recognition of a duty. In *Khan and Khan* [1998] Crim. L.R. 830, two drug dealers appealed from convictions of manslaughter arising out of their supply of heroin to the deceased and their failure to summon medical assistance when she went into a coma following her consumption of the drug. In quashing their convictions Swinton Thomas LJ stated:

"To extend the duty to summon medical assistance to a drug dealer who supplies heroin to a person who subsequently dies on the facts of this case would undoubtedly enlarge the class of persons to whom, on previous authority, such a duty may be owed. It may be correct to hold that such a duty does arise . . . Unfortunately, the question as to the existence or otherwise of [such] a duty . . . was not at any time considered by the Judge, and the jury was given no direction in relation to it."

The Court of Appeal took the view that it was for the judge to rule whether the facts were capable of giving rise to a duty and, if so, for the jury to decide whether there was such a duty. The danger with this approach is that the jury may be unduly influenced by the fact of death and conclude that there must have been a duty to prevent such a death. In a later case, *Singh (Gurphal)* [1999] Crim. L.R. 582, the Court of Appeal affirmed the trial judge's decision that whether a situation gave rise to a duty was a question of law for the judge to determine which, it is submitted, is the better view.

One such situation arose in *Ruffell* [2003] EWCA Crim 122. D was convicted of manslaughter following his failure to render assistance to V who had lapsed into unconsciousness after taking a mixture of cocaine and heroin. V was at D's house and having seen V become unconscious, D made some efforts to revive him by splashing water on his face, placing him by a radiator, placing him by a window for air and wrapping him in towels. D telephoned V's mother, informing her that V was sick because of drinking alcohol and that V was sitting on the doorstep. V's mother asked D to take V inside and cover him with a blanket. D said he would but instead, he simply went to bed and slept. V died due to the combined effects of hypothermia and opiate intoxication. The Court of Appeal approved the trial judge's direction to the jury that they could find that D had assumed a duty of care from the fact that V was a guest in D's house and that D had made some efforts to revive V after the drug taking.

Where a person is under a duty to care for another, whether due to relationship or because the duty is imposed as a result of care rendered to a helpless or infirm person, the question arises whether that person may be released from that duty. See the next case.

AIREDALE NHS TRUST V BLAND

[1993] A.C. 789 HL

Bland had been in a persistent vegetative state for three-and-a-half years being fed artificially and mechanically by a nasogastric tube. The doctors were unanimously of the opinion that there was no hope of recovery or improvement of any kind. The consultant, supported by other distinguished medical experts, was of the opinion that treatment and feeding should cease which would result in death within one to two weeks. The health authority applied for declarations that it and the doctors could lawfully discontinue all life-sustaining treatment (namely artificial feeding and antibiotic drugs) except for such as would be required to enable him to die without pain or distress. The parents and family of Bland supported the application. The judge granted the applications and the Official Solicitor appealed to the Court of Appeal and from its decision to the House of Lords contending that such a withdrawal of life-sustaining treatment would be a breach of the doctor's duty to care for his patient and would constitute a crime.

LORD BROWNE WILKINSON

If I am right so far in my analysis, the critical decision to be made is whether it is in the best interests of Anthony Bland to continue the invasive medical care involved in artificial feeding. That question is not the same as, 'Is it in Anthony Bland's best interests that he should die?' The latter question assumes that it is lawful to perpetuate the patient's life; but such perpetuation of life can only be achieved if it is lawful to continue to invade the bodily integrity of the patient by invasive medical care. Unless the doctor has reached the affirmative conclusion that it is in the patient's best interest to continue the invasive care, such care must cease.

LORD MUSTILL

6. Best Interests: the termination of treatment

After much expression of negative opinions I turn to an argument which in my judgment is logically defensible and consistent with the existing law. In essence it turns the previous argument on its head by directing the inquiry to the interests of the patient, not in the termination of life but in the continuation of his treatment. It runs as follows. (i) The cessation of nourishment and hydration is an omission not an act. (ii) Accordingly, the cessation will not be a criminal act unless the doctors are under a present duty to continue the regime. (iii) At the time when Anthony Bland came into the care of the doctors decisions had to be made about his care which he was unable to make for himself. In accordance with *F v West Berkshire Health Authority* [1990] 2 A.C. 1 these decisions were to be made in his best interests. Since the possibility that he might recover still existed his best interests required that he should be supported in the hope that this would happen. These best interests justified the application of the necessary regime without his consent. (iv) All hope of recovery has now been abandoned. Thus, although the termination of his life is not in the best interests of Anthony Bland, his best interests in being kept alive have also disappeared, taking with them the justification for the non-consensual regime and the correlative duty to keep it in being. (v) Since there is no longer a duty to provide nourishment and hydration a failure to do so cannot be a criminal offence.

My Lords, I must recognise at once that this chain of reasoning makes an unpromising start by transferring the morally and intellectually dubious distinction between acts and omissions into a context where the ethical foundations of the law are already open to question. The opportunity for anomaly and excessively fine distinctions, often depending more on the way in which the problem happens to be stated than on any real distinguishing features . . . .. All this being granted, we are still forced to take the law as we find it and try to make it work. Moreover, although in cases near the borderline the categorisation of conduct will be exceedingly hard, I believe that nearer the periphery there will be many instances which fall quite clearly into one category rather than the other. In my opinion the present is such a case, and in company with Compton J. in *Barber v Superior Court of Los Angeles County* (1983) 147 Cal App (3d) 1006 at 1017 amongst others I consider that the proposed conduct will fall into the category of omissions.

I therefore consider the argument to be soundly based. Now that the time has come when Anthony Bland has no further interest in being kept alive, the necessity to do so, created by his inability to make a choice, has gone; and the justification for the invasive care and treatment together with the duty to provide it have also gone. Absent a duty, the omission to perform what had previously been a duty will no longer be a breach of the criminal law.

Note

Their Lordships were at pains to distinguish cases such as the present which they categorised as omissions (there being no continuing duty to act due to the futility of the treatment) from those where positive acts are involved, such as the administration of lethal drugs, to bring about a patient's death. They found it difficult to justify the distinction, Lord Browne-Wilkinson confessing:

> "Finally, the conclusion I have reached will appear to some to be almost irrational. How can it be lawful to allow a patient to die slowly, though painlessly, over a period of weeks from lack of food but unlawful to produce his immediate death by a lethal injection, thereby saving his family from yet another ordeal to add to the tragedy that has already struck them? I find it difficult to find a moral answer to that question. But it is undoubtedly the law and nothing I have said casts doubt on the proposition that the doing of a positive act with the intention of ending life is and remains murder."

They also sought to explain why the administration of drugs which had a medicinal purpose, such as pain relief, but which inevitably accelerated death, would not give rise to criminal liability on the basis of what was in the patient's best interests. Lord Goff stated:

"It is this principle too which, in my opinion, underlies the established rule that a doctor may, when caring for a patient who is, for example, dying of cancer, lawfully administer painkilling drugs despite the fact that he knows that an incidental effect of that application will be to abbreviate the patient's life. Such a decision may properly be made as part of the care of the living patient, in his best interests; and, on this basis, the treatment will be lawful. Moreover, where the doctor's treatment of his patient is lawful, the patient's death will be regarded in law as exclusively caused by the injury or disease to which his condition is attributable."

The distinctions are fine, even strained, but on such distinctions depend the classification of transactions as lawful or unlawful. Their Lordships could not avoid such distinctions as "active" euthanasia is unlawful and only legislation can change that, Lord Goff stating:

"[T]he law draws a crucial distinction between cases in which a doctor decides not to provide, or to continue to provide, for his patient treatment or care which could or might prolong his life and those in which he decides, for example by administering a lethal drug, actively to bring his patient's life to an end. As I have already indicated, the former may be lawful, either because the doctor is giving effect to his patient's wishes by withholding the treatment or care, or even in certain circumstances in which (on principles which I shall describe) the patient is incapacitated from stating whether or not he gives his consent. But it is not lawful for a doctor to administer a drug to his patient to bring about his death, even though that course is prompted by a humanitarian desire to end his suffering, however great that suffering may be: see *R. v Cox* (18 September 1992, unreported) per Ognall J in the Crown Court at Winchester. So to act is to cross the Rubicon which runs between on the one hand the care of the living patient and on the other hand euthanasia—actively causing his death to avoid or to end his suffering. Euthanasia is not lawful at common law. It is of course well known that there are many responsible members of our society who believe that euthanasia should be made lawful; but that result could, I believe, only be achieved by legislation which expresses the democratic will that so fundamental a change should be made in our law, and can, if enacted, ensure that such legalised killing can only be carried out subject to appropriate supervision and control. It is true that the drawing of this distinction may lead to a charge of hypocrisy, because it can be asked why, if the doctor, by discontinuing treatment, is entitled in consequence to let his patient die, it should not be lawful to put him out of his misery straight away, in a more humane manner, by a lethal injection, rather than let him linger on in pain until he dies. But the law does not feel able to authorise euthanasia, even in circumstances such as these, for, once euthanasia is recognised as lawful in these circumstances, it is difficult to see any logical basis for excluding it in others."

Questions

1. Is it simply fortuitous that in this case the transaction could be classified as an omission?
2. Is it possible that death itself may be in a patient's best interests? If so is there a moral difference between the situation where death results from the discontinuance of treatment (an omission) as opposed to the administration of a lethal drug (an act)?

    See further *R. (Burke) v General Medical Council* [2005] Q.B. 424.

(d) Duty arising from creation of a dangerous situation

R. V MILLER

[1983] 2 A.C. 161 HL

M, a vagrant who lived in an unoccupied house, awoke to find that a cigarette he had been smoking had set fire to the mattress on which he was lying. He did not attempt to extinguish the fire but moved to another room. The house caught fire. M was convicted of arson contrary to s.1(1) and (3) of the Criminal Damage Act 1971. The Court of Appeal dismissed his appeal against conviction and he appealed to the House of Lords.

LORD DIPLOCK

[T]he Court of Appeal certified that the following question of law of general public importance was involved:

> 'Whether the actus reus of the offence of arson is present when a defendant accidentally starts a fire and thereafter, intending to destroy or damage property belonging to another or being reckless as to whether any such property would be destroyed or damaged, fails to take any steps to extinguish the fire or prevent damage to such property by that fire?'

The first question to be answered where a completed crime of arson is charged is: 'Did a physical act of the accused start the fire which spread and damaged property belonging to another (or did his act cause an existing fire, which he had not started but which would otherwise have burnt itself out harmlessly, to spread and damage property belonging to another)?' I have added the words in brackets for completeness. They do not arise in the instant case; in cases where they do, the accused, for the purposes of the analysis which follows, may be regarded as having started a fresh fire.

The first question is a pure question of causation; it is one of fact to be decided by the jury in a trial upon indictment. It should be answered 'No' if, in relation to the fire during the period starting immediately before its ignition and ending with its extinction, the role of the accused was at no time more than that of a passive bystander. In such a case the subsequent questions to which I shall be turning would not arise.

If on the other hand the question, which I now confine to: 'Did a physical act of the accused start the fire which spread and damaged property belonging to another?' is answered 'Yes', as it was by the jury in the instant case, then for the purpose of the further questions the answers to which are determinative of his guilt of the offence of arson, the conduct of the accused, throughout the period from immediately before the moment of ignition to the completion of the damage to the property by the fire, is relevant; so is his state of mind throughout that period.

Since arson is a result-crime the period may be considerable, and during it the conduct of the accused that is causative of the result may consist not only of his doing physical acts which cause the fire to start or spread but also of his failing to take measures that lie within his power to counteract the danger that he has himself created. And if his conduct, active or passive, varies in the course of the period, so may his state of mind at the time of each piece of conduct. If at the time of any particular piece of conduct by the accused that is causative of the result, the state of mind that actuates his conduct falls within the description of one or other of the states of mind that are made a necessary ingredient of the offence of arson by section 1 (1) of the Criminal Damage Act 1971 (i.e. intending to damage property belonging to another or being reckless as to whether such property would be damaged) I know of no principle of English criminal law that would prevent his being guilty of the offence created by that subsection. Likewise I see no rational ground for excluding from conduct capable of giving rise to criminal liability, conduct which consists of failing to take measures that lie within one's power to counteract a danger that one has oneself created, if at the time of such conduct one's state of mind is such as constitutes a necessary ingredient of the offence. I venture to think that the habit of lawyers to talk of 'actus reus', suggestive as it is of action rather than inaction, is responsible for any erroneous notion that failure to act cannot give rise to criminal liability in English law.

No one has been bold enough to suggest that if, in the instant case, the accused had been aware at the time that he dropped the cigarette that it would probably set fire to his mattress and yet had taken no steps to extinguish it he would not have been guilty of the offence of arson, since he would have damaged property of another being reckless as to whether any such property would be damaged.

I cannot see any good reason why, so far as liability under criminal law is concerned, it should matter at what point of time before the resultant damage is complete a person becomes aware that he has done a physical act which, whether or not he appreciated that it would at the time when he did it, does in fact create a risk that property of another will be damaged; provided that, at the moment of awareness, it lies within his power to take steps, either himself or by calling for the assistance of the fire brigade if this be necessary, to prevent or minimise the damage to the property at risk.

My Lords, in the instant case the prosecution did not rely upon the state of mind of the accused as being reckless during that part of his conduct that consisted of his lighting and smoking a cigarette while lying on his mattress and falling asleep without extinguishing it. So the jury were not invited to make any finding as to this. What the prosecution did rely upon as being reckless was his state of mind during that part of his conduct after he awoke to find that he had set his mattress on fire and that it was smouldering, but did not then take any steps either to try to extinguish it himself or to send for the fire brigade, but simply went into the other room to resume his slumbers, leaving the fire from the already smouldering mattress to spread and to damage that part of the house in which the mattress was.

The recorder, in his lucid summing up to the jury (they took 22 minutes only to reach their verdict) told them that the accused having by his own act started a fire in the mattress which, when he became aware of its existence, presented an obvious risk of damaging the house, became under a duty to take some action to put it out. The Court of Appeal upheld the conviction, but their ratio decidendi appears to be somewhat different from that of the recorder. As I understand the judgment, in effect it treats the whole course of conduct of the accused, from the moment at which he fell asleep and dropped the cigarette on to the mattress until the time the damage to the house by fire was complete, as a continuous act of the accused, and holds that it is sufficient to constitute the statutory offence of arson if at any stage in that course of conduct the state of mind of the accused, when he fails to try to prevent or minimise the damage which will result from his initial act, although it lies within his power to do so, is that of being reckless as to whether property belonging to another would be damaged.

My Lords, these alternative ways of analysing the legal theory that justifies a decision which has received nothing but commendation for its accord with commonsense and justice, have, since the publication of the judgment of the Court of Appeal in the instant case, provoked academic controversy. Each theory has distinguished support. Professor J. C. Smith espouses the 'duty theory'; Professor Glanville Wiliams who, after the decision of the Divisional Court in *Fagan v Metropolitan Police Commissioner* (below p.534) appears to have been attracted by the duty theory, now prefers that of the continuous act. When applied to cases where a person has unknowingly done an act which sets in train events that, when he becomes aware of them, present an obvious risk that property belonging to another will be damaged, both theories lead to an identical result; and since what your Lordships are concerned with is to give guidance to trial judges in their task of summing up to juries, I would for this purpose adopt the duty theory as being the easier to explain to a jury; though I would commend the use of the word 'responsibility', rather than 'duty' which is more appropriate to civil than to criminal law, since it suggests an obligation owed to another person, i.e. the person to whom the endangered property belongs, whereas a criminal statue defines combinations of conduct and state of mind which render a person liable to punishment by the state itself.

So, while deprecating the use of the expression 'actus reus' in the certified question, I would answer that question 'Yes' and would dismiss the appeal.

Appeal dismissed

B. HOGAN, "OMISSIONS AND A DUTY MYTH" IN P. SMITH (ED), *CRIMINAL LAW: ESSAYS IN HONOUR OF J.C. SMITH* (LONDON: BUTTERWORTHS, 1987)

R. v. Miller holds, and with respect rightly, that one who inadvertently (or otherwise faultlessly, presumably) starts a chain of events causing harm may be properly held liable if, having become aware that he was the cause, he fails to take steps reasonably available to him to prevent or minimise the damage that will ensue . . .

Miller is interesting. One analysis of the case is to say that when the defendant became aware that he had caused (albeit inadvertently) the fire he was under a duty to take steps reasonably available to him to prevent or minimise further harm. Lord Diplock, with whom all their lordships agreed, expressed some support for the duty theory as having the merit of being easier to explain to the jury but then added that he would prefer 'responsibility' instead of duty. He thought that 'duty' was:

'. . . more appropriate to civil than to criminal law since it suggests an obligation owed to another person, i.e. the person to whom the endangered property belongs, whereas a criminal statute defines combinations of conduct and states of mind which render a person liable to punishment by the state itself.'

Quite what Lord Diplock is getting at here is not perhaps as clear as crystal, but two things may be said. The first is that he was right to say, if this is what he was saying, that there is no general duty to intervene to prevent or minimise harm to another's property. The second is, in the context of his speech read as a whole, that, having addressed his mind to the question whether it could be said that the defendant caused the fire and inevitably concluding that he did, he sees that it can make no sensible difference that mens rea was formed after the first event in the chain of events leading to the damage. Nor, with respect, can I. The defendant's causal contribution did not end when he inadvertently dropped the lighted cigarette. The fire was causally attributable to him from start to finish; he can hardly be heard sensibly to say that the only damage he caused was the scorch hole in the mattress. When he became aware that steps reasonably available to him would prevent further harm he was still causing the damage. The only difference between the damage caused before and after his awareness was that he was not criminally liable for the damage occurring before his awareness since he lacked mens rea but was liable for the damage he caused after his awareness since he now had mens rea . . .

So in *R. v Pittwood* it becomes fruitless to debate whether leaving open the level-crossing gates is to be characterised as omission or commission. The court characterised the conduct as misfeasance and in so doing, though the report is brief, appears to have looked at the totality of the defendant's conduct. And looking at the totality of his conduct it can easily be said that he created a situation of danger which caused harm to the victim.

It is true that in *R. v Pittwood* the court also said that a duty might arise out of a contract and the cases on 'omissions' are certainly littered with references to 'duty.' In my view these references to duty are unhelpful. The issue in *R. v Pittwood* was simply whether the defendant had *caused* the deaths of the victims with the relevant mens rea. Most assuredly he had no duty to take employment as a level-crossing keeper but once he did so he must not perform the office (in the same way as one must not drive a car or handle a gun) in such a way as to cause harm to others. No one has a duty to buy a car or a gun, or to obtain employment as a level-crossing keeper, or even to walk down the road to post a letter. But if they choose to do any of these things they must so conduct themselves so as not to cause harm, and if their conduct causes harm with the relevant mens rea they will fall foul of the criminal law. There is no need to complicate such cases by the search for duty.

There is perhaps a stronger case for imputing the duty concept in connection with domestic and similar relationships. So in *R. v Instan* where the niece failed to summon medical assistance for her aunt who died of gangrene, the court talks of a duty founded in moral obligation. In law, of course, and now as much as then, the niece had no duty whatever to look after her aunt. Had she been paying a casual visit to her aunt, noticed that her aunt would die without prompt medical attention, but had left without taking any measures of assistance then surely the case would have been decided differently. What was determinative in *R. v Instan* was that the niece had taken it upon herself to look after her aunt. She had no duty to do so, any more than the defendant in *R. v Pittwood* had any duty to take the job of level-crossing keeper, but having undertaken a certain task (and it is essentially on all fours with driving a car or using a gun or walking down the road to post a letter) it must be performed properly. If it is performed improperly and, with the relevant mens rea, causes harm to another, then criminal liability follows.

I see nothing wrong with the principle in *R. v Stone* which I take to be that if one chooses to assume the care and control of another then the self-imposed responsibility must be carried out with reasonable care and skill and that liability for manslaughter (or even murder) may be incurred if that responsibility is discharged in a grossly negligent (now reckless) manner. What is disturbing about *R. v Stone* is that the evidence hardly supported the inference that these two elderly incompetents had taken it upon themselves to discharge the onerous task of looking after the sister. Did they really *kill* the sister?

I am unhappy about the duty concept in the context of 'omission' It is likely to mislead a jury into thinking of duties in other than legal terms; into a consideration of the immorality of particular conduct; into convicting the defendant merely for his callousness. Better to put the issue as simply one of causation. For this purpose it is proper to look not merely at the last link in the causal chain, be it commission or omission, but all the relevant conduct of the defendant. The questions then become whether the *conduct* of the defendant caused the actus reus and whether he did so with mens rea. To introduce an imprecise, ill-defined concept of 'duty' into the equation only serves to confuse the issue.

Note

In *DPP v Santana-Bermudez* [2003] EWHC 2908 (Admin), D had placed hypodermic needles in his pockets. A police officer, prior to conducting a search of D's person, asked if he had any sharp or dangerous objects concealed upon him. D said he had not and the police officer then carried out the search. The officer was injured by one of the needles. D was charged with an assault occasioning actual bodily harm and was convicted. The Administrative Court upheld D's conviction, stating that where someone by act or word, or a combination thereof, creates a danger and thereby exposes another to the risk of injury which materialises, this can amount to the actus reus of assault.

R. V EVANS (GEMMA)

[2009] EWCA Crim 650

The appellant gave C, her half-sister, heroin. C then self-injected the heroin and then began to suffer the harmful effects of an overdose. The appellant recognised that C was in real distress but failed to summon any assistance because she was worried that C (and presumably herself) would get into trouble with the police. C later died from the effects of the overdose and the appellant was charged with manslaughter.

THE LORD CHIEF JUSTICE

The question in this appeal is not whether the appellant may be guilty of manslaughter for having been concerned in the supply of the heroin which caused the deceased's death. It is whether, notwithstanding that their relationship lacked the features of familial duty or responsibility which marked her mother's relationship with the deceased, she was under a duty to take reasonable steps for the safety of the deceased once she appreciated that the heroin she procured for her was having a potentially fatal impact on her health.

21 When omission or failure to act are in issue two aspects of manslaughter are engaged. Both are governed by decisions of the House of Lords. The first is manslaughter arising from the defendant's gross negligence. (*R v Adomako* [1995] 1 AC 171). The second arises when the defendant has created a dangerous situation and when, notwithstanding his appreciation of the consequent risks, he fails to take any reasonable preventative steps. (*R v Miller* [1983] 2 AC 161). Gross negligence manslaughter and unlawful act manslaughter are not necessarily mutually exclusive (*R v Willoughby*). The same applies to the aspects of manslaughter presently under consideration. Indeed care needs to be taken to avoid the risk of allowing the convenience of addressing the different circumstances in which manslaughter may arise to be converted into a compartmentalised, mutually isolated series of offences each inconveniently described by the same word, 'manslaughter'.

22 Miller's duty to act arose after he fell asleep in a squat while holding a lighted cigarette. He woke up and found that his mattress was smouldering. He left the room in which he had been asleep and went back to sleep in an adjoining room. He wholly ignored the smouldering mattress. The house caught fire. He was convicted of arson. In the House of Lords argument ranged over whether his omission to act engaged what was described as the 'duty theory' espoused by Professor J.C. Smith or whether his reckless omission to rectify the consequences of his earlier unintended act attracted the 'continuing act theory' supported by Professor Glanville Williams. It was submitted that there was no liability in criminal law for an omission unless there was a legal duty to act imposed by common law or by statute, and that no statutory provision imposed a duty neglect of which involved criminal liability, and no common law duty to extinguish an accidental fire or fire innocently started had previously been 'declared'.

23 The decision of the House of Lords was expressed in the single opinion of Lord Diplock. Both theories, he said, led to an identical result. The 'continuing act' basis for liability was not disavowed, but the duty theory was adopted only on the basis that it was easier to explain to a jury, provided the word 'responsibility' rather than 'duty' was used. In fact, the issue has continued to be addressed in the context of 'duty' rather than responsibility, and we shall continue to do so. More important, however, Lord Diplock observed that he could see:

'. . . no rational ground for excluding from conduct capable of giving rise to criminal liability, conduct which consists of failing to take measures that lie within one's power to counteract a danger that one has oneself created, if at the time of such conduct one's state of mind is such as constitutes a necessary ingredient of the offence . . . I cannot see any good reason why, so far as liability under criminal law is concerned, it should matter at what point of time before the resultant damage is complete a person becomes aware that he has done a physical act which, whether or not he appreciated that it would at the time when he did it, does in fact create a risk that property of another will be damaged: provided that at the moment of awareness, it lies within his power to take steps, either himself or by calling for the assistance of the fire brigade if this be necessary, to prevent or minimise the damage to the property at risk.'

24 The mens rea necessary for arson was, and thereafter the analysis focussed on, recklessness. But the reasoning in the decision does not exclude liability where a different mens rea is required. And if, for example, the result of the fire in Miller had included the death of a fellow squatter, it appears to us that Miller would properly have been convicted of manslaughter by gross negligence as well as arson. (*R v Willoughby*) . . .

25 Adomako was an anaesthetist and the deceased was his patient. He plainly owed him a duty of care. Lord Mackay of Clashfern LC in the only speech, expressed the opinion that:

'The ordinary principles of the law of negligence apply to ascertain whether or not the defendant has been in breach of a duty of care towards the victim who has died',

. . . He answered the certified question:

'In cases of manslaughter by criminal negligence involving a breach of duty, it is a sufficient direction to the jury to adopt the gross negligence test set out by the Court of Appeal in the present case . . .'

26 Our attention was drawn to a number of subsequent authorities. In *R v Khan and Khan*, unreported, 18 March 1998 a young woman was supplied by the appellants with heroin. This was probably the first occasion on which she had used heroin. She took 10 times the recommended therapeutic dosage and twice the amount likely to be taken even by an experienced user of heroin. She became 'obviously very ill'. She needed medical attention. The appellants, who were drug dealers, left her where she was and did nothing to assist. On the next day they returned and found that she was dead. If she had received medical attention she would probably have survived.

27 The jury was directed that they could consider a manslaughter verdict on the basis of omission. This could arise only if the appellants had set in train 'a chain of events' which gave rise to a risk of harm to the deceased. The relevant act was the supply of heroin to her. The second necessary ingredient was knowledge or awareness of the obvious risk that, having taken the heroin, the deceased would or might be harmed, and that they deliberately took no steps to rectify it. The effect of the direction was 'to extend the duty to summon medical assistance to a drug dealer who supplies heroin to a person who subsequently dies'. This court held that that might be correct, (sed quaere today, in the light of *Kennedy (No 2)*) but the issue needed to be closely addressed with the jury. The summing up in relation to manslaughter by omission was flawed. The convictions were quashed. The issue which arises in the present appeal was not directly addressed, although impliedly at any rate it appears that the court would not have rejected criminal liability on this basis.

28 *R v Sinclair, Johnson and Smith* raised similar issues. For these purposes the detailed facts need no narrative. Johnson's conviction for manslaughter was quashed on the basis that his conduct had not demonstrated a 'voluntary assumption of a legal duty of care'. What he had done was rather 'a desultory attempt to be of assistance'. The facts were not capable of giving rise to a legal duty of care in his case. Sinclair, however, was in a different position. He was a close friend of the deceased. They lived together, almost like brothers. Sinclair paid for and supplied the deceased with the first dose of methadone and helped him to obtain the second dose. He knew that the deceased was not an addict. He remained with the deceased throughout the period of his unconsciousness. For a long time he was the only person who was with him. On this basis there was material on which the jury, properly directed, could have found that Sinclair owed the deceased a legal duty of care. That accords with the present case.

29 In *R v Willoughby* the appellant was convicted of manslaughter on the basis of arson. He owned some premises which he decided to destroy by fire. He recruited a man called Drury to help him set fire to the premises. In an explosion the premises collapsed and Mr Drury died. The court accepted that a duty to look after the deceased did not arise merely because the appellant owned the premises which collapsed and in which he was killed. But that fact, taken together with the additional facts that the destruction of the premises was for his financial

benefit, that he enlisted the deceased to take part, and that his role was to spread petrol inside the premises, were sufficient, 'in conjunction' to be capable of giving rise to a duty of care.

30 In *R v Wacker* the appellant's convictions for manslaughter arose from the horrific deaths of 58 illegal immigrants hiding in a container loaded on to a trailer. The appellant was the lorry driver. It was suggested that he owed no duty of care to any of the deceased because they were parties to the same illegal purpose. The court had 'no difficulty in concluding that . . . the appellant did voluntarily assume the duty of care for those in the container', and he was aware that 'no one's actions other than his own could realistically prevent (them) from suffocating to death'. The appeal was dismissed on the basis that, once the jury decided that the appellant knew about those travelling in the container, it was a very plain case of gross negligence manslaughter.

31 These authorities are consistent with our analysis. None involved what could sensibly be described as manslaughter by mere omission and in each it was an essential requirement of any potential basis for conviction that the defendant should have failed to act when he was under a duty to do so. The duty necessary to found gross negligence manslaughter is plainly not confined to cases of a familial or professional relationship between the defendant and the deceased. In our judgment, consistently with Adomako and the link between civil and criminal liability for negligence, for the purposes of gross negligence manslaughter, when a person has created or contributed to the creation of a state of affairs which he knows, or ought reasonably to know, has become life threatening, a consequent duty on him to act by taking reasonable steps to save the other's life will normally arise.

The directions to the jury

(a) The ingredients of the offence

32 When directing the jury as to the constituents of manslaughter by gross negligence, the judge prepared a detailed note for the jury. He summarised the propositions in four questions.

'(1) Has the prosecution made you sure that that defendant . . . owed Carly Townsend a duty of care?

(2) If so has the prosecution made you sure that that defendant was in breach of that duty of care?

(3) If so, has the prosecution made you sure that the defendant's breach of that duty of care caused the death of Carly Townsend?

(4) If so, has the prosecution made you sure that that defendant's breach of that duty of care was such gross negligence as to amount to the crime of manslaughter?'

33 In his summing up the judge emphasised that the prosecution case against the appellant was based 'solely' on her omission 'to summon medical help when Carly . . . was suffering from a heroin overdose', and that the negligence alleged by the prosecution was not any positive act but omission, taking this form. He directed the jury that before they could convict on manslaughter by omission, 'there must be a pre-existing duty to act'.

34 The judge told the jury that he would direct them 'as to the circumstances in which such a duty can arise as a matter of law' but it would be for the jury to decide whether, on the facts they found, either or each of the defendants owed such a duty towards the deceased. In the case of the appellant he directed the jury that as a matter of law the blood relationship between the appellant and her half sister, who was a minor, did not 'of itself' give rise to a duty of care. He then directed the jury that they had heard that the appellant

'did perform some acts to assist Carly during the evening of 2nd May, in particular she and her mother placed Carly in the recovery position and they took turns to look to see if she was alright. However, I direct you that as a matter of law there is nothing in that course of conduct which is capable of amounting to an acceptance or an assumption by Gemma Evans of responsibility for Carly so as to give rise to a duty of care. In the present case, the only matter which in law is capable of giving rise to a duty of care owed by Gemma Evans to Carly Townsend would be if Gemma Evans did, on this occasion, as the prosecution allege, act as an intermediary, giving the drugs to Carly herself having first obtained them from Andrew Taylor. If the prosecution have made you sure that Gemma Evans did on this occasion act as an intermediary, giving the drugs to Carly herself, having first obtained them from Andrew Taylor, that is a matter which in law is capable of giving rise to a duty of care. It is for you to decide whether the prosecution has made you sure that such a duty of care has arisen on the facts found by you. . . if the prosecution has not made you sure that Gemma Evans did, on this occasion, act as an intermediary, giving the drugs to Carly herself having first obtained them from Andrew Taylor, then she cannot have owed a duty of care to Carly Townsend and you must find Gemma Evans not guilty. It is for you to decide, having regard to all the circumstances of this case as you find them to be, whether each defendant owed a duty of care towards Carly Townsend.'

35 In relation to the circumstances in which a duty of care might arise in this case, these observations must be seen in their context, which is that the only issue of fact which the jury had to decide was the supply issue. Unless the jury was sure of this fact, the remaining undisputed areas of appellant's involvement (summarised at paragraph 12) would, on the judge's directions, have been insufficient for the purposes of gross negligence manslaughter. Without her involvement in the supply of heroin, the jury was directed that there was no duty on the appellant to act even after she became aware of the serious adverse effect of the drug taking on Carly. If on the other hand she was so involved, that fact, taken with the other undisputed facts would, and on our analysis of the relevant principles did give rise to a duty on the appellant to act. In law the judge's directions about the ingredients of gross negligence manslaughter, as applied to this case, were correct.

36 We would merely record that the judge's direction that a duty to act did not arise from a voluntary assumption of risk by the appellant may have been appropriate in this case, but it would not be of universal application where, for example, a voluntary assumption of risk by the defendant had led the victim, or others, to become dependent on him to act.

Appeal dismissed

Questions

1.   Was Miller (see above p.37) found guilty because he had fallen asleep while smoking a cigarette or because, when he awoke, he failed to take reasonable steps to put out the fire caused by his lighted cigarette?

2.   The facts in the case involved damage to property; would Miller have been guilty of manslaughter if a fellow squatter sharing the mattress with him had died as a result of asphyxiation?

3.   Would Miller have been liable for arson/manslaughter if the fire had been caused by an electrical fault? Would it make any difference if the fellow squatter was his eight-year-old son?

4.   What is the general principle for which *Miller* is authority?

5.   What duty did the defendant in *Santana-Bermudez* owe to the police officer?

6.   Would it be more appropriate, as Hogan suggests (see above p.38) to simply ask whether or not D's conduct has caused the actus reus?

7.   Who really created the dangerous situation in *Evans*? Does *Evans* conflict with the principles of causation as discussed by the House of Lords in *Kennedy (No.2)* [2007] UKHL 38?

Note

The situations in which the courts have recognised liability for offences of commission arising from omissions depend on the existence of a duty to act. In the absence of such a duty there can be no liability. Accordingly, in the absence of a duty arising from relationship, a bystander may watch a child drowning in a puddle and will not be guilty of any criminal offence. Should there be a specific offence of failure to render assistance to a person in peril? See further A. Ashworth and E. Steiner, "Criminal omissions and public duties: the French experience" (1990) 10 Legal Studies 153, who discuss, inter alia, art.63(2) of the French Penal Code which provides:

"Any person who voluntarily fails to render assistance to a person in peril, which he or she could have given either personally or by calling for help, without personal danger or danger to others, is guilty of an offence and may be punished by imprisonment from three months to five years or by a fine of 360 francs to 20,000 francs or both."

If such a duty were to be imposed in England and Wales should it be in addition to or in place of the duties which give rise to liability on the basis of commission by omission?

See further *Salmon* (1994) 115 FLR, 70 A. Crim. R. 536; (1996) 20 Crim. L.J. 102.

LAW COMMISSION, *DRAFT CRIMINAL CODE BILL* (TSO, 1989), LAW COM. NO.177

Offences of omission and situational offences

16. For the purposes of an offence which consists wholly or in part of an omission, state of affairs or occurrence, references in this Act to an 'act' shall, where the context permits, be read as including references to the omission, state of affairs or occurrence by reason of which a person may be guilty of the offence, and references to a person's acting or doing an act shall be construed accordingly.

Causation

17.—(1) Subject to subsections (2) and (3), a person causes a result which is an element of an offence when—

(a) he does an act which makes a more than negligible contribution to its occurrence; or

(b) he omits to do an act which might prevent its occurrence and which he is under a duty to do according to the law relating to the offence.

Notes

1. Clause 16 is an interpretation clause which instructs the user of the Code inter alia that the requirement of proof of an "act" in Code offences may be satisfied "where the context permits" with proof of an omission. This will be appropriate where there is a recognised duty to act. The Code does not specify when there is such a duty relying on the situations which have already been recognised by the courts. This hardly makes for clarity in the law.

2. Clause 17(1)(b) represents a radical change in the law of causation. It seems that as it is difficult to establish that a consequence has occurred as the result of an omission, the Law Commission is proposing to make it easier to establish causation (or, to be precise, their version of causation) in the case of omissions. Causation will be established where the prosecution prove that the consequence might not have occurred had D acted in performance of his duty to act. By contrast, where an offence of commission is involved, the prosecution must prove that the consequence would not have occurred "but for" D's act. This appears to make criminal liability more stringent in the case of those who omit to act. The Law Commission provides the following illustration of the operation of cl.17(1)(b)—

    "17(ii) D, E's mistress, lives with E and P. E's child by his wife. While E is away P falls seriously ill. D, wishing P to die, fails to call a doctor. P dies. P's life might have been prolonged by medical attention. If D was under a duty to obtain medical attention for P she is guilty of murder. She has caused Ps death intending to cause death."

Questions

1. Is D guilty of murder because of the possibility that medical assistance might have prolonged P's life?

2. If the expert medical evidence was to the effect that swift medical attention might have prolonged P's life for an hour, will D be liable for murder?

3. In the above example if, instead of failing to call a doctor D had done so but the doctor was delayed and P was dead on his arrival, what was the cause of P's death? How does this differ from the situation where D fails to call a doctor? Would D's culpability not be adequately reflected in a conviction under s.1 of the Children and Young Persons Act 1933 of wilfully neglecting a child in a manner likely to cause injury to his health? (See *Sheppard*, below p.188).

4. Is it not the case that the current law imposing liability for omissions in respect of "result crimes" represents a policy decision whereby the existence of a duty combined with a failure to prevent a consequence occurring is treated as equivalent to causing that consequence?

LAW COMMISSION, *DRAFT CRIMINAL LAW BILL* (TSO, 1993), LAW COM. NO.218

Supervening fault

31. Where it is an offence to be at fault in causing a result and a person lacks the fault required when he does an act that may cause, or does cause, the result, he nevertheless commits the offence if—

(a) being aware that he has done the act and that the result may occur or, as the case may be, has occurred and may continue, and

(b) with the fault required,

he fails to take reasonable steps to prevent the result occurring or continuing and it does occur or continue.

Note

This clause restates and generalises the principle applied by the House of Lords in *Miller*. The clause also covers the facts of *Fagan v Metropolitan Police Commissioner*, below, p.534.

----

4. CAUSATION

P. BRETT AND L. WALLER, *CRIMINAL LAW TEXT AND CASES*, 4TH EDN (MELBOURNE: BUTTERWORTHS, 1978), P.145

Many philosophers have devoted great effort to elucidating the notion of causation. In particular, Hume and Mill have made great contributions in this field of enquiry, and from time to time one finds echoes of or borrowings from their work in judgments and legal writings. It is fair to say, however, that their views (and those of other philosophers also) are concerned with causal statements of general application, such as scientific laws. They are thus of comparatively slight value to lawyers, who are concerned with isolated events in the past which cannot be reproduced in the present or future . . .

For our purposes it is enough to say that when the law treats a particular act or omission as the cause of an event it makes a choice. It does so for the purpose of attributing the responsibility for that event to a particular person, or of denying that he is responsible for it.

This, however, leaves unanswered the question: how is the choice made? The currently fashionable answer (in many other legal contexts as well as in this) is that the judges resort to considerations of 'policy.' But that tells us very little, and it may indeed be positively misleading. For it conjures up a picture of the judge consciously considering various possible choices and selecting what he thinks to be the 'best' one ('best' here having some rather vague reference to notions of supposed social utility). And it is reasonably clear that this is not what the judge does, either consciously or (as some would argue) unconsciously.

We think that a more accurate way of answering the question is to say that the judges make use of the common sense notions of the ordinary man (Hart and Honoré, in their *Causation in the Law* (1959), adopt broadly the same view). Nor indeed, is there any good reason why they should not do so. The ordinary common sense notions of causation and responsibility can be shown to have, in most respects, a sound moral basis . . .

The cases and books make use of a number of phrases in the attempt to clarify these common sense notions. Many of these, however, do little more than state a conclusion which has been reached rather than the reasons for reaching it—as when it is said that the law looks to 'proximate' causes as opposed to 'remote' causes, the notions of proximity and remoteness being taken as self-explanatory, likewise it is sometimes said that the law seeks for the 'primary' cause, or even the 'legal' cause, or that it seeks for the *causa causans* (causing, or operative cause).

Williams (T.C.L., pp.379–382) elucidates the meaning of some of these phrases:

A convenient English equivalent of the term causation *sine qua non* is but-for causation (properly speaking, but-for . . . not causation). For a factor to be a but-for cause, one must be able to say that *but for* the occurrence of the antecedent factor the event would *not* have happened . . .

When causation is in issue, the defendant's act (or omission) must be shown to be not only a but-for cause but also an imputable or legal cause of the consequence. Imputable causes are some of the but-for causes. In other words, the defendant's act, being a but-for cause, must be sufficiently closely connected with the consequence to involve him in responsibility. The lawyer is interested in the causal parentage of events, not in their causal ancestry . . .

Several attempts have been made to find a suitable name for this second notion of cause. To call it the 'direct' or 'proximate' cause (as is often done) is misleading, because several stages may intervene between the so-called direct cause and the effect. D may send poisoned chocolates to V, who lives at the other side of the world; if V eats the chocolates and dies, the law will certainly regard D as responsible for the death, though his act was far removed in space and considerably removed in time from its effect. To call D's act the 'effective' cause is unhelpful because every cause must by definition be effective—if an act is not effective to produce a given result, it is not a cause of it. 'Substantial' is a less misleading adjective, but it is not illuminating.

Sometimes (looking at the situation backwards instead of forwards) imputable causation is stated in terms of "remoteness of consequence." To say that a particular consequence is 'too remote' is only another way of saying that the defendant's act (or omission) is not an imputable cause.

. . . When one has settled the question of but-for causation, the further test to be applied to the but-for cause in order to qualify it for legal recognition is not a test of causation but a moral reaction. The question is whether the result can fairly be said to be imputable to the defendant. If the term 'cause' must be used, it can best be distinguished as the 'imputable' or 'responsible' or 'blamable' cause, to indicate the value-judgment involved. The word 'imputable' is here chosen as best representing the idea. Whereas the but-for cause can generally be demonstrated scientifically, no experiment can be devised to show that one of a number of concurring but-for causes is more substantial or important than another, or that one person who is involved in the causal chain is more blameworthy than another.

The remainder of the discussion of causation is divided as follows:

i. Sine qua non (but-for causation)

ii. Imputability

    (a) Fright and flight
    (b) Weak or intractable victims
    (c) Intervening causes

iii. An alternative approach

i. Sine qua non

R. V CATO

[1976] 1 W.L.R. 110

C and his victim F, were friends. F invited C to have a "fix" of his heroin. Each filled his own syringe and then asked the other to inject it into him. This procedure was repeated several times during one night. F died the next morning. One of the grounds on which C appealed against his conviction for manslaughter concerned causation.

LORD WIDGERY CJ

It seems to us that the first and most important single factor to which counsel for the appellant directed our attention was concerned with causation, that is to say with the link alleged to exist between the injection of heroin and the death of Farmer . . .

He pointed out that the medical evidence did not at any point say 'This morphine killed Farmer'; the actual link of that kind was not present. The witnesses were hesitant to express such a view and often recoiled from it, saying it was not for them to state the cause of death. It is perfectly true . . . that the expert evidence did not in positive terms provide a link, but it was never intended to. The expert witnesses here spoke to factual situations, and the conclusions and deductions therefrom were for the jury. The first question was: was there sufficient evidence upon which the jury could conclude, as they must have concluded, that adequate causation was present?

When one looks at the evidence it is important to realise that no other cause of Farmer's death was supplied. Dr Robinson thought that there might have been another drug, and she said at one stage it might have been cocaine, but there was never any cocaine found in the body. The only cause of death actually supplied by the evidence was morphine. No natural disease was present and no other drug was identified. Furthermore, the symptoms and the external appearance of the body, and the nature of the final terminal cause, was consistent with poison by the administration of heroin in the way which was described . . .

Of course behind this whole question of the sufficiency of evidence of causation is the fact that it was not necessary for the prosecution to prove that the heroin was the only cause. As a matter of law, it was sufficient if the prosecution could establish that it was *a* cause, provided it was a cause outside the de minimis range, and effectively bearing upon the acceleration of the moment of the victim's death. When one has that in mind it is, we think, really possible to say that if the jury had been directed to look for heroin as a cause, not de minimis but a cause of substance, and they came back with a verdict of not guilty, the verdict could really be described as a perverse one. The whole background of the evidence was the other way and there certainly was ample evidence, given a proper direction, upon which a charge of manslaughter could be supported.

But what about the proper direction? [the jury had been asked: 'Did [the] injection of heroin by [the appellant] cause, contribute to or accelerate the death of Farmer?'] It will be noted that in none of the versions which I have quoted of the judge's direction on this point, nor in any of those which I have not quoted which appear in the summing up, is there any reference to it being necessary for the cause to be a substantial one. It is said in clear terms . . . that the jury can consider whether the administration of the heroin was a cause or contributed to or accelerated the death, and in precise terms the word 'contributed' is not qualified to show that a substantial contribution is required . . .

Before pursuing that, it is worth reminding oneself that some of the more recent dicta in the textbooks about this point do not support as strongly as was once the case the theory that the contribution must be substantial. In Smith and Hogan, *Criminal Law*, 3rd ed. (1973), p.217 there is this rather interesting extract:

'It is commonly said by judges and writers that, while the accused's act need not be the sole cause of the death, it must be a substantial one. This appears to mean only that a minute contribution to the cause of death will not entail responsibility. It may therefore be misleading to direct a jury that D is not liable unless his conduct was a "substantial" cause. Killing is merely an acceleration of death and factors which produce a very trivial acceleration will be ignored.'

Whether that be so or not, and we do not propose to give that passage the court's blessing today at all events, if one looks at the circumstances of the present case with any real sense of reality, we think there can be no doubt that when the judge was talking about contribution the jury knew perfectly well that he was talking about something more than the mere de minimis contribution. We have given this point particular care in our consideration of the case because it worried us to some extent originally, but we do feel in the end, having looked at all the circumstances, that there could not have been any question in this case of the jury making the mistake of thinking that the contribution would suffice if it were de minimis . . .

Appeal dismissed

ii. Imputability

R. V DALLOWAY

(1847) 2 Cox 273

A child ran in front of the defendant's cart and was killed. The reins were not in the defendant's hands but loose on the horse's back.

ERLE J

. . . in summing up to the jury, directed them that a party neglecting an ordinary caution, and, by reason of that neglect, causing the death of another, is guilty of manslaughter; that if the prisoner had reins, and by using the reins could have saved the child, he was guilty of manslaughter; but that if they thought he could not have saved the child by pulling the reins, or otherwise by their assistance, they must acquit him.

Not guilty

Note

This case could also be seen as illustrating the but-for principle. The difficulty here is that the presence of the cart *was* a sine qua non of the child's death but D's negligent driving was not.
Problems can also arise where D's act was not the direct cause of death (where, for example, fright exacerbates a medical condition or V dies escaping from D), or where D's act does not cause instantaneous death and a complex chain of causation develops (through, for example, negligent medical care).

(a) Fright and flight

Note

Death may ensue as a result of fright caused by D bringing about a physiological reaction in V, such as a heart attack, or it may occur where V, because he is frightened by D, seeks to flee from him and dies in the process. In *Watson* [1989] 2 All E.R. 865 the Court of Appeal accepted that a jury, properly directed, could have found that the appellants' acts of burgling V's house, wakening and verbally abusing him, V being a frail 87-year-old, caused his death when he died 90 minutes later from a heart attack. See further Busuttil and McCall Smith, "Fright, Stress and Homicide" (1990) 54 J. Crim. L. 257.

R. V HAYWARD

(1908) 21 Cox 692

The defendant returned home in a state of violent excitement. He was heard to express the intention of "giving his wife something" when she came in. When she did arrive there were sounds of an altercation and shortly afterwards the woman ran from the house into the road, closely followed by the defendant. She fell into the roadway and the accused kicked her on the left arm. She died and a medical examination showed that the bruise on her arm, caused by the kick, was not the cause of death. The deceased woman was in good health apart from a persistent thyrus gland. Medical evidence was given that a person subject to this condition might die from a combination of fright or strong emotion and physical exertion. The defendant was charged with manslaughter.

Ridley J directed the jury that if they believed the witnesses there was a sufficient chain of evidence to support a conviction of manslaughter. He pointed out that no proof of actual physical violence was necessary, but that death from fright alone, caused by an illegal act, such as threats of violence, would be sufficient. The abnormal state of the deceased's health did not affect the question whether the prisoner knew or did not know of it if it were proved to the satisfaction of the jury that the death was accelerated by the prisoner's illegal act.

Verdict: Guilty

R. V MACKIE

(1973) 57 Cr. App. R. 453

M was convicted of the manslaughter of a boy aged three whom he was looking after. It was alleged that the boy fell downstairs while running away in fear of being ill-treated.

STEPHENSON LJ

Where the injuries are not fatal, the attempt to escape must be the natural consequence of the assault charged, not something which could not be expected, but something which any reasonable and responsible man in the assailant's shoes would have foreseen. Where the injuries are fatal, the attempt must be the natural consequence of an unlawful act and that unlawful act 'must be such as all sober and reasonable people would inevitably recognise must subject the other person to, at least, the risk of some harm resulting therefrom, albeit not serious harm': *Church* [1966] 1 Q.B. 59 (below) . . .

In this case there were two complications: (1) the victim was a child of three and regard must be had to his age in considering whether his reaction was well-founded or well-grounded on an apprehension of immediate violence (in the language of the old cases appropriate to adults) and therefore reasonably to be expected. (2) This defendant was in the position of a parent, which may have entitled him to 'assault' the child by smacking or threatening him without breaking the law, and it was not every act which might be expected to cause slight harm to the boy that would be unlawful for a man in his parental position; he might have to do some act in the interests of the boy's own safety, for instance, to keep him away from the upstairs window. The purpose of correcting the child—and perhaps the sole justification for correcting a young child—is to deter; how else can the kind parent of a nervous child save it from danger than by in some degree hurting or frightening it? How far was it reasonable, and therefore lawful, for the appellant to go in punishing this child was one of the questions the jury had to decide. Whether the boy 'overreacted' (as Mr Back put it) in a way which the appellant could not reasonably be expected to have foreseen was another.

. . . At the end of the summing-up the judge came back to these questions in suggesting what the vital points might be: 'First, was the boy in fear of Mackie? Secondly, did that cause him to try to escape? Thirdly, if he was in fear, was that fear well-founded? If it was well-founded, was it caused by the unlawful conduct of the accused, that is, by conduct for which there was no lawful excuse even on the part of a man in the position of a father . . .'

We think that the judge directed the jury clearly and correctly as to the law laid down in the cases . . .

Appeal dismissed

Note

This approach to "manslaughter by 'flight'" was confirmed by the Privy Council in *DPP v Daley* [1979] 2 W.L.R. 239. Lord Keith of Kinkel summarised it thus:

> "[T]he essential ingredients of the prosecution's proof of a charge of manslaughter, laid upon the basis that a person has sustained fatal injuries while trying to escape from assault . . . are: (1) that the victim immediately before he sustained the injuries was in fear of being hurt physically; (2) that this fear was such that it caused him to try to escape; (3) that whilst he was trying to escape, and because he was trying to escape he met his death; (4) that his fear of being hurt there and then was reasonable and was caused by the conduct of the defendant; (5) that the defendant's conduct which caused the fear was unlawful; and (6) that his conduct was such as any sober and reasonable person would recognise as likely to subject the victim to at least the risk of some harm resulting from it, albeit not a serious harm. Their Lordships have to observe that it is unnecessary to prove the defendant's knowledge that his conduct was unlawful."

Daley was further considered in *Williams and Davis* [1992] 1 W.L.R. 380. V was a hitch-hiker who had been picked up by a car driven by W in which D was also a passenger. After about five miles, while the car was travelling at 30 miles per hour, V jumped from the car and died from head injuries. It appeared that he had been threatened if he did not hand over his money. The Court of Appeal quashed W's convictions for manslaughter and robbery because of misdirections on evidence, and quashed D's convictions as it regarded a direction based on *Daley* as insufficient where there was a real issue as to causation. Stuart-Smith LJ, after referring to the six ingredients in *Daley*, stated:

> "Where the unlawful act was a battery, there was no difficulty with the second ingredient. However, where the unlawful act was merely a threat unaccompanied and not preceded by actual violence, the position might be more difficult. The nature of the threat was important in considering both the foreseeability of harm to the victim from the threat and the question whether the deceased's conduct was proportionate to the threat, that is to say that it was within the ambit of reasonableness and not so daft as to make it his own voluntary act which broke the chain of causation. The jury should consider two questions: first whether it was reasonably foreseeable that some harm, albeit not serious harm, was likely to result from the threat itself; and second, whether the deceased's reaction in jumping from the moving car was within the range of responses which might be expected from a victim placed in his situation. The jury should bear in mind any particular characteristic of the victim and the fact that in the agony of the moment he might act without thought and deliberation."

In *Marjoram* [2000] Crim. L.R. 372, D argued on appeal that for the purposes of the question whether a reasonable person could have foreseen the victim's attempt to escape as a possible consequence of D's assault, the reasonable person should be the same age and sex as the defendant. In this case D was aged 16. The Court of Appeal ruled that as the issue concerned the effect of the defendant's conduct on the victim's mind, the test had to be objective to avoid the absurdity where there were two defendants of one being held not to have caused the injury because he had not foreseen the victim's flight, and the other being held to have caused it because he had foreseen the victim's flight.

(b) Weak or intractable victims

It is a general rule of criminal liability that defendants take their victims as they find them. Thus in *R. v Plummer* (1844) 1 C. & K. 600, where a husband had denied shelter to his wife who died soon afterwards, Gurney B. said:

> "It does not appear in evidence what her disease was, or that she was afflicted with that mortal illness under which she laboured, or that she was suffering from diarrhoea which caused her death; but he was, nevertheless, informed that she was very ill, and had no shelter. If you should be of opinion that her death was caused or accelerated by his conduct you will say that he is guilty (of manslaughter)."

And in *R. v Martin* (1832) 5 C. & P. 128 Parke J said:

> "It is said, that the deceased was in a bad state of health; but that is perfectly immaterial, as, if the prisoner was so unfortunate as to accelerate her death, he must answer for it."

This principle applies where, for religious or other reasons, the victim refuses medical help.

R. V BLAUE

[1975] 1 W.L.R. 1411

The appellant stabbed a woman; the wound penetrated her lung. At the hospital she was told that a blood transfusion and surgery were necessary to save her life. She refused to have a transfusion as it was contrary to her beliefs as a Jehovah's Witness. She died the next day. Medical evidence indicated that she would not have died had she accepted the medical treatment. The appellant was convicted of manslaughter on grounds of diminished responsibility.

LAWTON LJ

Towards the end of the trial and before the summing up started counsel on both sides made submissions as to how the case should be put to the jury. Counsel then appearing for the defendant invited the judge to direct the jury to acquit the defendant generally on the count of murder. His argument was that her refusal to have a blood transfusion had broken the chain of causation between the stabbing and her death. As an alternative he submitted that the jury should be left to decide whether the chain of causation had been broken. Mr. Herrod submitted that the judge should direct the jury to convict, because no facts were in issue and when the law was applied to the facts there was only one possible verdict, namely, manslaughter by reason of diminished responsibility.

When the judge came to direct the jury on this issue he did so by telling them that they should apply their common sense. He then went on to tell them they would get some help from the cases to which counsel had referred in their speeches. He reminded them of what Lord Parker C.J. had said in *R. v Smith* [1959] 2 Q.B. 35, 42 and what Maule J. had said 133 years before in *R. v Holland* (1841) 2 Mood. & R. 351, 352. He placed particular reliance on what Maule J. had said. The jury, he said, might find it 'most material and most helpful'. He continued:

> 'This is one of those relatively rare cases, you may think, with very little option open to you but to reach the conclusion that was reached by your predecessors as members of the jury in *R. v Holland*, namely, "yes" to the

question of causation that the stab was still, at the time of the girl's death, the operative cause of death—or a substantial cause of death. However, that is a matter for you to determine after you have withdrawn to consider your verdict.'

Mr Comyn has criticised that direction on three grounds: first, because *R. v Holland* should no longer be considered good law; secondly, because *R. v Smith*, when rightly understood, does envisage the possibility of unreasonable conduct on the part of the victim breaking the chain of causation; and thirdly, because the judge in reality directed the jury to find causation proved although he used words which seemed to leave the issue open for them to decide.

In *R. v Holland*, 2 Mood. & R. 351, the defendant in the course of a violent assault, had injured one of his victim's fingers. A surgeon had advised amputation because of the danger to life through complications developing. The advice was rejected. A fortnight later the victim died of lockjaw. Maule J. said, at p.352: 'the real question is, whether in the end the wound inflicted by the prisoner was the cause of death'. That distinguished judge left the jury to decide that question as did the judge in this case. They had to decide it as juries always do, by pooling their experience of life and using their common sense. They would not have been handicapped by a lack of training in dialectic or moral theology.

Maule J.'s direction to the jury reflected the common law's answer to the problem. He who inflicted an injury which resulted in death could not excuse himself by pleading that his victim could have avoided death by taking greater care of himself: see *Hales Pleas of the Crown* (1800 ed.), pp.427–28. The common law in Sir Matthew Hale's time probably was in line with contemporary concepts of ethics. A man who did a wrongful act was deemed *morally* responsible for the natural and probable consequence of that act. Mr Comyn asked us to remember that since Sir Matthew Hale's day the rigour of the law relating to homicide has been eased in favour of the accused. It has been—but this has come about through the development of the concepts of intent, not by reason of a different view of causation . . .

There have been two cases in recent years which have some bearing upon this topic: *R. v Jordan* (1956), [below p.54] and *R. v Smith* [below p.55]. The physical cause of death in this case was the bleeding into the pleural cavity arising from the penetration of the lung. This had not been brought about by any decision made by the deceased but by the stab wound.

Mr Comyn tried to overcome this line of reasoning by submitting that the jury should have been directed that if they thought the deceased's decision not to have a blood transfusion was an unreasonable one, then the chain of causation would have been broken. At once the question arises—reasonable by whose standards? Those of Jehovah's Witnesses? Humanists? Roman Catholics? Protestants of Anglo-Saxon descent? The man on the Clapham omnibus? But he might well be an admirer of Eleazar who suffered death rather than eat the flesh of swine (2 Maccabees, ch. 6, w. 18–31) or of Sir Thomas More who, unlike nearly all his contemporaries was unwilling to accept Henry VIII as Head of the Church of England. Those brought up in the Hebraic and Christian traditions would probably be reluctant to accept that these martyrs caused their own deaths.

As was pointed out to Mr Comyn in the course of argument, two cases, each raising the same issue of reasonableness because of religious beliefs, could produce different verdicts depending on where the cases were tried. A jury drawn from Preston, sometimes said to be the most Catholic town in England, might have different views about martyrdom to one drawn from the inner suburbs of London. Mr Comyn accepted that this might be so: it was, he said, inherent in trial by jury. It is not inherent in the common law as expounded by Sir Matthew Hale and Maule J. It has long been the policy of the law that those who use violence on other people must take their victims as they find them. This in our judgment means the whole man, not just the physical man. It does not lie in the mouth of the assailant to say that the victim's religious beliefs which inhibited him from accepting certain kinds of treatment were unreasonable. The question for decision is what caused her death. The answer is the stab wound. The fact that the victim refused to stop this end coming about did not break the causal connection between the act and death . . .

Appeal dismissed

WILLIAMS, "NOTE" (1976) C.L.J. 15

Although the case follows the precedents, . . . it fails to notice that all of them dated from a time when medical science was in its infancy, and when operations performed without hygiene carried great danger to life. It was therefore open to the court for the benefit of the defendant to consider the question afresh, and there were several reasons for doing so.

It had been held in the law of tort that the test of reasonable foresight applies to facts like those in *Blaue*, but the court refused to bring the criminal law into line. The criminal law should avoid the appearance of harshness, and to make it more stringent than the civil law in the matter of causation is surprising. Lawton L.J., speaking for the court, explained the difference between crime and tort by saying that 'the criminal law is concerned with the maintenance of law and order and the protection of the public generally'. This overlooks that Blaue was in any event punishable severely for wounding with intent. What social purpose is served by giving an attacker *extra* punishment because the person attacked unreasonably refused treatment?

Questions

1. Would the decision in *Blaue* have differed if V had refused treatment because she wanted to die so that Blaue would be charged with murder?

2. Is the decision in *Blaue* inconsistent with the "fright and flight" cases above where an "unreasonable flight" can break the chain of causation?

3. Would Blaue's moral culpability differ any if V had not been a Jehovah's Witness and had accepted a blood transfusion and survived or if V had died before a blood transfusion had been administered? If not is it arguable that the concentration of the criminal law on consequences in determining liability is misplaced given that the consequences of action often depend on chance circumstances which are not within the accused's control? See Gobert directly below.

J. GOBERT, "THE FORTUITY OF CONSEQUENCE" (1993) 4 CRIM. L.F. 1

[T]he moral culpability of Blaue's initial actions is in no way altered by subsequent events, and it is on these actions that his criminal responsibility should be based.

What appears to be happening in cases like *Blaue* is that judges are not prepared to allow a defendant to avoid full liability for morally culpable acts on the basis that the victim was in some way responsible for the ultimate result, whatever logical merit there may be to this argument in pure causation terms. After all, had Blaue's victim bled to death before her plight could be discovered, or had there been no blood of the appropriate type available for a transfusion, there would have been no question regarding his responsibility for the death, for there would have been no intervening cause.

Why should the result be different when there is an intervening cause? The answer to this conundrum is, however, not to say that you must take your victim as you find him but to define crimes so that results are not of criminological significance. Blaue's attack on his victim was intentional, deliberate, and vicious. His criminality should reflect these facts and not the fortuity of whether the victim happened to die. The strained reasoning in *Blaue* resulted from the need to satisfy the legal definition of a crime specified in terms of result and the inevitable corollary of whether the defendant's acts caused that result. Because the court thought that Blaue was morally responsible for his victim's death, it stretched legal principle to find him criminally responsible.

(c) Intervening causes

G. WILLIAMS, "FINIS FOR NOVUS ACTUS" (1989) C.L.J. 391

A person is primarily responsible for what he himself does. He is not responsible, not blameworthy, for what other people do. The fact that his own conduct, rightful or wrongful, provided the background for a subsequent voluntary and wrong act by another does not make him responsible for it. What he does may be a but-for cause of the injurious act, but he did not do it. His conduct is not an imputable cause of it. Only the later actor, the doer of the act that intervenes between the first act and the result, the final wielder of human autonomy in the matter, bears responsibility (along with his accomplices) for the result that ensues . . .

The autonomy doctrine, expressing itself through its corollary the doctrine of *novus actus inteveniens*, teaches that the individual's will is the autonomous (self-regulating) prime cause of his behaviour. Although this may sound unbelievably metaphysical, the doctrine is supported because it accords with our ideas of moral responsibility and just punishment, and serves social objectives. The first actor who starts on a dangerous or criminal plan will often be responsible for what happens if no one else intervenes; but a subsequent actor who has reached responsible years, is of sound mind, has full knowledge of what he is doing, and is not acting under intimidation or other pressure or stress resulting from the defendant's conduct, replaces him as the responsible actor. Such an intervening act is thought to break the moral connection that would otherwise have been perceived between the defendant's acts and the forbidden consequence.

Policy arguments in favour of novus actus

(1) The law should not saddle a person with liability for consequences that not only he but also the general public would blame on someone else. The intervention of the responsible actor diverts our retributive wrath from the first actor, who may, in the event, appear to be so much less culpable than the later actor; and this switching of retributive feeling from the first actor to the later actor is expressed in causal language.

(2) Sometimes we may feel that making people responsible for the subsequent behaviour of others, merely because they foresaw or could have foreseen that behaviour, would be too great a restriction upon liberty.

(3) The rule has the beneficial effect of restricting the number of persons made liable for a particular occurrence. Part of the object of the criminal trial is to dramatise society's rejection of the deed, and, generally speaking, this is adequately done by prosecuting the immediate author and his accomplices. No pressing necessity exists to regard more remote authors as responsible for causing the harm . . . though some of them may well be prosecuted for other offences, such as attempt, or in appropriate circumstances as accessories.

Note

A problem which has arisen in several cases is that of medical treatment of wounds inflicted by D on V. If the medical treatment is negligent will this break the chain of causation? Will D only be liable where the original wound is not healed and V dies from it? What happens if the original wound is healed and the medical treatment itself is the immediate cause of death; as D's wounding of V caused him to undergo medical treatment, can it be said that this was still a substantial cause of V's death?

R. V JORDAN

(1956) 40 Cr. App. R. 152

The appellant stabbed the deceased in the abdomen. The deceased was taken promptly to hospital and the wound was stitched. A few days later he died. Jordan was convicted of murder at Leeds Assizes and on appeal sought to adduce further medical evidence. This evidence disclosed that the wound, which had penetrated the intestine in two places, was mainly healed at the time of death. At the hospital terramycin was administered to prevent infection. The deceased was found to be intolerant to this antibiotic. A doctor who was unaware of this ordered its continuance. Two fresh witnesses also testified that abnormal quantities of liquid had been given intravenously. This caused the lungs to become waterlogged and pulmonary oedema was discovered.

HALLETT J

We are disposed to accept it as the law that death resulting from any normal treatment employed to deal with a felonious injury may be regarded as caused by the felonious injury, but we do not think it necessary to examine the cases in detail or to formulate for the assistance of those who have to deal with such matters in the future the correct test which ought to be laid down with regard to what is necessary to be proved in order to establish causal connection between the death and the felonious injury. Not only one feature, but two separate and independent features, of treatment were, in the opinion of the doctors, palpably wrong and these produced the symptoms discovered at the post-mortem examination which were the direct and immediate cause of death, namely, the pneumonia resulting from the condition of oedema which was found.

Conviction quashed

R. V SMITH

[1959] 2 Q.B. 35

The appellant, a soldier, was charged with, and convicted of, the murder of a fellow soldier during the course of a fight between the men of two regiments who shared the same barrack room. The deceased received two bayonet wounds, one in the arm and one in the back which pierced the lung and caused haemorrhage. Another soldier tried to carry the wounded man to the medical reception station. He twice dropped him on the ground. At the station the medical officer and his orderly were extremely busy. There were two other stabbed men to deal with as well as others with minor injuries. The medical staff did not know of the haemorrhage nor was the serious nature of the injury realised. A transfusion of saline solution was tried but failed and when breathing seemed impaired, oxygen and artificial respiration were given. This treatment was "thoroughly bad" and might well have affected his chance of recovery. There was medical evidence at the trial that haemorrhage of this type tends to stop. Had there been a blood transfusion available chances of recovery were assessed as high as 75 per cent, by a medical witness for the defence.

LORD PARKER CJ

In these circumstances Mr. Bowen urged that not only was a careful summing-up required, but that a correct direction to the court would have been that they must be satisfied that the death of Private Creed was a natural consequence and the sole consequence of the wound sustained by him and flowed directly from it. If there was, says Mr Bowen, any other cause, whether resulting from negligence or not, if, as he contends here, something happened which impeded the chance of the deceased recovering, then the death did not result from the wound. The court is quite unable to accept that contention. It seems to the court that if at the time of death the original wound is still an operating cause and a substantial cause, then the death can properly be said to be the result of the wound, albeit that some other cause of death is also operating. Only if it can be said that the original wounding is merely the setting in which another cause operates can it be said that the death did not result from the wound. Putting it another way, only if the second cause is so overwhelming as to make the original wound merely part of the history can it be said that the death does not flow from the wound . . .

Mr Bowen placed great reliance on a case decided in the Court of Criminal Appeal, *R. v Jordan* [above, p.54] and in particular on a passage in the headnote which says, '. . . that death resulting from any normal treatment employed to deal with a felonious injury may be regarded as caused by the felonious injury, but that the same principle does not apply where the treatment is abnormal.' Reading those words into the present case, Mr Bowen says that the treatment that this unfortunate man received from the moment that he was struck to the time of his death was abnormal. The court is satisfied that *Jordan's* case was a very particular case depending upon its exact facts. It incidentally arose on the grant of an application to call further evidence, and leave having been obtained, two well-known medical experts gave evidence that in their opinion death had not been caused by the stabbing but by the introduction of terramycin after the deceased had shown that he was intolerant to it, and by the intravenous introduction of abnormal quantities of liquid. It also appears that at the time when that was done the stab wound which had penetrated the intestine in two places had mainly healed. In those circumstances the court felt bound to quash the conviction because they could not say that a reasonable jury, properly directed, would not have been able on that to say that there had been a break in the chain of causation; the court could only uphold the conviction in that case if they were satisfied that no reasonable jury could have come to that conclusion.

In the present case it is true that the judge-advocate did not in his summing-up go into the refinements of causation. Indeed, in the opinion of this court he was probably wise to refrain from doing so. He did leave the broad question to the court whether they were satisfied that the wound had caused the death in the sense that the death flowed from the wound, albeit that the treatment he received was in the light of after-knowledge a bad thing. In the opinion of this court that was on the facts of the case a perfectly adequate summing-up on causation; I say 'on the facts of the case' because, in the opinion of the court, they can only lead to one conclusion: a man is stabbed in the back, his lung is pierced and haemorrhage results; two hours later he dies of haemorrhage from that wound; in the interval there is no time for a careful examination, and the treatment given turns out in the light of subsequent knowledge to have been inappropriate and, indeed, harmful. In those circumstances no reasonable jury or court could, properly directed, in our view possibly come to any other conclusion than that the death resulted from the original wound. Accordingly the court dismisses this appeal.

Appeal dismissed

R. V MALCHEREK AND R. V STEEL

[1981] 2 All E.R. 422

These two cases raised the same question. M stabbed his wife with a kitchen knife causing a deep abdominal wound. S was accused of attacking a girl causing grave head injuries. Both victims were put on life support machines during normal courses of treatment. In each case the machines were switched off after a number of tests indicated that brain death had occurred. Both M and S were convicted at their trials for murder. The ground of M's appeal and S's application for leave to appeal was that the judge should not have withdrawn the question of causation from the jury. S also sought leave to adduce further medical evidence that the doctors in each case had not complied with all the Medical Royal Colleges' and Faculties of the United Kingdom 1976 suggested criteria for establishing brain death.

LORD LANE CJ

[After stating the facts] . . . This is not the occasion for any decision as to what constitutes death . . . There is, it seems, a body of opinion in the medical profession that there is only one true test of death and that is the irreversible death of the brain stem, which controls the basic functions of the body such as breathing. When that occurs it is said the body has died, even though by mechanical means the lungs are being caused to operate and some circulation of blood is taking place . . .

The question posed for answer to this court is simply whether the judge in each case was right in withdrawing from the jury the question of causation. Was he right to rule that there was no evidence on which the jury could come to the conclusion that the assailant did not cause the death of the victim?

The way in which the submissions are put by counsel for Malcherek on the one hand and by counsel for Steel on the other is as follows: the doctors, by switching off the ventilator and the life support machine, were the cause of death or, to put it more accurately, there was evidence which the jury should have been allowed to consider that the doctors, and not the assailant, in each case may have been the cause of death.

In each case it is clear that the initial assault was the cause of the grave head injuries in the one case and of the massive abdominal haemorrhage in the other. In each case the initial assault was the reason for the medical treatment being necessary. In each case the medical treatment given was normal and conventional. At some stage the doctors must decide if and when treatment has become otiose. This decision was reached, in each of the two cases here, in circumstances which have already been set out in some detail . . .

There are two comparatively recent cases which are relevant to the consideration of this problem. [His Lordship then considered *R. v Smith*, above, p.55 and *R. v Jordan*, above p.54].

In the view of this court, if a choice has to be made between the decision in *R. v Jordan* and that in ft. *R. v Smith*, which we do not believe it does (*R. v Jordan* being a very exceptional case), then the decision in *R. v Smith* is to be preferred.

The only other case to which reference has been made, it having been drawn to our attention by counsel for Steel, is *R. v Blaue*, [above, p.51] . . .

The passage . . . is the last paragraph of the judgment of Lawton L. J. [1975] 1 W.L.R. 1411 at 1416:

'The issue of the cause of death in a trial for either murder or manslaughter is one of fact for the jury to decide. But if, as in this case, there is no conflict of evidence and all the jury has to do is apply the law to the admitted facts, the judge is entitled to tell the jury what the result of that application will be. In this case the judge would have been entitled to have told the jury that the appellant's stab wound was an operative cause of death. The appeal fails.'

There is no evidence in the present case here that at the time of conventional death, after the life support machinery was disconnected, the original wound or injury was other than a continuing, operating and indeed substantial cause of the death of the victim, although it need hardly be added that it need not be substantial to render the assailant guilty. There may be occasions, although they will be rare, when the original injury has ceased to operate as a cause at all, but in the ordinary case if treatment is given bona fide by competent and careful medical practitioners, then evidence will not be admissible to show that the treatment would not have been administered in the same way by other medical practitioners. In other words, the fact that the victim has died, despite or because of medical treatment for the initial injury given by careful and skilled medical practitioners, will not exonerate the original assailant from responsibility for the death. It follows that so far as the ground of appeal in each of these cases relates to the direction given on causation, that ground fails . . . Where a medical practitioner adopting methods which are generally accepted comes bona fide and conscientiously to the conclusion that the patient is for practical purposes dead, and that such vital functions as exist (for example, circulation) are being maintained solely by mechanical means, and therefore discontinues treatment, that does not prevent the person who inflicted the initial injury from being responsible for the victim's death. Putting it in another way, the discontinuance of treatment in those circumstances does not break the chain of causation between the initial injury and the death.

Appeal and applications dismissed

Note

In *Jordan* the original wound had healed whereas in *Smith* and *Malcherek* the original wounds were still operating at the time of death. In the case which follows the Court of Appeal had sought to move away from the simplistic analysis of whether or not the original wound had healed at the time of death, as concentration on this may lead to the wrong conclusion. The issue is whether D has caused the death of V not whether the wound D inflicted caused V's death. Even though the actual wound may have healed, D's act may still be an operating and substantial (in the sense of "more than minimal") cause of death.

R. V CHESHIRE

[1991] 1 W.L.R. 844

In December 1987, D shot V in the leg and the stomach. V underwent surgery and when respiratory complications arose a tracheotomy was performed, the tube remaining in place until early January 1988. In February, V developed difficulty in breathing which was diagnosed as being due to anxiety. On February 14, V complained of further problems with breathing. His condition deteriorated and despite attempts at resuscitation V died early on February 15. The cause of death was given as cardio-respiratory arrest due to a condition produced as a result of provision of an artificial airway in treatment of gunshot wounds. At D's trial for murder, the defence presented expert medical evidence that the gunshot wounds no longer threatened V's life and that the cause of death was the failure to correctly diagnose and treat the cause of V's breathlessness which was due to a narrowing of V's windpipe near the site of the tracheotomy scar. The trial judge directed the jury that in order to find that the chain of causation between the original wounding and V's death had been broken, they had to be satisfied that the medical treatment or lack of it was not merely negligent but reckless in the sense that the doctors had acted or failed to act "careless of the consequences, careless of the comfort and safety of another person."

BELDAM LJ

Whilst medical treatment unsuccessfully given to prevent the death of a victim with the care and skill of a competent medical practitioner will not amount to an intervening cause, it does not follow that treatment which falls below that standard of care and skill will amount to such a cause. As Professors Hart and Honoré comment, treatment which falls short of the standard expected of the competent medical practitioner is unfortunately only too frequent in human experience for it to be considered abnormal in the sense of extraordinary. Acts or omissions of a doctor treating the victim for injuries he has received at the hands of a defendant may conceivably be so extraordinary as to be capable of being regarded as acts independent of the conduct of the defendant but it is most unlikely that they will be.

[His Lordship referred to the cases of *Jordan*, *Smith* and *Malcherek*. Referring to the latter case he continued:]

[I]t was not suggested that the actions of the doctors in disconnecting the life support machines were other than competent and careful. The court did not have to consider the effect of medical treatment which fell short of the standard of care to be expected of competent medical practitioners . . .

[W]hen the victim of a criminal attack is treated for wounds or injuries by doctors or other medical staff attempting to repair the harm done, it will only be in the most extraordinary and unusual case that such treatment can be said to be so independent of the acts of the defendant that it could be regarded in law as the cause of the victim's death to the exclusion of the defendant's acts.

Where the law requires proof of the relationship between an act and its consequences as an element of responsibility, a simple and sufficient explanation of the basis of such relationship has proved notoriously elusive.

In a case in which the jury have to consider whether negligence in the treatment of injuries inflicted by the defendant was the cause of death we think it is sufficient for the judge to tell the jury that they must be satisfied that the Crown have proved that the acts of the defendant caused the death of the deceased adding that the defendant's acts need not be the sole cause or even the main cause of death it being sufficient that his acts contributed significantly to that result. Even though negligence in the treatment of the victim was the immediate cause of his death, the jury should not regard it as excluding the responsibility of the defendant unless the negligent treatment was so independent of his acts, and in itself so potent in causing death, that they regard the contribution made by his acts as insignificant.

It is not the function of the jury to evaluate competing causes or to choose which is dominant provided they are satisfied that the defendant's acts can fairly be said to have made a significant contribution to the victim's death. We think the word 'significant' conveys the necessary substance of a contribution made to the death which is more than negligible.

[His Lordship concluded that although the judge erred when he invited the jury to consider the degree of fault in the medical treatment rather than its consequences, no miscarriage of justice had occurred as he had correctly directed the jury that the prosecution did not have to prove that the bullets were the only cause of death but that they were one operative and substantial cause of death. His Lordship continued:]

Even if more experienced doctors than those who attended the deceased would have recognised the rare complication in time to have prevented the deceased's death, that complication was a direct consequence of the appellant's acts, which remained a significant cause of his death. We cannot conceive that, on the evidence given, any jury would have found otherwise.

Appeal dismissed

Note

The decision in *Cheshire* focuses on the acts of the accused in setting in motion a sequence of events which culminates in the victim's death, viz., had D not injured V, V would not have required medical treatment from which complications might arise which in turn might result in misdiagnosis by the doctor. The Court of Appeal is adamant that only in the most exceptional circumstances will negligent medical treatment relieve the accused of causal responsibility for the victim's death. While *Cheshire* has resolved some of the confusion arising from *Jordan* and *Smith*, the decision itself is not above criticism (see Ashworth directly below).

A. ASHWORTH, *PRINCIPLES OF CRIMINAL LAW*, 3RD EDN (OXFORD: OXFORD UNIVERSITY PRESS, 1999), P.132

No clear reason is offered for discounting the voluntary intervening act of the doctor. If the doctor administers a drug to which the patient is known to be intolerant, or gives some other wrong treatment, should the inappropriateness of the medical treatment affect the casual enquiry? The courts' reluctance to discuss the causal significance of the medical treatment probably stems from a desire to ensure the conviction of a culpable offender, and this suggests a strong attachment to a 'wrongful act' approach to causation, deciding the issue by reference to broader judgments of innocence and culpability. This appears to overlook the fact that D, who inflicted the original wound which gave rise to the need for medical attention, will still be liable for attempted murder or a serious wounding offence even if the medical treatment is held to negative his causal responsibility for the ensuing death. Perhaps, for adherents of the 'wrongful act' approach, this is insufficient: they want to see responsibility for the ultimate result pinned on the defendant. However, a court which declares that it is not the doctor who is on trial but the original wrongdoer is merely offering an unconvincing rationalization of its failure to apply the ordinary causal principle that a voluntary intervening act which accelerates death should relieve the original wrongdoer of liability for the result. If that causal principle is thought unsuitable for medical cases, should we not be absolutely clear about the reasons, and then look closely at a doctrine of clinical medical necessity?

Questions

1. If the facts of *Jordan* were to recur how might the question of causation be decided?
2. What would have happened in *Cheshire* if the doctor, having misdiagnosed V's condition, rather than giving no treatment had gone on to give him drugs which exacerbated his condition?

Note

In *McKechnie* [1992] Crim. L.R. 194, the Court of Appeal upheld D's conviction of manslaughter on the grounds of provocation, D having caused serious head injuries to V. V died not from the head injuries but five weeks later from a burst duodenal ulcer. When V was first admitted to hospital unconscious from the head injuries, the doctors decided that they dare not operate on the ulcer. V would not have died had he had an operation on the ulcer. D's act therefore did not cause V to undergo medical treatment but rather prevented him undergoing treatment that would have saved his life. The decision not to operate was not to be judged on its correctness but its reasonableness. On this basis it could not be considered "extraordinary and unusual" and was not "so independent of the acts of the accused that it could be regarded in law as the cause of the victim's death".

R. V PAGETT

(1983) 76 Cr. App. R. 279

P, while hiding behind V whom he was holding against her will and whose body he was using as a shield, fired a shotgun at police officers who were attempting to arrest him. The officers returned P's fire killing V. P was charged, inter alia, with murder. On the issue of causation the judge directed the jury that they had to be sure that P had fired first at the officers and that that act caused the officers to fire back with the result that V was killed, and that in doing so they had to be satisfied that the police acted reasonably either by way of self-defence or in the performance of their duties as police officers. If they were not sure of those facts then they should acquit P because the chain that linked his deliberate and unlawful acts to V's death would be broken. The jury acquitted P of murder and convicted him of manslaughter. P appealed.

ROBERT GOFF LJ

(for the court) . . . [Two of the] three specific points raised on behalf of the appellant were as follows (we quote from the grounds of appeal):

(1) The learned judge erred in law in directing that the jury must as a matter of law find that the appellant caused the death of the deceased, if they were satisfied as to the four matters of fact which he set out. The learned judge ought rather to have left it to the jury to determine as an issue of fact whether the defend-ant's act in firing at the police officers was a substantial, or operative, or imputable, cause of the death of the deceased.

(2) In the alternative, if the learned judge was correct in himself determining as a matter of law what facts would amount to causation of the death by the appellant, he ought to have held that the appellant had not in the circumstances of this case caused the death of the deceased. The learned judge, in directing himself upon the law, ought to have held that where the act which immediately resulted in fatal injury was the act of another party, albeit in legitimate self-defence, then the ensuing death was too remote or indirect to be imputed to the original aggressor . . .

The argument addressed to this Court by Lord Gifford on behalf of the appellant was concentrated primarily on the first and second grounds of appeal, and was as presented concerned with the issue of causation. We find it convenient to deal first with the second ground of appeal . . .

[I]t was pressed upon us by Lord Gifford [for the appellant] that there either was, or should be, a . . . rule of English law, whereby, as a matter of policy, no man should be convicted of homicide (or, we imagine, any crime of violence to another person) unless he himself, or another person acting in concert with him, fired the shot (or, we imagine, struck the blow) which was the immediate cause of the victim's death (or injury).

No English authority was cited to us in support of any such proposition, and we know of none. So far as we are aware, there is no such rule in English law; and, in the absence of any doctrine of constructive malice, we can see no basis in principle for any such rule in English law . . .

In our judgment, the question whether an accused person can be held guilty of homicide, either murder or manslaughter, of a victim the immediate cause of whose death is the act of another person must be determined on the ordinary principles of causation, uninhibited by any such rule of policy as that for which Lord Gifford has contended. We therefore reject the second ground of appeal.

We turn to the first ground of appeal, which is that the learned judge erred in directing the jury that it was for him to decide *as a matter of law* whether by his unlawful and deliberate acts the appellant caused or was a cause of Gail Kinchen's death. It is right to observe that this direction of the learned judge followed upon a discussion with counsel, in the absence of the jury . . .

In cases of homicide, it is rarely necessary to give the jury any direction on causation as such . . . [H]ow the victim came by his death is usually not in dispute . . .

Even where it is necessary to direct the jury's minds to the question of causation, it is usually enough to direct them simply that in law the accused's act need not be the sole cause, or even the main cause, of the victim's death, it being enough that his act contributed significantly to that result . . .

Occasionally, however, a specific issue of causation may arise. One such case is where, although an act of the accused constitutes a *causa sine qua non* of (or necessary condition for) the death of the victim, nevertheless the intervention of a third person may be regarded as the sole cause of the victim's death, thereby relieving the accused of criminal responsibility. Such intervention, if it has such an effect, has often been described by lawyers as a *novus actus interveniens* . . .

[The phrase is] a term of art which conveys to lawyers the crucial feature that there has not merely been an intervening act of another person, but that that act was so independent of the act of the accused that it should be regarded in law as the cause of the victim's death, to the exclusion of the act of the accused.

. . . Professors Hart and Honoré, *Causation in the Law* . . . consider the circumstances in which the intervention of a third person, not acting in concert with the accused, may have the effect of relieving the accused of criminal responsibility. The criterion which they suggest should be applied in such circumstances is whether the intervention is voluntary, i.e. whether it is 'free, deliberate and informed'. We resist the temptation of expressing the judicial opinion whether we find ourselves in complete agreement with that definition; though we certainly consider it to be broadly correct and supported by authority. Among the examples which the authors give of non-voluntary conduct, which is not effective to relieve the accused of responsibility, are two which are germane to the present case, *viz.*, a reasonable act performed for the purpose of self-preservation, and an act done in performance of a legal duty.

There can, we consider, be no doubt that a reasonable act performed for the purpose of self-preservation, being of course itself an act caused by the accused's own act, does not operate as a *novus actus interveniens*. If authority is needed for this almost self-evident proposition, it is to be found in such cases as *R. v Pitts* (1842) C. & M. 284, and *R. v Curley* (1909) 2 Cr.App.R. 96. In both these cases, the act performed for the purpose of self-preservation consisted of an act by the victim in attempting to escape from the violence of the accused, which in fact resulted in the victim's death. In each case it was held as a matter of law that, if the victim acted in a reasonable attempt to escape the violence of the accused, the death of the victim was caused by the act of the accused. Now one form of self-preservation is self-defence; for present purposes, we can see no distinction in principle between an attempt to escape the consequences of the accused's act, and a response which takes the form of self-defence. Furthermore, in our judgment, if a reasonable act of self-defence against the act of the accused causes the death of a third party, we can see no reason in principle why the act of self-defence, being an involuntary act caused by the act of the accused, should relieve the accused from criminal responsibility for the death of the third party . . .

No English authority was cited to us, nor we think to the learned judge, in support of the proposition that an act done in the execution of a legal duty, again of course being an act itself caused by the act of the accused, does not operate as *novus actus interveniens* . . . Even so, we agree with the learned judge that the proposition is sound in law, because as a matter of principle such an act cannot be regarded as a voluntary act independent of the wrongful act of the accused. A parallel may be drawn with the so-called 'rescue' cases in the law of negligence, where a wrongdoer may be held liable in negligence to a third party who suffers injury in going to the rescue of a person who has been put in danger by the defendant's negligent act. Where, for example, a police officer in the execution of his duty acts to prevent a crime, or to apprehend a person suspected of a crime, the case is surely a *fortiori*. Of course, it is inherent in the requirement that the police officer, or other person, must be acting in the execution of his duty that his act should be reasonable in all the circumstances; see section 3 of the Criminal Law Act 1967 . . .

The principles which we have stated are principles of law. It follows that where, in any particular case, there is an issue concerned with what we have for convenience called *novus actus interveniens*, it will be appropriate for the judge to direct the jury in accordance with these principles. It does not however follow that it is accurate to state broadly that causation is a question of law. On the contrary, generally speaking causation is a question of fact for the jury . . .

But that does not mean that there are no principles of law relating to causation, so that no directions on law are ever to be given to a jury on the question of causation. On the contrary, we have already pointed out one familiar direction which is given on causation, which is that the accused's act need not be the sole, or even the main, cause of the victim's death for his act to be held to have caused the death.

[His Lordship then cited the principle in *R. v Blaue*, above, p.51 as an example of a *statement of legal principle* on causation.]

Likewise, in cases where there is an issue whether the act of the victim or of a third party constituted a *novus actus interveniens*, breaking the causal connection between the act of the accused and the death of the victim, it would be appropriate for the judge to direct the jury, of course in the most simple terms, in accordance with the legal principles which they have to apply. It would then fall to the jury to decide the relevant factual issues which, identified with reference to those legal principles, will lead to the conclusion whether or not the prosecution have established the guilt of the accused of the crime of which he is charged.

In the light of these principles, we do not consider that any legitimate criticism can be made, on behalf of the appellant, of the direction given by the learned judge to the jury on the issue of causation in the present case . . .

For these reasons, we are unable to accept Lord Gifford's argument based on the first ground of appeal.

Appeal dismissed

Questions

1.   Would the outcome have been the same if the victim had been an innocent passer-by?
2.   Would P have been guilty of wounding if V had not died?
3.   Would P have been guilty if V had escaped from his hold and run in the line of police fire?

Notes

1.   In *Pagett*, Robert Goff L.J. spoke of novus actus interveniens conveying the idea that there has not merely been an intervening act of another person, but that that act was so independent of the act of the accused that it should be regarded in law as the cause of the relevant consequence to the exclusion of the act of the accused, accepting as broadly correct and supported by authority the Hart and Honoré criterion of whether the intervention is voluntary, i.e. "free, deliberate and informed". Consider whether the following cases can be reconciled with this criterion.

2.   In *Kennedy* [2005] EWCA Crim 685, D supplied a syringe filled with heroin to V who paid him and injected it and subsequently died. D was convicted of manslaughter. It was not contended that V was an adult of sound mind who, having received the syringe from D, injected himself. At D's first appeal, reported at [1999] Crim. L.R. 65, the Court of Appeal placed considerable emphasis on the fact that D's supply of the syringe amounted to encouragement to V to inject himself. A person who encourages another to commit an offence may be liable as an accessory to that offence because of the encouragement offered, but not because the encouragement causes the relevant consequence—it is the principal who causes it (see Ch.6). In the instant case, however, V, being the deceased, could not be the principal to manslaughter, only D could be that but V's self-injection with heroin was the immediate cause of death (see further *Dalby*, Ch.8, below p.498). In *Dias* [2001] EWCA Crim 2986 on similar facts to *Kennedy*, the Court of Appeal quashed D's conviction for manslaughter on the basis that there was no offence committed by the self-injecting victim and thus no offence which D could have encouraged. The Court also expressed the view that the deceased's self injection may well have been seen as an intervening act breaking the chain of causation but was content, without further elaboration, to say that this could be left to the jury to determine.

The case of *Kennedy* was referred back to the Court of Appeal by the Criminal Cases Review Commission following the view expressed in *Dias* and other similar cases that threw doubt on the correctness of Kennedy's conviction. After again upholding the conviction, the matter finally reached the House of Lords in *R. v Kennedy (No.2)* [2007] UKHL 38, where it was held that the act of self-injection by V did break the chain of causation. (The full impact of this case is considered at Chs 6 and 8, below p.498).

Note

In *Environment Agency v Empress Car Co (Abertillery)* [1999] 2 A.C. 22, D Co had on its land a diesel tank which had an outlet pipe connected to it which led to a drum. The outlet pipe was controlled by a tap which was not locked. An unknown person opened the tap resulting in the contents of the tank draining into the drum, overflowing and polluting a river. The appellant was charged with causing polluting matter to enter controlled waters contrary to s.85(1) of the Water Resources Act 1991. D Co denied causing pollution but was convicted. The House of Lords dismissed D Co's appeal. The leading judgment by Lord Hoffmann drew no distinction between deliberate acts of third parties and interventions of nature stating that:

> "The true common sense distinction is, in my view, between acts and events which, although not necessarily foreseeable in the particular case, are in the generality a normal and familiar fact of life, and acts or events which are abnormal and extraordinary. Of course an act or event which is in general terms a normal fact of life may also have been foreseeable in the circumstances of the particular case, but the latter is not necessary for the purposes of liability. There is nothing extraordinary or abnormal about leaky pipes or lagoons as such: these things happen, even if the particular defendant could not reasonably have foreseen that it would happen to him. There is nothing unusual about people putting unlawful substances into the sewage system and the same, regrettably, is true about ordinary vandalism. So when these things happen, one does not say: that was an extraordinary coincidence, which negatived the causal connection between the original act of accumulating the polluting substance and its escape. In the context of section 85(1), the defendant's accumulation has still caused the pollution. On the other hand, the example I gave of the terrorist attack would be something so unusual that one would not regard the defendant's conduct as having caused the escape at all."

It appears that in cases involving pollution, at least, the free, deliberate, informed and malicious act of a third party will not constitute a novus actus as it is not extraordinary. In *Kennedy (No.2)* [2007] UKHL 38, the House of Lords confined the authority of *Empress* to strict liability offences involving pollution overruling a number of Court of Appeal decisions which purported to apply *Empress* to the offence of manslaughter (see further Ch.8, below p.498).

In *Hughes* [2013] UKSC 56 the Supreme Court observed that "the meaning of causation is heavily context-specific and that Parliament (or in some cases the courts) may apply different legal rules of causation in different situations".

Questions

1. What is the difference between a natural occurring event that produces a consequence and the action of a third-party that produces a consequence? Is it ever justifiable to impose liability in the latter?

2. Is the statement of the Supreme Court in *Hughes* (see note above) merely judicial recognition that causation is, in reality, determined by a moral reaction?

----

iii. An Alternative Approach

G.P. FLETCHER, *RETHINKING CRIMINAL LAW* (BOSTON: LITTLE, BROWN, 1978), PP.362, 368

It would be plausible to define a law protecting life in terms that made the occurrence of death irrelevant. The critical issue would be an act endangering life. An attempt to kill, particularly if manifested unequivocally in the actor's behaviour, would be treated the same as an actual killing. Conduct highly dangerous to human life would be treated as equivalent to reckless homicide. The rationale for eliminating the issues of causation and death would be that the purpose of the law should be to punish and to deter blameworthy assaults on the interest in life. The actual occurrence of death and its causal attribution are irrelevant to the sets of acts that should be deterred, and it is also irrelevant to the criteria rendering the accused blameworthy for his conduct. The man who shoots at an apparently alive but dead patient, is arguably no less blameworthy than the assassin who has the bad luck to shoot and kill a living patient . . .

There is no easy solution to the problem of causation. The metaphysics of proximate cause, degrees of contribution and intervening causes will continue to affect even the most rational penal system. The reasons are several. First, the inquiry into causation is categorical. A death is attributable to someone or it is not. There is no room for a compromise verdict as there is in the assessment of culpability for criminal homicide. Secondly, the issue of causation, along with the elements of acting and the occurrence of death, goes to the foundation of liability . . .

The third significant factor is that the courts are bound to render these appellate decisions in an all-or-nothing fashion without having a general theory to guide their assessment whether in close cases they should find for the defendant or the prosecution . . .

Rooted in the practice of tainting, the causal inquiry bears neither on the definition of conduct that should be deterred nor on the criteria for justly blaming someone who endangers human life.

Question

Consider whether any of the above cases would have been decided differently had the question not been one of causation but of an act endangering life, as suggested by Fletcher.

LAW COMMISSION, *DRAFT CRIMINAL CODE BILL* (TSO, 1989), LAW COM. NO.177

Causation

17.—(1)
(2) A person does not cause a result where, after he does such an act or makes such an omission, an act or event occurs—

(a) which is the immediate and sufficient cause of the result;

(b) which he did not foresee, and

(c) which could not in the circumstances reasonably have been foreseen.

(3) A person who procures, assists or encourages another to cause a result that is an element of an offence does not himself cause that result so as to be guilty of the offence as a principal except when—

(a) section 26(1)(c) applies; or

(b) the offence itself consists in the procuring, assisting or encouraging another to cause the result.

5. COINCIDENCE OF ACTUS REUS AND MENS REA

Note

Where an offence requires mens rea the prosecution must prove that D had mens rea at the time he did the act which caused the actus reus.

R. V JAKEMAN

(1983) 76 Cr. App. R. 223

J booked two cases containing cannabis on a flight from Accra to Rome and from there to London. The flight was diverted from Rome to Paris. J did not claim her cases in Paris but flew on to Rome and then to London. Officials in Paris sent the cases to London where they were not collected. The cannabis was discovered and J was charged with being knowingly concerned in the fraudulent evasion of the restriction on the importation of cannabis contrary to s.170(2) of the Customs and Excise Act 1979. J's defence was that on boarding the aircraft she repented of her original intention and tore up the baggage tags. The judge ruled that this provided no defence. J appealed.

WOOD J

Mr Mansfield . . . submits that for the offence under section 170(2) of the 1979 Act, the participation of the applicant and her *mens rea* must continue throughout the offence—in this case at least until the wheels of the aircraft touched down at Heathrow Airport

The following propositions are supported by decisions of this court. First, that the importation takes place when the aircraft . . .bringing the goods lands at an airport in this country, see *R. v Smith (Donald)*; [1973] Q.B. 924, 935G. Secondly, acts done abroad in order to further the fraudulent evasion of a restriction on importation into this country are punishable under this section, see *R. v Wall (Geoffrey)* [1974] 1 W.L.R. 930, 934C.

For guilt to be established the importation must, of course, result as a consequence, if only in part, of the activity of the accused. If, for example, in the present case the applicant had taken her two suitcases off the carousel at Charles de Gaulle airport in Paris, removed all the luggage tags, placed the suitcases in a left luggage compartment and thrown the key of that compartment into the Seine, and then subsequently, in a general emergency, all left luggage compartments had been opened, a well-known English travel label had been found on her suitcase and those suitcases had been sent to the Travel Agents' agency, care of Customs and Excise at Heathrow, then that undoubted importation would not be the relevant one for the purposes of a charge against the applicant

Although the importation takes place at one precise moment—when the aircraft lands—a person who is concerned in the importation may play his part before or after that moment. Commonly, the person responsible for despatching the prohibited drugs to England acts fraudulently and so does the person who removes them from the airport at which they have arrived. Each is guilty . . .

There is no doubt, that . . . the applicant had a guilty mind when at Accra she booked her luggage to London. By that act, she brought about the importation through the instrumentation of innocent agents. In this way, she caused the airline to label it to London, and the labels were responsible for the authorities in Paris sending it on to London.

What is suggested is that she should not be convicted unless her guilty state of mind subsisted at the time of importation. We see no reason to construe the Act in this way. If a guilty mind at the time of importation is an essential, the man recruited to collect the package which has already arrived and which he knows contains prohibited drugs commits no offence. What matters is the state of mind at the time the relevant acts are done, i.e. at the time the defendant is concerned in bringing about the importation. This accords with the general principles of common law. To stab a victim in a rage with the necessary intent for murder or manslaughter leads to criminal responsibility for the resulting death regardless of any repentance between the act of stabbing and the time of death, which may be hours or days later. This is so even if, within seconds of the stabbing, the criminal comes to his senses and does everything possible to assist his victim. Only the victim's survival will save him from conviction for murder or manslaughter.

The applicant alleged that she repented as soon as she boarded the aircraft; that she deliberately failed to claim her luggage in Paris, that she tore up the baggage tags attached to her ticket and so on, but none of this could have saved her from being held criminally responsible for the importation which she had brought about by deliberate actions committed with guilty intent. Thus, the learned judge was right in the ruling he made.

Appeal dismissed

Questions

1.   If checking in the cases at Accra amounted to an "act which is more than merely preparatory to the commission of the offence" (Criminal Attempts Act 1981 s.1(1)), would removal of the luggage in Paris, in the manner suggested by the judge, have provided an answer to a charge of attempted fraudulent evasion of importation restrictions?

2.   If checking in the cases at Accra did not amount to "an act which is more than merely preparatory to the commission of the offence," should such an intention be sufficient for conviction of the completed offence which unexpectedly occurs at a time when mens rea no longer exists?

Note

Where an actus reus may be brought about by a continuing act, it is sufficient that the accused had mens rea during its continuance even though he did not have mens rea at its inception (see *Fagan v Metropolitan Police Commissioner*, below, p.534; see also *Kaitamaki* [1985] A.C. 147). A problem which has arisen in relation to homicide, is that of death resulting from a series of acts performed by the accused only some of which were performed with mens rea.

THABO MELI V THE QUEEN

[1954] 1 W.L.R. 228

The deceased was taken to a hut by the appellants where he was struck over the head with intent to kill him. His unconscious body was then rolled over a small cliff to make the death appear to be an accident. Medical evidence indicated that the appellants had not succeeded in killing the deceased in the hut but that he had died from exposure.

LORD REID

The point of law which was raised in this case can be simply stated. It is said that two acts were necessary and were separable: first, the attack in the hut; and, secondly, the placing of the body outside afterwards. It is said that, while the first act was accompanied by *mens rea*, it was not the cause of death; but that the second act, while it was the cause of death, was not accompanied by *mens rea*; and on that ground it is said that the accused are not guilty of any crime, except perhaps culpable homicide.

It appears to their Lordships impossible to divide up what was really one transaction in this way. There is no doubt that the accused set out to do all these acts in order to achieve their plan and as parts of their plan; and it is too refined a ground of judgment to say that, because they were under a misapprehension at one stage and thought that their guilty purpose had been achieved before in fact it was achieved, therefore they are to escape the penalties of the law . . .

Notes

1. In the next chapter the issue of mistake will be considered. In *Thabo Meli* the appellants made a mistake; they thought they were disposing of a corpse when they threw the victim over the cliff. An intention to destroy or dispose of a corpse is not sufficient mens rea for murder; what is required is an intention to kill or to cause grievous bodily harm. Thus, in strict legal principle, the appellants' mistake meant that they did not have the mens rea of murder at the time they caused death. If they were to be convicted of murder, the court would have to extend the law on policy grounds to cover this situation where there was no contiguity between the actus reus and mens rea. As G. Williams states in *Criminal Law, The General Part*, 2nd edn (1961), pp.174–175:

    "In [this case of *Thabo Meli*] the accused intends to kill and does kill; his only mistake is as to the precise moment of death and as to the precise act that effects death. Ordinary ideas of justice and common sense require that such a case shall be treated as murder. If so it is necessary to make an exception to the general principle [that mistake as to an element of the actus reus negatives mens rea], and to hold that although the accused thinks that he is dealing with a corpse, still his act is murder if his mistaken belief that it is a corpse is the result of what he has done in pursuance of his murderous intent. If a killing by the first act would have been manslaughter, a later destruction of the supposed corpse should also be manslaughter."

2. In the case of *Church* [1966] 1 Q.B. 59 below, p.496, the problem of the supposed corpse arose in relation to a conviction of manslaughter. The appellant struck and attempted to strangle a woman. She fell unconscious and the appellant, believing her dead following his extremely cursory examination of her, threw her into a river where she drowned. He was convicted of manslaughter and on appeal that conviction was upheld. The Court of Criminal Appeal appears to have upheld the conviction on the basis of gross negligence manslaughter although it also made comments on the "series of acts" doctrine in *Thabo Meli*. It adopted "as sound" Williams's view as expressed in the final sentence of the passage above. The court was of opinion that the judge should have directed the jury that—

    ". . . they were entitled (if they thought fit) to regard the conduct of the appellant in relation to Mrs Nott [the deceased] as constituting throughout a series of acts which *culminated in her death*, and that, if that was how they regarded the accused's behaviour, it mattered not whether he believed her to be alive or dead when he threw her in the river." (emphasis added) (at 71).

    The problem with this approach is that it begs a question; was it such a series of acts that would have led to conviction under the *Thabo Meli* approach? In *Thabo Meli* the acts of attack and disposal were part of a concerted plan to kill the accused and then dispose of the corpse. There was no such plan in *Church* (nor could there be in a case of manslaughter unless it arose as a result of a plea of diminished responsibility), so were the acts of original attack and the act of disposal part of a series? In *Thabo Meli* the acts formed a series, not because the act of disposal followed sequentially on the attack, but because they were concerted acts in pursuance of a plan. In speaking of *Thabo Meli* the Court of Criminal Appeal stated that, with regard to the charge of murder against *Church* (of which he was acquitted),

    ". . . the jury should have been told that it was still open to them to convict of murder, notwithstanding that the appellant may have thought his blows and attempt at strangulation had actually produced death when he threw the body into the river, if they regarded the appellant's behaviour from the moment he first struck her to the moment when he threw her into the river as a series of acts designed to cause death or grievous bodily harm." (at 67)

This statement talks of a "series of acts designed to cause death" whereas, in respect of manslaughter, the court talked of a "series of acts which culminated in . . . death". It is difficult to follow the court's reasoning when it talks of a series of acts designed to cause death as the act of disposal is for the purpose of disposing of a *body*, it being the actor's belief that death had occurred already. Such a direction would be inherently illogical.

In *S v Masilela* 1968 (2) S.A. 558 the Supreme Court of South Africa (Appellate Division) held that a conviction of murder could be returned where death resulted from the act of disposal by the assailant even though there was no preconceived plan. In the case which follows there was neither a preconceived plan nor did the accused believe he was dealing with a corpse.

R. V LE BRUN

[1991] 3 W.L.R. 653

D and W (his wife) argued in the street, W refusing to go home. D struck W rendering her unconscious. He dragged her from the street either to get her into the house where she did not want to go or to conceal his previous assault and in so doing W's head struck the pavement, fracturing her skull and death resulted. D was convicted of manslaughter and appealed.

LORD LANE CJ

The question can be perhaps framed in this way. There was here an initial unlawful blow to the chin delivered by the appellant. That, again on what must have been the jury's finding, was not delivered with the intention of doing really serious harm to the wife. The guilty intent accompanying that blow was sufficient to have rendered the appellant guilty of manslaughter, but not murder, had it caused death. But it did not cause death. What caused death was the later impact when the wife's head hit the pavement. At the moment of impact the appellant's intention was to remove her, probably unconscious, body to avoid detection. To that extent the impact may have been accidental. May the earlier guilty intent be joined with the later non-guilty blow which caused death to produce in the conglomerate a proper verdict of manslaughter?

It has usually been in the previous decisions in the context of murder that the problem has arisen. We have had our attention directed to a Privy Council case, *Meli v The Queen* [1954] 1 W.L.R. 228 . . . That decision of course is not binding upon us. It is of very persuasive authority and it was adopted by another division of this court in 1975 in *R. v Moore* [1975] Crim.L.R. 229.

However, it will be observed that the present case is different from the facts of those two cases in that death here was not the result of a preconceived plan which went wrong, as was the case in those two decisions which we have cited. Here the death, again assuming the jury's finding to be such as it must have been, was the result of an initial unlawful blow, not intended to cause serious harm, in its turn causing the appellant to take steps possibly to evade the consequences of his unlawful act. During the taking of those steps he commits the actus reus but without the mens rea necessary for murder or manslaughter. Therefore the mens rea is contained in the initial unlawful assault, but the actus reus is the eventual dropping of the head on to the ground.

Normally the actus reus and mens rea coincide in point of time. What is the situation when they do not? Is it permissible, as the prosecution contend here, to combine them to produce a conviction for manslaughter?

The answer is perhaps to be found in the next case to which we were referred, and that was *R. v Church* [1966] 1 Q.B. 59.

[His Lordship quoted Edmund Davies J's judgment where he stated that a manslaughter verdict would have been returned on the basis of a "series of acts which culminated in death", and continued:]

It seems to us that where the unlawful application of force and the eventual act causing death are parts of the same sequence of events, the same transaction, the fact that there is an appreciable interval of time between the two does not serve to exonerate the defendant from liability. That is certainly so where the appellant's subsequent actions which caused death, after the initial unlawful blow, are designed to conceal his commission of the original unlawful assault . . .

In short, in circumstances such as the present, which is the only concern of this court, the act which causes death, and the necessary mental state to constitute manslaughter, need not coincide in point of time . . .

[His Lordship concluded that the judge's direction to the jury was satisfactory in so far as it related to manslaughter.]

Appeal dismissed

Questions

1. In all the earlier cases D killed in the course of covering up the homicide he mistakenly believed he had already committed. Is the true principle the following: that D is liable for homicide (murder or manslaughter depending on his mens rea) where he performs a series of acts which culminate in death, mens rea existing either (a) at the time of the initial act, or (b) at some stage during the transaction? (see *Attorney General's Reference (No.4 of 1980)*, directly below).

2. Lord Lane CJ also sought to support the conviction of manslaughter in *Le Brun* on the basis of causation. He stated:

    "It would be possible to express the problem as one of causation. The original unlawful blow to the chin was a cause sine qua non of the later actus reus. It was the opening event in a series which was to culminate in death: the first link in the chain of causation, to use another metaphor. It cannot be said that the actions of the appellant in dragging the victim away with the intention of evading liability broke the chain which linked the initial blow with the death."

Was the initial assault a substantial cause of death? Could the conviction be supported solely on this causation basis without the "series of acts" doctrine being applied? If it can be supported solely on causation what was the mens rea at the time of "the later actus reus"?

Note

A problem which the Court of Appeal did not address in *Le Brun* is that which arose in the following case where it was impossible to tell which act caused death.

ATTORNEY GENERAL'S REFERENCE (NO.4 OF 1980)

[1981] 2 All E.R. 617

D and V were arguing. D slapped V causing her to fall backwards down a flight of stairs head first onto the floor where she lay motionless. D tied a rope around her neck and dragged her upstairs, placed her in the bath, cut her throat to let out her blood, and then cut her up and disposed of the pieces. The body was never found so the cause of death could not be determined. V died either from the fall, from being strangled by the rope or from having her throat cut. The defence submitted that there was no case to go to the jury and the judge withdrew the case directing an acquittal on the basis that the Crown had failed to prove the cause of death. The Attorney General sought the court's opinion on the following point of law: whether a person who has committed a series of acts against another culminating in the death of that person, each act in the series being either unlawful and dangerous or an act of gross criminal negligence, is entitled to be acquitted of manslaughter on the ground that it cannot be shown which of such acts caused the death of the deceased.

ACKNER LJ

On the above facts this reference raises a single and simple question, *viz.*, if an accused kills another by one or other of two or more different acts each of which, if it caused the death, is a sufficient act to establish manslaughter, is it necessary in order to found a conviction to prove which act caused the death? The answer to the question is No, it is not necessary to found a conviction to prove which act caused the death. No authority is required to justify this answer, which is clear beyond argument, as was indeed immediately conceded by counsel on behalf of the accused.

What went wrong in this case was that counsel made jury points to the judge and not submissions of law. He was in effect contending that the jury should not convict of manslaughter if the death had resulted from the 'fall', because the push which had projected the deceased over the handrail was a reflex and not a voluntary action, as a result of her digging her nails into him. If, however, the deceased was still alive when he cut her throat, since he then genuinely believed her to be dead, having discovered neither pulse nor sign of breath, but frothy blood coming from her mouth, he could not be guilty of manslaughter because he had not behaved with gross criminal negligence. What counsel and the judge unfortunately overlooked was that there was material available to the jury which would have entitled them to have convicted the accused of manslaughter, whichever of the two sets of acts caused her death. It being common ground that the deceased was killed by an act done to her by the accused and it being conceded that the jury could not be satisfied which was the act which caused the death, they should have been directed in due course in the summing up, to ask themselves the following questions: (i) 'Are we satisfied beyond reasonable doubt that the deceased's "fall" downstairs was the result of an intentional act by the accused which was unlawful and dangerous?' If the answer was No, then they would acquit. If the answer was Yes, then they would need to ask themselves a second question, namely: (ii) 'Are we satisfied beyond reasonable doubt that the act of cutting the girl's throat was an act of gross criminal negligence?' If the answer to that question was No, then they would acquit, but if the answer was Yes, then the verdict would be guilty of manslaughter. The jury would thus have been satisfied that, whichever act had killed the deceased, each was a sufficient act to establish the offence of manslaughter.

The facts of this case did not call for 'a series of acts direction' following the principle in *Thabo Meli v R.* [above, p.66]. We have accordingly been deprived of the stimulating questions whether the decision in *R. v Church* [below, p.496] correctly extended that principle to manslaughter, in particular to 'constructive manslaughter' and if so whether that view was part of the ratio decidendi.

Determination accordingly

Questions

1. If the jury are satisfied that D, with mens rea, committed an unlawful and dangerous act in hitting V, could they, applying *Le Brun* (which approved the direction on manslaughter in *Church* based on a series of acts culminating in death), convict of manslaughter even though the cause of death is not determined? Has *Le Brun* rendered nugatory the decision in *Attorney General's Reference*?

2. Should the dual test articulated by Ackner LJ be applied if the charge is one of murder or should the "series of acts" doctrine in *Le Brun* be extended to cover murder?

3   MENS REA

Criminal liability is generally not based solely on the commission of acts and their attendant consequences or the commission of acts in particular circumstances. Generally (but see Strict Liability) liability only arises where an autonomous rational individual performs the act which causes the consequence, or performs the act in the particular prohibited circumstances, with the requisite mens rea (i.e. fault requirement) for the offence. Mens rea builds on ideas of individual autonomy in that an individual should only be liable to the extent that s/he chose to act as s/he did: (i) either intending the consequence to occur or being aware of the risk of the consequence occurring; or (ii) knowing or believing the relevant circumstance(s) to exist. Mens rea is a means by which responsible actors are identified for the purpose of attributing blame and imposing punishment. But there are a number of problems which arise in analysing mens rea. First, is blame or culpability dependent only on the state of mind of the accused when the relevant act was performed or does the incidence of harm resulting from the accused's act raise the degree to which s/he is culpable, that is, is blame a product of state of mind or of the harm caused plus the state of mind? Secondly, where mens rea indicators of blame are absent may blame arise from other factors such as intoxication for which the accused is responsible (see Ch.4)? Thirdly, what is the effect on mens rea of exculpatory factors such as impaired capacity (e.g. due to insanity, see Ch.4), impaired freedom of choice (e.g. due to duress or necessity, see Ch.5), or justifications such as self-defence (see Ch.5)? Finally what do the various terms which import mens rea into offences actually mean?

1. THE REQUIREMENT OF MENS REA

G. WILLIAMS, *CRIMINAL LAW: THE GENERAL PART* (STEVENS & SONS, 1961), P.30

Nature of the requirement of mens rea
There is no need to go into the remote history of *mens rea*; suffice it to say that the requirement of a guilty state of mind (at least for the most serious crimes) had been developed by the time of Coke, which is as far back as the modern lawyer needs to go. 'If one shoot at any wild fowl upon a tree, and the arrow killeth any reasonable creature afar off, without any evil intent in him, this is *per infortunium*.'

It may be said that any theory of criminal punishment leads to a requirement of some kind of *mens rea*. The deterrent theory is workable only if the culprit has knowledge of the legal sanction; and if a man does not foresee the consequence of his act he cannot appreciate that punishment lies in store for him if he does it. The retributive theory presupposes moral guilt; incapacitation supposes social danger; and the reformative aim is out of place if the offender's sense of values is not warped.

However, the requirement as we have it in the law does not harmonise perfectly with any of these theories. It does not fit the deterrent theory, because a man may have *mens rea* although he is ignorant of the law. On the deterrent theory, ignorance of the law should be a defence; yet it is not. Again, the requirement does not quite conform to the retributive theory, because the *mens rea* of English law does not necessarily connote an intention to engage in moral wrongdoing. A crime may be committed from the best of motives and yet remain a crime. (In this respect the phrase *mens rea* is somewhat misleading). There are similar difficulties with incapacitation and reform.

What, then, does legal *mens rea* mean? It refers to the mental element necessary for the particular crime, and this mental element may be either *intention* to do the immediate act or bring about the consequence or (in some crimes) *recklessness* as to such act or consequence. In different and more precise language, *mens rea* means intention or recklessness as to the elements constituting the *actus reus*. These two concepts, intention and recklessness, hold the key to the understanding of a large part of criminal law. Some crimes require intention and nothing else will do, but most can be committed either intentionally or recklessly. Some crimes require particular kinds of intention or knowledge.

Outside the class of crimes requiring *mens rea* there are some that do not require any particular state of mind but do require negligence. Negligence in law is not necessarily a state of mind; and thus these crimes are best regarded as not requiring *mens rea*. However, negligence is a kind of legal fault, and in that respect they are akin to crimes requiring *mens rea*.

Yet other crimes do not even require negligence. They are crimes of strict or vicarious responsibility, and, like crimes of negligence, they constitute exceptions to the adage *Actus non facit reum nisi mens sit rea*.

Note

Williams regards intention and recklessness as basic mens rea in that a defendant's culpability should be dependent on his awareness of the relevant circumstances surrounding, and consequences of, his conduct. The Law Commission in their *Draft Criminal Code Bill* recognised recklessness as the "presumed minimum requirement for criminal liability" and by cl.20(1) created a presumption for Code offences and offences created subsequent to the Code's enactment:

> "Every offence requires a fault element of recklessness with respect to each of its elements other than fault elements, unless otherwise provided."

Is mens rea a merely descriptive term or does it serve other purposes? The extracts which follow address this problem.

A.T.H. SMITH, "ON ACTUS REUS AND MENS REA" IN P. GLAZEBROOK (ED.), *RESHAPING THE CRIMINAL LAW* (LONDON: SWEET & MAXWELL, 1978), P.103

The idea that *mens rea* is in some sense a basic or indispensable ingredient of criminal liability is deeply rooted. For example, Stroud stated that:

> the guilt of an act charged against a prisoner must always depend upon two conditions . . . [which] . . . may be called the condition of illegality (*Actus Reus*) and the condition of culpable intentionality (*Mens Rea*). (*Mens Rea*) (London, 1914), p.7.)

Kenny's view was that:

> no external conduct, however serious or even fatal its consequences may have been, is ever punished unless it is produced by some form of *mens rea*. (*Outlines of Criminal Law* (2nd ed.) (Cambridge, 1904), p.39).

These writers explicitly discount the phenomenon of strict liability, and they should not be taken to task for failing to elucidate matters with which they were not concerned. Nevertheless, by insisting that *mens rea* is a necessary constituent of crime, they distort the function that that concept really performs. A fully descriptive account of criminal responsibility would be forced to acknowledge that there are many instances where liability is imposed without proof of *mens rea* as to at least some elements in the *actus reus*.

It may be helpful to identify three of the purposes for which the expression *mens rea* is used. It is, first, an expositional tool, when used in sentences such as 'the *mens rea* of X offence is Y', where Y might be (depending on the offence in question) intention, recklessness, malice, dishonesty, an intent to defraud or deceive. We could substitute the expression 'mental element' without any change of meaning. This is the use to which Stephen referred when he said that:

> the maxim about '*mens rea*' means no more than that the definition of all or nearly all crime contains not only an outward and visible element, but a mental element, varying according to the different nature of different crimes. (*A History of The Criminal Law of England* (London, 1883), vol. ii, p.95).

In addition the term is used, as has already been seen, to denote traditional *mens rea*, a catalogue of more or less blameworthy mental states of intention, recklessness and negligence from which the legislator, in defining crime, is free to pick and choose to suit his requirements.

The expression *mens rea* performs, however, another function by acting as an ideal towards which the legal system should evolve. A balance of modern opinion favours imposing liability on the basis of fault, subjectively assessed, and a considerable body of literature criticises such strict liability and constructive liability for deviating from this ideal. Such criticisms are premised on a view of criminal responsibility which has fault as its basis. But when traditional *mens rea* is referred to as the 'fault' element, this fault principle and a purely technical usage are conflated. The two by no means necessarily coincide, since traditional *mens rea* refers only to awareness of circumstances and to the contemplation of particular results. It does not follow that, because a person foresees or intends he is necessarily at fault: the intention may have been formed in a variety of exculpating circumstances such as under provocation, duress or necessity. As the expression of a fault principle, then, traditional *mens rea* is no more than a rule of thumb. Even as a description of the present law, it is necessary to look for a more embracing fault principle within which the existing excuses can be subsumed. This more fundamental principle has been formulated by Professor Hart in these terms:

> unless a man has the capacity and a fair opportunity or chance to adjust his behaviour to the law its penalties ought not to be applied to him. (*Punishment and Responsibility* (Oxford, 1968), p.181).

This, he argues, is not only a rationale for most of the excuses which the law already admits; it might also act as a critical principle to ask of the law more than it already concedes.

An account of criminal liability that treats traditional *mens rea* as a necessary fault requirement is thus deficient in two respects. It overlooks the phenomenon of strict liability, and it takes no account of a number of efficacious excuses which do not negative the element of awareness or cognition.

G.P. FLETCHER, *RETHINKING CRIMINAL LAW* (BOSTON: LITTLE, BROWN, 1978), PP.396–397

Descriptive and Normative Uses of the Same Terms

One of the persistent tensions in legal terminology runs between the descriptive and normative uses of the same terms. Witness the struggle over the concept of malice. The term has a high moral content, and when it came into the law as the benchmark of murder, it was presumably used normatively and judgmentally. Yet Fitzjames Stephen and succeeding generations of English jurists have sought to reduce the concepts of malice to the specific mental states of intending and knowing. California judges, in contrast, have stressed the normative content of malice in a highly judgmental definition, employing terms like 'base, anti-social purpose' and 'wanton disregard for human life'. For the English, malice is a question of fact: did the actor have a particular state of consciousness (intention or knowledge)? In California, malice is a value judgment about the actor's motives, attitudes and personal capacity.

If the English have tried to reduce the normative concept of malice to a state of fact, other commentators and courts seek to invest nominally descriptive terms with moral force. Though the terms 'intent', 'state of mind,' and 'mental state' appear to be descriptive, legislators and courts use these terms to refer to issues that require normative judgment . . .

The confusion between normative and descriptive language is so pervasive in Anglo-American criminal law that it affects the entire language of discourse. There appear to be very few terms that are exempt from the ambiguity. The term 'intent' may refer either to a state of intending (regardless of blame) or it may refer to an intent to act under circumstances (such as failing to inquire about the age of a sexual partner) that render an act properly subject to blame. The term 'criminal intent' does not resolve the ambiguity, for a criminal intent may simply be the intent to do the act, which, according to the statutory definition, renders the act 'criminal', i.e. punishable under the law. There may be nothing morally blameworthy in keeping a pair of brass knuckles as a conversation piece, yet that intent renders the act punishable and, in this sense, is a criminal intent.

It is obvious that the very word 'criminal' is affected by the same tension between descriptive and normative illocutionary force. When used normatively, 'criminal' refers to the type of person who by virtue of his deeds deserves to be branded and punished as a criminal. When used descriptively, as in the phrase 'criminal act' it may refer simply to any act that the legislature has declared to be 'criminal'. Thus the term 'criminal intent' may mean the intent to act under circumstances that make it just to treat the actor as a criminal in the pejorative sense. But it is equally plausible to use the term 'criminal intent' to refer to the intent or knowledge sufficient to commit a crime as defined by the legislature. The adjective 'criminal' in this context simply means that the intent is sufficient to render the act punishable under the statute . . .

There is no term fraught with greater ambiguity than that venerable Latin phrase that haunts Anglo-American criminal law: *mens rea*. Glanville Williams defines *mens rea* to mean 'the mental element necessary for the particular crime'. Of course, the term 'mental element' may be employed either descriptively or normatively, yet in this context it seems clear that Williams means to refer to a factual state of affairs. Intent, used descriptively, is an example of a required 'mental element'. In another passage, Williams argues that the issue of duress should not be seen as negating either intention or *mens rea*. Thus he would conclude, . . . that someone who was acquitted on grounds of duress nonetheless acted with *mens rea*. However prestigious this line of analysis might be, the courts fortunately remain unimpressed. Engaged as they are in the processes of judgment and condemnation, the courts repeatedly stress the normative content of *mens rea*, . . .

This tension between descriptive and normative usage carries significance for the structuring of issues in the criminal law. Descriptive theorists, like Stephen, Turner, Williams and others in the English tradition, are apt to see problems of insanity, duress and mistake as extrinsic to the analysis of *mens rea* and criminal intent. Normative theorists, in contrast, are able to integrate these 'defensive' issues into their formulation of the minimum conditions for liability. If *mens rea* raises a normative issue of just and appropriate blame, then there is no *mens rea* or 'criminal intent' when the intentional commission of the offence is excused by reason of duress, insanity, or reasonable mistake about an attendant circumstance.

A. ASHWORTH, "TAKING THE CONSEQUENCES" IN S. SHUTE, J. GARDNER AND J. HORDER (EDS), *ACTION AND VALUE IN CRIMINAL LAW* (OXFORD: CLARENDON PRESS, 1993), P.107

The consequences of one's acts do not always turn out in the way anticipated. What might be described as the expected result of one's conduct . . . may be overtaken by unexpected contingencies . . . and might therefore be followed by quite unusual consequences . . . Would it be right if one were blamed for these consequences?

We will focus here on outcome-luck, and begin by enquiring whether there is a plausible distinction between act and result which might be useful in this sphere. In an earlier essay I argued that the only element of an action which lies within the agent's control is the trying, the doing of all the acts which the agent reasonably believes necessary to achieve the desired end. Thus, if A and B each shoot at their victims from a distance of ten yards and A hits but B misses, the argument would be that intrinsically their actions are the same. Each of them tried to kill, and it is that trying alone which is sufficiently within their control, whereas what happens in the physical world thereafter may be affected by other forces and circumstances . . . It therefore seems possible, for some types of case at least, to identify intrinsic elements of an action which are independent of outcome-luck.

Separating the act of trying from the consequences is purely an analytical device. It is a prelude to, but does not establish, the proposition that it is wrong to blame people for unintended (or at least, unforeseeable) consequences . . . On this question of moral assessment two opposing positions have been urged, and they have been termed the subjectivist and the objectivist. Let us return to the example of A and B who each shoot at an intended victim, and suppose that A narrowly misses because the intended victim moves suddenly, but that B succeeds in killing his or her intended victim. On the subjectivist view, A and B are equally culpable, and the difference between them in terms of outcomes is purely a matter of chance. Their moral guilt ought to depend on the choices they make (which are sufficiently within their control), not on chance outcomes (which are not). As Duff himself has expressed it [*Intention, Agency and Criminal Liability*, p.113]:

It is through the intentions with which I act that I engage in the world as an agent, and relate myself most closely to the actual and potential effects of my actions; and the central or fundamental kind of wrongdoing is to direct my actions towards evil—to intend and to try to do what is evil.

On this view, the consequences are not significant for moral blame. By way of contrast, the objectivist view treats the consequences flowing from conduct as part of the act itself, and regards any separation between act and consequences as unconvincing. For the objectivist, the consequences must be taken into account when assessing moral responsibility.

How can the conflict between subjectivist and objectivist views be resolved?

[I]n terms of moral theory there may be distinct questions of at least three kinds—causal responsibility, responsibility to compensate, and moral blame—and that the arguments for one may not conclude the case for the others.

[Duff argues that a] leading function of the criminal law and punishment is the communicative or censuring function, and a law which drew no distinction between completed and merely attempted offences would imply that the actual causing of harm is unimportant. Since this is morally the wrong message to convey, the presence or absence of harmful consequences should be marked. This argument crosses the boundary from moral theory to legal theory, and raises questions about the differences (if any) between moral and legal responsibility. It is to these that we must now turn . . .

Without attempting a general survey of the differences between responsibility in a moral sense and responsibility under the law, a few relevant distinctions can be identified. One is that, even though it may not be entirely true that legal responsibility is concerned only with the more serious wrongs, it is certainly the case that legal responsibility can give rise to the application of the coercive powers of the State. Moral sanctions may take the form of verbal criticism, or social ostracism, or even expulsion from a family home or a club, whereas legal sanctions may impose compulsory payments, exclusion from premises or from occupying a certain position, compulsory supervision, and even incarceration. A second distinction is that legal responsibility is declared by a court in public, as a result of the machinations of a formal system. This lends an authoritative and, where the proceedings are criminal, an official censuring element to the judgment which is unlikely to form part of most moral judgments. Largely because of the declaratory or stigmatizing effect of legal processes and the powerful impact of legal sanctions, fairness is generally thought to require that there be reasonably precise rules which are announced in advance: these are elements of the concept of the 'rule of law' . . .

It is not merely that citizens should be able to discover in advance whether their conduct amounts to an offence. It is also that the degree of censure should be proportioned to the degree of wrongdoing, because that both respects the offender as a choosing individual and serves to structure the official response of the courts rather than leaving it as a matter of discretion. It would be manifestly inadequate for a legal system to have a single offence stating that anyone who behaves in a way that is contrary to the good of society may be liable to conviction and punishment of up to life imprisonment. Its communicative function would be intolerably vestigial, its censuring function would be hopelessly vague, and the discretion left at the sentencing stage would confer enormous power on the courts on what would then be the key issue. This suggests that a principle of fair labelling should form part of a system of criminal law, so as to ensure that each offence is defined and labelled in a way which conveys the relative seriousness of the offence, and which confines the court's sentencing powers appropriately. Of course this principle does not dictate particular formulae, and there is room for argument whether a system of criminal law which has a single, compendious offence of damage to property might also have a single, compendious offence of harm to individuals, or ought fairly to distinguish between minor assaults and serious woundings, for example. But this may illustrate a further difference between moral and criminal responsibility: in criminal law the behaviour has to be fitted into a pre-existing category which will specify certain elements and not others, whereas in moral discourse the blame may be expressed in a narrative and more individuated form.

[Ashworth goes on to examine the differences between civil and criminal liability.]

Just as criminal conviction may be followed by punishment, so civil liability may be followed by an award of compensation. Now the very idea of compensation is to provide the person who suffers loss, harm, or damage with 'a full and perfect equivalent', something which 'makes good' the harm . . .

The criminal law and punishment are differently directed. They are much more concerned with culpability, since their function is to censure, and that should be restricted to those who deserve it, to the extent that they deserve it. Most of the serious offences require proof of intention or recklessness, whereas the normal minimum for compensation through civil law is proof of negligence. More especially, the criminal law would regard attempted murder as a very serious crime, even though the conduct might not have given rise to any claim for compensation at all . . .

The reason why attempted murder is treated as a serious offence is that the attempter *tried* to commit murder, which is the highest crime—and, in many cases, the failure arose from factors not intended by the attempter (e.g. someone else intervened, the aim was slightly inaccurate, the victim moved). The problem of attempts is hardly peripheral to criminal liability: it is crucial to an understanding of the difference between that and civil liability. It demonstrates the central significance of culpability in the criminal law, where the purpose is to censure and the punishment may restrict or deprive of liberty. It also indicates a difference between the concepts of harm used in criminal law and in the civil law: whereas there is no civil liability unless there is proof of harm, the criminal law is composed only partly of 'result-crimes', and many other crimes impose liability on the basis of conduct which is preliminary to the infliction of harm, merely because of the intention with which the person acted.

The preoccupation with the mental or fault element in serious criminal offences has other manifestations. The culpable causing of a death will give rise, let us assume, to a right to compensation in the civil courts. The amount of compensation is unlikely to differ according to the degree of the harm-doer's culpability. But in the criminal courts the dispute will be over the classification of the conduct as murder, manslaughter, or some other grade of homicide. Murder will have the most stringent fault element and the highest sentence, whilst the other grade(s) of homicide will have lower fault elements and lower sentences. The criminal law is chiefly concerned with desert, that is, with whether or not the person deserves to be labelled as a criminal and, if so, what level of offence is fairly applicable. Once again, culpability is a crucial issue.

[Ashworth goes on to examine liability for manslaughter which may arise where the accused commits a battery which harbours the risk of harm but death occurs due to an unforeseen and unlucky turn of events. He continues that the accused does not deserve to be convicted of manslaughter which bears a heavily condemnatory label when his culpability is minor.]

The fault and the result are simply too far apart for a manslaughter label to communicate anything other than the misfortune which befell both the victim and [the accused]. The criminal law is a censuring institution. It should censure people for wrongs, not misfortunes, and should censure them fairly and propor-tionately . . .

CONCLUSIONS
The attraction of the subjectivist or the objectivist approach to outcome-luck rests largely on intuitions about fairness. But there are supporting arguments that can be tested, and much of this essay has been devoted to an examination of the arguments invoked by objectivists in favour of the view that wrongdoers should 'take the consequences'—or not—of their conduct. Some objectivists place considerable emphasis on the concordance of their approach with popular sentiments and public opinion. If intuitions lie at the foundation of both the rival approaches, this will be a significant consideration. But it cannot be conclusive unless it is also claimed that moral and legal responsibility should follow popular sentiments even when they can be shown to harbour elements of irrationality.

Three related difficulties with objectivism have been identified here. First, in some versions it fails to distin-guish adequately between issues of causation, of liability to compensate, and of moral blame and criminal liability. Indeed, some expressions of popular sentiment perpetrate a gross confusion between punishment and compensation. If it can be shown that the intuitions, or at least what is inferred from feelings of unfair-ness, are tainted with confusion, their strength as guides to ethical principle is much diminished. Second, objectivists seem to underestimate the censuring function of the criminal law, and to neglect the pivotal importance of culpability in both liability and sentencing. Third, whilst their insistence on the communica-tive function of the criminal law is right, it does not follow that the criminal law should always communicate what people wish to hear, as it were. The communicative function might be regarded as educative, where it is clear that popular sentiments are tainted by confusion. Political paternalism of this kind is open to abuse, of course . . .

The legal implications of favouring subjectivism in matters of outcome-luck have been tested here in rela-tion to three types of case: attempts and completed crimes; death resulting from a minor assault and battery; and dangerous driving. If a subjectivist were drafting a new criminal code, all these cases would be made to depend on the defendant's culpability rather than the outcome in the particular case. The effect of this on the form of the criminal law would be quite radical, since many offences are currently defined by reference to the result . . .

2. THE MEANING OF MENS REA

Note

While there may be differences in theoretical approach, a more pressing problem for any student of criminal law is the bewildering array of words and phrases with which the mental element in offences may be indicated. Lord Simon of Glaisdale in *DPP for Northern Ireland v Lynch* [1975] A.C. 653 at 688, speaking in a wider context than the issue of duress, with which the case was primarily concerned, said:

> "A principal difficulty in this branch of the law is the chaotic terminology, whether in judgments, academic writings or statutes. Will, volition, motive, purpose, object, view, intention, intent, specific intent or intention, wish, desire; necessity, coercion, compulsion, duress—such terms which do indeed overlap in certain contexts, seem frequently to be used interchangeably, without definition, and regardless that in some cases the legal usage is a term of art differing from the popular usage. As if this were not enough, Latin expressions which are themselves ambiguous, and often overlap more than one of the English terms, have been freely used—especially animus and (most question-begging of all) mens rea."

For this obfuscation of the law, the judges must carry a large share of the blame.

E. GRIEW, "CONSISTENCY, COMMUNICATION AND CODIFICATION: REFLECTIONS ON TWO MENS REA WORDS" IN P. GLAZEBROOK (ED), *RESHAPING THE CRIMINAL LAW* (STEVENS & SONS, 1978), PP.57–59

A striking feature of English criminal law has been the casual, erratic quality of the use of key terms in its technical language. This has been most marked in the case of important words that Parliament or the judges have used to express aspects of the mental element of crimes: words like 'malice' and 'maliciously' (examples of ancient casualness), 'wilfully' (a once-popular statutory adverb that has left a legacy of confusion), 'intention' and 'recklessness' (the most discussed of the criminal 'states of mind'). Judges in particular, but Parliament as well, have on the whole seemed to care little about achieving consensus or consistency in this department of the legal vocabulary. This indifference in the matter of language has been part of a larger indifference to criminal law analysis as a whole . . .

There has recently arisen a judicial practice of disposing of problems in the criminal law—some would say, of escaping from them—by explicit reliance on the linguistic competence of the common man. To the extent that consensus about the meaning of a word in a particular context is in the nature of language possible, it can arise in two broad ways. One of these occurs when, as it might be put, 'everyone knows what the word means'. If, however, there is no such spontaneous consensus, or if a special use is to be made of the word, the required consensus must be imposed by authority. The authority stipulates a meaning. Legal authority in this connection is legislature or court. In relation both to general concepts in the criminal law and to words in particular contexts, the courts have tended to make a virtue of refraining from 'stipulative definition'—from imposing consensus by saying what words are to be understood to mean. This tendency has been reinforced by the proposition, which has recently enjoyed a powerful vogue in appellate criminal courts, that the meaning of an ordinary word of the English language is not a question of law. Those courts have been very ready—though not consistently so—to find that statutory words whose application is in question before them are 'ordinary words', and have 'approved of trial judges' restraint in the explication of the words for their juries' assistance . . . The result is that even though there is in fact no spontaneous consensus about the meaning of a word, the courts proceed on the fiction that 'everyone knows what it means'. Parliament too has so far been silent in this field. In short, authority has not yet asserted itself in the stipulation of criminal law definitions . . .

Concern for language, whether as an aspect of the criminal law as a whole or in the expression of particular rules, is a concern for principle and for substance. If lawyers are not involved in understanding and expounding the theory of the criminal law, their operations will tend towards mere ritual. Theory depends upon the development and accurate deployment of a self-consistent language, through the medium of which legal statements may tellingly respond to discriminations of policy and to the relationships between relevant concepts. The theory and its servant language are not matters for the legislator alone. Lawyers and judges are vital participants in the business of communication by which legislative intention is translated into acts of adjudication. Where legislation is wanting, or where it lacks 'definition', the task of making or clarifying the law is with the courts. That task has, by its nature, to be performed as occasion arises and only to the extent demanded by the occasion. When occasion does not arise, the court's contribution ought to be made with two considerations (among others) in mind. One is the larger picture—the total body of criminal law theory into which the court's decision and the language that embodies it must fit; indifference to theory and principle involves the danger of particularistic decision and in the long run of incoherence. The second consideration is that criminal law rules are of general application. To deny explanation of them as required, on the ground that it is not the court's job to explain 'ordinary words', is to risk all upon the assumption that the word, being ordinary, is within the lexical equipment of the adult population at large and understood (if not used) by everyone in the same sense. This is in fact a set of uniformly unsafe assumptions about people's linguistic competence, about the sociology of language, and about the composition of tribunals of fact. The assumptions upon which, for safety, we should proceed, are: that very low levels of linguistic competence are quite general in the adult population; that even 'ordinary' words (and especially abstract words) are variously understood—everyone may 'know what they mean' but, without knowing it, use them with different meanings; and that the decisions of two benches or juries could depend upon quite different collective senses of how the law is using the same undefined abstract word.

i. Intention

"Intention" is the mens rea term which conveys the highest level of culpability of an offender. If a person intends to cause a result he is more culpable than a person who acts recklessly, that is, who acts recognising that the result might occur. It is important to define the boundary between intention and recklessness not only to determine the degree of culpability of the offender for sentencing purposes, but also to determine in many cases whether the offender is liable to conviction where the offence charged is one which requires intention to be proved. The *Concise Oxford Dictionary* defines "intend" as "have as one's purpose" and "intention" as "intending, one's purpose . . . object . . . ultimate aim". The law, however, does not always attribute to words their dictionary meaning. "Intention" is such a word.

G. WILLIAMS, "OBLIQUE INTENTION" (1987) 46 C.L.J. 417

Why is it that intention, or intent, one of the basic concepts of the criminal law, remains so unclear? Judges decline to define it, and they appear to adjust it from one case to another.

Part of the trouble is the disagreement on the subject of intention among jurists generally. The philosophers who have lately arrived on the scene, hoping to help the lawyers to solve their legal problems, in fact give only limited assistance. Their philosophical interest stems from the fact that intention is an important ethical concept, but they do not relate their discussions to any particular ethical theory, and they do not sufficiently consider the specific requirements of the criminal law. Indeed, they mix up the ordinary meaning of the word 'Intention' with its desirable legal meaning. To be sure, the meaning of intention as a technical term of the law ought to be close to the literary and popular one, but there are sound reasons for saying that the two should not always be identical.

Added to the confusion of counsel is the fact that judges sometimes wrap up excuses into the meaning of intention, though rationally excuses should have nothing to do with the matter.

Judges reject the proposition that the legal concept of intention in relation to the consequences of action necessarily involves desire of the consequence. This is quite right, and a useful beginning; but the recent pronouncements of the lords get no further. They do not acknowledge the truth that intention generally does involve desire, and they do not say when it does not.

Note

What, then, is the possible meaning of "intention" in the criminal law? Does "doing an act with foresight of its consequences" amount to the same as "doing an act intending to bring about that consequence"? To answer this question it is necessary to examine the various states of mind that might constitute intention. The states of mind competing to be included within the compass of the term *intention* may be illustrated as follows—

Scenario
D has insured V's life. He decides to kill V in order to obtain the insurance money. D's *desire* is to kill V and his *motive* is to obtain the insurance money. What is his *intention*?

Case (a) D intends a consequence if it is his *aim* or *objective*. If D shoots at V in order to kill him, the consequence, V's death, is both desired and *intended* by D.

Case (b) D intends a consequence if he foresees it as certain to result from his conduct.
So D wishing to kill V shoots at V who is standing behind a window.

In this case D knows that in order to kill V the bullet must pass through the window. With regard to the window, D intends to break it although he does not desire to do so for its own sake; breaking the window is a necessary precondition to shooting V, that is, it is a means to that end. As Lord Hailsham said in *Hyam* [1975] A.C. 55 at 74, "intention [includes] the means as well as the end and the inseparable consequences of the end as well as the means". In the circumstances as they exist, it is not possible for D to kill V without breaking the window. Thus it can be said that D has a *direct* intention regarding V and an *oblique* intention regarding the window; breaking the window is his subsidiary or secondary aim which must be achieved if he is to achieve his ultimate or primary aim.

Does D *desire* to break the window? This depends on the width of the definition of desire. Duff, "The Obscure Intentions of the House of Lords" [1986] Crim. L.R. 773, argues that a person may intend to do various unpleasant things without desiring them. For example, a person with toothache visits the dentist; he does not like visiting dentists and thus does not want or desire to go but he does go intentionally. Williams questions this conclusion.

G. WILLIAMS, "OBLIQUE INTENTION" (1987) 46 C.L.J. 417–421

What the courts ought to hold appears to me to be clear. (1) Except in one type of case, intention as to a consequence of what is done requires desire of the consequence. Of course, intention, for the lawyer, is not a bare wish; it is a combination of wish and act (or other external element). With one exception, an act is intentional as to a consequence if it is done with (motivated by) the wish, desire, purpose or aim (all synonyms in this context) of producing the result in question. (2) The one type of case in which it is reasonable to say that an undesired consequence can be intended in law is in respect of known certainties. A person can be held (but will not always be held) to intend an undesired event that he knows for sure he is bringing about.

(1) The first proposition is disputed by some writers, particularly the two philosophers, [Alan White and R. A. Duff], who have taken an interest in the English criminal law. Their principal argument is that one can intend to do various unpleasant things, e.g. visiting the dentist; therefore intention need not involve desire. I would have thought that the error in this is too obvious to need stating. The premise is true, but the conclusion does not follow. Obviously, people go to the dentist in order to get certain benefits (relief from pain or the preservation of the teeth). To get these benefits, the possibility of pain or discomfort is accepted. It is accepted not as an end in itself but as part of the package, and the package as a whole is desired—otherwise one would not go to the dentist. The pain taken by itself is not desired, but the proposition was not that the patient intends the pain but that he intends to visit (intentionally visits) the dentist.

The writers who deny the relevance of desire replace it with the word 'purpose'. But does not purpose imply desire? One can have an undeclared purpose, but not a undesired purpose. 'Undesired purpose' is a contradiction in terms.

(2) The second proposition seemed to be on its way to legal acceptance until recent pronouncements of the lords. Perhaps the lords intended to negative it. Or perhaps they did not. More of this later.

In one application, at least, the second proposition is accepted as almost universally true. Where the defendant desires result x, and anyone can see, by merely considering x, that another result, y (forbidden by law), will also be involved, as the direct consequence of x and almost as part and parcel of it, then the defendant will be taken to intend both x and y.

Three men accidentally killed a girl in horseplay. Being frightened, they hid the body under a pile of stones. It was held that they were guilty of conspiracy to prevent the burial of a corpse [*Hunter* [1974] Q.B. 95]. The Court of Appeal upheld a direction that 'if the defendants agreed to conceal the body and the concealment in fact prevented burial, then the offence was made out, although prevention of burial was not the object of the agreement.'

A result that is either witnessed or foreseen as certain is almost always regarded as sharing the intentional nature of an act where it is either the contemporaneous (concurrent) result or the immediate consequence of the act. A person will normally be taken to intend something that he is consciously doing, or that follows under his nose from what he is then doing . . .

Using the word 'intention' in this way admittedly involves an extension beyond its normal meaning in the language. The normal meaning connotes desire. [White] writes: 'What I do knowing I am doing it need not be done intentionally, as when I know that I am hurting your feelings but not doing so intentionally.' The remark is true for ordinary speech, and true in law for offences involving the 'hurting of feelings'; but the law is much more concerned with hurting bodies than with hurting feelings. If I drive over you because I am in a hurry and you will not get out of the way, I drive over you intentionally, and it would be no use my saying that my sole intention was to make progress. For legal purposes the meaning of intention has to be widened to this extent.

Similarly, a surgeon intentionally wounds his patient when he inserts the scalpel. He does not, of course, commit a crime of intention, but that is because he has the justification of consent. Lord Hailsham on one occasion denied this, and put the surgeon's defence on lack of intent; this is an example of the judicial tendency already mentioned, to bring in defences under the heading of lack of intention. In the unlikely case of a surgeon kidnapping his recalcitrant patient and making various incisions in him, entirely for the patient's benefit, the surgeon would be guilty of the offence of wounding with intent; yet his intention to make the incisions would be the same as in an ordinary medical operation.

The law should generally be the same where the defendant is aware that a consequence in the future is the certain (though undesired) result of what he does. He is liable for a crime of intention if the foreseen though undesired consequence is inseparably bound up with the desired consequence. This opinion has been supported by some writers, though not all. More importantly, it has been accepted by several of the major reform bodies of the common-law world. If such a variety of intention is accepted we need a name for it, the best being Bentham's coinage of 'oblique intention'. Direct intention is where the consequence is what you are aiming at. Oblique intention is something you see clearly, but out of the corner of your eye. The consequence is (figuratively speaking) not in the straight line of your purpose, but a side-effect that you accept as an inevitable or 'certain' accompaniment of your direct intent (desire-intent). There are twin consequences of the act, x and y; the doer wants x, and is prepared to accept its unwanted twin y. Oblique intent is, in other words, a kind of knowledge or realisation.

When one speaks of the unwanted consequence as being 'certain', one does not, of course, mean certain. 'Nothing is certain save death and taxes.' For example, a person who would otherwise have been the victim of the criminal's act may be warned in time, or providentially happen to change his plans, and so escape what would otherwise have been his fate. Certainty in human affairs means certainty as a matter of common sense—certainty apart from unforeseen events or remote possibilities. Realisation of practical certainty is something higher in the scale than appreciation of high probability.

Case (c) D intends a consequence if it is a virtual, practical or moral certainty that it will result from his actions—in other words, he intends a result where he acts being aware that the result will occur in the ordinary course of events if he succeeds in achieving his purpose.

So D places a bomb under V's seat timed to kill him in mid-flight as he pilots a plane.

In this case D does not desire to kill the crew or passengers but if he realises that their deaths are a *virtual, practical or moral certainty*, that is, that they will die in the ordinary course of events, he obliquely intends their deaths. The deaths of the crew or passengers are not a pre-condition to killing V but, in the ordinary course of events, they are the inevitable *by-product* of D's killing V; they are an inseparable consequence of that end. If, miraculously, the crew and passengers survive, D will not have failed in achieving his purpose, that is, killing V. This does not necessarily mean that D did not desire their deaths, if desire is given a wider meaning. Norrie is a supporter of the view that an act is intended where it is seen by the actor as having some "desirable characteristic". While agreeing that "intention" should include oblique intention he disagrees that obliquely intended consequences are undesired; this conclusion involves attributing a wider meaning to "desire".

A. NORRIE, "OBLIQUE INTENTION AND LEGAL POLITICS" [1989] CRIM. L.R. 793, 794–796

2. Defining oblique intention

I agree with Williams that intention ought to be defined to include desire but, so long as it is so defined, disagree with his claim that the concept of oblique intention 'involves an extension beyond its normal meaning in the language'. That is not to say that the legal usage of oblique intention corresponds wholly with the ordinary usage.

Intention and desire
Duff argued, I believe correctly, in an earlier paper that the idea of an intended act includes the notion of a desire to bring the act about, using the term 'desire' (or 'want')

> 'as the most general term of volition, covering attitudes normally contrasted with "wanting", like seeing an action as a duty, as the lesser of two evils, or as an unpleasant but necessary means to a desired end. To intend an action is to see it as having some "desirable characteristic" . . .'

But he later rejected this view:

> 'It is unnecessary, since it adds nothing to an analysis which talks only of the agent believing that her action might bring X about, and acting because of that belief. Indeed we may ascribe a desire for X to the agent only *because* we realise she intends to bring X about, rather than taking her to intend it because we realise that she desires it. It may be misleading, since it may lead us to treat desire as an independent ingredient or criterion of intention. We may then forget to distinguish the philosophers' use of "desire" (according to which it is an empty truism that all intended results are desired) from its ordinary use (according to which intention need not involve desire).'

The 'philosophers' use', however, is not an empty truism. Desire is analytically distinct from the narrow view of intention proposed by Duff. We may understand that the agent intended to bring X about either by deduction from the patterns of her action *or* by reference to her expressed wishes prior to the action or her *post facto* explanation of why she did it. Desire need not simply be tacked onto an already pre-established deduction of intention. Secondly, it is a moot point whether what Duff regards as ordinary use is not rather narrowly conceived. Take the standard illustration of the person with toothache who, in Duff's view, intends but does not want to go to the dentist. As Williams points out, there is no logical barrier to saying in a real (not technical) sense that the person *does* more broadly want to go to the dentist—as a means to an end, as part of a 'package' which has the ultimate end of removal of the pain at its heart. There seems no objection to saying both 'I didn't want to go to the dentist, but . . .' and 'I wanted to go to the dentist (but only) in order to . . .' Duff's original conception of a 'desirability characteristic' is valuable, and while the recognition of narrow and broader definitions of desire may entail complexity, it does not thereby entail confusion.

Intention, desire and oblique intention
The relevance of this philosophical discussion becomes apparent when we consider the rationale for a doctrine of oblique intent. Oblique intention only becomes a problem for ordinary usage if one separates intention from desire, for one then loses the possibility of seeing what was intended as being that which possesses a 'desirability characteristic', as being part of a 'package' of desires. Williams is wrong to say that oblique intention involves a departure from the ordinary usage of 'intention', for oblique intention can quite naturally be seen as a species of intention once one realises that what is intended is that which is desired in the broad 'package' sense of the term. Williams writes: 'If I drive over you because I am in a hurry and you will not get out of the way, I drive over you intentionally, and it would be no use my saying that my sole intention was to make progress.' Indeed not, but Williams gives the example to illustrate a situation where desire does not go with intent, whereas given his

espousal of the 'package' view of desire, it does. I want to drive over you as part of a package which includes my making progress. Your injury is not my direct desire, but it has a 'desirability characteristic' in the broader context. Oblique intention, which includes the intention of means necessary to ends and of necessary side consequences to ends, connotes desire in the broad sense outlined above.

Two further points may be made. First, to identify oblique intention with desire in this way makes good sense for it does away with the need for alternative artificial strategies to cover what normal usage requires. Duff suggests that obliquely intended actions may be intentional but not intended. He writes that 'if I know that my action will cause death, I surely cause that death intentionally, even if I do not act with the intention of causing it: for I voluntarily make myself its agent'. This circuitry could have been avoided had he followed the logic of the broad 'philosophers' sense of desire outlined earlier in the same article, for his definition of 'intentional' action corresponds to the 'philosophers' usage, rendering this distinction unnecessary.

Secondly, the so-called 'test of failure' is only relevant to the narrow sense of intention outlined above and has the effect of artificially constricting commonsensical usage. Where I intend to bring X about and am sure that Y is a necessary corollary, but it turns out that X happens without Y, I have failed to produce the necessary corollary but not failed in my intention. Therefore Y was not part of my intention. But Y *was* part of my intention in that I was prepared to accept its necessity as a means to my end or as a side-consequence of it. I may not directly have wanted Y to happen, but I wanted X sufficiently to will the existence of Y too. I may be quite happy that X occurs without Y, but that does not mean to say the bringing about of Y was not part of my initial intention . . .

The 'test of failure' is too constricting because it only tests direct intention, and not surrounding circumstances, means to ends, and necessary side-consequences . . . [It] is only relevant if one has already defined intention in the narrow direct sense, and constrains commonsensical usage.

Case (d) D intends a consequence if he foresees it as a probable or likely consequence of his actions.

So D shoots at V, while he is driving a bus, in order to kill him. D foresees that it is probable that the passengers on the bus or other road users will also be killed.

In this case D does not desire the deaths of the passengers or other road users and will have been successful in his objective if only X dies. Does his foresight of their probable deaths amount to *intention* or does it only constitute *recklessness*?

If there are different states of mind which may be classed as *intention* or *intentional* (as the examples above illustrate), how have the courts dealt with this definitional problem?

Their approach has been far from consistent.

R. V STEANE

[1947] K.B. 997

The appellant, a British film actor, was employed in Germany when war broke out. He was arrested and entered the service of the German broadcasting system reading news bulletins and helping to produce films. He gave evidence that this was done under the pressure of beatings and of threats and with a view to saving his wife and children from a concentration camp. After the war he was convicted of doing acts likely to assist the enemy, with intent to assist the enemy, contrary to reg.2A of the Defence (General) Regulations 1939. On appeal it was argued by the Crown that the saving of his wife and children from a concentration camp might have been the motive for his act, but that this was irrelevant on the issue whether he acted with the intent alleged.

LORD GODDARD CJ

The difficult question that arises, however, is in connexion with the direction to the jury with regard to whether these acts were done with the intention of assisting the enemy. The case as opened, and indeed, as put by the learned judge appears to this court to be this: A man is taken to intend the natural consequences of his acts; if, therefore, he does an act which is likely to assist the enemy, it must be assumed that he did it with the intention of assisting the enemy . . .

While no doubt the motive of a man's act and his intention in doing the act are, in law, different things, it is, none the less, true that in many offences a specific intention is a necessary ingredient and the jury have to be satisfied that a particular act was done with that specific intent, although the natural consequences of the act might, if nothing else were proved, be said to show the intent for which it was done . . ... The important thing to notice in this respect is that where an intent is charged in the indictment, the burden of proving that intent remains throughout on the prosecution. No doubt, if the prosecution prove an act the natural consequence of which would be a certain result and no evidence or explanation is given, then a jury may, on a proper direction, find that the prisoner is guilty of doing the act with the intent alleged, but if on the totality of the evidence there is room for more than one view as to the intent of the prisoner, the jury should be directed that it is for the prosecution to prove the intent to the jury's satisfaction, and if, on a review of the whole evidence, they either think that the intent did not exist or they are left in doubt as to the intent, the prisoner is entitled to be acquitted . . ...

In this case the court cannot but feel that some confusion arose with regard to the question of intent by so much being said in the case with regard to the subject of duress. Duress is a matter of defence where a prisoner is forced by fear of violence or imprisonment to do an act which in itself is criminal. If the act is a criminal act, the prisoner may be able to show that he was forced into doing it by violence, actual or threatened, and to save himself from the consequences of that violence. There is very little learning to be found in any of the books or cases on the subject of duress and it is by no means certain how far the doctrine extends, though we have the authority both of Hale and of Fitzjames Stephen, that while it does not apply to treason, murder and some other felonies, it does apply to misdemeanors; and offences against these regulations are misdemeanors. But here again, before any question of duress arises, a jury must be satisfied that the prisoner had the intention which is laid in the indictment. Duress is a matter of defence and the onus of proving it is on the accused. As we have already said, where an intent is charged on the indictment, it is for the prosecution to prove it, so the onus is the other way.

Now, another matter which is of considerable importance in this case, but does not seem to have been brought directly to the attention of the jury, is that very different considerations may apply where the accused at the time he did the acts is in subjection to an enemy power and where he is not. British soldiers who were set to work on the Burma road or, if invasion had unhappily taken place, British subjects who might have been set to work by the enemy digging trenches would undoubtedly be doing acts likely to assist the enemy. It would be unnecessary surely in their cases to consider any of the niceties of the law relating to duress, because no jury would find that merely by doing this work they were intending to assist the enemy. In our opinion it is impossible to say that where an act was done by a person in subjection to the power of others, especially if that other be a brutal enemy, an inference that he intended the natural consequences of his act must be drawn merely from the fact that he did it. The guilty intent cannot be presumed and must be proved. The proper direction to the jury in this case would have been that it was for the prosecution to prove the criminal intent, and that while the jury would be entitled to presume that intent if they thought that the act was done as the result of the free uncontrolled action of the accused, they would not be entitled to presume it, if the circumstances showed that the act was done in subjection to the power of the enemy, or was as consistent with an innocent intent as with a criminal intent, for example, the innocent intent of a desire to save his wife and children from a concentration camp. They should only convict if satisfied by the evidence that the act complained of was in fact done to assist the enemy, and if there was doubt about the matter, the prisoner was entitled to be acquitted.

Appeal allowed
Conviction quashed

Questions

1. Is it true to say that Steane had no intention to assist the enemy, or is it not the case that he intended to assist the enemy in order to save his family from the concentration camp? (See A.K.W. Halpin, "Intended Consequences and Unintended Fallacies" (1987) 7 O.J.L.S. 104, 110–111).

2. Is Glanville Williams correct when he states that "a more satisfactory way of deciding the case would have been to say that the accused did in law intend to assist the enemy but that duress was a defence?"

(See G. Williams, *Criminal Law: The General Part* (1961) s.18.)

Note

Following confusion created by *DPP v Smith* [1961] A.C. 290, the first point raised in *Steane* as to how intention might be proved has been clarified by Parliament by s.8 of the Criminal Justice Act 1967 which provides:

A court or jury, in determining whether a person has committed an offence,—

(a) shall not be bound in law to infer that he intended or foresaw a result of his actions by reason only of its being a natural and probable consequence of those actions; but

(b) shall decide whether he did intend or foresee that result by reference to all the evidence, drawing such inferences from the evidence as appear proper in the circumstances.

As to the meaning of "intention", *Steane* is the leading authority against the view that intention includes foresight of certainty. There are authorities, however, that suggest the opposite. In *R. v Lemon* [1979] A.C. 617 at 638, Lord Diplock, although dissenting on the question whether blasphemous libel required a mental element beyond the intention to publish, stated:

"The fear that, by retaining as a necessary element of the mens rea of the offence the intention of the publisher to shock and arouse resentment among believing Christians, those who are morally blameworthy will be unjustly acquitted appears to me to manifest a judicial distrust of the jury's capability of appreciating the meaning which in English criminal law is ascribed to the expression 'intention' of the accused. When Stephen was writing in 1883, he did not then regard it as settled law that, where intention to produce a particular result was a necessary element of an offence, no distinction is to be drawn in law between the state of mind of one who does an act because he desires it to produce that particular result and the state of mind of one who, when he does the act, is aware that it is likely to produce that result but is prepared to take the risk that it may do so, in order to achieve some other purpose which provided his motive for doing what he did. It is by now well-settled law that both states of mind constitute 'intention' in the sense in which that expression is used in the definition of a crime whether at common law or in a statute. Any doubts on this matter were finally laid to rest by the decision of this House in *R. v Hyam* [1975] A.C. 55."

R. V MOLONEY

[1985] 1 A.C. 905 HL

The appellant, a soldier, and his stepfather had been drinking heavily. His stepfather challenged him to a competition to see who could load, draw and fire a shotgun in the shortest time. The outcome was that the appellant shot his stepfather and was charged with murder. The appellant testified that he had no intention to kill and had not aimed his gun at his stepfather. In summing-up the judge gave the following direction on intent:

"When the law requires that something must be proved to have been done with a particular intent it means this: a man intends the consequences of his voluntary act (a) when he desires it to happen, whether or not he foresees that it will probably happen; and (b) when he foresees that it will probably happen, whether he desires it or not."

He appealed against conviction of murder.

LORD BRIDGE OF HARWICH

delivered the following opinion with which the remainder of their Lordships agreed . . . The fact that, when the appellant fired the gun, the gun was pointing directly at his stepfather's head at a range of about six feet was not, and could not be, disputed. The sole issue was whether, when he pressed the trigger, this fact and its inevitable consequence were present to the appellant's mind. If they were, the inference was inescapable, using words in their ordinary, everyday meaning, that he intended to kill his stepfather. The undisputed facts that the appellant loved his stepfather and that there was no premeditation or rational motivation, could not, as any reasonable juror would understand, rebut this inference . . .

The definition of intent on which Stephen Brown J. based his initial direction to the jury in this case and which first appeared in the 40th edition but now appears virtually unchanged in the 41st edition of *Archbold Criminal Pleading Evidence & Practice* published in 1982, is, as previously stated, clothed with the spurious authority of quotation marks. I will repeat it here for clarity (para. 17–13, p.995):

'In law a man intends the consequence of his voluntary act, (a) when he desires it to happen, whether or not he foresees that it probably will happen, or (b) when he foresees that it will probably happen, whether he desires it or not.'

Although in its terms applicable to any offence of specific intent, this so-called definition must be primarily derived from *R. v Hyam* [1975] A.C. 55. The text embodies a reference to Viscount Dilhorne's opinion, implicit in the passage cited above from p.82 of the report, that in *R. v Hyam* itself, as in the vast majority of cases, an explanation of intent was unnecessary and notes the endorsement of this view to which I have already referred in *R. v Beer*, 63 Cr.App.R. 222. Apart from copious references to *R. v Hyam*, the ensuing citation in support of the claim that the definition 'is in accordance with the great preponderance of authority', refers to many decided cases in which there are to be found obiter dicta on the subject. But looking on their facts at the decided cases where a crime of specific intent was under consideration, including *R. v Hyam* itself, they suggest to me that the probability of the consequence taken to have been foreseen must be little short of overwhelming before it will suffice to establish the necessary intent. Thus, I regard the *Archbold* definition of intent as unsatisfactory and potentially misleading and one which should no longer be used in directing juries.

The golden rule should be that, when directing a jury on the mental element necessary in a crime of specific intent, the judge should avoid any elaboration or paraphrase of what is meant by intent, and leave it to the jury's good sense to decide whether the accused acted with the necessary intent, unless the judge is convinced that, on the facts and having regard to the way the case has been presented to the jury in evidence and argument, some further explanation or elaboration is strictly necessary to avoid misunderstanding. In trials for murder or wounding with intent, I find it very difficult to visualise a case where any such explanation or elaboration could be required, if the offence consisted of a direct attack on the victim with a weapon, except possibly the case where the accused shot at A and killed B, which any first year law student could explain to a jury in the simplest of terms. Even where the death results indirectly from the act of the accused, I believe the cases that will call for a direction by reference to foresight of consequences will be of extremely rare occurrence. I am in full agreement with the view expressed by Viscount Dilhorne that, in *R. v Hyam* [1975] A.C. 55, 82 itself, if the issue of intent had been left without elaboration, no reasonable jury could have failed to convict. I find it difficult to understand why the prosecution did not seek to support the conviction, as an alternative to their main submission, on the ground that there had been no actual miscarriage of justice.

I do not, of course, by what I have said in the foregoing paragraph, mean to question the necessity, which frequently arises, to explain to a jury that intention is something quite distinct from motive or desire. But this can normally be quite simply explained by reference to the case before the court or, if necessary, by some homely example. A man who, at London Airport, boards a plane which he knows to be bound for Manchester, clearly intends to travel to Manchester, even though Manchester is the last place he wants to be and his motive for boarding the plane is simply to escape pursuit. The possibility that the plane may have engine trouble and be diverted to Luton does not affect the matter. By boarding the Manchester plane, the man conclusively demonstrates his intention to go there, because it is a moral certainty that that is where he will arrive.

I return to the two uncertainties by the Criminal Law Revision Committee in the Report referred to above as arising from *R. v Hyam*, which still remain unresolved. I should preface these observations by expressing my view that the differences of opinion to be found in the five speeches in *R. v Hyam* have, as I believe, caused some confusion in the law in an area where, as I have already indicated, clarity and simplicity are, in my view, of paramount importance. I believe it also follows that it is within the judicial function of your Lordships' House to lay down new guidelines which will achieve those desiderata, if we can reach broad agreement as to what they should be . . .

Starting from the proposition established by *R. v Vickers* [1957] 2 Q.B. 664, as modified by *D.P.P. v Smith* that the mental element in murder requires proof of an intention to kill or cause really serious injury, the first fundamental question to be answered is whether there is any rule of substantive law that foresight by the accused of one of those eventualities as a probable consequence of his voluntary act, where the probability can be defined as exceeding a certain degree, is equivalent or alternative to the necessary intention. I would answer this question in the negative. Here I derive powerful support from the speech of my noble and learned friend. Lord Hailsham of St Marylebone L.C., in *R. v Hyam* [1975] A.C. 55. He said, at p.75:

> 'I do not, therefore, consider, as was suggested in argument, that the fact that a state of affairs is correctly foreseen as a highly probable consequence of what is done is the same thing as the fact that the state of affairs is intended.'

And again, at p.77:

> 'I do not think that foresight as such of a high degree of probability is at all the same thing as intention, and, in my view, it is not foresight but intention which constitutes the mental element in murder.'

I am firmly of opinion that foresight of consequences, as an element bearing on the issue of intention in murder, or indeed any other crime of specific intent, belongs, not to the substantive law, but to the law of evidence. Here again I am happy to find myself aligned with my noble and learned friend, Lord Hailsham of St. Marylebone L.C., in *R. v Hyam*, where he said, at p.65: 'Knowledge or foresight is at the best material which entitles or compels a jury to draw the necessary inference as to intention.' A rule of evidence which judges for more than a century found of the utmost utility in directing juries was expressed in the maxim: 'A man is presumed to intend the natural and probable consequences of his acts.' In *D.P.P. v Smith* your Lordships' House, by treating this rule of evidence as creating an irrebuttable presumption and thus elevating it, in effect, to the status of a rule of substantive law, predictably provoked the intervention of Parliament by section 8 of the Criminal Justice Act 1967 to put the issue of intention back where it belonged, viz., in the hands of the jury, 'drawing such inferences from the evidence as appear proper in the circumstances'. I do not by any means take the conjunction of the verbs 'intended or foresaw' and 'intend or foresee' in that section as an indication that Parliament treated them as synonymous; on the contrary, two verbs were needed to connote two different states of mind.

I think we should now no longer speak of presumptions in this context but rather of inferences. In the old presumption that a man intends the natural and probable consequences of his acts the important word is 'natural'. This word conveys the idea that in the ordinary course of events a certain act will lead to a certain consequence unless something unexpected supervenes to prevent it. One might almost say that, if a consequence is natural, it is really otiose to speak of it as also being probable.

Section 8 of the Criminal Justice Act 1967 leaves us at liberty to go back to the decisions before that of this House in *D.P.P. v Smith* and it is here, I believe, that we can find a sure, clear, intelligible and simple guide to the kind of direction that should be given to a jury in the exceptional case where it is necessary to give guidance as to how, on the evidence, they should approach the issue of intent.

I know of no clearer exposition of the law than that in the judgment of the Court of Criminal Appeal (Lord Goddard C.J., Atkinson and Cassels JJ.) delivered by Lord Goddard C.J. in *R. v Steane* [1947] K.B. 997 [above] where he said, at p.1004:

> 'No doubt, if the prosecution prove an act the natural consequence of which would be a certain result and no evidence or explanation is given, then a jury may, on a proper direction, find that the prisoner is guilty of doing the act with the intent alleged, but if on the totality of the evidence there is room for more than one view as to the intent of the prisoner, the jury should be directed that it is for the prosection to prove the intent to the jury's satisfaction, and if, on a review of the whole evidence, they either think that the intent did not exist or they are left in doubt as to the intent, the prisoner is entitled to be acquitted.'

In the rare cases in which it is necessary to direct a jury by reference to foresight of consequences, I do not believe it is necessary for the judge to do more than invite the jury to consider two questions. First, was death or really serious injury in a murder case (or whatever relevant consequence must be proved to have been intended in any other case) a natural consequence of the defendant's voluntary act? Secondly, did the defendant foresee that consequence as being a natural consequence of his act? The jury should then be told that if they answer yes to both questions it is a proper inference for them to draw that he intended that consequence . . .

Appeal allowed

Questions

1. Lord Bridge spoke of a result being a "natural consequence". Does this mean that a consequence must be substantially more likely than one which is described as being probable if the inference of intention is to be drawn; or does this phrase create an ambiguity in that a consequence may be considered a *natural consequence* by the fact that it causally follows on directly from the original act?

2. Lord Bridge stated with regard to the term "natural consequences" that "the probability of the consequence taken to have been foreseen must be little short of overwhelming before it will suffice to establish the necessary intent". Was Lord Bridge really speaking of "oblique" intention in the sense in which Glanville Williams uses this term? (See above.)

3. Lord Bridge sought to distinguish *intention* from *foresight of consequences*; the latter is relevant only as *evidence* of intention. Lord Bridge also sought to distinguish *intention* from *motive* or *desire*. Stannard J in "Mens Rea in the Melting Pot" [1986] 37 N.I.L.Q. 61, accordingly concludes that *intention* must be equivalent to *purpose*. He states that the "failure test" distinguishes intended consequences from those that are merely foreseen. In the Manchester plane example, if the plane had been diverted from Manchester to Leeds, would the escapee have failed in his purpose?

4. Lord Bridge declared that he knew no clearer exposition of the law than that in *Steane*. Given his Manchester plane example and the expressed outcome, should Lord Bridge not regard Steane's intention as having been to assist the enemy?

Note

Lord Bridge's judgment in *Moloney*, far from clarifying the law, created its own problems which quickly surfaced in *R. v Hancock and Shankland* [1986] 1 A.C. 455. The appellants, who were striking miners, were charged with the murder of a taxi-driver who was killed taking a miner to work. The appellants pushed a concrete post and concrete block from a bridge over a three-lane highway on to the taxi travelling below. They claimed that they had intended only to block the road and frighten the miner as they believed the block was positioned over the middle lane and the taxi was in the nearside lane. The judge gave a direction to the jury based on Lord Bridge's speech in *Moloney* and the jury convicted. The Court of Appeal quashed the murder convictions substituting convictions for manslaughter holding that the *Moloney* guidelines were misleading. The Crown appealed but the House of Lords dismissed the appeal affirming the decision below that the phrase "natural consequence" used by Lord Bridge required amplification if it was not to mislead. Lord Scarman stated (at 473):

"[Lord Bridge] omitted any reference in his guidelines to probability. He did so because he included probability in the meaning which he attributed to 'natural.' My Lords, I very much doubt whether a jury without further explanation would think that 'probable' added nothing to 'natural.' I agree with the Court of Appeal that the probability of a consequence is a factor of sufficient importance to be drawn specifically to the attention of the jury and to be explained. In a murder case where it is necessary to direct a jury on the issue of intent by reference to foresight of consequences the probability of death or serious injury resulting from the act done may be critically important. Its importance will depend on the degree of probability: if the likelihood that death or serious injury will result is high, the probability of that result may . . . be seen as overwhelming evidence of the existence of the intent to kill or injure . . . In my judgment, therefore, the Moloney guidelines as they stand are unsafe and misleading. They require a reference to probability. They also require an explanation that the greater the probability of a consequence the more likely it is that the consequence was foreseen and that if that consequence was foreseen the greater the probability is that that consequence was also intended. But juries also require to be reminded that the decision is theirs to be reached upon a consideration of all the evidence."

Lord Scarman's focus appears to be on the means by which intention (in its direct sense) may be proved rather than on clarifying any broader conception of intention to incorporate oblique intent. It is arguable that Lord Bridge's ill-framed direction was concerned with the latter. It fell to the Court of Appeal to seek to make sense of the contradictory pronouncements of their Lordships in the case of *Nedrick* below.

Questions

1. In *Moloney* Lord Bridge, while declining to define what *intention* means, did provide guidelines for the jury on how to discover it. Lord Scarman deprecated the use of such guidelines because of the danger that they would be followed slavishly. He opined that the jury should "exercise practical common sense" and base their decision upon a consideration of all the evidence, stating that whereas the law is for the judge to define, the facts are for the jury to decide. But what is the law in relation to intention? Is *intention* an ordinary word with an ordinary meaning known to all? If, rather, it is a word with a technical meaning, what is that technical meaning?

2. If foresight of the probability of a consequence is simply evidence from which intention may be inferred, what is the further mental element the jury must find before they can conclude that the accused intended that consequence? (See R.A. Duff, "The Obscure Intentions of the House of Lords" [1986] Crim. L.R. 771, 772).

Note

In *Nedrick* (below) the Court of Appeal sought to draw together various threads contained in the speeches in *Moloney* and *Hancock* and *Shankland* to provide some guidance for trial judges.

R. V NEDRICK

[1986] 1 W.L.R. 1025

The appellant had a grudge against a woman. He poured paraffin through the letter box and on to the front door of her house and ignited it without giving any warning. A child died in the ensuing fire. The appellant admitted starting the fire but claimed he only wished to frighten the woman and did not want anyone to die. He was convicted of murder following a direction to the jury which equated foresight with intention.

LORD LANE CJ

read the following judgment of the court . . . That direction was given before the publication of the speeches in the House of Lords in *R. v Moloney* and *R. v Hancock*. In the light of those speeches it was plainly wrong. The direction was based on a passage in *Archbold Criminal Pleading Evidence & Practice*, 41st ed. (1982), p.994, paragraph 17–13, which has been repeated in the 42nd ed. (1985), p.1162, paragraph 17–13. That passage was expressly disapproved in *R. v Moloney*, in that it equates foresight with intention, whereas 'foresight of consequences, as an element bearing on the issue of intention in murder . . . belongs, not to the substantive law, but to the law of evidence', *per* Lord Bridge of Harwich, at [1985] A.C. 928. The judge was in no way to blame of course for having directed the jury in this way.

What then does a jury have to decide so far as the mental element in murder is concerned? It simply has to decide whether the defendant intended to kill or do serious bodily harm. In order to reach that decision the jury must pay regard to all the relevant circumstances, including what the defendant himself said and did.

In the great majority of cases a direction to that effect will be enough, particularly where the defendant's actions amounted to a direct attack upon his victim, because in such cases the evidence relating to the defendant's desire or motive will be clear and his intent will have been the same as his desire or motive. But in some cases, of which this is one, the defendant does an act which is manifestly dangerous and as a result someone dies. The primary desire or motive of the defendant may not have been to harm that person, or indeed anyone. In that situation what further directions should a jury be given as to the mental state which they must find to exist in the defendant if murder is to be proved? . . .

It may be advisable first of all to explain to the jury that a man may intend to achieve a certain result whilst at the same time not desiring it to come about. In *R. v Moloney* Lord Bridge gave an illustration of the distinction [the example of the man boarding a plane bound for Manchester to escape pursuit.] . . .

In *R. v Hancock* the House decided that the *R. v Moloney* guidelines require a reference to probability. Lord Scarman said, at p.473:

'They also require an explanation that the greater the probability of a consequence the more likely it is that the consequence was foreseen and that if that consequence was foreseen the greater the probability is that that consequence was also intended.'

When determining whether the defendant had the necessary intent, it may therefore be helpful for a jury to ask themselves two questions. (1) How probable was the consequence which resulted from the defendant's voluntary act? (2) Did he foresee that consequence?

If he did not appreciate that death or serious harm was likely to result from his act, he cannot have intended to bring it about. If he did, but thought that the risk to which he was exposing the person killed was only slight, then it may be easy for the jury to conclude that he did not intend to bring about that result. On the other hand, if the jury are satisfied that at the material time the defendant recognised that death or serious harm would be virtually certain (barring some unforeseen intervention) to result from his voluntary act, then that is a fact from which they may find it easy to infer that he intended to kill or do serious bodily harm, even though he may not have had any desire to achieve that result.

As Lord Bridge of Harwich said in *R. v Moloney*: 'the probability of the consequence taken to have been foreseen must be little short of overwhelming before it will suffice to establish the necessary intent'. At p.926 he uses the expression 'moral certainty'; he said, at p.929 'will lead to a certain consequence unless something unexpected supervenes to prevent it'.

Where the charge is murder and in the rare cases where the simple direction is not enough, the jury should be directed that they are not entitled to infer the necessary intention, unless they feel sure that death or serious bodily harm was a virtual certainty (barring some unforeseen intervention) as a result of the defendant's actions and that the defendant appreciated that such was the case.

Where a man realises that it is for all practical purposes inevitable that his actions will result in death or serious harm, the inference may be irresistible that he intended that result, however little he may have desired or wished it to happen. The decision is one for the jury to be reached upon a consideration of all the evidence.

Appeal allowed.
Conviction quashed.
Conviction of manslaughter substituted.

Note

Lord Lane CJ appeared to confine the situations in which a jury could infer intention to those where the consequence (in a murder case death or serious bodily harm) was foreseen as virtually certain. He did not, however, equate such foresight with intention making it clear that whether or not such an inference was to be drawn was a matter for the jury. Speaking extra-judicially, however, in the House of Lords' debate on the *Report of the Select Committee of the House of Lords on Murder and Life Imprisonment* (HL Deb., Vol.512 col.480) he stated:

> "It is right to say that the decision in *Nedrick* . . . endeavoured to provide a satisfactory defini-
> tion of the word 'intention' . . . It is equally true to say . . . that in *Nedrick* the court was obliged
> to phrase matters as it did because of earlier decisions in your Lordships' House by which it
> was bound. We had to tread gingerly indeed in order not to tread upon your Lordships' toes.
> As a result *Nedrick* was not as clear as it should have been. However, I agree respectfully
> with the conclusions of the committee that 'intention' should be defined in the terms set
> out in paragraph 195 of the report on page 50. [The Committee adopted cl.18(b) of the Law
> Commission draft Criminal Code which states that 'a person acts intentionally with respect
> to . . . a result when he acts either in order to bring it about or being aware that it will occur
> in the ordinary course of events.'] That seems to express clearly what in *Nedrick* we failed
> properly to explain."

This seems to go much further than the Court of Appeal sought to go in *Nedrick* as it defines "inten-tion" rather than providing a test from which a jury may *infer* intention. In the case which follows the House of Lords revisited this problem.

R. V WOOLLIN

[1999] A.C. 82 HL

The appellant was charged with the murder of his three-month-old son having lost his temper and thrown him on to a hard surface fracturing his skull from which injury he died. The trial judge initially had directed the jury that they could infer that the accused intended to kill (or cause serious bodily harm) if they were satisfied that he appreciated that death or serious bodily harm was virtually certain to result from his actions. Later in his summing up the judge said that if they were satisfied, he appre-ciated that there was a substantial risk of causing serious injury to his son they could find from this that he intended to do so. The jury convicted and the Court of Appeal dismissed his appeal against conviction.

LORD STEYN

The Court of Appeal certified the following questions as of general importance:

'1. In murder, where there is no direct evidence that the purpose of a defendant was to kill or to inflict serious injury on the victim, is it necessary to direct the jury that they may only infer an intent to do serious injury if they are satisfied (a) that serious bodily harm was a virtually certain consequence of the defendant's voluntary act and (b) that the defendant appreciated that fact? 2. If the answer to question 1 is "Yes," is such a direction necessary in all cases or is it only necessary in cases where the sole evidence of the defendant's intention is to be found in his actions and their consequence to the victim?'

On appeal to your Lordships' House the terrain of the debate covered the correctness in law of the direction recommended by Lord Lane C.J. in *Nedrick* and, if that direction is sound, whether it should be used only in the limited category of cases envisaged by the Court of Appeal. And counsel for the appellant renewed his submission that by directing the jury in terms of substantial risk the judge illegitimately widened the mental element of murder.

The directions of the judge on the mental element
His Lordship outlined the trial judge's initial direction to the jury which followed the *Nedrick* recommended direction. After an overnight adjournment the judge continued his summing up but did not use the *Nedrick* direction, instead referring to appreciation of a substantial risk of serious injury.

It is plain, and the Crown accepts, that a direction posing an issue as to appreciation of a 'substantial risk' of causing serious injury is wider than a direction framed in terms of appreciation of a 'virtual certainty (barring some unforeseen intervention).' If Lord Lane C.J. correctly stated the law in *Nedrick*, the judge's direction in terms of substantial risk was wrong. But the Crown argued, as I have indicated, that *Nedrick* was wrongly decided or, alternatively, that the principle as enunciated by Lord Lane does not apply to the present case.

The problem facing the Court of Appeal in Nedrick
. . . [His Lordship quoted extensively from *Nedrick* but highlighted the following passage as the critical part of Lord Lane CJ's direction:]

'. . . Where the charge is murder and in the rare cases where the simple direction is not enough, the jury should be directed that they are not entitled to infer the necessary intention, unless they feel sure that death or serious bodily harm was a virtual certainty (barring some unforeseen intervention) as a result of the defendant's actions and that the defendant appreciated that such was the case . . . .'

The effect of the critical direction is that a result foreseen as virtually certain is an intended result.

The direct attack on Nedrick
It is now possible to consider the Crown's direct challenge to the correctness of *Nedrick*. First, the Crown argued that *Nedrick* prevents the jury from considering all the evidence in the case relevant to intention. The argument is that this is contrary to the provisions of section 8 of the Act of 1967. This provision reads:

'A court or jury, in determining whether a person has committed an offence—(a) shall not be bound in law to infer that he intended or foresaw a result of his actions by reasons only of its being a natural and probable consequence of those actions; but (b) shall decide whether he did intend or foresee that result by reference to all the evidence, drawing such inferences from the evidence as appear proper in the circumstances.'

Paragraph (*a*) is an instruction to the judge and is not relevant to the issues on this appeal. The Crown's argument relied on paragraph (*b*) which is concerned with the function of the jury. It is no more than a legislative instruction that in considering their findings on intention or foresight the jury must take into account all relevant evidence: see Professor Edward Griew, 'States of Mind, Presumptions and Inferences,' in *Criminal Law: Essays in Honour of J. C. Smith* (1987), pp. 68, 76–77. *Nedrick* is undoubtedly concerned with the mental element which is sufficient for murder. So, for that matter, in their different ways were *Smith, Hyam, Moloney* and *Hancock*. But, as Lord Lane C.J. emphasised in the last sentence of *Nedrick*, at p.1028: 'The decision is one for the jury to be reached upon a consideration of all the evidence.' *Nedrick* does not prevent a jury from considering all the evidence: it merely stated what state of mind (in the absence of a purpose to kill or to cause serious harm) is sufficient for murder. I would therefore reject the Crown's first argument.

In the second place the Crown submitted that Nedrick is in conflict with the decision of the House in *Hancock*. Counsel argued that in order to bring some coherence to the process of determining intention Lord Lane C.J. specified a minimum level of foresight, namely virtual certainty. But that is not in conflict with the decision in *Hancock* which, apart from disapproving Lord Bridge's 'natural consequence' model direction, approved *Moloney* [1985] A.C. 905 in all other respects. And in *Moloney* Lord Bridge said, at p.925, that if a person foresees the probability of a consequence as little short of overwhelming, this 'will suffice to *establish* the necessary intent.' Nor did the House in *Hancock* rule out the framing of model directions by the Court of Appeal for the assistance of trial judges. I would therefore reject the argument that the guidance given in *Nedrick* was in conflict with the decision of the House in *Hancock*.

The Crown did not argue that as a matter of policy foresight of a virtual certainty is too narrow a test in murder. Subject to minor qualifications, the decision in *Nedrick* was widely welcomed by distinguished academic writers: see Professor J. C. Smith Q.C.'s commentary on *Nedrick* [1986] Crim.L.R. 742, 743–744; Glanville Williams, 'The Mens Rea for Murder: Leave it Alone' (1989) 105 L.Q.R. 387; J. R. Spencer, 'Murder in the Dark: A Glimmer of Light?' [1986] C.L.J. 366–367; *Ashworth, Principles of Criminal Law*, 2nd ed. (1995), p.172. It is also of interest that it is very similar to the threshold of being aware 'that it *will* occur in the ordinary course of events' in the Law Commission's draft Criminal Code (see Criminal Law: Legislating the Criminal Code: Offences against the Person and General Principles, Law Com. No. 218 (1993) (Cm. 2370), Appendix A (Draft Criminal Law Bill with Explanatory Notes), pp.90–91): compare also Professor J. C. Smith Q.C., 'A Note on Intention' [1990] Crim.L.R. 85, 86. Moreover, over a period of 12 years since *Nedrick* the test of foresight of virtual certainty has apparently caused no practical difficulties. It is simple and clear. It is true that it may exclude a conviction of murder in the often cited terrorist example where a member of the bomb disposal team is killed. In such a case it may realistically be said that the terrorist did not foresee the killing of a member of the bomb disposal team as a virtual certainty. That may be a consequence of not framing the principle in terms of risk-taking. Such cases ought to cause no substantial difficulty since immediately below murder there is available a verdict of manslaughter which may attract in the discretion of the court a life sentence. In any event, as Lord Lane C.J. eloquently argued in a debate in the House of Lords, to frame a principle for particular difficulties regarding terrorism 'would produce corresponding injustices which would be very hard to eradicate:' Hansard (H.L. Debates), November 6, 1989, col. 480. I am satisfied that the *Nedrick* test, which was squarely based on the decision of the House in *Moloney*, is pitched at the right level of foresight.

The argument that Nedrick has limited application

The Court of Appeal [1997] 1 Cr.App.R. 97, 107 held that the phrase a 'virtual certainty' should be confined to cases where the evidence of intent is limited to admitted actions of the accused and the consequences of those actions. It is not obligatory where there is other evidence to consider. The Crown's alternative submission on the appeal was to the same effect. This distinction would introduce yet another complication into a branch of the criminal law where simplicity is of supreme importance. The distinction is dependent on the vagaries of the evidence in particular cases. Moreover, a jury may reject the other evidence to which the Court of Appeal refers. And in preparing his summing up a judge could not ignore this possibility. If the Court of Appeal's view is right, it might compel a judge to pose different tests depending on what evidence the jury accepts. For my part, and with the greatest respect, I have to say that this distinction would be likely to produce great practical difficulties. But, most importantly, the distinction is not based on any principled view regarding the mental element in murder. Contrary to the view of the Court of Appeal, I would also hold that section 8 (*b*) of the Act of 1967 does not compel such a result.

In my view the ruling of the Court of Appeal was wrong. It may be appropriate to give a direction in accordance with *Nedrick* in any case in which the defendant may not have desired the result of his act. But I accept the trial judge is best placed to decide what direction is required by the circumstances of the case.

The disposal of the present appeal

It follows that the judge should not have departed from the *Nedrick* direction. By using the phrase 'substantial risk' the judge blurred the line between intention and recklessness, and hence between murder and manslaughter. The misdirection enlarged the scope of the mental element required for murder. It was a material misdirection. At one stage it was argued that the earlier correct direction 'cured' the subsequent incorrect direction. A misdirection cannot by any means always be cured by the fact that the judge at an earlier or later stage gave a correct direction. After all, how is a jury to choose between a correct and an incorrect direction on a point of law? If a misdirection is to be corrected, it must be done in the plainest terms: *Archbold, Criminal Pleading, Evidence & Practice*, 1998 ed., p.411, para.4–374.

That is, however, not the end of the matter. For my part, I have given anxious consideration to the observation of the Court of Appeal that, if the judge had used the phrase 'a virtual certainty,' the verdict would have been the same. In this case there was no suggestion of any other ill treatment of the child. It would also be putting matters too high to say that on the evidence before the jury it was an open-and-shut case of murder rather than manslaughter. In my view the conviction of murder is unsafe. The conviction of murder must be quashed.

The status of Nedrick

In my view Lord Lane C.J.'s judgment in *Nedrick* provided valuable assistance to trial judges. The model direction is by now a tried-and-tested formula. Trial judges ought to continue to use it. On matters of detail I have three observations, which can best be understood if I set out again the relevant part of Lord Lane's judgment. It was:

'(A) When determining whether the defendant had the necessary intent, it may therefore be helpful for a jury to ask themselves two questions. (1) How probable was the consequence which resulted from the defendant's voluntary act? (2) Did he foresee that consequence? If he did not appreciate that death or serious harm was likely to result from his act, he cannot have intended to bring it about. If he did, but thought that the risk to which he was exposing the person killed was only slight, then it may be easy for the jury to conclude that he did not intend to bring about that result. On the other hand, if the jury are satisfied that at the material time the defendant recognised that death or serious harm would be virtually certain (barring some unforeseen intervention) to result from his voluntary act, then that is a fact from which they may find it easy to infer that he intended to kill or do serious bodily harm, even though he may not have had any desire to achieve that result . . . (B) Where the charge is murder and in the rare cases where the simple direction is not enough, the jury should be directed that they are not entitled to infer the necessary intention, unless they feel sure that death or serious bodily harm was a virtual certainty (barring some unforeseen intervention) as a result of the defend-ant's actions and that the defendant appreciated that such was the case. (C) Where a man realises that it is for all practical purposes inevitable that his actions will result in death or serious harm, the inference may be irresistible that he intended that result, however little he may have desired or wished it to happen. The decision is one for the jury to be reached upon a consideration of all the evidence.' (Lettering added.)

First, I am persuaded by the speech of my noble and learned friend, Lord Hope of Craighead, that it is unlikely, if ever, to be helpful to direct the jury in terms of the two questions set out in (A). I agree that these questions may detract from the clarity of the critical direction in (B). Secondly, in their writings previously cited Glanville Williams, Professor Smith and Andrew Ashworth observed that the use of the words 'to infer' in (B) may detract from the clarity of the model direction. I agree. I would substitute the words 'to find.' Thirdly, the first sentence of (C) does not form part of the model direction. But it would always be right for the judge to say, as Lord Lane C.J. put it, that the decision is for the jury upon a consideration of all the evidence in the case.

The certified questions
Given my conclusions the certified questions fall away.

Appeal allowed.
Conviction of murder quashed.
Conviction of manslaughter substituted.
Cause remitted to Court of Appeal (Criminal Division) for sentencing.

R. V MATTHEWS; R. V ALLEYNE

[2003] EWCA Crim 192

The appellants were convicted, inter alia, of murder. The victim had been thrown into a river from a bridge. The trial judge gave a direction to the jury, in relation to intent to kill, in the following terms: "With regard to proving an *intent to kill*, the prosecution will only succeed in proving this intent *either*:

(i) by making you sure that this specific intention was actually in the mind/s of the defendants, *or*

(ii) (a) by making you are sure that [the deceased's] death was a virtual certainty (barring some attempts to save him), and

   (b) the defendant whose case you are considering appreciated at the time [the deceased] was thrown off the bridge that this was the case, *and* he then had no intention of saving him, and knew or realised that the others did not intend to save him either."

The appellants contended, inter alia, that that was a misdirection because the alternative (ii) was put as a substantive rule of law rather than as a rule of evidence.

RIX LJ

23. . . . [The trial judge's] direction was regarded as incorporating what has become known as the *Nedrick* or *Woollin* direction, after the cases of *R. v Nedrick* (1986) 83 Cr App R 267, [1986] 1 WLR 1025 and *R. v Woollin* [1999] 1 Cr App R 8, [1999] 1 A.C. 82. The classic form of that direction, repeated in the JSB model direction, is as follows:

'Where the charge is murder and in the rare cases where the simple direction is not enough, the jury should be directed that they are not entitled to *find* the necessary intention, unless they feel sure that death [or serious bodily harm] was a virtual certainty (barring some unforeseen intervention) as a result of the defendant's actions and that the defendant appreciated that such was the case.'

24. We have emphasised the word *find* in that direction, because the original direction of Lord Lane CJ in Nedrick contained the word 'infer'. The only change made by the House of Lords in Woollin was to substitute *find* for *infer* (see Lord Steyn at pp.20 and 96H and Lord Hope of Craighead at pp.21 and 97D). The essential ground of appeal argued on behalf of both Alleyne and Matthews is that the judge's direction on intent was a misdirection, and that in consequence their convictions for murder are unsafe . . .

39. Mr Coker for the Crown on this appeal submits that in *Woollin* the House of Lords has finally moved away from a rule of evidence to a rule of substantive law. In this connection he drew attention to a sentence in Lord Steyn's speech at pp.17 and 93F where he says, immediately after setting out Lord Lane's observations in *Nedrick*, that—'The effect of the critical direction is that a result foreseen as virtually certain is an intended result.'

40. He also relies on what Professor Sir John Smith has to say in his note on *R. v Woollin* [1998] Crim.L.R 890 and in Smith & Hogan, Criminal Law, 10th edition, at 70ff. Thus in the former, Professor Smith said this:

'A jury might still fairly ask 'We are all quite sure that D knew that it was virtually certain that his act would cause death. You tell us we are entitled to find that he intended it. Are we bound to find that? Some of us want to and some do not. How should we decide?' The implication appears to be that, even now, they are not so bound. But why not? At one point Lord Steyn says of *Nedrick* "The effect of the critical direction is that a result foreseen as virtually certain is an intended result." If that is right, the only question for the jury is, "Did the defendant foresee the result as virtually certain?" If he did, he intended it. That, it is submitted is what the law should be; and it now seems that we have at last moved substantially in that direction. The *Nedrick* formula, however, even as modified ("entitled to find"), involves some ambiguity with the hint of the existence of some ineffable, undefinable, notion of intent, locked in the breasts of the jurors.'

41. Moreover, in the latter treatise (at 72) Professor Smith cites Lord Lane speaking in the debate on the report of the House of Lords Select Committee on Murder (HL Paper, 78-I, 1989) as follows:

'in *Nedrick* the court was obliged to phrase matters as it did because of earlier decisions in your Lordships' House by which it was bound. We had to tread very gingerly indeed in order not to tread on your Lordships' toes. As a result, *Nedrick* was not as clear as it should have been. However, I agree with the conclusions of the committee that "intention" should be defined in the terms set out in para.195 of the report on p.50. That seems to me to express clearly what in *Nedrick* we failed properly to explain.'

42. The definition referred to, as Smith & Hogan goes on to explain, is that stated in cl.18(b) of the Draft Code (itself referred to by Lord Steyn in *Woollin*) as follows:

'A person acts "intentionally" with respect to . . . a result when he acts either in order to bring it about or being aware that it will occur in the ordinary course of events.'

43. In our judgment, however, the law has not yet reached a *definition* of intent in murder in terms of appreciation of a virtual certainty. Lord Lane was speaking not of what was decided in *Nedrick* (or in the other cases which preceded it) nor of what was thereafter to be decided in *Woollin*, but of what the law in his opinion should be, as represented by the cl.18(b) definition. Similarly, although the law has progressively moved closer to what Professor Smith has been advocating, we do not regard *Woollin* as yet reaching or laying down a substantive rule of law. On the contrary, it is clear from the discussion in *Woollin* as a whole that *Nedrick* was derived from the existing law, at that time ending in *Moloney* and *Hancock*, and that the critical direction in *Nedrick* was approved, subject to the change of one word . . .

45. Having said that, however, we think that, once what is required is an appreciation of virtual certainty of death, and not some lesser foresight of merely probable consequences, there is very little to choose between a rule of evidence and one of substantive law. It is probably this thought that led Lord Steyn to say that a result foreseen as virtually certain is an intended result . . .

Appeal dismissed

Questions

1. If on a trial for murder the evidence indicates that the accused may not have intended the result of death in the sense of that being his aim or purpose, is the trial judge obliged to give the revised *Nedrick* direction?

2. If a jury consider that the accused did foresee the result of death as virtually certain, are they bound to find that he intended that result?

3. If D in **Case (d)** (above, p.82) believed that death of the bus passengers was virtually certain to result from his actions of shooting the driver (even though in reality it was only a probability), and one of the passengers does die, could a jury convict D of murder if they strictly followed the revised *Nedrick* direction?

4. If D has a good motive for acting, even though death is virtually certain to ensue if he achieves his primary purpose, is the judge in the trial of D for murder obliged to give the revised *Nedrick* direction and, if so, is the jury, if it concludes that D foresaw death as virtually certain, obliged to convict? (See the cases in the next section).

----

ii. Motive and Intention

Note

In seeking to discover the meaning of "intention" a useful starting place is to distinguish it from a concept with which it is often confused, namely *motive*.

G. WILLIAMS, *TEXTBOOK OF CRIMINAL LAW*, 2ND EDN (STEVENS & SONS, 1983), P.75

In ordinary speech, 'intention' and 'motive' are often convertible terms. For the lawyer, the word 'motive' generally refers to some further intent which forms no part of the legal rule.

If we say that a man shot and killed his aunt with the motive of benefiting under her will, the immediate intent, which makes the act murder, is the intention or desire to kill, while the further intent or motive, which forms no part of the definition of the crime of murder, is the intention or desire to benefit under the will. Other motives are the desire to obtain the satisfaction of revenge, or to get rid of a rival, or to promote a political object. (Such motives may also be expressed in abstract terms: 'he killed her from a motive of greed/revenge/jealousy,' Motive in this sense is irrelevant to responsibility (guilt or innocence), though it may be relevant to proof, or to the quantum of punishment. The prosecution may prove a motive for the crime if it helps them to establish their case, as a matter of circumstantial evidence; but they are not legally bound to prove motive, because a 'motiveless' crime is still a crime. Conversely, the defendant may adduce evidence of his good motive in order to reduce his punishment, perhaps to vanishing-point.

Exceptionally, the term 'motive' is used in a sense relevant to responsibility in the crime of libel. Also, crimes of ulterior intent require two intents, one lying behind the other, and the second may be called motive. The crime of burglary is committed where a person enters a building or part of a building by way of trespass with intent to commit one of certain crimes therein. There is an intentional entry, with the ulterior intent of committing a crime in the house; this ulterior intent is the motive of the entry, and is sometimes referred to as such, yet here it forms part of the legal definition.

Note

Exceptionally, a motive may be made an element of an offence. For example, the Crime and Disorder Act 1998 provides for an enhanced penalty where certain offences are racially or religiously aggravated, such as assaults, criminal damage or public order offences. An offence is racially aggravated where it "is motivated (wholly or partly) by hostility towards members of a racial group, based on their membership of that group" (see s.28(l)(b)). But generally motive is irrelevant to liability, even where that motive may be good (see, for example, *Smith* [1960] 2 Q.B. 423; *Chandler v DPP* [1964] A.C. 763).

The position that a good motive does not absolve a person from criminal liability has been affirmed recently by both the Privy Council and the House of Lords in two cases involving claims of entrapment. In the first, *Yip Chiu-Cheung v R.* [1994] 3 W.L.R. 514, the appellant had been convicted in Hong Kong of conspiracy to traffic in heroin contrary to common law and the Dangerous Drugs Ordinance. The other party to the conspiracy was an American undercover drug enforcement agent who (with the agreement of the Hong Kong authorities) was to meet the appellant and take delivery of the heroin which he was then to take to Australia. The appellant argued that the agent could not be a co-conspirator as he lacked the necessary mens rea for conspiracy. Lord Griffiths stated (at 518):

> "The crime of conspiracy requires an agreement between two or more persons to commit an unlawful act with the intention of carrying it out. It is the intention to carry out the crime that constitutes the necessary *mens rea* for the offence."

On this basis his Lordship concluded that even though the agent was "acting courageously and with the best of motives", he intended to commit the offence of drug trafficking regardless of whether he would be prosecuted.

On similar facts the House of Lords in *R. v Latif* [1996] 1 All E.R. 353 expressed the view that a customs officer, who brought heroin to England as part of an operation designed to catch a major trafficker, had the necessary intention to evade the prohibition on the importation of heroin and would have been guilty of an offence contrary to s.50(3) of the Customs and Excise Management Act 1979.

In both *Yip Chiu-Cheung* and *Latif* the statements concerning motive and intention came in the context of appeals by what might be regarded as appellants for whom there would be little moral sympathy. The problem, however, which remains is those actors for whom there would be considerable moral sympathy but whose conduct may appear to fall within the strict letter of the law on intention if it is rigidly applied. There are two antagonistic tensions at play: first, the logic of the *Nedrick/ Woollin* test for oblique intention if applied without moderation could catch those whose motive for pursuing their primary purpose is morally inconsistent with the mens rea for the offence, the actus reus of which was the side-effect of achieving their primary purpose (cf. *Steane*, above, *Moor*, below, and *Gillick v West Norfolk & Wisbech AHA*, below p.263); and secondly, the reluctance of judges to frame a defence (whether based in justification or excuse) to cover those who act from a good motive. This problem is set in even starker contrast when the virtually certain side effect of D achieving his morally commendable primary purpose is death and thus, prima facie, could amount to murder, whereas the accepted mens rea for murder does not cover, for example, the terrorist bomber who displays "wicked recklessness" towards the bomb disposal team but does not foresee death as a virtual certainty.

Question

P is terminally ill and suffering extreme pain. D, a doctor, prescribes a course of pain relieving treatment involving the administration of diamorphine. The pain relieving treatment involves gradually increasing the amount of diamorphine administered. D knows that diamorphine in large doses eventually kills. After several days of diamorphine treatment, P dies. Assuming D is prosecuted for murder should the trial judge give the jury the revised *Nedrick* direction? If so would D's motive provide the jury with a reason for not finding intention should they be satisfied that D foresaw death as being virtually certain to ensue from the administration of diamorphine? Reconsider your answer after reading the following extracts from jury directions in two trials for attempted murder and murder respectively of two doctors. Consider also whether the effect of the two directions is to create a special defence for doctors to protect them from a rigid application of the *Nedrick* test.

R. V COX

(1992) 12 B.M.L.R. 38

Dr Cox, a consultant rheumatologist, was charged with the attempted murder of his patient, Mrs Lilian Boyes, who was suffering from rheumatoid arthritis and other conditions. She was dying and suffering extreme pain and pleading for help to die. A short time before her death Dr Cox administered to her an injection of potassium chloride in a quantity which could have no therapeutic purpose. Dr Cox admitted the injection and its quantity. The only issue of contention was his intent in giving it. The prosecution alleged that in administering it Dr Cox's intention was to end her life. The defence argued that his primary purpose was to relieve pain and that there was no intent to kill. Dr Cox was charged with attempted murder as Mrs Boyes' body had been cremated and thus the actual cause of death could not be established—that is whether she died from the effects of the potassium chloride injection or whether she died of natural causes before it took effect.

OGNALL J

directed the jury . . . We all appreciate that some medical treatment, whether of a positive, therapeutic character or solely of an analgesic kind—by which I mean designed solely to alleviate pain and suffering—some treatment carries with it a serious risk to the health or even the life of the patient. Doctors are frequently confronted with, no doubt, distressing dilemmas. They have to make up their minds as to whether the risk, even to the life of their patient, attendant upon their contemplated form of treatment, is such that the risk is, or is not, medically justified. If a doctor genuinely believes that a certain course is beneficial to his patient, either therapeutically or analgesically, then even though he recognises that that course carries with it a risk to life, he is fully entitled, nonetheless, to pursue it. If in those circumstances the patient dies, nobody could possibly suggest that in that situation the doctor was guilty of murder or attempted murder.

The problem is obviously particularly acute in the case of those who are terminally ill and in considerable pain, if not agony. Such was the case of Lillian Boyes. It was plainly Dr Cox's duty to do all that was medically possible to alleviate her pain and suffering, even if the course adopted carried with it an obvious risk that, as a side effect of that treatment, her death would be rendered likely or even certain.

There can be no doubt that the use of drugs to reduce pain and suffering will often be fully justified notwithstanding that it will, in fact, hasten the moment of death. What can never be lawful is the use of drugs with the primary purpose of hastening the moment of death.

And so, in deciding Dr Cox's intention, the distinction the law requires you to draw is this. Is it proved that in giving that injection, in that form and in those amounts, Dr Cox's primary purpose was to bring the life of Lillian Boyes to an end?

If it was, then he is guilty. If, on the other hand, it was, or may have been, his primary purpose in acting as he did to alleviate her pain and suffering, then he is not guilty. That is so even though he recognised that, in fulfilling that primary purpose, he might or even would hasten the moment of her death . . .

Disposition: Guilty

R. V MOOR

Unreported 11 May 1999 (Newcastle Crown Court)

Dr Moor, a General Practitioner, was charged with murdering a patient by administering a large dose of diapmorphine to him. The patient, George Liddell was 85 and suffering from bowel cancer which, according to the hospital, had been operated on successfully. However, Mr Liddell, on leaving hospital and going to live with his daughter, became depressed, immobile and appeared to be in severe pain. He went into decline and Dr Moor, who had been prescribing diamorphine (5mgms later increased to 10mgms) for him for some days gave him a much increased dose (30mgms)—all were administered by a syringe driver (this releases the diamorphine into the patient's bloodstream gradually over a 24-hour period). The following day Dr Moor administered a larger dose (at least 60mgms) by injection when he attended Mr Liddell who was in a coma and breathing in the manner of a person close to death. He claimed his purpose in doing so was to make sure that the patient suffered no break through pain. Within 20 minutes Mr Liddell died.

The case became the subject of an investigation because Dr Moor stated in an article in a Sunday newspaper that he had helped patients to die with large doses of diamorphine. A post-mortem was carried out on Mr Liddell revealing abnormally large levels of diamorphine. This also revealed that he was not terminally ill from cancer, as Dr Moor had thought on the basis of his acute pain. Defence experts, however, gave evidence that he had a serious heart condition which had been missed by the hospital and this was almost certainly responsible for his very sick, terminal, appearance. They also expressed the view that the cancer which remained after the operation could have caused acute pain.

HOOPER J

directed the jury as follows on the question of murder:
Question 1 Has the prosecution satisfied you so that you are sure that the . . . injection given by Dr Moor to George Liddell contained significantly more than 60 mgms (2 ampoules of 30mg). If the answer to question 1 is 'No', your verdict must be 'not guilty'. If the answer to question 1 is 'Yes', go on to question 2.

Question 2 Has the prosecution satisfied you so that you are sure that the defendant caused the death of George Liddell. If the answer to question 2 is 'No', your verdict must be 'not guilty'. If the answer to question 2 is 'Yes', go to question 3.

A person causes the death of another if his act, in this case the intramuscular injection containing morphine, contributed significantly to the death. It does not have to be the sole or principal cause of death.

Question 3 Has the prosecution satisfied you so that you are sure that Dr Moor's purpose in giving the intramuscular injection was not to give treatment which he believed in the circumstances (as he understood them) to be proper treatment to relieve George Liddell's pain and suffering? If the answer to question 3 is 'No', your verdict must be 'not guilty'. If the answer to question 3 is 'Yes', go to question 4.

Bear in mind that there is no dispute that Dr Moor believed that George Liddell would die shortly of natural causes. In other words of another judge [Devlin J, *R. v Adams*, Central Criminal Court, April 9, 1957]:

'A doctor aiding the sick or dying does not have to calculate in minutes or hours or weeks the effect on a patient's life of the medicines which he administers. If the first purpose of medicine, the restoration of health, can no longer be achieved there is still much for the doctor to do and he is entitled to do all that is proper and necessary to relieve the pain and suffering even if measures he takes may incidentally shorten life.'

Question 4 Has the prosecution satisfied you so that you are sure that the defendant when he gave the intramuscular injection intended to kill George Liddell. If the answer to question 4 is 'No', your verdict must be 'not guilty'. If the answer to question 4 is 'Yes', then your verdict must be one of 'guilty'.

A person intends to kill another person if he does an act, in this case giving the injection, for the purpose of killing that person. If Dr Moor thought or may have thought that it was only highly probable that death would follow the injection, then the prosecution would not have proved that he intended to kill and he would be not guilty.

Disposition: Not Guilty

Note

Hooper J effectively adopted the special defence approach used in *Cox*—if D's purpose is proper medical treatment (pain relief would be such) his purpose is not to kill and he should be acquitted (even though he may realise that death is virtually certain). If, however, his purpose is not proper medical treatment, the question for the jury is whether his intention was to kill. Hooper J framed the questions in the most generous way possible for Dr Moor. The jury acquitted. We do not know how far they proceeded in their deliberations on the questions (cf. *Gillick v West Norfolk & Wisbech AHA* [1986] A.C. 112, below, p.263).

Questions

1. In what way might the direction to the jury and the outcome of the case have differed if Dr Cox had administered a large dose of diamorphine to Mrs Boyes and she had died as a result?

2. Consider how a judge might direct the jury in the following circumstances:

    D is a retired General Practitioner. P, her husband, is terminally ill from cancer and in excruciating pain. He begs to be allowed to die. P's GP has prescribed diamorphine which is being administered by a syringe driver at a rate which will not prove fatal and which also is not controlling the pain. D alters the setting of the syringe driver to increase the rate at which the diamorphine is administered with the result that P dies. D admits that she knew from her experience that this would be the inevitable outcome but also claims that her purpose was to relieve P's suffering.

3. Should the way in which a judge directs a jury on intention be dependent upon the professional capacity in which an accused acts?

4. Is the criminal law creeping closer towards the recognition of a general justificatory defence based on good motive? (See further *Re A (Children) (Conjoined Twins: Medical Treatment) (No.1)* [2000] 4 All E.R. 961, below p.271.)

----

iii. Knowledge

LAW COMMISSION CONSULTATION PAPER, *A NEW HOMICIDE ACT FOR ENGLAND AND WALES?* (2005), LAW COM. NO.177

8.10 'Knowingly': knowledge and 'wilful blindness'
[T]he state of mind which is to be assimilated to 'actual knowledge' for the purposes of criminal liability is that of so-called 'wilful blindness'. English criminal law has commonly treated a person as knowing something if, being pretty sure that it is so, he deliberately avoids making an examination or asking questions that might confirm the fact—he avoids taking advantage of an available means of 'actual knowledge'. It is this state of mind which, we believe, has to be captured by a short form of words. Clause 18(a) therefore treats a person as acting 'knowingly' with respect to a circumstance 'not only when he is aware that it exists or will exist, but also when he avoids taking steps that might confirm his belief that it exists or will exist.'

Note

Statute may require knowledge expressly by use of that word or one of its variants. But even where an express requirement of knowledge is not included in the statute, the courts have frequently implied such a requirement: see, e.g. *Sweet v Parsley* (below, p.147). In *Roper v Taylor's Central Garages* [1951] 2 T.L.R. 284, Devlin J stated that "knowingly" only says expressly what is normally implied. He went on to explain that there are different degrees of knowledge:

"There are, I think, three degrees of knowledge which it may be relevant to consider in cases of this kind. The first is actual knowledge, which the justices may find because they infer it from the nature of the act done, for no man can prove the state of another man's mind; and they may find it even if the defendant gives evidence to the contrary. They may say, 'We do not believe him; we think that this was his state of mind.' They may feel that the evidence falls short of that, if they do they have then to consider what might be described as knowledge of the second degree; whether the defendant was, as it has been called, shutting his eyes to an obvious means of knowledge. Various expressions have been used to describe that state of mind. I do not think it necessary to look further, certainly not in cases of this type, than the phrase which Lord Hewart CJ used in a case under this section, *Evans v Dell* (1937) 53 T.L.R. 310, where he said (at p.313): . . . 'the respondent deliberately refrained from making inquiries, the results of which he might not care to have.'

The third kind of knowledge is what is generally known in law as constructive knowledge: it is what is encompassed by the words 'ought to have known' in the phrase 'knew or ought to have known.' It does not mean actual knowledge at all; it means that the defendant had in effect the means of knowledge. When, therefore, the case of the prosecution is that the defendant failed to make what they think were reasonable inquiries it is, I think, incumbent on them to make it plain which of the two things they are saying. There is a vast distinction between a state of mind which consists of deliberately refraining from making inquiries the result of which the person does not care to have, and a state of mind which is merely neglecting to make such inquiries as a reasonable and prudent person would make. If that distinction is kept well in mind I think that justices will have less difficulty than this case appears to show they have had in determining what is the true position. The case of shutting the eyes is actual knowledge in the eyes of the law: the case of merely neglecting to make inquiries is not knowledge at all—it comes within the legal conception of constructive knowledge, a conception which, generally speaking, has no place in the criminal law."

Where knowledge is required a court may be satisfied that wilful blindness suffices. In *Westminster City Council v Croyalgrange Ltd* [1986] 2 All E.R. 353 at 359, Lord Bridge stated:

> "[I]t is always open to the tribunal of fact, when knowledge on the part of a defendant is required to be proved, to base a finding of knowledge on evidence that the defendant had deliberately shut his eyes to the obvious or refrained from inquiry because he suspected the truth but did not want to have his suspicion confirmed."

How precise must a person's knowledge be if he is to be liable for knowingly committing a specified offence? See the case which follows.

R. V TAAFFE

[1984] A.C. 539 HL

On his arraignment on a charge of having been knowingly concerned in the fraudulent evasion of the prohibition on the importation of cannabis resin, contrary to s.170(2) of the Customs and Excise Management Act 1979 and the Misuse of Drugs Act 1971, T pleaded not guilty. No evidence having been called, the recorder was asked to rule on the question whether T's version of events, if accepted by the jury, would entitle him to be acquitted. T's version was: (i) that he had been enlisted by a third party in Holland to import a substance from that country into England in fraudulent evasion of the prohibition on its importation and had so imported it; (ii) the substance had in fact been cannabis, importation of which was prohibited by the 1971 Act; (iii) T had mistakenly believed the substance to be currency; (iv) currency was not subject to any such prohibition; (v) T believed that it was. The recorder ruled that, even on T's version of events, he would be obliged to direct the jury to convict. Thereupon T pleaded guilty and was sentenced. T appealed and the Court of Appeal quashed his conviction. The Crown appealed.

LORD SCARMAN delivered the following opinion with which the remainder of their Lordships agreed:

My Lords, the certified question in this appeal by the Crown from the decision of the Court of Appeal quashing the respondent's conviction in the Crown Court at Gravesend, neatly summarises the assumed facts upon which the learned recorder ruled that, even if they were proved to the satisfaction of a jury, the respondent would not be entitled to be acquitted. The question is in these terms:

> 'When a defendant is charged with an offence, contrary to section 170(2) of the Customs and Excise Management Act 1979, of being knowingly concerned in the fraudulent evasion of the prohibition on the importation of a controlled drug—Does the defendant commit the offence where he: (a) imports prohibited drugs into the United Kingdom; (b) intends fraudulently to evade a prohibition on importation; but (c) mistakenly believes the goods to be money and not drugs; and (d) mistakenly believes that money is the subject of a prohibition against importation?'

In effect, the learned recorder answered the question in the affirmative and the Court of Appeal in the negative . . .

Lord Lane C.J. [in the Court of Appeal] construed the section under which the respondent was charged as creating not an offence of absolute liability but an offence of which an essential ingredient is a guilty mind. To be 'knowingly concerned' meant, in his judgment, knowledge not only of the existence of a smuggling operation but also that the substance being smuggled into the country was one the importation of which was prohibited by statute. The respondent thought he was concerned in a smuggling operation but believed that the substance was currency. The importation of currency is not subject to any prohibition. Lord Lane C.J. concluded, at p.631:

'[The respondent] is to be judged against the facts that he believed them to be. Had this indeed been currency and not cannabis, no offence would have been committed.'

Lord Lane C.J. went on to ask this question:

'Does it make any difference that the [respondent] thought wrongly that by clandestinely importing currency he was committing an offence?'

The Crown submitted that it does. The court rejected the submission: the respondent's mistake of law could not convert the importation of currency into a criminal offence: and importing currency is what it had to be assumed that the respondent believed he was doing.

My Lords, I find the reasoning of the Lord Chief Justice compelling. I agree with his construction of section 170(2) of the Act of 1979: and the principle that a man must be judged upon the facts as he believes them to be is an accepted principle of the criminal law when the state of a man's mind and his knowledge are ingredients of the offence with which he is charged.

Appeal dismissed

Question

Could T have been convicted of attempt to evade the prohibition on importation contrary to s.170(2) of the 1979 Act? (See Ch.7, below.)

Note

Statute prohibits the importation of many different substances and the penalties available vary depending upon the substance illegally imported. This raises the question whether D believing he is importing prohibited goods the penalty for which is light, may be convicted of, and sentenced for, importing a prohibited substance the penalty for which is heavy? In *Ellis, Street and Smith* (1987) 84 Cr. App. R. 235, the appellants were convicted of being knowingly concerned in the fraudulent evasion of the prohibition on importation of a controlled drug, namely cannabis, contrary to s.170(2) of the Customs and Excise Management Act 1979. Cannabis is a Class B drug and the maximum penalty for its importation is 14 years' imprisonment. The appellants actually believed that they were importing pornographic materials which carries a maximum penalty of two years. The Court of Appeal upheld their convictions following the decision in *Hennessey* (1979) 68 Cr. App. R. 419 (approved in *Shivpuri* [1987] A.C. 1 HL) that all that the accused had to know was that he was importing prohibited goods; he need not know their nature. Thus if D believes he is importing prohibited pornography or prohibited birds eggs in a sealed container when, in fact, it contains heroin, he will be guilty of the offence of importing a Class A drug which carries a maximum sentence of life imprisonment even though, had he known the true facts, he would never have considered doing so.

Questions

1. Is D truly knowingly concerned in the fraudulent evasion of the prohibition on the importation of a controlled drug where he knows he is engaging in a smuggling operation but is mistaken as to the substance being smuggled? Why should he not be judged according to the facts as he believed them to be and be convicted of attempting to commit the offence he believed he was committing?

2. Is knowledge previously acquired but subsequently forgotten sufficient to support a conviction? See the case which follows.

R. V RUSSELL

(1984) 81 Cr. App. R. 315

Police officers stopped D's car and found a cosh under the driver's seat. D was convicted of possessing an offensive weapon in a public place. His defence had been that he had forgotten that he had put the cosh there. D appealed arguing that the trial judge had failed to direct the jury that it was for the prosecution to prove that D had the cosh with him "knowingly."

JUPP J

We were referred to the case of *Cugullere* (1961) 45 Cr.App.R. 108; [1961] 1 W.L.R. 858, brought under the same section of the Prevention of Crime Act 1953, in which the Court of Criminal Appeal said, at the bottom of p.110 and p.860 respectively: 'This court is clearly of the opinion that the words "has with him in any public place" must mean "knowingly has with him in any public place". If some innocent person has a cosh slipped into his pocket by an escaping rogue, he would not be guilty of having it with him within the meaning of the section, because he would be quite innocent of any knowledge that it had been put into his pocket. In the judgment of this court, the section cannot apply in circumstances such as those. It is, therefore, extremely important in any case under this section for the judge to give a careful direction to the jury on the issue of possession. The first thing the jury have to be satisfied about, and it is always a question for the jury, is whether the accused person knowingly had with him the alleged offensive weapon.' . . .

The appellant's defence in the present case is not that, having had a cosh slipped under his driving seat by some third party, he was innocent of any knowledge that it had been put there. It is that he himself put the cosh under the driving seat, but until the police found and showed it him, he had forgotten all about it. Whether or not the jury would have accepted it, this defence should have been properly left to the jury, but it was not.

It was submitted on behalf of the Crown in this Court that there is a distinction between 'not knowing' and 'having forgotten'. The appellant, it is said, always knew how he came to put the cosh under the driving seat, although he only recalled it when the police confronted him with the cosh, and asked him to explain it.

In our judgment, the Court in *Cugullere*, in saying that the words of the statute must be construed as 'knowingly had with him', were not merely dealing with the situation where a defendant has an offensive weapon put within his reach by a stranger without his knowing it. They were applying the general principle of criminal responsibility which makes it incumbent on the prosecution to prove full *mens rea*. The well-known observations of Lord Reid in *Sweet v Parsley* (1969) 53 Cr.App.R. 221, 225, [1970] A.C. 132, are relevant here: 'It is firmly established by a host of authorities that *mens rea* is an essential ingredient of every offence unless some reason can be found for holding that that is not necessary. It is also firmly established that the fact that other sections of the Act expressly require *mens rea*, for example because they contain the word "knowingly", is not in itself sufficient to justify a decision that a section which is silent as to *mens rea* creates an absolute offence. In the absence of a clear indication in the Act that an offence is intended to be an absolute offence, it is necessary to go outside the Act and examine all relevant circumstances in order to establish that this must have been the intention of Parliament. I say "must have been", because it is a universal principle that if a penal provision is reasonably capable of two interpretations, that interpretation which is most favourable to the accused must be adopted'.

It would in our judgment be wrong to hold that a man knowingly has a weapon with him if his forgetfulness of its existence or presence in his car is so complete as to amount to ignorance that it is there at all. This is not a defence which juries would in the ordinary way be very likely to accept, but if it is raised it should be left to them for their decision.

Appeal allowed
Conviction quashed

iv. Recklessness

Note

Most crimes may be committed *intentionally* or *recklessly*. As recklessness provides the baseline for liability in most offences it is important that the term be clearly defined. However, as with *intention*, *recklessness* has thrown up definitional problems in the last twenty years or so. The word *reckless* (and its variants) has only been used in statutes in recent years, e.g. the Criminal Damage Act 1971. Formerly the word *maliciously* was used. This was defined as meaning *intention* or *recklessness*.

In *Criminal Law: The General Part* (1961), Glanville Williams defined recklessness to mean *advertent negligence* as opposed to *inadvertent negligence*.

WILLIAMS, *CRIMINAL LAW: THE GENERAL PART* (1961), S.24

Negligence is of two kinds, being either advertent negligence (commonly called recklessness) or inadvertent negligence. Both advertent and inadvertent negligence may be found either as to surrounding circumstances, or as to consequences. Here, we are concerned with advertent negligence (recklessness) in relation to consequences . . .

Recklessness as to consequence occurs when the actor does not desire the consequence, but foresees the possibility and consciously takes the risk. In inadvertent negligence, on the other hand, there is no such foresight . . .

Convenience requires a narrow use of the term 'negligence' to signify inadvertent negligence unless the context concludes this meaning. Recklessness can thus be contrasted with negligence, though in a more general sense both are species of the same genus.

If the actor foresaw the probability of the consequence he is regarded as reckless, even though he fervently desired and hoped for the exact opposite of the consequence, and even though he did his best (short of abandoning his main project) to avoid it. Judges in speaking of recklessness frequently insert words to the effect that the defendant 'did not care whether he caused damage or not', but the better view is that this is irrelevant. Recklessness is any determination to pursue conduct with knowledge of the risks involved though without a desire that they should eventuate . . ..

Although this meaning of recklessness is now generally accepted, three factors imperil its stability. The first results from the etymology of the word in the English language. A man who is reckless is literally a man who does not reck, that is to say one who does not care; on this line of reasoning, reckless and careless become synonyms. This would matter little if 'careless' kept its primary meaning of one who does not care, but in fact 'careless' has come to be applied to persons who may care very much about the harmful result of their acts but are constitutionally incapable of preventing those results. It is only too easy for this widened meaning of 'careless' to infect the word 'reckless'.

The etymological similarity of 'reckless' and 'careless' is the more unfortunate because of a second factor, the constant pressure to extend the reach of the criminal law on account of the supposed policy of the individual case. Judges sometimes wish to punish a particular defendant who is thought to have been guilty of improper conduct, without remembering an even more imperative requirement of public policy: that the technical terms of the law should retain unequivocal meanings. To allow 'reckless' and 'careless' to become interchangeable would leave us without adequate means to differentiate two concepts.

The third inflationary factor results from another linguistic association, namely in the formulas commonly used to instruct juries. The need for a formula arises from the difficulty of proving recklessness. If the issue is whether the defendant was reckless as to a given consequence, the question is whether he foresaw the possibility of that consequence; but he will probably deny that he foresaw it, and it is impossible to look directly into his mind to know whether he is speaking the truth. Usually the question will have to be solved by examining the defendant's conduct and his opportunities of knowledge. Yet conduct is by no means so certain a guide to the issue of recklessness as it is to that of intention. When a man bends himself to secure a result, he will often leave evidence of telltale pieces of behaviour which are inexplicable except on the assumption that he intended the result. But recklessness may be a mere passing realisation, instantly dismissed, which leaves no mark upon conduct. Also, a man is capable of self-deception: he may decide that an unpleasant result is not likely because he does not want it to be likely.

On the issue of recklessness, these considerations may be put before the jury. There is no objection to instructing the jury to consider whether the defendant *must* have foreseen the consequence, but it is fatally easy to confuse this with the question whether the defendant *ought* as a reasonable man to have foreseen it. The latter question presupposes an objective test of the reasonable man, and the accused person's actual foresight is immaterial. The former question is directed exclusively to the accused's actual foresight, and the test of what a reasonable man would have foreseen is merely a step in reasoning. For example, it may be shown that the accused is mentally subnormal, or that on the occasion in question he was drunk, or suffering from some fear, anger, or other excitement which deprived him of the ability to look circumspectly to the probable outcome of his conduct. These facts would not, according to the usual view, be relevant to an issue of inadvertent negligence, if that were before the court; but they are very relevant to the issue of recklessness. They may lead the tribunal to decide that the accused did not foresee the consequence, even though a person somewhat differently situated would have foreseen it. In short, a judgment of inadvertent negligence rests merely on a comparison between the conduct of the accused and that of a reasonable man, while a judgment of recklessness uses the concept of the reasonable man only as a guide to what went on in the accused's mind, and only so long as it can plausibly be assumed that the accused's mind accorded with the normal at the time of his act.

It must be confessed that, defined in this way, recklessness is not a concept that is likely to secure many convictions, if the law is properly administered. Recklessness as a form of *mens rea* is some enlargement upon the requirement of intention, but not a considerable one. This, at least, is true for recklessness as to the consequence of conduct. There is, however, another application of the concept of recklessness, namely as to the existence of present facts, i.e. the circumstances surrounding conduct. A person is said to be reckless as to a surrounding circumstance if he is aware of the possibility that such a circumstance exists and does an act regardless of it.

Question

Williams spoke of three factors which could imperil the stability of the meaning of recklessness; to what extent do the cases which follow establish the prophetic quality of Williams' comments?

Note

The courts originally gave recklessness a subjective meaning.

R. V CUNNINGHAM

[1957] 2 Q.B. 396

C stole a gas meter from the cellar of a house and in doing so fractured a gas pipe. Gas escaped, percolated through the cellar wall to the adjoining house, and entered a bedroom with the result that W, when she was asleep, inhaled a considerable quantity of the gas. C was convicted of unlawfully and maliciously causing W to take a noxious thing, so as thereby to endanger her life contrary to s.23 of the Offences Against the Person Act 1861. The judge directed the jury that "maliciously" meant "wickedly"—doing "something which he has no business to do and perfectly well knows it".

BYRNE J read the judgment of the court

The act of the appellant was clearly unlawful and therefore the real question for the jury was whether it was also malicious within the meaning of section 23 of the Offences Against the Person Act 1861.

Before this court Mr Brodie has taken three points, all dependent upon the construction of that section. Section 23 provides: 'Whosoever shall unlawfully and maliciously administer to or cause to be administered to or taken by any other person any poison or other destructive or noxious thing, so as thereby to endanger the life of such person, or so as thereby to inflict upon such person any grievous bodily harm, shall be guilty of felony . . .'

Mr Brodie argued, first, that mens rea of some kind is necessary. Secondly that the nature of the mens rea required is that the appellant must intend to do the particular kind of harm that was done, or, alternatively, that he must foresee that that harm may occur yet nevertheless continue recklessly to do the act. Thirdly, that the judge misdirected the jury as to the meaning of the word 'maliciously'. He cited the following cases: *R. v Pembliton* [below, p.139], *R. v Latimer* [below, p.140] and *R. v Faulkner* (1877) 13 Cox C.C. 550. In reply, Mr Snowden, on behalf of the Crown, cited *R. v Martin* (1881) 8 Q.B.D. 54.

We have considered those cases, and we have also considered, in the light of those cases, the following principle which was propounded by the late Professor C. S. Kenny in the first edition of his *Outlines of Criminal Law* published in 1902 and repeated in 1952: 'In any statutory definition of crime, malice must be taken not in the old vague sense of wickedness in general but as requiring either (1) An actual intention to do the particular kind of harm that in fact was done; or (2) recklessness as to whether such harm should occur or not (i.e. the accused has foreseen that the particular kind of harm might be done and yet has gone on to take the risk of it). It is neither limited to nor does it indeed require any ill will towards the person injured.' The same principle is repeated by Mr Turner in his 10th edition of *Russell on Crime* at p.1592.

We think that this is an accurate statement of the law. It derives some support from the judgments of Lord Coleridge C.J. and Blackburn J. in *Pembliton* s case (1874) L.R. 2 C.C.R. 119. In our opinion the word 'maliciously' in a statutory crime postulates foresight of consequence . . .

With the utmost respect to the learned judge, we think it is incorrect to say that the word 'malicious' in a statutory offence merely means wicked. We think the judge was, in effect, telling the jury that if they were satisfied that the appellant had acted wickedly—and he had clearly acted wickedly in stealing the gas meter and its contents—they ought to find that he had acted maliciously in causing the gas to be taken by Mrs Wade so as thereby to endanger her life.

In our view it should have been left to the jury to decide whether, even if the appellant did not intend the injury to Mrs Wade, he foresaw that the removal of the gas meter might cause injury to someone but nevertheless removed it. We are unable to say that a reasonable jury, properly directed as to the meaning of the word 'maliciously' in the context of section 23, would without doubt have convicted.

In these circumstances this court has no alternative but to allow the appeal and quash the conviction.

Appeal allowed

Notes

1.   For further consideration of "maliciously" see Ch.9 on Non-Fatal Offences Against the Person.

2.   The Law Commission, in Working Paper No.31, *Codification of the Criminal Law, General Principles: The Mental Element in Crime* (TSO, 1970) and in its Report, *The Mental Element in Crime* (TSO, 1978), Law Com. No.89, attributed a subjective meaning to *recklessness*. The Criminal Damage Act 1971 resulted from the work of the Law Commission (*Criminal Law Report on Offences of Damage to Property* (TSO, 1970), Law Com. No.29). The Act sought to revise and simplify the law in relation to offences of damage to property. The term *reckless* as used in s.1 of the Act was construed by the Court of Appeal to mean *subjective recklessness*; the clearest statement of principle was given by Geoffrey Lane LJ in *R. v Stephenson* [1979] Q.B. 695. D, who suffered from schizophrenia, crept into a hollow in a large haystack and lit a fire to keep warm. The stack caught fire resulting in £3,500 of damage. Medical evidence was given that D might not have had the same ability to foresee or appreciate risks as the mentally normal person. The trial judge directed the jury that they could find D guilty if satisfied that he had closed his mind to the obvious fact of risk from his act and that schizophrenia might be a reason which made a person close his mind to the obvious fact of risk. In effect he was directing the jury to convict if the risk of damage would have been obvious to a reasonable person. The Court of Appeal quashed the conviction, Geoffrey Lane LJ stating:

"A man is reckless when he carries out the deliberate act appreciating that there is a risk that damage to property may result from his act. It is however not the taking of every risk which could properly be classed as reckless. The risk must be one which it is in all the circumstances unreasonable for him to take.

Proof of the requisite knowledge in the mind of the defendant will in most cases present little difficulty. The fact that the risk of some damage would have been obvious to anyone in his right mind in the position of the defendant is not conclusive proof of the defendant's knowledge, but it may well be and in many cases doubtless will be a matter which will drive the jury to the conclusion that the defendant himself must have appreciated the risk. The fact that he may have been in a temper at the time would not normally deprive him of knowledge or foresight of the risk. If he had the necessary knowledge or foresight and his bad temper merely caused him to disregard it or put it to the back of his mind not caring whether the risk materialised, or if it merely deprived him of the self-control necessary to prevent him from taking the risk of which he was aware, then his bad temper will not avail him. We wish to make it clear that the test remains subjective, that the knowledge or appreciation or risk of some damage must have entered the defendant's mind even though he may have suppressed it or driven it out."

Note

In 1981 the House of Lords had cause to consider the definition of recklessness as used in the Criminal Damage Act 1971. In *R. v Caldwell* [1982] A.C. 341, D got drunk and set fire to a hotel. The guests were evacuated from the hotel when the fire was discovered and the resulting damage was, in fact, relatively minor. D was indicted on two counts of arson. He pleaded guilty to the first count of intentionally or recklessly damaging property to another contrary to s.1(1) of the 1971 Act but pleaded not guilty to the second count of damaging property with intent to endanger life or being reckless whether life would be endangered contrary to s.1(2) of the 1971 Act. He claimed that he was so drunk that the thought that he might endanger life had never entered his mind. Accordingly, he claimed, he could not have been reckless having never appreciated any risk. The trial judge directed the jury that drunkenness is not a defence to this type of offence. He was convicted and the appeal eventually reached the House of Lords. The House approved of the trial judge's direction to the jury that drunkenness is not a defence as this is an offence of "basic intent" (see Ch.4 below, Intoxication). This conclusion should have been enough to dispose of the appeal but the House took the opportunity to redefine recklessness. The majority of the House stated the test of recklessness as follows:

"In my opinion, a person charged with an offence under s.1(1) of the 1971 Act is 'reckless as to whether or not property would be destroyed or damaged' if (1) he does an act which in fact creates an obvious risk that property will be destroyed or damaged and (2) when he does the act he either has not given any thought to the possibility of there being any such risk or has recognised that there was some risk involved and has none the less gone on to do it."

The requirement in s.1(2) introduced an objective element into the concept of recklessness. Recognising a risk and taking it equates with the established *Cunningham* test of recklessness but the newly introduced alternative of *not giving thought to the possibility of a risk* broke new ground. After *Caldwell*, there followed much confusion and the decision was heavily criticised. The matter was again addressed by the House of Lords in the following case.

R. V G

[2003] UKHL 50

G, aged 11, and R, aged 12, were out at night without their parents' permission. They set fire to some newspapers under a wheelie bin behind a supermarket and left the fire burning. The fire spread to the bin and the supermarket and surrounding buildings resulting in £1m worth of damage. G and R were charged with arson contrary to s. 1(1) and (3) of the Criminal Damage Act 1971. In their defence they contended that they had expected the newspapers to burn out and had not appreciated any risk of the fire spreading to the wheelie bin and buildings. The Crown did not contest their assertions adopting the position that they did not represent a defence in law. The trial judge directed the jury in accordance with the test for recklessness laid down in *Caldwell* while expressing his own reservations about the harshness of that test. G and R were convicted and on appeal the Court of Appeal upheld their convictions on the basis that the law in *Caldwell* had been correctly applied. The Court of Appeal certified a point of law of general importance for consideration by the House of Lords.

LORD BINGHAM OF CORNHILL

. . . [1] My Lords, the point of law of general public importance certified by the Court of Appeal to be involved in its decision in the present case is expressed in this way:

'Can a defendant properly be convicted under section 1 of the Criminal Damage Act 1971 on the basis that he was reckless as to whether property was destroyed or damaged when he gave no thought to the risk but, by reason of his age and/or personal characteristics the risk would not have been obvious to him, even if he had thought about it?'.

The appeal turns on the meaning of 'reckless' in that section. This is a question on which the House ruled in *R. v Caldwell* [1982] AC 341, a ruling affirmed by the House in later decisions. The House is again asked to reconsider that ruling.
. . . [Having set out the facts of the case, the judge's directions to the jury and the background to the 1971 Act, his Lordship continued:]
The 1971 Act
[14] Enactment of the 1971 Act did not at once affect the courts' approach to the causing of unintentional damage. In *R. v Briggs (Note)* [1977] 1 WLR 605 the defendant had been charged under section 1(1) of the 1971 as a result of damage caused to a car and the appeal turned on the trial judge's direction on the meaning of 'reckless'. The appeal succeeded since the judge had not adequately explained that the test to be applied was that of the defendant's state of mind. The Court of Appeal (James LJ, Kenneth Jones and Pain JJ) ruled (at page 608):

'A man is reckless in the sense required when he carries out a deliberate act knowing that there is some risk of damage resulting from that act but nevertheless continues in the performance of that act.'

This definition was adopted but modified in *R. v Parker (Daryl)* [1977] 1 WLR 600 where the defendant in a fit of temper had broken a telephone by smashing the handset violently down on to the telephone unit and had been convicted under section 1(1) of the 1971 Act. The court (Scarman and Geoffrey Lane LJJ and Kenneth Jones J) readily followed *R. v Briggs (Note)* (page 603) but held that the defendant had been fully aware of all the circumstances (page 603) and that if (page 604)

'he did not know, as he said he did not, that there was some risk of damage, he was, in effect, deliberately closing his mind to the obvious—the obvious being that damage in these circumstances was inevitable.'

The court accordingly modified the *Briggs* definition in this way (page 604):

'A man is reckless in the sense required when he carried [*sic*] out a deliberate act knowing or closing his mind to the obvious fact that there is some risk of damage resulting from that act but nevertheless continuing in the performance of that act.'

This modification made no inroad into the concept of recklessness as then understood since, as pointed out by Professor Glanville Williams, *Textbook of Criminal Law* (1978), page 79, cited by Lord Edmund-Davies in his dissenting opinion in *R. v Caldwell* [1982] AC 341, 358,

'A person cannot, in any intelligible meaning of the words, close his mind to a risk unless he first realises that there is a risk; and if he realises that there is a risk, that is the end of the matter.'

[15] The meaning of 'reckless' in section 1(1) of the 1971 Act was again considered by the Court of Appeal (Geoffrey Lane LJ, Ackner and Watkins JJ) in *R. v Stephenson* [1979] QB 695. The defendant had tried to go to sleep in a hollow he had made in the side of a haystack. Feeling cold, he had lit a fire in the hollow which had set fire to the stack and damaged property worth £3500. He had been charged and convicted under section 1(1) and (3) of the 1971 Act. The defendant however had a long history of schizophrenia and expert evidence at trial suggested that he may not have had the same ability to foresee or appreciate risks as the mentally normal person. Giving the reserved judgment of the court, Geoffrey Lane LJ (at pages 700–703) reviewed the definition of recklessness in the Law Commission's Working Paper No 31, the acceptance of that definition by the leading academic authorities and the House of Lords' adoption of a subjective meaning of recklessness in tort in *Herrington v British Railways Board* [1972] AC 877. The court (at page 703) thought it fair to assume that those who were responsible for drafting the 1971 Act were intending to preserve its legal meaning as described in Kenny and expressly approved in *R. v Cunningham* [1957] 2 QB 396. The court then continued:

'What then must the prosecution prove in order to bring home the charge of arson in circumstances such as the present? They must prove that (1) the defendant deliberately committed some act which caused the damage to property alleged or part of such damage; (2) the defendant had no lawful excuse for causing the damage; these two requirements will in the ordinary case not be in issue; (3) the defendant either (a) intended to cause the damage to the property, or (b) was reckless as to whether the property was damaged or not. A man is reckless when he carries out the deliberate act appreciating that there is a risk that damage to property may result from his act. It is however not the taking of every risk which could properly be classed as reckless. The risk must be one which it is in all the circumstances unreasonable for him to take. Proof of the requisite knowledge in the mind of the defendant will in most cases present little difficulty. The fact that the risk of some damage would have been obvious to anyone in his right mind in the position of the defendant is not conclusive proof of the defendant's knowledge, but it may well be and in many cases doubtless will be a matter which will drive the jury to the conclusion that the defendant himself must have appreciated the risk.'

The appeal was accordingly allowed. But the court recognised that what it called the subjective definition of recklessness produced difficulties. One of these was where a person by self-induced intoxication deprived himself of the ability to foresee the risks involved in his actions. The court suggested that a distinction was to be drawn between crimes requiring proof of specific intent and those, such as offences under section 1(1) of the 1971 Act, involving no specific intent:

'Accordingly it is no defence under the Act of 1971 for a person to say that he was deprived by self-induced intoxication of the ability to foresee or appreciate an obvious risk' (page 704).

[16] In the 1979 (40th) edition of Archbold *Pleading, Evidence and Practice in Criminal Cases*, on which jury directions were no doubt routinely based at the time, the better view was said (page 958, paragraph 1443c) to be

'that whereas "intent" requires a desire for consequences or foresight or probable consequences, "reckless" only requires foresight of possible consequences coupled with an unreasonable willingness to risk them.'

R. v Caldwell
R. v Caldwell [1982] AC 341 was a case of self-induced intoxication. The defendant, having a grievance against the owner of the hotel where he worked, got very drunk and set fire to the hotel where guests were living at the time. He was indicted upon two counts of arson. The first and more serious count was laid under section 1(2) of the 1971 Act, the second count under section 1(1). He pleaded guilty to the second count but contested the first on the ground that he had been so drunk at the time that the thought there might be people in the hotel had never crossed his mind. His conviction on count 1 was set aside by the Court of Appeal which certified the following question:

'Whether evidence of self-induced intoxication can be relevant to the following questions—(a) Whether the defendant intended to endanger the life of another; and (b) Whether the defendant was reckless as to whether the life of another would be endangered, within the meaning of section 1(2)(b) of the Criminal Damage Act 1971.'

In submitting that the two questions should be answered (a) Yes and (b) No, counsel for the Crown did not challenge the correctness of *R. v Briggs (Note)* [1977] 1 WLR 605 or *R. v Stephenson* [1979] QB 695.

[18] In a leading opinion with which Lord Keith of Kinkel and Lord Roskill agreed, but from which Lord Wilberforce and Lord Edmund-Davies dissented, Lord Diplock discounted Professor Kenny's statement of the law approved in *R. v Cunningham* [1957] 2 QB 396 as directed to the meaning of 'maliciously' in the 1861 Act and having no bearing on the meaning of 'reckless' in the 1971 Act: page 351. It was, he held, no less blameworthy for a man whose mind was affected by rage or excitement or drink to fail to give his mind to the risk of damaging property than for a man whose mind was so affected to appreciate that there was a risk of damage to property but not to appreciate the seriousness of the risk or to trust that good luck would prevent the risk occurring: page 352. He observed:

'My Lords, I can see no reason why Parliament when it decided to revise the law as to offences of damage to property should go out of its way to perpetuate fine and impracticable distinctions such as these, between one mental state and another. One would think that the sooner they were got rid of, the better.'

Reference was made to *R. v Briggs (Note)* [1977] 1 WLR 605, *R. v Parker (Daryl)* [1977] 1 WLR 600 and *R. v Stephenson* [1979] QB 695, but Lord Diplock saw no warrant for assuming that the Act of 1971, whose declared purpose was to revise the law of damage to property, intended 'reckless' to be interpreted as 'maliciously' had been: page 353. He preferred the ordinary meaning of 'reckless' which (pages 353–354):

'surely includes not only deciding to ignore a risk of harmful consequences resulting from one's acts that one has recognised as existing, but also failing to give any thought to whether or not there is any such risk in circumstances where, if any thought were given to the matter, it would be obvious that there was.

    If one is attaching labels, the latter state of mind is neither more nor less "subjective" than the first. But the label solves nothing. It is a statement of the obvious; mens rea is, by definition, a state of mind of the accused himself at the time he did the physical act that constitutes the actus reus of the offence; it cannot be the mental state of some non-existent hypothetical person.'

To decide whether a person had been reckless whether harmful consequences of a particular kind would result from his act it was necessary to consider the mind of 'the ordinary prudent individual' (page 354). In a passage which has since been taken to encapsulate the law on this point, and which has founded many jury directions (including that in the present case) Lord Diplock then said (at page 354):

'In my opinion, a person charged with an offence under section 1(1) of the Criminal Damage Act 1971 is "reckless as to whether any such property would be destroyed or damaged" if (1) he does an act which in fact creates an obvious risk that property will be destroyed or damaged and (2) when he does the act he either has not given any thought to the possibility of there being any such risk or has recognised that there was some risk involved and has nonetheless gone on to do it. That would be a proper direction to the jury; cases in the Court of Appeal which held otherwise should be regarded as overruled.'

On the facts Lord Diplock concluded that the defendant's unawareness, owing to his self-induced intoxication, of the risk of endangering the lives of hotel residents was no defence if that risk would have been obvious to him had he been sober (page 355). He held that evidence of self-induced intoxication was relevant to a charge under section 1(2) based on intention but not to one based on recklessness (page 356).

[19] In his dissenting opinion Lord Edmund-Davies expressed 'respectful, but profound, disagreement' with Lord Diplock's dismissal of Professor Kenny's statement which was 'accurate not only in respect of the law as it stood in 1902 but also as it has been applied in countless cases ever since, both in the United Kingdom and in other countries where the common law prevails' (page 357). Lord Edmund-Davies drew attention to the Law Commission's preparation of the 1971 Act and its definition of recklessness in Working Paper No 31 (pages 357–358) and continued:

'It was surely with this contemporaneous definition and the much respected decision of *R. v Cunningham* [1957] 2 QB 396 in mind that the draftsman proceeded to his task of drafting the Criminal Damage Act 1971.'

He observed (page 358):

'In the absence of exculpatory factors, the defendant's state of mind is therefore all-important where reckless-ness is an element in the offence charged, and section 8 of the Criminal Justice Act 1967 has laid down that:

"A court or jury, in determining whether a person has committed an offence,? (a) shall not be bound in law to infer that he intended *or foresaw* a result of his actions by reason only of its being a natural and probable consequence of those actions; but (b) shall decide whether he did intend *or foresee* that result by reference to all the evidence, drawing such inferences from the evidence as appear proper in the circumstances.".'

Lord Edmund-Davies differed from the majority on the relevance of evidence of self-induced intoxication: in his opinion such evidence was relevant to a charge under s.1(2) whether the charge was based on intention or recklessness (page 361) . . .

[23] . . . In *Elliott v C* [1983] 1 WLR 939 the defendant was a 14-year old girl of low intelligence who had entered a shed in the early morning, poured white spirit on the floor and set it alight. The resulting fire had flared up and she had left the shed, which had been destroyed. She was charged under s.1(1) of the 1971 Act and at her trial before justices the prosecution made plain that the charge was based not on intention but on recklessness. The justices sought to apply the test laid down in *R. v Caldwell* but inferred that in his reference to 'an obvious risk' Lord Diplock had meant a risk which was obvious to the particular defendant. The justices acquitted the defend-ant because they found that the defendant had given no thought at the time to the possibility of there being a risk that the shed and contents would be destroyed, and this risk would not have been obvious to her or appreciated by her if she had thought about the matter (page 945). The prosecutor's appeal was allowed. Glidewell J, giving the first judgment, accepted the submission (pages 945–947) that:

'if the risk is one which would have been obvious to a reasonably prudent person, once it has also been proved that the particular defendant gave no thought to the possibility of there being such a risk, it is not a defence that because of limited intelligence or exhaustion she would not have appreciated the risk even if she had thought about it.'

Robert Goff LJ felt constrained by the decisions of the House in *R. v Caldwell* . . . to agree, but he expressed his unhappiness in doing so and plainly did not consider the outcome to be just. A petition for leave to appeal against this decision was dismissed by an appeal committee.

[24] The defendant in *R. v Stephen Malcolm R* (1984) 79 CrAppR 334 had thrown petrol bombs at the outside wall of the bedroom of a girl who he believed had informed on him in relation to a series of burglaries. He had admitted throwing the bombs but claimed he had done so to frighten the girl and without realising that if a bomb had gone through the window it might have killed her. He was charged with arson under s.1(2) of the 1971 Act, on the basis of recklessness. At trial, it was submitted on the defendant's behalf that when considering reckless-ness the jury could only convict him if he did an act which created a risk to life obvious to someone of his age and with such of his characteristics as would affect his appreciation of the risk (page 337). On the trial judge ruling against that submission the defendant changed his plea and the issue in the Court of Appeal (Ackner LJ, Bristow and Popplewell JJ) was whether the ruling had been correct. The court held that it had: if the House had wished to modify the *R. v Caldwell* principle to take account of, for instance, the age of the defendant, the opportunity had existed in *Elliott v C* [1983] 1 WLR 939 and it had not been taken. Although concerned at the principle it was required to apply, the court had little doubt that on the facts of the case the answer would have been the same even if the jury had been able to draw a comparison with what a boy of the defendant's age would have appreciated

[26] In *R. v Coles* [1995] 1 CrAppR 157 a 15 year old defendant convicted under s.1(2) of the 1971 Act on the basis of recklessness again challenged, unsuccessfully, the rule laid down by Lord Diplock in *R. v Caldwell* [1982] AC 341. Since recklessness was to be judged by the standard of the reasonable prudent man, it followed that expert evidence of the defendant's capacity to foresee the risks which would arise from his setting fire to hay in a barn had been rightly rejected.

[27] In the present case the Court of Appeal (Dyson LJ, Silber J and His Honour Judge Beaumont QC) reviewed the authorities but was in no doubt that the *Caldwell* test had been rightly applied: [2002] EWCA Crim 1992,

[2003] 3 All ER 206, paragraph 18. It acknowledged that the *Caldwell* test had been criticised and had not been applied in a number of Commonwealth jurisdictions and saw great force in these criticisms but held that it was not open to the Court of Appeal to depart from it.

Conclusions

[28] The task confronting the House in this appeal is, first of all, one of statutory construction: what did Parliament mean when it used the word 'reckless' in s.1(1) and (2) of the 1971 Act? . . .

[29] . . . Since a statute is always speaking, the context or application of a statutory expression may change over time, but the meaning of the expression itself cannot change. So the starting point is to ascertain what Parliament meant by 'reckless' in 1971. Section 1 as enacted followed, subject to an immaterial addition, the draft proposed by the Law Commission. It cannot be supposed that by 'reckless' Parliament meant anything different from the Law Commission. The Law Commission's meaning was made plain both in its Report (Law Com No 29) and in Working Paper No 23 which preceded it. These materials (not, it would seem, placed before the House in *R. v Caldwell*) reveal a very plain intention to replace the old-fashioned and misleading expression 'maliciously' by the more familiar expression 'reckless' but to give the latter expression the meaning which *R. v Cunningham* [1957] 2 QB 396 and Professor Kenny had given to the former. In treating this authority as irrelevant to the construction of 'reckless' the majority fell into understandable but clearly demonstrable error. No relevant change in the mens rea necessary for proof of the offence was intended, and in holding otherwise the majority misconstrued section 1 of the Act.

[30] That conclusion is by no means determinative of this appeal. For the decision in *R. v Caldwell* was made more than 20 years ago. Its essential reasoning was unanimously approved by the House in *R. v Lawrence* [1982] AC 510. Invitations to reconsider that reasoning have been rejected. The principles laid down have been applied on many occasions, by Crown Court judges and, even more frequently, by justices. In the submission of the Crown, the ruling of the House works well and causes no injustice in practice. If Parliament had wished to give effect to the intention of the Law Commission it has had many opportunities, which it has not taken, to do so. Despite its power under *Practice Statement (Judicial Precedent)* [1966] 1 WLR 1234 to depart from its earlier decisions, the House should be very slow to do so, not least in a context such as this.

[31] These are formidable arguments, deployed by Mr Perry with his habitual skill and erudition. But I am persuaded by Mr Newman QC for the appellants that they should be rejected. I reach this conclusion for four reasons, taken together.

[32] First, it is a salutary principle that conviction of serious crime should depend on proof not simply that the defendant caused (by act or omission) an injurious result to another but that his state of mind when so acting was culpable. This, after all, is the meaning of the familiar rule *actus non facit reum nisi mens sit rea*. The most obviously culpable state of mind is no doubt an intention to cause the injurious result, but knowing disregard of an appreciated and unacceptable risk of causing an injurious result or a deliberate closing of the mind to such risk would be readily accepted as culpable also. It is clearly blameworthy to take an obvious and significant risk of causing injury to another. But it is not clearly blameworthy to do something involving a risk of injury to another if (for reasons other than self-induced intoxication: *R. v Majewski* [1977] AC 443) one genuinely does not perceive the risk. Such a person may fairly be accused of stupidity or lack of imagination, but neither of those failings should expose him to conviction of serious crime or the risk of punishment.

[33] Secondly, the present case shows, more clearly than any other reported case since *R. v Caldwell*, that the model direction formulated by Lord Diplock (see paragraph 18 above) is capable of leading to obvious unfairness. As the excerpts quoted in paragraphs 6–7 reveal, the trial judge regretted the direction he (quite rightly) felt compelled to give, and it is evident that this direction offended the jury's sense of fairness. The sense of fairness of 12 representative citizens sitting as a jury (or of a smaller group of lay justices sitting as a bench of magistrates) is the bedrock on which the administration of criminal justice in this country is built. A law which runs counter to that sense must cause concern. Here, the appellants could have been charged under s.1(1) with recklessly damaging one or both of the wheelie-bins, and they would have had little defence. As it was, jury might have inferred that boys of the appellants' age would have appreciated the risk to the building of what they did, but it seems clear that such was not their conclusion (nor, it would appear, the judge's either). On that basis the jury thought it unfair to convict them. I share their sense of unease. It is neither moral nor just to convict a defendant (least of all a child) on the strength of what someone else would have apprehended if the defendant himself had no such apprehension. Nor, the defendant having been convicted, is the problem cured by imposition of a nominal penalty.

[34] Thirdly, I do not think the criticism of *R. v Caldwell* expressed by academics, judges and practitioners should be ignored. A decision is not, of course, to be overruled or departed from simply because it meets with

disfavour in the learned journals. But a decision which attracts reasoned and outspoken criticism by the leading scholars of the day, respected as authorities in the field, must command attention. One need only cite (among many other examples) the observations of Professor John Smith ([1981] CrimLR 392, 393–396) and Professor Glanville Williams ('Recklessness Redefined' (1981) 40 CLJ 252). This criticism carries greater weight when voiced also by judges as authoritative as Lord Edmund-Davies and Lord Wilberforce in *R. v Caldwell* itself, Robert Goff LJ in *Elliott v C* [1983] 1 WLR 939 and Ackner LJ in *R. v Stephen Malcolm R* (1984) 79 CrAppR 334. The reservations expressed by the trial judge in the present case are widely shared. The shopfloor response to *R. v Caldwell* may be gauged from the editors' commentary, to be found in the 41st edition of *Archbold* (1982): paragraph 17–25, pages 1009–1010. The editors suggested that remedial legislation was urgently required.

[35] Fourthly, the majority's interpretation of 'reckless' in section 1 of the 1971 Act was, as already shown, a misinterpretation. If it were a misinterpretation that offended no principle and gave rise to no injustice there would be strong grounds for adhering to the misinterpretation and leaving Parliament to correct it if it chose. But this misinterpretation is offensive to principle and is apt to cause injustice. That being so, the need to correct the misinterpretation is compelling.

[36] It is perhaps unfortunate that the question at issue in this appeal fell to be answered in a case of self-induced intoxication. For one instinctively recoils from the notion that a defendant can escape the criminal consequences of his injurious conduct by drinking himself into a state where he is blind to the risk he is causing to others. In *R. v Caldwell* it seems to have been assumed that the risk would have been obvious to the defendant had he been sober. Further, the context did not require the House to give close consideration to the liability of those (such as the very young and the mentally handicapped) who were not normal reasonable adults. The overruling by the majority of *R. v Stephenson* [1979] QB 695 does however make it questionable whether such consideration would have led to a different result.

[37] In the course of argument before the House it was suggested that the rule in *R. v Caldwell* might be modified, in cases involving children, by requiring comparison not with normal reasonable adults but with normal reasonable children of the same age. This is a suggestion with some attractions but it is open to four compelling objections. First, even this modification would offend the principle that conviction should depend on proving the state of mind of the individual defendant to be culpable. Second, if the rule were modified in relation to children on grounds of their immaturity it would be anomalous if it were not also modified in relation to the mentally handicapped on grounds of their limited understanding. Third, any modification along these lines would open the door to difficult and contentious argument concerning the qualities and characteristics to be taken into account for purposes of the comparison. Fourth, to adopt this modification would be to substitute one misinterpretation of section 1 for another. There is no warrant in the Act or in the *travaux préparatoires* which preceded it for such an interpretation.

[38] A further refinement, advanced by Professor Glanville Williams in his article 'Recklessness Redefined' (1981) 40 CLJ 252, 270–271, adopted by the justices in *Elliott v C* [1983] 1 WLR 939 and commented upon by Robert Goff LJ in that case is that a defendant should only be regarded as having acted recklessly by virtue of his failure to give any thought to an obvious risk that property would be destroyed or damaged, where such risk would have been obvious to him if he had given any thought to the matter. This refinement also has attractions, although it does not meet the objection of principle and does not represent a correct interpretation of the section. It is, in my opinion, open to the further objection of over-complicating the task of the jury (or bench of justices). It is one thing to decide whether a defendant can be believed when he says that the thought of a given risk never crossed his mind. It is another, and much more speculative, task to decide whether the risk would have been obvious to him if the thought had crossed his mind. The simpler the jury's task, the more likely is its verdict to be reliable. Robert Goff LJ's reason for rejecting this refinement was somewhat similar (*Elliott v C*, page 950).

[39] I cannot accept that restoration of the law as understood before *R. v Caldwell* would lead to the acquittal of those whom public policy would require to be convicted. There is nothing to suggest that this was seen as a problem before *R. v Caldwell*, or before the 1971 Act. There is no reason to doubt the common sense which tribunals of fact bring to their task. In a contested case based on intention, the defendant rarely admits intending the injurious result in question, but the tribunal of fact will readily infer such an intention, in a proper case, from all the circumstances and probabilities and evidence of what the defendant did and said at the time. Similarly with recklessness: it is not to be supposed that the tribunal of fact will accept a defendant's assertion that he never thought of a certain risk when all the circumstances and probabilities and evidence of what he did and said at the time show that he did or must have done.

[40] In his printed case, Mr Newman advanced the contention that the law as declared in *R. v Caldwell* was incompatible with article 6 of the European Convention on Human Rights. While making no concession, he forebore to address legal argument on the point. I need say no more about it.

[41] For the reasons I have given I would allow this appeal and quash the appellants' convictions. I would answer the certified question obliquely, basing myself on clause 18(c) of the Criminal Code Bill annexed by the Law Commission to its Report 'A Criminal Code for England and Wales Volume 1: Report and Draft Criminal Code Bill' (Law Com No 177, April 1989):

'A person acts recklessly within the meaning of section 1 of the Criminal Damage Act 1971 with respect to—

    (i)   a circumstance when he is aware of a risk that it exists or will exist;
    (ii) a result when he is aware of a risk that it will occur;

and it is, in the circumstances known to him, unreasonable to take the risk.'

LORD STEYN

[45] In my view the very high threshold for departing from a previous decision of the House has been satisfied in this particular case. In summary I would reduce my reasons to three propositions. First, in *Caldwell* the majority should have accepted without equivocation that before the passing of the 1971 Act foresight of consequences was an essential element in recklessness in the context of damage to property under section 51 of the Malicious Damage Act 1861. Secondly, the matrix of the immediately preceding Law Commission recommendations shows convincingly that the purpose of section 1 of the 1971 Act was to replace the out of date language of 'maliciously' causing damage by more modern language while not changing the substance of the mental element in any way. Foresight of consequences was to remain an ingredient of recklessness in regard to damage to property. Thirdly, experience has shown that by bringing within the reach of s.1(1) cases of inadvertent recklessness the decision in *Caldwell* became a source of serious potential injustice which cannot possibly be justified on policy grounds . . .

Justice and policy

[52] . . . In the case before the House the two boys were 11 and 12 respectively. Their escapade of camping overnight without their parents' permission was something that many children have undertaken. But by throwing lit newspapers under a plastic wheelie bin they caused £1m of damage to a shop. It is, however, an agreed fact on this appeal that the boys thought there was no risk of the fire spreading in the way it eventually did. What happened at trial is highly significant. The jury were perplexed by the *Caldwell* directions which compelled them to treat the boys as adults and to convict them. The judge plainly thought this approach was contrary to common sense but loyally applied the law as laid down in *Caldwell*. The view of the jurors and the judge would be widely shared by reasonable people who pause to consider the matter. The only answer of the Crown is that where unjust convictions occur the judge can impose a lenient sentence. This will not do in a modern criminal justice system. Parliament certainly did not authorise such a cynical strategy . . .

[57] The surest test of a new legal rule is not whether it satisfies a team of logicians but how it performs in the real world. With the benefit of hindsight the verdict must be that the rule laid down by the majority in *Caldwell* failed this test. It was severely criticized by academic lawyers of distinction. It did not command respect among practitioners and judges. Jurors found it difficult to understand: it also sometimes offended their sense of justice. Experience suggests that in *Caldwell* the law took a wrong turn. That brings me to the question whether the subjective interpretation of recklessness might allow wrongdoers who ought to be convicted of serious crime to escape conviction. Experience before *Caldwell* did not warrant such a conclusion. In any event, as Lord Edmund-Davies explained, if a defendant closes his mind to a risk he must realise that there is a risk and, on the evidence, that will usually be decisive: 358D. One can trust the realism of trial judges, who direct juries, to guide juries to sensible verdicts and juries can in turn be relied on to apply robust common sense to the evaluation of ridiculous defences. Moreover, the endorsement by Parliament of the Law Commission proposals could not seriously have been regarded as a charter for the acquittal of wrongdoers . . .

[59] In my view the case for departing from *Caldwell* has been shown to be irresistible. I agree with the reasons given by Lord Bingham of Cornhill.

[Lord Browne-Wilkinson and Lord Rodger of Earlsferry agreed with Lord Bingham. Lord Hutton delivered an opinion agreeing with Lord Bingham and Lord Steyn].

Note

In the absence of an express statutory provision to the contrary, it is difficult to imagine how the objective approach of *Caldwell* could be revived. In *Attorney General's Reference (No.3 of 2003)* [2004] EWCA Crim 868, the Court of Appeal applied the subjective test of recklessness to the common law offence of misfeasance in public office indicating that the courts will now demand a subjective approach generally to all criminal offences.

----

v. Wilfulness

ARROWSMITH V JENKINS

[1963] 2 Q.B. 561

The defendant addressed a public meeting on the highway and was convicted on an information alleging wilful obstruction of the highway, by standing on it and causing others to congregate.

LORD PARKER CJ

The sole question here is whether the defendant has contravened s.121(1) of the Highways Act 1959. That section provides: 'If a person, without lawful authority or excuse, in any way wilfully obstructs the free passage along a highway he shall be guilty of an offence and shall be liable in respect thereof to a fine not exceeding forty shillings.'

I am quite satisfied that section 121(1) of the Act of 1959, on its true construction, is providing that if a person, without lawful authority or excuse, intentionally as opposed to accidentally, that is, by an exercise of his or her free will, does something or omits to do something which will cause an obstruction or the continuance of an obstruction, he or she is guilty of an offence. Mr Wigoder, for the defendant, has sought to argue that if a person—and I think that this is how he puts it—acts in the genuine belief that he or she has lawful authority to do what he or she is doing then, if an obstruction results, he or she cannot be said to have wilfully obstructed the free passage along a highway.

Quite frankly, I do not fully understand that submission. It is difficult, certainly, to apply in the present case. I imagine that it can be put in this way: that there must be some *mens rea* in the sense that a person will only be guilty if he knowingly does a wrongful act. I am quite satisfied that that consideration cannot possibly be imported into the words 'wilfully obstructs' in section 121(1) of the Act of 1959. If anybody, by an exercise of free will, does something which causes an obstruction, then an offence is committed. There is no doubt that the defendant did that in the present case.

Appeal dismissed

Notes

Cf. *Eaton v Cobb* [1950] 1 All E.R. 1016.

LEWIS V COX

[1985] Q.B. 509

The defendant's friend was arrested for being drunk and disorderly and placed in the back of a police vehicle. The defendant opened the rear door of the vehicle to ask his friend where he was being taken but a police constable closed the door warning him that he would be arrested for obstruction if he opened it again. When the constable returned to the driver's seat of the vehicle the defendant opened the door once more, whereupon the constable arrested him for obstructing him. The defendant was charged with wilfully obstructing a police constable in the execution of his duty, contrary to s.51(3) of the Police Act 1964. The justices acquitted the defendant and the prosecution appealed.

WEBSTER J

. . . The justices found as a fact that the opening of the rear door of the van by the defendant was not aimed at the police, and that he did not intend to obstruct the police.

It was accepted by counsel on behalf of the defendant that the arrest of Marsh was lawful, and that the defendant's conduct in opening the door on the second occasion in fact obstructed the police because it prevented the prosecutor from driving the police vehicle away, which he would have done had the defendant not opened the door. The contention before the justices, which was substantially the same as the contention made on his behalf before this court, was that the defendant did not wilfully obstruct the police because his actions were not aimed at the police. The expression 'aimed at the police' is an expression taken from the judgment of Griffiths L.J. in *Hills v Ellis* [1983] Q.B. 680, 685, to which I will refer more fully later in this judgment.

The justices considered that the principle laid down by the decision in that case was that a person is guilty of wilful obstruction of a police constable in the execution of his duty if he deliberately does some act which is aimed at the police and if that act, viewed objectively, obstructs the police. They concluded that on the evidence before them the defendant had done no deliberate aggressive act which was aimed at the police, but that his sole aim was to ask Marsh where he was to be taken and that, as the actions of the defendant were not aimed at the police, the justices were of the opinion that they could not convict him of the offence, and they accordingly dismissed the charge against him.

The question which they ask for the opinion of this court is whether the principles applied by them were those laid down in *Hills v Ellis*; they also ask whether, given the evidence in the case, the decision to dismiss the charge was perverse and unreasonable. For the moment I will consider only the first of those two questions.

For my part, I approach this question, in the first place, by disregarding any decision as to the meaning of the words 'wilful' or 'wilfully' in any context other than that of the section in question. This is because whereas, for instance, this court has held in *Arrowsmith v Jenkins* [above] that the wilful obstruction of a highway, contrary to section 121 of the Highways Act 1959, does not import *mens rea* in the sense that a person will only be guilty of that offence if he knowingly did a wrongful act, there is a line of authority, to which I will turn, that the word 'wilfully' in the context of section 51(3) of the Police Act 1964 connotes an element of *mens rea*. I find it necessary to consider this line of authority, although not every case in it, in some detail because it cannot, in my view, confidently be asserted that the test, whether the actions of the defendant are 'aimed at the police,' is the definitive and authoritative test.

It can, however, in my view be confidently stated, as I have already mentioned, that the word 'wilfully' imports an element of *mens rea*. In *Betts v Stevens* [1910] 1 K.B. 1 . . . Darling J., dealing with the question of intention, said, at p.8: 'The gist of the offence to my mind lies in the intention with which the thing is done.'

In *Willmott v Atack* [1977] Q.B. 498 . . . Croom-Johnson J., who gave the first judgment, said, at pp.504–505.

'When one looks at the whole context of s.51, dealing as it does with assaults upon constables in subsection (1) and concluding in subsection (3) with resistance and wilful obstruction in the execution of the duty, I am of the view that the interpretation of this subsection for which the defendant contends is the right one. It fits the words "wilfully obstructs" in the context of the subsection, and in my view there must be something in the nature of a criminal intent of the kind which means that it is done with the idea of some form of hostility to the police with the intention of seeing that what is done is to obstruct, and that it is not enough merely to show that he intended to do what he did and that it did in fact have the result of the police being obstructed.'

May J. agreed . . .
Lord Widgery C.J . . .. [also] agreed . . .
In *Moore v Green* [1983] 1 All E.R. 663, . . . McCullough J. said at p.665:

'I do not understand the reference to 'hostility' to indicate a separate element of the offence. I understand the word to bear the same meaning as the phrase which Croom-Johnson J. used immediately afterwards, namely "the intention of seeing that what is done is to obstruct" . . .'

Griffiths L.J. agreed with the judgment of McCullough J.

Finally, on this aspect of the matter, I return to *Hills v Ellis* . . .

Griffiths L.J. cited the same passage from the judgment of Croom-Johnson J. in *Willmott v Atack* and continued, at p.685:

'The defendant's counsel argues from that passage that as the motive here was merely to correct an officer's error, it cannot be said that he, the defendant, was acting with any hostility towards the police. But in my view, the phrase 'hostility to the police' in that passage means no more than that the actions of the defendant are aimed at the police. There can be no doubt here that his action in grabbing the officer's arm was aimed at that officer. It was an attempt to get that officer to desist from the arrest that he was making. In my view, this is as clear a case as we can have of obstructing a police officer in the course of his duty, and the justices came to the right decision.'

McCullough J. agreed with the judgment of Griffiths L.J., and added, at p.686:

'I am uncertain what Croom-Johnson J. had in mind when he used the word "hostility" . . . Hostility suggests emotion and motive, but motive and emotion are alike irrelevant in criminal law. What matters is intention, that is, what state of affairs the defendant intended to bring about. What motive he had while so intending is irrelevant. What is meant by "an intention to obstruct?" I would construe "wilfully obstructs" as doing deliberate actions with the intention of bringing about a state of affairs which, objectively regarded, amount to an obstruction as that phrase was explained by Lord Parker C.J. in *Rice v Connolly* [1966] 2 Q.B. 414, 419B, that is, making it more difficult for the police to carry out their duty. The fact that the defendant might not himself have called that state of affairs an obstruction is, to my mind, immaterial. That is not to say that it is enough to do deliberate actions which, in fact, obstruct; there must be an intention that those actions should result in the further state of affairs to which I have been referring.'

Lord Parker C.J. on the same page of his judgment in *Rice v Connolly* said that 'wilful' in the context of this section 'not only in my judgment means "intentional" but something which is done without lawful excuse;' and his explanation of 'wilfully obstructs' as being something which makes it more difficult for the police to carry out their duties was taken by him from the judgment of Lord Goddard C.J. in *Hinchliffe v Sheldon* [1955] 1 W.L.R. 1207, where Lord Goddard C.J. said, at p.1210; 'Obstructing, for the present purpose, means making it more difficult for the police to carry out their duties.'

For my part I conclude that, although it may not be unhelpful in certain cases to consider whether the actions of a defendant were aimed at the police, the simple facts which the court has to find are whether the defendant's conduct in fact prevented the police from carrying out their duty, or made it more difficult for them to do so, and whether the defendant intended that conduct to prevent the police from carrying out their duty or to make it more difficult to do so.

In the present case the test which the justices applied was whether the defendant had deliberately done some act which was aimed at the police, they found that his actions were not aimed at the police and they accordingly dismissed the charge. In my view, for the reasons which I have given, the justices did not ask themselves the right question for the purposes of the present case, or the whole of the right question.

I turn, therefore, to the second question which they ask, which is whether, given the evidence in the case, the decision to dismiss the charge was perverse and unreasonable . . .

For my part I conclude . . . that if the justices had directed themselves properly in the way in which I have set out they must, on the evidence, have decided that the defendant, when he opened the door on the second occasion, intended to make it more difficult for the police to carry out their duties, even though that was not his predominate intention, and they ought, therefore, to have convicted him of the charge against him.

My answer to the second part of the question, therefore, is that given the evidence in the case, the justices' decision to dismiss the charge was perverse and unreasonable, and I would accordingly allow this appeal and remit the case to the justices with a direction to them to convict.

KERR LJ

I agree with Webster J.'s analysis of the authorities. The *actus reus* is the doing of an act which has the effect of making it impossible or more difficult for the police to carry out their duty. The word 'wilfully' clearly imports an additional requirement of *mens rea*. The act must not only have been done deliberately, but with the knowledge and intention that it will have this obstructive effect. But in the absence of a lawful excuse, the defendant's purpose or reason for doing the act is irrelevant, whether this be directly hostile to, or 'aimed at', the police, or whether he has some other purpose or reason.

Appeal allowed
Case remitted with direction to convict

Questions

1.   Is the word "wilfully" in s.121(1) of the Highways Act 1959 (now s.137(1) of the Highways Act 1980) redundant? cf. *Lewis v Dickson* [1976] Crim.L.R 442.

2.   How does the interpretation of "wilfully" in *Arrowsmith v Jenkins* differ from that in *Lewis v Cox*?

Note

The courts have also struggled in their search for an appropriate interpretation of "wilful" in the context of "wilful neglect" under the Children and Young Persons Act 1933.

R. V SHEPPARD

[1980] 3 All E.R. 899 HL

The youngest child of Mr and Mrs S died at the age of 16 months from malnutrition and hypothermia. Three appointments to see a paediatrician had been made by the Health Visitor but the appellants had failed to attend. They were convicted of causing cruelty by wilful neglect under s.1 of the Children and Young Persons Act 1933. The Court of Appeal felt bound by authority to uphold the direction of the trial judge that no element of foresight of harm was necessary for the offence, but granted leave to appeal to the House of Lords.

LORD DIPLOCK

. . . In the light of the trial judge's instructions given to the jury as to the law applicable to the offence charged, it can safely be inferred from the verdicts of guilty that the jury found (1) that injury to Martin's health had in fact been caused by the failure of each of the parents to have him examined by a doctor in the period prior to his death and (2) that any reasonable parents, i.e. parents endowed with ordinary intelligence and not indifferent to the welfare of their child, would have recognised from the manifest symptoms of serious illness in Martin during that period that a failure to have him examined by a doctor might well result in unnecessary suffering or injury to his health . . .

Their real defence, if it were capable of amounting to a defence in law was that they did not realise that the child was ill enough to need a doctor; they had observed his loss of appetite and failure to keep down his food, but had genuinely thought that this was due to some passing minor upset to which babies are prone, from which they recover naturally without medical aid and which medical treatment can do nothing to alleviate or to hasten recovery.

We do not know whether the jury would have thought that this explanation of the parents' failure to have Martin examined by a doctor might be true. In his instructions the judge had told the jury that to constitute the statutory offence with which the parents were charged it was unnecessary for the Crown to prove that at the time when it was alleged the parents should have had the child seen by a doctor either they in fact knew that their failure to do so involved a risk of causing him unnecessary suffering or injury to health or they did not care whether this was so or not . . .

The Court of Appeal, regarding themselves as bound by the same line of authority, felt compelled to dismiss the parents' appeal . . . but certified as the point of law of general public importance involved in their decision to dismiss the appeal:

'What is the proper direction to be given to a jury on a charge of wilful neglect of a child under s.1 of the Children and Young Persons Act 1933 as to what constitutes the necessary mens rea of the offence?'

The relevant provisions of section 1 are in the following terms:

'(1) If any person who has attained the age of sixteen years and has the custody, charge, or care of any child or young person under that age, wilfully assaults, ill-treats, neglects, abandons, or exposes him, or causes or procures him to be assaulted, ill-treated, neglected, abandoned, or exposed, in a manner likely to cause him unnecessary suffering or injury to health (including injury to or loss of sight, or hearing, or limb, or organ of the body, and any mental derangement), that person shall be guilty of a misdemeanour, and shall be liable—(a) on conviction on indictment, to a fine, or alternatively, or in addition thereto, to imprisonment for any term not exceeding two years . . .
  (2) For the purposes of this section—(a) a parent or other person legally liable to maintain a child or young person shall be deemed to have neglected him in a manner likely to cause injury to his health if he has failed to provide adequate food, clothing, medical aid or lodging for him, or if, having been unable otherwise to provide such food, clothing, medical aid or lodging, he has failed to take steps to procure it to be provided under enactments applicable in that behalf . . .'

. . . My Lords, the language in which the relevant provisions of the 1933 Act are drafted consists of ordinary words in common use in the English language. If I were to approach the question of their construction untrammelled (as the House is) by authority I should have little hesitation in saying that where the charge is one of wilfully neglecting to provide a child with adequate medical aid, which in appropriate cases will include precautionary medical examination, the prosecution must prove (1) that the child did in fact need medical aid at the time at which the parent is charged with having failed to provide it and (2) either that the parent was aware at that time that the child's health might be at risk if it were not provided with medical aid or that the parent's unawareness of this fact was due to his not caring whether the child's health were at risk or not.
In view of the previous authorities, however, which reach a different conclusion, it becomes necessary to analyse more closely the wording and structure of sections 1(1) and (2)(a) . . .
The presence of the adverb 'wilfully' qualifying all five verbs, 'assaults, ill-treats, neglects, abandons, or exposes', makes it clear that any offence under section 1 requires *mens rea*, a state of mind on the part of the offender directed to the particular act or failure to act that constitutes the *actus reus* and warrants the description 'wilful'. The other four adverbs refer to positive acts, 'neglect' refers to failure to act, and the judicial explanation of the state of mind denoted by the statutory expression 'wilfully' in relation to the doing of a positive act is not necessarily wholly apt in relation to a failure to act at all. The instant case is in the latter category, so I will confine myself to considering what is meant by wilfully neglecting a child in a manner likely to cause him unnecessary suffering or injury to health . . .
The *actus reus* of the offence with which the accused were charged in the instant case does not involve construing the verb 'neglect' for the offence fell within the deeming provision; and the only question as respects the *actus reus* was: did the parents fail to provide for Martin in the period before his death medical aid that was in fact adequate in view of his actual state of health at the relevant time? This, as it seems to me, is a pure question of objective fact to be determined in the light of what has become known *by the date of the trial* to have been the child's actual state of health at the relevant time. It does not depend on whether a reasonably careful parent, with knowledge of those facts only which such a parent might reasonably be expected to observe for himself, would have thought it prudent to have recourse to medical aid . . . If failure to use the hypothetical powers of observation, ratiocination and foresight of consequences [of the reasonable man] is to constitute an ingredient of a criminal offence it must surely form part not of the *actus reus* but of the *mens rea*.
It does not, however, seem to me that the concept of the reasonable parent . . . has any part to play in the *mens rea* of an offence in which the description of the *mens rea* is contained in the single adverb 'wilfully'. In the context of doing a child a positive act (assault, ill-treat, abandon or expose) that is likely to have specified consequences (to cause him unnecessary suffering or injury to health), 'wilfully', which must describe the state of mind of the actual doer of the act, may be capable of bearing the narrow meaning that the wilfulness required extends only to the doing of the physical act itself which in fact results in the consequences

described, even though the doer thought that it would not and would not have acted as he did had he foreseen a risk that those consequences might follow. Although this is a possible meaning of 'wilfully', it is not the natural meaning even in relation to positive acts defined by reference to the consequences to which they are likely to give rise; and, in the context of the section, if this is all the adverb 'wilfully' meant it would be otiose. Section 1(1) would have the same effect if it were omitted; for even in absolute offences (unless vicarious liability is involved) the physical act relied on as constituting the offence must be wilful in the limited sense, for which the synonym in the field of criminal liability that has now become the common term of legal art is 'voluntary.'

So much for 'wilfully' in the context of a positive act. To 'neglect' a child is to omit to act, to fail to provide adequately for . . . its physical needs . . . For reasons already given the use of the verb 'neglect' cannot, in my view, of itself import into the criminal law the civil law concept of negligence. The *actus reus* in a case of wilful neglect is simply a failure, for whatever reason, to provide the child whenever it in fact needs medical aid with the medical aid it needs. Such a failure as it seems to me could not be properly described as 'wilful' unless the parent *either* (1) had directed his mind to the question whether there was some risk (though it might fall far short of a probability) that the child's health might suffer unless he were examined by a doctor and provided with such curative treatment as the examination might reveal as necessary, and had made a conscious decision, for whatever reason, to refrain from arranging for such medical examination, *or* (2) had so refrained because he did not care whether the child might be in need of medical treatment or not.

As regards the second state of mind, this imports the concept of recklessness which is a common concept in *mens rea* in criminal law. It is not to be confused with negligence in the civil law of tort (see *Andrews v Director of Public Prosecutions* [1937] A.C. 576 at 582–583). In speaking of the first state of mind I have referred to the parent's knowledge of the existence of some risk of injury to health rather than of probability. The section speaks of an act or omission that is 'likely' to cause unnecessary suffering or injury to health. The word is imprecise. It is capable of covering a whole range of possibilities from 'it's on the cards' to 'it's more probable than not'; but, having regard to the parent's lack of skill in diagnosis and to the very serious consequences which may result from failure to provide a child with timely medical attention, it should in my view be understood as excluding only what would fail to be described as highly unlikely . . .

To give to s.1(1) of the 1933 Act the meaning which I suggest it bears would not encourage parents to neglect their children nor would it reduce the deterrent to child neglect provided by the section. It would afford no defence to parents who do not bother to observe their children's health or, having done so, do not care whether their children are receiving the medical examination and treatment that they need or not; it would involve the acquittal of those parents only who through ignorance or lack of intelligence are genuinely unaware that their child's health may be at risk if it is not examined by a doctor to see if it needs medical treatment. And, in view of the abhorrence which magistrates and juries feel for cruelty to helpless children, I have every confidence that they would not readily be hoodwinked by false claims by parents that it did not occur to them that an evidently sick child might need medical care.

In the instant case it seems likely that on the evidence the jury, if given the direction which I have suggested as correct, would have convicted one or both of the accused; but I do not think it possible to say with certainty that they would. It follows that in my opinion these appeals must be allowed and that the certified question should be answered: 'The proper direction to be given to a jury on a charge of wilful neglect of a child under s.1 of the Children and Young; Persons Act 1933 by failing to provide adequate medical aid is that the jury must be satisfied (1) that the child did in fact need medical aid at the time at which the parent is charged with failing to provide it (the *actus reus*) and (2) either that the parent was aware at that time that the child's health might be at risk if it was not provided with medical aid or that the parent's unawareness of this fact was due to his not caring whether his child's health was at risk or not (the *mens rea*).'

[Lord Keith and Lord Edmund—Davies delivered opinions in which they agreed with Lord Diplock; Lord Scarman and Lord Fraser delivered dissenting opinions].

Questions

1.   Do you agree with Lord Diplock that, if the word "wilfully" were given a narrow meaning extending only to the doing of the positive act, and not its consequences, it would be otiose in s.1(1)? Is a parent who admonishes a child with a slap committing a voluntary act? Is it therefore a "wilful" assault? Or is it not an assault at all because it is "lawful"?

2. If the parent in question 1 is not committing an assault because parents are allowed to use reasonable disciplinary measures, is Lord Diplock right to assert it is only in the "mens rea" of an offence that the reasonable man concept will be found?

3. Both Lord Fraser and Lord Scarman believed that the deterrent effect of the offence would be reduced if the prosecution had to prove foresight of the consequences of neglect. Can this hypothesis be tested?

4. In *Sheppard* (above), Lord Diplock stated: "Such a failure . . . could not be properly described as 'wilful' unless the parent either (1) had directed his mind to the question whether there was some risk . . . or (2) had so refrained *because he did not care* . . .". Could this be interpreted as *Caldwell* type recklessness?

    (See *Attorney General's Reference (No.3 of 2003)* [2004] EWCA Crim 868, where the Court of Appeal concluded that the test should be interpreted subjectively not objectively).

----

vi. Proposals for Reform

In the *Draft Criminal Code Bill*, the Law Commission used the term *fault element* in preference to the common law phrase mens rea. In cl.18 it defined the *fault terms* "knowingly", and "intentionally" and "recklessly". Clause 18 provided that "a person acts—

"(a) 'knowingly' with respect to a circumstance not only when he is aware that it exists or will exist, but also when he avoids taking steps that might confirm his belief that it exists or will exist;"

Since drawing up the Draft Code the Law Commission has taken the pragmatic decision that the best chance of implementing it is through "a series of Bills, each of which will be complete in itself and will contain proposals for the immediate reform and rationalisation of a major, discrete area of the criminal law" (*Legislating the Criminal Code: Offences Against the Person and General Principles*, para.1.3). Following some criticisms of its definition of intention in the Draft Criminal Code Bill the Law Commission has revised the definition of intention in the Bill appended to Law Com. No.218. It has also included some minor revisions of the definition of "recklessly".

LAW COMMISSION, *DRAFT CRIMINAL LAW BILL* (TSO, 1993), LAW COM. NO.218

Definition of fault terms
   1.—For the purposes of this Part a person acts—

   (b) 'recklessly' with respect to—

      (i)   a circumstance, when he is aware of a risk that it exists or will exist, and
      (ii) a result, when he is aware of a risk that it will occur,

      and it is unreasonable, having regard to the circumstances known to him, to take that risk;

and related expressions shall be construed accordingly.

3. MISTAKE

Notes

An area of the law that has been in an unsatisfactory state for some time is that of mistake. What effect does a mistake have on the liability of a defendant where his mistake relates to an element of the actus reus of the offence with which he is charged?

There are many mistakes which a defendant may make, some of which may be relevant to his ultimate liability. A mistake may be such as to negate the mens rea of the defendant in respect of a circumstance of the offence (i.e. an actus reus element). However, if mens rea is not required in respect of a particular circumstance, a mistake thereto may be of no relevance. A mistake may also be made with regard to circumstances which justify or excuse the commission of an offence such as pleas of self-defence or duress.

A question which has taxed judicial minds over the last century is whether a mistake must be a reasonable one before it serves to relieve a defendant of liability. Unfortunately the judicial answers to this question have differed, lacking consistency and coherent exposition of principle.

There are two basic categories into which mistakes may be grouped: *relevant* mistakes and *irrelevant* mistakes. Most uncertainty and inconsistency has arisen in respect of the first category.

----

i. Relevant Mistakes

A mistake is *relevant* where it relates to either a definitional element of the offence (i.e. an actus reus element) or a possible justificatory or excusatory claim (more generally referred to as defences). At one time, if a mistake was to operate to negate liability, it had to be a reasonable one. The House of Lords in *DPP v Morgan* (below) opened the way for mistakes which were simply honest, although unreasonable, to operate to negate liability in certain circumstances. The effect of this decision, and the offspring it has generated, is that the category of relevant mistakes must now be divided into two sub-categories: mistakes which relate to definitional matters and those which relate to non-definitional matters.

(1) Mistake as to a definitional element of the offence

(a) Mistake negating mens rea

Where an offence requires intention or recklessness on the part of the defendant, may he be convicted if he makes a mistake as to one of the required circumstances of the offence, i.e. the definitional facts? In other words, does the mens rea requirement apply only to the doing of the act or does it also apply to the surrounding circumstances? Several cases established that where the word "wilfully" was used to define the mens rea requirement, a mistake as to the surrounding circumstances would act to negate the defendant's mens rea (see *Eaton v Cobb* [1950] 1 All E.R. 1016; *Wilson v Inyang* [1951] 2 K.B. 799; *Bullock v Turnbull* [1952] 2 Lloyd's Rep. 303; *Willmott v Atack* [1977] Q.B. 498; *Ostler v Elliott* [1980] Crim. L.R. 584; but cf. *Cotterill v Penn* [1936] 1 K.B. 53).

Would the same result ensue where a statute required intention or recklessness?

James LJ, giving judgment in *R. v Smith (David)* [1974] Q.B. 354, said of s.1(1) of the Criminal Damage Act 1971:

"Construing the language of [the] section we have no doubt that the *actus reus* is 'destroying or damaging any property belonging to another.' It is not possible to exclude the words 'belonging to another' which describe the 'property.' Applying the ordinary principles of *mens rea*, the intention and recklessness and the absence of lawful excuse required to constitute the offence have reference to property belonging to another. It follows that, in our judgment, no offence is committed under this section if a person destroys or causes damage to property belonging to another if he does so in the honest though mistaken belief that the property is his own, and provided that the belief is honestly held it is irrelevant to consider whether or not it is a justifiable belief."

Shortly after the decision in *Smith* the House of Lords was faced with the issue of which parts of the definition of an offence (all or some) are qualified by the requirement of a mental element, and whether a mistake as to such part must be *reasonable* if it is to affect the defendant's liability.

DPP V MORGAN

[1976] A.C. 182 HL

The appellant invited three friends to have intercourse with his wife telling them that her signs of resistance were not to be interpreted as lack of consent: she enjoyed it better that way. In fact she was not consenting and offered considerable resistance to her assailants who in turn used a considerable degree of force to overcome her resistance. The friends were charged with rape, the appellant with aiding and abetting. They appealed against the direction of the trial judge that their belief in her consent must be reasonable. The Court of Appeal dismissed their appeals but gave leave to appeal to the House of Lords certifying the following question: "Whether in rape a defendant can properly be convicted notwithstanding that he in fact believed the woman consented, if such belief was not based on reasonable grounds."

LORD HAILSHAM OF ST MARYLEBONE

. . . If it be true, as the learned judge says [in his summing up to the jury] 'in the first place,' that the prosecution have to prove that

'each defendant intended to have sexual intercourse without her consent, not merely that he intended to have intercourse with her but that he intended to have intercourse without her consent',

the defendant must be entitled to an acquittal if the prosecution fail to prove just that. The necessary mental ingredient will be lacking and the only possible verdict is 'not guilty'. If, on the other hand, as is asserted in the passage beginning 'secondly', it is necessary for any belief in the woman's consent to be 'a reasonable belief' before the defendant is entitled to an acquittal, it must either be because the mental ingredient in rape is not 'to have intercourse and to have it without her consent' but simply 'to have intercourse' subject to a special defence of 'honest and reasonable belief', or alternatively to have intercourse without a reasonable belief in her consent. Counsel for the Crown argued for each of these alternatives, but in my view each is open to insuperable objections of principle. No doubt it would be possible, by statute, to devise a law by which intercourse, voluntarily entered into, was an absolute offence, subject to a 'defence' or belief whether honest or honest and reasonable, of which the 'evidential' burden is primarily on the defence and the 'probative' burden on the prosecution. But in my opinion such is not the crime of rape as it has hitherto been understood. The prohibited act in rape is to have intercourse without the victim's consent. The minimum *mens rea* or guilty mind in most common law offences, including rape, is the intention to do the prohibited act, and that is correctly stated in the proposition stated 'in the first place' of the judge's direction . . .

The only qualification I would make to the direction of the learned judge's 'in the first place' is the refinement for which . . . there is both Australian and English authority, that if the intention of the accused is to have intercourse *nolens volens*, that is recklessly and not caring whether the victim be a consenting party or not, that is equivalent on ordinary principles to an intent to do the prohibited act without the consent of the victim.

The alternative version of the learned judge's direction would read that the accused must do the prohibited act with the intention of doing it without an honest and reasonable belief in the victim's consent. This in effect is the version which took up most of the time in argument, and although I find the Court of Appeal's judgment difficult to understand, I think it the version which ultimately commended itself to that court. At all events I think it the more plausible way in which to state the learned judge's 'secondly'. In principle, however, I find it unacceptable. I believe that '*mens rea*' means 'guilty or criminal mind', and if it be the case, as seems to be accepted here, that mental element in rape is not knowledge but intent, to insist that a belief must be reasonable to excuse is to insist that either the accused is to be found guilty of intending to do that which in truth he did not intend to do, or that his state of mind, though innocent of evil intent, can convict him if it be honest but not rational . . .

I believe the law on this point to have been correctly stated by Lord Goddard C.J. in *R. v Steane* [1947] K.B. 997, 1004, [above] when he said:

'. . . if on the totality of the evidence there is room for more than one view as to the intent of the prisoner, the jury should be directed that it is for the prosecution to prove the intent to the jury's satisfaction, and if, on a review of the whole evidence, they either think that the intent did not exist or they are left in doubt as to the intent, the prisoner is entitled to be acquitted.'

That was indeed, a case which involved a count where a specific, or, as Professor Smith has called it, an ulterior, intent was, and was required to be, charged in the indictment. But, once it be accepted that an intent of whatever description is an ingredient essential to the guilt of the accused I cannot myself see that any other direction can be logically acceptable. Otherwise a jury would in effect be told to find an intent where none existed or where none was proved to have existed. I cannot myself reconcile it with my conscience to sanction as part of the English law what I regard as logical impossibility, and, if there were any authority which, if accepted would compel me to do so, I would feel constrained to declare that it was not to be followed. However for reasons which I will give, I do not see any need in the instant case for such desperate remedies.

The beginning of wisdom in all the '*mens rea*' cases to which our attention was called is, as pointed out by Stephen J. in *R. v Tolson* (1889) 23 Q.B.D. 168, that '*mens rea*' means a number of quite different things in relation to different crimes . . . It follows from this, surely, that it is logically impermissible, as the Crown sought to do in this case, to draw a necessary inference from decisions in relation to offences where *mens rea* means one thing, and cases where it means another, and in particular from decisions on the construction of statutes, whether these be related to bigamy, abduction or the possession of drugs, and decisions in relation to common law offences. It is equally impermissible to draw direct or necessary inferences from decisions where the *mens rea* is, or includes, a state of opinion, and cases where it is limited to intention (a distinction I referred to in *R. v Hyam* or between cases where there is a special 'defence,' like self-defence or provocation and cases where the issue relates to the primary intention which the prosecution has to prove.

Once one has accepted, what seems to be abundantly clear, that the prohibited act in rape is non-consensual sexual intercourse, and that the guilty state of mind is an intention to commit it, it seems to me to follow as a matter of inexorable logic that there is no room either for a 'defence' of honest belief or mistake, or of a defence of honest and reasonable belief or mistake. Either the prosecution proves that the accused had the requisite intent, or it does not. In the former case it succeeds, and in the latter it fails. Since honest belief clearly negatives intent, the reasonableness or otherwise of that belief can only be evidence for or against the view that the belief and therefore the intent was actually held, and it matters not whether, to quote Bridge J. in the passage cited above, 'the definition of a crime includes no specific element beyond the prohibited act'. If the mental element be primarily an intention and not a state of belief it comes within his second proposition and not his third. Any other view, as for insertion of the word 'reasonable' can only have the effect of saying that a man intends something which he does not.

By contrast, the appellants invited us to overrule the bigamy cases from *R. v Tolson* onwards and perhaps also *R. v Prince*, L.R. 2 C.C.R. 154 (the abduction case) as wrongly decided at least in so far as they purport to insist that a mistaken belief must be reasonable . . .

Although it is undoubtedly open to this House to reconsider *R. v Tolson* and the bigamy cases, and perhaps *R. v Prince* which may stand or fall with them, I must respectfully decline to do so in the present case. Nor is it necessary that I should. I am not prepared to assume that the statutory offences of bigamy or abduction are necessarily on all fours with rape, and before I was prepared to undermine a whole line of cases which have been accepted as law for so long, I would need argument in the context of a case expressly relating to the relevant offences. I am content to rest my view of the instant case on the crime of rape by saying that it is my opinion that the prohibited act is and always has been intercourse without consent of the victim and the mental element is and always has been the intention to commit that act, or the equivalent intention of having intercourse willy-nilly not caring whether the victim consents or no. A failure to prove this involves an acquittal because the intent, an essential ingredient, is lacking. It matters not why it is lacking if only it is not there, and in particular it matters not that the intention is lacking only because of a belief not based on reasonable grounds. I should add that I myself am inclined to view *R. v Tolson* as a narrow decision based on the construction of a statute, which prima facie seemed to make an absolute statutory offence, with a proviso, related to the seven-year period of absence, which created a statutory defence. The judges in *R. v Tolson* decided that this was not reasonable, and, on general jurisprudential principles, imported into the statutory offence words which created a special 'defence' of honest and reasonable belief of which the 'evidential' but not the probative burden lay on the defence. I do not think it is necessary to decide this conclusively in the present case. But if this is the true view there is a complete distinction between *Tolson* and the other cases based in statute and the present.

I may also add that I am not impressed with the analogy based on the decision in *Wilson v Inyang* [1951] 2 K.B. 799, 803 which has attracted the attention of some academic authors. That clearly depends on the construction of the words 'wilfully and falsely' where they are used in the relevant statute. Also, though I get some support from what I have been saying from the reasoning of the decision in *R. v Smith (David)*, I nevertheless regard that case as a decision on the Criminal Damage Act 1971, rather than a decision covering the whole law of criminal liability.

For the above reasons I would answer the question certified in the negative, but would apply the proviso to the Criminal Appeal Act on the ground that no miscarriage of justice has or conceivably could have occurred.

Appeal dismissed

Note

Whilst the principle in *Morgan*, that an honest mistake in respect of a definitional element of the offence of rape negates mens rea, the law relating to consent in sexual offences has subsequently changed. The Sexual Offences Act 2003 provides that for a belief in consent to be effective, then it must be reasonable. (See Ch.9 below.)

B (A MINOR) V DIRECTOR OF PUBLIC PROSECUTIONS

[2000] 2 A.C. 428 HL

B, aged 15, sat next to a girl aged 13 on a bus and asked her several times to perform oral sex with him which she refused to do. He was charged with inciting a girl under the age of 14 to commit an act of gross indecency with him, contrary to s.1(1) of the Indecency with Children Act 1960. B honestly believed the girl was over 14 but when the justices ruled that this was no defence to the charge he changed his plea to guilty. On a case stated by the justices, the Divisional Court of the Queen's Bench Division dismissed B's appeal. The Divisional Court certified, inter alia, that the following point of law of general public importance was involved in its decision, namely, "Is a defendant entitled to be acquitted of the offence of inciting a child aged under 14 to commit an act of gross indecency . . . if he may hold an honest belief that the child in question was aged 14 years or over?"

LORD NICHOLLS OF BIRKENHEAD

. . . [O]ver the last quarter of a century there have been several important cases where a defence of honest but mistaken belief was raised. In deciding these cases the courts have placed new, or renewed, emphasis on the subjective nature of the mental element in criminal offences. The courts have rejected the reasonable belief approach and preferred the honest belief approach. When mens rea is ousted by a mistaken belief, it is as well ousted by an unreasonable belief as by a reasonable belief. In the pithy phrase of Lawton L.J. in *Reg. v Kimber* [1983] 1 W.L.R. 1118, 1122, it is the defendant's belief, not the grounds on which it is based, which goes to negative the intent. This approach is well encapsulated in a passage in the judgment of Lord Lane C.J. in *Reg. v Williams (Gladstone)* [1987] 3 All E.R. 411, 415:

> 'The reasonableness or unreasonableness of the defendant's belief is material to the question of whether the belief was held by the defendant at all. If the belief was in fact held, its unreasonableness, so far as guilt or innocence is concerned, is neither here nor there. It is irrelevant. Were it otherwise, the defendant would be convicted because he was negligent in failing to recognise that the victim was not consenting . . . and so on.'

Considered as a matter of principle, the honest belief approach must be preferable. By definition the mental element in a crime is concerned with a subjective state of mind, such as intent or belief . . . . I turn to the recent authorities. The decision which heralded this development in the criminal law was the decision of your Lordships' House in *Reg. v Morgan* [1976] A.C. 182. This was a case of rape. By a bare majority the House held that where a defendant had sexual intercourse with a woman without her consent but believing she did consent, he was not guilty of rape even though he had no reasonable grounds for his belief. The intent to commit rape involves an intention to have intercourse without the woman's consent or with a reckless indifference to whether she consents or not. It would be inconsistent with this definition if an honest belief that she did consent led to an acquittal only when it was based on reasonable grounds. One of the minority, Lord Edmund-Davies, would have taken a different view had he felt free to do so. In *Reg. v Kimber*, a case of indecent assault, the Court of Appeal applied the approach of the majority in Morgan's case. The guilty state of mind was the intent to use personal violence to a woman without her consent. If the defendant did not so intend, he was entitled to be found not guilty. If he did not so intend because he believed she was consenting, the prosecution would have failed to prove the charge, irrespective of the grounds for the defendant's belief. The court disapproved of the suggestion made in the earlier case of *Reg. v Phekoo* [1981] 1 W.L.R. 1117, 1127, that this House intended to confine the views expressed in Morgan's case to cases of rape. This reasoning was taken a step further in *Reg. v Williams* (Gladstone) [1987] 3 All E.R. 411. There the Court of Appeal, presided over by Lord Lane C.J., adopted the same approach in a case of assault occasioning actual bodily harm. The context was a defence that the defendant believed that the person whom he assaulted was unlawfully assaulting a third party. In *Beckford v The Queen* [1988] A.C. 130a similar issue came before the Privy Council on an appeal from Jamaica in a case involving a defence of self-defence to a charge of murder. The Privy Council applied the decisions in Morgan's case and Williams's case. Lord Griffiths said, at p.144:

> 'If then a genuine belief, albeit without reasonable grounds, is a defence to rape because it negatives the necessary intention, so also must a genuine belief in facts which if true would justify self-defence be a defence to a crime of personal violence because the belief negatives the intent to act unlawfully.'

Lord Griffiths also observed, at a practical level, that where there are no reasonable grounds to hold a belief it will surely only be in exceptional circumstances that a jury will conclude that such a belief was or might have been held. Finally in this summary, in *Blackburn v Bowering* [1994] 1 W.L.R. 1324, the Court of Appeal, presided over by Sir Thomas Bingham M.R., applied the same approach to the exercise by the court of its contempt jurisdiction in respect of an alleged assault on officers of the court while in the execution of their duty.

The Crown advanced no suggestion to your Lordships that any of these recent cases was wrongly decided. This is not surprising, because the reasoning in these cases is compelling . . . In principle, an age-related ingredient of a statutory offence stands on no different footing from any other ingredient. If a man genuinely believes that the girl with whom he is committing a grossly indecent act is over 14, he is not intending to commit such an act with a girl under 14.

LORD STEYN

. . . In *Reg. v Morgan* [1976] A.C. 182 the House of Lords held by a majority of three to two that when a defendant had sexual intercourse with a woman without her consent, genuinely believing that she did consent, he was not guilty of rape, even if he had no reasonable grounds for his belief. The importance of this decision for the coherent development of English law was not immediately appreciated. The next stage in the development was the decision of the Court of Appeal in *Reg. v Williams (Gladstone)* [1987] 3 All E.R. 411. The charge was assault. The defendant argued that he used force in the honest belief that he was protecting somebody else from an unlawful assault. Holding that the jury had been materially misdirected, the Court of Appeal, applying the logic of Morgan's case, held that if the defendant believed, reasonably or not, in the existence of facts which would justify the force used in self-defence, he did not intend to use *unlawful* force. The decision in Williams's case was followed and approved and applied by the Privy Council in *Beckford v The Queen* [1988] A.C. 130. It was held that if the defendant honestly believed the circumstances to be such as would, if true, justify his use of force to defend himself from attack and the force was no more than reasonable to resist the attack, he was entitled to be acquitted of murder, since the intent to act unlawfully would be negatived by his belief, however mistaken or unreasonable. Morgan's case was described, at p.145, as 'a landmark decision in the development of the common law.' There has been a general shift from objectivism to subjectivism in this branch of the law. It is now settled as a matter of general principle that mistake, whether reasonable or not, is a defence where it prevents the defendant from having the mens rea which the law requires for the crime with which he is charged . . .

Appeal allowed

(b) Mistake as to a justificatory claim

Where a defendant has, prima facie, committed the offence charged, having brought about the actus reus with the requisite mens rea, will a claim of justification serve to negate his liability where it is based upon a mistaken belief. For example, if D intentionally wounds X in the mistaken belief that X is about to attack him, will his plea of self-defence succeed to negate his liability where it is an honestly held belief or must the belief also be a reasonable one?

In *Albert v Lavin* [1982] A.C. 546, the Divisional Court held that a mistaken belief on the part of the defendant that his act was justified on the basis of self-defence, had to be based on reasonable grounds. Is a claim of justification something separate from the definitional elements of an offence? If so there might be some reason in principle for requiring such mistakes to be reasonable. Alternatively, is the absence of a justificatory claim part of the definitional elements of the offence? If so, does *Morgan* apply or is it to be confined to rape and kindred offences? Glanville Williams has been a strong proponent of the second view.

G. WILLIAMS, *TEXTBOOK OF CRIMINAL LAW*, 2ND EDN (STEVENS & SONS, 1983), P.138

No other rule of the substantive criminal law distinguishes between the definitional and defence elements of a crime, and it is a distinction that it is impossible to draw satisfactorily. A rule creating a *defence* merely supplies additional details of the scope of the *offence*. To regard the offence as subsisting independently of its limitations and qualifications is unrealistic. The defence is a negative condition of the offence, and is therefore an integral part of it. What we regard as part of the offence and what as part of a defence depends only on traditional habits of thought or accidents of legal drafting; it should have no bearing on the important question of criminal liability. For example, it is purely a matter of convenient drafting whether a statute says, on the one hand, that damaging the property of another without his consent is a crime, or, on the other hand, that damaging the property of another is a crime but that his consent is a defence. In fact we regard the non-consent of the owner as a definitional element, but there is no particular reason why this should be so, and the question of guilt or innocence should not depend on it (see 2 Leg.Stud. 233).

This view was echoed in the Court of Appeal in the following case.

R. V WILLIAMS (GLADSTONE)

(1984) 78 Cr. App. R. 276

Mason saw a youth rob a woman. He chased and caught him but the youth broke free. The appellant then witnessed Mason catch the youth again and knock him to the ground. Mason told the appellant that he was a police officer (which was untrue) and that he was arresting the youth for mugging a woman. The appellant asked to see his warrant card. When Mason failed to produce one, a struggle ensued, during which the appellant punched Mason in the face. He was charged with assault occasioning actual bodily harm. He claimed that he honestly believed that the youth was being unlawfully assaulted by Mason and that he was trying to rescue him. As Mason was acting lawfully, the appellant had made a mistake. The jury were directed that his mistake would be relevant if it was honest and based on reasonable grounds. He was convicted and appealed on the ground that the judge had misdirected the jury.

LORD LANE CJ gave the judgment of the court

'Assault' . . . is an act by which the defendant, intentionally or recklessly, applies unlawful force to the complainant. There are circumstances in which force may be applied to another lawfully. Taking a few examples: first, where the victim consents, as in lawful sports, the application of force to another will, generally speaking, not be unlawful. Secondly, where the defendant is acting in self-defence: the exercise of any necessary and reasonable force to protect himself from unlawful violence is not unlawful. Thirdly, by virtue of section 3 of the Criminal Law Act 1967, a person may use such force as is reasonable in the circumstances in the prevention of crime or in effecting or assisting in the lawful arrest of an offender or suspected offender or persons unlawfully at large. In each of those cases the defendant will be guilty if the jury are sure that first of all he applied force to the person of another, and secondly that he had the necessary mental element to constitute guilt.

The mental element necessary to constitute guilt is the intent to apply unlawful force to the victim. We do not believe that the mental element can be substantiated by simply showing an intent to apply force and no more.

What then is the situation if the defendant is labouring under a mistake of fact as to the circumstances? What if he believes, but believes mistakenly, that the victim is consenting, or that it is necessary to defend himself, or that a crime is being committed which he intends to prevent? He must then be judged against the mistaken facts as he believes them to be. If judged against those facts or circumstances the prosecution fail to establish his guilt, then he is entitled to be acquitted.

The next question is, does it make any difference if the mistake of the defendant was one which, viewed objectively by a reasonable onlooker, was an unreasonable mistake? . . .

It is upon this point that the large volume of historical precedent . . . is concerned. But in our judgment the answer is provided by the judgment of this Court in *Kimber* [above] by which . . . we are bound . . .

We respectfully agree with what Lawton L.J. said [in *Kimber*] with regard both to the way in which the defence should have been put and also with regard to his remarks as to the nature of the defence. The reasonableness or unreasonableness of the defendant's belief is material to the question of whether the belief was held by the defendant at all. If the belief was in fact held, its unreasonableness, so far as guilt or innocence is concerned, is neither here nor there. It is irrelevant. Were it otherwise, the defendant would be convicted because he was negligent in failing to recognise that the victim was not consenting or that a crime was not being committed and so on. In other words the jury should be directed first of all that the prosecution have the burden or duty of proving the unlawfulness of the defendant's actions; secondly, if the defendant may have been labouring under a mistake as to the facts, he must be judged according to his mistaken view of the facts; thirdly, that is so whether the mistake was, on an objective view, a reasonable mistake or not.

In a case of self-defence, where self-defence or the prevention of crime is concerned, if the jury came to the conclusion that the defendant believed, or may have believed, that he was being attacked or that a crime was being committed, and that force was necessary to protect himself or to prevent the crime, then the prosecution have not proved their case. If however the defendant's alleged belief was mistaken and if the mistake was an unreasonable one, that may be a powerful reason for coming to the conclusion that the belief was not honestly held and should be rejected.

Even if the jury come to the conclusion that the mistake was an unreasonable one, if the defendant may genuinely have been labouring under it, he is entitled to rely upon it.

We have read the recommendations of the Criminal Law Revision Committee, Part IX, paragraph 72(a), in which the following passage appears: 'The common law defence of self-defence should be replaced by a statutory defence providing that a person may use such force as is reasonable in the circumstances as he believes them to be in the defence of himself or any other person.' In the view of this Court that represents the law as expressed in *DPP v Morgan* and in *Kimber* and we do not think that the decision of the Divisional Court in *Albert v Lavin* from which we have cited can be supported.

Appeal allowed
Conviction quashed

Williams was considered in *R. v O'Grady* [1987] 3 W.L.R. 321 CA (below, p.225). The Judicial Committee of the Privy Council reviewed the whole area in the following case.

BECKFORD V R.

[1988] A.C. 130

At the appellant's trial for murder the judge directed the jury that if the appellant had a *reasonable* belief that his life was in danger or that he was in danger of serious bodily injury he was entitled to be acquitted on the grounds of self-defence.

LORD GRIFFITHS

. . . It is accepted by the prosecution that there is no difference on the law of self-defence between the law of Jamaica and the English common law and it therefore falls to be decided whether it was correctly decided by the Court of Appeal in *R. v Williams* [above] that the defence of self-defence depends upon what the accused 'honestly' believed the circumstances to be and not upon the reasonableness of that belief—what the Court of Appeal in Jamaica referred to as the 'honest belief' and 'reasonable belief' schools of thought.

There can be no doubt that prior to the decision of the House of Lords in *R. v Morgan* [above] the whole weight of authority supported the view that it was an essential element of self-defence not only that the accused believed that he was being attacked or in imminent danger of being attacked but also that such belief was based on reasonable grounds.

The question then is whether the present Lord Chief Justice, Lord Lane, in *R. v Williams*, was right to depart from the law as declared by his predecessors in the light of the decision of the House of Lords in *R. v Morgan* . . .

The common law recognises that there are many circumstances in which one person may inflict violence upon another without committing a crime, as for instance, in sporting contests, surgical operations or in the most extreme example judicial execution. The common law has always recognised as one of these circumstances the right of a person to protect himself from attack and to act in the defence of others and if necessary to inflict violence on another in so doing. If no more force is used than is reasonable to repel the attack such force is not unlawful and no crime is committed. Furthermore a man about to be attacked does not have to wait for his assailant to strike the first blow or fire the first shot; circumstances may justify a pre-emptive strike.

It is because it is an essential element of all crimes of violence that the violence or the threat of violence should be unlawful that self-defence, if raised as an issue in a criminal trial, must be disproved by the prosecution. If the prosecution fail to do so the accused is entitled to be acquitted because the prosecution will have failed to prove an essential element of the crime namely that the violence used by the accused was unlawful.

If then a genuine belief, albeit without reasonable grounds, is a defence to rape because it negatives the necessary intention, so also must a genuine belief in facts which if true would justify self-defence be a defence to a crime of personal violence because the belief negates the intent to act unlawfully. Their Lordships therefore approve . . . *R. v Williams*, as correctly stating the law of self-defence . . .

Looking back, *R. v Morgan* can now be seen as a landmark decision in the development of the common law returning the law to the path upon which it might have developed but for the inability of an accused to give evidence on his own behalf . . .

There may be a fear that the abandonment of the objective standard demanded by the existence of reasonable grounds for belief will result in the success of too many spurious claims of self-defence. The English experience has not shown this to be the case. The Judicial Studies Board with the approval of the Lord Chief Justice has produced a model direction on self-defence which is now widely used by judges when summing up to juries. The direction contains the following guidance:

> 'Whether the plea is self-defence or defence of another, if the defendant may have been labouring under a mistake as to the facts, he must be judged according to his mistaken belief of the facts: that is so whether the mistake was, on an objective view, a reasonable mistake or not.'

Their Lordships have heard no suggestion that this form of summing up has resulted in a disquieting number of acquittals. This is hardly surprising for no jury is going to accept a man's assertion that he believed that he was about to be attacked without testing it against all the surrounding circumstances. In assisting the jury to determine whether or not the accused had a genuine belief the judge will of course direct their attention to those features of the evidence that make such a belief more or less probable. Where there are no reasonable grounds to hold a belief it will surely only be in exceptional circumstances that a jury will conclude that such a belief was or might have been held.

Their Lordships therefore conclude that the summing up in this case contained a material misdirection and . . . the test to be applied for self-defence is that a person may use such force as is reasonable in the circumstances as he honestly believes them to be in the defence of himself or another.

Appeal allowed

Note

See further the discussion of *Scarlett* [1994] 3 All E.R. 629, below and *Owino* [1995] Crim. L.R. 743, below.

(c) The Problem of Tolson

The offence of bigamy under s.57 of the Offences Against the Person Act 1861 is committed where a person "being married, shall marry any other person during the life of the former husband or wife". A proviso to the section provides that it shall not extend to a person marrying a second time where their "husband or wife shall have been continually absent from such person for the space of seven years then last past, and shall not have been known by such person to be living within that time" or where the first marriage has been annulled or dissolved. In *Tolson* (1889) 23 QBD 168, a wife remarried five years after last seeing her husband whom she believed to have been lost at sea. She was charged with bigamy when it was discovered that he was still alive. She was convicted as she did not come within the proviso although the jury found that she believed on reasonable grounds and in good faith that he was dead. The Court for Crown Cases Reserved by a majority quashed her conviction importing into the statute a defence based on honest and reasonable belief. Cave J stated (at 181):

"At common law an honest and reasonable belief in the existence of circumstances, which, if true, would make the act for which a prisoner is indicted an innocent act has always been held to be a good defence."

The defence would apply to statutory offences unless excluded expressly or by necessary implication. In *Gould* [1968] 2 Q.B. 65, it was held that a reasonable belief that the first marriage had been dissolved was also a defence. The effect is to make bigamy an offence of strict liability in respect of the element of "being married" to which a defence of "no negligence" may be raised.

When a statute creates an offence it does not recapitulate all the defences traditionally allowed by the criminal law; yet it must have been the intention of Parliament that these defences should apply. Similarly, since the requirement of mens rea is a traditional principle of law, for serious crimes, it is reasonable to suppose that Parliament meant it to govern the statute.

Stephen J stated this argument in a much-quoted passage. It is too long to reproduce, but may be summarised. The judge begins by saying that "the full definition of every crime contains a proposition as to a state of mind". Then he spells this out again by saying that if the mental element is absent there is no crime; and he clearly means this proposition to apply to crimes created by statute as well as at common law, so that all alike require a mental element. There follows a series of instances showing that where a person does not know a fact required for the crime he lacks the mental element and so cannot be guilty. Finally, however, the judge confines his proposition to cases where the defendant's belief that the facts were innocent was not merely in good faith but was based on reasonable grounds. This implies that if the defendant genuinely but unreasonably believed in the existence of justifying facts he has no defence, even though in that case he lacked the mental element that is supposed to be required. The reference to reasonable grounds departs from the purely subjective element that the judge has hitherto been propounding, and introduces an objective test. There is, therefore, a basic contradiction in the judgment . . .

Stephen J is assuming that the mental element required for a crime is knowledge of a particular fact, which we may call A (e.g. "I am still married"). The defendant's defence is that he believed that the fact present was not-A ("I am not now married"). A defence of belief in not-A is of course the same thing as denying knowledge of A. But Stephen J says that belief in not-A is no defence unless it is reasonable. If it is unreasonable, the defendant is convicted although he believed not-A, i.e. although he did not know A. Yet the judge says that the defendant must know A. So he contradicts himself: QED. His judgment would make a person guilty of bigamy although the only mental element was that of intending to enter into a valid marriage—a state of mind that almost all of us possess at some time in our lives.

Although the question of reasonable belief was not before the court in *Tolson*, and although Stephen J and some other members of the court were clearly guilty of self-contradiction, the idea started in *Tolson* was perpetuated in later bigamy cases. Time and again the judges have said that a mistake of fact, to be a defence to a charge of bigamy, must be reasonable.

Questions

1.   In *Morgan* Lord Fraser said "bigamy does not involve any intention except the intention to go through a marriage ceremony"; if this is correct, wherein lies the guilty state of mind in bigamy which distinguishes a bigamist from every other person who marries?

2.   Is there any justification in convicting a person of bigamy who mistakenly believes he or she is free to marry?

Note

In *Sweet v Parsley* [1970] A.C. 132 (below p.147), Lord Diplock referred to a general principle of construction of statutory offences in terms similar to those used in *Tolson* stating (at 163):

"a general principle of construction of any enactment, which creates a criminal offence, [is] that, even where the words used to describe the prohibited conduct would not in any other context connote the necessity for any particular mental element, they are nevertheless to be read as subject to the implication that a necessary element in the offence is the absence of a belief, held honestly and upon reasonable grounds, in the existence of facts which, if true, would make the act innocent."

In *B (A Minor) v DPP* [2000] 2 W.L.R. 452 (above), the House of Lords had to answer the following questions certified by the Divisional Court as points of law of general public importance:

"1. Is a defendant entitled to be acquitted of the offence of inciting a child aged under 14 to commit an act of gross indecency, contrary to section 1(1) of the Indecency with Children Act 1960, if he may hold an honest belief that the child in question was aged 14 years or over? 2. If yes, (a) must the belief be held on reasonable grounds? (b) On whom does the burden of proof lie?"

Their Lordships answered question 1. in the affirmative, question 2.(a) in the negative and question 2.(b) the prosecution. Lord Nicholls of Birkenhead referred to *Tolson* but did not overrule it. Both Lord Nicholls and Lord Steyn referred to Lord Diplock's dictum in *Sweet v Parsley* which they considered in light of the later decisions in *Morgan, Kimber, Williams (Gladstone)* and *Beckford* and concluded that his formulation of the common law presumption was out of step with these cases in so far as it required that a mistaken belief had to be based on reasonable grounds. Lord Nicholls stated (at 457–8):

"This seems to be a relic from the days before a defendant in a criminal case could give evidence in his own defence. It is not surprising that in those times juries judged a defendant's state of mind by the conduct to be expected of a reasonable person.

[T]he traditional formulation of the common law presumption must now be modified appropriately. Otherwise the formulation would not be an accurate reflection of the current state of the criminal law regarding mistakes of fact. Lord Diplock's dictum . . . must in future be read as though the reference to reasonable grounds were omitted."

Lord Steyn stated (at 471):

"There has been a general shift from objectivism to subjectivism in this branch of the law. It is now settled as a matter of general principle that mistake, whether reasonable or not, is a defence where it prevents the defendant from having the mens rea which the law requires for the crime with which he is charged. It would be in disharmony with this development now to rule that in respect of a defence under s.1(1) of the Act of 1960 the belief must be based on reasonable grounds. Moreover, if such a special solution were to be adopted, it would almost certainly create uncertainty in other parts of the criminal law. It would be difficult to confine it on a principled basis to section1(1)."

Tolson appears to be an aberrant decision, limited to bigamy, and awaiting the right circumstances to arise for it to be overruled.

It is, perhaps regrettable that in neither *B v DPP* nor *DPP v K* did the House take the opportunity to overrule *Tolson*.

----

(2) Mistake as to a non-definitional element, i.e. as to an excusatory claim

PETER ALLDRIDGE, "THE COHERENCE OF DEFENCES" [1983] CRIM. L.R. 665–666

The basis of a claim of justification is that it speaks to the act, a claim of excuse to whether the actor is properly regarded as responsible for it. A claim of justification involves saying, 'I am responsible for what was done, but I am not an appropriate object for punishment because what was done, although an invasion of an interest of another which is generally protected by the criminal law, was done in circumstances which gave me a legal right to do it.' The reason for there being such a legal right is that the behaviour was such as should be encouraged (carrying out the order of the court, arresting offenders, preventing crime, some instances of necessity, consent), or at the very least legally tolerated (self-defence, other cases of consent). The claim of excuse is a different sort of claim altogether. Here D admits, 'There was an unjustified invasion of a legally protected interest.' But s/he says, 'the normal inference from the fact that my action caused the invasion to the conclusion that I am responsible for it ought not to be drawn: some factor operates which makes that normal inference unwarranted.'

[A]n exculpatory defence must be an excuse or justification but cannot be both. The point of the claim of justification is that D was a responsible actor. Knowledge of sufficient circumstances to make the invasion of P's interest tolerable, and thus establish the right to invade it, is itself a prerequisite of that right. The point of a claim of excuse is that D was not a responsible actor. A coherent defence cannot contain elements the rationale of which is that D was a responsible actor, together with elements whose rationale is that D was not.

G.P. FLETCHER, *RETHINKING CRIMINAL LAW* (BOSTON: LITTLE, BROWN, 1978), PP.798–800, 810–812

THE THEORY OF EXCUSES

Interposing a claim of excuse concedes that there is a wrong to be excused. The claim challenges the attribution of the wrongdoing to the actor. If the excuse is valid, then, as a matter of definition, the actor is not accountable or culpable for the wrongful act. The focus of the excuse is not on the act in the abstract, but on the circumstances of the act and the actor's personal capacity to avoid either an intentional wrong or the taking of an excessive risk. Insanity and involuntary intoxication are paradigmatic excuses. Duress and necessity are regarded as excuses in some legal systems, but not in others . . .

In a case of justified conduct, the act typically reflects well on the actor's courage or devotion to the public interest. If he disables an aggressor in order to save the life of another, his conduct speaks well for his courage; if as a police officer he disables a felon seeking to escape, his conduct testifies at least to his devotion to duty. Justifications require good reasons for violating the prohibitory norm; someone who chooses to act on these reasons is likely to deserve respect and praise rather than blame.

The distinguishing feature of excusing conditions is that they preclude an inference from the act to the actor's character. Typically, if a bank teller opens a safe and turns money over to a stranger, we can infer that he is dishonest. But if he does all this at gunpoint, we cannot infer anything one way or the other about his honesty. Typically, if a driver knowingly runs over someone lying in the roadway, we might infer something about the driver's indifference to human life. But we cannot make that inference if the choice open to the driver was going over a cliff or continuing down the incline and running over someone lying in the roadway. Similarly, if someone violates a legal prohibition under an unavoidable mistake about the legality of his conduct, we cannot infer anything about his respect for law and the rights of others. The same breakdown in the reasoning from conduct to character occurs in cases of insanity, for it is implicit in the medical conception of insanity that the actor's true character is distorted by his mental illness . . .

The single most difficult point in the theory of excuses is the relationship between excuses and the norms that govern our conduct. The nature of a justification is that the claim is grounded in an implicit exception to the prohibitory norm. The 'right' of self-defence carves out a set of cases in which violation of the norm is permissible. When the principles of justification are rendered concrete in particular cases, the result is a precedent that other people may properly rely upon in similar cases. If a court recognises a privilege, based on necessity, to shoot a rabies-stricken dog in order to protect children in the neighbourhood, the result modifies the norm against the destruction of property. If deadly force is adjudged permissible against a threatened rape, the norm against homicide is pro tanto contracted. In similar cases arising in the future, similarly situated actors may rely on these recognised privileges in planning their conduct. The only requirement for claiming the precedent is the general legal rule that the new case may not be significantly different in its relevant facts.

Excuses bear a totally different relationship to prohibitory norms. They do not constitute exceptions or modifications of the norm, but rather a judgment in the particular case that an individual cannot be fairly held accountable for violating the norm. This fundamental difference means that cases acknowledging that conduct in a particular situation is excused do not generate precedents that other people may rely on in the future. This is obvious in cases of mistake of law, for the judgment of the court serves to advise the public of the rule in question, and therefore in the future there is even less excuse for ignorance of the particular law . . .

Excuses have this peculiar quality, for they occupy a hiatus between two concepts of law. Law in the narrow sense consists solely of the norms prohibiting conduct and laying down the criteria of justification. Law in the broad sense encompasses the total set of criteria that affects the outcomes of particular case. In the ring between these two circles of law, one finds the criteria of excuses as well as other conditions—such as criteria of immunity and the statute of limitations—that affect the outcome of particular cases.

(See further, Glanville Williams, "The Theory of Excuses" [1982] Crim. L.R. 732.)

R. V GRAHAM

(1981) 74 Cr. App. R. 235

LORD LANE CJ

[I]n general, if a mistake is to excuse what would otherwise be criminal, the mistake must be a reasonable one . . .

The correct approach [is] (1) Was the defendant, or may he have been, impelled to act as he did because, as a result of what he reasonably believed [X] had said or done, he had good cause to fear that if he did not so act [X] would kill him or (if this is to be added) cause him serious physical injury? (2) If so, have the prosecution made the jury sure that a sober person of reasonable firmness, sharing the characteristics of the defendant, would not have responded to whatever he reasonably believed [X] said or did by taking part in the killing?

Note

Lord Lane CJ's dicta were approved by the House of Lords in *R. v Howe and Bannister* [1987] 2 W.L.R. 568. In neither case was mistake an issue, so what was said was strictly obiter. Subsequent cases have accepted that in duress or duress of circumstances the issue is one of reasonable belief (see, for example, *Abdul-Hussain* [1999] Crim. L.R. 570; *Cairns* [1999] 2 Cr. App. R. 137; *Safi* [2003] EWCA Crim 1809). It should be noted, however, that *Cairns* was misconstrued in *Martin* [2000] 2 Cr. App. R. 42 as having held that the test in duress was subjective thereby creating further uncertainty.

Questions

1. Is there any basis in principle why a mistake in respect of an excusatory claim must be based on reasonable grounds when a mistake in respect of a justificatory claim need not be?

2. Is it possible to reconcile Lord Lane's statement in *Williams*, that a defendant must be judged on the basis of the facts as he believed them to be, with his pronouncement in *Graham*?

----

ii. Irrelevant Mistakes

(1) Mistake and Strict Liability

(2) Ignorance of the Law

(3) Transferred Malice

Mistakes can only be relevant in crimes which require proof of some mental element. As the preceding sections indicate, the courts, in allocating mistake to one category or another, are making decisions as to what that mental element is and to what parts of the actus reus it is to apply. The rules deduced from the cases can be stated without reference to mistake as such. Thus of bigamy it can be said that proof of intention is necessary for the act of getting married while as to the circumstances of being married only negligence is needed. Where an offence is interpreted as not even requiring negligence as to an element of the actus reus it is said to be an offence of strict liability. *Prince*, below, illustrates how the creation of such an offence renders the mistake of no legal consequence.

The converse of the opening statement of the above paragraph is not true: mistakes are sometimes irrelevant in mens rea crimes. Ignorance of the law is often no defence. In these cases, as in *Prince*, the mistake is *rendered* irrelevant by the law even though, had things been as the defendant supposed, there would have been no offence. However, in cases of transferred malice, the mistake is legally irrelevant because it is immaterial to D's culpability whether the victim is the intended one or someone else.

(1) Mistake and strict liability

R. v Miller [1975] 1 W.L.R. 1222: The offence of driving a motor vehicle on a road while disqualified under s.99(6) of the Road Traffic Act 1972 (now s.103 of the Road Traffic Act 1988) was held to have been committed despite the defendant's belief that he was driving on a private road. James LJ at 1226: "[W]e have reached the clear conclusion that section 99 . . . provides an offence which is proved once the prosecution establish the facts which were not disputed in the present case, namely, that there was driving by a person who was at that time disqualified . . . and that it is not relevant for a defendant to raise the question of his state of mind in order to show . . . a mistaken belief as to the nature of the place where the driving was taking place."

R. v Howells [1977] 2 W.L.R. 716: It is an offence under s.1 of the Firearms Act 1968 to possess a revolver without a firearm certificate. Under s.58(2) this does not apply to antique firearms, "purchased . . . or possessed as a curiosity or ornament." D thought he possessed an antique; in fact it was a modern reproduction. His appeal against conviction was dismissed by the Court of Appeal, Brown LJ at 725: "This court has reached the decision that s.1 should be construed strictly . . . to allow a defence of honest and reasonable belief that the firearm was an antique and therefore excluded would be likely to defeat the clear intention of the Act."

L.H. LEIGH, *STRICT AND VICARIOUS LIABILITY* (LONDON: SWEET & MAXWELL, 1982), PP.58–61

. . . Lord Diplock in *Sweet v Parsley* suggested that a general due diligence defence might be possible at common law. [S]uch a defence [exists] in Australia and Canada. It is appropriate at this juncture to examine its antecedents and extent, before considering the question upon what basis it might be introduced into English law.

The Australian formulation derives from *Proudman v Dayman* (1943) 67 C.L.R. 536). The charge was that the accused permitted a person, not being the holder of a licence for the time being in force, to drive a motor vehicle on a public road. The question arose whether the accused could raise a defence of honest and reasonable mistake to the charge. Although on the facts there was no basis for such a defence, Dixon J. held that reasonable mistake might be raised as a defence to a charge of a strict liability offence. The reasoning adopted by His Honour was that a holding that the prosecution need not prove intention or recklessness to procure a conviction does not imply that fault has no part in the case. His Honour thus states:

> 'It is one thing to deny that a necessary ingredient of the offence is positive knowledge of the fact that the driver holds no subsisting licence. It is another to say that an honest belief founded on reasonable grounds that he is licensed cannot exculpate a person who permits him to drive. As a general rule an honest and reasonable belief in a state of facts which, if they existed, would make the defendant's act innocent affords an excuse for doing what would otherwise be an offence.' (at 540)

From this it followed that, save in an exceptional case where liability is truly intended to be absolute, the accused might defend himself by showing that he exercised due diligence to comply with the law. The affinity of this thought to those English cases which insisted that an absence of *metis rea* words simply shifted the burden of proof is plain.

The result of this approach is to create three categories of statutory offences: those in which the prosecution must prove full *mens rea*: those in which it need not prove *mens rea* but the accused may raise as a defence to a charge that he or she exercised all due diligence: and those in which liability is absolute. In this latter case, the legislature must make it clear that absolute liability is intended.

It is impossible to indicate what view English courts will ultimately take of the place of fault as a common law principle. In *Sweet v Parsley* Lords Reid, Pearce and Diplock intimated that the question of due diligence defences may not be entirely foreclosed by authority. In *R. v Warner*, Lord Guest had thought that the half-way house represented by the Australian cases was blocked by the decision in *Woolmington v D.P.P.* that the Crown must prove, beyond a reasonable doubt, all the elements of the case. In *Sweet v Parsley*, Lord Diplock intimates that this point may need to be reconsidered: *Woolmington*, his Lordship states, is no bar to the use of honest and reasonable mistake as a solvent of strict liability cases since it only decides that where there is evidence of a defence, a jury must consider it and acquit the accused unless they are sure that the accused did not hold a particular belief, or there are no reasonable grounds for it.

Dicta in *Morgan* also suggest that a common law no fault defence is possible, but they are very confused. The *ratio* of the case is that in rape, an honest mistake as to the existence of the elements of the offence is a defence. The House of Lords was, however, obliged to explain away a series of cases on bigamy which held that a mistake had both to be honest and reasonable to afford a defence. Lord Cross drew a distinction between offences which require *mens rea* and those which do not. Some *mens rea* offences specify the mental element required for the offence: in respect of them, mistake need only be honest. Other *mens rea* offences do not specify any mental element: in their case, mistake must be both honest and reasonable. Where no *mens rea* is required at all, mistake will not excuse the defendant. On this view, a mistake defence would only be available where a court was prepared to construe an offence which is silent as to the mental element, as involving *mens rea*. Why there should be a difference between two classes of *mens rea* offences is obscure. Lord Hailsham took a different view of the bigamy cases. He treated the leading case, *Tolson*, as a narrow decision based on the construction of a statute which *prima facie* appeared to create an absolute offence subject to a statutory defence related to a seven year period of absence. His Lordship suggests this explanation:

> 'The judges . . . decided that this was not reasonable, and, on general jurisprudential principles, imported into the statutory offence words which created a special "defence" of honest and reasonable belief of which the "evidential", but not the probative burden lay on the defence.'

If Lord Hailsham's suggestion were adopted, there would be no reason why honest and reasonable mistake, or a showing by the accused that he used due diligence to comply with the law, should not afford a defence to crimes of strict liability generally, subject always to the power of Parliament to legislate so as to exclude it. If the general jurisprudential principle referred to (whatever it may be) can be invoked to prevent injustice in one case, there seems no reason why it could not be invoked in another. No doubt a tendency to do so would be most marked where a penalty of imprisonment was available and sometimes imposed for the offence, or where the stigma attaching to conviction for that offence was very considerable. Where the usual penalty was a fine, an inference that no such defence was intended might well be drawn, as it might where an adequate statutory scheme of defences was already provided. But all these are possibilities latent in *dicta* in leading cases; no court has sought to build upon them. It cannot be said with certainty therefore, whether the courts will continue to recognise defences based upon particular statutory words, or whether they will take the further step of creating a general due diligence defence which would be displaced only where a particular scheme made it clear that no such defence was intended.

Question

Would the defence of honest and reasonable belief stated by Dixon J in *Proudman v Dayman* have availed the defendants in *Prince, Miller* and *Howells*, above, if it had existed in English common law?

----

(3) Ignorance of the law

R. v Smith and *R. v Gould* [1968] 1 All E.R. 849 indicate that mistake of civil law can preclude a person from having the requisite mental element for a particular offence.

SECRETARY OF STATE FOR TRADE AND INDUSTRY V HART

[1982] 1 All E.R. 817

Hart acted as the auditor of two companies although as a director of each company he was disqualified from so doing by virtue of s.161(2) of the Companies Act 1948. He was charged with acting as an auditor of a company knowing that he was disqualified for appointment as auditor, contrary to s.161(2) of the 1948 Act and s.13(5) and (6) of the Companies Act 1976. Hart submitted that as he did not know of the statutory provisions disqualifying him, he could not be guilty. The magistrate dismissed the case because of Hart's ignorance of the law and the Secretary of State appealed.

WOOLF J

. . . The fact that Mr Hart, during the relevant period, had acted as auditor of those companies, at a time when he was disqualified as alleged in the information, was not in dispute before the stipendiary magistrate. The only matter that was in issue was whether or not Mr Hart had the necessary *mens rea* to constitute the offences which were alleged . . .

In subs. (2) [of section 161] it is stated:

'None of the following persons shall be qualified for appointment as auditor of a company—(*a*) an officer or servant of the company; (*b*) a person who is a partner of or in the employment of an officer or servant of the company; (*c*) a body corporate.'

The term 'officer' is defined in s.455 of that Act as including a director, manager or secretary. So clearly, because of the provisions of subs. (2), although Mr Hart had been authorised to act as an auditor, he was not qualified to hold the appointment in a company in respect of which he was a director or secretary . . .

Subsection (5) [of section 13 of the 1976 Act] provides:

'No person shall act as auditor of a company at a time when he knows that he is disqualified for appointment to that office; and if an auditor of a company to his knowledge becomes so disqualified during his term of office he shall thereupon vacate his office and give notice in writing to the company that he has vacated it by reason of such disqualification.'

Subsection (5) therefore creates the disqualification which arises as a result of persons holding particular offices . . .

Subsection (6) of s.13 of the 1976 Act widens the categories of persons who could be guilty of a criminal offence in relation to this matter. It provides:

'Any person who acts as auditor in contravention of subsection (5) above or fails without reasonable excuse to give notice of vacating his office as required by that subsection shall be guilty of an offence and liable on conviction on indictment to a fine and on summary conviction to a fine not exceeding £40 for every day during which the contravention continues.'

It is subss. (5) and (6) of s.13 of the 1976 Act that this court is primarily concerned with in answering the question posed by this appeal. Counsel on behalf of the Secretary of State argues that when subs. (5) and (6) are read together the position is one where a person is guilty of an offence under those provisions if he knows the facts or circumstances which cause him to be disqualified but nonetheless acts as an auditor. He contends that it is not necessary for a person charged with an offence under those subsections also to know as a matter of law he is disqualified. He submits that it is sufficient if he knows the facts and circumstances, because like anyone else a person acting as an auditor should be aware of the provisions of the law which deal with the disqualification for an appointment to the office of auditor.

This is, however, as I have already pointed out, a criminal offence which is created by s.13(5) and (6). In my view it is at least equally consistent with the ordinary meaning of the words which are used in those subsections, that their effect is that a person is not guilty of an offence and is not disqualified from acting as an auditor unless he in fact knows not only the relevant facts but also that in consequence of the facts he is disqualified by the law for appointment to the office. The words in their ordinary interpretation are wholly consistent with a view of the subsections which means that a person in the position of Mr Hart must be aware of the statutory restrictions which exist against his holding the appointment . . .

[T]he wording we have to consider, introduced by s.13 of the Companies Act 1976, clearly requires some form of *mens rea*, and clearly requires it expressly . . . Counsel for the Secretary of State concedes that the offence here created is not an absolute offence . . . However, he wishes to introduce a limited form of knowledge as being necessary. In my view it would be wrong to introduce such a limitation, bearing in mind the express words here are open to the interpretation which I have indicated. Because it is wrong, and would be an undesirable limitation on the normal principles of statutory construction in relation to a criminal offence, to qualify what is required as *mens rea*, it is my view that the stipendiary magistrate in this case came to the right decision.

ORMROD LJ

[After referring to subs.(5) and (6) of s.13 of the 1976 Act] [T]he offence, as was correctly set out in the information, is that Mr Hart acted as an auditor of a company at a time when he knew that he was disqualified for that appointment. And interpreting the language quite simply, it seems to me to indicate that Mr Hart is not guilty of a criminal offence unless he knew that he was disqualified.

If that means that he is entitled to rely on ignorance of the law as a defence, in contrast to the usual practice and the usual rule, the answer is that the section gives him that right . . .

Appeal dismissed

Question

Would the result have been different if Mr Hart's submission had been that while he knew he was disqualified under the Companies Acts from acting as an auditor, he did not know that this constituted a criminal offence?

Note

Compare the outcome in *Hart* with *Grant v Borg* [1982] 1 W.L.R. 638, where the accused (a non-patrial with limited leave to remain in the UK) was charged with knowingly remaining beyond the time limited by the leave, contrary to s.24(1)(b)(i) of the Immigration Act 1971. On the issue whether a mistake, as to whether "leave to remain" had expired, was relevant, Lord Bridge stated:

> "The principle that ignorance of the law is no defence in crime is so fundamental that to construe the word 'knowingly' in a criminal statute as requiring not merely knowledge of the facts material to the offender's guilt, but also knowledge of the relevant law, would be revolutionary and, to my mind, wholly unacceptable."

Ignorance of the law in the sense of not realising that a particular act is prohibited is rarely a defence. People are presumed to know the law. Two justifications have been advanced for this constructive knowledge:

Oliver Wendell Holmes, *The Common Law* (1881), p.48:

> "[T]o admit the excuse at all would be to encourage ignorance . . . and justice to the individual is rightly outweighed by the larger interests on the other side of the scales."

Jerome Hall, *General Principles of Common Law* (1947), p.382:

"If that plea [mistake of law] were valid, the consequence would be: wherever a defendant in a criminal case thought the law was thus and so, he is to be treated as though the law were thus and so, i.e. *the law actually is thus and so*. But such a doctrine would contradict the essential requisites of a legal system . . ." (italics in original).

Hall's view seems logically attractive but does any defence of mistake, whether of fact or law, alter either factual reality or the law itself? In any case, this view fails to recognise that ignorance of the law does sometimes affect culpability. When an offence is confined to a particular class of prohibited persons and the means of discovering who is in that class are obscure, ignorance may be excused: Lord Evershed in *Lim Chin Aik v The Queen* [1963] A.C. 160 at 171, below: "[T]he maxim [ignorance of the law is no excuse] cannot apply to such a case as the present where it appears that there is . . . no provision . . . for the publication in any form of an order of the kind made in the present case or any other provision designed to enable a man by appropriate inquiry to find out what 'the law' is." The United States' Supreme Court has allowed a defence of ignorance to an offence of "failing to register as a convicted person": *Lambert v California* 355 U.S. 225 (1957). The court drew a distinction between crimes of commission, where ignorance could never be a defence, and crimes of omission, where it may be, unless the failure to act is under circumstances which should alert the doer to the consequences of such failure. Mr Justice Douglas said, at 232: "Were it otherwise, the evil would be as great as it is when the law is written in print too fine to read, or in language foreign to the community." Can this be reconciled with Holmes's statement above? See, generally, A.J. Ashworth, "Excusable Mistake of Law" [1974] Crim. L.R. 652.

----

(4) Transferred malice

Note

Where D makes a mistake as to the identity of his victim, for example he thinks that B is A and he shoots him intending to kill him, his mistake is irrelevant as he intended to kill a person and he did kill a person.

   Where some chance factor alters the result from that which D intended, his liability will depend on whether the result amounts to the same offence which D had intended. This is illustrated by the two cases which follow.

R. V PEMBLITON

(1874) L.R. 2 C.C.R. 119

The defendant was a member of a group who were fighting outside the public-house called The Grand Turk. He picked up a large stone and threw it at those with whom he had been fighting. The stone passed over their heads and broke a window of the public-house. The defendant was indicted for "unlawfully and maliciously" committing damage under the Malicious Damage Act 1861 s.51. The jury found that he had intended to strike the persons at whom he aimed the stone and that he did not intend to break the window.

LORD COLERIDGE CJ

I am of the opinion that the evidence does not support the conviction. The indictment is under [Malicious Damage Act 1861 s.51] which deals with malicious injuries to property, and the section expressly says that the act is to be unlawful and malicious. There is also the fifty-eighth section, which makes it immaterial whether the offence has been committed from malice against the owner of the property or otherwise, that is, from malice against someone not the owner of the property. In both these sections it seems to me that what is intended by the statute is a wilful doing of an intentional act. Without saying that if the case had been left to them in a different way the conviction could not have been supported, if, on these facts, the jury had come to the conclusion that the prisoner was reckless of the consequence of his act, and might reasonably have expected that it would result in breaking the window, it is sufficient to say that the jury have expressly found the contrary . . .

BLACKBURN J

We have not now to consider what would be malice aforethought to bring a given case within the common law definition of murder; here the statute says that the act must be unlawful and malicious, and malice may be defined to be 'where any person wilfully does an act injurious to another without lawful excuse'. Can this man be considered, on the case submitted to us, as having wilfully broken a pane of glass? The jury might perhaps have found on this evidence that the act was malicious, because they might have found that the prisoner knew that the natural consequence of his act would be to break the glass, and although that was not his wish, yet that he was reckless whether he did it or not; but the jury have not so found, and I think it is impossible to say in this case that the prisoner has maliciously done an act which he did not intend to do.

Conviction quashed

R. V LATIMER

(1886) 17 Q.B.D. 359

L, who was quarrelling with C in a public house aimed a blow at C with his belt. The belt glanced off C and severely injured R. In answer to questions by the recorder the jury found that the striking of R was purely accidental and not such a consequence of the blow as the prisoner ought to have expected to follow. They also found that the blow was unlawful and malicious. L was found guilty of unlawful and malicious wounding.

LORD COLERIDGE CJ

We are of opinion that this conviction must be sustained. It is common knowledge that a man who has an unlawful and malicious intent against another, and, in attempting to carry it out, injures a third person, is guilty of what the law deems malice against the person injured, because the offender is doing an unlawful act, and has that which the judges call general malice, and that is enough . . . So, but for *R. v Pembliton* (above), there would not have been the slightest difficulty. Does that case make any difference? I think not, and, on consideration, that it was quite rightly decided. But it is clearly distinguishable, because the indictment in *R. v Pembliton* was on the Act making unlawful and malicious injury to property a statutory offence punishable in a certain way, and the jury expressly negatived, the facts expressly negatived, any intention to do injury to property, and the court held that under the Act making it an offence to injure any property there must be an intent to injure property. *R. v Pembliton*, therefore, does not govern the present case, and on no other ground is there anything to be said for the prisoner.

Conviction affirmed

(See also *R. v Mitchell* [1983] 2 W.L.R. 938.)

Question

If the facts of *Pembliton* recurred today with what offence(s) could he be charged?

Note

The Law Commission in *Legislating the Criminal Code: Offences Against the Person and General Principles* favours the retention of transferred fault. In the article which follows the author argues that the doctrine of "transferred fault" is misconceived providing a solution to a perceived problem which does not truly arise if the principles of actus reus and mens rea are understood and applied.

I.H.E. PATIENT, "TRANSFERRED MALICE—A MISLEADING MISNOMER" (1990) 54 J.C.L. 116–124

Assume that X aims a shot at A, intending to kill A. The shot misses the intended victim, but hits and kills B instead. There are two ways of looking at this situation.

The first approach is based on the notion that one must distinguish between a 'killing of victim A' and a 'killing of victim B'. As to A, the intended killing did not succeed. Hence, there might be a charge of attempted murder. As to B, there was no intention to kill 'B', hence no murder of B. However, a lesser form of homicide, namely manslaughter, might be given, either in the form of constructive manslaughter (the unlawful act need not be directed against the eventual victim) or in the form of reckless killing (if B stood close to A there would be at least an obvious risk that B might be hit).

Alternatively, one might ignore the particular identity of the victim. The *actus reus* of homicide is not the 'killing of A' or the 'killing of B', but in more general terms the 'killing of a human being'. Accordingly, the required intention is that of 'killing a human being'. On that basis, X, in our example, has committed a murder of B, for he killed a human being (namely B) and he did so with the required intention of killing a human being (namely A). This second, more streamlined, solution is capable of avoiding certain practical difficulties, especially of proof, and moreover represents, it is submitted, the more correct approach in principle, provided it is clearly seen as resting on the application of the general principles of *actus reus* and *mens rea*. Unfortunately, it is often rationalised in a different manner, namely as an instance of so called 'transferred malice'. In other words, the case is seen as one where the intention to kill victim A is 'transferred' to victim B. Such a view must be based on the assumption that the *mens rea* for murder is the killing (or causing of grievous bodily harm) to a particular victim, namely, in our case, an 'intention to kill A' as opposed to an 'intention to kill B', so that the required intention can then be 'transferred' from one victim to the other. This kind of thinking seems to be, consciously or otherwise, influenced by a preoccupation with the form of the indictment, where, of course, the particular victim is referred to. Now that the principles of *actus reus* and *mens rea* have become more clearly established, not least as the direct and indirect result of increasing codification, such a misleading way of thinking must be challenged, in order to curb the creation of avoidable difficulties. Significantly, one of the early leading cases, *R. v Latimer* [above, p.140], which is often relied upon as an authority for the notion of transferred malice, in fact rejects that concept and adopts the approach described above of simply applying the principles of *actus reus* and *mens rea*. The facts of the case were these: the prisoner, X, aimed a blow at A with his belt. The belt bounded off and struck B, who stood close by, and caused wounds to her (B's) face. X was convicted under section 20 of the Offences Against the Person Act 1861. An appeal was taken on the ground that X could not be guilty of injuring B, as he did not intend to injure her.

This argument could only be conceived on the implied assumption that the offence in question was the wounding of a particular victim, namely B, as opposed to the wounding of another victim, A. The court made short shrift of this idea. The *actus reus* of the offence in section 20 is the inflicting of grievous bodily harm upon *any other person* and the prisoner had the necessary *general malice*. It was, therefore, not a question of establishing an intention to injure a particular victim, which would then be 'transferred' to another victim. Rather, the accused had the necessary 'general' *metis rea* of intending to inflict grievous bodily harm upon any (other) person. Whether that person was A or B, was irrelevant . . .

To summarise the argument so far: In the cases under discussion, the original plan misfires in that a target, other than that envisaged, is affected . . . Whether there is liability concerning the substituted target, turns solely on whether the necessary *mens rea* relating to the *actus reus* in question, is given. There is no transfer of any kind involved. If the *actus reus* is described as the 'wounding of any other person' (s.20 Offences Against the Person Act 1861), then an intention to wound another person constitutes the required *mens rea*, irrespective of whether the intention relates to a person called 'A' or 'B'. To use the terminology of the new Draft Criminal Code Bill, A, as much as B, is 'capable of being the victim of the offence', since he is capable of coming under the description 'any other person'. Hence, if X, intending to wound A, wounds B by mistake, X can be guilty of wounding B. He wounds another person and he intends to do so. Both *actus reus* and *mens rea* of the relevant offence are given. Anyone who sees this as involving a transfer, can do so only on the basis of a distorted, artificially narrowed view of *mens rea*. He must assume that section 20 requires an 'intention to wound B' as opposed to an 'intention to wound A', so that, B having actually been injured in place of A, the intention relating to A can be 'transferred' to B. That, as has been explained above, is *not* the approach in the relevant cases. By way of contrast, let it be assumed that B, the substitute-victim in our example, is a police constable and that X is charged with assaulting a constable in the execution of his duty under section 51(1) of the Police Act 1964. X's intention to assault a non-policeman, A, cannot—it is submitted—constitute the necessary *mens rea* for the charge. For the *actus reus* in section 51 requires not 'any person', but 'a constable' and A, not being a constable, is in the words of clause 24 of the Draft Code, not capable of being the victim of the offence in section 51. Thus, it is entirely a matter of testing the *mens rea* against the wording of the relevant *actus reus*. To see this as a situation where a 'transfer from one victim to another is impossible' would be inappropriate and distorting. The victim of the offence in section 51 cannot be A in the first place.

Note

In the case which follows the doctrine of transferred malice arose for consideration in a novel way.

ATTORNEY GENERAL'S REFERENCE (NO.3 OF 1994)

[1998] A.C. 245 HL

B stabbed his pregnant girlfriend in the abdomen. No injury to the foetus was detected. Subsequently the child was born prematurely and it was discovered that she had received a wound while in the womb. The child died subsequently not from the knife wound but due to complications arising from her premature birth. B was charged with murder. The trial judge directed an acquittal on the ground that no conviction for either murder or manslaughter was possible in law. The Attorney General referred the matter to the Court of Appeal which, applying the doctrine of transferred malice, arrived at a contrary conclusion to that of the trial judge holding that murder or manslaughter could be committed where unlawful injury is deliberately inflicted either to a child in utero or to a mother carrying a child in utero where the child was subsequently born alive, existed independently of the mother and then died, the injuries in utero either having caused or made a substantial contribution to the death. The requisite intent which had to be proved in the case of murder is an intention to kill or to cause really serious bodily injury to the mother, the foetus before birth being viewed as an integral part of the mother. The case, at B's request, was referred to the House of Lords.

LORD MUSTILL

[His Lordship stated five rules which, regardless of their justice or logic, are undeniable features of the criminal law.]

1. *It is sufficient to raise a prima facie case of murder (subject to entire or partial excuses such as self-defence or provocation) for it to be proved that the defendant did the act which caused the death intending to kill the victim or to cause him at least grievous bodily harm . . . .*

2. *If the defendant does an act with the intention of causing a particular kind of harm to X, and unintentionally does that kind of harm to Y, then the intent to harm X may be added to the harm actually done to Y in deciding whether the defendant has committed a crime towards Y . . . .*

3. *Except under statute an embryo or foetus in utero cannot be the victim of a crime of violence. In particular, violence to the foetus which causes its death in utero is not a murder . . .*

4. *The existence of an interval of time between the doing of an act by the defendant with the necessary wrongful intent and its impact on the victim in a manner which leads to death does not in itself prevent the intent, the act and the death from together amounting to murder, so long as there is an unbroken causal connection between the act and the death . . ..*

5. *Violence towards a foetus which results in harm suffered after the baby has been born alive can give rise to criminal responsibility even if the harm would not have been criminal (apart from statute) if it had been suffered in utero . . ..*

[His Lordship went on to reject the proposition accepted by the Court of Appeal that a foetus is part of the mother concluding that a foetus is a separate organism to which existing principles could not necessarily be applied. His Lordship also expressed his dislike of the rule that an intent to cause grievous bodily harm is sufficient mens rea for murder albeit that the rule was too long established for the House of Lords to abolish it.]

I turn to the second rule, of 'transferred malice.' For present purposes this is more important and more difficult. Again, one must look at its origins to see whether they provide a theme which can be applied today. Three of them are familiar. [The first] explanation of [the rule is] founded on the notion of risk. The person who committed a crime took the chance that the outcome would be worse than he expected . . ..

Secondly, there is the reversed burden of proof whereby the causing of death is prima facie murder, unless it falls within one of the extenuating categories recognised by the institutional writers. Again, this concept is long out of date. Nobody could seriously think of using it to make new law.

Thirdly, there was the idea of 'general malice,' of an evil disposition existing in the general and manifesting itself in the particular, uniting the aim of the offender and the result which his deeds actually produced. According to this theory, there was no need to 'transfer' the wrongful intent from the intended to the actual victim; for since the offender was . . . 'an enemy to all mankind in general,' the actual victim was the direct object of the offender's enmity. Plainly, this will no longer do, for the last vestiges of the idea disappeared with the abolition of the murder/felony doctrine.

What explanation is left: for explanation there must be, since the 'transferred malice' concept is agreed on both sides to be sound law today?

[His Lordship discussed the cases of *Pembliton*, above, and *Latimer*, above.]

My Lords, I find it hard to base a modern law of murder on these two cases. The court in *R. v Latimer* was, I believe, entirely justified in finding a distinction between their statutory backgrounds and one can well accept that the answers given, one for acquittal, the other for conviction, would be the same today. But the harking back to a concept of general malice, which amounts to no more than this, that a wrongful act displays a malevolence which can be attached to any adverse consequence, has long been out of date. And to speak of a particular malice which is 'transferred' simply disguises the problem by idiomatic language. The defendant's malice is directed at one objective, and when after the event the court treats it as directed at another object it is not recognising a 'transfer' but creating a new malice which never existed before. As Dr. Glanville Williams pointed out (*Criminal Law: The General Part*, 2nd ed. (1961), p.184) the doctrine is 'rather an arbitrary exception to general principles.' Like many of its kind this is useful enough to yield rough justice, in particular cases, and it can sensibly be retained notwithstanding its lack of any sound intellectual basis. But it is another matter to build a new rule upon it . . ..

I turn to deal more briefly with the remaining rules. The third rule, it will be recalled, is that a foetus cannot be the victim of murder. I see no profit in an attempt to treat the medieval origins of this rule. It is sufficient to say that is established beyond doubt for the criminal law, as for the civil law (*Burton v Islington Health Authority* [1993] Q.B. 204) that the child en ventre sa mére does not have a distinct human personality, whose extinguishment gives rise to any penalties or liabilities at common law.

The fourth rule is an exception to the generally accepted principle that actus reus and mens rea must coincide. A continuous act or continuous chain of causes leading to death is treated by the law as if it happened when first initiated. The development of this into the fifth rule, which links an act and intent before birth with a death happening after a live delivery, causes a little more strain, given the incapacity of the foetus to be the object of homicide. If, however, it is possible to interpret the situation as one where the mental element is directed, not to the foetus but to the human being when and if it comes into existence, no fiction is required.

My Lords, the purpose of this inquiry has been to see whether the existing rules are based on principles sound enough to justify their extension to a case where the defendant acts without an intent to injure either the foetus or the child which it will become. In my opinion they are not. To give an affirmative answer requires a double 'transfer' of intent: first from the mother to the foetus and then from the foetus to the child as yet unborn. Then one would have to deploy the fiction (or at least the doctrine) which converts an intention to commit serious harm into the mens rea of murder. For me, this is too much. If one could find any logic in the rules I would follow it from one fiction to another, but whatever grounds there may once have been have long since disappeared. I am willing to follow old laws until they are overturned, but not to make a new law on a basis for which there is no principle.

Moreover, even on a narrower approach the argument breaks down. The effect of transferred malice, as I understand it, is that the intended victim and the actual victim are treated as if they were one, so that what was intended to happen to the first person (but did not happen) is added to what actually did happen to the second person (but was not intended to happen), with the result that what was intended and what happened are married to make a notionally intended and actually consummated crime. The cases are treated as if the actual victim had been the intended victim from the start. To make any sense of this process there must, as it seems to me, be some compatibility between the original intention and the actual occurrence, and this is, indeed, what one finds in the cases. There is no such compatibility here. The defendant intended to commit and did commit an immediate crime of violence to the mother. He committed no relevant violence to the foetus, which was not a person, either at the time or in the future, and intended no harm to the foetus or to the human person which it would become. If fictions are useful, as they can be, they are only damaged by straining them beyond their limits. I would not overstrain the idea of transferred malice by trying to make it fit the present case.

Accordingly, . . . on the presumed facts the judge was right to direct an acquittal on the count of murder.

[His Lordship, adopting the reasoning of Lord Hope of Craighead, went on to conclude that had the trial judge directed the jury on the question of manslaughter, B could have been convicted without the need to resort to the doctrine of transferred malice.]

LORD HOPE OF CRAIGHEAD

. . . It was submitted that, since the foetus was not at the time of the unlawful act a living person, the offence of manslaughter could not be committed; and that, in any event, what constitutes a 'dangerous act' for the purposes of the law of manslaughter has always been defined by reference to what all sober and reasonable people would recognise was dangerous towards persons who were alive when the danger manifests itself . . . For the foetus, life lies in the future, not the past. It is not sensible to say that it cannot ever be harmed, or that nothing can be done to it which can ever be dangerous. Once it is born it is exposed, like all other living persons, to the risk of injury. It may also carry with it the effects of things done to it before birth which, after birth, may prove to be harmful. It would seem not to be unreasonable therefore, on public policy grounds, to regard the child in this case, when she became a living person, as within the scope of the mens rea which B. had when he stabbed her mother before she was born . . . .

I think, then, that the position can be summarised in this way. The intention which must be discovered is an intention to do an act which is unlawful and dangerous. In this case the act which had to be shown to be an unlawful and dangerous act was the stabbing of the child's mother. There can be no doubt that all sober and reasonable people would regard that act, within the appropriate meaning of this term, as dangerous. It is plain that it was unlawful as it was done with the intention of causing her injury. As B. intended to commit that act, all the ingredients necessary for mens rea in regard to the crime of manslaughter were established, irrespective of who was the ultimate victim of it. The fact that the child whom the mother was carrying at the time was born alive and then died as a result of the stabbing is all that was needed for the offence of manslaughter when actus reus for that crime was completed by the child's death. The question, once all the other elements are satisfied, is simply one of causation. The defendant must accept all the consequences of his act, so long as the jury are satisfied that he did what he did intentionally, that what he did was unlawful and that, applying the correct test, it was also dangerous. The death of the child was unintentional, but the nature and quality of the act which caused it was such that it was criminal and therefore punishable. In my opinion that is sufficient for the offence of manslaughter. There is no need to look to the doctrine of transferred malice for a solution to the problem raised by this case so far as manslaughter is concerned.

Questions

1. Is the doctrine of transferred malice based on the fact that the difference between the way in which the actus reus occurred and the way D intended it to occur is immaterial, or is it, as Lord Mustill believes, based on a fiction?

2. Lord Mustill stated with regard to *Pembliton* and *Latimer* that he found it "hard to base a modern law of murder on these two cases". Is the law of murder based on them?

3. Lord Mustill expressed dislike for both the doctrine of transferred malice and the rule that intent to cause grievous bodily harm is sufficient mens rea for murder if the victim dies. Had B intended to kill his pregnant girlfriend and the baby had been born alive but died subsequently due to injuries she had sustained in the stabbing of her mother, would Lord Mustill have countenanced a conviction of B for murder of the baby?

4. Is the outcome that B could be convicted of manslaughter but not murder not incongruous where B had the mens rea for murder, a human being was killed as a result of his acts, and the killing was accepted by their Lordships as being an unlawful homicide?

----

4. STRICT LIABILITY

If mens rea or negligence need not be proved in respect of one or more elements of the actus reus of an offence, that offence is one of strict liability. JUSTICE, the British Section of the International Commission of Jurists, estimated that of the 7,200 separate offences listed in *Stones Justices' Manual* for 1975, over half did not require proof of a mental element. (JUSTICE, *Breaking the Rules* (London, 1980)).

i. The evolution of strict liability

SAYRE, "PUBLIC WELFARE OFFENCES" (1933) 33 COL.L.R. 55

The growth of a distinct group of offences punishable without regard to any mental element dates from about the middle of the nineteenth century. Before this, convictions for crime without proof of a *mens rea* are to be found only occasionally, chiefly among the nuisance cases. In the early days newspaper proprietors might also be punished . . . for libel without proof of *mens rea*, for in libel prosecutions actual criminal knowledge on the part of the owners or publishers of newspapers would often be a matter so difficult to ascertain as to make proof well-nigh impossible. Yet to treat as criminal newspaper owners who were altogether innocent of any criminal intent seemed so harsh and unjust a doctrine and so out of accord with established legal principles that in 1836 an act of Parliament was passed to make this no longer possible [Lord Campbell's Act: s.7 allowed a newspaper proprietor to escape liability by proving that the publication was made 'without his authority, consent or knowledge.'] But apart from exceptional isolated cases criminal liability depended upon proof of a criminal intent . . .

The decisions permitting convictions of light police offences without proof of a guilty mind came just at the time when the demands of an increasingly complex social order required additional regulation of an administrative character unrelated to questions of personal guilt; the movement also synchronised with the trend of the day away from nineteenth century individualism toward a new sense of the importance of collective interests. The result was almost inevitable. The doctrine first evolved in the adulterated food and liquor cases came to be recognized as a special class of offence for which no *metis rea* was required . . . The interesting fact that the same development took place in both England and the United States at about the same time strongly indicates that the movement has been not merely an historical accident but the result of the changing social conditions and beliefs of the day . . .

The problem is how to draw the line between those offences which do and those which do not require *mens rea*. Clearly, it will not depend on whether the crime happens to be a common law or statutory offence . . . Some courts have suggested that the line depends upon the distinction between *mala in se* and *mala prohibita*; and this seems to depend essentially upon whether or not the offence is inherently immoral. But this also is . . . unsound . . . Many offences which are held not to require proof of *mens rea* are highly immoral; and many requiring it are not inherently immoral at all . . .

Neither can the dividing line be drawn according to the gravity or the lightness of the offence. Petty larceny is a much lighter and less dangerous offence than selling narcotics or poisoned food, yet the former requires *mens rea* and the latter not . . .

How then can one determine practically which offences do and which do not require *mens rea*, when the statute creating the offence is . . . silent?

. . . [T]wo cardinal principles stand out upon which the determination must turn.

The first relates to the character of the offence. All criminal enactments in a sense serve the double purpose of singling out wrongdoers for the purpose of punishment or correction and of regulating the social order. But often the importance of the one far outweighs the other . . .

The second criterion depends upon the possible penalty. If this be serious . . . the individual interest of the defendant weighs too heavily to allow conviction without proof of a guilty mind Crimes punishable with prison sentences, therefore, ordinarily require proof of a guilty intent.

ii. Identifying offences of strict liability

If Parliament did its job properly there should never be any room for doubt whether or not an offence is one of strict liability. However, many offences are created without there being a clear indication whether liability is to be strict or whether the absence of words which impose a requirement of proving mens rea is simply the result of oversight. Sometimes Parliament makes its intention clear as in the provision which follows.

CONTEMPT OF COURT ACT 1981

Strict liability

1. In this Act 'the strict liability rule' means the rule of law whereby conduct may be treated as a contempt of court as tending to interfere with the course of justice in particular legal proceedings regardless of intent to do so.

2.—(1) The strict liability rule applies only in relation to publications, and for this purpose 'publication' includes any speech, writing, . . . or other communication in whatever form, which is addressed to the public at large or any section of the public.

(2) The strict liability rule applies only to a publication which creates a substantial risk that the course of justice in the proceedings in question will be seriously impeded or prejudiced.

(3) The strict liability rule applies to a publication only if the proceedings in question are active within the meaning of this section at the time of the publication.

(4) Schedule 1 applies for determining the times at which proceedings are to be treated as active within the meaning of this section.

Defence of innocent publication or distribution

3.—(1) A person is not guilty of contempt of court under the strict liability rule as the publisher of any matter to which that rule applies if at the time of publication (having taken all reasonable care) he does not know and has no reason to suspect that relevant proceedings are active.

(2) A person is not guilty of contempt of court under the strict liability rule as the distributor of a publication containing any such matter if at the time of distribution (having taken all reasonable care) he does not know that it contains such matter and has no reason to suspect that it is likely to do so.

(3) The burden of proof of any fact tending to establish a defence afforded by this section to any person lies upon that person.

In the absence of such express language courts when interpreting penal provisions have to discover the intention of Parliament. Certain factors or considerations may assist the courts in this exercise. However, the weight to be attributed to any factor is more difficult to assess with the result that it is very difficult to predict how a court will construe a particular provision.

(1) The presumption of mens rea

SWEET V PARSLEY

[1970] A.C. 132 HL

Miss Sweet, a teacher, let rooms in a farmhouse to students. She did not reside in the farmhouse but retained one room for her own use for occasional overnight stays when she visited to collect the rent and check the property. After the police had searched the premises, finding evidence that cannabis had been smoked there, Miss Sweet was convicted by magistrates of being concerned in the management of premises which were used for the purpose of smoking cannabis, contrary to s.5(b) of the Dangerous Drugs Act 1965. The magistrates found that Miss Sweet did not exercise any control over her tenants and that she had no knowledge that the house was being used for the purpose of smoking cannabis. Her appeal to the Divisional Court was dismissed and she appealed to the House of Lords.

LORD REID

A Divisional Court dismissed her appeal, holding that she had been concerned in the management of those premises. The reasons given for holding that she was managing the property were that she was in a position to choose her tenants: that she could put them under as long or as short a tenancy as she desired and that she could make it a term of any letting that smoking of cannabis was not to take place. All these reasons would apply to every occupier who lets out parts of his house or takes in lodgers or paying guests. But this was held to be an absolute offence following the earlier decision in *Yeandel v Fisher* [1966] 1 Q.B. 440.

How has it come about that the Divisional Court has felt bound to reach such an obviously unjust result? It has in effect held that it was carrying out the will of Parliament because Parliament has chosen to make this an absolute offence. And, of course, if Parliament has so chosen the courts must carry out its will, and they cannot be blamed for any unjust consequences. But has Parliament so chosen?

I dealt with this matter at some length in *Warner v Metropolitan Police Commissioner* [1969] 2 A.C. 256. On reconsideration I see no reason to alter anything which I there said. But I think that some amplification is necessary. Our first duty is to consider the words of the Act: if they show a clear intention to create an absolute offence that is an end of the matter. But such cases are very rare. Sometimes the words of the section which creates a particular offence make it clear that *mens rea* is required in one form or another. Such cases are quite frequent. But in a very large number of cases there is no clear indication either way. In such cases there has for centuries been a presumption that Parliament did not intend to make criminals of persons who were in no way blameworthy in what they did. That means that whenever a section is silent as to *mens rea* there is a presumption that, in order to give effect to the will of Parliament, we must read in words appropriate to require *mens rea*. . . [I]t is firmly established by a host of authorities that *mens rea* is an essential ingredient of every offence unless some reason can be found for holding that that is not necessary.

It is also firmly established that the fact that other sections of the Act expressly require *mens rea*, for example because they contain the word 'knowingly' is not in itself sufficient to justify a decision that a section which is silent as to *mens rea* creates an absolute offence. In the absence of a clear indication in the Act that an offence is intended to be an absolute offence, it is necessary to go outside the Act and examine all relevant circumstances in order to establish that this must have been the intention of Parliament. I say 'must have been' because it is a universal principle that if a penal provision is reasonably capable of two interpretations, that interpretation which is most favourable to the accused must be adopted.

What, then, are the circumstances which it is proper to take into account? In the well-known case of *Sherras v. De Rutzen* [below], Wright J. only mentioned the subject-matter with which the Act deals. But he was there dealing with something which was one of a class of acts which 'are not criminal in any real sense, but are acts which in the public interest are prohibited under a penalty.' It does not in the least follow that when one is dealing with a truly criminal act it is sufficient merely to have regard to the subject-matter of the enactment. One must put oneself in the position of a legislator. It has long been the practice to recognise absolute offences in this class of quasi-criminal acts, and one can safely assume that, when Parliament is passing new legislation dealing with this class of offences, its silence as to *mens rea* means that the old practice is to apply. But when one comes to acts of a truly criminal character, it appears to me that there are at least two other factors which any reasonable legislator would have in mind. In the first place a stigma still attaches to any person convicted of a truly criminal offence, and the more serious or more disgraceful the offence the greater the stigma. So he would have to consider whether, in a case of this gravity, the public interest really requires that an innocent person should be prevented from proving his innocence in order that fewer guilty men may escape. And equally important is the fact that fortunately the Press in this country are vigilant to expose injustice and every manifestly unjust conviction made known to the public tends to injure the body politic by undermining public confidence in the justice of the law and of its administration. But I regret to observe that, in some recent cases where serious offences have been held to be absolute offences, the court has taken into account no more than the wording of the Act and the character and seriousness of the mischief which constitutes the offence.

The choice would be much more difficult if there were no other way open than either *mens rea* in the full sense or an absolute offence; for there are many kinds of case where putting on the prosecutor the full burden of proving *mens rea* creates great difficulties and may lead to many unjust acquittals. But there are at least two other possibilities. Parliament has not infrequently transferred the onus as regards *mens rea* to the accused so that, once the necessary facts are proved, he must convince the jury that on balance of probabilities he is innocent of any criminal intention. I find it a little surprising that more use has not been made of this method: but one of the bad effects of the decision of this House in *Woolmington v D.P.P* [1935] A.C. 462 may have been to discourage its use. The other method would be in effect to substitute in appropriate classes of cases gross negligence for *mens rea* in the full sense as the mental element necessary to constitute the crime. It would often be much easier to infer that Parliament must have meant that gross negligence should be the necessary mental element than to infer that Parliament intended to create an absolute offence. A variant of this would be to accept the view of Cave J. in *R. v Tolson* [above p.125]. This appears to have been done in Australia where authority appears to support what Dixon J. said in *Proudman v Dayman* (1941) 67 C.L.R. 536, 540: 'As a general rule an honest and reasonable belief in a state of facts which, if they existed, would make the defendant's act innocent affords an excuse for doing what would otherwise be an offence.' It may be that none of these methods is wholly satisfactory but at least the public scandal of convicting on a serious charge persons who are in no way blameworthy would be avoided.

If this section means what the Divisional Court have held that it means, then hundreds of thousands of people who sublet part of the premises or take in lodgers or are concerned in the management of residential premises or institutions are daily incurring a risk of being convicted of a serious offence in circumstances where they are in no way to blame. For the greatest vigilance cannot prevent tenants, lodgers or inmates or guests whom they bring in from smoking cannabis cigarettes in their own rooms. It was suggested in argument that this appellant brought this conviction on herself *because it is found as a* fact that when the police searched the premises there were people there of the 'beatnik fraternity'. But surely it would be going a very long way to say that persons managing premises of any kind ought to safeguard themselves by refusing accommodation to all who are of slovenly or exotic appearance or who bring in guests of that kind. And unfortunately drug taking is by no means confined to those of unusual appearance.

Speaking from a rather long experience of membership of both Houses, I assert with confidence that no Parliament within my recollection would have agreed to make an offence of this kind an absolute offence if the matter had been fully explained to it. So, if the court ought only to hold an offence to be an absolute offence where it appears that that must have been the intention of Parliament, offences of this kind are very far removed from those which it is proper to hold to be absolute offences.

I must now turn to the question what is the true meaning of section 5 of the 1965 Act . . . is the 'purpose' the purpose of the smoker or the purpose of the management? . . . It is clear that the purpose is the purpose of the management . . . So if the purpose is the purpose of the management, the question whether the offence . . . is absolute can hardly arise.

I would allow the appeal and quash the appellant's conviction.

LORD PEARCE

My Lords, the prosecution contend that any person who is concerned in the management of premises where cannabis is in fact smoked even once, is liable, though he had no knowledge and no guilty mind. This is, they argue, a practical act intended to prevent a practical evil. Only by convicting some innocents along with the guilty can sufficient pressure be put upon those who make their living by being concerned in the management of premises. Only thus can they be made alert to prevent cannabis being smoked there. And if the prosecution have to prove knowledge or mens rea, many prosecutions will fail and many of the guilty will escape. I find that argument wholly unacceptable.

The notion that some guilty mind is a constituent part of crime and punishment goes back far beyond our common law. And at common law mens rea is a necessary element in a crime. Since the Industrial Revolution the increasing complexity of life called into being new duties and crimes which took no account of intent. Those who undertake various industrial and other activities, especially where these affect the life and health of the citizen, may find themselves liable to statutory punishment regardless of knowledge or intent, both in respect of their own acts or neglect and those of their servants. But one must remember that normally mens rea is still an ingredient of any offence. Before the court will dispense with the necessity for mens rea it has to be satisfied that Parliament so intended. The mere absence of the word 'knowingly' is not enough. But the nature of the crime, the punishment, the absence of social obloquy, the particular mischief and the field of activity in which it occurs, and the wording of the particular section and its context, may show that Parliament intended that the act should be prevented by punishment regardless of intent or knowledge.

Viewing the matter on these principles, it is not possible to accept the prosecution's contention. Even granted that this were in the public health class of case, such as, for instance, are offences created to ensure that food shall be clean, it would be quite unreasonable. It is one thing to make a man absolutely responsible for all his own acts and even vicariously liable for his servants if he engages in a certain type of activity. But it is quite another matter to make him liable for persons over whom he has no control . . .

[His Lordship concluded that the "purpose" which had to be proved was that of the person concerned in the management of the premises. Since the appellant had no knowledge of the use being made of the premises, he concluded the appeal had to be allowed.]

Appeal allowed

[The Misuse of Drugs Act 1971 incorporated "knowingly" in this offence.]

Questions and Note

1. How is a court to distinguish between a "truly criminal" offence to which stigma attaches and "quasi-criminal" acts which are prohibited in the public interest? Would no stigma attach to a farmer whose leaking slurry tank pollutes a nearby river killing hundreds of salmon or to a butcher who sells meat unfit for human consumption if in each case the parties had acted with due vigilance?

2. Would a better solution to the position of stark choice between mens rea and strict liability be the middle ground of providing a "due diligence" defence for the accused to prove as in *Proudman v Dayman* (1941) 67 C.L.R. 536 and *R. v City of Sault Ste Marie* (1978) 85 D.L.R. (3d) 161. See also Misuse of Drugs Act 1971 ss.8 and 28.

3. Unlike the High Court of Australia in *Proudman v Dayman* and the Supreme Court of Canada in *R. v City of Sault Ste Marie*, English courts have not developed a general due diligence (or "no negligence") defence to offences of strict liability, although Lord Diplock did suggest in *Sweet v Parsley* that it might be possible at common law. However, Parliament often does provide for a due diligence defence: see e.g. Offices, Shops and Railway Premises Act 1963 s.67; Trade Descriptions Act 1968 s.24(3); Weights and Measures Act 1985 s.34. A refinement of the due diligence defence in many statutes is the imposition of the requirement that the accused not only prove due diligence but that he also prove that the contravention was due to the act or default of a third party: see e.g. Food Safety Act 1990 s.21(2); Medicines Act 1968 s.121. Some statutes merely require disclosure of the identity of the third party alleged to have been responsible for the contravention: see e.g. Consumer Safety Act 1978 s.2(6).

Note

The presumption of mens rea is merely the starting point in the courts' analysis of statutory provisions. In determining whether the presumption is to be upheld or rebutted in a particular instance the courts will look at other relevant factors.

----

(2) The statutory context

In construing a particular section of an Act courts may obtain assistance by considering the presence or absence of mens rea words in other sections of the Act and by determining the purpose of the provision in question.

CUNDY V LE COCQ

(1884) 13 Q.B.D. 207

C, a licensed victualler, sold liquor to a person who was drunk. C was unaware of the drunkenness, but he was nevertheless convicted of unlawfully selling liquor to a drunken person, contrary to s.13 of the Licensing Act 1872. C appealed to the Divisional Court.

STEPHEN J

I am of opinion that this conviction should be affirmed. Our answer to the question put to us turns upon this, whether the words of the section under which this conviction took place, taken in connection with the general scheme of the Act, should be read as constituting an offence only where the licensed person knows or has means of knowing that the person served with intoxicating liquor is drunk, or whether the offence is complete where no such knowledge is shown. I am of opinion that the words of the section amount to an absolute prohibition of the sale of liquor to a drunken person, and that the existence of a bona fide mistake as to the condition of the person served is not an answer to the charge, but is a matter only for mitigation of the penalties that may be imposed. I am led to that conclusion both by the general scope of the Act, which is for the repression of drunkenness, and from a comparison of the various sections under the head 'offences against public order'. Some of these contain the word 'knowingly', as for instance section 14, which deals with keeping a disorderly house, and section 16, which deals with the penalty for harbouring a constable. Knowledge in these and other cases is an element in the offence; but the clause we are considering says nothing about the knowledge of the state of the person served. I believe the reason for making this prohibition absolute was that there must be a great temptation to a publican to sell liquor without regard to the sobriety of the customer, and it was thought right to put upon the publican the responsibility of determining whether his customer is sober. Against this view we have had quoted the maxim that in every criminal offence there must be a guilty mind; but I do not think that maxim has so wide an application as it is sometimes considered to have. In old time and as applicable to the common law or to earlier statutes, the maxim may have been of general application; but a difference has arisen owing to the greater precision of modern statutes. It is impossible now, as illustrated by the cases of *R. v Prince* and *R. v Bishop* (1880) 5 Q.B.D. 259, to apply the maxim generally to all statutes, and the substance of all the reported cases is that it is necessary to look at the object of each Act that is under consideration to see whether and how far knowledge is of the essence of the offence created. Here, as I have already pointed out, the object of this part of the Act is to prevent the sale of intoxicating liquor to drunken persons, and it is perfectly natural to carry that out by throwing on the publican the responsibility of determining whether the person supplied comes within that category.

I think, therefore, the conviction was right and must be affirmed.

Conviction affirmed

SHERRAS V DE RUTZEN

[1895] 1 Q.B. 918

S, a licensed victualler, was convicted under s.16(2) of the Licensing Act 1872, for having unlawfully supplied liquor to a police constable on duty without having the authority of a superior officer of such constable for so doing. S reasonably believed that the constable was off duty. He appealed to quarter sessions and thence to the Divisional Court.

DAY J

I am clearly of opinion that this conviction ought to be quashed. This police constable comes into the appellant's house without his armlet, and with every appearance of being off duty. The house was in the immediate neighbourhood of the police-station, and the appellant believed, and he had very natural grounds for believing, that the constable was off duty. In that belief he accordingly served him with liquor. As a matter of fact, the constable was on duty—but does that fact make the innocent act of the appellant an offence? I do not think it does. He had no intention to do a wrongful act; he acted in the bona fide belief that the constable was off duty. It seems to me that the contention that he committed an offence is utterly erroneous. An argument has been based on the appearance of the word 'knowingly' in subsection (1) of section 16, and its omission in subsection (2). In my opinion the only effect of this is to shift the burden of proof. In cases under subsection (1) it is for the prosecution to prove the knowledge, while in cases under subsection (2) the defendant has to prove that he did not know. That is the only inference I draw from the insertion of the word 'knowingly' in the one subsection and its omission in the other.

It appears to me that it would be straining the law to say that this publican, acting as he did in the bona fide belief that the constable was off duty, and having reasonable grounds for that belief, was nevertheless guilty of an offence against the section for which he was liable both to a penalty and to have his licence indorsed.

WRIGHT J

I am of the same opinion. There are many cases on the subject, and it is not very easy to reconcile them. There is a presumption that *mens rea*, an evil intention, or a knowledge of the wrongfulness of the act, is an essential ingredient in every offence; but that presumption is liable to be displaced either by the words of the statute creating the offence or by the subject-matter with which it deals, and both must be considered: *Nichols v Hall* (1873) L.R. 8 C.P. 322. One of the most remarkable exceptions was in the case of bigamy. It was held by all the judges, on the statute 1 Jac. 1, c. 11, that a man was rightly convicted of bigamy who had married after an invalid Scotch divorce, which had been obtained in good faith, and the validity of which he had no reason to doubt: *Lolly's Case* (1812) R. & R. 237. Another exception, apparently grounded on the language of a statute, is *Prince's Case* (1875) L.R. 2 C.C.R. 154, where it was held by 15 judges against one that a man was guilty of abduction of a girl under 16, although he believed, in good faith and on reasonable grounds, that she was over that age. Apart from isolated and extreme cases of this kind, the principal classes of exceptions may perhaps be reduced to three. One is a class of acts which, in the language of Lush J. in *Davies v Harvey* (1874) L.R. 9 Q.B. 433, are not criminal in any real sense, but are acts which in the public interest are prohibited under a penalty . . . Another class comprehends some, and perhaps all, public nuisances . . . Lastly, there are many cases in which, although the proceeding is criminal in form, it is really only a summary mode of enforcing a civil right . . . But, except in such cases as these, there must in general be guilty knowledge on the part of the defendant, or of someone whom he has put in his place to act for him, generally, or in the particular matter, in order to constitute an offence. It is plain that if guilty knowledge is not necessary, no care on the part of the publican could save him from a conviction under section 16, subsection (2), since it would be as easy for the constable to deny that he was on duty when asked, or to produce a forged permission from his superior officer, as to remove his armlet before entering the public-house. I am, therefore, of opinion that this conviction ought to be quashed.

Conviction quashed

Question

Do the two cases above represent a conflict of authority, as Glanville Williams suggests in *Criminal Law: The General Part* (1961), p.223? Or can a rationale be found in the distinction between the risk of serving a drunk, and that of serving a constable on duty?

Note

In the case that follows, the discussion centres on s.1(1) of the Indecency with Children Act 1960, together with the Sexual Offences Act 1956. These were repealed and replaced by the Sexual Offences Act 2003 (see Ch.9, below). On the central issue of the presumption of mens rea however, the decision (together with *R. v K* [2001] UKHL 41; [2001] 3 W.L.R. 471) remains the principal authority.

B (A MINOR) V DIRECTOR OF PUBLIC PROSECUTIONS

[2000] 2 W.L.R. 452 HL

B, aged 15, sat next to a girl aged 13 on a bus and asked her several times to perform oral sex with him which she refused to do. He was charged with inciting a girl under the age of 14 to commit an act of gross indecency with him, contrary to s.1(1) of the Indecency with Children Act 1960. B honestly believed the girl was over 14 but when the justices ruled that this was no defence to the charge he changed his plea to guilty. On a case stated by the justices, the Divisional Court of the Queen's Bench Division dismissed B's appeal. The Divisional Court certified, inter alia, that the following point of law of general public importance was involved in its decision, namely, "Is a defendant entitled to be acquitted of the offence of inciting a child aged under 14 to commit an act of gross indecency . . . if he may hold an honest belief that the child in question was aged 14 years or over?"

LORD NICHOLLS OF BIRKENHEAD

[His Lordship referred to the common law presumption that mens rea is an essential ingredient of an offence unless Parliament has indicated the contrary intention either expressly or by necessary implication.]

The question, therefore, is whether, although not expressly negatived, the need for a mental element is negatived by necessary implication. 'Necessary implication' connotes an implication which is compellingly clear. Such an implication may be found in the language used, the nature of the offence, the mischief sought to be prevented and any other circumstances which may assist in determining what intention is properly to be attributed to Parliament when creating the offence.

I venture to think that there is no great difficulty in this case. The section created an entirely new criminal offence, in simple unadorned language. The offence so created is a serious offence. The more serious the offence, the greater is the weight to be attached to the presumption, because the more severe is the punishment and the graver the stigma which accompany a conviction. Under section 1 conviction originally attracted a punishment of up to two years' imprisonment. This has since been increased to a maximum of ten years' imprisonment. The notification requirements under Part I of the Sex Offenders Act 1997 now apply, no matter what the age of the offender: see Schedule 1, paragraph 1(1)(b). Further, in addition to being a serious offence, the offence is drawn broadly ('an act of gross indecency'). It can embrace conduct ranging from predatory approaches by a much older paedophile to consensual sexual experimentation between precocious teenagers of whom the offender may be the younger of the two. The conduct may be depraved by any acceptable standard, or it may be relatively innocuous behaviour in private between two young people. These factors reinforce, rather than negative, the application of the presumption in this case.

The purpose of the section is, of course, to protect children. An age ingredient was therefore an essential ingredient of the offence. This factor in itself does not assist greatly. Without more, this does not lead to the conclusion that liability was intended to be strict so far as the age element is concerned, so that the offence is committed irrespective of the alleged offender's belief about the age of the 'victim' and irrespective of how the offender came to hold this belief.

Nor can I attach much weight to a fear that it may be difficult sometimes for the prosecution to prove that the defendant knew the child was under fourteen or was recklessly indifferent about the child's age . . ..

Similarly, it is far from clear that strict liability regarding the age ingredient of the offence would further the purpose of section 1 more effectively than would be the case if a mental element were read into this ingredient. There is no general agreement that strict liability is necessary to the enforcement of the law protecting children in sexual matters. For instance, the draft criminal code bill prepared by the Law Commission in 1989 proposed a compromise solution. Clauses 114 and 115 of the bill provided for committing or inciting acts of gross indecency with children aged under thirteen or under sixteen. Belief that the child is over sixteen would be a defence in each case: see the Law Commission, Criminal Law, A Criminal Code for England and Wales, vol 1, Report and draft Criminal Code Bill, p.81 (Law Com. No.177).

Is there here a compellingly clear implication that Parliament should be taken to have intended that the ordinary common law requirement of a mental element should be excluded in respect of the age ingredient of this new offence? Thus far, having regard especially to the breadth of the offence and the gravity of the stigma and penal consequences which a conviction brings, I see no sufficient ground for so concluding.

Indeed, the Crown's argument before your Lordships did not place much reliance on any of the matters just mentioned. The thrust of the Crown's argument lay in a different direction: the statutory context. This is understandable, because the statutory background is undoubtedly the Crown's strongest point. The Crown submitted that the law in this field has been regarded as settled for well over one hundred years, ever since the decision in *Reg v Prince* (1875) L.R. 2 C.C.R. 154. That well known case concerned the unlawful abduction of a girl under the age of sixteen. The defendant honestly believed she was over sixteen, and he had reasonable grounds for believing this. No fewer than fifteen judges held that this provided no defence. Subsequently, in *R. v Maughan* (1934) 24 Cr.App.R. 130 the Court of Criminal Appeal (Lord Hewart C.J., Avory and Roche JJ.) held that a reasonable and honest belief that a girl was over sixteen could never be a defence to a charge of indecent assault. The court held that this point had been decided in *Rex v Forde* (1923) 17 Cr.App.R. 99. The court also observed that in any event the answer was to be found in *Prince*'s case. Building on this foundation Mr. Scrivener Q.C. submitted that the Sexual Offences Act 1956 was not intended to change this established law, and that section 1 of the Indecency with Children Act 1960 was to be read with the 1956 Act. The preamble to the 1960 Act stated that its purpose was to make 'further' provision for the punishment of indecent conduct towards young people. In this field, where Parliament intended belief as to age to be a defence, this was stated expressly: see, for instance, the 'young man's defence' in section 6(3) of the 1956 Act.

This is a formidable argument, but I cannot accept it . . .. Where the Crown's argument breaks down is that the motley collection of offences, of diverse origins, gathered into the Sexual Offences Act 1956 displays no satisfactorily clear or coherent pattern. If the interpretation of section 1 of the Act of 1960 is to be gleaned from the contents of another statute, that other statute must give compelling guidance. The Act of 1956 as a whole falls short of this standard. So do the two sections, sections 14 and 15, which were the genesis of section 1 of the Act of 1960.

Accordingly, I cannot find, either in the statutory context or otherwise, any indication of sufficient cogency to displace the application of the common law presumption. In my view the necessary mental element regarding the age ingredient in section 1 of the Act of 1960 is the absence of a genuine belief by the accused that the victim was fourteen years of age or above. The burden of proof of this rests upon the prosecution in the usual way. If Parliament considers that the position should be otherwise regarding this serious social problem, Parliament must itself confront the difficulties and express its will in clear terms. I would allow this appeal.

LORD STEYN

. . . [His Lordship examined the history of s.1(1) offence and the relationship of the Act of 1960 to the Sexual Offences Act 1956.]

The correct approach

My Lords, it will be convenient to turn to the approach to be adopted to the construction of section 1(1) of the Act of 1960. While broader considerations will ultimately have to be taken into account, the essential point of departure must be the words of section 1(1). The language is general and nothing on the face of section 1(1) indicates one way or the other whether section 1(1) creates an offence of strict liability. In enacting such a provision Parliament does not write on a blank sheet. The sovereignty of Parliament is the paramount principle of our constitution. But Parliament legislates against the background of the principle of legality. In *Reg. v Secretary of State for the Home Department, Ex parte Pierson* [1998] A.C. 539 many illustrations of the application of the principle were given in the speech of Lord Browne-Wilkinson and in my speech: 573G–575D, 587C–590A. Recently, in *Reg. v Secretary of State for the Home Department, Ex parte Simms* [1999] 3 W.L.R. 328 the House applied the principle to subordinate legislation: see in particular the speeches of Lord Hoffmann at p.341F–G, myself, at p.340G–H, and Lord Browne-Wilkinson, at p.330E. In *Ex parte Simms* Lord Hoffmann explained the principle as follows, at p.341:

'But the principle of legality means that Parliament must squarely confront what it is doing and accept the political cost. Fundamental rights cannot be overridden by general or ambiguous words. This is because there is too great a risk that the full implications of their unqualified meaning may have passed unnoticed in the democratic process. In the absence of express language or necessary implication to the contrary, the courts therefore presume that even the most general words were intended to be subject to the basic rights of the individual.'

This passage admirably captures, if I may so, the rationale of the principle of legality. In successive editions of his classic work Professor Sir Rupert Cross cited as the paradigm of the principle the '"presumption" that mens rea is required in the case of statutory crimes': *Statutory Interpretation* 3 ed. (1995), p.166. Sir Rupert explained that such presumptions are of general application and are not dependent on finding an ambiguity in the text. He said they

'not only supplement the text, they also operate at a higher level as expressions of fundamental principles governing both civil liberties and the relations between Parliament, the executive and the courts. They operate as constitutional principles which are not easily displaced by a statutory text.'

In other words, in the absence of express words or a truly necessary implication, Parliament must be presumed to legislate on the assumption that the principle of legality will supplement the text. This is the theoretical framework against which section 1(1) must be interpreted.

[His Lordship examined *Sweet v Parsley* placing emphasis on the speech of Lord Reid.]

Concentrating still on the wording of section 1(1) of the Act of 1960, I now address directly the question whether the presumption is prima facie applicable. Two distinctive features of section 1(1) must be taken in to account. First, the actus reus is widely defined. Unlike the position under sections 14 and 15 of the Act of 1956, an assault is not an ingredient of the offence under section 1(1). Any act of gross indecency with or towards a child under the age of 14, or incitement to such an act, whether committed in public or private, is within its scope. The subsection is apt to cover acts of paedophilia and all responsible citizens will welcome effective legislation in respect of such a great social evil. But it also covers any heterosexual or homosexual contact between teenagers if one of them is under 14. And the actus reus extends to incitement of a child under 14: words are enough. The subsection therefore extends to any verbal sexual overtures between teenagers if one of them is under 14: see the telling examples given by Brooke L.J. in the instant case [1999] 3 W.L.R. 116, 128H–129C. For the law to criminalise such conduct of teenagers *by offences of strict liability* would be far reaching and controversial. The second factor is that section 1(1) creates an offence of a truly criminal character. It was initially punishable on indictment by a custodial term of up to two years and by subsequent amendment the maximum term has been increased to ten years' imprisonment. Moreover, as Lord Reid observed in *Sweet v Parsley* (at 146H) 'a stigma still attaches to any person convicted of a truly criminal offence, and the more serious or more disgraceful the offence the greater the stigma.' Taking into account the cumulative effect of these two factors, I am persuaded that, if one concentrates on the language of section 1(1), the presumption is *prima facie* applicable.

[His Lordship examined the arguments of the Crown which sought to rebut the presumption but found no merit in them. He answered the certified question in the affirmative.]

Note

The Sexual Offences Act 2003 contains a number of offences that are intended to protect children from various forms of sexual abuse (see further Ch.9, below). For serious offences such as rape of a child under 13, sexual assault of a child under 13, and other similar offences, a child under 13 is presumed incapable of giving consent. It is clear that Parliament intended that liability in respect of the circumstance of the child's age should be strict and, accordingly, it should be no defence that D believed the child to be over 13.

A range of (relatively) less serious offences apply where the age of the child is over 13 but under 16 and here, D may plead as a defence that he *reasonably* believed the child to be over 16 at the relevant time (see ss.9 and 10). It is clear that liability is strict where the age of the child is under 13 but where the child is over 13, then D can defend himself by demonstrating his reasonably held belief that the child was over 16 at the relevant time. Another way of viewing this would be to say that negligence is required where D seeks to show that he reasonably believed the child to be over 16. In other words, D could not have a reasonable belief that the child was over 16 because he was negligent in reaching that conclusion. The sections are silent as to the mental element in respect of age. It might be argued that because the more serious offences relating to a child under 13 are strict, the less serious offences ought to be construed as requiring mens rea. The presumption of mens rea will only be displaced if the necessary implication for this result is compellingly clear. The overlap between the more serious and less serious offences would appear to militate against that conclusion. The outcome remains to be seen.

----

(3) The social context

Courts have sought to distinguish between offences which involve moral obloquy or stigma and those which do not. If an offence is of a regulatory nature it is more likely to fall into this latter category. In determining whether the presumption of mens rea has been rebutted, two factors are of particular relevance, namely (1) whether the offence is of general application to all members of the public or confined to a specific class of persons engaged in a particular activity, trade or profession, and (2) the nature of the social danger which the offence is aimed at preventing. If the offence applies only to a particular class of persons the courts will more readily hold the presumption has been rebutted. (See Lord Diplock's speech in *Sweet v Parsley*, above).

PHARMACEUTICAL SOCIETY OF GREAT BRITAIN V STORKWAIN LTD

[1986] 2 All E.R. 635 HL

The respondents brought information against the appellants alleging they were guilty of offences under s.58(2)(a) and s.67(2) of the Medicines Act 1968, having sold on prescription medicines to customers who had presented prescriptions which proved to be forgeries. The appellants believed in good faith and on reasonable grounds that the prescriptions were valid. The magistrates dismissed the information. The Divisional Court allowed the appeal of the respondents. The appellants appealed to the House of Lords.

LORD GOFF OF CHIEVELEY

My Lords, this appeal is concerned with a question of construction of section 58 of the Medicines Act 1968 . . . The Divisional Court certified the following point of law as being of general public importance:

'Whether the prosecution have to prove mens rea where an information is laid under Section 58(2)(a) of the Medicines Act 1968 where the allegation is that the supply of "prescription only" drugs was made by the [defendant] in accordance with a forged prescription and without fault on [his] part.'

. . . For the appellants, counsel submitted [*inter alia*] that there must, in accordance with the well-recognised presumption, be read into section 58(2)(a) words appropriate to require *mens rea* in accordance with *R. v Tolson* [above, p.130]; in other words, to adopt the language of Lord Diplock in *Sweet v Parsley* [1970] A.C. 132 at 163, the subsection must be read subject to the implication that a necessary element in the prohibition (and hence in the offence created by the subsection together with section 67(2) of the 1968 Act) is the absence of belief, held honestly and on reasonable grounds, in the existence of facts which, if true, would make the act innocent . . .

I am unable to accept counsel's submission, for the simple reason that it is, in my opinion, clear from the 1968 Act that Parliament must have intended that the presumption of *mens rea* should be inapplicable to section 58(2)(a). First of all, it appears from the 1968 Act that, where Parliament wished to recognise that *mens rea* should be an ingredient of an offence created by the Act, it has expressly so provided. Thus, taking first of all offences created under provisions of Pt. II of the 1968 Act, express requirements of *mens rea* are to be found both in section 45(2) and section 46(1), (2) and (3) of the Act. More particularly, in relation to offences created by Pt. III and Pts. V and VI of the 1968 Act, section 121 makes detailed provision for a requirement of *mens rea* in respect of certain specified sections of the act, including sections 63 to 65 (which are contained in Pt. III), but significantly not section 58, nor indeed sections 52 and 53 . . . It is very difficult to avoid the conclusion that, by omitting section 58 from those sections to which section 121 is expressly made applicable, Parliament intended that there should be no implication of a requirement of *mens rea* in section 58(2)(*a*). This view is fortified by subss. (4) and (5) of section 58 itself. Subsection (4) (*a*) provides that any order made by the appropriate ministers for the purposes of section 58 may provide that section 58(2)(*a*) or (*b*), or both, shall have effect subject to such exemptions as may be specified in the order. From this subsection alone it follows that the ministers, if they think it right, can provide for exemption where there is no *mens rea* on the part of the accused. Subsection (5) provides that any exemption conferred by an order in accordance with subsection (4)(*a*) may be conferred subject to such conditions or limitations as may be specified in the order. From this it follows that, if the ministers, acting under subs. (4), were to confer an exemption relating to sales where the vendor lacked the requisite *mens rea*, they may nevertheless circumscribe their exemption with conditions and limitations which render the exemption far narrower than the implication for which counsel for the appellants contends should be read into the statute itself. I find this to be very difficult to reconcile with the proposed implication.

It comes as no surprise to me, therefore, to discover that the relevant order in force at that time, the Medicines (Prescriptions Only) Order 1980, is drawn entirely in conformity with the construction of the statute which I favour . . .

For these reasons, which are substantially the same as those which are set out in the judgments of Farquharson and Tudor Price JJ. in the Divisional Court, I am unable to accept the submissions advanced on behalf of the appellants. I gratefully adopt as my own the following passage from the judgment of Farquharson J. ([1985] 3 All E.R. 4 at 10):

'. . . it is perfectly obvious that pharmacists are in a position to put illicit drugs and perhaps other medicines on the market. Happily this rarely happens but it does from time to time. It can therefore be readily understood that Parliament would find it necessary to impose a heavier liability on those who are in such a position, and make them more strictly accountable for any breaches of the Act.'

I would therefore answer the certified question in the negative, and dismiss the appeal with costs.

Certified question answered in negative.
Appeal dismissed

Questions

1.   What measures would it be necessary for pharmacists to adopt to ensure that drugs were not dispensed on a forged prescription and would any such measures be practicable?

2. If the purpose of the legislation was to encourage pharmacists to take care when dispensing drugs, could this purpose have been achieved in any other way without imposing strict liability?

Note

Courts are vigilant to protect public safety. Where this consideration is weighty the courts may find that the presumption of mens rea has been rebutted. This is more likely to be the result where the court considers that the imposition of strict liability will encourage greater vigilance on the part of those regulated by the statute.

ALPHACELL LTD V WOODWARD

[1972] A.C. 824 HL

In the course of their business the appellants produced large quantities of polluted effluent which they pumped into a settling tank near a river bank. Pumps were installed in the tank to pump out excess water to prevent the tank from overflowing. The pumps were shielded by filters to prevent solid matter from blocking them. They were also regularly inspected. Despite these precautions the pumps became blocked by brambles, leaves and other vegetable matter causing the tank to overflow and polluted effluent to enter the river. The appellants were convicted under s.2(l) of the Rivers (Prevention of Pollution) Act 1951 which made it an offence if a person "causes or knowingly permits to enter a stream any poisonous, noxious or polluting matter". The question certified for the House of Lords was:

"Whether the offence of causing polluting matter to enter a stream contrary to section 2 of the Rivers (Prevention of Pollution) Act 1951 can be committed by a person who has no knowledge of the fact that polluting matter is entering the stream and has not been negligent in any relevant respect."

LORD SALMON

My Lords, I agree that this appeal should be dismissed and I wish to add only a few brief observations of my own. It is undisputed that the river on the banks of which stands the appellants' Mount Sion Works was polluted by contaminated effluent which flowed from those works into the river. The vital question is whether the appellants caused that pollution within the meaning of section 2 (1) of the Rivers (Prevention of Pollution) Act 1951. The nature of causation has been discussed by many eminent philosophers and also by a number of learned judges in the past. I consider, however, that what or who has caused a certain event to occur is essentially a practical question of fact which can best be answered by ordinary common sense rather than by abstract metaphysical theory.

It seems to me that, giving the word 'cause' its ordinary and natural meaning, anyone may cause something to happen intentionally or negligently or inadvertently without negligence and without intention . . ..

The appellants clearly did not cause the pollution intentionally and we must assume that they did not do so negligently. Nevertheless, the facts so fully and clearly stated by my noble and learned friend Viscount Dilhorne to my mind make it obvious that the appellants in fact caused the pollution. If they did not cause it, what did? There was no intervening act of a third party nor was there any act of God to which it could be attributed. The appellants had been responsible for the design of the plant; everything within their works was under their control; they had chosen all the equipment. The process which they operated required contaminated effluent being pumped round their works until it came to rest in an open tank which they sited on the river bank. If the pumps which they had installed in this tank failed to operate efficiently the effluent would necessarily overflow into the river. And that is what occurred. It seems plain to me that the appellants caused the pollution by the active operation of their plant. They certainly did not intend to cause pollution but they intended to do the acts which caused it.

The appellants contend that, even if they caused the pollution, still they should succeed since they did not cause it intentionally or knowingly or negligently. Section 2(1)(a) of the Rivers (Prevention of Pollution) Act 1951 is undoubtedly a penal section. It follows that if it is capable of two or more meanings then the meaning most favourable to the subject should be adopted. Accordingly, so the argument runs, the words 'intentionally' or 'knowingly' or 'negligently' should be read into the section immediately before the word 'causes'. I do not agree. It is of the utmost public importance that our rivers should not be polluted. The risk of pollution, particularly from the vast and increasing number of riparian industries, is very great. The offences created by the Act of 1951 seem to me to be prototypes of offences which 'are not criminal in any real sense, but are acts which in the public interest are prohibited under a penalty': *Sherras v De Rutzen* [1895] 1 Q.B. 918, *per* Wright J. at p.922, referred to with approval by my noble and learned friends, Lord Reid and Lord Diplock, in *Sweet v Parsley* [1970] A.C. 132, 149, 162. I can see no valid reason for reading the word 'intentionally', 'knowingly' or 'negligently' into section 2(1)(a) and a number of cogent reasons for not doing so. In the case of a minor pollution such as the present, when the justices find that there is no wrongful intention or negligence on the part of the defendant, a comparatively nominal fine will no doubt be imposed. This may be regarded as a not unfair hazard of carrying on a business which may cause pollution on the banks of a river. The present appellants were fined £20 and ordered to pay, in all, £24 costs. I should be surprised if the costs of pursuing this appeal to this House were incurred for the purpose of saving these appellants £44.

If this appeal succeeded and it were held to be the law that no conviction could be obtained under the Act of 1951 unless the prosecution could discharge the often impossible onus of proving that the pollution was caused intentionally or negligently, a great deal of pollution would go unpunished and undeterred to the relief of many riparian factory owners. As a result, many rivers which are now filthy would become filthier still and many rivers which are now clean would lose their cleanliness. The legislature no doubt recognised that as a matter of public policy this would be most unfortunate. Hence section 2 (1) (a) which encourages riparian factory owners not only to take reasonable steps to prevent pollution but to do everything possible to ensure that they do not cause it.

I do not consider that the appellants can derive any comfort (as they seek to do) from the inclusion in section 2 (1) (a) of the words 'knowingly permits' nor from the deeming provision against local authorities in relation to sewage escaping into a river from sewers or sewage disposal units [section 2 (1)]. The creation of an offence in relation to permitting pollution was probably included in the section so as to deal with the type of case in which a man knows that contaminated effluent is escaping over his land into a river and does nothing at all to prevent it. The inclusion of the word 'knowingly' before 'permits' is probably otiose and, if anything, is against the appellants, since it contrasts with the omission of the word 'knowingly' before the word 'causes'. The deeming provision was probably included to meet what local authorities might otherwise have argued was a special case and cannot, in my opinion, affect the plain and unambiguous general meaning of the word 'causes'.

For these reasons I would dismiss the appeal with costs.

[Lords Wilberforce, Pearson, Cross of Chelsea and Viscount Dilhorne made speeches dismissing the appeal.]

Appeal dismissed with costs

GAMMON (HONG KONG) LTD V ATTORNEY GENERAL OF HONG KONG

[1954] 2 All E.R. 503

The appellants were respectively the registered contractor, the project manager and the site agent for building works on a site in Hong Kong. Part of a temporary lateral support system collapsed. The company was charged with a material deviation from an approved plan in contravention of subs.(2A)(b) of s.40 of the Hong Kong Building Ordinance 1981 (revised edn), and with carrying out works in a manner likely to cause risk of injury or damage in contravention of subs.(2B)(b). The project manager and the site engineer were charged under subs.(2B)(b), respectively, with carrying out works, and permitting them to be carried on in a manner likely to cause risk of injury or damage.

LORD SCARMAN DELIVERED THE JUDGMENT OF THE BOARD:. . .

i. The general law

. . . The question in the appeal is whether the ordinance, correctly interpreted, provides a sound reason for holding that the offences created by subss. (2A)(*b*) and (2B)(*b*) of section 40 of the ordinance are offences of strict liability . . .

In their Lordships' opinion, the law relevant to this appeal may be stated in the following propositions: (1) there is a presumption of law that *mens rea* is required before a person can be held guilty of a criminal offence; (2) the presumption is particularly strong where the offence is 'truly criminal' in character; (3) the presumption applies to statutory offences, and can be displaced only if this is clearly or by necessary implication the effect of the statute; (4) the only situation in which the presumption can be displaced is where the statute is concerned with an issue of social concern; public safety is such an issue; (5) even where a statute is concerned with such an issue, the presumption of *mens rea* stands unless it can also be shown that the creation of strict liability will be effective to promote the objects of the statute by encouraging greater vigilance to prevent the commission of the prohibited act.

ii. The ordinance

Their Lordships turn to consider the purpose and subject matter of the ordinance. Its overall purpose is clearly to regulate the planning, design and construction of the building works to which it relates in the interests of safety. It covers a field of activity where there is, especially in Hong Kong, a potential danger to public safety. And the activity which the ordinance is intended to regulate is one in which citizens have a choice whether they participate or not. Part IV (section 40) of the ordinance makes it very clear that the legislature intended that criminal sanctions for contraventions of the ordinance should be a feature of its enforcement. But it is not to be supposed that the legislature intended that any of the offences created by the ordinance should be offences of strict liability unless it is plain, from a consideration of the subject-matter of the ordinance and of the wording of the particular provision creating the offence, that an object of the ordinance, e.g. the promotion of greater vigilance by those having responsibility under the ordinance, would be served by the imposition of strict liability.

The appellants submit that there is no necessity for strict liability in respect of any of the offences charged. Their first submission is that strict liability would not promote greater vigilance. If the persons charged had no knowledge of an essential fact, what could they have done to avoid its occurrence? Their second submission is more comprehensive. They submit that strict liability in respect of any offence created by the ordinance would run counter to the structure and character of the ordinance. The ordinance, it is submitted, relies not on criminal liability but on the elaborate and stringent provisions for the registration of persons qualified to ensure that its requirements are met.

So far as the first submission is concerned, their Lordships are satisfied that strict liability would help to promote greater vigilance in the matters covered by the two offenders with which this appeal is concerned (the material deviation under subs. (2A)(*b*) and the risk of injury or damage under subs. (2B)(*b*). The second submission is more formidable. Their Lordships, however, reject it also. Their Lordships agree with the view expressed by the Court of Appeal as to the purpose and subject-matter of the ordinance. The Court of Appeal saw no injustice in the imposition of heavy penalties for offences under the ordinance 'whether resulting from intentional infringement of the law, negligence or incompetence.' They made this powerful comment:

'Any large scale building operation will almost inevitably produce circumstances in which a departure from the generally accepted standards (whether of work or materials) will be likely to cause danger. Indeed, the extent of the danger and of the damage which may be done will frequently be enormous. It therefore behoves the incompetent to stay away and the competent to conduct themselves with proper care. A building contractor who delegates his legal responsibilities to an agent can fairly be held liable if he appoints an agent who is incompetent or careless: he should regulate his business in such a way as to avoid, on the one hand, the appointment of incompetent agents and, on the other, the consequences of any carelessness by a competent agent. Only if he is made responsible for seeing that the statutory standards are maintained can the purpose of the legislature be attained and in such a case as this the presumption of strict liability displaces the ordinary presumption of mens rea: see *Lim Chin Aik v R*. [below].'

Important as are the provisions of the ordinance for the registration, disqualification and discipline of persons qualified, authorised and registered to perform the duties and obligations required by the ordinance, the legislature by enacting Pt. IV (section 40) of the ordinance clearly took the view that criminal liability and punishment were needed as a deterrent against slipshod or incompetent supervision, control or execution of building works. The imposition of strict liability for some offences clearly would emphasise to those concerned the need for high standards of care in the supervision and execution of work. The view that their Lordships have reached, after the thorough review of the ordinance and history . . . is that, where the ordinance provides for an offence in terms which are silent or ambiguous as to the need for full *mens rea* covering all its essential ingredients, the wording of the particular provision must be carefully examined against the background and in the context of the ordinance to determine whether it is necessary to interpret the silence or resolve the ambiguity in favour of *mens rea* or of strict liability.

Put in positive terms, the conclusion of the Board is that it is consistent with the purpose of the ordinance in its regulation of the works to which it applies that at least some of the criminal offences which it creates should be of strict liability. It is a statute the subject matter of which may properly be described as—

'the regulation of a particular activity involving potential danger to public health [and] safety . . . in which citizens have a choice whether they participate or not. . .'

(See [1970] A.C. 132 at 163 per Lord Diplock.)

Whether, therefore, a particular provision of the statute creates an offence of full *mens rea* or of strict liability must depend on the true meaning of the words of the particular provision construed with reference to its subject-matter and to the question whether strict liability in respect of all or any of the essential ingredients of the offence would promote the object of the provision . . .

iii. Subsections (2A) and (2B)

Their Lordships now turn to consider the two subsections in detail and separately; for it does not follow that, if one subsection should create an offence of strict liability, the other must also do so. But first a few observations on certain features common to both.

The first common feature is that both subsections have a characteristic of which Lord Reid spoke in *Sweet v Parsley* [1970] A.C. 132 at 149. The specific provisions subsections (2A)(*b*) and (2B)(*b*) belong to that:

'multitude of criminal enactments where the words of the Act simply make it an offence to do certain things but where everyone agrees that there cannot be a conviction without proof of mens rea in some form.'

Each provision clearly requires a degree of *mens rea*, but each is silent whether it is required in respect of all the facts which together constitute the offence created. The issue here is, therefore, a narrow one. Does subs. (2A)(*b*) require knowledge of the materiality of the deviation? Does subs. (2B)(*b*) require knowledge of the likelihood of risk of injury or damage?

The second common feature is that each provision appears in a section which creates many other offences, the wording of some, though not all, of which clearly requires full *mens rea*.

A third common feature is that the maximum penalties for the offences which they create are heavy: a fine of $250,000 and imprisonment for three years. There is no doubt that the penalty indicates the seriousness with which the legislature viewed the offences.

The first of these features raises the determinative question in the appeal. Their Lordships will, therefore, consider it later in respect of each subsection.

The second feature, in their Lordships' opinion, proves nothing. One would expect a wide range of very different offences in a statute which establishes a comprehensive system of supervision and control over a great range of complicated works in diverse circumstances. And it can be said with equal force that a feature of section 40 is that in many cases where *mens rea* is required it expressly says so, and that, where a defence of reasonable excuse or lack of knowledge is to be available, it makes express provision to that end; examples may be seen in subss. (IB), (10), (2A)(*c*), (2C), (6), (7) and (7A).

The severity of the maximum penalties is a more formidable point. But it has to be considered in the light of the ordinance read as a whole. For reasons which their Lordships have already developed, there is nothing inconsistent with the purpose of the ordinance in imposing severe penalties for offences of strict liability. The legislature could reasonably have intended severity to be a significant deterrent, bearing in mind the risks to public safety arising from some contraventions of the ordinance. Their Lordships agree with the view on this point of the Court of Appeal. It must be crucially important that those who participate in or bear responsibility for the carrying out of works in a manner which complies with the requirements of the ordinance should know that severe penalties await them in the event of any contravention or non-compliance with the ordinance by themselves or by anyone over whom they are required to exercise supervision or control.

Subsection (2A)

. . . The wording of paragraph (*b*) clearly requires knowledge of the approved plan and of the fact of deviation. But in their Lordships' view it would be of little use in promoting public safety if it also required proof of knowledge of the materiality of the deviation. As it was put on behalf of the Attorney-General, if the offence requires knowledge of the materiality of the deviation to be proved, the defendant is virtually judge in his own cause. The object of the provision is to assist in preventing material deviations from occurring. If a building owner, an authorised person or a registered person is unaware of the materiality of the deviation which he authorises (and knowledge of the deviation is necessary), he plainly ought to be. He is made liable to criminal penalties because of the threat to public safety arising from material deviations from plans occurring within the sphere of his responsibility. The effectiveness of the ordinance would be seriously weakened if it were open to such a person to plead ignorance of what was material. In the words already quoted of the Court of Appeal, '. . . it behoves the incompetent to stay away and the competent to conduct themselves with proper care.'

Subsection (2B)

The construction of subsection (2B)(*b*) is more difficult, but their Lordships are satisfied that it imposes strict liability for substantially the same reasons as those which have led them to this conclusion in respect of subsection (2A)(*b*). The offence created clearly requires a degree of *metis rea*. A person cannot carry out works or authorise or permit them to be carried out in a certain manner unless he knows the manner which he is employing, authorising or permitting . . .

Their Lordships find some support for their view that subsection (2B)(*b*) is an offence of strict liability in the wording of the offence created by subsection (2B)(*a*). The wording of paragraph (*a*) points to strict liability, once injury or damage has in fact been caused. Anyone who has carried out, authorised or permitted work to be carried out in a manner which has in fact caused injury or damage is caught.

Conclusion

For these reasons their Lordships conclude that to the extent indicated the offences charged against the appellants are of strict liability.

Appeal dismissed: case remitted to magistrate

Question

In *Alphacell* and *Gammon* the defendants were companies engaging in commercial activities in spheres which involved risk to public safety. With the exception of road traffic offences where the danger to the public is grave, and a few other activities such as possessing firearms (see *R. v Howells* [1972] 2 W.L.R. 716, above) individuals rarely engage in activities which involve serious risks to public safety. Corporate entities do not suffer the stigma which individuals may suffer when convicted of a criminal offence. Professor Andrew Ashworth in *Principles of Criminal Law*, 3rd edn (Oxford: Oxford University Press, 1999), p.169 states that "the conflict between social welfare and fairness to defendants should be resolved differently according to whether the defendant is a private individual or a large corporation". Do you agree?

----

(4) Promoting the enforcement of the law

REYNOLDS V GH AUSTIN & SONS LTD

[1951] 2 K.B. 135

A women's guild organised an outing and arranged with a company, who carried on the business of operating motor-coaches, to convey in a motor-coach a party at a fixed price per person. The organiser of the outing caused to be exhibited in a shop an advertisement giving particulars of the trip which stated "Few tickets left. Apply within." The company had no knowledge and no reasonable means of discovering that any such advertisement had been made. The outing took place and the company, who held no road service licence covering the journey in question, were charged with having used the motor-coach in contravention of s.72 of the Act of 1930 on the ground that by the condition of s.25 subs.(1)(b) of the Act of 1934, such journey "must be made without previous advertisement to the public of the arrangements therefore." The information was dismissed and the prosecutor appealed.

DEVLIN J

. . . The main weight of the case for the prosecutor rests on the contention that this statute belongs to a class in which *mens rea* should be dispensed with. There is no doubt that some of the provisions of the Road Traffic Acts do fall within that class: see, for example, *Griffiths v Studebakers Ltd* [1924] 1 K.B. 102. It may seem, on the face of it, hard that a man should be fined, and, indeed, made subject to imprisonment, for an offence which he did not know that he was committing. But there is no doubt that the legislature has for certain purposes found that hard measure to be necessary in the public interest . . . Thus a man may be made responsible for the acts of his servants, or even for defects in his business arrangements, because it can be fairly said that by such sanctions citizens are induced to keep themselves and their organisations up to the mark. Although, in one sense, the citizen is being punished for the sins of others, it can be said that, if he had been more alert to see that the law was observed, the sin might not have been committed. But if a man is punished because of an act done by another, whom he cannot reasonably be expected to influence or control, the law is engaged, not in punishing thoughtlessness or inefficiency, and thereby promoting the welfare of the community, but in pouncing on the most convenient victim. Without the authority of express words, I am not willing to conclude that Parliament can intend what would seem to the ordinary man (as plainly it seemed to the justices in this case) to be the useless and unjust infliction of a penalty . . .

I think it a safe general principle to follow (I state it negatively, since that is sufficient for the purposes of this case), that where the punishment of an individual will not promote the observance of the law either by that individual or by others whose conduct he may reasonably be expected to influence then, in the absence of clear and express words, such punishment is not intended.

Appeal dismissed

LIM CHIN AIK V THE QUEEN

[1963] A.C. 160

The appellant was charged with and convicted of contravening s.6(2) of the Immigration Ordinance 1952 of the State of Singapore by remaining in Singapore (after having entered) when he had been prohibited from entering by an order made by the Minister under s.9. At the trial there was no evidence from which it could properly be inferred that the order had in fact come to the notice or attention of the appellant. He appealed, ultimately to the Privy Council.

LORD EVERSHED

That proof of the existence of a guilty intent is an essential ingredient of a crime at common law is not at all in doubt. The problem is of the extent to which the same rule is applicable in the case of offences created and defined by statute or statutory instrument . . .

Mr Gratiaen founded his argument upon the formulation of the problem contained in the judgment of Wright J. in *Sherras* case (above). The language of that learned and experienced judge was as follows: 'There is a presumption that *mens rea*, or evil intention or knowledge of the wrongfulness of the act, is an essential ingredient in every offence, but that presumption is liable to be displaced either by the words of the statute creating the offence or by the subject-matter with which it deals, and both must be considered.' . . .

Their Lordships accept as correct the formulation cited from the judgment of Wright J . . . What should be the proper inferences to be drawn from the language of the statute or statutory instrument under review—in this case of sections 6 and 9 of the Immigration Ordinance? More difficult, perhaps, still what are the inferences to be drawn in a given case from the 'subject-matter with which [the statute or statutory instrument] deals'?

Where the subject-matter of the statute is the regulation for the public welfare of a particular activity—statutes regulating the sale of food and drink are to be found among the earliest examples—it can be and frequently has been inferred that the legislature intended that such activities should be carried out under conditions of strict liability. The presumption is that the statute or statutory instrument can be effectively enforced only if those in charge of the relevant activities are made responsible for seeing that they are complied with. When such a presumption is to be inferred, it displaces the ordinary presumptions of *mens rea* . . .

But it is not enough in their Lordships' opinion merely to label the statute as one dealing with a grave social evil and from that to infer that strict liability was intended. It is pertinent also to inquire whether putting the defendant under strict liability will assist in the enforcement of the regulations. That means that there must be something he can do, directly or indirectly, by supervision or inspection, by improvement of his business methods or by exhorting those whom he may be expected to influence or control, which will promote the observance of the regulations. Unless this is so, there is no reason in penalising him, and it cannot be inferred that the legislature imposed strict liability merely in order to find a luckless victim. This principle has been expressed and applied in *Reynolds v G. H. Austin & Sons Ltd* (above, p.161) and *James & Son Ltd v Smee* [1955] 1 Q.B. 78. Their Lordships prefer it to the alternative view that strict liability follows simply from the nature of the subject-matter and that persons whose conduct is beyond any sort of criticism can be dealt with by the imposition of a nominal penalty . . . But though a nominal penalty may be appropriate in an individual case where exceptional lenience is called for, their Lordships cannot, with respect, suppose that it is envisaged by the legislature as a way of dealing with offenders generally. Where it can be shown that the imposition of strict liability would result in the prosecution and conviction of a class of persons whose conduct could not in any way affect the observance of the law, their Lordships consider that, even where the statute is dealing with a grave social evil, strict liability is not likely to be intended.

Their Lordships apply these general observations to the Ordinance in the present case. The subject-matter, the control of immigration, is not one in which the presumption of strict liability has generally been made. Nevertheless, if the courts of Singapore were of the view that unrestricted immigration is a social evil which it is the object of the Ordinance to control most rigorously, their Lordships would hesitate to disagree. That is a matter peculiarly within the cognisance of the local courts. But Mr Le Quesne was unable to point to anything that the appellant could possibly have done so as to ensure that he complied with the regulations. It was not, for example, suggested that it would be practicable for him to make continuous inquiry to see whether an order had been made against him. Clearly one of the objects of the Ordinance is the expulsion of prohibited persons from Singapore, but there is nothing that a man can do about it if, before the commission of the offence, there is no practical or sensible way in which he can ascertain whether he is a prohibited person or not . . . It seems to their Lordships that, where a man is said to have contravened an order or an order of prohibition, the common sense of the language presumes that he was aware of the order before he can be said to have contravened it. Their Lordships realise that this statement is something of an over-simplification when applied to the present case; for the 'contravention' alleged is of the unlawful act, prescribed by subsection (2) of the section, of remaining in Singapore after the date of the order of prohibition. Nonetheless it is their Lordships' view that, applying the test of ordinary sense to the language used, the notion of contravention here alleged is more consistent with the assumption that the person charged had knowledge of the order than the converse. But such a conclusion is in their Lordships' view much reinforced by the use of the word 'remains' in its context. It is to be observed that if the respondent is right a man could lawfully enter Singapore and could thereafter lawfully remain in Singapore until the moment when an order of prohibition against his entering was made; that then, instanter, his purely passive conduct in remaining—that is, the mere continuance, quite unchanged, of his previous behaviour, hitherto perfectly lawful—would become criminal. These considerations bring their Lordships clearly to the conclusion that the sense of the language here in question requires for the commission of a crime thereunder *mens rea* as a constituent of such crime; or at least there is nothing in the language used which suffices to exclude the ordinary presumption. Their Lordships do not forget . . . the fact that the word 'knowingly' or the phrases 'without reasonable cause' or 'without reasonable excuse' are found in various sections of the Ordinance (as amended) but find no place in the section now under consideration . . . In their Lordships' view the absence of such a word or phrase in the relevant section is not sufficient in the present case to prevail against the conclusion which the language as a whole suggests. In the first place, it is to be noted that to have inserted such words as 'knowingly' or 'without lawful excuse' in the relevant part of section 6(3) of the Act would in any case not have been sensible.

Further, in all the various instances where the word or phrase is used in the other sections of the Ordinance before-mentioned the use is with reference to the doing of some specific act or the failure to do some specific act as distinct from the mere passive continuance of behaviour theretofore perfectly lawful. Finally, their Lordships are mindful that in the Sherras case itself the fact that the word 'knowingly' was not found in the subsection under consideration by the court but was found in another subsection of the same section was not there regarded as sufficient to displace the ordinary rule.

Appeal allowed

(5) Human Rights

It has been suggested that imposing strict liability may infringe art.6 of the European Convention on Human Rights, enshrined into English law by the Human Rights Act 1998 (see Ch.1, above). The case which follows suggests that merely because an offence is one of strict liability that fact, of itself, will not infringe art.6.

SALABIAKU V FRANCE

(1991) 13 E.H.R.R. 379

The applicant complained of a violation of art.6(2). He had been charged both with the criminal offence of unlawful importation of narcotics and with the customs offence of smuggling prohibited goods. Although he was awarded the benefit of doubt on the first charge and acquitted, he was convicted on the second. A presumption of criminal liability was laid down in art.392(1) of the Customs Code for every person who was found in possession of prohibited goods.

JUDGMENT OF THE COURT

The applicant relied on paragraphs 1 and 2 of Art.6 of the Convention, which are worded as follows:

1. 'In the determination . . . of any criminal charge against him, everyone is entitled to a fair . . . hearing . . . by a . . . tribunal . . .
2. Everyone charged with a criminal offence shall be presumed innocent until proved guilty according to law.'
. . . In particular, and again in principle, the Contracting States may, under certain conditions, penalise a simple or objective fact as such, irrespective of whether it results from criminal intent or from negligence. Examples of such offences may be found in the laws of the Contracting States.

This shift from the idea of accountability in criminal law to the notion of guilt shows the very relative nature of such a distinction. It raises a question with regard to Art.6(2) of the Convention . . . Presumptions of fact or of law operate in every legal system. Clearly, the Convention does not prohibit such presumptions in principle. It does, however, require the Contracting States to remain within certain limits in this respect as regards criminal law. If, as the Commission would appear to consider, paragraph 2 of Art.6 merely laid down a guarantee to be respected by the courts in the conduct of legal proceedings, its requirements would in practice overlap with the duty of impartiality imposed in paragraph 1. Above all, the national legislature would be free to strip the trial court of any genuine power of assessment and deprive the presumption of innocence of its substance, if the words 'according to law' were construed exclusively with reference of domestic law. Such a situation could not be reconciled with the object and purpose of Art.6, which, by protecting the right to a fair trial and in particular the right to be presumed innocent, is intended to enshrine the fundamental principle of the rule of law . . . Art.6(2) does not therefore regard presumptions of fact or of law provided for in the criminal law with indifference. It requires States to confine them within reasonable limits which take into account the importance of what is at stake and maintain the rights of the defence . . .

Held, by the Court, unanimously that on the facts, Article 6(2) had not been violated

Question

Does the decision in *Salabiaku* mean that in no circumstances will offences of strict liability breach art.6? If, not, in what circumstances might a breach occur?

Reliance was sought to be placed on the proposition in *Salabiaku* in the following case.

R. V G

[2008] UKHL 37

LORD HOFFMAN:

1. On 20 April 2005 the appellant pleaded guilty to the offence of rape of a child under 13, contrary to section 5 of the Sexual Offences Act 2003:

(1) A person commits an offence if—

    (a) he intentionally penetrates the vagina, anus or mouth of another person with his penis; and

    (b) the other person is under 13.

(2) A person guilty of an offence under this section is liable, on conviction on indictment, to imprisonment for life.

2. For the purpose of sentence, the prosecution accepted the appellant's version of the facts, namely, that the accused was 15 at the time of the offence, the complainant had consented to intercourse and she had told him that she was 15. On 8 July 2005 Judge Hone sentenced him to a 12 month detention and training order. The appellant appealed on the grounds that (1) the conviction violated his right to a fair trial and the presumption of innocence under article 6 of the Convention, because it was an offence of strict liability, and (2) it violated his right to privacy under article 8 because it was disproportionate to charge him with rape under section 5 when he could have been charged with a less serious offence under section 13, which deals with sex offences committed by persons under 18. The Court of Appeal dismissed the appeal against conviction but allowed an appeal against sentence and substituted a conditional discharge. It certified two questions as being of general public importance:

(1) May a criminal offence of strict liability violate article 6(1) and/or 6(2) . . .?

(2) Is it compatible with a child's rights under article 8 . . . to convict him of rape contrary to section 5 . . . in circumstances where the agreed basis of plea establishes that his offence fell properly within the ambit of section 13 . . .?

3. The mental element of the offence under section 5, as the language and structure of the section makes clear, is that penetration must be intentional but there is no requirement that the accused must have known that the other person was under 13. The policy of the legislation is to protect children. If you have sex with someone who is on any view a child or young person, you take your chance on exactly how old they are. To that extent the offence is one of strict liability and it is no defence that the accused believed the other person to be 13 or over.

4. Article 6(1) provides that in the determination of his civil rights or any criminal charge, everyone is entitled to a 'fair and public hearing' and article 6(2) provides that everyone charged with a criminal offence 'shall be presumed innocent until proved guilty according to law'. It is settled law that Article 6(1) guarantees fair procedure and the observance of the principle of the separation of powers but not that either the civil or criminal law will have any particular substantive content: see *Matthews v Ministry of Defence* [2003] UKHL 4; [2003] 1 AC 1163. Likewise, article 6(2) requires him to be presumed innocent of the offence but does not say anything about what the mental or other elements of the offence should be. In the case of civil law, this was established (after a moment of aberration) by *Z v United Kingdom* (2001) 34 EHRR 97. There is no reason why the reasoning should

not apply equally to the substantive content of the criminal law. In *R. v Gemmell* [2002] EWCA Crim 1992; [2003] 1 Cr. App. R. 343, 356, para 33 Dyson L.J. said:

> 'The position is quite clear. So far as Article 6 is concerned, the fairness of the provisions of the substantive law of the Contracting States is not a matter for investigation. The content and interpretation of domestic substantive law is not engaged by Article 6.'

5. The only authority which is said to cast any doubt upon this proposition is the decision of the Strasbourg court in *Salabiaku v France* (1988) 13 EHRR 379 and in particular a statement in paragraph 28 (at p.388) that 'presumptions of fact or of law' in criminal proceedings should be confined 'within reasonable limits'. No one has yet discovered what this paragraph means but your Lordships were referred to a wealth of academic learning which tries to solve the riddle.

6. My Lords, I think that judges and academic writers have picked over the carcass of this unfortunate case so many times in attempts to find some intelligible meat on its bones that the time has come to call a halt. The Strasbourg court, uninhibited by a doctrine of precedent or the need to find a ratio decidendi, seems to have ignored it. It is not mentioned in *Z v United Kingdom* (2001) 34 EHRR 97. I would recommend your Lordships to do likewise.

LORD HOPE OF CRAIGHEAD

13. Section 5 of the Sexual Offences Act 2003, which makes sexual intercourse with a child under 13 a crime of strict liability irrespective of the age of the defendant and calls it rape, has given rise to some important and difficult questions: see J R Spencer, *The Sexual Offences Act 2003: (2) Child and Family Offences* [2004] Crim L R 347, 360. Section 13 of the same Act, read with section 9(1)(c)(ii), makes it an offence for a person under 18 to have sexual intercourse with a child under 13. Unlike section 5, it does not attach the label of rape to this offence. What behaviour then should the criminal law prohibit, and what should it not? To what extent is it is reasonable to leave it to the police and other authorities to decide when to prosecute and, where there is a choice, for which offence? These questions have been brought out into the real world by this case.

14. There is no doubt that when section 5 of the 2003 Act was enacted the protection of children was one of the primary concerns of the legislature. Furthermore, as Rose L.J. said in *R v Corran* [2005] EWCA Crim 192, para 6, its purpose is to protect children under 13 from themselves as well as from others who are minded to prey upon them. But the creation of an unqualified offence of this kind carries with it the risk of stigmatising as rapists children who engage in a single act of mutual sexual activity. A heavy responsibility has been placed on the prosecuting authorities, where both parties are of a similar young age, to discriminate between cases where the proscribed activity was truly mutual on the one hand and those where the complainant was subjected to an element of exploitation or undue pressure on the other. In the former case more harm than good may be done by prosecuting. In the latter case the threshold will have been crossed and prosecution is likely to be inevitable. But if in the former case it is decided to prosecute, a decision still has to be made about the section under which the perpetrator is to be prosecuted.

15. Of course, the prosecuting authorities can only work on what they have got. As Mr Perry QC for the respondent put it, they can only engage with the complainer's account of events. No criticism can be made of the decision to prosecute under section 5 in this case in view of the account which the complainant gave when she was interviewed by the police. At the time of the events complained of the appellant was aged 15 and the complainant was aged 12. She said that he had vaginal intercourse with her despite the fact that, alarmed by what was to happen, she made clear her objections. Then the situation changed. The complainant accepted that she had told the appellant that she was 15 and she was reluctant to attend court to give evidence. The appellant pleaded guilty to a contravention of section 5 of the 2003 Act on the basis that the complainant willingly agreed to have sexual intercourse with him and that he believed at the time that she was 15. The appeal arises from the fact that the prosecution informed the court that they had decided to accept his plea of guilty on this basis as one of guilty to the offence charged under section 5.

16. The judge sentenced the appellant to a twelve months' detention and training order. But the appellant had been in custody for about five months before he was granted bail on being granted permission to appeal against his sentence. So there were grounds for regarding the sentence as excessive. It was quashed by the Court of Appeal and replaced with an immediate conditional discharge for a period of twelve months: [2006] EWCA Crim 821, [2006] 1 WLR 2052. As the court pointed out in para 52 of its judgment, if the appellant committed no offence during that period the notification requirement imposed by Part 2 of the 2003 Act would end with it and he would not thereafter be deemed to have had a conviction.

17. Mr Owen QC for the appellant maintained nevertheless that the full impact of his conviction for rape under section 5 was, is and will continue to be substantial. He was morally blameless, but he would carry the stigma of a conviction for rape with him for the rest of his life. His argument was that the conviction under that section on the agreed basis was a violation of his rights under article 6(2) of the European Convention on Human Rights and that, in any event, it was not compatible with his right to respect for his private life under article 8 of the Convention. He submitted that the prosecution ought to have been discontinued, or alternatively that the prosecutor should have sought a conviction under section 13 of the 2003 Act, read with section 9(1)(c)(ii), which would not have carried with it the stigma of a conviction for rape.

The alternative offences

18. Section 5 of the 2003 Act is headed 'Rape of a child under 13'. A person commits an offence under that section if he intentionally penetrates the vagina, anus or mouth of another person with his penis and the other person is under 13. He is liable on conviction on indictment to imprisonment for life. It replaced section 5 of the Sexual Offences Act 1956 which bore the side note 'Intercourse with girl under thirteen' and provided: 'It is a felony for a man to have unlawful sexual intercourse with a girl under the age of thirteen.' . . . The alteration in the way section 5 is described from the description which was applied to its predecessor is significant.

19. Section 5 of the 2003 differs from the provision which it replaced in three respects. The first, as I have just said, is its heading. The offence contrary to section 5 of the 1965 was commonly described as 'statutory rape'. Now this is its official designation. Rape is an apt description of any kind of coercive penetrative sexual activity. It is not if the sexual activity was truly consensual. It has been applied to section 5 because at common law a girl under 13 cannot consent to sexual intercourse. Second, it applies to offences against boys under the age of 13 as well as girls. Third, it applies to the use of the penis to penetrate the mouth as well as the vagina or the anus of the complainant. So the scope of the protection has been extended, to keep pace with current trends in sexual behaviour. There is no upper or lower limit to the age of the person by whom the offence may be committed. The fact that a contravention of rape under this section may attract a sentence of life imprisonment is an indication of the gravity of the offence.

20. The actus reus of the offence created by section 5 is the penetration by the penis of the vagina, anus or mouth of a complainer who is under the age of 13. Mens rea as to the age of the complainer is not required. The mens rea is using the penis deliberately to penetrate the relevant orifice. . .

21. In this case the requirement of mens rea has not been wholly eliminated. The offence which the section creates is one of strict liability in the sense that proof of the intentional penetration of a child under 13 is all that is needed for a conviction. Mistake as to age is a defence in the case of offences committed against older children. In the case of children under 13 it is not. This must be taken to have been a deliberate choice by Parliament which, under domestic law, it was entitled to take. The principle which has been applied is that intentional sexual activity of the proscribed kind with children below that age should not be permitted in any circumstances. In *R v Hess; R v Nguyen* [1990] 2 SCR 906 McLachlin J said, at p 948, that the protection of children from the evils of intercourse is multi-faceted and so obvious as not to require formal demonstration. Sections 5 to 8 were designed to protect children under 13 of both sexes from sexual conduct perpetrated against them by anyone.

22. This, however, is not the only way in which sexual activity between children may be prosecuted. A group of sections, sections 9 to 15, is headed 'Child sex offences'. Section 9 is headed 'Sexual activity with a child'. It criminalises intentional touching of a sexual nature, including penetration of the complainer's vagina, anus or mouth. It applies where the person accused of the offence is over 18. If the other person is under 16, it is a defence that the person accused reasonably believed that the other person was 16 or over. If the other person is under 13 the offence is one of strict liability, as it is in section 5: section 9(1)(c)(ii). The defence of mistaken belief in age is not available. Section 13 extends its reach to protect children from sexual assaults by other young people. It provides that a person under 18 commits an offence if he does anything which would be an offence under any of sections 9 to 12 if he were aged 18. He may be prosecuted either on indictment or summarily. The maximum sentence on indictment is 5 years' imprisonment.

23. Conduct of the kind that was the basis of the appellant's decision to plead guilty in this case was within the reach of section 9(1)(c)(ii) as extended by section 13 to acts committed by persons under 18. . . The choice as to which of sections 5 or 13 to employ is left by the statute entirely to the prosecutor. The context suggests however that a child under 18 ought not to be prosecuted under section 5 for performing a sexual act with a child under 13 of the kind to which that section applies unless the circumstances are such as to indicate that it plainly was an offence of such gravity that prosecution under section 13 would not be appropriate. It suggests that a child under 18 (and more especially a child as young as 15) should not be prosecuted under section 5 (rape of a child under 13) if the complainer says that he or she consented to sexual intercourse. The problem revealed by this case is the

familiar one which faces every prosecutor. The complainer's account of events may change. The appellant seeks to find a solution under sections 6 and 7 of the Human Rights Act 1998 to the way he was dealt with in this case.

Article 6(2)

24. Mr Owen's primary submission was that the offence which section 5 creates, interpreted as one of strict liability, is incompatible with article 6(2) of the Convention, which provides that everyone charged with a criminal offence shall be presumed innocent until proved guilty according to law. He sought support for this argument in the observations of the European Court in *Salabiaku v France* (1988) 13 EHRR 379. In paras 27-28 of its judgment the court said:

'27. As the Government and the Commission have pointed out, in principle the Contracting States remain free to apply the criminal law to an act where it is not carried out in the normal exercise of one of the rights protected under the Convention and, accordingly, to define the constituent elements of the resulting offence. In particular, and again in principle, the Contracting States may, under certain conditions, penalise a simple or objective fact as such, irrespective of whether it results from criminal intent or from negligence. Examples of such offences may be found in the laws of the Contracting States . . .. 28. . . .. Presumptions of fact or of law operate in every legal system. Clearly, the Convention does not prohibit such presumptions in principle. It does, however, require the Contracting States to remain within certain limits in this respect as regards criminal law . . .. Article 6(2) does not therefore regard presumptions of fact or of law provided for in the criminal law with indifference. It requires States to confine them within reasonable limits which take into account the importance of what is at stake and maintain the rights of the defence.'

25. Mr Owen sought to apply what he described as the reasonable limits test to the offence that section 5 creates. The effect of any offence of strict liability, he said, was to create a presumption that the accused had done something of which he was innocent. So the creation of strict criminal liability will always engage a consideration of compatibility with the presumption of innocence in article 6(2). The conduct to which the appellant had pleaded guilty in this case was morally blameless, as the complainant willingly agreed to have sexual intercourse with him. It was difficult to distil from *Salabiaku* a clear principle that strict criminal liability was always free from regulation under article 6(2). The European Court said in para 27 that the Contracting States could penalise a simple or objective fact as such irrespective of whether there was criminal intent. But it had made it clear that it could only do so under certain conditions. This was to be read as applying not just to matters of procedure. The substance of an offence could be examined too, and it would violate article 6(2) if it failed properly to recognise that the accused is to be presumed innocent until proven guilty of the conduct which it was intended to deter.

. . .

27. This argument seems me to read far too much into the wording of article 6(2) and to the Court's reasoning in *Salabiaku*. Article 6(2), like article 6(3), must be read in the context of article 6(1). The article as a whole is concerned essentially with procedural guarantees to ensure that there is a fair trial, not with the substantive elements of the offence with which the person has been charged. As has been said many times, article 6 does not guarantee any particular content of the individual's civil rights. It is concerned with the procedural fairness of the system for the administration of justice in the contracting states, not with the substantive content of domestic law: *Matthews v Ministry of Defence* [2003] 1 AC 1163, para 3, per Lord Bingham of Cornhill, paras 30-35 per Lord Hoffmann, para 142, per Lord Walker of Gestingthorpe; *R (Kehoe) v Secretary of State for Work and Pensions* [2005] UKHL 48; [2006] 1 AC 42, para 41. The approach which the article takes to the criminal law is the same. Close attention is paid to the requirements of a fair trial. But it is a matter for the contracting states to define the essential elements of the offence with which the person has been charged. So when article 6(2) uses the words 'innocent' and 'guilty' it is dealing with the burden of proof regarding the elements of the offence and any defences to it. It is not dealing with what those elements are or what defences to the offence ought to be available.

28. The observations in paras 27-28 of *Salabiaku* are not inconsistent with this analysis. As the Court of Appeal noted in para 31 of its decision, that case was decided, in accordance with the practice of the Strasbourg court, on its own facts. The principles which it was seeking to enunciate are set out in rather general terms, which that court has not so far attempted to enlarge upon. But the key to a proper understanding of the passage as a whole is to be found in the first sentence of para 27. It contains a clear affirmation of the principle that the contracting states are free to apply the criminal law to any act, so long as it is not one which is carried out in the exercise of one of the rights protected under the Convention. Accordingly they are free to define the constituent elements of the offence that results from that act. So when the court said in the next sentence that the contracting states

may 'under certain conditions' penalise a simple or objective fact as such, irrespective of whether it results from criminal intent or negligence, it was reaffirming the same principle. As in the previous sentence, the certain conditions that are referred to indicate that objection could be taken if the offence was incompatible with other articles of the Convention. But they have no wider significance. If there is no such incompatibility, the definition of the constituents of the offence is a matter for domestic law.

29. *Salabiaku* is not easy to construe, as my noble and learned friend Lord Hoffmann points out. But I do not agree with him that we should simply ignore it. Read in the way I have indicated, it continues to offer guidance about the extent of the guarantee that is afforded by article 6(2). Dyson LJ's remarks in *R v Gemmell* [2003] 1 Cr. App. R., 343, 356, para 33 with which I too agree, are consistent with that guidance. The substantive content of the criminal law does not raise issues of fairness of the kind to which that article is directed.

30. I would therefore respectfully endorse the conclusion which the Court of Appeal drew from the reasoning in *Salabiaku*. It said in para 33:

'An absolute offence may subject a defendant to conviction in circumstances where he has done nothing blameworthy. Prosecution for such an offence and the imposition of sanctions under it may well infringe articles of the Convention other than article 6. The legislation will not, however, render the trial under which it is enforced unfair, let alone infringe the presumption of innocence under article 6(2).'

It follows that I would not attach the significance to the decision in *Hansen v Denmark* that Mr Owen sought to attach to it. The offence in that case was one of strict liability. But, as the court noted, the burden of proof of all its elements was throughout on the prosecution. As it said, there was nothing to indicate that the courts in fulfilling their functions started from the assumption that the applicant was liable. This passage in its judgment is consistent with the view that article 6(2) does not proscribe offences of strict liability, so long as the prosecution bears the burden of proof of all the elements that constitute the offence.

31. That requirement is plainly met in this case. So I would hold that section 5 of the 2003 Act is not incompatible with article 6(2) of the Convention and that the prosecutor's act in prosecuting the appellant under that section was not unlawful in that respect.

[Lord Mance and Baroness Hale concurred with Lords Hope and Hoffman on the art.6 issues.]

Question

1. Was "rape" an appropriate and fair label that accurately described G's conduct?

----

iii. Critique

It is evident from the cases in the preceding section that a number of justifications are advanced for the imposition of strict liability, such as improved standards of prevention (i.e. the public will be better protected from the inherent risks in certain activities), and greater administrative efficiency (i.e. that efficacious enforcement is only possible where there is no burden on the prosecution to prove a mental element). On their own both these arguments could be used to favour the abolition of mens rea in all crimes. (See Wootton, below.)

Two further glosses are thus added. On the one hand it is suggested that strict liability does not eliminate fault as a basis of liability but that the fault element is determined at an earlier stage of the criminal process. Such an argument can lead to different conclusions. (See Paulus, Thomas and Smith, below.) On the other hand, it is said that, since these offences are not "true" crimes, the concept of mens rea is not required to prevent the injustice of punishing the "morally" innocent. This approach leads to difficulties in deciding whether it is the nature of the prohibited activity or the fact that no mental element is required which renders these "quasi'" crimes. A vicious circle may arise in which strict liability is imposed to protect the public from the risks inherent in certain activities, while that protection is undermined by sentencing lightly defendants who, by virtue of the use of discretionary enforcement policies, have at the very least been negligent. (See Walker, below.) At a different level of analysis, it can be questioned whether either strict liability or negligence acts as an incentive to greater safety precautions (Hutchinson, below).

INGEBORG PAULUS, "STRICT LIABILITY: ITS PLACE IN PUBLIC WELFARE OFFENCES"

(1978) 20 Crim.L.Q. 445

Theoretical legal reasoning repeatedly stresses that strict liability . . . is unjust and holds persons liable for offences for which they are morally blameless. Yet empirical researchers assessing the law in action are not alarmed about strict liability offences and their enforcement . . . [W]henever studies have been made investigating the workings of strict liability, the persons involved in the administration of public welfare offences, especially those concerning food and drug laws, have stressed that strict liability generally does not penalise offenders who are not also clearly guilty . . . [T]he personnel in charge of enforcement rarely prosecute unless they find an element of fault or *mens rea* present in the offence. But the *availability* of strict liability prosecutions greatly facilitates their work.

[The studies referred to are: Smith and Pearson, "The Value of Strict Liability" [1969] Crim. L.R. 5; W.G. Carson, "Some Sociological Aspects of Strict Liability and the Enforcement of Factory Legislation" (1970) 33 M.L.R. 396; F.J. Remington, et al., "Liability Without Fault Criminal Statutes" [1965] Wis. L.R. 625. To these can be added: Law Commission, Published Working Paper No.30, *Strict Liability and the Enforcement of the Factories Act 1961* (TSO, 1970); and Law Reform Commission of Canada, *Studies in Strict Liability* (Ottawa, 1974).]

D.A. THOMAS, "FORM AND FUNCTION IN CRIMINAL LAW" IN P. GLAZEBROOK, *RESHAPING THE CRIMINAL LAW* (STEVENS & SONS, 1978), P.30

The effect of imposing strict liability is not necessarily to eliminate fault as a requirement of liability, but to delegate to the enforcer both the responsibility of deciding what kind of fault will in general justify a prosecution (with the certainty of conviction) and the right to determine whether in the circumstances of the particular case that degree of fault is present. The main objections to the concept of strict liability are thus procedural rather than substantive, and the questions to be addressed to the proponent of a statute creating an offence of strict liability are: 'Why is it not possible to incorporate into the definition of the offence the nature of the fault which is likely in practice to be required as a condition precedent to prosecution, and why is it not possible for the existence of this fault to be determined in accordance with the normal processes of the law?' At the very least, there can be no justification for enacting an offence of strict liability which is not balanced by a provision allowing the question whether fault existed or not to be raised in the trial as an affirmative defence, and any offence of strict liability where the gravity of the offence would be enhanced by the offender's knowledge of the relevant circumstances should be the lowest step in a hierarchy of offences including similar offences requiring proof of knowledge or intent.

J. C. Smith [1966] Crim.L.R. 505, commenting on *Lockyer v Gibb* [1967] 2 Q.B. 243, a case on possession of drugs where the defendant did not know that what she possessed *was* a drug:

The interpretation of statutes so as to create offences of strict liability in fact creates difficulties of sentencing which have not been faced up to by the courts. Take a case in which the accused is tried on indictment. The judge tells the jury to convict if they are satisfied that (i) D knew he was in possession of the thing, and (ii) the thing is a dangerous drug. They convict. If these are the only facts proved against D it would be quite scandalous to do other than give him an absolute discharge. If D ought to have known the thing was a drug, then he is in some degree blameworthy; if he in fact knew it was a drug, he is more blameworthy. But the jury need not consider these questions. How does the judge know on what basis he should sentence? He is discouraged from asking the jury the question at all. The judge presumably makes up his own mind. His view of the facts may differ completely from that of the jury—if they have a view. Thus what is really the fundamental issue of fact in the case is withdrawn from the jury and decided by the judge alone. The position in the case of a magistrates' court is a little easier because the magistrates at least know on what facts the conviction is based; but it is unsatisfactory that they may come to the sentencing stage without having considered whether the accused bears any moral responsibility whatever for the 'offence' which has been committed. This question must be considered before a sentence can be imposed. Presumably it is dealt with in the informal way in which other findings of fact relating only to sentence are handled. But this is hardly satisfactory, when it is really the most fundamental issue of fact in the case which is being considered. On what basis was the fine of £10 in the present case imposed? The magistrate must have thought that the defendant was in some degree blameworthy or he would presumably have granted an absolute discharge. Yet he was evidently not satisfied beyond reasonable doubt that the defendant knew that the substance was a dangerous drug. Did he then fine her because she ought to have known? Or was he satisfied with a lower degree of proof (she probably knew)?

ALLAN C. HUTCHINSON, "NOTE ON SAULT STE MARIE" (1979) 17 OSGOODE HALL LAW JOURNAL 415, 429 (FN.78)

An application of the presently favoured 'economic perspective,' as represented by Richard A. Posner and other members of the so-called Chicago School, to the problem offers some interesting insights into the relative efficiency of strict liability and negligence as methods of combating the type of harm and safeguarding the interests that public welfare offences are intended to protect. According to such an analysis, where the primary object of an offence is accident prevention, as is the case with public welfare offences, there is little to choose between strict liability and negligence. Whichever basis of liability is employed, the standard of care taken by the potential injurer is likely to be influenced almost exclusively by the result of balancing the cost of precautions against the predicted cost of the penalty. If the preventive costs are lower, then precautions will be taken whether the offence is one of negligence or strict liability. But if the penalty is lower, then neither negligence nor strict liability is likely to encourage the taking of precautions. Therefore, the choice of liability standards has no effect on the level of safety achieved. Moreover, it is possible, yet surprising to many, that if either basis of liability is to bring about some long term effect, the imposition of strict liability is more likely than negligence to result in an improvement in accident prevention. As regards negligence, liability is usually determined on the existing state of sophistication of the technology of accident prevention and, as such, presents little or no incentive to advance such knowledge by investing in its research and development. On the other hand, strict liability may engender greater safety, as there is more of an incentive to encourage and engage in the research into and the development of precautionary measures:

> 'If [for example, a railroad company] were liable for all accidents . . ., it would compare the liability that it could not avoid by means of existing safety precautions without the feasibility of developing new precautions that would reduce that liability. If safety research and development seemed likely to reduce accident costs by more than the cost of research and development, the [company] would undertake it . . .' (Posner, *The Economic Analysis of Law* (2nd ed., Boston: Little, Brown, 1977) at 138).

Such an approach is overly simplistic. The validity of the argument is contingent on two dubious assumptions: that penalties will remain minimal and unrealistic, and that the intangible costs (i.e. loss of reputation in the community, political embarrassment, unsettling of shareholders) will be negligible. Moreover, it fails to take into account the possible and positive gains that are available if the polluter shows himself to be a morally and socially responsible member of the community. There is much more to law and life than the cold and relentless logic of economic reasoning.

iv. Proposals for Reform

In contrast to the general trend one commentator has ardently advocated the increase in crimes of strict liability:

BARONESS WOOTTON, *CRIME AND THE CRIMINAL LAW,* 2ND EDN (STEVENS, 1981), PP.46–48

If, however, the primary function of the courts is conceived as the prevention of forbidden acts, there is little cause to be disturbed by the multiplication of offences of strict liability. If the law says that certain things are not to be done, it is illogical to confine this prohibition to occasions on which they are done from malice aforethought: for at least the material consequences of an action, and the reasons for prohibiting it, are the same whether it is the result of sinister malicious plotting, of negligence or of sheer accident. A man is equally dead and his relatives equally bereaved whether he was stabbed or run over by a drunken motorist or by an incompetent one; and the inconvenience caused by the loss of your bicycle is unaffected by the question whether or not the youth who removed it had the intention of putting it back, if in fact he had not done so at the time of his arrest. It is true, of course, as Professor Hart has argued, that the material consequences of an action by no means exhaust its effects. If one person hits another, the person struck does not think of the other as *just* a cause of pain to him . . . If the blow was light but deliberate, it has a significance for the person struck quite different from an accidental much heavier blow.' To ignore this difference, he argues, is to outrage 'distinctions which not only underlie morality, but pervade the whole of our social life'. That these distinctions are widely appreciated and keenly felt no one would deny. Often perhaps they derive their force from a purely punitive or retributive attitude; but alternatively they may be held to be relevant to an assessment of the social damage that results from a criminal act. Just as a heavy blow does more damage that a light one, so also perhaps does a blow which involves psychological injury do more damage than one in which the hurt is purely physical.

The conclusion to which this argument leads is, I think, not that the presence or absence of the guilty mind is unimportant, but that *mens rea* has, so to speak—and this is the crux of the matter—*got into the wrong place.* Traditionally, the requirement of the guilty mind is written into the actual definition of a crime. No guilty intention, no crime, is the rule. Obviously this makes sense if the law's concern is with wickedness: where there is no guilty intention, there can be no wickedness. But it is equally obvious, on the other hand, that an action does not become innocuous merely because whoever performed it meant no harm. If the object of the criminal law is to prevent the occurrence of socially damaging actions, it would be absurd to turn a blind eye to those which were due to carelessness, negligence or even accident. The question of motivation is *in the first instance* irrelevant.

But only in the first instance. At a later stage, that is to say, after what is now known as conviction, the presence or absence of guilty intention is all-important for its effect on the appropriate measures to be taken to prevent a recurrence of the forbidden act. The prevention of accidental deaths presents different problems from those involved in the prevention of wilful murders. The results of the actions of the careless, the mistaken, the wicked and the merely unfortunate may be indistinguishable from one another, but each case calls for a different treatment. Tradition, however, is very strong, and the notion that these differences are relevant only after the fact has been established that the accused committed the forbidden act seems still to be deeply abhorrent to the legal mind. Thus Lord Devlin, discussing the possibility that judges might have taken the line that all 'unintentional' criminals might be dealt with simply by the imposition of a nominal penalty, regards this as the 'negation of law'. 'It would,' [Devlin, Lord, *Samples of Law Making* (OUP, 1962) p.73] he says, 'confuse the function of mercy which the judge is dispensing when imposing the penalty with the function of justice. It would have been to deny to the citizen due process of law because it would have been to say to him, in effect: 'Although we cannot think that Parliament intended you to be punished in this case because you have really done nothing wrong, come to us, ask for mercy, and we shall grant mercy' . . . In all criminal matters the citizen is entitled to the protection of the law . . . and the mitigation of penalty should not be adopted as the prime method of dealing with accidental offenders.'

Within its own implied terms of reference the logic is unexceptionable. If the purpose of the law is to dispense punishment tempered with mercy, then to use mercy as a consolation for unjust punishment is certainly to give a stone for bread. But these are not the implied terms of reference of strict liability. In the case of offences of strict liability the presumption is not that those who have committed forbidden actions must be punished, but that appropriate steps must be taken to prevent the occurrence of such actions.

J.C. SMITH, "RESPONSIBILITY IN CRIMINAL LAW" IN BEAN AND WHYNES (EDS), *BARBARA WOOTTON, ESSAYS IN HER HONOUR* (TAVISTOCK PUBLICATIONS, 1986), PP.141 AND 153

This brings me to what I regard as the major difficulty in Lady Wootton's theory. It is essentially a practical one. The only question for the court of trial is to be 'Did he do it?' Whether he did it intentionally, recklessly, negligently, or by sheer accident is irrelevant. In any event the person who did it is to be passed on to the 'sentencer' who will consider what should be done to ensure that he does not do it again. Now if the court of trial has to disregard the question of fault, so too surely do the police and the prosecuting authority (or whatever takes its place). If we allow the police or prosecutor to decide to proceed or not on the basis of whether or not the defendant was at fault, we do indirectly what we will not permit to be done directly. We allow the crucial decision which is now made formally and openly on proper evidence in court to be made informally, privately, and on whatever evidence the prosecutor, in his wisdom, or lack of it, considers relevant. The logic of the system requires the prosecution of *all* cases because even if the forbidden result has resulted from 'sheer accident,' the sentencer is under a duty to consider whether there is anything to be done to ensure that the 'offender' does not have such accidents again. Everyone who causes injury to another person, everyone who damages another's property, could, and should, be brought to court. Every buyer or seller of goods who makes an innocent misrepresentation, every bona-fide purchaser of goods in fact stolen, the surgeon whose patient dies on the operating table, the Good Samaritan who innocently gives help to a person escaping after committing an arrestable offence—all these have brought about the harm which it is the object of the law to prevent; so they should be subject to process of law so as to ensure that they do not cause the harm again. The business of the courts would be enormously multiplied. And to what purpose? What is to be done with all those who (like Ball and Mrs Tolson) have behaved reasonably and have had the misfortune to cause the forbidden result by sheer accident—except to tell them to continue to behave reasonably?

It is reasonably safe to assume that what would in fact happen is that, however illogically, the fault test would be applied at the police or prosecution stage. This would be prompted, not only by the natural sense of justice of those operating the system, but also by their realization of the futility of invoking legal process against one who has behaved entirely reasonably.

A further practical difficulty is that the system would put enormous discretion into the hands of the sentencer. He would apparently have the same power in law over one who caused death accidentally as over a murderer. It is difficult to believe that such a large discretion would be tolerable. It would dilute, if not destroy, the criminal law as a moral force and that at a time when the decline of religious belief has, as Lady Wootton herself says, created a dangerous vacuum. The shift from punishment to prevention may be intended to remove the moral basis of the law; but if, as some believe, one of the major reasons why people do not commit crimes is the sense of guilt which attaches to them, should not the aim be to enhance the sense of guilt rather than otherwise? To remove the element of fault is to empty the law of moral content. If murder were, in law, no different from accidental death, should we be so inhibited from committing murder as most of us are?

4 MENTAL INCAPACITY

In this chapter defences which relate to the defendant's mental capacity will be considered. Duress, necessity and self-defence are considered in Ch.5.

In a criminal case, the defendant's mental state at three separate times may be relevant:

(i) the time when the actus reus is committed;

(ii) the time when the defendant is called to plead to the charge against him;

(iii) the time when the court comes to consider the appropriate sentence where the defendant stands convicted.

In this book (i) will be considered in detail. On (ii) see J. Sprack, *A Practical Approach to Criminal Procedure*, 14th edn (Oxford: Oxford University Press, 2012), Ch.16; on (iii) see A. Ashworth, Sentencing and Criminal Justice, 6th edn (Cambridge: Cambridge University Press, 2015)

There are three ways in which the issue of the defendant's mental state may be raised as relevant when the actus reus was committed:

(a) on a plea of insanity;

(b) a plea that the defendant was acting in a state of automatism;

(c) on a plea of diminished responsibility where the charge is one of murder (see Ch.8, below p.477).

1. INSANITY

A successful plea of insanity provides a complete defence to a charge where the defendant was insane at the time the actus reus of the offence was committed. The principal justification for this is the obvious injustice of punishing an actor who is not responsible for his actions. It may, of course, be necessary to subject the insane person to compulsory detention but it is neither just nor appropriate to stigmatise the sick with a criminal conviction.

Previously the defence carried with it the consequence that the defendant would be ordered by the court to be admitted to a mental hospital under s.37 of the Mental Health Act 1983 subject to restriction without limit of time under s.41. The defendant would be detained until the Home Secretary or a Mental Health Tribunal ordered his release on being satisfied that detention was no longer necessary for the protection of the public. Unsurprisingly perhaps, this automatic committal to a mental hospital for an indefinite period was a strong deterrent against pleading insanity as a defence. It was not uncommon to hear of defendants choosing to plead guilty instead of relying on the defence of insanity even though the defence was available to them. In this way, they would at least receive a determinate sentence which might, in many circumstances, be preferable to the uncertainty of indefinite confinement in a mental hospital. Between 1975 and 1989 there was a total of 52 verdicts of "not guilty by reason of insanity", with the number in any single year ranging from one to six (see R.D. Mackay, *Mental Condition Defences in the Criminal Law* (Oxford: Clarendon Press, 1995), p.102). The Criminal Procedure (Insanity and Unfitness to Plead) Act 1991 has now altered this position significantly. Section 3 substitutes a new s.5 of the Criminal Procedure (Insanity) Act 1964 providing the judge with discretion in the disposal he chooses. No longer is a judge compelled to commit an insane person to indefinite detention in a mental hospital. The substituted s.5 provides—

"**5.**—(1) This section applies where—

(a) a special verdict is returned that the accused is not guilty by reason of insanity; or
(b) findings are recorded that the accused is under a disability and that he did the act or made the omission charged against him.

(2) Subject to subsection (3) below, the court shall either—

(a)   make an order that the accused be admitted, in accordance with the provisions of Schedule 1 to the Criminal Procedure (Insanity and Unfitness to Plead) Act 1991, to such hospital as may be specified by the Secretary of State; or
(b)   where they have the power to do so by virtue of s.5 of that Act, make in respect of the accused such one of the following orders as they think most suitable in all the circumstances of the case, namely—

 (i) a guardianship order within the meaning of the Mental Health Act 1983;
 (ii) a supervision and treatment order within the meaning of Schedule 2 to the said Act of 1991; and
 (iii) an order for his absolute discharge.

(3) Paragraph (b) of subsection (2) above shall not apply where the offence to which the special verdict or findings relate is an offence the sentence for which is fixed by law."

In the five years immediately following the coming into force of the Criminal Procedure (Insanity) Act 1991 there were 44 findings of "not guilty by reason of insanity" (see Mackay and Kearns, "More Fact(s) about the Insanity Defence" [1999] Crim. L.R. 714, 716). The authors speculate that the reason for this increase is that "the new legislation has started to become more widely known by lawyers and psychiatrists as it has permeated the body of medico-legal knowledge. This in turn may have led to an appreciation that the 1991 Act has removed the more glaring disincentives inherent within the 1964 Act of running a defence of [not guilty by reason of insanity]". The vast majority of offences in respect of which the special verdict was returned were offences of violence. In 17 cases the disposal was as it would have been prior to the passage of the 1991 Act, a restriction order without limit of time. However in 23 cases a community-based disposal was utilised. The authors speculate that this fact will, itself, stimulate greater use of the insanity defence. The fact remains, however, that the 1991 Act has not removed the stigmatising label of "insane" which may still deter some defendants from raising the insanity defence. In addition, the Act does not address the problem of the legal definition of insanity which remains grossly outdated and fails to recognise developments in medical knowledge.

In July 2013, the Law Commission issued a Discussion Paper concerned with insanity and automatism. The Law Commission identified problems with these defences and made a number of proposals for reform.

The Paper, together with a summary of the recommendations, can be viewed in full at *http://www.lawcom.gov.uk/document/insanity-and-automatism-discussion-paper/*
The current law will now be examined.

M'NAGHTEN'S CASE

(1843) 10 Cl. & R 200; 8 E.R. 718

M'Naghten was indicted for murder and acquitted on the ground of insanity. In consequence debates took place in the House of Lords, and it was decided to take the opinion of the judges as to the nature and extent of the unsoundness of mind which would excuse the commission of a felony of this sort. Five questions were put to the judges in the terms set out in the following extract from their opinions.

TINDAL CJ

(Delivering the opinion of all the judges except Maule J): The first question proposed by your Lordships is this: 'What is the law respecting alleged crimes committed by persons afflicted with insane delusion in respect of one or more particular subjects or persons: as, for instance, where at the time of the commission of the alleged crime the accused knew he was acting contrary to law, but did the act complained of with a view, under the influence of insane delusion, of redressing or revenging some supposed grievance or injury, or of producing some supposed public benefit?'

In answer to which question, assuming that your Lordships' inquiries are confined to those persons who labour under such partial delusions only, and are not in other respects insane, we are of opinion that, notwithstanding the party accused did the act complained of with a view, under the influence of insane delusion, of redressing or revenging some supposed grievance or injury, or of producing some public benefit, he is nevertheless punishable according to the nature of the crime committed, if he knew at the time of committing such crime that he was acting contrary to law; by which expression we understand your Lordships to mean the law of the land.

Your Lordships are pleased to inquire of us, secondly, 'What are the proper questions to be submitted to the jury, where a person alleged to be afflicted with insane delusion respecting one or more particular subjects or persons, is charged with the commission of a crime (murder, for example), and insanity is set up as a defence?'

And, thirdly, 'In what terms ought the question to be left to the jury as to the prisoner's state of mind at the time when the act was committed?' And as these two questions appear to us to be more conveniently answered together, we have to submit our opinion to be, that the jurors ought to be told in all cases that every man is to be presumed to be sane, and to possess a sufficient degree of reason to be responsible for his crimes, until the contrary be proved to their satisfaction; and that to establish a defence on the ground of insanity, it must be clearly proved that, at the time of the committing of the act, the party accused was labouring under such a defect of reason, from disease of the mind, as not to know the nature and quality of the act he was doing; or, if he did know it, that he did not know he was doing what was wrong. The mode of putting the latter part of the question to the jury on these occasions has generally been, whether the accused at the time of doing the act knew the difference between right and wrong: which mode, though rarely, if ever, leading to any mistake with the jury, is not, as we conceive, so accurate when put generally and in the abstract, as when put with reference to the party's knowledge of right and wrong in respect of the very act with which he is charged. If the question were to be put as to the knowledge of the accused solely and exclusively with reference to the law of the land, it might tend to confound the jury, by inducing them to believe that an actual knowledge of the law of the land was essential in order to lead to a conviction: whereas the law is administered upon the principle that everyone must be taken conclusively to know it, without proof that he does know it. If the accused was conscious that the act was one which he ought not to do, and if that act was at the same time contrary to the law of the land, he is punishable: and the usual course therefore has been to leave the question to the jury, whether the party accused had a sufficient degree of reason to know that he was doing an act that was wrong: and this course we think is correct, accompanied with such observations and explanations as the circumstances of each particular case may require.

The fourth question which your Lordships have proposed to us is this: 'If a person under an insane delusion as to existing facts, commits an offence in consequence thereof, is he thereby excused?' To which question the answer must, of course, depend on the nature of the delusion: but, making the same assumption as we did before, namely, that he labours under such partial delusion only, and is not in other respects insane, we think he must be considered in the same situation as to responsibility as if the facts with respect to which the delusion exists were real. For example, if under the influence of his delusion he supposes another man to be in the act of attempting to take away his life, and he kills that man, as he supposes, in self-defence, he would be exempt from punishment. If this delusion was that the deceased had inflicted a serious injury to his character and fortune, and he killed him in revenge for such supposed injury, he would be liable to punishment.

Question

Do you agree that the three questions a jury must consider under the M'Naghten Rules are principally concerned with mens rea?

C. WELLS "WHITHER INSANITY?" [1983] CRIM. L.R. 787–788 AND 793–794

Insanity, along with the related defences of automatism and intoxication, raises very clearly the social protection role of the criminal law. The recent cases of *Bailey* [below, p197] and *Sullivan* [below, p182] illustrate this point. At one level they merely confirm the status quo—epilepsy is a 'disease of the mind', diabetes is not. At another, they give an insight into the difficulty of pursuing the dual models of individual responsibility and social protection. In neither case is there any attempt to locate the argument within a theoretical context. And yet unless there is more clarity as to whether insanity is treated as a condition, like infancy, barring the jurisdiction of the court, or as an excuse for the particular act, the operation of the defence and its effect on other defences such as automatism and intoxication will continue to confound . . .

Very few defendants choose to avail themselves of the insanity defence. Although nominally an acquittal, the special verdict of 'not guilty by reason of insanity' is little less than 'a direction to punish but not to punish criminally.' . . . The choice therefore for mentally disordered defendants is that between conviction (and the possibility at least of a determinate sentence) and a rather double-edged acquittal. Some defendants may be able to argue that they were in a state of automatism and thus add the possibility of a full acquittal. Because this represents a more attractive choice it is not surprising that it is in this sort of case that the courts have most often been asked to draw a line between the sane and the insane. But not infrequently the decision can also become entwined with the intoxication defence. The possibility of conceptual confusion on a large scale is thus opened—from insanity as a precluding or excusing condition through automatism on the basis of the 'no act' plea to the qualification of that plea by the doctrine of self-induced automatism. The issue then becomes one of whether to apply the rationale of the intoxication defence to the automaton whose condition is self-induced other than through drink or drugs. This may seem a long way from insanity. The paradigm mad person and the paradigm drunk may have little in common but appeal cases rarely deal with the unitary paradigm. *Bailey* (the case of the diabetic) is no exception. Considered with *Sullivan* (the epilepsy case), it confronts the problematic issue of when automatism should be treated as insanity. *Bailey* also raises the important, related, question of the limitations on automatism as a defence when it is self induced . . .

> 'It has for centuries been recognised that if a person was, at the time of his unlawful act, mentally so disordered that it would be unreasonable to impute guilt to him, he ought not to be held liable for conviction and punishment.'

This type of 'reason is since reason long has been' argument was employed also by the Butler Committee and is of course a somewhat inadequate starting point for an inquiry into insanity, particularly in view of changing ideas about criminal responsibility. And, as with much discussion in this area, it skates over the dual effect of the insanity verdict, concentrating only on the absolvent quality and ignoring its concomitant of indefinite detention.

One view prevalent in the English literature is that insanity excuses because it negatives the mental element in crime. There are two problems with this. Unless *mens rea* is here being given the wider normative meaning of 'the state of mind stigmatised as wrongful by the criminal law', it is not easy to see that insanity does necessarily negative *mens rea*. It only does so if *mens rea* consists of a subjective mental element. Where it is an objective form of recklessness or negligence, or where there is a crime of strict liability, then the argument that insanity excuses because it precludes *mens rea* breaks down. And if one took the wider normative view of *mens rea*, then the argument would be somewhat tautologous; it would amount to saying that an insane person is not responsible because the stigmatised wrongful state of mind includes only the sane.

The other problem with the *mens rea* view of insanity is that it is an implicit acknowledgement that the insanity defence is about disposal rather than responsibility. A sane person who lacks *mens rea* is normally acquitted. If insanity is a 'defence' because it amounts to lack of *mens rea*, then it is otiose.

Thus an exploration of insanity and responsibility has either to go beyond *mens rea*, or, if a normative view is taken, it has to justify the exclusion of the insane.

Notes

1. *M'Naghten* places the burden of proof on the defendant. It was held in *R. v Sodeman* [1936] 2 All E.R. 1138 that this requires proof on a balance of probability. Both the Criminal Law Revision Committee, *11th Report* (TSO, 1972), Cmnd.4991, s.1.40) and the Butler Committee on Mentally Abnormal Offenders (TSO, 1975), Cmnd.6244, s.18.39 recommended that this burden should be on the prosecution. In the Draft Criminal Code cl.35, either the defence or prosecution may prove mental disorder on a balance of probabilities.

2. Where the issue of insanity is raised during a trial, the prosecution are relieved of the duty of proving mens rea as the 1883 Act only requires it to be proved that the accused "did the act or made the omission charged" (see *Attorney General's Reference (No.3 of 1998)* [1999] 3 W.L.R. 1994).

3. There is a problem with placing a burden of proof on the accused in cases where the effect of the defect of reason is that he did not know the nature and quality of the act he was doing. In such a case he is being asked to prove on a balance of probabilities something the contrary of which the prosecution have not proved. If the prosecution prove beyond reasonable doubt that he knew what he was doing, and thus had mens rea that would be an end of the matter. But if they fail to prove this it seems superfluous, and indeed illogical, to require the accused to prove the contrary on a balance of probabilities. The opportunity to confront this problem arose in the context of the next case but was ignored by the Court of Appeal which focused its attention on whether a trial judge may raise the issue of insanity and leave it to the jury.

R. V THOMAS (SHARON)

[1995] Crim. L.R. 314

D was charged with burglary and robbery. At the time of the alleged offences she was drunk. Medical evidence was called on her behalf at the trial to the effect that she had a mental condition, hypomania, which was aggravated by drink, and which, if aggravated, would render her so confused that she would be unable to form the specific intent required for the offences. The trial judge intervened and put questions to D's doctor which elicited answers to the effect that hypomania was a disease of the mind and D would not have been aware of the nature and quality of her acts. The judge raised the question of leaving the defence of insanity to the jury but counsel for D submitted that it should not be so left. The judge directed the jury on insanity. D was convicted of burglary and appealed arguing, inter alia, that (1) where medical evidence was called to the effect that D could not have formed the specific intent for the offence, the judge erred in leaving to the jury, against the wishes of D's counsel, the defence of insanity and in ruling he was obliged to do so; (2) to leave such a defence over complicated the case: it failed to differentiate between the ability to form a specific intent and the ability to appreciate the nature and quality of her acts.

ROCH LJ

. . . The judge's decision to raise the issue of insanity and his direction to the jury on the matter were, in the judgment of this Court, material irregularities for several reasons. First, insanity was not a defence raised by the appellant or her counsel. Her defence was simply that by reason of her hypomania, and the drink that she had taken, the jury could not be sure that she had been capable of forming, and had formed, the specific intents required by Counts 1 and 2 in the indictment. She was entitled, on the evidence . . . to raise that issue. That issue being raised by the defence, it was for the Crown to satisfy the jury that the appellant had had the ability to form, and had formed, one or other of the two specific intents required.

The judge clearly thought that he had a duty to raise the issue of insanity, and that it provided an additional defence for the appellant in this case. In our judgment, it did not, as a practical matter, raise an additional defence for this appellant.

It may well be that a judge has a duty in an appropriate case to raise defences open to a defendant where the burden of disproving that defence rests on the prosecution. However, in our judgment, the situation is not the same where the defence places a burden of proof upon a defendant. In those cases, in our view, the principle is correctly stated in *Archbold*, current edition, Volume 2 at para. 17–111 in these terms:

> 'In certain exceptional circumstances, a judge can of his own volition raise an issue of insanity and leave the issue to the jury providing there is evidence embracing all the relevant considerations in the M'Naghten Rules.'

The editors of *Archbold* then go on to set out what a judge must do if he is minded to take such a course. That statement is consistent with the views expressed by this Court in the case of *R v Dickie* (1984) 79 Cr.App.R. 213, in the judgment given by Watkins LJ where, at page 218, the court said:

> 'We have come to the conclusion that we are unable to say there are no circumstances in which a judge may of his own volition raise an issue of insanity and leave it to a jury, provided that if he chooses to do so there is relevant evidence which goes to all the factors involved in the M'Naghten test. We envisage, however, that circumstances in which a judge will do that will be exceptional and very rare.'

Then his Lordship went on to consider the procedural steps that a judge would have to take if a judge decided that he had before him an exceptional and very rare case in which he should take that initiative.

There may be cases, for example, cases of homicide, where an accused has raised a defence of, say, diminished responsibility where a judge would be entitled, of his own volition to raise the issue of insanity with the jury. However, it would have to be a rare and exceptional case. This was not such a case in our judgment.

The evidence of possible insanity arose in answer to questions put by the judge after the cross-examination of Dr O'Riordan had been completed. It is to be regretted, in our view, that the judge chose to ask those questions. A serious consequence of those questions was that the jury may well have supposed that the appellant would only have been incapable of forming the necessary specific intentions if she had been legally insane.

In the . . . summing-up, the judge had correctly indicated that the jury could not find the appellant to have been legally insane unless it was shown to be more probable than not that she had been unaware of the nature and quality of her acts, and that that had been caused by a disease of the mind. This may well have misled the jury as to the burden of proof on the second issue left to them, namely, had the appellant had the necessary intent to support a charge of robbery or, alternatively, a charge of burglary.

These unsatisfactory features were added to by the judge's references on more than one occasion to the uncomfortable consequences of this line of defence. The issue of insanity was, in our view, a complication which the judge should have avoided and from which the jury should have been spared. Leaving the issues raised on behalf of the appellant, and only those issues to the jury, was not simplistic. It was, in the circumstances of this case, the correct thing for the judge to have done.

In our judgment, that first matter was a material irregularity which justifies the quashing of the appellant's conviction.

Appeal allowed and conviction quashed

Note

In the above case, D was not pleading automatism or insanity but raising the possibility that due to her intoxication she did not have the requisite intention for the offence. Had she pleaded automatism the judge would have been free to determine as a question of law whether the alleged cause of that condition was a disease of the mind in which case the plea would have been one of insane automatism (see *Sullivan*, below p.182).

----

i. Disease of the Mind

R. V KEMP

[1957] 1 Q.B. 399

The defendant was charged with causing grievous bodily harm to his wife. He suffered from arterio-sclerosis which had not given rise to general mental trouble but caused temporary loss of consciousness during which state the attack was made. He did not plead insanity.

DEVLIN J

. . . In this case it is conceded that everything [in the third and fourth answers in *M'Naghten's Case*] applies here, except for 'disease of the mind . . .' The law is not concerned with the brain but with the mind, in the sense that 'mind' is ordinarily used, the mental faculties of reason, memory and understanding. If one read for 'disease of the mind' 'disease of the brain', it would follow that in many cases pleas of insanity would not be established because it could not be proved that the brain had been affected in any way, either by degeneration of the cells or in any other way. In my judgment the condition of the brain is irrelevant and so is the question of whether the condition of the mind is curable or incurable, transitory or permanent. There is no warranty for introducing those considerations into the definition in the M'Naghten Rules. Temporary insanity is sufficient to satisfy them. It does not matter whether it is incurable and permanent or not.

I think that the approach of Mr Lee (for the Crown) to the definition in the Rules is the right one. He points out the order of the words 'a defect of reason, from disease of the mind'. The primary thing that has to be looked for is the defect of reason. 'Disease of the mind' is there for some purpose, obviously, but the prime tiling is to determine what is admitted here, namely, whether or not there is a defect of reason. In my judgment, the words 'from disease of the mind' are not to be construed as if they were put in for the purpose of distinguishing between diseases which have a mental origin and diseases which have a physical origin, a distinction which in 1843 was probably little considered. They were put in for the purpose of limiting the effect of the words 'defect of reason'. A defect of reason is by itself enough to make the act irrational and therefore normally to exclude responsibility in law. But the Rule was not intended to apply to defects of reason caused simply by brutish stupidity without rational power. It was not intended that the defence should plead 'although with a healthy mind he nevertheless had been brought up in such a way that he had never learned to exercise his reason, and therefore he is suffering from a defect of reason'. The words ensure that unless the defect is due to a diseased mind and not simply to an untrained one there is insanity within the meaning of the Rule.

Hardening of the arteries is a disease which is shown on the evidence to be capable of affecting the mind in such a way as to cause a defect, temporarily or permanently, of its reasoning, understanding and so on, and so as is my judgment a disease of the mind which comes within the meaning of the Rules.

Verdict: Guilty but insane

R. V SULLIVAN

[1984] A.C. 156 HL

The appellant was charged with inflicting grievous bodily harm on P. At his trial he admitted the act but asserted by way of defence that he had done so while in an epileptic seizure. The trial judge ruled that this amounted to a defence of insanity rather than a defence of automatism. The appellant then changed his plea to guilty of assault occasioning actual bodily harm and was convicted of that offence. He appealed against the conviction but the Court of Appeal upheld the judge's ruling and dismissed the appeal. He appealed to the House of Lords.

LORD DIPLOCK

The evidence as to the pathology of a seizure due to psychomotor epilepsy can be sufficiently stated for the purposes of this appeal by saying that after the first stage, the prodram, which precedes the fit itself, there is a second stage, the ictus, lasting a few seconds, during which there are electrical discharges into the temporal lobes of the brain of the sufferer. The effect of these discharges is to cause him in the post-ictal stage to make movements which he is not conscious that he is making, including, and this was a characteristic of previous seizures which Mr Sullivan had suffered, automatic movements of resistance to anyone trying to come to his aid. These movements of resistance might, though in practice they very rarely would, involve violence . . .

[His Lordship reviewed the M'Naghten rules and *Bratty*, below p.191 and continued.] In the instant case, as in *Bratty*, the only evidential foundation that was laid for any finding by the jury that Mr. Sullivan was acting unconsciously and involuntarily when he was kicking Mr Payne, was that when he did so he was in the post-ictal stage of a seizure of psychomotor epilepsy. The evidential foundation in the case of Bratty, that he was suffering from psychomotor epilepsy at the time he did the act with which he was charged, was very weak and was rejected by the jury; the evidence in Mr Sullivan's case, that he was so suffering when he was kicking Mr Payne, was very strong and would almost inevitably be accepted by a properly directed jury. It would be the duty of the judge to direct the jury that if they did accept that evidence the law required them to bring in a special verdict and none other. The governing statutory provision is to be found in section 2 of the Trial of Lunatics Act 1883. This says 'the jury *shall* return a special verdict . . .'

My Lords, I can deal briefly with the various grounds on which it has been submitted that the instant case can be distinguished from what constituted the ratio decidendi in *Bratty v Attorney-General for Northern Ireland* [1963] A.C. 386, and that it falls outside the ambit of the M'Naghten Rules.

First, it is submitted the medical evidence in the instant case shows that psychomotor epilepsy is not a disease of the mind, whereas in *Bratty* it was accepted by all the doctors that it was. The only evidential basis for this submission is that Dr Fenwick said that in medical terms to constitute a 'disease of the mind' or 'mental illness', which he appeared to regard as interchangeable descriptions, a disorder of brain functions (which undoubtedly occurs during a seizure in psychomotor epilepsy) must be prolonged for a period of time usually more than a day; while Dr Taylor would have it that the disorder must continue for a minimum of a month to qualify for the description 'a disease of the mind'.

The nomenclature adopted by the medical profession may change from time to time; Bratty was tried in 1961. But the meaning of the expression 'disease of the mind' as the cause of 'a defect of reason' remains unchanged for the purposes of the application of the M'Naghten Rules. I agree with what was said by Devlin J. in *R. v Kemp* [above, p181], that 'mind' in the M'Naghten Rules is used in the ordinary sense of the mental faculties of reason, memory and understanding. If the effect of a disease is to impair these faculties so severely as to have either of the consequences referred to in the latter part of the rules, it matters not whether the aetiology of the impairment is organic, as in epilepsy, or functional, or whether the impairment itself is permanent or is transient and intermittent, provided that it subsisted at the time of commission of the act. The purpose of the legislation relating to the defence of insanity, ever since its origin in 1800, has been to protect society against recurrence of the dangerous conduct. The duration of a temporary suspension of the mental faculties of reason, memory and understanding, particularly if, as in Mr Sullivan's case, it is recurrent, cannot on any rational ground be relevant to the application by the courts of the M'Naghten Rules, though it may be relevant to the course adopted by the Secretary of State, to whom the responsibility for how the defendant is to be dealt with passes after the return of the special verdict of 'not guilty by reason of insanity'.

To avoid misunderstanding I ought perhaps to add that in expressing my agreement with what was said by Devlin J. in *Kemp*, where the disease that caused the temporary and intermittent impairment of the mental faculties was arteriosclerosis, I do not regard that learned judge as excluding the possibility of non-insane automatism (for which the proper verdict would be a verdict of 'not guilty') in cases where temporary impairment (not being self-induced by consuming drink or drugs) results from some external physical factor such as a blow on the head causing concussion or the administration of an anaesthetic for therapeutic purposes. I mention this because in *R. v Quick* [1973] Q.B. 910, Lawton L.J. appears to have regarded the ruling in *Kemp* as going as far as this. If it had done, it would have been inconsistent with the speeches in this House in *Bratty*, below, p191) where *Kemp* was alluded to without disapproval by Viscount Kilmuir L.C. at p.403, and received the express approval of Lord Denning, at p.411. The instant case, however, does not in my view afford an appropriate occasion for exploring possible causes of non-insane automatism.

The only other submission in support of Mr Sullivan's appeal which I think is necessary to mention is that, because the expert evidence was to the effect that Mr Sullivan's acts in kicking Mr Payne were unconscious and thus 'involuntary' in the legal sense of that term, his state of mind was not one dealt with by the M'Naghten Rules at all, since it was not covered by the phrase 'as not to know the nature and quality of the act he was doing.' Quite apart from being contrary to all three speeches in this House in *Bratty v A.-G. for Northern Ireland* this submission appears to me, with all respect to counsel, to be quite unarguable. Dr Fenwick himself accepted it as an accurate description of Mr Sullivan's mental state in the post-ictal stage of a seizure. The audience to whom the phrase in the M'Naghten Rules was addressed consisted of peers of the realm in the 1840's when certain orotundity of diction had not yet fallen out of fashion. Addressed to an audience of jurors in the 1980's it might more aptly be expressed as 'He did not know what he was doing.'

My Lords, it is natural to feel reluctant to attach the label of insanity to a sufferer from psychomotor epilepsy of the kind to which Mr Sullivan was subject, even though the expression in the context of a special verdict of 'not guilty by reason of insanity' is a technical one which includes a purely temporary and intermittent suspension of the mental faculties of reason, memory and understanding resulting from the occurrence of an epileptic fit. But the label is contained in the current statute, it has appeared in this statute's predecessors ever since 1800. It does not lie within the power of the courts to alter it. Only Parliament can do that. It has done so twice; it could do so once again.

Sympathise though I do with Mr Sullivan, I see no other course open to your Lordships than to dismiss this appeal.

[The other Law Lords agreed with Lord Diplock's speech.]

Appeal dismissed

Questions

1.   If, as Lord Diplock stated, the purpose of the M'Naghten Rules is "to protect society against the recurrence of the dangerous conduct," was this purpose furthered by the procedure followed in *Sullivan* when the guilty plea was accepted? Was it furthered by the outcome in *R. v Thomas* (above, p179) (see E. Lederman, "Non-Insane and Insane Automatism: Reducing the Significance of a Problematic Distinction" (1985) 34 I.C.L.Q. 819).

2.   Did Sullivan's conviction serve any other purpose such as deterring other epileptics from injuring others while in an epileptic seizure?

3.   Does the distinction between external physical factors and internal organic or functional factors provide a sound basis for identifying those who are dangerous and from whom society needs to be protected? (See further *Parks*, below, p185.)

4.   Do, and if so should, the M'Naghten Rules apply to defendants who suffer from retarded development, i.e. is mental deficiency a disease of the mind?

5.   If the facts of *Sullivan* were to recur with the difference that the victim dies and on a trial for murder the judge refuses to accept a plea of guilty to manslaughter, and the jury return a verdict

of not guilty by reason of insanity resulting in the accused's compulsory indefinite detention in a secure mental hospital, could the accused appeal against this outcome on the grounds that s.5 of the Criminal Procedure (Insanity) Act 1964 is incompatible with his rights under art.5 of the European Convention of Human Rights? (See n.1 directly below.)

Notes

1. Article 5 of the European Convention of Human Rights states:

> "1. Everyone has the right to liberty and security of person.
> No one shall be deprived of his liberty save in the following cases and in accordance with a procedure prescribed by law; . . . (e) the lawful detention . . . of persons of unsound mind . . ."

In the leading case before the European Court of Human Rights, *Winterwerp v Netherlands* (1979) 2 E.H.R.R. 387, the Court stated at para.39:

> "In the Court's opinion, except in emergency cases, the individual concerned should not be deprived of his liberty unless he has been reliably shown to be of 'unsound mind'. The very nature of what has to be established before the competent national authority—that is, a true mental disorder—calls for objective medical expertise. Further, the mental disorder must be of a kind or degree warranting compulsory confinement. What is more, the validity of the continued confinement depends upon the persistence of such a disorder."

It is doubtful whether conditions such as diabetes, epilepsy, or somnambulism would be classified by objective medical experts as mental disorders. Certainly they would not fall within the definition of "mental disorder" in s.1 of the Mental Health Act 1983 which governs the conditions for civil commitment to a mental hospital and covers "mental illness, arrested or incomplete development of mind, psychopathic disorder and any other disorder or disability of mind". Detention of such a person who is not of "unsound mind" would be a breach of art.5. This form of challenge to the law of insanity, however, will be of limited utility as it will be an option only where a special verdict results in detention and the condition from which the accused suffers is not a mental disorder. If any other disposal under s.5 of the 1964 Act is used, it will not breach art.5 however much one might consider that, for example, a diabetic should not be labelled as being insane. In *R. v H* [2003] H.R.L.R. 19, the House of Lords rejected an argument that the unfitness to plead procedure violated the European Convention on Human Rights.
. . .In the *Supplementary Material to the Scoping Paper* (TSO, 2012), the Law Commission concluded that the defence of insanity breaches art.6(2) of the ECHR by placing the burden of proof on the accused. They also articulated additional concerns:

> "1.35 We also have concerns about potential violations of the right to life (article 2), and to private and family life (article 8) of potential victims if the law does not adequately distinguish between those who may fairly be held responsible for what they do and those who, due to their condition, may not. In addition, the unsuitability of the current definition of the insanity defence leads to some people being detained in custody when a fair test would lead to the conclusion that they were not criminally responsible. In consequence, they are at greater risk of imprison-

ment rather than treatment and hence at greater risk of suicide and self-harm, and the state, which owes duties to those held in custody, risks violations of their right to life (article 2) and the right not to be subjected to inhuman and degrading treatment (article 3)."

3. In *Bratty v Attorney General for Northern Ireland* [1963] A.C. 386 (below, p191) Lord Denning stated at 412:

> "It seems to me that any mental disorder which has manifested itself in violence and is prone to recur is a disease of the mind. At any rate it is the sort of disease for which a person should be detained in hospital rather than be given an unqualified acquittal."

This dictum was not approved in *Sullivan* which focused on the cause of the defect of reason rather than the consequences flowing from it. In *Burgess* [1991] 2 W.L.R. 1206, the accused sought to plead automatism due to sleep walking on a charge of wounding with intent to do grievous bodily harm contrary to s.18 of the Offences Against the Person Act 1861. The trial judge ruled that this was a plea of insanity. The appellant appealed against the finding of the jury that he was not guilty by reason of insanity. The Court of Appeal expressed its approval of Lord Denning's "definition" of "disease of the mind". Lord Lane CJ adding this qualification (at 1212):

> "It seems to us that if there is a danger of recurrence that may be an added reason for catego-rising the condition as a disease of the mind. On the other hand, the absence of the danger of recurrence is not a reason for saying that it cannot be a disease of the mind."

This revival of Lord Denning's dictum is hardly helpful (nor was it necessary for deciding the appeal). First, mental disorders may manifest themselves in other ways which do not involve violence, for example, pyromania or kleptomania; if these conditions are due to an internal cause they will be labelled diseases of the mind. In *Hennessy* [1989] 1 W.L.R. 287, D, whilst in a hyperglycaemic episode due to failure to take insulin which he claimed was due to stress, anxiety and depression, took a motor vehicle without author-ity and drove whilst disqualified. The offences were not violent but the Court of Appeal held that D's plea was one of insanity as diabetes being an internal factor amounted to a disease of the mind. Stress, anxiety and depression, while they may be caused by external factors, were not themselves external factors. Secondly, there are conditions which manifest themselves in violence which do not fall within the defini-tion of disease of the mind approved in *Sullivan* as the case of *Quick* (below, p192) discloses.
2. The Court of Appeal has recently confirmed that voluntary intoxication will not be regarded as a disease of the mind (*Coley* [2013] EWCA Crim 233)—see also *Quick* (below, p192).

The Supreme Court of Canada has taken a rather more pragmatic and explicitly policy oriented approach to the "disease of the mind" test.

R. V PARKS

(1992) 95 D.L.R. (4th) 27

D was charged with murder and raised the defence of automatism based on somnambulism. Medical evidence indicated that D had been under stress, had been getting very little sleep and that there was a family history of sleep disorders. The medical witnesses also testified that somnambulism is not a disease of the mind in the sense of being a neurological, psychiatric or other illness but rather a disorder of sleep. They testified that a sleep-walker's ability to control voluntarily even complex behaviour is severely limited or not available and that aggression while sleep-walking is quite rare and repetition of violence is unheard of. The trial judge directed the jury that if D was in a state of somnambulism at the time of the killing he was entitled to be acquitted on the basis of non-insane automatism. The jury acquitted and the prosecution appealed.

LAMER CJC

. . . For a defence of insanity to have been put to the jury, together with or instead of a defence of automatism, as the case may be, there would have had to have been in the record evidence tending to show that sleep-walking was the cause of the respondent's state of mind . . . [T]hat is not the case here. This is not to say that sleep-walking could never be a disease of the mind, in another case on different evidence.

LA FOREST J

. . . In part because of the imprecision of medical science in this area the legal community reserves for itself the final determination of what constitutes a 'disease of the mind'. This is accomplished by adding the 'legal or policy component' to the inquiry.

A review of the cases on automatism reveals two distinct approaches to the policy component of the 'disease of the mind' inquiry. These may be labelled the 'continuing danger' and 'internal cause' theories . . . At first glance these approaches may appear to be divergent, but in fact they stem from a common concern for public safety . . .

The 'continuing danger' theory holds that any condition likely to present a recurring danger to the public should be treated as insanity. The 'internal cause' theory suggests that a condition stemming from the psychological or emotional make-up of the accused, rather than some external factor should lead to a finding of insanity. The two theories share a common concern for recurrence, the latter holding that an internal weakness is more likely to lead to recurrent violence than automatism brought on by some intervening external cause.

The 'internal cause' approach has been criticized as an unfounded development of the law . . . These criticisms have particular validity if the 'internal cause' theory is held out as the definitive answer to the disease of the mind inquiry. However, it is apparent from the cases that the theory is really meant to be used only as an analytical tool, and not as an all-encompassing methodology . . . [S]omnambulism is an example of a condition that is not well suited to analysis under the 'internal cause' theory. The poor fit arises because certain factors can legitimately be characterized as either internal or external sources of automatistic behaviour. For example, the Crown in this case argues that the causes of the respondent's violent sleepwalking were entirely internal, a combination of genetic susceptibility and the ordinary stresses of everyday life (lack of sleep, excessive afternoon exercise, and a high stress level due to personal problems). These 'ordinary stresses' were ruled out as external factors by this court in *Rabey* (1980) 54 C.C.C. (2d) 1 (although by a narrow majority). However, the factors that for a waking individual are mere ordinary stresses can be differently characterized for a person who is asleep, unable to counter with his conscious mind the onslaught of the admittedly ordinary strains of life. One could argue that the particular amalgam of stress, excessive exercise, sleep deprivation and sudden noises in the night that causes an incident of somnambulism is, for the sleeping person, analogous to the effect of concussion upon a waking person, which is generally accepted as an external cause of non-insane automatism. In the end the dichotomy between internal and external causes becomes blurred in this context, and is not helpful in resolving the inquiry . . .

In this case, then, neither of the two leading policy approaches determines an obvious result. It is clear from the evidence that there is almost no likelihood of recurrent violent somnambulism. A finding of insanity is therefore less likely, but the absence of a continuing danger does not mean that the respondent must be granted an absolute acquittal. At the same time, the 'internal cause' theory is not readily applicable in this case. It is therefore necessary to look further afield.

. . . [citing additional policy considerations in *Rabey*]

It seems unlikely that the recognition of somnambulism as non-insane automatism will open the floodgates to a cascade of sleep-walking defence claims . . . Moreover, it is very difficult to feign sleep-walking—precise symptoms and medical histories beyond the control of the accused must be presented to the trier of fact, and as in this case, the accused will be subjected to a battery of medical tests . . .

As I noted at the outset, it is apparent that the medical evidence in this case is not only significant in its own right, but also has an impact at several stages of the policy inquiry. As such, I agree with the Chief Justice that in another case with different evidence sleep-walking might be found to be a disease of the mind . . .

Appeal dismissed

Note

While Parks may be celebrating his good fortune to have been tried in Canada, one puzzle for other Canadians will be to work out which cases of somnabulism might fall within insane rather than non-insane automatism!

----

ii. Defect of Reason

Note

The basis of the M'Naghten Rules is "defect of reason" (not emotion or will) and the result of the defect of reason must be that the accused either did not know what he was doing or did not know that what he was doing was wrong.

R. V CODERE

(1917) 12 Cr. App. R. 21

The appellant had been convicted of murder. Insanity was the only defence raised at the trial. Under s.5(4) of the Criminal Appeal Act 1907, the Court of Criminal Appeal have power to quash the sentence and order the appellant to be detained as insane.

LORD READING CJ

. . . Mr Foote (on behalf of Codere) has addressed an argument to us based on *M'Naghten's Case*, which is the classic authority on the subject, which in substance resolved itself into this, that we must assume that when the law says that the question is whether the accused was labouring under such a defect of reason, from disease of the mind, as not to know the nature and quality of the act he was doing, we must read 'nature' to have reference to the physical act, and 'quality' to refer to the morality of the act, and that therefore the jury should be asked if he knew he was doing wrong. The argument advanced is that the judge ought to tell the jury that 'quality' means, 'Did the accused person know that the act was immoral?' and when one stops and asks the meaning of 'immoral' we get to the first of the difficulties which faced Mr Foote.

It is said that 'quality' is to be regarded as characterising the moral, as contrasted with the physical, aspect of the deed. The court cannot agree with that view of the meaning of the words 'nature and quality.' The court is of opinion that in using the language 'nature and quality' the judges were only dealing with the physical character of the act, and were not intending to distinguish between the physical and moral aspects of the act. That is the law as it has been laid down by judges in many directions to juries, and as the court understands it to be at the present time.

We then come to the second branch of the test, namely, if he knew the physical nature of the act did he know that he was doing wrong? Mr Foote has argued that it is not enough that he knew the act was contrary to law and punishable by law, and that, even if he did know that . . . yet the jury ought to have been told that they must find a special verdict (of guilty but insane) . . . unless they came to the conclusion that he knew that the act was morally wrong. The question of the distinction between morally and legally wrong opens wide doors. In a case of this kind, namely, killing, it does not seem debatable that the appellant could have thought that the act was not morally wrong, judged by the ordinary standards, when the act is punishable by law, and is known by him to be punishable by law. It was suggested at one time in the course of argument that the question should be judged by the standard of the accused, but it is obvious that this proposition is wholly untenable, and would tend to excuse crimes without number, and to weaken the law to an alarming degree. It is conceded now that the standard to be applied is whether according to the ordinary standard adopted by reasonable men the act was right or wrong . . . Once it is clear that the appellant knew that the act was wrong in law, then he was doing an act which he was conscious he ought not to do, and as it was against the law, it was punishable by law; assuming, therefore, that he knew the nature and quality of the act, he was guilty of murder, and was properly convicted.

The difficulty no doubt arises over the words 'conscious that the act was one which he ought not to do', but, looking at all the answers in *M'Naghten's Case*, it seems that if it is punishable by law it is an act which he ought not to do, and that is the meaning in which the phrase is used in that case. There may be minor cases before a court of summary jurisdiction where that view may be open to doubt, but in cases such as these the true view is what we have just said.

Application dismissed

Question

Under an insane delusion that his wife is possessed by evil, D decides to kill her and does so. Does his delusion relate to the nature and quality of his act entitling him to plead insanity?

R. V WINDLE

[1952] 2 Q.B. 826

The appellant gave his wife a fatal dose of aspirin. He admitted that he had done so, and said he supposed he would hang for it. The appellant's only defence was that of insanity. At the trial, Devlin J ruled that there was no evidence to go to the jury on the defence of insanity.

LORD GODDARD CJ

The point we have to decide in this case can be put into a very small compass. We are asked to review what are generally known as the M'Naghten Rules, and possibly to make new law . . .. The argument before us has really been on what is the meaning of the word 'wrong' . . . Mr Shawcross (for Windle) . . . suggested that the word 'wrong' as it was used in the M'Naghten Rules, did not mean contrary to law but has some kind of qualified meaning, such as morally wrong, and that if a person was in such a state of mind through a defect of reason that, although he knew that what he was doing was wrong in law, he thought that it was beneficial or kind or praiseworthy, that would excuse him.

Courts of law can only distinguish between that which is in accordance with law and that which is contrary to law. There are many acts which, to use an expression which is to be found in some of the old cases, are contrary to the law of God and man. For instance, in the Decalogue will be found the laws 'Thou shalt not kill' and 'Thou shalt not steal'. Those acts are contrary to the law of man and also to the law of God. If the seventh commandment is taken, 'Thou shalt not commit adultery,' although that is contrary to the law of God, so far as the criminal law is concerned it is not contrary to the law of man. That does not mean that the law encourages adultery; I only say that it is not a criminal offence. The law cannot embark on the question, and it would be an unfortunate thing if it were left to juries to consider whether some particular act was morally right or wrong. The test must be whether it is contrary to law . . .

In the opinion of the court there is no doubt that in the M'Naghten Rules 'wrong' means contrary to law and not 'wrong' according to the opinion of one man or of a number of people on the question of whether a particular act might or might not be justified. In the present case, it could not be challenged that the appellant knew that what he was doing was contrary to law, and that he realised what punishment the law provided for murder.

Appeal dismissed

Questions

1. Consider the questions raised by these last two cases. Is what is legally wrong always morally wrong? In *Codere* the judge was prepared to conceive of a negative answer only in minor crimes dealt with by courts of summary jurisdiction.

2. Would D be entitled to rely on the insanity defence if he believed his act was morally wrong although because of a disease of the mind he failed to appreciate that it was contrary to law? (Note that the Court of Appeal in *Johnson* [2007] EWCA Crim 1978 held that knowledge of illegality was the sole criterion of what was wrong and compare the approach of the High Court of Australia in *Stapleton v R.* (1952) 86 C.L.R. 358 with *Windle*.)

3. *Codere* approves the test "the ordinary standard adopted by reasonable men", *Windle* indicates that the test is "whether it is contrary to law". Does this alter the law? Was the creation of a new test essential for the decision in *Windle*?

4. If the test is one of insanity is an objective test of any sort appropriate? Consider the passage in *Codere* which indicates that a subjective standard would "weaken the law to an alarming degree".

Note

In practice it appears that psychiatrists pay little heed to the arcane distinctions drawn in *Windle* and *Codere* as the following extracts discloses.

R.D. MACKAY AND G. KEARNS, "MORE FACT(S) ABOUT THE INSANITY DEFENCE" [1999] CRIM. L.R. 714, 722–723

Perhaps the most interesting finding is in the way that the 'wrongness' limb of M'Naghten continues to be interpreted by psychiatrists. In previous research it was remarked that 'the general impression gained from reading the documentation in these cases was that the wrongness issue was being treated in a liberal fashion by all concerned, rather than in the strict manner regularly depicted by legal commentators'. [See Mackay, R. D., 'Fact and Fiction about the Insanity Defence' [1990] Crim.L.R. 247 at 251. The strict manner referred to is that the defendant did not know that his action was legally wrong, [see *Windle*.] Within the current research sample it was found that in 25 reports (18 cases) the psychiatrists specifically used the term that the defendant did not know that his act was 'wrong'. However, it is safe to say the vast majority of these reports made no reference to knowledge of legal wrongness. Rather in most of the case reports the 'wrongness' limb was interpreted widely to cover whether the defendant thought his/her actions were morally justified, and/or whether the actions were in perceived self-defence of themselves or others, in the sense of protecting their physical or spiritual well-being. [The factual scenarios in many of these cases involved religious delusions relating to the victim being possessed by the devil or concerning the need to save the world . . ..] Indeed, when we include the reports which supported these arguments (but where the phrase contained in the M'Naghten rules 'did not know that it was wrong' was not actually referred to) then we find that 35 reports (25 cases) utilised the 'wrongness' limb in agreeing that the defendant was NGRI. In short, the overwhelming impression is that the question the majority of psychiatrists are addressing is: if the delusion that the defendant was experiencing at the time of the offence was in fact reality, then would the defendant's actions be morally justified?—rather than the narrow cognitive test of legal wrongness required by the M'Naghten rules . . .

It seems clear, therefore, that the 'wrongness' limb continues to be preferred in psychiatric reports as indicated in the earlier research. In so doing, it may be argued that psychiatrists in many respects are adopting a common sense or folk psychology approach and that the courts by accepting this interpretation are, in reality, expanding the scope of the M'Naghten Rules.

More recently, in *R. v Johnson* [2007] EWCA Crim 1978, the Court of Appeal confirmed that, despite the observations made by Mackay and Kearns in the extract above, knowledge of illegality was the *sole* criterion of what was wrong.

iii. Uncontrollable Impulse

Notes

1. Will an individual be able to rely on the insanity defence where he appreciates the nature and quality of his conduct and knows that it is contrary to the law but, because of a defect of reason due to a disease of the mind, is unable to prevent himself from acting as he did? When the defence of uncontrollable impulse was raised in *Sodeman v R.* [1936] 2 All E.R. 1138, the Privy Council (at 1140), rejected the proposition "that the rules in *M'Naghten's Case* are no longer to be treated as an exhaustive statement of the law with regard to insanity, and that there is to be engrafted upon those rules another rule that where a man knows that he is doing what is wrong, nonetheless he may be held to be insane if he is caused to do the act by an irresistible impulse produced by disease."

    This was further explained in *Attorney General for South Australia v Brown* [1960] A.C. 432 where, in an appeal to the Privy Council, Lord Tucker said (at 449) "At various times in the past attempts have been made to temper the supposed harshness or unscientific nature of the M'Naghten Rules. These attempts were supported by the high authority of Sir James Fitz-James Stephen, but in the end the Rules remain in full force and their harshness has in this country been to some extent alleviated by the recent legislative enactment affording the defence of diminished responsibility . . .

    > Their Lordships must not, of course, be understood to suggest that in a case where evidence has been given (and it is difficult to imagine a case where such evidence would be other than medical evidence) that irresistible impulse is a symptom of the particular disease of the mind from which a prisoner is said to be suffering and as to its effect on his ability to know the nature and quality of his act or that his act is wrong it would not be the duty of the judge to deal with the matter in the same way as any other relevent evidence given at the trial."

    For the way in which "irresistible impulse" has been treated in the defence of diminished responsibility, see *R. v Byrne*, below, p479.

2. The "defect of reason" must arise "from a disease of the mind". The question may arise whether a person's state of automatism (where clearly reason is not only defective but completely absent) arises from a disease of the mind. These cases are dealt with in the next section. A similar problem can be seen in the section on intoxication, below.

----

2. AUTOMATISM

The defence of automatism arises initially as one form of denial that the prosecution has proved that the actus reus was voluntary (see, Ch.2). But acquittal will not necessarily follow. If the origin of the automatic state is a disease of the mind, a finding of insanity will result. *Kemp*, *Bratty*, *Quick* and *Bailey*, below, illustrate the problems facing the courts in this borderland between the two defences. Where the origin is self-induced intoxication, the defendant is subject to the limitations of that defence: see *Majewski*, below, p203. Even where the defendant's state is attributable to neither of those factors a person who is at fault in losing the capacity for voluntary control of his or her actions cannot rely on this defence: *Quick* and *Bailey*, below, pp.192 & 197. This imports a similar notion to that which qualifies intoxication as a denial of mens rea: self-induced incapacity may be culpable.

Thus it is only in extremely confined circumstances that the defence can be successfully raised. See G. Williams, *Textbook of Criminal Law*, 2nd edn (1983), pp.662–666 for a description of the common causes of automatism.

BRATTY V ATTORNEY GENERAL FOR NORTHERN IRELAND

[1963] A.C. 386 HL

The appellant strangled a girl. He said in a statement to the police that when he was with her he had "a terrible feeling" and "a sort of blackness" came over him. At the trial there was medical evidence that he might have been suffering from psychomotor epilepsy. To a charge of murder he raised three defences: automatism, lack of intent for murder, and insanity. The judge refused to leave the first two to the jury, and they rejected the plea of insanity. This was affirmed by the Court of Criminal Appeal in Northern Ireland. He appealed to the House of Lords.

Viscount Kilmuir and Lord Morris of Borth-Y-Gest delivered speeches dismissing the appeal with which Lords Tucker and Hodson agreed.

LORD DENNING

My Lords, in the case of *Woolmington v D.P.P.* A.C. 462, 482, Viscount Sankey L.C said that 'when dealing with a murder case the Crown must prove (a) death "as a result of a voluntary act of the accused", and (b) malice of "the accused"'. The requirement that it should be a voluntary act is essential, not only in a murder case, but also in every criminal case. No act is punishable if it is done involuntarily: and an involuntary act in this context—some people nowadays prefer to speak of it as 'automatism'—means an act which is done by the muscles without any control by the mind, such as a spasm, a reflex action or a convulsion; or an act done by a person who is not conscious of what he is doing, such as an act done whilst suffering from concussion or whilst sleep-walking . . .

The term 'involuntary act' is, however, capable of wider connotations: and to prevent confusion it is to be observed that in the criminal law an act is not to be regarded as an involuntary act simply because the doer does not remember it. When a man is charged with dangerous driving, it is no defence to him to say 'I don't know what happened. I cannot remember a "thing"', see *Hill v Baxter* [1958] 1 Q.B. 277. Loss of memory afterwards is never a defence in itself, so long as he was conscious at the time . . . see *Russell v H.M. Advocate* 1946 S.C.(J.) 37; *R. v Podola* [1960] 1 Q.B. 325. Nor is an act to be regarded as an involuntary act simply because the doer could not control his impulse to do it. When a man is charged with murder, and it appears that he knew what he was doing, but he could not resist it, then his assertion 'I couldn't help myself' is no defence in itself, see *A.-G. for South Australia v Brown* (1960) A.C. 432: though it may go towards a defence of diminished responsibility, in places where that defence is available [see *R. v Byrne*, below, p.479]: but it does not render his act involuntary so as to entitle him to an unqualified acquittal. Nor is an act to be regarded as an involuntary act simply because it is unintentional or its consequences are unforeseen. When a man is charged with dangerous driving, it is no defence for him to say, however truly, 'I did not mean to drive dangerously . . .' But even though it is absolutely prohibited, nevertheless he has a defence if he can show that it was an involuntary act in the sense that he was unconscious at the time and did not know what he was doing . . .

Another thing to be observed is that it is not every involuntary act which leads to a complete acquittal. Take first an involuntary act which proceeds from a state of drunkenness. If the drunken man is so drunk that he does not know what he is doing, he has a defence to any charge, such as murder or wounding with intent, in which a specific intent is essential, but he is still liable to be convicted of manslaughter or unlawful wounding for which no specific intent is necessary, see *Beard* [1920] A.C 479.

Again, if the involuntary act proceeds from a disease of the mind, it gives rise to a defence of insanity, but not to a defence of automatism. Suppose a crime is committed by a man in a state of automatism or clouded consciousness due to a recurrent disease of the mind. Such an act is no doubt involuntary, but it does not give rise to an unqualified acquittal, for that would mean that he would be let at large to do it again. The only proper verdict is one which ensures that the person who suffers from the disease is kept secure in a hospital so as not to be a danger to himself or others. That is a verdict of guilty but insane.

Once you exclude all the cases I have mentioned, it is apparent that the category of involuntary acts is very limited . . .

My Lords, I think that Devlin J. was quite right in *Kemp*'s case in putting the question of insanity to the jury, even though it had not been raised by the defence. When it is asserted that the accused did an involuntary act in a state of automatism, the defence necessarily puts in issue the state of mind of the accused man: and thereupon it is open to the prosecution to show what his true state of mind was. The old notion that only the defence can raise a defence of insanity is now gone. The prosecution are entitled to raise it and it is their duty to do so rather than allow a dangerous person to be at large . . .

Upon the other point discussed by Devlin J., namely, what is a 'disease of the mind' within the M'Naghten Rules, I would agree with him that this is a question for the judge. The major mental diseases, which the doctors call psychoses, such as schizophrenia, are clearly diseases of the mind. But in *Charlson* [1955] 1 W.L.R. 317, . . ., Barry J. seems to have assumed that other diseases such as epilepsy or cerebral tumour are not diseases of the mind, even when they are such as to manifest themselves in violence. I do not agree with this. It seems to me that any mental disorder which has manifested itself in violence and is prone to recur is a disease of the mind. At any rate it is the sort of disease for which a person should be detained in hospital rather than be given an unqualified acquittal . . .

I am clearly of opinion that, if the act of George Bratty was an involuntary act, as the defence suggested, the evidence attributed it solely to a disease of the mind and the only defence open was the defence of insanity. There was no evidence of automatism apart from insanity. There was, therefore, no need for the judge to put it to the jury. And when the jury rejected the defence of insanity, they rejected the only defence disclosed by the evidence . . .

I would, therefore, dismiss the appeal.

Appeal dismissed

R. V QUICK AND PADDISON

[1973] Q.B. 910

The appellant, who was a diabetic, was a psychiatric nurse. He was charged with assaulting a patient at the hospital where he worked. He said he could not remember the incident but that on the day it occurred he had taken his prescribed insulin, a small breakfast, some whisky, a quarter of a bottle of rum, and had no lunch. Medical evidence showed he was suffering at the time from hypoglycaemia, a deficiency of blood sugar after an injection of insulin. The appellant changed his plea to guilty after the judge rejected his defence of automatism on the grounds that the only defence open to him was insanity.

LAWTON LJ   for the court

In its broadest aspects these appeals raise the question what is meant by the phrase 'a defect of reason from disease of the mind' within the meaning of the M'Naghten Rules. More particularly the question is whether a person who commits a criminal act whilst under the effects of hypoglycaemia can raise a defence of automatism, as the appellants submitted was possible, or whether such a person must rely on a defence of insanity if he wishes to relieve himself of responsibility for his acts, as Bridge J. ruled . . .

Our examination of such authorities as there are must start with *Bratty v A.-G. for Northern Ireland, supra*, because the judge ruled as he did in reliance on that case. The House of Lords . . . accepted that automatism as distinct from insanity could be a defence if there was a proper foundation in the evidence for it. In this case, if Quick's alleged condition could have been caused by hypoglycaemia Bridge J.'s ruling was right. The question remains, however, whether a mental condition arising from hypoglycaemia does amount to a disease of the mind.

All their Lordships based their speeches on the basis that such medical evidence as there was pointed to Bratty suffering from a 'defect of reason from disease of the mind' and nothing else. Lord Denning discussed in general terms what constitutes a disease of the mind [His Lordship then quoted the passage on 'disease of the mind', above].

If this opinion is right and there are no restricting qualifications which ought to be applied to it, Quick was setting up a defence of insanity. He may have been at the material time in a condition of mental disorder manifesting itself in violence. Such manifestations had occurred before and might recur. The difficulty arises as soon as the question is asked whether he should be detained in a mental hospital? No mental hospital would admit a diabetic merely because he had a low blood sugar reaction; and common sense is affronted by the prospect of a diabetic being sent to such a hospital when in most cases the disordered mental condition can be rectified quickly by pushing a lump of sugar or a teaspoonful of glucose into the patient's mouth.

The 'affront to common sense' argument, however, has its own inherent weakness, as counsel for the Crown pointed out. If an accused is shown to have done a criminal act whilst suffering from a 'defect of reason from disease of the mind', it matters not 'whether the disease is curable or incurable . . . temporary or permanent' (see R. v Kemp [above, p181], per Devlin J.). If the condition is temporary, the Secretary of State may have a difficult problem of disposal; but what happens to those found not guilty by reason of insanity is not a matter for the courts.

In R. v Kemp, where the violent act was alleged to have been done during a period of unconsciousness arising from arteriosclerosis, counsel for the accused submitted that his client had done what he had during a period of mental confusion arising from a physical, not a mental disease. Devlin J. rejected this argument saying:

'It does not matter, for the purposes of the law, whether the defect of reasoning is due to a degeneration of the brain or to some other form of mental derangement. That may be a matter of importance medically, but it is of no importance to the law, which merely has to consider the state of mind in which the accused is, not how he got there.'

Applied without qualification of any kind, Devlin J.'s statement of the law would have some surprising consequences. Take the not uncommon case of the rugby player who gets a kick on the head early in the game and plays on to the end in a state of automatism. If, whilst he was in that state, he assaulted the referee it is difficult to envisage any court adjudging that he was not guilty by reason of insanity. Another type of case which could occur is that of the dental patient who kicks out whilst coming round from an anaesthetic. The law would be in a defective state if a patient accused of assaulting a dental nurse by kicking her whilst regaining consciousness could only excuse himself by raising the defence of insanity . . . [His Lordship referred to Hill v Baxter [1958] 1 Q.B. 277, D.C., and Watmore v Jenkins [1962] 2 Q.B. 572.]

In this case, had the jury been left to decide whether the appellant Quick at the material time was insane, or in a state of automatism or just drunk, they probably would not have any difficulty in making up their minds.

[His Lordship then referred to some Commonwealth cases].

. . .

In this quagmire of law seldom entered nowadays save by those in desperate need of some kind of defence, Bratty v A.-G. for Northern Ireland, supra, provides the only firm ground. Is there any discernible path? We think there is—judges should follow in a common sense way their sense of fairness. This seems to have been the approach of the New Zealand Court of Appeal in R. v Cottle [1958] N.Z.L.R. 999, and of Sholl J. in R. v Carter [1959] V.R. 105. In our judgment no help can be obtained by speculating (because that is what we would have to do) as to what the judges who answered the House of Lords' questions in 1843 meant by disease of the mind, still less what Sir Matthew Hale meant in the second half of the 17th century [(1682) Vol. J, Ch. IV.] A quick backward look at the state of medicine in 1843 will suffice to show how unreal it would be to apply the concepts of that age to the present time . . .. Our task has been to decide what the law means now by the words 'disease of the mind.' In our judgment the fundamental concept is of a malfunctioning of the mind caused by disease. A malfunctioning of the mind of transitory effect caused by the application to the body of some external factor such as violence, drugs including anaesthetics, alcohol and hypnotic influences cannot fairly be said to be due to disease. Such malfunctioning, unlike that caused by a defect of reason from disease of the mind, will not always relieve an accused from criminal responsibility. A self-induced incapacity will not excuse—see R. v Lipman [1970] 1 Q.B. 152, nor will one which could have been reasonably foreseen as a result of either doing, or omitting to do something, as, for example, taking alcohol against medical advice after using certain prescribed drugs, or failing to have regular meals whilst taking insulin. From time to time difficult borderline cases are likely to arise. When they do, the test suggested by the New Zealand Court of Appeal in *R. v Cottle* is likely to give the correct result, *viz.* can this mental condition be fairly regarded as amounting to or producing a defect of reason from disease of the mind?

In this case Quick's alleged mental condition, if it ever existed, was not caused by his diabetes but by his use of insulin prescribed by his doctor. Such malfunctioning of the mind as there was, was caused by an external factor and not by a bodily disorder in the nature of a disease which disturbed the working of his mind. It follows in our judgment that Quick was entitled to have his defence of automatism left to the jury and that Bridge J.'s ruling as to the effect of the medical evidence called by him was wrong. Had the defence of automatism been left to the jury, a number of questions of fact would have to be answered. If he was in a confused mental condition, was it due to a hypoglycaemic episode or to too much alcohol? If the former, to what extent had he brought about his condition by not following his doctor's instructions about taking regular meals? Did he know that he was getting into a hypoglycaemic episode? If Yes, why did he not use the antidote of eating a lump of sugar as he had been advised to do? On the evidence which was before the jury Quick might have had difficulty in answering these questions in a manner which would have relieved him of responsibility for his acts. We cannot say, however, with the requisite degree of confidence, that the jury would have convicted him. It follows that this conviction must be quashed on the ground that the verdict was unsatisfactory.

Appeal allowed

Questions

1. Lawton LJ stated that the law should not give the words "defect of reason from disease of the mind" a meaning which would be regarded with incredulity outside the court. Is it arguable that the distinction between automatism arising from intrinsic causes and that arising from extrinsic causes, itself affronts common sense in that, implicit in the distinction is the conclusion that diabetes is a disease of the mind?

2. Quick's hypoglycaemic condition arose from taking insulin, drinking alcohol and not eating suf-ficient food. The opposite condition, hyperglycaemia (excess blood-sugar) arises where insulin is missing from the blood; this condition can have similar effects to hypoglycaemia. If Quick had committed the assault in a hyperglycaemic episode, what would have been the result under the principles expounded by the Court of Appeal? (See *Hennessy*, and *Bingham* [1991] Crim. L.R. 433.)

3. What would be the position of D, an epileptic, who fails to take drugs which completely suppress epileptic seizures, and who, in the course of a seizure, thrashes violently injuring V? Would it make any difference if D knew that such failure could lead to seizures and violence on his part? (See *Bailey*, below p.197.)

4. If the criterion for sane automatism is that it is due to an extrinsic cause, how would the courts react to an automatic act due to the effects of a disease caused by a bacterial or viral infection? For example, D suffering from bacterial meningitis and in a convulsive fit, hits V. On a charge of causing grievous bodily harm D pleads automatism; would he succeed? E, who is suffering from arteriosclerosis, falls into an autonomic state and hits X. On a charge of causing grievous bodily harm E pleads automatism; would he succeed? If the outcome in each case differs, can this be justified on any logical and substantive basis?

Note

Stress, anxiety or depression which lead to impaired consciousness are not themselves external physical factors, but where they are due to an external physical factor and they lead to impaired consciousness, automatism may be pleaded successfully (see *R. v T* [1990] Crim. L.R. 256, where the issue of automatism was left to the jury on the basis of medical evidence that D was acting in a dissociative state when she committed a robbery and caused actual bodily harm due to post traumatic stress disorder as a result of being raped three days previously. cf. *Rabey* (1977) 37 C.C.C. (2d) 461.) See further Horder, "Pleading Involuntary Lack of Capacity", directly below, who engages in a critique of the non-insane automatism plea, particularly as used in cases such as *T*.

J. HORDER, "PLEADING INVOLUNTARY LACK OF CAPACITY" (1993) 52 CAMB. LJ. 298

Defendants may plead involuntary lack of capacity on a number of grounds that raise different theoretical problems. They may claim that the harm complained of was done by them when they were sleepwalking or under hypnosis. Alternatively they may claim that the causing of the harm was linked to an abnormal state of mind induced in them by, for example, Post Traumatic Stress Disorder (PTSD), pre-menstrual tension (PMT), or an unexpectedly violent allergic reaction to food or alcohol of a certain kind. There is, however, a fundamental difference between these two groups of cases. In the sleepwalking and hypnosis cases, the defendants' pleas amount to a claim that they were not truly acting at all . . . In the latter group of cases, the defendant's pleas amount to a claim that they were not (or not fully) in control of what were admittedly their actions . . .

We may engage with the world through causing things to happen, through voluntary conduct, or through evaluated conduct. A system of criminal law based solely on causation could not give rise to any difficulties concerning a plea of lack of capacity, for such a plea could gain no purchase . . . Our system of criminal law is not based . . . on principles of brute deterrence, and presupposes that to become criminals people must be responsible for harm, and not just cause it.

This brings us to the second means by which we may engage with the world, namely through conduct . . . Under the voluntary conduct model of criminal responsibility, it becomes possible to distinguish between accidents which are attributable to me and those which are not, and (a related point) to plead lack of capacity as a complete denial of responsibility . . . If . . . voluntary conduct is one of the benchmarks of responsibility (putting aside questions about blame) it becomes possible to distinguish between cases on the grounds of lack of capacity; it becomes possible to distinguish between mere causers of harm, like sleepwalkers, and unwitting agents of harm, like those who leap without looking. The former will lack capacity, whereas the latter will not . . .

[I]t is the voluntary conduct model of engagement with the world that the criminal law claims to adopt in analysing responsibility, as opposed to blame. Lord Denning's classic definition of non-insane automatism in *Bratty* [above, p.191] reveals this:

> 'Automatism—means an act which is done by the muscles without any control by the mind such as a spasm, a reflex action or a convulsion; or an act done by a person who is not conscious of what he is doing such as an act done whilst suffering from concussion or whilst sleepwalking.'

In other words, it is only where defendants are agents and not mere causers of harm that they are to be regarded as responsible for causing that harm, a finding of responsibility being an essential precondition (absent questions of voluntary intoxication) for investigation into *mens rea* or blame . . . This is as clear an endorsement of the voluntary conduct model of responsibility . . . as one could wish to find.

Despite the fact that, in theory at least, the voluntary conduct model is the model of engagement with the world which underpins the criminal law's conception of responsibility, there are troublesome cases. The law regards young children as beyond (or beneath) criminal responsibility even when they do harm intentionally, and mitigates the offence of intentional killers suffering from diminished responsibility, even though they may unquestionably be voluntary agents rather than mere causers of harm . . .

Under the evaluated conduct model of engagement with the world, what counts as significant engagement by me is conduct which was or could have been influenced by critical evaluation before I embarked or decided to go ahead . . . [I]f we return to our troublesome examples, it is the fact that the influence of critical evaluation on an agent's conduct is (virtually) impossible that qualifies the agent's capacities for engagement with the world and enables them to deny (full) responsibility.

In the case of very young children, their exemption from criminal liability might be justified on a number of grounds, such as the wish to avoid undue harshness in the application of criminal process and sanctions. Nonetheless, what gives grounds such as this their force is that, whilst even very young children are quite capable of engaging in intentionally harmful conduct, they do not have developed moral characters as to which such conduct can be related. It is the possession of such a character that makes possible the formation of and action upon an intelligent conception of the good (in) life, and hence makes it possible to subject one's (potential) conduct to critical moral evaluation, and shape it in the light of that evaluation.

By way of contrast, engagement in nothing more than voluntary and intentional conduct does not presuppose the possession of a moral character . . .

[Analysing the case of *R. v T*. Horder goes on to state:]

The defendant's condition points clearly in the direction of acquittal or substantial mitigation of the offence on the grounds of non-insane automatism, but non-insane automatism is a plea shaped by the voluntary conduct model of responsibility, which seeks to do no more than distinguish agents from mere causers of harm; and like the victim of post hypnotic suggestion, T seems most plausibly to have been an agent, albeit a morally unwitting agent, and not a mere causer of harm.

There are other agents who may lack capacity under the evaluated conduct model of responsibility but who, in virtue of being voluntary agents, may have difficulty pleading non-insane automatism. Examples are provided by those whose moods are radically affected by PMT or by the violently allergic reaction, even to small quantities of alcohol, known as Pathological Alcoholic Intoxication. The law is forced into an inconsistent attitude to such defendants when they do harm as a result of their violent mood changes. Since they engage in voluntary conduct, the general applicability of the law's voluntary conduct model of responsibility dictates that the presumption of rational capacity has not been displaced, and they must rely on a lack of *mens rea* (that is unless, of course, they are as fortunate as T in persuading the judge that they might have been in a state akin to sleepwalking and thus were indeed not engaged in voluntary conduct). Yet if it should happen that such defendants kill intentionally, and they plead diminished responsibility, the grounding of this plea . . . in the evaluated conduct model of responsibility means that their plea of partial lack of capacity stands a good chance of success, despite the admittedly voluntary character of their conduct . . .

[W]here defendants may have intentionally done harm through some voluntary conduct of theirs [such as cases concerning PTSD, PMT, Pathological Alcoholic Intoxication and hypoglycaemia], . . . their inability to evaluate conduct ought to excuse them . . . These are cases best dealt with through the broadening out of diminished responsibility into a general defence. [This would require the creation of] an intermediate 'diminished responsibility' verdict . . . distinct from finding the defendant guilty or not guilty. The verdict would indicate nothing more or less than that defendants had voluntarily caused harm whilst unable to evaluate their conduct or control it through moral evaluation. Such a finding would have the effect of giving the trial judge the power to make an order in lieu of punishment or outright acquittal, an order which might conceivably be one ranging from absolute or conditional discharge, through supervision and treatment, to an order for detention in a secure institution for exceptional cases where the defendant's condition makes them, albeit temporarily, a vivid and violent danger . . .

It is important to recognise, though that allowing people to plead lack of moral capacity as an excuse, when they are suffering from the kinds of (temporary) disorders discussed above, need not give rise to the possibility of unjust leniency for the person who claims 'I could not help it; it's just the way I am.' Consider someone whose violent nature is attributable to the violent abuse they themselves witnessed, or suffered, in their formative childhood years. Such a person is tragically unlucky but nonetheless fully responsible for their conduct. There are many things for which we must take responsibility even though we did not deliberately or even carelessly bring them about, and our moral character is one of these. The victim of abuse who turns abuser *exhibits* their moral character in the abuse they inflict, and they must take responsibility for this just because the moral character exhibited is *theirs*. Those who are violent or dangerous due to PMT, PTSD, Pathological Alcoholic Intoxication or hypoglycaemia, however, are not morally responsible for their actions precisely because they are estranged from their moral characters when they act.

Self-induced automatism

Note

If non-insane automatism leads to a complete acquittal based on the doctrine of voluntariness, will this principle lead to the same outcome where it can be shown that the autonomic state was self-induced?

In *Quick* Lawton LJ stated:

> "A self-induced incapacity will not excuse . . . nor will one which could have been reasonably foreseen as a result of either doing, or omitting to do something, as, for example, taking alcohol against medical advice after using certain prescribed drugs, or failing to have regular meals while taking insulin."

On the basis of this dictum *Quick's* autonomic state appears to have been self-induced by not eating or taking a lump of sugar when the first signs of hypoglycaemia manifested themselves. However, his conviction was quashed as his defence of automatism had not been left to the jury. The effect of *Quick*, however, appeared categorically to rule out the defence of automatism where it was self-induced.

R. V BAILEY

[1983] 1 W.L.R. 760

The appellant was charged with wounding with intent and with an alternative count of unlawful wounding contrary to ss.18 and 20 respectively of the Offences Against the Person Act 1861. His defence was automatism caused by hypoglycaemia which was due to his failure to take sufficient food after taking insulin, although he had taken some sugar and water. He claimed, accordingly, that he lacked the specific intent required for the purpose of s.18 and the basic intent required for the purpose of s.20. The judge directed the jury that as the appellant's incapacity was self-induced he could not plead automatism. The appellant was convicted of causing grievous bodily harm with intent, contrary to s.18. He appealed.

GRIFFITHS LJ

. . . But in [*Quick*] [t]he Court of Appeal held that [the ruling upon which the present trial judge had based his direction] was wrong and that the malfunctioning caused by the hypoglycaemia was not a disease of the mind and that the appellant was entitled to have his defence considered by the jury . . .

But in that case, the offence, assault occasioning actual bodily harm, was an offence of basic intent. No specific intent was required. It is now quite clear that even if the incapacity of mind is self-induced by the voluntary taking of drugs or alcohol, the specific intent to kill or cause grievous bodily harm may be negatived: see *R. v Majewski* [1977] A.C. 443 [below, p.203]. This being so, as it is conceded on behalf of the Crown, the direction to which we have referred cannot be correct so far as the offence under section 18 is concerned.

But it is also submitted that the direction is wrong or at least in too broad and general terms, so far as the section 20 offence is concerned. If . . . *Quick* correctly represents the law, then the direction given by the recorder was correct so far as the second count was concerned even though the appellant may have had no appreciation of the consequences of his failure to take food and even though such failure may not have been due to deliberate abstention but because of his generally distressed condition. In our judgment the passage from Lawton L.J.'s judgment was obiter and we are free to re-examine it.

Automatism resulting from intoxication as a result of a voluntary ingestion of alcohol or dangerous drugs does not negative the mens rea necessary for crimes of basic intent, because the conduct of the accused is reckless and recklessness is enough to constitute the necessary mens rea in assault cases where no specific intent forms part of the charge: see *R. v Majewski*.

The same considerations apply where the state of automatism is induced by the voluntary taking of dangerous drugs: see *R. v Lipman* [1970] Q.B. 152 where a conviction for manslaughter was upheld, the appellant having taken L.S.D. and killed his mistress in the course of an hallucinatory trip. It was submitted on behalf of the Crown that a similar rule should be applied as a matter of public policy to all cases of self-induced automatism. But it seems to us that there may be material distinctions between a man who consumes alcohol or takes dangerous drugs and one who fails to take sufficient food after insulin to avert hypoglycaemia.

It is common knowledge that those who take alcohol to excess or certain sorts of drugs may become aggressive or do dangerous or unpredictable things, they may be able to foresee the risks of causing harm to others but nevertheless persist in their conduct. But the same cannot be said without more of a man who fails to take food after an insulin injection. If he does appreciate the risk that such a failure may lead to aggressive, unpredictable and uncontrollable conduct and he nevertheless deliberately runs the risk or otherwise disregards it, this will amount to recklessness. But we certainly do not think that it is common knowledge, even among diabetics, that such is a consequence of a failure to take food and there is no evidence that it was known to this appellant. Doubtless he knew that if he failed to take his insulin or proper food after it, he might lose consciousness, but as such he would only be a danger to himself unless he put himself in charge of some machine such as a motor car, which required his continued conscious control.

In our judgment, self-induced automatism, other than that due to intoxication from alcohol or drugs, may provide a defence to crimes of basic intent. The question in each case will be whether the prosecution have proved the necessary element of recklessness. In cases of assault, if the accused knows that his actions or inaction are likely to make him aggressive, unpredictable or uncontrolled with the result that he may cause some injury to others and he persists in the action or takes no remedial action when he knows it is required, it will be open to the jury to find that he was reckless.

Turning again to *R. v Quick* and the passage we have quoted, we think that notwithstanding the unqualified terms in which the proposition is stated, it is possible that the court may not have intended to lay down such an absolute rule. In the following paragraph Lawton L.J. considers a number of questions, which are not necessarily exhaustive, which the jury might have wanted to consider if the issue had been left to them. One such question was whether the accused knew that he was getting into a hypoglycaemic episode and if so why he did not use the antidote of taking sugar which he had been advised to do. These questions suggest that even if the hypoglycaemia was induced by some action or inaction by the accused his defence will not necessarily fail.

In the present case the recorder never invited the jury to consider what the appellant's knowledge or appreciation was of what would happen if he failed to take food after his insulin or whether he realised that he might become aggressive. Nor were they asked to consider why the appellant had omitted to take food in time. They were given no direction on the elements of recklessness. Accordingly, in our judgment there was also a misdirection in relation to the second count in the indictment of unlawful wounding.

But we have to consider whether, notwithstanding these misdirections, there has been any miscarriage of justice and whether the jury properly directed could have failed to come to the same conclusion. As Lawton L.J. said in *Quick*'s case at p.922, referring to the defence of automatism, it is a 'quagmire of law seldom entered nowadays save by those in desperate need of some kind of a defence . . .' This case is no exception. We think it very doubtful whether the appellant laid a sufficient basis for the defence to be considered by the jury at all. But even if he did we are in no doubt that the jury properly directed must have rejected it. Although an episode of sudden transient loss of consciousness or awareness was theoretically possible it was quite inconsistent with the graphic description that the appellant gave to the police both orally and in his written statement. There was abundant evidence that he had armed himself with the iron bar and gone to Mr Harrison's house for the purpose of attacking him because he wanted to teach him a lesson and because he was in the way.

Moreover the doctor's evidence to which we have referred showed it was extremely unlikely that such an episode could follow some five minutes after taking sugar and water. For these reasons we are satisfied that no miscarriage of justice occurred and the appeal will be dismissed.

Appeal dismissed

Questions

1. A drunkard has no defence to a crime of basic intent (see below, p.203). As a result of *Bailey* an automaton who has brought about his own state of automatism may have a defence. Is this difference one which can be justified on grounds of policy or principle?

2. The court in *Bailey* did not presume recklessness because of the absence of common knowledge amongst diabetics that failure to take food after insulin might result in aggressive behaviour. How might a court come to such a conclusion? What would happen if directions on prescriptions of insulin were to include such a warning?

3. M.E. Schiffer, in *Mental Disorder and the Criminal Trial Process* (Butterworths, 1978), gives examples of statistical studies which show that "(1) violent behaviour of any sort is unusual in epileptic automatisms; (2) the vast majority of epileptics have never experienced fugue state automatism; and (3) amongst those who do . . . it is a relatively rare occurrence" (p.93). In light of the fact that a person in hypoglycaemic coma though unconscious may still perform normal functions, as if a robot, is it tenable to conclude (as a reading of *Bailey and Sullivan* would seem to dictate) that epileptics represent a greater danger to the public than diabetics? If not, is the distinction between external and internal organic causes, a fatuous one? (cf. *Parks*, above, p.185)

4. Schiffer (p.100) states that hypoglycaemic coma may be caused by overproduction of insulin by the pancreas. How would the courts have treated Bailey if his automatism had resulted from this cause?

----

3. PROPOSALS FOR REFORM

LAW COMMISSION

Criminal Liability: Insanity and Automatism

Discussion Paper (July 2013)

POSSIBLE NEW DEFENCES

1.84 Although the practical evidence does not make reform of the defences of insanity and automatism urgent, it is still needed. Respondents to the Scoping Paper told us they find them outmoded, inappropriate, and complicated, and they supported several of the academic criticisms. It therefore seems to us that it is valuable for us to contribute to the public debate by publishing ideas about how the insanity and automatism defences could be reformed.

1.85 Professor Ronnie Mackay, a member of our Advisory Board, has described our provisional proposals for the reform of the insanity defence as 'radical', and stated that in his view 'a "radical" change to the M'Naghten Rules is precisely what is needed'. We agree.

New defence and special verdict of 'not criminally responsible by reason of recognised medical condition'

1.86 We provisionally propose that the common law rules on the defence of insanity be abolished.

1.87 We provisionally propose the creation of a new defence of 'not criminally responsible by reason of recognised medical condition'. This would be a defence founded on complete loss of capacity; mere impaired capacity, even substantially impaired capacity, would not be enough for the defence to succeed. This is such a significant 'bright line' that a court would address it first: if the accused could not adduce sufficient credible evidence that he or she had wholly lacked a relevant capacity as a result of a recognised medical condition, then the court would not allow the defence to go forward.

1.88 As just noted, the lack of capacity must arise out of a 'recognised medical condition'. Determining what constitutes a 'recognised medical condition' here involves a question of law, not of medicine. It is a term of art and an essential component of the defence. It is therefore a term to be interpreted by the court.

1.89 Not all medical conditions will qualify as a 'recognised medical condition'. There are, in our view, good policy reasons for some medical conditions not to qualify as criminal defences. For example, the criminal law has already developed rules to deal with the criminal liability of those who are intoxicated, and it would not be right for a defence of non-responsibility to undermine those rules.

1.90 Similarly, it would also not be right for a person to be able to rely on this defence if the accused's condition consists of a personality disorder characterised solely or principally by abnormally aggressive or seriously irresponsible behaviour; in other words, the evidence for the condition is simply evidence of what might broadly be called criminal behaviour.

1.91 We provisionally conclude that these two conditions should be explicitly excluded from the proposed new defence.

1.92 There are no doubt other kinds of condition which may be diagnosed for medical purposes but which would not qualify as the foundation for a defence of nonresponsibility.

We provisionally conclude that the best approach is for the courts to have discretion, with the guidance of the Court of Appeal, to decide whether any condition which is not specifically excluded is nevertheless not a qualifying condition. We see this approach as preferable to the alternatives, such as providing an exhaustive list of qualifying conditions, which we regard as unworkable, or not excluding any conditions from the proposed defence, thus leaving interpretation solely to the courts in all cases, risking the possibility of inconsistent decision-making.

1.93 In sum, the party seeking to raise the defence must adduce evidence from at least two experts that at the time of the alleged offence the defendant wholly lacked the capacity:

 (i) rationally to form a judgment about the relevant conduct or circumstances;

 (ii) to understand the wrongfulness of what he or she is charged with having done; or

 (iii) to control his or her physical acts in relation to the relevant conduct or circumstances as a result of a qualifying recognised medical condition.

1.94 In other words, a defendant should not be held responsible where he or she could not have reasoned rationally about what he or she was doing, could not have understood that it was wrong, or could not have controlled his or her physical actions. The defence would not apply where the accused simply found it difficult to do any of those things.

1.95 The defence would be available in relation to any type of offence, not just those which require proof of mens rea, and it would be available in the magistrates' courts and the Crown Court.

1.96 The relevant expert from whom evidence would be required before the defence could even get off the ground need not be a medical practitioner, but where the relevant expert is a psychiatrist, he or she should continue to be one who is 'approved' under the Mental Health Act 1983 ('the 1983 Act').

Reformed defence of automatism

1.109 We propose reforming the defence of automatism and putting it into statutory form.

1.110 We provisionally propose a defence of automatism where at the time of the alleged offence the accused suffered a total loss of capacity to control his or her actions which was not caused by a recognised medical condition. If the defence succeeds (which means if the accused adduces enough evidence to put it in issue and it is not disproved by the prosecution) then the accused will be simply acquitted.

1.111 Given that our proposed defence of recognised medical condition will apply to some cases which would currently fall within the automatism defence under the current law, we anticipate that the new automatism defence would apply in a narrower range of cases than the current automatism defence.

1.112 A small number of defendants who under the current law would be able to plead automatism and avoid any stigmatising verdict, would under our proposals fall instead within the recognised medical condition defence, and so be subject to the special verdict. In our view, that is the right outcome: if the loss of capacity is the result of a recognised medical condition such as sleep apnoea or diabetes causing sudden loss of consciousness, then the verdict should reflect that fact.

As regards disposal, the court would have the power to order a disposal which offers the possibility of greater protection of the public, in contrast with a simple acquittal. Our proposed new verdict would not have the same negative connotations as a verdict of 'not guilty by reason of insanity'.

1.113 Thus, for instance, where the accused is charged with causing death by dangerous driving and claims to have had no warning of a hypoglycaemic episode, the jury might convict if they are sure that the accused should have anticipated the medical emergency. However if they accept he had a hypoglycaemic episode but are not sure he had warning of it, they will reach the new special verdict, and not acquit. The new special verdict would be apt for those who should bear 'no moral blame'.

1.114 If a person's defence is based on a recognised medical condition, then the automatism defence would not be available to him or her, irrespective of whether it is a qualifying recognised medical condition defence. So, for example, if D says that he lost all capacity to control his actions because of his acute intoxication, he or she will not be able to rely on the automatism defence or the recognised medical condition defence.

Prior fault and intoxication

1.115 Those who work in the criminal justice system will know that offenders with mental disorder will often also have a background of alcohol or drug abuse, and either or both of those factors may have played a part in the commission of an offence. It is therefore essential for us to consider how our proposals would work in practice alongside relevant common law rules governing those who commit crimes when voluntarily intoxicated or otherwise incapacitated.

1.116 The interaction of insanity, automatism and intoxication was considered in C. There is in the common law a supervening principle of prior fault: the accused is generally liable for any basic intent offence where he or she was culpable in inducing his or her loss of capacity. Lord Justice Hughes restated this principle as follows:

> In most, but not all, intoxication cases, the intoxication will be possibly
> relevant to a serious offence allegedly committed but will afford no
> defence to a lesser offence constituted by the same facts: for
> example causing grievous bodily harm with intent . . . and causing
> grievous bodily harm without such intent . . . , or of course murder and
> manslaughter. In the development of the common law, intoxication
> was historically regarded chiefly as an aggravation of offending,
> rather than as an excuse for it. For all the reasons explained in
> *Majewski*, the law refuses as a matter of policy to afford a general
> defence to an offender on the basis of his own voluntary intoxication.
> The pressing social reasons for maintaining this general policy of the
> law are certainly no less present in modern conditions of substance
> abuse than they were in the past.

1.117 The policy for this is readily understood: while it may be fair for a person to be acquitted where he or she completely lost control of his or her actions, it is not fair for there to be an acquittal where the accused may be blamed for whatever led to the loss of control. For example, a driver who loses control of the car when a stone comes through the windscreen is not to be held responsible, but a driver who knows he is on the verge of a hypoglycaemic coma but who drives anyway will fairly be held responsible.

1.118 This principle, and the case law, will continue to be relevant to the proposed new defence of recognised medical condition and to the proposed reformed defence of automatism..

1.119. . ..

1.120 . . . we identify a potential anomaly in the current law which we need to address. A diabetic who, without fault, fails to take insulin and then commits an allegedly criminal act would be categorised as 'insane' under the current law. In contrast, a diabetic who took insulin in accordance with a medical prescription, but who then had an unexpected reaction to it and committed an allegedly criminal act, would be acquitted. In our view, the appropriate verdict in both cases should be "not criminally responsible by reason of recognised medical condition" because in both cases it is the underlying condition which has given rise to the conduct constituting an offence. Achieving this result requires an amendment to the rules on intoxication, and so we propose that a person 'D' shall be treated as pleading the recognised medical condition defence and not involuntary intoxication where:

D suffered from a recognised medical condition, and

D took a properly authorised or licensed medicine or drug for the treatment of that condition, and

D took the medicine or drug in accordance with a prescription, with advice given by a suitably qualified person, or in accordance with the instructions accompanying the medicine or drug in the case of over-thecounter medicines, or, if D did not take it in accordance with instructions, it was nevertheless reasonable for D to take it in the way he or she did in the circumstances, and

D had no reason to believe that he or she would have an adverse reaction to that medicine which would cause him or her to act in that way and

the taking of that medicine or drug caused D totally to lack the relevant criminal capacity.

Question

How would these proposals improve the current law?

----

4. INTOXICATION

A person may become intoxicated through the consumption of drink or drugs. Whatever the cause of the intoxication, the law treats the intoxicated offender the same. Intoxication is not per se a defence;

rather, a defendant who relies on intoxication is saying that because of his intoxication he did not have the necessary mens rea for the offence. Thus, if D, although intoxicated (whether voluntarily or involuntarily) has formed the necessary intent for the crime he will be guilty. See *Kingston*, below p. 217. If D's intoxication leaves him incapable of forming the mens rea for the offence with which he is charged, or if he claims that he did not form the mens rea for the offence because he was intoxicated, he will not necessarily be acquitted; the outcome will hinge on whether the offence is one of specific or basic intent.

i. Specific and Basic Intent

DPP V MAJEWSKI

[1976] 2 W.L.R. 623 HL

M appealed against convictions of assault occasioning actual bodily harm and assault of a police constable in the execution of his duty on the ground that he was too intoxicated, through a combination of drugs and alcohol, to form the appropriate mens rea. M was a drug addict who, over the previous two days, had consumed a large quantity of amphetamines and barbiturates before spending an evening drinking at the pub where the offences were committed. M admitted that he had sometimes "gone paranoid" but this was the first time he had "completely blacked out". Medical evidence was given that such a state of "pathological intoxication" was uncommon and that automatism due to the ingestion of alcohol together with either amphetamines or barbiturates was unlikely; it was more likely for a person intoxicated in this way to know what he was doing at the time but to suffer an "amnesic patch" later.

LORD ELWYN-JONES LC

The Court of Appeal dismissed the appeal against conviction but granted leave to appeal to your Lordships' House certifying that the following point of law of general public importance was involved:

'Whether a defendant may properly be convicted of assault notwithstanding that, by reason of his self-induced intoxication, he did not intend to do the act alleged to constitute the assault . . .'

If a man consciously and deliberately takes alcohol and drugs not on medical prescription, but in order to escape from reality, to go 'on a trip', to become hallucinated, whatever the description may be, and thereby disables himself from taking the care he might otherwise take and as a result by his subsequent actions causes injury to another—does our criminal law enable him to say that because he did not know what he was doing he lacked both intention and recklessness and accordingly is entitled to an acquittal?

Originally the common law would not and did not recognise self-induced intoxication as an excuse. Lawton L.J. spoke of the 'merciful relaxation' to that rule which was introduced by the judges during the 19th century, and he added:

'Although there was much reforming zeal and activity in the 19th century Parliament never once considered whether self-induced intoxication should be a defence generally to a criminal charge. It would have been a strange result if the merciful relaxation of a strict rule of law had ended, without any Parliamentary intervention, by whittling it away to such an extent that the more drunk a man became, provided he stopped short of making himself insane, the better chance he had of acquittal . . . The common law rule still applied but there were exceptions to it which Lord Birkenhead L.C., *D.P.P. v Beard* [1920] A.C. 479, tried to define by reference to specific intent.'

There are, however, decisions of eminent judges in a number of Commonwealth cases in Australia and New Zealand (but generally not in Canada nor in the United States), as well as impressive academic comment in this country, to which we have been referred supporting the view that it is illogical and inconsistent with legal principle to treat a person who of his own choice and volition has taken drugs and drink, even though he thereby creates a state in which he is not conscious of what he is doing, any differently from a person suffering from the various medical conditions like epilepsy or diabetic coma and who is regarded by the law as free from fault. However, our courts have for a very long time regarded in quite another light the state of self-induced intoxication. The authority which for the last half century has been relied on in this context has been the speech of Lord Birkenhead L.C. in *D.P.P. v Beard*, at 494:

> 'Under the law of England as it prevailed until early in the nineteenth century voluntary drunkenness was never an excuse for criminal misconduct; and indeed the classic authorities broadly assert that voluntary drunkenness must be considered rather an aggravation than a defence. This view was in terms based upon the principle that a man who by his own voluntary act debauches and destroys his will power, shall be no better situated in regard to criminal acts than a sober man.'

Lord Birkenhead L.C. made an historical survey of the way the common law from the 16th century on dealt with the effect of self-induced intoxication on criminal responsibility. This indicates how, from 1819 on, the judges began to mitigate the severity of the attitude of the common law in such cases as murder and serious violent crime when the penalties of death or transportation applied or where there was likely to be sympathy for the accused, as in attempted suicide. Lord Birkenhead L.C, at 499, concluded that (except in cases where insanity was pleaded) the decisions he cited—

> 'establish that where a specific intent is an essential element in the offence, evidence of a state of drunkenness rendering the accused incapable of forming such an intent should be taken into consideration in order to determine whether he had in fact formed the intent necessary to constitute the particular crime. If he was so drunk that he was incapable of forming the intent required he could not be convicted of a crime which was committed only if the intent was proved . . . In a charge of murder based upon intention to kill or to do grievous bodily harm, if the jury are satisfied that the accused was, by reason of his drunken condition, incapable of forming the intent to kill or to do grievous bodily harm . . . he cannot be convicted of murder. But nevertheless unlawful homicide has been committed by the accused, and consequently he is guilty of unlawful homicide without malice aforethought, and that is manslaughter: *per* Stephen J. in *Doherty's Case* (1887) 16 Cox C.C. 306, 307. [He concluded the passage:] the law is plain beyond all question that in cases falling short of insanity a condition of drunkenness at the time of committing an offence causing death can only, when it is available at all, have the effect of reducing the crime from murder to manslaughter.'

From this it seemed clear—and this is the interpretation which the judges have placed on the decision during the ensuing half-century—that it is only in the limited class of cases requiring proof of specific intent that drunkenness can exculpate. Otherwise in no case can it exempt completely from criminal liability . . .

[His Lordship quoted Lord Denning in *Gallagher*, below p.222 and in *Bratty*, above p.191.]

In no case has the general principle of English law as described by Lord Denning in *Gallagher's* case and exposed again in *Bratty's* case been overruled in this House and the question now to be determined is whether it should be.

I do not for my part regard that general principle as either unethical or contrary to the principles of natural justice. If a man of his own volition takes a substance which causes him to cast off the restraints of reason and conscience, no wrong is done to him by holding him answerable criminally for any injury he may do while in that condition. His course of conduct in reducing himself by drugs and drink to that condition in my view supplies the evidence of mens rea, of guilty mind certainly sufficient for crimes of basic intent. It is a reckless course of conduct and recklessness is enough to constitute the necessary mens rea in assault cases: see *R. v Venna* [below, p.537], *per* James L.J. The drunkenness is itself an intrinsic, an integral part of the crime, the other part being the evidence of the unlawful use of force against the victim. Together they add up to criminal recklessness. On this I adopt the conclusion of Stroud that:

> 'It would be contrary to all principle and authority to suppose that drunkenness [and what is true of drunkenness is equally true of intoxication by drugs] can be a defence for crime in general on the ground that 'a person cannot be convicted of a crime unless the *mens* was *rea*.' By allowing himself to get drunk and thereby putting

himself in such a condition as to be no longer amenable to the law's commands, a man shows such regardless-ness as amounts to *mens rea* for the purpose of all ordinary crimes.'

This approach is in line with the American Model Code, s.2.08(2),

'When recklessness establishes an element of the offence, if the actor, due to self-induced intoxica-tion, is unaware of a risk of which he would have been aware had be been sober, such unawareness is immaterial.'

. . . The final question that arises is whether s.8 of the Criminal Justice Act 1967 has had the result of abrogating or qualifying the common law rule. That section emanated from the consideration the Law Commission gave to the decision of the House in *D.P.P. v Smith* [1961] A.C. 290. Its purpose and effect was to alter the law of evidence about the presumption of intention to produce the reasonable and probable consequences of one's acts. It was not intended to change the common law rule. In referring to 'all the evidence' it meant all the *relevant* evidence. But if there is a substantive rule of law that in crimes of basic intent, the factor of intoxication is irrelevant (and such I hold to be the substantive law), evidence with regard to it is quite irrelevant. Section 8 does not abrogate the substantive rule and it cannot properly be said that the continued application of that rule contravenes the section. For these reasons, my conclusion is that the certified question should be answered Yes, that there was no misdirection in this case and that the appeal should be dismissed.

My noble and learned friends and I think it may be helpful if we give the following indication of the general lines on which in our view the jury should be directed as to the effect on the criminal responsibility of the accused of drink or drugs or both, whenever death or physical injury to another person results from something done by the accused for which there is no legal justification and the offence with which the accused is charged is manslaugh-ter or assault at common law or the statutory offence of unlawful wounding under s.20, or of assault occasioning actual bodily harm under s.47 of the Offences Against the Person Act 1861.

In the case of these offences it is no excuse in law that, because of drink or drugs which the accused himself had taken knowingly and willingly, he had deprived himself of the ability to exercise self-control, to realise the pos-sible consequences of what he was doing or even to be conscious that he was doing it. As in the instant case, the jury may be properly instructed that they 'can ignore the subject of drink or drugs as being in any way a defence to' charges of this character.

[Lord Diplock agreed with the speech of Lord Elwyn-Jones and with Lord Russell's explanation of *Beard*.]

Lord Simon also agreed but added 'by way of marginal comment': . . . a considerable difficulty in this branch of the law arises from the terminology which has been used . . . [I]t is desirable that the terms used should be defined, unambiguous and used consistently

But, in order to understand this branch of the law in general and *D.P.P. v Beard* in particular, it is desirable to have further tools of analysis. A term that appears frequently in discussion of this aspect of the law and crucially in *Beard* is 'specific intent.' . . .

I would not wish it to be thought that I consider 'ulterior intent' as I defined it in *Morgan* [above, p.123] as interchangeable with 'specific intent' as that term was used by Stephen, for example, in his Digest, by Lord Birken-head L.C. in *Beard* or by Lord Denning and others in commenting on *Beard*. 'Ulterior intent', which I can here summarily describe as a state of mind contemplating consequences beyond those defined in the actus reus, is merely one type of 'specific intent' as that term was used by Lord Birkenhead L.C., etc. 'Ulterior intent' does not accurately describe the state of mind in the crime of doing an act likely to assist the enemy (*R. v Steane* [1947] K.B. 997, above, p.82) or causing grievous bodily harm with intent to do some grievous bodily harm (Offences Against the Person Act 1861, s.18, as amended by the Criminal Law Act 1967) or even murder. None of these requires by its definition contemplation of consequences extending beyond the actus reus.

I still have the temerity to think that the concept of 'crime of basic intent' is a useful tool of analysis; and I explained what I meant by it in the passage in *Morgan* generously cited by my noble and learned friend, Lord Elwyn-Jones L.C. It stands significantly in contrast with 'crime of specific intent' as that term was used by Stephen's Digest and by Lord Birkenhead L.C. in Beard. The best description of 'specific intent' in this sense that I know is contained in the judgement of Fauteux J. in *R. v George* (1960) 128 Can. Crim. Cas. 289, 301:

'In considering the question of *mens rea*, a distinction is to be made between (i) intention as applied to acts considered in relation to their purposes and (ii) intention as applied to acts apart from their purposes. A general intent attending the commission of an act is, in some cases, the only intent required to constitute the crime while, in others, there must be, in addition to that general intent, a specific intent attending the purpose for the commission of the act.'

In short, where the crime is one of 'specific intent' the prosecution must in general prove that the purpose for the commission of the act extends to the intent expressed or implied in the definition of the crime . . .

As I have ventured to suggest, there is nothing unreasonable or illogical in the law holding that a mind rendered self-inducedly insensible (short of *M'Naghten* insanity), through drink or drugs, to the nature of a prohibited act or to its probable consequences is as wrongful a mind as one which consciously contemplates the prohibited act and foresees its probable consequences (or is reckless whether they ensue). The latter is all that is required by way of mens rea in a crime of basic intent. But a crime of specific intent requires something more than contemplation of the prohibited act and foresight of its probable consequences. The mens rea in a crime of specific intent requires proof of a purposive element. This purposive element either exists or not; it cannot be supplied by saying that the impairment of mental powers by self-induced intoxication is its equivalent, for it is not. So that the 19th century development of the law as to the effect of self-induced intoxication on criminal responsibility is juristically entirely acceptable; and it need be a matter of no surprise that Stephen stated it without demur or question.

LORD SALMON

. . . [A]n assault committed accidentally is not a criminal offence . . .. A man who by voluntarily taking drink and drugs gets himself into an aggressive state in which he does not know what he is doing and then makes a vicious assault can hardly say with any plausibility that what he did was a pure accident which should render him immune from any criminal liability. Yet this in effect is precisely what counsel for the appellant contends that the learned judge should have told the jury.

A number of distinguished academic writers support this contention on the ground of logic. As I understand it, the argument runs like this. Intention, whether special or basic (or whatever fancy name you choose to give it), is still intention. If voluntary intoxication by drink or drugs can, as it admittedly can, negative the special or specific intention necessary for the commission of crimes such as murder and theft, how can you justify in strict logic the view that it cannot negative a basic intention, e.g. the intention to commit offences such as assault and unlawful wounding? The answer is that in strict logic this view cannot be justified. But this is the view that has been adopted by the common law of England, which is founded on common sense and experience rather than strict logic. There is no case in the 19th century when the courts were relaxing the harshness of the law in relation to the effect of drunkenness on criminal liability in which the courts ever went so far as to suggest that drunkenness, short of drunkenness producing insanity, could ever exculpate a man from any offence other than one which required some special or specific intent to be proved.

[His Lordship then discussed *Beard*.]

As I have already indicated, I accept that there is a degree of illogicality in the rule that intoxication may excuse or expunge one type of intention and not another. This illogicality is, however, acceptable to me because the benevolent part of the rule removes undue harshness without imperilling safety and the stricter part of the rule works without imperilling justice. It would be just as ridiculous to remove the benevolent part of the rule (which no one suggests) as it would be to adopt the alternative of removing the stricter part of the rule for the sake of preserving absolute logic. Absolute logic in human affairs is an uncertain guide and a very dangerous master. The law is primarily concerned with human affairs. I believe that the main object of our legal system is to preserve individual liberty. One important aspect of individual liberty is protection against physical violence . . .

My Lords, for these reasons, I would dismiss the appeal.

[Lord Edmund-Davies and Lord Russell of Killowen delivered speeches in favour of dismissing the appeal.]

Appeal dismissed

Questions

1. Lord Elwyn-Jones states that self-induced intoxication is "a reckless course of conduct" and that "recklessness is enough to constitute the necessary *mens rea* in assault cases." In what sense(s) is the word "reckless" being used in these two statements? (See further A. Ashworth and J. Horder, *Principles of Criminal Law*, 7th edn (Oxford: Oxford University Press, 2013).)

2. Although Lord Simon agreed with Lord Elwyn-Jones he also said "*Mens rea* is . . . the state of mind stigmatised as wrongful by the criminal law . . . There is no juristic reason why mental incapacity . . . brought about by self-induced intoxication, to realise what one is doing should not be such a state of mind stigmatised as wrongful." Is this compatible with describing such intoxication as "reckless"?

3. Lord Salmon and Lord Edmund-Davies admitted that the decision was illogical. Do you agree? See Dashwood: "Logic and the Lords in Majewski" [1977] Crim. L.R. 532 and 591; and Sellers: "*Mens Rea* and the Judicial Approach to Bad Excuses" (1978) 41 M.L.R. 245.

4. Barlow in "Drug Intoxication and the Principle of *Capacitas Rationalis*" (1984) 100 L.Q.R. 639, 646 states:

   "Given that self induced intoxication creates a risk that harmful conduct of some diverse kind may result, it would almost always be forensically impossible to demonstrate that a specific risk was known and ignored, at the point before the drug was used. Can it really be said that the accused in *DPP v Majewski* soberly foresaw on Sunday morning before he began intoxicating himself with amphetamines, barbiturates and alcohol that he might consequently commit an assault on Monday evening? The most he could have foreseen at that point was that intoxication might create a wide range of risks to other people or their property. That he might become irrational and might be reduced to a socially dangerous entity. That is not the essence of criminal recklessness."

   Do you agree?

Notes

1. It is clear from *Garlick* [1981] Crim. L.R. 178 that when intoxication is raised as a defence to a crime of specific intent the question in issue is not whether the defendant was incapable of forming the intent but whether, even if still capable, he or she did form that intent.

2. The onus of proof remains on the prosecution to prove beyond reasonable doubt that regardless of the alleged intoxication, D had the requisite intent (see *Sheehan and Moore* (1974) 60 Cr. App. R. 308; *Pordage* [1975] Crim. L.R. 575).

3. Where on a charge of an offence of specific intent evidence of intoxication emerges during the trial which might lead a reasonable jury to conclude that there is a reasonable possibility that D did not form the intent, whether or not D expressly raises it, the judge is under an obligation to direct the jury on this matter as intent is an essential element of the offence which the Crown has to prove (see *Bennett* [1995] Crim. L.R. 877; *Brown and Stratton* [1998] Crim. L.R. 485).

4. Unfortunately a line of cases has developed which is undermining the clarity of the above position largely due to two mistakes which are becoming prevalent in judicial reasoning. The first is the assertion (with *Beard* [1920] A.C. 479 being cited as the authority) that evidence of intoxication

must be to the effect that it rendered D incapable of forming the requisite intent. This ignores *Garlick, Sheehan and Moore* and *Pordage*. Secondly, there is a tendency to regard intoxication as a defence requiring proof by the accused (again due to reliance on dicta in Beard which were made before the leading case on the burden of proof, *Woolmington* [1935] A.C. 462, was decided) when, in fact, it is simply a denial that the Crown has discharged its burden of proving beyond reasonable doubt that D had the requisite intent. Both these mistakes were made by the Court of Appeal in *McKnight, The Times*, 5 May 2000 where Henry LJ placed considerable reliance on the Privy Council case of *Sooklal v The State of Trinidad and Tobago* [1999] 1 W.L.R. 2011, where both mistakes were also made. In *McKnight*, a murder case, the Court of Appeal held that the trial judge is obliged to direct the jury to consider the question of the accused's claim that he was intoxicated and did not form the necessary intent only where there is a sufficient factual basis established in the evidence for the claim that D was so drunk as to be incapable of forming the intent or was so drunk as not to know what she was doing. Henry LJ cited with approval the speech of Lord Hope of Craighead in *Sooklal* where he stated (at 2017):

"Whenever reduction of a charge of murder on the ground of self-induced intoxication is in issue, the ultimate question is whether the defendant formed the mens rea for the crime charged . . . What is required is specific evidence that the defendant was so intoxicated that he lacked the specific intent which is essential for murder: that is the intent to kill or to inflict grievous bodily harm upon the victim . . .

This test is not satisfied by evidence that the defendant had consumed so much alcohol that he was intoxicated. Nor is it satisfied by evidence that he could not remember what he was doing because he was drunk. The essence of the defence is that the defendant did not have the guilty intent because his mind was so affected by drink that he did not know what he was doing at the time when he did the act with which he was charged. The intoxication must have been of such a degree that it prevented him from foreseeing or knowing what he would have foreseen or known had he been sober . . ."

There is little excuse for senior judges making such basic errors which have the unfortunate effect of leaving the law in a state of uncertainty.

Note

Section 1(2) of the Criminal Damage Act 1971 provides:

"A person who without lawful excuse destroys or damages any property, whether belonging to himself or another

(*a*)   intending to destroy or damage any property or being reckless as to whether any property should be destroyed or damaged; and

(*b*)   intending by the destruction or damage to endanger the life of another or being reckless as to whether the life of another would be thereby endangered;

shall be guilty of an offence."

In *R. v Caldwell*, the House of Lords held that whether this is a crime of specific or basic intent depends on the basis of the charge.

R. V CALDWELL

[1981] 2 All E.R. 961 HL; [1982] A.C. 341

The certified question was as follows:

"Whether evidence of self-induced intoxication can be relevant to the following questions—(a) Whether the defendant intended to endanger the life of another; and (b) Whether the defendant was reckless as to whether the life of another would be endangered, within the meaning of section '(2)(b) of the Criminal Damage Act 1971."

LORD DIPLOCK

As respects the charge under section 1(2) the prosecution did not rely upon an actual intent of the respondent to endanger the lives of the residents but relied upon his having been reckless whether the lives of any of them would be endangered . . .

If the only mental state capable of constituting the necessary *mens rea* for an offence under section 1(2) were that expressed in the words 'intending by the destruction or damage to endanger the life of another', it would have been necessary to consider whether the offence was to be classified as one of 'specific' intent for the purposes of the rule of law which this House affirmed and applied in *R. v Majewski*, and this it plainly is. But this is not, in my view, a relevant inquiry where 'being reckless as to whether the life of another would be thereby endangered' is an alternative mental state that is capable of constituting the necessary *mens rea* of the offence with which he is charged.

The speech of the Lord Chancellor in *Majewski* with which Lord Simon of Glaisdale, Lord Kilbrandon and I agreed, is authority that self-induced intoxication is no defence to a crime in which recklessness is enough to constitute the necessary *mens rea* . . .

Reducing oneself by drink or drugs to a condition in which the restraints of reason and conscience are cast off was held to be a reckless course of conduct and an integral part of the crime. The Lord Chancellor accepted as correctly stating English law the provision in section 2.08 of the American Model Penal Code:

'When recklessness establishes an element of the offence, if the actor, due to self-induced intoxication, is unaware of a risk of which he would have been aware had he been sober, such unawareness is immaterial.'

So, in the instant case, the fact that the respondent was unaware of the risk of endangering the lives of residents in the hotel owing to his self-induced intoxication, would be no defence if that risk would have been obvious to him had he been sober.

. . . [T]he Court of Appeal in the instant case regarded the case as turning upon whether the offence under section 1(2) was one of 'specific' intent or 'basic' intent. Following a recent decision of the Court of Appeal by which they were bound, *R. v Orpin* (1980) 70 Cr.App.R. 306, they held that the offence under s.1(2) was one of 'specific' intent in contrast to the offence under s.1(1) which was of basic intent. This would be right if the only *mens tea* capable of constituting the offence were an actual intention to endanger the life of another. For the reasons I have given, however, classification into offences of 'specific' and 'basic' intent is irrelevant where being reckless as to whether a particular harmful consequence will result from one's act is a sufficient alternative *mens rea*. I would give the following answers to the certified questions:

(a) If the charge of an offence under s.1(2) of the Criminal Damage Act 1971 is framed so as to charge the defendant only with '*intending* by the destruction or damage' [of the property] 'to endanger the life of another,' evidence of self-induced intoxication can be relevant to his defence.

(b) If the charge is, or includes, a reference to his 'being reckless as to whether the life of another would thereby be endangered,' evidence of self-induced intoxication is not relevant.

Lords Keith of Kinkel and Roskill agreed with this statement of the law. Lord Wilberforce agreed with Lord Edmund-Davies.

LORD EDMUND-DAVIES

[T]he view expressed by my noble and learned friend Lord Diplock 'that the speech of the Lord Chancellor in *Majewski* is authority that self-induced intoxication is no defence to a crime in which recklessness is enough to constitute the necessary *mens rea*' . . . is a view which, with respect, I do not share. In common with all noble and learned Lords hearing that appeal, Lord Elwyn-Jones L.C. adopted the well-established (though not universally favoured) distinction between basic and specific intents. *Majewski* related solely to charges of assault, undoubtedly an offence of basic intent, and the Lord Chancellor made it clear that his observations were confined to offences of that nature . . . My respectful view is that *Majewski* accordingly supplies no support for the proposition that, in relation to crimes of specific intent (such as section 1(2) of the 1971 Act) incapacity to appreciate the degree and nature of the risk created by his action which is attributable to the defendant's self-intoxication is an irrelevance. The Lord Chancellor was dealing simply with crimes of basic intent, and in my judgment it was strictly within that framework that he adopted the view expressed in the American Penal Code [s.2.08] and recklessness as an element in crimes of specific intent was, I am convinced, never within his contemplation . . .

Appeal dismissed

Note

Mitchell, "The Intoxicated Offender—Refuting the Legal and Medical Myths" (1988) Int. J. Law & Psych. 77, argues that scientific evidence supports a simple subjective test for the effect of intoxication on mens rea in all cases, making the following points:

1. Modern day judicial assumptions about the effects of drugs and alcohol stem from Victorian medical opinion.

2. There is a lack of consensus among scientists as to a link between aggression and psychoactive drugs (including alcohol).

3. Research and scientific literature indicate that intoxicated people almost always know what they are doing and do exactly what they intend; the assumption by the courts that intoxication both causes aggression and negatives intent is anomalous—aggression is necessarily directed and targeted.

4. His research had uncovered no genuine case where intoxication caused an automatic or involuntary act.

5. Medical testimony about intoxication is "biased, inaccurate, harmful and unnecessary".

Mitchell's views would tend to suggest that the *Majewski* rule is unnecessary and that the only question for a jury in any case should be "did D, whatever his state of intoxication, perform a voluntary act and do so with the mens rea for the crime with which he is charged?" The need to distinguish between offences of basic and specific intent disappears. This is the position adopted in the non-Code Australian States (see *O'Connor* (1981) 146 C.L.R. 64) and in New Zealand (see *Kamipeli* [1975] 2 N.Z.L.R. 610). In "Surviving without Majewski—A View from Down Under" [1993] Crim. L.R. 427, 429, Orchard states:

"In these jurisdictions complete acquittal as a result of intoxication raising doubt as to a required state of mind is not unknown, but it is very unusual. This may in part be due to juries and judges being unwilling to give effect to what they regard as an unmeritorious principle, but it also reflects the reality that while intoxication may often contribute to and explain intentional offending it will seldom result in the absence of the modest mental requirements of intention, awareness and foresight that generally suffice for *mens rea*. Advocacy and expert speculation might obscure this, but it can be appropriately brought home to the jury. In *Kamipeli* it was recognised that it is proper, and often it will be necessary, for the jury to be warned that absence of intent because of intoxication 'is a conclusion not to be lightly reached', and the issue may be removed from the jury's consideration if there is no evidence which could reasonably support such a conclusion."

Note

Majewski is authority for the proposition that "self-induced intoxication is no defence to a crime in which recklessness is enough to constitute the necessary mens rea". This dictum indicates that offences which may be committed recklessly are not crimes of specific intent but does not precisely determine how offences of specific intent should be identified. The matter was revisited by the Court of Appeal in the case which follows.

R. V HEARD

[2007] EWCA Crim 125

D was heavily intoxicated and exposed his penis, rubbing it against the thigh of a police officer. He was arrested and charged with sexual assault contrary to s.3 of the Sexual Offences Act 2003. The section which creates this offence provides as follows:

'3 Sexual assault
(1) A person (A) commits an offence if

(a)   he intentionally touches another person (B),
(b)   the touching is sexual,
(c)   B does not consent to the touching, and
(d)   A does not reasonably believe that B consents.'

At trial D claimed to have no recollection of the incident owing to his intoxication. He sought to plead in his defence that his voluntary intoxication was a complete defence as it prevented him from having the intention to touch the other person which was required by s.3(1)(a). The trial judge ruled that the offence was one of basic intent and that voluntary intoxication was not a defence.

LORD JUSTICE HUGHES

[After reciting the facts and reviewing the trial judge's direction His Lordship continued . . .]
    10. The appellant contends that the Judge's ruling was wrong. The offence is, it is said, one requiring proof of a specific intent and the jury should have been directed to consider whether the drink which the appellant had taken meant that he did not have the intention to touch. The Crown on the other hand contends that the offence is one of basic intent and that evidence of self-induced intoxication is simply irrelevant.
    11. In a little more detail, Mr Stern's argument for the appellant runs like this:

i)   The correct reading of *Majewski* and subsequent cases is that voluntary intoxication is incapable of being a defence only where recklessness suffices as the mens rea of the offence; it is such offences which are properly described as those of 'basic intent'.

ii)   The present offence is one for which reckless touching will not suffice; only intentional touching will do.

iii) Therefore this is an offence of specific and not of basic intent. Voluntary intoxication is a relevant factor to consider when asking whether the appellant did or did not have the intention to touch required by the section.

12. For the Crown, Mr Perry's argument, similarly summarised, runs as follows:

i) The *Majewski* concept of crimes of basic intent, in which voluntary intoxication cannot be advanced as a defence, is not limited to those where recklessness suffices; the correct distinction is between crimes requiring ordinary intent (where voluntary intoxication cannot be relied upon), and those requiring specific or purposive intent (where it can).

ii) There is however no universally logical test for distinguishing between crimes in which voluntary intoxication can be advanced as a defence and those in which it cannot; there is a large element of policy; categorisation is achieved on an offence by offence basis.

iii) Before the Sexual Offences Act 2003, indecent assault could only be committed by intentional touching; yet voluntary intoxication was not a defence, as it was also not to rape. The decisions of *Woods* (1982) 74 Cr.App.R. 312 and *R v C* [1992] Crim.L.R. 642 are relied upon. The new Act was not intended to change the law in this respect; on the contrary its object was to improve the protection of potential victims of sexual interference. To treat sexual assault as a crime of specific intent would mean treating similarly the very many other sexual offences created by the 2003 Act which are structured in the same way, including rape (section 1), assault by penetration (section 2) and most of the child sex offences. In sexual assault (and in rape and other similar offences) a defendant's belief in consent is said by the statute to provide a defence only if it is reasonable, and that must mean that a drunken belief cannot be relied upon.

iv) Where it applies, the rule that voluntary intoxication cannot be relied upon is a rule of substantive law; accordingly in sexual assault and other similarly structured sexual offences under the 2003 Act voluntarily taken intoxicants are simply to be ignored for all purposes when considering whether the offence has been committed.

v) Although the requirement that the touching be intentional means that it must be deliberate, if accident is suggested the question whether what happened was accidental or not must be answered as if the defendant had been sober, even though he was not.

Discussion

13. The present case concerns alcohol. The same however must apply to intoxication or otherwise altered state of mind resulting from the voluntary taking of drugs or other substances. Indeed the mind-altering effects of some drugs, especially hallucinogenic ones, may be more far-reaching than the effects of alcohol. *Majewski* itself was a drugs case. When we refer to 'voluntary intoxication' we mean to include all such cases.

14. The first thing to say is that it should not be supposed that every offence can be categorised simply as either one of specific intent or of basic intent. So to categorise an offence may conceal the truth that different elements of it may require proof of different states of mind. In the law of rape, as it stood immediately before the passing of the Sexual Offences Act 2003, rape was sexual intercourse with a woman who did not in fact consent, by a man who either knew she did not or was reckless as to whether she did. No-one doubted that the act of intercourse could only be committed intentionally. But when it came to the defendant's state of mind as to the woman's lack of consent, either knowledge or recklessness sufficed for guilt: section 1 Sexual Offences (Amendment) Act 1976. Many other examples of the point could be cited. The current legislative practice of itemising separately different elements of offences created by statute, which is much exhibited in the Sexual Offences Act 2003, may occasionally have the potential to complicate matters for a jury, but it demonstrates the impossibility of fitting an offence into a single pigeon-hole, whether it be labelled 'basic intent' or 'specific intent'.

15. The offence of sexual assault, with which this case is concerned, is an example. The different elements of the offence, identified in paragraphs (a) to (d) of section 3, do not call for proof of the same state of mind. Element (a), the touching, must by the statute be intentional. Element (b), the sexual nature of the touching, takes one to section 78. By that section the primary question is a purely objective one, as set out in s.78(a). If, however, the act itself is objectively equivocal, the purpose of the Defendant may be a relevant consideration, as provided by s.78(b), and that must be a reference to his own (subjective) purpose. The state of mind in a defendant which must be proved in relation to element (c), the absence of consent, is expressly stipulated by element (d) and by s.3(2), and the stipulation is in terms which make it clear that the test is substantially objective; a belief in consent which

was induced largely by drink would be most unlikely to be reasonable. It is accordingly of very limited help to attempt to label the offence of sexual assault, as a whole, one of either basic or specific intent, because the state of mind which must be proved varies with the issue. For this reason also, it is unsafe to reason (as at one point the Crown does) directly from the state of mind required in relation to consent to the solution to the present question.

16. Since it is only the touching which must be intentional, whilst the sexual character of the touching is, unless equivocal, to be judged objectively, and a belief in consent must be objectively reasonable, we think that it will only be in cases of some rarity that the question which we are posed in this appeal will in the end be determinative of the outcome.

17. We do not think that it determines this appeal. On the evidence the appellant plainly did intend to touch the policeman with his penis. That he was drunk may have meant either:

i)   that he was disinhibited and did something which he would not have done if sober; and/or

ii) that he did not remember it afterwards.

But neither of those matters (if true) would destroy the intentional character of his touching. In the homely language employed daily in directions to juries in cases of violence and sexual misbehaviour, 'a drunken intent is still an intent.' And for the memory to blot out what was intentionally done is common, if not perhaps quite as common as is the assertion by offenders that it has done so. In the present case, what the appellant did and said at the time, and said in interview afterwards, made it perfectly clear that this was a case of drunken intentional touching. Although the Judge directed the jury that drink was no defence, he also directed the jury that it must be sure that the touching was deliberate. That amounted to a direction that for conviction the appellant's mind (drunken or otherwise) had to have gone with his physical action of touching. Mr Stern realistically conceded that he could not hope to improve upon that direction.

18. We do not attempt the notoriously unrealistic task of foreseeing every possible permutation of human behaviour which the future may reveal. But it nevertheless seems to us that in the great majority of cases of alleged sexual assault, or of comparable sexual crimes, as in the present case, the mind will have gone with the touching, penetration or other prohibited act, albeit in some cases a drunken mind.

19. It is, however, possible to envisage the exceptional case in which there is a real possibility that the intoxication was such that the mind did not go with the physical act. In *Lipman* (1969) 55 Cr.App.R. 600 the defendant contended that when he killed his victim by stuffing bedclothes down her throat he was under the illusion, induced by hallucinatory drugs voluntarily taken, that he was fighting for his life against snakes. If an equivalent state of mind were (assumedly genuinely) to exist in someone who committed an act of sexual touching or penetration, the question which arises in this appeal would be directly in point.

20. A different situation was also put to us in the course of argument. Its formulation probably owes much to Professor Ormerod's current edition of Smith and Hogan's Criminal Law (11th edition, page 624). It is that of the intoxicated person whose control of his limbs is uncoordinated or impaired, so that in consequence he stumbles or flails about against another person, touching him or her in a way which, objectively viewed, is sexual for example because he touches a woman on her private parts. Can such a person be heard to say that what happened was other than deliberate when, if he had been sober, it would not have happened?

21. In the present case the Judge directed the jury that drunkenness was not a defence, although coupling with it the direction that the touching must be deliberate. Whether or not the jury's decision was likely to be that the appellant had acted intentionally (albeit drunkenly), the Judge had to determine whether or not it was necessary for the jury to investigate the suggestion that the appellant was so drunk that his mind did not go with his act. That question may also face judges and juries, as it seems to us, in many cases where a defendant wishes to contend that he was thus intoxicated, and scientific or medical evidence can say no more than that in an extreme case drink or drugs are capable of inducing a state of mind in which a person believes that what he is doing is something different to what he in fact does. In those circumstances, and in deference to the full argument which we have heard, we have concluded that we should address the issue, rather than confine ourselves to saying that this conviction is safe.

22. We are in the present case concerned with element (a), the touching. The Act says that it must be intentional. We regard it as clear that a reckless touching will not do. The Act plainly proceeds upon the basis that there is a difference between 'intentionally' and 'recklessly'. Where it wishes to speak in terms of recklessness, the Act does so: see for example sections 63(1), 69(1)(c) & (2)(c) and 70(1)(c). It is not necessary to decide whether or not it is possible to conceive of a reckless, but unintentional, sexual touching. Like their Lordships in *Court* [1989] 1 AC 28, we think that such a possibility is a remote one, but we are unable wholly to rule it out. One theoretical

possible example might be a Defendant who intends to avoid (just) actual physical contact, but realises that he may touch and is reckless whether he will.

23. Because the offence is committed only by intentional touching, we agree that the Judge's direction that the touching must be deliberate was correct. To flail about, stumble or barge around in an uncoordinated manner which results in an unintended touching, objectively sexual, is not this offence. If to do so when sober is not this offence, then nor is it this offence to do so when intoxicated. It is also possible that such an action would not be judged by the jury to be objectively sexual, on the basis that it was clearly accidental, but whether that is so or not, we are satisfied that in such a case this offence is not committed. The intoxication, in such a situation, has not impacted on intention. Intention is simply not in question. What is in question is impairment of control of the limbs. Accordingly we reject Mr Perry's submission number (v) see paragraph 12 above. We would expect that in some cases where this was in issue the Judge might well find it useful to add to the previously-mentioned direction that 'a drunken intent is still an intent', the corollary that 'a drunken accident is still an accident'. To the limited, and largely theoretical, extent that a reckless sexual touching is possible the same would apply to that case also. Whether, when a defendant claims accident, he is doing so truthfully, or as a means of disguising the reality that he intended to touch, will be what the jury has to decide on the facts of each such case.

24. The remaining question is whether the Judge was also correct to direct the jury that drunkenness was not a defence.

25. We do not agree with Mr Stern's submission for the appellant that the fact that reckless touching will not suffice means that voluntary intoxication can be relied upon as defeating intentional touching. We do not read the cases, including *Majewski*, as establishing any such rule. As we shall show, we would hold that it is not open to a defendant charged with sexual assault to contend that his voluntary intoxication prevented him from intending to touch. The Judge was accordingly correct, not only to direct the jury that the touching must be deliberate, but also to direct it that the defence that voluntary drunkenness rendered him unable to form the intent to touch was not open to him. Our reasons are as follows.

26. In *Majewski* the rival contentions before the House of Lords were these. For the appellant it was contended that if intoxication affected the mind of the defendant it was illogical and unethical to distinguish between its effect on one state of mind and on another; it was capable of destroying any state of mind which is required as a component of a criminal offence. There was thus, it was argued, no permissible distinction between offences of basic intent and those of specific intent. The Crown contended that that distinction had nevertheless represented the law of England for many years. The House upheld the Crown's contention. It did so in the full knowledge that it was not perfectly logical. It so held, in large measure, on grounds of policy. As was observed by several of their Lordships, historically the law of England regarded voluntary intoxication as an aggravation rather than a potential excuse and the development of the law had been by way of a partial, but only a partial, relaxation of that common law rule where a specific intent was required. Both Lord Elwyn-Jones LC (at 471H) and Lord Edmund-Davies (at 494F) approved what Lawton LJ had said in the Court of Appeal:

'Although there was much reforming zeal and activity in the 19th century, Parliament never once considered whether self-induced intoxication should be a defence generally to a criminal charge. It would have been a strange result if the merciful relaxation of a strict rule of law had ended, without any Parliamentary intervention, by whittling it away to such an extent that the more drunk a man became, provided it stopped short of making him insane, the better chance he had of an acquittal. The common law rule still applied but there were exceptions to it which Lord Birkenhead LC tried to define by reference to specific intent.'

Lord Simon (at 476F) added this:

'One of the primary purposes of the criminal law, with its penal sanctions, is the protection from certain proscribed conduct of persons who are pursuing their lawful lives. Unprovoked violence has from time immemorial been a significant part of such proscribed conduct. To accede to the argument on behalf of the appellant would leave the citizen legally unprotected from unprovoked violence where such violence was the consequence of drink or drugs having obliterated the capacity of the perpetrator to know what he was doing or what were its consequences.'

Lord Salmon (at 482E) said this of the distinction between basic and specific intent which the House upheld:

'The answer is that in strict logic this view cannot be justified. But this is the view that has been adopted by the common law of England, which is founded on common sense and experience rather than strict logic. There is no case in the nineteenth century when the courts were relaxing the harshness of the law in relation to the effect of drunkenness upon criminal liability in which the courts ever went so far as to suggest that drunkenness, short of drunkenness producing insanity, could ever exculpate a man from any offence other than one which require some special or specific intent to be proved.'

27. Mr Stern's proposition that *Majewski* decides that it is only where recklessness suffices that voluntary intoxication cannot be relied upon derives from a part of the speech of Lord Elwyn-Jones LC in *Majewski* and some observations, obiter, of Lord Diplock in the subsequent case of *Caldwell* 1982] AC 341. In *Majewski*, Lord Elwyn-Jones, having approved the distinction between crimes of specific and of basic intent, said this at page 474H:

'I do not for my part regard that general principle as either unethical or contrary to the principles of natural justice. If a man of his own volition takes a substance which causes him to cast off the restraints of reason and conscience, no wrong is done to him by holding him answerable criminally for any injury he may do whilst in that condition. His course of conduct in reducing himself by drugs and drink to that condition in my view supplies the evidence of mens rea, of guilty mind certainly sufficient for crimes of basic intent. It is a reckless course of conduct and recklessness is enough to constitute the necessary mens rea in assault cases: see *Venna* [1976] QB 421 per James LJ at p 429. The drunkenness is itself an intrinsic and integral part of the crime, the other part being the evidence of the unlawful use of force against the victim. Together they add up to criminal recklessness.'

28. In *Caldwell*, Lord Diplock added this, at page 355F

'The speech of Lord Elwyn-Jones LC in *Majewski* . . . is authority that self-induced intoxication is no defence to a crime in which recklessness is enough to constitute the necessary mens rea. Reducing oneself by drink or drugs to a condition in which the restraints of reason and conscience are cast off was held to be a reckless course of conduct and an integral part of the crime.'

29. In *Caldwell* the charge was of arson, being reckless as to the endangering of life, contrary to s 1(2)(b) Criminal Damage Act 1971. The defendant accepted that he had deliberately set the fire, but claimed that his drunken state prevented him from appreciating the risk that people might be present and their lives be put in danger. The majority held, through the speech of Lord Diplock, that for the purposes of the use of the word in a criminal statute, recklessness was made out not only by the man who appreciated a risk yet ran it unreasonably anyway, but also by the man who failed to appreciate an objectively obvious risk.
30. There are a number of difficulties about extracting Mr Stern's proposition from the passages cited.

  i) Lord Elwyn-Jones was addressing the submission made on behalf of the appellant in Majewski that it was unprincipled or unethical to distinguish between the effect of drink upon the mind in some crimes and its effect upon the mind in others. In rejecting that submission, and upholding the distinction between crimes of basic and of specific intent, he was drawing attention to the fact that a man who has got himself into a state of voluntary intoxication is not, by ordinary standards, blameless. Both the Lord Chancellor and others of their Lordships made clear their view that to get oneself into such a state is, viewed broadly, as culpable as is any sober defendant convicted of a crime of basic intent, whether because he has the basic intent or because he is reckless as to the relevant consequence or circumstance. Throughout *Majewski* it is clear that their Lordships regarded those latter two states of mind as equivalent to one another for these purposes. It therefore does not follow from the references to recklessness that the same rule (that voluntary intoxication cannot be relied upon) does not apply also to basic intent; on the contrary, it seems to us clear that their Lordships were treating the two the same.

  ii) The new analysis of recklessness in *Caldwell* may have led readily to the proposition that voluntary intoxication is broadly equivalent to recklessness, thus defined. But that analysis and definition of recklessness have now been reversed by the House of Lords in *G* [2004] 1 AC 1034. As now understood, recklessness requires actual foresight of the risk.

  iii) Since the majority in *Caldwell* held that it was enough for recklessness that the risk was obvious objectively (thus, to the sober man) no question of drink providing a defence could arise; it follows that the explanation of *Majewski* which was advanced was plainly obiter.

  iv) Lord Diplock's proposition in *Caldwell* attracted a vigorous dissent from Lord Edmund-Davies, who, like

Lord Diplock, had been a party to *Majewski*, and with whom Lord Wilberforce agreed. They dissented not only from the new definition of recklessness, but also from the analysis of *Majewski*. Their view was that arson being reckless as to the endangering of life is an offence of specific, not of basic, intent; that would seem to have been because the state of mind went to an ulterior or purposive element of the offence, rather than to the basic element of causing damage by fire.

v)   There were, moreover, many difficulties in the proposition that voluntary intoxication actually supplies the mens rea, whether on the basis of recklessness as re-defined in *Caldwell* or on the basis of recklessness as now understood; if that were so the drunken man might be guilty simply by becoming drunk and whether or not the risk would be obvious to a sober person, himself or anyone else. That reinforces our opinion that the proposition being advanced was one of broadly equivalent culpability, rather than of drink by itself supplying the mens rea.

31. It is necessary to go back to *Majewski* in order to see the basis for the distinction there upheld between crimes of basic and of specific intent. It is to be found most clearly in the speech of Lord Simon, at pages 478B to 479B. Lord Simon's analysis had been foreshadowed in his speech in *Morgan* [1976] AC 182, 216 (dissenting in the result), which analysis was cited and approved in *Majewski* by Lord Elwyn-Jones (at 471). It was that crimes of specific intent are those where the offence requires proof of purpose or consequence, which are not confined to, but amongst which are included, those where the purpose goes beyond the actus reus (sometimes referred to as cases of 'ulterior intent'). Lord Simon put it in this way at 478H:

> 'The best description of "specific intent" in this sense that I know is contained in the judgment of Fauteux J. in *Reg v George* (1960) 128 Can CC 289, 301
> "In considering the question of mens rea, a distinction is to be made between (i) intention as applied to acts considered in relation to their purposes and (ii) intention as applied to acts apart from their purposes. A general intent attending the commission of an act is, in some cases, the only intent required to constitute the crime while, in others, there must be, in addition to that general intent, a specific intent attending the purpose for the commission of the act."'

That explanation of the difference is consistent with the view of Lord Edmund-Davies that an offence contrary to s.1(2)(b) Criminal Damage Act is one of specific intent in this sense, even though it involves no more than recklessness as to the endangering of life; the offence requires proof of a state of mind addressing something beyond the prohibited act itself, namely its consequences. We regard this as the best explanation of the sometimes elusive distinction between specific and basic intent in the sense used in *Majewski*, and it seems to us that this is the distinction which the Judge in the present case was applying when he referred to the concept of a 'bolted-on' intent. By that test, element (a) (the touching) in sexual assault contrary to s.3 Sexual Offences Act 2003 is an element requiring no more than basic intent. It follows that voluntary intoxication cannot be relied upon to negate that intent.

32. We therefore accept Mr Perry's submission number (i) (see paragraph 12 above). We also, however, recognise the accuracy of submission number (ii). There is a great deal of policy in the decision whether voluntary intoxication can or cannot be relied upon. We have already referred to one of several passages in *Majewski* where the rule is firmly grounded upon common sense, whether purely logical or not. We agree that it is unlikely that it was the intention of Parliament in enacting the Sexual Offences Act 2003 to change the law by permitting reliance upon voluntary intoxication where previously it was not permitted. *R v Woods*, relied upon by the Crown, does not entirely resolve the question which we are now addressing. What was there decided was that a defendant charged with rape could not rely on voluntary drunkenness when the question was whether he was reckless as to whether the woman consented. By the statute then in force, the presence or absence of reasonable grounds for belief in consent was made a factor to be taken into account. There are now separate, and differently expressed, statutory provisions as to belief in consent, which make it clear that belief must not only be held in fact but be objectively reasonable. As we have said in paragraph 15 above, it does not necessarily follow that the rule need be the same for different elements of the offence, especially given the new restrictive rules as to belief in consent. That said, the following observation of Griffiths L.J. in *Woods* seems to us to be as relevant to this case now as it was to that case then:

> 'If Parliament had meant to provide in future that a man whose lust was so inflamed by drink that he ravished a woman, should nevertheless be able to pray in aid his drunken state to avoid the consequences we would have expected them to have used the clearest words to express such a surprising result, which we believe

would be utterly repugnant to the great majority of people. We are satisfied that Parliament had no such intention.'

The decision in *R v C* is more clearly in point. The Defendant had penetrated a child's vagina with his finger when drunk. That, like the present, was a clear case of drunken intent, with possible absence of memory. The decision of this Court, presided over by Lord Woolf C.J., was that indecent assault remained a crime of basic intent for these purposes, at least unless the act was an equivocal one so that the purpose of the defendant had to be examined. We are wholly satisfied that there is no basis for construing the new Sexual Offences Act as having altered the law so as to make voluntary intoxication available as a defence to the allegation that the defendant intentionally touched the complainant.

33. For all these reasons, this conviction is in no sense unsafe. Further, our view is that the Judge's directions were substantially correct. Sexual touching must be intentional, that is to say deliberate. But voluntary intoxication cannot be relied upon as negating the necessary intention. If, whether the Defendant is intoxicated or otherwise, the touching is unintentional, this offence is not committed.

34. As we announced at the hearing, this appeal is in consequence dismissed.

Note

The re-interpretation of *Majewski* in *Heard* appears to decide that evidence of voluntary intoxication is only relevant and admissible where the offence is one of "ulterior" intent (e.g. burglary) or where the required intention relates to a prohibited consequence (e.g. murder). If the required intention relates only to the performance of the prohibited act, in this case touching, then the offence remains one of basic intent for the purposes of intoxication.

Questions

1. If *Heard* is followed will the offence of criminal damage being reckless as to whether life is endangered be categorised as an offence of specific or basic intent?

2. Why do you believe the Court of Appeal in *Heard* abandoned the orthodox understanding of *Majewski* which would have classified the offence of sexual assault under s.3 as being one of specific intent?

----

ii. Involuntary Intoxication

R. V KINGSTON

[1994] 3 W.L.R. 519 HL

D, who had paedophiliac tendencies, was convicted of indecent assault on a 15-year-old boy. The defence was that he had been drugged by his co-defendant who had intended to blackmail him and that he would not otherwise have committed the offence. He appealed against the trial judge's ruling that involuntary intoxication could only serve as a defence if, as a result, the defendant had not formed the necessary mens rea for the offence. The Court of Appeal allowed his appeal against conviction, holding that if a surreptitiously administered intoxicant causes a person to lose his self-control and so form an intent he would not otherwise have formed, the law should exculpate him as the operative fault is not his. The following point of law was certified as being of general public importance:

"Whether if it is proved that the necessary intent was present when the necessary act was done by him, a defendant has open to him a defence of involuntary intoxication?" On appeal by the Crown:

LORD MUSTILL

. . . [T]he general nature of the case is clear enough. In ordinary circumstances the respondent's paedophiliac tendencies would have been kept under control, even in the presence of the sleeping or unconscious boy on the bed. The ingestion of the drug (whatever it was) brought about a temporary change in the mentality or personality of the respondent which lowered his ability to resist temptation so far that his desires overrode his ability to control them. Thus we are concerned here with a case of disinhibition. The drug is not alleged to have created the desire to which the respondent gave way, but rather to have enabled it to be released . . .

On these facts there are three grounds on which the respondent might be held free from criminal responsibility. First, that his immunity flows from general principles of the criminal law. Secondly, that this immunity is already established by a solid line of authority. Finally, that the court should, when faced with a new problem acknowledge the justice of the case and boldly create a new common law defence.

It is clear from the passage already quoted that the Court of Appeal adopted the first approach. The decision was explicitly founded on general principle. There can be no doubt what principle the court relied upon, for at the outset the court [1994] Q.B. 81, 87, recorded the submission of counsel for the respondent:

'the law recognises that, exceptionally, an accused person may be entitled to be acquitted if there is a possibility that although his act was intentional, the intent itself arose out of circumstances for which he bears no blame.'

The same proposition is implicit in the assumption by the court that if blame is absent the necessary mens rea must also be absent.

My Lords, with every respect I must suggest that no such principle exists or, until the present case, had ever in modern times been thought to exist. Each offence consists of a prohibited act or omission coupled with whatever state of mind is called for by the statute or rule of the common law which creates the offence. In those offences which are not absolute the state of mind which the prosecution must prove to have underlain the act or omission—the 'mental element'—will in the majority of cases be such as to attract disapproval. The mental element will then be the mark of what may properly be called a 'guilty mind.' The professional burglar is guilty in a moral as well as a legal sense; he intends to break into the house to steal, and most would confidently assert that this is wrong. But this will not always be so. In respect of some offences the mind of the defendant, and still less his moral judgment, may not be engaged at all. In others, although a mental activity must be the motive power for the prohibited act or omission the activity may be of such a kind or degree that society at large would not criticise the defendant's conduct severely or even criticise it at all. Such cases are not uncommon. Yet to assume that contemporary moral judgments affect the criminality of the act, as distinct from the punishment appropriate to the crime once proved, is to be misled by the expression 'mens rea,' the ambiguity of which has been the subject of complaint for more than a century. Certainly, the 'mens' of the defendant must usually be involved in the offence; but the epithet 'rea' refers to the criminality of the act in which the mind is engaged, not to its moral character . . .

I would therefore reject that part of the respondent's argument which treats the absence of moral fault on the part of the appellant as sufficient in itself to negative the necessary mental element of the offence . . .

[I]t is impossible to consider the exceptional case of involuntary intoxication without placing it in the context of intoxication as a whole . . .

As I understand the position it is still the law that in the exceptional case where intoxication causes insanity the M'Naghten Rules (*M'Naghten's Case* (1843) 10 Cl. & F. 200) apply: see *Director of Public Prosecutions v Beard* [1920] A.C. 479, 501 and *Attorney-General for Northern Ireland v Gallagher* [below, p.222]. Short of this, it is no answer for the defendant to say that he would not have done what he did had he been sober, provided always that whatever element of intent is required by the offence is proved to have been present. As was said in *Reg. v Sheehan* [1975] 1 W.L.R. 739, 744C, 'a drunken intent is nevertheless an intent.' As to proof of intent, it appears that at least in some instances self-induced intoxication can be taken into account as part of the evidence from which the jury draws its conclusions; but that in others it cannot. I express the matter in this guarded way because it has not yet been decisively established whether for this purpose there is a line to be drawn between offences of 'specific' and of 'basic' intent. That in at least some cases a defendant cannot say that he was so drunk that he could not form the required intent is however clear enough. Why is this so? The answer must I believe be the same as that given in other common law jurisdictions: namely that such evidence is excluded as a matter of policy. As Mason J. put the matter in *Reg. v O'Connor* (1980) 146 C.L.R. 64, 110:

'the view is taken that the act charged is voluntary notwithstanding that it might not be ordinarily considered so by reason of the condition of the perpetrator, because his condition proceeds from a voluntary choice made by him. These cases therefore constitute an exception to the general rule of criminal responsibility.'

There remains the question by what reasoning the House put this policy into effect. As I understand it two different rationalisations were adopted. First that the absence of the necessary [intent] is cured by treating the intentional drunkenness (or more accurately, since it is only in the minority of cases that the drinker sets out to make himself drunk, the intentional taking of drink without regard to its possible effects) as a substitute for the mental element ordinarily required by the offence. The intent is transferred from the taking of drink to the commission of the prohibited act. The second rationalisation is that the defendant cannot be heard to rely on the absence of the mental element when it is absent because of his own voluntary acts. Borrowing an expression from a far distant field it may be said that the defendant is estopped from relying on his self-induced incapacity.

Your Lordships are not required to decide how these two explanations stand up to attack, for they are not attacked here. The task is only to place them in the context of an intoxication which is not voluntary. Taking first the concept of transferred intent, if the intoxication was not the result of an act done with an informed will there is no intent which can be transferred to the prohibited act, so as to fill the gap in the offence. As regards the 'estoppel' there is no reason why the law should preclude the defendant from relying on a mental condition which he had not deliberately brought about. Thus, once the involuntary nature of the intoxication is added the two theories of *Majewski* fall away, and the position reverts to what it would have been if *Majewski* had not been decided, namely that the offence is not made out if the defendant was so intoxicated that he could not form an intent. Thus, where the intoxication is involuntary *Majewski* does not *subtract* the defence of absence of intent; but there is nothing in *Majewski* to suggest that where intent is proved involuntary intoxication *adds* a further defence.

[His Lordship referred to some Scottish cases and continued.]

My Lords, making due allowance for the differences between the laws of the two jurisdictions these cases are clear authority against the proposition that mere disinhibition is sufficient to found a defence.

[His Lordship referred to the American Law Institute's Model Penal Code and continued.]

My Lords, I cannot find in this material any sufficient grounds for holding that the defence relied upon is already established by the common law, any more than it can be derived from general principles. Accordingly I agree with the analysis of Professor Griew, *Archbold News*, 28 May 1993, pp.4–5:

'What has happened is that the Court of Appeal has recognised a new *defence* to criminal charges in the nature of an exculpatory excuse. It is precisely because the defendant acted in the prohibited way with the intent (the mens rea) required by the definition of the offence that he needs this defence.'

To recognise a new defence of this type would be a bold step. The common law defences of duress and necessity (if it exists) and the limited common law defence of provocation are all very old. Since counsel for the appellant was not disposed to emphasise this aspect of the appeal the subject was not explored in argument, but I suspect that the recognition of a new general defence at common law has not happened in modern times. Nevertheless, the criminal law must not stand still, and if it is both practical and just to take this step, and if judicial decision rather than legislation is the proper medium, then the courts should not be deterred simply by the novelty of it. So one must turn to consider just what defence is now to be created. The judgment under appeal implies five characteristics.

1. The defence applies to all offences, except perhaps to absolute offences. It therefore differs from other defences such as provocation and diminished responsibility.

2. The defence is a complete answer to a criminal charge. If not rebutted it leads to an outright acquittal, and unlike provocation and diminished responsibility leaves no room for conviction and punishment for a lesser offence. The underlying assumption must be that the defendant is entirely free from culpability.

3. It may be that the defence applies only where the intoxication is due to the wrongful act of another and therefore affords no excuse when, in circumstances of no greater culpability, the defendant has intoxicated himself by mistake (such as by shortsightedly taking the wrong drug). I say that this may be so, because it is not clear whether, since the doctrine was founded in part on the dictum of Park J. in *Pearson's Case*, 2 Lew. 144, the 'fraud or stratagem of another' is an essential element, or whether this was taken as an example of a wider principle.

4. The burden of disproving the defence is on the prosecution.

5. The defence is subjective in nature. Whereas provocation and self-defence are judged by the reactions of the reasonable person in the situation of the defendant, here the only question is whether this particular defendant's inhibitions were overcome by the effect of the drug. The more susceptible the defendant to the kind of temptation presented, the easier the defence is to establish . . .

[T]he defence appears to run into difficulties at every turn. In point of theory, it would be necessary to reconcile a defence of irresistible impulse derived from a combination of innate drives and external disinhibition with the rule that irresistible impulse of a solely internal origin (not necessarily any more the fault of the offender) does not in itself excuse although it may be a symptom of a disease of the mind: *Attorney-General for South Australia v Brown* [1960] A.C. 432. Equally, the state of mind which founds the defence superficially resembles a state of diminished responsibility, whereas the effect in law is quite different. It may well be that the resemblance is misleading, but these and similar problems must be solved before the bounds of a new defence can be set.

On the practical side there are serious problems. Before the jury could form an opinion on whether the drug might have turned the scale witnesses would have to give a picture of the defendant's personality and susceptibilities, for without it the crucial effect of the drug could not be assessed; pharmacologists would be required to describe the potentially disinhibiting effect of a range of drugs whose identity would, if the present case is anything to go by, be unknown; psychologists and psychiatrists would express opinions, not on the matters of psychopathology familiar to those working within the framework of the Mental Health Acts but on altogether more elusive concepts. No doubt as time passed those concerned could work out techniques to deal with these questions. Much more significant would be the opportunities for a spurious defence. Even in the field of road traffic the 'spiked' drink as a special reason for not disqualifying from driving is a regular feature. Transferring this to the entire range of criminal offences is a disturbing prospect. The defendant would only have to assert, and support by the evidence of well-wishers, that he was not the sort of person to have done this kind of thing, and to suggest an occasion when by some means a drug might have been administered to him for the jury to be sent straight to the question of a possible disinhibition. The judge would direct the jurors that if they felt any legitimate doubt on the matter—and by its nature the defence would be one which the prosecution would often have no means to rebut—they must acquit outright, all questions of intent, mental capacity and the like being at this stage irrelevant . . .

For these reasons I consider that both the ruling and the direction of the learned judge were correct. Accordingly I would answer the first certified question in the negative and would allow the appeal.

[Lords Keith of Kinkel, Goff of Chieveley, Browne-Wilkinson and Slynn of Hadley agreed with the speech of Lord Mustill.]

Appeal allowed

R. V HARDIE

[1985] 1 W.L.R. 64

When the relationship with the woman with whom he had been living broke down, the appellant became upset and took several Valium tablets belonging to the woman. He was unaware of the effect the tablets might have. Several hours later he started a fire in the bedroom of the flat while the woman and her daughter were in the sitting room. He was charged with damaging property with intent to endanger life or being reckless whether life would be endangered contrary to s.1(2) of the

Criminal Damage Act 1971. He argued in his defence that the effect of the Valium had been to prevent him having mens rea. The judge directed the jury that this could not provide a defence as he had voluntarily self-administered the drug. He appealed on grounds of misdirection.

PARKER LJ

. . . It is clear from *R. v Caldwell* [1982] A.C. 341 that self-induced intoxication can be a defence where the charge is only one of specific intention. It is equally clear that it cannot be a defence where, as here, the charge included recklessness. Hence, if there was self-intoxication in this case the judge's direction was correct. The problem is whether, assuming that the effect of the Valium was to deprive the appellant of any appreciation of what he was doing it should properly be regarded as self-induced intoxication and thus no answer . . .

R. v Majewski was a case of drunkenness resulting from alcoholic consumption by the accused whilst under the influence of non-medically prescribed drugs. *R. v Caldwell* was a case of plain drunkenness. There can be no doubt that the same rule applies both to self-intoxication by alcohol and intoxication by hallucinatory drugs, but this is because the effects of both are well-known and there is therefore an element of recklessness in the self-administration of the drug. *R. v Lipman* [1970] 1 Q.B. 152 is an example of such a case.

'Intoxication' or similar symptoms may, however, arise in other circumstances. In *R. v Bailey* [above, p.197] this court had to consider a case where a diabetic had failed to take sufficient food after taking a normal dose of insulin and struck the victim over the head with an iron bar. The judge directed the jury that the defence of automatism, i.e. that the mind did not go with the act, was not available because the incapacity was self-induced. It was held that this was wrong on two grounds (a) because on the basis of *R. v Majewski* it was clearly available to the offence embodying specific intent and (b) because although self-induced by the omission to take food it was also available to negative the other offence which was of basic intent only.

[Having referred to the judgment of Griffiths LJ, his Lordship continued:]

In the present instance the defence was that the Valium was taken for the purpose of calming the nerves only, that it was old stock and that the appellant was told it would do him no harm. There was no evidence that it was known to the appellant or even generally known that the taking of Valium in the quantity taken would be liable to render a person aggressive or incapable of appreciating risks to others or have other side effects such that its self-administration would itself have an element of recklessness. It is true that Valium is a drug and it is true that it was taken deliberately and not taken on medical prescription, but the drug is, in our view, wholly different in kind from drugs which are liable to cause unpredictability or aggressiveness. It may well be that the taking of a sedative or soporific drug will, in certain circumstances, be no answer, for example in a case of reckless driving, but if the effect of a drug is merely soporific or sedative the taking of it, even in some excessive quantity, cannot in the ordinary way raise a *conclusive* presumption against the admission of proof of intoxication for the purpose of disproving mens rea in ordinary crimes, such as would be the case with alcoholic intoxication or incapacity or automatism resulting from the self-administration of dangerous drugs.

In the present case the jury should not, in our judgment, have been directed to disregard any incapacity which resulted or might have resulted from the taking of Valium. They should have been directed that if they came to the conclusion that, as a result of the Valium, the appellant was, at the time, unable to appreciate the risks to property and persons from his actions they should then consider whether the taking of the Valium was itself reckless. We are unable to say what would have been the appropriate direction with regard to the elements of recklessness in this case for we have not seen all the relevant evidence, nor are we able to suggest a model direction, for circumstances will vary infinitely and model directions can sometimes lead to more rather than less confusion. It is sufficient to say that the direction that the effects of Valium were necessarily irrelevant was wrong.

Appeal allowed

Questions

1. To which drugs does the *Majewski* rule apply and which fall under the *Hardie* exception?

2. If, instead of taking the drug himself, Hardie's drink had been drugged with a proscribed drug leading to the same outcome, what would have been the judge's instruction to the jury?

----

iii. Becoming Intoxicated "With Intent"—the "Dutch Courage" Problem

If D drinks to give himself "Dutch courage" to commit an offence, may he rely on his intoxication in defence to support a plea that when he committed the offence he was so drunk that he either did not form or was incapable of forming the necessary intent? See the next case.

ATTORNEY GENERAL FOR NORTHERN IRELAND V GALLAGHER

[1963] A.C. 349 HL

The respondent was convicted of the murder of his wife. The defence was that of insanity under the M'Naghten Rules or, in the alternative, that at the time of the commission of the crime the respondent was by reason of drink incapable of forming the intent required in murder and was therefore guilty only of manslaughter. The respondent had indicated an intention to kill his wife before taking the alcohol. The Court of Criminal Appeal in Northern Ireland allowed an appeal on the ground that the judge in his summing-up directed the jury to apply the tests laid down in the M'Naghten Rules to the time when alcohol was taken and not to the time when the actual murder was committed.

LORD DENNING

My Lords, this case differs from all others in the books in that the accused man, whilst sane and sober, before he took to the drink, had already made up his mind to kill his wife. This seems to me to be far worse—and far more deserving of condemnation—than the case of a man who, before getting drunk has no intention to kill, but afterwards in his cups, whilst drunk, kills another by an act which he would not dream of doing when sober. Yet by the law of England in this latter case his drunkenness is no defence even though it has distorted his reason and his will-power. So why should it be a defence in the present case? And is it made any better by saying that the man is a psychopath?

The answer to the question is, I think, that the case falls to be decided by the general principle of English law that, subject to very limited exceptions, drunkenness is no defence to a criminal charge, nor is a defect of reason produced by drunkenness. This principle was stated by Sir Matthew Hale in his *Pleas of the Crown*, I, p.32, in words which I would repeat here. 'This vice' (drunkenness) 'doth deprive men of the use of reason, and puts many men into a perfect, but temporary, phrenzy . . . By the laws of England such a person shall have no privilege by this voluntary contracted madness, but shall have the same judgment as if he were in his right senses.' . . .

The general principle which I have enunciated is subject to two exceptions:

1. If a man is charged with an offence in which a specific intention is essential (as in murder, though not in manslaughter), then evidence of drunkenness, which renders him incapable of forming that intention, is an answer: see *Beard*'s case. This degree of drunkenness is reached when the man is rendered so stupid by drink that he does not know what he is doing (see *R. v Moore* (1852) 3 C. & K. 153), as where, at a christening, a drunken nurse put the baby behind a large fire, taking it for a log of wood (*Gentleman's Magazine*, 1748, p.570); and where a drunken man thought his friend (lying in his bed) was a theatrical dummy placed there and stabbed him to death (*The Times*, January 13, 1951). In each of those cases it would not be murder. But it would be manslaughter.

2. If a man by drinking brings on a distinct disease of the mind such as delirium tremens, so that he is temporarily insane within the M'Naghten Rules, that is to say, he does not at the time know what he is doing or that it is wrong, then he has a defence on the ground of insanity: see *R. v Davis* (1881) 14 Cox 563 and *Beard*'s case.

Does the present case come within the general principle or the exceptions to it? It certainly does not come within the first exception. This man was not incapable of forming an intent to kill. Quite the contrary. He knew full well what he was doing. He formed an intent to kill, he carried out his intention and he remembered afterwards what he had done. And the jury, properly directed on the point, have found as much, for they found him guilty of murder. Then does the case come within the second exception? It does not, to my mind, for the simple reason that he was not suffering from a disease of the mind brought on by drink. He was suffering from a different disease altogether. As the Lord Chief Justice observed in his summing-up: 'If this man was suffering from a disease of the mind, it wasn't of a kind that is produced by drink.' . . .

My Lords, I think the law on this point should take a clear stand. If a man, whilst sane and sober, forms an intention to kill and makes preparation for it, knowing it is a wrong thing to do, and then gets himself drunk so as to give himself Dutch courage to do the killing, and whilst drunk carries out his intention, he cannot rely on this self-induced drunkenness as a defence to a charge of murder, nor even as reducing it to manslaughter. He cannot say that he got himself into such a stupid state that he was incapable of an intent to kill. So also when he is a psychopath, he cannot by drinking rely on his self-induced defect of reason as a defence of insanity. The wickedness of his mind before he got drunk is enough to condemn him, coupled with the act which he intended to do and did do. A psychopath who goes out intending to kill knowing it is wrong, and does kill, cannot escape the consequences by making himself drunk before doing it. That is, I believe, the direction which the Lord Chief Justice gave to the jury and which the Court of Criminal Appeal found to be wrong. I think it was right and for this reason I would allow the appeal.

I would agree, of course, that if before the killing he had discarded his intention to kill or reversed it—and then got drunk—it would be a different matter. But when he forms the intention to kill and without interruption proceeds to get drunk and carry out his intention, then his drunkenness is no defence and nonetheless so because it is dressed up as a defence of insanity. There was no evidence in this case of any interruption and there was no need for the Lord Chief Justice to mention it to the jury.

I need hardly say, of course, that I have here only considered the law of Northern Ireland. In England a psychopath such as this man might now be in a position to raise a defence of diminished responsibility under s.2 of the Homicide Act 1957 . . .

Appeal allowed

iv. Intoxication and Defences

JAGGARD V DICKINSON

[1980] 3 All E.R. 716 QBD

The appellant went to a house late one night. She was drunk. She thought it was a house belonging to a friend. She believed, correctly, that her friend would not object to her breaking in. It was the wrong house. She appealed against a conviction under s.1(1) of the Criminal Damage Act 1971, on the ground that, despite her intoxication, she was entitled to rely on the defence of lawful excuse under s.5(2) and (3) of the Act (below).

MUSTILL J

. . . It is convenient to refer to the exculpatory provisions of s.5(2) as if they created a defence while recognising that the burden of disproving the facts referred to by the subsection remains on the prosecution. The magistrates held that the appellant was not entitled to rely on s.5(2) since the belief relied on was brought about by a state of self-induced intoxication.

In support of the conviction counsel for the respondent advanced an argument which may be summarised as follows (i) Where an offence is one of 'basic intent', in contrast to one of 'specific intent', the fact that the accused was in a state of self-induced intoxication at the time when he did the acts constituting the actus reus does not prevent him from possessing the mens rea necessary to constitute the offence: see *D.P.P. v Morgan* [above, p.123], *D.P.P. v Majewski* [above, p.203]. (ii) Section 1(1) of the 1971 Act creates an offence of basic intent: see *R. v Stephenson* [1979] Q.B. 695. (iii) Section 5(3) has no bearing on the present issue. It does not create a separate defence, but is no more than a partial definition of the expression 'without lawful excuse' in s.1(i)). The absence of lawful excuse forms an element in the mens rea: see *R. v Smith* [below]. Accordingly, since drunkenness does not negative mens rea in crimes of basic intent, it cannot be relied on as part of a defence based on s.5(2).

Whilst this is an attractive submission, we consider it to be unsound, for the following reasons. In the first place, the argument transfers the distinction between offences of specific and of basic intent to a context in which it has no place. The distinction is material where the defendant relies on his own drunkenness as a ground for denying that he had the degree of intention or recklessness required in order to constitute the offence. Here, by contrast, the appellant does not rely on her drunkenness to displace an inference of intent or recklessness; indeed she does not rely on it at all. Her defence is founded on the state of belief called for by s.5(2). True, the fact of the appellant's intoxication was relevant to the defence under s.5(2) for it helped to explain what would otherwise have been inexplicable, and hence lent colour to her evidence about the state of her belief. This is not the same as using drunkenness to rebut an inference of intention or recklessness. Belief, like intention or recklessness, is a state of mind; but they are not the same states of mind.

. . . Parliament has specifically required the court to consider the defendant's actual state of belief, not the state of belief which ought to have existed. This seems to us to show that the court is required by s.5(3) to focus on the existence of the belief, not its intellectual soundness; and a belief can be just as much honestly held if it is induced by intoxication as if it stems from stupidity, forgetfulness or inattention.

It was, however, urged that we could not properly read s.5(2) in isolation from s.1(l), which forms the context of the words 'without lawful excuse' partially defined by s.5(2). Once the words are put in context, so it is maintained, it can be seen that the law must treat drunkenness in the same way in relation to lawful excuse (and hence belief) as it does to intention and recklessness, for they are all part of the mens rea of the offence. To fragment the mens rea, so as to treat one part of it as affected by drunkenness in one way and the remainder as affected in a different way, would make the law impossibly complicated to enforce.

In these circumstances, I would hold that the magistrates were in error when they decided that the defence furnished to the appellant by s.5(2) was lost because she was drunk at the time. I would therefore allow the appeal.

Appeal allowed
Conviction quashed

Question

Is there any reason in principle or policy why a drunken defendant who believes that property belonging to P is his own and damages it, should be convicted whereas a drunken D who destroys P's property believing it belongs to Q and that Q would consent, will be acquitted because his drunken belief is covered by s.5(2)?

Note

In *Young* [1984] 1 W.L.R. 654, the appellant was charged with possessing a controlled drug with intent to supply. His defence, based on s.28(3) of the Misuse of Drugs Act 1971, was that because of intoxication he "neither believed nor suspected nor had reason to suspect that the substance . . . in question was a controlled drug." The Courts-Martial Appeal Court accepted that where there is an exculpatory statutory defence of honest belief, self-induced intoxication is a factor which must be considered in the context of a subjective consideration of the individual state of mind. However, with regard to the phrase *"nor had reason to suspect"* in s.28(3) the court held that this was not a matter which was entirely personal and individual calling for subjective consideration; rather it involved the concept of objective rationality to which self-induced intoxication is irrelevant.

R. V O'GRADY

(1987) Q.B. 995

A was convicted of manslaughter having been charged with murder. A and V, a friend, had been drinking heavily and spent the night at A's flat. During the night they fought. A claimed that he had been attacked by V while asleep and that he had fought to subdue him, stating to the police, "If I had not hit him I would be dead myself." The judge directed the jury that if, due to his intoxication, A mistakenly thought he was under attack, he would be entitled to defend himself but he was not entitled to go beyond what was reasonable because of his mind being affected by drink. A appealed on the grounds that: (1) the judge was wrong to limit the reference to mistake as to the existence of an attack; he should have included the possibility of mistake as to the severity of an attack; and (2) the judge in effect divorced the reasonableness of A's reaction from his state of mind at the time.

LORD LANE CJ

. . . As to the first two grounds, these require an examination of the law as to intoxication in relation to mistake . . . As McCullough J., when granting leave, pointed out helpfully in his observations for the benefit of the court:

'Given that a man who *mistakenly* believes he is under attack is entitled to use reasonable force to defend himself, it would seem to follow that, if he is under attack and mistakenly believes the attack to be more serious than it is, he is entitled to use reasonable force to defend himself against an attack of the severity he believed it to have. If one allows a mistaken belief induced by drink to bring this principle into operation, an act of gross negligence (viewed objectively) may become lawful even though it results in the death of the innocent victim. The drunken man would be guilty of neither murder nor manslaughter.'

How should the jury be invited to approach the problem? One starts with the decision of this court in *R. v Williams (Gladstone)* (1983) 78 Cr.App.R. 276 [above, p.127], namely, that where the defendant might have been labouring under a mistake as to the facts he must be judged according to that mistaken view, whether the mistake was reasonable or not. It is then for the jury to decide whether the defendant's reaction to the threat, real or imaginary, was a reasonable one. The court was not in that case considering what the situation might be where the mistake was due to voluntary intoxication by alcohol or some other drug.

We have come to the conclusion that where the jury are satisfied that the defendant was mistaken in his belief that any force or the force which he in fact used was necessary to defend himself and are further satisfied that the mistake was caused by voluntarily induced intoxication, the defence must fail. We do not consider that any distinction should be drawn on this aspect of the matter between offences involving what is called specific intent, such as murder, and offences of so called basic intent, such as manslaughter. Quite apart from the problem of directing a jury in a case such as the present where manslaughter is an alternative verdict to murder, the question of mistake can and ought to be considered separately from the question of intent. A sober man who mistakenly believes he is in danger of immediate death at the hands of an attacker is entitled to be acquitted of both murder and manslaughter if his reaction in killing his supposed assailant was a reasonable one. What his intent may have been seems to us to be irrelevant to the problem of self-defence or no. Secondly, we respectfully adopt the reasoning of McCullough J. already set out.

This brings us to the question of public order. There are two competing interests. On the one hand the interest of the defendant who has only acted according to what he believed to be necessary to protect himself, and on the other hand that of the public in general and the victim in particular who, probably through no fault of his own, has been injured or perhaps killed because of the defendant's drunken mistake. Reason recoils from the conclusion that in such circumstances a defendant is entitled to leave the Court without a stain on his character . . .

Finally we draw attention to the decision of this court in *R. v Lipman* [1970] 1 Q.B. 152 itself. The defence in that case was put on the grounds that the defendant, because of the hallucinatory drug which he had taken, had not formed the necessary intent to found a conviction for murder, thus resulting in his conviction for manslaughter. If the appellant's contentions here are correct, Lipman could successfully have escaped conviction altogether by raising the issue that he believed he was defending himself legitimately from an attack by serpents. It is significant that no one seems to have considered that possibility . . .

We have therefore come to the conclusion that a defendant is not entitled to rely, so far as self-defence is concerned, upon a mistake of fact which has been induced by voluntary intoxication . . .

Appeal dismissed

Questions

1. Under the rule in *Majewski*, D can only use evidence of voluntary intoxication to establish lack of mens rea if the offence is one of "specific intent", but D may be convicted of an offence of basic intent. This promotes the policy of protecting the public from those who, by becoming intoxicated, render themselves a danger to society. As *O'Grady* had been convicted of the basic intent offence of manslaughter, was there any need for the court to abandon the *Majewski* rule in relation to a defence of self-defence? Would the court have promoted the policy of protecting the public against the intoxicated offender by applying the Majewski rule and upholding *O'Grady*'s conviction?

2. In *Gladstone Williams* (above, p.127), in respect of assault, Lord Lane CJ stated that:

    "the mental element necessary to constitute guilt is the intent to apply unlawful force to the victim. We do not believe that the mental element can be substantiated by simply showing an intent to apply force and no more."

    In *Beckford v R*. [1987] 3 W.L.R. 611 Lord Griffiths stated that "it is an essential element of all crimes of violence that the violence or threat of violence should be unlawful". If this reasoning is followed, is it not the case that a drunken defendant who pleads self-defence is saying that, by reason of his mistake, he did not intend to use unlawful violence but rather he believed he was justified in using force in self-defence? If so, should not *Majewski* be applied thereby providing for acquittal where the offence is one of specific intent but, if it is one of basic intent, recklessness in becoming intoxicated might be substituted for recklessness in respect of using unlawful violence?

3. In *Gladstone Williams* the Court of Appeal, under Lord Lane CJ, adopted the recommendations of the Criminal Law Revision Committee on *Offences Against the Person* in its 14th Report (TSO, 1980), Cmnd.7844, declaring that they represented the existing law. Is it not surprising that in the present case, where the law was unclear, the Court of Appeal, again under Lord Lane CJ, ignored the C.L.R.C.'s further recommendations (*Offences Against the Person*, Cmnd.7844 para.277) which stated that the defence of self-defence should be available for offences of specific intent where the mistake was wholly or partly induced by drink or drugs, but not for offences of basic intent?

4. If the situation in *O'Grady* arises now will the defendant be convicted of murder or manslaughter?

Note

In *O'Connor* [1991] Crim. L.R. 135, the Court of Appeal treated the obiter decision in *O'Grady* as binding on them. D, who was drunk, was arguing with V in a public house. In the course of the argument D head-butted V about three times as a result of which V died. D was convicted of murder having argued in his defence that he believed he was acting in self-defence. The Court of Appeal held that the trial judge was correct to conclude that intoxication was irrelevant on the question whether D believed he was acting in self-defence. The conviction for murder was quashed, however, as the trial judge had not directed the jury to take account of D's intoxication when considering whether he had formed the specific intent to cause grievous bodily harm. The decision in *O'Connor* highlights the illogicality of the decision in *O'Grady*; the jury must ignore D's intoxication when considering whether he believed he was acting in self-defence but they must take it into account in deciding whether he intended to kill or cause grievous bodily harm. It will be surprising if juries are not left confused by such a direction.

In *R. v Hatton* [2005] EWCA Crim 2951, the Court of Appeal confirmed that where a defendant sought to establish the defence of self defence, it was not open to him to rely on a mistake induced by voluntary intoxication irrespective of whether the charge was murder or manslaughter.

Question

D and E are drunk and as a prank they seize V, their friend, and hold him over a balcony believing that he is consenting to their dangerous horseplay. V falls and sustains several broken bones. D and E are charged with unlawfully and maliciously inflicting grievous bodily harm (GBH) contrary to s.20 of the Offences Against the Person Act 1861. Will D and E be able to rely in their defence on their drunken belief that V consented to their prank?

Notes

1. You may be surprised to learn that in *Richardson and Irwin* [1999] 1 Cr. App. R. 392, the Court of Appeal held on the facts in the question above that D's and E's convictions should be quashed as the trial judge should have directed the jury that when considering the question of consent they should have taken account of evidence that the defendants' minds were affected by alcohol. Section 20 is an offence of basic intent and one would have expected the Court to rule that intoxication is irrelevant on such a charge. This decision, however, gives rise to the strange anomaly that D's intoxication relieves the prosecution of the need to prove foresight of some harm but does not relieve them of the need to prove absence of a belief in consent. This decision is consistent with the questionable authority of *Aitken* (1992) 95 Cr. App. R. 304 but the Court of Appeal did not consider the cases of *O'Grady* (1987) Q.B. 995 (above, p.225) nor did it refer to the cases on rape where the Court of Appeal had disallowed reliance on intoxicated beliefs in consent (see *Woods* (1982) 74 Cr. App. R. 312; *Fotheringham* (1988) 88 Cr. App. R. 206). The authority of *Richardson and Irwin*, accordingly must be open to doubt. It is certainly difficult to find any policy reason to support the decision particularly when one considers that had D and E not been drunk they would not have made the mistake regarding V's consent and most probably would not have engaged in such potentially dangerous horseplay.

2. Where D seeks to plead either loss of control or diminished responsibility in defence to a charge of murder, his voluntary intoxication at the time of the killing has no relevance to either defence (see *Asmelash* [2013] EWCA Crim 157 in respect of loss of control, below, p.452; and *Dowds* [2012] EWCA Crim 281 in respect of diminished responsibility, below, p.477).

----

v. Proposals for Reform

LAW COMMISSION, *INTOXICATION AND CRIMINAL LIABILITY* (TSO, 2009), LAW COM. NO.314, CM.7526

VOLUNTARY INTOXICATION

Recommendation 1: the Majewski rule

5.1 There should be a general rule that:

(1) if D is charged with having committed an offence as a perpetrator;

(2) the fault element of the offence is not an integral fault element (for example, because it merely requires proof of recklessness); and

(3) D was voluntarily intoxicated at the material time;

then, in determining whether or not D is liable for the offence, D should be treated as having been aware at the material time of anything which D would then have been aware of but for the intoxication.
[para.3.35]

Recommendation 2: the rule for integral fault elements

5.2 If the subjective fault element in the definition of the offence, as alleged, is one to which the justification for the *Majewski* rule cannot apply, then the prosecution should have to prove that D acted with that relevant state of mind.
[para.3.42]

Recommendation 3: the integral fault elements

5.3 The following subjective fault elements should be excluded from the application of the general rule and should, therefore, always be proved:

(1) intention as to a consequence;

(2) knowledge as to something;

(3) belief as to something (where the belief is equivalent to knowledge as to something);

(4) fraud; and

(5) dishonesty.

[para.3.46]

Recommendation 4 (defences and mistaken beliefs)

5.4 D should not be able to rely on a genuine mistake of fact arising from self-induced intoxication in support of a defence to which D's state of mind is relevant, regardless of the nature of the fault alleged. D's mistaken belief should be taken into account only if D would have held the same belief if D had not been intoxicated.
[para.3.53]

Recommendation 5 ('honest belief' provisions)

5.5 The rule governing mistakes of fact relied on in support of a defence (recommendation 4) should apply equally to 'honest belief' provisions which state how defences should be interpreted.
[para.3.80]

Recommendation 6 (negligence and no-fault offences)

5.6 If the offence charged requires proof of a fault element of failure to comply with an objective standard of care, or requires no fault at all, D should be permitted to rely on a genuine but mistaken belief as to the existence

of a fact, where D's state of mind is relevant to a defence, only if D would have made that mistake if he or she had not been voluntarily intoxicated.
[para.3.84]

Recommendation 7 (secondary liability generally)
    5.7 For the doctrine of secondary liability generally (where no joint enterprise is alleged):

(1) if the offence is one which always requires proof of an integral fault element, then the state of mind required for D to be secondarily liable for that offence should equally be regarded as an integral fault element;

(2) if the offence does not always require proof of an integral fault element, then the (*Majewski*) rule on voluntary intoxication should apply in determining D's secondary liability for the offence.

[para.3.92]

Recommendation 8 (secondary liability – joint enterprises)
    5.8 Our proposed rule on the relevance of voluntary intoxication to secondary liability generally should apply equally to cases of alleged joint enterprise.
[para.3.99]

Recommendation 9 (inchoate liability)
    5.9 If D is charged under Part 2 of the Serious Crime Act 2007 with an offence of encouraging or assisting another person to commit a crime ('the crime'), then if the crime is one which would always require proof of an integral fault element for a perpetrator to be liable, and the allegation against D requires the prosecution to prove that D was 'reckless' for the purposes of section 47(5) of the Act, the state of mind of being 'reckless' should be treated as an integral fault element.
[para.3.104]

INVOLUNTARY INTOXICATION

Recommendation 10 (the general rule)
    5.10 D's state of involuntary intoxication should be taken into consideration:

(1) in determining whether D acted with the subjective fault required for liability, regardless of the nature of the fault element; and

(2) in any case where D relies on a mistake of fact in support of a defence to which his or her state of mind is relevant.

[para.3.121]

Recommendation 11 (species of involuntary intoxication)
    5.11 There should be a non-exhaustive list of situations which would count as involuntary intoxication:

(1) the situation where an intoxicant was administered to D without D's consent;

(2) the situation where D took an intoxicant under duress;

(3) the situation where D took an intoxicant which he or she reasonably believed was not an intoxicant;

(4) the situation where D took an intoxicant for a proper medical purpose.

    5.12 D's state of intoxication should also be regarded as involuntary if, though not entirely involuntary, it was *almost* entirely involuntary.
    [paras 3.125–3.126]

Questions

1.   How do these proposals affect the current law on intoxication?
2.   Do these proposals improve the present law?

5   DEFENCES

1. DEFENCES IN GENERAL

After the prosecution have adduced their evidence in an effort to prove that the accused committed the actus reus of the offence together with the relevant mens rea, the accused may still be able to avoid conviction by relying on a defence. He may, for example, in response to a charge of intentionally assaulting the victim, claim that he acted under duress or, perhaps, that he acted in self-defence.

There is some disagreement amongst lawyers as to what should or should not be properly classified as a defence. If, for example, the accused claims to have been acting under an honest mistake this may, in reality, amount to no more than an assertion by the accused that the actus reus or mens rea of the office has not been established. So where the accused mistakenly (but nonetheless honestly) believes that the property he took was his own, he has not committed an act of theft because he has not acted *dishonestly* in respect of property that *belongs to another*. A mens rea element of the offences (*dishonesty*) in relation to part of the actus reus (that the *property belongs to another*) is negated (see s.1 of the Theft Act 1968). In this sense, mistake is not properly classified as a general defence even though it is common for such explanations to be referred to as defences.

On other occasions, the accused may concede that he has committed the actus reus of the offence together with the necessary mens rea but seeks to be excused from conviction and punishment because of the particular circumstances. An example would be the general defence of duress. This section examines and considers those defences which have been properly and most frequently classified as general defences.

A.T.H. SMITH, "ON ACTUS REUS AND MENS REA" IN P. GLAZEBROOK (ED), *RESHAPING THE CRIMINAL LAW* (STEVENS & SONS, 1978), PP.97–101

When speaking colloquially lawyers are inclined to call any reason advanced by a defendant in support of an acquittal a 'defence'. These include such explanations as alibi, infancy, mistake, accident, and insanity. When they use the term more precisely, they point out that automatism—for example—is not really a defence at all, but a denial that the prosecution has proved part of its case: the prosecution has failed to show that the defendant acted with *mens rea*. It has now been accepted by no less a body than the House of Lords that, where the definition of any particular crime includes intention or recklessness, any mistake that has the effect of preventing the formation of these states of mind must exculpate, whether it be a reasonable mistake or not. This is so because mistake prevents the formation of the particular *mens rea* which must be established as part of the prosecution case. Duress, necessity, self-defence, and infancy, on the other hand, are said to be properly described as 'defences', because they do not negative either traditional *mens rea* or *actus reus*, but operate in some way independently . . .

It is possible to make a distinction between defences which are justificatory in character, and those which are excuses. It has not found much favour in Anglo-American jurisprudence, partly no doubt because of Stephen's emphatic assertion that it 'involves no legal consequences,' a reproach guaranteed to deprive it of any significance it might otherwise have enjoyed. Briefly stated, the distinction is that we excuse the actor because he is not sufficiently culpable or at fault, whereas we justify an act because we regard it as the most appropriate course of action in the circumstances, even though it may result in harm that would, in the absence of the justification, amount to a crime. It does not follow that, because the distinction between the two is not formally taken in our law that it is altogether without significance, particularly where the law is in a state of flux. The reasons why, and the circumstances in which, we are prepared to excuse may be altogether different from the corresponding reasons for justification. We admit excuses as 'an expression of compassion for one of our kind caught in a maelstrom of circumstances'. A plea of justification, by contrast, is founded upon the law's preference, in social and policy terms, for one course of action rather than another.

Where a defendant successfully pleads a defence such as prevention of crime or self-defence, he argues that what he did was not unlawful, and he is able to point to a specific rule—in the one case of statutory origin, and in the other, in common law—to substantiate his plea. It may be, however, that a plea of justification has not crystallised into one of these specific defences, but is of a more nebulous sort.

For example, although it appears that there is no general defence of necessity in that there is no rule to which a defendant can appeal to justify his having chosen to bring about a proscribed harm, there is nevertheless a principle infiltrating the legal system, given efficacy through a variety of legal inlets, that where a person is placed by force of circumstance in the position of having to choose between two evils, his act is justified if he chooses the lesser one. In that somewhat fitful sense, necessity operates as a 'defence'. Some would say that a person who commits a prima facie unlawful act as a result of necessity is not blameworthy or at fault and hence lacks *mens rea*. But it does not necessarily follow that we exculpate him for that reason. An alternative explanation is that where the act done is the lesser of two evils, it is justified or lawful—that there was no *actus reus* notwithstanding that the conduct falls literally within the terms of the definition of the offence.

Analysis of crime in terms of *actus reus* and *mens rea*, and the mechanical application of statutes, tend to obscure the principles of harm and illegality on which criminal liability is based. Unless these principles find expression either in the definition of the crime itself (e.g. by the inclusion of 'unlawfully') or in some express exculpatory rule, it seems that our legal system is incapable of giving effect to them. Whereas the judges are adept at interpreting legislation in such a way as to introduce traditional *mens rea*, if necessary by reading words into the statutes, they will only infrequently allow considerations of principle to override the plain words of a statute. Only by providing in a code for a defence of necessity, therefore, is it possible to ensure that this principle is preserved in a form in which it will invariably prevail.

See also G. Williams, "The Theory of Excuses" [1982] Crim. L.R. 732.

2. DURESS

WASIK, "DURESS AND CRIMINAL RESPONSIBILITY" [1977] CRIM. L.R. 453

There seems to be general agreement among lawyers that criminal responsibility should follow when an individual chooses to perform an act proscribed by the criminal law, when he has both the capacity and a fair opportunity or chance to adjust his behaviour to conform with the law. It follows that no individual should be held responsible if he had no opportunity to choose an alternative to breaking the law. As the philosophers put it: there should be no ascription of responsibility to the accused unless 'he could have acted otherwise'. Much attention has been paid to this requirement by philosophers but lawyers, by contrast, have not shown a great deal of interest. Perhaps the main reason for this is the practical rarity of such problems. It is much more common for an accused to plead mistake or lack of intention as an excuse than to plead that he had no choice but to act as he did. Cases in which the defence of duress is raised are probably the most frequent of this small group . . .

A comparison has sometimes been made between the defence of duress and that of automatism. The suggestion is that in duress, the accused claims that there was no act by *him*; in automatism the accused claims that there was no *act* by him. Both defences are then seen as containing what may in loose terminology be called 'an involuntary act' on the part of the accused. But this is misleading, as the element of voluntariness is quite different in the two excuses. Where the defence of automatism succeeds, the accused has had no opportunity at all to exercise choice with regard to the performing of the act, and thus he cannot be held responsible for it . . . By contrast, in duress, there is an issue of choice. If a man is threatened with physical injury unless he assists in a criminal enterprise, he has the choice (albeit a difficult one) of assisting in the crime or facing the consequences. The question here is whether the accused had a fair opportunity to make the choice.

i. An imminent threat of death or serious injury

R. V HUDSON AND TAYLOR

[1971] 2 Q.B. 202

H and T who were aged 17 and 19 respectively, were charged with perjury in a case in which they were witnesses to an unlawful wounding incident. They admitted that they had given false evidence but raised the defence of duress. This took the form of threats before the trial that unless they did so they would be "cut up". The recorder directed the jury that the defence was not available since the threat was not immediate. On appeal the Crown contended that the plea should have failed on the additional ground that they should have sought police protection before the trial.

LORD WIDGERY CJ

. . . it is clearly established that duress provides a defence in all offences including perjury (except possibly treason or murder as a principal) if the will of the accused has been overborne by threats of death or serious personal injury so that the commission of the alleged offence was no longer the voluntary act of the accused. This appeal raises two main questions: first, as to the nature of the necessary threat and, in particular, whether it must be 'present and immediate'; secondly, as to the extent to which a right to plead duress may be lost if the accused has failed to take steps to remove the threat as, for example, by seeking police protection.

It is essential to the defence of duress that the threat shall be effective at the moment when the crime is committed. The threat must be a 'present' threat in the sense that it is effective to neutralise the will of the accused at that time. Hence an accused who joins a rebellion under the compulsion of threats cannot plead duress if he remains with the rebels after the threats have lost their effect and his own will has had a chance to re-assert itself (*McCrowther's Case* (1746) Fost. 13; and *A.-G. v Whelan* [1934] I.R. 518). Similarly a threat of future violence may be so remote as to be insufficient to overpower the will at the moment when the offence was committed, or the accused may have elected to commit the offence in order to rid himself of a threat hanging over him and not because he was driven to act by immediate and unavoidable pressure. In none of these cases is the defence of duress available because a person cannot justify the commission of a crime merely to secure his own peace of mind.

When, however, there is no opportunity for delaying tactics, and the person threatened must make up his mind whether he is to commit the criminal act or not, the existence at that moment of threats sufficient to destroy his will ought to provide him with a defence even though the threatened injury may not follow instantly, but after an interval. This principle is illustrated by *Subramaniam v Public Prosecutor* [1956] 1 W.L.R. 965, when the appellant was charged in Malaya with unlawful possession of ammunition and was held by the Privy Council to have a defence of duress, fit to go to the jury, on his plea that he had been compelled by terrorists to accept the ammunition and feared for his safety if the terrorists returned.

In the present case the threats of Farrell were likely to be no less compelling, because their execution could not be effected in the court room, if they could be carried out in the streets of Salford the same night. Insofar, therefore, as the recorder ruled as a matter of law that the threats were not sufficiently present and immediate to support the defence of duress we think that he was in error. He should have left the jury to decide whether the threats had overborne the will of the appellants at the time when they gave the false evidence.

Counsel for the Crown, however, contends that the recorder's ruling can be supported on another ground, namely, that the appellants should have taken steps to neutralise the threats by seeking police protection either when they came to court to give evidence, or beforehand. He submits on grounds of public policy that the accused should not be able to plead duress if he had the opportunity to ask for protection from the police before committing the offence and failed to do so. The argument does not distinguish cases in which the police would be able to provide effective protection, from those when they would not, and it would, in effect, restrict the defence of duress to cases where the person threatened had been kept in custody by the maker of the threats, or where the time interval between the making of the threats and the commission of the offence had made recourse to the police impossible. We recognise the need to keep the defence of duress within reasonable bounds but cannot accept so severe a restriction on it. The duty, of the person threatened, to take steps to remove the threat does not seem to have arisen in an English case but in full review of the defence of duress in the Supreme Court of Victoria (*R. v Hurley, R. v Murray* [1967] V.R. 526), a condition of raising the defence was said to be that the accused 'had no means, with safety to himself, of preventing the execution of the threat.'

In the opinion of this court it is always open to the Crown to prove that the accused failed to avail himself of some opportunity which was reasonably open to him to render the threat ineffective, and that on this being established the threat in question can no longer be relied on by the defence.

In our judgment the defence of duress should have been left to the jury in the present case, as should any issue raised by the Crown and arising out of the appellants' failure to seek police protection. The appeals will, therefore, be allowed and the convictions quashed.

Appeals allowed

Notes

1. In *Abdul-Hussain* [1999] Crim. L.R. 570, the Court of Appeal followed the approach adopted in *Hudson and Taylor*. The appellants were Shiite Muslims from Iraq who had fled to Sudan. They were over-stayers in Sudan and feared being arrested and returned to Iraq where they expected they would be tortured and executed. They hijacked an aeroplane at Khartoum Airport and forced the pilot to fly to London where they sought political asylum. They pleaded duress of circumstances (see below) to charges of hijacking an aeroplane. The trial judge ruled that this defence would not be left to the jury as death or injury would not have immediately followed had they not hijacked the aeroplane. The Court of Appeal quashed their convictions holding that the defence should have been left to the jury as the issue for them to consider was whether the threat of imminent death or injury was operating on the mind of the accused so as to overbear his will when he committed the crime and not whether the execution of the threat was immediately in prospect. Rose LJ stated:

    "[I]f Anne Frank had stolen a car to escape from Amsterdam and been charged with theft, the tenets of English law would not . . . have denied her a defence of duress of circumstances, on the ground that she should have waited the Gestapo's knock on the door."

2. In *Batchelor* [2013] EWCA Crim 2638 the Court of Appeal considered the issue of imminence and immediacy in the context of a series of crimes. D appealed against his conviction for cheating the public revenue by means of a series of VAT frauds over many months. D claimed that he committed the offences to raise funds to pay off a debt having been threatened and intimidated by John, the person to whom he was indebted. The trial judge refused to leave duress to the jury on the basis, inter alia, that D had ample opportunity over many months to go to the police. The Court of Appeal affirmed this decision stating (at para.15):

    "The appellant could have gone to the police at any time over a period of two and a half years. Moreover, he was not placed under such fear that he was being forced immediately to pay John . . .. That is not to say, as the judge pointed out in his sentencing remarks, that the appellant may not have been subject to some deeply unpleasant intimidation, but even if his account was true in all the particulars, the appellant could not reasonably believe that the execution of the threat was imminent and immediate. The law requires a certain degree of fortitude to be shown by victims in circumstances such as these."

3. In *R. v McDonald* [2003] EWCA Crim 1170, it was confirmed that it is not enough that there was, in fact, an opportunity for the accused to escape the threat; it is necessary to prove that the accused both appreciated the opportunity to escape and rejected it, it being one which a reasonable

person in a like situation would have taken. However, in *R. v Hasan* [2005] UKHL 22 (see further below) doubts were expressed over the decision in *R. v Hudson and Taylor*. Lord Bingham of Cornhill said (at [27] and [28]):

> "I can understand that the Court of Appeal . . . had sympathy with the predicament of the young appellants but I cannot, consistently with principle, accept that a witness testifying in the Crown Court at Manchester has no opportunity to avoid complying with a threat incapable of execution then or there . . ..
>
>   It should . . . be made clear to juries that if the retribution threatened against the defendant or his family or a person for whom he reasonably feels responsible is not such as he reasonably expects to follow immediately or almost immediately . . . there may be little if any room for doubt that he could have taken evasive action, whether by going to the police or in some other way, to avoid the crime . . ."

4. In *R. v Valderrama-Vega* [1985] Crim. L.R. 220 CA, the appellant was charged with the importation of prohibited drugs from Colombia. He pleaded duress on the basis that a Mafia-type organisation had threatened injury or death to himself and his family. In addition he said that he needed money as he was under severe financial pressure and he had also been threatened with disclosure of his homosexuality. The Court of Appeal held that it was wrong to direct the jury that duress was a defence only where the defendant acted "*solely* as the result of threats of death or serious injury to himself or his family". Rather these threats must be a sine qua non of the defendant's decision to commit the offence although he may have had other motives.

5. It is not enough that a defendant felt threatened or under pressure; the threat must be of death or serious physical injury. In *A* [2012] EWCA Crim 434, Lord Judge CJ stated:

> "64. . . . Duress cannot and should not be confused with pressure. The circumstances in which different individuals are subject to pressures, or perceive that they are under pressure, are virtually infinite. Such pressures may indeed provide powerful mitigation. . . Dealing with it very broadly duress involves pressure which arises in extreme circumstances, the threat of death or serious injury, which for the avoidance of any misunderstanding, we have no doubt would also include rape, and which cannot reasonably be evaded."

6. While not having to make a final determination on the matter, the Court of Appeal indicated in *Dao* [2012] EWCA Crim 1717 that a threat of false imprisonment would not be sufficient on its own to support a defence of duress.

7. Most of the cases have involved threats to kill or injure the accused. Will threats to kill or injure others be sufficient to found the defence of duress? In *R. v Ortiz* (1986) 83 Cr. App. R. 173, the Court of Appeal assumed that a threat to injure the accused's wife or family could do so. This is confirmed by *Martin* [1989] 1 All E.R. 652. In *Conway* [1989] Q.B. 290 a threat to the passenger in the accused's car was sufficient. In *R. v Hasan* [2005] UKHL 22, the House of Lords, obiter, approved the Judicial Studies Board specimen direction (also approved by the Court of Appeal in *R. v Wright* [2000] Crim. L.R. 510) which specified that the threat must be directed against the defendant, a member of his immediate family, or a person "for whose safety the defendant would reasonably regard himself as responsible".

Questions

1.   If X threatens to kill D's child unless D commits a crime and D has the opportunity to report this threat to the police, will the defence of duress be denied? (See *R. v Hasan* at n.2 above.)

2.   What is meant by the word "responsibility" in the Judicial Studies Board specimen direction approved by the House of Lords in *R. v Hasan*? (See n.4 above.)

----

ii. The test for duress

R. V GRAHAM

[1982] 1 W.L.R. 294

G, a practising homosexual, lived with his wife (W) and K, another homosexual. G took Valium for an anxiety state and this made him susceptible to bullying. K was a violent man. One night K attacked W with a knife but G intervened. The next day W left home; K and G remained drinking heavily and G took more Valium than was prescribed. K suggested killing W and at K's suggestion G telephoned her luring her back to the flat. When she arrived K put a flex round her neck and told G to take hold of the other end of the flex and pull on it. He did so, he claimed, only because he was afraid of K. He was convicted of murder, the Crown having conceded that duress could be raised as a defence. G appealed on the ground that the judge had misdirected the jury.

LORD LANE CJ

The prosecution at the trial conceded that, on those facts, it was open to the defence to raise the issue of duress. In other words, they were not prepared to take the point that the defence of duress is not available to a principal in the first degree to murder. Consequently, the interesting question raised by the decisions in *D.P.P. for Northern Ireland v Lynch* [1975] A.C. 653 and *Abbott v The Queen* [1977] A.C. 755 was not argued before us. We do not have to decide it. We pause only to observe that the jury would no doubt have been puzzled to learn that whether the appellant was to be convicted of murder or acquitted altogether might depend on whether the plug came off the end of the percolator flex when he began to pull it . . .

The direction which the judge gave to the jury required them to ask themselves two questions. First, a subjective question which the judge formulated:

'Was this man at the time of the killing taking part . . . because he feared for his own life (or) personal safety as a result of the words or the conduct . . . on the part of King, either personally experienced by him, or genuinely believed in by him . . .'

Neither side in the present appeal has taken issue with the judge on this question. We feel, however, that, for purposes of completeness, we should say that the direction appropriate in this particular case should have been in these words: 'Was this man at the time of the killing taking part because he held a well-grounded fear of death (or serious physical injury) as a result of the words or conduct on the part of King?' The bracketed words may be too favourable to the defendant. The point was not argued before us.

The judge then went on to direct the jury that if the answer to that first question was 'yes', or 'he may have been', the jury should then go on to consider a second question importing an objective test of reasonableness. This is the issue which arises in this appeal. Mr. Kennedy for the appellant contends that no second question arises at all; the test is purely subjective. He argues that if the appellant's will was in fact overborne by threats of the requisite cogency, he is entitled to be acquitted and no question arises as to whether a reasonable man, with or without his characteristics, would have acted similarly.

Mr Sherrard, for the Crown, on the other hand, submits that such dicta as can be found on the point are in favour of a second test; this time an objective test. He argues that public policy requires this and draws an analogy with provocation.

[Having considered dicta in *Lynch* (above), *Archbold Criminal Pleading & Practice*, edited by S.G. Mitchell, 40th edn (London: Sweet & Maxwell, 1979), J.C. Smith & B. Hogan, *Criminal Law*, 4th edn (London: Butterworths, 1978); and the Law Commission, *Report on Defences of General Application* (TSO, 1977), Law Com. No.83 para.2.28, his Lordship continued:]

As a matter of public policy, it seems to us essential to limit the defence of duress by means of an objective criterion formulated in terms of reasonableness. Consistency of approach in defences to criminal liability is obviously desirable. Provocation and duress are analogous. In provocation the words or actions of one person break the self-control of another. In duress the words or actions of one person break the will of another. The law requires a defendant to have the self-control reasonably to be expected of the ordinary citizen in his situation. It should likewise require him to have the steadfastness reasonably to be expected of the ordinary citizen in his situation. So too with self-defence, in which the law permits the use of no more force than is reasonable in the circumstances. And, in general, if a mistake is to excuse what would otherwise be criminal, the mistake must be a reasonable one.

It follows that we accept Mr Sherrard's submission that the direction in this case was too favourable to the appellant. The Crown having conceded that the issue of duress was open to the appellant and was raised on the evidence, the correct approach on the facts of this case would have been as follows. (1) Was the defendant, or may he have been, impelled to act as he did because, as a result of what he reasonably believed King had said or done, he had good cause to fear that if he did not so act King would kill him or (if this is to be added) cause him serious physical injury? (2) If so, have the prosecution made the jury sure that a sober person of reasonable firmness, sharing the characteristics of the defendant, would not have responded to whatever he reasonably believed King said or did by taking part in the killing? The fact that a defendant's will to resist has been eroded by the voluntary consumption of drink or drugs or both is not relevant to this test.

We doubt whether the Crown were right to concede that the question of duress ever arose on the facts of this case. The words and deeds of King relied on by the defence were far short of those needed to raise a threat of the requisite gravity. However, the Crown having made the concession, the judge was right to pose the second objective question to the jury. His only error lay in putting it too favourably to the appellant.

The appeal is dismissed.

Appeal dismissed

Question

Lord Lane stated that "consistency of approach in defences to criminal liability is obviously desirable". Has Lord Lane been consistent in his approach with regard to the issue of mistake in respect of the facts upon which a defence is based?

Notes

1. Lord Lane's formulation of the test for duress was approved by the House of Lords in *R. v Howe*, below.

2. For duress to be raised as a defence there must be a nexus between the threats made and the offence committed by the accused as a result of the threats. In *Cole* [1994] Crim. L.R. 582, the accused appealed against his conviction for robbery committed as a result of threats of violence made by moneylenders if he did not repay the money he had borrowed. The Court of Appeal upheld the conviction, holding that the defence of duress by threats can only apply where the offence charged is the very offence nominated by the person making the threats. In this case, the moneylenders had not stipulated that the accused commit robbery to meet their demands and the defence was therefore not available to him. In *Ali* [1995] Crim. L.R. 303 the Court of Appeal assumed that a threat "to get the money from a bank or building society" . . . or else, without

specifying a particular place, was sufficient to found a defence of duress by threats to a charge of robbery.

----

iii. Characteristics attributable to the person of reasonable firmness

There is some uncertainty as to which of the accused's characteristics may be relevant to the objective test. In *Graham*, above, Lord Lane CJ stated that the law requires a defendant "to have the steadfastness reasonably to be expected of the ordinary citizen in his situation". This would suggest that for duress, perhaps with the exception of age and sex in so far as they may be relevant to steadfastness, it is only those characteristics which render the threat more grave to the defendant than the ordinary citizen which should be taken into account. For example, a threat to break D's arm would be more grave to D than the ordinary citizen if D only has one arm. In the case which follows the Court of Appeal attempts to state the relevant principles having examined the earlier cases of *Emery* (1993) 14 Cr. App. R. (S) 394; *Hegarty* [1994] Crim. L.R. 353; *Horne* [1994] Crim. L.R. 584; and *Hurst* [1995] 1 Cr. App. R. 82.

R. V BOWEN

[1996] 2 Cr. App. R. 157 CA

D was convicted of obtaining services by deception, having obtained numerous goods on credit over a six-month period and then failed to make payments. He claimed he was acting under duress having been threatened by two men that if he did not obtain the goods for them he and his family would be petrol-bombed. He was told that if he went to the police his family would be attacked. The judge excluded from the jury's consideration evidence that D was abnormally suggestible and vulnerable. On appeal the question of D's low IQ was also raised.

STUART-SMITH LJ read the judgement of the Court

But the question remains, what are the relevant characteristics of the accused to which the jury should have regard in considering the second objective test? This question had given rise to considerable difficulty in recent cases. It seems clear that age and sex are, and physical health or disability may be, relevant characteristics. But beyond that it is not altogether easy to determine from the authorities what others may be relevant . . .

[His Lordship referred to *Emery*, *Hegarty*, *Home*, *Hurst*, *Graham*, *Camplin* and *Morhall*, below.]

Questions of duress and provocation are similar, in that the two-fold test applies in each case . . . In the case of duress, the question is: would an ordinary person sharing the characteristics of the defendant be able to resist the threats made to him?

What principles are to be derived from these authorities? We think they are as follows:

(1) The mere fact that the accused is more pliable, vulnerable; timid or susceptible to threats than a normal person are not characteristics with which it is legitimate to invest the reasonable/ordinary person for the purpose of considering the objective test.

(2) The defendant may be in a category of persons who the jury may think less able to resist pressure than people not within that category. Obvious examples are age, where a young person may well not be so robust as a mature one; possibly sex, though many women would doubtless consider they had as much moral courage to resist pressure as men; pregnancy, where there is added fear for the unborn child; serious physical disability, which may inhibit self-protection; recognised mental illness or psychiatric condition, such as post-traumatic stress disorder leading to learned helplessness.

(3) Characteristics which may be relevant in considering provocation, because they relate to the nature of the

provocation, itself will not necessarily be relevant in cases of duress. Thus homosexuality may be relevant to provocation if the provocative words or conduct are related to this characteristic; it cannot be relevant in duress, since there is no reason to think that homosexuals are less robust in resisting threats of the kind that are relevant in duress cases.

(4) Characteristics due to self-induced abuse, such as alcohol, drugs or glue-sniffing, cannot be relevant.

(5) Psychiatric evidence may be admissible to show that the accused is suffering from some mental illness, mental impairment or recognised psychiatric condition provided persons generally suffering from such condition may be more susceptible to pressure and threats and thus to assist the jury in deciding whether a reasonable person suffering from such a condition might have been impelled to act as the defendant did. It is not admissible simply to show that in the doctor's opinion an accused, who is not suffering from such illness or condition, is especially timid, suggestible or vulnerable to pressure and threats. Nor is medical opinion admissible to bolster or support the credibility of the accused.

(6) Where counsel wishes to submit that the accused has some characteristic which falls within (2) above, this must be made plain to the judge. The question may arise in relation to the admissibility of medical evidence of the nature set out in (5). If so, the judge will have to rule at that stage. There may, however, be no medical evidence, or, as in this case, medical evidence may have been introduced for some other purpose, e.g. to challenge the admissibility or weight of a confession. In such a case counsel must raise the question before speeches in the absence of the jury, so that the judge can rule whether the alleged characteristic is capable of being relevant. If he rules that it is, then he must leave it to the jury.

(7) In the absence of some direction from the judge as to what characteristics are capable of being regarded as relevant, we think that the direction approved in *Graham* without more will not be as helpful as it might be, since the jury may be tempted, especially if there is evidence, as there was in this case, relating to suggestibility and vulnerability, to think that these are relevant. In most cases it is probably only the age and sex of the accused that is capable of being relevant. If so, the judge should, as he did in this case, confine the characteristics in question to these.

How are these principles to be applied in this case? Miss Levitt accepts, rightly in our opinion, that the evidence that the appellant was abnormally suggestible and a vulnerable individual is irrelevant. But she submits that the fact that he had, or may have had, a low I.Q. of 68 is relevant since it might inhibit his ability to seek the protection of the police. We do not agree. We do not see how low I.Q., short of mental impairment or mental defectiveness, can be said to be a characteristic that makes those who have it less courageous and less able to withstand threats and pressure.

Appeal dismissed

Questions

1. In *Hudson and Taylor*, above, the Court of Appeal stated that the defence of duress would be denied to the defendant if he "failed to avail himself of some opportunity which was reasonably open *to him* to render the threat ineffective" (emphasis added). If because of his low IQ, D is not capable of recognising such an opportunity, is it not the case that evidence of his IQ is relevant to the subjective question rather than the objective question?

2. As questions whether something constitutes a "mental illness, mental impairment or recognised psychiatric condition" are both matters of degree and opinion on which psychiatrists may differ, would it not be better either (a) to abandon the objective question (see Professor Smith's Commentary below); or (b) to abandon attempts to identify relevant and non-relevant characteristics when considering liability and leave these matters to the judge to taken into account when sentencing?

PROFESSOR SIR JOHN SMITH, "R. V BOWEN, COMMENTARY" [1996] CRIM. L.R. 577, 579

Clearly a characteristic which has no bearing on ability to resist threats of the kind which have been made in the particular case is irrelevant. If a person of low I.Q. is as well able to resist the threats as a person of high I.Q., the fact that the defendant has a low I.Q. is irrelevant for this purpose. It appears that this is a question for the judge. The court seems to have ruled it out as a matter of law in the present case. Similarly in *Flatt*, [1996] Crim. L.R. 576, with reference to drug addiction. If, however, the defendant is in a 'category of persons who the jury may think less able to resist pressure than people not within that category', then the defendant's membership of that category is relevant; *but* the merely pliable, vulnerable and timid are not a category for this purpose. Those suffering from 'recognised mental illness or psychiatric condition, such as post-traumatic stress disorder leading to learned helplessness' apparently are. A jury may have some difficulty with the question: 'Would a woman, displaying the firmness reasonably to be expected of a woman suffering from learned helplessness, have yielded to the threat?' Effectively, this seems to eliminate the objective test for this category of persons. The elimination of the objective test might in principle be a good thing but, if so, it should be done generally and not for limited categories.

   The opinion of the court on this last point seems to be based on its interpretation of *Emery*. It is submitted that it is not the correct interpretation . . . In *Emery* Lord Taylor C.J. said '. . . the question for the doctors was whether a woman of reasonable firmness with the characteristics of Miss Emery, if abused in the manner which she said, would have had her will crushed so that she could not have protected the child.' Lord Taylor cannot have envisaged anything so absurd as 'a woman of reasonable firmness suffering from a condition of dependent helplessness', and that is not what he says. The jury were to consider whether a woman of reasonable firmness *would have been reduced* to a condition of dependent helplessness. If so, the will of the reasonably firm woman would obviously have been overborne. The point surely is that the history of violence which was alleged in that case to have produced the condition of dependent helplessness was part of the duress. The jury have to envisage an ordinary woman of reasonable firmness before the history of the violence begins and consider whether, by the time of the final threat, her will would be so overborne that she would fail to resist it.

Note

In the extract below Professor K.J.M. Smith argues that the requirement of reasonable steadfastness is superfluous as the defence already has a "non-variable threshold" by requiring a threat of death or serious harm.

K.J.M. SMITH, "DURESS AND STEADFASTNESS: IN PURSUIT OF THE UNINTELLIGIBLE" [1999] CRIM. L.R. 363, 370

It is within these initial objective boundaries that the current law's additional, separate requirement of reasonable steadfastness has to be considered. Just what is its function alongside a fixed minimum level of threat?

   Judicial comments suggest it to be a particular manifestation of the ever-present concern over eroding the universal expectation, reinforced by the threat of sanctions, that the law is to be observed. Only exceptionally will the law compromise this expectation. In Lord Lane's frequently quoted words: it was a 'matter of public policy . . . to limit the defence . . . by means of an objective criterion formulated in terms of reasonableness'. [*Graham*, [1982] 1 All E.R. 801 at 806] But does not the fixed qualifying standard of the threat of serious harm or death perform this role? It is being maintained that, when faced with a belief in the threat of death or serious harm, the question is, *should* that defendant have capitulated bearing in mind their personal characteristics? In other words, does the reasonable steadfastness test envisage some defendants of strong emotional or physical disposition who will be denied a defence of duress and who must not choose self-preservation? Unless some curious, morally unsustainable variability exists in the standard of self-sacrifice or self-preservation expected of a defendant *in extremis*, no coherent function can be assigned to the steadfastness requirement.

   In suggesting this, a fundamental and vital distinction must be drawn between the emotional impact of a threat of at least serious harm on the defendant (how personally disturbing or intimidating it was), and what the defendant might have done in the circumstances to avoid or neutralise the threat, or how much credibility the threat should have been given. It is with respect to these two latter factors, where reasonableness of response is demanded by the law, that the defendant's personal characteristics could plausibly be drawn into the wider question of whether the defendant has behaved reasonably. However, undoubtedly, this was not Lord Lane's intended role for 'steadfastness'. Moreover, most subsequent judicial wrangles over just what personal characteristics may legitimately be admitted in determining 'reasonable steadfastness' were clearly concerned with the issue of the emotional impact on the defendant's ability to resist threats as distinct from the reasonableness of a belief in the threat's existence or ways of avoiding it. Thus, these cases would seem to accept that even where the threat of serious harm is credible and where there is no reasonable prospect of escape open to the defendants, the jury must still consider, in effect, whether the defendant's choice of self-preservation was morally acceptable bearing in mind his personal characteristics; in other words, in the jury's view did the defendant deserve to be excused? . . .

Arguably, steadfastness is a superfluous objective test, pointlessly adding to the complexity of the defence. Steadfastness is superfluous when set alongside duress's fixed minimum standard of the threat of at least serious harm. Subject to other distinct requirements, this threat condition marks the threshold of qualifying coercion, submission to which is deemed to be the fitting basis for excusing a defendant because it constitutes acceptable 'human frailty' or self-preference. Moreover, it can hardly be accidental that the Model Penal Code's duress provisions, whilst incorporating a 'reasonable firmness' condition, do not specify a fixed universal minimum level of threat. To this extent, the Model Penal Code formulation of duress implicitly requires juries to balance the level of threat against the offence committed—a proportionality requirement. Secondly, the presence of a steadfastness test deflects attention away from legitimate defence conditions relating to the neutralization or avoidance of threats. Contrary to an implicit view persisting in an extensive body of case law from *Graham* onwards (and explicit Law Commission opinion), the steadfastness requirement cannot coherently relate to anything other than the distinct conditions that defendants take all reasonable opportunities to escape from or neutralise an aggressor's threat. This is true both for duress *per minas* and duress of circumstances. It is in satisfying these objective conditions of the reasonableness of the defendant's capitulation to threats that reference may plausibly be made to the defendant's characteristics and capacities.

Just what characteristics *ought* to be admissible remains problematic, even when steadfastness is employed in this defensible fashion. As pointed out, the question is very much akin to that arising in self-defence (and prevention of crime) and as yet lacks authoritative resolution. For both defences the question is what characteristics, beyond those of physical attributes, ought to be regarded as relevant to the defendant's ability to make a reasonable effort to avoid or neutralise a threat of harm. In both duress and self-defence the outstanding question may be reduced to whether, besides physical limitations, evidence of anything less than medically recognised mental impairment affecting the defendant's competence to cope with a threat should [be] admissible in determining whether the defendant acted reasonably . . .. [T]he inherent difficulty entailed in a jury weighing up a defendant's moral resilience alone argues against admitting such evidence. But beyond such practical problems, deeper conceptual objections exist. Allowing evidence of character to influence the ascription of criminal responsibility would be a unique departure from orthodox principles of liability. Drawing into the calculation of reasonableness the defendant's character traits would be to reduce the issue to something approaching whether the defendant could have acted otherwise

Jettisoning the steadfastness standard, except in relation to matters of escape from or avoidance of a threat, would be a worthwhile simplification.

Note

In determining the first question in duress (whether the accused, because of what he reasonably believed the duressor had said or done, had good cause to fear death or GBH) it was believed that any condition from which D suffered which may have affected his perception should not be taken into account in determining the reasonableness of his belief. In *Martin* [2000] 2 Cr. App. R. 42, D suffered from schizoid-affective disorder which meant that he was more likely than others to regard things said to him as threatening and to believe that such threats would be carried out. The trial judge ruled that evidence of this condition was irrelevant in relation to the first question. The Court of Appeal held that duress and self-defence being analogous (relying on Lord Lane's dictum to this effect in *Graham*), the same subjective approach should be taken in respect of the accused's belief. In other words, D's psychiatric conditions may provide the explanation for his mistaken belief and thus were relevant to the jury's consideration of the first question. While this may be seen by some as a welcome development, the reasoning of the Court of Appeal is difficult to support. Lord Lane's dictum in *Graham* pre-dated his decision in *Williams (Gladstone)* (1984) 78 Cr. App. R. 276 (above), which established the subjective approach for self-defence. Secondly, the Court of Appeal placed reliance on the duress of circumstances case of *Cairns* [1999] 2 Cr. App. R. 137 reading this as having established a subjective test for duress of circumstances. However, that case did not establish such a test; the case concerned a direction by the trial judge that the defence could only be availed of where the perceived threat was "an actual or real threat". The Court of Appeal held this to be a misdirection, the issue being whether the accused reasonably perceived a threat of serious injury or death. In *R. v Safi* [2003] EWCA Crim 1809, the Court of Appeal confirmed that it is not necessary to establish that there actually was a threat, it being sufficient that the defendant believed there was a threat. The Court, however, did not resolve the issue of whether or not the defendant's belief must be reasonable or merely genuine. In *R. v Hasan* [2005] UKHL 22, Lord Bingham of Cornhill stated:

> "But the words used in *R. v Graham* and approved in *R. v Howe* were 'he reasonably believed'. It is of course essential that the defendant should genuinely, i.e. actually, believe in the efficacy of the threat by which he claims to have been compelled. But there is no warrant for relaxing the requirement that the belief must be reasonable as well as genuine."

Consequently it is unclear whether *Martin* has amended the first question to dispense with the requirement that D's belief be a reasonable one or whether the test remains as it was but D's mental condition is to be treated as relevant to the question, that is, whether his belief was reasonable or not was to be judged against the reasonable man having that particular condition.

----

iv. Voluntary association with criminal organisation

R. V SHARP

[1987] 1 Q.B. 853

A was convicted of manslaughter and pleaded guilty to robbery and attempted robbery. He had joined a gang of robbers which carried out a series of armed robberies of sub-post offices. This series culminated in the offence which resulted in the death of the sub-postmaster who was shot by H. A was tried on a count charging murder and submitted that he had acted under duress as he had only taken part in the last robbery because a gun had been pointed at his head by H who threatened to blow it off if he did not participate. The trial judge rejected this submission and A appealed.

LORD LANE CJ

No one could question that if a person can avoid the effects of duress by escaping from the threats, without damage to himself, he must do so. In other words if there is a moment at which he is able to escape, so to speak, from the gun being held at his head by Hussey, or the equivalent of Hussey, he must do so. It seems to us to be part of the same argument, or at least to be so close to the same argument as to be practically indistinguishable from it, to say that a man must not voluntarily put himself in a position where he is likely to be subjected to such compulsion.
    . . . But we are fortified in the view . . . that this is part of the common law and always has been, by certain matters which appear in the speeches of their Lordships in *D.P.P. for Northern Ireland v Lynch* [1975] A.C. 653. Although Lynch's case has been the subject of certain adverse comment since the date of those speeches, nevertheless the passages to which we wish to refer have not, as far as we know, been the subject of criticism.

First of all in the speech of Lord Morris of Borth-y-Gest appears this passage, at p.668:

'Where duress is in issue many questions may arise such as whether threats are serious and compelling or whether (as on the facts of the present case may specially call for consideration) a person the subject of duress could reasonably have extricated himself or could have sought protection or had what has been called a "safe avenue of escape". Other questions may arise such as whether a person is only under duress as a result of being in voluntary association with those whom he knew would require some course of action. In the present case, as duress was not left to the jury, we naturally do not know what they thought of it at all.'

A little later Lord Morris of Borth-y-Gest again said, at p.670:

'In posing the case where someone is "really" threatened I use the word "really" in order to emphasise that duress must never be allowed to be the easy answer of those who can devise no other explanation of their conduct nor of those who readily could have avoided the dominance of threats nor of those who allow themselves to be at the disposal and under the sway of some gangster-tyrant. Where duress becomes an issue courts and juries will surely consider the facts with care and discernment.'

Here, of course, I interpolate, Hussey was the archetypal gangster-tyrant.
I turn from Lord Morris of Borth-y-Gest to the speech of Lord Wilber-force, at p.679:

'It is clear that a possible case of duress, on the facts, could have been made. I say "a possible case" because there were a number of matters which the jury would have had to consider if this defence had been left to them. Among these would have been whether Meehan, though uttering no express threats of death or serious injury, impliedly did so in such a way as to put the appellant in fear of death or serious injury; whether, if so, the threats continued to operate throughout the enterprise; whether the appellant had voluntarily exposed himself to a situation in which threats might be used against him if he did not participate in a criminal enterprise (the appellant denied that he had done so); whether the appellant had taken every opportunity open to him to escape from the situation of duress. In order to test the validity of the judge's decision to exclude this defence, we must assume on this appeal that these matters would have been decided in favour of the appellant.'

Finally, so far as the passages in favour of the contention which we are supporting are concerned, in the speech of Lord Simon of Glaisdale appears this passage, at p.687:

'I spoke of the social evils which might be attendant on the recognition of a general defence of duress. Would it not enable a gang leader of notorious violence to confer on his organisation by terrorism immunity from the criminal law? Every member of his gang might well be able to say with truth, It was as much as my life was worth to disobey/Was this not in essence the plea of the appellant? We do not, in general, allow a superior officer to confer such immunity on his subordinates by any defence of obedience to orders: why should we allow it to terrorists? Nor would it seem to be sufficient to stipulate that no one can plead duress as a defence who had put himself into a position in which duress could be exercised on himself.'

We draw assistance from the fact that common law jurisdictions as well as Commonwealth jurisdictions throughout the world have adopted this rule almost unanimously (although the wording in their various statutes differs the one from the other), which is an indication to us that this may well have been, and indeed was, throughout a principle of the common law.

[His Lordship referred to *R. v Hurley and Murray* [1967] V.R. 526.]

We are therefore, in the light of that persuasive authority and the indications in their Lordships' speeches in *D.P.P. for Northern Ireland v Lynch* [1975] A.C. 653 of the opinion that the judge, Kenneth Jones J., was correct in the decision which he reached.
We are further fortified in that view by the judgment of Lord Lowry C.J. of Northern Ireland, in *R. v Fitzpatrick* [1977] N.I. 20. Let me read the brief headnote once again in order to indicate the nature of the decision. It runs as follows:

'If a person by joining an illegal organisation or a similar group of men with criminal objectives and coercive methods, voluntarily exposes and submits himself to illegal compulsion, he cannot rely on the duress to which he has voluntarily exposed himself as an excuse either in respect of the crimes he commits against his will or in respect of his continued but unwilling association with those capable of exercising upon him the duress which he calls in aid.'

. . . In other words, in our judgment, where a person has voluntarily, and with knowledge of its nature, joined a criminal organisation or gang which he knew might bring pressure on him to commit an offence and was an active member when he was put under such pressure, he cannot avail himself of the defence of duress. Mr Mylne concedes that such a ruling is the end of his appeal. The appeal is therefore dismissed.

Appeal dismissed

Question

Would the joining of a criminal organisation or gang automatically disentitle a defendant from raising duress as a defence or must the organisation or gang be one which he knew used violence to enforce its discipline? See next case.

R. V HASAN

[2005] UKHL 22

The defendant had worked as a driver and minder for T, who ran an escort agency and was involved in prostitution. In about August 1999, according to the defendant, S became T's boyfriend and also her minder in connection with her prostitution business. He had, the defendant said, the reputation of being a violent man and a drug dealer. The second count of aggravated burglary in the indictment against the defendant related to an incident on January 23, 2000. The defendant admitted at trial that he had forced his way into the house, armed with a knife, and had attempted to steal the contents of the safe, but claimed that he had acted under duress exerted by S, who had fortified his reputation for violence by talking of three murders he had recently committed. On the day in question, the defendant claimed, he had been ambushed outside his home by S and an unknown black man whom he described as a "lunatic yardie". S demanded that the defendant get the money from the safe, and told the defendant that the black man would go with him to see that this was done. S said that, if the defendant did not do it, he and his family would be harmed. The defendant claimed that he had no chance to escape and go to the police. The black man drove the defendant to the house and gave him a knife, saying that he himself had a gun. The defendant then broke into the house and tried unsuccessfully to open and then to remove the safe. The black man was in the vicinity throughout, and drove him away when the attempt failed. The jury convicted him on the second count and he was sentenced to nine years' imprisonment.

LORD BINGHAM OF CORNHILL

[1] My Lords, this appeal by the Crown against the decision of the Criminal Division of the Court of Appeal raises two questions. The first concerns the meaning of 'confession' for the purposes of s.76(1) of the Police and Criminal Evidence Act 1984. The second concerns the defence of duress. I shall confine this opinion to the issue of duress. On that issue the judge put four questions to the jury: . . . [After stating the first three questions His Lordship continued:] . . .

'Question 4: Did the defendant voluntarily put himself in the position, in which he knew he was likely to be subjected to threats? You look to judge that in all the circumstances. If he had stopped associating with S after August, would he have ever found himself in this predicament? It is for you to decide. It is right to say he says he did stop associating but S kept finding him. It may not be wholly straightforward. It is for you to consider and it is a relevant consideration because if someone voluntarily associates with the sort of people who he knows are likely to put pressure on him, then he cannot really complain, if he finds himself under pressure. If you are sure that he did voluntarily put himself in such a position, the defence fails and he was guilty. If you are not sure and you have not been sure about all of the other questions, then you would find him not guilty.'

On his appeal to the Court of Appeal the defendant criticised the judge's directions on the . . . fourth question.
    Having considered a number of authorities, the Court of Appeal also concluded that there was a misdirection in the judge's formulation of question 4:

'and that he should have directed the jury to consider whether the [defendant] knew that he was likely to be subjected to threats to commit a crime of the type [with] which he was charged.'

In this appeal to the House, the Crown seek to establish that the judge's directions on the fourth question involved no misdirection . . ..

[After reviewing general principles relating to the law of duress His Lordship continued:]

[29] The judge's direction to the jury on question 4 quoted above and, as recorded in para 15, the Court of Appeal ruled that this was a misdirection because the judge had not directed the jury to consider whether the defendant knew that he was likely to be subjected to threats to commit a crime of the type of which he was charged. It is this ruling which gives rise to the certified question on this part of the case, which is:

'Whether the defence of duress is excluded when as a result of the accused's voluntary association with others:

  (i)   he foresaw (or possibly should have foreseen) the risk of being subjected to any compulsion by threats of violence, or
  (ii) only when he foresaw (or should have foreseen) the risk of being subjected to compulsion to commit criminal offences, and, if the latter,
  (iii) only if the offences foreseen (or which should have been foreseen) were of the same type (or possibly of the same type and gravity) as that ultimately committed.'

The Crown contend for answer (i) in its objective form. The defendant commends the third answer, omitting the first parenthesis . . .
    [32] . . . The trial judge's direction which was challenged on appeal is fully quoted in *R. v Shepherd* (1987) 86 Cr.App.R. 47, 51, and was to this effect:

'. . . but in my judgment the defence of duress is not available to an accused who voluntarily exposes and submits himself to illegal compulsion. It is not merely a matter of joining in a criminal enterprise; it is a matter of joining in a criminal enterprise of such a nature that the defendant appreciated the nature of the enterprise itself and the attitudes of those in charge of it, so that when he was in fact subjected to compulsion he could fairly be said by a jury to have voluntarily exposed himself and submitted himself to such compulsion.'

The Court of Appeal upheld that direction in *R. v Sharp*, expressing the principle at p.861:

'where a person has voluntarily, and with knowledge of its nature, joined a criminal organisation or gang which he knew might bring pressure on him to commit an offence and was an active member when he was put under such pressure, he cannot avail himself of the defence of duress.'

In *R. v Shepherd* the criminal activity was of a less serious kind: the question which the jury should have been (but were not) directed to consider was 'whether the appellant could be said to have taken the risk of P's violence simply by joining a shoplifting gang of which he [P] was a member'.

[33] *R. v Ali* is summarised at [1995] Crim.L.R. 303, but the ratio of the decision more clearly appears from the transcript of the judgment given by the Court of Appeal on 14 November 1994. The appellant claimed to have become involved in drug dealing and to have become indebted to his supplier, X, who (he said) had given him a gun and told him to obtain the money from a bank or building society the following day, failing which he would be killed. The appellant accordingly committed the robbery of which he was convicted. In directing the jury on the defence of duress advanced by the defendant the trial judge had said:

'The final question is this: did he, in obtaining heroin from Mr X and supplying it to others for gain, after he knew of Mr X's reputation for violence, voluntarily put himself in a position where he knew that he was likely to be forced by Mr X to commit a crime?'

It was argued by the appellant that the judge should have said 'forced by Mr X to commit armed robbery', but this was rejected, and the court held that by 'a crime' the jury could only have understood the judge to be referring to a crime other than drug dealing. The principle stated by the court was this:

'The crux of the matter, as it seems to us, is knowledge in the defendant of either a violent nature to the gang or the enterprise which he has joined, or a violent disposition in the person or persons involved with him in the criminal activity he voluntarily joined. In our judgment, if a defendant voluntarily participates in criminal offences with a man "X", whom he knows to be of a violent disposition and likely to require him to perform other criminal acts, he cannot rely upon duress if 'X' does so.'

(In this case, as in *R. v Cole*, above, it would seem that the defence of duress should in any event have failed, for lack of immediacy, since the threat was not to be executed until the following day, and therefore the defendant had the opportunity to take evasive action).

[34] In its Working Paper No.55 of 1974, the Law Commission in para.26 favoured

'a limitation upon the defence [of duress] which would exclude its availability where the defendant had joined an association or conspiracy which was of such a character that he was aware that he might be compelled to participate in offences of the type with which he is charged.'

This reference to 'offences of the type with which he is charged' was, in substance, repeated in the Law Commission's 'Report on Defences of General Application' (Law Com No.83) of 1977, paras 2.38 and 2.46(8), in clause 1(5) of the draft bill appended to that report, in clause 45(4) of the draft bill appended to the Law Commission's Report on 'Codification of the Criminal Law' (Law Com No.143) of 1985, as explained in para.13.19 of the Report, and in clause 42(5) of the Law Commission's draft 'Criminal Code Bill' (Law Com No.177) published in 1989. But there was no warrant for this gloss in any reported British authority until the Court of Appeal gave judgment in *R. v Baker and Ward* [1999] 2 Cr.App.R.335. The facts were very similar to these in *R. v Ali*, above, save that the appellants claimed that they had been specifically instructed to rob the particular store which they were convicted of robbing. The trial judge had directed the jury (p.341):

'A person cannot rely on the defence of duress if he has voluntarily and with full knowledge of its nature joined a criminal group which he was aware might bring pressure on him of a violent kind or require him if necessary to commit offences to obtain money where he himself had defaulted to the criminal group in payment to the criminal group.'

This was held to be a misdirection (p.344):

'What a defendant has to be aware of is the risk that the group might try to coerce him into committing criminal offences of the type for which he is being tried by the use of violence or threats of violence.'

At p.346 this ruling was repeated:

'The purpose of the pressure has to be to coerce the accused into committing a criminal offence of the type for which he is being tried.'

The appeals were accordingly allowed and the convictions quashed.

[35] Counsel for the defendant in the present case contends (as the Court of Appeal accepted) that this ruling was correct and that the trial judge in the present case misdirected the jury because he did not insist on the need for the defendant to foresee pressure to commit the offence of robbery of which he was convicted.

[36] In *R. v Heath* [2000] Crim.L.R. 109 the appellant again claimed that he had become indebted to a drug supplier, and claimed that he had been compelled by threats of physical violence to collect the consignment of drugs which gave rise to his conviction. His defence of duress failed at trial, rightly as the Court of Appeal held. In its judgment, Kennedy L.J. said:

'The appellant in evidence conceded that he had put himself in the position where he was likely to be subjected to threats. He was therefore, in our judgment, not entitled to rely on those same threats as duress to excuse him from liability for subsequent criminal conduct.'

The court found it possible to distinguish *R. v Baker and Ward*, observing:

'It is the awareness of the risk of compulsion which matters. Prior awareness of what criminal activity those exercising compulsion may offer as a possible alternative to violence is irrelevant.'

The facts in *R. v Harmer* [2002] Crim.L.R. 401 were very similar to those in *R. v Heath*, which the court followed. It does not appear from the court's judgment given by Goldring J whether *R. v Baker and Ward* was directly cited, but it would seem that counsel for the appellant did not rely on it. He argued that the appellant did not foresee that he might be required to commit crimes for the supplier. But the court did not accept this argument:

'We cannot accept that where a man voluntarily exposes himself to unlawful violence, duress may run if he does not foresee that under the threat of such violence he may be required to commit crimes. There is no reason in principle why that should be so.'

[37] The principal issue between the Crown on one side and the appellant and the Court of Appeal on the other is whether *R. v Baker and Ward* correctly stated the law. The defendant is seeking to be wholly exonerated from the consequences of a crime deliberately committed. The prosecution must negative his defence of duress, if raised by the evidence, beyond reasonable doubt. The defendant is, *ex hypothesi*, a person who has voluntarily surrendered his will to the domination of another. Nothing should turn on foresight of the manner in which, in the event, the dominant party chooses to exploit the defendant's subservience. There need not be foresight of coercion to commit crimes, although it is not easy to envisage circumstances in which a party might be coerced to act lawfully. In holding that there must be foresight of coercion to commit crimes of the kind with which the defendant is charged, *R. v Baker and Ward* mis-stated the law.

[38] There remains the question, which the Court of Appeal left open in para.75 of their judgment, whether the defendant's foresight must be judged by a subjective or an objective test: i.e. does the defendant lose the benefit of a defence based on duress only if he actually foresaw the risk of coercion or does he lose it if he ought reasonably to have foreseen the risk of coercion, whether he actually foresaw the risk or not? I do not think any decided case has addressed this question, and I am conscious that application of an objective reasonableness test to other ingredients of duress has attracted criticism: see, for example, Elliott, *'Necessity, Duress and Self-Defence'* [1989] Crim.L.R. 611, 614–615, and the commentary by Professor Ashworth on *R. v Safi* [2003] Crim.L.R. 721, 723. The practical importance of the distinction in this context may not be very great, since if a jury concluded that a person voluntarily associating with known criminals ought reasonably to have foreseen the risk of future coercion they would not, I think, be very likely to accept that he did not in fact do so. But since there is a choice to be made, policy in my view points towards an objective test of what the defendant, placed as he was and knowing what he did, ought reasonably to have foreseen. I am not persuaded otherwise by analogies based on self-defence or provocation . . . The policy of the law must be to discourage association with known criminals, and it should be slow to excuse the criminal conduct of those who do so. If a person voluntarily becomes or remains associated with others engaged in criminal activity in a situation where he knows or ought reasonably to know that he may be the subject of compulsion by them or their associates, he cannot rely on the defence of duress to excuse any act which he is thereafter compelled to do by them.

[39] I would answer this certified question by saying that the defence of duress is excluded when as a result of the accused's voluntary association with others engaged in criminal activity he foresaw or ought reasonably to have foreseen the risk of being subjected to any compulsion by threats of violence.

Conclusion

[40] The judge's direction to the jury on question 4 involved no misdirection. It was based on the JSB specimen direction current at the time, save that it omitted the qualification made to reflect the erroneous ruling in *R. v Baker and Ward*. The ruling was, on the law as I have stated it, too favourable to the defendant, but he cannot complain of that. It is desirable that the content, and perhaps even the order, of the current JSB directions should be reconsidered in the light of this opinion, but that is not a task which the House should undertake. I would accordingly answer the certified question as indicated, allow the Crown's appeal, set aside the Court of Appeal's order, restore the defendant's conviction and remit this matter to the Court of Appeal so that the defendant may surrender to his bail.

Appeal allowed
Conviction restored

R. V ALI

[2008] EWCA Crim 716

The appellant was convicted of robbery. It was not disputed that the appellant had been involved in robbing V of a car. The defence case was that the appellant acted under duress, the threats being administered by H. The defence case was that when the appellant first met H he did not know that he was a criminal. He was later threatened and driven to commit the offence by threats that he received from H. The sole issue for the jury was whether or not the appellant had been acting under duress.

DYSON LJ

[After reviewing the facts and the trial judge's directions His Lordship continued . . .]

10 The effect of voluntary association on duress was considered by the House of Lords in [R v *Hasan*] [2005] UKHL 22. In that case the trial judge had included the following direction in his summing-up (we refer to paragraph 14 of Lord Bingham's speech):

'Did the defendant voluntarily put himself in the position, in which he knew he was likely to be subjected to threats? You look to judge that in all the circumstances . . . It is for you to decide. It is right to say he says he did stop associating but Sullivan kept finding him. It may not be wholly straightforward. It is for you to consider and it is a relevant consideration because if someone voluntarily associates with the sort of people who he knows are likely to put pressure on him, then he cannot really complain, if he finds himself under pressure. If you are sure that he did voluntarily put himself in such a position, the defence fails and he was guilty. If you are not sure and you have not been sure about all of the other questions, then you would find him not guilty.'

11 The certified question of law in that case was set out by Lord Bingham at paragraph 29:

'Whether the defence of duress is excluded when as a result of the accused's voluntary association with others:

(i)   He foresaw (or possibly should have foreseen) the risk of being subjected to any compulsion by threats of violence, or

(ii)   Only when he foresaw (or should have foreseen) the risk of being subjected to compulsion to commit criminal offences, and, if the latter,

(iii) Only if the offences foreseen (or which should have been foreseen) were of the same type (or possibly of the same type and gravity) as that ultimately committed.'

Lord Bingham answered that question at paragraph 39 in these terms:

'I would answer this certified question by saying that the defence of duress is excluded when as a result of the accused's voluntary association with others engaged in criminal activity he foresaw or ought reasonably to have foreseen the risk of being subjected to any compulsion by threats of violence.'

At paragraph 40 Lord Bingham said that the judge's direction, to which we have referred, 'involved no misdirection.'

12 The current Judicial Studies Board specimen direction reflects the decision in *R v Hasan*. The relevant part of the direction is to be found at paragraph 7 in these terms:

'Did D voluntarily put himself in a position in which he foresaw or ought reasonably to have foreseen the risk of being subjected to any compulsion by threats of violence? The prosecution say that he did, by [joining a criminal group the members of which might make such threats] [getting involved with crime and thus with other criminals who might make such threats if he let them down or came to owe them money]. But it is for you to decide. If you are sure that D did voluntarily put himself in such a position, the defence of duress does not apply [and D is guilty]. However, if you are not sure that he did so, the defence of duress does apply and you must find D not guilty.'

It is true that Lord Bingham refers at paragraph 39 to a voluntary association with others 'engaged in criminal activity'. That is not surprising because in most cases where A subjects B to compulsion by threats of violence, A is engaged in criminal activity. But as the Judicial Studies Board specimen directions makes clear, the core question is whether the defendant voluntarily put himself in the position in which he foresaw or ought reasonably to have foreseen the risk of being subjected to any compulsion by threats of violence. As a matter of fact, threats of violence will almost always be made by persons engaged in a criminal activity; but in our judgment it is the risk of being subjected to compulsion by threats of violence that must be foreseen or foreseeable that is relevant, rather than the nature of the activity in which the threatener is engaged. As further support for this, we point out that the direction given by the trial judge in *Hasan* made no reference to the nature of the activity in which the threatener was engaged and yet Lord Bingham said in terms that there was no misdirection.

13 With those observations in mind we turn to the directions of which complaint is made in this case. We agree that if the judge had simply said that the appellant could not rely on duress, if he may have been acting under the compulsion of threats from H in circumstances where the jury considered that the appellant had chosen to join 'very bad company', that would have been an insufficient direction. But the judge did not say that. Before he made his reference to 'bad company' he said:

'The defence of duress does not apply, does not apply, if the defendant chooses voluntarily to associate with others where he ought to foresee that he might be subjected to compulsion by threats of violence.'

He repeated this direction twice at the end of the summing-up. In our judgment that is not a misdirection. In substance it is the same as the first sentence of the Judicial Studies Board specimen direction which, as we have said, contains the core requirement. Moreover, with a substitution of 'might be' or 'likely' the direction is not materially different from that given by the trial judge in *Hasan*. Furthermore, in the sentence which contains the reference to 'bad company' the judge added:

'. . . such bad company that you can foresee that you are going to be liable to threats of some kind to do things . . .'

Again, although expressed slightly differently, these words capture the essence of the point that has to be made to the jury. . . Accordingly we dismiss the . . . appeal.

Appeal dismissed

Questions

1. Does D lose the defence of duress only where he joins an established criminal gang or also if he joins with any others whom he ought to have realized might subject him to threats of violence?

2. D is addicted to gambling. He associates with X, a loan shark. If X threatens D with death or serious injury unless he commits theft to repay loans X gave him for gambling, will D be able to rely on duress?

----

v. Duress and murder

R. V HOWE

[1987] 1 A.C. 417 HL

H and B, with C and M, participated in the assault and then killing of two victims. On the first occasion H and B were principals in the second degree. On the second occasion they jointly strangled the victim. On a third occasion the intended victim escaped. At their trial on two counts of murder and one of conspiracy to murder they pleaded duress claiming that they had feared for their own lives if they had not done as M directed. The judge left the defence of duress to the jury in respect of the first murder and the conspiracy charge but not in respect of the second murder. The appellants were convicted on all three counts.

LORD HAILSHAM OF MARYLEBONE LC

[The first of the three questions certified by the Court of Appeal is as follows:] '(I) Is duress available as a defence to a person charged with murder as a principal in the first degree (the actual killer)?' . . . In my opinion, this must be decided on principle and authority, and the answer must in the end demand a reconsideration of the two authorities of *D.P.P. for Northern Ireland v Lynch* and *Abbott v The Queen* . . .

I therefore consider the matter first from the point of view of authority. On this I can only say that at the time when *Lynch* was decided on the balance of weight in an unbroken tradition of authority dating back to Hale and Blackstone seems to have been accepted to have been that duress was not available to a defendant accused of murder. I quote only from Hale and Blackstone. Thus *Rale's Pleas of the Crown* (1736), vol. 1, p.51:

'if a man be desperately assaulted, and in peril of death, and cannot otherwise escape, unless to satisfy his assailant's fury he will kill an innocent person then present, the fear and actual force will not acquit him of the crime and punishment of murder, if he commit the fact; for he ought rather to die himself, than kill an innocent: . . .'

Blackstone, Commentaries on the Laws of England (1857 ed.), vol. 4, p.28 was to the same effect. He wrote that a man under duress: 'ought rather to die himself than escape by the murder of an innocent.' . . .

Before I leave the question of reported authority I must refer to . . . *R. v Dudley and Stephens* (below, p.269). That is generally and, in my view correctly, regarded as an authority on the availability of the supposed defence of necessity rather than duress. But I must say frankly that, if we were to allow this appeal, we should, I think, also have to say that *Dudley and Stephens* was bad law. There is, of course, an obvious distinction between duress and necessity as potential defences; duress arises from the wrongful threats of violence of another human being and necessity arises from any other objective dangers threatening the accused. This, however, is, in my view a distinction without a relevant difference, since on this view duress is only that species of the genus of necessity which is caused by wrongful threats. I cannot see that there is any way in which a person of ordinary fortitude can be excused from the one type of pressure on his will rather than the other . . .

I do not think that the decision in *Lynch* can be justified on authority and that, exercising to the extent necessary, the freedom given to us by the *Practice Statement (Judicial Precedent)* [1966] 1 W.L.R. 1234 which counsel for the respondent urged us to apply, I consider that the right course in the instant appeal is to restore the law to the condition in which it was almost universally thought to be prior to *Lynch* . . .

This brings me back to the question of principle. I begin by affirming that, while there can never be a direct correspondence between law and morality, an attempt to divorce the two entirely is and has always proved to be, doomed to failure, and, in the present case, the overriding objects of the criminal law must be to protect innocent lives and to set a standard of conduct which ordinary men and women are expected to observe if they are to avoid criminal responsibility . . .

In general, I must say that I do not at all accept in relation to the defence of murder it is either good morals, good policy or good law to suggest, as did the majority in *Lynch* and the minority in *Abbott* that the ordinary man of reasonable fortitude is not to be supposed to be capable of heroism if he is asked to take an innocent life rather than sacrifice his own. Doubtless in actual practice many will succumb to temptation, as they did in *Dudley and Stephens*. But many will not, and I do not believe that as a 'concession to human frailty' the former should be exempt from liability to criminal sanctions if they do. I have known in my own lifetime of too many acts of heroism by ordinary human beings of no more than ordinary fortitude to regard a law as either 'just or humane' which withdraws the protection of the criminal law from the innocent victim and casts the cloak of its protection upon the coward and the poltroon in the name of a 'concession to human frailty.'

I must not, however, underestimate the force of the arguments on the other side, advanced as they have been with such force and such persuasiveness by some of the most eminent legal minds, judicial and academic, in the country.

First, amongst these is, perhaps, the argument from logic and consistency. A long line of cases, it is said, carefully researched and closely analysed, established duress as an available defence in a wide range of crimes, some at least, like wounding with intent to commit grievous bodily harm, carrying the heaviest penalties commensurate with their gravity. To cap this, it is pointed out that at least in theory, a defendant accused of this crime under section 18 of the Offences Against the Person Act 1861, but acquitted on the grounds of duress, will still be liable to a charge of murder if the victim dies within the traditional period of one year and a day. I am not, perhaps, persuaded of this last point as much as I should. It is not simply an anomaly based on the defence of duress. It is a product of the peculiar *mens rea* allowed on a charge of murder which is not confined to an intent to kill. More persuasive, perhaps, is the point based on the availability of the defence of duress on a charge of attempted murder, where the actual intent to kill is an essential prerequisite. It may be that we must meet this casus omissus in your Lordships' House when we come to it. It may require reconsideration of the availability of the defence in that case too.

I would, however, prefer to meet the case of alleged inconsistency head on. Consistency and logic, though inherently desirable, are not always prime characteristics of a penal code based like the common law on custom and precedent. Law so based is not an exact science. All the same, I feel I am required to give some answer to the question posed. If duress is available as a defence to some crimes of the most grave why, it may legitimately be asked, stop at murder, whether as accessory or principal and whether in the second or the first degree? But surely I am entitled to believe that some degree of proportionality between the threat and the offence must, at least to some extent, be a prerequisite of the defence under existing law. Few would resist threats to the life of a loved one if the alternative were driving across the red lights or in excess of 70 m.p.h. on the motorway. But . . . it would take rather more than the threat of a slap on the wrist or even moderate pain or injury to discharge the evidential burden even in the case of a fairly serious assault. In such a case the 'concession to human frailty' is no more than to say that in such circumstances a reasonable man of average courage is entitled to embrace as a matter of choice the alternative which a reasonable man would regard as the lesser of two evils. Other considerations necessarily arise where the choice is between the threat of death or *a fortiori* of serious injury and deliberately taking an innocent life. In such a case a reasonable man might reflect that one innocent human life is at least as valuable as his own or that of his loved one. In such a case a man cannot claim that he is choosing the lesser of two evils. Instead he is embracing the cognate but morally disreputable principle that the end justifies the means.

I am not so shocked as some of the judicial opinions have been at the need, if this be the conclusion, to invoke the availability of administrative as distinct from purely judicial remedies for the hardships which might otherwise occur in the most agonising cases. Even in *Dudley and Stephens* in 1884 when the death penalty was mandatory and frequently inflicted, the prerogative was used to reduce a sentence of death by hanging to one of six months in prison. In murder cases the available mechanisms are today both more flexible and more sophisticated. The trial judge may make no minimum recommendation. He will always report to the Home Secretary, as he did in the present case of Clarkson and Burke. The Parole Board will always consider a case of this kind with a High Court judge brought into consultation. In the background is always the prerogative and, it may not unreasonably be suggested, that is exactly what the prerogative is for. If the law seems to bear harshly in its operation in the case of a mandatory sentence on any particular offender there has never been a period of time when there were more effective means of mitigating its effect than at the present day . . .

During the course of argument it was suggested that there was available to the House some sort of half way house between allowing these appeals and dismissing them. The argument ran that we might treat duress in murder as analogous to provocation, or perhaps diminished responsibility, and say that, in indictments for murder, duress might reduce the crime to one of manslaughter. I find myself quite unable to accept this. The cases show that duress, if available and made out, entitles the accused to a clean acquittal, without, it has been said, the 'stigma' of a conviction. Whatever other merits it may have, at least the suggestion makes nonsense of any pretence of logic or consistency in the criminal law. It is also contrary to principle. Unlike the doctrine of provocation, which is based on emotional loss of control, the defence of duress, as I have already shown, is put forward as a 'concession to human frailty' whereby a conscious decision, it may be coolly undertaken, to sacrifice an innocent human life is made as an evil lesser than a wrong which might otherwise be suffered by the accused or his loved ones at the hands of a wrong doer. The defence of diminished responsibility (which might well, had it then been available to *Dudley and Stephens*, have prevailed there) is statutory in England though customary in Scotland, the law of its origin. But in England at least it has a conceptual basis defined in the Homicide Act 1957 which is totally distinct from that of duress if duress be properly analysed and understood. Provocation (unique to murder and not extending even to 'section 18' offences) is a concession to human frailty due to the extent that even a reasonable man may, under sufficient provocation temporarily lose his self control towards the person who has provoked him enough. Duress, as I have already pointed out, is a concession to human frailty in that it allows a reasonable man to make a conscious choice between the reality of the immediate threat and what he may reasonably regard as the lesser of two evils. Diminished responsibility as defined in the Homicide Act 1957 depends on abnormality of mind impairing mental responsibility. It may overlap duress or even necessity. But it is not what we are discussing in the instant appeal.

LORD GRIFFITHS

. . . There are surprisingly few reported decisions on duress but it cannot be gainsaid that the defence has been extended, particularly since the second war, to a number of crimes. I think myself it would have been better had this development not taken place and that duress had been regarded as a factor to be taken into account in mitigation as Stephen suggested in his *History of the Criminal Law of England* (1883) vol. 2, p.108. However, as Lord Morris of Borth-y-Gest said in *D.P.P. for Northern Ireland v Lynch* [1975] A.C. 653, 670, it is too late to adopt that view. And the question now is whether that development should be carried a step further and applied to a murderer who is the actual killer, and if the answer to this question is no, whether there is any basis upon which it can be right to draw a distinction between a murderer who did the actual killing and a murderer who played a different part in the design to bring about the death of the victim . . .

[A]re there any present circumstances that should impel your Lordships to alter the law that has stood for so long and to extend the defence of duress to the actual killer? My Lords, I can think of none. It appears to me that all present indications point in the opposite direction. We face a rising tide of violence and terrorism against which the law must stand firm recognising that its highest duty is to protect the freedom and lives of those that live under it. The sanctity of human life lies at the root of this ideal and I would do nothing to undermine it, be it ever so slight.

On this question your Lordships should, I believe, accord great weight to the opinion of the Lord Chief Justice [Lord Lane in *Graham*, above] . . . and the judges who sat with him, and decline to extend the defence to the actual killer. If the defence is not available to the killer what justification can there be for extending it to others who have played their part in the murder. I can, of course, see that as a matter of commonsense one participant in a murder may be considered less morally at fault than another. The youth who hero-worships the gang leader and acts as lookout man whilst the gang enter a jeweller's shop and kill the owner in order to steal is an obvious example. In the eyes of the law they are all guilty of murder, but justice will be served by requiring those who did the killing to serve a longer period in prison before being released on licence than the youth who acted as lookout. However, it is not difficult to give examples where moral fault may be thought to attach to a participant in murder who was not the actual killer; I have already mentioned the example of a contract killing, when the murder would never have taken place if a contract had not been placed to take the life of the victim. Another example would be an intelligent man goading a weakminded individual into a killing he would not otherwise commit.

It is therefore neither rational nor fair to make the defence dependent upon whether the accused is the actual killer or took some other part in the murder. I have toyed with the idea that it might be possible to leave it to the discretion of the trial judge to decide whether the defence should be available to one who was not the killer, but I have rejected this as introducing too great a degree of uncertainty into the availability of the defence. I am not troubled by some of the extreme examples cited in favour of allowing the defence to those who are not the killer such as a woman motorist being highjacked [sic] and forced to act as getaway driver, or a pedestrian being forced to give misleading information to the police to protect robbery and murder in a shop. The short, practical answer is that it is inconceivable that such persons would be prosecuted; they would be called as the principal witnesses for the prosecution.

As I can find no fair and certain basis upon which to differentiate between participants to a murder and as I am firmly convinced that the law should not be extended to the killer, I would depart from the decision of this House in *D.P.P. for Northern Ireland v Lynch* and declare the law to be that duress is not available as a defence to a charge of murder, or to attempted murder. I add attempted murder because it is to be remembered that the prosecution have to prove an even more evil intent to convict of attempted murder than in actual murder.

Attempted murder requires proof of an intent to kill, whereas in murder it is sufficient to prove an intent to cause really serious injury.

It cannot be right to allow the defence to one who may be more intent upon taking a life than the murderer. This leaves, of course, the anomaly that duress is available for the offence of wounding with intent but not to murder if the victim dies subsequently. But this flows from the special regard that the law has for human life, it may not be logical but it is real and has to be accepted.

I do not think that your Lordships should adopt the compromise solution of declaring that duress reduces murder to manslaughter. Where the defence of duress is available it is a complete excuse. This solution would put the law back to lines upon which Stephen suggested it should develop by regarding duress as a form of mitigation. English law has rejected this solution and it would be yet another anomaly to introduce it for the crime of murder alone. I would have been more tempted to go down this road if the death penalty had remained for murder. But the sentence for murder although mandatory and expressed as imprisonment for life, is in fact an indefinite sentence, which is kept constantly under review by the parole board and the Home Secretary with the assistance of the Lord Chief Justice and the trial judge. I have confidence that through this machinery the respective culpability of those involved in a murder case can be fairly weighed and reflected in the time they are required to serve in custody.

LORD MACKAY OF CLASHFERN

. . . The first question . . . that arises in this appeal is whether any distinction can be made between this case and the *Lynch* case . . . While . . . *Lynch* was decided by reasoning which does not extend to the present case, the question remains whether there is a potential distinction between this case and that of *Lynch* by which to determine whether or not the defence of duress should be available . . .

I have not found any satisfactory formulation of a distinction which would be sufficiently precise to be given practical effect in law and at the same time differentiate between levels of culpability so as to produce a satisfactory demarcation between those accused of murder, who should be entitled to resort to the defence of duress and those who were not.

The House is therefore, in my opinion, faced with the unenviable decision of either departing altogether from the doctrine that duress is not available in murder or of departing from the decision of this House in *Lynch*. While a variety of minor attacks on the reasoning of the majority were mounted by counsel for the Crown in the present case, I do not find any of these sufficiently important to merit departing from *Lynch* on these grounds. I do, however, consider that having regard to the balance of authority on the question of duress as a defence to murder prior to *Lynch*, for this House now to allow the defence of duress generally in response to a charge of murder would be to effect an important and substantial change in the law. In my opinion too, it would involve a departure from the decision in the famous case of *R. v Dudley and Stephens*. The justification for allowing a defence of duress to a charge of murder is that a defendant should be excused who killed as the only way of avoiding death himself or preventing the death of some close relation such as his own well-loved child. This essentially was the dilemma which Dudley and Stephens faced and in denying their defence the court refused to allow this consideration to be used in a defence to murder. If that refusal was right in the case of Dudley and Stephens it cannot be wrong in the present appeals. Although the result of recognising the defence advanced in that case would be that no crime was committed and in the case with which we are concerned that a murder was committed and a particular individual was not guilty of it (subject to the consideration of the second certified question) that does not distinguish the two cases from the point of view now being considered.

To change the law in the manner suggested by counsel for the appellants in the present case would, in my opinion, introduce uncertainty over a field of considerable importance . . .

[His Lordship referred to uncertainties in the defence of duress such as, whether a threat of loss of liberty suffices or whether the threatened harm must be to D or extends to his family, which would require further definition, or to any person.]

To say that a defence in respect of which so many questions remain unsettled should be introduced in respect of the whole field of murder is not to promote certainty in the law . . .

In my opinion, we would not be justified in the present state of the law in introducing for the first time into our law the concept of duress acting to reduce the charge to one of manslaughter even if there were grounds on which it might be right to do so. On that aspect of the matter the Law Commission took the view that where the defence of duress had been made out it would be unjust to stigmatise the person accused with a conviction and there is clearly much force in that view . . . It seems to me plain that the reason that it was for so long stated by writers of authority that the defence of duress was not available in a charge of murder was because of the supreme importance that the law afforded to the protection of human life and that it seemed repugnant that the law should recognise in any individual in any circumstances, however extreme, the right to choose that one innocent person should be killed rather than another. In my opinion, that is the question which we still must face. Is it right that the law should confer this right in any circumstances, however extreme? While I recognise fully the force of the reasoning which persuaded the majority of this House in *Lynch* to reach the decision to which they came in relation to a person not the actual killer, it does not address directly this question in relation to the actual killer. I am not persuaded that there is good reason to alter the answer which Hale gave to this question. No development of the law or progress in legal thinking which have taken place since his day have, to my mind, demonstrated a reason to change this fundamental answer. In the circumstances which I have narrated of a report to Parliament from the Law Commission concerned *inter alia* with this very question it would seem particularly inappropriate to make such a change now. For these reasons, in my opinion, the first certified question should be answered in the negative.

It follows that, in my opinion, the House should decline to follow the decision in *Lynch* . . . Up to the present time, the courts have been declining to allow an actual killer to plead the defence of duress while allowing it to a person charged with murder who was not the actual killer as is illustrated in the circumstances of these appeals. Lord Lane C.J. in *R. v Graham*, illustrated how technical and puzzling in practice the distinction could be. In my opinion, it would not be right to allow this state of affairs to continue. I recognise that this decision leaves certain apparent anomalies in the law but I regard these as consequences of the fact that murder is a result related to crime with a mandatory penalty. Consequently no distinction is made in penalty between the various levels of culpability. Differentiation in treatment once sentence has been pronounced depends upon action by the Crown advised by the executive government although that may be affected by a recommendation which the court is empowered to make. Where a person has taken a minor part in a wounding with intent and is dealt with on that basis he may receive a very short sentence. If sufficiently soon after that conviction the victim dies, on the same facts with the addition of the victim's death caused by the wounding he may be sentenced to life imprisonment. This is simply one illustration of the fact that very different results may follow from a set of facts together with the death of a victim from what would follow the same facts if the victim lived.

[Lord Bridge of Harwich and Lord Brandon of Oakbrook made speeches dismissing the appeal.]

Appeals dismissed

Questions

1. Lord Hailsham, knowing of many acts of heroism by ordinary people, concluded that a law which protected the "coward and the poltroon" could not be regarded as either "just or humane". Is there a general duty in the criminal law to be a hero? Against what standard is a defendant usually judged? (See self-defence, below and *Miller*, above.) Does Lord Hailsham provide any clear refutation of the statement by Wechsler and Michael in "A rationale of the law of homicide" (1937) 37 Col.L.R. 738, that "when a third person's life is also at stake even the path of heroism is obscure"?

2. Lord Griffiths stated "I would do nothing to undermine [the sanctity of human life], be it ever so slight." Does the criminal law unequivocally protect this ideal? (See self-defence, mistake and loss of control (previously known as provocation).)

3. Lord Griffiths supported the view of Lord Lane CJ in the Court of Appeal that the defence should not be afforded to a murderer as the "defence of duress is so easy to raise and may be so difficult for the prosecution to disprove." If this is the case, does not the same criticism apply to all defences? Is Lord Griffiths' view reconcilable with Lord Hailsham's view that "juries have been commendably robust" in rejecting the defence where appropriate (which they did in the case

before their Lordships)? Bearing in mind their Lordships' approval of Lord Lane's statement of the test for duress in *Graham*, whereby the defendant will be judged against the standard of the "sober person of reasonable firmness sharing the defendant's characteristics," is it any more likely that the unmeritorious defendant would succeed on a defence of duress where the charge is one of murder as opposed to theft or wounding or any other offence?

4. Lords Hailsham and MacKay placed considerable emphasis on the precedent of *Dudley and Stephens*, below, in dictating the result of the instant appeals. Is it true, as Lord Hailsham asserted, that that case has met with "very wide acceptance"? Is the defence of necessity wholly analogous to duress? Is necessity based on excuse or justification? Is it available for all offences (except murder)?

5. Lords Hailsham, Griffiths and MacKay placed considerable emphasis on the writers of the past (all of whom could be traced back to Hale) who stated that duress was not available as a defence to a charge of murder. Was this approach to be commended in light of the counsel of Lords Wilberforce and Edmund-Davies in *Abbott* at 771, where they stated:

> "Great stress has been laid by the majority of their Lordships upon the apparent unanimity with which great writers of the past have rejected duress as a defence, but, on any view, they have to be read with circumspection in these days, for the criminal courts have long accepted duress as an available defence to a large number of crimes from which those same writers withheld it."?

6. Lord Bridge stated that it is "by legislation alone . . . that the scope of the defence of duress can be defined with the degree of precision which, if it is to be available in murder at all, must surely be of critical importance". Lord MacKay also believed the defence was too uncertain for it to be extended to cover an actual killer. As duress is a common law defence (like self-defence and provocation) how did it develop in the first place? If duress is uncertain, is it not also uncertain in relation to other offences? What role do their Lordships envisage for judges if it is not to develop and clarify the common law? Is it arguable, as Milgate states in "Duress and the criminal law: another about turn by the House of Lords" (1988) 47 C.L.J. 61, that *Howe* is "a major piece of judicial legislation, based on an apparently cursory examination of principle and policy"?

7. Lord MacKay, having rejected the idea that, in relation to a murder charge, duress should operate like the defence of provocation and reduce the charge to one of manslaughter, sought to support his view by quoting from Law Commission, *Criminal Law Report on Defences of General Application* that "where the defence of duress had been made out it would be unjust to stigmatise the person accused with a conviction". Is Lord MacKay's reasoning convincing in light of the decision in *Howe* and the proposals of the Law Commission?

8. Lords Hailsham and Griffiths expressed the view that the issue of duress in murder would best be dealt with by the Executive through the agency of the Parole Board or Royal Pardon. Do you agree?

9. Lord Griffiths was of the opinion that duress should not be available on a charge of attempted murder. Would duress also need to be removed as a potential defence to charges under s.18 of the Offences Against the Person Act 1861? What would happen if, after an acquittal following a defence of duress on a charge under s.18, the victim died from the injuries inflicted by D?

Note

The decision in *Howe* left unresolved the question whether duress was a defence to attempted murder. This question arose for decision in the following case.

R. V GOTTS

[1992] 2 W.L.R. 284 HL

A, aged 16, was threatened with death by his father unless he killed his mother who had fled the matrimonial home. A followed his mother and stabbed her in the street but was restrained by bystanders so that, although she sustained serious injuries, she did not die. A pleaded duress on a charge of attempted murder. The trial judge ruled that duress was not available on a charge of attempted murder whereupon A pleaded guilty and an order of three years probation was made against him. The Court of Appeal dismissed A's appeal against his conviction.

LORD JAUNCEY OF TULLICHETTLE (with whom Lords Templeman and Browne-Wilkinson agreed):

[His Lordship, having referred to M. Hale, *The History of the Pleas of the Crown* (1736); W. Blackstone, *Commentaries on the Laws of England* (1776); H.L.C. Stephen, *History of the Criminal Law of England* (1883); and C.S. Kenny, *Outlines of Criminal Law*, 13th edn (Cambridge: Cambridge University Press, 1929) concluded:]

My Lords, there is nothing in the writings to which I have referred which leads me to conclude that at common law duress is or is not a defence to attempted murder. In arriving at this conclusion or lack of it I am fortified by the fact that Lord Lane C.J. [1991] 1 Q.B. 660, 667 came to a similar view where he said:

'In these circumstances we are not constrained by a common law rule or by authority from considering whether the defence of duress does or does not extend to the offence of attempted murder.' . . .

[His Lordship referred to *Lynch*, *Abbott* and *Howe* and concluded that these cases did not decide the question whether duress is available on a charge of attempted murder.]

As the question is still open for decision by your Lordships it becomes a matter of policy how it should be answered. It is interesting to note that there is no uniformity of practice in other common law countries. The industry of Mr Miskin who appeared with Mr Farrer disclosed that in Queensland, Tasmania, Western Australia, New Zealand and Canada duress is not available as a defence to attempted murder but that it is available in almost all of the states of the United States of America. The reason why duress has for so long been stated not to be available as a defence to a murder charge is that the law regards the sanctity of human life and the protection thereof as of paramount importance. Does that reason apply to attempted murder as well as to murder? As Lord Griffiths pointed out in [*Howe*, at p.303] an attempt to kill must be proved in the case of attempted murder but not necessarily in the case of murder. Is there logic in affording the defence to one who intends to kill but fails and denying it to one who mistakenly kills intending only to injure? If I may give two examples:

(1a) A stabs B in the chest intending to kill him and leaves him for dead. By good luck B is found whilst still alive and rushed to hospital where surgical skill saves his life.

(1b) C stabs D intending only to injure him and inflicts a near identical wound. Unfortunately D is not found until it is too late to save his life.

I see no justification or logic or morality for affording a defence of duress to A who intended to kill when it is denied to C who did not so intend.

(2a) E plants in a passenger aircraft a bomb timed to go off in midflight. Owing to bungling it explodes while the aircraft is still on the ground with the result that some 200 passengers suffer physical and mental injuries of which many are permanently disabling, but no one is killed.

(2b) F plants a bomb in a light aircraft intending to injure the pilot before it takes off but in fact it goes off in mid-air killing the pilot who is the sole occupant of the airplane.

It would in my view be both offensive to common sense and decency that E if he established duress should be acquitted and walk free without a stain on his character notwithstanding the appalling results which he has achieved, whereas F who never intended to kill should, if convicted in the absence of the defence, be sentenced to life imprisonment as a murderer.

It is of course true that withholding the defence in any circumstances will create some anomalies but I would agree with Lord Griffiths (*R. v Howe* [1987] A.C. 417, 444A) that nothing should be done to undermine in any way the highest duty of the law to protect the freedom and lives of those that live under it. I can therefore see no justification in logic, morality or law in affording to an attempted murderer the defence which is withheld from a murderer. The intent required of an attempted murderer is more evil than that required of a murderer and the line which divides the two offences is seldom, if ever, of the deliberate making of the criminal. A man shooting to kill but missing a vital organ by a hair's breadth can justify his action no more than can the man who hits that organ. It is pure chance that the attempted murderer is not a murderer and I entirely agree with what Lord Lane C.J. [1991] 1 Q.B. 660, 667 said: that the fact that the attempt failed to kill should not make any difference. For the foregoing reasons I have no doubt that the Court of Appeal reached the correct conclusion and that the appeal should be dismissed.

LORD LOWRY

(with whom Lord Keith of Kinkel agreed): . . . The basic proposition for the appellant is that at common law duress has always been a defence for those charged with every crime except murder, most forms of treason and possibly (for a short time) robbery and that to add attempted murder to the exceptions would not be justified. The trial judge, whose words I have cited earlier, may seem to have adopted the first part of this proposition but not the second. The answer by the Crown I suggest, has to be that attempted murder *is* at common law an exception to the general rule and was an exception at the time when the appellant tried to kill his mother . . .

The foundation of the Crown's argument is that, accepting the sanctity of human life as the basis for denying the defence of duress in murder, both logic and morality demand that that defence must be withheld from one who tried (albeit unsuccessfully), and therefore *intended*, to kill, when one considers that in murder the defence is withheld not only from the deliberate killer but also from the killer who intended only to inflict very serious injury and from all principals in the second degree, whatever their mens rea . . .

I sympathise with the proposition that attempted murder should be recognised as an exempted crime. But from the point of view of deterrence this idea holds no special attraction. If one makes the somewhat artificial assumption (without which the principle of deterrence has no meaning) that a potential offender will know when the defence of duress is not available, one then has to realise that, whatever the law may be about *attempted* murder, one who sets out to kill under threat will be guilty of murder if he succeeds. Therefore the deterrent is in theory operative already. The moral position, too, is clouded, because *Director of Public Prosecutions for Northern Ireland v Lynch* [1975] A.C. 653, in this respect alone affirming the majority opinion of the Court of Criminal Appeal in Northern Ireland, affirmed that the offender, even when acting under duress, intends to commit the crime (of murder, not attempted murder). But his guilty intent is of a special kind: 'coactus voluit,' as the Latin phrase has it. Thus the denial of the duress defence, based on moral principles, is not straightforward. It may not be just a case of the law saying: 'Although you did not succeed, you intended to kill. Therefore you cannot rely on duress.' The law might equally well say: 'As with other offenders who allege duress, your guilty intent was caused by threats. Therefore, since the intended victim did not die, you, like other offenders, can rely on those threats as a defence. If the victim had died in circumstances amounting to murder or if treason had been the crime, it would of course have been different.' This emphasises the point that murder is a result-related crime.

The choice is between the two views propounded by Lord Lane C.J. [1991] 1 Q.B. 660, 664f–g and 667b: (1) *if* the common law recognised that murder and treason were the only excepted crimes, then we are bound to accept that as the law, whether it seems a desirable conclusion or not; the fact that there is no binding decision on the point does not weaken a rule of the common law which has stood the test of time; or (2) we are not constrained by a common law rule or by authority from considering whether the defence of duress does or does not extend to the offence of attempted murder.

I consider that the view to be preferred is that which is contained in the first of these propositions and that to adopt the second would result in an unjustified judicial change in the law. It is only with diffidence that I would express an opinion on the criminal law which conflicts with that of such highly respected authorities as the present Lord Chief Justice and my noble and learned friend, Lord Griffiths, but on this occasion I feel obliged to do so. I proceed to give my reasons for this conclusion.

Both judges and textwriters have pointed out that the law on the subject is vague and uncertain . . . But, in my opinion, this vagueness ought not to encourage innovation which makes a departure from the received wisdom even if that wisdom is imperfect. This is particularly true if the innovation is retrospective in effect, to the prejudice of an accused person . . .

To withhold in respect of *every* crime the defence of duress, leaving it to the court (or, in relation to fixed penalty crimes, the executive) to take mitigating circumstances into account, seems logical. But to withhold that defence only from a selected list of serious crimes (some of which incur variable penalties) is questionable from a sentencing point of view, as indeed the sentence in the present case shows. The defence is withheld on the ground that the crime is so odious that it must not be palliated; and yet, if circumstances are allowed to mitigate the punishment, the principle on which the defence of duress is withheld has been defeated.

The fact that the sentence for attempted murder is at large is, with respect to those who think otherwise, no justification for withholding the defence of duress. Quite the reverse, because it is the theoretical inexcusability of murder and treason which causes those crimes (the fixed penalty for which can be mitigated only by the executive) to be deprived of the duress defence . . .

Having referred in the Court of Appeal's judgment [1991] 1 Q.B. 660 to the wise observations of Lord Griffiths in *R. v Howe* [1987] A.C. 417 on the undesirability of making available the defence of duress to any person who has deliberately killed, Lord Lane C.J. said [1991] 1 Q.B. 660, 667: 'It seems to us that if those considerations are well founded, the fact that the attempt failed to kill *should* not make any difference.' (Emphasis supplied.) But in my submission everything except the turpitude of attempted murder points away from saying that that offence is already at common law outside the ambit of the duress defence. And I further suggest that actual wickedness is not shown to be a dominant factor in the calculation compared with the result.

As I have said, your Lordships are concerned to say what the law is and not what it ought to be. So far from clearing the way for judges to declare that attempted murder is an excepted crime, the uncertainty and vagueness surrounding duress ought to induce caution before deciding to reject the received wisdom on the subject. What we can be clear about is that the common law regards duress as *generally available* but not available in cases of murder and treason, and the statutory codes treat duress as generally available except as expressly mentioned . . .

If the common law has had a policy towards duress heretofore, it seems to have been to go by the result and not primarily by the intent and, if a change of policy is needed with regard to criminal liability, it must be made prospectively by Parliament and not retrospectively by a court.

I am not influenced in favour of the appellant by the supposed illogicality of distinguishing between attempted murder on the one hand and conspiracy and incitement to murder on the other and I agree on this point with the view of Lord Lane C.J.: short of murder itself, attempted murder is a special crime. But I am not swayed in favour of the Crown by the various examples of the anomalies which are said to result from holding that the duress defence applies to attempted murder. As Lord Lane CJ. said, at p.668B, it would be possible to suggest anomalies wherever the line is drawn. The real logic would be to grant or withhold the duress defence universally.

Attempted murder, however heinous we consider it, was a misdemeanour. Until 1861 someone who shot and missed could suffer no more than two years' imprisonment and I submit that, when attempted murder became a felony, that crime, like many other serious felonies, continued to have available the defence of duress.

My Lords, having considered all the arguments on either side, I am of the opinion that your Lordships *are* constrained by a common law rule (though not by judicial authority) from holding that the defence of duress does not apply to attempted murder. Accordingly, I would allow the appeal, quash the conviction and set aside the probation order but, in the special circumstances of this case, I would not propose that a new trial be ordered.

Appeal dismissed

Questions

1.   Was the decision of the majority one of principle or policy?

2.   J. Raz in "The rule of law and its virtue" (1977) 93 L.Q.R. 195, 198–199 states:

"*All laws should be prospective, open and clear.* One cannot be guided by a retroactive law. It does not exist at the time of action . . .. The law must be open and adequately publicised. If it is to guide people they must be able to find out what it is. For the same reason its meaning must be clear. An ambiguous, vague, obscure or imprecise law is likely to mislead or confuse at least some of those who desire to be guided by it."

Were these principles observed by the majority in *Gotts*? If someone seeking to know the law in advance of action inquired whether duress is a defence to the offences of wounding with intent contrary to s.18 of the Offences Against the Person Act 1861, or incitement to kill or conspiracy to murder, would it be possible to provide a clear answer?

3.   Lord Keith of Kinkel stated at pp.285–286:

"The principal argument against allowing the defence of duress to a charge of attempted murder appears to be what is said to be the illogicality of denying the defence to one who has killed while intending only to wound with intent to inflict grievous bodily harm, while admitting it in the case of one who has intended to kill but chanced to fail to do so. Considering that the intent is more evil in the latter case than in the former, so it is claimed, the person who has intended to kill but failed should not be treated more leniently. But I find it difficult to accept that a person acting under duress had a truly evil intent. He does not actually desire the death of the victim. In the case of a man who is compelled by threats against his wife and children to drive a vehicle loaded with explosives into a checkpoint, the object being to kill those manning it, but that object having fortunately failed, the driver is likely to be as relieved at the outcome as anyone else. It would be hard to condemn him as having had an evil intent. The logical solution may be to withhold the defence in the case of all crimes, leaving the circumstances of the duress to be taken into account in mitigation. But that solution is not open to the court in the present state of the law. It could only be brought about by Parliament."

Is it likely that the argument in future may move to the meaning of intent with an accused charged with attempted murder who seeks to plead duress relying on authorities such as *Steane* [1947] K.B. 997 (above); and *Gillick v West Norfolk & Wisbech AHA* [1986] A.C. 112 (below p.263)? See the extract from his commentary on Howe by J.C. Smith which follows.

J.C. SMITH, "COMMENTARY" [1987] CRIM. L.R. 483–484

. . . *Duress and intent* Lord Hailsham agreed with the opinions of Lords Kilbrandon and Edmund-Davies in *Lynch* that duress does not negative intention. Where the defence of duress is allowed, this is notwithstanding the fact that the defendant intended to commit the crime. It is submitted that this is right—but it is surely inconsistent with *Steane* [1947] K.B. 997, recently accepted as rightly decided by the House in *Moloney* [1985] A.C. 905. Steane, of course, knew that he was doing an act of assistance to the enemy war effort but was held not to intend to assist the enemy because his purpose was to avert the threat of the concentration camp to himself and his family. If that negatived intention, so surely does a purpose of saving one's own life. The present case suggests that *Steane* would have been more properly acquitted on the ground that he acted with intent to assist the enemy under duress. Unfortunately, however, it is likely to continue to bedevil discussion of the meaning of intention.

There is a similar problem with *Gillick's* case [1986] A.C. 112 and the matter of the *mens rea* of an aider and abettor of crime. The reason why a doctor who gives contraceptive advice to a girl under the age of 16 is not guilty of aiding and abetting the commission of an offence under section 6 of the Sexual Offences Act 1956 is nowhere clearly spelt out in the speeches of the majority, but one view for which there is considerable support is that he lacks the necessary intent. But if it is said that the hypothetical doctor, doing an act which he knows will promote, encourage or facilitate the commission of an offence, is not guilty because his real intention is to protect the girl, how can it be said that a person intends to aid and abet murder when his real object is to save himself or others from death? If that object does not negative intention to aid and abet, surely, *a fortiori*, the object of protecting the girl cannot do so.

Note

While *Gotts* dealt with the problem of attempted murder, further anomalies remain unresolved. In *Gotts*, Lord Lane CJ opined that duress would be available on a charge of conspiracy to murder or incitement to murder as they are one stage further away from the completed offence than is attempt. In *Ness and Awan* [2011] Crim. L.R. 645, McCombe J left the defence of duress to the jury for their consideration in a case of conspiracy to murder. This approach seems to ignore the fact that for D to be convicted of conspiracy to murder it must be proved he had an intention that V be killed; this is the same mens rea that was used by the House of Lords in *Gotts* to justify denying the defence in attempted murder.

----

vi. Proposals for Reform

Note

In *Legislating the Criminal Code: Offences Against the Person and General Principles* (Law Com No.218), the Law Commission recommended that the burden of proving the defence of duress should be placed on D on a balance of probabilities, and that the defence should be available in respect of a charge of murder or attempted murder, thereby reversing the House of Lords' decisions in *Howe* and *Gotts*. The change in the burden of proof was presented partly as a trade-off to make the availability of the defence to murder more acceptable (see paras 33.2 and 33.3). In addition, the Law Commission regarded the defence of duress by threats as "wholly exceptional, depending on factors unique to that defence which distinguish it from all others" (para.33.5) as "it is much more likely than any other defence to depend on assertions which are peculiarly difficult for the prosecution to investigate or disprove" (para.33.6). In particular, in duress "the circumstances on which the defence is founded will characteristically have occurred well before, and quite separately from, the actual commission of the offence" (para.33.7).

In the subsequent Report, *Murder, Manslaughter and Infanticide* (Law Com No.304; http://www.lawcom.gov.uk/wp-content/uploads/2015/03/lc304_Murder_Manslaughter_and_Infanticide_Report.pdf [Accessed 17 March 2016]), where the Law Commission recommended that murder be reformed to create two offences of first degree murder and second degree murder, they further recommended that:

(1) duress should be a full defence to first degree murder, second degree murder and attempted murder;

(2) for duress to be a defence to first degree murder, second degree murder and attempted murder, the threat must be one of death or life-threatening harm;

(3) the defendant should bear the legal burden of proving the qualifying conditions of the defence on a balance of probabilities.

At paras 6.43 and 6.44 the Law Commission provide the following explanation for this recommendation:

> 6.43 The argument that duress should be a full defence to first degree murder has a moral basis. It is that the law should not stigmatise a person who, on the basis of a genuine and reasonably held belief, intentionally killed in fear of death or life-threatening injury in circumstances where a jury is satisfied that an ordinary person of reasonable fortitude might have acted in the same way. If a reasonable person might have acted as D did, then the argument for withholding a complete defence is undermined. In the words of Professor Ormerod, 'if the jury find that the defendant has, within the terms of the defence, acted reasonably, it seems unfair to treat him as a second degree murderer or even a manslaughterer'.
>
> 6.44 Further, the option also accords with the way that duress operates as a complete defence in relation to other offences and it is, therefore, conducive to coherence and consistency. . .

The Law Commission, however, reaffirmed their commitment to the burden of proof resting upon the defendant where duress is pleaded in respect of murder, adopting the position of Lord Bingham of Cornhill in *Hasan* that duress is "peculiarly difficult for the prosecution to investigate and disprove beyond reasonable doubt". As the Law Commission's recommendations relating to murder have not been implemented, it is unlikely that their proposals in relation to duress will be implemented.

----

3. NECESSITY

i. A defence of necessity?

Note

Criminal lawyers have for a considerable time debated the question whether a general defence of necessity exists in English law. Duress by threats relates to the situation where a person commits an offence to avoid a greater evil of death or serious injury to himself or another threatened by a third party. The defence operates to excuse him from criminal liability. Necessity relates to the situation where a person commits an offence to avoid a greater evil to himself or another which would ensue from the circumstances in which he or that other are placed. It was thought that if the defence of necessity existed it operated as a justification rendering the accused's conduct lawful. The dicta in the cases both as to the existence of the defence and its operation as either an excuse or justification are scant and contradictory.

Early writers on English law such as Bracton, Coke and Hale all quoted maxims which conceded that necessity might justify conduct which would otherwise be unlawful. In *Moore v Hussey* (1609) Hob 96, Hobart J stated:

> "All laws admit certain cases of just excuse, when they are offended in the letter, and where the offender is under necessity, either of compulsion or inconvenience."

The examples of necessity these writers supplied were pulling down a house to prevent a fire spreading, a prisoner escaping from a burning jail although statute made prison-breach a felony, jettisoning cargo to save a vessel in a storm (see *Mouse's Cases* (1620) 12 Co. Rep. 63). Obiter dicta in 20th century cases have been inconclusive. In *Buckoke v GLC* [1971] Ch. 655 at 668 Lord Denning stated:

"During the argument I raised the question: Might not the driver of a fire engine be able to raise the defence of necessity? I put this illustration: A driver of a fire engine with ladders approaches the traffic lights. He sees 200 yards down the road a blazing house with a man at an upstairs window in extreme peril. The road is clear in all directions. At that moment the lights turn red. Is the driver to wait for 60 seconds, or more, for the lights to turn green? If the driver waits for that time, the man's life will be lost. I suggested to both counsel that the driver might be excused in crossing the lights to save the man. He might have the defence of necessity. Both counsel denied it. They would not allow him any defence in law. The circumstances went to mitigation, they said, and did not take away his guilt. If counsel are correct—and I accept that they are—nevertheless such a man should not be prosecuted. He should be congratulated."

[The particular question in this case is of academic interest only since drivers of fire engines, police cars and ambulances are now allowed in emergencies to regard red traffic lights as warnings to give way (Traffic Signs Regulations 2002 (SI 2002/3113) reg.33). They are also permitted to exceed speed limits (Road Traffic Regulation Act 1984 s.87).]

Similarly in *London Borough of Southwark v Williams* [1971] 2 All E.R. 175 at 179, Lord Denning stated:

"[I]f hunger were once allowed to be an excuse for stealing, it would open a way through which all kinds of disorder and lawlessness would pass. So here. If homelessness were once admitted as a defence to trespass, no one's house could be safe. Necessity would open a door which no man could shut. It would not only be those in extreme need who would enter. There would be others who would imagine that they were in need, or would invent a need, so as to gain entry. Each man would say his need was greater than the next man's. The plea would be an excuse for all sorts of wrongdoing. So the courts must, for the sake of law and order, take a firm stand. They must refuse to admit the pleas of necessity to the hungry and the homeless; and trust that their distress will be relieved by the charitable and the good."

Edmund Davies LJ considered that there was a defence of necessity but it would not avail the squatters in the instant case as the defence was dependent on there being "an urgent situation of imminent peril".

In several traffic cases there are obiter dicta to the effect that there is a defence of necessity. In *Johnson v Phillips* [1976] 1 W.L.R. 65, a motorist was instructed by a police officer to reverse the wrong way down a narrow one-way street in order to allow ambulances access to injured persons further up the street. On his refusal he was charged with wilful obstruction of a constable in the execution of his duty. Wien J at 69:

"The precise question that has to be answered in the instant case may be put thus: has a constable in purported exercise of his power to control traffic on a public road the right under common law to disobey a traffic regulation such as going the wrong way along a one-way street? If he himself has that right then it follows that he can oblige others to comply with his instructions to disobey such a regulation. If, for example, a bomb had been planted in The Windsor public house and the exit from Cannon Street had in some way been blocked, could he lawfully reverse a police vehicle and oblige any other motorist then present in the road to reverse his own vehicle? The answer is yes, provided that in the execution of his duty he was acting to protect life or property: see *Hoffman v Thomas* [1974] 1 W.L.R. 374, 379 . . . In the judgment of this court a constable would be entitled, and indeed under a duty, to give such instruction if it were reason-ably necessary for the protection of life or property."

In *Wood v Richards* [1977] R.T.R. 201, Eveleigh J stated:

"In so far as the defence of necessity is relied on . . . [t]here is no evidence at all in this case of the nature of the emergency to which the defendant [a police officer] was being summoned. As the defence of necessity to the extent that it exists must depend on the degree of emergency or the alternative danger to be averted, it is quite impossible in the present case to express the view that the defence was open to the defendant."

This view suggests that had there been evidence of the nature of the emergency the defence could have been considered by weighing that emergency against the manner in which the defendant drove his car which had given rise to the charge of careless driving. See also *R. v O'Toole* (1971) Cr. App. R. 206.

More recently, cases involving driving offences have given rise to the recognition of the defence of duress of circumstances (see below).

In *DPP v Harris* [1995] 1 Cr. App. R. 170, the Divisional Court spoke in terms of the common law defence of necessity being available to a charge of reckless driving, but held that it was not available on a charge of careless driving in the instant case, being excluded by the terms of the Traffic Signs Regulations which relates to the circumstances in which a police vehicle may ignore a traffic light showing red. In another Divisional Court case, *Cichon v DPP* [1994] Crim. L.R. 918, the court held that a defence of necessity was not available on a charge of allowing a pit bull terrier to be in a public place without being muzzled, contrary to s.1(2)(d) of the Dangerous Dogs Act 1991, as the offence was an absolute one and Parliament could not have intended that it should apply.

In several other cases the decisions appear to have been based on necessity although that term was not used. In *R. v Bourne*, a surgeon in a London hospital performed an abortion on a 14-year-old rape victim. He was charged with *unlawfully* using an instrument with intent to procure a miscarriage, con-trary to s.58 of the Offences Against the Person Act 1861. Macnaghten J, in directing the jury, defined the word "unlawfully" to mean an act "not done in good faith for the purpose only of preserving the life of the mother." As necessity is a defence of justification, and justification renders lawful an act which would otherwise be unlawful, was Macnaghten J impliedly directing the jury on necessity? (See Lord Edmund-Davies in *Southwark London Borough Council v Williams* [1971] Ch. 734 at 746.)

In *Gillick v West Norfolk & Wisbech AHA* [1986] A.C. 112, the House of Lords stated that where a doctor prescribed contraceptives for a girl under 16, he would not be guilty of aiding, abetting, coun-selling or procuring the offence of unlawful sexual intercourse committed by her with a man provided certain circumstances pertained. These were detailed by Lord Scarman as follows:

"Clearly a doctor who gives a girl contraceptive advice or treatment not because in his clinical judgment the treatment is medically indicated for the maintenance or restoration of her health but with the intention of facilitating her having unlawful sexual intercourse may well be guilty of a criminal offence. It would depend, as my noble and learned friend, Lord Fraser of Tullybelton, observes, upon the doctor's intention—a conclusion hardly to be wondered at in the field of the criminal law . . . He may prescribe only if she has the capacity to consent or if exceptional cir-cumstances exist which justify him in exercising his clinical judgment without parental consent. The adjective 'clinical' emphasises that it must be a medical judgment based upon what he honestly believes to be necessary for the physical, mental, and emotional health of his patient.

The bona fide exercise by a doctor of his clinical judgment must be a complete negation of the guilty mind which is an essential ingredient of the criminal offence of aiding and abetting the commission of unlawful sexual intercourse."

Question

If a doctor knows that contraceptives will encourage an underage girl to engage in sexual intercourse but he prescribes them to protect her physically, emotionally and mentally from the trauma of unwanted pregnancy or even abortion, how can his motive in prescribing the contraceptives negate his guilty mind? Is this not in reality a defence of necessity providing a justification for the doctor's act which otherwise would be criminal?

In the case which follows, necessity was given recognition by the House of Lords.

RE F (MENTAL PATIENT: STERILISATION)

[1990] 2 A.C. 1 HL

(For the facts of this case see below.)

LORD GOFF OF CHIEVELEY

That there exists in the common law a principle of necessity which may justify action which would otherwise be unlawful is not in doubt. But historically the principle has been seen to be restricted to two groups of cases, which have been called cases of public necessity and cases of private necessity. The former occurred in the Great Fire of London in 1666. The latter cases occurred when a man interfered with another man's property in the public interest—for example (in the days before we could dial 999 for the fire brigade) the destruction of another man's house to prevent the spread of a catastrophic fire, as indeed occurred when a man interfered with another's property to save his own person or property from imminent danger—for example, when he entered upon his neighbour's land without his consent, in order to prevent the spread of fire onto his own land.

There is, however, a third group of cases, which is also properly described as founded upon the principle of necessity and which is more pertinent to the resolution of the problem in the present case. These cases are concerned with action taken as a matter of necessity to assist another person without his consent. To give a simple example, a man who seizes another and forcibly drags him from the path of an oncoming vehicle, thereby saving him from injury or even death, commits no wrong. But there are many emanations of this principle, to be found scattered through the books. These are concerned not only with the preservation of the life or health of the assisted person, but also with the preservation of his property (sometimes an animal, sometimes an ordinary chattel) and even with certain conduct on his behalf in the administration of his affairs. Where there is a pre-existing relationship between the parties, the intervenor is usually said to act as an agent of necessity on behalf of the principal in whose interests he acts, and his action can often, with not too much artificiality, be referred to the pre-existing relationship between them. Whether the intervenor may be entitled either to reimbursement or to remuneration raises separate questions which are not relevant in the present case.

We are concerned here with action taken to preserve the life, health or well-being of another who is unable to consent to it. Such action is sometimes said to be justified as arising from an emergency; in *Prosser and Keeton, Handbook on Torts*, 5th ed. (1984), p.117, the action is said to be privileged by the emergency. Doubtless, in the case of a person of sound mind, there will ordinarily have to be an emergency before such action taken without consent can be lawful; for otherwise there would be an opportunity to communicate with the assisted person and to seek his consent. But this is not always so; and indeed the historical origins of the principle of necessity do not point to emergency as such as providing the criterion of lawful intervention without consent. The old Roman doctrine of negotiorum gestio presupposed not so much an emergency as a prolonged absence of the dominus from home as justifying intervention by the gestor to administer his affairs. The most ancient group of cases in the common law, concerned with action taken by the master of a ship in distant parts in the interests of the shipowner, likewise found its origin in the difficulty of communication with the owner over a prolonged period of time—a difficulty overcome today by modern means of communication. In those cases, it was said that there had to be an emergency before the master could act as agent of necessity; though the emergency could well be of some duration. But when a person is rendered incapable of communication either permanently or over a considerable period of time (through illness or accident or mental disorder), it would be an unusual use of language to describe the case as one of 'permanent emergency'—if indeed such a state of affairs can properly be said to exist. In truth, the relevance of an emergency is that it may give rise to a necessity to act in the interests of the assisted person, without first obtaining his consent. Emergency is however not the criterion or even a pre-requisite; it is simply a frequent origin of the necessity which impels intervention. The principle is one of necessity, not of emergency.

We can derive some guidance as to the nature of the principle of necessity from the cases on agency of necessity in mercantile law. When reading those cases, however, we have to bear in mind that it was there considered that (since there was a pre-existing relationship between the parties) there was a duty on the part of the agent to act on his principal's behalf in an emergency. From these cases it appears that the principle of necessity connotes that circumstances have arisen in which there is a necessity for the agent to act on his principal's behalf at a time when it is in practice not possible for him to obtain his principal's instructions so to do. In such cases, it has been said that the agent must act bona fide in the interests of his principal: see *Prager v Blatspiel Stamp & Heacock Ltd* [1924] 1 K.B. 566, 572 per McCardie J. A broader statement of the principle is to be found in the advice of the Privy Council delivered by Sir Montague Smith in *Australasian Steam Navigation Co. v Morse* (1872) L.R. 4 P.C. 222, 230, in which he said.

> 'when by the force of circumstances a man has the duty cast upon him of taking some action for another, and under that obligation, adopts the course which, to the judgment of a wise and prudent man, is apparently the best for the interest of the persons for whom he acts in a given emergency, it may properly be said of the course so taken, that it was, in a mercantile sense, necessary to take it.'

In a sense, these statements overlap. But from them can be derived the basic requirements, applicable in these cases of necessity, that, to fall within the principle, not only (1) must there be a necessity to act when it is not practicable to communicate with the assisted person, but also (2) the action taken must be such as a reasonable person would in all the circumstances take, acting in the best interests of the assisted person.

(For further extracts from Lord Goff's speech see below.)

Question

1. Did Lord Goff recognise necessity as an excuse or justification?
2. The three categories of situation which give rise to a defence of necessity are quite narrow; would the doctors in *Bourne* or *Gillick* be able to bring themselves within any of these categories if charged with a criminal offence?

Notes

1. In *R. v Bournewood Community and Mental Health NHS Trust* [1998] 3 All E.R. 289, the defence of necessity was recognised and applied by the House of Lords to justify the informal detention and treatment of a mentally incompetent person who had become a danger to himself. The formal procedures under the Mental Health Act 1983 had not been invoked but the House of Lords held that the common law doctrine of necessity applied, Lord Goff of Chieveley stating:

> "I have no doubt that all the steps in fact taken . . . were in fact taken in the best interests of Mr. L and, in so far as they might otherwise have constituted an invasion of his civil rights, were justified on the basis of the common law doctrine of necessity."

While this case is an example of the defence of necessity being applied, the reasoning of their Lordships does not supply any further explanation of the rationale underpinning the defence nor any further guidance on its ambit and operation.

2. In *R. (Nicklinson) v Ministry of Justice* [2012] EWHC 2381 (Admin), the Divisional Court ruled that the defence of necessity would not be available to any person who might assist the claimant, a sufferer of "locked-in" syndrome, to end his life. The Court recognised the difference between a doctor not seeking to prolong life and positively acting to end life; the former would not involve any criminal liability as was recognised in *Airedale NHS Trust v Bland* (above, p.34) but extending the law to cover the latter would involve a major change, rather than an incremental development, involving controversial matters of social policy which it was for Parliament to resolve rather than the courts.

----

ii. Duress of circumstances

Note

The categories of situation giving rise to a defence of necessity are very narrow. In recent years, however, the defence of duress has been widened to cover an imminent threat of death or serious injury arising from the circumstances in which the accused finds himself. The earlier cases all involved driving offences where the accused has driven recklessly (see *Willer* (1986) 83 Cr. App. R. 225; *Conway* [1988] 3 All E.R. 1025) or has driven whilst disqualified from driving (see *Martin* [1989] 1 All E.R. 652) or has driven with excess alcohol (see *DPP v Bell* [1992] Crim. L.R. 176) in order to avoid a threat of death or serious injury to himself or a third party. In *R. v Pommell* [1995] 2 Cr. App. R. 607 the Court of Appeal confirmed that the defence is not so limited and applies to all crimes except murder, attempted murder and some forms of treason. In cases of duress by threats the party issuing the threats dictates the criminal offence the accused must commit to avoid the threatened harm (see *Cole*, above); in the cases of duress of circumstances which have arisen the accused has chosen to commit a particular crime to avoid the threatened harm but the defence does not appear to be limited to such situations. In *Conway*, Woolf LJ explained the rationale of the defence in the following terms (at 1029):

> "As the learned editors point out in Smith and Hogan *Criminal Law* (6th edn. 1988) p.225, to admit a defence of 'duress of circumstances' is a logical consequence of the existence of the defence of duress as that term is ordinarily understood, ie 'do this or else'. This approach does no more than recognise that duress is an example of necessity. Whether 'duress of circumstances' is called 'duress' or 'necessity' does not matter. What is important is that, whatever it is called, it is subject to the same limitations as the 'do this or else' species of duress. As Lord Hailsham LC said in his speech in *R. v Howe* [1987] 1 All ER 771 at 777, [1987] AC 417 at 429:
>
> There is, of course, an obvious distinction between duress and necessity as potential defences: duress arises from the wrongful threats or violence of another human being and necessity arises from any other objective dangers threatening the accused. This, however, is, in my view a distinction without a relevant difference, since on this view duress is only that species of the genus of necessity which is caused by wrongful threats. I cannot see that there is any way in which a person of ordinary fortitude can be excused from the one type of pressure on his will rather than the other."

In *Martin*, Simon Brown J sought to summarise the principles relating to duress of circumstances (at 653–654):

"The principles may be summarised thus: first, English law does, in extreme circumstances, recognise a defence of necessity. Most commonly this defence arises as duress, that is pressure on the accused's will from the wrongful threats or violence of another. Equally however it can arise from other objective dangers threatening the accused or others. Arising thus it is conveniently called 'duress of circumstances'.

Second, the defence is available only if, from an objective standpoint, the accused can be said to be acting reasonably and proportionately in order to avoid a threat of death or serious injury.

Third, assuming the defence to be open to the accused on his account of the facts, the issue should be left to the jury, who should be directed to determine these two questions: first, was the accused, or may he have been, impelled to act as he did because as a result of what he reasonably believed to be the situation he had good cause to fear that otherwise death or serious physical injury would result; second, if so, would a sober person of reasonable firmness, sharing the characteristics of the accused, have responded to that situation by acting as the accused acted? If the answer to both those questions was Yes, then the jury would acquit; the defence of necessity would have been established.

That the defence is available in cases of reckless driving is established by *R. v Conway* itself and indeed by an earlier decision of the court in *R. v Wilier* (1986) 83 Cr.App.R. 225. *R. v Conway* is authority also for the proposition that the scope of the defence is no wider for reckless driving than for other serious offences. As was pointed out in the judgment, 'reckless driving can kill' (see [1988] 3 All E.R. 1025 at 1029, [1988] 3 W.L.R. 1238 at 1244).

We see no material distinction between offences of reckless driving and driving whilst disqualified so far as the application and scope of this defence is concerned. Equally we can see no distinction in principle between various threats of death; it matters not whether the risk of death is by murder or by suicide or indeed by accident. One can illustrate the latter by considering a disqualified driver being driven by his wife, she suffering a heart attack in remote countryside and he needing instantly to get her to hospital."

In *Cole* (see above) the Court of Appeal stated that a "situation of imminent peril" is a necessary precondition to the defence arising (see further *Abdul-Hussain*, above). It is clear, too, that the accused must desist from the commission of the crime as soon as he reasonably can. In *Pommell* the accused was convicted of possessing a prohibited weapon without a firearms certificate. He raised the defence of duress of circumstances, alleging that he had persuaded X, who had visited him in the night, to give him the gun in order to prevent X shooting people who had killed his friend. The trial judge ruled that the accused's failure to take the gun to the police immediately deprived him of the defence. The Court of Appeal held that the question of the reasonableness of the accused's actions, taking into account the surrounding circumstances, ought to have been left to the jury, particularly where, as here, some explanation was offered for the delay in desisting from committing the offence. Only where the delay is such as to make it clear that the duress must have ceased to operate is the judge entitled to withdraw the defence from the jury (see also *DPP v Bell* (1992) R.T.R. 335; and *DPP v Jones* (1990) R.T.R. 33).

While the principles applying in duress and duress of circumstances cases are the same, the Court of Appeal in *Abdul-Hussain* (see above) drew attention to one issue, proportionality, which may be of greater significance in cases of duress of circumstances where D chooses the offence he commits in response to the perceived threat rather than it being specified by a duressor. The jury have to consider whether the offence D committed was a reasonable and proportionate response to the threat perceived in the circumstances. This forms part of the objective question whether a reasonable person would have done as D did.

A further limitation on pleading duress of circumstances is that the threat D perceives must come from an extraneous source. In *Rodger & Rose* [1998] 1 Cr. App. R. 143, the appellants sought to raise the defence of duress of circumstances on charges of breaking prison claiming they had done so as they had become suicidal in prison. The Court of Appeal affirmed the trial judge's decision not to leave the defence to the jury as the source of the threat was "the thought processes and emotions of the offenders themselves" and not some extraneous to them. To allow such a development "could amount to a licence to commit crime dependent on the personal characteristics and vulnerability of the offender."

Questions

1. The facts of *Pommell* do not disclose any relationship between the accused and those against whom the threatened harm was directed. Is it appropriate to use the language of duress and speak of D's will being overborne in such a case? Would it not be more correctly approached as a defence of necessity? See J.C. Smith [1994] Crim. L.R. 918.

2. When Lord Hailsham stated that "duress is only that species of genus of necessity which is caused by wrongful threats" was he correct and is this statement reconcilable with Lord Goff's speech in *Re F*, i.e. can a genus which is a justification give birth to a species which is an excuse?

3. The Divisional Court in *DPP v Harris* [1995] 1 Cr. App. R. 170 when applying the *Martin* test stated that a court must "look at all the circumstances, including the nature and extent of the emergency, in order to determine objectively whether in driving as he did a defendant acted reasonably and proportionately". McCowan LJ went on to consider the potential evil "to be put into the scales". Are these not elements of the defence of necessity in which D makes a rational judgment rather than a test to be applied to the defence of duress?

4. Will the existence of the defence of duress of circumstances assist or obstruct the future development of a general defence of necessity based on the concept of balancing of harms?

5. D, driving his car approaches a traffic light which changes to red. Further along the road he sees a child fall into a river. D drives on both ignoring the traffic light and breaking the speed limit to effect a rescue of the child. On being tried for both driving offences could D plead in his defence either necessity or duress of circumstances (cf. Lord Denning in *Buckoke* and *Conway* and *Martin*)?

----

iii. Necessity, duress of circumstances and homicide

Duress by threats is no defence to a charge of murder (see *Howe*, above) and the same applies to duress of circumstances (see Woolf LJ in *Conway*, above). Is there a residual defence of necessity to a charge of homicide?

R. V DUDLEY AND STEPHENS

(1884) 14 QBD 273

D and S and a boy were cast away from a ship on the high seas and drifted for 20 days in an open boat. They had hardly any food or water during that time, and fearing they would all die soon unless they obtained some sustenance D and S killed the boy, who was likely to die first anyway, and ate his flesh. Four days later they were rescued, and were subsequently indicted for the boy's murder. The jury found the facts of the case in a special verdict and the case was adjourned for argument before five judges.

LORD COLERIDGE CJ

. . . Now it is admitted that the deliberate killing of this unoffending and unresisting boy was clearly murder, unless the killing can be justified by some well-recognised excuse admitted by the law. It is further admitted that there was in this case no such excuse, unless the killing was justified by what has been called 'necessity'. But the temptation to the act which existed here was not what the law has ever called necessity. Nor is this to be regretted. Though law and morality are not the same, and many things may be immoral which are not necessarily illegal, yet the absolute divorce of law from morality would be of fatal consequence; and such divorce would follow if the temptation to murder in this case were to be held by law an absolute defence of it. It is not so. To preserve one's life is generally speaking a duty, but it may be the plainest and the highest duty to sacrifice it. War is full of instances in which it is a man's duty not to live, but to die. The duty, in case of shipwreck, of a captain to his crew, of the crew to the passengers, of soldiers to women and children, as in the noble case of the *Birkenhead*; these duties impose on man the moral necessity, not of the preservation, but of the sacrifice of their lives for others, from which in no country, least of all, it is to be hoped, in England, will men shrink, as indeed, they have not shrunk. It is not correct, therefore, to say that there is any absolute or unqualified necessity to preserve one's life. 'Necesse est ut earn, non ut vivam', is a saying of a Roman officer quoted by Lord Bacon himself with high eulogy in the very chapter on necessity to which so much reference has been made. It would be a very easy and cheap display of commonplace learning to quote from Greek and Latin authors, from Horace, from Juvenal, from Cicero, from Euripides, passage after passage, in which the duty of dying for others has been laid down in glowing and emphatic language as resulting from the principles of heathen ethics; it is enough in a Christian country to remind ourselves of the Great Example whom we profess to follow. It is not needful to point out the lawful danger of admitting the principle which has been contended for. Who is to be the judge of this sort of necessity? By what measure is the comparative value of lives to be measured? Is it to be strength or intellect, or what? It is plain that the principle leaves to him who is to profit by it to determine the necessity which will . . . justify him in deliberately taking another's life to save his own. In this case the weakest, the youngest, the most unresisting, was chosen. Was it more necessary to kill him than one of the grown men? The answer must be 'No' . . .

It must not be supposed that in refusing to admit temptation to be an excuse for crime it is forgotten how terrible the temptation was; how awful the suffering; how hard in such trials to keep the judgment straight and the conduct pure. We are often compelled to set up standards we cannot reach ourselves, and to lay down rules which we could not ourselves satisfy. But a man has no right to declare temptation to be an excuse, though he might himself have yielded to it, nor allow compassion for the criminal to change or weaken in any manner the legal definition of the crime. It is therefore our duty to declare that the prisoners' act in this case was wilful murder, that the facts as stated in the verdict are no legal justification of the homicide; and to say that in our unanimous opinion the prisoners are upon this special verdict guilty of murder.

Sentence of death
Commuted later to six months' imprisonment

Question

Consider and compare the following examples often found in textbooks:

A shipwrecked sailor, clinging to a plank which will only support the weight of one man, prevents another from grasping the plank, so that that other dies by drowning.

The man on the plank is pushed off by the swimmer, who takes his place, leaving him to drown.

The lower of two roped rock-climbers slips and falls. The upper is not strong enough to hold him and to save himself from a certain fall, cuts the lower man free, so that he falls to his death.

X, Y and Z are stranded at the foot of a cliff with the tide coming in. A rope ladder is lowered to them which X starts to ascend but fearing heights he stops and clings to it petrified refusing to move up or down. Y, fearing that he and Z will drown, tells Z, who is immediately below X on the ladder, to pull X off. Z does so and X falls to the rocks below where he dies from drowning while Y and Z climb to safety.

Note

In *US v Holmes* (1842) 25 Fed.Cas. 360, the accused was convicted of the manslaughter of 16 passengers whom he had thrown out of an overcrowded lifeboat. The judge would, it seems, have allowed a defence of necessity if the choice had been made by the drawing of lots.

The extracts below illustrate the moral and philosophical challenge which necessity as a defence to homicide presents.

CROSS "MURDER UNDER DURESS" (1978) 28 U.T.L.J. 369, 377

Speaking of the hypothetical case of the two shipwrecked mariners struggling for a plank only large enough for one, [Kant] said: 'A penal law applying to such a situation could never have the effect intended, for the threat of an evil that is still uncertain (being condemned to death by a judge) cannot outweigh the fear of an evil that is certain (being drowned). Hence we must judge that, although an act of self-preservation through violence is not inculpable, it is still unpunishable.' . . .

[I]n the context, I find myself wholly unable to distinguish this defence from that of duress, and I feel bound to say that the English Law Commission has achieved the apotheosis of absurdity by recommending that our proposed criminal code should provide for a defence of duress while excluding any general defence of necessity. Surely Lord Simon of Glais-dale was speaking in unanswerable terms when he said in the course of his dissenting speech in *Lynch* [above, p.77] 'It would be a travesty of justice and an invitation to anarchy to declare that an innocent life may be taken with impunity if the threat to one's own life is from a terrorist but not when from a natural disaster like ship- or plane-wreck.'

A.P. KENNY, *FREEWILL AND RESPONSIBILITY* (ROUTLEDGE & KEGAN PAUL, 1978), PP.36–38

In everyday language people are often said to be compelled to do things when no actual force is used but the actions are performed to avert the threat of violent action or imminent disaster. These are cases where it will be natural for the agent to say that he 'had no choice' . . . but in fact the action is a voluntary one, arising out of a choice between evils. When the choice . . . is posed as a result of the wrongful threats of another, lawyers speak of 'duress'; when it arises through the operation of natural causes, they prefer to speak of 'necessity' . . . To me the decision [in *Dudley & Stephens*] seems ethically sound . . . The principle that one should never intentionally take innocent life would be contested by supporters of euthanasia . . . The decision in *Dudley and Stephens* can be justified by the narrower principle that one should not take innocent life in order to save one's own life. This principle seems to me, as it did to Lord Coleridge in 1884, to be correct: it seems likely to reduce the overall number of innocent deaths. Certainly I would rather be in an open boat with companions who accepted the principle than in company with lawyers who accepted necessity as a defence to murder.

G. WILLIAMS, *CRIMINAL LAW: THE GENERAL PART* (1961), S.237

. . . Where it is merely a case of life for life, the doctrine of necessity must generally be silent, because the two lives must be accounted equal in the eye of the law and there is nothing to choose between them. Necessity cannot justify in such circumstances; but they may go so strongly in alleviation that the accused is discharged without punishment (where this is possible) or pardoned. The technical conviction merely records that in the eye of the law the act was wrongful. The necessary and reasonable consequence of this view is that resistance to the act on the part of the victim is lawful.

It seems that the position is different where the killing results in a net saving of life. Here it seems that the killing should be regarded as not merely excusing from punishment but as legally justifying. We need a general rule, and one allowing necessity as a defence to homicide where the minority are killed to preserve the majority is on the whole more satisfactory than the opposite.

A strong instance of this kind of justification is the action of a ship's captain in a wreck. He can determine who are to enter the first lifeboat; he can forbid overcrowding; and it makes no difference that the passengers who are not allowed to enter the lifeboat will inevitably perish with the ship. The captain, in choosing who are to live, is not guilty of killing those who remain. He would not be so guilty even though he kept some of the passengers back from the boat at revolver-point . . .

AMERICAN LAW INSTITUTE, *MODEL PENAL CODE* (1962), S.3.02

Conduct which the actor believes necessary to avoid a harm or evil to himself or another is justifiable provided that (1) the harm or evil sought to be avoided by such conduct is greater than that sought to be prevented by the law defining the offence charged . . .

See also H.A. Gross, *A Theory of Criminal Justice* (1979), pp.26, 27.

Note

The problem of killing in order to save life arose in unusual and traumatic circumstances in the case *Re A (Children) (Conjoined Twins: Medical Treatment) (No.1)* [2000] 4 All E.R. 961, involving the twins Jodie and Mary. The court had to consider whether it would be lawful for doctors to perform an operation to separate the twins the effect of which would be the inevitable death of Mary. The twins shared a common aorta which enabled Jodie's heart to pump the blood she oxygenated through Mary's body as Mary's heart and lungs were deficient and incapable of sustaining her life. Mary's brain was also not fully developed. If an operation to separate them were not performed both twins were expected to die within six months due to the strain being placed on Jodie's heart. If separated the prospects for Jodie's survival were good albeit that she would suffer some disabilities and require further surgery. Mary was incapable of independent existence.

The Court of Appeal was faced with three problems: first, what was in the best interests of the children; secondly, if those interests were in conflict, could that conflict be resolved so as to allow one to prevail; and, thirdly, if the prevailing interest was in favour of the operation, could the operation be performed lawfully. The first two questions raised family law issues, the third related to the criminal law. Ward LJ with whom Brooke LJ agreed, concluded that while it was in Jodie's best interests for the operation to take place, this was not in Mary's best interests as it would mean her death. He stated that her life "desperate as it is, still has its own ineliminable value and dignity". This conclusion derived from the sanctity of life doctrine which, he said, "compels me to accept that each life has inherent value in itself and the right to life, being universal, is equal for all of us." By contrast Walker LJ concluded that the operation would be in Mary's best interests as continued life would hold nothing for her except possible pain and discomfort whereas the operation would restore to her, albeit in death, the bodily integrity and autonomy which is her right. For Ward LJ and Brooke LJ the court's task, where the best interests of the children were in conflict, was to balance the welfare of each child against the other to find the "least detrimental alternative". This balancing exercise would not involve valuing each life but rather the "worthwhilenss" of the proposed treatment. For Mary the treatment was not worthwhile as she had always been "designated for death" due to her disabilities. She was only alive because she was sucking "the lifeblood out of Jodie" and by so doing would ultimately kill her. Only the doctors could save Jodie whereas Mary was beyond help. In those circumstances the balance weighed heavily in Jodies's favour, Ward LJ stating:

> "The best interests of the twins is to give the chance of life to the child whose actual bodily condition is capable of accepting the chance to her advantage even if that has to be at the cost of the sacrifice of the life which is so unnaturally supported. I am wholly satisfied that the least detrimental choice, balancing the interests of Mary against Jodie and Jodie against Mary, is to permit the operation to be performed."

Turning to the criminal law there were two main issues: first, whether the operation to separate the twins would involve the intentional killing of Mary; and, secondly, if so whether this could be justified. Both Ward LJ and Brooke LJ concluded that the doctors performing the operation would, following the decision of the House of Lords in *Woollin* [1999] 1 A.C. 82, intend to kill Mary, however much they might not desire that result, as they would recognise her death as being the virtually certain consequence of their acts. (By contrast Walker LJ adopted the reasoning of Lord Scarman in *Gillick*, above, p.263, that the bona fide exercise by a doctor of his clinical judgment would negate the guilty mind required for a criminal offence.) The dilemma for the doctors, however, was not just a moral or social one but also a legal one as the failure to operate could amount to a breach of their duty to act in Jodie's best interests. This raised the crucial question in the case, originally framed by Lord Mackay in *Howe* [1987] 1 A.C. 417 whether "the law should recognise in any individual in any circumstances, however extreme, the right to choose that one innocent person should be killed rather than another"? As the doctors' duties to Jodie and Mary were in conflict Ward LJ concluded that "the law must allow an escape through choosing the lesser of two evils" in which case, the operation being justified would involve no unlawful act. Furthermore, as the reality of the situation was that Mary was slowly killing Jodie (even though this unique situation could not be classed as unlawful), the doctors were entitled to come to Jodie's defence to remove the threat of fatal harm Mary presented. Ward LJ was, however, concerned to point out the very limited extent to which this decision should be regarded as a precedent emphasising the uniqueness of the case. He stated:

> "Lest it be thought that this decision could become authority for wider propositions, such as that a doctor, once he has determined that a patient cannot survive, can kill the patient, it is important to restate the unique circumstances for which this case is authority. They are that it must be impossible to preserve the life of X. without bringing about the death of Y., that Y. by his or her very continued existence will inevitably bring about the death of X. within a short period of time, and that X. is capable of living an independent life but Y. is incapable under any circumstances (including all forms of medical intervention) of viable independent existence."

Brooke LJ expressly framed the issue as one of necessity. He conducted a comprehensive review of the history and case law relating to this defence concluding that there was no need for an emergency to exist nor need the threat which constitutes the harm be unlawful or constitute "unjust aggression". He overcame the problem of *Dudley and Stephens* and *Howe* which would render necessity unavailable as a defence to murder stating:

"I have considered very carefully the policy reasons for the decision in *R v Dudley and Stephens*, supported as it was by the House of Lords in *R v Howe*. These are, in short, that there were two insuperable objections to the proposition that necessity might be available as a defence for the Mignonette sailors. The first objection was evident in the court's questions: Who is to be the judge of this sort of necessity? By what measure is the comparative value of lives to be measured? The second objection was that to permit such a defence would mark an absolute divorce of law from morality.

In my judgment, neither of these objections are dispositive of the present case. Mary is, sadly, self-designated for a very early death. Nobody can extend her life beyond a very short span. Because her heart, brain and lungs are for all practical purposes useless, nobody would have even tried to extend her life artificially if she had not, fortuitously, been deriving oxygenated blood from her sister's bloodstream.

It is true that there are those who believe most sincerely—and the Archbishop of Westminster is among them—that it would be an immoral act to save Jodie, if by saving Jodie one must end Mary's life before its brief allotted span is complete . . . But there are also those who believe with equal sincerity that it would be immoral not to assist Jodie if there is a good prospect that she might live a happy and fulfilled life if this operation is performed. The court is not equipped to choose between these competing philosophies. All that a court can say is that it is not at all obvious that this is the sort of clear-cut case, marking an absolute divorce from law and morality, which was of such concern to Lord Coleridge and his fellow judges."

Brooke LJ adopted the tests for necessity which Sir James Stephen provided in his *Digest of Criminal Law* (MacMillan, 1887):

"(i)   the act is needed to avoid inevitable and irreparable evil;
(ii)   no more should be done than is reasonably necessary for the purpose to be achieved;
(iii)   the evil inflicted must not be disproportionate to the evil avoided."

He concluded that as the principles of family law "point irresistibly to the conclusion that the interests of Jodie must be preferred to the interests of Mary, I consider that all these requirements are satisfied in this case." Walker LJ was also prepared, if necessary, to extend the defence of necessity to cover the instant case. Brooke LJ's adoption of the *Stephen* test would suggest a more broadly based defence of necessity more closely related to a balancing of harms test as provided in the American Law Institute's *Model Penal Code* (above p.271).

As regards the Human Rights Act 1998 and art.2 of the European Convention, the Court of Appeal was satisfied that the operation would not constitute a breach. Ward LJ took the view that the rights of each child being in conflict and a solution being required, it was inconceivable that the court in Strasbourg would arrive at a different conclusion to the Court of Appeal. Brooke LJ and Walker LJ took the view that art.2(1) which protects individuals from being "intentionally" deprived of life, was not infringed as "intentionally" in this context had to be given its natural and ordinary meaning and thus applied "only to cases where the purpose of the prohibited action is to cause death". Thus as the doctors' purpose would be to save the life of Jodie rather than to cause the death of Mary, the operation would not constitute a violation of art.2.

Questions

1. Reconsider the questions that follow *R. v Dudley and Stephens*, in light of the decision in *A (Children)*.

2. A, a twin, is terminally and incurably ill having been diagnosed by doctors to have four to six months to live. A is in a coma but is not connected to a life support machine. B, A's twin brother, is also terminally ill having been diagnosed to have only weeks to live but he could be saved provided a suitable donor of a healthy liver is found. A tissue match is carried out indicating that A's tissue is an exact match for B and further tests establish that A's liver is perfectly healthy. The removal of A's liver would lead to his immediate death but would offer the prospect of saving B's life. Before falling into a coma A signed a consent form to his organs being used for transplant purposes. The doctors treating B apply to the High Court seeking a declaration that an operation to remove A's liver would not be unlawful. How might the court decide such an application? Would it make any difference if A's heart and kidneys were also to be used to save other lives?

3. Ed and Frank are climbing in the Peak District when Frank is hit by a falling rock which knocks him unconscious causing him to slip and fall. He is attached to Ed who loses his foothold and also falls. Miraculously the rope snags on a gnarled tree growing in a crack in the rock face leaving both climbers suspended in space. Dan, a lone climber climbing on the same rock face sees their plight and traverses the rock face to seek to offer assistance. He discovers that the tree is beginning to give way under the strain of the combined weight of the climbers. Dan realises that he will be unable to save both climbers, particularly as Frank is unable to do anything to help himself. Dan determines that he must cut the rope in order to save Ed. He does so resulting in Frank falling to his death but Ed is rescued. Consider whether Dan would be liable for the murder of Frank.

----

iv. Necessity by Circumstance

R. V QUAYLE; ATTORNEY GENERALS' REFERENCE (NO.2 OF 2004)

[2005] EWCA Crim 1415; [2005] 2 Cr. App. R. 34 CA

The Court heard a number of related appeals together with a reference by the Attorney General. The principal issue was whether the common law defence of "necessity by circumstance" was available in respect of offences concerned with the possession, cultivation and supply of cannabis where the defendant genuinely and reasonably believed that the activities were necessary to avoid pain arising from a medical condition.

MANCE LJ

. . . The most basic defence in this area of the law is duress by human threats. The defence is potentially available where, through fear of wrongful violence or threats by another, a person's will is so overborne that he or she, reasonably and proportionately, acts in a way which would otherwise be unlawful in order to avoid a perceived risk of death or serious injury induced by such fear. The defence was recently considered by the House of Lords in *R. v Hasan* (sub nom *R. v Z*); [2005] UKHL 22; [2005] 2 Cr.App.R. 314; [2005] 2 W.L.R. 709. Lord Bingham said in *Hasan* at para.19 that 'the only criminal defences which have any close affinity with duress are necessity, where the force or compulsion is exerted not by human threats but by extraneous circumstances, and, perhaps, marital coercion under s.47 of the Criminal Justice Act 1925'. Necessity by circumstances is the defence relied on in the present appeals and reference.

36. In *Hasan* Lord Bingham said at para.24 that it was 'unsurprising' that the law in England and elsewhere 'should have been developed so as to confine the defence of duress within narrowly defined limits'. In this respect, we note in passing that he was also echoing a thought expressed in an early case by Lord Denning M.R., who said that the doctrine 'must be carefully circumscribed. Else necessity would open the door to many an excuse', and by Edmund Davies L.J. (*Southwark LBC v Williams* [1971] Ch. 734 at 743H and 745). Lord Bingham went on to identify certain features of duress, namely that it operates as a complete defence excusing what would otherwise be criminal conduct in relation to an innocent victim, that the onus is on the Crown to disprove duress and that, citing Prof. Sir John Smith Q.C., 'duress is a unique defence in that it is so much more likely than any other to depend on assertions which are peculiarly difficult for the prosecution to investigate or subsequently to disprove'. Later, Lord Bingham said that these features 'incline me, where policy choices have to be made, towards tightening rather than relaxing the conditions to be met before duress may be successfully relied on'; and cited words of Dickson J. in *Perka v R.* [1984] 2 S.C.R. 232, at 250:

'If the defence of necessity is to form a valid and consistent part of our criminal law it must, as has been universally recognised, be strictly and scrupulously limited to situations which correspond to its underlying rationale.'

37. Lord Bingham also pointed out at para.22 that 'If it appears at trial that a defendant acted in response to a degree of coercion but in circumstances where the strict requirements of duress were not satisfied, it is always open to the judge to adjust his sentence to reflect his assessment of the defendant's true culpability'. This point was made in the context of the defence of duress by threats, but may be compared with other earlier judicial statements in *R. v Howe* (1987) 85 Cr.App.R. 32 at 43 [1987] A.C. 417 at 433, *per* Lord Hailsham (in a similar vein in the context of murder), in *R. v Pommell* [1995] 2 Cr.App.R. 607 at 613–4, *per* Kennedy L.J. (in an opposite sense in a case where it was arguable that the defendant was fulfilling the underlying legislative policy) and in *Re A (Children) (Conjoined Twins: Surgical Separation) (No.1)* [2001] Fam. 147 at 234, *per* Brooke L.J. At its lowest, in our view, the point made by Lord Bingham points to a need to consider the appropriateness of recognising any suggested defence of necessity in the context in which it is raised.

38. The most important limitations of duress identified in para. 21 by Lord Bingham were these: (1) duress does not, despite the logic of the opposite argument, afford a defence to murder, attempted murder and, perhaps, some forms of treason; (2) the threat relied on must be to cause death or serious injury; (3) the threat must be directed against the defendant or his immediate family or someone close to him—in this regard, although the point was not in issue in Hasan, it appeared to Lord Bingham that the Judicial Studies Board's specimen direction was 'if strictly applied, . . . consistent with the rationale of the defence exception' in suggesting 'that the threat must be directed, if not to the defendant or a member of his immediate family, to a person for whose safety the defendant would reasonably regard himself as responsible'; (4) the relevant tests have been stated largely objectively—thus, for example, the threat must induce a belief in its efficacy that is reasonable as well as genuine (para.23); (5) the defence is available only where the criminal conduct which it is sought to excuse has been directly caused by the threats relied upon; (6) there must have been no evasive action the defendant could reasonably have been expected to take—an 'important limitation' which Lord Bingham considered to have been unduly weakened in recent years, in particular by the decisions in *R. v Hudson and Taylor* (1972) 56 Cr.App.R. 1; [1971] 2 Q.B. 202) and, so far as it purported to follow *Hudson and Taylor* on this point, *R. v Abdul-Hussain*, December 17, 1998, [1999] Crim.L.R. 570; and (7) the defendant must not voluntarily have laid himself open to the duress relied upon.

39. In the context of point (6) Lord Bingham emphasised in paras 27 and 28 'the requirement that execution of a threat must be reasonably believed to be imminent and immediate if it is to support a plea of duress', saying that juries should be directed that 'if the retribution threatened . . . is not such as [the defendant] expects to follow immediately or almost immediately on his failure to comply with the threat, there may be little if any room for doubt that he could have taken evasive action . . .'

40. Turning to the defence of necessity where the force or compulsion is exerted not by human threats but by extraneous circumstances, a convenient starting point is the decision in *R. v Martin* (1989) 88 Cr.App.R. 343. A husband, whilst disqualified, drove his son to work. His explanation was that his son had overslept and was at risk of losing his job if he arrived late, and that his wife had suicidal tendencies and had threatened to commit suicide if he did not do as he did. A court of appeal, presided over by the Lord Chief Justice, held that, however sceptically one might view that defence, it should have been left to the jury. Simon Brown J., giving the judgment, said at p.345:

'The principles may be summarised thus. First, English law does, in extreme circumstances, recognise a defence of necessity. Most commonly this defence arises as duress, that is pressure upon the accused's will from the wrongful threats or violence of another. Equally, however, it can arise from other objective dangers threatening the accused or others. Arising thus it is conveniently called 'duress of circumstances.'

Secondly, the defence is available only if, from an objective standpoint, the accused can be said to be acting reasonably and proportionately in order to avoid a threat of death or serious injury. Thirdly, assuming the defence to be open to the accused on his account of the facts, the issue should be left to the jury, who should be directed to determine these two questions: first, was the accused, or may he have been, impelled to act as he did because, as a result of what he reasonably believed to be the situation, he had good cause to fear that otherwise death or serious physical injury would result? Secondly, if so, may a sober person of reasonable firmness, sharing the characteristics of the accused, have responded to that situation by acting as the accused acted? If the answer to both those questions was "Yes", then the jury would acquit: the defence of necessity would have been established. That the defence is available in cases of reckless driving is established by Conway (supra) itself, and indeed by an earlier decision of the court in *R. v Willer* (1986) 83 Cr.App.R. 225. Conway is authority also for the proposition that the scope of the defence is no wider for reckless driving than for other serious offences. As was pointed out in the judgment, (1988) 88 Cr.App.R. 159 at 164, [1988] 3 All E.R. at 1029h: "reckless driving can kill".

We see no material distinction between offences of reckless driving and driving whilst disqualified so far as the application of the scope of this defence is concerned. Equally we can see no distinction in principle between various threats of death: it matters not whether the risk of death is by murder or by suicide or, indeed, by accident. One can illustrate the matter by considering a disqualified driver driven by his wife, she suffering a heart attack in remote countryside and he needing instantly to get her to hospital.'

41. In *Pommell* the court was concerned with a defence to a charge to possession of a loaded shotgun found in bed with the defendant. The defendant said that he had, during the night, persuaded someone to give him the gun to prevent him shooting some other people who had killed a friend, and that he intended in the morning to give the gun to his brother to hand in to the police. It was held that this proposed defence should have been left to the jury. Kennedy L.J., giving the judgment, said at p.613 that: 'The strength of the argument that a person ought to be permitted to breach the letter of the criminal law in order to prevent a greater evil befalling himself of others has long been recognised, . . . but it has, in English law, not given rise to a recognised general defence of necessity, and in relation to the charge of murder, the defence has been specifically held not to exist.' However, he continued: 'that does not really deal with the situation where someone commendably infringes a regulation in order to prevent another person from committing what everyone would accept as being a greater evil with a gun.' After referring to Martin, Kennedy L.J. went on to agree with a commentary on *Director of Public Prosecutions v Bell* [1992] R.T.R. 335 in which Prof. Sir John Smith Q.C. said (at [1992] Crim.L.R. 176) that the defence was not limited to road traffic offences, but, on the contrary, 'being closely related to the defence of duress by threats, appears to be general, applying to all crimes except murder, attempted murder and some forms of treason'.

42. In *R. v Abdul-Hussain* December 17, 1998, Rose L.J., giving the judgment of this Court, referred to Pommell in stating the first of 11 propositions, which was that 'the defence of duress, whether by threats or from circumstances, is generally available in relation to all substantive crimes, except murder, attempted murder and some forms of treason'. But he went on, in seeking to summarise the legal position, to say, as proposition 2, that: 'The courts have developed the doctrine on a case by case basis, notably during the last 30 years. Its scope remains imprecise.' He also observed, as proposition 7, that:

'All the circumstances of the peril, including the number, identity and status of those creating it, and the opportunities (if any) which exist to avoid it are relevant, initially for the judge, and, in appropriate cases, for the jury, when assessing whether the defendant's mind was affected as in 4 above [that is so as to overbear his will].'

This test is, at the least, suggestive of a situation which the judge and jury can assess on the basis of objectively ascertainable and available material.

43. The Crown relies before us upon this Court's decision in *R. v Rodger and Rose* [1998] 1 Cr.App.R. 143. The facts there involved a break-out from Parkhurst Prison which the two defendants sought to excuse on the basis that the Home Secretary had increased their original tariffs and they had become suicidal. The prosecution was prepared to concede that the break-outs were because of contemplated suicide, which would have taken place had the break-outs not occurred. The Court, in a judgment given by Russell L.J., held that no such defence was available. It distinguished all previous cases, including, *R. v Martin* (1989) 88 Cr.App.R. 343, *R. v Conway* (1989)

88 Cr.App.R. 159, and *R. v Pommell* [1995] 2 Cr.App.R. 607, as having one factor not present in Rodger and Rose, namely that the feature causative of the defendant committing the offence was in all these cases (p.145):

'extraneous to the offender himself. In contrast, in these appeals it was solely the suicidal tendencies, the thought processes and the emotions of the offenders themselves which operated as duress. That factor introduces an entirely subjective element not present in the authorities . . . if these appeals were to succeed it would involve an extension of the law upon this topic as hitherto reflected in authority and would introduce an entirely subjective element divorced from any extraneous influence.

We do not consider that such a development of the law would be justified, nor do we think that such an extension would be in the public interest. If allowed it would amount to a licence to commit crime dependent on the personal characteristics and vulnerability of the offender. As a matter of policy that is undesirable and in our view it is not the law and should not be the law.'

44. *Rodger and Rose* does not mean that the defence of necessity of circumstances is never available in respect of prison-breach. As long ago as 1500, it was said in argument that a prisoner might justify an escape from a burning gaol which was necessary to save his life 'for he is not to be hanged because he did not stay to be burnt' (Cf. *Southwark LBC v Williams* [1971] Ch. 734 at 746B, *per* Edmund Davies L.J., citing Glanville Williams). On behalf of the appellants and Mr Ditchfield it is submitted that, in so far as it excluded suicide, *Rodger and Rose* can be regarded as a decision based purely on public policy considerations in the particular context of prison sentences. It is also submitted that it only relates to suicide by the defendant him or herself, and attention is drawn to *Martin* as a case where a threat of suicide by a third party was regarded by this Court as capable of giving rise to a potential defence of necessity. It is submitted that, at all events outside the content of prison-breach, there is no logical or satisfactory distinction between action necessary to avoid one's own and someone else's suicide.

45. The appellants also rely on this Court's judgment in *R. v Shayler* [2001] EWCA Crim 1977, [2001] 1 W.L.R. 2206, CA; on appeal [2002] UKHL 11, [2003] 1 A.C. 247, HL. In giving the Court of Appeal's judgment, Lord Woolf C.J. said that any definition of the precise limits of the defence of duress and necessity was fraught with difficulty, because its development had been closely related to the particular facts of the different cases which had come before the courts (para.46). But he went on seek to identify the 'core ingredients' by reference to *inter alia Martin* and *Abdul-Hussain*. Commenting on Brooke L.J.'s distinction in Re A (Children) between cases of duress by threats or circumstances and cases of real choice (para.52 below), Lord Woolf said at para.55: 'None the less the distinction between duress of circumstances and necessity has, correctly, been by and large ignored or blurred by the courts.' However, he recognised that In re F (Mental Patient: Sterilisation) [1990] 2 A.C. 1 was another case in which they were treated as different.

46. A number of other points arise from Lord Woolf's judgment in *Shayler*. *Abdul-Hussain* is cited as making clear that the harm threatened need not be immediate but should be imminent; however, that statement itself needs care in the light of Lord Bingham's speech in *Hasan*. Secondly, the question addressed whether the alleged harm that the defendant seeks to avoid has to involve a danger to life or of serious injury, or whether it can simply be harm greater than the act done which seeks to avoid such harm. Lord Woolf answered that question by citing (at para.58) Smith & Hogan's statement (9th ed.) p.247, that 'There are some cases where what was in substance a defence of necessity was allowed without identifying a threat to life or serious injury', coupled with reference to *Gillick v West Norfolk and Wisbech Area Health Authority* [1986] A.C. 112 and In re F. He then said at para 59: 'However, any extension of the defence here is slight: protection of the physical and mental well-being of a person from serious harm is still being required.' If this were read as a general acceptance in all circumstances of such harm as sufficient to justify a defence of necessity, it would seem open to question, particularly in the light of Lord Bingham's approach in *Hasan*.

47. Thirdly, however, the Court of Appeal concluded that at para. 66 that Mr Shayler did not have available to him any potential defence of necessity because:

'it is inherent in the defence that it has ingredients which Mr Shayler is not in a position to establish. He cannot identify the action by some external agency which is going to create the imminent (if not immediate) threats to the life and limb of members of the general public as a result of the security service's alleged abuses and blunders. This is a fundamental ingredient of the defence. Without it, it is impossible to test whether there was sufficient urgency to justify the otherwise unlawful intervention. It is also impossible to apply the proportionality test. Furthermore, if it is possible to identify the members of the public at risk this will only be by hindsight. This creates difficulty over the requirement of responsibility. Mr Shayler's justification for what he did lacks the required degree of precision. There is no close nexus between his disclosure and the possible injury to members of the public. Putting it simply there was no necessity or duress as those words are ordinarily understood.'

The reference to a need for 'action by some external agency' in our view reflects thinking similar to that in *Rodger and Rose*, although that case was not mentioned. The duress or necessity on which a defendant relies must be capable of objective assessment. According to this Court's decision in *R. v Safi (Ali Ahmed)* [2003] EWCA Crim 1809, [2004] 1 Cr.App.R. 157 (although this case was not, we note, commented upon in Hasan) a reasonable and well-founded belief in a threat or other danger may suffice. But, even assuming that that qualification is to be added, a requirement that the belief be 'well-founded' imports a need for it to have been manifested externally and an ability to measure and assess it accordingly.

48. The general reasoning in *Shayler* on the subject of necessity remains open to review in the light of the House of Lords' treatment of the subject in the same case. Lord Bingham, at para.17, thought it 'a little unfortunate' that the Court of Appeal had followed the judge and 'ventured into this vexed and uncertain territory' when Mr Shayler had raised no question of necessity or duress of circumstances before the judge. He said:

'I should not for my part be taken to accept all that the Court of Appeal said on these difficult topics, but in my opinion it is unnecessary to explore them in this case.'

Mr Shayler's only defence was that he had acted in the public and national interest, and Lord Bingham did not think that it was 'within measurable distance of affording him a defence of necessity or duress of circumstances'. However, nothing was said specifically casting doubt on the statements in the passage quoted in para.47 above, in which we see much force. . .

. . .

51. With regard to the references in the authorities to a need for a threat to life or of serious injury, the appellants submit that the avoidance of severe pain should be equated with the avoidance of serious injury; Mr Fitzgerald Q.C., for Mr Quayle and Mr Wales, invokes in this connection caselaw concerning medical treatment and general considerations of principle. The caselaw include *R. v Bourne* [1939] 1 K.B. 687, *Gillick v West Norfolk and Wisbech AHA* [1986] 1 A.C. 112, *F (Mental Patient: Sterilisation), Re* [1990] 2 A.C. 1 and *In re A*. In *Bourne* Macnaghten J. directed the jury that the inclusion of the word 'unlawfully' in the statutory definition of the offence of procuring a miscarriage with intent, made it incumbent on the Crown to prove that the act was not 'done in good faith for the purpose only of preserving the life of the mother', and further that, in considering whether there was any clear line of distinction between danger to health and to life, the jury should take 'a reasonable view' of the latter words. He was assisted in his interpretation by an express proviso in a parallel statute (the Infant Life (Preservation) Act 1929) dealing with the situation of children after birth. In *Gillick* the House held that doctors could in certain circumstances be justified in giving contraceptive advice and treatment to under 16 year olds without parental consent (even in exceptional cases those not yet sufficiently mature to give their own consent), where this was justified as necessary in the child's best interests to avoid physical and/or mental suffering. In In re F the House held that doctors are, on the ground of necessity, entitled (and may even be under a duty to their patients) to act in the best interests of the lives, physical or mental health of adults unable to give consent to medical treatment, who would otherwise be deprived of the medical care to which they were entitled. In both *Gillick* and In re *F* the issue was whether doctors could act in the best interests of persons for whose treatment they were medically responsible, in circumstances where those persons could not decide for themselves. That is a very different situation from the present.

52. In *Bourne* the issue could also be viewed as involving competing interests of the parent and an as yet unborn child. In *In re A* doctors owing duties to both conjoined twins faced the clinical dilemma that any chance of saving the life of the one (Jodie) over a longer period involved an operation which would positively invade the bodies of both and necessarily end the life of the other (Mary) at once. Brooke L.J.'s comprehensive discussion described the 'species of the genus of necessity which is caused by wrongful threats' in terms tending to equate it with 'the newly identified defence of "duress of circumstances"', which he exemplified by reference to, *inter alia*, *Martin*. He distinguished both from 'cases of pure necessity where the actor's mind is not irresistibly overborne by external pressures' but 'the claim is that his or her conduct was not harmful because on a choice between two evils the choice of avoiding the greater harm was justified' (pp.232C–236B). Brooke L.J. treated this situation at least as one where the law might speak of conduct as justified (compare Lord Bingham's statement in Hasan at para. 18 that, in the context of duress by threats, the law is concerned with no more than a potential excuse). Robert Walker L.J. at pp.253H–255E also found in the previous cases concerning duress of circumstances no real assistance or clear principle or analogy applicable to the situation of clinical dilemma faced by the doctors

In re A. Recognising that in the absence of parliamentary intervention the law had to develop on a case by case basis, as indicated by Rose L.J. in *Abdul-Hussain*, he concluded that, on the particular facts, where Mary was, on the evidence, bound to die soon in any event, the doctors' fundamental duty to protect the life of Jodie justified the medical operation to separate the twins, despite its inevitably fatal effect for Mary. This reasoning in our view underlines the danger of Mr Fitzgerald Q.C.'s approach, in so far as that seeks to extract from cases from the very different area of medical intervention general principles to be applied across the whole area of duress by threats or necessity by circumstances.

53. In the light of these authorities, we are not persuaded by Mr Fitzgerald Q.C.'s attempts to derive from individual authorities in different areas a coherent over-arching principle applicable in all cases of necessity. Such an attempt appears to us to pay too little attention to the particular context of individual decisions, and not to correspond with the case-by-case approach suggested by the authorities. However, there is a recognised defence of duress by threats, to which it is clear that the defence of necessity by circumstances bears a close affinity. Save that, in the present cases at least, the offences in question are not readily seen as involving any individual victim, the arguments which Lord Bingham mentioned in Hasan in favour of a confined definition appear to us applicable to any defence of necessity by circumstances . . .

71. Apart from the general considerations addressed in paras 54–58 above, there are also detailed requirements of any defence of necessity which are indicated by the common law authorities and which the present cases in our view lack.

Extraneous circumstances

72. Lord Bingham spoke in Hasan of the need for 'a just and well-founded fear', while accepting that threats of death or serious injury will suffice. He noted that the relevant requirements had been defined objectively, and went on (with the majority of the House) to apply the same approach when he decided that the defence was not available if the defendant ought reasonably to have foreseen the risk of coercion. It is by 'the standards of honest and reasonable men' therefore that the existence or otherwise of such a fear or such threats falls to be decided. We have observed that Lord Bingham did not address or comment on the case of *Safi*, in which this Court held that what matters is not whether there was actually a threat of torture, but whether there was a reasonable perception of such a threat. But that still involves an objective test based on external events, conduct or words about which evidence would have to be produced or given. It is also notable that Lord Bingham described the criminal defence which he thought had a close affinity with duress by threats as 'necessity . . . by extraneous circumstances'.

73. There is therefore considerable authority pointing towards a need for extraneous circumstances capable of objective scrutiny by judge and jury and as such, it may be added, more likely to be capable of being checked and, where appropriate, met by other evidence. Lord Bingham's dictum fits in this regard with dicta in *Abdul-Hussain*, the decision in *Rodger & Rose* and Lord Woolf C.J.'s dicta in *Shayler* speaking of a 'fundamental ingredient' of 'some external agency' as well as with the non-counsel decision in *Brown*.

74. The appellants' objection to any such distinction is that it means, for example, that the commission of an offence could be excused if it was to avoid the realisation of a danger of one's wife committing suicide (*Martin*), but not if in that case it had been the wife herself who, realising that she would commit suicide unless she drove her son to school, had driven while disqualified (*Rodger & Rose*). Likewise, they suggest, the distinction could deny a defence of necessity to a person at risk of serious injury or perhaps pain, but allow it potentially to a parent or carer responsible for the well-being of such a person; and in circumstances like those in *Rodger & Rose*, a compassionate warder with responsibility for the prisoner, could release the prisoner, if he was able to detect the risk of suicide in time; while in cases such as the present, a person in or at risk of serious injury or pain could not himself engage in cultivation, possession or use of cannabis for medical purposes, but a parent or carer responsible for his upkeep could cultivate or obtain and administer cannabis to him or her for such purposes. The appellants suggest that none of these distinctions can stand scrutiny, so that *Rodger & Rose* must be regarded as a special case based on policy considerations.

75. We accept that it is right to remember the context of the decision in *Rodger & Rose*. Any court was, we think, bound to recognise the incongruous penal results and the risk of abuse that would result from recognising a defence of necessitous escape from prison based on danger that the prisoner escaping would commit suicide if he remained in custody. But, on that basis, the suggestion that a prison officer in a situation like that in *Rodger & Rose* might legitimately free a prisoner is we think likely to run into problems at a more basic level of legislative policy, which in our view the cases before us also present (see paras 54–58 above). Nevertheless, although the court in *Rodger & Rose* adverted to considerations of policy when it said that the suggested defence was undesirable, it did so not to justify a particular exception in this context to the defence,

but in support of a generally expressed common law exception, based on the undesirability of introducing 'an entirely subjective element divorced from any extraneous influence' into the defence. On the authorities (para. 73 above), the requirement of an objectively ascertainable extraneous cause has a considerable, and in our view understandable, basis. It rests on the pragmatic consideration that the defence of necessity, which the Crown would carry the onus to disprove, must be confined within narrowly defined limits or it will become an opportunity for almost untriable and certainly peculiarly difficult issues, not to mention abusive defences. On that basis, we consider that the Crown's first narrow point, namely that, for the defence of necessity of circumstances to be potentially available, there must be extraneous circumstances capable of objective scrutiny by judge and jury, is valid.

Pain

76. It is, however, submitted on behalf of Messrs. Quayle, Wales and Kenny that any such test is satisfied in all their cases both because of the objectively ascertainable facts giving rise to the pain they suffer actually, or would suffer if they were not to use cannabis, whether from their afflictions or from taking alternative lawful medicaments, and because pain is capable of some degree of objective scrutiny and is not wholly subjective. In addressing this submission, we do not gain any real assistance from cases from other areas of the law, where distinctions may or may not have been drawn between injury and harm or pain.

77. The reason why we would not accept the submission is that the law has to draw a line at some point in the criteria which it accepts as sufficient to satisfy any defence of duress or necessity. Courts and juries have to work on evidence. If such defences were to be expanded in theory to cover every possible case in which it might be felt that it would be hard if the law treated the conduct in question as criminal, there would be likely to be arguments in considerable numbers of cases, where there was no clear objective basis by reference to which to test or determine such arguments. It is unlikely that this would lead overall to a more coherent result, or even necessarily to a more just disposition of any individual case. There is, on any view, a large element of subjectivity in the assessment of pain not directly associated with some current physical injury. The legal defences of duress by threats and necessity by circumstances should in our view be confined to cases where there is an imminent danger of physical injury. In reaching these conclusions, we recognise that hard cases can be postulated, but these, as Lord Bingham said, can and should commonly be capable of being dealt with in other ways. The nature of the sentences passed in the cases before us is consistent with this.

78. It is also submitted that the present cases involve not merely pain, but a risk of serious physical or psychological injury as a result of pain, or as a result of the alternative medicines which would have to be taken if cannabis was not. We have in the case of Quayle already given our reasons for rejecting on the facts Mr Fitzgerald Q.C.'s submission that there was any relevant risk of suicide in that case (para.2(vi) above). In the case of Wales, the judge is criticised for failing to explain that serious pain could amount to serious injury because of its psychological consequences, but there does not appear to have been any evidence which could have justified such a case. Mr Wales did describe the pain he suffered as 'life-threatening' and the judge reminded the jury of this, although it does not appear to have been Mr Wales's case that there was an actual risk of suicide. His case on the facts was that cannabis helped him cope with the pain, without side effects, while the prescribed medicines had side-effects (stopping him eating) and, on the expert evidence that he called, also involved medical risks such as a general risk of peritonitis. We do not see in the evidence any basis on which a jury could be asked to conclude that Mr Wales faced any imminent risk of serious injury sufficient to justify him taking cannabis on a regular basis. Further, if there was such a case, it was left to the jury. Finally, in the case of Kenny, the evidence did not suggest any risk other than that of pain, and the criticism is that that risk should have been left to the jury.

Imminence and immediacy

79. We consider that these requirements represent another reason why, even at the detailed level, it is difficult to accept that there could be any successful defence of necessity in the cases of Quayle, Wales and Kenny. Their defences amount to saying that it is open to defendants on a continuous basis to plan for and justify breaches of the law. However, we need not express a view whether that would have alone justified a judge in refusing to leave their defences to a jury. The requirements of imminence and immediacy mean, in any event, in our view that the judge was right to refuse to leave any defence of necessity to the jury in Taylor and Lee, and that the defence should not have been left to the jury in *Ditchfield*. In each of these three cases, the defendant was taking a deliberately considered course of conduct over a substantial period of time, involving continuous or regular breaches of the law. In each case, the defendant was not the immediate sufferer and had every opportunity to reflect and to desist. The compassionate grounds which may well have motivated Mr Taylor and Ms Lee and which the jury

evidently accepted did motivate Mr Ditchfield cannot avoid the fact that they deliberately chose to act contrary to the law on a continuous basis.

80. We note in passing that the court in *Southwark L.B.C. v Williams* [1971] Ch. 734 refused to recognise a defence of necessity raised by squatters in answer to a claim to recover possession of properties owned by the council. The evidence was that there were no homes for the squatters, they had been living in 'quite deplorable conditions' and the empty council properties in which they then squatted had been vandalised by the council to make them unfit for habitation, but that they had entered and lived there in an orderly way and repaired them after entry. Nevertheless, the court upheld summary possession orders, 'for the sake of law and order', as Lord Denning M.R. put it, and because the circumstances 'do not . . . constitute the sort of emergency to which the plea [of necessity] applies', as Edmund Davies L.J. said. Megaw L.J. agreed with both judgments on this aspect. The case is an old one, and the law has developed, so that we need not consider it further. But the underlying theme, that a continuous and deliberate course of otherwise unlawful self-help is unlikely to give rise to the defence has itself, in our view, continuing relevance.

81. The point made in paras 79–80 may also be viewed in another way. Where there is no imminent or immediate threat or peril, but only a general assertion of an internal motivation to engage in prohibited activities in order to prevent or alleviate pain, it is also difficult to identify any extraneous or objective factors by reference to which a jury could be expected to measure whether the motivation was such as to override the defendant's will or to force him to act as he did. If the response is that the defendant was not forced, but chose to act as he did, then the considerations mentioned in the previous paragraph apply.

Conclusions

82. It follows both from the general objection identified in paras 54–58 and, independently, from the more detailed points addressed in paras 71–81 read in each case with paras 59–70 above, that none of the defendants in any of the cases before us was in our view able to rely at trial on any facts which could at common law give him or her any defence of necessity. The judicial rulings to that effect in the cases of Quayle, Taylor, Lee and Kenny were correct in the result, even though not in every case in their reasoning. The judges in Wales and in the Attorney General's Reference in *Ditchfield* were wrong to leave the defence of necessity to the jury. In the case of Wales, the jury anyway convicted, but in the case of *Ditchfield* the jury acquitted. It follows that all the appeals will be dismissed, and the question of law on which this court's opinion is sought by the Attorney General in the reference will be answered in the negative.

Appeals dismissed
Attorney General's question answered in the negative

The Court of Appeal certified, under s.33(2) of the Criminal Appeal Act 1968, that a point of law of general public importance was involved in its decision, namely: 'Whether a defence of necessity is available to a defendant in respect of an offence of: (a) possession, cultivation or production of cannabis, contrary to the Misuse of Drugs Act 1971, for the purpose of alleviating a defendant's own serious pain arising from a pre-existing medical condition or from conventional medicine that he would otherwise resort to in order to reduce his pain; and/or (b) importation of cannabis, contrary to the Customs and Excise Management Act 1979 and/or possession with intent to supply cannabis, contrary to the Misuse of Drugs Act 1971, for the purpose of alleviating the serious pain of others arising from a pre-existing medical condition or from conventional medicine that they would otherwise resort to in order to reduce their pain.'

Leave to appeal to the House of Lords refused

Question

Are there now any distinctions between the defences of duress and necessity?

----

v. Proposals for Reform

LAW COMMISSION, *DRAFT CRIMINAL LAW BILL* (TSO, 1993), LAW COM. NO.218

26.—(1) No act of a person constitutes an offence if the act is done under duress of circumstances.

(2) A person does an act under duress of circumstances if—

(a) he does it because he knows or believes that it is immediately necessary to avoid death or serious injury to himself or another, and

(b) the danger that he knows or believes to exist is such that in all the circumstances (including any of his personal characteristics that affect its gravity) he cannot reasonably be expected to act otherwise.

It is for the defendant to show that the reason for his act was such knowledge or belief as is mentioned in paragraph (a).

(3) This section applies in relation to omissions as it applies in relation to acts.

(4) This section does not apply to a person who knowingly and without reasonable excuse exposed himself to the danger known or believed to exist.

If the question arises whether a person knowingly and without reasonable excuse exposed himself to that danger, it is for him to show that he did not.

(5) This section does not apply to—

(a) an act done in the knowledge or belief that a threat has been made to cause death or serious injury to himself or another (see s.25), or

(b) the use of force within the meaning of section 27 or 28, or an act immediately preparatory to the use of force, for the purposes mentioned in section 27(1) or 28(1).

4. SELF-DEFENCE AND KINDRED DEFENCES

Note

This section covers those situations where force is used by a defendant to protect himself, or his property, or others or to prevent crime. Pleas based on these grounds are not strictly "defences" in the sense that duress is a defence; a successful plea means that the accused's conduct was justified and thus lawful. However the term defence will be used as it appears in the cases and textbooks.

G. WILLIAMS, "THE THEORY OF EXCUSES" [1982] CRIM. L.R. 732, 739

At any rate, for present English law private defence is clearly a matter of justification, not merely of according mercy to a defender. (Lord MacDermott C.J. referred to it as a 'plea of justification' in *Devlin v Armstrong* [1971] N.I. 13). If the choice is between injury to an aggressor and injury to a defender, it is better that the injury be suffered by the aggressor, for two reasons. First, it is the aggressor who is the prime cause of the mischief. Secondly, a rule allowing defensive action tends to inhibit aggression, or at least to restrain its continuance, as a rule forbidding defensive action would tend to promote it. It follows that if a person acts against a wrongdoer in the actual necessity of private defence, no one who assists him should be guilty as bringing about a wrongful act, whatever may have been the reason why he lent his assistance.

Winn L.J. stated in *R. v Wheeler* [1967] W.L.R. 1531, at p.1533:

'. . . wherever there has been a killing, or indeed the infliction of violence not proving fatal, in circumstances where the defendant puts forward a justification such as self-defence, . . . such as resistance to a violent felony, it is very important and indeed quite essential that the jury should understand, and that the matter should be so put before them that there is no danger of their failing to understand, that none of those issues of justification are properly to be regarded as defences: unfortunately there is sometimes a regrettable habit of referring to them as, for example, the defence of self-defence. In particular, where a judge does slip into the error or quasi error of referring to such explanations as defences, it is particularly important that he should use language which suffices to make it clear to the jury that they are not defences in respect of which any onus rests upon the accused, but are matters which the prosecution must disprove as an essential part of the prosecution case before a verdict of guilty is justified.'

(Reiterated in *R. v Abraham* [1973] 1 W.L.R. 1270.)

If D's account of the facts includes matters which, if accepted, could raise a prima facie case of self-defence, that issue should be left to the jury even where D. has not formally relied on self-defence (see *D.P.P. v Bailey* [1995] 1 Cr.App.R. 257).

i. Scope of the defences

(a) Self-defence

R. V SCULLY

(1824) C. & P. 319; 171 E.R. 1213

The defendant was set to watch his master's premises. He saw a man on the garden wall and hailed him. This man said to another, "Tom, why don't you fire?". The defendant hailed the man on the wall again and he said, "Shoot and be d—d," whereupon he shot at the man on the wall, aiming at his legs. He missed and shot the deceased whom he had not seen. The defendant was charged with manslaughter.

GARROW B

Any person set by his master to watch a garden or yard, is not at all justified in shooting at or injuring in any way persons who may come into those premises, even in the night: and if he saw them go into his master's hen roost, he would still not be justified in shooting them. He ought first to go and see if he could not take measures for their apprehension. But here the life of the prisoner was threatened and if he considered his life in actual danger, he was justified in shooting the deceased as he had done; but, if not considering his own life in danger, he rashly shot that man, who was only a trespasser, he would be guilty of manslaughter.

Verdict: Not guilty

(b) Defence of others

R. V ROSE

(1884) 15 Cox 540

The defendant was a weakly young man of 22; his father was a powerful man. Recently the father had been drinking excessively and whilst intoxicated he was of the opinion that his wife had been unfaithful to him. He had threatened her life and she was so frightened that she had frequently hidden everything in the house that could be used as a weapon. On the night in question the family had retired to separate bedrooms when the father had started abusing and arguing with his wife, threatening to murder her. He rushed from his room, seized his wife, and forced her up against the balusters in such a way as to give the impression that he was cutting her throat. The daughter and the mother shouted "murder", whereupon the defendant ran from his room. He is said to have fired a gun to frighten his father—no trace of his shot was found, and then he fired again, hitting his father in the eye and killing him. On arrest he said, "Father was murdering mother. I shot on one side to frighten him: he would not leave her, so I shot him." He was charged with murder.

LOPES J

Homicide is excusable if a person takes away the life of another in defending himself, if the fatal blow which takes away life is necessary for his preservation. The law says not only in self-defence such as I have described may homicide be excusable, but also it may be excusable if the fatal blow inflicted was necessary for the preservation of life. In the case of parent and child, if the parent had reason to believe that the life of a child is in imminent danger by reason of an assault by another person, and that the only possible, fair and reasonable means of saving the child's life is by doing something which will cause the death of that person, the law excuses that act. It is the same of a child with regard to a parent; it is the same in the case of husband and wife. Therefore, I propose to lay the law before you in this form: If you think, having regard to the evidence, and drawing fair and proper inferences from it, that the prisoner at the Bar acted without vindictive feeling towards his father when he fired the shot, if you think that at the time he fired that shot he honestly believed, and had reasonable grounds for the belief, that his mother's life was in imminent peril, and that the fatal shot which he fired was absolutely necessary for the preservation of her life, then he ought to be excused, and the law will excuse him, from the consequences of the homicide. If, however, on the other hand, you cannot come to this conclusion, if you think, and think without reasonable doubt, that it is not a fair inference to be drawn from the evidence, but are clearly of opinion that he acted vindictively, and had not such a belief as I have described to you, or had not reasonable grounds for such a belief, then you must find him guilty of murder.

Verdict: Not guilty

R. V DUFFY

[1967] 1 Q.B. 63

The appellant's sister was fighting. It was the appellant's case that she went to rescue her sister and that this was justifiable as self-defence. They were both convicted of unlawful wounding.

EDMUND-DAVIES J

. . . defending counsel throughout relied upon the plea that the appellant was acting in self-defence, a plea which he submitted extended to the action of the appellant in seeking to rescue her sister. It is established that such a defence is not restricted to the person attacked. It has been said to extend to 'the principal civil and natural relations.' Hale's Pleas of the Crown, Vol. 1, p.484, gives as instances master and servant, parent and child, and husband and wife who, if they even kill an assailant in the necessary defence of each other, are excused, the act of the relative assisting being considered the same as the act of the party himself. But no reported case goes outside the relations indicated, although the editor of Kenny's Outlines of Criminal Law, 18th ed. (1962), p.198, says that '. . . perhaps the courts will now take a still more general view of this duty of the strong to protect the weak.' Be that as it may, the judge seems to have found himself limited by the fact that no reported decision extended self-defence to a case where, as here, a sister went to the rescue of a sister, and the direction given to the jury as far as this appellant is concerned was this: 'So far as I can see, members of the jury, in this case, the defence of self-defence is not open to Lilian Duffy. There is no suggestion whatever that she personally was attacked and it is my direction to you to approach this case on the footing that it is no defence for Lilian Duffy to say she was going to the assistance of her sister . . .'

The source of error in this case, as it appears to this court is, as we have said, that everyone, including counsel at the trial and again before us, seems to have overlooked that in reality and in law the case of Lilian Duffy was not trammelled by any technical limitations on the application of the plea of self-defence, and this court is not here concerned to consider what those limitations are. Quite apart from any special relations between the person attacked and his rescuer, there is a general liberty even as between strangers to prevent a felony. That is not to say, of course, that a newcomer may lawfully join in a fight just for the sake of fighting. Such conduct is wholly different in law from that of a person who in circumstances of necessity intervenes with the sole object of restoring the peace by rescuing a person being attacked. That, credible or otherwise, was the basic defence advanced by the appellant. She herself tied no lawyer's label to her tale. It is true that the judge said: 'I need only remind you again that it is Lilian Duffy's case that she was going to the rescue of her sister and that was why she hit Akbar with a bottle, she could not get him off her sister.' But his earlier directions had indicated that such a case afforded no defence in law. We think that this was a misdirection. The necessity for intervening at all and the reasonableness or otherwise of the manner of intervention were matters for the jury. It should have been left to them to say whether, in view of the appellant's proved conduct, such a defence could possibly be true, they being directed that the intervener is permitted to do only what is necessary and reasonable in all the circumstances for the purpose of rescue . . .

Appeal allowed

See also *Devlin v Armstrong*, below.

(c) Defence of property

R. V HUSSEY

(1924) 18 Cr. App. R. 160

The appellant given an invalid notice to quit his rooms by his landlady, refused to do so. The landlady with two friends, armed with a hammer, a spanner, a poker and a chisel, tried to break down the door to the appellant's room which he had barricaded. A panel of the door was broken and the appellant fired through the hole wounding the friends of the landlady. He was charged with unlawfully wounding them and convicted. He appealed on the ground that the distinction between self-defence and defence of one's house had not been drawn to the attention of the jury.

LORD HEWART CJ

No sufficient notice had been given to the appellant to quit his room, and therefore he was in the position of a man who was defending his house. In Archbold's Criminal Pleading, Evidence and Practice, 26th ed., p.887, it appears that: 'In defence of a man's house, the owner or his family may kill a trespasser who would forcibly dispossess him of it, in the same manner as he might, by law, kill in self-defence a man who attacks him personally; with the distinction, however, that in defending his home he need not retreat, as in other cases of self-defence, for that would be giving up his house to his adversary.' That is still the law, but not one word was said about that distinction in the summing-up, which proceeded on the foundation that the defence was the ordinary one of self-defence. The jury, by their verdict, negatived felonious intent, and with a proper direction they might have come to a different conclusion. The appeal must therefore be allowed.

Conviction quashed

Note

The landlady in *Hussey*, above, would now be committing an offence under the Protection from Eviction Act 1977 s.1, and under the Criminal Law Act 1977 s.6. Had the case arisen today, Hussey could have relied on the defence of prevention of crime.

(d) Prevention of crime

CRIMINAL LAW ACT 1967 S.3

(1) A person may use such force as is reasonable in the circumstances in the prevention of crime, or in effecting or assisting in the lawful arrest of offenders or suspected offenders or of persons unlawfully at large.

(2) Subsection (1) above shall replace the rules of common law on the question when force used for a purpose mentioned in the subsection is justified by that purpose.

Question

Did s.3(1) supersede the common law defences of self-defence, defence of others and defence of property?

A. ASHWORTH, *PRINCIPLES OF CRIMINAL LAW*, 3RD EDN (OXFORD UNIVERSITY PRESS, 1999), PP.141–144

(d) The Rules and the Principles

A precise statement of English law on the justifications is difficult to locate. The Criminal Law Act 1967, s.3, states that 'a person may use such force as is reasonable in the circumstances in the prevention of crime . . .'. The section was not intended to supplant the common law rules on self-defence, and the courts have continued to develop those rules. It is true that in most situations of self-defence it could be said that the person was preventing crime (i.e. preventing an attack which constituted a crime), but that would still leave certain cases untouched—notably, attacks by a child under 10, by a mentally disordered person, or by a person labouring under a mistake of fact. Such aggressors would commit no offence, and so it is the law of self-defence, not the prevention of crime, which governs.

The English law of self-defence, as it is applied by the courts, turns on two requirements: the force must have been necessary, and it must have been reasonable. In dealing with particular cases, however, the courts have, as we shall see, reached decisions which suggest certain sub-rules, but they have generally been reluctant to refer to them as such, preferring to make use of the broad flexibility of the concept of reasonableness . . .

Both the legislation and judicial decisions prefer to state the law in terms of what is 'reasonable' or 'reasonable and necessary' . . .

(e) The Proportionality Standard

The requirement that the use of force must be necessary . . . should be combined with a further requirement that the amount of force must be proportionate to the value being upheld. This shows respect for the rights of the attacker in self-defence cases, and for the rights of suspected offenders in relation to the other justifications. The standard cannot be a precise one: probably the best way of defining it is in terms of what is reasonably proportionate to the amount of harm likely to be suffered by the defendant, or likely to result if the forcible intervention is not made. What is crucial is that it should rule out the infliction or risk of considerable physical harm merely to apprehend a fleeing thief, to stop minor property loss or damage, etc . . . [T]he proper approach is to compare the relative value of the rights involved, and not to give special weight to the rights of the property owner simply because the other party is in the wrong (i.e. committing a crime) . . .

(f) Aspects of the Necessity Requirement

The necessity requirement forms part of most legal regimes on justifiable force. The first question to be asked is: necessary for what? We have seen that force may be justified for any one of several lawful purposes. The necessity must be judged according to the lawful purpose which the defendant was trying to pursue: for self-defence, purely defensive force will often be all that is necessary; in order to apprehend a suspected offender, on the other hand, a police officer or citizen will need to behave proactively. These differences may become particularly important in cases where there is a suspicion or allegation that the force was used by way of revenge or retaliation rather than in pursuit of a lawful purpose.

Question

D, a nurse in a mental hospital, is attacked by X a patient wielding a meat cleaver. X had escaped from a secure ward for the violently insane. D knowing this nevertheless defends himself with a crutch. He hits X over the head fracturing his skull. If self-defence has been swallowed up by s.3 of the Criminal Law Act 1967, could D plead prevention of crime on a charge under s.20 of the Offences Against the Person Act 1861 of unlawfully and maliciously inflicting grievous bodily harm?

Notes

1. Smith and Hogan suggest that although s.3 has swallowed up self-defence, in point of policy D in the above situation should have a defence. What would this defence be? Would it be the common law defence of self-defence?

2. The case below is interesting as it raises not only the issue of the relationship between the common law and s.3 of the Criminal Law Act 1967 (or its Northern Irish equivalent), but also other issues such as the imminence of the threat and defence of others. (This case must be read in light of *R. v Gladstone Williams*, above.)

DEVLIN V ARMSTRONG

[1971] N.I. 13

The case arose out of serious disturbances in Londonderry in August 1969. The appellant exhorted a crowd of people, who had been stoning the police, to build barricades and to fight the police with petrol bombs. Her grounds of appeal against four convictions of riotous behaviour and incitement to riotous behaviour were that she reasonably believed that the police were about to act unlawfully in assaulting people and damaging property and so her behaviour was justified.

LORD MACDERMOTT LCJ

with whom Curran and McKeigh L.JJ. agreed, after describing the events in some detail:

The findings of the case indicate that the state of disorder which I have described involved a violent and aggressive resistance to constitutional authority, and if the relevant facts and considerations ended with the tale of events already told, the inescapable conclusion would be that the appellant and those associated with her opposing the police by the means described were participants in a riot and guilty of riotous behaviour.

As I have stated, the answer to this, as advanced on behalf of the appellant, is one of justification. She did what she did, it was submitted, because she believed honestly and reasonably that the police were about to assault people and damage property in the Bogside. . . [F]or present purposes that in fact, the appellant did honestly and reasonably believe that the police were about to behave unlawfully in the manner mentioned. Thus arises what I have called the principal issue. Does this plea of justification afford a defence to the charges? . . .

The conclusion I have reached on this issue is against the appellant. In my opinion the submission under discussion fails as an answer to any of the charges. Since there is a dearth of authority on the point and various principles have been invoked on one side and the other, I shall enumerate the reasons which, separately and in conjunction, have led me to this view.

1. At any rate one common purpose of the rioters and the appellant was, beyond any question, to keep the police from entering or establishing themselves in the Bogside and to achieve this by force. The appellant's contention that the honesty and reasonableness of her apprehensions (as I have assumed them to be for the sake of the argument) robbed her actions of the *mens rea* necessary to constitute the offences charged must, to my mind, fail once the nature of this common purpose has been demonstrated. If it were conceded that her apprehensions supplied a motive for her actions and incitements, that in itself would fall well short of neutralising her intentions as manifested by the manner of her participation.

2. Reliance was also placed upon the doctrine of self-defence. The general nature of this doctrine may be taken as described in Russell on Crime, 12th ed. (1964) vol. I, p.680, thus:

'The use of force is lawful for the necessary defence of self or others or of property; but the justification is limited by the necessity of the occasion, and the use of unnecessary force is an assault.'

The plea of self-defence may afford a defence where the party raising it uses force, not merely to counter an actual attack, but to ward off or prevent an attack which he has honestly and reasonably anticipated. . .

That there was a distinction between the right of self-defence and the right to prevent a felony appears from *R. v Duffy*, but the latter right has gone with the abolition of the distinctions between felony and misdemeanour and its place is now taken in this jurisdiction by s.3 of the Criminal Law Act (Northern Ireland), 1967, subsection (1) which says:

'a person may use such force as is reasonable in the circumstances in the prevention of crime . . .'

I find it impossible to hold that the danger she anticipated was sufficiently specific or imminent to justify the actions she took as measures of self-defence. The police were then in the throes of containing a riot in the course of their duty, and her interventions at that juncture were far too aggressive and premature to rank as justifiable effort to prevent the prospective danger of the police getting out of hand and acting unlawfully which, as I have assumed, she anticipated.

3. Where force is used either in exercise of the right of self-defence or, under s.3 of the Act of 1967, in the prevention of crime, it must be reasonable in the circumstances. This consideration alone seems to me fatal to the appellant's plea of justification. Whatever her fears and however genuine they may have been, to organise and encourage the throwing of petrol bombs was, I would hold, an utterly unwarranted and unlawful reaction. The night of August 12 had demonstrated the capacity of these lethal weapons to injure and destroy and nothing that had happened or was likely to happen could excuse the appellant in facilitating and encouraging their use.

4. The plea of justification, whether based on the doctrine of self-defence or the statutory right to prevent crime, appears to me to place a further difficulty when the offence sought to be justified is that of inciting others to riotous behaviour. While there was evidence of a general fear of the police amongst people of the Bogside, there is nothing in the findings or facts of the case to show that those who were exhorted by the appellant to riot were actuated by any honest and reasonable apprehension of unlawful violence on the part of the police such as she is assumed to have had. Her incitements were, therefore, directed to encouraging others to do what for them was prima facie unlawful. It cannot be taken for granted that those she addressed were opposing the police for what she says were her reasons, and this all the more as the rioting had started in opposition to the parade and before the police had entered the Bogside. In my opinion the plea of self-defence cannot be availed of where what is sought to be justified is an incitement to unjustifiable crime. I know of no authority to the contrary, and on this ground as well I would hold that the plea fails.

. . .6. The ambit of the doctrine of self-defence may be wider than it once was, but when considered apart from the statutory right to which I have referred, some special nexus or relationship between the party relying on the doctrine to justify what he did in aid of another, and that other, would still appear to be necessary. Without attempting to define that factor, I cannot accept, on the material available, that it existed as between the appellant and the people of the Bogside. There is nothing to suggest that she belonged to or had property or a home in that district, and her status as a Member of Parliament would not, of itself, afford her protection by supplying a special relationship. It would seem as though she came in as a visitor and made common cause with the rioters, but I cannot regard that as an adequate relationship on which to found a defence of justification by way of self-defence.

7. Finally, the outbreak of rioting on August 12 and 13 imposed a duty on more than the constabulary. The private citizen has authority in law to help in the suppression of riots, and it is his common law duty to assist the constabulary to this end: see Russell on Crime, 12th ed. (1964), pp.270 *et seq.*, and, in particular, the *Bristol Riots* case (1832) 3 St.Tr. (N.S.) 1 at 4 and 5, and *R. v Pinney* (1832) 3 St.Tr. (N.S.) 11. That obligation, which rested upon the appellant as well as others, made it impossible, in my opinion, for her to find any legal justification for her conduct in aiding and encouraging the rioters as she undoubtedly did.

Appeals dismissed

Notes

1.   Following a pledge made at the Labour Party Conference in 2007, s.76 of the Criminal Justice and Immigration Act 2008 was enacted. This simply placed on a statutory basis certain principles established in the case law. The legislation was a knee-jerk response to tabloid newspaper stories about "have-a-go heroes" arrested and prosecuted for intervening and assisting people being attacked on the street. The problem police officers face in such circumstances is seeking

to determine what the true facts might be where witnesses' accounts of what happened may be inconsistent and contradictory. In addition, even if this can be determined, it may not resolve matters as determining what force is reasonable is context-specific and that context includes not only the external circumstances but also D's perception and belief in relation to those circumstances. Sometimes the only way to determine whether a "have-a-go hero" was acting reasonably in self-defence or to prevent a crime, rather than unreasonably to exact revenge or as a vigilante, may be to prosecute him for an offence against the person and leave the jury to determine the issue.

2. Following the enactment of s.76 problems continued to arise relating to the degree of force that might be considered reasonable. Several cases involving householders using force against burglars presented particular problems which provoked considerable coverage in the tabloid press. In response s.148 of the Legal Aid, Sentencing and Punishment of Offenders Act 2012 was enacted making amendments to s.76 (see subs.(2)(aa) and subs.(6A).

3. But no sooner had these amendments been made than further problems arose leading to s.43 of the Crime and Courts Act 2013 making further amendments specifically to deal with what are referred to as "householder cases" (see s.76(5A)) where D (not being a trespasser—see s.76(8A)) in, or partly in, a building which is a dwelling uses force against V whom he believes to be in, or entering, the building as a trespasser. These "householder cases" are distinguished from other cases involving the use of force as the use of force by D is not to be regarded as having been reasonable in the circumstances as D believed them to be if it was *grossly disproportionate* in those circumstances. This suggests that it may be reasonable for householders to use disproportionate force to defend themselves in their homes.

4. Many more subsections are then required ((8A) − (8F)) to define what is a "householder" case resulting in immense complexity which ultimately a lay jury will have to resolve!

CRIMINAL JUSTICE AND IMMIGRATION ACT 2008 S.76

Reasonable force for purposes of self-defence etc.

(1) This section applies where in proceedings for an offence—

(a) an issue arises as to whether a person charged with the offence ('D') is entitled to rely on a defence within subsection (2), and

(b) the question arises whether the degree of force used by D against a person ('V') was reasonable in the circumstances.

(2) The defences are—

(a) the common law defence of self-defence;

(aa) the common law defence of defence of property; and

(b) the defences provided by section 3(1) of the Criminal Law Act 1967 or section 3(1) of the Criminal Law Act (Northern Ireland) 1967 . . ..

(3) The question whether the degree of force used by D was reasonable in the circumstances is to be decided by reference to the circumstances as D believed them to be, and subsections (4) to (8) also apply in connection with deciding that question.

(4) If D claims to have held a particular belief as regards the existence of any circumstances—

(a) the reasonableness or otherwise of that belief is relevant to the question whether D genuinely held it; but

(b) if it is determined that D did genuinely hold it, D is entitled to rely on it for the purposes of subsection (3), whether or not—

    (i)   it was mistaken, or

    (ii) (if it was mistaken) the mistake was a reasonable one to have made.

(5) But subsection (4)(b) does not enable D to rely on any mistaken belief attributable to intoxication that was voluntarily induced.

(5A) In a householder case, the degree of force used by D is not to be regarded as having been reasonable in the circumstances as D believed them to be if it was grossly disproportionate in those circumstances.

(6) In a case other than a householder case, the degree of force used by D is not to be regarded as having been reasonable in the circumstances as D believed them to be if it was disproportionate in those circumstances.

(6A) In deciding the question mentioned in subsection (3), a possibility that D could have retreated is to be considered (so far as relevant) as a factor to be taken into account, rather than as giving rise to a duty to retreat.

(7) In deciding the question mentioned in subsection (3) the following considerations are to be taken into account (so far as relevant in the circumstances of the case)—

(a) that a person acting for a legitimate purpose may not be able to weigh to a nicety the exact measure of any necessary action; and

(b) that evidence of a person's having only done what the person honestly and instinctively thought was necessary for a legitimate purpose constitutes strong evidence that only reasonable action was taken by that person for that purpose.

(8A) For the purposes of this section "a householder case" is a case where —0

    (a)   the defence concerned is the common law defence of self-defence,

    (b)   the force concerned is force used by D while in or partly in a building, or part of a building, that is a dwelling or is forces accommodation (or is both),

    (c)   D is not a trespasser at the time the force is used, and

    (d)   at that time D believed V to be in, or entering, the building or part as a trespasser.

(8B) Where —

    (a)   a part of a building is a dwelling where D dwells,

    (b)   another part of the building is a place of work for D or another person who dwells in the first part, and

    (c)   that other part is internally accessible from the first part,

that other part, and any internal means of access between the two parts, are each treated for the purposes of subsection (8A) as a part of a building that is a dwelling.

(8C) Where —

    (a)   a part of a building is forces accommodation that is living or sleeping accommodation for D,

    (b)   another part of the building is a place of work for D or another person for whom the first part is living or sleeping accommodation, and

    (c)   that other part is internally accessible from the first part,

that other part, and any internal means of access between the two parts, are each treated for the purposes of subsection (8A) as a part of a building that is forces accommodation.

(8D)Subsections (4) and (5) apply for the purposes of subsection (8A)(d) as they apply for the purposes of subsection (3).

(8E) The fact that a person derives title from a trespasser, or has the permission of a trespasser, does not prevent the person from being a trespasser for the purposes of subsection (8A).

(8F) In subsections (8A) to (8C)—

"building" includes a vehicle or vessel, and

"forces accommodation" means service living accommodation for the purposes of Part 3 of the Armed Forces Act 2006 by virtue of section 96(1)(a) or (b) of that Act.

(9) This section, except so far as making different provision for householder cases, is intended to clarify the operation of the existing defences mentioned in subsection (2).

(10) In this section—

(a) "legitimate purpose" means—

(i) the purpose of self-defence under the common law, or
(ii) the prevention of crime or effecting or assisting in the lawful arrest of persons mentioned in the provisions referred to in subsection (2)(b);

(b) references to self-defence include acting in defence of another person; and

(c) references to the degree of force used are to the type and amount of force used.

Questions

1. How, if at all, does s.76 legislate for matters not already established in the case law?

2. How, if at all, does s.76 assist a jury who are considering whether or not the amount of force used by D was unreasonable in the circumstances?

3. Where it is a "householder case" will a jury necessarily hold that force which was disproportionate, but not grossly so, was reasonable force? If not, in what way does s.76(5A) provide any greater guidance to jurors' deliberations, or to unfortunate householders confronted in the dead of night by an intruder, than that which existed prior to its enactment?

4. D's house has a covered veranda with some garden seats on it. He confronts V on the veranda attempting to open a window and, concluding that V is a burglar, hurls him over the veranda railing on to a concrete patio below fracturing V's skull. Is this a "householder case"? In what way would your answer differ if D, while inside, had confronted V trying to climb through the window to (a) D's motorhome parked on the driveway; (b) D's summerhouse which contains a camp-bed for use by occasional visitors; (c) D's garage which is integrated into his house; (d) D's detached garage; (e) D's detached garage above which is a games room; and (f) D's garden shed?

5. Does s.76 offer any guidance on the use of pre-emptive force or on unknown circumstances of justification?

Note

The five principles put into statutory form in s.76 are:

(1) the question whether D's use of force was reasonable in the circumstances is to be decided on the basis of the circumstances D believed to exist (s.76(3)), even if his belief was mistaken and unreasonable (s.76(4));

(2) D cannot rely on any mistaken belief attributable to intoxication that was voluntarily induced (s.76(5));

(3) the degree of force used by D is not to be regarded as having been reasonable in the circumstances as D believed them to be if it was disproportionate in those circumstances (s.76(6)) (in a householder case the test is whether it was "grossly disproportionate" (s.76(5A));

(4) in deciding the question in (1) above, a possibility that D could have retreated is to be considered (so far as relevant) as a factor to be taken into account, rather than as giving rise to a duty to retreat (s.76(6A));

(5) a person acting for a "legitimate purpose" (i.e. self-defence, defence of property, prevention of crime, or lawful arrest) may not be able to weigh to a nicety the exact measure of any necessary action (s.76(7)(a)) and evidence of his only having done what he honestly and instinctively thought was necessary for a legitimate purpose constitutes strong evidence that only reasonable action was taken by him for that purpose (s.76(7)(b)).

----

ii. The Issues of Imminence and the Pre-Emptive Strike

ATTORNEY GENERAL'S REFERENCE (NO.2 OF 1983)

[1984] Q.B. 456

The defendant's shop in Toxteth had been attacked and damaged by rioters. Fearing further attacks he made some petrol bombs which he intended to use purely as a last resort to repulse raiders from his shop. He was charged with an offence under s.4 of the Explosive Substances Act 1883, namely, of having made an explosive substance in such circumstances as to give rise to a reasonable suspicion that he had not made it for a lawful object. He pleaded that his lawful object was self-defence and the jury acquitted. The Attorney General referred for the court's opinion the question whether the defence of self-defence was available to a defendant charged with an offence under s.4 of the 1883 Act.

LORD LANE CJ

. . . Counsel for the Crown argued at trial that self-defence did not provide a valid defence to the respondent on this charge because such a plea is available only to justify actual violence by a defendant. Mr Hill contends that it does not exist as a justification for preliminary and premeditated acts anticipatory of an act of violence by the defendant in the absence of any express statutory provision therefor . . .

Mr Hill submits that to allow a man to justify in advance his own act of violence for which he has prepared runs wholly contrary to the principle and thinking behind legitimate self-defence and legitimate defence of property. Both are defences which the law allows to actual violence by a defendant, and both are based on the principle that a man may be justified in extremis in taking spontaneous steps to defend himself, others of his family and his property against actual or mistakenly perceived violent attack. It was argued that if a plea of self-defence is allowed to section 4 of the Act of 1883 the effect would be that a man could write his own immunity for unlawful acts done in preparation for violence to be used by him in the future. Rather than that, goes on the argument, in these circumstances a man should protect himself by calling on the police or by barricading his premises or by guarding them alone or with others, but not with petrol bombs . . .

[In *R. v Fegan* [1972] N.I. 80, Lord MacDermott CJ said at 87:]

'Possession of a firearm for the purpose of protecting the possessor or his wife or family from acts of violence, *may* be possession for a lawful object. But the lawfulness of such a purpose cannot be founded on a mere fancy, or on some aggressive motive. The threatened danger must be reasonably and genuinely anticipated, must appear reasonably imminent, and must be of a nature which could not reasonably be met by more pacific means. A lawful object in this particular field therefore falls within a strictly limited category and cannot be such as to justify going beyond what the law may allow in meeting the situation of danger which the possessor of the firearm reasonably and genuinely apprehends.'

. . . In our judgment, approaching *a priori* the words 'lawful object' it might well seem open to a defendant to say, 'My lawful object is self-defence.' The respondent in this case said that his intentions were to use the petrol bombs purely to protect his premises should any rioters come to his shop. It was accordingly open to the jury to find that the respondent has made them for the reasonable protection of himself and his property against this danger. The fact that in manufacturing and storing the petrol bombs the respondent committed offences under the [Explosives] Act of 1875 [which prohibits the manufacture and storage of explosives without a licence] did not necessarily involve that when he made them his object in doing so was not lawful. The means by which he sought to fulfil that object were unlawful, but the fact that he could never without committing offences reach the point where he used them in self-defence did not render his object in making them for that purpose unlawful. The object or purpose or end for which the petrol bombs were made was not itself rendered unlawful by the fact that it could not be fulfilled except by unlawful means. The fact that the commission of other offences was unavoidable did not result in any of them becoming one of the respondent's objects . . .

In the judge's summing up the threatened danger was assumed, as was the respondent's anticipation of it. Also assumed, no doubt upon the basis of the evidence led, was the imminence of the danger. What the judge upon the facts of the case before him left to the jury was the reasonableness of the means adopted for the repulsion of raiders . . .

In our judgment a defendant is not left in the paradoxical position of being able to justify acts carried out in self-defence but not acts immediately preparatory to it. There is no warrant for the submission on behalf of the Attorney-General that acts of self-defence will only avail a defendant when they have been done spontaneously. There is no question of a person in danger of attack 'writing his own immunity' for violent future acts of his. He is not confined for his remedy to calling in the police or boarding up his premises.

He may still arm himself for his own protection, if the exigency arises, although in so doing he may commit other offences. That he may be guilty of other offences will avoid the risk of anarchy contemplated by the reference. It is also to be noted that although a person may 'make' a petrol bomb with a lawful object, nevertheless if he remains in possession of it after the threat has passed which made his object lawful, it may cease to be so. It will only be very rarely that circumstances will exist where the manufacture or possession of petrol bombs can be for a lawful object.

For these reasons the point of law referred by Her Majesty's Attorney-General for the consideration of this court is answered by saying: the defence of lawful object is available to a defendant against whom a charge under section 4 of the Act of 1883 has been preferred, if he can satisfy the jury on balance of probabilities that his object was to protect himself or his family against imminent apprehended attack and to do so by means which he believed were no more than reasonably necessary to meet the force used by the attackers.

Opinion accordingly

J.C. SMITH, "COMMENTARY" [1984] CRIM. L.R. 290

If the respondent intended to use the bombs only in circumstances in which it would have been lawful to do so, then it seems to follow inevitably that he had them in his possession 'for a lawful object,' and so was not guilty of the offence under the Explosives Substances Act 1883. In determining whether the object was lawful, the court was looking forward to the contemplated actual use of the weapons, so it was not really necessary to decide whether the preparatory acts were lawful or not. So regarded, the decision is a narrow one; and indeed, it seems to have accepted that the respondent was committing an offence of manufacturing and storing explosives without a licence, contrary to the Explosives Act 1875. Nor does any doubt seem to have been cast on *Evans v Wright* [1964] Crim.L.R. 466 and the other cases under the Prevention of Crime Act 1953 which hold that there is no lawful authority or reasonable excuse for carrying an offensive weapon in a public place for purposes of self-defence, unless there is 'an imminent particular threat affecting the particular circumstances in which the weapon was carried': *Evans v Hughes* [1972] 3 All E.R. 412 at 415. A person who intends to use an offensive weapon only in reasonable defence has it 'for a lawful object'; yet it seems to be accepted that, unless there is an 'imminent' threat, he commits an offence under the 1953 Act. A taxi-driver might be justified in using the two feet of rubberhose with a piece of metal inserted in the end which he carries for the purposes of self-defence, when he is the victim of a violent attack; but he was committing an offence, at least until the moment when the attack was imminent, by having the article with him in a public place: *Grieve v Macleod* 1967, S.L.T. 70.

The reasons of policy for such an approach are obvious. The court does not want to create a situation in which the manufacture and carrying of weapons will proliferate. The court says, however, that in their judgment, a defendant was not left in the paradoxical position of being able to justify acts carried out in self-defence but not acts immediately preparatory to it; but the justification is somewhat illusory if, as the court also says, he might at the same time commit other offences.

Self-defence is a defence at common law. It applies not only to common law offences but also to statutory offences, although the statutory definition gives no hint of the existence of any such defence—see, for example, ss 18 and 20 of the Offences Against the Person Act 1861. If the common law defence applies to these offences, why not to other offences such as those under the Explosive Substances Act 1875? If I am being shot at by a dangerous criminal and I pick up the revolver which has been dropped by a wounded policeman and fire it in self-defence, am I really guilty of an offence under the Firearms Act 1968, s.1, of being in possession of firearms without holding a firearm certificate? It seems strange that the circumstances might justify me in killing my assailant with the revolver and yet not justify me in being in possession of it. If self-defence is justifiable, it surely ought to be a defence to all crimes. If it is not justifiable, it is a defence to none.

Because the only question in the present case was whether the respondent was in possession for a 'lawful object', the question whether the preliminary acts were justifiable did not really arise; but the better view seems to be that at least those acts which are immediately preparatory to the use of reasonable force in self-defence are justifiable to the same extent as the actual use of force.

Question

In the bank robbery example, if Professor Smith was charged with an offence under s.1 of the Firearms Act 1968, could he now plead duress of circumstances?

Notes

1.   In *Beckford v The Queen* [1988] 1 A.C. 130, Lord Griffiths stated at 144:

> "The common law recognises that there are many circumstances in which one person may inflict violence upon another without committing a crime, as for instance, in sporting contests, surgical operations or in the most extreme example judicial execution. The common law has always recognised as one of these circumstances the right of a person to protect himself from attack and to act in the defence of others and if necessary to inflict violence on another in so doing. If no more force is used than is reasonable to repel the attack such force is not unlawful and no crime is committed. Furthermore a man about to be attacked does not have to wait for his assailant to strike the first blow or fire the first shot; circumstances may justify a pre-emptive strike.
>
>   It is because it is an essential element of all crimes of violence that the violence or the threat of violence should be unlawful that self-defence, if raised as an issue in a criminal trial, must be disproved by the prosecution. If the prosecution fail to do so the accused is entitled to be acquitted because the prosecution will have failed to prove an essential element of the crime namely that the violence used by the accused was unlawful."

2.   Section 76 does not address the issues of imminence and pre-emptive strike.

----

iii. Is there a duty to retreat?

R. V BIRD

[1985] 1 W.L.R. 816 CA

The appellant was charged with unlawful wounding having lunged at a young man with a glass in her hand, injuring him. She claimed that he had slapped and pushed her so that her back was to the wall and that she acted in self-defence without realising until later that she had been holding the glass in her hand. She was convicted.

LORD LANE CJ

. . . The relevant passages in the summing up are these—first, towards the beginning of the direction to the jury:

'You cannot wrap up an attack in the cloak of self-defence and it is necessary that a person claiming to exercise a right of self-defence should demonstrate by her action that she does not want to fight. At one time it was thought that in order to demonstrate that, that the person seeking to raise a question of self-defence had to retreat. That is not so any longer at all, but there is an obligation to see whether the person claiming to exercise the right of self-defence should have demonstrated that she does not want to fight at all.'

Towards the end of the summing up the judge used these words:

'You will have to consider whether in the circumstances of this case self-defence has any application at all. Does it look to you that this lady, who was behaving in this fashion, had demonstrated that she did not want to fight and if she had demonstrated that she did not want to fight, was the use of the glass with a hard blow which broke it, reasonable in the circumstances? All these are matters for you and not for me.'

Those words were taken very largely from a decision of this court in *R. v Julien* [1969] 1 W.L.R. 839. That was an ex tempore judgment by Widgery L.J. to which I was a party as was Karminski L.J. The passage from which the words are taken reads, at p.842:

'The third point taken by Mr McHale is that the deputy chairman was wrong in directing the jury that before the appellant could use force in self-defence he was required to retreat. The submission here is that the obligation to retreat before using force in self-defence is an obligation which only arises in homicide cases. As the court understands it, it is submitted that if the injury results in death then the accused cannot set up self-defence except on the basis that he had retreated before he resorted to violence. On the other hand, it is said that where the injury does not result in death (as in the present case) the obligation to retreat does not arise . . .

It is not, as we understand it, the law that a person threatened must take to his heels and run in the dramatic way suggested by Mr McHale, but what is necessary is that he should demonstrate by his actions that he does not want to fight. He must demonstrate that he is prepared to temporise and disengage and perhaps to make some physical withdrawal: and that that is necessary as a feature of the justification of self-defence is true, in our opinion, whether the charge is a homicide charge or something less serious. Accordingly, we reject Mr McHale's third submission.'

That decision was to some extent followed later in *R. v McInnes* [1971] 1 W.L.R. 1600 . . .
The court in *R. v Julien* was anxious to make it clear that there was no duty, despite earlier authorities to the contrary, actually to turn round or walk away from the scene. But reading the words which were used in that judgment, it now seems to us that they placed too great an obligation upon a defendant in circumstances such as those in the instant case, an obligation which is not reflected in the speeches in *Palmer v The Queen* [1971] A.C. 814.
The matter is dealt with accurately and helpfully in *Smith and Hogan Criminal Law*, 5th ed. (1983), p.327:

'There were formerly technical rules about the duty to retreat before using force, or at least fatal force. This is now simply a factor to be taken into account in deciding whether it was necessary to use force, and whether the force was reasonable. If the only reasonable course is to retreat, then it would appear that to stand and fight must be to use unreasonable force. There is, however, no rule of law that a person attacked is bound to run away if he can; but it has been said that—". . . what is necessary is that he should demonstrate by his actions that he does not want to fight. He must demonstrate that he is prepared to temporise and disengage and perhaps to make some physical withdrawal." [*R. v Julien* [1969] 1 W.L.R. 839, 842]. It is submitted that it goes too far to say that action of this kind is *necessary*. It is scarcely consistent with the rule that it is permissible to use force, not merely to counter an actual attack, but to ward off an attack honestly and reasonably believed to be imminent. A demonstration by [the defendant] at the time that he did not want to fight is, no doubt, the best evidence that he was acting reasonably and in good faith in self-defence; but it is no more than that. A person may in some circumstances so act without temporising, disengaging or withdrawing; and he should have a good defence.'

We respectfully agree with that passage. If the defendant is proved to have been attacking or retaliating or revenging himself, then he was not truly acting in self-defence. Evidence that the defendant tried to retreat or tried to call off the fight may be a cast-iron method of casting doubt on the suggestion that he was the attacker or retaliator or the person trying to revenge himself. But it is not by any means the only method of doing that.

It seems to us therefore that in this case the judge—we hasten to add through no fault of his own—by using the word 'necessary' as we did in the passages in the summing up to which we have referred, put too high an obligation upon the appellant.

Appeal allowed
Conviction quashed

Note

Section 76(6A) of the Criminal Justice and Immigration Act 2008 gives statutory force to the principle established in *Bird*.

----

iv. Unknown circumstances of justification

If circumstances actually exist which would justify the use of force against V, must D know of or believe in the existence of these circumstances if he is to plead self-defence or prevention of crime or lawful arrest in respect of a charge arising from his use of force? This problem of "unknown circumstances of justification" arose in *Dadson* (1850) 4 Cox C.C. 358. D, a constable, was on duty watching a copse from which wood had been stolen. V emerged from the copse carrying wood which had been stolen. He ran away when D called to him and D shot him so that he could arrest him. D was convicted of shooting at V with intent to cause him grievous bodily harm. D had sought to raise the justification that he was shooting to arrest an escaping felon. Stealing wood was only a felony where the thief had two previous convictions for that offence. In fact V had several such convictions and thus was a felon but D did not know this. Ds conviction was upheld as he was not justified in shooting V as the fact that V was committing a felony was not known to him at the time.

When the Criminal Law Act 1967 was passed it was argued by some that ss.2 and 3 had the effect of reversing *Dadson*. (The Police and Criminal Evidence Act 1984 s.24(4) replaced s.2.) It was argued that if a person actually had committed an arrestable offence an arrest of him would be lawful even though the arresting officer did not know nor suspect on reasonable grounds that he had committed that offence. The Law Commission in its reports on *Codification of the Criminal Law* (TSO, 1985 and 1989),Law Com. Nos 143 and 177, recommended that an accused should be able to rely on unknown circumstances of justification in any case where the use of force was necessary and reasonable (contra, see Hogan, "The *Dadson* principle" [1989] Crim. L.R. 679). In *Chapman* (1988) 89 Cr. App. R. 190, the Divisional Court effectively reaffirmed *Dadson* pointing out that if a person is unaware of circumstances justifying an arrest he cannot perform a lawful arrest as he will not be able to comply with s.28(3) of the Police and Criminal Evidence Act 1984 which requires that he inform the suspect of the grounds for the arrest. If an arrest is unlawful it follows that any force used to effect it is likewise unlawful.

Question

D, looking out from his bedroom, spies the head and shoulders of V, his life-long sworn enemy, protruding above a wall 50m away. D takes aim with his rifle and shoots V wounding him. Unknown to D, V was about to depress a plunger wired to an explosive charge below where D was standing which, if it had exploded, would have killed D. D is charged with wounding with intent to do grievous bodily harm contrary to s.18 of the Offences Against the Person Act 1861. Will D succeed on a plea of self-defence or prevention of crime?

----

v. To which offences do the defences apply?

R. V RENOUF

[1986] 1 W.L.R. 522 CA

The appellant was charged with reckless driving. He had driven his car in pursuit of another vehicle, the occupants of which had assaulted him and damaged his car, he forced the vehicle off the road and rammed it. He was convicted after the trial judge directed that s.3(1) of the Criminal Law Act 1967 was incapable of affording a defence to the charge of reckless driving. He appealed.

LAWTON LJ

. . . The evidence relating to edging the Volvo off the road was what the prosecution alleged amounted to the reckless driving as charged. It did create an obvious and serious risk of causing physical harm to the occupants of the Volvo and of damage to it. On the evidence this was the only risk upon which the allegation of recklessness could be based. There was no risk to oncoming traffic; and nothing more than a tenuous suggestion that there might have been a risk to any traffic there may have been (and there was none) on a side road nearby . . .

This case has to be considered in the light of the evidence which was said to have amounted to reckless driving. This evidence had two facets: one was what the prosecution alleged to be the acts of recklessness; and the other was that these same acts amounted to the use of reasonable force for the purpose of assisting in the lawful arrest of offenders. In our judgment it is only when evidence has these two facets that section 3(1) of the Criminal Law Act 1967 can apply. This being so, the occasions for relying on that section will be rare, certainly not when the reckless acts were antecedent to the use of force. In our judgment the alleged presence of these two facets in the appellant's evidence concerning why he did the acts which the prosecution said were reckless was capable of providing him with a defence. It is no answer for the prosecution to submit, as Mr Clark did, that the wording of ss 1 and 2 of the Road Traffic Act 1972 shuts out any possibility of such a defence because they contained no words such as 'lawful excuse'. Nor does s.20 of the Offences Against the Persons Act 1861; but section 3(1) had been used to provide a defence to charges under that section.

The only other point which calls for consideration is whether what the appellant said he did amounted to the use of 'force'. That word is one of ordinary usage in English and does not require judicial interpretation. In that usage a jury might consider that the appellant had forced the Volvo off the road on to the grass verge. The trial judge used the word 'force' in this sense in the course of his summing up.

In our judgment, on the unusual evidence in case, the judge should have left to the jury the appellant's defence based on section 3(1) of the Act of 1967. They might have accepted it because they found the appellant not guilty of causing criminal damage to the Volvo when he rammed it in order to stop it moving. They could only have done so because of his defence of 'lawful excuse'.

Appeal allowed

vi. Reasonable Force

Note

If the prosecution prove beyond reasonable doubt that there was no necessity to use force this will be an end of the matter unless D brings forward some evidence that he was operating under a mistake. Several different situations need to be distinguished. First, if D makes a mistake as to the necessity to use force, the force used is necessarily objectively unreasonable, i.e. no force being necessary, any force used would be unreasonable. For example, V in an April Fools Day prank wears a mask, carries an imitation gun and stages an ambush on his friend D who is stalking deer. D, believing V is an armed robber and that his life is at risk, shoots V with his rifle. *R. v Williams (Gladstone)* and *Beckford v The Queen* established that in such circumstances D must be judged according to his mistaken view of the facts (see s.76(3) and (4)) of the Criminal Justice and Immigration Act 2008). Evidence that D suffered from a psychiatric condition affecting his perception would be relevant to the question whether he held a genuine belief that he was under threat (see *Press and Thompson* [2013] EWCA 2514). (But where the belief in the need to use force arises from a delusion, the correct defence is that of insanity: see *Oye* [2013] EWCA Crim 1725.) If D used only such force as was reasonable in the circumstances as he believed them to be, the effect of D's mistake is that he did not intend to use unlawful force and thus lacked the *mens rea* for the offence with which he is charged. Secondly, in any case where force is necessary (or the prosecution have not satisfied the jury that it was not), the reasonableness of that force is to be judged objectively by the jury, see *Palmer v The Queen*, below; and *Attorney General for Northern Ireland's Reference (No.1 of 1975)*, below. If the force used is excessive the defence will fail. Thirdly, D may make a mistake not as to the need to use force but as to the extent of the necessity, believing that more force is required than the circumstances objectively require—e.g. V attacks D with a knife and D hits V on the head with a brick—the knife, in fact, was a theatrical knife where the blade retracts into the handle when pressure is applied to its tip. There was an assault and probably a battery on D therefore justifying D in using reasonable force to defend himself. The problem is that D anticipated greater danger to himself and used force which would have been appropriate in those anticipated circumstances. In such a situation D believes he is using reasonable force but in fact he is using excessive force. Again, D will be judged according to the circumstances as he believed them to be, see *Scarlett*, below; and *Owino*, below. But if D uses more force than is reasonable, his belief that the degree of force he used was reasonable will not be determinative of the issue, see *Owino*. For example, V steals chocolate from D's shop and runs off. D takes a gun from under the counter and shouts at him to stop. V continues running and D shoots him in the back killing him. D asserts in his defence that he believes the use of deadly force is reasonable to apprehend shoplifters.

PALMER V THE QUEEN

[1971] A.C. 814

A group of men, including the appellant went to buy ganja. The accused had a gun. A dispute arose and the men left with the ganja but without paying. A chase ensued and a man was shot.

The appellant was charged with murder and claimed self-defence. He was convicted of murder and appealed.

LORD MORRIS OF BORTH-Y-GEST

. . . On behalf of the appellant it was contended that if where self-defence is an issue in a case of homicide a jury came to the conclusion that an accused person was intending to defend himself then an intention to kill or to cause grievous bodily harm would be negatived: so it was contended that if in such a case the jury came to the conclusion that excessive force had been used the correct verdict would be one of manslaughter: hence it was argued that in every case where self-defence is left to a jury they must be directed that there are the three possible verdicts, viz. guilty of murder, guilty of manslaughter, and not guilty. But in many cases where someone is intending to defend himself he will have had an intention to cause serious bodily injury or even to kill, and if the prosecution satisfy the jury that he had one of these intentions in circumstances in which or at a time when there was no justification or excuse for having it—then the prosecution will have shown that the question of self-defence is eliminated. All other issues which on the facts may arise will be unaffected.

An issue of self-defence may of course arise in a range and variety of cases and circumstances where no death has resulted. The tests as to its rejection or its validity will be just the same as in a case where death has resulted. In its simplest form the question that arises is the question: Was the defendant acting in necessary self-defence? If the prosecution satisfy the jury that he was not then all other possible issues remain.

. . . In their Lordships' view the defence of self-defence is one which can be and will be readily understood by any jury. It is a straightforward conception. It involves no abstruse legal thought. It requires no set words by way of explanation. No formula need be employed in reference to it. Only common sense is needed for its understanding. It is both good law and good sense that a man who is attacked may defend himself. It is both good law and good sense that he may do, but may only do what is reasonably necessary. But everything will depend upon the particular facts and circumstances. Of these a jury can decide. It may in some cases be only sensible and clearly possible to take some simple avoiding action. Some attacks may be serious and dangerous. Others may not be. If there is some relatively minor attack it would not be common sense to permit some action of retaliation which was wholly out of proportion to the necessities of the situation. If an attack is serious so that it puts someone in immediate peril then immediate defensive action may be necessary. If the moment is one of crisis for someone in imminent danger he may have to avert the danger by some instant reaction. If the attack is all over and no sort of peril remains then the employment of force may be by way of revenge or punishment or by way of paying off an old score or may be pure aggression. There may no longer be any link with a necessity of defence. Of all these matters the good sense of a jury will be the arbiter. There are no prescribed words which must be employed in or adopted in a summing up. All that is needed is a clear exposition, in relation to the particular facts of the case, of the conception of necessary self-defence. If there has been no attack then clearly there will have been no need for defence. If there has been attack so that defence is reasonably necessary it will be recognised that a person defending himself cannot weigh to a nicety the exact measure of his necessary defensive action. If a jury thought that in a moment of unexpected anguish a person attacked had only done what he honestly and instinctively thought was necessary that would be most potent evidence that only reasonable defensive action had been taken. A jury will be told that the defence of self-defence, where the evidence makes its raising possible, will only fail if the prosecution show beyond doubt that what the accused did was not by way of self-defence. But their Lordships consider, in agreement with the approach in the *De Freitas* case (1960) 2 W.I.R. 523, that if the prosecution have shown that what was done was not done in self-defence then that issue is eliminated from the case. If the jury consider that an accused acted in self-defence or if the jury are in doubt as to this then they will acquit. The defence of self-defence either succeeds so as to result in an acquittal or it is disproved in which case as a defence it is rejected. In a homicide case the circumstances may be such that it will become an issue as to whether there was provocation so that the verdict might be one of manslaughter. Any other possible issues will remain. If in any case the view is possible that the intent necessary to constitute the crime of murder was lacking then that matter would be left to the jury.

Appeal dismissed

Does it follow that because the defendant honestly believed that the force which he used was necessary, a jury will always find that the degree of force which he used was reasonably necessary?

Palmer was followed by the Court of Appeal in *McInnes* [1971] 1 W.L.R. 1600. In the *Attorney General for Northern Ireland's Reference (No.1 of 1975)* [1977] A.C. 105, Lord Dilhorne said that where death results from the use of excessive force in prevention of crime or in effecting an arrest, and the accused intended to kill or do grievous bodily harm, he would be guilty of murder and not manslaughter.

In *R. v Clegg* [1995] 1 A.C. 482, the House of Lords confirmed this position expressing their regret that this was the law but considering that any change in the law was a matter for the legislature. Following this decision the Home Secretary announced a review of the law in this area on 24 January 1995 (see below).

In the case of *R. v Mackay* [1957] V.R. 560, the Supreme Court of Victoria recognised a qualified defence to murder based on the excessive use of force in circumstances where some force would have been lawful. A killing in such circumstances would result in a manslaughter verdict. This defence was confirmed by the High Court of Australia in *R. v Howe* (1958) 100 C.L.R. 448 and again in *Viro v The Queen* (1978) 141 C.L.R. 88. In *Palmer* the Privy Council considered these authorities but decided not to follow them. However, in *Zecevic v DPP* (1987) 61 A.L.J.R. 375, by a majority of five to two, the High Court of Australia abolished the defence. The majority were motivated by a desire first, to simplify the defence of self-defence to make it more readily understandable by juries; secondly, to make for consistency between homicide and other crimes; and thirdly, to bring Australian common law into line with *Palmer*, English common law and the law of the Code States of Australia. Prior to this development there was a rising tide of support in England for the Australian qualified defence; both Smith and Hogan, *Criminal Law*, 8th edn (1996); and Glanville Williams, *Textbook of Criminal Law*, 2nd edn (1983), pp.546–547 are in favour of the importation of the defence into the English common law; while the Criminal Law Revision Committee on *Offences Against the Person* in its 14th Report para.288 and the Law Commission, *Draft Criminal Code Bill*, cl.59 and the Select Committee of the House of Lords on *Murder and Life Imprisonment* (HL Paper 78–1 session 1988–89), para.83 recommended the introduction of a defence similar to the Australian qualified defence.

ATTORNEY GENERAL FOR NORTHERN IRELAND'S REFERENCE

[1977] A.C. 105 HL

The reference was based on a case in which a soldier was charged with murder after shooting at the deceased in the mistaken belief that he was a member of the IRA, a proscribed organisation.

LORD DIPLOCK

To kill or wound another person is *prima facie* unlawful. There may be circumstances, however, which render the act of shooting and any killing which results from it lawful; and an honest and reasonable belief by the accused in the existence of facts which if true would have rendered his act lawful is a defence to any charge based on the shooting. So for the purposes of the present reference one must ignore the fact that the deceased was an entirely innocent person and must deal with the case as if he were a member of the Provisional I.R.A. and a potentially dangerous terrorist, as the accused honestly and reasonably believed him to be . . .

What amount of force is 'reasonable in the circumstances' for the purpose of preventing crime is, in my view, always a question for the jury in a jury trial, never a 'point of law' for the judge.

The form in which the jury would have to ask themselves the question in trial for an offence against the person in which this defence was raised by the accused, would be: Are we satisfied that no reasonable man a) with knowledge of such facts as were known to the accused or reasonably believed by him to exist b) in the circumstances and time available to him for reflection c) could be of the opinion that the prevention of the risk of harm to which others might be exposed if the suspect were allowed to escape justified exposing the suspect to the risk of harm to him that might result from the kind of force that the accused contemplated using?

To answer this the jury would have first to decide what were the facts that did exist and were known to the accused to do so and what were mistakenly believed by the accused to be facts. In respect of the latter the jury would have had to decide whether any reasonable man on the material available to the accused could have shared that belief . . .

The jury would have also to consider how the circumstances in which the accused had to make his decision whether or not to use force and the shortness of the time available to him for reflection, might affect the judgment of a reasonable man. In the facts that are to be assumed for the purposes of the reference there is material upon which a jury might take the view that the accused had reasonable grounds for apprehension of imminent danger to himself and other members of the patrol if the deceased were allowed to get away and join armed fellow-members of the Provisional I.R.A. who might be lurking in the neighbourhood, and that the time available to the accused to make up his mind what to do was so short that even a reasonable man could only act intuitively. This being so, the jury in approaching the final part of the question should remind themselves that the postulated balancing of risk against risk, harm against harm, by the reasonable man is not undertaken in the calm analytical atmosphere of the court-room after counsel with the benefit of hindsight have expounded at length the reasons for and against the kind of degree of force that was used by the accused; but in the brief second or two which the accused had to decide whether to shoot or not and under all the stresses to which he was exposed.

Note

Part a) of the question to be left to the jury must now be read in light of s.76 (3) and (4) Criminal Justice and Immigration Act 2008 which reflects *R. v Gladstone Williams* and the cases which follow. This modification has no impact on the remainder of Lord Diplock's judgment.

R. V SCARLETT

(1994) 98 Cr. App. R. 290 CA

D, the landlord of a public house, was convicted of an unlawful act of manslaughter following his use of force to eject a drunk from the premises. The jury were directed that if they concluded that D had used unnecessary and unreasonable force, this was unlawful force and that if that caused V to fall and strike his head, he was guilty of manslaughter. D appealed on the ground that this was a misdirection.

BELDAM LJ

Where one of the issues for the jury is whether the accused is guilty of the unlawful act of assault in circumstances in which he is entitled to use reasonable force either in self-defence or for the purpose of preventing crime, or as here in removing a trespasser, the need for a careful direction was stressed by Lord Lane C.J. in *Williams (Gladstone)*, (above).

[His Lordship quoted the first two paragraphs from Lord Lane CJ's judgment reproduced above, p.128 and continued:]

The issue in the case of *Williams (Gladstone)* was whether the accused was entitled to be acquitted if he mistakenly believed that he was justified in using force. The court held that, even if the jury came to the conclusion that the mistake was an unreasonable one, if the defendant may genuinely have been labouring under it, he was entitled to rely upon it.

The reason why he was entitled to be acquitted is because he did not intend to apply unlawful force. The principle we have quoted that the mental element necessary to constitute guilt of an assault is the intent to apply unlawful force to the victim was approved by the Board of the Privy Council in the case of *Beckford v R*.

If the mental element necessary to prove an assault is an intention to apply unlawful force to the victim, and the accused is to be judged according to his mistaken view of the facts whether that mistake was on an objective view reasonable or not, we can see no logical basis for distinguishing between a person who objectively is not justified in using force at all but mistakenly believes he is and another who is in fact justified in using force but mistakenly believes that the circumstances call for a degree of force objectively regarded as unnecessary.

Where, as in the present case, an accused is justified in using some force and can only be guilty of an assault if the force used is excessive, the jury ought to be directed that he cannot be guilty of an assault unless the prosecution prove that he acted with the mental element necessary to constitute his action an assault, that is: '. . . that the defendant intentionally or recklessly applied force to the person of another', *per* James L.J. in *Venna* (1975) 61 Cr.App.R. 310, [1976] Q.B. 421.

Further, they should be directed that the accused is not to be found guilty merely because he intentionally or recklessly used force which they consider to have been excessive. They ought not to convict him unless they are satisfied that the degree of force used was plainly more than was called for by the circumstances as he believed them to be, and, provided he believed the circumstances called for the degree of force used, he is not to be convicted even if his belief was unreasonable.

In this case, the learned judge gave no direction to the jury that the prosecution, to establish an assault, had to prove that the appellant intentionally or recklessly applied excessive force in seeking to evict the deceased. On the contrary, the jury were simply left to say what in the circumstances they considered was reasonable force and directed that if they concluded that what was done involved an unnecessary and unreasonable degree of force they then only had to consider whether the act of unlawful and unnecessary force actually caused the deceased to fall down the steps. And again later:

'So you are left with the situation: how did he meet his death and are you sure that it was the accused's conduct which directly produced it by his unlawful act?'

We are of the opinion that the directions to the jury in the circumstances of this case were inadequate to support a verdict of guilty of manslaughter. The appellant had given clear evidence that he only intended to use sufficient force to remove the deceased from the bar, an act he was lawfully entitled to do. It was not contended, nor were submissions made to the jury on the basis, that he acted recklessly. The direction to the jury was based on the assertion that it was sufficient if they found the force used by the appellant excessive in the circumstances. The learned judge seems to have assumed that this was sufficient to prove that what the appellant did amounted to an assault.

Appeal allowed
Conviction quashed

R. V OWINO

[1996] 2 Cr. App. R. 128 CA

D was convicted of assaulting his wife occasioning actual bodily harm. His defence was that the injuries were caused by the use of reasonable force to restrain her and to prevent her from assaulting him. D appealed against his conviction on the ground that the judge had failed to direct the jury that the test of reasonable force was subjective.

COLLINS J

. . . Mr Mendelle [for the appellant] essentially submits that [the trial judge] failed to direct the jury, as he ought to have done, that any force used must be unlawful, in the sense that it must have been excessive—more than was reasonable for self-defence; and further, that the test of what was reasonable was subjective, in the sense that the defendant could not be convicted unless he intended to use force which was more than was necessary for lawful self-defence. He relies on the authority of *Scarlett* to support that proposition.

Before I come to the case of *Scarlett* specifically, it is our view that the law does not go as far as Mr Mendelle submits that it does. The essential elements of self-defence are clear enough. The jury have to decide whether a defendant honestly believed that the circumstances were such as required him to use force to defend himself from an attack or a threatened attack. In this respect a defendant must be judged in accordance with his honest belief, even though that belief may have been mistaken. But the jury must then decide whether the force used was reasonable in the circumstances as he believed them to be.

Scarlett was a case where a landlord of a public house had been ejecting, and perfectly lawfully and properly ejecting, a drunken customer from his public house. The allegation was that he had used excessive force in the course of ejecting him so that the customer fell down the steps of the entrance to the pub and unfortunately hit his head and was killed. What Mr Mendelle relies upon in the case of *Scarlett* is a passage . . . where Beldam L.J., giving the judgement of the Court, said this:

'Where, as in the present case, an accused is justified in using some force and can only be guilty of an assault if the force used is excessive, the jury ought to be directed that he cannot be guilty of an assault unless the prosecution prove that he acted with the mental element necessary to constitute his action an assault, that is "that the defendant intentionally or recklessly applied force to the person of another". Further, they should be directed that the accused is not to be found guilty merely because he intentionally or recklessly used force which they consider to have been excessive. They ought not to convict him unless they are satisfied that the degree of force used was plainly more than was called for by the circumstances as he believed them to be and, provided he believed the circumstances called for the degree of force used, he is not to be convicted even if his belief was unreasonable.

In this case the learned judge gave no direction to the jury that the prosecution, to establish an assault, had to prove that the appellant intentionally or recklessly applied excessive force in seeking to evict the deceased.'

The passage which we have cited could, if taken out of context, give rise to a suggestion that the submission by Mr Mendelle is well-founded. But what, in the context, the learned Lord Justice was really saying was, in our view, this: he was indicating that the elements of an assault involved the unlawful application of force. In the context of an issue of self-defence or reasonable restraint, which was what *Scarlett* was essentially about, then clearly a person would not be guilty of an assault unless the force used was excessive; and in judging whether the force used was excessive, the jury had to take account of the circumstances as he believed them to be. That is what is made clear in the first part of the sentence, which we will isolate and read again:

'They ought not to convict him unless they are satisfied that the degree of force used was plainly more than was called for by the circumstances as he believed them to be and, provided be believed the circumstances called for the degree of force used, he is not to be convicted even if his belief was unreasonable.'

So far as the second half of the sentence is concerned, what we understand the learned Lord Justice to have been saying was that, in judging what he believed the circumstances to be, the jury are not to decide on the basis of what was objectively reasonable; and that even if he, the defendant, was unreasonable in his belief, if it was an honest belief and honestly held, that he is not to be judged by reference to the true circumstances. It is in that context that the learned Lord Justice talks about '[belief] that the circumstances called for the degree of force used', because clearly you cannot divorce completely the concept of degree of force and the concept of the circumstances as you believe them to be. In our judgment, that is effectively all that the learned Lord Justice was saying.

What he was not saying, in our view (and indeed if he had said it, it would be contrary to authority) was that the belief, however ill-founded, of the defendant that the degree of force he was using was reasonable, will enable him to do what he did. As Kay J. indicated in argument, if that argument was correct, then it would justify, for example, the shooting of someone who was merely threatening to throw a punch, on the basis that the defendant honestly believed, although unreasonably and mistakenly, that it was justifiable for him to use that degree of force. That clearly is not, and cannot be, the law.

In truth, in the view of this Court, the law was properly and adequately set out in the case of *Williams* (1984) 78 Cr.App.R. 276, (1983) 3 All E.R. 411, which was cited and referred to in *Scarlett* and the Court in *Scarlett* was not going beyond what it set out in *Williams*.

[His Lordship quoted the last three paragraphs of Lord Lane CJ's judgment reproduced above, p.128 and concluded that the trial judge's direction had gone further in favour of the defence than the law made necessary.]

Appeal dismissed

vii. Fatal Force and the European Convention on Human Rights

Note

Article 2 of the European Convention on Human Rights provides:

"1.   Everyone's right to life shall be protected by law. No on shall be deprived of his life intentionally save in the execution of a sentence of a court following his conviction of a crime for which this penalty is provided by law.

2.   Deprivation of life shall not be regarded as inflicted in contravention of this Article when it results from the use of force which is no more than absolutely necessary:

(a)   in the defence of any person from unlawful violence;

(b)   In order to effect a lawful arrest or to prevent the escape of a person lawfully detained;

(c)   in action lawfully taken for the purpose of quelling a riot or insurrection."

The State could be in contravention of art.2 where a state official, for example a police officer or a soldier, uses force in circumstances not covered by the exceptions listed in art.2(2). These exceptions amount to an exhaustive list and in each case the degree of force permitted to be used must be "no more than absolutely necessary in the circumstances". In contrast s.3 of the Criminal Law Act 1967 provides for force being used inter alia "in the prevention of crime" and both this provision and the common law on self-defence permit the use of "such force as is reasonable in the circumstances". It is this latter test which may have to be reconsidered by domestic courts following the enactment of the Human Rights Act 1998 when considering fatal force used by state officials. The English case law on the use of force does not distinguish between force used by state officials and that used by private individuals. This will have to reconsidered in several respects in light of European Convention case law. In *McCann v United Kingdom* (1996) 21 E.H.R.R. 97, the United Kingdom was found to be in breach of art.2. Following intelligence information received that a Provisional IRA active service unit was planning a terrorist bomb attack on Gibraltar, SAS soldiers were sent to assist the Gibraltar authorities to arrest them. Three members of the unit were intercepted after they had crossed from Spain into Gibraltar and parked a car. They were shot and killed by the SAS soldiers who believed that they had planted a car bomb which could be detonated by a radio controlled trigger and thus shot them repeatedly to ensure they were unable to trigger the bomb. In fact there was no bomb (although explosives were subsequently discovered in Spain at a property they had rented) nor any radio controlled trigger nor were they armed. The Court emphasised that art.2 was one of the most fundamental provisions in the Convention. They stated that art.2(2) did not provide exceptions where it is permissible intentionally to kill but rather instances where it is permissible to use force which may result in the deprivation of life. The crucial point, however, was that the use of force must be no more than "absolutely necessary" for the achievement of one of the purposes set out in art.2(2). This test would be applied strictly and the Court would scrutinise not only the actions of the individuals who use that force but also all the surrounding circumstances including such matters as the planning and control of the operation to see whether it was organised so as "to minimise, to the greatest extent possible, recourse to lethal force". The Court concluded that in light of the information they had and the instructions they had received, the soldiers did honestly believe, for good reasons, that lethal force was necessary. However, the planning and control of the operation amounted to a breach of art.2 as there were errors in the intelligence gathering and the assumptions made about the attack, insufficient allowance had been made for alternative possibilities, and the training of the soldiers giving rise to immediate reflex actions which necessarily did not involve assessments of whether less force might be sufficient, "lacks the degree of caution in the use of firearms to be expected from law enforcement personnel in a democratic society, even when dealing with dangerous terrorists".

The Convention requirement that force be "absolutely necessary" is much more exacting than the domestic test of "reasonable in the circumstances". Where the official using force makes a mistake, the Convention as interpreted in *McCann* (see also *Andronicou and Constantinou v Cyprus* (1998) 25 E.H.R.R. 491) requires that the beliefs on which the official acted must be based on "good reason" which again is more exacting than the subjective test of honest belief required by *Gladstone Williams* and *Beckford*. In *R. (Bennett) v HM Coroner for Inner London* [2006] EWHC Admin 196, the coroner directed a jury that they had to determine "whether the force used was reasonable, having regard to the circumstances which were believed to exist". Mr Bennett had been shot and killed by a police officer. It was argued that the test of reasonableness did not comply with art.2 which, it was stated, requires that the use of force be "absolutely necessary". Collins J ruled that the use of fatal force can only be reasonable in all the circumstances where it is absolutely necessary. The court will not make a hindsight assessment whether force was, in fact, absolutely necessary. A police officer on the ground is only able to make his assessment based on his perception of the circumstances that exist. If he is mistaken, fatal force is not actually necessary but to constrain him by such concerns would harbour the potential to be to the detriment of their own lives and the lives of others. It follows that the decision to use fatal force must be assessed according to the circumstances as he perceived them to be at the time; an honest but mistaken belief, therefore, can provide a "good reason".

6   DEGREES OF RESPONSIBILITY

1. ACCOMPLICES

i. Principals and Secondary Parties

Notes

The actual perpetrator of a crime or part of a crime, or one who effects it through an innocent agent, is guilty of the crime as principal. A person is the perpetrator if his act is the most immediate cause of the actus reus of the offence. One who does not perpetrate a crime but participates in it is punishable as a secondary party if he aids, abets, counsels or procures the principal offender to commit the crime. See Accessories and Abettors Act 1861 s.8, in the judgment of Lord Widgery CJ in *Attorney General's Reference (No.1 of 1975)*, below, p.309, and as to summary offences, Magistrates' Courts Act 1980 s.44. His punishment is the same as that of the principal.

The words "aid and abet, counsel and procure" may all be used together to charge a person who is alleged to have participated in a crime otherwise than as the principal or as accessory after the fact; *Re Smith* (1858) 3 H. & N. 227; *Ferguson v Weaving*, below, p.323. Such a person may also be charged as a principal: see *Maxwell v DPP for Northern Ireland*, below, p.325. Indeed if two persons are present at the scene of a crime and it is not clear which committed the act and which did no more than help, it is not necessary to show which was the actual perpetrator in order to convict them both: see *Mohan v R.*, below, p.308. A person charged as an accessory may be convicted as a principal: see *R. v Cogan & Leak*, below, p.314.

The terminology has changed over the years, and several terms used in cases before 1967 are now obsolete, a fact which must be borne in mind in reading such cases. The actual perpetrator was called the first principal, or the principal in the first degree. Secondary parties were of two kinds, in felonies principals in the second degree or accessories before the fact, in misdemeanours aiders and abettors, or counsellors and procurers. The technical distinction between the two kinds of secondary party still exists but is not important.

Although principal and secondary party are equally guilty, the distinction between them is still of importance because: (1) the definition of a crime is almost always in terms applicable only to a principal, and the liability of a secondary party follows from the terms of the Accessories and Abettors Act 1861 s.8, or Magistrates' Courts' Act 1980 s.44; (2) the mens rea required of a secondary party is different from that of a principal; and (3) not all secondary parties who participate with the appropriate mens rea are liable for the offence.

One who aids a criminal *after* the commission of a crime to avoid detection or arrest or trial is not technically a party, although the old term for such a person was accessory after the fact. He may be guilty of one of several offences against the administration of justice, of which the most prominent is assisting an offender, contrary to s.4 of the Criminal Law Act 1967.

MOHAN V R.

[1967] 2 A.C. 187

D was quarrelling with M, when R, who was D's father, ran out of his house and attacked M with a cutlass. While R was chasing M, D went off and returned with another cutlass. Both struck many blows at M, who collapsed and later died. He was found to be wounded in the back and in the leg. It appeared that death was caused only by the leg wound. D and R were convicted of murder, and appealed on the ground that, as there was no evidence of a pre-arranged plan to attack M, the Crown must show which of them struck the fatal blow.

LORD PEARSON

[The appellants' argument] will be considered on the hypothesis that the death may have been caused solely by the leg wound. The question then arises whether each of the appellants can be held responsible for the leg wound, when it may have been inflicted by the other of them. There is conflicting evidence as to which of them struck the blow on M's leg, the evidence for the prosecution tending to show that the appellant D struck it and the evidence for the defence tending to show that the appellant R struck it. There is uncertainty on that point.

Also it cannot be inferred with any certainty from the evidence that the appellants had a pre-arranged plan for their attack on M.

It is, however, clear from the evidence for the defence as well as from the evidence for the prosecution, that at the material time both the appellants were armed with cutlasses, both were attacking M, and both struck him. It is impossible on the facts of this case to contend that the fatal blow was outside the scope of the common intention. The two appellants were attacking the same man at the same time with similar weapons and with the common intention that he should suffer grievous bodily harm. Each of the appellants was present, and aiding and abetting the other of them in the wounding of M.

That is the feature which distinguishes this case from cases in which one of the accused was not present or not participating in the attack or not using any dangerous weapon, but may be held liable as a conspirator or an accessory before the fact or by virtue of a common design if it can be shown that he was party to a pre-arranged plan in pursuance of which the fatal blow was struck. In this case one of the appellants struck the fatal blow, and the other of them was present aiding and abetting him. In such cases the prosecution do not have to prove that the accused were acting in pursuance of a prearranged plan.

Appeals dismissed

Note

The principle in this case does not apply if it is not proved that both were involved in some capacity or other. "Where two people were jointly indicted, and the evidence did not point to one rather than the other, they both ought to be acquitted because the prosecution had not proved its case. The uncertainty could not be resolved by convicting both": *Collins & Fox v Chief Constable of Merseyside* [1988] Crim. L.R. 247 (DC). But where the prosecution can prove that one of the accused committed the offence and the other aided or abetted him, it does not matter that they cannot establish who performed which role: see *R. v Forman and Ford* [1988] Crim. L.R. 677.

----

ii. Aiding, Abetting, Counselling or Procuring

ATTORNEY GENERAL'S REFERENCE (NO.1 OF 1975)

[1975] Q.B. 773 CA

The facts appear in the judgment.

LORD WIDGERY CJ:

This case comes before the court on a reference from the Attorney-General, under s.36 of the Criminal Justice Act 1972, and by his reference he asks the following question:

'Whether an accused, who surreptitiously laced a friend's drinks with double measures of spirits when he knew that his friend would shortly be driving his car home, and in consequence his friend drove with an excessive quantity of alcohol in his body and was convicted of the offence under s.6(1) of the Road Traffic Act 1972, is entitled to a ruling of no case to answer on being later charged as an aider and abettor, counsellor and procurer, on the ground that there was no shared intention between the two, that the accused did not by accompanying him or otherwise positively encourage the friend to drive, or on any other ground'

. . . The present question has no doubt arisen because in recent years there have been a number of instances where men charged with driving their motor cars with an excess quantity of alcohol in the blood have sought to excuse their conduct by saying that their drinks were 'laced,' as the jargon has it; that is to say, some strong spirit was put into an otherwise innocuous drink and as a result the driver consumed more alcohol than he had either intended to consume or had the desire to consume. The relevance of all that is not that it entitles the driver to an acquittal because such driving is an absolute offence, but that it can be relied on as a special reason for not disqualifying the driver from driving. Hence no doubt the importance which has been attached in recent months to the possibility of this argument being raised in a normal charge of driving with excess alcohol.

The question requires us to say whether on the facts posed there is a case to answer and, needless to say, in the trial from which this reference is derived the judge was of the opinion that there was no case to answer and so ruled. We have to say in effect whether he is right.

The language in the section which determines whether a 'secondary party', as he is sometimes called, is guilty of a criminal offence committed by another embraces the four words 'aid, abet, counsel or procure'. The origin of those words is to be found in s.8 of the Accessories and Abettors Act 1861, which provides:

'Whosoever shall aid, abet, counsel or procure the commission of any misdemeanor, whether the same be a misdemeanour at common law or by virtue of any Act passed or to be passed, shall be liable to be tried, indicted and punished as a principal offender'.

Thus, in the past, when the distinction was still drawn between felony and misdemeanor, it was sufficient to make a person guilty of a misdemeanour if he aided, abetted, counselled or procured the offence of another. When the difference between felonies and misdemeanors was abolished in 1967, s.1 of the Criminal Law Act 1967 in effect provided that the same test should apply to make a secondary party guilty either of treason or felony.

Of course it is the fact that in the great majority of instances where a secondary party is sought to be convicted of an offence there has been a contact between the principal offender and the secondary party. Aiding and abetting almost inevitably involves a situation in which the secondary party and the main offender are together at some stage discussing the plans which they may be making in respect of the alleged offence, and are in contact so that each knows what is passing through the mind of the other.

In the same way it seems to us that a person, who counsels the commission of a crime by another, almost inevitably comes to a moment when he is in contact with that other, when he is discussing the offence with that other and when, to use the words of the statute, he counsels the other to commit the offence.

The fact that so often the relationship between the secondary party and the principal will be such that there is a meeting of minds between them caused the trial judge in the case from which this reference is derived to think that this was really an essential feature of proving or establishing the guilt of the secondary party and, as we understand his judgment, he took the view that in the absence of some sort of meeting of minds, some sort of mental link between the secondary party and the principal, there could be no aiding, abetting or counselling of the offence within the meaning of the section.

So far as aiding, abetting and counselling is concerned we would go a long way with that conclusion. It may very well be, as I said a moment ago, difficult to think of a case of aiding, abetting or counselling when the parties have not met and have not discussed in some respects the terms of the offence which they have in mind. But we do not see why a similar principle should apply to procuring. We approach s.8 of the Act of 1861 on the basis that the words should be given their ordinary meaning, if possible. We approach the section on the basis also that if four words are employed here, 'aid, abet, counsel or procure', the probability is that there is a difference between each of those four words and the other three, because, if there were no such difference, then Parliament would be wasting time in using four words where two or three would do. Thus, in deciding whether that which is assumed to be done under our reference was a criminal offence we approach the section on the footing that each word must be given its ordinary meaning.

To procure means to produce by endeavour. You procure a thing by setting out to see that it happens and taking the appropriate steps to produce that happening. We think that there are plenty of instances in which a person may be said to procure the commission of a crime by another even though there is no sort of conspiracy between the two, even though there is no attempt at agreement or discussion as to the form which the offence should take. In our judgment the offence described in this reference is such a case.

If one looks back at the facts of the reference: the accused surreptitiously laced his friend's drink. This is an important element and, although we are not going to decide today anything other than the problem posed to us, it may well be that, in similar cases where the lacing of the drink or the introduction of the extra alcohol is known to the driver quite different considerations may apply. We say that because, where the driver has no knowledge of what is happening, in most instances he would have no means of preventing the offence from being committed. If the driver is unaware of what has happened, he will not be taking precautions. He will get into his car seat, switch on the ignition and drive home, and, consequently, the conception of another procuring the commission of the offence by the driver is very much stronger where the driver is innocent of all knowledge of what is happening, as in the present case where the lacing of the drink was surreptitious.

The second thing which is important in the facts set out in our reference is that, following and in consequence of the introduction of the extra alcohol, the friend drove with an excess quantity of alcohol in his blood. Causation here is important. You cannot procure an offence unless there is a causal link between what you do and the commission of the offence, and here we are told that in consequence of the addition of this alcohol the driver, when he drove home, drove with an excess quantity of alcohol in his body.

Giving the words their ordinary meaning in English, and asking oneself whether in those circumstances the offence has been procured, we are in no doubt that the answer is that it has. It has been procured because, unknown to the driver and without his collaboration, he has been put in a position in which in fact he has committed an offence which he never would have committed otherwise. We think that there was a case to answer and that the trial judge should have directed the jury that an offence is committed if it is shown beyond reasonable doubt that the defendant knew that his friend was going to drive, and also knew that the ordinary and natural result of the additional alcohol added to the friend's drink would be to bring him above the recognised limit of 80 milligrammes per 100 millilitres of blood

Our decision on the reference is that the question posed by the Attorney-General should be answered in the negative.

Opinion accordingly

Question

How is this decision likely to affect the frequency of the "my drink was laced" plea?

Notes

1.   "To procure means to produce by endeavour." If the charge is of procuring only, intention in the accused that the offence shall be committed must be shown, but if the charge is of aiding, abetting, counselling and procuring (as it usually is) recklessness as to the commission of the offence is sufficient: see *Blakely v DPP* [1991] R.T.R. 405 DC.

2. In *R. v Calhaem* [1985] Q.B. 808 CA it was held that "counselling," unlike "procuring" needs no causal connection between the counselling and the offence.

3. In *Ferguson v Weaving* (for facts, see below, p.323), the defendant, although "absent", was charged with aiding, abetting, counselling and procuring. Lord Goddard CJ:

    "At the hearing an application was made to amend the information against the respondent by the deletion of the words 'aid and abet' so that the information charged her only with counselling and procuring the commission of the offences. Before us it was contended on her behalf that, even if the facts on which the prosecution relied were accepted, they could only establish a case of aiding and abetting, and that there was no evidence that the respondent in any way counselled or procured the commission of the said offences. It is well known that the words 'aid and abet' are apt to describe the action of a person who is present at the time of the commission of an offence and takes some part therein. He is then described as an aider and abettor, whereas the words 'counsel and procure' are appropriate to a person who, though not present at the commission of the offence, is an accessory before the fact. That all these words may be used together to charge a person who is alleged to have participated in an offence otherwise than as a principal in the first degree was established by *Re Smith* (1858) 3 H. & N. 227. Whether, where the words 'counsel and procure' alone are used, there must be a proof of something more than would establish a case of being an accessory before the fact is not one which we feel necessary to decide in this case . . . As we are satisfied that the respondent cannot be convicted as a participant, to use a compendious expression, in the offences charged against the persons who consumed the intoxicating liquor, we give no decision on it."

4. J.C. Smith, "Aid, Abet, Counsel or Procure" in P. Glazebrook (ed), *Reshaping the Criminal Law* (London: Stevens, 1978), p.125 states:

    "It is submitted that the true position is as follows. The distinction between 'aiding and abetting' and 'counselling and procuring', like that between principal and accessory, depends on one consideration only, namely whether the defendant was present (again in the large sense in which the common law understood that term) or absent. Notwithstanding the ordinary meaning of the words, the distinction does not turn in any way on the nature of the acts done by the defendant. Any act which would amount to 'aiding and abetting' if done while present at the crime would amount to 'counselling and procuring' if done while absent. Any act which would amount to 'counselling and procuring' when done in the absence of the principal would amount to 'aiding and abetting' if done while present at the crime . . . If it is right to regard the words 'aid and abet' as indicative of the liability of a person present and the words 'counsel and procure' as indicative of the liability of a person absent, it is obvious that these are highly technical terms. It is inconsistent so to treat the words in one context and yet to regard them as words of ordinary meaning in another."

5. Until 1987, there was one case where a party's liability turned on whether he was present or *absent*. One who was absent could not be convicted of a greater crime than the principal: *R. v Richards* [1974] Q.B. 776. However this case was overruled by the House of Lords in *R. v Howe* [1987] A.C. 417, below, p.317.

6. An unusual example of aiding and abetting is provided by the case of *Gnango* [2011] UKSC 59. G, armed with a gun, was searching for B at a car park; B apparently, owed him some money. Upon B

appearing he shot at G who took cover behind a car and fired several shots in return. B continued shooting and one of his shots hit V, a passer-by, killing her. The point of law certified by the Court of Appeal for consideration by the Supreme Court was:

"If (1) D1 and D2 voluntarily engage in fighting each other, each intending to kill or cause grievous bodily harm to the other and each foreseeing that the other has the reciprocal intention, and if (2) D 1 mistakenly kills V in the course of the fight, in what circumstances, if any, is D2 guilty of the offence of murdering V?"

The Supreme Court restored G's conviction for murder (which the Court of Appeal had quashed) on the basis that G and B had agreed to shoot and be shot at by the other, each having an intent to kill the other. In the direction to the jury, the trial judge had made it clear that if there was a plan it did not matter whether the plan had been made beforehand or simply on the spur of the moment when G and B saw each other. In their jointly written opinion Lord Phillips and Lord Judge stated (at [58]–[59]):

"[The] direction did not permit the jury to convict if they believed that one of the protagonists might have been the aggressor and the other merely responding in self-defence. It was an unequivocal direction that the jury could convict only if they were satisfied that the protagonists had formed a mutual plan or agreement to have a gun fight in which each would attempt to kill or seriously injure the other. If the jury were satisfied of this, the consequence in law was that each of the protagonists was party, not merely to his own attempt to kill or seriously injure the other, but to the other's attempt to kill or seriously injure him. Contrary to the finding of the Court of Appeal, the direction of the judge required the jury to consider whether they were satisfied that the respondent and [B] had a common plan or agreement to shoot at each other and be shot at. If they were so satisfied, and their verdict indicates that they were, this was a proper basis for finding that the respondent was guilty of murder.

In arguing at the close of the prosecution case that there was a case of simple aiding and abetting to go to the jury Mr Altman [prosecution counsel] sought to draw an analogy with a duel. There is indeed a close analogy between a consensual gunfight and a duel. In the case of a duel all who are present and who lend encouragement to the duel will be guilty of aiding and abetting each of the protagonists in his attempt to kill or injure the other. If one is killed, all who gave encouragement will be guilty of murder, and this includes the seconds on each side—see *R v Young and Webber* (1838) 8 C & P 644. It logically follows that each protagonist will be party to the violence, or attempted violence, inflicted on himself by his opponent. The same is true of a prize fight. In *R v Coney* (1882) 8 QBD 534 each protagonist was held guilty of assaulting the other and a number of bystanders were held to have encouraged, and thus to have been guilty of aiding and abetting, the assaults of both. Once again each protagonist could properly have been held guilty of aiding and abetting the assault by the other upon himself."

The intent B had was transferred (see above, p.139) when B killed V having done so with encouragement from G (through his shooting at B thereby encouraging him to shoot back at G). G, accordingly, had encouraged B's act of murdering V. It had been argued by the respondent before the Supreme Court that a conviction for murder in the circumstances would not accord with the public's sense of justice. Lord Phillips and Lord Judge responded (at [61]):

"We have considered whether to hold the respondent guilty of murder would be so far at odds with what the public would be likely to consider the requirements of justice as to call for a reappraisal of the application of the doctrine in this case. We have concluded to the contrary. On the jury's verdict the respondent and Bandana Man had chosen to indulge in a gunfight in a public place, each intending to kill or cause serious injury to the other, in circumstances where there was a foreseeable risk that this result would be suffered by an innocent bystander. It was a matter of fortuity which of the two fired what proved to be the fatal shot. In other circumstances it might have been impossible to deduce which of the two had done so. In these circumstances it seems to us to accord with the demands of justice rather than to conflict with them that the two gunmen should each be liable for [V's] murder."

----

iii. Proving the principal offence

Note

If B aids or encourages A to commit the actus reus of a crime, it may be that A, for some reason personal to himself, is not guilty of the crime. The question of B's liability arises. If A is the "principal" and commits no crime, it would appear that there is no crime to which B can be a secondary party. Sometimes the logic of that has to be accepted: see *Thornton v Mitchell*, directly below. In other cases, the logic is avoided by holding that B is the principal, since he used A as an innocent agent to commit what would be a crime if done by B: see *R. v Cogan & Leak*, below, p.314. In other cases, it is possible to convict B by holding that although A is not guilty, or not prosecutable, a crime was nevertheless committed by him, in which B was a secondary party: see *R. v Bourne, R. v Austin*, below, p.316. Finally, A may be guilty of a lesser offence which has the same actus reus as the more serious offence of which B may be convicted: see *Howe*, below, p.317.

THORNTON V MITCHELL

[1940] 1 All E.R. 339

A bus driver reversed his bus according to the signals of his conductor, who failed to notice some persons standing behind the bus. The driver could not possibly see behind the bus and had to rely on the signals of the conductor. The persons standing behind the bus were injured. The driver was charged with careless driving, and the conductor with aiding and abetting, counselling and procuring the commission of that offence. The charge against the driver was dismissed, but the conductor was convicted. He appealed.

LORD HEWART CJ

[The justices] say in paragraph 8: 'We being of opinion that the conductor [had been very negligent] held that he was guilty of aiding, abetting, counselling and procuring the said Hollindrake to drive without due care and attention, and accordingly we inflicted a fine.' In my opinion, this case is *a fortiori* on *Morris v Tolman* [1923] 1 K.B. 166, to which our attention has been directed. I will read one sentence from the judgment of Avory J. at p.171: '. . . in order to convict, it would be necessary to show that the respondent was aiding and abetting the principal, but a person cannot aid another in doing something which that other has not done.'
    That I think is the very thing which these justices have decided that the bus conductor did. In one breath they say that the principal did nothing which he should not have done and in the next breath they hold that the bus

conductor aided and abetted the driver in doing something which had not been done or in not doing something which he ought to have done. I really think that, with all respect to the ingenuity of counsel for the respondent, the case is too plain for argument.

Appeal allowed

Note

The reason why the bus conductor could not be convicted of careless driving as principal was because it was impossible to construe the word "drive" in the relevant section of the Road Traffic Act as referring to the conduct of anyone other than the immediate driver. There would seem to be limits beyond which the concept of agency will not stretch, i.e. wherever a crime needs personal action by the offender. Rape would appear to be such a crime, but see next case.

R. V COGAN AND LEAK

[1976] 1 Q.B. 217

L forced his wife to have sexual intercourse with C. C was charged with rape and L was charged with aiding, abetting, counselling and procuring C to commit rape. C was acquitted of rape on it appearing that he did not know that L's wife was not consenting to the intercourse. L was convicted and appealed.

LAWTON LJ

. . . Leak's appeal against conviction was based on the proposition that he could not be found guilty of aiding and abetting Cogan to rape his wife if Cogan was acquitted of that offence as he was deemed in law to have been when his conviction was quashed: see s.2(3) of the Criminal Appeal Act 1968. Leak's counsel, Mr Herrod, conceded however, that his proposition had some limitations. The law on this topic lacks clarity as a perusal of some of the textbooks shows: see *Smith and Hogan, Criminal Law*, 3rd ed. (1973), pp.106–109; *Glanville Williams, Criminal Law*, 2nd ed. (1961), pp.386–390, 406–408; *Russell on Crime*, 12th ed. (1964), vol. 1, p.128. We do not consider it appropriate to review the law generally because, as was said by this court in *R. v Quick* [1973] Q.B. 910, 923, when considering this kind of problem:

'The facts of each case . . . have to be considered and in particular what is alleged to have been done by way of aiding and abetting.'

The only case which Mr Herrod submitted had a direct bearing upon the problem of Leak's guilt was *Walters v Lunt* [1951] 2 All E.R. 645. In that case the respondents had been charged, under s.33(1) of the Larceny Act 1916, with receiving from a child aged seven years, certain articles knowing them to have been stolen. In 1951, a child under eight years was deemed in law to be incapable of committing a crime: it followed that at the time the charge had not been proved. That case is very different from this because here one fact is clear—the wife had been raped. Cogan had had sexual intercourse with her without her consent. The fact that Cogan was innocent of rape because he believed that she was consenting does not affect the position that she was raped.

Her ravishment had come about because Leak had wanted it to happen and had taken action to see that it did by persuading Cogan to use his body as the instrument for the necessary physical act. In the language of the law the act of sexual intercourse without the wife's consent was the *actus reus*: it had been procured by Leak who had the appropriate *mens rea*, namely, his intention that Cogan should have sexual intercourse with her without her consent. In our judgment it is irrelevant that the man whom Leak had procured to do the physical act himself did not intend to have sexual intercourse with the wife without her consent. Leak was using him as a means to procure a criminal purpose.

Before 1861 a case such as this, pleaded as it was in the indictment, might have presented a court with problems arising from the old distinctions between principals and accessories in felony. Most of the old law was swept away by s.8 of the Accessories and Abettors Act 1861 and what remained by s.1 of the Criminal Law Act 1967. The modern law allowed Leak to be tried and punished as a principal offender. In our judgment he could have been indicted as a principal offender. It would have been no defence for him to submit that if Cogan was an 'innocent' agent, he was necessarily in the old terminology of the law a principal in the first degree, which was a legal impossibility as a man cannot rape his own wife during cohabitation. The law no longer concerns itself with niceties of degrees in participation in crime; but even if it did Leak would still be guilty. The reason a man cannot by his own physical act rape his wife during cohabitation is because the law presumes consent from the marriage ceremony: see Hale, *Pleas of the Crown* (1778), vol. 1, p.629. There is no such presumption when a man procures a drunken friend to do the physical act for him. Hale C.J. put this case in one sentence, at p.629:

'. . . tho in marriage she hath given up her body to her husband, she is not to be by him prostituted to another': see *loc. cit.*

Had Leak been indicted as a principal offender, the case against him would have been clear beyond argument. Should he be allowed to go free because he was charged with 'being aider and abettor to the same offence'? If we are right in our opinion that the wife had been raped (and no one outside a court of law would say that she had not been), then the particulars of offence accurately stated what Leak had done, namely, he had procured Cogan to commit the offence. This would suffice to uphold the conviction. We would prefer, however, to uphold it on a wider basis. In our judgment convictions should not be upset because of mere technicalities of pleading in an indictment. Leak knew what the case against him was and the facts in support of that case were proved. But for the fact that the jury thought that Cogan in his intoxicated condition might have mistaken the wife's sobs and distress for expressions of her consent, no question of any kind would have arisen about the form of pleading. By his written statement Leak virtually admitted what he had done. As Judge Chapman said in *R. v Humphreys* [1965] 3 All E.R. 689, 692:

'It would be anomalous if a person who admitted to a substantial part in the perpetration of a misdemeanour as aider and abettor could not be convicted on his own admission merely because the person alleged to have been aided and abetted was not or could not be convicted.'

In the circumstances of this case it would be more than anomalous: it would be an affront to justice and to the common sense of ordinary folk. It was for these reasons that we dismissed the appeal against conviction

Appeal against conviction dismissed

Notes

1. At the date of this case, a husband could not ordinarily be guilty of personally raping his wife. This ceased to be the case following the insertion of a new s.1 to the Sexual Offences Act 1956 by s.142 of the Criminal Justice and Public Order Act 1994 which placed on a statutory footing the effect of the House of Lords decision in *R. v R.* [1992] A.C. 599. Rape is now defined in s.1(1) of the Sexual Offences Act 2003. (See below, p.576.)

2. In *R. v Bourne* (1952) 36 Cr. App. R. 125, the Criminal Court of Appeal upheld a conviction of a husband for aiding and abetting his wife to commit buggery with a dog, although the facts showed that the wife, who was the only possible principal, would have been able to raise the defence of duress had she been charged with committing buggery with the dog. The reason given was that a plea of duress admits the crime but prays to be excused punishment on the grounds of duress.

3. In *Millward*, [1994] Crim. L.R. 527, M instructed H to drive a tractor and trailer. M knew, but H did not know, that the hitch mechanism was dangerously defective. As H was driving, the trailer

became detached causing a fatal accident. H was acquitted of causing death by reckless driving but M was convicted as he had procured the actus reus. While it was not M's purpose to bring about the death, it was his purpose to bring about the reckless driving. The requirement to prove purpose on the part of a procurer seems to be confined to purpose as to the initiating cause of a consequence.

Note

The doctrine employed in *R. v Bourne*, above, that although the principal actor may have a complete defence, there is nonetheless a crime, to which secondary participants can be parties, is sometimes less artificial than it was in that case. See the next case.

R. V AUSTIN

[1981] 1 All E.R. 374

A child of three years was in the lawful custody of her mother JK. RK, the father, got an order from a Maryland Court awarding control of the child to him, which order was not enforceable in England. RK employed A and others to help him take the child by force. RK snatched the child from JK in a street in Winchester, and while A and others confused the pursuit, reached Heathrow and was able to leave the country with the child. A and others were convicted of child stealing and appealed.

WATKINS LJ

At the close of the case for the Crown in the Crown Court at Winchester counsel for the appellants . . . made a number of concessions on behalf of the appellants. He has repeated them to this court. They are: (1) that each of these appellants aided and abetted King in taking Lara away from the possession of her mother; (2) that the child was taken by King by the use of force on the mother and the child. It was also conceded that they all knew the child was in the lawful possession of the mother, since there was no order in this country which affected her right to that at the material time and the order of the American court could not affect it in any practical way. It was also admitted that they had the intention to deprive the mother of possession of the child.

Having regard to those admissions and the background of this affair, one looks at s.56 of the 1861 [Offences Against the Person] Act which provides:

'Whosoever shall unlawfully . . . by force . . . take away . . . any child under the age of fourteen years, with intent to deprive any parent . . . of the possession of such child . . . shall be liable, at the discretion of the court to be imprisoned: Provided, that no person who shall have claimed any right to the possession of such child, or shall be the mother or shall have claimed to be the father of an illegitimate child, shall be liable to be prosecuted by virtue hereof on account of the getting possession of such child . . .'

. . . A parent who seeks, especially when there is no order of a court in existence affecting the ordinary common law right of possession of parents to a child, to take away that child from the other parent by force will inevitably commit the offence of child stealing under s.56, unless it be shown that at the time there was lawful excuse for the use of the force as a means of taking the child away. Accordingly, apart from the proviso, King on the known facts could have had no defence if charged with this offence.

Undoubtedly King could properly have claimed a right of possession to the child and so have gained the protection of the proviso. What would have been the effect of that? The effect would have been that, although he had committed the offence of child stealing, because he was the child's father and could claim a right to possession of the child, he would not have been prosecuted. It is submitted on the appellant's behalf that the proviso also protects a class of persons wide enough to include those who aid a person such as the father of the child in gaining possession of his child by force. They become his agents for the purpose. Many persons have from time to time the temporary possession of a child as agents of parents. Why are they not protected to the same extent as parents when regaining possession as agents of parents?

In our view the only sensible construction of the proviso allows of its protection being granted to a small class of persons only, which includes the father and the mother of the child, whether the child be legitimate or illegitimate or a guardian appointed by a testamentary document, or by an order conferring the status of guardianship, or a person to whom is granted an order conferring some form of care, control, custody or access. We can think of no other who could claim exemption from prosecution by reason of the proviso.

What of these appellants? They had no good reason for doing what they did. They had no right to assert, and no interest in, the possession of the child. They were the paid hirelings of King to aid him in the commission of a criminal offence, namely stealing a child, and with him they committed it as aiders and abettors. While King may shelter behind the proviso, there is no room there for them. Parliament in its wisdom undoubtedly decided that the mischiefs of matrimonial discord which are unhappily so widespread should not give rise to wholesale criminal prosecutions arising out of disputes about children, about who should have possession and control of them. That and that alone is the reason for the existence of the proviso to s.56. Thus, as we have said, its application is confined to the select class of persons we have endeavoured to define . . .

Appeals dismissed

R. V HOWE

[1987] A.C. 417 HL

LORD MACKAY OF CLASHFERN: . . .

I turn now to the second certified question [:Can the one who incites or procures by duress another to kill or to be a party to a killing be convicted of murder if that other is acquitted by reason of duress?] In the view that I take on question one the second does not properly arise. However, I am of opinion that the Court of Appeal reached the correct conclusion upon it as a matter of principle.

Giving the judgment of the Court of Appeal Lord Lane CJ. said [1986] Q.B. 626, 641–642:

'The judge based himself on a decision of this court in *Reg. v Richards* [1974] Q.B. 776. The facts in that case were that Mrs Richards paid two men to inflict injuries on her husband which she intended should 'put him in hospital for a month/ The two men wounded the husband but not seriously. They were acquitted of wounding with intent but convicted of unlawful wounding. Mrs. Richards herself was convicted of wounding with intent, the jury plainly, and not surprisingly, believing that she had the necessary intent, though the two men had not. She appealed against her conviction on the ground that she could not properly be convicted as accessory before the fact to a crime more serious than that committed by the principals in the first degree. The appeal was allowed and the conviction for unlawful wounding was substituted. The court followed a passage from *Hawkins' Pleas of the Crown*, vol. 2. c. 29, para. 15: "I take it to be an uncontroverted rule that [the offence of the accessory can never rise higher than that of the principal]; it seeming incongruous and absurd that he who is punished only as a partaker of the guilt of another, should be adjudged guilty of a higher crime than the other."

James L.J. delivering the judgment in *Reg. v Richards* [1974] Q.B. 776 said, at p.780: If there is only one offence committed, and that is the offence of unlawful wounding, then the person who has requested that offence to be committed, or advised that that offence be committed, cannot be guilty of a graver offence than that in fact which was committed.' The decision in *Reg. v Richards* has been the subject of some criticism—see for example Smith & Hogan, *Criminal Law*, 5th ed. (1983), p.140. Counsel before us posed the situation where A hands a gun to D informing him that it is loaded with blank ammunition only and telling him to go and scare X by discharging it. The ammunition is in fact live, as A knows, and X is killed. D is convicted only of manslaughter, as he might be on those facts. It would seem absurd that A should thereby escape conviction for murder. We take the view that *Reg. v Richards* [1974] Q.B. 776 was incorrectly decided, but it seems to us that it cannot properly be distinguished from the instant case.'

I consider that the reasoning of Lord Lane CJ. is entirely correct and I would affirm his view that where a person has been killed and that result is the result intended by another participant, the mere fact that the actual killer may be convicted only of the reduced charge of manslaughter for some reason special to himself does not, in my opinion in any way, result in a compulsory reduction for the other participant.

Note

Section 2(4) of the Homicide Act 1957 specifically provides that the fact that one party to a killing is not liable to be convicted of murder because of diminished responsibility does not affect the question whether the killing amounted to murder in the case of any other party to it. Section 54 of the Coroners and Justice Act 2009, which replaced the defence of provocation with the defence of "loss of control" provides that "the fact that one party to a killing is by virtue of this section not liable to be convicted of murder does not affect the question whether the killing amounted to murder in the case of any other party to it" (s.54(8)).

----

iv. Mens Rea of a secondary party

Note

The secondary party must have intentionally supplied help or encouragement to the principal: see *R. v Clarkson*, directly below. It is sufficient if he knew that the principal was likely to commit the crime; he need not have desired him to do so: see *NCB v Gamble*, below, p.320. He must have known of the circumstances which made the principal's act criminal, even in the case of a strict liability offence: see *Ferguson v Weaving*, below, p.323. He need not have foreseen the precise circumstances, e.g. time and place of commission, provided that the crime which happened was within his contemplation: see *Maxwell v DPP for Northern Ireland*, below.

(a) Help or encouragement intentionally supplied

R. V CLARKSON

[1971] 1 W.L.R. 1402

The accused were charged with aiding and abetting three offences of rape. The evidence was that the accused, who had been drinking heavily, heard a disturbance in a room. They went in and stood watching whilst a woman was raped. They gave neither physical assistance nor verbal encouragement. They were convicted and appealed.

MEGAW LJ

. . . Let it be accepted, and there was evidence to justify this assumption, that the presence of those two defendants in the room where the offence was taking place was not accidental in any sense and that it was not by chance, unconnected with the crime, that they were there. Let it be accepted that they entered the room when the crime was committed because of what they had heard, which indicated that a woman was being raped, and they remained there.
    R. v Coney (1882) 8 Q.B.D. 534, decided that non-accidental presence at the scene of the crime is not conclusive of aiding and abetting. The jury has to be told by the judge, or in this case the court-martial has to be told by the judge advocate, in clear terms what it is that has to be proved before they can convict of aiding and abetting; what it is of which the jury or the court-martial, as the case may be, must be sure as matters of inference before they can convict of aiding and abetting in such a case where the evidence adduced by the prosecution is limited to non-accidental presence.

What has to be proved is stated in *R. v Coney* by Hawkins J. in a well-known passage in his judgment, at p.557:

'In my opinion, to constitute an aider and abettor some active steps must be taken by word, or action, with the intent to instigate the principal, or principals. Encouragement does not of necessity amount to aiding and abetting, it may be intentional or unintentional, a man may unwittingly encourage another in fact by his presence, by misinterpreted words, or gestures, or by his silence, or non-interference or he may encourage intentionally by expressions, or gestures, or actions intended to signify approval. In the latter case he aids and abets, in the former he does not. It is no criminal offence to stand by, a mere passive spectator of a crime, even of a murder. Non-interference to prevent a crime is not itself a crime. But the fact that a person was voluntarily and purposely present witnessing the commission of a crime, and offered no opposition to it, though he might reasonably be expected to prevent and had the power so to do, or at least to express his dissent, might under some circumstances, afford cogent evidence upon which a jury would be justified in finding that he wilfully encouraged and so aided and abetted. But it would be purely a question for the jury whether he did so or not.'

It is not enough, then, that the presence of the accused has, in fact, given encouragement. It must be proved that the accused intended to give encouragement; that he *wilfully* encouraged. In a case such as the present, more than in many other cases where aiding and abetting is alleged, it was essential that that element should be stressed; for there was here at least the possibility that a drunken man with his self-discipline loosened by drink, being aware that a woman was being raped, might be attracted to the scene and might stay on the scene in the capacity of what is known as a voyeur; and, while his presence and the presence of others might in fact encourage the rapers or discourage the victim, he, himself, enjoying the scene or at least standing by assenting, might not intend that his presence should offer encouragement to rapers and would-be rapers or discouragement to the victim; he might not realise that he was giving encouragement; so that, while encouragement there might be, it would not be a case in which, to use the words of Hawkins J., the accused person 'wilfully encouraged.'

A further point is emphasised in passages in the judgment of the Court of Criminal Appeal in *R. v Allan* [1965] 1 Q.B. 130, 135, 138. That was a case concerned with participation in an affray. The court said, at p.135:

'in effect, it amounts to this: that the judge thereby directed the jury that they were duty bound to convict an accused who was proved to have been present and witnessing an affray if it was also proved that he nursed an intention to join in if help was needed by the side he favoured and this notwithstanding that he did nothing by words or deeds to evince his intention and outwardly played the role of a purely passive spectator. It was said that, if that direction is right, where A and B behave themselves to all outward appearances in an exactly similar manner, but it be proved that A had the intention to participate if needs be, whereas B had no such intention, then A must be convicted of being a principal in the second degree to the affray, whereas B should be acquitted. To do that, it is objected, would be to convict A on his thoughts, even though they found no reflection in his actions.'

The other passage in the judgment is at p.138:

'In our judgment, before a jury can properly convict an accused person of being a principal in the second degree to an affray, they must be convinced by the evidence that, at the very least, he by some means or other encouraged the participants. To hold otherwise would be, in effect, as the appellants' counsel rightly expressed it, to convict a man on his thoughts, unaccompanied by any physical act other than the fact of his mere presence.'

From that it follows that mere intention is not in itself enough. There must be an intention to encourage; and there must also be encouragement in fact, in cases such as the present case.

So we come to what was said by the judge advocate . . . This court has come to the conclusion that the court might have misunderstood the relevant principles that ought to be applied. It might have been left under the impression that it could find these two defendants guilty on the basis of their continuing, non-accidental presence, even though it was not sure that the necessary inferences to be drawn from the evidence included (i) an intention to encourage and (ii) actual encouragement. While we have no doubt that those inferences could properly have been drawn in respect of each defendant on each count, so that verdicts of guilty could properly have been returned, we cannot say that the court-martial, properly directed, would necessarily have drawn those inferences. Accordingly the convictions of the defendants Clarkson and Carroll must be quashed.

Appeals allowed

Questions

1. If B is able to control A's behaviour, and does not do so, with the result, expected by B, that A commits a crime, what is the significance, on a charge of aiding, abetting, counselling or procuring A's crime, of B's failure?

2. Ought it to make any difference whether B's power to control A is a legal one or merely a physical or psychological one? See *Cassady v Morris* [1975] Crim. L.R. 398; *Du Cros v Lambourne* [1907] 1 K.B. 40; *R. v Harris* [1964] Crim. L.R. 54.

3. B's wife A tells him that she is going to kill herself and their infant children. B protests but does nothing to stop A, who throws her children into a river and jumps in herself, so that they are all drowned. Has B aided, abetted, counselled or procured: (i) the murder of the children; (ii) the suicide of A? See Suicide Act 1961 s.2(l) (cf. *R. v Russell* [1933] V.L.R. 59).

(b) Knowledge enough

NATIONAL COAL BOARD V GAMBLE

[1959] 1 Q.B. 11

The National Coal Board had an instalment contract with the Central Electricity Authority for a supply of coal to be delivered at a colliery into lorries sent by a carrier on behalf of the authority. In pursuance of this contract W Ltd, a carrier, sent a lorry in the charge of its servant M into the colliery. The method of loading was for a lorry-driver to place his lorry under the Board's hopper and tell the hopper operator to stop when the driver thought he had enough coal on his lorry. The lorry was then driven to the colliery weighbridge which was in the charge of H, a servant of the Board. H, after weighing the lorry and its load, would give the driver a ticket showing the weight of coal loaded, which ticket operated as a delivery note, so that the sale of the load of coal was then complete and the property in the coal passed from the Board to the purchaser.

M went through this procedure, but when H weighed his lorry and load he discovered that they together exceeded the maximum permitted weight for a vehicle being driven on a road. H drew M's attention to this fact, and there was also a large notice at the door of the weighbridge office warning drivers that the Board was not responsible for the use of any vehicle on a road which was loaded beyond its authorised capacity. On being asked by H if he intended to take this load (which he could easily have offloaded) M said that he would risk it. H then handed M the weighbridge ticket and M drove the overloaded lorry out of the colliery onto a road, thereby committing an offence against the Motor Vehicles (Construction and Use) Regulations 1955.

The Board were charged with and convicted of aiding, abetting, counselling and procuring the carrier W Ltd to commit the offence under the Regulations. The Board appealed.

DEVLIN J

A person who supplies the instrument for a crime or anything essential to its commission aids in the commission of it; and if he does so knowingly and with intent to aid, he abets it as well and is therefore guilty of aiding and abetting. I use the word 'supplies' to comprehend giving, lending, selling or any other transfer of the right of property. In a sense a man who gives up to a criminal a weapon which the latter has a right to demand from him aids in the commission of the crime as much as if he sold or lent the article. But this has never been held to be aiding in law: see *R. v Bullock* [1955] 1 W.L.R. 1. The reason, I think, is that in the former case there is in law a positive act and in the latter only a negative one. In the transfer of property there must be either a physical delivery or a positive act of assent to a taking. But a man who hands over to another his own property on demand, although he may physically be performing a positive act, in law is only refraining from detinue. Thus in law the former act is one of assistance voluntarily given and the latter is only a failure to prevent the commission of the crime by means of forcible detention, which would not even be justified except in the case of felony. Another way of putting the point is to say that aiding and abetting is a crime that requires proof of *mens rea*, that is to say, of intention to aid as well as of knowledge of the circumstances, and proof of the intent involves proof of a positive act of assistance voluntarily done.

These considerations make it necessary to determine at what point the property in the coal passed from the Board and what the Board's state of knowledge was at that time. If the property had passed before the Board knew of the proposed crime, there was nothing they could legally do to prevent the driver of the lorry from taking the overloaded lorry out onto the road. If it had not, then they sold the coal with knowledge that an offence was going to be committed. (His Lordship repeated the facts as found in the case).

In these circumstances, the property in the coal passed on delivery to the carrier in accordance with Rule 5 of s.18 of the Sale of Goods Act, 1893. If the delivery was complete after loading and before weighing, the Board has not until after delivery any knowledge that an offence had been committed. But where weighing is necessary for the purpose of the contract, as, for example, in order to ascertain the price of an instalment, the property does not pass until the weight has been agreed . . .

It was contended on behalf of the Board that H had no option after weighing but to issue a ticket for the amount then in the lorry. I think this contention is unsound. In the circumstances of this case the loading must be taken as subject to adjustment; otherwise, if the contract were for a limited amount, the seller might make an over-delivery or an under-delivery which could not thereafter be rectified and the carrier might be contractually compelled to carry away a load in excess of that legally permitted. I think that delivery of the coal was not completed until after the ascertained weight had been assented to and some act was done signifying assent and passing the property. The property passed when H asked M whether he intended to take the load and M said he would risk it and when mutual assent was, as it were, sealed by the delivery and acceptance of the weighbridge ticket. He could, therefore, after he knew of the overload, have refused to transfer the property in the coals.

This is the conclusion to which the justices came. Mr Thompson submits on behalf of the Board that it does not justify a verdict of guilty of aiding and abetting. He submits, first, that even if knowledge of the illegal purpose had been acquired before delivery began, it would not be sufficient for the verdict; and secondly, that if he is wrong about that, the knowledge was acquired too late and the Board was not guilty of aiding and abetting simply because H failed to stop the process of delivery after it had been initiated.

On his first point Mr Thompson submits that the furnishing of an article essential to the crime with knowledge of the use to which it is to be put does not of itself constitute aiding and abetting; there must be proved in addition a purpose or motive of the defendant to further the crime or encourage the criminal. Otherwise, he submits, there is no *mens rea*.

I have already said that in my judgment there must be proof of an intent to aid . . .

No doubt evidence of an interest in the crime or of an express purpose to assist it will greatly strengthen the case of the prosecution. But an indifference to the result of the crime does not of itself negative abetting. If one man deliberately sells to another a gun to be used for murdering a third, he may be indifferent about whether the third man lives or dies and interested only in the cash profit to be made out of the sale, but he can still be an aider and abettor. To hold otherwise would be to negative the rule that *mens rea* is a matter of intent only and does not depend on desire or motive.

The authorities, I think, support this conclusion, though none has been cited to us in which the point has been specifically argued and decided . . .

The same principle has been applied in civil cases where the seller has sued upon a contract for the supply of goods which he knew were to be used for an illegal purpose. In some of the authorities there is a suggestion that he could recover on the contract unless it appeared that in addition to knowledge of the purpose he had an interest in the venture and looked for payment to the proceeds of the crime. But in *Pearce v Brooks* (1866) L.R. 1 Ex. 213, Pollock C.B. stated the law as follows:

'I have always considered it as settled law that any person who contributes to the performance of an illegal act by supplying a thing with the knowledge that it is going to be used for that purpose, cannot recover the price of the thing so supplied. If, to create that incapacity, it was ever considered necessary that the price should be bargained or expected to be paid out of the fruits of the illegal act (which I do not stop to examine), that proposition has been overruled by the cases I have referred to, and has now ceased to be law.' . . .

As to Mr Thompson's alternative point, I have already expressed the view that the facts show an act of assent made by H after knowledge of the proposed illegality and without which the property would not have passed. If some positive act to complete delivery is committed after knowledge of the illegality, the position in law must, I think, be just the same as if the knowledge had been obtained before the delivery had been begun. Of course, it is quite likely that H was confused about the legal position and thought that he was not entitled to withhold the weighbridge ticket. There is no *mens rea* if the defendant is shown to have a genuine belief in the existence of circumstances which, if true, would negative an intention to aid; see *Wilson v Inyang* [1951] 2 K.B. 799; but this argument, which might have been the most cogent available to the defence, cannot now be relied upon, because H was not called to give evidence about what he thought or believed.

Appeal dismissed

Notes

1.   Lord Goddard CJ delivered a concurring judgment. Slade J dissented on the ground that the alleged aider must have assisted or encouraged the principal offender:

"It is not sufficient that the alleged abettor should be proved to have done some act, or to have made some omission, without which the principal offender would not have committed the offence; nor is it sufficient that such act or omission had the effect of facilitating the commission of the offence or that it in fact operated on the mind of the principal offender so as to decide him to commit it. The prosecution must prove that the act or omission upon which they rely as constituting the alleged aiding and abetting was done or made with a view to assisting or encouraging the principal offender to commit the offence or, in other words, with the motive of endorsing the commission of the offence."

His Lordship considered that the facts found by the magistrates did not support the inference that H meant to encourage M in any way. (See further *Bryce* [2004] EWCA Crim 1231.)

2.   Devlin J's discussion becomes heavily involved with the civil law of sale, the passing of property, and the ability of a seller to sue on a contract tainted by illegality. It seems inappropriate for the criminal law to be entangled with the civil law this way. Perhaps Slade J's solution, requiring a positive motive of endorsing the commission of the offence, is too lax, at any rate where a serious crime is *substantially* facilitated by the accessory's act. But in other cases, the law perhaps ought to excuse an "indifferent" provider of assistance (i.e. one who knows that a crime may be committed but does not wish it to happen). In *Gillick v West Norfolk & Wisbech AHA* [1986] A.C. 112, the question arose whether a doctor who provided contraceptives to a girl under 16 years of age, knowing that that would facilitate her having sexual intercourse with a man, would necessarily be an accessory to the man's offence if that intercourse took place. Lord Scarman (at 190) thought that if the provision was a bona fide exercise of his clinical judgment "it must be a complete negation of the guilty mind which is an essential ingredient of the criminal offence of aiding and abetting the commission of unlawful sexual intercourse". Lord Bridge (at 194) agreed with the trial judge that the doctor would not be guilty either because the provision was not directly assisting the offence, or because the doctor's knowledge of the circumstances of the proposed offence was not sufficiently specific. (On specificity of knowledge, see, below, p.325.)

Questions

Would it be practicable for the law to excuse some "indifferent" helpers because:

(a) the principal offence is trivial?

(b) the aid supplied is trivial and could easily be got from others?

(c) the aid supplied was in the normal course of a legitimate business?

(d) the secondary party makes known his disapproval of the offence?

(e) the secondary party was merely "refraining from detinue" (see Devlin J, directly above)? On this note *Garrett v Arthur Churchill (Glass) Ltd* [1969] 2 All E.R. 1141. The question was whether B was knowingly concerned in the export of a valuable goblet without an export licence. B was holding the goblet as agent for A, who was in America. B told A that the export needed a licence; but A said that his agency was terminated and ordered him to hand over the goblet to a courier at Heathrow. B did so and the courier took the goblet out of the country. It was held that, "albeit there was a legal duty in ordinary circumstances to hand over the goblet once the agency was determined, I do not think that an action would lie for breach of that duty, if the handing over would constitute the offence of being knowingly concerned in its exportation": per Lord Parker CJ, at 1145.

FERGUSON V WEAVING

[1951] 1 K.B. 814

Section 4 of the Licensing Act 1921, made it an offence for any person, except during the permitted hours, to consume on licensed premises any intoxicating liquor. In a large public house managed by W, customers were found consuming liquor outside permitted hours and were convicted of an offence under the section. There was no evidence that W knew that the liquor was being consumed, which had been supplied by waiters employed by her who had neglected to collect the glasses in time. A charge against W of counselling and procuring the customers' offence was dismissed and the prosecutor appealed.

LORD GODDARD CJ

There can be no doubt that this court has more than once laid it down in clear terms that before a person can be convicted of aiding and abetting the commission of an offence, he must at least know the essential matters which constitute the offence . . . The magistrate in this case has acquitted the licensee of any knowledge of the matters which constituted the principal offence, but it is said that the cases established that the knowledge of her servants must be imputed to her . . .. We now turn to [these] cases . . . It is unnecessary to go through them all because the principle which applies was laid down, not for the first time, in *Linnett v Metropolitan Police Commissioner* [1946] K.B. 290. All the cases on the subject were quoted, and, in giving judgment, I said: 'The principle underlying these decisions does not depend upon the legal relationship existing between master and servant or between principal and agent; it depends on the fact that the person who is responsible in law, as, for example, a licensee under the licensing Acts, has chosen to delegate his duties, powers and authority to another.'

We will assume for the purpose of this case that the licensee had delegated to the waiters the conduct and management of the concert room, and if the Act had made it an offence for a licensee knowingly to permit liquor to be consumed after hours, then the fact that she had delegated management and control of the concert room to the waiters would have made their knowledge her knowledge. In this case there is no substantive offence in the licensee at all. The substantive offence is committed only by the customers. She can aid and abet the customers if she knows that the customers are committing the offence, but we are not prepared to hold that knowledge can be imputed to her so as to make her not a principal offender, but an aider and abettor. So to hold would be to establish a new principle in criminal law and one for which there is no authority. If Parliament had desired to make a licensee guilty of an offence by allowing persons to consume liquor after hours it would have been perfectly easy so to provide in the section. But a doctrine of criminal law that a licensee who has knowledge of the facts is liable as a principal in the second degree is no reason for holding that if she herself has no knowledge of the facts but that someone in her employ and to whom she may have entrusted the management of the room did know them, this makes her an aider and abettor. As no duty is imposed on her by the section to prevent the consumption of liquor after hours there was no duty in this respect that she could delegate to her employees. While it may be that the waiters could have been prosecuted for aiding and abetting the consumers, as to which we need express no opinion, we are clearly of opinion that the licensee could not be. To hold to the contrary would, in our opinion, be an unwarranted extension of the doctrine of vicarious responsibility in criminal law.

Appeal dismissed

Notes

1.   For vicarious liability, see, below, p.347.

2.   *Callow v Tillstone* (1900) 83 L.T. 411 (QBD). B, a veterinary surgeon, negligently examined a carcase and certified it as fit for human consumption, when it was not, as B ought to have known. A, a butcher, was convicted of exposing for sale meat unfit for human consumption. *Held*, B was not guilty of aiding and abetting A's offence.

Question

B's intentional act has facilitated the commission by A of the offence of driving over the blood/alcohol limit.

   (i)   He knows (intends) that A shall drive, but is merely reckless as to whether he is over the limit.

   (ii)   He knows that A is over the limit, but is merely reckless as to whether he will drive while in that state. Is there a relevant difference between these two cases? See *Carter v Richardson* [1974] R.T.R. 314 as to (i); and *Blakely v DPP* [1991] R.T.R. 405 as to (ii); and see, below, as to recklessness as to circumstance in attempts

(c) Scope of the Common Design

Note

Where D2 counsels or procures D1 to commit a particular crime, D2 necessarily knows the type of offence involved as the commission of the offence is D2's purpose. For example, if D2 writes to D1 encouraging him to kill V, D2 will know that if D1 does so he will commit murder as he will have done so with the necessary mens rea. Where D2 aids or abets D1 to commit an offence, commission of the offence may not be D2's purpose or object. For example, D2 may supply D1 with equipment or assistance knowing that D1 intends to commit an offence but being unaware of the exact nature of the offence. The House of Lords dealt with this problem in the case which follows.

MAXWELL V DPP FOR NORTHERN IRELAND

[1978] 1 W.L.R. 1350 HL

The facts are set out in the speech of Lord Hailsham.

LORD HAILSHAM OF ST MARYLEBONE

My Lords, in my opinion this appeal should be dismissed. The applicant was the owner and driver of the guide car in what subsequently turned out to be a terrorist attack by members of the criminal and illegal organisation known as the Ulster Volunteer Force (UVF) on a public house owned by a Roman Catholic licensee at 40, Grange Road, Toomebridge and known as the Crosskeys Inn. The attack was carried out on the night of January 3,1976 by the occupants of a Cortina car and took the form of throwing a pipe bomb containing about five pounds of explosive into the hallway of the public house. The attack failed because the son of the proprietor had the presence of mind to pull out the burning fuse and detonator and throw it outside the premises where the detonator exploded either because the fuse had reached the detonator or on contact with the ground.

The appellant was tried on October 13, 1976, on an indictment containing four counts to two of which he pleaded guilty. This appeal is concerned with the remaining two counts (numbered 1 and 2) on which he was convicted at the Belfast City Commission by MacDermott J. sitting without a jury . . .

The only substantial matter to be discussed in the appeal is the degree of knowledge required before an accused can be found guilty of aiding, abetting, counselling, or procuring. To what extent must the accused be proved to have particular knowledge of the crime in contemplation at the time of his participation and which was ultimately committed by its principal perpetrators? For myself I am content for this purpose to adopt the words of Lord Parker C.J. in *R. v Bainbridge* [1960] 1 Q.B. 129 when, after saying that it is not easy to lay down a precise form of words which will cover every case, he observed at p.134 '. . . there must not be merely suspicion but knowledge that a crime of the type in question was intended . . .' and the words of Lord Goddard C.J. in *Johnson v Youden* [1950] 1 K.B. 544, 546, endorsed by this House in *Churchill v Walton* [1967] 2 A.C. 224, 236 that 'Before a person can be convicted of aiding and abetting the commission of an offence he must at least know the essential matters which constitute that offence.' The only question in debate in the present appeal is whether the degree of knowledge possessed by the appellant was of the 'essential matters constituting' the offence in fact committed, or, to put what in the context of the instant case is exactly the same question in another form, whether the appellant knew that the offence in which he participated was 'a crime of the type' described in the charge.

For that purpose I turn to two passages in the findings of fact of the learned judge. The first is as follows: 'In my judgment, the facts of this case make it clear to me that the accused knew the men in the Cortina car were going to attack the Inn and had the means of attacking the Inn with them in their car. The accused may not, as he says, have known what form the attack was going to take, but in my judgment he knew the means of the attack, be they bomb, bullet or incendiary device, were present in that car.'

In the second passage MacDermott J. said: 'In my judgment, the accused knew that he was participating in an attack on the Inn. He performed an important role in the execution of that attack. He knew that the attack was one which would involve the use of means which would result in danger to life or damage to property. In such circumstances, where an admitted terrorist participates actively in a terrorist attack, having knowledge of the type of attack intended, if not of the weapon chosen by his colleagues, he can in my view be properly charged with possession of the weapon with which it is intended that life should be endangered or premises seriously damaged.'

The learned judge also found *inter alia* that the word 'job' (as used in the appellant's statements) is 'synonymous with military action which raises, having regard to the proven activities of the UVF, the irresistible inference [that] the attack would be one of violence in which people would be endangered or premises seriously damaged.'

There was no dispute that there was ample evidence to support all these findings and it follows that the only question is whether the passages contain some self-misdirection in point of law. As to this I agree with the opinion of Sir Robert Lowry C.J. (in the Court of Criminal Appeal for Northern Ireland) when he said [1978] 1 W.L.R. 1363, 1375: 'The facts found here show that the appellant, as a member of an organisation which habitually perpetrates sectarian acts of violence with firearms and explosives, must, as soon as he was briefed for his role, have contemplated the bombing of the Crosskeys Inn as not the only possibility but one of the most obvious possibilities among the jobs which the principals were likely to be undertaking and in the commission of which he was intentionally assisting. He was therefore in just the same situation, so far as guilty knowledge is concerned, as a man who had been given a list of jobs and told that one of them would be carried out.'

The only argument attacking this passage of any substance directed to your Lordships on the part of the appellant was to the effect that since at the time of the commission of the offence there was no generalised offence of terrorism as such the state of ignorance which must be assumed in favour of the accused as to the precise weapon (e.g. bomb, bullets, or incendiary device) or type of violence to be employed in the concerted 'job' contemplated was such as to make him ignorant of some or all of the 'essential ingredients' of the two offences charged in the particulars of offence in which a 'pipe bomb' is specified, and one at least of which, had it been committed, would or at least might have been laid under a separate penal provision.

I regard this point as frankly unarguable. I would consider that bullet, bomb, or incendiary device, indeed most if not all types of terrorist violence, would all constitute offences of the same 'type' within the meaning of *R. v Bainbridge* and that so far as *mens rea* is concerned 'the essential ingredients' of all and each of the offences within the other authorities I have cited were each and all contained within the guilty knowledge of the appellant at the time of his participation. The fact that, in the event, the offence committed by the principals crystallised into one rather than the other of the possible alternatives within his contemplation only means that in the event he was accessory to that specific offence rather than one of the others which in the event was not the offence committed. Obviously there must be limits to the meaning of the expression 'type of offence' and a minimum significance attached to the expression 'essential ingredients' in this type of doctrine, but it is clear that if an alleged accessory is perfectly well aware that he is participating in one of a limited number of serious crimes and one of these is in fact committed he is liable under the general law at least as one who aids, abets, counsels or procures that crime even if he is not actually a principal. Otherwise I can see no end to the number of unmeritorious arguments which the ingenuity of defendants could adduce. This disposes of the present appeal, which seems to me to be as lacking in serious plausibility as it is wholly devoid of substantial merits . . .

LORD SCARMAN

My Lords, I also would dismiss this appeal. The question it raises is as to the degree of knowledge required by law for the attachment of criminal responsibility to one who assists another (or others) to commit or attempt crime . . .

I think *R. v Bainbridge* was correctly decided. But I agree with counsel for the appellant that in the instant case the Court of Criminal Appeal in Northern Ireland has gone further than the Court of Criminal Appeal for England and Wales found it necessary to go in *R. v Bainbridge*. It is not possible in the present case to declare that it is proved, beyond reasonable doubt, that the appellant knew a bomb attack upon the Inn was intended by those whom he was assisting. It is not established, therefore, that he knew the particular type of crime intended. The Court, however, refused to limit criminal responsibility by reference to knowledge by the accused of the type or class of crime intended by those whom he assisted. Instead, the Court has formulated a principle which avoids the uncertainties and ambiguities of classification. The guilt of an accessory springs, according to the Court's formulation, 'from the fact that he contemplates the commission of one (or more) of a number of crimes by the principal and he intentionally lends his assistance in order that such a crime will be committed': *per* Sir Robert Lowry C.J. 'The relevant crime,' the Lord Chief Justice continues, 'must be within the contemplation of the accomplice, and only exceptionally would evidence be found to support the allegation that the accomplice had given the principal a completely blank cheque.'

The principle thus formulated has great merit. It directs attention to the state of mind of the accused—not what he ought to have in contemplation, but what he did have: it avoids definition and classification while ensuring that a man will not be convicted of aiding and abetting any offence his principal may commit, but only one which is within his contemplation. He may have in contemplation only one offence, or several: and the several which he contemplates he may see as alternatives. An accessory who leaves it to his principal to choose is liable, provided always the choice is made from the range of offences from which the accessory contemplates the choice will be made. Although the court's formulation of the principle goes further than in the earlier cases, it is a sound development of the law and in no way inconsistent with them. I accept it as good judge-made law in a field where there is no statute to offer guidance.

Appeal dismissal

(d) Joint enterprise and a wrong turning in the law

Note

Where two parties, D1 and D2, embark on an agreed criminal venture to commit a particular offence, they have a common criminal purpose. If, in the course of that venture, D1 commits another, incidental,offence, will D2 be liable for this incidental offence as a secondary party? This situation has been referred to in the case law as "joint enterprise". More recently, a new term, was coined, "parasitic accessory liability", which was considered to be more accurate—the accessory's liability for the incidental offence is parasitic upon his participation in agreed criminal venture. The problem is most acute where the incidental offence is murder. For example, D1 and D2 set out to commit a burglary to steal jewellery. They are unexpectedly disturbed by V, the householder, and D1 draws a knife and kills V. While there may be no problem establishing D1's intent to kill, what is it that must be proved in terms of D2's contemplation or intention for him to be convicted as a secondary party to murder? The circumstances in which killings may take place may be even more complicated than this example. Often violence erupts spontaneously and individuals may find themselves embroiled in an affray where punches and kicks are exchanged. If D2 is assisting D1 in an altercation with V, involving punches and kicks and D1 produces a knife and stabs V killing him, how is D2's criminal liability to be determined?

IN *ANDERSON AND MORRIS* [1966] 2 Q.B. 110 AT 118–119, LORD PARKER CJ STATED:

'. . . where two persons embark on a joint enterprise . . . that includes liability for unusual consequences if they arise from the execution of the agreed joint enterprise but (and this is the crux of the matter) . . . if one of the adventurers goes beyond what has been tacitly agreed as part of the common enterprise, his co-adventurer is not liable for the consequences of that unauthorised act. Finally . . . it is for the jury in every case to decide whether what was done was part of the joint enterprise, or went beyond it and was in fact an act unauthorised by that joint enterprise.'

Where two or more parties embark on a criminal venture, their individual liability would thus be limited to what they agreed whether expressly or tacitly. The question for juries would be to determine what it was that D2 was intending to assist or encourage D1 to do; if D1's act went beyond the common design, D2 should not be liable for this independent venture. But, if the commission of the common design resulted in an unusual consequence, both would be liable for this consequence as, for example, where D1 and D2 agree to assault V, D1 punches V and V falls hitting his skull and dies. Each would be liable for unlawful act manslaughter (see p.494.).

Unfortunately, matters became somewhat complicated following the decision of the Privy Council in *Chan Wing-Siu* [1985] 1 A.C. 168. As often happens, a misconceived defence argument and ground of appeal can result in a distortion of law. In this case D1, D2 and D3, armed with knives, went to a flat intending to steal from V, the occupant. V refused to hand over any money whereupon he was stabbed to death. D1, D2 and D3 were charged with murder. D2 claimed he was not involved in the killing as he was restraining V's wife in another room when D1 and D3 killed V. D2 argued at trial, and again on appeal, that it had to be proved that he foresaw that death or grievous bodily would *probably* result from the joint enterprise if a contingency in which a weapon might be used by one of his companions eventuated. In dealing with this argument the trial and appeal courts appear to have misled themselves. The trial judge directed the jury that each party was guilty if proved to have contemplated that a knife *might* be used on the occasion by one of his accomplices with the intention of inflicting serious bodily harm. All three were convicted and ultimately appealed to the Privy Council. Dismissing the appeals, Sir Robin Cooke stated (at 175):

"[A] secondary party is criminally liable for acts by the primary offender of a type which the former foresees but does not necessarily intend. . . .. [This principle] turns on contemplation or, putting the same idea in other words, authorisation, which may be express but is more usually implied. It meets the case of a crime foreseen as a possible incident of the common unlawful enterprise. The criminal culpability lies in participating in the venture with that foresight."

The first point to recognise is that contemplating something as a possible outcome is not the same as authorising it. But more importantly, foreseeing a possible outcome is not the same as intending it. However, in a string of cases which followed, the courts focused more and more on foresight and appeared to lose sight of the fact that the mens rea for an accessory was intention and, in particular, the intention to assist or encourage the commission of the offence the principal ultimately committed. The focus should always have been on what the common design was and whether D2 intended to assist or encourage D1 and D3 to achieve it. In *R v Powell and R v English* [1999] 1 A.C. 1, Lord Hutton stated (at 18):

"[T]here is a strong line of authority that where two parties embark on a joint enterprise to commit a crime, and one party foresees that in the course of the enterprise the other party may carry out, with the requisite mens rea, an act constituting another crime, the former is liable for that crime if committed by the latter in the course of the enterprise."

In the three decades since *Chan Wing-Siu* was decided, the incidence of gang violence and the use of guns and knives has increased. There have been many convictions for murder on the basis of parasitic accessory liability and many of those convicted have been juveniles. Campaigns have been conducted to have the law of joint enterprise abolished or, at least, reformed. A major plank in the arguments put forward has been that it is unjust to convict an accessory of murder on the basis of foresight of a possibility that the principal may kill with the intent for murder where the principal may only be convicted where it is proved that he had the intent to kill or cause grievous bodily harm. Arcane and complex arguments were raised in numerous appeals as to what had to be contemplated by D2 and whether D1's actions may have involved a "fundamental departure" from the common purpose. With each passing year the law became more complicated and the job of trial judges in directing juries, and juries in determining their verdicts, more difficult.

In the case which follows the Supreme Court has revisited parasitic accessory liability and concluded that the Privy Council and House of Lords took a wrong turning in their reasoning in *Chan Wing-Siu* and *Powell and English*.

R. V JOGEE

[2016] UKSC 8 Supreme Court

J and H spent the evening drinking and taking drugs, becoming increasingly intoxicated and aggressive. Around midnight they went to N's house but she told them to leave before her boyfriend, F, returned. J and H said they were not scared of him and would sort him out. They left but later H returned and was there when F arrived. N phoned J and told him to fetch H, which he did. Not long afterwards, however, J and H returned to N's house, which H entered and an angry confrontation with F occurred. H seized a knife from the kitchen while J remained outside with a bottle damaging a car. F tried to persuade H to leave. J shouted threats at F of what he would do with the bottle if he could reach him and shouted to H to do something to him. H stabbed F in the throat killing him. Both H and J were convicted of murder. The judge had directed the jury, consistent with Chan Wing-Siu and Powell and English, that they could convict J if satisfied that he participated in the attack on the deceased, by encouraging H, and realised when doing so that H might use the knife to stab the deceased with intent to cause him really serious harm. J's appeal against conviction was dismissed. J appealed to the Supreme Court.

LORD HUGHES AND LORD TOULSON: (with whom Lord Neuberger, Lady Hale and Lord Thomas agree)

1. In the language of the criminal law a person who assists or encourages another to commit a crime is known as an accessory or secondary party. The actual perpetrator is known as a principal, even if his role may be subordinate to that of others. It is a fundamental principle of the criminal law that the accessory is guilty of the same offence as the principal. The reason is not difficult to see. He shares the physical act because even if it was not his hand which struck the blow, ransacked the house, smuggled the drugs or forged the cheque, he has encouraged or assisted those physical acts. Similarly he shares the culpability precisely because he encouraged or assisted the offence. No one doubts that if the principal and the accessory are together engaged on, for example, an armed robbery of a bank, the accessory who keeps guard outside is as guilty of the robbery as the principal who enters with a shotgun and extracts the money from the staff by threat of violence. Nor does anyone doubt that the same principle can apply where, as sometimes happens, the accessory is nowhere near the scene of the crime. The accessory who funded the bank robbery or provided the gun for the purpose is as guilty as those who are at the scene. Sometimes it may be impossible for the prosecution to prove whether a defendant was a principal or an accessory, but that does not matter so long as it can prove that he participated in the crime either as one or as the other. These basic principles are long established and uncontroversial.

2. In the last 20 years a new term has entered the lexicon of criminal lawyers: parasitic accessory liability. The expression was coined by Professor Sir John Smith in a lecture later published in the Law Quarterly Review (*Criminal liability of accessories: law and law reform* [1997] 113 LQR 453). He used the expression to describe a doctrine which had been laid down by the Privy Council in *Chan Wing-Siu v The Queen* [1985] AC 168 and developed in later cases, including most importantly the decision of the House of Lords in *R v Powell and R v English* [1999] 1 AC 1. In *Chan Wing-Siu* it was held that if two people set out to commit an offence (crime A), and in the course of that joint enterprise one of them (D1) commits another offence (crime B), the second person (D2) is guilty as an accessory to crime B if he had foreseen the possibility that D1 might act as he did. D2's foresight of that possibility plus his continuation in the enterprise to commit crime A were held sufficient in law to bring crime B within the scope of the conduct for which he is criminally liable, whether or not he intended it.

3. . . . [T]he court has been asked to review the doctrine of parasitic accessory liability and to hold that the court took a wrong turn in *Chan Wing-Siu* and the cases which have followed it. . .

History

. . .

7. Although the distinction is not always made in the authorities, accessory liability requires proof of a conduct element accompanied by the necessary mental element. Each element can be stated in terms which sound beguilingly simple, but may not always be easy to apply.

8. The requisite conduct element is that D2 has encouraged or assisted the commission of the offence by D1.

9. Subject to the question whether a different rule applies to cases of parasitic accessory liability, the mental element in assisting or encouraging is an intention to assist or encourage the commission of the crime and this requires knowledge of any existing facts necessary for it to be criminal: *National Coal Board v Gamble* [1959] 1 QB 11, applied for example in *Attorney General v Able* [1984] QB 795, *Gillick v West Norfolk and Wisbech Area Health Authority* [1986] AC 112 and *Director of Public Prosecutions for Northern Ireland v Maxwell* [1978] 1 WLR 1350 per Lord Lowry at 1374G-1375E, approved in the House of Lords at 1356A; 1358F; 1359E; 1362H and echoed also at 1361D.

10. If the crime requires a particular intent, D2 must intend to assist or encourage D1 to act with such intent. D2's intention to assist D1 to commit the offence, and to act with whatever mental element is required of D1, will often be co-extensive on the facts with an intention by D2 that the offence be committed. Where that is so, it will be seen that many of the cases discuss D2's mental element simply in terms of intention to commit the offence. But there can be cases where D2 gives intentional assistance or encouragement to D1 to commit an offence and to act with the mental element required of him, but without D2 having a positive intent that the particular offence will be committed. That may be so, for example, where at the time that encouragement is given it remains uncertain what D1 might do; an arms supplier might be such a case.

11. With regard to the conduct element, the act of assistance or encouragement may be infinitely varied. Two recurrent situations need mention. Firstly, association between D2 and D1 may or may not involve assistance or encouragement. Secondly, the same is true of the presence of D2 at the scene when D1 perpetrates the crime. Both association and presence are likely to be very relevant evidence on the question whether assistance or encouragement was provided. . .

12. Once encouragement or assistance is proved to have been given, the prosecution does not have to go so far as to prove that it had a positive effect on D1's conduct or on the outcome: *R v Calhaem* [1985] QB 808. . .

14. With regard to the mental element, the intention to assist or encourage will often be specific to a particular offence. But in other cases it may not be. D2 may intentionally assist or encourage D1 to commit one of a range of offences, such as an act of terrorism which might take various forms. If so, D2 does not have to 'know' (or intend) in advance the specific form which the crime will take. It is enough that the offence committed by D1 is within the range of possible offences which D2 intentionally assisted or encouraged him to commit (*Maxwell*). . .

16. The decision in *Maxwell* did not derogate from the principle identified in para 9 that an intention to assist or encourage the commission of an offence requires knowledge by D2 of any facts necessary to give the principal's conduct or intended conduct its criminal character. . .

17. Secondary liability does not require the existence of an agreement between the principal and the secondary party to commit the offence. If a person sees an offence being committed, or is aware that it is going to be committed, and deliberately assists its commission, he will be guilty as an accessory. But where two or more parties agree on an illegal course of conduct (or where one party encourages another to do something illegal), the question has often arisen as to the secondary party's liability where the principal has allegedly gone beyond the scope of what was agreed or encouraged.

. . .

26. The evidential relevance of the carrying of a weapon on a criminal venture has been a common theme in the case law. Its evidential strength depends on the circumstances. . .

27. In a line of cases the courts recognised that even where there was a joint intent to use weapons to overcome resistance or avoid arrest, the participants might not share an intent to cause death or really serious harm. If the principal had that intent and caused the death of another he would be guilty of murder. Another party who lacked that intent, but who took part in an attack which resulted in an unlawful death, would be not guilty of murder but would be guilty of manslaughter, unless the act which caused the death was so removed from what they had agreed as not to be regarded as a consequence of it: *R v Smith (Wesley)* [1963] 1 WLR 1200, *R v Betty* (1964) 48 Cr App R 6, *R v Anderson and R v Morris* [1966] 2 QB 110 and *R v Reid* (1976) 62 Cr App R 109.

28. In *Wesley Smith* (see pp 1205–1206) the trial judge directed the jury:

'Manslaughter is unlawful killing without an intent to kill or do grievous bodily harm. Anybody who is party to an attack which results in an unlawful killing which results in death is a party to the killing.

. . . a person who takes part in or intentionally encourages conduct which results in a criminal offence will not necessarily share the exact guilt of the one who actually strikes the blow. His foresight of the consequences will not necessarily be the same as that of the man who strikes the blow, the principal assailant, so that each may have a different form of guilty mind, and that may distinguish their respective criminal liability. Several persons, therefore, present at the death of a man may be guilty of different degrees of crime – one of murder, others of unlawful killing, which is manslaughter. *Only he who intended that unlawful and grievous bodily harm should be done is guilty of murder. He who intended only that the victim should be unlawfully hit and hurt will be guilty of manslaughter if death results.*' (Emphasis added.)

29. Smith was convicted of manslaughter. Because he appealed against that conviction, it fell to a Court of Criminal Appeal of five judges to consider the direction as a whole, including the passage relating to murder. They praised the judge for his clear summing-up, which they described as 'legally unassailable'. They added that it was possible to hypothesise a case where what was done was wholly beyond the defendant's contemplation, but that could not be said in that case, where the death resulted from use of a knife which the appellant knew that the principal offender was carrying. . .

30. In *Betty* Lord Parker CJ quoted the passage from the summing-up in *Wesley Smith* emphasised above and noted that the court of five judges had approved it.

31. In *Anderson and Morris*, a fatal stabbing resulted in the conviction of Anderson for murder and Morris for manslaughter. The evidence of Morris's role, if any, in the attack was unclear. The judge directed the jury that if there was a common design to attack the victim, but without any intent by Morris to kill or cause grievous bodily harm, and if Anderson, acting outside the common design, produced a knife about which Morris had no knowledge and used it to kill the victim, Morris was liable to be convicted of manslaughter. The defendants' appeal was heard by a Court of Criminal Appeal of five judges, presided over by Lord Parker CJ. Mr Geoffrey Lane, QC for Morris submitted that the authorities from about 1830 onwards established the principle that (see p 118):

'. . . where two persons embark on a joint enterprise, each is liable for the acts done in pursuance of that joint enterprise, that that includes liability for unusual consequences if they arise from the execution of the agreed joint enterprise but (and this is the crux of the matter) that, if one of the adventurers goes beyond what has been tacitly agreed as part of the common enterprise, his co-adventurer is not liable for the consequences of that unauthorised act.' (Emphasis added)

32. It was submitted that the judge had therefore misdirected the jury in saying that Morris could be liable if Anderson had acted outside the common design. Accepting counsel's proposition as set out above and allowing Morris' appeal, Lord Parker said at p 120:

'It seems to this court that to say that adventurers are guilty of manslaughter when one of them has departed completely from the concerted action of the common design and has suddenly formed an intent to kill and has used a weapon and acted in a way which no party to that common design could suspect is something which would revolt the conscience of people today . . .

Considered as a matter of causation there may well be an overwhelming supervening event which is of such a character that it will relegate into history matters which would otherwise be looked on as causative factors.'

33. The court in that case did not call into question what had been said in *Wesley Smith*, and Lord Parker noted that it had been approved by the court in *Betty*. The court was not therefore resiling from the general statement that where a person takes part in an unlawful attack which results in death, he will be guilty either of murder or of manslaughter according to whether he had the *mens rea* for murder. But the court recognised that there could be cases where the actual cause of death was not simply an escalation of a fight but 'an overwhelming supervening event'. That there had been such an event in *Anderson and Morris* may have been a charitable view on the facts, but the principle was endorsed by the court in *Reid* (of which the former Mr Geoffrey Lane QC was a member).

[Their Lordships proceeded to discuss Chan Wing-Siu and Powell and English and various Court of Appeal, House of Lords and Privy Council cases which followed them.]

Analysis
. . .
62. From our review of the authorities, there is no doubt that the Privy Council laid down a new principle in *Chan Wing-Siu* when it held that if two people set out to commit an offence (crime A), and in the course of it one of them commits another offence (crime B), the second person is guilty as an accessory to crime B if he foresaw it as a possibility, but did not necessarily intend it. We have referred (at paras 31–33 and 39–45) to the authorities on which the Privy Council placed reliance in laying down that principle. . .
64. In *Anderson and Morris* the Court of Appeal affirmed *Wesley Smith* including the rule that if an adventurer departed completely from what had been tacitly agreed as part of an agreed joint enterprise his co-adventurer would not be liable for the consequences of that unauthorised act. In such a situation, the effect of the overwhelming supervening event is that any assistance is spent. The issue was whether that applied to Morris. The court did not otherwise address the question of what is necessary to establish joint responsibility, and specifically whether what is required is intention to assist or mere foresight of what D1 might do. Still less did it address the meaning of contemplation (foresight) and authorisation. It provided no foundation for the rule in *Chan Wing-Siu*.
65. The Privy Council judgment, moreover, elided foresight with authorisation, when it said that the principle 'turns on contemplation or, putting the same idea in other words, authorisation, which may be express but is more usually implied'. But as Professor Smith observed, contemplation and authorisation are not the same at all.
66. Nor can authorisation of crime B automatically be inferred from continued participation in crime A with foresight of crime B. As Lord Brown accurately pointed out in *R v Rahman* [2008] UKHL 45 at para 63, the rule in *Chan Wing-Siu* makes guilty those who foresee crime B but never intended it or wanted it to happen. There can be no doubt that if D2 continues to participate in crime A with foresight that D1 may commit crime B, that is evidence, and sometimes powerful evidence, of an intent to assist D1 in crime B. But it is evidence of such intent (or, if one likes, of 'authorisation'), not conclusive of it.
. . .
68. In *Powell and English* Lord Hutton placed considerable reliance on *Wesley Smith*, which had been cited

in *Chan Wing-Siu* but was not mentioned in the judgment. Lord Hutton said that he considered that in *Wesley Smith* 'the Court of Appeal recognised that the secondary party will be guilty of unlawful killing committed by the primary party with a knife if he contemplates that the primary party may use such a weapon' (p 19). But the unlawful killing to which the Court of Appeal was referring was manslaughter, not murder, and it is very important to understand its reasoning. The defendant in *Wesley Smith* was one of a group of four men who became involved in a row in a public house. He and one other went outside and threw bricks at the building. One of the two who remained inside stabbed the barman with a knife which Smith knew he carried. Smith was acquitted of murder but convicted of manslaughter.

69. The question in *Wesley Smith* was whether his conviction for manslaughter was unsafe in the light of his acquittal of murder. The starting point was that anyone who takes part in an unlawful and violent attack on another person which results in death is guilty (at least) of manslaughter. There might conceivably have been an intervening act by another person of such a character as to break any connection between the defendant's conduct and the victim's death (as, for example, in *Anderson and Morris*); but the fact that it must have been within Smith's contemplation that the principal might act in the way that he did was fatal to the argument that he was not guilty even of manslaughter. (See para 96 below).

70. Although Lord Hutton quoted part of the judge's summing-up in *Wesley Smith* he ended his quotation with the first part of the passage set out at para 28 above. ('Anybody who is party to an attack which results in an unlawful killing . . . is a party to the killing'.) He did not go on to refer to the critical passage which followed, including the statement:

'Only he who intended that unlawful and grievous bodily harm should be done is guilty of murder. He who intended only that the victim should be unlawfully hit and hurt will be guilty of manslaughter if death results.'

71. Moreover, as we have explained at para 29, the Court of Appeal had explicitly praised the summing-up as a correct statement of the law. Far from supporting the *Chan Wing-Siu* principle, *Wesley Smith* was an authority contrary to it.

72. *Wesley Smith* was not the only authority inconsistent with the *Chan Wing-Siu* principle. We have referred to other authorities from *Collison* (1831) 4 Car & P 565 to *Reid*, which were not cited in *Chan Wing-Siu*. *Reid* was cited in *Powell and English*, but it was not mentioned in any of the judgments, although it was a reserved judgment of a strong Court of Appeal which reiterated that a secondary party could not be convicted of murder unless he had the *mens rea* for murder.

73. In *Chan Wing-Siu* Sir Robin Cooke referred, at p 176, to the 'modern emphasis on subjective tests of criminal guilt'. There has indeed been a progressive move away from the historic tendency of the common law to presume as a matter of law that the 'natural and probable consequences' of a man's act were intended, culminating in England and Wales in its statutory removal by section 8 of the Criminal Justice Act 1967. Since then in England and Wales the foreseeability of the consequences has been a matter of evidence from which intention may be, but need not necessarily be, inferred . . . But in any event the proper subjective counterpart to Foster's objective test (whether 'the events, although possibly falling out beyond his original intention, were in the ordinary course of things the probable consequence of what B did under the influence, and at the instigation of A') would have been intention, as was held to be necessary in *Wesley Smith* and *Reid*. Foresight may be good evidence of intention but it is not synonymous with it, as Lord Steyn acknowledged in *Powell and English* at p 13.

74. It was, of course, within the jurisdiction of the courts in *Chan Wing-Siu* and *Powell and English* to change the common law in a way which made it more severe, but to alter general principles which have stood for a long time, especially in a way which has particular impact on a subject as difficult and serious as homicide, requires caution; and all the more so when the change involved widening the scope of secondary liability by the introduction of new doctrine (since termed parasitic accessory liability). In *Chan Wing-Siu* the Privy Council addressed the policy argument for the principle which it laid down in two sentences . . . The statement at p 177 'Where a man lends himself to a criminal enterprise knowing that potentially murderous weapons are to be carried, and in the event they in fact are used by his partner with an intent sufficient for murder, he should not escape the consequences . . .' may be thought to oversimplify the question of what is the enterprise to which he has intentionally lent himself, but it also implies that he would escape all criminal liability but for the *Chan Wing-Siu* principle. On the facts postulated, if the law remained as set out in *Wesley Smith* and *Reid* he would be guilty of homicide in the form of manslaughter, which carries a potential sentence of life imprisonment. The dangers of escalation of violence where people go out in possession of weapons to commit crime are indisputable, but they were specifically referred to by the court in *Reid*, when explaining why it was right that such conduct should result in

conviction for manslaughter if death resulted, albeit that the initial intention may have been nothing more than causing fright. There was no consideration in *Chan Wing-Siu*, or in *Powell and English*, of the fundamental policy question whether and why it was necessary and appropriate to reclassify such conduct as murder rather than manslaughter. Such a discussion would have involved, among other things, questions about fair labelling and fair discrimination in sentencing.

75. In *Powell and English* Lord Hutton referred to the need to give effective protection to the public against criminals operating in gangs (at p 25), but the same comments apply. There does not appear to have been any objective evidence that the law prior to *Chan Wing-Siu* failed to provide the public with adequate protection. A further policy reason suggested by Lord Hutton for setting a lower *mens rea* requirement for the secondary party than for the principal was that the secondary party has time to think before taking part in a criminal enterprise like a bank robbery, whereas the principal may have to decide on the spur of the moment whether to use his weapon. But the principal has had an earlier choice whether to go armed or not. As for the secondary party, he may have leisure to think before going out to rob a bank, but the same is not true in many other cases (for example, of young people who become suddenly embroiled in a fight in a bar and may make a quick decision whether or not to help their friends).

76. We respectfully differ from the view of the Australian High Court, supported though it is by some distinguished academic opinion, that there is any occasion for a separate form of secondary liability such as was formulated in *Chan Wing-Siu*. As there formulated, and as argued by the Crown in these cases, the suggested foundation is the contribution made by D2 to crime B by continued participation in crime A with foresight of the possibility of crime B. We prefer the view expressed by the Court of Appeal in *Mendez* [2011] QB 876, at para 17, and by textbook writers including Smith and Hogan's *Criminal Law*, 14th ed (2015), p 260 that there is no reason why ordinary principles of secondary liability should not be of general application.

77. The rule in *Chan Wing-Siu* is often described as 'joint enterprise liability'. However, the expression 'joint enterprise' is not a legal term of art. As the Court of Appeal observed in *R v A* [2011] QB 841, para 9, it is used in practice in a variety of situations to include both principals and accessories. As applied to the rule in *Chan Wing-Siu*, it unfortunately occasions some public misunderstanding. It is understood (erroneously) by some to be a form of guilt by association or of guilt by simple presence without more. It is important to emphasise that guilt of crime by mere association has no proper part in the common law.

78. As we have explained, secondary liability does not require the existence of an agreement between D1 and D2. Where, however, it exists, such agreement is by its nature a form of encouragement and in most cases will also involve acts of assistance. The long established principle that where parties agree to carry out a criminal venture, each is liable for acts to which they have expressly or impliedly given their assent is an example of the intention to assist which is inherent in the making of the agreement. Similarly, where people come together without agreement, often spontaneously, to commit an offence together, the giving of intentional support by words or deeds, including by supportive presence, is sufficient to attract secondary liability on ordinary principles. We repeat that secondary liability includes cases of agreement between principal and secondary party, but it is not limited to them.

79. It will be apparent from what we have said that we do not consider that the *Chan Wing-Siu* principle can be supported, except on the basis that it has been decided and followed at the highest level. In plain terms, our analysis leads us to the conclusion that the introduction of the principle was based on an incomplete, and in some respects erroneous, reading of the previous case law, coupled with generalised and questionable policy arguments. We recognise the significance of reversing a statement of principle which has been made and followed by the Privy Council and the House of Lords on a number of occasions. We consider that it is right to do so for several reasons.

80. Firstly, we have had the benefit of a much fuller analysis than on previous occasions when the topic has been considered. . .

81. Secondly, it cannot be said that the law is now well established and working satisfactorily. It remains highly controversial and a continuing source of difficulty for trial judges. It has also led to large numbers of appeals.

82. Thirdly, secondary liability is an important part of the common law, and if a wrong turn has been taken, it should be corrected.

83. Fourthly, in the common law foresight of what might happen is ordinarily no more than evidence from which a jury can infer the presence of a requisite intention. It may be strong evidence, but its adoption as a test for the mental element for murder in the case of a secondary party is a serious and anomalous departure from the basic rule, which results in over-extension of the law of murder and reduction of the law of manslaughter. Murder already has a relatively low *mens rea* threshold, because it includes an intention to cause serious injury, without intent to kill or to cause risk to life. The *Chan Wing-Siu* principle extends liability for murder to a secondary party

on the basis of a still lesser degree of culpability, namely foresight only of the possibility that the principal may commit murder but without there being any need for intention to assist him to do so. It savours, as Professor Smith suggested, of constructive crime.

84. Fifthly, the rule brings the striking anomaly of requiring a lower mental threshold for guilt in the case of the accessory than in the case of the principal.

85. As to the argument that even if the court is satisfied that the law took a wrong turn, any correction should now be left to Parliament, the doctrine of secondary liability is a common law doctrine (put into statutory form in section 8 of the 1861 Act) and, if it has been unduly widened by the courts, it is proper for the courts to correct the error.

86. It is worth attention that the Westminster Parliament has legislated over inchoate criminal liability in the Serious Crime Act 2007. Section 44 provides:

'(1)   A person commits an offence if -

(a)   he does an act capable of encouraging or assisting the commission of an offence; and
(b)   he intends to encourage or assist its commission. >c1i41<

(2)   But he is not to be taken to have intended to encourage or assist the commission of an offence merely because such encouragement or assistance was a foreseeable consequence of his act.'

Section 45 creates a parallel offence if a person does such an act believing that the offence will be committed and that his act will encourage or assist his commission, but both sections are subject to a statutory defence if the defendant acted reasonably in the circumstances as he believed them to be. It is a noteworthy feature of the present law in England and Wales that Parliament has provided that foresight is not sufficient *mens rea* for the offence of intentionally encouraging or assisting another to commit an offence; whilst at present under *Chan Wing-Siu* if that other person goes on to commit the offence, such foresight is sufficient *mens rea* for the second-ary party to be regarded as guilty of the full offence at common law. The correction of the error in *Chan Wing-Siu* brings the common law back into recognition of the difference between foresight and intent, consistently with Parliament's approach in section 44(2) of the 2007 Act and more generally in section 8 of the Criminal Justice Act 1967 (referred to at para 73 above).

87. It would not be satisfactory for this court simply to disapprove the *Chan Wing-Siu* principle. Those who are concerned with criminal justice, including members of the public, are entitled to expect from this court a clear statement of the relevant principles. We consider that the proper course for this court is to re-state, as nearly and clearly as we may, the principles which had been established over many years before the law took a wrong turn. The error was to equate foresight with intent to assist, as a matter of law; the correct approach is to treat it as evidence of intent. The long-standing pre *Chan Wing-Siu* practice of inferring intent to assist from a common criminal purpose which includes the further crime, if the occasion for it were to arise, was always a legitimate one; what was illegitimate was to treat foresight as an inevitable yardstick of common purpose. . .

Restatement of the principles

88. We have summarised the essential principles applicable to all cases in paras 8 to 12 and 14 to 16. In some cases the prosecution may not be able to prove whether a defendant was principal or accessory, but it is sufficient to be able to prove that he participated in the crime in one way or another.

89. In cases of alleged secondary participation there are likely to be two issues. The first is whether the defend-ant was in fact a participant, that is, whether he assisted or encouraged the commission of the crime. Such participation may take many forms. It may include providing support by contributing to the force of numbers in a hostile confrontation.

90. The second issue is likely to be whether the accessory intended to encourage or assist D1 to commit the crime, acting with whatever mental element the offence requires of D1 (as stated in para 10 above). If the crime requires a particular intent, D2 must intend (it may be conditionally) to assist D1 to act with such intent. To take a homely example, if D2 encourages D1 to take another's bicycle without permission of the owner and return it after use, but D1 takes it and keeps it, D1 will be guilty of theft but D2 of the lesser offence of unauthorised taking, since he will not have encouraged D1 to act with intent permanently to deprive. In cases of concerted physical attack there may often be no practical distinction to draw between an intention by D2 to assist D1 to act with the intention of causing grievous bodily harm at least and D2 having the intention himself that such harm be caused. In such cases it may be simpler, and will generally be perfectly safe, to direct the jury (as suggested in *Wesley*

Smith and *Reid*) that the Crown must prove that D2 intended that the victim should suffer grievous bodily harm at least. However, as a matter of law, it is enough that D2 intended to assist D1 to act with the requisite intent. That may well be the situation if the assistance or encouragement is rendered some time before the crime is committed and at a time when it is not clear what D1 may or may not decide to do. Another example might be where D2 supplies a weapon to D1, who has no lawful purpose in having it, intending to help D1 by giving him the means to commit a crime (or one of a range of crimes), but having no further interest in what he does, or indeed whether he uses it at all.

91. It will therefore in some cases be important when directing juries to remind them of the difference between intention and desire.

92. In cases of secondary liability arising out of a prior joint criminal venture, it will also often be necessary to draw the jury's attention to the fact that the intention to assist, and indeed the intention that the crime should be committed, may be conditional. The bank robbers who attack the bank when one or more of them is armed no doubt hope that it will not be necessary to use the guns, but it may be a perfectly proper inference that all were intending that if they met resistance the weapons should be used with the intent to do grievous bodily harm at least. The group of young men which faces down a rival group may hope that the rivals will slink quietly away, but it may well be a perfectly proper inference that all were intending that if resistance were to be met, grievous bodily harm at least should be done.

93. Juries frequently have to decide questions of intent (including conditional intent) by a process of inference from the facts and circumstances proved. The same applies when the question is whether D2, who joined with others in a venture to commit crime A, shared a common purpose or common intent (the two are the same) which included, if things came to it, the commission of crime B, the offence or type of offence with which he is charged, and which was physically committed by D1. A time honoured way of inviting a jury to consider such a question is to ask the jury whether they are sure that D1's act was within the scope of the joint venture, that is, whether D2 expressly or tacitly agreed to a plan which included D1 going as far as he did, and committing crime B, if the occasion arose.

94. If the jury is satisfied that there was an agreed common purpose to commit crime A, and if it is satisfied also that D2 must have foreseen that, in the course of committing crime A, D1 might well commit crime B, it may in appropriate cases be justified in drawing the conclusion that D2 had the necessary conditional intent that crime B should be committed, if the occasion arose; or in other words that it was within the scope of the plan to which D2 gave his assent and intentional support. But that will be a question of fact for the jury in all the circumstances.

95. In cases where there is a more or less spontaneous outbreak of multi-handed violence, the evidence may be too nebulous for the jury to find that there was some form of agreement, express or tacit. But, as we have said, liability as an aider or abettor does not necessarily depend on there being some form of agreement between the defendants; it depends on proof of intentional assistance or encouragement, conditional or otherwise. If D2 joins with a group which he realises is out to cause serious injury, the jury may well infer that he intended to encourage or assist the deliberate infliction of serious bodily injury and/or intended that that should happen if necessary. In that case, if D1 acts with intent to cause serious bodily injury and death results, D1 and D2 will each be guilty of murder.

96. If a person is a party to a violent attack on another, without an intent to assist in the causing of death or really serious harm, but the violence escalates and results in death, he will be not guilty of murder but guilty of manslaughter. So also if he participates by encouragement or assistance in any other unlawful act which all sober and reasonable people would realise carried the risk of some harm (not necessarily serious) to another, and death in fact results: *R v Church* [1965] 1 QB 59, approved in *Director of Public Prosecutions v Newbury* [1977] AC 500 and very recently re-affirmed in *R v F (J) & E (N)* [2015] EWCA Crim 351; [2015] 2 Cr App R 5. The test is objective. As the Court of Appeal held in *Reid*, if a person goes out with armed companions to cause harm to another, any reasonable person would recognise that there is not only a risk of harm, but a risk of the violence escalating to the point at which serious harm or death may result. Cases in which D2 intends some harm falling short of grievous bodily harm are a fortiori, but manslaughter is not limited to these.

97. The qualification to this (recognised in *Wesley Smith*, *Anderson and Morris* and *Reid*) is that it is possible for death to be caused by some overwhelming supervening act by the perpetrator which nobody in the defendant's shoes could have contemplated might happen and is of such a character as to relegate his acts to history; in that case the defendant will bear no criminal responsibility for the death.

98. This type of case apart, there will normally be no occasion to consider the concept of 'fundamental departure' as derived from *English*. What matters is whether D2 encouraged or assisted the crime, whether it be murder or some other offence. He need not encourage or assist a particular way of committing it, although

he may sometimes do so. In particular, his intention to assist in a crime of violence is not determined only by whether he knows what kind of weapon D1 has in his possession. The tendency which has developed in the application of the rule in *Chan Wing-Siu* to focus on what D2 knew of what weapon D1 was carrying can and should give way to an examination of whether D2 intended to assist in the crime charged. If that crime is murder, then the question is whether he intended to assist the intentional infliction of grievous bodily harm at least, which question will often, as set out above, be answered by asking simply whether he himself intended grievous bodily harm at least. Very often he may intend to assist in violence using whatever weapon may come to hand. In other cases he may think that D1 has an iron bar whereas he turns out to have a knife, but the difference may not at all affect his intention to assist, if necessary, in the causing of grievous bodily harm at least. Knowledge or ignorance that weapons generally, or a particular weapon, is carried by D1 will be evidence going to what the intention of D2 was, and may be irresistible evidence one way or the other, but it is evidence and no more.

99. Where the offence charged does not require mens rea, the only *mens rea* required of the secondary party is that he intended to encourage or assist the perpetrator to do the prohibited act, with knowledge of any facts and circumstances necessary for it to be a prohibited act: *National Coal Board v Gamble*.

. . .

Jogee

. . .

105. Mr John McGuinness QC on behalf of the prosecution properly accepted that the appellant's conviction could not stand if we were to conclude, as we do, that the *Chan Wing-Siu* principle was wrong.

106. Ms Felicity Gerry QC submitted on behalf of the appellant that he could not properly have been convicted either of murder or of manslaughter.

107. We regard that submission as hopeless. The jury's verdict means that it was sure, at the very least, that the appellant knew that Hirsi had the knife and appreciated that he might use it to cause really serious harm. In returning to the house . . . the appellant and Hirsi were clearly intent on some form of violent confrontation. The appellant was brandishing a bottle, striking the car and shouting encouragement to his co-defendant at the scene. There was a case fit to go to the jury that he had the *mens rea* for murder. At a minimum, he was party to a violent adventure carrying the plain objective risk of some harm to a person and which resulted in death; he was therefore guilty of manslaughter at least. The choice of disposal is whether to quash the appellant's conviction for murder and order a re-trial or whether to quash his conviction for murder and substitute a conviction for manslaughter. We invite the parties' written submissions on that question.

Notes

1.   In *Jogee* at para.37 their Lordships, referring to *Chan Wing-Siu*, stated:

"There was an overwhelming case for inferring that the appellants foresaw the likelihood of resistance and that their plan included the possible use of knives to cause serious harm. However, the Privy Council upheld the convictions on a different basis."

At para.100 they stated:

"The error identified, of equating foresight with intent to assist rather than treating the first as evidence of the second, is important as a matter of legal principle, but it does not follow that it will have been important on the facts to the outcome of the trial or to the safety of the conviction."

In practice, the reversion to the position which pre-dated the decision in *Chan Wing-Siu* may not lead to much difference in the outcomes of trials in the future. It is also unlikely to lead to many convictions arrived at in the intervening 30 years being overturned on appeal. But the decision does much to restore the law in this area to a principled state reaffirming that the mens rea of the secondary party is intent and that foresight of a possible outcome is simply evidence which may lead a jury to infer that the secondary party had the necessary intent to assist or encourage the principal to commit that offence, but it need not necessarily do so.

2. Following the decision in *Powell and English* a body of case law, of ever increasing complexity, developed to deal with the issue of "fundamental departure" where, for example, D1 kills V using a weapon different to the one D2 contemplated might be used and, or, with an intent to kill when D2 contemplated an intent to do serious injury. The Supreme Court has consigned this body of case law to a siding and do not expect it to be revisited. The focus is to be on the crime D2 encouraged or assisted rather than the method or weapon by which it was committed, and whether or not D2 had the requisite intent, unless the departure from the criminal venture in which D1 and D2 were engaged involves death being caused by some overwhelming supervening act by D1 which nobody in D2's shoes could have contemplated might happen and is of such a character as to relegate his acts to history.

(e) Acts beyond the Common Design

Notes and Questions

1. Where A incidentally commits a different offence in performing the common design, B will be liable for this offence. For example, A and B agree that they will burgle a factory and that A will hit V the night-watchman over the head with a cosh to knock him unconscious. If V dies as a result both A and B will be liable for unlawful act manslaughter (see *Baldessare* (1930) 22 Cr. App. R. 70; *Anderson and Morris* [1966] 2 Q.B. 110).

2. Where A deliberately departs from the common design B will not be liable. Hawkins stated the principle as follows (2 P.C. c.29 s.21):

    "But if a man command another to commit a felony on a particular person or thing and he do it on another; as to kill A and he kill B or to burn the house of A and he burn the house of B or to steal an ox and he steal a horse; or to steal such an horse and he steal another; or to commit a felony of one kind and he commit another of quite a different nature; . . . it is said that the commander is not an accessory because the act done varies in substance from that which was commanded."

    In *Saunders and Archer* (1573) 2 Plowd 473, S desired to kill his wife and sought the assistance of A who supplied him with poison. S put the poison in an apple and gave it to his wife who ate a little but gave the remainder to their daughter. S witnessed this but did not intervene and his daughter ate the apple and died. S was convicted of murder but A was acquitted as S's failure to intervene amounted to a deliberate variation in substance from the common design. If the same situation arose today, would S's actions fall within the ambit of an "overwhelming supervening act"?

3. D1 and D2 agree to commit a robbery. D2 instructs D1 that they should only use mild force if any resistance is offered. D1 ends up hitting V repeatedly over the head with the intention of killing him after V offers token resistance to D1 and D2's demands for his wallet. Could D2 be convicted of manslaughter if D1 is convicted of murder? In *Lovesey and Peterson* [1970] 1 Q.B. 352 Lord Widgery CJ stated (at 356):

"It is clear that a common design to use unlawful violence, short of the infliction of grievous bodily harm, renders all co-adventurers guilty of manslaughter if the victim's death is an unexpected consequence of the carrying out of that design. Where, however, the victim's death is not the product of the common design but is attributable to one of the co-adventurers going beyond the scope of that design, by using violence which is intended to cause grievous bodily harm, the others are not responsible for that unauthorised act."

Will this approach still be followed following the decision in *Jogee* and the reference therein to an "overwhelming supervening act" by D1? How might your answer differ if there was evidence to show that D2 knew from past experience that D1 was easily riled and could erupt using extreme and gratuitous violence on his robbery victims?

4.   Situations arise where there is a divergence in the mens rea of the participants in a criminal venture albeit that they agree on the act that will be performed. In *Gilmour* [2000] 2 Cr. App. R. 407 the Northern Ireland Court of Appeal approved the following hypothetical (originally posed in *Blackstone's Criminal Practice* 1996):

"Suppose P and A agree that P will post a specific incendiary device to V, A contemplating only superficial injuries to V when he opens it but P foreseeing and hoping that the injuries will be serious or fatal. If V is killed as a result, P will clearly be guilty of murder, A is clearly not guilty of murder as an accessory but should be guilty of manslaughter because the act done by P is precisely what was envisaged. The fact that P happens also to have the mens rea of murder is irrelevant because it does not change the nature of the act that he does or the manner in which he does it."

5.   Because murder may be committed with an intent to kill or the lesser intent to cause grievous bodily harm, and grievous bodily harm covers serious injuries which may not be life threatening as well as those which may threaten life, further complications may arise in delineating the ambit of the common design. A good example of the problems that may arise is the case of *Gamble* [1989] N.I. 268. A and B were parties to what they thought was going to be a punishment beating and contemplated that it might involve, at worst, "knee-capping" V (i.e. shooting V through his knee-caps). The other participants, C and D, however, murdered V in an attack which involved multiple stab wounds, gunshot wounds, and blows to the head and body. Two of the gunshot wounds would have been fatal had death not been caused by cutting V's throat. Carswell J, sitting without a jury in the Crown Court of Northern Ireland, convicted A and B of wounding with intent to inflict grievous bodily harm. Counsel for the Crown had argued that as A and B had both intended GBH and that this was sufficient mens rea for murder, they should be convicted of murder. In response Carswell J stated (at 284):

"Although the rule remains well entrenched that an intention to inflict grievous bodily harm qualifies as the mens rea of murder, it is not in my opinion necessary to apply it in such a way as to fix an accessory with liability for a consequence which he did not intend and which stems from an act which he did not have within his contemplation."

In the language of *Jogee* the murder of V was an "overwhelming supervening act" as clearly there was no evidence from which an intention to encourage or assist C and D in murder could be inferred.

(f) Withdrawal

R. V BECERRA

(1975) 62 Cr. App. R. 212 CA

B broke into a house with C and G, intending to steal. B gave a knife to C to use if necessary on anyone interrupting them. The tenant of the upstairs flat L came down to investigate the noise. B said, "There's a bloke coming. Let's go," jumped out of the window and ran away. C stabbed L with the knife, killing him. At his trial for murder, B contended that he had withdrawn from the joint adventure before the attack on L. The jury were directed that his words and departure through the window were insufficient to constitute a withdrawal. B was convicted, and sought leave to appeal.

ROSKILL LJ

Mr Owen [for the appellant] says that in that passage which I have just read, the learned judge in effect, though perhaps not in so many words, withdrew the defence of 'withdrawal' from the jury, because the learned judge was saying to the jury that the only evidence of Becerra's suggested 'withdrawal' was the remark, if it were made, 'Come on let's go', coupled with the fact of course that Becerra then went out through the window and ran away and that that could not in those circumstances amount to 'withdrawal' and therefore was not available as a defence, even if they decided the issue of common design against Becerra. It is upon that passage in the summing-up that Mr Owen has principally focused his criticism.

It is necessary, before dealing with that argument in more detail, to say a word or two about the relevant law. It is a curious fact, considering the number of times in which this point arises where two or more people are charged with criminal offences, particularly murder or manslaughter, how relatively little authority there is in this country upon the point. But the principle is undoubtedly of long standing.

Perhaps it is best first stated in *R. v Saunders and Archer* [above, p.337], in a note by *Plowden*, p.476, thus: '. . . for if I command one to kill J.S. and before the Fact done I go to him and tell him that I have repented, and expressly charge him not to kill J.S. and he afterwards kills him, there I shall not be Accessory to this Murder, because I have countermanded my first Command, which in all Reason shall discharge me, for the malicious Mind of the Accessory ought to continue to do ill until the Time of the Act done, or else he shall not be charged; but if he had killed J.S. before the Time of my Discharge or Countermand given, I should have been Accessory to the Death, notwithstanding my private Repentance.'

The next case to which I may usefully refer is some 250 years later, but over 150 years ago: *R. v Edmeads and Others* (1828) 3 C. & P. 390, where there is a ruling of Vaughan B. at a trial at Berkshire Assizes, upon an indictment charging Edmeads and others with unlawfully shooting at game keepers. At the end of his ruling the learned Baron said on the question of common intent, at p.392, 'that is rather a question for the jury; but still, on this evidence, it is quite clear what the common purpose was. They all draw up in lines, and point their guns at the game-keepers, and they are all giving their countenance and assistance to the one of them who actually fires the gun. If it could be shewn that either of them separated himself from the rest, and showed distinctly that he would have no hand in what they were doing, the objection would have much weight in it.'

I can go forward over 100 years. Mr Owen (to whose juniors we are indebted for their research into the relevant Canadian and United States cases) referred us to several Canadian cases, to only one of which is it necessary to refer in detail, a decision of the Court of Appeal of British Columbia in *R. v Whitehouse* (alias *Savage*) (1941) 1 W.W.R. 112. I need not read the headnote. The Court of Appeal held that the trial judge concerned in that case, which was one of murder, had been guilty of misdirection in his direction to the jury on this question of 'withdrawal'. The matter is, if I may most respectfully say so, so well put in the leading judgment of Sloan J.A., that I read the whole of the passage at pp.115 and 116: 'Can it be said on the facts of this case that a mere change of mental intention and a quitting of the scene of the crime just immediately prior to the striking of the fatal blow will absolve those who participate in the commission of the crime by overt acts up to that moment from all the consequences of its accomplishment by the one who strikes in ignorance of his companions' change of heart? I think not. After a crime has been committed and before a prior abandonment of the common enterprise may be found by a jury there must be, in my view, in the absence of exceptional circumstances, something more than a mere mental change of intention and physical change of place by those associates who wish to dissociate themselves from the consequences attendant upon their willing assistance up to the moment of the actual commission of that crime. I would not attempt to define too closely what must be done in criminal matters involving participation in a common unlawful purpose to break the chain of causation and responsibility. That must depend upon the circumstances of each case but it seems to me that one essential element ought to be established in a case of this kind: Where practicable and reasonable there must be timely communication of the intention to abandon the common purpose from those who wish to dissociate themselves from the contemplated crime to those who desire to continue in it. What is 'timely communication' must be determined by the facts of each case but where practicable and reasonable it ought to be such communication, verbal or otherwise, that will serve unequivocal notice upon the other party to the common unlawful cause that if he proceeds upon it he does so without the further aid and assistance of those who withdraw. The unlawful purpose of him who continues alone is then his own and not one in common with those who are no longer parties to it nor liable to its full and final consequences.' The learned judge then went on to cite a passage from 1 Hale's *Pleas of the Crown* 618 and the passage from *R. v Saunders and Archer* to which I have already referred.

In the view of each member of this Court, that passage, if we may respectfully say so, could not be improved upon and we venture to adopt it in its entirety as a correct statement of the law which is to be applied in this case.

The last case, an English one, is *R. v Croft* [1944] 1 K.B. 295, a well known case of a suicide pact where, under the old law, the survivor of a suicide pact was charged with and convicted of murder. It was sought to argue that he had withdrawn from the pact in time to avoid liability (as the law then was) for conviction for murder.

The Court of Criminal Appeal, comprising Lawrence J. (as he then was), Lewis and Wrottesley JJ. dismissed the appeal and upheld the direction given by Humphreys J. to the jury at the trial. Towards the end of the judgment Lawrence J. said (pp.297 and 298): '. . . counsel for the appellant complains—although I do not understand that the point had ever been taken in the court below—that the summing-up does not contain any reference to the possibility of the agreement to commit suicide having been determined or countermanded. It is true that the learned judge does not deal expressly with that matter except in a passage where he says: 'Even if you accept his statement in the witness-box that the vital and second shot was fired when he had gone through the window, he would still be guilty of murder if she was then committing suicide as the result of an agreement which they had mutually arrived at that that should be fate of both of them, and it is no answer for him that he altered his mind after she was dead and did not commit suicide himself' . . . The authorities, such as they are, show in our opinion, that where a person has acted as an accessory before the fact, he must give express and actual countermand or revocation of the advising, counselling, procuring, or abetting which he had given before.'

It seems to us that those authorities make plain what the law is which has to be applied in the present case.

We therefore turn back to consider the direction which the learned judge gave in the present case to the jury and what was the suggested evidence that Becerra had withdrawn from the common agreement. The suggested evidence is the use by Becerra of the words 'Come on let's go', coupled, as I said a few moments ago, with his act in going out through the window. The evidence, as the judge pointed out, was that Cooper never heard that nor did the third man. But let it be supposed that that was said and the jury took the view that it was said.

On the facts of this case, in the circumstances then prevailing, the knife having already been used and being contemplated for further use when it was handed over by Becerra to Cooper for the purpose of avoiding (if necessary) by violent means the hazards of identification, if Becerra wanted to withdraw at that stage, he would have to 'countermand', to use the word that is used in some of the cases or 'repent' to use another word so used, in some manner vastly different and vastly more effective than merely to say 'Come on, let's go' and go out through the window.

It is not necessary, on this application, to decide whether the point of time had arrived at which the only way in which he could effectively withdraw, so as to free himself from joint responsibility for any act Cooper thereafter did in furtherance of the common design, would be physically to intervene so as to stop Cooper attacking Lewis, as the judge suggested, by interposing his own body between them or somehow getting in between them or whether some other action might suffice. That does not rise for decision here. Nor is it necessary to decide whether or not the learned judge was right or wrong, on the facts of this case, in that passage which appears at the bottom of p.206, which Mr Owen criticised: 'and at least take all reasonable steps to prevent the commission of the crime which he had agreed the others should commit.' It is enough for the purposes of deciding this application to say that under the law of this country as it stands, and on the facts (taking them at their highest in favour of Becerra), that which was urged as amounting to withdrawal from the common design was not capable of amounting to such withdrawal. Accordingly Becerra remains responsible, in the eyes of the law, for everything that Cooper did and continued to do after Becerra's disappearance through the window as much as if he had done them himself.

Application refused

Notes

"A declared intent to withdraw from a conspiracy to dynamite a building is not enough, if the fuse has been set; he must step on the fuse", per McDermott J in *Eldredge v US*, 62 F. 2nd 449 (1932). That leaves the question of what will be enough if it is timely. Roskill LJ appears to indicate that at some stage a point of time will be reached where only physical prevention of the crime, or at least all reasonable steps to prevent it, will exculpate the accessory, leaving open the question of what will suffice before that point of time is reached.

R. v Grundy [1977] Crim. L.R. 543: Six weeks before a burglary, A gave information to the burglars about the premises to be attacked, the habits of the owner and other matters. For two weeks before the burglary, "he had been trying to stop them breaking in" [although it does not appear that he warned the householder or the police]. *Held*, his defence of withdrawal should have been left to the jury.

R. v Whitefield (1983) 79 Cr. App. R. 36 CA; W told G that the occupant of the flat next to his was away; he agreed to break in with G by way of his own flat's balcony and to divide the spoils. Later he told G he would take no part, but on the night in question, he heard G breaking in via the coal chute, and took no steps to stop him. "In this case there was . . . evidence . . . that he had served unequivocal notice on G. that if he proceeded with the burglary he would do so without the aid or assistance of the appellant. In his ruling the judge stated that such notice was not enough, and that in failing to communicate with the police or take any other steps to prevent the burglary he remained 'liable in law for what happened, for everything that was done that night' In the judgment of the court, in making that statement the judge fell into an error of law" (at 40).

In *Mitchell* [1999] Crim. L.R. 496, M, N and D having desisted from a spontaneous attack on V, D returned to administer a further beating to V as a result of which V died. In quashing the convictions of M and N for murder and ordering a retrial, the Court of Appeal sought to draw a distinction between joint enterprises involving pre-planned violence and those involving spontaneous violence. In the former *Becerra* remains the authority, but in the latter the Court of Appeal suggested that mere withdrawal from the scene without communication could be sufficient. Professor Smith in his *Commentary* on the case was critical of the decision as withdrawal from the scene does not necessarily cancel out the encouragement already offered to the principal by the secondary party's participation in the enterprise up to that point, particularly if the principal is unaware of the secondary party's withdrawal.

In *Robinson* [2000] 5 Archbold News 2 CA, D and a group of youths had followed V taunting him. The group looked to D for leadership and called on him to hit V. D did so, whereupon the group joined in the attack. D stood back while they did so but when the attack appeared to be going further than he intended, he intervened and the attack ceased. The Court of Appeal followed *Becerra* holding that in the instant case where violence was not spontaneous communication of withdrawal was necessary. Furthermore, Otton LJ stated:

> "There is a clear line of authority that where a party has given encouragement to others to commit an offence it cannot be withdrawn once the offence has commenced. (See *R v Whitefield* [1984] 79 CAR. 36, *R v Rook* [1993] 97 CAR. 327 and *R v Pearman* [1996] 1 CAR. p.24)."

His Lordship, who also gave the judgment of the Court in *Mitchell*, quoted from Professor Smith's *Commentary to Mitchell* with approval, and made it clear that *Mitchell* was an exceptional case stating:

> "It can only be in exceptional circumstances that a person can withdraw from a crime he has initiated. Similarly in those rare circumstances communication of withdrawal must be given in order

to give the principal offenders the opportunity to desist rather than complete the crime. This must be so even in situations of spontaneous violence unless it is not practicable or reasonable so to communicate as in the exceptional circumstances pertaining in *Mitchell* where the accused threw down his weapon and moved away before the final and fatal blows were inflicted."

Dealing with the question of withdrawing where encouragement had been offered, Otton LJ stated:

"The trial judge's direction that encouragement once given, cannot be withdrawn once the offence has commenced, is in accordance with principle. Once the jury found as a fact that the defendant had encouraged the commission of the violence that ensued it was an accurate direction that by the time the appellant had given his encouragement he had played his part and thereafter he could not escape liability by attempting to withdraw at that stage.

   We have no hesitation in reaching the conclusion that there is no basis upon which it can be said that the verdict of the jury was unsafe. Indeed it would be a very curious state of our law if a person who had encouraged or incited violence by initiating the attack, could stand aside when he was aware that those who were to continue the violence might form the necessary intention to commit (and did commit) an offence of grievous bodily harm and could thereafter escape all responsibility except for assault occasioning actual bodily from the initial blow. Commonsense and the Common Law go hand in hand."

The effect of this judgment appeared to limit withdrawal where encouragement has been offered to the period prior to the commencement of the offence. If the attack on the victim which D has initiated commences, it will be too late for him to withdraw and avoid liability.

   Unfortunately, in *O'Flaherty* [2004] EWCA Crim 526, the Court of Appeal in obiter comments (not having had the benefit of being referred to *Robinson*) expressed approval of the decision in *Mitchell* that "while communication of withdrawal is a necessary precondition for disassociation from pre-planned violence it is not necessary when violence is spontaneous". The damage which the obiter comments in *O'Flaherty* may have done may have been undone by recent equally obiter comments in *Mitchell and Ballantyne* [2009] EWCA Crim 2552 where the Court of Appeal referred with approval to *Robinson*. Thus, even in cases of spontaneous violence communication of withdrawal must be given unless in exceptional circumstances it is not practicable or reasonable to do so.

   In *O'Flaherty*, however, the Court of Appeal did not confine its obiter comments to this situation as they also expressed approval of the decisions in *Grundy* and *Whitefield*. Mantell LJ stating (at [60]) that where assistance has been given it is not necessary for reasonable steps to be taken to prevent the crime in order to withdraw, timely communication of withdrawal being enough. The situation, accordingly, remains confused and, it is contended, unduly generous to persons in positions such as *Grundy* and *Whitefield* who have offered assistance which remains of benefit to the principal even after they have communicated their decision to withdraw from the enterprise.

Questions

1. What ought to be the law's objectives in this area? To encourage repentance, or to encourage efforts to undo the harm done by the initial encouragement?

2. If the latter, is it likely that "unequivocal notice to the principal that if he goes on it will be without the aid or assistance of the accessory" will often be a significant undoing of the harm done by the initial encouragement?

3. If in *Whitefield*, the telling of G that the flat was unoccupied without any promise of assistance in the actual break-in would be enough to implicate W, why should the making and later withdrawal of the promise make any difference to his liability?

4. Whichever object is to be preferred, need notice to the principal be insisted on if steps are taken to frustrate the enterprise?

5. Ought the requirements for withdrawal to be different if the accessory has supplied the principal with the means for committing the crime? Might it have made a difference in *Becerra* if B had not supplied C with the knife?

Note

See D. Lanham, "Accomplices and Withdrawal" (1981) 97 L.Q.R. 575.

----

v. Secondary party not convictable as a principal

SAYCE V COUPE

[1953] 1 Q.B. 1

C was charged with aiding, abetting, counselling and procuring a person unknown to sell tobacco otherwise than as a licensed retailer of tobacco contrary to s.13 of the Tobacco Act 1842 as amended. It appeared that C had purchased the tobacco from a person who was not a licensed retailer. The magistrates dismissed the charge, and the prosecutor appealed.

LORD GODDARD CJ

[Counsel for the accused] has argued that because the statute does not make it an offence to buy, but only makes it an offence to sell, we ought to hold that the offence of aiding and abetting the sale ought not to be preferred or could not be preferred. It is obvious that it can be preferred. The statute does not make it an offence to buy, but obviously, on ordinary general principles of criminal law, if in such case a person knows the circumstances and knows, therefore, that an offence is being committed and takes part in, or facilitates the commission of the offence, he is guilty as a principal in the second degree, for it is impossible to say that a person who buys does not aid and abet the sale.

Appeal allowed

R. V TYRRELL

[1894] 1 Q.B. 710

Tyrrell, a girl aged between 13 and 16, was convicted of aiding and abetting one Ford to commit the misdemeanour of having unlawful carnal knowledge of her, which was an offence under Criminal Law Amendment Act 1885 s.5. (See now, Sexual Offences Act 2003 s.9.)

Counsel for the accused—Under [the Offences Against the Person Act 1861], s.58, a woman is not indictable for administering poison or other noxious thing to herself with intent to procure abortion, unless she is with child when she does so; but she is liable to conviction and punishment if, with the same intent, she administers poison, etc. to another woman, though the other be not with child . . . *R. v Whitchurch* (1890) 24 Q.B.D. 420 . . . therefore has no application here. It is impossible that the legislature, in passing the Criminal Law Amendment Act 1885, can have intended that the women and girls for whose protection it was passed should be liable to prosecution and punishment under it. Part I, in which s.5 comes, is headed 'Protection of Women and Girls'. A girl under 16 is treated as of so immature a mind as not to be capable of consenting. The Act assumes that she has no *mens rea*, and she cannot, therefore, be treated as capable of aiding and abetting. If a girl is liable to be convicted of aiding and abetting an offence under s.5 she is also liable to conviction for aiding and abetting the felony made punishable by s.4, and she would then be liable to be sentenced to penal servitude for life, because an accessory before the fact to a felony may be punished as a principal. The result would be to render the Act inoperative, because girls would not come forward to give evidence. The Criminal Law Amendment Act, 1885, s.5, created no new offence, and for 600 years it has never been suggested that such an offence as that charged against the defendant could be committed at common law.

LORD COLDERIDGE CJ

The Criminal Law Amendment Act, 1885, was passed for the purpose of protecting women and girls against themselves. At the time it was passed there was a discussion as to what point should be fixed as the age of consent. That discussion ended in a compromise, and the age of consent was fixed at 16. With the object of protecting women and girls against themselves the Act of Parliament has made illicit connection with a girl under that age unlawful; if a man wishes to have such illicit connection he must wait until the girl is 16, otherwise he breaks the law; but it is impossible to say that the Act, which is absolutely silent about aiding and abetting or soliciting or inciting, can have intended that the girls for whose protection it was passed should be punishable under it for the offences committed upon themselves. I am of opinion that this conviction ought to be quashed.

MATHEW J

I am of the same opinion. I do not see how it would be possible to obtain convictions under the statute if the contention for the Crown were adopted, because nearly every section which deals with offences in respect of women and girls would create an offence in the woman or girl. Such a result cannot have been intended by the legislature. There is no trace in the statute of any intention to treat the woman or girl as criminal.

Conviction quashed

Notes

1. The rationale of *Tyrrell* appears to be that the statute never meant to include underage girls, because it was passed for their protection. Other reasons apart from the protection principle could in appropriate cases be advanced for concluding that a statute was not intended to cover particular classes of people, e.g. that in penalising the unlicensed sale of tobacco, Parliament must have had both parties to the sale in mind, and the fact that it did not penalise the seller is an indication that it did not want him to be punished. However English law appears, on this question, to take no account of any reason other than the protection principle, see *Sayce v Coupe*, above, p.343.

2. In Law Com. No.305, *Participating in Crime* (TSO, 2007) the Law Commission proposed to preserve and refine the *Tyrrell* exemption recommending that D should not be held liable as a secondary party or as a principal offender by virtue of innocent agency if:

    (1)   the principal offence is one that exists for the protection of a particular category of person;

    (2)   D falls within that category; and

    (3)   D is the victim of the principal offence.

3. In *Gnango* [2011] UKSC 59, the Supreme Court made it clear that the victim rule only operates where an offence is created specifically to protect the victim; it does not operate generally where a person happens to be an actual or intended victim of the offence. In this case the fact that G was engaged in a gunfight with B and could have been murdered by him did not serve to shield G

from conviction for murder as an accessory when V, a passer-by, was accidentally shot by B who was liable to conviction as principal on the basis of the doctrine of transferred malice (see above, pp.311 and 139).

4. On the law as it is at present, apart from the rule of statutory exclusion involved in *R. v Tyrrell* and *R. v Whitehouse*, and the rule that a victim cannot be guilty of conspiracy, (see s.?(1) of the Criminal Law Act 1977, below, p.412) there is no *general* rule that a victim cannot be a party to an offence. For example if A allows B to inflict bodily harm on him without what the law regards as a good reason, he will be an accessory to that crime: see below. But where consent is a defence to the crime, the "Victim's" participation may mean that no crime has been committed.

----

vi. Proposals for Reform

In its Report, *Participating in Crime*, the Law Commission accepts that secondary liability for participation in an offence committed by a principal offender should be retained. It does, however, recommend a series of reforms designed to make the law more rational and fair. The Law Commission propose in cl.1 of their Draft Bill (see directly below) that D should be liable for aiding and abetting (which will be called under the new scheme "assisting and encouraging") the commission of an offence by P only if D does his act of assistance or encouragement with the intention that P will thereby commit the offence. Foresight/contemplation will not be enough. Separate provision is made in cl.2 of the Draft Bill (see directly below) for joint venture cases is also proposed which will be based on foresight on the part of D of what P might do when, for example, they embark on a joint criminal venture, such as burglary, in the course of which P kills V.

1 Assisting or encouraging an offence

(1) Where a person (P) has committed an offence, another person (D) is also guilty of the offence if—
  (a) D did an act with the intention that one or more of a number of other acts would be done by another person,
  (b) P's criminal act was one of those acts,
  (c) D's behaviour assisted or encouraged P to do his criminal act, and
  (d) subsection (2) or (3) is satisfied.
(2) This subsection is satisfied if D believed that a person doing the act would commit the offence.
(3) This subsection is satisfied if D's state of mind was such that had he done the act he would have committed the offence.

2 Participating in a joint criminal venture

(1) This section applies where two or more persons participate in a joint criminal venture.
(2) If one of them (P) commits an offence, another participant (D) is also guilty of the offence if P's criminal act falls within the scope of the venture.
(3) The existence or scope of a joint criminal venture may be inferred from the conduct of the participants (whether or not there is an express agreement).
(4) D does not escape liability under this section for an offence committed by P at a time when D is a participant in the venture merely because D is at that time—

(a) absent,
(b) against the venture's being carried out, or
(c) indifferent as to whether it is carried out.

The Law Commission explain the nature of cl.2 as follows:

"'JOINT CRIMINAL VENTURE'

A.17 The Bill does not define 'joint criminal venture'. However, the expression is employed to describe cases where D and P share a common intention to commit an offence. The obvious example of a shared common intention is where D and P are both party to an express agreement to commit an offence. In addition, clause 2(3) makes it clear that a joint criminal venture (in the sense of a shared common intention) may also be inferred from the conduct of D and P regardless of whether they are parties to an express agreement to commit an offence.

A.18 Accordingly, clause 2 of the Bill is wide enough to address three categories of joint venture:

(1) the type of venture which is preceded by a conspiracy to commit the offence ultimately committed by P;
(2) the less formal type of venture, where D and P tacitly agree (perhaps on the spur of the moment) that the offence ultimately committed by P should be committed; and
(3) the type of spontaneous venture where it would be difficult to infer a tacit agreement, but it would be possible to infer a shared common intention, such as where a number of youths spontaneously involve themselves in an attack on a person outside a public house."

Under the Law Commission's proposals, procuring will cease to be a basis of secondary liability instead proposing to cover such situations by its clauses 4 and 5 on innocent agency and causing the commission of a no-fault offence.

The Law Commission Report has received praise and criticism in equal measure: see W. Wilson, "A Rational Scheme of Liability for Participation in Crime" [2008] Crim. L.R. 3; G. R. Sullivan, "Participating in Crime" [2008] Crim. L.R. 19; R. D. Taylor, "Procuring, Causation, Innocent Agency and the Law Commission [2008] Crim. L.R. 32; R. Buxton, "Joint Enterprise" [2009] Crim. L.R. 233.

In the Ministry of Justice's Consultation Paper, *Murder, manslaughter and infanticide: proposals for reform of the law* (2008),CP 19/08, the Government sets out its proposals for reform of the law on complicity in homicide accepting much of the Law Commission's analysis and recommendations. The proposal was to create a new statutory offence of intentionally assisting or encouraging murder and a statutory offence of murder where P is guilty of manslaughter owing to a lack of mens rea and D assisted or encouraged intending P to kill or cause serious injury. The Law Commission's recommendation to retain a broad offence of murder in the context of a joint criminal venture was also adopted. Reform to the "fundamental difference" principle was also proposed seeking greater flexibility based on whether P's act was within the scope of the joint criminal venture: it would be where the act did not go far beyond that which was planned, agreed to or foreseen by the secondary party. In 2009, however, following responses to the consultation, the Government announced that it would not press ahead with reform to the law of complicity to murder. It accepted that any such reform should take place in the context of reform of the general law relating to complicity (see

Murder, manslaughter and infanticide: proposals for reform of the law: Summary of responses and Government position (2009), CP(R) 19/08).

2. VICARIOUS LIABILITY

R. V HUGGINS

(1730) 2 Strange 869

H, the Warden of the Fleet prison was charged with aiding and abetting B, a turnkey, in the murder of A, a prisoner who was so neglected by B that he died. The jury found a special verdict and the case was argued before all the judges.

It is a point not to be disputed but that in criminal cases the principal is not answerable for the act of the deputy, as he is in civil cases; they must each answer for their own acts and stand or fall by their own behaviour. All the authors that treat of criminal proceedings, proceed on the foundation of this distinction; that to affect the superior by the act of the deputy, there must be the command of the deputy, which is not found in this case. The duress in this case consisted in the first taking him against his consent, and putting him in that room, and the keeping him there so long without necessaries, which was the occasion of his death. Now none of these circumstances are found as against the prisoner. The jury does not say he directed his being put into the room; that he knew how long he had been there, that he was without the necessaries in the indictment, or was ever kept there after the time the prisoner saw him, which was fifteen days before his death. . .

Judgment: Not guilty

MOUSELL BROS V LONDON AND NORTH WESTERN RAILWAY

[1917] 2 K.B. 836 at 845

ATKIN J

I think that the authorities cited . . . make it plain that while prima facie a principal is not to be made criminally responsible for the acts of his servants, yet the legislature may prohibit an act or enforce a duty in such words as to make the prohibition or the duty absolute; in which case the principal is liable if the act is in fact done by his servants. To ascertain whether a particular Act of Parliament has that effect or not regard must be had to the object of the statute, the words used, the nature of the duty laid down, the person upon whom it is imposed, the person by whom it would in ordinary circumstances be performed, and the person upon whom the penalty is imposed.

Notes

1. Discovering the parliamentary intention involves first asking whether strict liability was intended (on this, see above, p.309) because on the whole if mens rea is required for a conviction, a guiltless master cannot be convicted (although *Mousell's* case is itself an exception, the offence being "giving a false account with intent to avoid tolls," which was held to import vicarious liability). If the statute contains such words as "knowingly", "maliciously", "fraudulently", the master is not usually fixed with the knowledge, malice or fraud of his servant. And if the offence consists of "permitting", "suffering" or "allowing" something to happen, a master does not do so merely because his servant permits, suffers or allows: see *James & Son v Smee* [1955] 1 Q.B. 78.

2. Even if the offence is one of strict liability, much depends on the key verb used in the statute to describe the conduct prohibited: some activities by a servant can be attributed to the master with more plausibility than others. "Using" is apt for vicarious liability, so if a servant uses a vehicle on his master's business, the master will often be held to be using it: see *James & Son v Smee* [1955] 1 Q.B. 78; *John Henshall (Quarries) Ltd v Harvey* [1965] 2 Q.B. 233. Compare "driving"—only the actual driver can be said to be doing this: cf. *Thornton v Mitchell*, above, p.313.

NATIONAL RIVERS AUTHORITY V ALFRED MCALPINE HOMES EAST LTD

[1994] 4 All E.R. 286

The respondent company were building houses on a residential development. The NRA inspected a stream close to the building site and discovered a number of dead and distressed fish. Cement had been washed into a stream from the building site. The company's site agent and site manager both accepted responsibility for the pollution. The NRA brought an information against the company alleging that it had caused polluting matter to enter controlled waters contrary to s.85 of the Water Resources Act 1991 which provides:

> "A person contravenes this section if he causes or knowingly permits any poisonous, noxious or polluting matter . . . to enter any controlled waters."

The justices held that there was no case to answer and dismissed the information holding that while s.85 appeared to create an offence of strict liability, the NRA had failed to show that the company itself was liable because neither the site agent nor site manager were of a sufficiently senior standing within the company to fall within the category of those whose acts were the acts of the company. The NRA appealed arguing that s.85 could be construed as imposing vicarious liability on the company.

SIMON BROWN LJ

[Counsel for the company argued, inter alia, that:]

(1) A company can only be criminally liable in one of two ways, either (a) by being held vicariously liable for the acts of its servants or agents, or (b) by being identified with individuals held to represent its controlling mind and will—the acts and state of mind of these individuals being deemed to be those also of the company itself.

(2) *Alphacell* [above, p.157] is properly to be regarded as a category (b) case.

(3) This case is distinguishable from *Alphacell*, there being nothing equivalent here to the storage system designed and operated by the controlling officers of the defendant company there.

(4) Given, as all accept, that neither the site agent nor the site manager can possibly be regarded as exercising the respondent company's con trolling mind and will, it can accordingly only be found criminally liable were this court (for the first time, it is suggested) to determine that s.85 of the 1991 Act should be construed so as to impose vicarious liability upon companies—liability, that is, for their servants or agents . . .

To my mind the difficulty with this whole elaborate argument is that it breaks down at least as early as stage (2). Assuming, without deciding, that the dichotomy suggested at stage (1) is both sound and absolute, I for my part see *Alphacell* as an illustration of vicarious liability rather than a case where the House of Lords concluded that those representing the directing mind and will of the company had themselves personally caused the polluting matter to escape. The failure in the pumps which was the immediate cause of the pollution was unexplained; but there was certainly nothing to link it to any senior officer in the company. True, none of their Lordships' speeches specifically referred to the company's servants or agents as such; nor did they expressly use the language of vicarious liability. But to my mind the whole tenor of the judgments is consistent only with that approach. How else distinguish *Moses v Midland Railway Co* (1915) 84 L.J.K.B. 2181 in the way they did? Why else, in discussing *Impress (Worcester) Ltd v Rees* [1971] 2 All E.R. 357, does Lord Wilberforce speak of 'some unauthorised person' having opened the valve 'for purposes unconnected with the appellant's business', and 'the act of a third person' having interrupted 'the chain of causation initiated by the person who owns or operates the installation or plant from which the flow took place'; and Lord Salmon refer to 'the active intervention of a stranger, the risk of which could not reasonably have been foreseen'? Why do the speeches stress the clear analogy between this statutory offence of causing pollution and the common law public nuisance cases which plainly recognise a master's liability for his servant's acts? Why, similarly, does Lord Salmon speak of the section as one 'which encourages riparian factory owners not only to take reasonable steps to prevent pollution but to do everything possible to ensure that they do not cause it'?

And only such an approach seems to me consistent too with later decisions of the Divisional Court directed to subsequent enactments of this same provision. Take Lloyd LJ's judgment in the Divisional Court in *Welsh Water Authority v Williams Motors (Cymdu) Ltd* (1988) Times, 5 December, with regard to s. 32(l)(a) of the Control of Pollution Act 1974. There, a delivery company, whilst filling the defendants' storage tank with diesel oil, spilled some oil, which eventually found its way into controlled waters. In upholding the defendants' acquittal, Lloyd LJ said this:

> '[The delivery company] were independent contractors . . . They were not in any sense under the control of the respondents in the way they carried out and fulfilled their functions under the contract . . . It was no different from that of an ordinary domestic householder who finds that his tank has been overfilled by the oil company . . . Giving the word 'cause' its ordinary common sense meaning, as Lord Wilberforce says we must, I can find no positive act in any chain of operations by the respondents here which could be said to have caused the pollution.'

The implication from these various dicta is surely unmistakable: an employer is liable for pollution resulting from its own operations carried out under its essential control, save only where some third party acts in such a way as to interrupt the chain of causation.

Is the present case then properly distinguishable from *Alphacell Ltd v Woodward* [1972] 2 All E.R. 475, [1972] A.C. 824 in point of fact? I believe not, at least not on the evidence as it stood before the justices at the close of the authority's case. I see no difference in principle between the design and maintenance of a storage tank for pollutants (*Alphacell*), and the carrying on of building operations involving the use of pollutants (here, cement to construct a water feature), each occurring on land adjacent to controlled waters. Either system, if ineffectively devised or operated, can result equally in the escape of polluting material into the adjacent stream.

It accordingly seems to me nothing to the point that those in the company's head office here may well have had no direct part in determining the precise system of construction which allowed this cement to wash into the Ditton Stream. It is sufficient that those immediately responsible on site (those who in the event acknowledged what had occurred) were employees of the company and acting apparently within the course and scope of that employment. Certainly it could not be said of them (in contradistinction to the independent contractors responsible for the pollution in the *Welsh Water Authority case*) that 'they were not in any sense under the control of the [company] in the way they carried out and fulfilled their functions under the contract'. In my judgment, therefore, unless and until the company were themselves to call evidence displacing the clear inference otherwise arising from the facts found—that the pollution resulted directly from the company's own operation in constructing the water feature—it seems to me that the justices could not properly find here no case to answer. On the contrary, there appears to me to have been the clearest possible case.

MORLAND J

. . . Despite the skill and cogency of Mrs Kennedy-McGregor's arguments and her attempt to distinguish *Alphacell Ltd v Woodward* [1972] 2 All E.R. 475, [1972] A.C. 824 on the basis of the inherent design fault in the pumping system (see Viscount Dilhorne's speech [1972] 2 All E.R. 475 at 479, [1972] A.C. 824 at 836) and that thus the causative act of pollution was by the controlling mind and will of the company, in my judgment, her arguments are fallacious if the relevant words of s. 85(1) of the 1991 Act are given a purposive interpretation.

The object of the relevant words of s. 85(1) and the crime created thereby is the keeping of streams free from pollution for the benefit of mankind generally and the world's flora and fauna. Most significantly deleterious acts of pollution will arise out of industrial, agricultural or commercial activities. The damage occasioned may take years to repair and often at a cost running into thousands or millions of pounds. The act or omission by which the polluting matter enters a stream may result from negligence or may not. It does not matter. In almost all cases the act or omission will be that of a person such as a workman, fitter or plant operative in a fairly low position in the hierarchy of the industrial, agricultural or commercial concern.

In my judgment, to make the offence an effective weapon in the defence of environmental protection, a company must by necessary implication be criminally liable for the acts or omissions of its servants or agents during activities being done for the company. I do not find that this offends our concept of a just and fair criminal legal system, having regard to the magnitude of environmental pollution, even though no due diligence defence was provided for.

In my judgment, the dicta in *Alphacell Ltd v Woodward* entirely support this interpretation, although the question for the House was whether 'knowingly' qualified 'causes' in the earlier 1951 Act . . .

It can be strongly argued that the respondents by their activities directly caused the flow of polluting matter into the stream. It is difficult to see in principle why it should matter whether those activities are essentially mechanical by their plant or essentially manual by their servants or agents. The forbidden result is the same . . .

Lord Salmon said ([1972] 2 All E.R. 475 at 491, [1972] A.C. 824 at 848–849):

> 'If this appeal succeeded and it were held to be the law that no conviction could be obtained under the [Rivers (Prevention of Pollution) Act 1951] unless the prosecution could discharge the often impossible onus of proving that the pollution was caused intentionally or negligently, a great deal of pollution would go unpunished and undeterred to the relief of many riparian factory owners. As a result, many rivers which are now filthy would become filthier still and many rivers which are now clean would lose their cleanliness. The legislature no doubt recognised that as a matter of public policy this would be most unfortunate. Hence s.2(l)(a) which encourages riparian factory owners not only to take reasonable steps to prevent pollution but to do everything possible to ensure that they do not cause it.'

Although Lord Salmon was dealing with an entirely different point, 'mens rea', in my judgment, if, to succeed in such prosecutions, the authorities had to prove that the company by its 'controlling mind and will' caused the pollution rather than criminal liability vicariously by some human intervention by their servants or agents in the company's activities, the effectiveness of the relevant part of s. 85(1) of the 1991 Act would be lost and the filthiness of rivers increased.

I see no reason why Parliament as a matter of policy should not have placed on principals, whether companies or others, the responsibility of environmental protection. They are best placed to ensure that streams are not polluted during their activities by their servants or agents. They can do this by training, discipline, supervision and the highest standard of maintenance of plant . . .

In my judgment if the magistrates had directed themselves correctly in law they must have found a case to answer.

I would allow the appeal and order that the case be reheard by a fresh bench of magistrates.

Appeal allowed

G. WILLIAMS, *CRIMINAL LAW: THE GENERAL PART* (STEVENS & SONS, 1961), S.96, P.281 (CITATIONS OMITTED)

. . . It seems we are now to witness the compiling of a new 'judicial dictionary' which will distinguish between those verbs in respect of which the servant's conduct can be regarded as the master's, and those in which it cannot. We must take it as settled by authority that a sale or use or (perhaps) presentation of a play by a servant, if within the general scope of his authority (though forbidden in the precise circumstances), is a sale or use or presentation by the master. On the other hand, it has been held that a representation made by the servant in the course of selling is not a representation by the master. A servant's 'ill-treating' of an animal cannot be attributed to his master. A receiving by a servant does not make his master guilty of 'receiving' stolen goods. So also a giving of credit by a servant is not a giving of credit by the master, and a demand for an illegal premium by a servant is not a demand by the master. Although the point has not been expressly decided, it seems that a master could not be convicted of an offence of 'driving' a vehicle through his servant, for in law it is only the actual driver who drives. Yet it has been held that a bus company 'carries' its passenger and is apparently responsible for an offence in relation to carriage committed by the conductor . . .

To make the law more difficult still, the same verb may possibly be construed to create vicarious responsibility in a 'public welfare offence' but not in one of the traditional crimes. Thus when a servant is in *de facto* possession of a thing on behalf of his master, the possession may be attributed to the master for the purpose of a public welfare offence, and yet not attributed to him for the purpose of the crime of receiving stolen goods. This way of reconciling the authorities may lead to the somewhat surprising conclusion that the presentation of an unlicensed stage play is a 'public welfare offence'. Again, the context of the verb may modify its meaning: for example, the word 'use' may be restricted by the purport of the section to persons of a particular class.

Notes

1. Where vicarious responsibility is held to exist, it is not, in the absence of some express provision in the statute, any defence to show that the act of the servant was in defiance of the master's instructions: *Coppen v Moore (No.2)* [1898] 2 Q.B. 306.

2. Except when the master is a company and the servant a director (as to which see below), whether or not the offence is one where vicarious liability is held to be intended, it seems that in no case will a master be primarily or vicariously liable for *aiding and abetting* an offence, without personal knowledge of the essential matters constituting the offence. On such a charge, the knowledge of the servant is not imputed to the master (see *Ferguson v Weaving*, above, p.323. *NCB v Gamble*, above, p.320 is not an authority to the contrary because there the master invited the court to identify him with the servant whose acts and knowledge constituted the aiding and abetting: see [1959] 1 Q.B. 11 at 26.

----

3. CORPORATIONS

Notes

1. According to the Interpretation Act 1978 s.5 Sch.1, in every Act, unless the contrary intention appears, "person" includes a body of persons corporate or unincorporate.

2. A corporation is *vicariously* liable to exactly the same extent as a natural person: see last section. However a corporation is also directly liable for acts performed by some natural persons who are identified with it. In such a case the acts and intentions of those who control the corporation are deemed to be those of the corporation itself. There are, however, two limitations to corporate liability identified in *R. v ICR Haulage Ltd* [1944] K.B. 551. First, there are certain offences which, from their very nature, cannot be committed by corporations, for example, bigamy, rape, incest and perjury. Secondly, a corporation will not be convicted of an offence where the only punishment which may be imposed is physical. Where a corporation is convicted of an offence it will be punished by the imposition of a fine and/or a compensation order.

TESCO SUPERMARKETS LTD V NATTRASS

[1972] A.C. 153 HL

TS Ltd was charged with an offence under the Trade Descriptions Act 1968. It sought to raise a defence under s.24(1) on the grounds that the commission of the offence was due to the act or default of another person, namely the manager of the store at which it was committed, and it exercised all due diligence to avoid the commission of the offence. The magistrates found that the company had set up a proper system, so it had exercised all due diligence; but the manager, who had failed to carry out his part under the system, was not "another person". The company, on conviction, appealed to the Divisional Court which held that the manager was "another person" but the company had not exercised all due diligence. The company appealed to the House of Lords.

LORD REID

My Lords, the appellants own a large number of supermarkets in which they sell a wide variety of goods. The goods are put out for sale on shelves or stands, each article being marked with the price at which it is offered for sale. The customer selects the articles he wants, takes them to the cashier, and pays the price. From time to time the appellants, apparently by way of advertisement, sell 'flash packs' at prices lower than the normal price. In September 1969 they were selling Radiant washing powder in this way. The normal price was 3s. 11d. but these packs were marked and sold at 2s. 11d. Posters were displayed in the shops drawing attention to this reduction in price.

These prices were displayed in the appellants' shop at Northwich on September 26. Mr Coane, an old age pensioner, saw this and went to buy a pack. He could only find packs marked 3s. 11d. He took one to the cashier who told him that there were none in stock for sale at 2s. 11d. He paid 3s. 11d. and complained to an inspector of weights and measures. This resulted in a prosecution under the Trade Descriptions Act 1968 and the appellants were fined £25 and costs.

Section 11(2) provides:

'If any person offering to supply any goods gives, by whatever means, any indication likely to be taken as an indication that the goods are being offered at a price less than that at which they are in fact being offered he shall, subject to the provisions of this Act, be guilty of an offence.'

It is not disputed that that section applies to this case. The appellants relied on s.24(1) which provides:

'In any proceedings for an offence under this Act it shall, subject to subsection (2) of this section, be a defence for the person charged to prove—(a) that the commission of the offence was due to a mistake or reliance on information supplied to him or to the act or default of another person, an accident or some other cause beyond his control; and (b) that he took all reasonable precautions and exercised all due diligence to avoid the commission of such an offence by himself or any person under his control.'

The relevant facts as found by the magistrates were that on the previous evening a shop assistant, Miss Rogers, whose duty it was to put out fresh stock found that there were no more of the specially marked packs in stock. There were a number of packs marked with the ordinary price so she put them out. She ought to have told the shop manager, Mr Clement, about this, but she failed to do so. Mr Clement was responsible for seeing that the proper packs were on sale, but he failed to see to this although he marked his daily return 'all special offers O.K.' The magistrates found that if he had known about this he would either have removed the poster advertising the reduced price or given instructions that only 2s. 11d. was to be charged for the packs marked 3s. 11d.

Section 24(2) requires notice to be given to the prosecutor if the accused is blaming another person and such notice was duly given naming Mr Clement.

In order to avoid conviction the appellants had to prove facts sufficient to satisfy both parts of s.24(1) of the Act of 1968. The magistrates held that they

'had exercised all due diligence in devising a proper system for the operation of the said store and by securing so far as was reasonably practicable that it was fully implemented and thus had fulfilled the requirements of s.24(l)(b).'

But they convicted the appellants because in their view the requirements of s.24(1)(a) had not been fulfilled: they held that Clement was not 'another person' within the meaning of that provision.

Where a limited company is the employer difficult questions do arise in a wide variety of circumstances in deciding which of its officers or servants is to be identified with the company so that his guilt is the guilt of the company.

I must start by considering the nature of the personality which by a fiction the law attributes to a corporation. A living person has a mind which can have knowledge or intention or be negligent and he has hands to carry out his intentions. A corporation has none of these: it must act through living persons, though not always one or the same person. Then the person who acts is not speaking or acting for the company. He is acting as the company and his mind which directs his acts is the mind of the company. There is no question of the company being vicariously liable. He is not acting as a servant, representative, agent or delegate. He is an embodiment of the company or, one could say, he hears and speaks through the persona of the company, within his appropriate sphere, and his mind is the mind of the company. If it is a guilty mind then that guilt is the guilt of the company. It must be a question of law whether, once the facts have been ascertained, a person in doing particular things is to be regarded as the company or merely as the company's servant or agent. In that case any liability of the company can only be a statutory or vicarious liability.

In *Lennard's Carrying Co. Ltd v Asiatic Petroleum Co. Ltd* [1915] A.C. 705 the question was whether damage had occurred without the 'actual fault or privity' of the owner of a ship. The owners were a company. The fault was that of the registered managing owner who managed the ship on behalf of the owners and it was held that the company could not dissociate itself from him so as to say that there was no actual fault or privity on the part of the company. Viscount Haldane L.C. said, at pp.713, 714:

'For if Mr Lennard was the directing mind of the company, then his action must, unless a corporation is not to be liable at all, have been an action which was the action of the company itself within the meaning of s.502 . . . It must be upon the true construction of that section in such a case as the present one that the fault or privity is the fault or privity of somebody who is not merely a servant or agent for whom the company is liable upon the footing respondent superior, but somebody for whom the company is liable because his action is the very action of the company itself.'

Reference is frequently made to the judgment of Denning L.J. in *HL Bolton (Engineering) Co. Ltd v T.J. Graham & Sons Ltd* [1957] 1 Q.B. 159. He said, at p.172:

'A company may in many ways be likened to a human body. It has a brain and nerve centre which controls what it does. It also has hands which hold the tools and act in accordance with directions from the centre. Some of the people in the company are mere servants and agents who are nothing more than hands to do the work and cannot be said to represent the mind or will. Others are directors and managers who represent the directing mind and will of the company, and control what it does. The state of mind of these managers is the state of mind of the company and is treated by the law as such.'

In that case the directors of the company only met once a year: they left the management of the business to others, and it was the intention of those managers which was imputed to the company. I think that was right. There have been attempts to apply Lord Denning's words to all servants of a company whose work is brain work, or who exercise some managerial discretion under the direction of superior officers of the company. I do not think that Lord Denning intended to refer to them. He only referred to those who 'represent the directing mind and will of the company, and control what it does'.

I think that is right for this reason. Normally the board of directors, the managing director and perhaps other superior officers of a company carry out the functions of management and speak and act as the company. Their subordinates do not. They carry out orders from above and it can make no difference that they are given some measure of discretion. But the board of directors may delegate some part of their functions of management giving to their delegate full discretion to act independently of instructions from them. I see no difficulty in holding that they have thereby put such a delegate in their place so that within the scope of the delegation he can act as the company. It may not always be easy to draw the line but there are cases in which the line must be drawn. *Lennard's* case was one of them.

In some cases the phrase alter ego has been used. I think it is misleading. When dealing with a company the word alter is I think misleading. The person who speaks and acts as the company is not alter. He is identified with the company. And when dealing with an individual no other individual can be his alter ego. The other individual can be a servant, agent, delegate or representative but I know of neither principle nor authority which warrants the confusion (in the literal or original sense) of two separate individuals . . .

In the next two cases a company was accused and it was held liable for the fault of a superior officer. In *D.P.P. v Kent and Sussex Contractors Ltd* [1944] K.B. 146 he was the transport manager. In *R. v I.C.R. Haulage Ltd* [1944] K.B. 551 it was held that a company can be guilty of common law conspiracy. The act of the managing director was held to be the act of the company. I think that a passage in the judgment is too widely stated, at p.559:

'Where in any particular case there is evidence to go to a jury that the criminal act of an agent, including his state of mind, intention, knowledge or belief is the act of the company, and, in cases where the presiding judge so rules, whether the jury are satisfied that it has been proved, must depend on the nature of the charge, the relative position of the officer or agent, and the other relevant facts and circumstances of the case.'

. . . I think that the true view is that the judge must direct the jury that if they find certain facts proved then as a matter of law they must find that the criminal act of the officer, servant or agent including his state of mind, intention, knowledge or belief is the act of the company. I have already dealt with the considerations to be applied in deciding when such a person can and when he cannot be identified with the company. I do not see how the nature of the charge can make any difference. If the guilty man was in law identifiable with the company then whether his offence was serious or venial his act was the act of the company but if he was not so identifiable then no act of his, serious or otherwise, as the act of the company itself.

In *John Henshall (Quarries) Ltd v Harvey* [1965] 2 Q.B. 233 a company was held not criminally responsible for the negligence of a servant in charge of a weighbridge. In *Magna Plant v Mitchell* (unreported) April 27, 1966, the fault was that of a depot engineer and again the company was held not criminally responsible. I think these decisions were right. In the *Magna Plant* case Lord Parker C.J. said:

'. . . knowledge of a servant cannot be imputed to the company unless he is a servant for whose actions the company are criminally responsible, and as the cases show, that only arises in the case of a company where one is considering the acts of responsible officers forming the brain, or in the case of an individual, a person to whom delegation in the true sense of the delegation of management has been passed.'

I agree with what he said with regard to a company. But delegation by an individual is another matter. It has been recognised in licensing cases but that is in my view anomalous. . .

What good purpose could be served by making an employer criminally responsible for the misdeeds of some of his servants but not for those of others? It is sometimes argued—it was argued in the present case—that making an employer criminally responsible, even when he has done all that he could to prevent an offence, affords some additional protection to the public because this will induce him to do more. But if he has done all he can how can he do more? I think that what lies behind this argument is a suspicion that magistrates too readily accept evidence that an employer has done all he can to prevent offences. But if magistrates were to accept as sufficient a paper scheme and perfunctory efforts to enforce it they would not be doing their duty—that would not be 'due diligence' on the part of the employer.

Then it is said that this would involve discrimination in favour of a large employer like the appellants against a small shopkeeper. But that is not so. Mr Clement was the 'opposite number' of the small shopkeeper and he was liable to prosecution in this case. The purpose of this Act must have been to penalise those at fault, not those who were in no way to blame.

The Divisional Court decided this case on a theory of delegation. In that they were following some earlier authorities. But they gave far too wide a meaning to delegation. I have said that a board of directors can delegate part of their functions of management so as to make their delegate an embodiment of the company within the sphere of the delegation. But here the board never delegated any part of their functions. They set up a chain of command through regional and district supervisors, but they remained in control. The shop managers had to obey their general directions and also take orders from their superiors. The acts or omissions of shop managers were not acts of the company itself.

In my judgment the appellants established the statutory defence. I would therefore allow this appeal.

[Lord Morris of Borth-y-Gest, Viscount Dilhorne, Lord Pearson and Lord Diplock delivered speeches agreeing that the appeal should be allowed.]

Appeal allowed

Notes

There are several problems arising from the principle of identification.

1. The larger and more diverse a company is, the more likely it is that it will be able to avoid liability. Tesco had hundreds of branches; a branch manager would have no control over the company's affairs. In a small company the controlling officers are much closer to the action which may involve the commission of offences.

2. The principle in *Tesco* does not fit well with many regulatory offences which do not require mens rea but for which defences (e.g. due diligence) exist to mitigate the harshness of strict liability. Such offences might more appropriately be dealt with under the vicarious liability approach. In another case involving Tesco, *Tesco Stores Ltd v Brent LBC* [1993] 2 All E.R. 718, T was convicted of supplying an "18" classified video to a person under that age contrary to s.11(1) of the Video Recordings Act 1984. Under s.11(1)(b) it was a defence for the accused to prove that he "neither knew nor had reasonable grounds to believe that the person concerned had not attained that age". T argued that the directing minds of the company (who would be directors in the London headquarters) had no means of knowing the age of the purchaser. The justices found that the cashier had reasonable grounds to believe that the purchaser was under 18 and convicted T. The Divisional Court dismissed T's appeal holding that it was impracticable to suppose that those who controlled a large company would have knowledge or information about the age of the purchaser, but that as the person who supplied the video was under T's control and she had such knowledge or information, the defence was not available to the company. This effectively meant that the offence was one of vicarious liability (see also *R. v British Steel Plc* [1995] I.C.R. 587).

3. The identification principle has also been diluted by the decision of the Privy Council in *Meridian Global Funds Management Asia Ltd v Securities Commission* [1995] 3 All E.R. 918. In this case, the Privy Council attributed knowledge to the company for the purposes of determining their liability for the offence of failing to make a disclosure under the New Zealand Securities Act 1988 where the facts required to be disclosed were known to the senior investment team. This team did not constitute the "directing mind" of the company. The Privy Council upheld the company's conviction on the basis of its interpretation of the statute, taking into account the statutory language, its contents and the underlying policy which would be defeated if knowledge on the part of those who constituted the "directing mind" of the company was required to be proved. This special rule of attribution would apply where a court considers that a statute was intended to apply to companies and application of the identification principle would defeat the purpose of the statute.

4. A company will only be liable if the person identified with it is, himself, individually liable in that he had the mens rea for the offence. Where there are several superior officers involved, each may not have the requisite degree of knowledge to constitute the mens rea of the offence. In the area of safety, for example, there may be many failures within a corporation at different levels which may coalesce to result in a major disaster resulting in loss of life. Different individuals may know, or do, or fail to do different things. But, if a company is a legal person, and the knowledge of its officials is its knowledge, should not that knowledge be aggregated and, in the aggregate, constitute the mens rea for a crime? This particular question has been considered in the context of manslaughter. For a time it was thought that manslaughter was an offence of which a corporation could not be convicted. This view was rejected in *P&O European Ferries Ltd* (1990) 93 Cr. App. R. 72. Following the decision of the House of Lords in *Seymour* [1983] 2 A.C. 493, manslaughter demanded proof of recklessness in the *Caldwell/Lawrence* sense. In this context the aggregation principle was rejected in *R. v HM Coroner for East Kent, Ex p. Spooner* (1989) 88 Cr. App. R. 10; and

P&O European Ferries Ltd as no controlling mind cold be shown to have mens rea. Since the decision of the House of Lords in *Adomako* [1995] 1 A.C. 171 (see below, p.510), however, manslaughter by gross negligence is not an offence requiring mens rea. This being so, it should have been possible to aggregate the negligence of individuals within a corporation to arrive at a finding of gross negligence on the part of the corporation. In *Kite and OLL Ltd* Unreported 8 December 1994 (Winchester Crown Court), the company was convicted of manslaughter but this followed on the conviction of its managing director, the company being a one-man concern. In *Attorney General's Reference (No.2 of 1999)* [2000] 1 Cr. App. R. 207, the issue of aggregation was directly addressed. A high speed train crashed into a freight train at Southall killing seven people and injuring many others. The company operating the high speed train was indicted for manslaughter but the trial judge ruled that a non-human defendant could only be convicted where guilt of a human being with whom it could be identified was also established. As no such individual was indicted the charges against the company were dismissed. Two questions were referred to the Court of Appeal by the Attorney General:

(a) Can a defendant be properly convicted of manslaughter by gross negligence in the absence of evidence as to that defendant's state of mind?

(b) Can a non-human defendant be convicted of the crime of manslaughter by gross negligence in the absence of evidence establishing the guilt of an identified human individual for the same crime?

The Court of Appeal answered the first question "Yes". Its reasoning in respect of, and answer to, the second question is set out below. Insofar as this reasoning relates to the issue of aggregation generally, it remains authoritative.

ATTORNEY GENERAL'S REFERENCE (NO.2 OF 1999)

[2000] 1 Cr. App. R. 207

THE VICE PRESIDENT, ROSE LJ

As to question 2, Mr Lissack accepted that policy considerations arise. Large companies should be as susceptible to prosecution for manslaughter as one-man companies. Where the ingredients of a common law offence are identical to those of a statutory offence there is no justification for drawing a distinction as to liability between the two and the public interest requires the more emphatic denunciation of a company inherent in a conviction for manslaughter. He submitted that the ingredients of the offence of gross negligence man slaughter are the same in relation to a body corporate as to a human being, namely grossly negligent breach of a duty to a deceased causative of his death. It is, he submitted, unnecessary and inappropriate to enquire whether there is an employee in the company who is guilty of the offence of man slaughter who can be properly be said to have been acting as the embodiment of the company. The criminal law of negligence follows the civil law of negligence as applied to corporations: the only difference is that, to be criminal, the negligence must be gross. Of the three theories of corporate criminal liability, namely vicarious liability, identification and personal liability, it is personal liability which should here apply. In the present case, it would have been open to the jury to convict if they were satisfied that the deaths occurred by reason of a gross breach by the defendant of its personal duty to have a safe system of train operation in place. The identification theory, attributing to the company the mind and will of senior directors and managers, was developed in order to avoid injustice: it would bring the law into disrepute if every act and state of mind of an individual employee was attributed to a company which was entirely blameless (see *per* Lord Reid in *Tesco Supermarkets Ltd v Nattrass* 1972 A.C. 153 at 169 and *per* Estey J. of the Supreme Court of Canada in *Canadian Dredge Co v The Queen*) 19 D.L.R. 314 at 342). Its origins lay in the speech of Viscount Haldane L.C.

in *Lennard's Carrying Co Ltd v Asiatic Petroleum Co Ltd* 1915 AC 705 at 713, and it was developed by the judg-ment of Denning L.J. in *Bolton Engineering v T J Graham & Sons* 1957 1 Q.B. 159 at 172 and [Lord Reid in] *Tesco Supermarkets Ltd v Nattrass . . ..*

Before turning to Mr Lissack's submission in relation to personal liability it is convenient first to refer to the speech of Lord Hoffmann in *Meridian Global Funds Management v Securities Commission* [1995] 2 A.C. 500 on which Mr Lissack relied as the lynch pin of this part of his argument. It was a case in which the chief investment officer and senior portfolio manager of an investment management company, with the company's authority but unknown to the board of directors and managing director, used funds managed by the company to acquire shares, but failed to comply with a statutory obligation to give notice of the acquisition to the Securities Commission. The trial judge held that the knowledge of the officer and manager should be attributed to the company and the Court of Appeal of New Zealand upheld the decision on the basis that the officer was the directing mind and will of the company. The Privy Council dismissed an appeal. In a passage at 506C Lord Hoffmann, giving the judgment of the Privy Council, said that the company's primary rules of attribution were generally found in its constitution or implied by company law. But, in an exceptional case, where the application of those principles would defeat the intended application of a particular provision to companies, it was necessary to devise a special rule of attribution. At 507B Lord Hoffmann said:

'For example, a rule may be stated in language primarily applicable to a natural person and require some act or state of mind on the part of that person "himself", as opposed to his servants or agents. This is generally true of the rules of the criminal law, which ordinarily impose liability only for the *actus reus* and *mens rea* of the defendant himself. How is such a rule to be applied to a company? One possibility is that the court may come to the conclusion that the rule was not intended to apply to companies at all; for example, a law which created an offence for which the only penalty was community service. Another possibility is that the court might interpret the law as meaning that it could apply to a company only on the basis of its primary rules of attribution i.e. if the act giving rise to liability was specifically authorised by a resolution of the board or an unanimous agreement of the shareholders. But there will be many cases in which neither of these solutions is satisfactory; in which the court considers that the law was intended to apply to companies and that, although it excludes ordinary vicari-ous liability, insistence on the primary rules of attribution would in practice defeat that intention. In such a case, the court must fashion a special rule of attribution for the particular substantive rule. This is always a matter of interpretation: given that it was intended to apply to a company, how was it intended to apply? Whose act (or knowledge, or state of mind) was *for this purpose* intended to count as the act etc of the company? One finds the answer to this question by applying the usual canons of interpretation, taking into account the language of the rule (if it is a statute) and its content and policy'.

Lord Hoffmann then referred to *Tesco Supermarkets Ltd v Nattrass* and *In re. Supply of Ready Mixed Concrete (No.2)* [1995] 1 AC 456, Viscount Hald-ane's speech in *Lennards Co* and Denning L.J's judgment in *Bolton v Graham*. Having at 511A referred to the concept of directing mind and will, he went on to say:

'It will often be the most appropriate description of the person designated by the relevant attribution rule, but it might be better to acknowledge that not every such rule has to be forced into the same formula. Once it is appreciated that the question is one of construction rather than metaphysics the answer in this case seems to their Lordships to be . . . the policy of s20 of the Securities Amendment Act 1988 is to compel, in fast-moving markets, the immediate disclosure of the identity of persons who become substantial security holders in public issuers . . . What rule should be implied as to the person whose knowledge for this purpose is to count as the knowledge of the company? Surely the person who, with the authority of the company, acquired the relevant interest. Otherwise the policy of the Act would be defeated . . . The company knows that it has become a sub-stantial security holder when that is known to the person who had authority to do the deal. It is then obliged to give notice'. Lord Hoffmann went onto comment that it was not necessary in that case to inquire whether the chief investment officer could be described as the 'directing mind and will' of the company. At 511H he said 'It is a question of construction in each case as to whether the particular rule requires that the knowledge that an act has been done, or the state of mind in which it was done, should be attributed to the company'.

Mr Lissack's submission that personal liability on the part of the company is capable of arising in the present case was based on a number of authorities in addition to *Meridian*. In *R v British Steel Plc* [1995] 1 W.L.R. 1356 the defendant was prosecuted, as was the present defendant, for a breach of ss.3.(1) and 33(1)(a) of the Health and Safety at Work Act 1974. A worker was killed because of the collapse of a steel platform during a re-positioning operation which a competent supervisor would have recognised was inherently dangerous. The defence was that the workmen had disobeyed instructions and, even if the supervisor was at fault, the company at the level of its directing mind had taken reasonable care. An appeal against conviction was dismissed by the Court of Appeal Criminal Division. The judgment was given by Steyn LJ who said this at 1362H

'Counsel for British Steel Plc concedes that it is not easy to fit the idea of corporate criminal liability only for acts of the "directing mind" of the company into the language of s.3(l). We would go further. If it be accepted that Parliament considered it necessary for the protection of public health and safety to impose, subject to the defence of reasonable practicability, absolute criminal ability, it would drive a juggernaut through the legislative scheme if corporate employers could avoid criminal liability where the potentially harmful event is committed by someone who is not the directing mind of the company, that would emasculate the legislation'.

. . . Mr Lissack also relied on *In re-supply of Ready Mixed Concrete (No.2)* where the House of Lords held companies liable for a breach of the restrictive trade practices legislation where their local managers had entered into price fixing and market sharing agreements in defiance of clear instructions from the board of directors and without their knowledge. Lord Templeman said, at 465B, that to permit a company to escape liability by forbidding its employees to do the acts in question would allow it

'to enjoy the benefit of restriction outlawed by Parliament and the benefit of arrangements prohibited by the courts, provided that the restrictions were accepted and implemented and the arrangements negotiated by one or more employees who had been forbidden to do so by some superior employee, identified in argument as a member of the higher management of the company, or by one or more of the directors of the company identified in argument as the guiding will of the company'.

In *R v Associated Octel* [1996] 1 W.L.R. 1543, in a prosecution under s.3 of the Health and Safety at Work Act 1974 the defendant's conviction was upheld by the House of Lords. Lord Hoffmann, in a speech with which the other members of the House agreed, said, at 1547B, that s.3 imposed a duty towards persons not in employment on the employer himself defined by the conduct of his undertaking. In *R v Gateway Foodmarkets* [1997] 2 Cr.App.R. 40 the Court of Appeal Criminal Division reached a similar conclusion in relation to s2(l) of the same Act in relation to employees.

Mr Lissack submitted that, in accordance with the speech of Lord Hoffmann in *Meridian*, the choice of the appropriate theory depends on the ingredients of the offence itself; and the requirements of both retribution and deterrence point to corporate liability where death is caused through the company's gross negligence. He relied on a passage in Steyn L.J's judgment in the *British Steel* case at 1364A where there is reference to the promotion of 'a culture of guarding against the risks to health and safety by virtue of hazardous industrial operations'.

Mr Lissack advanced two subsidiary submissions. First, if, contrary to his primary submission, a corporation cannot be convicted unless an employee embodying the company can be identified as guilty of manslaughter, the presence of such an employee can be inferred: he relied on a passage in the speech of Lord Hoffmann in *Meridian* at 51 OH which seems to us to afford no support whatever for this submission. We reject it. Secondly, he suggested that aggregation has a role to play i.e. where a series of venial management failures are aggregated and cumulatively amount to gross negligence, a company may be convicted. There is a tentatively expressed passage in Smith and Hogan 9th Edition at p.186, based on an analogy with civil negligence, which supports this suggestion. But there is no supporting and clear contrary judicial authority—see per Bingham L.J. in *R v HM Coroner Ex.p Spooner* 88 Cr.App.R. 10 at 16: 'A case against a personal defendant cannot be fortified by evidence against another defendant. The case against a corporation can only be made by evidence properly addressed to showing guilt on the part of the corporation as such'. The Law Commission 237 at para. 7.33 are against introducing the concept of aggregation. We reject the suggestion that aggregation has any proper role to play.

For the defendant, Mr Caplan submitted, in relation to question 2, that *Adomako* was not concerned with corporate liability. It is necessarily implicit in the Law Commission's recommendation, in L.C. 237, that Parliament should enact a new offence of corporate killing, that the doctrine of identification still continues to apply to gross negligence manslaughter since *Adomako*. *Tesco v Nattrass* is still authoritative (see *Seaboard Offshore v Secretary of State for Transport* [1994] 1 W.L.R. 541) and it is impossible to find a company guilty unless its alter ego is identified. None of the authorities since *Tesco v Nattrass* relied on by Mr Lissack supports the demise of the doctrine of identification: all are concerned with statutory construction of different substantive offences and the appropriate rule of attribution was decided having regard to the legislative intent, namely whether Parliament intended companies to be liable. There is a sound reason for a special rule of attribution in relation to statutory offences rather than common law offences, namely there is, subject to a defence of reasonable practicability, an absolute duty imposed by the statutes. The authorities on statutory offences do not bear on the common law principle in relation to manslaughter. Lord Hoffmann's speech in *Meridian* is a re-statement not an abandonment of existing principles: see, for example, Lord Diplock in *Tesco v Nattrass* at 200H: 'There may be criminal statutes which upon their true construction ascribe to a corporation criminal responsibility for the acts of servants and agents who would be excluded by the test that I have stated' (viz those exercising the powers of the company under its articles of association). The Law Commission's proposals were made after *Meridian* and the *British Steel* case. Identification is necessary in relation to the actus reus i.e. whose acts or omissions are to be attributed to the company and *Adomako's* objective test in relation to gross negligence in no way affects this. Furthermore, the civil negligence rule of liability for the acts of servants or agents has no place in the criminal law—which is why the identification principle was developed. That principle is still the rule of attribution in criminal law whether or not mens rea needs to be proved.

Finally Mr Caplan relied on the speech of Lord Lowry in *C. v DPP* [1996] 1 A.C. 1 and invited this court to reject the prosecution's argument for extending corporate liability for manslaughter. At page 28C Lord Lowry said, with regard to the propriety of judicial law making '(1) If the solution is doubtful, the judges should beware of imposing their own remedy. (2) Caution should prevail if Parliament has rejected opportunities of clearing up a known difficulty or has legislated, while leaving the difficulty untouched. (3) Disputed matters of social policy are less suitable areas for judicial intervention than purely legal problems. (4) Fundamental legal doctrines should not be lightly set aside. (5) Judges should not make a change unless they can achieve finality and certainty'. Each of these considerations, submitted Mr Caplan, is pertinent in the present case.

There is, as it seems to us, no sound basis for suggesting that, by their recent decisions, the courts have started a process of moving from identification to personal liability as a basis for corporate liability for manslaughter. In *Adomako* the House of Lords were, as it seems to us, seeking to escape from the unnecessarily complex accretions in relation to recklessness arising from *Lawrence* [1982] A.C. 510 and *Caldwell* [1982] A.C. 341. To do so, they simplified the ingredients of gross negligence manslaughter by re-stating them in line with *Bateman*. But corporate liability was not mentioned anywhere in the submissions of counsel or their Lordship's speeches. In any event, the identification principle is in our judgment just as relevant to the actus reus as to mens rea. In *Tesco v Nattrass* at 173D Lord Reid said 'The judge must direct the jury that if they find certain facts proved then, as a matter of law, they must find that the criminal act of the officer, servant or agent, including his state of mind, intention, knowledge or belief is the act of the Company.' In *R v HM Coroner Ex.p Spooner* Bingham L.J. at 16 said 'For a company to be criminally liable for manslaughter . . . it is required that the mens rea and the *actus reus* of manslaughter should be established . . . against those who were to be identified as the embodiment of the company itself.' In *R. v P & O European Ferries* 93 CAR. 72 Turner J., in his classic analysis of the relevant principles, said at 83 'Where a corporation through the controlling mind of one of its agents, does an act which fulfils the pre-requiste of the crime of manslaughter, it is properly indictable for the crime of manslaughter.' In our judgment, unless an identified individual's conduct, characterisable as gross criminal negligence, can be attributed to the company the company is not, in the present state of the common law, liable for manslaughter. Civil negligence rules e.g. as enunciated in *Wilsons & Clyde Coal Co v English* [1938] A.C. 57 are not apt to confer criminal liability on a company.

None of the authorities relied on by Mr Lissack as pointing to personal liability for manslaughter by a company supports that contention. In each, the decision was dependent on the purposive construction that the particular statute imposed, subject to a defence of reasonable practicability, liability on a company for conducting its undertaking in a manner exposing employees or the public to health and safety risk. In each case there was an identified employee whose conduct was held to be that of the company. In each case it was held that the concept of directing mind and will had no application when construing the statute. But it was not suggested or implied that the concept of identification is dead or moribund in relation to common law offences. Indeed, if that were so, it might have been expected that Lord Hoffmann, in *Associated Octel*, would have referred to the ill health of the doctrine in the light of his own speech, less than a year before, in *Meridian*. He made no such reference, nor was *Meridian* cited in *Associated Octel*. It therefore seems safe to conclude that Lord Hoffmann (and, similarly, the members of the Court of Appeal Criminal Division in *British Steel* and in *Gateway Food Market*) did not think that the common law principles as to the need for identification have changed. Indeed, Lord Hoffmann's speech in *Meridian*, in fashioning an additional special rule of attribution geared to the purpose of the statute, proceeded on the basis that the primary 'directing mind and will' rule still applies although it is not determinative in all cases. In other words, he was not departing from the identification theory but re-affirming its existence.

This approach is entirely consonant with the Law Commission's analysis of the present state of the law and the terms of their proposals for reform in their Report No 237 published in March 1996. In this report, both the House of Lords decision in *Adomako* and the Privy Council's decision in *Meridian* were discussed. In the light of their analysis, the Law Commission concluded (para. 6.27 and following and para. 7.5) that, in the present state of the law, a corporation's liability for manslaughter is based solely on the principle of identification and they drafted a Bill to confer liability based on management failure not involving the principle of identification (see clause 4 of the Draft Bill annexed to their Report). If Mr Lissack's submissions are correct there is no need for such a Bill and, as Scott Baker J put it, the Law Commission have missed the point. We agree with the judge that the Law Commission have not missed the point and Mr Lissack's submissions are not correct: the identification principle remains the only basis in common law for corporate liability for gross negligence manslaughter.

We should add that, if we entertained doubt on the matter, being mindful of the observations of Lord Lowry in *C. v D.P.P* at page 28C, we would not think it appropriate for this court to propel the law in the direction which Mr Lissack seeks. That, in our judgment, taking into account the policy considerations to which Mr Lissack referred, is a matter for Parliament, not the courts. For almost 4 years, the Law Commission's draft Bill has been to hand as a useful starting point for that purpose. It follows that, in our opinion, the answer to question 2 is 'No'.

Questions

1. Is Rose LJ correct when he states that Bingham LJ's view in *Spooner* is "clear, contrary judicial authority" to the proposition of aggregation in a case of gross negligence manslaughter when the authority governing Bingham LJ was *Seymour* and the prosecution would have been for reckless manslaughter?

2. Rose LJ states:

    "unless an identified individual's conduct, characterisable as gross criminal negligence, can be attributed to the company the company is not, in the present state of the common law, liable for manslaughter. Civil negligence rules . . . are not apt to confer criminal liability on a company."

    But in *Adomako* Lord Mackay stated that "the ordinary principles of the law of negligence apply to ascertain whether or not the defendant has been in breach of a duty of care towards the victim who has died." Next the jury had to consider causation and then whether the breach was gross enough to constitute a crime. If the operation system was not safe, is Rose LJ suggesting that this could not amount to civil negligence unless an actual individual was proved to be negligent? If not, why should there be a difference in applying the criminal law to companies as opposed to private individuals? Is there a danger that the more neglectful of safety individuals within a company are (i.e. they do nothing rather than simply doing something incompetently) the less likely the company is to be convicted of manslaughter if death ensues from its operations?

REFORM AND THE CORPORATE MANSLAUGHTER AND CORPORATE HOMICIDE ACT 2007

Notes

1. Under the previous law, based on the identification principle, a company could be convicted of manslaughter only where a "directing mind" of the organisation was also guilty of the offence, that is some senior individual who embodies the company in his actions and decisions. Where no such senior individual was liable, it was not possible to convict the company even though a series of errors by individuals within the company, when aggregated together, might be sufficient to establish gross breach of duty on the part of the company. In 1996 the Law Commission in its

Report *Legislating the Criminal Code: Involuntary Manslaughter* (TSO, 1996), Law Com. No.237, proposed a new offence of "corporate killing". Following this Report the Government published a Consultation Paper, *Reforming the Law on Involuntary Manslaughter: the Government's Proposals* (2000) which endorsed the proposal for a new offence. In March 2005 a *Draft Corporate Manslaughter Bill* (TSO, 2005), Cm.6497 was published setting out the Government's proposals for reform. The Draft Bill was subject to pre-legislative scrutiny by the Home Affairs and Work and Pensions Committees whose report was published in December 2005 (HC 540 I–III). In March 2006, the Government responded in *The Government Reply to the First Joint Report from the Home Affairs and Work and Pensions Committees Session 2005–06 HC 540* (TSO, 2006), Cm.6755.

2.   In July 2006, the *Corporate Manslaughter Bill* received its First Reading in the House of Commons. It did not complete its stages in the 2005–06 session and was re-introduced in November 2006. This became the Corporate Manslaughter and Corporate Homicide Act 2007 which largely came into force on 6 April 2008.

3.   The important aspects of the new Act are that it dispenses with the need to find a controlling or directing mind that is also personally guilty of manslaughter (the identification principle) and it also greatly reduces the scope for Crown immunity which previously existed. The offence applies to bodies corporate which covers companies and public bodies such as NHS trusts and local authorities. It also applies to Government departments and the police (but certain exclusions apply to public policy decisions, military activities, policing and law enforcement, emergencies, child protection, and probation functions, see ss.3–7).The offence also covers a partnership, a trade union or employers' association, which is an employer.

4.   The new offence is defined in s.1; s.2 defines the "relevant duty of care" and s.8 provides detailed guidance on the issues a jury should consider in arriving at the decision whether or not a death was caused by a gross breach of duty.

"1 The offence

(1)   An organisation to which this section applies is guilty of an offence if the way in which its activities are managed or organised—

(a)   causes a person's death, and

(b)   amounts to a gross breach of a relevant duty of care owed by the organisation to the deceased.

(2)   The organisations to which this section applies are—

(a)   a corporation;

(b)   a department or other body listed in Schedule 1;

(c)   a police force;

(d)   a partnership, or a trade union or employers' association, that is an employer.

(3)   An organisation is guilty of an offence under this section only if the way in which its activities are managed or organised by its senior management is a substantial element in the breach referred to in subsection (1).

(4)   For the purposes of this Act—

(a)   'relevant duty of care' has the meaning given by section 2, read with sections 3 to 7;

(b)   a breach of a duty of care by an organisation is a "gross" breach if the conduct alleged to amount to a breach of that duty falls far below what can reasonably be expected of the organisation in the circumstances;

(c) 'senior management', in relation to an organisation, means the persons who play significant roles in—
  (i) the making of decisions about how the whole or a substantial part of its activities are to be managed or organised, or
  (ii) the actual managing or organising of the whole or a substantial part of those activities.

2 Meaning of 'relevant duty of care'

(1) A 'relevant duty of care', in relation to an organisation, means any of the following duties owed by it under the law of negligence—
  (a) a duty owed to its employees or to other persons working for the organisation or performing services for it;
  (b) a duty owed as occupier of premises;
  (c) a duty owed in connection with—
    (i) the supply by the organisation of goods or services (whether for consideration or not),
    (ii) the carrying on by the organisation of any construction or maintenance operations,
    (iii) the carrying on by the organisation of any other activity on a commercial basis, or
    (iv) the use or keeping by the organisation of any plant, vehicle or other thing;
  (d) a duty owed to a person who, by reason of being a person within subsection (2), is someone for whose safety the organisation is responsible.
(2) A person is within this subsection if—
  (a) he is detained at a custodial institution or in a custody area at a court or police station;
  (b) he is detained at a removal centre or short-term holding facility;
  (c) he is being transported in a vehicle, or being held in any premises, in pursuance of prison escort arrangements or immigration escort arrangements;
  (d) he is living in secure accommodation in which he has been placed;
  (e) he is a detained patient.
(3) Subsection (1) is subject to sections 3 to 7.
(4) A reference in subsection (1) to a duty owed under the law of negligence includes a reference to a duty that would be owed under the law of negligence but for any statutory provision under which liability is imposed in place of liability under that law.
(5) For the purposes of this Act, whether a particular organisation owes a duty of care to a particular individual is a question of law.
  The judge must make any findings of fact necessary to decide that question.
(6) For the purposes of this Act there is to be disregarded—
  (a) any rule of the common law that has the effect of preventing a duty of care from being owed by one person to another by reason of the fact that they are jointly engaged in unlawful conduct;
  (b) any such rule that has the effect of preventing a duty of care from being owed to a person by reason of his acceptance of a risk of harm.
  . . .

8 Factors for jury

(1) This section applies where—

    (a) it is established that an organisation owed a relevant duty of care to a person, and

    (b) it falls to the jury to decide whether there was a gross breach of that duty.

(2) The jury must consider whether the evidence shows that the organisation failed to comply with any health and safety legislation that relates to the alleged breach, and if so—

    (a) how serious that failure was;

    (b) how much of a risk of death it posed.

(3) The jury may also—

    (a) consider the extent to which the evidence shows that there were attitudes, policies, systems or accepted practices within the organisation that were likely to have encouraged any such failure as is mentioned in subsection (2), or to have produced tolerance of it;

    (b) have regard to any health and safety guidance that relates to the alleged breach.

(4) This section does not prevent the jury from having regard to any other matters they consider relevant.

(5) In this section 'health and safety guidance' means any code, guidance, manual or similar publication that is concerned with health and safety matters and is made or issued (under a statutory provision or otherwise) by an authority responsible for the enforcement of any health and safety legislation."

Notes and Questions

1. The offence builds on key aspects of the offence of gross negligence manslaughter. The important development, however, is that liability for the new offence is dependent upon a finding of gross negligence in the way in which the activities of the organisation are run rather than being contingent upon the guilt of an individual "directing mind". The offence is committed where, in particular circumstances, an organisation owes a relevant duty of care and the way in which the activities of the organisation have been managed or organised amounts to a gross breach of that duty and causes a person's death. A substantial element of the gross breach must be the way in which the activities were managed or organised by the senior management. A breach is gross if it falls far below what could reasonably have been expected of the organisation in the circumstances (s.2(4)(b). Senior management comprises those who play a significant role in the management of the whole or a substantial part of the organisation's activities. This covers those in the direct chain of management at an operational level and those with strategic or regulatory compliance roles. This approach allows for collective rather than just individual failure to be assessed, unlike the current offence. Consider the facts in *Attorney General's Reference (No.2 of 1999)* above, p.356. Would a successful prosecution for corporate manslaughter now be a realistic possibility were similar circumstances to arise?

2. The duties are fault based as they must be duties "under the law of negligence". Thus the new offence does not impose new duties which are not already part of the civil law. Doubtless the duties which will most often lead to prosecutions under the new Act will be those of employers and occupiers. The focus is upon senior management failures where a corporation has inadequate practices or systems for managing a particular activity which results in a death. For a prosecution

to succeed, however, the way in which an organisation's activities are managed or organised by its senior management must be a substantial element in the breach of a relevant duty of care. Is there a danger that this requirement will become as difficult to prove as previously where fault had to be established on the part of a "directing mind" of the company?

3. NB: regarding "relevant duty of care" s.2(1)(d) relates to persons in custody whether as arrested suspects, prisoners (convicted or on remand), asylum/immigration detainees, and detained mental patients. This was a very contentious amendment to the Bill introduced in the Lords by the former Chief Inspector of Prisons, Lord Ramsbotham, because of concerns over deaths in custody. At one point it looked as if the whole Bill might fail owing to Government objections to this amendment. The compromise negotiated was that the commencement for this part of the Act would require approval of both Houses of Parliament under the affirmative resolution procedure. At the time of writing s.2(1)(d) has not commenced.

4. Whether a duty of care is owed in a particular situation is a matter of law for the judge to decide (s.2(5)). It is then for the jury to determine whether death was caused by a gross breach of duty. The common law rules preventing a duty of care being owed (a) by one person to another because they are both engaged in unlawful conduct; and (b) to a person by reason of his acceptance of a risk of harm, are to be disregarded (s.2(6)).

5. The task for a jury in any trial for the new offence will not be an easy one; nor will it be easy for the prosecution to jump through all the hoops which the Act sets up in order to reach the point where there could be a reasonable prospect of securing a conviction. It is unlikely that there will be many more prosecutions under the new Act than under the old law. Trials, if they take place, will undoubtedly be lengthy and complex. At the end, if convicted, the only penalty the court will be able to impose is that of a fine (as well as a possible order under s.9 to take specified steps to remedy the breach and under s.10 to publicise their conviction).

6. In the first case that was successfully prosecuted under the Act, a fine of £385,000 (representing 250 per cent of the annual turnover of the company) was imposed on a small company in full recognition that it would inevitably force the company into administration with its employees losing their jobs (see *Cotswold Geotechnical Holdings* [2011] 1 Cr. App. R.(S.) 153). In these circumstances not only was the employee who died because of a grossly unsafe system of work a victim, but all the employees of the company become victims to its negligence. Is this really what the legislature intended when enacting the 2007 Act?

7 INCHOATE OFFENCES

The criminal law is not broken simply by having evil thoughts; to plan in one's mind to commit an offence is not unlawful. Where, however, a person moves from planning to taking steps towards putting that plan into effect by committing a substantive offence, he may, in the process, commit one of the inchoate offences of encouraging or assisting an offence (previously incitement), conspiracy or attempt. If the criminal law could only bite once a substantive offence had been committed, it would be seriously deficient in protecting persons and property from harm. The inchoate offences provide for intervention at an earlier stage where a person moves from planning an offence to performing acts in furtherance of that intention whether that be by encouraging another to commit the offence, agreeing with another to commit the offence, or attempting to commit the offence.

ASHWORTH, *PRINCIPLES OF CRIMINAL LAW*, 3RD EDN (OXFORD: OXFORD UNIVERSITY PRESS, 1999), P.460

THE CONCEPT OF AN INCHOATE OFFENCE

The word 'inchoate', not much used in ordinary discourse, means 'just begun', 'undeveloped'. The common law has given birth to three general offences which are usually termed 'inchoate' or 'preliminary' crimes—attempt, conspiracy, and incitement. A principal feature of these crimes is that they are committed even though the substantive offence (i.e. the offence it was intended to bring about) is not completed and no harm results. An attempt fails, a conspiracy comes to nothing, words of incitement are ignored—in all these instances, there may be liability for the inchoate crime.

Note

Attempt is now defined and punished in the Criminal Attempts Act 1981, and conspiracy in Pt I of the Criminal Law Act 1977, as amended by the Criminal Attempts Act 1981. Incitement remains a common law offence.

1. ATTEMPTS

CRIMINAL ATTEMPTS ACT 1981 SS.1, 4(3), 6(1)

Section 1: (1) If, with intent to commit an offence to which this section applies, a person does an act which is more than merely preparatory to the commission of the offence, he is guilty of attempting to commit the offence.

(2) A person may be guilty of attempting to commit an offence to which this section applies even though the facts are such that the commission of the offence is impossible.

(3) In any case where—

(a) apart from this subsection a person's intention would not be regarded as having amounted to an intent to commit an offence; but

(b) if the facts of the case had been as he believed them to be, his intention would be so regarded,

then, for the purposes of subsection (1) above, he shall be regarded as having had an intent to commit that offence.

(4) This section applies to any offence which, if it were completed, would be triable in England and Wales as an indictable offence, other than—

(a) conspiracy (at common law or under s.1 of the Criminal Law Act 1977 or any other enactment);

(b) aiding, abetting, counselling, procuring or suborning the commission of an offence;

(c) offences under section 4(1) (assisting offenders) or 5 (1) (accepting or agreeing to accept consideration for not disclosing information about an arrestable offence) of the Criminal Law Act 1967.

Section 4: (3) Where, in proceedings against a person for an offence under s.1 above, there is evidence sufficient in law to support a finding that he did an act falling within subsection (1) of that section, the question whether or not his act fell within that subsection is a question of fact.

Section 6: (1) The offence of attempt at common law and any offence at common law of procuring materials for crime are hereby abolished for all purposes not relating to acts done before the commencement of this Act.

Note

1. Section 1 applies to indictable offences only. An attempt to commit a summary offence is only an offence if the statute creating the offence specifically makes it so. In deciding whether such an attempt has been committed, a court will work to the same definition as for an attempt to commit an indictable offence: see s.3(4), (5).

2. In the common law of attempt existing before August 1981, there was much uncertainty surrounding the definition of the actus reus, especially in cases where the crime attempted was, for one reason or another, impossible to commit. Some uncertainty also attached to the mens rea. The difficulties are outlined in the Law Commission's *Attempt, and Impossibility in Relation to Attempt, Conspiracy and Incitement* (TSO, 1980), Law Com. No.102. The Law Commission's proposals for dealing with those difficulties were reproduced, although not exactly, in the Act. The common law of attempt was abolished: s.6(1), above. However this did not at first prevent the courts from referring to many of the pre-Act authorities.

ASHWORTH, *PRINCIPLES OF CRIMINAL LAW*, 6TH EDN (OXFORD: OXFORD UNIVERSITY PRESS, 2009), PP.439–440

The rationale for criminalizing attempts can best be appreciated by drawing a theoretical distinction (which the law itself does not draw) between two kinds of attempt. First, there are incomplete attempts, which are cases in which the defendant has set out to commit an offence but has not yet done all the acts necessary to bring it about. [For] example, . . . X put[s] petrol-soaked paper through the door of V's house . . .: he has still to strike a match and light the paper. Contrast this with the second kind of attempt, which will be called a complete attempt. Here the defendant has done all that he intended, but the desired result has not followed—Y has driven [a] car at V, intending to injure V, but he failed; and Z has smuggled [a] package into the country, believing it to be cannabis when in fact it is a harmless and worthless substance.

It is easier to justify the criminalization of complete attempts than incomplete attempts, and the two sets of justifications have somewhat different emphases. The justification for punishing complete attempts is that the defendant has done all the acts intended, with the beliefs required for the offence, and is therefore no less blameworthy than a person who is successful in committing the substantive offence. The complete 'attempter' is thwarted by some unexpected turn of events which, to him, is a matter of pure chance—the intended victim jumped out of the way, or the substance was not what it appeared to be. These are applications of . . . 'subjective' principles . . ., the essence of which is that people's criminal liability should be assessed on what they were trying to do, intended to do, and believed they were doing rather than on the actual consequences of their conduct. Rejection of this approach would lead to criminal liability always being judged according to the actual outcome, which would allow luck to play too great a part in the criminal law. Of course luck and chance play a considerable role in human affairs . . .

However, there is no reason why a human system for judging and formally censuring the behaviour of others should be a slave to the vagaries of chance. The 'subjective principle' would also be accepted by the consequentialist as a justification for criminalizing complete attempts: the defendant was trying to break the law, and therefore constitutes a source of social danger no less (or little less) than that presented by 'successful' harm-doers.

What about incomplete attempts? The subjective principle does have some application here, inasmuch as the defendant has given some evidence of a determination to commit the substantive offence—though the evidence is likely to be less conclusive than in cases of complete attempts. There is one distinct factor present in incomplete attempts, which is the social importance of authorizing official intervention before harm is done. Since the prevention of harm has a central place in the justifications for criminal law, there is a strong case for stopping attempts before they result in the causing of harm . . .

Once this point has been reached, then the agents of law enforcement may intervene to stop attempts before they go further. The culpability of the incomplete attempter may be less than that of the complete attempter because there remains the possibility that there would have been voluntary repentance at some late stage: after all, it may take greater nerve to do the final act which triggers the actual harm than to do the preliminary acts. But so long as it is accepted that the incomplete attempter has evinced a settled intention to continue, and to commit the substantive offence by doing some further acts, there is sufficient ground for criminalization.

Note

In the Law Commission's view, punishable preparatory acts should be limited to those which a layman would describe as trying to commit an offence (Law Com. No.102, para.2.8). This philosophy, embodied in the use of the ordinary word "attempt" as the name for the offence, confines the ambit of the law more narrowly than some might think desirable from the point of view of public protection.

----

i. Mental Element

R. V MOHAN

[1976] Q.B. 1

M drove his car straight at a policeman, who managed to jump out of the way. M was convicted of attempting by wanton driving to cause bodily harm to the policeman. The jury were directed that it was sufficient for the prosecution to prove that he was reckless as to whether bodily harm would be caused by his driving. M appealed.

JAMES LJ

for the Court: Mr Bueno's argument for the Crown was that the judge was right in his direction that the Crown did not have to prove, in relation to count 2, any intention in the mind of the defendant. His argument was that where the attempt charged is an attempt to commit a crime which itself involves a specific state of mind, then to prove the attempt the Crown must prove that the accused had that specific state of mind, but where the attempt relates to a crime which does not involve a specific state of mind, the offence of attempt is proved by evidence that the accused committed an act or acts proximate to the commission of the complete offence and which unequivocally point to the completed offence being the result of the act or acts committed. Thus to prove a charge of attempting to cause grievous bodily harm with intent there must be proof that the accused intended to cause grievous bodily harm at the time of the act relied on as the attempt. But, because the offence of causing bodily harm by wanton or furious driving, prescribed by s.35 of the Offences against the Person Act 1861, does not require proof of any intention or other state of mind of the accused, proof of attempt to commit that crime does not involve proof of the accused's state of mind, but only that he drove wantonly and that the wanton driving was proximate to, and pointed unequivocally to, bodily harm being caused thereby.

The attraction of this argument is that it presents a situation in relation to attempts to commit a crime which is simple and logical, for it requires in proof of the attempt no greater burden in respect of mens rea than is required in proof of the completed offence. The argument in its extreme form is that an attempt to commit a crime of strict liability is itself a strict liability offence. It is argued that the contrary view involves the proposition that the offence of attempt includes mens rea when the offence which is attempted does not and in that respect the attempt takes on a graver aspect than, and requires an additional burden of proof beyond that which relates to, the completed offence.

Mr Glass, for the defendant, does not shrink from this anomalous situation. His argument was expressed in words which he cited from *Smith and Hogan, Criminal Law*, 3rd ed. (1973), p.191.

'Whenever the definition of the crime requires that some consequence be brought about by (the defendant's) conduct, it must be proved, on a charge of attempting to commit that crime, that (the defendant) intended that consequence; and this is so even if, on a charge of committing the complete crime, recklessness as to that consequence—or even some lesser degree of mens rea—would suffice.'

That, Mr Glass argued, is an accurate statement of the law.
In support of his argument he cited the words of Lord Goddard C.J. in *R. v Whybrow* (1951) 35 Cr.App.R. 141, 146:

'Therefore, if one person attacks another, inflicting a wound in such a way that an ordinary, reasonable person must know that at least grievous bodily harm will result, and death results, there is the malice aforethought sufficient to support the charge of murder. But, if the charge is one of attempted murder, the intent becomes the principal ingredient of the crime. It may be said that the law, which is not always logical, is somewhat illogical in saying that, if one attacks a person intending to do grievous bodily harm and death results, that is murder, but that if one attacks a person and only intended to do grievous bodily harm, and death does not result, it is not attempted murder, but wounding with intent to do grievous bodily harm. It is not really illogical because, in that particular case, the intent is the essence of the crime while, where the death of another is caused, the necessity is to prove malice aforethought, which is supplied in law by proving intent to do grievous bodily harm.'

[After citations from *R. v Hyam* [1975] A.C. 55.]
We do not find in the speeches of their Lordships in *R. v Hyam* anything which binds us to hold that mens rea in the offence to attempt is proved by establishing beyond reasonable doubt that the accused knew or correctly foresaw that the consequences of his act unless interrupted would 'as a high degree of probability', or would be 'likely' to, be the commission of the complete offence. Nor do we find authority in that case for the proposition that a reckless state of mind is sufficient to constitute the mens rea in the offence of attempt.

Prior to the enactment of section 8 of the Criminal Justice Act 1967, the standard test in English law of a man's state of mind in the commission of an act was the forseeable or natural consequence of the act. Therefore it could be said that when a person applied his mind to the consequences that did happen and foresaw that they would probably happen he intended them to happen, whether he wanted them to happen or not. So knowledge of the foreseeable consequence could be said to be a form of 'intent'. Section 8 reads:

'A court or jury, in determining whether a person has committed an offence, (a) shall not be bound in law to infer that he intended or foresaw a result of his actions by reason only of its being a natural and probable consequence of those actions; but (b) shall decide whether he did intend or foresee that result by reference to all the evidence, drawing such inferences from the evidence as appear proper in the circumstances.'

Thus, upon the question whether or not the accused had the necessary intent in relation to a charge of attempt, evidence tending to establish directly, or by inference, that the accused knew or foresaw that the likely consequence, and, even more so, the highly probable consequence, of his act—unless interrupted—would be the commission of the completed offence, is relevant material for the consideration of the jury. In our judgment, evidence of knowledge of likely consequences, or from which knowledge of likely consequences can be inferred, is evidence by which intent may be established but it is not, in relation to the offence of attempt, to be equated with intent. If the jury find such knowledge established they may and, using common sense, they probably will find intent proved, but it is not the case that they must do so.

An attempt to commit a crime is itself an offence. Often it is a grave offence. Often it is as morally culpable as the completed offence which is attempted but not in fact committed. Nevertheless it falls within the class of conduct which is preparatory to the commission of a crime and is one step removed from the offence which is attempted. The court must not strain to bring within the offence of attempt conduct which does not fall within the well-established bounds of the offence. On the contrary, the court must safeguard against extension of those bounds save by the authority of Parliament. The bounds are presently set requiring proof of specific intent, a decision to bring about, in so far as it lies within the accused's power, the commission of the offence which it is alleged the accused attempted to commit, no matter whether the accused desired that consequence of his act or not.

In the present case the final direction was bad in law.

Appeal allowed

Note

1. *Narrow meaning of Intention*: In rejecting foresight of probable consequences as "intention" in respect of Attempts, the Court distinguished *Hyam v DPP* [1975] A.C. 55, a murder case which laid down that such foresight generally is intention. But see now *R. v Woollin*, above, which differs from *Hyam v DPP* on this.

2. *Intention as to Context*: According to James LJ, attempt requires specific intent, "a decision to bring about, in so far as it lies in the accused's power, the commission of the offence which it is alleged the accused attempted to commit". The Law Commission, adopting this dictum, paraphrased it as "an intent to commit the crime attempted", and accordingly s.1 of the Criminal Attempts Act 1981 uses that expression. However, the phrase is ambiguous, because if an offence requires intention for the *result* of D's conduct but is satisfied by recklessness as to the context (i.e. circumstances) in which the conduct takes place, it can be questioned whether D "intends to commit the offence", if he is intentional as to the result but only reckless as to context. But see the next case.

R. V KHAN

[1990] 2 All E.R. 783

Seven men were charged with rape and attempted rape of V, a 16-year-old girl. It appeared that some of them had not succeeded in having intercourse with her. The trial judge directed the jury that they could convict of attempt if they found that a defendant tried but failed to have sexual intercourse with V knowing she did not consent, or being reckless whether or not she consented. (Recklessness was sufficient mens rea for rape but it had been thought that for attempted rape it would have to be proved that a defendant knew V did not consent, knowledge being equivalent to intention.) Three defendants were convicted of rape. The four appellants were convicted of attempted rape and appealed:

RUSSELL LJ for the Court

These appeals raise the short but important point of whether the offence of attempted rape is committed when the defendant is reckless as to the woman's consent to sexual intercourse. The appellants submit that no such offence is known to the law . . .

The impact of the words of s.1 of the 1981 Act and in particular the words 'with intent to commit an offence' has been the subject matter of much debate amongst distinguished academic writers. We were referred to and we have read and considered an article by Professor Glanville Williams entitled 'The Problem of Reckless Attempts' [1983] Crim.L.R. 365. The argument there advanced is that recklessness can exist within the concept of attempt and support is derived from *R. v Pigg* [1982] 2 All E.R. 591, [1982] 1 W.L.R. 762, albeit that authority was concerned with the law prior to the 1981 Act. The approach also receives approval from Smith and Hogan, *Criminal Law* (6th ed., 1988) pp.287–289.

Contrary views, however, have been expressed by Professor Griew and Mr Richard Buxton QC, who have both contended that the words 'with intent to commit an offence' involve an intent as to every element constituting the crime.

Finally, we have had regard to the observations of Mustill LJ giving the judgment of the Court of Appeal, Criminal Division in *R. v Millard and Vernon* [1987] Crim.L.R. 393. That was a case involving a charge of attempting to damage property . . .

Mustill L.J. said (and we read from the transcript):

'. . . We have come to the conclusion that there does exist a problem in this field [of attempts], and that it is by no means easy to solve, but also that it need not be solved for the purpose of deciding the present appeal. In our judgment two different situations must be distinguished. The first exists where the substantive offence consists simply of the act which constitutes the actus reus (which for present purposes we shall call the "result") coupled with some element of volition, which may or may not amount to a full intent. Here the only question is whether the "intent" to bring about the result called for by s.1(1) [of The Criminal Attempts Act 1981] is to be watered down to such a degree, if any, as to make it correspond with the mens rea of the substantive offence. The second situation is more complicated. It exists where the substantive offence does not consist of one result and one mens rea, but rather involves not only the underlying intention to produce the result, but another state of mind directed to some circumstance or act which the prosecution must also establish in addition to proving the result. The problem may be illustrated by reference to the offence of attempted rape. As regards the substantive offence the "result" takes the shape of sexual intercourse with a woman. But the offence is not established without proof of an additional circumstance (namely that the woman did not consent), and a state of mind relative to that circumstance (namely that the defendant knew she did not consent, or was reckless as to whether she consented). When one turns to the offence of attempted rape, one thing is obvious, that the result, namely the act of sexual intercourse, must be intended in the full sense. Also obvious is the fact that proof of something about the woman's consent, and something about the defendant's state of mind in relation to that consent. The problem is to decide precisely what that something is. Must the prosecution prove not only that the defendant intended the act, but also that he intended it to be non-consensual? Or should the jury be directed to consider two different states of mind, intent as to the act and recklessness as to the circumstances? Here the commentators differ: contrast Smith and Hogan *Criminal Law* (5th ed., 1983) p.255 ff. with a note on the Act by Professor Griew in *Current Law Statutes 1981*.'

We must now grapple with the very problem that Mustill L.J. identifies in the last paragraph of the passage cited.

In our judgment an acceptable analysis of the offence of rape is as follows: (1) the intention of the offender is to have sexual intercourse with a woman: (2) the offence is committed if, but only if, the circumstances are that (a) the woman does not consent *and* (b) the defendant knows that she is not consenting or is reckless as to whether she consents.

Precisely the same analysis can be made of the offence of attempted rape: (1) the intention of the offender is to have sexual intercourse with a woman: (2) the offence is committed if, but only if, the circumstances are that (a) the woman does not consent *and* (b) the defendant knows that she is not consenting or is reckless as to whether she consents.

The only difference between the two offences is that in rape sexual intercourse takes place whereas in attempted rape it does not, although there has to be some act which is more than preparatory to sexual intercourse. Considered in that way, the intent of the defendant is precisely the same in rape and in attempted rape and the mens rea is identical, namely an intention to have intercourse plus a knowledge of or recklessness as to the woman's absence of consent. No question of attempting to achieve a reckless state of mind arises; the attempt relates to the physical activity; the mental state of the defendant is the same. A man does not recklessly have sexual intercourse, nor does he recklessly attempt it. Recklessness in rape and attempted rape arises not in relation to the physical act of the accused but only in his state of mind when engaged in the activity of having or attempting to have sexual intercourse.

If this is the true analysis, as we believe it is, the attempt does not require any different intention on the part of the accused from that for the full offence of rape. We believe this to be a desirable result which in the instant case did not require the jury to be burdened with different directions as to the accused's state of mind, dependent on whether the individual achieved or failed to achieve sexual intercourse.

We recognise, of course, that our reasoning cannot apply to all offences and all attempts. Where, for example as in causing death by reckless driving or reckless arson, no state of mind other than recklessness is involved in the offence, there can be no attempt to commit it.

In our judgment, however, the words 'with intent to commit an offence' to be found in s.1 of the 1981 Act mean, when applied to rape, 'with intent to have sexual intercourse with a woman in circumstances where she does not consent and the defendant knows or could not care less about her absence of consent'. The only 'intent', giving that word its natural and ordinary meaning, of the rapist is to have sexual intercourse. He commits the offence because of the circumstances in which he manifests that intent, i.e. when the woman is not consenting and he either knows it or could not care less about the absence of consent.

Accordingly, we take the view that in relation to the four appellants the judge was right to give the directions that he did when inviting the jury to consider the charges of attempted rape.

Appeals against conviction dismissed

Notes

1. The definition of rape is now to be found in s.1(1) of the Sexual Offences Act 2003, below, p.576.

2. As often happens, this appeal arose from the decision of the Crown Prosecution Service to charge attempted rape broadly. Had the indictment alleged attempted rape based upon knowledge that the complainant did not consent, and the appellants had been convicted, they would have had no basis upon which to appeal and the Court of Appeal would not have been tempted to dilute the mens rea of attempt to uphold the convictions. In the context of a gang rape where three defendants had already been convicted it might be considered highly unlikely that any defendant could have successfully raised a doubt in the jury's mind that they did not know that the complainant, a sixteen-year-old virgin, was not consenting to intercourse. It was also open to the prosecution to seek to pursue convictions for rape on the part of any defendant on the basis that they were secondary parties present aiding and abetting those who did succeed in having intercourse with V. So many problems in the criminal law arise from prosecutors over-playing their hand and from appellate courts yielding to the temptation to stretch principle to patch up the prosecutor's error rather than quashing the convictions of undeserving appellants. But less damage would have been caused to the law of attempts had the Court of Appeal quashed these convictions and ordered a retrial.

3. In the *A-G's Reference (No.3 of 1992)* [1994] 1 W.L.R. 409, the Court of Appeal, while affirming *Khan*, went further in stretching the realm of liability for attempt by accepting that a person may be convicted of attempt where *Caldwell* recklessness suffices for the full offence. Although the House of Lords declared in *G* [2003] UKHL 50 that the decision in *Caldwell* was wrong, the issues as to the mens rea of attempt to which the case gives rise remain problematic. The respondents

were in a moving car from which a lighted petrol bomb was thrown at an occupied car beside a pavement on which persons were standing. The bomb passed over the car and hit a wall adjacent to the pavement. They were charged with attempted aggravated arson, contrary to s.1 of the Criminal Damage Act 1971. The trial judge ruled that there was no evidence on which the jury could find an intent to endanger life and that on a true construction of the Act, the danger to the life of another was a consequence of the intended damage and as such required a specific intent in relation to that element recklessness being insufficient. Accordingly she directed that the respondents be acquitted. The Attorney General referred the following point of law for the opinion of the Court of Appeal:

"Whether on a charge of attempted arson in the aggravated form contemplated by s.1(2) of the Criminal damage Act 1971, in addition to establishing a specific intent to cause damage by fire, it is sufficient to prove that the defendant was reckless as to whether life would thereby be endangered."

The Court of Appeal analysed the policy of attempt as requiring punishment of those who have done their best to supply the element missing from the completed offence. Schiemann J stated (at 416):

If, on a charge of attempting to commit the offence, the prosecution can show not only the state of mind required for the completed offence but also that the defendant intended to supply the missing physical element of the completed offence, that suffices for a conviction. That cannot be done merely by the prosecution showing him to be reckless. The defendant must intend to damage property, but there is no need for a graver mental state than is required for the full offence.

Question referred answered in affirmative

Questions

1. In s.1(1) of the Criminal Attempts Act 1981 a person is stated to be guilty of attempt where he does a more than merely preparatory act "with intent to commit an offence". Is this the same as an intent "to supply the missing physical element of the completed offence"?

2. Would it be fair to say that the decisions in *Khan* and *Attorney General's Reference (No.3 of 1992)* have the effect of treating s.1(1) of the Criminal Attempts Act 1981, as if it read:

    "If, with [the mens rea for] an offence to which this section applies, a person [intentionally] does an act which is more than merely preparatory to the commission of the offence, he is guilty of attempting to commit the offence"?

3. If the answer to 2. is in the affirmative, does this raise the possibility that D could be guilty of attempt where strict liability suffices in respect of a circumstance of the actus reus of the substantive offence?

Notes

1. In "The mens rea of criminal attempts" (2015) 131 L.Q.R. 169, Professor Simester contends that the "missing element" analysis of attempts adopted in *A-G's Reference (No.3 of 1992)* is incorrect. He states:

"It is . . . inconsistent with ordinary language. To 'attempt' to do something is to try to do it. If only for the sake of speaking clearly to the citizens it is meant to guide, a law criminalising the 'attempt' to do something should mean what it says, i.e. that trying to do the thing is a crime. Once this is accepted, we can see why the missing element analysis is wrong in principle. Consider the law of rape. Under s.1 of the Sexual Offences Act 2003, it suffices for the full offence that D lacks a reasonable belief about V's consent. Rightly so. But no-one could describe D, however blameworthy he may be, as trying to rape someone whom he genuinely yet negligently believes to be consenting to sex. Attempts cannot be made inadvertently. Ordinary language does not allow that conclusion. Neither does s.1(1) of the 1981 Act. And that means the missing element analysis must fail."

2.   In the case that follows the issue of the mental element for attempt arose once more. Once again, the prosecution overplayed their hand by charging the offence too broadly; on this occasion, however, the Court of Appeal resisted the temptation to stretch principle in order to uphold the convictions. The Court of Appeal adopted an approach which is inconsistent with that adopted in *Khan* and *A-G's Reference (No.3 of 1992)* but which does seek to be true to the wording of the statute.

R. V PACE AND ROGERS

[2014] EWCA Crim 186

P and R were scrap metal merchants who were targeted by undercover police officers in a sting operation. Two officers visited the scrap metal yard and offered to sell metal which they said was stolen. The metal was purchased and P and R were charged with attempting to conceal, disguise or convert criminal property. (As the metal was not stolen P and R could not be charged with the substantive offence of concealing, disguising or converting criminal property contrary to s.327(1) of the Proceeds of Crime Act 2002.) The prosecution presented their case on the basis that P and R suspected that the metal they purchased from the undercover officers was criminal property. The trial judge rejected the defendant's submission of no case to answer, holding that as suspicion was sufficient for the substantive offence it would be sufficient to constitute the mens rea for attempt and that proof of knowledge that the property was criminal property was not required. On appeal from their convictions P and R contended that s.1 of the Criminal Attempts Act 1981 required that a defendant intend to commit an offence and therefore precluded suspicion from being the applicable mens rea.

DAVIS LJ:

Introduction
1 The principal issue raised on these two appeals relates to the mental element required for criminal attempt. . .

The appeals
    36 . . .[O]ne might have thought that other charges—such as, for example, conspiracy to handle or attempted handling—would have been the more obvious charges to bring. Moreover, the legal problems arising in the present case would not have been likely to have arisen had the offences been so charged. So why have they been so charged? It is difficult not to think, by way of an answer, that the decision to charge in this way (viz attempting to convert criminal property) was primarily prompted by the consideration that under section 327 and section 340(3) [of the Proceeds of Crime Act 2002], the state of mind applicable to the substantive offence is 'knowledge or suspicion': whereas, of course, in cases of handling it would be, by section 22(1) of the Theft Act 1968,

'knowledge or belief'. Plainly suspicion involves a lesser state of awareness than belief. Thus it has been judicially observed that 'to suspect something to be so is by no means to believe it to be so: it is to believe only that it may be so'.

The parties' submissions

37 Mr Stein [counsel for Mr Pace], in his excellent and carefully considered submissions (submissions which Mr Reilly [counsel for Mr Rogers] adopted), emphasised that the prosecution case at trial of attempting to convert criminal property had been put, so far as the mental element was concerned, on the basis of suspicion. He went on to submit that, on its true construction, section 1 of the 1981 Act, which required that a defendant intend to commit an offence, precluded suspicion from being the applicable mens rea. He accepted that suspicion could be the applicable mens rea where the substantive offence of converting was charged and where there was in fact criminal property: that is, property constituting or representing benefit from criminal conduct. But there was, he submitted, no reason in principle at all why the mens rea for criminal attempt should be required to be the same mens rea as that applicable to the underlying substantive offence. On the contrary, he said, there are a number of cases which illustrate that the contrary can be the case.

38 He sought to support his argument by relying on what he said were the analogous principles relating to offences of criminal conspiracy under section 1 of the 1977 Act. He submitted that knowledge and intent was required under section 1 of the 1977 Act in situations such as these: and one would expect no different outcome for cases where attempt had been charged.

39 Mr Stein accepted that, under section 1(2)(3) of the 1981 Act, it is possible to attempt to commit an 'impossible' offence. But where that situation arises, section 1(3)(b) makes clear, he says, that the applicable mens rea is one of belief: it is not one of suspicion.

Legal authorities. . .

46 A convenient starting point is this. Where the substantive criminal offence specifically requires the consequence of an act, it is well established that an attempt to commit that offence ordinarily requires proof of intent as to that consequence. To take a familiar example, the required intent for murder is either an intent to kill or an intent to cause really serious injury. The required consequence of the act is, of course, death. Accordingly, for a charge of attempted murder to be made out the intent which must be proved is an intent to kill: see *R. v Whybrow* (1951) 35 Cr. App. R. 141. That remains the case since the 1981 Act. Of course, that is an offence different from the present case. But Mr Stein is at least entitled to make the point that that case is an illustration of the proposition that the mental element required to make a person guilty of an attempted offence may well be different from, and at a higher level than, that applicable to the substantive offence itself.

47 The same point can be made with regard to *R. v Mohan* [1976] QB 1 [see p.367 above] . . .

48 We next turn to the decision in *R. v Khan (Mohammed Iqbal)* [1990] 2 All E.R. 783. . .

52 . . .In *R. v Khan* . . .the defendants were charged with attempted rape solely because they had not succeeded in penetrating the victim, which is what they had intended to do. Had they succeeded in that act, as they had intended, the full offence of rape would have been made out. But that is not so in the present case. The two defendants here could never have been guilty of the substantive offence of converting criminal property: just because the property in question did not constitute or represent benefit from criminal conduct. Furthermore, the court in R v Khan had been careful to say, at p 819:

> 'We recognise, of course, that our reasoning cannot apply to all offences and all attempts. Where, for example, as in causing death by reckless driving or reckless arson, no state of mind other than recklessness is involved in the offence, there can be no attempt to commit it.'

53 We were also referred to . . . *Attorney General's Reference (No 3 of 1992)* [1994] 1 WLR 409 [by the Crown]. . .. But Mr Stein himself was in a position to seek to cull from the decision at least some support for his own argument. For Schiemann J then went on to say this, at p 417:

> 'If the facts are that, although the defendant has one of the appropriate states of mind required for the complete offence, but the physical element required for the commission of the complete offence is missing, the defendant is not to be convicted unless it can be shown that he intended to supply the physical elements.'

And at p 419 he likewise said: 'In order to succeed in a prosecution for attempt, it must be shown that the defendant intended to achieve that which was missing from the full offence.' Mr Stein's submission was that the 'physical element' in the present case which was missing was conversion of criminal property: and it was the 'supply' of that which had to be shown to be intended.

54 This, at all events, leads on to another line of authority which also bears on the present problem. That relates to cases where the attempt is to commit the 'impossible'—the position here. . . .

57 [In] *R. v Shivpuri* [1987] AC 1 [see below p.432] . . . Lord Bridge said, at p 22: 'What turns what would otherwise, from the point of view of the criminal law, be an innocent act into a crime is the intent of the actor to commit the offence.'

58 For an offence of converting criminal property the property must in fact be criminal property: section 340(3)(a) of the 2002 Act makes that clear. Indeed, in *R. v Montila* [2004] 1 WLR 3141 . . . Lord Hope of Craighead, giving the opinion of the committee, stated in terms in para 37: 'the fact that the property in question had its origin in drug trafficking or criminal conduct Is an essential part of the actus reus of the offence.' . .

Disposition

60 Against that citation of authority we turn to the disposal of these two appeals.

61 The starting point has to be section 1(1) of the 1981 Act: indeed, as Mr Stein pointed out, it is by reference to that statutory provision that the statement of offence in the indictment is framed. Mr Farrell [for the Crown] did at one stage of his argument, if we understood it aright, suggest that section 1(3) of the 1981 Act of itself provided a complete answer in favour of the Crown. But that cannot be right. That subsection only applies where 'the facts of the case' had been as the accused had believed them to be. But in the present proceedings the Crown's case had been put not on the basis of belief but on the basis of suspicion. Accordingly, one has to revert to section 1(1). That said, we would at least agree with Mr Farrell's acceptance that the 'intention' referred to in section 1(3) must be the same as the intention referred to in section 1(1): that is to say, an intent to commit the offence.

62 Turning, then, to section 1(1) we consider that, as a matter of ordinary language and in accordance with principle, an 'intent to commit an offence' connotes an intent to commit all the elements of the offence. We can see no sufficient basis, whether linguistic or purposive, for construing it otherwise.

63 Once that is appreciated, the fault line in the Crown's argument is revealed. A constituent element of the offence of converting criminal property is, as we have said, that the property in question is criminal property. That is an essential part of the offence. Accordingly, an intent to commit the offence involves, in the present case, an intent to convert criminal property: and that connotes an intent that the property should be criminal property. But the Crown's argument glosses over that. Its argument connotes that the property in question which it is intended to be converted is property known or suspected to constitute or represent benefit from criminal conduct. It ignores the requirement for the substantive offence that the property concerned must be criminal property (as defined). The Crown, in effect, thus seeks to make it a criminal offence to intend to convert property suspecting, if not knowing, that it is stolen. But that is not what section 327, read with section 340(3), provides. [Section 340(3) states:

'(3) Property is criminal property if—(a) it constitutes a person's benefit from criminal conduct or it represents such a benefit . . ., and (b) the alleged offender knows or suspects that it constitutes or represents such a benefit.]

64 Reflecting this difficulty in the Crown's argument, there is this further point to be made. For the purpose of the substantive offence, a person may in point of fact convert property intending and believing that it is criminal property: yet he will not be guilty of the substantive offence if, in fact, it is not criminal property: *R. v Montila* . . .. It is most odd that, on the Crown's case, such a person who cannot on such a scenario be liable for the substantive offence can nevertheless be made liable, where his state of mind is one of suspicion only, if what is charged is, instead, an attempt to commit the offence. We have the greatest difficulty in seeing that the provisions of section 1 of the 1981 Act were designed to bring about such a result.

Conspiracy

65 We further consider, and accepting Mr Stein's submission on this, that such a conclusion is supported by the approach of Parliament taken to conspiracy cases as enunciated in section 1 of the 1977 Act, as amended, and as interpreted by the courts. Mr Farrell objected that an offence of criminal conspiracy is different from an offence of criminal attempt. So it is. But that does not preclude us, and should not preclude us, from having regard to the provisions of the 1977 Act (as amended) in assessing the reach of the 1981 Act.

66 We say that for the following reasons. (i) First, the provisions of section 1 of the 1977 Act, as amended, were introduced by the 1981 Act itself. One would therefore be predisposed to anticipate a coherence of approach in the relevant provisions of the two statutes in this regard. (ii) Second, offences of criminal attempt and offences of criminal conspiracy are both inchoate offences. Both have in common that they are looking to what is planned for the future. That remains so even if counts formulated as conspiracy counts are commonly sought to be proved by proof of the commission of substantive offences. (iii) Third, it is not difficult to envisage scenarios—not least,

as it happens, in money laundering cases—where what may be charged as an attempt would be capable of being charged as conspiracy, and vice versa.

67 In this regard, we think that the approach taken by the courts to section 1 of the 1977 Act is most revealing.

68 Thus in *R. v Harmer* [2005] 2 Cr App R 23 the defendant was, with another, charged with conspiracy to convert or transfer money which, it was alleged, they had reasonable grounds to suspect represented another person's proceeds of criminal conduct or drug trafficking. It was accepted by the prosecution that it could not prove that the money in fact represented proceeds of crime or drug trafficking (and therefore the substantive charge could not be made out). Accordingly, it was not, and could not be, alleged that the defendant knew that the money represented another person's proceeds of crime or drug trafficking.

69 A constitution of the Court of Appeal held that the allegation of conspiracy required proof of an intention that the property represented the proceeds of crime, for the purposes of section 1(1)(a) of the 1977 Act. It was further held that the defendant could only be guilty of conspiracy in such a case if he intended or knew that the money would be the proceeds of crime when the agreement was made. See in particular para 26 of the judgment of the court given by May LJ, where he said this:

'he is not to be guilty of conspiracy unless he and at least one other party to the agreement intend or know that the money will be the proceeds of crime when the agreed conduct takes place . . . If the prosecution cannot prove that the money was the proceeds of crime they cannot prove that the defendant knew that it was. So section 1(2) of the 1977 Act applies and is not satisfied . . .'

It is further to be noted that having so decided May LJ went on to say, at para 28:

'It may possibly be that to charge attempt would save a prosecutor who could establish that the relevant proceeds were illicit, but could not establish whether they derived from drug trafficking or criminal conduct. It could not, we think, save a prosecutor who, as in the present case, cannot establish that they are the proceeds of any crime. The same difficulty arises with section 6(4) of the 1967 Act as with section 1(1) of the 1977 Act. The prosecution have to prove that what was attempted was an offence—see also section 1(1)(2) of the Criminal Attempts Act 1981, where there are equivalent problems.'

70 That approach of the Court of Appeal accords with the majority decision of the House of Lords in the subsequent case *R. v Saik* [2007] 1 AC 18 [see p.391 below]. In that case the charge of conspiracy under the 1977 Act was by reference to the underlying provisions of the Criminal Justice Act 1988. It was accepted that, for the purposes of the substantive offence under those statutory provisions, reasonable grounds for suspicion that the property represented the proceeds of crime sufficed. But it was held that in a case of conspiracy, and where the provisions of section 1(2) of the 1977 Act came into play, it had to be proved that the conspirator knew that the property was in fact the proceeds of crime or intended that it should be. Suspicion thus would not suffice.

71 In the course of his speech, Lord Nicholls of Birkenhead emphasised that the offence of conspiracy lay in making an agreement: and that section 1(1) of the 1977 Act implicitly required that the parties intended to carry out their agreement. The offence was complete at that stage. Under section 1(1) the mental element comprised the intention to pursue conduct which would necessarily involve the commission of the crime in question: and the conspirators must intend to do the prohibited act with the intent prescribed for the substantive offence.

72 Lord Nicholls then turned to section 1(2) of the 1977 Act. Having referred to its terms, and made observations on its ambit, he said, at para 8:

'It follows from this requirement of intention or knowledge that proof of the mental element needed for the commission of a substantive offence will not always suffice on a charge of conspiracy to commit that offence. In respect of a material fact or circumstance conspiracy has its own mental element. In conspiracy this mental element is set as high as "intend or know". This subsumes any lesser mental element, such as suspicion, required by the substantive offence in respect of a material fact or circumstances. In this respect the mental element of conspiracy is distinct from and supersedes the mental element in the substantive offence. When this is so, the lesser mental element in the substantive offence becomes otiose on a charge of conspiracy. It is an immaterial averment. To include it in the particulars of the offence of conspiracy is potentially confusing and should be avoided.'

He went on to observe that the mental element of an offence is not itself a 'fact or circumstance' for the purpose of section 1(2). He then said this, at para 20 of his speech:

'"intend" is descriptive of a state of mind which is looking to the future. This is to be contrasted with the language of substantive offences. Generally, references to "knowingly" or the like in substantive offences are references to a past state of affairs . . . Thus on a charge of conspiracy to handle stolen property where the property has not been identified when the agreement is made, the prosecution must prove that the property which was the subject of the conspiracy would be stolen property.'

He then referred to the principle established by *R. v Montila* . . . that the provenance of the property was a required ingredient of the substantive offence. Overall, by that process of reasoning, he concluded, in the case of conspiracy to commit a money laundering offence under the Criminal Justice Act 1988, that where the property had not been identified when the agreement was made the prosecution must prove that the conspirator intended that the property would be the proceeds of criminal conduct: para 23. Where on the other hand the property in question was identified, the prosecution must prove that the conspirator knew that the property was the proceeds of crime: para 25. Mr Stein's pithy consequential submission was accordingly that, just as you cannot 'intend to suspect' or 'agree to suspect' in conspiracy cases, so you cannot 'attempt to suspect' in attempt cases.

74 Overall, then, this authority establishes that a conspiracy to commit an offence under section 327 of the 2002 Act (no less than an offence under the Criminal Justice Act 1988) can require a higher level of mens rea than that applicable to the actual commission of the substantive offence itself. True it is that the language of section 1 of the 1977 Act is not precisely the same as section 1 of the 1981 Act. Even so, as we have indicated, section 1 of the 1977 Act can properly be read so as to take account of the 1981 Act, and vice versa. Accordingly it makes it, in our view, all the more principled to conclude that likewise in the case of attempt a higher level of mens rea may be required under section 1(1) than is applicable to the substantive offence itself: and thus that, in the present case, proof of suspicion will not suffice on a count of attempted money laundering.

75 Further, if that interpretation is to be said to involve a narrow reading of the section 1 of the 1981 Act—although we are not sure if it is to be styled a narrow reading—then, given that the context is one of a criminal statute imposing criminal liability, reading the statute narrowly is not a vice.

Conclusion
78 For the reasons we have given, we conclude that the appeals must be allowed. For the purposes of a count of attempted money laundering proof of a mental element of suspicion (only) does not suffice. We therefore think that the judge erred in his approach in his ruling on the submission of no case to answer; and, in consequence, also erred in the instruction he gave to the jury in his summing up. In so holding, we intend no disrespect to the judge, who plainly had sought to consider the matter carefully. But since we are not able to agree with his conclusions the consequence is that we cannot consider these convictions to be safe.

79 We do appreciate the anxieties of the Crown in this context of money laundering. Such cases are by no means always easy of proof: and the choice of Parliament to set suspicion as an available mental element for the purposes of the substantive offences indicates a policy that the reach of the provisions is designed to be wide. But, as we have sought to say, the policy behind the substantive offences of money laundering cannot be allowed to distort the meaning of section 1 of the 1981 Act relating to attempts.

80 As to the pending trials and the forthcoming cases of the present kind, involving substantively impossible attempts to convert scrap metal—impossible, because the scrap metal will not have been stolen—it will be for the Crown to decide how best hereafter to proceed. We apprehend that the effect of this judgment will preclude, in such cases, the efficacy of charges of attempting to convert criminal property if (as here) the Crown considers that it is not in a position to allege more than suspicion on the part of the accused that the property was stolen.

81 That may or may not create problems for prosecutors. However, we observe that there in any event may well be, in an appropriate case, other charges potentially available: such as, for example, attempted handling. Those necessarily will, we appreciate, require proof of a higher level of mens rea than suspicion: and of course defendants can be expected to be astute to emphasise that to a jury. Even so, as observed by Lord Hope in para 62 of his speech in *R. v Saik* . . ., the margin between knowledge and suspicion is perhaps not all that great, at all events where the person has reasonable grounds for his suspicion. Where a defendant can be shown deliberately to have turned a blind eye to the provenance of goods and deliberately to have failed to ask obvious questions, then that can be capable, depending on the circumstances, of providing evidence going to prove knowledge or belief. However, all this will be something for the prosecutors to consider in the pending cases by reference to the circumstances of those cases.

Appeals allowed.
Convictions quashed.

Note

1. In *Pace and Rogers* the Court of Appeal accepted that a charge of attempted handling could have been brought by the Crown. For an offence of handling to be proved a defendant must know or believe goods to be stolen. If such a mens rea could suffice for attempted handling this must be because knowledge or belief (in the sense of settled belief with no significant doubt) are, as regards circumstances, equivalent to intention as regards consequences. The Court arrived at this position by the simple stratagem of applying s.1(3) of the 1981 Act where intention is presumed if it would have been found to exist under the facts as D believed them to be.

2. In "In Defence of *Pace and Rogers*" (2015) 8 Arch. Rev. 6, Bruneau and Taylor describe the operation of s.1(3) as follows:

    "On facts similar to Pace, the provision appears to work as follows: if the goods in question were indeed stolen, and the defendant believed them so to be, then the defendant would know them to be stolen, since, for these purposes, the law defines 'knowledge' as 'true belief' [see Saik]. If they were not in fact stolen, but the defendant believed them so to be, then 'on the facts as he believed them to be,' he would know them to be stolen. Section 1(3) thus acts as a deeming provision, turning belief into knowledge. Such a provision is consistent with Lord Brown's reasoning in Saik . . . that, in certain contexts, the law ought to see no difference between belief and knowledge. . . As Simester notes [(2015) 131 LQR 169, 171] '[w]hen applied to circumstance elements within an actus reus, the mens rea requirement of "intention" has always been understood – translated – to mean its cognitive equivalent, i.e. knowledge or settled belief (with no significant doubt).' This conclusion is eminently sensible; when a defendant intentionally acts in order to bring about some consequence in circumstances he knows to be the case and such conduct, consequences and circumstances constitute a crime there can be little doubt that he or she intended to commit the crime."

3. If the approach adopted in *Pace and Rogers* is followed more generally a repetition of the facts as pleaded in *Khan* would result in an acquittal of the defendants. Bruneau and Taylor suggest that this should not cause alarm as:

    "Following Pace, a defendant should be liable for attempted rape only if he did the relevant act intending or believing that the victim did not consent. On the facts of Khan – a gang rape in which only three of the defendants succeeded in penetration – it is almost certain that this burden would have been met. In other cases, facts which might fail to produce a successful conviction for attempted rape could be charged as a sexual assault, or as secondary liability for rape or sexual assault. Facts which fail to satisfy any of these or similar charges are surely undeserving of criminal conviction."

----

ii. Actus Reus

Note

There may be many stages between the formulation of an intention to commit a crime and the actual commission of it. At some stage after formulation of intention and before actual commission, the point will be reached at which the actor can be said to have attempted it and so be guilty of the crime of attempt. The common law never succeeded in what is probably an impossible task, namely, formulating a general test which would, on being applied to any set of facts, infallibly indicate whether the crucial point had been reached. About the only two propositions which could be taken as settled were: (1) that not all things done on the way to commission of an intended crime were attempts at it (some early steps were regarded as too remote); and (2) that if the accused had done the last act which he knew was needed for full commission, it was an attempt by him.

Various tests were suggested in the cases or in writings, such as the first step on the road to full commission, the final step before full commission (sometimes qualified by the view that even a final step was not enough if the accused could still withdraw from full commission); the doing of an act which unequivocally showed what crime was intended; the taking of a substantial step towards commission of the offence. (For a review of these theories, see Law Commission, *Attempt, and Impossibility in Relation to Attempt, Conspiracy and Incitement* ½ 2.22–2.37.) None of them yielded satisfactory results across the whole band of possible cases. The only general test consistently quoted in the authorities was that formulated in *R. v Eagleton* (1855) 6 Cox C.C. 559 at 571 by Parke B:

> "The mere intention to commit a misdemeanour is not criminal. Some act is required and we do not think that all acts towards committing a misdemeanour are indictable. Acts remotely leading towards the commission of the offence are not to be considered as attempts to commit it, but acts immediately connected with it are . . ."

This was usually called the proximity test. Proximity was accepted by the House of Lords in *DPP v Stonehouse* (1978) A.C. 55 as the true test, although there was little agreement on how to define the concept more exactly, and of course without more exact definition the test is so vague as to be of but limited use. Lord Diplock, while approving *Eagleton*, added (at 68): "In other words the offender must have crossed the Rubicon and burnt his boats"—which suggests having reached a point of no return. This would set the hurdle extremely high and was not accepted in the reform proposals leading to the 1981 Act.

A. ASHWORTH, *PRINCIPLES OF CRIMINAL LAW*, 6TH EDN (OXFORD: OXFORD UNIVERSITY PRESS, 2009), PP.442–443

Since the effect of the law of attempts is to extend the criminal sanction further back than the definition of substantive offences, the question of the minimum conduct necessary to constitute an attempt has great importance. The issue concerns incomplete attempts: when has a person gone far enough to justify criminal liability? Two schools of thought may be outlined here. First, there is the fault-centred approach, arguing that the essence of an attempt is trying to commit a crime, and that all the law should require is proof of the intention plus any act designed to implement that intention. The reasoning is that any person who has gone so far as to translate a criminal intention into action has crossed the threshold of criminal liability, and deserves punishment . . .

Secondly, there is the act-centred approach, of which two types may be distinguished. One type bases itself on the argument that one cannot be sure that the deterrent effect of the criminal law has failed until D has done all the acts necessary, since one could regard the law as successful if D did stop before the last act out of fear of detection and punishment. This suggests that only acts close to the substantive crime should be criminalised. The other type of act-centred approach is adopted by those who see great dangers of oppressive official action— to the detriment of individual liberties—if the ambit of the law of attempts is not restricted tightly. If *any* overt act were to suffice as the conduct element in attempts, wrongful arrests might be more numerous; convictions would turn largely on evidence of D's intention, so the police might be tempted to exert pressure in order to obtain a confession; and miscarriages of justice might increase, especially when inferences from silence are permissible . . . To safeguard the liberty of citizens and to assure people that justice is being fairly administered, the law should require proof of an unambiguous act close to the commission of the crime before conviction of an attempt. Otherwise, we would be risking a world of thought crimes and thought police.

The choices for the conduct element in attempts might therefore be ranged along a continuum. The least requirement would be 'any overt act', but that would be objectionable as risking oppressive police practices and as leaving little opportunity for an attempter to withdraw voluntarily. The most demanding requirement would be the last act' or 'final stage', but that goes too far in the other direction, leaving little time for the police to intervene to prevent the occurrence of harm and allowing the defence to gain an acquittal by raising a doubt as to whether D had actually done the very last act.

LAW COMMISSION, *ATTEMPT, AND IMPOSSIBILITY IN RELATION TO ATTEMPT, CONSPIRACY AND INCITEMENT* (TSO, 1980), LAW COM. NO.102

(Footnotes as in the original)

3. Recommendations as to the actus reus

§ 2.45 In the light of the case law, the opinions of writers and the various approaches to the *actus reus* already described, we must make it clear that in our view there is no magic formula which can now be produced to define precisely what constitutes an attempt . . . Of the various approaches, only the 'proximity' test has produced results which may be thought broadly acceptable. Its disadvantages are that hitherto it has not worked well in some cases, and that it is imprecise. It shares the latter disadvantage with all other approaches but its flexibility does enable difficult cases to be reconsidered and their authority questioned. Further, where cases are so dependent on what are sometimes fine differences of degree, we think it is eminently appropriate for the question whether the conduct in a particular case amounts to an attempt to be left to the jury. This suggests that a relatively similar definition based on the 'proximity' approach is the best which can be hoped for.

(a) Content of the Actus Reus
§ 2.46 The first element in a statutory test of proximity should be the drawing of the distinction between acts of preparation and acts which are sufficiently proximate to the offence. This is a truism repeated in many cases including the most recent. It is nonetheless useful because it recognises that certain forms of conduct, in almost all circumstances which can be envisaged, do not amount to an attempt. Possession of implements for the purpose of committing an offence is an obvious example which, as we have noted, is at present dealt with by other means. Reconnoitring the place contemplated for the commission of the intended offence is another example of conduct which it is difficult to regard as more than an act of preparation: it would not ordinarily be called an attempt.

§ 2.47 The definition of sufficient proximity must be wide enough to cover two varieties of cases; first, those in which a person has taken all the steps towards the commission of a crime which he believes to be necessary as far as he is concerned for that crime to result, This is on the assumption that he is the actual perpetrator; if his part in the commission is a minor one, none of his acts may get beyond the state of preparation: see *D.P.P. v Stonehouse* [1978] A.C. 55, 86, *per* Lord Edmund-Davies. such as firing a gun at another and missing. Normally such cases cause no difficulty. Secondly, however, the definition must cover those instances where a person has to take some further step to complete the crime, assuming that there is evidence of the necessary mental element on his part to commit it; for example, when the defendant has raised the gun to take aim at another but has not yet squeezed the trigger. We have reached the conclusion that, in regard to these cases, it is undesirable to recommend anything more complex than a rationalisation of the present law.

§ 2.48 In choosing the words to be used to describe this rationalisation of the present law, we have had to bear in mind that they will be the subject of consideration and interpretation by the courts. For this reason we have rejected a number of terms which have already been used with some frequency in reported cases, such as acts which are 'proximate to', or 'closely connected' or 'immediately connected' with the offence attempted. The literal meaning of 'proximate' is 'nearest, next before or after (in place, order, time, connection of thought, causation, etc.).' Thus, were this term part of a statutory description of the *actus reus* of attempt, it would clearly be capable of being interpreted to exclude all but the 'final act'; this would not be in accordance with the policy outlined above. The term 'immediately connected' is in our view inappropriate for the same reason. And acts which may be 'closely connected' in the sense that they have advanced a considerable way towards the completed offence may nonetheless bear no qualitative resemblance to the acts required for completion. For example, it is arguable that what the appellant in *R. v Robinson* below, had done had no close qualitative connection with that remainder to be done—making a claim on the insurance company even though in terms of quantity his conduct as a whole had advanced far towards his objective. This potential ambiguity therefore precludes use of that term.

§ 2.49 The foregoing considerations lead us to recommend as the most appropriate form of words to define the *actus reus* of attempt any act which goes so far towards the commission of the offence attempted as to be more than an act of mere preparation.

(b) Issues of Law and Fact
§ 2.50 The final element of the offence of attempt which requires consideration in the present context is the respective functions of the judge and jury. We have noted that the 'substantial step' approach would require the judge to direct the jury as a matter of law as to whether particular conduct, if proved, constitutes a substantial step. (§ 2.30) . . . Since then, the majority in *D.P.P. v Stonehouse* has, as we have noted, approved the decision in *R. v Cook* in which Lord Parker C.J. stated that, 'while in every case it is for the judge to rule whether there is any evidence capable of constituting an attempt, it is always for the jury to say whether they accept it as amounting to an attempt. That involves . . . a careful direction in every case on the general principle with regard to what acts constitute attempts': (1963) 48 Cr.App.R. 98,102. We agree with this view: as factual situations may be infinitely varied and the issue of whether an accused's conduct has passed beyond mere preparation to commit an offence may depend upon all the surrounding circumstances, it is appropriate to leave the final issue to be decided as a question of fact, although 'the judge may sum up in such a way as to make it plain that he considers that the accused is guilty and should be convicted.' *D.P.P. v Stonehouse* [1978] A.C. 55, 80, *per* Lord Salmon. Furthermore, this division of function between judge and jury is in accord with the principle that it is for the judge to tell the jury what the law is, but for the jury to say whether on the facts the accused has been brought within the provisions of the offence with which he has been charged. If the conduct is such that in law it cannot constitute more than an act of preparation the judge must direct the jury to acquit . . .

Note

R. v Robinson and *Comer v Bloomfield* were criticised by the Law Commission as cases where the result, to the man in the street, appears to be contrary to common sense (§ 2.39). Nevertheless, in this scene-setting type of case, the dangers of inconsistent verdicts may have receded, in that the Court of Appeal seems to take the view, contrary to that of the Law Commission, that such cases are not capable of being attempts in law.

R. v Robinson [1915] 2 K.B. 342. D, a jeweller, insured his stock against theft and contrived to be found tied up, with his safe empty. He told the policeman who found him that he had been the victim of a burglary. Later he confessed that his object was to make a false claim on his insurers. He did not submit any claim. Held (CA) no attempt at obtaining money by false pretences, the acts done being too remote.

Comer v Bloomfield (1970) 55 Cr. App. R. 305. D drove his vehicle into the depths of a wood and reported it stolen. He enquired of insurers whether a claim would lie for its loss, but did not make a claim. Held (Div. Ct), no attempt to obtain money by deception. See also *R. v Ilyas* (1983) 78 Cr. App. R. 17, which was decided after the Criminal Attempts Act had been passed but on facts which required to be judged at common law. The facts were on all fours with those in *Comer v Bloomfield* and the result was the same.

R. v Widdowson (1985) 82 Cr. App. R. 314. D, wishing to obtain a van on hire-purchase terms but knowing that he would not be accepted as creditworthy, filled in a credit enquiries form in the name of another person. Held (CA) not an attempt to obtain services (the hire-purchase of a van) by deception:

> "Assuming that the finance company had responded favourably to proposal, it still remained for the appellant to seek a hire purchase deal from them. To our minds it is that step which would constitute an attempt to obtain the services relied upon in this case. If one asks whether this

appellant had carried out every step which it was necessary for him to perform to achieve the consequences alleged to have been attempted, the answer must be that he did not.

Equally, it seems to us, this appellant's acts cannot be described as immediately rather than merely remotely connected with the specific offence alleged to have been attempted. Thus whichever of the tests described in *Ilyas* is applied, what the appellant did cannot reasonably be described as more than merely preparatory."

R. V GULLEFER

[1990] 3 All E.R. 882

The appellant was convicted of attempted theft. During a race at a greyhound racing stadium the appellant had climbed on to the track in front of the dogs and in an attempt to distract them had waved his arms. His efforts were only marginally successful and the stewards decided it was unnecessary to declare "no race". Had they done so the bookmakers would have had to repay the amount of his stake to any punter, but would not have been liable to pay any winnings to those punters who would have been successful had the race been valid. The appellant told the police he had attempted to stop the race because the dog on which he had staked £18 was losing. He had hoped for a "no race" declaration and the recovery of his stake. The appellant's main ground of appeal was that the acts proved to have been carried out by the appellant were not "sufficiently proximate to the completed offence of theft to be capable of comprising an attempt to commit theft".

LORD LANE CJ FOR THE COURT

[His Lordship referred to ss.1(1) and 4(3) of the 1981 Act:]

Thus the judge's task is to decide whether there is evidence on which a jury could reasonably come to the conclusion that the defendant had gone beyond the realm of mere preparation and had embarked on the actual commission of the offence. If not, he must withdraw the case from the jury. If there is such evidence, it is then for the jury to decide whether the defendant did in fact go beyond mere preparation. That is the way in which the judge approached this case. He ruled that there was sufficient evidence. Counsel for the appellant submits that he was wrong in so ruling.

The first task of the court is to apply the words of the 1981 Act to the facts of the case. Was the appellant still in the stage of preparation to commit the substantive offence, or was there a basis of fact which would entitle the jury to say that he had embarked on the theft itself? Might it properly be said that when he jumped on to the track he was trying to steal £18 from the bookmaker?

Our view is that it could not properly be said that at that stage he was in the process of committing theft. What he was doing was jumping onto the track in an effort to distract the dogs, which in its turn, he hoped, would have the effect of forcing the stewards to declare 'no race', which would in its turn give him the opportunity to go back to the bookmaker and demand the £18 he had staked. In our view there was insufficient evidence for it to be said that he had, when he jumped onto the track, gone beyond mere preparation.

So far at least as the present case is concerned, we do not think that it is necessary to examine the authorities which preceded the 1981 Act, save to say that the sections we have already quoted in this judgment seem to be a blend of various decisions, some of which were not easy to reconcile with others.

However, in deference to the arguments of counsel, we venture to make the following observations. Since the passing of the 1981 Act, a division of this court in *R. v Ilyas* (1983) 78 Cr.App.R. 17 has helpfully collated the authorities. As appears from the judgment in that case, there seem to have been two lines of authority. The first was exemplified by the decision in *R. v Eagleton* (1855) Dears CC 515. . .

The other line of authority is based on a passage in *Stephen's Digest of the Criminal Law* (5th edn, 1894) art 50:

'An attempt to commit a crime is an act done with intent to commit that crime, and forming part of a series of acts which would constitute its actual commission if it were not interrupted.'

As Lord Edmund-Davies points out in *D.P.P. v Stonehouse* at 85–86, that definition has been repeatedly cited with judicial approval . . . [but it] falls short of defining the exact point of time at which the series of acts can be said to begin.

It seems to us that the words of the 1981 Act seek to steer a midway course. They do not provide, as they might have done, that the *R. v Eagleton* test is to be followed, or that, as Lord Diplock suggested, the defendant must have reached a point from which it was impossible for him to retreat before the actus reus of an attempt is proved. On the other hand the words give perhaps as clear a guidance as is possible in the circumstances on the point of time at which *Stephen's* 'series of acts' begins. It begins when the merely preparatory acts come to an end and the defendant embarks on the crime proper. When that is will depend of course on the facts in any particular case . . .

Appeal allowed: Conviction quashed

R. V JONES

[1990] 3 All E.R. 886

J was convicted of attempted murder of his former girlfriend's new boyfriend, F. J bought a shotgun, shortened the barrel, disguised himself, jumped into the rear seat of F's car, pointed the gun at F and said "You are not going to like this". F managed to grab the gun and escape with it from the car. It was not established whether J's finger was on the trigger when he pointed the gun at F. J appealed on the ground that the correct test of an attempt was whether the defendant had committed the last act prior to the full offence being committed.

TAYLOR LJ

At the end of the prosecution case, after the above facts had been given in evidence, a submission was made to the judge that the charge of attempted murder should be withdrawn from the jury. It was argued that since the appellant would have had to perform at least three more acts before the full offence could have been completed, i.e. remove the safety catch, put his finger on the trigger and pull it, the evidence was insufficient to support the charge. . . After hearing full argument, the judge ruled against the submission and allowed the case to proceed on count 1. Thereafter, the appellant gave evidence. In the result, the jury convicted him unanimously of attempted murder. It follows that they found that he intended to kill the victim.

The sole ground of appeal is that the judge erred in law in his construction of s.1(1) and ought to have withdrawn the case

Counsel for the appellant puts forward three broad propositions. First, he says that for about a century, two different tests as to the actus reus of attempt have been inconsistently applied by the courts . . ..

The second proposition of counsel for the appellant is that s 1(1) of the 1981 Act has not resolved the question which is the appropriate test. Third, he submits that the test deriving from *R. v Eagleton* should be adopted.

This amounts to an invitation to construe the statutory words by reference to previous conflicting case law. We believe this to be misconceived. The 1981 Act is a codifying statute. It amends and sets out completely the law relating to attempts and conspiracies. In those circumstances the correct approach is to look first at the natural meaning of the statutory words, not to turn back to earlier case law and seek to fit some previous test to the words of the section . . .

This approach was adopted by Lord Lane C.J. presiding over this court in *R. v Gullefer* . . .

[After quoting the last paragraph reproduced above at p.383, Lord Taylor L.J. continued.] We respectfully adopt those words. We do not accept counsel's contention that s.1(1) of the 1981 Act in effect embodies the 'last act' test derived from *R. v Eagleton*. Had Parliament intended to adopt that test, a quite different form of words could and would have been used.

It is of interest to note that the 1981 Act followed a report from the Law Commission on *Attempt, and Impossibility in Relation to Attempt, Conspiracy and Incitement* (Law. Com. no. 102). [His Lordship quoted paras 2.47, 2.48, above p.380].

Clearly, the draftsman of s.1(1) must be taken to have been aware of the two lines of earlier authority and of the Law Commission's report. The words 'an act which is more than merely preparatory to the commission of the offence' would be inapt if they were intended to mean 'the last act which lay in his power towards the commission of the offence.'

Looking at the plain natural meaning of s.1(1) in the way indicated by Lord Lane C.J., the question for the judge in the present case was whether there was evidence from which a reasonable jury, properly directed, could conclude that the appellant had done acts which were more than merely preparatory. Clearly his actions in obtaining the gun, in shortening it, in loading it, in putting on his disguise and in going to the school could only be regarded as preparatory acts. But, in our judgment, once he had got into the car, taken out the loaded gun and pointed it at the victim with the intention of killing him, there was sufficient evidence for the consideration of the jury on the charge of attempted murder. It was a matter for them to decide whether they were sure that those acts were more than merely preparatory. In our judgment, therefore, the judge was right to allow the case to go to the jury, and the appeal against conviction must be dismissed.

Appeal against conviction dismissed

K.J.M. SMITH, "PROXIMITY IN ATTEMPT: LORD LANE'S MIDWAY COURSE" [1991] CRIM. L.R. 576, 577

. . . Lord Lane CJ. saw pre-Act case law as amply illustrating the 'difficulties which abound in this branch of the criminal law,' but that the 'present law is . . . now enshrined in the Criminal Attempts Act . . .' Are we then to take it that references to pre-Act decisions should never cross the lips of counsel in future attempt cases? Well not quite, for a few paragraphs later Lord Lane qualifies his earlier comment by noting: 'So far as the *present* case is concerned, we do not think it is necessary to examine the authorities which preceded the Act of 1981'; the implication being that in some (unspecified) situations admission of common law authorities would be permissible for some (unspecified) purposes. There is little doubt that the subsequent Court of Appeal judgment in *Jones* construed *Gullefer's* relegation of pre-Act cases in this modified sense: 'the correct approach is to look *first* at the natural meaning of the statutory words.' . . .

It, therefore, seems that pre-Act authorities may still be enlisted in *some* circumstances to assist a court in settling what acts may be 'more than merely preparatory.' However, no direct clues are offered by the Court of Appeal in *Gullefer* or *Jones* as to when such earlier case law may be prayed in aid, and to what effect. Yet, if anything is of 'doubtful import', surely the unforthcoming formula set out in the 1981 Act takes a lot of beating: doubt on the proximity question lurks in relation to almost any activity falling short of the unsuccessful defendant's 'last act'.

R. v Campbell [1991] Crim. L.R. 268 (C.A.): C appealed against a conviction of attempted robbery. Police had information leading them to believe that an attempt might be made to rob a sub-post office, and watched the premises. On the day in question, C was seen lurking in the vicinity. He rode a motor cycle along the road and walked around. He wore a crash helmet and gloves. He was seen to put on sunglasses and then put his right hand into a pocket which seemed to contain something heavy. He stopped about 30 yards from the post office and took off his sunglasses. He looked around before turning away. Half an hour later he walked back towards the post office. He was arrested in front of the post office. He was searched and an imitation gun, sunglasses and a threatening note were found on him. He admitted that he had been reconnoitring the post office and had intended using the note to frighten the person behind the counter. The trial judge rejected a submission of no case to answer. *Held*, quashing his conviction, the judge should not have made any reference to the previous law; moreover, since several acts remained to be done by C and he had not even gained the place where he would be in a position to carry out the offence, the judge should have withdrawn the case from the jury.

R. v Geddes, The Times, July 16, 1996 (C.A.): D. entered a school and, on being found in the boys' toilet by a teacher, he ran away, leaving behind a rucksack containing a knife, lengths of rope and tape. He appealed against his conviction for attempted false imprisonment arguing that the evidence was insufficient in law to support a finding that he had done an act which was more than merely preparatory to the commission of an offence. *Held*: An accurate paraphrase of the statutory test was to ask whether the available evidence, if accepted, could show that a defendant had done an act which showed that he was actually trying to commit the act in question or whether he had only got ready or put himself in a position or equipped himself to do so. Had he moved from the role of intention, preparation and planning into the area of execution or implementation? The court answered in the negative, allowing the appeal and quashing the conviction.

R. v Tosti [1997] Crim.L.R. 746 (CA): D. and E. appealed against convictions of attempted burglary. They had concealed oxyacetylene equipment in a hedge, approached the door of a barn they were intending to burgle and examined the padlock on the door before being arrested. Held, upholding the convictions, that the question is one of degree: how close to, and necessary for, the commission of the offence were the acts which the accused did? The acts were not merely preparatory but were essentially first steps in the commission of the offence.

Notes

1. The line to be drawn between preparation and commission appears to be an exceedingly fine one. In *Tosti* examining the padlock appears to have amounted to a crossing of that line even though no attempt was made to break the lock and the oxyacetylene equipment was still hidden in the hedge. It is difficult to see how this differs from *Campbell* but if the line is correctly drawn in *Tosti*, it would appear to have been incorrectly drawn in *Geddes*. In any event, a repetition of Geddes' acts now would fall foul of s.63 of the Sexual Offences Act 2003, trespass with intent to commit a sexual offence.

2. A further problem, however, is that D's act may be more than merely preparatory to more than one offence. In such circumstances it is important to determine what D's intent was; this requires evidence to support any inference that the prosecution may ask a jury to draw. The temptation to over-charge a defendant should be resisted as is clear from the following case.

R V FERRITER

[2012] EWCA Crim 2211

F was the last remaining customer in the pub where C was the barmaid. CCTV footage showed F go behind the bar, wrestle C to the floor and get on top of her. C continued to struggle and managed to break free and escape. At F's trial for attempted rape C testified that he had tried repeatedly to pull her trousers down before she managed to break free. F pleaded to two counts of theft (having stolen money and alcohol after C escaped) but pleaded Not Guilty to counts of attempted rape or, in the alternative, attempted assault. The jury convicted F of attempted rape and he appealed.

THE VICE PRESIDENT, HUGHES LJ

1. This defendant was convicted of attempted rape. His appeal as originally formulated was founded on the submission which was made to the judge that there was insufficient evidence to leave to the jury that what he did was more than a merely preparatory act. However, as the argument has developed it has become apparent that there is a second line to the submission, which is that there was insufficient evidence to leave to the jury to justify the inference that, even assuming there was a more than merely preparatory act, the intent was not merely to assault the complainant sexually, but to commit the specific offence of rape.

   . . .

6. It is a commonplace that attempted rape requires proof of two things. The first is an intention to rape, rather than to do anything else, and the second thing that must be proved is actions which are more than mere preparation for committing the offence. To borrow the language of Lord Bingham in *R v Geddes* [1996] Crim LR 894, it is often helpful to invite the jury to consider whether the defendant has done an act which shows that he has actually tried to commit the offence in question, or whether he has only got ready or put himself into a position or equipped himself to do so in future.

7. Mr Oscroft [for the appellant] has referred us to a decision of this court in *Beaney* [2010] EWCA Crim. 2551. That was a case in which the defendant accosted a woman who was leaving a railway station at night. He put some kind of weapon to her neck and pushed her into some bushes. She went to the ground but was able to break free and run away, leaving her bag behind. The defendant took her bag and was found later in possession of her i-Pod which had been in it. In due course his case was that it had been simple robbery or theft but there was no sexual motive at all. This court held that on the facts of that case there was insufficient evidence of an intent to rape, as distinct from an intent to commit a lesser sexual assault. For that reason the conviction for attempted rape was quashed and a conviction for attempted sexual assault was substituted.

8. It is essential to separate in the analysis of this case, as it was in *Beaney*, the evidence as to the defendant's intention on the one hand and whether there was more than mere preparation on the other. As we have said, the

principal submission advanced to the judge and initially the principal submission advanced to us, focused on the second of those questions. But logically it makes sense to consider first the question of intention.

9. The defendant's case here, rather as Mr Beaney's case, was that there was nothing sexual in his mind at all. His case was that what he wanted to do was to take the money out of the tills behind the bar. Indeed it was his case that he told the unfortunate complainant that that is what he was after—in effect that he said to her that she need not fear anything worse, he was only after the money. The evidence however belied that assertion. First, she said he had said no such thing and she would undoubtedly have heard it if he had. The jury plainly believed her and did not believe him. Secondly, her evidence, plainly accepted by the jury, was that he had tried while they were struggling on the ground, on something like three or perhaps four occasions, to pull her trousers down. True it was that because she was wearing a top coat the part of the trousers that he was able to get his hand on were at or about knee level, or possibly below, but that is what was accessible. Whilst it was of course a perfectly proper submission to make to the jury on his behalf, for Mr Oscroft to contend that he might simply have been trying to prevent her from getting up and running away, rather than actually trying to remove her trousers, the jury was quite entitled to take the view that that was not so, and plainly it did.

10. The first question in the case is accordingly whether there was evidence from which the jury could safely infer a sexual intent rather than the intent to rob which the defendant asserted. We are entirely satisfied that the jury had ample material on which to conclude that the intention was sexual molestation as distinct from robbery. If he had wanted the money, he would have said so and he did not. The attempt to remove her trousers, which the jury clearly accepted, is wholly inconsistent with robbery and only consistent with sexual intent. Her handbag which was over her shoulder and likely to contain something of some value was not touched. When he came in behind the bar he went straight to her, rather than to the tills, and when she ran away it was some little time before he went anywhere near the tills and then only after he can plainly be seen deliberating for some time whether to pour himself a glass from one of the optics or to take, as in the end he did, one of the bottles down.

11. The next question is however more difficult. It is whether there was material on which the jury could safely infer that the sexual intention which the defendant plainly had was to commit the specific offence of rape with all that that entails, rather than something unpleasant and sexual but not necessarily the particular kind of penetration which is rape.

12. We sympathise with the judge in leaving the entire case to the jury because it is not at all clear to us that the submission which we have just articulated was ever clearly made to the judge. But the answer of Mr Connor for the Crown to the simply expressed but penetrating question of my Lord, Popplewell J, is revealing. Was there, my Lord asked, any evidence or activity which was capable of justifying the conclusion which pointed to an intent to commit rape rather than, for example, an intent to molest her sexually under her clothes in some other way? Mr Connor's frank answer was that there was not, and he is right. In those circumstances we are, we think, driven to the conclusion that the conviction for attempted rape is unsafe.

13. Before we come to the consequences of that, we need to address the third question which is: was this a case in which the jury was entitled to say, assuming an intent either to rape or to commit some other sexual offence, that the activity of the defendant went beyond mere preparation into trying to do it? We have not the slightest doubt that his actions did go well beyond mere preparation and into trying to do it. He was engaged in the act of molesting the unfortunate complainant physically and trying to remove her trousers. If that is not more than mere preparation we are not at all sure that we know what is. We observe that in the case of Beaney this court reached a similar conclusion in relation to activities on the part of that defendant which were a good deal less explicit than the activities of this one. What had there been done was no more than to reach out a hand towards the complainant's leg.

14. The result therefore is that we are left with a case in which there was ample evidence of an intent to commit a serious sexual assault, involving the removal of the lady's trousers and thus, plainly, an assault directed at her private parts unclothed. The jury must, on the findings that it made, have concluded that that was his intent and they must in those circumstances, had they gone on to consider count 2, have concluded that there was in this case a sexual assault. There was clearly a physical assault and by section 78 of the Sexual Offences Act 2003, touching or other activity is sexual if a reasonable person would consider that the act is of its nature sexual, but also if such a person would consider that, whilst of its nature it was equivocal, yet because of the purpose of the perpetrator it was sexual. This is a case of the second of those alternatives without, in our view, the slightest doubt.

. . .

17. In those circumstances, section 3 of the Criminal Appeal Act 1968 plainly applies and the right course for this court to take is, whilst quashing the conviction for attempted rape, to substitute a conviction of sexual assault. [The Court went on to reduce the sentence of four years' imprisonment to three-and-a-half years.]

iii. Reform

The Law Commission published a Consultation Paper, *Conspiracy and Attempts* (TSO, 2007), No.183 which identified a number of problems with the law on attempts and proposed several changes. Their thesis was that completed attempts (where D has failed to commit the offence) should be distinguished from incomplete attempts and that two separate offences should be created to deal with these different situations—first, the offence of attempt for those performing the last acts towards committing a substantive offence and, secondly, an offence of "criminal preparation" for conduct occurring before D actually completes or all-but completes an attempt to commit an offence. They proposed that any final report should contain examples which could then be used by judges interpreting new legislation. The proposals met with considerable opposition. In their Report, *Conspiracy and Attempts* (TSO, 2009), Law Com. No.318, the Law Commission accepted that there was no pressing case for reform. While they considered that there were sound responses to be made to most of the objections raised to their proposals, the 10th objection they identified was highly persuasive and led them to conclude that they should not recommend the repeal of the law on attempts and its replacement with two new offences. They did, however, make some recommendations for amending the existing law.

LAW COMMISSION, *CONSPIRACY AND ATTEMPT* (TSO, 2009), LAW COM. NO.318

REFORMING THE CRIMINAL ATTEMPTS ACT 1981 IN OTHER RESPECTS

8.83 In the following paragraphs we consider the issues we addressed in the CP, in relation to the offence of attempt, which are incidental to the principal proposals considered above. These issues are free-standing and therefore continue to be relevant despite our decision not to carry those proposals forward into recommendations.

8.84 We now consider these issues on the basis that section 1(1) of the 1981 Act remains unchanged. . .

8.85 There are eight issues which fall to be considered:

(1) the meaning of the word 'intent' in section 1(1) of the 1981 Act;

(2) the elements of the relevant substantive offence to which D's intent should relate;

(3) whether proof of subjective recklessness as to a circumstance element in the definition of the intended substantive offence should be sufficient for attempt where recklessness (as to that circumstance) is sufficient for D to be liable for the substantive offence;

(4) whether proof of subjective recklessness as to a circumstance element in the definition of the intended substantive offence should be required for attempt where proof of a lesser degree of fault (or no proof of fault) as to that circumstance is required for D to be liable for the substantive offence;

(5) whether proof of a fault element as to a circumstance which is higher than subjective recklessness (such as knowledge) should be required for attempt where it is required for D to be liable for the substantive offence;

(6) whether the word 'act' in section 1(1) of the 1981 Act should be replaced to encompass omissions (where the substantive offence is capable of being committed by an omission);

(7) whether it should be permissible to bring a prosecution in a magistrates' court for attempting to commit an offence which can be tried only summarily; and

(8) whether the respective roles of the trial judge and jury should be revised, in cases where D is tried on indictment in the Crown Court.

[The first five issues related to the fault element of the offence of attempt. The Law Commission made three recommendations to deal with these issues. They made a further recommendation to deal with the issue of omissions but made no recommendations in respect of the remaining two issues.]

9.17 We recommend that the Criminal Attempts Act 1981 be amended to provide that, for the purposes of section 1(1), an intent to commit an offence includes a conditional intent to commit it.

9.18 We recommend that for substantive offences which have a circumstance requirement but no corresponding fault requirement, or which have a corresponding fault requirement which is objective (such as negligence), it should be possible to convict D of attempting to commit the substantive offence only if D was subjectively reckless as to the circumstance at the relevant time.

9.19 We recommend that where a substantive offence has fault requirements not involving mere negligence (or its equivalent) in relation to a fact or circumstance, it should be possible to convict D of attempting to commit the substantive offence if D possessed those fault requirements at the relevant time.

9.20 We recommend that the Criminal Attempts Act 1981 be amended so that D may be convicted of attempted *murder* if (with the intent to kill V) D failed to discharge his or her legal duty to V (where that omission, unchecked, could have resulted in V's death).

2. CONSPIRACY

DPP v Nock [1978] A.C. 979:

"Lord Tucker [in *BOT v Owen* (below, p. 412)] by stressing the 'auxiliary' nature of the crime of conspiracy, and by explaining its justification as being to prevent the commission of substantive offence, has placed the crime firmly in the same class and category as attempts to commit a crime. Both are criminal because they are steps towards the commission of a substantive offence. The distinction between the two is that whereas a 'proximate' act is that which constitutes the crime of attempt, agreement is the necessary ingredient in conspiracy. The importance of the distinction is that agreement may, and usually will, occur well before the first step which can be said to be an attempt. The law of conspiracy thus makes possible an earlier intervention by the law to prevent the commission of the substantive offence." per Lord Scarman.

Note

Conspiracy was a common law offence, consisting of "the agreement of two or more to do an unlawful act, or to do a lawful act by unlawful means" per Willes J in *Mulcahy v R*. (1868) L.R. 3 HL 306. "Unlawful" in this context covered all crimes, even summary offences, some torts, fraud, the corruption of public morals and the outraging of public decency. The aim of the Law Commission, *Conspiracy and Criminal Law Reform* (TSO, 1976), Law Com. No.76 § 1.111, was to confine conspiracy to agreements to commit crimes. This aim was partially achieved by ss.1 and 5 of the Criminal Law Act 1977 (see below). However, pending a comprehensive review of offences of fraud and of the law relating to obscenity and indecency, conspiracies to defraud, and to corrupt public morals or outrage public decency, were preserved.

----

i. Common elements to common law and statutory conspiracies

Notes

Agreement

1. The essence of conspiracy is an agreement between two or more persons to effect the particular prohibited purpose. The agreement may be express or implied, but whatever form it takes, the offence of conspiracy is complete as soon as the parties agree whether or not they put the agreement into effect or whether or not all the details of the agreement are settled.

2. It is not necessary to prove that a conspirator knew all the details of the scheme to which he

attached himself; it is enough that he and the other conspirators shared a common criminal purpose (*Clark* [2012] EWCA Crim 1220).

3.   A conspiracy will continue to subsist as long as the parties agree and will only terminate on its completion by performance or by abandonment or frustration (see *DPP v Doot* [1973] A.C. 807). As conspiracy is a continuing offence, other persons may join an existing conspiracy and become parties to it and there is no requirement for all conspirators to know or be in contact with each other. What is necessary is that all the parties to the conspiracy have a common purpose communicated to at least one other party to the conspiracy (see *Ardalan* [1972] 2 All E.R. 257; *Scott* (1979) 68 Cr. App. R. 164).

Parties

4.   There must be at least two parties to the agreement; agreements with certain persons may not suffice to establish the offence of conspiracy. For example, a director of a company who is solely responsible for the conduct of the company's business who decides to commit an offence in the company's name, cannot be convicted of conspiring with the company as only one mind was involved albeit that the company has a separate legal personality (see *McDonnell* [1966] 1 Q.B. 233). But where a director conspires in the course of the company's business with other persons or companies, the company may be indicted as a party to that conspiracy (see *R. v ICR Haulage Ltd* [1944] K.B. 551).

5.   Where the only parties to an agreement are husband and wife they cannot be guilty of conspiracy, whether statutory (s.2(2) of the Criminal Law Act 1977) or common law (*Mawji v R.* [1957] A.C. 126). However, a husband and wife can be convicted of conspiracy where a third party is also involved (*Whitehouse* (1852) 6 Cox C.C. 38; *Chrastny* [1991] 1 W.L.R. 1381), or where the agreement was entered into before they married (*R. v Robinson* (1746) 1 Leach 37).

6.   Where the only other party to an agreement to commit an offence is a child under the age of criminal responsibility, D will not be guilty of conspiracy (s.2(2)). Where the only other party to an agreement to commit an offence is an intended victim of that offence, D will not be guilty of conspiracy (s.2(2)). The intended victim of the offence will not be guilty of conspiracy regardless of the number of persons involved in the conspiracy (s.2(1)).

7.   Exemption from liability for commission of an offence as a principal (for example a woman cannot commit rape) does not exempt a person from liability for conspiracy to commit that offence.

8.   Where a person is exempt both as a principal and an accessory, liability for conspiracy will depend upon an assessment of the purpose of the statute and whether it would be defeated by holding an exempt person liable for conspiracy or whether its purpose requires the extension of the exemption to cover conspiracy. In *Burns* (1984) 79 Cr. App. R. 173, the Court of Appeal upheld the conviction of a father of a child of conspiracy with others to steal it from the mother, although he was exempt from prosecution for the substantive offence under s.56 of the Offences Against the Person Act 1861 (s.56 has since been repealed by the Child Abduction Act 1984). Watkins LJ stated the considerations which influenced the court in its decision as follows (at 179):

"We find [no authority] that leads us to say that it is in any way wrong or unjust for a person who is exempt, in the sense that James Burns was, from prosecution for the substantive offence to be proceeded against for the crime of conspiracy.

The dangers of permitting a father of children to collect a posse of men and suddenly launch a siege of the home of his erstwhile wife, to break in and then snatch away sleeping children are surely self-evident. The criminal law does not in our view permit that sort of conduct. When a father who is exempt under s. 56 behaves in that way, it is, in our judgment, not only lawful but right and just that the prosecution should be free to bring a charge of conspiracy against him."

----

ii. Statutory conspiracy

CRIMINAL LAW ACT 1977, AS AMENDED

1   (1) Subject to the following provisions of this Part of this Act, if a person agrees with any other person or persons that a course of conduct shall be pursued which, if the agreement is carried out in accordance with their intentions, either—

   (a) will necessarily amount to or involve the commission of any offence or offences by one or more parties to the agreement, or

   (b) would do so but for the existence of facts which render the commission of the offence or any offences impossible, he is guilty of conspiracy to commit the offence or offences in question.

  (2) Where liability for any offence may be incurred without knowledge on the part of the person committing it of any particular fact or circumstance necessary for the commission of the offence, a person shall nevertheless not be guilty of conspiracy to commit that offence by virtue of subsection (1) above unless he and at least one other party to the agreement intend or know that that fact or circumstance shall or will exist at the time when the conduct constituting the offence is to take place.

As conspiracy is an offence which centres on the agreement between the parties, which involves a meeting of minds, it is difficult to divide the offence into *actus reus* and *mens rea*. It is proposed, therefore, to analyse the separate ingredients contained in s. 1(1) which go to make up the offence.

(a) Course of conduct

Notes

1.   The essence of conspiracy is that the parties agree upon a course of conduct to be pursued which if pursued in accordance with their intentions, must necessarily amount to or involve the commission of an offence by one or more of the conspirators. Where the agreement is to commit a "result crime" the phrase "course of conduct" cannot be divorced from the consequences of those actions. For example, if A and B agree to kill V by placing poison in a bottle of milk in his fridge, this will not necessarily result in murder as V may not drink the milk. If the phrase "course of conduct" covered only the parties' physical acts, A and B would not be guilty of conspiracy to murder. This phrase must therefore include the intended consequences of those actions which, in this case, are the death of V. Thus the course of conduct agreed includes not only the actions intended to be taken but also the consequences of those actions.

2.   If "course of conduct" includes intended consequences, these must be determined as the parties' liability will be limited to these. In *Siracusa* (1990) 90 Cr. App. R. 340, the accused were charged, inter alia, with conspiracy to import heroin contrary to s.170(2)(b) of the Customs and Excise Management Act 1979. This provision prohibits the fraudulent evasion of the prohibition on the importation of controlled drugs. Case law established that a person may be convicted of the substantive offence even though mistaken as to the drugs he is involved in importing. Thus, D could be convicted if the drugs are heroin even though he believed they were cannabis. On a charge of conspiracy, however, the Court of Appeal made it clear that the intention and the actual nature of the drugs must coincide, O'Connor LJ stating (at 350):

"The mens rea sufficient to support the commission of a substantive offence will not necessarily be sufficient to support a charge of conspiracy to commit that offence. An intent to cause grievous bodily harm is sufficient to support the charge of murder, but is not sufficient to support a charge of conspiracy to murder or of attempt to murder. . . [I]f the prosecution charge a conspiracy to contravene s.170(2) of the Customs and Excise Management Act by the importation of heroin, then the prosecution must prove that the agreed course of conduct was the importation of heroin. This is because the essence of the crime of conspiracy is the agreement and in simple terms, you do not prove an agreement to import heroin by proving an agreement to import cannabis."

3.   Where the course of conduct agreed also includes any facts or circumstance necessary for the commission of the substantive offence, D cannot be convicted of conspiracy unless he and at least one other party to the agreement intend or know that such fact or circumstance shall or will exist at the time when the conduct constituting the offence is to take place (s.1(2)). Even though recklessness or negligence suffice with respect to a fact or circumstance of the substantive offence or strict liability applies thereto, D may be convicted of conspiracy to commit such an offence only where he and another party to the agreement intend that the circumstance shall exist or know that it will exist at the time the offence is to take place. See case of *Saik* below. Where a person was charged with an offence of money-laundering contrary to s.93C of the Criminal Justice Act 1988 (now superseded by the Proceeds of Crime Act 2002), it was sufficient to establish liability that he had reasonable grounds to suspect the money was the proceeds of criminal conduct. Their Lordships embarked on a thorough analysis of the mental element in conspiracy including dealing with the problem of conditional intent.

R. V SAIK

[2006] UKHL 18

Saik ran a bureau de change. He was charged with conspiracy to launder money having reasonable grounds to suspect it was the proceeds of criminal conduct. Saik appealed his conviction on the basis that this was not enough to sustain a charge of conspiracy.

LORD NICHOLLS OF BIRKENHEAD

1. . . The issue before your Lordships is whether the offence . . . is an offence known to law. Reasonable grounds for suspicion are enough for the substantive offence of laundering money. But are they enough for a conspiracy to commit that offence?
2. . . The best way to tackle this conundrum is to consider first the ingredients of criminal conspiracy, then apply this approach to a conspiracy to commit the substantive offence of laundering. . .

The statutory offence of criminal conspiracy . . .
3. The Criminal Law Act 1977 redefined conspiracy and put it on a statutory footing. . .
The offence therefore lies in making an agreement. Implicitly, the subsection requires also that the parties intend to carry out their agreement. The offence is complete at that stage. The offence is complete even if the parties do not carry out their agreement. The offence is complete even if the substantive offence is not thereafter committed by any of the conspirators or by anyone else.
4. Thus . . . the mental element of the offence, apart from the mental element involved in making an agreement, comprises the intention to pursue a course of conduct which will necessarily involve commission of the crime in question by one or more of the conspirators. The conspirators must intend to do the act prohibited by the substantive offence. The conspirators' state of mind must also satisfy the mental ingredients of the substantive

offence. If one of the ingredients of the substantive offence is that the act is done with a specific intent, the conspirators must intend to do the prohibited act and must intend to do the prohibited act with the prescribed intent. A conspiracy to wound with intent to do grievous bodily harm contrary to section 18 of the Offences of the Person Act 1861 requires proof of an intention to wound with the intent of doing grievous bodily harm. The position is the same if the prescribed state of mind regarding the consequence of the prohibited act is recklessness. Damaging property, being reckless as to whether life is endangered thereby, is a criminal offence: Criminal Damage Act 1971, section 1(2). Conspiracy to commit this offence requires proof of an intention to damage property, and to do so recklessly indifferent to whether this would endanger life.

5. An intention to do a prohibited act is within the scope of section 1(1) even if the intention is expressed to be conditional on the happening, or non-happening, of some particular event. The question always is whether the agreed course of conduct, if carried out in accordance with the parties' intentions, would necessarily involve an offence. A conspiracy to rob a bank tomorrow if the coast is clear when the conspirators reach the bank is not, by reason of this qualification, any less a conspiracy to rob. In the nature of things, every agreement to do something in the future is hedged about with conditions, implicit if not explicit. In theory if not in practice, the condition could be so far-fetched that it would cast doubt on the genuiness of a conspirator's expressed intention to do an unlawful act. If I agree to commit an offence should I succeed in climbing Mount Everest without the use of oxygen, plainly I have no intention to commit the offence at all. Fanciful cases apart, the conditional nature of the agreement is insufficient to take the conspiracy outside section 1(1).

6. Section 1(2) qualifies the scope of the offence created by section 1(1). This subsection is more difficult. Its essential purpose is to ensure that strict liability and recklessness have no place in the offence of conspiracy. . .

7. Under this subsection conspiracy involves a third mental element: intention or knowledge that a fact or circumstances necessary for the commission of the substantive offence will exist. Take the offence of handling stolen goods. One of its ingredients is that the goods must have been stolen. That is a fact necessary for the commission of the offence. Section 1(2) requires that the conspirator must intend or know that this fact will exist when the conduct constituting the offence takes place.

8. It follows from this requirement of intention or knowledge that proof of the mental element needed for the commission of a substantive offence will not always suffice on a charge of conspiracy to commit that offence. In respect of a material fact or circumstance conspiracy has its own mental element. In conspiracy this mental element is set as high as 'intend or know'. This subsumes any lesser mental element, such as suspicion, required by the substantive offence in respect of a material fact or circumstances. In this respect the mental element of conspiracy is distinct from and supersedes the mental element in the substantive offence. When this is so, the lesser mental element in the substantive offence becomes otiose on a charge of conspiracy. It is an immaterial averment. To include it in the particulars of the offence of conspiracy is potentially confusing and should be avoided.

9. The phrase 'fact or circumstance necessary for the commission of the offence' is opaque. Difficulties have sometimes arisen in its application. The key seems to lie in the distinction apparent in the subsection between 'intend or know' on the one hand and any particular 'fact or circumstance necessary for the commission of the offence' on the other hand. The latter is directed at an element of the actus reus of the offence. A mental element of the offence is not itself a 'fact or circumstance' for the purposes of the subsection.

10. This contrast can be illustrated by the offence of entering into an arrangement whereby the retention by another person (A) of A's proceeds of crime is facilitated, knowing or suspecting A has been engaged in crime: section 93A of the Criminal Justice Act 1988, now repealed. The requirement that the defendant must know or suspect A's criminal history is an element of the offence, but it is a mental element. The need for the defendant to have this state of mind is not a fact or circumstance within section 1(2). Another ingredient of the offence is that the property involved must be the proceeds of crime. That is a fact necessary for the commission of the offence and section 1(2) applies to that fact.

. . .

13. The rationale underlying this approach is that conspiracy imposes criminal liability on the basis of a person's intention. This is a different harm from the commission of the substantive offence. So it is right that the intention which is being criminalised in the offence of conspiracy should itself be blameworthy. This should be so, irrespective of the provisions of the substantive offence in that regard.

14. Against that background I turn to some issues concerning the scope and effect of section 1(2). The starting point is to note that this relieving provision is not confined to substantive offences attracting strict liability. The subsection does not so provide. Nor would such an interpretation of the subsection make sense. It would make no sense for section 1(2) to apply, and require proof of intention or knowledge, where liability for the substantive offence is absolute but not where the substantive offence has built into it a mental ingredient less than knowledge, such as suspicion.

15. So much is clear. A more difficult question arises where an ingredient of the substantive offence is that the defendant must know of a material fact or circumstance. On its face section 1(2) does not apply in this case. The opening words of section 1(2), on their face, limit the scope of the subsection to cases where a person may commit an offence without knowledge of a material fact or circumstance.

16. Plainly Parliament did not intend that a person would be liable for conspiracy where he lacks the knowledge required to commit the substantive offence. That could not be right. Parliament could not have intended such an absurd result. Rather, the assumption underlying section 1(2) is that, where knowledge of a material fact is an ingredient of a substantive offence, knowledge of that fact is also an ingredient of the crime of conspiring to commit the substantive offence.

17. There are two ways this result might be achieved. One is simply to treat section 1(2) as inapplicable in this type of case. This would mean that the knowledge requirement in the substantive offence would survive as a requirement which must also be satisfied in respect of a conspiracy. In the same way as a conspirator must intend to do the prohibited act with any specific intent required by the substantive offence, so he must intend to do the prohibited act having the knowledge required by the substantive offence. Accordingly, on this analysis, where knowledge of a fact is an ingredient of the substantive offence, section 1(2) is not needed.

18. The other route is to adopt the interpretation of section 1(2) suggested by Sir John Smith. The suggestion is that section 1(2) applies in such a case despite the opening words of the subsection. Section 1(2) is to be read as applicable even 'where liability for an offence may be incurred without knowledge [etc]'. It is difficult to see what other function the word 'nevertheless' has in the subsection. This may seem a slender peg on which to hang a conclusion of any substance, but it is enough: see 'Some Answers' [1978] Crim LR 210.

19. The first route accords more easily with the language of section 1(2), but I prefer the second route for the following reason. A conspiracy is looking to the future. It is an agreement about future conduct. When the agreement is made the 'particular fact or circumstance necessary for the commission' of the substantive offence may not have happened. So the conspirator cannot be said to know of that fact or circumstance at that time. Nor, if the happening of the fact or circumstance is beyond his control, can it be said that the conspirator will know of that fact or circumstance.

20. Section 1(2) expressly caters for this situation. The conspirator must 'intend or know' that this fact or circumstance 'shall or will exist' when the conspiracy is carried into effect. Although not the happiest choice of language, 'intend' is descriptive of a state of mind which is looking to the future. This is to be contrasted with the language of substantive offences. Generally, references to 'knowingly' or the like in substantive offences are references to a past state of affairs. No doubt this language could be moulded appropriately where the offence charged is conspiracy. But the more direct and satisfactory route is to regard section 1(2) as performing in relation to a conspiracy the function which words such as 'knowingly' perform in relation to the substantive offence. That approach accords better with what must be taken to have been the parliamentary intention on how the phrase 'intend or know' in section 1(2) would operate in this type of case. Thus on a charge of conspiracy to handle stolen property where the property has not been identified when the agreement is made, the prosecution must prove that the conspirator intended that the property which was the subject of the conspiracy would be stolen property.

21. In my view, therefore, the preferable interpretation of section 1(2) is that the subsection applies to all offences. It applies whenever an ingredient of an offence is the existence of a particular fact or circumstance. The subsection applies to that ingredient.

The Criminal Justice Act 1988, section 93C

22. I must now take this a step further and confront another difficulty. I can do this most readily by reference to the substantive offence relevant in the present case: section 93C of the Criminal Justice Act 1988. This section was inserted into the 1988 Act by section 31 of the Criminal Justice Act 1993. It has now been superseded. Section 93C(2) provided:

'A person is guilty of an offence if, knowing or having reasonable grounds to suspect that any property is, or in whole or in part directly or indirectly represents, another person's proceeds of criminal conduct, he—

(a) conceals or disguises that property; or
(b) converts or transfers that property or removes it from the jurisdiction,

for the purpose of assisting any person to avoid prosecution for an offence to which this Part of this Act applies or the making or enforcement in his case of a confiscation order.'

23. The acts prohibited by this offence are listed in paragraphs (a) and (b): concealing or disguising the property, or converting or transferring the property or taking it abroad. Thus a conspiracy to commit this offence involves an agreement to do one or more of these acts. Further, the agreement must be an agreement to do one or more of these acts for one or more of the stated purposes. Another ingredient of the substantive offence is that the property in question must emanate from a crime: *R. v Montila* [2004] 1 WLR 3141. The criminal provenance of the property is a fact necessary for the commission of the offence. This fact falls within section 1(2). So, applying section 1(2) to that fact, the prosecution must prove the conspirator intended or knew that fact would exist when the conspiracy was carried out. Hence, where the property has not been identified when the conspiracy agreement is reached, the prosecution must prove the conspirator intended that the property would be the proceeds of criminal conduct.

24. If these ingredients are established the offence of conspiracy is made out. In this type of case, namely, where the conspiracy related to unidentified property, there is no question of having to prove that the property was the proceeds of criminal conduct. In this type of case that is not possible. It is not possible because the property which was the subject of the conspiracy had not been identified when the conspiracy was entered into. Despite this, the crime of conspiracy will be committed. It will be committed even if the property never material-ises or never exists. . .

25. What, however, if the property to which the conspiracy relates was specifically identified when the con-spirators made their agreement? In that event the prosecution must prove the conspirators 'knew' the property was the proceeds of crime. This is the next point of difficulty in the interpretation of section 1(2). Does 'know' in this context have the meaning attributed to it in the Montila case when considering the substantive offence? If it does, the identified property to which the conspiracy related must actually be or represent the proceeds of crime, and the conspirator must be aware of this. Or does 'know' in this context mean 'believe', as seems to be suggested in *R. v Ali* [2006] 2 WLR 316, 335, para 98? On the ordinary use of language a person cannot 'know' whether property is the proceeds of crime unless he participated in the crime. He can only believe this is so, on the basis of what he has been told. Adopting this approach would mean that, so far as section 93C is concerned, equating knowledge with belief in the case of identified property would achieve a measure of symmetry with the requirement of intention in the case of unidentified property. It would mean that in both cases what matters is the conspirator's state of mind: the actual provenance of the property would not be material.

26. I do not think the latter approach can be accepted. The phrase under consideration ('intend or know') in section 1(2) is a provision of general application to all conspiracies. In this context the word 'know' should be interpreted strictly and not watered down. In this context knowledge means true belief. Whether it covers wilful blindness is not an issue arising on this appeal. As applied to section 93C(2) it means that, in the case of identified property, a conspirator must be aware the property was in fact the proceeds of crime. The prosecution must prove the conspirator knew the property was the proceeds of criminal conduct.

LORD HOPE OF CRAIGHEAD . . .

The meaning of the words used
57. In *R. v Churchill* [1967] 2 AC 224 it was held that if on the facts known to them at the time of their agreement what the parties agreed to was lawful, they were not rendered guilty of conspiracy to commit an offence by the existence of other facts not known to them which gave a different and criminal quality to the act or course of conduct that they had agreed on: Viscount Dilhorne, p 237. The offence that was in issue in that case was an offence of strict liability. Section 1(2) codifies this principle. It does so in language which was designed to make it clear that, while ignorance of the law was no excuse, full knowledge of the consequences of the agreement was required: see the Law Commission's Report, *Conspiracy and Criminal Law Reform* (Law Com No 76), 1976, paras 1.39–1.41. It was designed also to exclude recklessness as to the consequences. In para 1.41 the Law Commission recognised that the mental element which their proposals required was a stringent one, adding this explanation:

'However, we think that the stringency we recommend is fully justified by the fact that conspiracy is essentially an inchoate offence which is committed before any prohibited event has in fact taken place.'

58. A provision to give effect to this proposal was included in clause 1(3) of the draft Bill appended to the report. Section 1(2) does not follow its language precisely, but the requirement that the defendant and at least one other party to the agreement must 'intend or know' that the fact or circumstance 'shall or will exist' at the time when the conduct constituting the offence is to take place was taken directly from the draft Bill. There is no doubt that the requirement was designed to eliminate the risk that someone could be guilty of conspiracy just because he was reckless as to the existence or otherwise of the circumstances that would make the conduct criminal. In his

commentary on this subsection in *Current Law Statute*, Professor Edward Griew of Leicester University, noted that offences that might be committed without knowledge of the facts that gave the act a criminal quality are not confined to offences of strict liability. They include offences where recklessness as to some fact was a minimum but sufficient requirement:

'There are many offences, for example, which require knowledge or recklessness as to the falsity of some statement. But only knowledge of the falsity will ground liability for conspiracy to commit such an offence. All this is as the Law Commission intended: Law Com Report, paras 1.39 et seq.'

. . .

80. But in this case all we know is that the appellant suspected that the money 'was' the proceeds of crime. . . He suspected that he was being asked to convert the proceeds of criminal conduct. But he did not know that this was the origin of the money that was actually being given to him. He was prepared to go ahead and convert the money without knowing that it was in fact the proceeds of crime. It would not be quite right to say that he was reckless. All he was to do was simply to convert money from one currency into another—an everyday transaction which involves no risk to anyone. But he was willing to go ahead with this without troubling to find out whether or not what he was proposing to do was criminal. A person who is in that state of mind cannot be said to intend that the fact or circumstance that makes his act criminal should exist. That being the position I would hold that, although he was suspicious, the appellant cannot be said to have intended that the money should be the proceeds of crime when he came to deal with it.

Conclusion

81. . . I see no escape from the conclusion that the appellant's case is caught by section 1(2) of the 1977 Act. He cannot be said to be guilty of the conspiracy to commit the substantive offence under section 93C(2) because he did not know, and therefore did not intend, that the money which he agreed to convert would be the proceeds of crime when at some future date he came to perform his part of the agreement. I would allow the appeal and set aside the conviction.

Appeal allowed.
Conviction quashed

(b) If the agreement is carried out

Note

The agreement need not be to the effect that the course of conduct must necessarily be carried out; only to the effect that, if it is carried out, it will necessarily involve a crime. The fact that the agreement will only be carried out if some condition precedent, e.g. it is safe, necessary, expedient, etc. is satisfied, is nothing to the point.

In *Jackson* [1985] Crim. L.R. 444, the appellants' convictions of conspiracy to pervert the course of justice were upheld by the Court of Appeal. The appellants had agreed with W, then on trial for burglary, that if he was convicted they would shoot him in the leg as they considered that the court would then deal with him more leniently. The Court of Appeal held that:

"Planning was taking place for a contingency and if that contingency occurred the conspiracy would necessarily involve the commission of an offence. 'Necessarily' is not to be held to mean that there must inevitably be the carrying out of the offence; it means, if the agreement is carried out in accordance with the plan, there must be the commission of the offence referred to in the conspiracy count."

In *O'Hadhmaill* [1996] Crim. L.R. 509 a conviction of conspiracy to cause an explosion was upheld where, during the IRA ceasefire, members of the IRA agreed to make bombs to be used if the ceasefire came to an end. If the ceasefire continued the bombs would not be used.

Contrast these situations with the situation where the object of the agreement is not the commission of a particular offence but the attainment of some other objective, albeit the parties may contemplate the commission of an offence to attain that end. The following example was given in *Reed* [1982] Crim. L.R. 819, and approved in *Jackson*:

> A and B agree to drive from London to Edinburgh in a time which can be achieved without exceeding the speed limits, but only if the traffic which they encounter is exceptionally light. Their agreement will not necessarily involve the commission of any offence, even if it is carried out in accordance with their intentions, and they do drive from London to Edinburgh within the agreed time. Accordingly the agreement does not constitute the offence of statutory conspiracy or indeed of any offence.

Driving from London to Edinburgh within a particular time was an object which could be attained without the commission of any offence; if the speed limit was broken, this was incidental to the main object of the agreement. In *Reed* the Court of Appeal contrasted the driving example with that of A and B who agree to rob a bank, if when they arrive at the bank it seems safe to do so. "Their agreement will necessarily involve the commission of the offence of robbery if it is carried out in accordance with their intentions. Accordingly, they are guilty of the statutory offence of conspiracy". The object of their agreement was robbery; the commission of the offence was not incidental to any other object.

What if A and B agree to rob the bank and to kill anyone who seeks to prevent their escape? Are they guilty of conspiracy to murder? The driving example might appear to suggest that they are not, as the main object of their agreement is to rob the bank and this can be attained without necessarily killing anyone. But if this agreement to kill is isolated from the agreement to rob, there is little to distinguish it from *Jackson* as it is an agreement to kill subject to a condition precedent. If no one seeks to prevent their escape the course of conduct will not be pursued, but if anyone does seek to prevent their escape, the agreed course of conduct will necessarily involve the commission of murder. Perhaps the correct approach to this problem is to separate the elements of the agreement from each other. The result is two separate agreements to pursue two courses of conduct: first, the agreement to rob the bank, and secondly the agreement, if a particular contingency occurs, to kill. The driving example is not severable in this way; there is one agreement to pursue one course of conduct which may or may not involve the commission of an offence.

Compare the robbery example with one used by Baroness Hale of Richmond in *Saik*: A and B consider having sex with a woman, V, and agree that they will do so *even if* it turns out that V does not consent. Baroness Hale states: (at [99]):

> "[I]t is important to distinguish between what happens when the substantive offence is committed—when the men have intercourse with the woman whether or not she consents—and what happens when they agree to do so. When they agree, they have thought about the possibility that she may not consent. They have agreed that they will go ahead *even if at the time when they go ahead they know that she is not consenting*. If so, that will not be recklessness; that will be intent to rape. Hence they are guilty of conspiracy to rape."

Notes

1. In *Saik* reference was made to the problem of handling stolen goods. For example, A and B agree to handle particular goods. Several situations may arise: (i) they know at the time of their

agreement that the goods are stolen; or (ii) the goods may not yet be stolen but it is their intention that when they are stolen they will handle them; or (iii) they may not know the provenance of the goods but their agreement is to handle them whether they be stolen goods or goods from a legitimate source.

In situations (i) and (ii) there should generally not be a problem; in (i) A and B know the provenance of the goods at the time they enter into their agreement while in (ii) the purpose of their agreement is to handle stolen goods (see Lord Nicholls below).

Situation (iii), however, involves conditional intention; A and B have agreed to pursue a course of conduct which, if carried out *in accordance with their intentions*, may, or may not, depending on the provenance of the goods they ultimately handle, involve the commission of the substantive offence of handling. The issue did not strictly arise in *Saik* (on the facts the defendants had only agreed to transfer cash being suspicious as to its provenance—they had not agreed to transfer it *even if* it turned out to be the proceeds of crime) and the majority do not provide a clear answer.

(See further iii. Reform below where the Law Commission in its Report, *Conspiracy and Attempt* (TSO, 2009) are critical of the decision in *Saik* and have made recommendations (3 and 4) to deal with problems to which it gives rise.)

2. If only one of the parties to the agreement has the relevant knowledge or intention there is no conspiracy. For example, if A and B agree to purchase a particular consignment of goods from C, A knowing them to be stolen and B having no such knowledge or belief, neither will be liable for conspiracy to handle stolen goods even though the agreed course of action, if pursued, would necessarily have involved the offence of handling stolen goods by A. Similarly, where the parties differ as to the intended consequences, this will affect their liability for conspiracy. For example, if A and B agree to wound V and A intends that V should die but B only intends that he should sustain grievous bodily harm, there is no conspiracy to kill but there is a conspiracy to cause grievous bodily harm.

(c) In accordance with their intentions

At common law the prosecution had to prove not only an agreement to carry out an unlawful purpose but also an intention on the part of any alleged conspirator to carry out the unlawful purpose (see *Thomson* (1965) 50 Cr. App. R. 1). The Law Commission did not recommend any change in the law. In Law Commission, *Conspiracy and Criminal Law Reform* (TSO, 1976), it stated (at para.7.2):

> "A person should be guilty of conspiracy if he agrees with another person that an offence shall be committed. Both must intend that any consequence specified in the definition of the offence will result and both must know of the existence of any state of affairs which it is necessary for them to know in order to be aware that the course of conduct agreed upon will amount to the offence."

The implication of this view was that if A did not intend the substantive offence to be committed he could not be liable for conspiracy, and if there were only two parties to the alleged agreement, the other party likewise could not be guilty of conspiracy. The Law Commission's intention was frustrated by the next case.

R. V ANDERSON

[1986] A.C. 27 HL

D and A, in custody in relation to entirely unconnected offences, spent one night in the same cell. D, who was expecting to be released soon, agreed with A to participate in a scheme to secure A's escape from prison. D was to meet A's brother and another man and supply diamond wire, which they would then smuggle in to A. D was also to do further acts to facilitate the escape. He was to be paid £20,000 for his assistance. He received £2,000 on account from A's brother, but was injured in a road accident before anything further happened. He did not supply the wire, and took no further part in the scheme. D admitted that he had intended to supply the wire on payment of another £10,000 on account, but said he would then have gone abroad and taken no further part in the plan, which he believed was doomed to failure. His submission that he lacked the mental element for conspiracy to effect an escape, in that he did not intend or expect the plan to be carried into effect, was rejected by the judge and by the Court of Appeal, which also held that, even if he was not a principal in conspiracy he could be convicted of aiding abetting counselling and procuring the conspiracy of the other two men (see 80 Cr. App. R. 64 at 77). On appeal to the House of Lords on both of these questions:

LORD BRIDGE OF HARWICH

The Act of 1977, subject to exceptions not presently material, abolished the offence of conspiracy at common law. It follows that the elements of the new statutory offence of conspiracy must be ascertained purely by inter-pretation of the language of s.1(1) of the Act of 1977. For purposes of analysis it is perhaps convenient to isolate the three clauses each of which must be taken as indicating an essential ingredient of the offence as follows: (1) 'if a person agrees with any other person or persons that a course of conduct shall be pursued' (2) 'which will necessarily amount to or involve the commission of any offence or offences by one or more of the parties to the agreement' (3) 'if the agreement is carried out in accordance with their intentions'.

Clause (1) presents, as it seems to me, no difficulty. It means exactly what it says and what it says is crystal clear. To be convicted, the party charged must have agreed with one or more others that 'a course of conduct shall be pursued.' What is important is to resist the temptation to introduce into this simple concept ideas derived from the civil law of contract. Any number of persons may agree that a course of conduct shall be pursued without undertaking any contractual liability. The agreed course of conduct may be a simple or an elaborate one and may involve the participation of two or any larger number of persons who may have agreed to play a variety of roles in the course of conduct agreed.

Again, clause (2) could hardly use simpler language. Here what is important to note is that it is not necessary that more than one of the participants in the agreed course of conduct shall commit a substantive offence. It is, of course, necessary that any party to the agreement shall have assented to play his part in the agreed course of conduct, however innocent in itself, knowing that the part to be played by one or more of the others will amount to or involve the commission of an offence.

It is only clause (3) which presents any possible ambiguity. The heart of the submission for the appellant is that in order to be convicted of conspiracy to commit a given offence the language of clause (3) requires that the party charged should not only have agreed that a course of conduct shall be pursued which will necessarily amount to or involve the commission of that offence by himself or one or more other parties to the agreement, but must also be proved himself to have intended that that offence should be committed. Thus, it is submitted here that the appellant's case that he never intended that Andaloussi should be enabled to escape from prison raised an issue to be left to the jury, who should have been directed to convict him only if satisfied that he did so intend. I do not find it altogether easy to understand why the draftsman of this provision chose to use the phrase 'in accordance with their intentions'. But I suspect the answer may be that this seemed a desirable alternative to the phrase 'in accordance with its terms' or any similar expression, because it is a matter of common experience in the criminal courts that the 'terms' of a criminal conspiracy are hardly ever susceptible of proof. The evidence from which a jury may infer a criminal conspiracy is almost invariably to be found in the conduct of the parties. This was so at common law and remains so under the statute. If the evidence in a given case justifies the infer-ence of an agreement that a course of conduct should be pursued, it is a not inappropriate formulation of the test of the criminality of the inferred agreement to ask whether the further inference can be drawn that a crime would necessarily have been committed if the agreed course of conduct had been pursued in accordance with the *several* intentions of the parties. Whether that is an accurate analysis or not, I am clearly driven by consideration of the diversity of roles which parties may agree to play in criminal conspiracies to reject any construction of the statutory language which would require the prosecution to prove an intention on the part of each conspirator that the criminal offence or offences which will necessarily be committed by one or more of the conspirators if the agreed course of conduct is fully carried out should in fact be committed. A simple example will illustrate the absurdity to which this construction would lead. The proprietor of a car hire firm agrees for a substantial payment to make available a hire car to a gang for use in a robbery and to make false entries in his books relating to the hiring to which he can point if the number of the car is traced back to him in connection with the robbery. Being fully aware of the circumstances of the robbery in which the car is proposed to be used he is plainly a party to the conspiracy to rob. Making his car available for use in the robbery is as much a part of the relevant agreed course of conduct as the robbery itself. Yet, once he has been paid, it will be a matter of complete indifference to him whether the robbery is in fact committed or not. In these days of highly organised crime the most serious statutory conspiracies will frequently involve an elaborate and complex agreed course of conduct in which many will consent to play necessary but subordinate roles, not involving them in any direct participation in the commission of the offence or offences at the centre of the conspiracy. Parliament cannot have intended that such parties should escape conviction of conspiracy on the basis that it cannot be proved against them that they intended that the relevant offence or offences should be committed.

There remains the important question whether a person who has agreed that a course of conduct will be pursued which, if pursued as agreed, will necessarily amount to or involve the commission of an offence is guilty of statutory conspiracy irrespective of his intention, and, if not, what is the *mens rea* of the offence. I have no hesitation in answering the first part of the question in the negative. There may be many situations in which perfectly respectable citizens, more particularly those concerned with law enforcement, may enter into agreements that a course of conduct shall be pursued which will involve commission of a crime without the least intention of playing any part in furtherance of the ostensibly agreed criminal objective, but rather with the purpose of exposing and frustrating the criminal purpose of the other parties to the agreement. To say this is in no way to encourage schemes by which police act, directly or through the agency of informers, as agents provocateurs for the purpose of entrapment. That is conduct of which the courts have always strongly disapproved. But it may sometimes happen, as most of us with experience in criminal trials well know, that a criminal enterprise is well advanced in the course of preparation when it comes to the notice either of the police or of some honest citizen in such circumstance that the only prospect of exposing and frustrating the criminal is that some innocent person should play the part of an intending collaborator in the course of criminal conduct proposed to be pursued. The *mens rea* implicit in the offence of statutory conspiracy must clearly be such as to recognise the innocence of such a person, notwithstanding that he will, in literal terms, be obliged to agree that a course of conduct be pursued involving the commission of an offence.

I have said already, but I repeat to emphasise its importance, that an essential ingredient in the crime of conspiring to commit a specific offence or offences under s.1(1) of the Act of 1977 is that the accused should agree that a course of conduct be pursued which he knows must involve the commission by one or more of the parties to the agreement of that offence or those offences. But, beyond the mere fact of agreement, the necessary *mens rea* of the crime is, in my opinion, established if, and only if, it is shown that the accused, when he entered into the agreement, intended to play some part in the agreed course of conduct in furtherance of the criminal purpose which the agreed course of conduct was intended to achieve. Nothing less will suffice; nothing more is required.

Applying this test to the facts which, for the purposes of the appeal, we must assume, the appellant, in agreeing that a course of conduct be pursued that would, if successful, necessarily involve the offence of effecting Andaloussi's escape from lawful custody, clearly intended, by providing diamond wire to be smuggled into the prison, to play a part in the agreed course of conduct in furtherance of that criminal objective. Neither the fact that he intended to play no further part in attempting to effect the escape, nor that he believed the escape to be impossible, would, if the jury had supposed they might be true, have afforded him any defence.

In the result, I would answer the first part of the certified question in the affirmative and dismiss the appeal. Your Lordships did not find it necessary to hear argument directed to the second part of the certified question and it must, therefore, be left unanswered.

Lords Scarman, Diplock, Keith and Brightman agreed.

Appeal dismissed

Question

If a person may be convicted of conspiracy "irrespective of his intention", what then is the mens rea of conspiracy?

Notes

1. The House of Lords could have avoided the need to tinker with the mens rea of conspiracy if they had upheld D's conviction on the basis that he had aided and abetted the conspiracy as the others involved clearly had the intention that the substantive offence be committed.

2. ". . . An essential ingredient in the crime of conspiring to commit a specific offence . . . is that the accused shall agree that a course of conduct be pursued which he knows must involve the commission by one or more parties to the agreement of that offence . . . But, beyond the mere fact of agreement, the necessary mens rea of the crime . . . is established if, and only if, it is shown that the accused, when he entered into the agreement, intended to play some part in the agreed course of conduct in furtherance of the criminal purpose which the agreed course of conduct was intended to achieve. Nothing less will suffice, nothing more is required."

    This dictum was considered and "explained" by the Court of Appeal in *R. v Siracusa* (1989) 90 Cr. App. R. 340. There was a large and complicated agreement to import various prohibited drugs at various times. The parties were charged with conspiracy to contravene s.170(2)(b) of the Customs and Excise Management Act 1979, which prohibits the import of various classes of drugs with various penalties attached. In *R. v Shivpuri* [1987] A.C. 1 (below, p.432), the House of Lords held that for this offence the mens rea required was an intention to import any prohibited drug, not necessarily one of the class actually imported. In the course of dismissing the appeals in the present case, O'Connor LJ said:

    > "[The dictum above quoted] must be read in the context of that case. We think it obvious that Lord Bridge cannot have been intending that the organiser of a crime who recruited others to carry it out would not himself be guilty of conspiracy unless it could be proved that he intended to play some active part himself thereafter . . . Participation in a conspiracy is infinitely variable; it can be active or passive. If the majority shareholder and director of a company consents to the company being used for drug smuggling carried out in the company's name by a fellow director and minority shareholder, he is guilty of conspiracy. Consent, that is the agreement or adherence to the agreement, can be inferred if it is proved that he knew what was going on and the intention to participate in the furtherance of the criminal purpose is also established by his failure to stop the unlawful activity.
    >
    > . . . The mens rea sufficient to support the commission of a substantive offence will not necessarily be sufficient to support a charge of conspiracy to commit that offence. An intent to cause grievous bodily harm is sufficient to support a charge of murder, but it is not sufficient to support a charge of conspiracy to murder, or of attempt to murder. We have come to the conclusion that if the prosecution charge a conspiracy to contravene s.170(2) of the Customs and Excise Management Act by the importation of heroin, then the prosecution must prove that the agreed course of conduct was the importation of heroin. This is because the essence of the crime of conspiracy is the agreement and, in simple terms, you do not prove an agreement to import heroin by proving an agreement to import cannabis."

3. The defendant must know that what is projected is a crime, otherwise it cannot be said that he agreed to a course of conduct involving the commission of a crime. This is the position even if the *offence* can be committed without full knowledge of a fact or circumstance which makes the conduct criminal. Section 1(2) of the Criminal Law Act 1977, above, p.390, provides that in such a case, to be guilty of *conspiring* to commit the offence, D and at least one other party must intend or know that that fact or circumstance shall or will exist at the time when the conduct constituting the offence is to take place. Thus, it is an offence to use in a vehicle fuel on which the appropriate duty has not been paid; to convict D of this offence it is not necessary to show that he knew that the duty had not been paid. But if D is charged with conspiracy to use in a vehicle fuel on which duty has not been paid, it must be shown that he and at least one other party knew that the duty had not been paid. (see also *Ali* [2005] EWCA Crim 87 for conspiracies to launder the proceeds of crime) (Compare the similar rule in aiding and abetting, above, p.313.)

4. But, according to Lord Bridge in *Anderson*, it is not necessary that D should intend that the crime should be carried out; it is sufficient if he knows that another party to the agreement intends to commit it.

Question

The brother of A and B had been murdered, apparently on the orders of P, a dangerous criminal. A and B agreed to meet near P's house on 14 June, when they knew that P would be away, and reconnoitre a place to ambush him; on 16 June they would return, lie in wait for P and kill him. At the time of the agreement, each privately thought that the enterprise was too dangerous, and resolved not to be present on the 16th. In order not to appear too fainthearted, each intended to be present on the 14th and assist in fixing a place of ambush, but each intended to arrange some pressing business to keep him away on the day of the attack, which each expected the other to carry out alone. Are they guilty of conspiracy to murder?

Note

The authority of *Anderson* has been thrown further into doubt by the Privy Council decision in *Yip Chiu-Cheung v R.*, below, which, although not binding on English courts, is highly persuasive particularly as the committee comprised Lords Griffiths, Browne-Wilkinson, Mustill, Jauncey of Tullichettle and Slynn of Hadley. *Siracusa* was not cited but their Lordships addressed issues raised in *Anderson*. The case arose in Hong Kong where conspiracy is an offence contrary to common law. There is no apparent distinction between the Hong Kong common law definition of conspiracy and the statutory definition in s.1(1) of the 1977 Act.

YIP CHIU-CHEUNG V THE QUEEN

[1995] 1 A.C. 111

D had been convicted of conspiracy to traffic in heroin contrary to common law and to s.4 of the Dangerous Drugs Ordinance. The conspiracy concerned an agreement between D and N, an American undercover drug enforcement agent, that he would meet D in Hong Kong where he would receive from him the supply of heroin which N would take to Australia. The authorities were aware of the plan and had agreed not to prevent N proceeding to Australia as his aim was to identify the others in the drugs ring. N however, missed his flight to Hong Kong and the plan was abandoned. D argued on appeal that N could not be a co-conspirator as he lacked the necessary mens rea for conspiracy.

LORD GRIFFITHS

delivered the judgment of their Lordships:

. . . On the principal ground of appeal it was submitted that the trial judge and the Court of Appeal were wrong to hold that Needham, the undercover agent, could be a conspirator because he lacked the necessary mens rea or guilty mind required for the offence of conspiracy. It was urged upon their Lordships that no moral guilt attached to the undercover agent who was at all times acting courageously and with the best of motives in attempting to infiltrate and bring to justice a gang of criminal drug dealers. In these circumstances it was argued that it would be wrong to treat the agent as having any criminal intent, and reliance was placed upon a passage in the speech of Lord Bridge of Harwich in *R. v Anderson (William Ronald)* [1986] A.C 27, 38–39; but in that case Lord Bridge was dealing with a different situation from that which exists in the present case. There may be many cases in which undercover police officers or other law enforcement agents pretend to join a conspiracy in order to gain information about the plans of the criminals, with no intention of taking any part in the planned crime but rather with the intention of providing information that will frustrate it. It was to this situation that Lord Bridge was referring in *R. v Anderson*. The crime of conspiracy requires an agreement between two or more persons to commit an unlawful act with the intention of carrying it out. It is the intention to carry out the crime that constitutes the necessary mens rea for the offence. As Lord Bridge pointed out, an undercover agent who has no intention of committing the crime lacks the necessary mens rea to be a conspirator.

The facts of the present case are quite different. Nobody can doubt that Needham was acting courageously and with the best of motives; he was trying to break a drug ring. But equally there can be no doubt that the method he chose and in which the police in Hong Kong acquiesced involved the commission of the criminal offence of trafficking in drugs by exporting heroin from Hong Kong without a licence. Needham intended to commit that offence by carrying the heroin through the customs and on to the aeroplane bound for Australia.

Neither the police, nor customs, nor any other member of the executive have any power to alter the terms of the Ordinance forbidding the export of heroin, and the fact that they may turn a blind eye when the heroin is exported does not prevent it from being a criminal offence . . .

Naturally, Needham never expected to be prosecuted if he carried out the plan as intended. But the fact that in such circumstances the authorities would not prosecute the undercover agent does not mean that he did not commit the crime albeit as part of a wider scheme to combat drug dealing.

The judge correctly directed the jury that they should regard Needham as a conspirator if they found that he intended to export the heroin.

Appeal dismissed

Note

Although *Yip Chiu-Cheung* concerned common law conspiracy, it is difficult to see any distinction between this and statutory conspiracy. The signs clearly are that if the issue comes before the Supreme Court *Anderson* will not be followed; that much has been hinted at by the Court of Appeal in *King* [2012] EWCA Crim 805. Where there appears to be an agreement between parties to commit an offence but, in fact, none of them intend to carry the agreement out and it is nothing more than a fantasy, there is not a conspiracy; there needs to be some credible evidence of "executory intent" for the case to be left to the jury (see *Goddard* [2012] EWCA Crim 1756). The Law Commission in its Report, *Conspiracy and Attempt* (TSO, 2009) have made recommendations to neutralise the decision in *Anderson* (see iii Reform below).

(d) Necessarily amount to or involve the commission of any offence

If the course of conduct agreed upon is carried out in accordance with the parties' intentions, will it necessarily amount to or involve the commission of an offence? Two situations may arise.

First, if A and B agree upon a course of conduct which they believe will amount to an offence but it is not an offence, their belief will not convert their agreement into the offence of conspiracy. For example, believing that it is illegal to import lace into England, A and B agree to smuggle some lace into the country. In fact, there is no restriction on the importation of lace, so the agreement, if executed, will not involve the commission of any offence.

Secondly, the agreement, when executed, must involve one or more of the parties to the agreement in the commission of an offence. Will participation as an aider, abettor, counsellor, or procurer of an offence suffice? In *Hollinshead* [1985] 1 All E.R. 850, the Court of Appeal held that an agreement to aid and abet an offence was not sufficient; a charge of conspiracy would only be sustainable where the agreement envisaged the commission of the offence as a principal by one or more of the parties. On the appeal hearing of that case in the House of Lords, *Hollinshead* [1985] A.C. 975, their Lordships did not address this question, they upheld the convictions of the accused for common law conspiracy to defraud and considered it unnecessary to decide whether a statutory conspiracy to aid and abet an offence was possible. The wording of s.1(1) and the fact that their Lordships did not decide that there was a statutory conspiracy seem to imply that a conspiracy to aid and abet is not possible (see also *Kenning* [2008] EWCA 1534). Thus "commission" in s.1(1) means commission as a principal.

It should be noted, however, that there are a few statutory offences, whose actus reus consists of aiding and abetting or procuring something, for example aiding, abetting, counselling or procuring another's suicide. In these cases the aider and abettor is the principal so that it is possible to conspire to aid and abet a suicide (see *Reed* [1982] Crim. L.R. 819).

iii. Reform

The Law Commission published a Consultation Paper No.183, *Conspiracy and Attempts* (2007)[1] which identified a number of problems with the law on conspiracy and proposed several changes. In their Report, *Conspiracy and Attempt* (TSO, 2009), the Law Commission made their final recommendations for reforming the law.[2] These recommendations involved an attempt to bring the law of conspiracy into line with the law of attempts particularly as regards mens rea regarding circumstance elements. However, since 2009 the Court of Appeal has, in the context of attempts, responded to the decision of the House of Lords in *Saik* (see *Pace and Rogers*, p.373 above) with the result that the law of attempts has been re-aligned with the law of conspiracy so the premises upon which some of the recommendations are based no longer pertain.

---

1 See: http://www.lawcom.gov.uk/project/conspiracy-and-attempts/#conspiracy-and-attempts-2
2 For the summary of their reasoning see: http://www.lawcom.gov.uk/wp-content/uploads/2015/03/lc318_Conspiracy_and_Attempts_Report.pdf

LAW COMMISSION, *CONSPIRACY AND ATTEMPT* (TSO, 2009), LAW COM. NO.318

LIST OF RECOMMENDATIONS

CONSPIRACY

9.1 We recommend that a conspiracy must involve an agreement by two or more persons to engage in the conduct element of an offence and (where relevant) to bring about any consequence element of the substantive offence. (**Recommendation 1** . . .)

9.2 We recommend that a conspirator must be shown to have intended that the conduct element of the offence, and (where relevant) the consequence element (or other consequences), should respectively be engaged in or brought about. (**Recommendation 2** . . .)

9.3 We recommend that an alleged conspirator must be shown at the time of the agreement to have been reckless whether a circumstance element of a substantive offence (or other relevant circumstance) would be present at the relevant time, when the substantive offence requires no proof of fault, or has a requirement for proof only of negligence (or its equivalent), in relation to that circumstance. (**Recommendation 3** . . .)

9.4 We recommend that where a substantive offence has fault requirements not involving mere negligence (or its equivalent), in relation to a fact or circumstance element, an alleged conspirator may be found guilty if shown to have possessed those fault requirements at the time of his or her agreement to commit the offence. (**Recommendation 4** . . .)

9.5 We recommend that it should be possible for a defendant to deny that he or she possessed the fault element for conspiracy because of intoxication, whether voluntary or involuntary, even when the fault element in question is recklessness (or its equivalent). (**Recommendation 5** . . .)

9.6 We recommend that agreements comprising a course of conduct which, if carried out, will amount to more than one offence with different fault as to circumstance elements or to which different penalties apply, should be charged as more than one conspiracy in separate counts on an indictment. (**Recommendation 6** . . .)

9.7 We recommend that the present requirement for the Director of Public Prosecutions to give consent if proceedings to prosecute a conspiracy to commit a summary offence are to be initiated need not be retained. (**Recommendation 7** . . .)

9.8 We recommend that the immunity for spouses and civil partners provided for by section 2(2)(a) of the Criminal Law Act 1977 should be abolished. (**Recommendation 8** . . .)

9.9 We recommend that the present exemption for a non-victim co-conspirator should be abolished but that the present exemption for a victim (D) should be retained if:

(a) The conspiracy is to commit an offence that exists wholly or in part for the protection of a particular category of persons;

(b) D falls within the protected category; and

(c) D is the person in respect of whom the offence agreed upon would have been committed.

(**Recommendation 9** . . .)

9.10 We recommend that the rule that an agreement involving a person of or over the age of criminal responsibility and a child under the age of criminal responsibility gives rise to no criminal liability for conspiracy should be retained. (**Recommendation 10** . . .)

9.11 We recommend that the defence of acting reasonably provided for by section 50 of the Serious Crime Act 2007[see p.421 below] should be applied in its entirety to the offence of conspiracy. (**Recommendation 11** . . .)

9.12 We recommend that it should be possible to convict D of conspiracy to commit a substantive offence regardless of where any of D's relevant conduct (or any other party's relevant conduct) occurred so long as D knew or believed that the conduct or consequence element of the intended substantive offence might occur, whether wholly or in part, in England or Wales. (**Recommendation 12** . . .)

9.13 We recommend that it should be possible to convict D of conspiracy to commit a substantive offence, regardless of where any other party's conduct occurred, if: D's relevant conduct occurred in England or Wales; D knew or believed that the conduct or consequence element of the intended substantive offence might be committed wholly or partly in a place outside England and Wales; and the substantive offence, if committed in that place, would also be an offence under the law in force in that place (however described in that law). (**Recommendation 13** . . .)

9.14 We recommend that it should be possible to convict D of conspiracy to commit a substantive offence, regardless of where any other party's relevant conduct occurred, if: D's relevant conduct occurred in England or Wales; D knew or believed that the intended substantive offence might occur wholly or partly in a place outside England and Wales; and the substantive offence, if committed in that place, would be an offence triable in England and Wales (or would be so triable if committed by a person satisfying relevant citizenship, nationality or residence conditions). (**Recommendation 14** . . .)

9.15 We recommend that it should be possible to convict D of conspiracy to commit a substantive offence, where D's relevant conduct occurred outside England and Wales, if: D knew or believed that the intended substantive offence might occur wholly or partly in a place outside England and Wales and D could be tried in England and Wales (as the perpetrator) if he or she committed the substantive offence in that place. (**Recommendation 15** . . .)

9.16 We recommend that the consent of the Attorney General should be obtained for a prosecution for conspiracy to proceed, in a case where it cannot be proved that D knew or believed that the intended substantive offence might be committed wholly or partly in England or Wales. (**Recommendation 16** . . .)

iv. Common Law Conspiracies

CRIMINAL LAW ACT 1977

Section 5: *Abolitions, savings, transitional provisions, consequential amendments and repeals.*

(1) Subject to the following provisions of this section, the offence of conspiracy at common law is hereby abolished.

(2) Subsection (1) above shall not affect the offence of conspiracy at common law so far as relates to conspiracy to defraud. [As amended by Criminal Justice Act 1987 s.12, below].

(3) Subsection (1) above shall not affect the offence of conspiracy at common law if and in so far as it may be committed by entering into an agreement to engage in conduct which—

(a) tends to corrupt public morals or outrages public decency, but
(b) would not amount to or involve the commission of an offence if carried out by a single person otherwise than in pursuance of an agreement.

(7) Incitement to commit the offence of conspiracy (whether the conspiracy incited would be the offence at common law or under s.1 above or any other enactment) shall cease to be offences. [As amended by Criminal Attempts Act 1981 s.10.]

CRIMINAL JUSTICE ACT 1987

Section 12: *Charges of and penalty for conspiracy to defraud.*

(1) If—
(a) a person agrees with any other person or persons that a course of conduct shall be pursued; and
(b) that course of conduct will necessarily amount to or involve the commission of any offence or offences by one or more of the parties to the agreement if the agreement is carried out in accordance with their intentions,

the fact that it will do so shall not preclude a charge of conspiracy to defraud being brought against any of them in respect of the agreement.

(2) In s.5 (2) of the Criminal Law Act 1977, the words from 'and' to the end are hereby repealed.

(3) A person guilty of conspiracy to defraud is liable on conviction on indictment to imprisonment for a term not exceeding 10 years or a fine or both.

(a) Conspiracy to defraud

SCOTT V METROPOLITAN POLICE COMMISSIONER

[1975] A.C. 819 HL

S agreed with employees of cinema owners temporarily to abstract, without permission of the owners, films, without the knowledge or consent of the copyright owners, for the purpose of making infringing copies and distributing them on a commercial basis. He was convicted of conspiracy to defraud the copyright owners, and appealed.

VISCOUNT DILHORNE

The Court of Appeal certified that a point of law of general public importance was involved in the decision to dismiss the appeal against conviction on count one, namely,

> 'Whether on a charge of conspiracy to defraud, the Crown must establish an agreement to deprive the owners of their property by deception; or whether it is sufficient to prove an agreement to prejudice the rights of another or others without lawful justification and in circumstances of dishonesty.'

Before the House Mr Blom-Cooper put forward three contentions, his main one being that which he advanced unsuccessfully before the Court of Appeal and Judge Hines that there could not be a conspiracy to defraud without deceit . . .

Mr Blom-Cooper's main submission was based on the well known dicta of Buckley J. in *Re London and Globe Finance Corporation Ltd* [1903] 1 Ch. 728, 732:

> 'To deceive is, I apprehend, to induce a man to believe that a thing is true which is false, and which the person practising the deceit knows or believes to be false. To defraud is to deprive by deceit: it is by deceit to induce a man to act to his injury. More tersely it may be put, that to deceive is by falsehood to induce a state of mind; to defraud is by deceit to induce a course of action.'

Mr Blom-Cooper, while not submitting that an intent to defraud necessarily includes an intention to deceive, nevertheless submitted that a man could not be defrauded unless he was deceived. Buckley J.'s definition was, he said, exhaustive and as the conspiracy charged in count one did not involve any deceit of the companies and persons who owned the copyright and the distribution rights of the films which had been copied, the conviction on that count could not, he submitted, stand.

In a great many and it may be the vast majority of fraud cases the fraud has been perpetrated by deceit and in many cases Buckley J.'s dicta have been quoted in charges to juries. It does not, however, follow that it is an exhaustive definition of what is meant by 'defraud'. Buckley J. had to decide when a prima facie case had been shown 'of doing some or one of the acts' mentioned in ss.83 and 84 of the Larceny Act 1861 'with intent to deceive or defraud.' He did not have to make or to have to attempt to make an exhaustive definition of what was meant by 'defraud.'

Stephen, History of the Criminal Law of England (1883), vol. 2, contains the following passage, at p.121:

> 'Fraud—There has always been a great reluctance amongst lawyers to attempt to define fraud, and this is not unnatural when we consider the number of different kinds of conduct to which the word is applied in connection with different branches of it. I shall not attempt to construct a definition which will meet every case which might be suggested, but there is little danger in saying that whenever the words 'fraud' or 'intent to defraud' or 'fraudulently' occur in the definition of a crime two elements at least are essential to the commission of the crime: namely, first, deceit or an intention to deceive or in some cases mere secrecy; and, secondly, either actual injury or possible injury or an intent to expose some person either to actual injury or to a risk of possible injury by means of that deceit or secrecy.'

Stephen thus recognises that a fraud may be perpetrated without deceit by secrecy and that an intent to defraud need not necessarily involve an intent to deceive . . .

In the course of the argument many cases were cited. It is not necessary to refer to all of them. Many were cases in which the conspiracy alleged was to defraud by deceit. Those cases do not establish that there can only be a conspiracy to defraud if deceit is involved and there are a number of cases where that was not the case.

[After citing various cases] Indeed, in none of these cases was it suggested that the conviction was bad on the ground that the conspiracy to defraud did not involve deceit of the person intended to be defrauded. If that had been a valid ground for quashing the conviction it is, I think, inconceivable that the point would not have been taken, if not by counsel, by the court . . .

In the course of delivering the judgment of the Court of Appeal in *R. v Sinclair* [1968] 1 W.L.R. 1246, where the defendants had been convicted of conspiracy to cheat and defraud a company, its shareholders and creditors by fraudulently using its assets for purposes other than those of the company and by fraudulently concealing such use, James J. said at p.1250:

'To cheat and defraud is to act with deliberate dishonesty to the prejudice of another person's proprietary right.'

Again, one finds in this case no support for the view that in order to defraud a person that person must be deceived.

One must not confuse the object of a conspiracy with the means by which it is intended to be carried out. In the light of the cases to which I have referred, I have come to the conclusion that Mr Blom-Cooper's main contention must be rejected. I have not the temerity to attempt an exhaustive definition of the meaning of 'defraud'. As I have said, words take colour from the context in which they are used, but the words 'fraudulently' and 'defraud' must ordinarily have a very similar meaning. If as I think, and as the Criminal Law Revision Committee appears to have thought, 'fraudulently' means 'dishonestly', then 'to defraud' ordinarily means, in my opinion, to deprive a person dishonestly of something which is his or of something to which he is or would or might but for the perpetration of the fraud be entitled . . .

In this case the accused bribed servants of the cinema owners to secure possession of films in order to copy them and in order to enable them to let the copies out on hire. By so doing Mr Blom-Cooper conceded they inflicted more than nominal damage to the goodwill of the owners of the copyright and distribution rights of the films. By so doing they secured for themselves profits which but for their actions might have been secured by those owners just as in *R. v Button* (1848) 3 Cox C.C. 229, the defendants obtained profits which might have been secured by their employer. In the circumstances it is, I think, clear that they inflicted pecuniary loss on those owners.

Reverting to the questions certified by the Court of Appeal, the answer to the first question is in my opinion in the negative. I am not very happy about the way in which the second question is phrased although the word 'prejudice' has been not infrequently used in this connection. If by 'prejudice' is meant 'injure', then I think that an agreement by two or more by dishonesty to deprive a person of something which is his or to which he is or would be or might be entitled and an agreement by two or more by dishonesty to injure some proprietory right of his, suffices to constitute the offence of conspiracy to defraud.

In my opinion this appeal should be dismissed.

Appeal dismissed

Notes

1. Just as deceit is not necessary for a conspiracy to defraud, neither is an intent (in the sense of purpose) that the victim shall suffer injury in some proprietary right. In *Wai Yu-Tsang v R.* [1991] 4 All E.R. 664, the following direction by a trial judge was approved by the Privy Council, when upholding a conviction of conspiracy to defraud:

    "It is fraud if it is proved that there was the dishonest taking of a risk which there was no right to take, which—to [D's] knowledge at least—would cause detriment or prejudice to another, detriment or prejudice to the economic or proprietary rights of another. That detriment or prejudice to somebody else is very often incidental to the purpose of the fraudsman himself. The prime object of the fraudsmen is usually to gain some economic advantage for themselves, any detriment or prejudice to somebody else is often secondary to that objective, but nonetheless is a contemplated or predictable outcome of what they do. If the interests of some other person— the economic or proprietary interests of some other person are imperilled, that is sufficient to constitute fraud even though no loss is actually suffered and even though the fraudsman himself did not desire to bring about any loss."

In *Adams v The Queen* [1995] 1 W.L.R. 52, D, a director of E.H.L. agreed with his co-defendants, who comprised the investment team, to set up a complex system by which share transactions could be conducted thereby making for themselves a profit which they concealed from E.H.L. The Privy Council dismissed D's appeal against conviction for conspiracy to defraud, Lord Jauncey of Tullichettle stating (at 65):

"Since a company is entitled to recover from directors secret profits made by them at the company's expense, it would follow that any dishonest agreement by directors to impede a company in the exercise of its right of recovery would constitute a conspiracy to defraud. In their Lordship's view a person can be guilty of fraud when he dishonestly conceals information from another which he was under a duty to disclose to that other or which that other was entitled to require him to disclose."

Affirming *Wai Yu-Tsang* he stated (at 64) that "A person is not prejudiced if he is hindered in inquiring into the source of moneys in which he has no interest. He can only suffer prejudice in relation to some right or interest which he possesses."

2. In *R. v Ayres* [1984] A.C. 447 at 455, Lord Bridge, dealing with s.5 as it existed before amendment by s.12 of the Criminal Justice Act 1987 said "According to the true construction of the Act, an offence which amounts to a common law conspiracy to defraud must be charged as such and not as a statutory conspiracy under s.1. Conversely a s.1 conspiracy cannot be charged as a common law conspiracy to defraud." The extreme width of conspiracy to defraud as defined in *Scott v MPC* covering agreements to commit crimes, e.g. theft or obtaining by deception, meant that these agreements must be charged as conspiracies to defraud, and not as conspiracies to steal, or obtain by deception. It was therefore held that the effect of s.5 was to cut down conspiracy to defraud to agreements which, if carried into effect, would not necessarily involve the commission of any substantive criminal offence by any of the conspirators: *R. v Ayres*, above. The effect of s.12 of the Criminal Justice Act 1987, above, p.405, is to restore the offence of conspiracy to defraud to what it was held to be in *Scott v MPC*. An agreement, e.g. to steal, is therefore both a statutory and a common law conspiracy and may be charged as either.

3. An agreement to deceive a public official into breaching his duty is a conspiracy to defraud: *DPP v Withers* [1975] A.C. 842.

4. The problem remains as to whether conspiracy to defraud could be abolished without leaving unacceptable gaps in the law. The Law Commission, returning to the matter in 1987, reached a provisional view that it could be, but that there would be lost significant procedural and practical advantages of being able to charge the offence, particularly in large scale fraud cases: W.P. 104. In its Report *Criminal Law: Conspiracy to Defraud* (TSO, 1994), Law Com. No.228, the Law Commission concluded that simple abolition of conspiracy to defraud, without replacement, would leave undesirable gaps in the law and that the offence should be retained pending the outcome of their comprehensive review of dishonesty offences. (For further discussion see J.C. Smith, "Conspiracy to Defraud: Some comments on the Law Commission's Report" [1995] Crim. L.R. 209.)

In its Report, *Fraud* (TSO, 2002), Law Com No.276, the Law Commission recommended the abolition of the offence.

FRAUD

Law Commission, Fraud (TSO, 2002), Law Com No.276

(footnotes omitted)

CONSPIRACY TO DEFRAUD

An anomalous crime

3.2 The concept of fraud, for the purposes of conspiracy to defraud, is wider than the range of conduct caught by any of the individual statutory offences involving dishonest behaviour. Thus it can be criminal for two people to *agree* to do something which it would not be unlawful for one person to do.

3.3 This anomaly has an historical basis. Before the Criminal Law Act 1977, a criminal conspiracy could be based on an agreement to commit an unlawful but non-criminal act, such as a tort or breach of contract. It appears that the justification for this was that there was a greater danger from people acting in concert than alone. As Professor Andrew Ashworth has explained:

> In legal terms, the reasoning seemed to be that acts which were insufficiently antisocial to justify criminal liability when done by one person could become sufficiently antisocial to justify criminal liability when done by two or more people acting in agreement. Such a combination of malefactors might increase the probability of harm resulting, might in some cases increase public alarm, and might in other cases facilitate the perpetration and concealment of the wrong [A. Ashworth, *Principles of Criminal Law*, 3rd edn (1999), p.472].

3.4 The 1977 Act was the implementation of our Report on Conspiracy and Criminal Law Reform, which "emphatically" concluded that the object of a conspiracy should be limited to the commission of a substantive offence and that there should be no place in a criminal code for a law of conspiracy extending beyond this ambit. An agreement should not be criminal where that which it was agreed should be done would not amount to a criminal offence if committed by one person [Law Commission, *Conspiracy and Criminal Law Reform* (TSO, 1976) para.1.9].

3.5 This Commission has repeated its adherence to this principle in subsequent Reports [see, e.g. Law Commission, *Conspiracy To Defraud* (TSO, 1994), Law Com. No.228 para 3.6] and we believe it commands very wide support. *Either* conspiracy to defraud is too wide in its scope (in that it catches agreements to do things which are rightly not criminal) *or* the statutory offences are too narrow (in that they fail to catch certain conduct which *should* be criminal)—or, which is our view, the problem is a combination of the two. On any view, the present position is anomalous and has no place in a coherent criminal law.

The definition of 'to defraud'

3.6 As we stated in paragraphs 2.4 to 2.6, the cases on the meaning of 'to defraud' have given it a broad meaning, so that any dishonest agreement to make a gain at another's expense could form the basis of conspiracy to defraud. We take the view that this definition is *too* broad. In a capitalist society, commercial life revolves around the pursuit of gain for oneself and, as a corollary, others may lose out, whether directly or indirectly. Such behaviour is perfectly legitimate. It is only the element of 'dishonesty' which renders it a criminal fraud. In other words, that element 'does all the work' in assessing whether particular facts fall within the definition of the crime.

3.7 In most cases it will be self-evident that the conduct alleged, if proved, would be dishonest, and the question will be whether that conduct has been proved. Nonetheless, in some cases, the defence will argue that the alleged conduct was not dishonest. There is no statutory definition of dishonesty, so the issue is determined with reference to *Ghosh*. In that case it was held that the fact-finders must be satisfied (a) that the defendant's conduct was dishonest according to the ordinary standards of reasonable and honest people, *and* (b) that the defendant must have realised that it was dishonest according to those standards (as opposed to his or her own standards).

3.8 Activities which would otherwise be legitimate can therefore become fraudulent if a jury is prepared to characterise them as dishonest. Not only does this delegate to the jury the responsibility for defining what conduct is to be regarded as fraudulent, but it leaves prosecutors with an uncommonly broad discretion when they are deciding whether to pursue a conspiracy to defraud case. If, for example, the directors of a company enter into 'industrial espionage' in order to gain the edge over a competitor, they could potentially be prosecuted for conspiracy to defraud, despite the absence of any statutory offence governing such activities. As *Smith and Hogan* states, the offence opens 'a very broad vista of potential criminal liability'.

3.9 In effect, conspiracy to defraud is a "general dishonesty offence", subject only to the irrational requirement of conspiracy. We consider the arguments for and against such offences in Part V below, where we conclude that their disadvantages outweigh their advantages.

In the Consultation Paper which preceded the passage of the Fraud Act 2006, *Fraud Law Reform: Consultation on Proposals for Legislation* (Home Office, 2004) the Government asked the question:

Question 6

Do you agree that all behaviour which is in practice rightly prosecuted as conspiracy to defraud can be prosecuted as fraud under the Bill (or under another existing law), and that conspiracy to defraud can be repealed?

The Government provided their response in May 2005.

HOME OFFICE CRIMINAL POLICY UNIT, *FRAUD LAW REFORM: GOVERNMENT RESPONSE TO CONSULTATIONS*

(2005)

(footnotes omitted)

Repeal of conspiracy to defraud (Question 6)

39. The repeal of Common Law Conspiracy to Defraud was the only proposal to which there was widespread opposition. It is normally fundamental to a codification exercise such as this, that the common law should be repealed in favour of the new statute. A large minority of respondents agreed with the Law Commission that it was illogical that what was legal for one person should be criminal for many, and that the offence is unfairly uncertain, and so wide it has the potential to catch behaviour that should not be criminal. They took the view that the new statutory offences, together with the possibility of charging statutory conspiracy to commit these new offences, and bearing in mind other possible charges—such as the new offence of cheating at gambling that is in the current Gambling Bill—cover all the behaviour that in practice should be covered by the criminal law.

40. However the repeal was opposed by the majority of consultees. The main argument was that, at least until we have experience of how the new offences operate in practice, it would be rash to repeal conspiracy to defraud as it provides flexibility in dealing with a wide variety of frauds. They argued that it was not clear that the new offences could successfully replace it in every case, especially bearing in mind developing technology and possible new types of fraud.

41. It was argued that conspiracy to defraud was well defined and is not tied to economic gain or loss, but only requires that the conduct prejudices another person's rights. That makes it particularly useful in intellectual property cases and in cases where no economic loss has been suffered. An example of the latter was *Terry* [1984] AC 374 HL where the defendants made use of vehicle excise licences in a fraudulent manner. It is also useful in dealing with cases where the fraudulent nature of a transaction only becomes apparent in the context of several other transactions.

42. Some respondents referred to limitations on statutory conspiracy (under the Criminal Law Act 1977)—in particular that the parties to it must intend that the substantive offence will be perpetrated by one or more of the conspirators. This is not required for conspiracy to defraud. In *Hollinshead* for example the defendants conspired to market devices for use by third parties to avoid paying for electricity used. The Court of Appeal held that this did not amount to a conspiracy to commit offences under section 2 of the 1978 Act, as the defendants themselves were not practising the fraud on the electricity companies, but it did constitute conspiracy to defraud. One respondent said that this situation often arose in cases involving intellectual property: for example a group of

people conspire to manufacture counterfeit goods but do not themselves commit any deception in selling them on to another person, who makes the actual public sale.

43. In their 2002 report, the Law Commission suggested that this issue is more appropriately dealt with in the context of their work on assisting and encouraging crime rather than in the Fraud Bill. This work is not yet complete, though it should be published early in 2005.

44. A compromise position was proposed, under which repeal would be enacted but not implemented until after a transitional period during which experience may show it is no longer being used, having been successfully replaced in practice by the new offences. We are not attracted by this approach, which is somewhat untidy and unlikely to work in the absence of a solution to the *Hollinshead* type of case.

45. Bearing in mind in particular the *Hollinshead* type of case, we decided to accept the view of the majority and retain common law conspiracy to defraud for the present. However it remains our long-term aim to repeal this common law crime and we will review the position in the context of the Law Commission's forthcoming report and any action to implement it. This should also allow any final decision to be made in the light of some experience of the Fraud Bill in operation.

In 2005 a major prosecution for conspiracy to defraud collapsed before the jury were asked to consider their verdicts, the trial by that stage having lasted for 21 months. The trial arose out of an investigation into allegations that personnel of London Underground had been corrupted, and that as a result the main defendants had dishonestly enriched themselves out of the public financing for the Jubilee Line extension. The Attorney General referred the case to HM Chief Inspector for the Crown Prosecution Service. In his Report, *Review of the Investigation and Criminal Proceedings Relating to the Jubilee Line Case* (2006) he stated (para. 11.88):

Conspiracy to defraud at common law is an extremely useful weapon for a fraud prosecutor and frequently a course of offending cannot be adequately reflected in an indictment without recourse to it. For example, such a charge avoids the difficulties associated with 'specimen' counts of substantive offences. Not surprisingly, it is frequently used and is the main charge in most SFO prosecutions. However, it can sometimes be resorted to in an attempt to sidestep significant difficulties in the proof of any substantive offence and bridge the gaps in an investigation which has failed to prove more specific offences of dishonesty. Furthermore, as happened in this case, the use of the charge, because of its great breadth, can make potentially relevant a very large body of documentary and other evidence which would not be relevant or admissible in relation to specific statutory offences. The charging of conspiracy to defraud needs therefore to be carefully considered in each case, not only to ensure that it is good in law, but also so as to anticipate the consequences of its use for the length and manageability of any ensuing trial. Conspiracy to defraud should only be used in preference to substantive offences when it can clearly be shown that the available substantive offences are significantly inadequate to reflect the real and demonstrable criminality of the case, as revealed unequivocally by the evidence gathered.

The Fraud Act was passed on November 8, 2006 and unsurprisingly did not abolish the common law offence of conspiracy to defraud (see Ch.11, below).

(b) Conspiracies to corrupt public morals or outrage public decency

Note

Agreements to do these things are certainly criminal conspiracies. They were common law conspiracies before the 1977 Act: see *Knuller v DPP* [1973] A.C. 435. According to s.5(3), above, an agreement to do either of them is still a common law conspiracy if and insofar as corrupting public morals or outraging public decency is a crime in its own right (i.e. a crime if done by one person without any agreement with someone else). If they are offences in their own right, agreements to commit them would be statutory conspiracies to commit those crimes; this was confirmed by the Court of Appeal in *Gibson* [1991] 1 All E.R. 439 as regards outraging public decency.

v. Jurisdiction

Note

Conspiracies are nowadays often international in character. Since "all crime is local" and "The jurisdiction over the crime belongs to the country where the crime is committed . . .": per Lord Haldane L.C. in *MacLeod v Attorney General for New South Wales* [1891] A.C. 455 at 458, and since the essence of conspiracy is the agreement, it might be thought that the only question on jurisdiction is whether the agreement was made in this country. However this is not so. For the purposes of discussion, "international" conspiracies may be divided into two classes: (a) Agreement here to do acts abroad; and (b) Agreement abroad to do acts here.

(a) Agreement here to do acts abroad

In *Board of Trade v Owen* [1957] A.C. 602, the House of Lords held that a conspiracy to commit a crime abroad is not indictable in this country unless the substantive offence, if committed, could be tried here. In the aftermath of the Omagh bombing on 25 August 1998, legislation was introduced primarily to deal with terrorism but also giving the courts jurisdiction to try for conspiracy those who plot in England and Wales to commit offences abroad. The Criminal Justice (Terrorism and Conspiracy) Act 1998 inserts a new s.1A into the Criminal Law Act 1977.

CRIMINAL LAW ACT 1977

1A.—(1) Where each of the following conditions is satisfied in the case of an agreement, this Part of this Act has effect in relation to the agreement as it has effect in relation to an agreement falling within s.1(1) above.

    (2) The first condition is that the pursuit of the agreed course of conduct would at some stage involve—

        (a)   an act by one or more of the parties, or
        (b)   the happening of some other event,
        intended to take place in a country or territory outside the United Kingdom.

    (3) The second condition is that that act or other event constitutes an offence under the law in force in that country or territory.

    (4) The third condition is that the agreement would fall within s.1(1) above as an agreement relating to the commission of an offence but for the fact that the offence would not be an offence triable in England and Wales if committed in accordance with the parties7 intentions.

    (5) The fourth condition is that—

        (a)   a party to the agreement, or a party's agent, did anything in England and Wales in relation to the agreement before its formation, or
        (b)   a party to the agreement became a party in England and Wales (by joining it either in person or through an agent), or
        (c)   a party to the agreement, or a party's agent, did or omitted anything in England and Wales in pursuance of the agreement.

(b) Agreement abroad to do acts here

The Criminal Law Act 1977 makes no specific reference to this, but see the next case.

R. V SANSOM

(1990) 92 Cr. App. R. 115 CA

S and others were convicted of conspiracy to evade the prohibition on the import of cannabis. The appeal was dealt with on the footing that they had agreed while abroad to import into Belgium from Morocco half a ton of cannabis resin. The consignment was to be shipped from Morocco in the vessel Lady Rose and trans-shipped in international waters from the Lady Rose into the fishing boat Danny Boy, on which it would be taken into Belgium. One of the conspirators chartered the Danny Boy in England and sailed it out to meet the Lady Rose. It was contended that on these facts the Court had no jurisdiction to try the appellants for conspiracy.

TAYLOR LJ

. . . A submission was made to the learned judge, and has been repeated on appeal, on behalf of Sansom and Williams that the court had no jurisdiction to try the count of conspiracy. The agreement was alleged to have been made abroad and it was contended that to constitute a triable offence in England there would have to be proven some unlawful act in England in pursuance of the conspiracy. If, as the defence alleged, the Danny Boy was arrested outside territorial waters, no such unlawful act could be proved. The learned judge rejected the submission, basing his decision on *D.P.P. v Boot* [1973] A.C.807. In that case the House of Lords held that a conspiracy entered into abroad could be prosecuted in England if the parties acted in England in concert and in pursuance of the agreement . . .
Lord Salmon said, at p.833F:

'Suppose a case in which evidence existed of a conspiracy hatched abroad by . . . drug pedlars to smuggle large quantities of dangerous drugs on to some stretch of the English coast. Suppose the conspirators came to England for the purpose of carrying out the crime and were detected by the police reconnoitring the place where they proposed to commit it, but doing nothing which by itself would be illegal, it would surely be absurd if the police could not arrest them then and there but had to take the risk of waiting and hoping to be able to catch them as they were actually committing or attempting to commit the crime. Yet that is precisely what the police would have to do if a conspiracy entered into abroad to commit a crime here were not in the circumstances postulated recognised by our law as a criminal offence which our courts had any jurisdiction to try.'

At p.835B–C Lord Salmon went further. There he said:

'It is, unfortunately, by no means unlikely that cases may arise in the future in which there will be conclusive evidence of persons having conspired abroad to commit serious crimes in England and then having done acts here in furtherance of the conspiracy and in preparation for the commission of those crimes yet none of these acts will in itself be unlawful. Although such a case would be very different from the present, if the reasoning upon which I have based this opinion is sound it follows that such persons could properly be arrested and tried for conspiracy in our courts.'

That view was supported by the learned authors of *Smith and Hogan on Criminal Law*, 6th ed. (1988), p.269. They say:

'Whether such a conspiracy is indictable if the parties take no steps in England to implement it has not been decided. It is submitted that the better view is that any of the parties entering the jurisdiction during the continuance of the agreement should be indictable at common law.'

In *Somchai Liangsiriprasert v The Government of the United States of America and Another* [1990] 3 W.L.R. 606, the Privy Council on July 2, 1990 upheld that view. The case concerned a conspiracy to import heroin to the United States from Thailand, the proceeds to be collected in Hong Kong. Lord Griffiths, giving the advice of the Board, stated that in general English criminal law is local in its effect and does not concern itself with crimes abroad. There are exceptions. At p.614 he said:

'There has as yet however been no decision in which it has been held that a conspiracy entered into abroad to commit a crime in England is a common law crime triable in English courts in the absence of any overt act pursuant to the conspiracy taking place in England. There are however a number of dicta in judgments and academic commentaries suggesting that it should be so.'

Lord Griffiths then reviewed the authorities and, at p.620, he continued:

'But why should an overt act be necessary to found jurisdiction? In the case of conspiracy in England the crime is complete once the agreement is made and no further overt act needs be proved as an ingredient of the crime. The only purpose of looking for an overt act in England in the case of a conspiracy entered into abroad can be to establish the link between the conspiracy and England or possibly to show the conspiracy is continuing. But if this can be established by other evidence, for example the taping of conversations between the conspirators showing a firm agreement to commit the crime at some future date, it defeats the preventative purpose of the crime of conspiracy to have to wait until some overt act is performed in pursuance of the conspiracy.

Unfortunately in this century crime has ceased to be largely local in origin and effect. Crime is now established on an international scale and the common law must face this new reality. Their Lordships can find nothing in precedent, comity or good sense that should inhibit the common law from regarding as justiciable in England inchoate crimes committed abroad which are intended to result in the commission of criminal offences in England. Accordingly a conspiracy entered into in Thailand with the intention of committing the criminal offence of trafficking in drugs in Hong Kong is justiciable in Hong Kong even if no overt act pursuant to the conspiracy has yet occurred in Hong Kong.'

Although not binding on this Court, the decision of the Privy Council has of course very strong persuasive force especially when coupled with the earlier *dicta* in *D.P.P. v Doot*. It was argued that *Somchai* referred only to the common law. The present conspiracy was charged as contrary to the Criminal Law Act 1977 which does not in terms deal with extraterritorial conspiracies. We reject that argument for three reasons. First, it cannot have been the intention of Parliament in enacting the 1977 Act to alter the common law rules as to extra-territorial conspiracies without specific words. Secondly, since conspiracies to defraud are not within the scope of the 1977 Act, the appellants' argument would produce the absurdity that the *Somchai* principle would apply to them but not to other conspiracies. Finally, we consider that the Privy Council, knowing that most conspiracies in English law are now covered by the 1977 Act, would specifically have indicated that the important principle they were enunciating in regard to conspiracy only applied to the restricted categories of common law conspiracy now surviving, had that been intended. In our judgment the principle propounded in *Somchai* by Lord Griffiths should now be regarded as the law of England on this point. In the present case there was clear evidence that one of the alleged conspirators, Wilkins, had acted in England in pursuance of the alleged conspiracy which was still subsisting by commissioning the Danny Boy and sailing in her to collect the cannabis from the Lady Rose . . . This ground of appeal therefore fails.

Sansom's Appeal allowed on other grounds

Note

Part I of the Criminal Justice Act 1993 expands the jurisdiction of courts in England and Wales to try most offences of fraud and dishonesty where an element of the actus reus occurs in England and Wales regardless of the whereabouts of the accused at that time. The Act applies to offences under ss.1, 17, 19, 21, 22 and 24A of the Theft Act 1968, ss.1, 6, 9 and 11 of the Fraud Act 2006 and ss.1 to 5, 14, 15, 16, 17, 20 and 21 of the Forgery and Counterfeiting Act 1981. The Act also asserts jurisdiction to try conspiracy (or attempt) to commit any of the above offences or conspiracy to defraud regardless of where the conspiracy (or attempt) takes place provided the court would have jurisdiction to try the substantive offence.

----

3. ENCOURAGING OR ASSISTING OFFENCES

Note

In cl.47 of the Law Commission's *Draft Criminal Code Bill*, which would have codified the existing common law, the Law Commission defined incitement as follows:

"(1) A person is guilty of incitement to commit an offence or offences if—

(a) he incites another to do or cause to be done an act or acts which, if done, will involve the commission of the offence or offences by the other; and

(b) he intends or believes that the other, if he acts as incited,

(c) shall, or will do so with the fault required for the offence or offences."

This would have been a fairly brief and simple definition of the offence of incitement involving little complexity. In their Report, *Inchoate Liability for Assisting and Encouraging Crime* (TSO, 2006), Law Com. No.300, the Law Commission proposed the abolition of the common law offence of incitement and its replacement with two new statutory inchoate offences which would prohibit assisting and encouraging crime.

LAW COMMISSION, *INCHOATE LIABILITY FOR ASSISTING AND ENCOURAGING CRIME* (TSO, 2006), LAW COM. NO.2006

(footnotes omitted)

1.1 The issue of criminal liability for encouraging or assisting another person to commit an offence is important, complex and difficult. It is important because it is very common for offences to involve two or more participants only some of whom are actual perpetrators of the offence as opposed to encouraging or assisting its commission.

1.2 The issue is also important because it is often the prime movers behind criminal ventures, for example drug or people traffickers, who take good care to distance themselves from the commission of the offences that they seek to encourage or assist. Recent advances in technology, together with the enhanced financial resources of career criminals, have facilitated this process.

1.3 This is the first of two reports in which we consider the circumstances in which a person ('D') ought to be criminally liable for encouraging or assisting another person ('P') to commit an offence. A substantial portion of this report focuses on what we consider to be a major defect of the common law. At common law if D *encourages* P to commit an offence that subsequently P does not commit or attempt to commit, D may nevertheless be criminally liable [by virtue of having committed the common law offence of incitement]. By contrast, if D *assists* P to commit an offence, D incurs no criminal liability at common law if subsequently P, for whatever reason, does not commit or attempt to commit the offence:

Example 1A
D, in return for payment, lends a van to P believing that P will use the van in order to commit a robbery. The police arrest P in connection with another matter before P can even attempt to commit the robbery.

D is not criminally liable despite the fact that he or she intended to bring about harm and, by lending the van to P, has manifested that intention. If, however, in addition to giving P the van, D had uttered words encouraging P to rob V, D would be guilty of incitement to commit robbery. The common law appears to treat words more seriously than deeds. Yet, it might be thought that seeking to bring about harm by assisting a person to commit an offence is as culpable as seeking to do so by means of encouragement.

1.4 Increasingly, the police, through the gathering of intelligence, are able to identify preliminary acts of assistance by D before P commits or attempts to commit the principal offence. Yet, the common law only partially reflects this significant development. As a result, if D assists but does not encourage P to commit an offence, the police may have to forego at least some of the advantages of more sophisticated and effective methods of investigation by having to wait until P commits or attempts to commit the offence before they can proceed against D. [It is different if P and D agree to commit an offence. D and P are guilty of conspiracy and the offence is committed as soon as the agreement is concluded. Accordingly, the police can arrest and charge both P and D without having to wait for the offence to be committed or attempted.]

1.5 In contrast to acts of assistance, if D encourages P to commit an offence which P does not go on to commit, D will be guilty of incitement provided he or she satisfies the fault element of the offence. However, the offence of incitement has a number of unsatisfactory features:

(1) there is uncertainty as to whether it must be D's purpose that P should commit the offence that D is inciting;

(2) the fault element of the offence has been distorted by decisions of the Court of Appeal [see *Curr* [1968] 2 Q.B. 944; *Shaw* [1994] Crim.L.R. 365]. These decisions have focused, wrongly, on the state of mind of P rather than on D's state of mind;

(3) there is uncertainty as to whether and, if so, to what extent it is a defence to act in order to prevent the commission of an offence or to prevent or limit the occurrence of harm;

(4) there is uncertainty as to the circumstances in which D is liable for inciting P to do an act which, if done by P, would not involve P committing an offence, for example because P is under the age of criminal responsibility or lacks a guilty mind;

(5) the rules governing D's liability in cases where D incites P to commit an inchoate offence have resulted in absurd distinctions;

(6) D may have a defence if the offence that he or she incites is impossible to commit whereas impossibility is not a defence to other inchoate offences, apart from common law conspiracies.

The offence of incitement is therefore in need of clarification and reform.

Note

A simple solution to the lacuna identified by the Law Commission would have been to introduce a new and simple offence of facilitation. Instead a more ambitious approach was adopted with questionable results. The Serious Crime Act was enacted on 30 October 2007. This does not adopt verbatim the Law Commission Draft Bill which accompanied its Report but it does replicate its complexity. Part 2, which came into force on 1 October 2008, abolishes the common law offence of incitement and replaces it with three new offences which will also deal with the lacuna (facilitation without encouragement) identified by the Law Commission. The Act also includes a defence and an exemption from liability.

Under the new offences, D's liability relates to the (hypothetical) offence he intended or believed would be committed by P. If the offence is committed D will be an accessory to it and additionally liable under the law on secondary liability. It is unfortunate that this provision has the effect of creating an extensive overlap with the law on secondary participation dealt with in Ch.6 above. Some of the confusion and overlap might have been mitigated had the Government enacted the Law Commission's recommendations in *Participating in Crime* (TSO, 2007), Law Com. No.305. The two reports were meant to form a package for the reform of incitement and secondary liability and would have led to the creation of a total of eight offences. The widening of liability under the offences of encouraging and assisting crime was to be counterbalanced by a narrowing of secondary liability. The piecemeal approach to reform adopted by the Government, however, is hardly desirable and will only lead to confusion in an area of law which is already confused. It is seriously disappointing that an enactment which seeks to reform and clarify one area of the law, incitement, should lead to confusion in another, secondary participation.

The main provisions offences and defences are outlined below. Sections 47 and 65–67 apply to all three offences but will be examined in detail only in relation to the s.44 offence. When considering the offences under ss.45 and 46, refer back to the analysis under s.44.

(a) Intentionally encouraging or assisting an offence

44 Intentionally encouraging or assisting an offence

(1) A person commits an offence if—

    (a) he does an act capable of encouraging or assisting the commission of an offence; and

    (b) he intends to encourage or assist its commission.

(2) But he is not to be taken to have intended to encourage or assist the commission of an offence merely because such encouragement or assistance was a foreseeable consequence of his act.

47 Proving an offence under this Part

(1) Sections 44, 45 and 46 are to be read in accordance with this section.

(2) If it is alleged under section 44(1)(b) that a person (D) intended to encourage or assist the commission of an offence, it is sufficient to prove that he intended to encourage or assist the doing of an act which would amount to the commission of that offence.

(3) If it is alleged under section 45(b) that a person (D) believed that an offence would be committed and that his act would encourage or assist its commission, it is sufficient to prove that he believed—

    (a) that an act would be done which would amount to the commission of that offence; and

    (b) that his act would encourage or assist the doing of that act.

(4) If it is alleged under section 46(1)(b) that a person (D) believed that one or more of a number of offences would be committed and that his act would encourage or assist the commission of one or more of them, it is sufficient to prove that he believed—

    (a) that one or more of a number of acts would be done which would amount to the commission of one or more of those offences; and

    (b) that his act would encourage or assist the doing of one or more of those acts.

(5) In proving for the purposes of this section whether an act is one which, if done, would amount to the commission of an offence—

    (a) if the offence is one requiring proof of fault, it must be proved that—

        (i) D believed that, were the act to be done, it would be done with that fault;

        (ii) D was reckless as to whether or not it would be done with that fault; or

        (iii) D's state of mind was such that, were he to do it, it would be done with that fault; and

    (b) if the offence is one requiring proof of particular circumstances or consequences (or both), it must be proved that—

        (i) D believed that, were the act to be done, it would be done in those circumstances or with those consequences; or

        (ii) D was reckless as to whether or not it would be done in those circumstances or with those consequences.

(6) For the purposes of subsection (5)(a)(iii), D is to be assumed to be able to do the act in question.

(7) In the case of an offence under section 44—

    (a) subsection (5)(b)(i) is to be read as if the reference to 'D believed' were a reference to 'D intended or believed'; but

    (b) D is not to be taken to have intended that an act would be done in particular circumstances or with particular consequences merely because its being done in those circumstances or with those consequences was a foreseeable consequence of his act of encouragement or assistance.

(8) Reference in this section to the doing of an act includes reference to—

    (a) a failure to act;

    (b) the continuation of an act that has already begun;

    (c) an attempt to do an act (except an act amounting to the commission of the offence of attempting to commit another offence).

(9) In the remaining provisions of this Part (unless otherwise provided) a reference to the anticipated offence is—

    (a) in relation to an offence under section 44, a reference to the offence mentioned in subsection (2); and

    (b) in relation to an offence under section 45, a reference to the offence mentioned in subsection (3).

65 Being capable of encouraging or assisting

(1) A reference in this Part to a person's doing an act that is capable of encouraging the commission of an offence includes a reference to his doing so by threatening another person or otherwise putting pressure on another person to commit the offence.

(2) A reference in this Part to a person's doing an act that is capable of encouraging or assisting the commission of an offence includes a reference to his doing so by—

    (a) taking steps to reduce the possibility of criminal proceedings being brought in respect of that offence;

    (b) failing to take reasonable steps to discharge a duty.

(3) But a person is not to be regarded as doing an act that is capable of encouraging or assisting the commission of an offence merely because he fails to respond to a constable's request for assistance in preventing a breach of the peace.

66 Indirectly encouraging or assisting

If a person (D1) arranges for a person (D2) to do an act that is capable of encouraging or assisting the commission of an offence, and D2 does the act, D1 is also to be treated for the purposes of this Part as having done it.

67 Course of conduct

A reference in this Part to an act includes a reference to a course of conduct, and a reference to doing an act is to be read accordingly.

Notes

1.   Whether or not D's act was "capable" of encouraging or assisting P to commit a crime, is a question of fact.

2.   What "encouraging or assisting" means will be a matter for the jury or magistrates to determine but s.65(1) makes clear that encouraging includes threatening or putting pressure on another person to commit an offence. The focus of the offence is on D's act or acts as the offence is committed when D does the relevant act which is capable of encouraging or assisting the commission of an offence with the necessary intent. There is no need for P to be aware of the encouragement or assistance or to have acted in response to it as liability arises where D's act is capable of encouraging or assisting. This extends the liability beyond that which the law of incitement covered as this offence required that the incitement be communicated to someone. For example, if D posts a letter to P encouraging him to commit an offence, or providing him with information that would assist him in committing an offence, but the letter never arrives, D will nonetheless be liable to conviction under s.44.

3.   "Act" includes a course of conduct (s.67). It also includes "taking steps to reduce the possibility

of criminal proceedings being brought in respect of that offence" (s.65(2)(a)) which, although the statute is silent on the matter, logic dictates must be an act done before the relevant offence is committed. For example, if D being aware that P is going burgle a house, arranges for a getaway car to be available for him and lets him know this before P enters the house, this would be an act capable of encouraging or assisting P in the commission of the burglary. By contrast if D comes out of the house having burgled it, and D assists him at that point in making his getaway by lending him his car, this act, having occurred after the burglary took place, could not be capable or encouraging or assisting P in the commission of the robbery.

4. The "act" requirement may also be satisfied by D "failing to take reasonable steps to discharge a duty" (s.65(2)(b)). An example given by the Law Commission is that of a disgruntled security guard, D, who omits to turn on a burglar alarm with the intention of assisting P to burgle the premises of D's employer. The fact the offence requires proof of an ulterior intent means that mere inadvertence, for example simply forgetting to switch the alarm on, will not give rise to liability on the part of D.

5. D may indirectly encourage or assist the commission of an offence where D arranges for another, E, to do an act capable of encouraging or assisting P to commit an offence, and E does so, then D will be treated as having done E's act (s.66). The Explanatory Notes give the example of a gang leader D who instructs a member of his gang E to encourage another person P to kill V.

6. D may encourage or assist the commission of another inchoate offence, for example D encourages E to solicit P to commit murder (soliciting murder is an offence under s.4 of the Offences Against the Person Act 1861).

7. This is an offence which requires direct intent; oblique intent will not suffice (see s.44(2)). Where the offence D assists or encourages is an offence requiring proof of fault it must be proved that D either: (i) intended believed that P would have the necessary fault; or (ii) was reckless whether or not P would have the necessary fault; or (iii) if D were to do the act himself he would have the necessary fault (s.47(5)(a)). Paragraph (iii) is designed to cover the situation where P may lack the requisite mens rea for the offence D has assisted or encouraged but D would have had the mens rea had he done the act himself. Where this limb is relied upon D is to be assumed to be able to do the relevant act (i.e. there is no defence of impossibility—see s.47(6)). The Explanatory Notes provide an example of these very particular circumstances which are designed to prevent D from evading liability purely because it is impossible for him/her to commit the offence (para.159):

    "D (a woman) encourages P to penetrate V with his penis (rape) and believes that if P were to do so, it would be without V's consent. P reasonably believes that V does consent so does not have the mental element required for conviction of rape. Therefore, D's fault is determined under section 47(5)(a)(iii) in that if she were to commit the act, she would do it with the fault required. However it is not possible for a woman to commit the act of penetration with a penis so were it not for this subsection, D would escape liability."

8. Where the offence D assists or encourages requires proof of particular consequences or circumstances, it must be proved that D either intended or believed that were the act to be done, it would be done in those circumstances or with those consequences, or D was reckless thereto (s.47(5)(b)). The Explanatory Notes to the Act further explain that requiring some degree of belief in relation to the circumstances ensures that D will not be guilty of an offence of encouraging

or assisting a strict liability offence unless he believes or is reckless as to whether those circumstances exist. The following example is provided (para.156):

> "D asks P to drive him home from the pub as he has had too much to drink. P is insured to drive D's car but unknown to D and P, P was disqualified from driving the day before. P is committing the principal offence of driving whilst disqualified, despite the fact he is not aware that he is disqualified, as this is an offence of strict liability. However it would not be fair to hold D liable in such circumstances."

In respect of consequences, the Explanatory Notes provide the following example (para.157):

> "D gives P a baseball bat and intends P to use it to inflict minor bodily harm on V. P however uses the bat to attack V and intentionally kills V. It would not be fair to hold D liable for encouraging and assisting murder, unless he also believes or is reckless as to whether V will be killed."

9. If D's act is capable of encouraging or assisting the commission of a number of offences, D can be charged with the s.44 offence in respect of each offence he intends to encourage or assist to be committed (s.49(2)).

(b) Encouraging or assisting an offence believing it will be committed

45 Encouraging or assisting an offence believing it will be committed

A person commits an offence if—

   (a) he does an act capable of encouraging or assisting the commission of an offence; and

   (b) he believes—

      (i) that the offence will be committed; and
      (ii) that his act will encourage or assist its commission.

Notes

1. This offence covers the situation where D may not intend that a particular offence be committed but he believes both that it will be committed and that his act will encourage or assist its commission. This would cover the situation where D supplies a weapon to P believing he is going to use it to commit murder but being quite indifferent whether or not he does as his sole concern is to make a profit from the sale.

2. If D's act is capable of encouraging or assisting the commission of a number of offences, D can be charged with the s.45 offence in respect of each offence he believes will be encouraged or assisted to be committed (s.49(2)). Thus where D lends P a crowbar believing D will use it to break into houses to steal, D could be liable for each separate burglary P commits.

3. D will not be liable for the s.45 offence where he does an act believing it will encourage or assist P to commit another inchoate offence (as listed in Sch.3; see s.49(4); see further Spencer and Virgo, below).

(c) Encouraging or assisting offences believing one or more will be committed

46 Encouraging or assisting offences believing one or more will be committed

(1) A person commits an offence if—

    (a) he does an act capable of encouraging or assisting the commission of one or more of a number of offences; and

    (b) he believes—

        (i) that one or more of those offences will be committed (but has no belief as to which); and

        (ii) that his act will encourage or assist the commission of one or more of them.

(2) It is immaterial for the purposes of subsection (1)(b)(ii) whether the person has any belief as to which offence will be encouraged or assisted.

Notes

1. This offence covers the situation where D may not intend that a particular offence be committed but he believes both that one or more offences will be committed and that his act will assist or encourage the commission or one or more of them. It does not matter whether he has any belief as to which offence his act will assist or encourage (s.46(2)). For example, where D drives P to V's house knowing that P is going to wreak revenge on V but not knowing whether he is going to beat up V, kill him or burn his house (cf. *Maxwell* v *DPP for Northern Ireland*, above, p.325).

2. The difference, however, from the *Maxwell* situation is that there a substantive offence is committed and D is charged as an accessory to it whereas for this offence no substantive offence is committed. The focus is upon D's mens rea—the offences he believed would be committed. In *Saddique* [2013] EWCA Crim 1150 D had supplied various chemical cutting agents knowing they would assist the recipient drug dealers in supplying Class A or Class B drugs without knowing (and perhaps not wanting to know) which. In charging D the prosecution were required toidentify each offence D's act was capable of encouraging or assisting and charge a separate count on the indictment in respect of each. For D to be convicted of any particular count it had be proved that he believed that that particular offence would be committed with the relevant fault; or that one or more of the specified offences would be committed but he had no belief as to which. Essentially D is leaving the decision as to which offence is committed to P whom he is assisting or encouraging. D may be convicted even though P has no intention to commit any offence provided D believes (even though wrongly) that P will commit an offence.

3. D will not be liable for the s.46 offence where he does an act believing it will encourage or assist P to commit one or more other inchoate offence (as listed in Sch.3; see s.49(4)).

(d) Defence of acting reasonably

50 Defence of acting reasonably

(1) A person is not guilty of an offence under this Part if he proves—

    (a) that he knew certain circumstances existed; and

    (b) that it was reasonable for him to act as he did in those circumstances.

(2) A person is not guilty of an offence under this Part if he proves—

(a)   that he believed certain circumstances to exist;
(b)   that his belief was reasonable; and
(c)   that it was reasonable for him to act as he did in the circumstances as he believed them to be.

(3) Factors to be considered in determining whether it was reasonable for a person to act as he did include—

(a)   the seriousness of the anticipated offence (or, in the case of an offence under section 46, the offences specified in the indictment);
(b)   any purpose for which he claims to have been acting;
(c)   any authority by which he claims to have been acting.

Note

It is difficult to conceive of circumstances where D charged with the s.44 offence which requires intention, could rely on this defence. It is notable that the Explanatory Notes to the Act provide no examples of when the defence could be raised. The Law Commission did not recommend the defence to be available for the s.44 offence. The Law Commission provided three examples (at para.A.63) of when reliance might be placed on the defence only one of which merits reproduction, the other two being bizarre:

> D, a motorist, changes motorway lanes to allow a following motorist (P) to overtake, even though D knows that P is speeding.

(e) Protective offences: victims not liable

51 Protective offences: victims not liable

(1) In the case of protective offences, a person does not commit an offence under this Part by reference to such an offence if—

(a)   he falls within the protected category; and
(b)   he is the person in respect of whom the protective offence was committed or would have been if it had been committed.

(2) 'Protective offence' means an offence that exists (wholly or in part) for the protection of a particular category of persons ('the protected category').

Note

This provision puts a statutory footing on the "*Tyrrell* principle" (see above, p.343). The Explanatory Notes provide the following example (para.180):

> D is a 12 year old girl and encourages P, a 40 year old man to have sex with her. P does not attempt to have sex with D. D cannot be liable of encouraging or assisting child rape despite the fact it is her intent that P have sexual intercourse with a child under 13 (child rape) because she would be considered the "victim" of that offence had it taken place and the offence of child rape was enacted to protect children under the age of 13.

(f) Jurisdiction

Notes

1. D may be found guilty of an offence under ss.44, 45 or 46 if he anticipates that the conduct he encourages or assists will take place wholly or partly in England and Wales regardless of where D is at the time (s.52(1)). The Explanatory Notes provide the following example (para.183):

    > D in Belgium sends a number of emails to P in London, encouraging him to plant a bomb on the tube. D can be prosecuted in England and Wales . . . despite the fact he was outside the jurisdiction when he did his act.

2. The opposite situation, of D being in England and Wales but encouraging or assisting the commission of an offence outside England and Wales, may give rise to liability (see s.52(2) and Sch.4). There are three situations specified. The first covers offences for which P could be tried in England and Wales (Sch.4 para.1). For example, D in England, communicates with P who is a British citizen living abroad, encouraging P to kill V living in the same country. Under English law (see s.9 of the Offences Against the Person Act 1861) murder committed by a British citizen is punishable in English courts wherever it is committed. The second situation applies where D acts wholly or partly in England and Wales and although the offence he encourages or assists might take place outside England and Wales, it is an offence under the law of that place (Sch.14 para.2). For example, D in England sends an email to P in Spain containing details of how to disarm an alarm system used by a bank in Madrid. D intends to assist P to rob the bank. The third situation arises where D, outside England and Wales, encourages or assists P to commit an offence (also outside England and Wales), but the courts in England and Wales would have jurisdiction if D had himself committed the anticipated offence (Sch.14 para.3). The Explanatory Notes give the following example (para.191):

    > D (a British citizen) in Canada sends a parcel of poison to P in France encouraging him to use it to murder V (also in France). It would be possible to try D in England because he is a British citizen and the anticipated principal offence (murder) is one which could be tried in England, Wales or Northern Ireland as it would be committed by a British citizen.

(g) Critique

Note

The new offences and ancillary provisions have not met with critical acclaim. It is fair to say that the provisions in the Serious Crime Act have been lambasted as some of the most ill-conceived pieces of recent criminal justice legislation. The following two extracts are examples of the criticism levelled at these new offences.

D. ORMEROD AND R. FORTSON, "SERIOUS CRIME ACT 2007: THE PART 2 OFFENCES"

[2009] Crim. L.R. 389, 414

We conclude that these provisions are some of the worst criminal provisions to fall from Parliament in recent years, a view shared by others: *Blackstone's Criminal Practice* (2009) describes them as containing 'inordinately complex interpretative, evidential, procedural, limitational, jurisdictional, consequential and sentencing provisions, spread over 18 sections and two schedules'. These are offences of breathtaking scope and complexity. They constitute both an interpretative nightmare and a prosecutor's dream.

Four possible outcomes of Pt 2 are, we submit, foreseeable: (1) that Pt 2 offences are frequently charged because their reach is too attractive for prosecutors to resist, (2) that Pt 2 offences are rarely charged by reason of their complexity, (3) that judges discourage the use of Pt 2 offences on the grounds that the language of that part is so impenetrable that it is preferable to make do with 'tried and tested' offences either in the form of secondary liability or in broad-ranging substantive offences where applicable, and (4) that an already overburdened appeal process is further burdened.

J. SPENCER AND G. VIRGO, "ENCOURAGING AND ASSISTING CRIME: LEGISLATE IN HASTE, REPENT AT LEISURE"

[2008] 9 Archbold News 7

The first and most obvious problem about this piece of legislation is that it is so long. To rewrite this area of the law, Part II of the Serious Crime Act employs 24 sections that use between them no less than 3,458 words—or 5,130 if you count the attendant Schedule: a block of text as big as an article in a law review, and over three times the size of the Criminal Attempts Act 1981.

The main reason for the daunting size of this piece of legislation is that the approach it takes to the problem it is supposed to solve is a complicated one: more complicated, surely, than was necessary.

The gap in the previous law that had been identified, and which this legislation was designed to fill, was the fact that whereas criminal liability existed at the inchoate level for incitement, there was no inchoate liability for facilitation. So if A said to B, 'Go and burgle X's house', A could be prosecuted for incitement, whether B then carried out the burglary or not; whereas if A obtained for B, whom he knew to be a burglar, a copy of X's keys, A could be prosecuted for no criminal offence unless the burglary was then committed, when he would be liable as an accessory to B's completed crime, If this gap in the law was worth filling, which it surely was, then the simple solution would have been to leave incitement well alone and just create a new inchoate offence of facilitation to supplement it. But instead of that, Part II of the Serious Crime Act has abolished the common law offence of incitement—which everybody understood and nobody much criticised—and has created a new form of inchoate liability that is designed to cover incitement and facilitation too. To make matters even more complicated, a number of statutory offences of inciting specific crimes are preserved.

And then to add to the complexity, the new form of inchoate liability does not consist of one offence, but three. . . . These three offences differ from each other not only by reason of the mental element involved, but also, and rather less obviously, by reason of the actus reus; because although the offence contained in s.44 is committed by encouraging or assisting any offence at all, the other two do not apply where what was encouraged or assisted was one of the offences set out in Sch.3: a list of 50 different offences, to which (of course!) the Act allows the Secretary of State to add or subtract at will. This distinction in the range of the three offences created by ss.44 to 45 is not obvious to the reader, because instead of being spelt out in the body of those sections, it is buried, almost out of sight, in the depths of s.49, which the marginal note entitles 'supplemental provisions'. . .

However, it is not only the tripartite scheme that makes this legislation less than 'user-friendly'. It is also the style of drafting, which is over-detailed, convoluted and unreadable. Of provisions that are hard to understand a number of examples could be given, but for present purposes two will do.

The first is s.56, which is entitled 'Persons who may be perpetrators or encouragers etc.', and is as follows:

(1) In proceedings for an offence under this Part ('the inchoate offence') the defendant may be convicted if—

    (a)   it is proved that he must have committed the inchoate offence or the anticipated offence; but
    (b)   it is not proved which of those offences he committed,

(2) For the purposes of this section, a person is not to be treated as having committed the anticipated offence merely because he aided, abetted, counselled or procured its commission,

(3) In relation to an offence under section 46. a reference in this section to the anticipated offence is to be read as a reference to an offence specified in the indictment

According to the Explanatory Note, 'This section sets out that If an anticipated offence has been committed and it cannot be proved whether the person has either encouraged or assisted the offence on the one hand, or committed the offence as a principal on the other, he can be convicted of an offence in section 44, 45 or 46'. If that is what is meant, then why could section 56 not have said so, in something like those words? And if the rule it lays down is a good one, why, one wonders, was it necessary to put beyond the reach of it the defendant who, at trial, is shown to be guilty of the 'anticipated offence', but as an accessory rather than as a principal?

The second and worse example of impenetrable drafting is section 47. Entitled 'Proving an offence under this Part', this section uses nine subsections and 587 words to (in effect) extend the reach of the offences created by sections 44 to 46, This it does, in essence, by saying that you are to be treated as encouraging or assisting the commission of an offence when you encourage or assist another person in the 'doing an act' that constitutes an *actus reus*, and to that end, attempts in s.47(8) to nail down the concept of 'the doing of an act'. This says:

(8) Reference in this section to the doing of an act includes reference to—

   (a)   a failure to act;
   (b)   the continuation of an act that has already begun;
   (c)   an attempt to do an act (except an act amounting to the commission of the offence of attempting to commit another offence).

Can any reader of this paper make sense of the wording of subsection (c)? The authors of this article cannot—and think that if anybody can, they deserve to win a prize.

The general complexity of the new legislation is further illustrated by the following hypothetical example, which also relates to s.47.

Andrew offers his girl-friend. Brenda, a necklace which he has stolen. Andrew thinks that Brenda believes he has acquired the necklace honestly, but in fact she knows he has stolen it.

Under the common law offence of incitement this is more or less straightforward. Andrew was not guilty because he did not think that Brenda would commit an offence of handling stolen goods when she received the necklace, because he thinks that she neither knows nor believes that the necklace is stolen. But under the Serious Crime Act the law is much more complex and produces what is surely an unsatisfactory result.

The mode of analysis now proceeds as follows, Andrew is encouraging Brenda to handle goods which are stolen, and at first sight he does not intend to encourage the offence of handling stolen goods under s.44 and neither does he believe that this offence will be committed under s.45.

However, s.47(2) states that, for the purposes of s.44 'it is sufficient to prove that he intended to encourage or assist the doing of an act which would amount to the commission of that offence'. Andrew does intend to encourage and assist Brenda to commit the act of handling stolen goods, so this provision applies. But it is then necessary to consider s.47(5) which identifies, with an extraordinary wealth of detail, what is meant by an act which 'would amount to the commission of an offence'. If the substantive offence is one requiring proof of fault then according to this provision it seems that three alternative mental states need to be considered—anyone of which, if present, would make Andrew guilty:

(1) Andrew believes that if Brenda does handle the goods she will know or believe that they are stolen. Andrew does not believe this.

(2) Andrew is reckless as to whether or not Brenda will know or believe that the goods are stolen. Andrew does not suspect this, so this will not be established either.

(3) Andrew's state of mind is such that, if he were to handle the stolen goods, he would know or believe that they are stolen. Andrew does know that they were stolen and so he will be guilty of the offence of encouraging or assisting a crime even though he does not intend the offence to be committed or believe that it will be committed.

So you can be guilty of intentionally encouraging or assisting an offence if you only intend the *actus reus* of the substantive offence to be committed and you have the *mens rea* for that offence, but you do not think the party you are encouraging or assisting will commit the offence. This is, surely, a piece of quite unnecessary criminalisation. Andrew will, anyway, presumably be the thief or will be guilty of handling stolen goods in his own right. Why is it necessary to expand his criminal liability like this? And, secondly, assuming it is necessary, why has Parliament chosen to do this in such a convoluted way? The task of the judge who has to direct the jury on provisions such as these will be anything but easy.

And yet for all its length and complication and excessive detail, Part II of the Serious Crime Act fails to deal with one important point of doubt, which is the issue of impossibility. At common law, it will be remembered, a defendant was not guilty of any of the three inchoate offences if the crime that he envisaged was impossible. So if, for example, the intended murder victim had, unknown to those who were compassing his death, already died, they could not be convicted of incitement to murder, or conspiracy to murder, or attempt to murder. In 1981, the Criminal Attempts Act explicitly reversed this rule in respect of conspiracy and attempt, but left the position with incitement as it was. That the 'impossibility rule' apparently continued to apply to incitement when it had been abolished for conspiracy and attempt was as an obvious anomaly, and was, indeed, one of the few points about the crime of incitement that was generally thought to be unsatisfactory. In the light of this, it might have been expected that legislation designed to replace the common law offence of incitement would make it plain beyond any doubt that the new inchoate offence, like the revamped offences of conspiracy and attempt, could be committed even where the offence in contemplation was impossible. But nowhere in Part II of the Serious Crime Act is such a provision to be found, and it is open to the defendant to argue that Parliament intended the 'impossibility rule' to apply to the new offences, as it did to the old one. . .

As the person who in 1987 identified the gap in the law that this legislation seeks to fill, the first author of this paper ought to be gratified that it has done so. But when he looks at this new law he feels, alas, like a man who learns in later life that the consequence of an unwise youthful one-night stand has been the birth of a juvenile delinquent.

4. IMPOSSIBILITY IN RELATION TO INCHOATE OFFENCES

Note

This section deals with the position where what D attempts to do, or conspires with another to do, or encourages or assists another to do is in some respects impossible. The question is, should that mean that D is not guilty as charged, even if all the other elements of attempt, incitement or conspiracy are present? It is evident that the answer, whatever it is, should not differ depending upon which inchoate offence is involved. The Law Commission's *Draft Criminal Code Bill*, cl.50(1) proposed, "A person may be guilty of incitement conspiracy or attempt to commit an offence, although the commission of the offence is impossible, if it would be possible in the circumstances which he believes or hopes exist or will exist at the relevant time." This does not reflect the present law, which has different answers for the various inchoate offences. This is because: (1) the leading case, *Haughton v Smith*, below, set out the law on impossible attempts in a way which was widely regarded as unsatisfactory; (2) it was subsequently decided that that unsatisfactory law applied to the other inchoate offences also; but (3) statutory attempts to rectify the position apply only to attempts and statutory conspiracy. Common law conspiracy continues to be governed by the principles enunciated in *Haughton v Smith*. The position in respect of encouraging or assisting offences appears to be that if D's act is incapable of providing encouragement or assistance to P, even though D intended to assist or encourage, he cannot be guilty of one of the Serious Crime Act 2007 offences.

i. Attempt

Note

No one attempts to do that which he knows to be impossible (the same can be said of conspiring). Anyone who appears to do so is therefore making a mistake of some sort. The kinds of mistake possibly involved are three.

1. He mistakes the criminal law, and assumes that it prohibits what he is aiming at. Since the criminal law is not interested in his projected conduct, it follows that it will not punish him for achieving what he desires; a fortiori if he merely goes some way towards achieving it. The fact that he believes he is defying the law can make no difference. There has never been any liability where this kind of mistake is involved, and that is still the position. An example would be where D, knowing he has English lace, and thinking the law prohibits the import of English lace without payment of duty, attempts to avoid the payment of duty on his lace.

2. Where, because of a mistake about the facts, D believes that the factual result he wishes is possible of attainment, it is necessary to distinguish two situations, namely, inadequacy of means and absolute impossibility. The former arises where, e.g. D tries to kill someone with a dose of poison which is too small to kill, or tries to shoot someone out of the range of his gun, or tries to break into a safe which is too strong for the tools he uses. In these cases of "inadequate means", there may be an attempt, but the House of Lords in *Haughton v Smith*, below denied that it could be an attempt if what D attempted was absolutely impossible, as where the subject matter did not exist or did not exist in the form he imagined, e.g. where D attempted to take money from a pocket or purse which contained no money, or where D attempted to deceive a person who knew the truth and could not be deceived.

3. Where because of a mistake about the facts, D believes that the factual result he wishes is criminal, e.g. D wishes to smuggle in French lace, on which he knows that duty is payable, but the lace in his possession is in fact English lace, on which no duty is payable; or D wishes to handle stolen goods, but the goods involved in his plan are not stolen. There was controversy about this class of mistake, and this handling non-stolen goods problem received different answers in cases from Commonwealth and American jurisdictions. This particular problem was involved in *Haughton v Smith*, and the House decided that that particular mistake, and all mistakes in this class, prevented D's conduct from being an attempt.

HAUGHTON V SMITH

[1975] A.C. 746 HL

A van load of stolen meat was intercepted by the police, and allowed to continue its journey with two policemen concealed inside. S later did acts amounting to handling the meat. On the view that the goods' restoration to lawful custody meant that they were no longer stolen (see below, p.718), S was not charged with handling stolen goods, but with attempting to handle stolen goods contrary to s.22 of the Theft Act 1968 (see below, p.717). He was convicted, his appeal was allowed by the Court of Appeal, and the prosecution further appealed.

LORD HAILSHAM OF ST. MARYLEBONE, LC

I was at first inclined to think that s.22 of the Theft Act 1968 was drafted in such a way as to permit the construction that to be stolen for the purpose of s.22(1) it was sufficient that the goods had been stolen without continuing to be stolen at the time of the handling, provided, of course, that the accused believed them at the time of the handling to be stolen. I thought that the expression 'believed' in the subsection aided the view that it could cover a state of facts where the defendant believed the goods to be stolen when they were not in fact still stolen at that moment of time. But, on consideration, I am sure that this would be a false construction, and that the expression 'believed' was inserted to guard against acquittals which had taken place under the former Larceny Act when it was necessary to prove knowledge that the goods were stolen and belief was not enough. If I were not already certain that this was the true meaning of s.22(1), the provisions of s.24, and, in particular, s.24(3), would, I think, clinch the matter. In my view, it is plain that, in order to constitute the offence of handling, the goods specified in the particulars of offence must not only be believed to be stolen, but actually continue to be stolen goods at the moment of handling. Once this is accepted as the true construction of the section, I do not think that it is possible to convert a completed act of handling, which is not itself criminal because it was not the handling of stolen goods, into a criminal act by the simple device of alleging that it was an attempt to handle stolen goods on the ground that at the time of handling the accused falsely believed them still to be stolen. In my opinion, this would be for the courts to manufacture a new criminal offence not authorised by the legislature.

This would be enough to decide the result of this appeal, but both counsel invited us to take a wider view of our obligations, and, since the question was discussed by the Court of Appeal in general terms and since I believe that the result of our decision is to overrule a number of decided cases, at least to some extent, I feel bound to accede to this invitation. The question certified by the Court of Appeal was:

'If stolen goods are returned to lawful custody and thus cease to be stolen by virtue of s.24(3) of the Theft Act 1968 can a person who subsequently dishonestly handles goods believing them to be stolen be guilty of the offence of attempting to handle stolen goods?'

I have already given a negative answer to this question, but the range of the discussion before us demands a wider consideration of the principles involved . . .

I note that in the New Zealand case of *R. v Donnelly* [1970] N.Z.L.R. 980, which, except in so far as it relates to the construction of the relevant New Zealand statutes, is very much on all fours with this, Turner J., adopts a six-fold classification. He says, at p.990:

'He who sets out to commit a crime may in the event fall short of the complete commission of that crime for any one of a number of reasons. *First*, he may, of course, simply change his mind before committing any act sufficiently overt to amount to an attempt. *Second*, he may change his mind, but too late to deny that he had got so far as an attempt. *Third*, he may be prevented by some outside agency from doing some act necessary to complete commission of the crime—as when a police officer interrupts him while he is endeavouring to force the window open, but before he has broken into the premises. *Fourth*, he may suffer no such outside interference, but may fail to complete the commission of the crime through ineptitude, inefficiency or insufficient means. The jemmy which he has brought with him may not be strong enough to force the window open. *Fifth*, he may find that what he is proposing to do is after all impossible—not because of insufficiency of means, but because it is for some reason physically not possible, whatever means be adopted. He who walks into a room intending to steal, say a specific diamond ring, and finds that the ring is no longer there, but has been removed by the owner to the bank, is thus prevented from committing the crime which he intended, and which, but for the supervening physical impossibility imposed by events he would have committed. *Sixth*, he may without interruption efficiently do every act which he set out to do, but may be saved from criminal liability by the fact that what he has done, contrary to his own belief at the time, does not after all amount in law to a crime.'

. . . Applying the three principles derived from my primary definitions, I would seek to obtain the following results. (1) In the first case no criminal attempt is committed. At the relevant time there was no *mens rea* since there had been a change of intention, and the only overt acts relied on would be preparatory and not immediately connected with the completed offence. (2) In the second case there is both *mens rea* and an act connected immediately with the offence. An example would be an attempted rape where the intended victim was criminally assaulted, but the attacker desisted at the stage immediately before he had achieved penetration. It follows that there is a criminal attempt. (3) The third case is more difficult because, as a matter of fact and degree, it will depend to some extent on the stage at which the interruption takes place, and the precise offence the attempt to commit which is the subject of the charge. In general, however, a criminal attempt is committed, assuming that the proximity test is passed. (4) In the fourth case there is ample authority for the proposition that, assuming the proximity test is passed, a criminal attempt is committed. But here casuistry is possible. Examples were given in argument of shots at an intended victim which fail because he is just out of range, or because, as in the case of the well known popular novel, *The Day of the Jackal*, the intended victim moves at the critical moment, or when a dose of poison insufficient to kill is administered with intent to murder. In all these cases the attempt is clearly criminal. (5) The fifth case is more complicated. It is clear that an attempt to obtain money by a false pretence which is not in fact believed, is criminal notwithstanding that the consequences intended were not achieved: see *R. v Hensler* (1870) 11 Cox C.C. 570. The same would be true of an attempted murder when the victim did not actually die for whatever reason. But I do not regard these as true, or at least not as typical, examples of the fifth class. They belong rather to the fourth, since the criminal had done all that he intended to do, and all that was necessary to complete the crime was an act or event wholly outside his control. *R. v M'Pherson* (1857) Dears. & B. 197 where the conviction was quashed, may be regarded as simply a case where a man was charged with one thing and convicted of another. But both the facts and the reasoning of the judges are much closer to the example postulated by Turner J. in *R. v Donnelly* as typical of the fifth class, though Turner J.'s own opinion to the effect that the attempt is criminal depends on the terms of the New Zealand statute and has no application to English law. In *R. v M'Pherson* the reasoning of the English judges on English law was to the contrary. Cockburn C.J. said, at p.201:

'Here the prisoner had the *intention* to steal before he went into the house; but when he got there the goods specified in the indictment were not there; how then could he *attempt* to steal those goods? There can be no attempt asportare unless there is something asportare.'

Bramwell B., anticipating the decisions in *R. v Collins* (1864) 9 Cox C.C. 497, said, at p.201:

'The argument that a man putting his hand into an empty pocket might be convicted of attempting to steal, appeared to me at first plausible; but suppose a man, believing a block of wood to be a man who was his deadly enemy, struck it a blow intending to murder, could he be convicted of attempting to murder the man he took it to be?'

And, in giving judgment, Cockburn C.J. said, at p.202:

'The word attempt clearly conveys with it the idea, that if the attempt had succeeded the offence charged would have been committed, and therefore the prisoner might have been convicted if the things mentioned in the indictment or any of them had been there; but attempting to commit a felony is clearly distinguishable from intending to commit it. An attempt must be to do that which, if successful, would amount to the felony charged; but here the attempt5 never could have succeeded, as the things which the indictment charges the prisoner with stealing had already been removed—stolen by somebody else.'

And Bramwell B. was equally emphatic.

Clearly Cockburn C.J. and Bramwell B. were of the view that Turner J.'s example of his fifth class of inchoate act was not a criminal attempt. *R. v M'Pherson*, was followed in *R. v Collins*, by a court which also included Cockburn C.J. and Bramwell B. and was the identical case postulated by Bramwell B. in the earlier case of a man putting his hand into an empty pocket . . .

It was not long, however, before the decision in *R. v Collins* was challenged by Lord Coleridge C.J. in *R. v Brown* (1889) 24 Q.B.D. 357,359 as 'no longer law', but without giving reasons and in *R. v Ring* (1892) 17 Cox C.C. 491,492 (an early 'mugging' case on the Metropolitan Railway) with even greater emphasis and even fewer reasons. Since then *R. v Collins* has generally been held to be bad law. On this I express no concluded opinion, but in general I regard the reasoning in *R. v M'Pherson* and *R. v Collins* as sound and in general I would consider that 'attempts' in Turner J.'s fifth class of case are not indictable in English law, and I consider that the purported overruling of J*R. V. Collins* needs further consideration. In addition to the reported cases, we postulated in argument a number of real and imaginary instances of this class. In *The Empty Room*, Sherlock Holmes' enemy, Colonel Maron, was induced to fire at a wax image of the detective silhouetted in the window, though Holmes prudently rejected Inspector Lestrade's advice to prefer a charge of attempted murder and so the matter was never tested; in *R. v*

White [1910] 2 K.B. 124, a man who put a small quantity of cyanide in a wine glass, too small to kill, was held guilty of attempted murder. This was an example of the fourth of Turner J.'s cases and therefore criminal. But *quaere*, what would have been the position if the glass administered had contained pure water, even though the accused believed falsely that it contained cyanide? We discussed the situation when a would-be murderer attempts to assassinate a corpse, or a bolster in a bed, believing it to be the living body of his enemy, or when he fires into an empty room believing that it contained an intended victim; and we had our attention drawn to an American case where the accused fired at a peephole in a roof believed to be in use by a watching policeman who was in fact a few yards away. In most of these cases, a statutory offence of some kind (e.g. discharging a firearm with intent to endanger life) would be committed in English law, but in general I would think that a charge of an attempt to commit the common law offence of murder would not lie since, if the contemplated sequence of actions had been completed (as in some of the supposed instances they were) no substantive offence could have been committed of the type corresponding to the charge of attempt supposed to be laid. I get some support for this view from the summing up of Rowlatt J. in *R. v Osborn* (1919) 84 J.P. 63. But I prefer to rest on the principle above stated, since *Osborn* was couched in more popular language than is appropriate to what has become a somewhat theoretical discussion. At the end of the day there must be a question of fact for the jury. The judge may direct them what facts, if established, could constitute an attempt, or would be evidence of an attempt. The jury alone can decide whether there was an attempt.

(6) Turner J.'s sixth class of case was where a man efficiently does 'without interruption every act which he set out to do, but may be saved from criminal liability by the fact that what he has done, contrary to his own belief at the time, does not after all amount to a crime.' . . . I have already explained that I consider that the present appeal fails on the proper construction of s.22 of the Theft Act 1968. But I think that this is a special example of a wider principle, and I agree with Turner J.'s conclusion about it.

'Suppose a man takes away an umbrella from a stand with intent to steal it, believing it not to be his own, but it turns out to be his own, could he be convicted of attempting to steal?'

In *R. v Villensky* [1892] 2 Q.B. 597 Lord Coleridge C.J. in circumstances not unlike the present, following *R. v Dolan* (1855) Dears. C.C. 436, held that prisoners could [not] be indicted under the old law for receiving stolen goods, and made no reference to the possibility of a conviction for attempt.

In *R. v Williams* [1893] 1 Q.B. 320, 321, the same Lord Chief Justice said that a boy below the age at which he could be properly indicted for rape could not be convicted on the same facts for an attempt. I do not agree with the contrary opinion of Hawkins J. in the same case, even though it was possibly supported by the rest of the court. The same reasoning would apply to a case of unlawful carnal knowledge (*Cf. R. v Waite* [1892] 2 Q.B. 600), whether, as there, it was the male who was by reason of age incapable in law of committing the offence, or the female who was in law incapable by reason of her age of having it committed against her, and it would not, in my view, matter in the latter case that the male falsely believed her to be under age. Support for his view is to be found in *D.P.P. v Head* [1959] A.C. 83, which was a charge of a completed offence in relation to a mental defective, but counsel for the respondent made considerable play with the argument a *silentio* to be derived from the fact that no one suggested the possibility of a conviction for an attempt. In my view, it is a general principle that Turner J.'s sixth class of attempts are not criminal, not because the acts are not proximate or because the intention is absent, but because the second of the three propositions I derive from the two judicial definitions I cited above is not satisfied. The acts are not part of a series 'which would constitute the actual commission of the offence if it were not interrupted.' In this event the often discussed question whether the legal impossibility derives from a mistake of fact or law on the part of the accused is hardly relevant.

This discussion enables me to deal with the cases cited in the judgment of the Court of Appeal. Like Lord Widgery C.J., I disagree with the decision in *People v Rojas* (1961) 10 Cal.Rptr. 465 and prefer the decisions in *R. v Donnelly* [1970] N.Z.L.R. 980 and *People v Jaffe* (1960) 185 N.Y. 496 (overruling the decisions in the lower courts, *Cf.* (1906) 98 N.Y.S. 406). I agree with the decision in *R. v Percy Dalton (London) Ltd* (1984) 33 Cr.App.R. 102, and particularly with the quotation from Birkett J. cited by Lord Widgery C.J. in the present case, where he said, at p.110:

'Steps on the way to the commission of what would be a crime, if the acts were completed, may amount to attempts to commit that crime, to which, unless interrupted, they would have led; but steps on the way to the doing of something, which is thereafter done, and which is no crime, cannot be regarded as attempts to commit a crime.'

I would add to the last sentence a rider to the effect that equally steps on the way to do something which is there-after *not* completed, but which if done would not constitute a crime cannot be indicted as attempts to commit that crime. It is, of course, true that, at least in theory, some villains will escape by this route. But in most cases they can properly be charged with something else—statutory offences like breaking and entering with intent etc., or loitering with intent etc., using an instrument with intent etc., discharging or possessing a firearm with intent etc., or as here, common law offences like conspiring to commit the same offence as that the attempt to commit which is charged, or even committing a substantive offence of a different kind, as here, stealing or attempting to steal.

[Lord Reid, Lord Morris and Viscount Dilhorne delivered speeches dismissing the appeal; Lord Salmon agreed with Lord Hailsham.]

Appeal dismissed

Note

1.   The Law Commission criticised the ratio of *Haughton v Smith*.

LAW COMMISSION, *ATTEMPT, AND IMPOSSIBILITY IN RELATION TO ATTEMPT, CONSPIRACY AND INCITEMENT* (TSO, 1980), LAW COM. NO.102

§ 2.96: We think it would be generally accepted that if a man possesses the appropriate *mens rea* and commits acts which are sufficiently proximate to the *actus reus* of a criminal offence, he is guilty of attempting to commit that offence. Where, with that intention, he commits acts which, if the facts were as he believed them to be, would have amounted to the *actus reus* of the full crime or would have been sufficiently proximate to amount to an attempt, we cannot see why this failure to appreciate the true facts should, in principle, relieve him of liability for the attempt. We stress that this solution to the problem does not punish people simply for their intentions. The necessity for proof of proximate acts remains.

2. As to the differences between "inadequate means" and absolute impossibility, one of its criticisms centred on the very fine distinctions it required the Court to draw.

LAW COMMISSION, ATTEMPT, AND IMPOSSIBILITY IN RELATION TO ATTEMPT, CONSPIRACY AND INCITEMENT (TSO, 1980), LAW COM. NO.102

§ 2.64: In *R. v Farrance* (1977) 67 Cr.App.R. 136, the defendant had been convicted of attempting to drive when he had a blood alcohol concentration above the prescribed limit contrary to section 6(1) of the Road Traffic Act 1972. The facts were that the clutch of his car had burnt out, so that although the defendant could operate the engine he could not drive the car. The Court of Appeal upheld the conviction on the grounds that a burnt out clutch was only an impediment to the commission of a crime, similar to the inadequate burglar's tool or the would-be poisoner's insufficient dose. It is not clear what the court's answer would have been if the car had had no petrol or if its transmission had completely seized up.

3. The Commission's proposals for rectifying the position were amended during the passage of the Act, and eventually emerged as s.1(2) and (3), above, p.366. In *Anderton v Ryan* [1985] A.C. 560, the House of Lords held that the statutory wording had not affected the *ratio* of *Haughton v Smith*, which was still of authority. However the House speedily reconsidered this position. See below.

R. V SHIVPURI

[1987] A.C. 1. HL

D was arrested in possession of a suitcase which he believed contained heroin or cannabis. Subsequently the substance in the suitcase was analysed and found to be harmless vegetable matter. D was convicted under s.1(1) of the Criminal Attempts Act 1981 of attempting to be knowingly concerned in dealing with and in harbouring prohibited drugs contrary to s.170(l)(b) of the Customs and Excise Management Act 1979. The Court of Appeal dismissed his appeal but certified the following point of law of general public importance:

> "Does a person commit an offence under Section 1, Criminal Attempts Act, 1981, where, if the facts were as at that person believed them to be, the full offence would have been committed by him, but where on the true facts the offence which that person set out to commit was in law impossible, e.g. because the substance imported and believed to be heroin was not heroin but a harmless substance?"

LORD BRIDGE OF HARWICH

The certified question depends on the true construction of the Criminal Attempts Act 1981. The Act marked an important new departure since, by s.6, it abolished the offence of attempt at common law and substituted a new statutory code governing attempts to commit criminal offences. It was considered by your Lordships' House last year in *Anderton v Ryan* after the decision in the Court of Appeal which is the subject of the present appeal . . .

[After reading s.1, above, p.365]. Applying this language to the facts of the case, the first question to be asked is whether the appellant intended to commit the offences of being knowingly concerned in dealing with and harbouring drugs of class A or class B with intent to evade the prohibition on their importation. Translated into more homely language the question may be rephrased, without in any way altering the legal significance, in the following terms: did the appellant intend to receive and store (harbour) and in due course pass on to third parties (deal with) packages of heroin or cannabis which he knew had been smuggled into England from India? The answer is plainly Yes, he did. Next, did he, in relation to each offence, do an act which was more than merely preparatory to the commission of the offence? The act relied on in relation to harbouring was the receipt and retention of the packages found in the lining of the suitcase. The act relied on in relation to dealing was the meeting at Southall station with the intended recipient of one of the packages. In each case the act was clearly more than preparatory to the commission of the *intended* offence; it was not and could not be more than merely preparatory to the commission of the *actual* offence, because the facts were such that the commission of the actual offence was impossible. Here then is the nub of the matter. Does the 'act which is more than merely preparatory to the commission of the offence' in section 1(1) of the 1981 Act (the *actus reus* of the statutory offence of attempt) require any more than an act which is more than merely preparatory to the commission of the offence which the defendant intended to commit? Section 1(2) must surely indicate a negative answer; if it were otherwise, whenever the facts were such that the commission of the actual offence was impossible, it would be impossible to prove an act more than merely preparatory to the commission of that offence and subsections (1) and (2) would contradict each other.

This very simple, perhaps over-simple, analysis leads me to the provisional conclusion that the appellant was rightly convicted of the two offences of attempt with which he was charged. But can this conclusion stand with *Anderton v Ryan*? The appellant in that case was charged with an attempt to handle stolen goods. She bought a video recorder believing it to be stolen. On the facts as they were to be assumed it was not stolen. By a majority the House decided that she was entitled to be acquitted. I have re-examined the case with care. If I could extract from the speech of Lord Roskill or from my own speech a clear and coherent principle distinguishing those cases of attempting the impossible which amount to offences under the statute from those which do not, I should have to consider carefully on which side of the line the instant case fell. But I have to confess that I can find no such principle.

Running through Lord Roskill's speech and my own in *Anderton v Ryan* is the concept of 'objectively innocent' acts which, in my speech certainly, are contrasted with 'guilty acts'. A few citations will make this clear. Lord Roskill said [1985] A.C. 560 at 580):

'My Lords, it has been strenuously and ably argued for the respondent that these provisions involve that a defendant is liable to conviction for an attempt even where his actions are innocent but he erroneously believes facts which, if true, would make those actions criminal, and further, that he is liable to such conviction whether or not in the event his intended course of action is completed.'

He proceeded to reject the argument. I referred to the appellant's purchase of the video recorder and said [1985] A.C. 560 at 582): 'Objectively considered, therefore, her purchase of the recorder was a perfectly proper commercial transaction.'
A further passage from my speech stated [1985] A.C. 560 at 582–583):

'The question may be stated in abstract terms as follows. Does s.1 of the 1981 Act create a new offence of attempt where a person embarks on and completes a course of conduct, which is objectively innocent, solely on the ground that the person mistakenly believes facts which, if true, would make the course of conduct a complete crime? If the question may be answered affirmatively it requires convictions in a number of surprising cases: the classic case, put by Bramwell B. in *R. v Collins* (1864) 9 Cox C.C. 497 at 498, of the man who takes away his own umbrella from a stand, believing it not to be his own and with intent to steal it; the case of the man who has consensual intercourse with a girl over 16 believing her to be under that age; the case of the art dealer who sells a picture which he represents to be and which is in fact a genuine Picasso, but which the dealer mistakenly believes to be a fake. The common feature of all these cases, including that under appeal, is that the mind alone is guilty, the act is innocent.'

I then contrasted the case of the man who attempts to pick the empty pocket, saying [1985] A.C. 560 at 583):

'Putting the hand in the pocket is the guilty act, the intent to steal is the guilty mind, the offence is appropriately dealt with as an attempt, and the impossibility of committing the full offence for want of anything in the pocket to steal is declared by [subs. (2)] to be no obstacle to conviction.'

If we fell into error, it is clear that our concern was to avoid convictions in situations which most people, as a matter of common sense, would not regard as involving criminality. In this connection it is to be regretted that we did not take due note of para.2.97 of the Law Commission Report, Criminal Law: Attempt and Impossibility in Relation to Attempt, Conspiracy and Incitement (1980) (Law Com. No. 102) which preceded the enactment of the 1981 Act, which reads:

'If it is right in principle that an attempt should be chargeable even though the crime which it is sought to commit could not possibly be committed, we do not think that we should be deterred by the consideration that such a change in our law would also cover some extreme and exceptional cases in which a prosecution would be theoretically possible. An example would be where a person is offered goods at such a low price that he believes that they are stolen, when in fact they are not; if he actually purchases them, upon the principles which we have discussed he would be liable for an attempt to handle stolen goods. Another case which has been much debated is that raised in argument by Bramwell B. in *R. v Collins*. If A takes his own umbrella, mistaking it for one belonging to B and intending to steal B's umbrella, is he guilty of attempted theft? Again, on the principles which we have discussed he would in theory be guilty, but in neither case would it be realistic to suppose that a complaint would be made or that a prosecution would ensue.'

The prosecution in *Anderton v Ryan* itself falsified the Commission's prognosis in one of the 'extreme and exceptional cases.' It nevertheless probably holds good for other such cases, particularly that of the young man having sexual intercourse with a girl over 16, mistakenly believing her to be under that age, by which both Lord Roskill and I were much troubled.
However that may be, the distinction between acts which are 'objectively innocent' and those which are not is an essential element in the reasoning in *Anderton v Ryan* and the decision, unless it can be supported on some other ground, must stand or fall by the validity of this distinction. I am satisfied on further consideration that the concept of 'objective innocence' is incapable of sensible application in relation to the law of criminal attempts. The reason for this is that any attempt to commit an offence which involves 'an act which is more than merely preparatory to the commission of the offence' but which for any reason fails, so that in the event no offence is committed, must *ex hypothesi*, from the point of view of the criminal law, be 'objectively innocent'. What turns what would otherwise, from the point of view of the criminal law, be an innocent act into a crime is the intent of the

actor to commit an offence. I say 'from the point of view of the criminal law' because the law of tort must surely here be quite irrelevant. A puts his hand into B's pocket. Whether or not there is anything in the pocket capable of being stolen, if A intends to steal his act is a criminal attempt; if he does not so intend his act is innocent. A plunges a knife into a bolster in a bed. To avoid the complication of an offence of criminal damage, assume it to be A's bolster. If A believes the bolster to be his enemy B and intends to kill him, his act is an attempt to murder B; if he knows the bolster is only a bolster, his act is innocent. These considerations lead me to the conclusion that the distinction sought to be drawn in *Anderton v Ryan* between innocent and guilty acts considered 'objectively' and independently of the state of mind of the actor cannot be sensibly maintained . . .

I am thus led to the conclusion that there is no valid ground on which *Anderton v Ryan* can be distinguished. I have made clear my own conviction, which as a party to the decision (and craving the indulgence of my noble and learned friends who agreed in it) I am the readier to express, that the decision was wrong. What then is to be done? If the case is indistinguishable, the application of the strict doctrine of precedent would require that the present appeal be allowed. Is it permissible to depart from precedent under the 1966 Practice Statement Note notwithstanding the especial need for certainty in the criminal law? The following considerations lead me to answer the question affirmatively. Firstly, I am undeterred by the consideration that the decision in *Anderton v Ryan* was so recent. The 1966 Practice Statement is an effective abandonment of our prevention to infallibility. If a serious error embodied in a decision of this House has distorted the law, the sooner it is corrected the better. Secondly, I cannot see how, in the very nature of the case, anyone could have acted in reliance on the law as propounded in *Anderton v Ryan* in the belief that he was acting innocently and now find that, after all, he is to be held to have committed a criminal offence. Thirdly, to hold the House bound to follow *Anderton v Ryan* because it cannot be distinguished and to allow the appeal in this case would, it seems to me, be tantamount to a declaration that the 1981 Act left the law of criminal attempts unchanged following the decision in *Haughton v Smith*. Finally, if, contrary to my present view, there is a valid ground on which it would be proper to distinguish cases similar to that considered in *Anderton v Ryan*, my present opinion on that point would not foreclose . . . the option of making such a distinction in some future case . . .

I would answer the certified question in the affirmative and dismiss the appeal.

Appeal dismissed

Note

Although the whole House agreed with Lord Bridge's speech overruling *Anderton v Ryan* (and therefore that Mrs Ryan was guilty of attempted handling), Lord Hailsham, with Lord Elwyn-Jones and Lord Mackay, also held that *Anderton v Ryan* was distinguishable on the ground that the sole intent of Shivpuri was to evade the prohibition on the import of drugs, whereas "the only intention of Mrs. Ryan was to buy a particular video cassette recorder at a knock-down price and the fact that she believed it to be stolen formed no part of that intention" (per Lord Hailsham, at 337).

It is misleading to describe her intention to buy this particular recorder at a low price as "her only intention", and to say that the fact that she believed it to be stolen was "no part of that intention". A crime is committed intentionally if the forbidden result is *desired* and the circumstances making it forbidden are *known* to the actor. (See Ch.3.) If the recorder had been stolen, her intention to buy that object knowing it to be stolen would be an intention to handle stolen goods. Section 1(3) provides that, since that would be her intention on the facts as she thinks them to be, it is her intention on the facts as they are.

But in any event s.1(3) is redundant. Intention is a state of mind which does not depend on the facts as they are. Otherwise, as has been pointed out by J.C. Smith [1986] Crim. L.R. 540, as often as the facts change, the defendant's intention will change even though he is unaware of the changes in the facts. His intention cannot be affected by situational changes of which he is unaware. If D intends to handle goods, which are, as he knows, stolen, he intends to handle stolen goods, and it cannot be said that that *intention* is no longer there if, unknown to him, they have ceased to exist as stolen goods.

On the difficulties involved in Lord Hailsham's suggested distinction, see J.C. Smith [1986] Crim. L.R. 539–541.

----

ii. Conspiracy

Note

In *DPP v Nock* [1978] A.C. 979, the defendants agreed to extract cocaine from a substance which, unknown to them, contained none. It was held by the House of Lords that "logic and justice seem to require that the question as to the effect of the impossibility of the substantive offence should be answered in the same way, whether the crime charged be conspiracy or attempt" (per Lord Scarman, at 997). The principles of *Haughton v Smith*, above, p.427, therefore applied and since the result agreed on by the defendants—extraction of cocaine—was absolutely impossible, their agreement was not punishable.

So far as concerns statutory conspiracies, s.1(1) of the Criminal Law Act 1977 (above, p.390) includes in the definition of conspiracy an agreement which would amount to or involve the commission of an offence but for the existence of facts which render the commission of the offence impossible. However common law conspiracies are unaffected by the section, and are still governed by *DPP v Nock* and, presumably, the principles laid down in *Haughton v Smith*.

8   HOMICIDE

Note

Causing another person's death in a culpable way is generally regarded as the most serious of criminal offences; death is the most serious harm which may be inflicted upon another person. There are several homicide offences: murder, manslaughter (both voluntary and involuntary), infanticide and causing death by dangerous driving. There are other offences closely approximating to homicide such as child destruction and abortion. Suicide was an offence until the Suicide Act 1961 but some aspects of the crime still remain.

1. THE ACTUS REUS OF HOMICIDE

Notes

1.   The common element in homicides is the actus reus, expressed by Coke as follows:

"Unlawfully killing a reasonable person who is in being and under the [Queen's] Peace, the death following within a year and a day" Coke, 3 Inst. 47.

2.   In Adebolajo [2014] EWCA Crim 2779, A, who had been convicted of the murder of Fusilier Lee Rigby having attacked him on the streets of Woolwich and attempted to decapitate him, renewed his application for leave to appeal contending that the trial judge was in error in rejecting his submission that he had not killed under "the Queen's Peace" based on his claim that he honestly believed he was a soldier fighting a war against the Queen and her forces. The trial judge ruled that the "Queen's Peace" requirement related to the victim of the offence not the perpetrator and his beliefs. On the renewed application for leave to appeal, Lord Thomas CJ, refusing leave to appeal, stated (at para 33):

"The law is now clear. An offender can generally be tried for murder wherever committed if he is a British subject, or, if not a British subject, the murder was committed within England and Wales. The reference to "the Queen's peace", . . . went essentially to jurisdiction. Although the Queen's Peace may play some part still in the elements that have to be proved for murder as regards the status of the victim (and it is not necessary to examine or define the ambit of that), it can only go to the status of the victim; it has nothing whatsoever to do with the status of the killer. The argument was completely hopeless. We have set out at some length why it was hopeless; it should never have been advanced. We dismiss this ground of appeal as entirely misconceived."

3.   The rule that death must occur within a year and a day became increasingly anachronistic. With the development of medical knowledge it is now possible to determine the cause of a person's death even though it may occur a long time after the original injury was inflicted by the defendant. In addition the use of life-support machines in hospitals has meant that patients who may otherwise have died relatively quickly may be kept alive for a considerable length of time in the hope of recovery. In such a case, however, a prosecution for homicide would be precluded if death occurred more than a year and a day after the act which caused it. The Criminal Law Revision Committee's 14th Report on Offences Against the Person (1980), Cmnd.7844 suggested that "it would be wrong for a person to remain almost indefinitely at risk of prosecution for murder. A line has to be drawn somewhere and in our opinion the present law operates satisfactorily" (s.39). In its Consultation Paper No.136, The Year and a Day Rule in Homicide (TSO, 1994) the Law Commission carried out a review of the rule highlighting both the advantages and disadvantages of its retention. The Law Commission recommended its abolition in its Report, Legislating the Criminal Code: The Year and a Day Rule in Homicide (TSO, 1995), Law Com. No.230. Parliament acted promptly in response to its recommendations and the Law Reform (Year and a Day Rule) Act 1996 was passed into law on 17 June 1996. To safeguard against oppressive prosecutions brought several years after the original act causing death was performed, or after the perpetrator has already been convicted of a non-fatal offence in respect of the same incident, the consent of Attorney General to a prosecution is required in certain circumstances (see s.2).

LAW REFORM (YEAR AND A DAY RULE) ACT 1996

Abolition of 'year and a day rule'

1. The rule known as the 'year and a day rule' (that is, the rule that, for the purposes of offences involving death and of suicide, an act or omission is conclusively presumed not to have caused a person's death if more than a year and a day elapsed before he died) is abolished for all purposes.

Restriction on institution of proceedings for a fatal offence

2. (1) Proceedings to which this section applies may only be instituted by or with the consent of the Attorney General.

(2) This section applies to proceedings against a person for a fatal offence if—

(a) the injury alleged to have caused the death was sustained more than three years before the death occurred, or

(b) the person has previously been convicted of an offence committed in circumstances alleged to be connected with the death.

(3) In subsection (2) 'fatal offence' means—

(a) murder, manslaughter, infanticide or any other offence of which one of the elements is causing a person's death, or

(b) the offence of aiding, abetting, counselling or procuring a person's suicide.

(4) No provision that proceedings may be instituted only by or with the consent of the Director of Public Prosecutions shall apply to proceedings to which this section applies.

Short title, commencement and extent

3. (1) This Act may be cited as the Law Reform (Year and a Day Rule) Act 1996.

(2) Section 1 does not affect the continued application of the rule referred to in that section to a case where the

act or omission (or the last of the acts or omissions) which caused the death occurred before the day on which this Act is passed.

(3) Section 2 does not come into force until the end of the period of two months beginning with the day on which this Act is passed; but that section applies to the institution of proceedings after the end of that period in any case where the death occurred during that period (as well as in any case where the death occurred after the end of that period).

(4) This Act extends to England and Wales and Northern Ireland.

Questions

1.   Should there be a legal definition of death? See *R. v Malcherek*, above p.56; G. Williams, *Textbook of Criminal Law* (1983), pp.279–285; and Criminal Law Revision Committee, *14th Report: Offences Against the Person* (1980), Cmnd.7844 p.37.

2.   What is a life in being? See the next case.

R. V POULTON

(1832) 5 C. & P. 330; 172 E.R. 997

The defendant had given birth to a child. Its body was found with a ligature round its neck. Three medical witnesses called for the prosecution all said that although the child had breathed they could not tell whether the child had been completely born, as breathing can take place during birth. The defendant was charged with murder.

LITTLEDALE J

With respect to birth the being born must mean that the whole body is brought into the world: and it is not sufficient that the child respires in the progress of the birth. Whether the child was born alive depends mainly upon the evidence of the medical man. None of them say that the child was born alive; they only say that it had breathed . . .

Not guilty of murder

Note

The period 1830–40 saw many cases on this point reported by Carrington and Payne, e.g. *R. v Brain* (1834) 6 C. & P. 349; *R. v Crutchley* (1837) 7 C & P. 814; and *R. v Reeves* (1839) 9 C. & P. 25, which last case added the point that the umbilical cord need not be severed for there to be a life in being. This legal test is not apparently in accord with medical opinion where the emphasis is on breathing; see Stanley B. Atkinson, "Life, Birth and Live Birth" (1904) 20 L.Q.R. 134, 141 and following. As long as the child has "lived" it does not matter that the injuries causing its death occurred while it was still in the womb: *R. v West* (1848) 2 Car. & Kir. 784; and see *Attorney General's Reference (No.3 of 1994)* [1998] A.C. 245, above, p.142.

----

2. MURDER

i. The Penalty for Murder

Note

"The punishment for murder in the old days was a mandatory death sentence; now, by a quirk of language, it was to be a mandatory life sentence" (G. Williams, *Textbook of Criminal Law* (1983), p.175). Capital punishment for murder was abolished by the Murder (Abolition of the Death Penalty) Act 1965 which replaced the unhappy compromise of partial abolition established by the Homicide Act 1957.

The unusual feature of the penalty for murder is that it is mandatory. The judge has no discretion other than to recommend that the convicted person be detained in prison for a specified minimum term of years (1965 Act s.1(2)). The *Report of the Select Committee of the House of Lords on Murder and Life Imprisonment* (HL Paper 78–1, 1989), para.118, recommended that the mandatory sentence for murder should be abolished (see also Prison Reform Trust, *Committee on the Penalty for Homicide* (1993)). The mandatory sentence, whether death or life, has been a crucial factor in the shaping of the law of homicide, insanity and diminished responsibility. Any discussion of reform of the law of homicide is forced to take account of this. See below.

----

ii. The Mental Element in Murder

R. GOFF, "THE MENTAL ELEMENT IN THE CRIME OF MURDER" (1988) 104 L.Q.R. 30, 33

I must emphasise that murder is a crime at common law; and that the definition of the mental element is therefore a common law, and not a statutory, definition . . . The mental element in the crime of murder used to be called 'malice aforethought'. This is, of course, thoroughly misleading; since neither premeditation nor malice towards the victim were necessary. Furthermore, there were three kinds of malice aforethought; express malice, implied malice, and constructive malice. Express malice was simple; that existed where the defendant actually intended to kill his victim. Implied malice existed when he intended to cause 'grievous bodily harm' to his victim and, by so doing, killed him. Constructive malice existed in two circumstances: first, when the defendant killed his victim in the course of, or in furtherance of, committing a felony (as a serious crime was then called); and second, when the defendant killed his victim in the course of, or for the purpose of, resisting an officer of justice, or resisting or avoiding or preventing a lawful arrest, or effecting or assisting an escape or rescue from legal custody. However, we need spend little time on constructive malice, because in English law this category of murder was abolished by section 1 of the Homicide Act 1957.

Note

If, therefore, "malice aforethought" is a technical term whose meaning implies neither ill-will nor premeditation, a person who kills out of motives of mercy or compassion to alleviate suffering may, nevertheless, be guilty of murder, just as a person who kills in the "heat of the moment" without prior planning may be guilty of murder. In *Inglis* [2010] EWCA Crim 2637, the Court of Appeal upheld the conviction for murder of a mother who killed her son by a heroin injection as he lay in a hospital bed seriously ill. She regarded the act as a mercy killing but the Court dismissed her appeal reiterating the position that all "mercy killings" are unlawful and any change in the law is a matter for Parliament Lord Judge CJ stating (at [37]):

"[W]e must underline that the law of murder does not distinguish between murder committed for malevolent reasons and murder motivated by familial love. Subject to well established partial defences, like [loss of self-control] or diminished responsibility, mercy killing is murder."

This was not a case of voluntary euthanasia as there was no evidence that the victim requested an assisted suicide; but even if he had, this would also have amounted to unlawful homicide (see also *R (Nicklinson) v Ministry of Justice* [2012] EWHC 2381 (Admin)).

Below the meaning of "malice aforethought" is explored.

HOMICIDE ACT 1957 S.1

(1) Where a person kills another in the course or furtherance of some other offence, the killing shall not amount to murder unless done with the same malice aforethought (express or implied) as is required for a killing to amount to murder when not done in the course or furtherance of another offence.

(2) For the purposes of the foregoing subsection, a killing done in the course or for the purpose of resisting an officer of justice or of resisting or avoiding or preventing a lawful arrest, or of affecting or assisting an escape or rescue from legal custody, shall be treated as a killing in the course or furtherance of an offence.

R. V VICKERS

[1957] 2 Q.B. 664

The appellant broke into a shop intending to steal. He was seen by the occupant of the living quarters above, an elderly woman of 72. He struck her many blows and kicked her in the face. She died as a result. The appellant was convicted of capital murder.

LORD GODDARD CJ

. . . The point that has been raised on the appellant's behalf turns entirely on section 1 (1) of the Homicide Act, 1957, which came into force this year.

The marginal note to that section (s.1(1)), which, of course, is not part of the section but may be looked at as some indication of its purpose, is: 'Abolition of "constructive malice".'

'Constructive malice' is an expression which I do not think will be found in any particular decision, but it is to be found in the textbooks, and is something different from implied malice. The expression 'constructive malice' is generally used where a person causes death during the course of carrying out a felony which involves violence—that always amounted to murder. There may be many cases in which a man is not intending to cause death, as, for instance, where he gives a mere push and a person falls and strikes his head or falls down the stairs and breaks his neck, and although the push would never have been considered in the ordinary way as an act which would be likely to cause death, yet if it was done in the course of carrying out a felony it would amount to murder. Another illustration of 'constructive malice' would be if a man raped a woman, and she died in the course of the struggle. The fact that he may only have used a moderate or even small degree of violence in the struggle would have been no defence to a charge of murder, because if he caused death, he did so during the commission of the felony of rape . . . Murder is, of course, killing with malice aforethought, but 'malice aforethought' is a term of art. It has always been defined in English law as, either an express intention to kill, as could be inferred when a person, having uttered threats against another, produced a lethal weapon and used it on a victim, or implied, where, by a voluntary act, the accused intended to cause grievous bodily harm to the victim and the victim died as the result. If a person does an act which amounts to the infliction of grievous bodily harm he cannot say that he only intended to cause a certain degree of harm. It is called *malum in se* in the old cases and he must take the consequences. If he intends to inflict grievous bodily harm and that person dies, that has always been held in English law, and was at the time this Act was passed, sufficient to imply the malice aforethought which is a necessary constituent of murder.

It will be observed that the section preserves implied malice as well as express malice, and the words 'Where a person kills another in the course or furtherance of some other offence' cannot, in our opinion, be referred to the infliction of the grievous bodily harm if the case which is made against the accused is that he killed a person by having assaulted the person with intent to do grievous bodily harm, and from the bodily harm he inflicted that person dies. The 'furtherance of some other offence' must refer to the offence he was committing or endeavouring to commit other than the killing, otherwise there would be no sense in it. It was always the English law, as I have said, that if death was caused by a person in the course of committing a felony involving violence that was murder. Therefore, in the present case it is perfectly clear that the words 'Where a person kills another in the course or furtherance of some other offence' must be attributed to the burglary he was committing. The killing was in the course or furtherance of that burglary. He killed that person in the course of the burglary because he realised that the victim recognised him and he therefore inflicted grievous bodily harm on her, perhaps only intending to render her unconscious, but he did intend to inflict grievous bodily harm by the blows he inflicted upon her and by kicking her in the face, of which there was evidence. The section goes on: 'the killing shall not amount to murder unless done with the same malice aforethought (express or implied) as is required for a killing to amount to murder when not done in the course or furtherance of another offence.' It would seem clear, therefore, that the legislature is providing that where one has a killing committed in the course or furtherance of another offence, that other offence must be ignored. What have to be considered are the circumstances of the killing, and if the killing would amount to murder by reason of the express or implied malice, then that person is guilty of capital murder. It is not enough to say he killed in the course of the felony unless the killing is done in a manner which would amount to murder ignoring the commission of felony. It seems to the court, therefore, that in the present case, a burglar attacked a householder to prevent recognition. The householder died as the result of blows inflicted upon her—blows or kicks or both—and if this section had not been passed there could be no doubt that the appellant would have been guilty of murder. He is guilty of murder because he has killed a person with the necessary malice aforethought being implied from the fact that he intended to do grievous bodily harm . . .

The court desires to say quite firmly that in considering the construction of section 1(1) it is impossible to say that the doing of grievous bodily harm is the other offence which is referred to in the first line and a half of the section. One has to show, independently of the fact that the accused is committing another offence, that the act which caused the death was done with malice aforethought as implied by law. The existence of express or implied malice is expressly preserved by the Act and, in our opinion, a perfectly proper direction was given by Hinchcliffe J. to the jury, and accordingly this appeal fails and is dismissed.

Appeal dismissed

DIRECTOR OF PUBLIC PROSECUTIONS V SMITH

[1961] A.C. 290 HL

The appellant was driving a car containing some stolen property when a policeman told him to draw into the kerb. Instead he accelerated and the constable clung on to the side of the car. The car followed an erratic course and the policeman fell in front of another car and was killed. The appellant drove on for 200 yards, dumped the stolen property, and then returned. He was charged with capital murder. The judge directed the jury to consider whether the appellant intended to cause the officer grievous bodily harm. He was convicted but the Court of Criminal Appeal quashed the conviction for capital murder and substituted one for manslaughter. The Crown appealed to the House of Lords, which restored the conviction for capital murder.

VISCOUNT KILMUIR LC

. . . The last criticism of the summing-up which was raised before your Lordships was in regard to the meaning which the learned judge directed the jury was to be given to the words 'grievous bodily harm'. The passages of which complaint is made are the following:

> 'When one speaks of an intent to inflict grievous bodily harm upon a person, the expression grievous bodily harm does not mean for that purpose some harm which is permanent or even dangerous. It simply means some harm which is sufficient seriously to interfere with the victim's health or comfort.'

'In murder the killer intends to kill, or to inflict some harm which will seriously interfere for a time with health or comfort.'

'If the accused intended to do the officer some harm which would seriously interfere at least for a time with his health and comfort, and thus perhaps enable the accused to make good his escape for the time being at least that would be murder too.'

The direction in these passages was clearly based on the well-known direction of Willes J. in *R. v Ashman* (1858) 1 F. & F. 88 and on the words used by Graham B. in *R. v Cox* (1818) R. & R. 362 (C.C.R.). Indeed, this is a direction which is commonly given by judges in trials for the statutory offence under section 18 of the Offences Against the Person Act 1861, and has on occasions been given in murder trials: cf. *R. v Vickers* (above, p 441).

My Lords, I confess that whether one is considering the crime of murder or the statutory offence, I can find no warrant for giving the words 'grievous bodily harm' a meaning other than that which the words convey in their ordinary and natural meaning. 'Bodily harm' needs no explanation, and 'grievous' means no more and no less than 'really serious' . . .

It was, however, contended before your lordships on behalf of the respondent, that the words ought to be given a more restricted meaning in considering the intent necessary to establish malice in a murder case. It was said that the intent must be to do an act 'obviously dangerous to life' or 'likely to kill'. It is true that in many of the cases the likelihood of death resulting has been incorporated into the definition of grievous bodily harm, but this was done, no doubt, merely to emphasise that the bodily harm must be really serious, and it is unnecessary, and I would add inadvisable, to add anything to the expression 'grievous bodily harm' in its ordinary and natural meaning.

To return to the summing-up in the present case, it is true that in the two passages cited the learned judge referred to 'grievous bodily harm' in the terms used by Willes J. in *R. v Ashman*, but in no less than four further passages, and in particular in the vital direction given just before the jury retired he referred to 'serious hurt' or 'serious harm'. Read as a whole, it is, I think, clear that there was no misdirection. Further, on the facts of this case it is quite impossible to say that the harm which the respondent must be taken to have contemplated could be anything but of a very serious nature coming well within the term of 'grievous bodily harm'.

Before leaving this appeal I should refer to a further contention which was but faintly adumbrated, namely, that section 1(1) of the Homicide Act 1957, had abolished malice constituted by a proved intention to do grievous bodily harm, and that, accordingly, *R. v Vickers* [above, p.441], which held the contrary, was wrongly decided. As to this it is sufficient to say that in my opinion the Act does not in any way abolish such malice. The words in parenthesis in section 1(1) of the Act and a reference to section 5(2) make this clear beyond doubt.

Appeal allowed

Note

For analysis of the meaning of "intention" see above, pp.78–95.

In *R. v Hyam* [1975] A.C. 55, the issue whether intention to cause grievous bodily harm constituted malice aforethought, was left in doubt as Lords Diplock and Kilbrandon held that it was not sufficient mens rea for murder. Lord Diplock stated:

"[T]he now familiar expression 'grievous bodily harm' appears to owe its place in the development of the English law of homicide to its use in 1803 in Lord Ellenborough's Act (43 Geo. 3, c. 58), which made it a felony to shoot at, stab or cut any other person 'with intent . . . to murder, . . . maim, disfigure, or disable, . . . or . . . do some other grievous bodily harm . . .' [section 1] . . . For my part, I am satisfied that the decision of this House in *DPP v Smith* was wrong in so far as it rejected the submission that in order to amount to the crime of murder the offender, if he did not intend to kill, must have intended or foreseen as a likely consequence of his act that human life would be endangered . . . I think the reason why this House fell into error was because it failed to appreciate that the concept of 'intention to do grievous bodily harm' only became relevant to the common law of murder as a result of the passing of Lord Ellenborough's Act in 1803 and the application to the new felony thereby created of the then current common law doctrine of constructive malice. This led this House to approach the problem as one of the proper construction of the words 'grievous bodily harm' which because, though *only* because, of the doctrine of constructive malice had over the past 100 years become part of the standard definition of *mens rea* in murder, as well as part of the statutory definition of *mens rea* in the statutory felony of causing grievous bodily harm with intent to cause grievous bodily harm. I do not question that in the statutory offence 'grievous bodily harm' bears the meaning ascribed to it by this House in *DPP v Smith* but the actual problem which confronted this House in *DPP v Smith* and the Court of Criminal Appeal in *R. v Vickers* was a much more complex one . . ."

Lord Hailsham and Viscount Dilhorne expressly approved *Vickers*. Viscount Dilhorne stated:

"I now turn to the second contention advanced on behalf of the appellant. This has two facets: first, that the reference to the intent to cause grievous bodily harm has been based on the law that killing in the course or furtherance of a felony is murder, and that when the Homicide Act 1957 was enacted abolishing constructive malice it meant that it no longer sufficed to establish intent to do grievous bodily harm; and, secondly, that, if intent to do grievous bodily harm still made a killing murder, it must be intent to do grievous bodily harm of such a character that life was likely to be endangered.

   Committing grievous bodily harm was for many, many years, and until all felonies were abolished, a felony. Consequently so long as the doctrine of constructive malice was part of the law of England, to secure a conviction for murder it was only necessary to prove that the death resulted from an act committed in the course of or in furtherance of the commission of grievous bodily harm. But when one looks at the cases and the old textbooks, one does not find any indication that proof of intent to do grievous bodily harm was an ingredient of murder only on account of the doctrine of constructive malice. Indeed, one finds the contrary . . .

This was recognised in the report of the Royal Commission on Capital Punishment (1953) (Cmnd. 8932). Their five propositions stated in paragraph 76 which were, so the report said, generally accepted to be properly included in the category of murder, were

'. . . all cases where the accused either *intended* to cause death or grievous bodily harm or *knew* that his act was likely to cause death or grievous bodily harm'.

The Royal Commission went on to recommend the abolition of constructive malice, and in paragraph 123 suggested a clause for inclusion in a Bill to bring that about.

   Section 1 of the Homicide Act 1957 is in all material respects similar to the clause proposed. It would, indeed, be odd if the Royal Commission by recommending the abolition of constructive malice had in fact proposed the abolition of intent to do grievous bodily harm as an ingredient of murder when the commission had not intended and did not recommend that. Parliament may, of course, do more by an Act than it intends but if, as in my opinion was the case, intent to do grievous bodily harm was entirely distinct from constructive malice, then the conclusion that Parliament did so by the Homicide Act 1957 must be rejected. In my opinion, *R. v Vickers* was rightly decided and this House was right in saying that that was so in *D.P.P. v Smith*.

   I now turn to the second facet of the appellant's contention, namely, that the words 'grievous bodily harm' are to be interpreted as meaning harm of such a character as is likely to endanger life . . .

Our task is to say what, in our opinion, the law is, not what it should be. In the light of what I have said, in my opinion, the words 'grievous bodily harm' must, as Viscount Kilmuir said [in *D.P.P. v Smith*] be given their ordinary and natural meaning and not have the gloss put on them for which the appellant contends . . .

To change the law to substitute 'bodily injury known to the offender to be likely to cause death' for 'grievous bodily harm' is a task that should . . . be left to Parliament if it thinks such a change expedient . . . I share the view of the majority of the Royal Commission that such a change would not lead to any great difference in the day-to-day administration of the law."

Note

Lord Cross was not prepared to decide on the issue as it had not been fully argued before the House. The matter was finally resolved in the following case:

R. V CUNNINGHAM

[1981] 2 All E.R. 863

The appellant suspected (wrongly) that the victim was associating with the woman he planned to marry. The victim died from blows struck by the appellant with a chair. He appealed against his conviction for murder on the grounds that to tell the jury that intending really serious harm was sufficient for murder was a misdirection. The Court of Appeal dismissed his appeal but certified that a point of law of general public importance was involved.

LORD HAILSHAM OF ST. MARYLEBONE LC

with whom Lords Wilberforce, Simon of Glaisdale and Bridge of Harwich agreed; . . . The real nerve of Lord Diplock's argument [in *R. v Hyam*]; however, does, as it seems to me, depend on the importance to be attached to the passing in 1803 of Lord Ellenborough's Act (43 Geo. 3 c. 58) by which, for the first time, wounding with the intent to inflict grievous bodily harm became a felony. This, Lord Diplock believes, rendered it possible to apply the doctrine of 'felony murder' as defined in Stephen's category (c), abolished in 1957, to all cases of felonious wounding, where death actually ensued from the wound. The abolition of 'felony murder' in 1957 was thus seen to enable the judiciary to pursue the mental element in murder behind the curtain imposed on it by the combined effect of the statutory crime of felonious wounding and the doctrine of constructive malice, and so to arrive at a position in which the mental element could be redefined in terms either of an intention to kill, or an intention actually to endanger human life, to correspond with the recommendations of the Fourth Report of Her Majesty's Commissioners on Criminal Law (March 8, 1839).

It seems to me, however, that this highly ingenious argument meets with two insuperable difficulties. I accept that it appears to be established that the actual phrase 'grievous bodily harm', if not an actual coinage by Lord Ellenborough's Act, can never be found to have appeared in print before it, though it has subsequently become current coin, and has passed into the general legal jargon of statute law, and the cases decided thereon. But counsel, having diligently carried us through the institutional writers on homicide, starting with Coke, and ending with East, with several citations from the meagre reports available, only succeeded in persuading me at least that, even prior to Lord Ellenborough's Act of 1803, and without the precise label 'grievous bodily harm', the authors and the courts had consistently treated as murder, and therefore unclergiable, any killing with intent to do serious harm, however described, to which the label 'grievous bodily harm', as defined by Viscount Kilmuir L.C. in *D.P.P. v Smith* [1961] A.C. 290 at 334 reversing the 'murder by pinprick' doctrine quantum of proof. [D.A. Thomas, 'Form and Function in Criminal Law' in There is a second difficulty in the way of treating Lord Ellenborough's Act as providing the kind of historical watershed demanded by Lord Diplock's speech and contended for in the instant appeal by the appellant's counsel. This consists in the fact that, though the nineteenth-century judges might in theory have employed the felony-murder rule to apply to cases where death ensued in the course of a felonious wounding, they do not appear to have done so in fact. No case was cited where they did so. On the contrary, there appears to be no historical discontinuity between criminal jurisprudence before and after 1803. Stephen never so treated the matter (either in his text, or except in the last few lines, in his Note XIV). It was not so treated in the Australian case of *La Fontaine v R*. (1976) 136 C.L.R. 62 (after *Hyam*, but in a skill, with no medical qualifications, and there is no pretence that it is done for the Counsel for the appellant used one further ground, not found in Lord Diplock's opinion, for supporting the minority view in *Hyam*. This was the difficulty which, as he suggested, a jury would find in deciding what amounted to an intention to inflict 'grievous bodily harm' or 'really serious bodily harm' as formulated in *Smith*. I do not find this argument convincing. For much more than a hundred years juries have constantly been required to arrive at the answer to precisely this question in cases falling short of murder e.g. the s.18 cases). I cannot see that the fact that death ensues should render the identical question particularly anomalous, or its answer, though admittedly more important, any more difficult. Nor am I persuaded that a reformulation of murder so as to confine the *mens rea* to an intention to endanger life instead of an intention to do really serious bodily harm would either improve the clarity of the law or facilitate the task of juries in finding the facts. On the contrary, in cases where death has ensued as the result of the infliction of really serious injuries I can see endless opportunity for fruitless and interminable discussion of the question whether the accused intended to endanger life and thus expose the victim to a probable danger of death, or whether he simply intended to inflict really serious injury . . . In my opinion, *Vickers* was a correct statement of the law as it was after amendment by the Homicide Act 1957, and in *Smith* and *Hyam* your Lordships were right to indorse *Vickers* . . .

LORD EDMUND-DAVIES

The minority dissents of Lord Diplock and Lord Kilbrandon, in Hyam, above, were based on their conclusions that the law as to intent in murder had been incorrectly stated by this House in *Smith* and that exposure of the error should lead to a quashing of Hyam's conviction for murder. In the present case, on the other hand, your Lordships have unanimously concluded and now reiterate that the law as to murderous intent was correctly stated in *R. v Vickers*. Even so, is now the time and is this House the place to reveal and declare (so as to 'avoid injustice') what ought to be the law and, in the light of that revelation, here and now to recant from its former adoption of *Vickers*?

My lords, I would give a negative answer to the question. I say this despite the fact that, after much veering of thought over a period of years, the view I presently favour is that there should be no conviction for murder unless an intent to kill is established, the wide range of punishment for manslaughter being fully adequate to deal with all less heinous forms of homicide. I find it passing strange that a person can be convicted of murder if death results from, say, his intentional breaking of another's arm, an action which, while undoubtedly involving the infliction of 'really serious harm' and, as such, calling for severe punishment, would in most cases be unlikely to kill. And yet, for the lesser offence of attempted murder, nothing less than an intent to kill will suffice. But I recognise the force of the contrary view that the outcome of intentionally inflicting serious harm can be so unpredictable that anyone prepared to act so wickedly has little ground for complaint if, where death results, he is convicted and punished as severely as one who intended to kill.

So there are forceful arguments both ways. And they are arguments of the greatest public consequence, particularly in these turbulent days when, as Lord Hailsham L.C. has vividly reminded us, violent crimes have become commonplace. Resolution of that conflict cannot, in my judgment, be a matter for your Lordships' House alone. It is a task for none other than Parliament, as the constitutional organ best fitted to weigh the relevant and opposing factors. Its solution has already been attempted extra-judicially on many occasions, but with no real success. My Lords, we can do none other than wait to see what will emerge when the task is undertaken by the legislature, as I believe it should be when the time is opportune . . .

Appeal dismissed

Note

Similar criticisms to those expressed by Lord Edmund-Davies concerning the grievous bodily harm rule have been made more recently in the House of Lords. In *Attorney General's Reference (No.3 of 1994)* [1998] A.C. 245 (above, p.441), Lord Mustill stated (at 258) that "the grievous harm rule is an outcropping of old law from which the surrounding strata of rationalisations have weathered away." In *Powell (Anthony)* [1999] A.C. 1, Lord Steyn said of the rule (at 15) that it turned "murder into a constructive crime . . . [resulting] in defendants being classified as murderers who are not in truth murderers . . . It results in the imposition of mandatory life sentences when neither justice nor the needs of society require the classification of the case as murder and the imposition of the mandatory life sentence." He went on to recommend that "a killing should be classified as murder if there is an intention to kill or an intention to cause really serious harm coupled with awareness of the risk of death". Their Lordships accepted, however, that the problem was one which only Parliament could resolve.

----

iii. Proposals for reform

Note

The stream of proposals for reform of the law of murder, and more widely homicide, seems endless. A recurrent theme is that any reform project needs to address first the penalty for murder which has a distorting effect upon the law of murder itself and the concomitant defences of diminished responsibility and loss of self-control (or previously provocation) and, secondly, the breadth of the offence incorporating in its mens rea an intent to cause grievous bodily harm. In 1978 D.A. Thomas, "Form and Function in Criminal Law", in P. Glazebrook (ed), *Reshaping the Criminal Law* (1978), p.21, commented:

> "A reconstruction of the law of homicide must begin with a decision on the nature of the sentencing structure which is to be attached to the offences concerned. It would clearly be absurd to design a series of definitions on the assumption that a mandatory sentence in some form will continue to exist for murder, and then enact those definitions against the background of a discretionary sentence. The present shape of the law of murder is the product of the process of reducing the scope of the death penalty; a new approach must start with sentencing structure and proceed to establish the graduations and degrees of liability necessary to the rational operation of that structure."

In the same year the Advisory Council on the Penal System reported.

REPORT OF THE ADVISORY COUNCIL ON THE PENAL SYSTEM, *SENTENCES OF IMPRISONMENT* (HOME OFFICE, 1978)

Section 224. Although murder has been traditionally and distinctively considered the most serious crime, it is not a homogeneous offence but a crime of considerable variety. It ranges from deliberate cold-blooded killing in pursuit of purely selfish ends to what is commonly referred to as 'mercy killing'. Instead of automatically applying a single sentence to such an offence, we believe that sentences for murder should reflect this variety with correspondingly variable terms of imprisonment or, in the exceptional case, even with a non-custodial penalty. This is primarily because we do not think that anyone should, without the most specific justification, be subjected to the disadvantages which we see in indeterminate sentencing (see paragraph 226). It is also because we cannot believe that the problems of predicting future behaviour at the time of conviction are inherently more difficult in a murder case than in any other case where there is a measure of instability, or that judges are any less able to make predictions or to assess degrees of culpability in murder cases than in any others. But it is also because efforts to alleviate the harshness of the mandatory penalty have led to complications in legal proceedings for which we believe there can be no proper justification.

Section 225. The efforts at alleviation to which we refer are, first of all, the two special defences of provocation and diminished responsibility which, if successful, reduce the conviction to manslaughter. Although a conviction for manslaughter may be considered less of a stigma than a conviction for murder, to the offender the important difference often is that the lesser conviction avoids the mandatory penalty. The jurisprudence that has developed out of this defence demonstrates the conceptual difficulties of seeking to mitigate a penal consequence via the substantive law. Provocation may be a factor in any crime; it can and does properly affect the sentence passed on the offender, but only in this one case does it reduce the finding of guilt to a lesser offence. Similarly, the legal concept which enables the defence of diminished responsibility, under section 2 of the Homicide Act 1957, to reduce the crime of murder to manslaughter, creates difficulties. If the mental incapacity is not sufficient to negative the requisite mental element for murder, there are problems in describing the offence as any other crime. If judges had discretion in sentencing, the issues of provocation and diminished responsibility could be considered in their proper place, as mitigating factors in the sentencing process.

REPORT OF THE SELECT COMMITTEE OF THE HOUSE OF LORDS ON MURDER AND LIFE IMPRISONMENT (HL PAPER 78–1, SESSION 1988–89), PARA.118

Opinion of the Committee

118. The Committee agree with the majority of their witnesses that the mandatory life sentence for murder should be abolished. Among the considerations which carried most weight with the Committee was the weight of judicial opinion in England and Wales. The Lord Chief Justice and 12 out of 19 judges of the High Court and the Court of Appeal were in favour of a discretionary sentence. The Committee also note that the great majority of judges who took part in the vote in the House of Lords in 1965 were in favour of the discretionary sentence.

Note

On 21 July 2005 the Home Office announced the terms of reference for a comprehensive review of the law of murder by the Law Commission. The terms of reference set out below indicated that despite the serious criticisms which may be levelled at the mandatory life sentence, this penalty was excluded from the terms of the review. The terms of reference were:

> To review the various elements of murder, including the defences and partial defences to it, and the relationship between the law of murder and the law relating to homicide (in particular manslaughter). The review will make recommendations that:
>
> - take account of the continuing existence of the mandatory life sentence for murder;
>
> - provide coherent and clear offences which protect individuals and society;
>
> - enable those convicted to be appropriately punished; and
>
> - are fair and non-discriminatory in accordance with European Convention on Human Rights and Human Rights Act 1998.

In December 2005, the Law Commission published their Consultation Paper No.177, *A New Homicide Act for England and Wales?* (TSO, 2005) and an accompanying *Overview*. The Law Commission followed this up with a Report in autumn 2006.

LAW COMMISSION, *MURDER, MANSLAUGHTER AND INFANTICIDE* (TSO, 2006), LAW COM NO.304

(footnotes omitted)

PART 1

WHY IS A NEW HOMICIDE ACT NEEDED?

THE EXISTING LAW AND THE PROBLEMS WITH IT

1.8 The law governing homicide in England and Wales is a rickety structure set upon shaky foundations. Some of its rules have remained unaltered since the seventeenth century, even though it has long been acknowledged that they are in dire need of reform. Other rules are of uncertain content, often because they have been constantly changed to the point that they can no longer be stated with any certainty or clarity. . . Moreover, certain piece meal reforms effected by Parliament, although valuable at the time, are now beginning to show their age or have been overtaken by other legal changes and, yet, have been left unreformed.

1.9 This state of affairs should not continue. The sentencing guidelines that Parliament has recently issued for murder cases presuppose that murder has a rational structure that properly reflects degrees of fault and provides appropriate defences. Unfortunately, the law does not have, and never has had, such a structure. Putting that right is an essential task for criminal law reform.

1.10 We will recommend that, for the first time, the general law of homicide be rationalised through legislation. Offences and defences specific to murder must take their place within a readily comprehensible and fair legal structure. This structure must be set out with clarity, in a way that will promote certainty and in a way that non-lawyers can understand and accept. . .

The current structure of offences

1.12 Two general homicide offences—murder and manslaughter—cover the ways in which someone might be at fault in killing. There are also a number of specific homicide offences, for example, infanticide and causing death by dangerous driving (the latter was not within our terms of reference for consideration).

1.13 Murder, which carries a mandatory life sentence, is committed when someone ('D') unlawfully kills another person ('V') with an intention either to kill V or to do V serious harm.

1.14 Manslaughter can be committed in one of four ways:

(1) killing by conduct that D knew involved a risk of killing or causing serious harm ('reckless manslaughter');

(2) killing by conduct that was grossly negligent given the risk of killing ('gross negligence manslaughter');

(3) killing by conduct taking the form of an unlawful act involving a danger of some harm to the person ('unlawful act manslaughter'); or

(4) killing with the intent for murder but where a partial defence applies, namely provocation, diminished responsibility or killing pursuant to a suicide pact.

The term 'involuntary manslaughter' is commonly used to describe a manslaughter falling within (1) to (3) while (4) is referred to as 'voluntary manslaughter'. . .

The serious harm rule

1.17 Under the current law, D is liable for murder not only if he or she kills intentionally but also if he or she kills while intentionally inflicting harm which the jury considers to have been serious. In our view, the result is that the offence of murder is too wide. Even someone who reasonably believed that no one would be killed by their conduct and that the harm they were intentionally inflicting was not serious, can find themselves placed in the same offence category as the contract or serial killer. Here is an example:

D intentionally punches V in the face. The punch breaks V's nose and causes V to fall to the ground. In falling, V hits his or her head on the curb causing a massive and fatal brain haemorrhage.

1.18 This would be murder if the jury decided that the harm that D intended the punch to cause (the broken nose) can be described as 'serious'. Whilst it is clear that a person who kills in these circumstances should be guilty of a serious homicide offence, it is equally clear to the great majority of our consultees that the offence should not be the top tier or highest category offence. . .

1.20 The inclusion of all intent-to-do-serious-harm cases within murder distorts the sentencing process for murder. The fact that an offender only intended to do serious harm, rather than kill, is currently regarded as a mitigating factor that justifies the setting of a shorter initial custodial period as part of the mandatory life sentence. On the face of it, this seems perfectly reasonable. However, there is a strong case for saying that when an offence carries a *mandatory* sentence, there should be no scope for finding mitigation in the way in which the basic or essential fault elements come to be fulfilled.

1.21 We have been informed by research, carried out by Professor Barry Mitchell, into public opinion about murder. This shows that the public assumes that murder involves an intention to kill or its moral equivalent, namely a total disregard for human life. The latter may not be evident in a case where someone has intentionally inflicted harm the jury regards as serious, as when D intentionally breaks someone's nose. Indeed, some members of the public regarded deaths caused by intentionally inflicted harm that was not inherently life threatening as being in some sense 'accidental'.

1.22 Having said that, we do not recommend that killing through an intention to do serious injury should simply be regarded as manslaughter. Manslaughter is an inadequate label for a killing committed with that degree of culpability. In any event, to expand the law of manslaughter still further would be wrong because manslaughter is already an over-broad offence.

1.23 We will be recommending that the intent-to-do-serious-injury cases should be divided into two. Cases where D not only intended to do serious injury but also was aware that his or her conduct posed a serious risk of death should continue to fall within the highest category or top tier offence. This is warranted by the kind of total disregard for human life that such Ds show. They are morally equivalent to cases of intentional killing. Cases where D intended to do serious injury but was unaware of a serious risk of killing should fall (along with some instances of reckless killing) into a new middle tier homicide offence.

Reckless manslaughter

1.24 The scope of murder is both too broad and too narrow. Where the scope of murder is too narrow, the scope of manslaughter is correspondingly too broad. In particular, the law is too generous to some who kill by 'reckless' conduct, that is those who do not intend to cause serious harm but do realise that their conduct involves an unjustified risk of causing death. The law is too generous in treating all those who realise that their conduct poses a risk of causing death but press on regardless as guilty only of manslaughter. Again, the problems have arisen from the way that periodic judicial development of the law in individual cases, albeit well-intentioned, has changed the boundaries of homicide offences.

. . .

The 'two category' structure of general homicide offences

1.32 The distinction between murder and manslaughter is almost certainly over 500 years old. No further general category of homicide has been developed over the intervening period. So, over the centuries, the two categories of murder and manslaughter have had to bear the strain of accommodating changing and deepening understandings of the nature and degree of criminal fault and the emergence of new partial defences. They have also had to satisfy demands that labelling and sentencing should be based on rational and just principles.

1.33 Further, the existence of the death penalty and, then, its successor the mandatory life sentence for murderers, has meant that the argument over who should be labelled a 'murderer' has become identified with who should receive the mandatory sentence for murder. Whilst in some respects understandable, the link with sentencing can distort the argument about labels. For example, it is arguable, and we will recommend that, although a person who kills intentionally in response to gross provocation does not deserve a mandatory sentence, he or she should still be labelled a 'murderer'.

1.34 Our consultees almost all agreed that the two-category structure of the general law of homicide is no longer fit for purpose. Consequently, we are proposing to replace the two-tier structure with a three-tier structure. Such a structure will be much better equipped to deal with the stresses and strains on the law and with the issues of appropriate labelling and sentencing. The three tiers in descending order of seriousness would be first degree murder, second degree murder and manslaughter.

1.35 Under our recommendations, first degree murder would encompass:

(1) intentional killing; or

(2) killing through an intention to do serious injury with an awareness of a serious risk of causing death.

1.36 Second degree murder would encompass:

(1) killing through an intention to do serious injury (even without an awareness of a serious risk of causing death); or

(2) killing where there was an awareness of a serious risk of causing death, coupled with an intention to cause either:

    (a) some injury;
    (b) a fear of injury; or
    (c) a risk of injury.

1.37 Second degree murder would also be the result when a partial defence of provocation, diminished responsibility or killing pursuant to a suicide pact is successfully pleaded to first degree murder.

1.38 Manslaughter would encompass:

(1) where death was caused by a criminal act intended to cause injury, or where the offender was aware that the criminal act involved a serious risk of causing injury; or

(2) where there was gross negligence as to causing death.

Note

The Law Commission proposed that the mandatory life sentence should be reserved for first degree murder while second degree murder and manslaughter would have a discretionary life sentence maximum penalty.

The Government responded to the Law Commission's proposals with its own Consultation Paper, *Murder, Manslaughter and Infanticide: Proposal for Reform of the Law* (CP19/08). In this it rejected the redefinition of the basis offence of murder but proposed to proceed with legislation in the areas of provocation, diminished responsibility, complicity and infanticide. The Government ignored the fact that the Law Commission's proposals in respect of these matters were posited upon its key proposal to reform murder and manslaughter as set out above. J.R. Spencer, "Messing up Murder" [2008] 8 Arch. News 5, observed, "The resulting structure, unfortunately, looks rather like a wheel without a hub." The Government pressed on, however, with legislation and the results in relation to provocation, diminished responsibility, infanticide and assisting or encouraging suicide are to be found in the Coroners and Justice Act 2009 which is examined below. Reform of the mess that is murder and involuntary manslaughter has been parked in a siding and appears as far off as it was in 1978.

----

3. VOLUNTARY MANSLAUGHTER

Notes

1. The offence of manslaughter generally covers all unlawful homicides which are not murder. The punishment for manslaughter is in the discretion of the court and may range from an absolute discharge to life imprisonment, reflecting the immense range of circumstances encompassed by the offence.

2. There are two types of manslaughter—voluntary and involuntary. Voluntary manslaughter is committed where D has killed with malice aforethought, and thus could be convicted of murder,

but there are mitigating circumstances present reducing his culpability such as loss of control, diminished responsibility or suicide pact. As the sentence for murder is mandatory life imprisonment, the only way to reflect such mitigating circumstances in sentence is by providing a defence which reduces the offence from murder to manslaughter and thereby provides the judge with discretion as regards sentence.

3.   In the sections which follow relating to loss of control and diminished responsibility, the law is in a post-reform state. The Coroners and Justice Act 2009 abolished the defence of provocation, replacing it with the defence of "loss of control" while also making major changes to the defence of diminished responsibility. These changes took effect on 4 October 2010 and apply to any murder which occurred on or after that date. The previous law applies to any murder which occurred prior to that date. This means that for many years to come lawyers will have to keep abreast of both the old law and the new law as prosecutions may take place many years after the murder occurred.

i. Loss of control

Note

In order to understand the changes that have been made by ss.54–56 of the Coroners and Justice Act 2009, a brief outline of the law of provocation is provided below.

(a) Provocation

Provocation is only a defence to a charge of murder reducing to manslaughter what, in the absence of provocation, would have been murder. If the jury are satisfied D killed with the requisite intent for murder they must convict of manslaughter if the accused may have been provoked. The burden of proof in respect of provocation is upon the prosecution (*Cascoe* [1970] 2 All E.R. 833); if there is evidence raising the possibility of provocation the burden is upon the prosecution to prove beyond reasonable doubt that the accused was not provoked. If there is any evidence of provocation, the judge must leave the defence to the jury. Section 3 of the Homicide Act 1957, provides:

> "Where on a charge of murder there is evidence on which the jury can find that the person charged was provoked (whether by things done or by things said or by both together) to lose his self-control, the question whether the provocation was enough to make a reasonable man do as he did shall be left to be determined by the jury; and in determining that question the jury shall take into account everything both done and said according to the effect which, in their opinion, it would have on a reasonable man."

There are two elements to the defence of provocation: first, the subjective question whether the accused was provoked to lose his self-control; and, secondly, the objective question whether a reasonable man would have been provoked to lose his self-control and do as he did. Because of the burden of proof being on the prosecution, the defence will succeed if the jury feel the accused may possibly have been provoked to lose his self-control and a reasonable man may possibly have lost his self-control and done as he did.

At common law words alone, except "in circumstances of a most extreme and exceptional character" could not amount to provocation (*Holmes v DPP* [1946] A.C. 588). With two exceptions, actual violence by the deceased upon the accused was required. The exceptions were discovery by a husband of his wife in the act of committing adultery and discovery by a father of someone committing sodomy on his son. The Act removed all such restrictions. The provocation need not be illegal or wrongful (see *Doughty* (1986) 83 Cr. App. R. 319) and may emanate from third parties (*Davies* [1975] Q.B. 691) or be directed at third parties (*Pearson* [1992] Crim. L.R. 193). What is crucial is that there is evidence that D was provoked to lose his self-control.

Loss of self-control does not have to be "complete" to the extent that the accused did not know what he was doing; it is sufficient that he may not have been able to restrain himself from doing what he did (*Richens* [1993] Crim. L.R. 384). In *Ibrams* (1981) 74 Cr. App. R. 154; and *Thornton* [1992] 1 All E.R. 306, the Court of Appeal approved the dictum of Devlin J in *Duffy* [1949] 1 All E.R. 932 that there must be "a sudden and temporary loss of self-control, rendering the accused so subject to passion as to make him or her for the moment not master of his mind". While there may have been a history of provocative acts or words, if at the time of the killing, D was not provoked to lose his self-control, he cannot rely on past provocation. In *Ahluwalia* [1992] 4 All E.R. 889 where D killed her husband after a long history of domestic violence by him, it was argued that in domestic violence "slow-burn" cases, where the accused only loses self-control after a prolonged period of provocation from the deceased, the Duffy test was inappropriate as a delay or "cooling-off period" between the last act of provocation and the killing might, in fact, cause the accused to react more strongly. While only Parliament could change the law, the Court accepted that delay would not as a matter of law negate provocation, provided that there was a "sudden and temporary loss of self-control".

The fact that D lost his self-control does not mean that his defence of provocation will succeed; the jury have then to consider the objective question. If the jury conclude that there is a reasonable possibility that the reasonable man might have done as D did, they must return a verdict of manslaughter. The purpose of the objective question is to set a standard of self-control against which D's actions are to be measured. The reasonable man standard was well established in the common law before s.3 of the 1957 Act was passed and was a purely objective standard. The reasonable man was an adult person with normal physical and mental attributes and not having any characteristics which would single him out from ordinary people. This was consistent with the common law rule that provocation was limited to acts of violence by the deceased upon the accused. Thus, if the accused was disfigured or impotent, taunts about these matters could not constitute provocation so there was no need to attribute these characteristics to the reasonable man.

Section 3 of the Homicide Act 1957 changed this by allowing words alone to constitute provocation. Taunts or insults might acquire a seriousness deriving from the fact that they focused on a particular characteristic of the accused. That this might necessitate a redefinition of the reasonable man was intimated by the requirement in s.3, that, in seeking to answer the objective question, the jury must "consider everything both done and said according to the effect which, in their opinion, it would have on a reasonable man". It would seem to be crucial, therefore, for the reasonable man to be placed in the same situation as the accused and thus to share such of the accused's characteristics, circumstances, history, or conditions as are pertinent to the provocation. Two particular problems presented themselves: first, D, due to his characteristics, history, or circumstances, may be particularly sensitive to the alleged provocative words or conduct; and secondly, D, due to his youthfulness or some mental impairment, may not be able to exercise the self-control to be expected of the ordinary adult. At a time before any appellate decisions were made on these issues, Professor Ashworth in "The Doctrine of Provocation" (1976) 35 C.L.J. 292, expressed the view (at 312) that the defence of provocation was for those who were mentally normal, whereas those suffering from a mental abnormality should rely on the defence of diminished responsibility under s.2 of the 1957 Act. In seeking to apply the objective test, Ashworth concluded (at 300) that a distinction had to be drawn between those "individual peculiarities which bear on the gravity of the provocation [which] should be taken into account, whereas individual peculiarities bearing on the accused's level of self-control should not".

In *Camplin* [1978] A.C. 705 Lord Diplock stated (at 717) that the reasonable man is:

"an ordinary person of either sex, not exceptionally excitable or pugnacious, but possessed of such powers of self-control as everyone is entitled to expect that his fellow citizens will exercise in society as it is today."

He accepted (at 714) that the reasonable man was the "embodiment of the standard of self-control required by the criminal law" but, following the 1957 Act, he could be attributed with those characteristics, or placed in those circumstances which would affect the gravity of the taunts or insults directed at the accused. In addition, age, which may be taken into account in assessing the gravity of the provocation (for example, a physical threat or assault may be graver due to the less developed physique of a young person), was also relevant when considering powers of self-control as "to require old heads upon young shoulders is inconsistent with the law's compassion to human infirmity". But other factors which might reduce or impair the accused's powers of self-control were not attributable. In *Morhall* [1996] A.C. 90, the House of Lords emphasised that the reasonable man test is not concerned with ratiocination nor with reasonable conduct; rather it represents a standard of self-control. When directing a jury the judge should refer them to the hypothetical person:

having the power of self-control to be expected of an ordinary person of the age and sex of the defendant, but in other respects sharing such of the defendant's characteristics as [the jury] think would affect the gravity of the provocation to him.

Things relevant to the gravity of the provocation should not be confined to characteristics but could include "the defendant's history or the circumstances in which he was placed at the time", and the characteristics, history, or circumstances did not cease to be relevant because they were discreditable (in the instant case D's addiction, which formed the focus for taunts, was the relevant characteristic). Furthermore, a characteristic could be something temporary or transitory if the subject of taunts or insults.

Despite these clear pronouncements in the House of Lords, the Court of Appeal throughout the 1980s and 1990s continued to intimate that the standard of self-control to be expected of the reasonable person might be modified to take account of the defendant's psychiatric idiosyncracies. The Privy Council considered those decisions in *Luc Thiet Thuan v R* [1996] 3 W.L.R. 45, concluding that a mental infirmity which impairs an accused's power of self-control was not to be taken into account as it is inconsistent with a person having the power of self-control of an ordinary person who features in the objective test. The mental infirmity of the accused could be taken into account if it was the subject of taunts by the deceased as this would go to the gravity of the provocation but otherwise it would be irrelevant. Lord Goff reasoned that this position preserved the distinction between diminished responsibility and provocation which it must have been the intention of the legislature in passing the Homicide Act 1957 to maintain. Lord Steyn, who had concurred in *Morhall*, dissented expressing the view that mental characteristics which gave rise to impaired self-control should be taken into account when considering whether a reasonable person might have done as the accused did. Lord Steyn's reading of the Court of Appeal decisions was endorsed, obiter, by Lord Bingham CJ in *Campbell* [1997] 1 Cr. App. R. 199. Lord Bingham's reasoning was itself adopted by the Court of Appeal in *Parker* [1997] Crim. L.R. 760 where the accused was a chronic alcoholic with some brain damage which made him more susceptible to provocation.

The House of Lords reconsidered the issue in *Smith (Morgan)* [2000] 3 W.L.R. 654, another case involving an alcoholic suffering from a depressive illness which impaired his ability to exercise self-control reducing his threshold for erupting with violence. The trial judge accepted the Crown's argument that this evidence was not relevant to the question whether a reasonable man might have lost his self-control. D was convicted of murder and appealed. The Court of Appeal allowed his appeal, substituting a verdict of manslaughter on the ground that his mental impairment was a characteristic to be attributed to the reasonable man not only in assessing the gravity of the provocation but also his reaction to it. The Crown appealed. The Court of Appeal granted leave to appeal and certified the following point of law of general public importance: "Are characteristics other than age and sex, attributable to the reasonable man, for the purpose of section 3 of the Homicide Act 1957, relevant not only to the gravity of the provocation to him but also to the standard of self-control to be expected?" Unbelievably their Lordships by a majority of three to two answered the question in the affirmative. The majority concluded that Lord Diplock did not intend to draw any distinction between "characteristics relevant to the gravity of the provocation and characteristics relevant to the power of self-control". In Lord Hoffmann's view it would be to trespass on the jury's territory to tell them to ignore any factor or characteristic as it is the right of the jury "to act upon its own opinion of whether the objective element of provocation has been satisfied".

Following Smith, the jury when considering the objective question had to take into account any condition from which the accused suffered which impaired his ability to exercise self-control. The test was "whether he has exercised the degree of self-control to be expected of someone in his situation" (per Lord Slynn at 661) i.e. someone with the same impaired powers of self-control; or whether his behaviour "fell below the standard which should reasonably have been expected of him" (per Lord Hoffmann at 677); or whether the accused had "made reasonable efforts to control himself within the limits of what he [was] reasonably able to do" (per Lord Clyde at 684). When one bears in mind the burden of proof on the prosecution to disprove provocation beyond reasonable doubt, there would be little chance of a jury scrupulously following a judge's direction in a case such as *Smith*, not returning a verdict of manslaughter if satisfied that the accused may have been provoked to lose his self-control: if the accused may have been provoked to act as he did, who could doubt that someone else suffering the same illness or condition which impaired his powers of self-control might not have done the same?

Following the decision of the House of Lords in *Smith* the Court of Appeal struggled to make sense of it. Their struggle, however, was short-lived as in a completely unprecedented judgment, *A-G for Jersey v Holley* [2005] UKPC 23, the Privy Council, sitting as a Board made up of nine serving Lords of Appeal in Ordinary, by a majority of six to three followed *Luc Thiet Thuan* and declared that *Morgan Smith* could not be regarded as an accurate statement of English law. The majority held that s.3 of the Homicide Act 1957 had altered the common law defence of provocation. The statutory reference to the "reasonable man" was intended to refer to the ordinary person, i.e. a person of ordinary self-control, and thereby it set an external standard of self-control. Lord Nicholls of Birkenhead, delivering the judgment of the majority, stated (at [22]):

"Whether the provocative act or words and the defendant's response met the 'ordinary person' standard prescribed by the statute is the question the jury must consider, not the altogether looser question of whether, having regard to all the circumstances, the jury consider the loss of self-control was sufficiently excusable. The statute does not leave each jury free to set whatever standard they consider appropriate in the circumstances by which to judge whether the defendant's conduct is 'excusable'."

The majority recognised that inherent in the use of a uniform standard applicable to all defendants is "the possibility that an individual defendant may be temperamentally unable to achieve this standard". While sex and age are relevant to the application of this standard, other abnormalities not found in a person having ordinary powers of self-control, are not. The majority considered that s.2, diminished responsibility, reflected Parliament's recognition of the potential harshness of s.3 if it stood alone. It would be wrong for the courts to distort s.3 to accommodate cases for which Parliament had expressly provided in enacting s.2.

While in terms of strict precedent the Privy Council cannot overrule a decision of the House of Lords, the nine person panel in *Holley* declared it as their purpose to resolve the conflict in the authorities and clarify definitively the present state of English law. In *James and Karimi* [2006] EWCA Crim 14, the Court of Appeal unusually sitting in a five-strong panel, held that in the exceptional circumstances which pertained as a result of the decision in *Holley*, the principle of law was to be found in the decision of the Privy Council.

Reform

In its Report, *Partial Defences to Murder* (TSO, 2004), Law Com. No.290, the Law Commission recommended that the defence of provocation should be reformed in accordance with the following principles (para.3.168):

"1) Unlawful homicide that would otherwise be murder should instead be manslaughter if the defendant acted in response to

    (a) gross provocation (meaning words or conduct or a combination of words and conduct which caused the defendant to have a justifiable sense of being seriously wronged); or

    (b) fear of serious violence towards the defendant or another; or

    (c) a combination of (a) and (b); and

a person of the defendant's age and of ordinary temperament, i.e. ordinary tolerance and self-restraint, in the circumstances of the defendant might have reacted in the same or a similar way.

2) In deciding whether a person of ordinary temperament in the circumstances of the defendant might have acted in the same or a similar way, the court should take into account the defendant's age and all the circumstances of the defendant other than matters whose only relevance to the defendant's conduct is that they bear simply on his or her general capacity for self-control.

3) The partial defence should not apply where

    (a) the provocation was incited by the defendant for the purpose of providing an excuse to use violence, or

    (b) the defendant acted in considered desire for revenge.

4) A person should not be treated as having acted in considered desire for revenge if he or she acted in fear of serious violence, merely because he or she was also angry towards the deceased for the conduct which engendered that fear.

5) The partial defence should not apply to a defendant who kills or takes part in the killing of another person under duress of threats by a third person.

6) A judge should not be required to leave the defence to the jury unless there is evidence on which a reasonable jury, properly directed, could conclude that it might apply."

The Law Commission took the view that the existing test for provocation leaves to the jury the decision as to "what are the legal standards which differentiate murder from manslaughter" (para.3.124). They considered this position to be unsatisfactory as the law should determine those standards and provide the jury with clear direction. In explaining their test they stated (at para.3.127):

"The test under our proposal is not whether the defendant's conduct was reasonable, but whether it was conduct which a person of ordinary temperament might have been driven to commit (not a bigot or a person with an unusually short fuse). We believe that a jury would be able to grasp and apply this idea in a common-sense way. Because the test is not whether the defendant's conduct was reasonable, there is no illogicality in providing only a partial defence."

The ink had barely dried on the Law Commission Report, *Partial Defences to Murder*, before its proposals underwent reconsideration. The proposal for there to be two degrees of murder (see above, p.457) led to a reconsideration of the ambit and the effect of a defence of provocation. In their Consultation Paper No.177, *A New Homicide Act for England and Wales?*, the Law Commission proposed that provocation should only be a defence to "first degree murder" with the effect of reducing it to "second degree murder". In their Report *Murder, Manslaughter and Infanticide*, the Law Commission affirmed these recommendations.

The Government responded to these proposals with its own Consultation Paper, *Murder, Manslaughter and Infanticide: Proposals for Reform of the Law* (CP19/08). Although it accepted the Law Commission's analysis of the problems, the Government proposed a different solution; it proposed the abolition of the defence of provocation and a new partial defence based on loss of self-control to replace it. As the Government also rejected the proposals in respect of murder, the new defence would, like provocation, operate to reduce the offence to manslaughter rather than to second degree murder. In January 2009 the Government published a summary of the responses to the consultation. It made alterations to several of the proposals. These alterations and some of the Government's reasoning in relation to other proposals are set out below.

MURDER, MANSLAUGHTER AND INFANTICIDE: PROPOSALS FOR REFORM OF THE LAW SUMMARY OF RESPONSES AND GOVERNMENT POSITION

Response to Consultation (CP(R)19/08)

Reform of the partial defence of provocation

To abolish the existing partial defence of *provocation* and replace it with two new partial defences of:

- *killing in response to a fear of serious violence*; and
- (to apply only in exceptional circumstances) *killing in response to words and conduct which caused the defendant to have a justifiable sense of being seriously wronged. . .*

Words and conduct

32. The proposals for the second limb of the partial defence, loss of control in response to words or conduct, received a mixed response.

33. A small number of respondents considered that this limb of the defence should not be available at all. They reasoned that killing in response to words or conduct should always be murder; they could not conceive of any circumstances in which it would be a justifiable defence that the defendant had killed someone because they were wronged by what had been said.

34. However, other respondents including a number of academics, did not support the Government's policy to restrict the current law. These respondents were concerned that deserving cases would be excluded, for example where the defendant killed out of grief or despair. Some of the concern about the injustice was linked to concerns about the mandatory life penalty.

35. In the middle there were a number of respondents who supported the Government's proposal to have a

narrowly available partial defence, on the basis that it would be for exceptional circumstances. This group agreed with the Government that complete abolition could lead to injustices in a small number of cases.

Government response

36. The Government recognises the diverging views about whether or not a partial defence should be available in exceptional circumstances where defendants kill in response to words or conduct. On balance, the Government believes that such a defence should remain.

37. In addition to the general views on the Government's policy, there were also concerns that the drafting would not achieve the policy as set out in the consultation document. The next few paragraphs look at comments on specific aspects of the definition of this limb of the proposed partial defence. Many respondents did not comment on any or all of them; the comments below are generally suggestions as to how the partial defence could be changed for the better.

Exceptional happening

38. A number of respondents did not think that the meaning of the term 'exceptional happening' is clear. . . There was also a concern that it relates solely to the frequency of an event. Related to this was a fear that cumulative abuse cases might be ruled out because the very nature of the frequent and cumulative abuse would mean that any final act which led to the loss of self-control would not be 'exceptional'.

Government response

39. It was always our intention that words and conduct which resulted in the loss of self-control might not be a single event but could be a series of words and/or conduct which, when taken together, amount to exceptional circumstances. We accept that the wording in the draft clause annexed to the consultation paper may not have conveyed this as well as desired.

40. We have therefore replaced the term 'exceptional happening' with 'circumstances of an extremely grave character'. This formulation should ensure that the defence is only available in a very narrow set of circumstances in which a killing in response to things said or done should rightly be classified as manslaughter rather than murder.

. . .

> To make clear that sexual infidelity on the part of the victim does not constitute grounds for reducing murder to manslaughter.

. . .

52. Some respondents thought that the drafting could have the effect that an act which should be capable of providing a basis for the defence might be excluded because it was also an act of sexual infidelity. For example, a partner raping a child should not be an act which is automatically excluded as a possible trigger for the loss of self-control on the basis that it was also infidelity.

53. Finally, a number of respondents thought that if there was an exclusion for sexual infidelity specifically on the face of the Act, there ought also to be an exclusion for honour killings.

Government response

54. The Government does not accept that sexual infidelity should ever provide the basis for a partial defence to murder. We therefore remain committed to making it clear—on the face of the statute—that sexual infidelity should not provide an excuse for killing.

55. We believe that where sexual infidelity is one part in a set of circumstances which led to the defendant losing self-control, the partial defence should succeed or fail on the basis of those circumstances disregarding the element of sexual infidelity. However, the Government has sought to improve the wording of the drafting in response to the concern raised in the paragraphs above.

56. The Government fully agrees that anyone involved in a so-called 'honour killing' should not be able to reduce a charge of murder to manslaughter on the basis of the victim's behaviour. The Government believes that the high threshold for the words and conduct limb of the partial defence will have the effect of excluding situations which might be characterised as 'honour killings' because such cases will not satisfy the requirements that the circumstances were of an extremely grave character and caused a justifiable sense of being seriously wronged. In addition we intend to introduce an exemption for cases where there is a 'considered desire for

revenge' which will also have a role to play in ensuring that so-called honour killings do not benefit from a partial defence (paragraph 74 below).

> To remove the existing common law requirement for loss of self-control in these circumstances to be 'sudden'.

57. Many respondents, including academics, legal practitioners and organisations supporting victims of violence, supported the proposal to remove the requirement that the loss of self-control should be sudden. However there were concerns that the drafting would not change the current law simply by abolishing the common law and that suddenness could be read back into the defence.

58. On the other side, there was concern on the part of some that the removal of the requirement of suddenness may open the door to revenge killings.

59. A number of respondents (particularly those representing victims of domestic abuse both in England and Wales and in Northern Ireland) thought that the Government should go further and abolish the requirement for a loss of self-control completely. The concern was that the need to show a loss of self-control at all could prevent some cases where the defendant had suffered long term domestic abuse from accessing the partial defence.

60. In addition, some academics and legal practitioners believed that the retention of the loss of self-control did not fit well with the intention for the partial defence to apply to cases of where a person overreacts to what they perceived as an imminent threat of serious violence. They argued that a defendant acting in self defence does so in a way that he or she believes is rational and therefore is inconsistent with a loss of self-control.

61. There was also a suggestion that loss of self-control should be replaced with 'extreme emotional disturbance', as a better description.

Government response

62. The Government believes that it is important that the partial defence is grounded in a loss of self control. We are not persuaded by the arguments for removing the requirement that the defendant must have lost self-control when they killed: we believe that the danger of opening this up to cold-blooded killing is too great.

63. In addition, we do not believe that the loss of self control requirement is inconsistent with situations where a person reacts to an imminent fear of serious violence. Indeed, loss of self control does not act as a bar to a full defence of self defence. This is particularly important where a loss of self control impairs a person's ability to accurately assess the degree of threat posed. The law has the flexibility to accommodate genuinely held, if mistaken beliefs, the like of which may well feature in cases where there has been a loss of self control.

64. Under the current law, a person claiming self defence is given a considerable degree of latitude. Defendants are not expected to weigh to a nicety the exact level of defensive force necessary in the situation, and when they honestly and instinctively do what they believe is necessary that is strong evidence that they have acted reasonably. The degree of force used should be proportionate to the *perceived* level of threat. Where the force used is judged unreasonable by these standards, the Government believes that it is right that the partial defence should only be available where a person is not in control of themselves.

65. In contrast the Government believes that if a defendant kills in full control of him or herself, then even if he or she fears serious violence there are insufficient grounds to reduce a murder charge to manslaughter.

66. We continue to believe that the right approach is to retain the requirement for control to have been lost but to remove the requirement for the loss to have been 'sudden' to make plain that situations where the defendant's reaction has been delayed or builds gradually are not excluded. However, we acknowledge the concerns that 'suddenness' could be read back into the law and therefore have decided to put the matter beyond doubt on the face of the statute. We also do not believe that it will be a bar to the partial defence applying in deserving cases of long-term abuse.

. . .

> To provide that the 'words and conduct' partial defence should not apply where the words and conduct were incited by the defendant for the purpose of providing an excuse to use violence.

Government response

68. As set out in more detail below, the Government considers that this exemption should be extended to the fear of serious violence limb of the defence, in order to ensure criminal gangs may not benefit from the defence if they have incited the violence in order to provide an excuse for killing.

    . . .

> To provide that neither partial defence should apply where criminal conduct on the part of the defendant is largely responsible for the situation in which he or she finds him or herself.

71. A number of respondents (including academics, legal practitioners and a campaigning organisation) were concerned that excluding all criminal conduct could lead to unjust outcomes in some cases, although they supported the underlying policy to exclude criminal gangs from the partial defence. The concern was that there are many criminal offences of varying degrees of seriousness and defendants could be excluded from the partial defence when that would be disproportionate to the criminality they were involved in. For example, there was a concern that a prostitute who killed an abusive and controlling pimp in response to a fear of serious violence might be excluded from the defence because of the very involvement in prostitution.

72. An alternative approach, suggested by one academic lawyer, would be to make criminal conduct a factor but not an absolute basis for exclusion from pleading the partial defence.

Government response

73. The Government believes that the drafting of the clause allowed for some flexibility in how criminal conduct would affect the defendant's access to the defence, as it excluded cases where the loss of self control was *predominantly* due to the criminality of the defendant. However, the Government accepts that there may be some cases where this test is met but it would nevertheless be disproportionate to bar the defendant from the defence, particularly where the criminality is at the lowest level of seriousness.

74. We therefore propose to remove this exclusion and replace it with two other safeguards to ensure that violence such as tit-for-tat gang killing is excluded from the defence:

- reinstating the exemption initially proposed by the Law Commission for those acting in considered desire for revenge;

- ensuring that those who incite violence, or the threat of it, in order to have an excuse for killing cannot use the defence. This was already exempted for the words and conduct limb of the defence but we will extend the exemption to the fear of serious violence limb also.

75. The Government recognises that there may be cases where individuals incite violence in legitimate circumstances. For example, the victim of a robbery might be said to incite violence from a robber by refusing to part with money. However, the extension will be to cases where the incitement was done for the purpose of providing an excuse for using violence, we therefore do not consider cases of legitimate incitement will be barred from the defence.

> To provide that these partial defences should apply only if a person of the defendant's sex and age, with a normal degree of tolerance and self-restraint and in the circumstances of the defendant, might have reacted in the same or in a similar way.

76. There were a number of comments about the inclusion of a test of 'reasonableness' in the partial defence. Some thought that the test for the partial defence should be entirely subjective, so that the fact that the defendant in fact lost self-control should be sufficient to form the basis of the defence. Others thought that the test was already too subjective.

77. Other views expressed were that the gender and age specific aspects are not helpful. One respondent was concerned that to include gender in the test could be seen as reinforcing sexism in the statute. Broken Rainbow, an organisation that provides support for lesbian, gay, bisexual and transgender people experiencing domestic violence, expressed concern about the ability of a 'typical jury' (one that is likely to be composed of a majority

of, if not entirely, heterosexual members) to empathise with a lesbian, gay, bisexual or transgender person. The concern about age was that it is arbitrary as not everyone matures at the same rate.

Government response

78. The Government believes that a test of 'reasonableness' is key to the partial defence, otherwise people with particularly short tempers could use that as an excuse for killing. On balance, and having considered carefully the views expressed, we are not persuaded of the arguments for removing references to gender and age in the test. . .

> To ensure that the judge should not be required to leave either of these defences to the jury unless there is evidence on which a reasonable jury properly directed could conclude that they might apply.

79. A number of respondents commented on this area and were concerned that judges would be able to withdraw a defence based on loss of self control in circumstances where the decision should be left to the jury.

Government response

80. These comments appear to show a misunderstanding of the Government's proposal. Under section 3 of the 1957 Act, where there is sufficient evidence that a person was provoked to lose their self-control, the defence of provocation must be put to the jury even in circumstances where no properly directed jury could reasonably conclude that the reasonableness requirement of the defence was made out. This is in contrast to the position that existed before the 1957 Act where the issue could be withdrawn from the jury if the judge considered that no reasonable jury could possibly conclude that a reasonable person would have done as the defendant did. An additional impact of the current law is that the judge must direct on provocation in circumstances where neither the prosecution *nor defence* have raised provocation as a defence, and indeed in cases where the defence would prefer for it not to be raised. This contrasts with the usual position whereby a judge need only direct on the defence when there is sufficient evidence that a jury might reasonably accept the defence. We think the general position for the defence, as it existed before the 1957 Act, is the appropriate one the new defence of loss of self control. We therefore accepted the Law Commission recommendation in this area to allow judges not to direct the jury on provocation where the evidence of the defence is very poor. Following concerns raised by the senior judiciary, we have amended the wording of the clause from that contained in the consultation paper to put the matter beyond doubt.

Note

The Government's proposals were quickly translated into legislation when the Coroners and Justice Act 2009 was enacted on 12 November 2009. The relevant provisions are ss.54–55 as set out below which came into force on 4 October 2010 applying to all murders on or after that date.

CORONERS AND JUSTICE ACT 2009

Partial defence to murder: loss of control

54   Partial defence to murder: loss of control

(1)   Where a person ('D') kills or is a party to the killing of another ('V'), D is not to be convicted of murder if—

  (a)   D's acts and omissions in doing or being a party to the killing resulted from D's loss of self-control,
  (b)   the loss of self-control had a qualifying trigger, and
  (c)   a person of D's sex and age, with a normal degree of tolerance and self-restraint and in the circumstances of D, might have reacted in the same or in a similar way to D.

(2) For the purposes of subsection (1)(a), it does not matter whether or not the loss of control was sudden.

(3) In subsection (1)(c) the reference to 'the circumstances of D' is a reference to all of D's circumstances other than those whose only relevance to D's conduct is that they bear on D's general capacity for tolerance or self-restraint.

(4) Subsection (1) does not apply if, in doing or being a party to the killing, D acted in a considered desire for revenge.

(5) On a charge of murder, if sufficient evidence is adduced to raise an issue with respect to the defence under subsection (1), the jury must assume that the defence is satisfied unless the prosecution proves beyond reasonable doubt that it is not.

(6) For the purposes of subsection (5), sufficient evidence is adduced to raise an issue with respect to the defence if evidence is adduced on which, in the opinion of the trial judge, a jury, properly directed, could reasonably conclude that the defence might apply.

(7) A person who, but for this section, would be liable to be convicted of murder is liable instead to be convicted of manslaughter.

(8) The fact that one party to a killing is by virtue of this section not liable to be convicted of murder does not affect the question whether the killing amounted to murder in the case of any other party to it.

55   Meaning of 'qualifying trigger'

(1) This section applies for the purposes of section 54.

(2) A loss of self-control had a qualifying trigger if subsection (3), (4) or (5) applies.

(3) This subsection applies if D's loss of self-control was attributable to D's fear of serious violence from V against D or another identified person.

(4) This subsection applies if D's loss of self-control was attributable to a thing or things done or said (or both) which—

    (a) constituted circumstances of an extremely grave character, and
    (b) caused D to have a justifiable sense of being seriously wronged.

(5) This subsection applies if D's loss of self-control was attributable to a combination of the matters mentioned in subsections (3) and (4).

(6) In determining whether a loss of self-control had a qualifying trigger—

    (a) D's fear of serious violence is to be disregarded to the extent that it was caused by a thing which D incited to be done or said for the purpose of providing an excuse to use violence;
    (b) a sense of being seriously wronged by a thing done or said is not justifiable if D incited the thing to be done or said for the purpose of providing an excuse to use violence;
    (c) the fact that a thing done or said constituted sexual infidelity is to be disregarded.

(7) In this section references to 'D' and 'V' are to be construed in accordance with section 54.

56   Abolition of common law defence of provocation

(1) The common law defence of provocation is abolished and replaced by sections 54 and 55.

(2) Accordingly, the following provisions cease to have effect—

    (a) section 3 of the Homicide Act 1957 (c. 11) (questions of provocation to be left to the jury);
    (b) section 7 of the Criminal Justice Act (Northern Ireland) 1966 (c. 20) (questions of provocation to be left to the jury).

Note

In the report which follows, the Court of Appeal considered three appeals together in order to provide significant guidance at an early stage on the interpretation of the new defence of loss of control. The Court makes it clear that this is a new defence and that resort should not be had to the case law under the old law of provocation. It also indicates that little assistance on interpretation is to be gleaned from the reports and recommendations of the Law Commission prior to the enactment of the 2009 Act as the Government differed in significant respects from those recommendations. The report provides useful guidance in the appeal by Parker on the way in which the defence of loss of control operates in practice; in particular, the judge's role in determining whether there is sufficient evidence of loss of self-control arising from a qualifying trigger to place a burden on the prosecution to disprove the defence and, if so, how the judge should sum up to the jury. The issue of sexual infidelity was also considered in detail in the appeal by Clinton. Section 55(6)(c) provides that when determining whether a loss of self-control had a qualifying trigger, "the fact that a thing done or said constituted sexual infidelity is to be disregarded". The Court sought to consider the limits of this provision and gave consideration to the questions whether the context in which a killing and loss of self-control occurred had to be looked at artificially ignoring any background of infidelity which might be con-nected to, or add colour to, other things said or done which might amount to a qualifying trigger and whether in considering the objective question in s.54(1)(c), D's circumstances should include contex-tual information pertaining to sexual infidelity. In the third appeal, Evans, a key issue was whether D had "acted in a considered desire for revenge". The judge directed the jury as follows:

"An act of retribution as a result of a deliberate and considered decision to get your own back, that is one that has been thought about. If you are sure that what the defendant did was to reflect on what had happened and the circumstances in which he found himself and decided to take his revenge on (his wife), that would not have been a loss of self-control as the law requires."

This direction was challenged on the basis that it did not provide the jury with a sufficient elucidation of the significance of the use of the word "considered" in its statutory context. The Court indicated that there was no need to rewrite the statute and that a direction to the jury using the words of the statute was not amenable to challenge whereas a reformulation of the statutory language harboured the potential for confusion. (Evans' case is not further considered below.)

R V CLINTON; R V PARKER; R V EVANS

[2012] EWCA Crim 2

THE LORD CHIEF JUSTICE OF ENGLAND AND WALES

Introduction

1. The difficulties of giving consistent effect to section 3 of the Homicide Act 1957, which encapsulated in statu-tory form the common law defence of provocation, were notorious. . . With effect from 4 October 2010 section 3 of the 1957 Act ceased to have effect. The ancient common law defence of provocation, reducing murder to manslaughter, was abolished and consigned to legal history books.

2. It was replaced by sections 54 and 55 of the Coroners and Justice Act 2009 (the 2009 Act) which created a new partial defence to murder, 'loss of control'. Just because loss of control was an essential ingredient of the

old provocation defence, the name is evocative of it. It therefore needs to be emphasised at the outset that the new statutory defence is self-contained. Its common law heritage is irrelevant. The full ambit of the defence is encompassed within these statutory provisions. Unfortunately there are aspects of the legislation which, to put it with appropriate deference, are likely to produce surprising results. . .

4. In these appeals the main focus of our attention is the controversial provision which relates to the impact on the 'loss of control' defence of what is described as 'sexual infidelity'. We looked, *de bene esse*, at the debates in Parliament prior to the enactment. Even on the most generous interpretation of *Pepper v Hart*, the debates did not reveal anything which assisted in the process of legislative construction. So we must ascertain the meaning of these provisions from their language. As we shall explain, however, the conclusion we have reached is consistent not only with the views which would have been expressed by those who were opposed to this provision in its entirety, but also with the views expressed by ministers responsible for the legislation during its passage through Parliament.

. . .

8. . . . There are cases, and Clinton was one, where the defences of loss of control and diminished responsibility will be raised in the same proceedings. The defence arises from an abnormality of mental functioning which

'. . . (b) substantially impaired D's ability to do one or more of the things mentioned in sub-section (1a) and . . .

(1A) those things are—

    (a)   to understand the nature of D's conduct;
    (b)   to form a rational judgment;
    (c)   to exercise self-control. . .'

9. The first feature of section 54 is that it identifies three statutory components (or ingredients) to the 'loss of control' defence. We begin by emphasising that each is integral to it. If one is absent, the defence fails. It is therefore inevitable that the components should be analysed sequentially and separately. However, it is worth emphasising that in many cases where there is a genuine loss of control, the remaining components are likely to arise for consideration simultaneously or virtually so, at or very close to the moment when the fatal violence is used. Further, the discussion will proceed in terms which suggest that the defendant seeking to advance the loss of control defence is not always male. This is because experience shows that women as well as men kill when they have lost self-control. In the legislation no special provision is made for the gender of the killer. Finally, by way of introduction, we do not overlook that the burden of disproof is on the prosecution.

The first component

10. For present purposes, subsection 1(a), which addresses the first ingredient, is self-explanatory. The killing must have resulted from the loss of self-control. The loss of control need not be sudden, but it must have been lost. That is essential. Before reaching the second ingredient, the qualifying trigger, there is a further hurdle, that the defendant must not have been acting in a 'considered' desire for revenge. The possible significance of 'considered' arises in the appeal of Evans. In the broad context of the legislative structure, there does not appear to be very much room for any 'considered' deliberation. In reality, the greater the level of deliberation, the less likely it will be that the killing followed a true loss of self-control.

The second component

11. The qualifying trigger provisions are self-contained in section 55. There is no point in pretending that the practical application of this provision will not create considerable difficulties. Sections 55(3) and (4) define the circumstances in which a qualifying trigger may be present. The statutory language is not bland. In section 55(3) it is not enough that the defendant is fearful of violence. He must fear *serious* violence. In subsection (4)(a) the circumstances must not merely be grave, but *extremely* so. In subsection (4)(b) it is not enough that the defendant has been caused by the circumstances to feel a sense of grievance. It must arise from a *justifiable* sense not merely that he has been wronged, but that he has been *seriously* wronged. By contrast with the former law of provocation, these provisions, as Mr Michael Birnbaum QC, on behalf of Clinton submitted, have raised the bar. We have been used to a much less prescriptive approach to the provocation defence.

12. Mr Birnbaum submitted, and we think correctly, that the defendant himself must have a sense of having been seriously wronged. However even if he has, that is not the end of it. In short, the defendant cannot invite the jury to acquit him of murder on the ground of loss of control because he personally sensed that he had been seriously wronged in circumstances which he personally regarded as extremely grave. The questions whether the

circumstances were extremely grave, and whether the defendant's sense of grievance was justifiable, indeed all the requirements of section 55(4)(a) and (b), require objective evaluation.

13. The process of objective evaluation in each individual case is hugely complicated by the prohibitions in section 55(6) which identifies a number of features which are expressly excluded from consideration as qualifying triggers. Thus the defendant, who, looking for trouble to the extent of inciting or exciting violence loses his control, does not qualify. In effect self-induced loss of control will not run. The most critical problem, however, which lies at the heart of the *Clinton* appeal, is subsection 6(c), 'sexual infidelity'.

14. This provision was described by Mr Andrew Edis QC, who acted for the prosecution in each of the appeals, as a 'formidably difficult provision': so indeed it is. On the face of the statutory language, however grave the betrayal, however humiliating, indeed however provocative in the ordinary sense of the word it may be, sexual infidelity is to be disregarded as a qualifying trigger. Nevertheless, other forms of betrayal or humiliation of sufficient gravity may fall within the qualifying triggers specified in section 55(4). What, therefore, is the full extent of the prohibition?

15. We highlight some of the matters raised in argument to illustrate some of the potential problems. This list is not comprehensive. The forensic analysis could have gone on much longer, and so, for that matter, could this judgment.

16. We immediately acknowledge that the exclusion of sexual infidelity as a potential qualifying trigger is consistent with the concept of the autonomy of each individual. Of course, whatever the position may have been in times past, it is now clearly understood, and in the present context the law underlines, that no one (male or female) owns or possesses his or her spouse or partner. . . Meanwhile experience over many generations has shown that, however it may become apparent, when it does, sexual infidelity has the potential to create a highly emotional situation or to exacerbate a fraught situation, and to produce a completely unpredictable, and sometimes violent response. . .

17. Mr Birnbaum drew attention to and adopted much of the illuminating and critical commentary by Professor Ormerod at pp.520–522 in Smith and Hogan's Criminal Law. To begin with, there is no definition of 'sexual infidelity'. Who and what is embraced in this concept? Is sexual infidelity to be construed narrowly so as to refer only to conduct which is related directly and exclusively to sexual activity? Only the words and acts constituting sexual activity are to be disregarded: on one construction, therefore, the effects are not. What acts relating to infidelity, but distinguishable from it on the basis that they are not 'sexual', may be taken into account? Is the provision directly concerned with sexual infidelity, or with envy and jealousy and possessiveness, the sort of obsession that leads to violence against the victim on the basis expressed in the sadly familiar language, 'if I cannot have him/her, then no one else will/can'? The notion of infidelity appears to involve a relationship between the two people to which one party may be unfaithful. Is a one-night-stand sufficient for this purpose?

18. Take a case like *R v Stingel* [1990] 171 CLR 312, an Australian case where a jealous stalker, who stabbed his quarry when he found her, on his account, having sexual intercourse. He does not face any difficulty with this element of the offence, just because, so far as the stalker was concerned, there was no sexual infidelity by his victim at all. Is the jealous spouse to be excluded when the stalker is not? In *R v Tabeel Lewis* . . . an 18 year old Jehovah's Witness killed his lover, a 63 year old co-religionist, because on one view, he was ashamed of the consequences, if she carried out her threat to reveal their affair to the community. She was not sexually unfaithful to him, but he killed her because he feared that she would betray him, not sexually, but by revealing their secret. Mr Birnbaum asked rhetorically, why should the law exclude one kind of betrayal by a lover but not another?

19. Mr Edis agreed that 'sexual infidelity' is not defined. He suggested that its ambit is not confined to 'adultery' and that no marriage or civil partnership ceremony or any formal arrangement is required to render the violent reaction of the defendant to the sexual infidelity of the deceased impermissible for the purposes of a qualifying trigger. He suggested however that the concept of 'infidelity' involves a breach of mutual understanding which is to be inferred within the relationship, as well as any of the more obvious expressions of fidelity, such as those to be found in the marriage vows. Notwithstanding their force, these considerations do not quite address the specific requirement that the infidelity to be disregarded must be 'sexual' infidelity. The problem was illustrated when Mr Edis postulated the example of a female victim who decided to end a relationship and made clear to her former partner that it was at an end, and whether expressly or by implication, that she regarded herself as free to have sexual intercourse with whomsoever she wanted. After the end of the relationship, any such sexual activity could not sensibly be called 'infidelity'. If so, for the purposes of any qualifying trigger, it would not be caught by the prohibition in section 55(6)(c). In such a case the exercise of what Mr Edis described as her sexual freedom might possibly be taken into account in support of the defence, if she was killed by her former partner, whereas, if notwithstanding her disillusionment with it, she had attempted to keep the relationship going, while from time to time having intercourse with others, it could not.

20. Mr Birnbaum and Mr Edis could readily have identified a large number of situations arising in the real world which, as a result of the statutory provision, would be productive of surprising anomalies. We cannot resolve them in advance. Whatever the anomalies to which it may give rise, the statutory provision is unequivocal: loss of control triggered by sexual infidelity cannot, on its own, qualify as a trigger for the purposes of the second component of this defence. This is the clear effect of the legislation.

21. The question however is whether it is a consequence of the legislation that sexual infidelity is similarly excluded when it may arise for consideration in the context of another or a number of other features of the case which are said to constitute an appropriate permissible qualifying trigger. The issue is complex.

22. To assist in its resolution, Mr Edis drew attention to the formal guidance issued by the Crown Prosecution Service on this issue. This provides that 'it is the issue of sexual infidelity that falls to be disregarded under subsection (6)(c). However certain parts of the case may still amount to a defence under section 55(4)'. The example is given of the defendant who kills her husband because he has raped her sister (an act of sexual infidelity). In such a case the act of sexual infidelity may be disregarded and her actions may constitute a qualifying trigger under section 55(4).

23. This example is interesting as far as it goes, and we understand it to mean that the context in which sexual infidelity may arise may be relevant to the existence of a qualifying trigger, but in truth it is too easy. Any individual who witnesses a rape may well suffer temporary loss of control in circumstances in which a qualifying trigger might well be deemed to be present, although in the case of a rape of a stranger, insufficient to cause the defendant to have a sense of being seriously wronged personally. A much more formidable and difficult example would be the defendant who kills her husband when she suddenly finds him having enthusiastic, consensual sexual intercourse with her sister. Taken on its own, the effect of the legislation is that any loss of control consequent on such a gross betrayal would be totally excluded from consideration as a qualifying trigger. Let us for the purposes of argument take the same example a little further. The defendant returns home unexpectedly and finds her spouse or partner having consensual sexual intercourse with her sister (or indeed with anyone else), and entirely reasonably, but vehemently, complains about what has suddenly confronted her. The response by the unfaithful spouse or partner, and/or his or her new sexual companion, is to justify what he had been doing, by shouting and screaming, mercilessly taunting and deliberately using hurtful language which implies that she, not he, is responsible for his infidelity. The taunts and distressing words, which do not themselves constitute sexual infidelity, would fall to be considered as a possible qualifying trigger. The idea that, in the search for a qualifying trigger, the context in which such words are used should be ignored represents an artificiality which the administration of criminal justice should do without. And if the taunts by the unfaithful partner suggested that the sexual activity which had just been taking place was infinitely more gratifying than any earlier sexual relationship with the defendant, are those insults – in effect using sexual infidelity to cause deliberate distress – to be ignored? On the view of the legislation advanced for our consideration by Mr Edis, they must be. Yet, in most criminal cases, as our recent judgment in the context of the riots and public order demonstrates, context is critical.

24. We considered the example of the wife who has been physically abused over a long period, and whose loss of self-control was attributable to yet another beating by her husband, but also, for the first time, during the final beating, taunts of his sexual activities with another woman or other women. And so, after putting up with years of violent ill-treatment, what in reality finally caused the defendant's loss of control was hurtful language boasting of his sexual infidelity. Those words were the final straw. Mr Edis invited us to consider (he did not support the contention) whether, on a narrow interpretation of the statutory structure, if evidence to that effect were elicited (as it might, in cross-examination), there would then be no sufficient qualifying trigger at all. Although the persistent beating might in a different case fall within the provisions for qualifying triggers in section 55(4)(a) and (b), in the case we are considering, the wife had endured the violence and would have continued to endure it but for the sudden discovery of her husband's infidelity. On this basis the earlier history of violence, as well as the violence on the instant occasion, would not, without reference to the claims of sexual infidelity, carry sufficient weight to constitute a qualifying trigger. Yet in the real world the husband's conduct over the years, and the impact of what he said on the particular occasion when he was killed, should surely be considered as a whole.

25. We addressed the same issue in discussion about the impact of the words 'things said' within subsection 55(6)(c). Everyone can understand how a thing done may constitute sexual infidelity, but this argument revolved around finding something 'said' which 'constituted' sexual infidelity. Mr Edis accepted that no utterance, as such, could constitute sexual infidelity, at any rate as narrowly construed. Professor Ormerod suggests the example of a defendant hearing a wife say to her lover, 'I love you'. On close examination, this may or may not provide evidence of *sexual* infidelity. However it does not necessarily 'constitute' it, and whether it does or not depends on the relationship between the parties, and the person by whom and to whom and the circumstances in which the endearment is spoken. It may constitute a betrayal without any sexual contact or intention. Mr Birnbaum raised

another question. He pointed out that in the case of Clinton, Mrs Clinton confessed to having had an affair on the day before she was killed, but earlier she boasted that she had had sex with five men. If the boast, intended to hurt, was simply untrue, how could those words 'constitute' infidelity?

26. We are required to make sense of this provision. It would be illogical for a defendant to be able to rely on an untrue statement about the victim's sexual infidelity as a qualifying trigger in support of the defence, but not on a truthful one. Equally, it would be quite unrealistic to limit its ambit to words spoken to his or her lover by the unfaithful spouse or partner during sexual activity. In our judgment things 'said' includes admissions of sexual infidelity (even if untrue) as well as reports (by others) of sexual infidelity. Such admissions or reports will rarely if ever be uttered without a context, and almost certainly a painful one. In short, the words will almost invariably be spoken as part of a highly charged discussion in which many disturbing comments will be uttered, often on both sides.

27. We must briefly return to the second example suggested by Professor Ormerod, that is the defendant telling his spouse or partner that he or she loves someone else. As we have said, this may or may not provide evidence of *sexual* infidelity. But it is entirely reasonable to assume that, faced with such an assertion, the defendant will ask who it is, and is likely to go on to ask whether they have already had an affair. If the answer is 'no' there would not appear to be any sexual infidelity. If the answer is 'yes', then obviously there has been. If the answer is 'no', but it is perfectly obvious that the departing spouse intends to begin a full relationship with the new partner, would that constitute sexual infidelity? And is there a relevant distinction between the defendant who believes that a sexual relationship has already developed, and one who believes that it has not, but that in due course it will. Situations arising from overhearing the other party to a relationship saying 'I love you', or saying to the defendant, 'I love someone else', simple enough words, will give rise to manifold difficulties in the context of the prohibition on sexual infidelity as a qualifying trigger.

28. This discussion of the impact of the statutory prohibition in section 55(6)(c) arises, we emphasise, in the context, not of an academic symposium, but a trial process in which the defendant will be entitled to give evidence. There is no prohibition on the defendant telling the whole story about the relevant events, including the fact and impact of sexual infidelity. To the contrary: this evidence will have to be considered and evaluated by the jury. That is because notwithstanding that sexual infidelity must be disregarded for the purposes of the second component if it stands alone as a qualifying trigger, for the reasons which follow it is plainly relevant to any questions which arise in the context of the third component, and indeed to one of the alternative defences to murder, as amended in the 2009 Act, diminished responsibility.

29. We shall return to the question whether, notwithstanding that it must be disregarded if it is the only qualifying trigger, a thing done or said which constitutes sexual infidelity is properly available for consideration in the course of evaluating any qualifying trigger which is not otherwise prohibited by the legislation.

The third component

30. Assuming that the qualifying trigger is present, the defence is still not complete. We must return from section 55 to section 54 (1)(c). This third ingredient is related to the requirement, that even faced with situations which may amount to a qualifying trigger, the defendant is nevertheless expected to exercise a degree of self-control. For this purpose the age and sex of the defendant is relevant. Perhaps a very immature defendant will be less likely to be able to exercise the self-control which might be exercised by an adult. The defendant's reaction (that is what he actually did, rather than the fact that he lost his self-control) may therefore be understandable in the sense that another person in his situation and the circumstances in which he found himself, might have reacted in the same or in a similar way.

31. For present purposes the most significant feature of the third component is that the impact on the defendant of sexual infidelity is not excluded. The exclusion in section 55(6)(c) is limited to the assessment of the qualifying trigger. In relation to the third component, that is the way in which the defendant has reacted and lost control, 'the circumstances' are not constrained or limited. Indeed, section 54(3) expressly provides that reference to the defendant's circumstances extends to 'all' of the circumstances except those bearing on his general capacity for tolerance and self-restraint. When the third component of the defence is examined it emerges that, notwithstanding section 55(6)(c), account may, and in an appropriate case, should be taken of sexual infidelity.

32. We must reflect briefly on the directions to be given by the judge to the jury. On one view they would require the jury to disregard any evidence relating to sexual infidelity when they are considering the second component of the defence, yet, notwithstanding this prohibition, would also require the same evidence to be addressed if the third component arises for consideration. In short, there will be occasions when the jury would be both disregarding and considering the same evidence. That is, to put it neutrally, counter intuitive.

Diminished responsibility

33. The situation for the jury, and the judge, is yet further complicated if and when, as sometimes happens, the defence is inviting the jury to consider possible verdicts of manslaughter both on the grounds of loss of control and diminished responsibility. If the defendant is suffering from a recognised medical condition, for example, serious and chronic depression, the discovery that a partner has been sexually unfaithful may, and often will be said to, impair the defendant's ability to form a rational judgment and exercise self-control. This situation is not all that uncommon. It arose in Clinton where one of the psychiatrists suggested that if Clinton was telling the truth, the effect of his 'depressed state' would have been that he would have been more likely to lose self-control following his wife's graphic account of sexual activity with other men and her taunts that he lacked the courage to commit suicide. Sexual infidelity may therefore require consideration when the jury is examining the diminished responsibility defence even when it has been excluded from consideration as a qualifying trigger for the purposes of the loss of control defence.

Sexual infidelity—conclusion

34. We must now address the full extent of the prohibition against 'sexual infidelity' as a qualifying trigger for the purposes of the loss of control defence. The question is whether or not sexual infidelity is wholly excluded from consideration in the context of features of the individual case which constitute a permissible qualifying trigger or triggers within section 55(3) and (4).

35. We have examined the legislative structure as a whole. The legislation was designed to prohibit the misuse of sexual infidelity as a potential trigger for loss of control in circumstances in which it was thought to have been misused in the former defence of provocation. Where there is no other potential trigger, the prohibition must, notwithstanding the difficulties identified earlier in the judgment, be applied.

36. The starting point is that it has been recognised for centuries that sexual infidelity may produce a loss of control in men, and, more recently in women as well as men who are confronted with sexual infidelity. The exclusion created by section 55(6) cannot and does not eradicate the fact that on occasions sexual infidelity and loss of control are linked, often with the one followed immediately by the other. Indeed on one view if it did not recognise the existence of this link, the policy decision expressly to exclude sexual infidelity as a qualifying trigger would be unnecessary.

37. In section 54(1)(c) and (3) the legislation further acknowledges the impact of sexual infidelity as a potential ingredient of the third component of the defence, when all the defendant's circumstances fall for consideration, and when, although express provision is made for the exclusion of some features of the defendant's situation, the fact that he/she has been sexually betrayed is not. In short, sexual infidelity is not subject to a blanket exclusion when the loss of control defence is under consideration. Evidence of these matters may be deployed by the defendant and therefore the legislation proceeds on the basis that sexual infidelity is a permissible feature of the loss of control defence.

38. The ambit of section 55(3) and (4) – the second component, the qualifying triggers – is clearly defined. Any qualifying trigger is subject to clear statutory criteria. Dealing with it broadly, to qualify as a trigger for the defendant's loss of control, the circumstances must be extremely grave and the defendant must be subject to a justifiable sense of having been seriously wronged. These are fact specific questions requiring careful assessment, not least to ensure that the loss of control defence does not have the effect of minimising the seriousness of the infliction of fatal injury. Objective evaluation is required and a judgment must be made about the gravity of the circumstances and the extent to which the defendant was seriously wronged, and whether he had a justifiable sense that he had been seriously wronged.

39. Our approach has, as the judgment shows, been influenced by the simple reality that in relation to the day to day working of the criminal justice system events cannot be isolated from their context. We have provided a number of examples in the judgment. Perhaps expressed most simply, the man who admits, 'I killed him accidentally', is never to be treated as if he had said 'I killed him'. That would be absurd. It may not be unduly burdensome to compartmentalise sexual infidelity where it is the only element relied on in support of a qualifying trigger, and, having compartmentalised it in this way, to disregard it. Whether this is so or not, the legislation imposes that exclusionary obligation on the court. However, to seek to compartmentalise sexual infidelity and exclude it when it is integral to the facts as a whole is not only much more difficult, but is unrealistic and carries with it the potential for injustice. In the examples we have given earlier in this judgment, we do not see how any sensible evaluation of the gravity of the circumstances or their impact on the defendant could be made if the jury, having, in accordance with the legislation, heard the evidence, were then to be directed to excise from their evaluation of the qualifying trigger the matters said to constitute sexual infidelity, and to put them into distinct compartments

to be disregarded. In our judgment, where sexual infidelity is integral to and forms an essential part of the context in which to make a just evaluation whether a qualifying trigger properly falls within the ambit of subsections 55(3) and (4), the prohibition in section 55(6)(c) does not operate to exclude it.

. . .

The responsibilities of the judge

(a) at the conclusion of the evidence

45. One of the responsibilities the trial judge in the context of the new defence is defined. Unless there is evidence sufficient to raise the issue of loss of control it should be withdrawn from consideration by the jury. If there is, then the prosecution must disprove it. In this context 'sufficient evidence' is explained by reference to well understood principles, that is, that a properly directed jury could 'reasonably conclude that the defence might apply'. In reaching this decision the judge is required to address the ingredients of the defence, as defined in section 54 and further amplified in section 55. There must be sufficient evidence to establish each of the ingredients defined in subsections 54(1)(a),(b) and (c), and this carries with it, evidence which satisfies the test in subsections 55(4)(a) and (b). In making the decision in accordance with the principles identified in this judgment the judge must exclude the specific matters which might otherwise be regarded as constituting possible justification in section 55(6)(b) and the express conditions to be disregarded in accordance with section 55(6)(a) and (c). In the end however, although the judge must bear these different features in mind when deciding whether the case should be left to the jury, and the task is far from straightforward, these statutory provisions reflect well established principles summarised in the phrase 'the evidential burden'. Sufficient evidence must be adduced to enable the judgment to be made that a jury could reasonably decide that the prosecution had failed to negate the defence of loss of control.

46. This requires a common sense judgment based on an analysis of all the evidence. To the extent that the evidence may be in dispute, the judge has to recognise that the jury may accept the evidence which is most favourable to the defendant, and reject that which is most favourable to the prosecution, and so tailor the ruling accordingly. That is merely another way of saying that in discharging this responsibility the judge should not reject disputed evidence which the jury might choose to believe. Guiding himself or herself in this way, the more difficult question which follows is the judgment whether the circumstances were sufficiently grave and whether the defendant had a justifiable grievance because he had been seriously wronged. These are value judgments. They are left to the jury when the judge concludes that the evidential burden has been satisfied.

47. When exercising these responsibilities, the judge is not, where there is no sufficient evidence to leave the loss of control defence to the jury, directing a conviction in the sense prohibited in *Wang* [2005] 1WLR 66. The statutory provision is clear. If there is evidence on which the jury could reasonably conclude that the loss of control defence might apply, it must be left to the jury: if there is no such evidence, then it must be withdrawn. Thereafter in accordance with the judge's directions the jury will consider and return its verdict.

48. The appeals of Clinton and Parker highlight these difficulties. In Clinton the defence was not left to the jury and it is argued that it should have been. In Parker the defence was left to the jury, and certainly had the prosecution suggested that the defence should be withdrawn, the judge might have felt it necessary to withdraw it from the jury.

(b) The Summing Up

49. Confining ourselves to the second component (the qualifying trigger or triggers under section 55), for the reasons already given, if the only potential qualifying trigger is sexual infidelity, effect must be given to the legislation. There will then be no qualifying trigger, and the judge must act accordingly. The more problematic situations will arise when the defendant relies on an admissible trigger (or triggers) for which sexual infidelity is said to provide an appropriate context (as explained in this judgment) for evaluating whether the trigger relied on is a qualifying trigger for the purposes of subsection 55(3) and (4). When this situation arises the jury should be directed:

   a)   as to the statutory ingredients required of the qualifying trigger or triggers;

   b)   as to the statutory prohibition against sexual infidelity on its own constituting a qualifying trigger;

   c)   as to the features identified by the defence (or which are apparent to the trial judge) which are said to constitute a permissible trigger or triggers;

d)   that, if these are rejected by the jury, in accordance with (b) above sexual infidelity must then be disregarded;

e)   that if, however, an admissible trigger may be present, the evidence relating to sexual infidelity arises for consideration as part of the context in which to evaluate that trigger and whether the statutory ingredients identified in (a) above may be established.

Jon-Jacques Clinton

50. We shall summarise the facts very briefly . . .. Mr and Mrs Clinton had lived together for 16 years. They had two children of school age. They married in 2001. Two weeks before her death, the appellant's wife had left him and the children of the family as they began what was described as a trial separation. She went to live with her parents. The couple continued to spend time together with the children as a family, and their mother would return to the family home to look after them on their return from school until the appellant returned home from work.

51. Mrs Clinton spent time in the family home on Saturday 13th November, and they went swimming and ate dinner together as a family on the next day. On that day Mrs Clinton told the appellant that she was having an affair.

52. That evening Mrs Clinton's Land Rover or Jeep (her most treasured possession) was stolen from outside her parent's home. On the following morning it was found in a burnt out condition. The jury was satisfied that the appellant was responsible for the removal and damage to the car. He was contacted by the police on the morning when the vehicle was found. He went over to see Mrs Clinton at her parent's home to tell her of the incident, and during a brief visit, arrangements were made for her to return to the family home to collect insurance documents relating to the vehicle. During the morning the appellant consumed drink and drugs, including a large amount of Codeine and he searched websites containing material dealing with suicide.

53. Mrs Clinton was dropped at the family home by her mother at about 14.00 hours. When her mother returned at 15.40 she found that the curtains were drawn and the door was barricaded. Police attended at about 17.10. They forced the front door. They found the body of Mrs Clinton on the living room floor semi naked. She had obvious head injuries. There was a ligature around her neck. She was pronounced dead. The appellant was found in the loft with a noose around his neck attached to the rafters.

54. The deceased had been beaten about the head with a wooden baton, strangled with a belt, and then a piece of rope had been tightened around her neck with the aid of the wooden baton. There were defensive injuries. The cause of death was head injury and asphyxia caused by a ligature compression of the neck. After he had killed her the appellant removed most of her clothes and having put her body into a number of different poses, took photographs of it and then sent text messages to Mr Montgomery, the man with whom she was having a relationship.

55. The prosecution case was that the appellant had set fire to the Land Rover out of spite and then, incensed when he found out that she was conducting an affair with another man, he had confronted her at the family home in the afternoon of 15th November. He had planned to kill her before she arrived at the house and had made preparations to do so. During the confrontation he beat her and strangled her to death. At a plea and case management hearing the appellant pleaded guilty to manslaughter, but not guilty to murder. Although responsible for his wife's death, either on the basis of 'loss of control' or 'diminished responsibility', he was not guilty of murder.

56. [The defendant gave evidence at his trial describing his depression, intention to commit suicide, the information he had obtained by reading his wife's Facebook entries describing her status as 'separated' and her affair (including messages replete with sexual innuendo between her and the man with whom she was having an affair), the confrontation that had taken place between them when she had come to the house relating to her affairs (including her graphic accounts of what she had done with other men), their children, his financial worries, his confession to burning her car, his intention to commit suicide, her dismissal of this, and his actions in attacking her with a piece of wood.]

. . .

76. At the conclusion of the evidence Judge Smith directed herself that there was no evidence that the loss of self-control necessary for the purposes of this defence was due to one of the qualifying triggers identified in the statute. She was required 'specifically' to disregard anything said or done that constituted sexual infidelity. The remarks allegedly made by the wife, challenged about her infidelity, to the effect that she had intercourse with five men were to be ignored. Removing that element of that evidence, what was left was the evidence when the wife saw that the appellant had visited the suicide site on the internet, she commented that he had 'not the balls to commit suicide' and that she also said, so far as the future was concerned, that he could have the children who

were then currently living with him at their home. The judge observed that she could not see that the circumstances were of an extremely grave character or that they would cause the defendant to have a justifiable sense of being seriously wrong. On this issue no sufficient evidence had been adduced. She could not find that a jury properly directed could reasonably conclude that the defence might apply. In due course she proceeded to her summing up, leaving diminished responsibility for the consideration of the jury.

77. In addressing these problems, Judge Smith did not have the advantage of the careful and detailed submissions made to us by leading counsel on behalf of the appellant and the Crown. On the basis that the remarks made by the wife had to be disregarded, her conclusion that the defence should be withdrawn from the jury was unassailable. In context, it was a characteristically courageous decision. For the reasons we have endeavoured to explain in this judgment, we have concluded that she misdirected herself about the possible relevance of the wife's infidelity. We have reflected whether the totality of the matters relied on as a qualifying trigger, evaluated in the context of the evidence relating to the wife's sexual infidelity, and examined as a cohesive whole, were of sufficient weight to leave to the jury. In our judgment they were. Accordingly the appeal against conviction will be allowed.

78. In the circumstances of this case, we shall order a new trial. The issues should be examined by a jury.

R v Steven Parker

79. The appellant and his wife, Jane, were both in their mid-twenties at the date of her death. They had been in a relationship for some 10 years, and they were married for the last 4 years. They had three children together.

80. During their marriage the appellant had a number of affairs, and his wife had a brief sexual relationship with another man. The appellant was unaware of this until after her death. During the year prior to her death she had confided in close friends and family that she was unhappy in her marriage and was seeking to separate from the appellant. She planned to leave him after the October half-term holiday in 2010, although she had not told the appellant.

81. On the night of 26th October 2010 in the course of an argument between them, he inflicted what was described as a 'fat lip' on her. On the following afternoon while she was at an activity centre with her children, Mrs Parker sent a text message to the applicant who was at home. Ignoring the text language it reads as follows:

'I'm sorry, Steve. I will always love you but you have hurt me too much now. I've never forgiven you for Claire, so think it's time for us to separate. Pack your stuff while I am here so kids don't see it all. And I'll drop car off in a bit for you to put your stuff in and go. Nothing you say or do will change my mind. x'

82. On leaving the activity centre her brother-in-law accompanied her to the matrimonial home. They arrived at the house between 15.54 and 15.58. Mrs Parker went into the house. The appellant locked the back door. Her brother-in-law was told to wait outside. Within a short period of her entering the house, the precise length of which was in dispute, Mrs Parker was attacked and repeatedly stabbed by the appellant. Her brother-in-law heard her screams and broke into the house. He wrestled the appellant off her and summoned the emergency services. Paramedics and the police arrived.

83. The deceased was found dead at the scene. It later emerged that the deceased had suffered 53 separate stab wounds to the body, which varied in severity, but also included 5 stab wounds to the neck, shoulder and face. There were superficial incised and stab wounds to the body, with defence incised wounds to the hands. The cause of death was blood loss from the stab wounds to the neck. . .

87. The case for the prosecution was straightforward. The appellant had decided to kill his wife before she arrived at the house and that this was why he asked her brother-in-law to remain outside. The crown alleged that he had locked the back door of the house. He had placed knives close to hand in preparation for the attack, which started almost as soon as she entered the house. The appellant was jealous and controlling and he resented Mrs Parker's newly found confidence and ambition, and, although not habitually violent, he was capable of being violent towards her, as indeed he had been on the previous night. He was guilty of murder.

88. The defence case was that the appellant was guilty of manslaughter, but not murder, on the basis of 'loss of control' within the 2009 Act. There was no pre-planning and that the loss of control resulted from a combination of the contents of the text message demanding that he leave the family home, which it was said came as a 'bolt from the blue', and from what she said to him and her manner when she returned to the house, and his realisation that she would have the children and that she had been planning this for a while with other people behind his back.

89. The appellant was a man of previous good character. In evidence he described various problems in the

relationship at an earlier stage, but by 2010 he thought the relationship was in good order. He knew nothing of any relationship in which she had become involved.

90. The argument on the evening of 26th October was about money. He said that he pushed her out of frustration as he walked past. The cup struck her in the mouth. He didn't realise she had an injury, and didn't mean to hurt her. She chucked it at him and its contents went everywhere. He cleared it up. He apologised. They had sexual intercourse together that night.

91. On the following morning she took him to work and then went with the children. They had a disagreement via text messages as to whether he had apologised for the incident the previous night, but he still thought that everything was all right between them. She collected him from work because he was unwell, dropped him off home, and then went back to the children.

92. The text message came as a 'bolt from the blue'. He was devastated. He used the small knife which was later found under Mrs Parker's body to self-harm, scratching his left forearm repeatedly but not deeply. He scored a love heart onto his ribs. He wrote a non-threatening letter to his wife, professing his love for her. He was really upset, distressed and crying, and not thinking clearly. He had never self-harmed before.

93. He said that he put that knife down in the kitchen and went upstairs to pack his belongings. He felt that he had no choice. He looked through a family photograph album which he happened to come across, and became increasingly upset. He texted her asking how long she would be. He wanted to be able to tell her that he loved her.

94. When she returned home, the car pulled up without the children. He realised it was all over between them, and that her actions had been pre-planned. He remembered going to the back door, but did not recall opening it or asking her brother-in-law to give them a minute, nor did he recall locking the back door, although he accepted that he must have done. Mrs Parker walked passed him into the kitchen. He followed and pleaded with her not to leave. He said that he loved her. With a smug look on her face she said that she did not love him anymore. He then lost it.

95. He said that he was upset and he 'snapped' and lashed out at her. He said that he did not recall doing it. He could not recall if he used the small knife. He had no recollection of the large knife or of the attack itself. The next thing he could recall was his brother-in-law with his arm around his neck shouting at him to drop the knife. . .

100. The main ground of appeal arises from the way in which the judge directed the jury on the loss of control issue. It is suggested that he failed to direct them adequately about the burden of proof, wrongly implying that the burden rested on the defendant. Alternatively, the summing-up on these issues was unclear and confusing and had the effect of reversing the burden of proof.

101. The criticisms of the judge's directions to the jury begin with his assertive failure to tell them what a 'loss of control' was, and what it amounted to, and the jury's attention was not drawn to all relevant matters in a coherent way.

102. Judge Mettyear began his directions to the jury in unequivocal terms. The burden of proof rested on the prosecution. It 'always, always rests' on the prosecution and never shifts. The Crown had to prove all the elements of the offence. The standard to be reached was that the jury had to be sure of guilt. The directions were given in unequivocal terms.

103. In his route to verdict (which was agreed by both counsel at trial), the judge directed the jury:

'The defendant has admitted unlawful killing of his wife Jane Parker. He is, on the facts of this case guilty of murder unless the killing resulted from his loss of self-control'.

Question 1. When he stabbed Jane had he lost self-control?

If you are sure he had not lost his self-control your verdict must be guilty of murder and you should proceed no further. Otherwise go to the next question.

Question 2. Was the defendant's loss of self-control caused by a qualifying trigger? (note. The qualifying triggers are things which you find to be said or done by Jane individually or in combination which

   a.   constitute circumstances of an extremely grave character and

   b.   which caused the defendant to have a justified sense of being seriously wronged. You should look at the whole of the evidence relating to the relationship between them including the events of the 27th October, when judging whether things said or done by Jane constituted circumstances which caused the defendant to have justifiable sense of being seriously wronged.

If you are sure that his loss of self-control was not caused by a qualifying trigger or triggers then your verdict must be guilty of murder and you should proceed no further. Otherwise go on to the next question.

Question 3. Might a man of the defendant's age with a normal degree of tolerance and self restraint have reacted in the same or in a similar way to the way that the defendant reacted?

If you are sure that such a person would not have reacted in the same or similar way to the defendant then your verdict must be guilty of murder. If you think such a person might have reacted in the same or a similar way your verdict must be not guilty of murder but guilty of manslaughter.

104. We have examined the document, and the judge's oral directions. On this particular point, taken in isolation, the answer to the second question could have been more felicitously expressed in relation to the burden of proof. However that may be, the remainder of the directions to the jury were impeccable. In particular, the references in the route to verdict plainly put the burden of proof where it rested. It carefully isolated the three ingredients of the 'loss of control' defence. We have examined the criticisms of the summing-up with care. We can discern no unfairness or lack of balance. It fairly reflected the available evidence. The defence was put before the jury in careful detail. We cannot identify any reason for concluding that this conviction was unsafe.

105. Before leaving the conviction appeal we propose to add one further observation. The judge was not invited to withdraw the 'loss of control' defence from the jury. With our increased understanding of the differences between the loss of control defence and the former provocation defence, we anticipate that such a submission would now be raised by the Crown for the judge to consider. He might well have concluded that the matters relied on by the appellant could not reasonably be treated by any jury as circumstances of an extremely grave character which caused him to have a justifiable sense that he had been seriously wronged.

106. The appeal against conviction is dismissed.

Questions

1. At para.18 Lord Judge CJ referred to the stalker in *Stingel* who would not be affected by s.55(6)(c) which disregards sexual infidelity as a qualifying trigger. Does the stalker have an unfair advantage over the betrayed spouse who loses control and kills, or does the stalker's claim to the defence of loss of control founder on the rocks of s.55(4)? Would the same outcome also apply to the example given in para.19?

2. The Court of Appeal ruled that Judge Smith, the trial judge, misdirected herself about the possible relevance of sexual infidelity to Clinton's defence. But the Court agreed that sexual infidelity on its own could not amount to a qualifying trigger, albeit that it might have relevance in the assessment of D's reaction to other words or conduct that might amount to a qualifying trigger, and as part of D's circumstances when applying the objective test in s.54(1)(c). However, absent Mrs Clinton's infidelity (which includes the Facebook entries and her graphic descriptions of her sexual exploits with others) what other evidence was there of words or conduct that could have amounted to a qualifying trigger (i.e. circumstances of an extremely grave character and which cause D to have a justifiable sense of being seriously wronged) the assessment of which might have differed had they been seen in the context of a background of sexual infidelity being discovered? Was there such evidence which might lead a jury, properly directed, to conclude that the defence of loss of control might apply? If there was not, why did the Court quash the conviction and order a re-trial as opposed to upholding the conviction as safe? (NB: On 3 September 2012, at his retrial at Reading Crown Court, Clinton pleaded guilty to murder suggesting thereby that both he and his lawyers, despite the Court of Appeal's favourable decision, could not identify any evidence of words or conduct to support a claim that his loss of control had a qualifying trigger.)

3. Where D fears violence from V and kills using more force than is reasonable for the purposes of a successful plea of self-defence, will the requirement in s.54(1) that D's acts resulted from a loss

of self-control so limit the availability of the new defence based on a fear of serious violence as to make it otiose?

4. D has suffered violence at the hands of her husband for many years. Finally one night she stabs him to death. Consider her liability in the following circumstances:

   (a) V returns home drunk and entering the kitchen demands sex from D threatening that otherwise he will beat her. D grabs a knife and lashes out at V severing his jugular vein resulting in his death.

   (b) V returns home drunk and falls asleep on the sofa. D seeing him in this state decides that she has had enough of the years of violence and stabs him as a result of which wound he dies.

   (c) As in (b) except that D, seeing V asleep, realises that when he wakens he will demand sex and beat her as he has done before. Recalling these many incidents D experiences mounting anger until eventually her self-control snaps and she overcomes the fear which usually paralyses her from acting. D seizes a knife from the kitchen and in blind rage stabs V repeatedly.

   (d) As in (b) except that as D makes to stab V he stirs and seeing her with the knife laughs in her face calling her a "pathetic bitch" and taunting her that she is too weak to do anything. D's self-control snaps and she stabs V to death.

   (e) As in (d) except that when V stirs and sees D with the knife he kicks at her. D fearing he will overpower her and beat and sexually abuse her, lashes out at V repeatedly until he lies dead.

5. D goes to the cinema leaving V, her husband and X, their daughter, at home. D does not enjoy the film so leaves after only thirty minutes and returns home. She goes upstairs and catches sight of V naked entering X's bedroom. Consider D's liability in the following circumstances:

   (a) D fearing V is about to rape X, grabs a heavy vase and smashes it over V's head killing him.

   (b) D, incensed by moral outrage at the thought of V and X having an incestuous relationship, smashes a vase over V's head killing him and does the same to X.

   (c) Would it make any difference in either case if D had suspected V of having sex with X and planned from the outset to return early from the cinema?

Notes

1. In *Dawes* [2013] EWCA Crim 322 the Court of Appeal emphasised that the focus of the new defence is not on D's view of the gravity of the circumstances nor is D's own sense of justification in feeling he had been seriously wronged the test for determining if there was a qualifying trigger. Lord Judge CJ stated (at para.61):

   "The presence, or otherwise, of a qualifying trigger is not defined or decided by the defendant and any assertions he may make in evidence, or any account given in the investigative process. S.55(3) directly engages the defendant's fear of serious violence. . . .[I]n this type of case s.55(4) will almost inevitably arise for consideration. Unless the defendant has a sense of being seriously wronged s.55(4) has no application. Even if it does, there are two distinctive further requirements. The circumstances must be extremely grave and the defendant's sense of being seriously wronged by them must be justifiable. In our judgment these matters require objective assessment by the judge at the end of the evidence and, if the defence is left, by the jury considering their verdict. If it were otherwise it would mean that a qualifying trigger would be present if the defendant were to give an account to the effect that, "the circumstances were extremely grave to me and caused me to have what I believed was a justifiable sense that I had been seriously wronged". If so, when it is clear that the availability of a defence based on the loss of control has been significantly narrowed, one would have to question the purpose of s.55(3) (4) and (5)."

2. If D has killed and sufficient evidence has been adduced to raise the defence of loss of control, he will succeed in his defence unless the prosecution disprove that "a person of D's sex and age, with a normal degree of tolerance and self-restraint and in the circumstances of D, might have reacted in the same of a similar way to D" (s.54(1)(c)). However, anything in D's circumstances which impairs his capacity to exercise the normal degree of tolerance and self-restraint to be expected of people living in England and Wales today, will not be attributed to the normal person (see s.54(3)). If D has extreme views colouring his tolerance for others whether based on their race, religion, gender, or sexual orientation, those views will not be attributed to the normal person. Similarly, if D's capacity for exercising self-restraint is impaired by, for example, mental illness or retarded development, these circumstances are not attributed to the normal person. If D's ability to exercise tolerance or self-restraint is substantially impaired, he may be able to rely on the defence of diminished responsibility (see below, p.483). In the case which follows the issue arose whether D could rely on his intoxication as affecting his capacity for tolerance and self-restraint and have this attributed to the person of D's sex and age under s.54(1)(c).

R V ASMELASH

[2013] EWCA Crim 157

D and V had spent much of the day drinking. An argument broke out between them, D claiming that V insulted his mother and him and exposed his penis at D before hitting him in the face with a beer can. D claimed he feared for his life, grabbed a knife and threatened V with it but that V continued insulting and assaulting him and that he then, through fear and anger, lost control and stabbed V killing him. The jury convicted D of murder rejecting his defence of loss of control. On appeal the question for decision was whether the voluntary consumption of alcohol falls within the ambit of s.54(1)(c), as amplified by s.54(3) of the Coroners and Justice Act 2009, when considering the question whether a person of the D's sex and age "with a normal degree of tolerance and self-restraint and in all of D's circumstances other than those whose only relevance to D's conduct is that they bear on D's general capacity for tolerance or self-restraint might have reacted in the same or a similar way to D?"

LORD JUDGE CJ

. . .

15. Addressing the loss of control defence, in the context of what were otherwise conventional directions which are not criticised, the judge directed the jury:

'Are you sure that a person of Dawit Asmelash's sex and age with a normal degree of tolerance and self restraint and in the same circumstances, but unaffected by alcohol, would not have reacted in the same or similar way?'

Amplifying this direction the judge told the jury that he had deliberately inserted the words 'unaffected by alcohol' into his written route to verdict, because, as he put it, the law had never said that the 'voluntary consumption of alcohol can assist a criminal offender. If it did, the flood gates – you may think – would be open and every violent drunk would say 'I must be judged against the standards of other violently disposed drunken people even though I may be like a lamb when I am sober.'

. . .

17. Focussing on the circumstances of D, Mr Davey [counsel for D] suggested that, assuming the provisions of s.54(1)(a) and (b) were engaged (and for present purposes we assume that they were) the fact that the appellant was drunk at the material time was one of his 'circumstances' to be considered in accordance with s.54(1)(c). The appellant should not be precluded from advancing the partial defence simply because, entirely coincidentally, he happened to be intoxicated. It would be otherwise if he had been drinking to give himself Dutch courage for some violent action, but the partial defence should be available so as to ensure that D would not be in any worse position than a sober person who might have acted as he did in similar circumstances. Mr Davey was not contending that the defendant should be entitled to take advantage of his self-induced intoxication, but that the fact of such intoxication should not of itself preclude him from advancing the partial defence. . .

19. Mr Andrew Edis QC [for the Crown] submitted that the judge's direction to the jury was correct, entirely in accordance with well understood principle. Everyone agreed that the appellant was drunk as the result of self-induced intoxication. No one suggested that this caused him to be mistaken about anything that was going on at the relevant time, or about what he was doing. Accordingly the only relevance of the drunkenness was that it affected the appellant's self-restraint, and caused him to act in a way in which he would not have acted if sober. Such drunkenness was an irrelevant consideration. It may have had some relevance to his general capacity for tolerance or self-restraint: but no more.

20. . . Mr Edis drew attention to the *Law Commission Report*. (Law Commission No. 34) on Murder, Manslaughter and Infanticide (published in 2006). He reminded us that the 2009 Act had not fully or faithfully followed all the recommendations of the Law Commission, and that in some respects, it had ignored them. Nevertheless in the present context the statutory provisions had followed the Law Commission recommendations very closely. At 5.41, where the report is directing attention to temporary intoxication rather than chronic alcoholism, the Law Commission reported that 'abnormal states of mind, such as intoxication or irritability, should also be left out, as should other factors that affect a general capacity to exercise adequate self-control'. This approach is consistent with very well understood policy considerations, robustly summarised by the observations of the trial judge in his summing up. In the absence of any express provision to the effect contended for by Mr Davey, the court should proceed on the basis that the law was unchanged. What is more, the issue of self-induced intoxication has already been considered in this court in the context of newly enacted provisions related to diminished responsibility in *R v Dowds* [2012] 1 Cr. App R 34, at para 35 [see below, p.485]. In that context, the defence could not be founded on voluntary intoxication, even if acute.

22. It has of course been long understood that the consumption of alcohol, or indeed the taking of drugs, may diminish the ability of an individual to control or restrain himself, so that, in drink, or affected by drugs, he may behave in a way in which he would not have behaved when sober or drug free. Although it may sometimes impact on the question whether the constituent elements of a crime, in particular in relation to the required intent, have been proved, self-induced intoxication does not provide a defence to a criminal charge. This principle was applied to the defence of provocation in *McCarthy* [1954] 2 QB 105, and in the context of the law of Jersey which corresponded with s.3 of the Homicide Act 1957, underlined in *Attorney General for Jersey v Holley* [2005] 580. Indeed for several decades now, judicial directions to the jury considering the provocation defence in the context of the voluntary consumption of alcohol, referred to the reasonable sober person in the position of the defendant. If Mr Davey's submission is correct, a remarkably benign development to the issue of alcohol has been adopted as part of the statutory ingredients of the loss of control defence when, simultaneously, the defence itself is in many ways much more restrictive than the former provocation defence. In *Dowds*, after a valuable analysis of the policy reasons underlining the approach of the criminal law to the issue of self-induced intoxication, headed *Voluntary Drunkenness in English Criminal Law*, the court observed:

'The exception which prevents a defendant from relying on his voluntary intoxication, save upon the limited question of whether a "specific intent" has been formed, is well entrenched and formed the unspoken backdrop for the new statutory formula. There has been no hint of any dissatisfaction with that rule of law. If Parliament had meant to alter it, or depart from it, it would undoubtedly have made its intention explicit.'

23. As Hughes LJ explained in *Dowds*, on occasions when recasting a defence in statutory form, express provision is made about the approach to self-induced drunkenness (see s.75(5) of the Criminal Justice and Immigration Act 2008 which put the law of self-defence into statutory form). On other occasions, however, a new

statute simply proceeded on the basis of the well established principles of law, and specific legislative provision was unnecessary.

24. In essence, therefore, Mr Davey's submission proceeds on the basis that in the absence of any express statutory provision, in the context of 'loss of control', a new approach to the issue of voluntary drunkenness is required. We disagree. We can find nothing in the 'loss of control' defence to suggest that Parliament intended, somehow, that the normal rules which apply to voluntary intoxication should not apply. If that had been the intention of Parliament, it would have been spelled out in unequivocal language. Moreover, faced with the compelling reasoning of this court in *Dowds* in the context of diminished responsibility, it is inconceivable that different criteria should govern the approach to the issue of voluntary drunkenness, depending on whether the partial defence under consideration is diminished responsibility or loss of control. Indeed, given that in a fair proportion of cases, both defences are canvassed before the jury, the potential for uncertainty and confusion which would follow the necessarily very different directions on the issue of intoxication depending on which partial defence was under consideration, does not bear contemplation.

25. Our conclusion does not bear the dire consequences suggested by Mr Davey. It does not mean that the defendant who has been drinking is deprived of any possible loss of control defence: it simply means, as the judge explained, that the loss of control defence must be approached without reference to the defendant's voluntary intoxication. If a sober individual in the defendant's circumstances, with normal levels of tolerance and self-restraint might have behaved in the same way as the defendant confronted by the relevant qualifying trigger, he would not be deprived of the loss of control defence just because he was not sober. And different considerations would arise if, a defendant with a severe problem with alcohol or drugs was mercilessly taunted about the condition, to the extent that it constituted a qualifying trigger, the alcohol or drug problem would then form part of the circumstances for consideration.

26. In our judgment the judge was right to direct the jury as he did. This ground of appeal fails.

Appeal dismissed

ii. Diminished Responsibility

Note

Section 52 of the Coroners and Justice Act 2009 came into force on 4 October 2010 replacing subs.(1) of section 2 of the Homicide Act 1957 with new subss.(1) and (1A).

The defence of diminished responsibility was created by s.2 of the Homicide Act 1957. Almost from the point of its enactment it was the subject of criticism and there have been various proposals for its reform. The Coroners and Justice Act 2009 has radically amended s.2 of the Homicide Act 1957 recasting the defence. The new defence applies to all murders committed on or after 4 October 2010. For murders committed prior to that date the original version of the defence applies. In order to understand the new defence it is necessary to understand the original defence and the reform proposals which led to its replacement.

(a) The original defence of diminished responsibility

The defence of diminished responsibility is not a general defence; it may only be pleaded in defence to a charge of murder. Its effect, if successfully raised, is in the nature of a partial excuse; the accused is acquitted of murder but is convicted of manslaughter.

The defence was introduced in response to the *Royal Commission on Capital Punishment* (TSO, 1949–1953), Cmnd.8932, which had argued for an expanded insanity defence. The Government accepted that the defence of insanity was limited and that injustices could occur in murder cases but considered that an expanded defence of insanity would cause major difficulties. The defence was created by s.2 of the Homicide Act 1957:

(1)   Where a person kills or is a party to the killing of another, he shall not be convicted of murder if he was suffering from such abnormality of mind (whether arising from a condition of

arrested or retarded development of mind or any inherent causes or induced by disease or injury) as substantially impaired his mental responsibility for his acts and omissions in doing or being a party to the killing.

(2) On a charge of murder, it shall be for the defence to prove that the person charged is by virtue of this section not liable to be convicted of murder.

(3) A person who but for this section would be liable, whether as principal or as accessory, to be convicted of murder shall be liable instead to be convicted of manslaughter.

As with insanity, the accused bears the burden of proving the defence (s.2(2)) on a balance of probabilities (*Dunbar* [1958] 1 Q.B. 1). In practice the accused is rarely put to his proof as a plea of guilty of manslaughter is accepted in about 80 per cent of the cases in which the defence of diminished responsibility is raised (see S. Dell, "Diminished responsibility reconsidered" [1982] Crim. L.R. 809). In *Vinagre* (1979) 69 Cr. App. R. 104, the Court of Appeal stated that pleas to manslaughter on the grounds of diminished responsibility should only be accepted when there is clear evidence of mental imbalance. The defence will generally be put to their proof where there is disagreement between the psychiatric reports or where these reports do not wholeheartedly support the defence. Where the accused raises the defence of diminished responsibility, and the prosecution have evidence that he is insane, it may adduce or elicit evidence tending to prove this (see s.6 of the Criminal Procedure (Insanity) Act 1964), but this power would appear to be rarely used. Section 6 also allows for the converse situation; the prosecution may, where the accused pleads insanity, contend that he was suffering from diminished responsibility. The trial judge has no power to raise the issue of diminished responsibility if the defence do not do so, but if he detects evidence of diminished responsibility he may point this out to defence counsel and leave it so that the defence can decide whether to raise this issue and seek to prove it before the jury (see *Campbell* (1987) 84 Cr. App. R. 255).

There are three elements to the defence. Medical evidence is crucial to the success of the defence (see *Dix* (1981) 74 Cr. App. R. 306) and a jury may not return a verdict of manslaughter on the ground of diminished responsibility unless there is medical evidence of an abnormality of mind arising from one of the specified causes. While the decision is ultimately for the jury, they must act on the evidence and if the medical evidence supporting a finding of diminished responsibility is unchallenged, and there is nothing in the facts or circumstances to cast doubt on it, they must accept it (see *Matheson* (1958) 42 Cr. App. R. 145; *Bailey* (1978) 66 Cr. App. R. 31). However, as Lord Parker CJ stated in *Byrne* [1960] 2 Q.B. 396 at 403, the jury "are not bound to accept the medical evidence if there is other material before them which, in their good judgment, conflicts with it and outweighs it" (see further *Eifinger* [2001] EWCA Crim 1855).

It is important to note that s.2 does not require proof that the abnormality of mind caused the killing (although in many cases such a causal link may be apparent); the section is framed in such a way as to indicate that it is sufficient to establish the defence that D's mind was abnormal at the time of the killing such that his mental responsibility for his acts was substantially impaired. Obviously, if the defence claims that D's ability to control his acts was impaired by his mental abnormality, this condition has causal significance. However, if the focus of the defence is on D's moral culpability for his acts (which could be diminished due to mental illness or D's arrested or retarded development of mind), there may be no causal connection between D's condition and the killing, but it does bear directly on the question of the extent to which he should be held responsible for it (see further G.R. Sullivan, "Intoxicants and Diminished Responsibility" [1994] Crim. L.R. 156).

It must be proved that the accused was suffering from an abnormality of mind at the material time. This is a question for the jury but medical evidence is important. The jury should weigh this up with all the other evidence "including acts or statements of the accused and his demeanour" (see *Byrne* [1960] 2 Q.B. 396). In *Byrne*, Lord Parker CJ defined "abnormality of mind" (at 403) as:

> "a state of mind so different from that of ordinary human beings that the reasonable man would term it abnormal. It appears to us to be wide enough to cover the mind's activities in all its aspects, not only the perception of physical acts and matters, and the ability to form a rational judgment as to whether an act is right or wrong, but also the ability to exercise will-power to control physical acts in accordance with that rational judgment."

In *Byrne* sexual psychopathy giving rise to violent perverted sexual desires which he found difficult, if not impossible, to control, amounted to an abnormality of mind. By contrast, in *Seers* (1984) 79 Cr. App. R. 261, D was convicted of the murder of his wife when suffering from chronic reactive depression which constituted an abnormality of mind.

Unless the abnormality of mind from which the accused is alleged to suffer is shown to arise from one of the causes specified in parenthesis in s.2(1), the defence will fail (see *King* [1965] 1 Q.B. 443 at 450). The aetiology of the abnormality of mind is a matter to be determined by medical evidence (*Byrne*). There is little guidance, however, on what is meant by the causes specified in parenthesis. They were meant to rule out emotions such as hatred, rage, or jealousy and external factors such as alcohol or drugs. There are cases, however, where jealousy (see *Miller*, *The Times*, 16 May 1972; *Asher*, *The Times*, 9 June 1981) and rage (see *Coles* (1980) 144 J.P.N. 528) have resulted in a s.2 verdict. In the Northern Irish case of *McQuade* [2005] NICA 2, the Court of Appeal were faced with the question whether or not "injury" (in this case psychological harm) resulting from years of sexual abuse was capable of amounting to an abnormality of the mind from one of the specified causes. The Court of Appeal, taking into account the decisions in *Ireland*, *Burstow*, and *Chan-Fook* which held that bodily harm or injury for the purposes of offences against the person included injury to the mind, held that the important question was whether the mind had been injured, not how it had been injured, i.e. by physical or psychological means.

Intoxication will not support a verdict of manslaughter but alcoholism (alcohol dependence syndrome) may give rise to an abnormality of mind arising from "disease or injury". There is no need to prove actual damage to the brain, although such damage may make it more likely to find there is an abnormality of the mind (*Wood* [2008] EWCA Crim 1305 where the Court of Appeal explained and limited the earlier decisions of *Tandy* (1988) 87 Cr. App. R. 45; and *Inseal* [1992] Crim. L.R. 35). The issue for the jury is whether the alcoholism has produced an abnormality of mind. It will only do so where there is gross impairment of judgement and emotional responses or the drinking was involuntary.

Temporary mental impairment lasting for several hours resulting from ingestion of a medically prescribed drug does not constitute an "injury" (*O'Connell* [1997] Crim. L.R. 683). Where the evidence suggests more than one cause for the abnormality of the mind, one of which is intoxication (or some other cause not specified in s.2), the judge should direct the jury to ignore the effect of the inadmissible causes and consider whether the effect of the admissible cause or causes was an abnormality of the mind such as to impair substantially the accused's mental responsibility (*Fenton* (1975) 61 Cr. App. R. 261; *Gittens* [1984] Q.B. 698).

It should be noted that the term "diminished responsibility" is not used in s.2; it appears in the marginal note. Section 2 is hardly a paradigm of legislative clarity as it appears to conflate two ideas, namely, those of impaired capacity and reduced liability. If the accused is to be convicted only of manslaughter rather than murder it is because his impaired capacity diminishes his moral culpability for his act. The question ultimately resolves itself into a moral one for the jury: whether they think that the accused deserves to be convicted of murder or manslaughter. The jury's response, however, may vary greatly depending on the extent of their sympathy for the accused and the nature of his offence. Thus manslaughter verdicts have been returned on the basis of very little evidence of abnormality, such as in cases of reactive depression or hysterical dissociation where a person kills in response to extreme anxiety, grief, or stress (often in the context of a "mercy killing"), whereas horrific killings by someone whom all the psychiatrists agreed suffered from a severe abnormality of the mind (paranoid schizophrenia) amounting to diminished responsibility, may result in a conviction of murder, as occurred in the case of Peter Sutcliffe (the "Yorkshire Ripper").

The crucial question in a case where diminished responsibility is raised in defence, is whether the abnormality was such as to impair substantially the accused's mental responsibility for his acts. "Substantial" means "less than total—more than trivial" (see *Lloyd* [1967] 1 Q.B. 175). In *Byrne* the Court of Appeal stated that "mental responsibility for his acts" pointed to "a consideration of the extent to which the accused's mind is answerable for his physical acts which must include a consideration of the extent of his ability to exercise will-power to control his physical acts". This was said to be a question of degree and essentially one for the jury. Lord Parker CJ stated (at 403):

"Medical evidence is, of course, relevant, but the question involves a decision not merely as to whether there was some impairment of the mental responsibility of the accused but whether such impairment can properly be called 'substantial', a matter upon which juries may quite legitimately differ from doctors."

Thus there is no absolute scientific measure; inability to resist impulses is clearly covered but where there is merely difficulty in resisting impulses, the issue of substantial impairment will depend on the degree of difficulty. While the question whether the accused's mental responsibility was substantially impaired is one for the jury to decide, in *Bailey* (1978) 66 Cr. App. R. 31, the Court of Appeal stated (at 32) that juries must accept and act on medical evidence if there is nothing before them in terms of facts or circumstances to throw doubts on it (see also *Sanders* (1990) 93 Cr. App. R. 245). If the medical evidence is weak or equivocal or if there is other evidence which tends to point to a contrary conclusion, the jury weigh that evidence and draw their own conclusions (see *Walton* [1978] A.C. 788).

Reform

Notes

1.   In its Report, *Partial Defences to Murder* (TSO, 2004) Law Com. No.290, the Law Commission recommended that for so long as the law of murder remains unreformed there should be no change to s.2 of the Homicide Act 1957. They did, however, put forward a formulation of diminished responsibility for consideration in the context of a full review of murder (see para.5.97):

"A person, who would otherwise be guilty of murder, is not guilty of murder but of manslaughter if, at the time of the act or omission causing death,
      (1) that person's capacity to:
        (a) understand events;
        (b) judge whether his actions were right of wrong; or
        (c) control himself,
was substantially impaired by an abnormality of mental functioning arising from an underlying condition and

(2) the abnormality was a significant cause of the defendant's conduct in carrying out or taking part in the killing.

'Underlying condition' means a pre-existing mental or physiological condition other than of a transitory kind."

2. In their Consultation Paper, *A New Homicide Act for England and Wales?*, the Law Commission made an additional proposal in respect of diminished responsibility, namely that special provision for children under 18 should be made to reflect their "developmental immaturity". In their Report, *Murder, Manslaughter and Infanticide*, the Law Commission affirmed this recommendation stating:

5.130   It is important to recognise the nature and limits of what we are suggesting. In England and Wales, criminal liability for murder can be imposed on an offender if he or she was at least 10 years of age at the time of the offence. We are not suggesting that imposing liability for murder on a child of this age is always unfair or inappropriate. Some 10-year-old killers may be sufficiently advanced in their judgement and understanding that such a conviction would be fair.

5.131   What we are suggesting is that it is unrealistic and unfair to assume that *all* children aged 10 or over who kill must have had the kind of developed sense of judgement, control and understanding that makes a first degree murder conviction the right result (provided the fault element was satisfied). Instead, our recommendation is that it should be for the jury to decide in the individual case whether D had such a sense of judgement, control, or understanding. Moreover, it will be for the D to prove that his or her capacity for judgement, control and understanding was substantially impaired by developmental immaturity.

5.132   D may wish to prove substantial impairment by developmental immaturity through appeal either to biological factors, or to social and environmental influences, or to a combination of both. For example, D may wish to give evidence that his or her power of control over his or her actions was substantially impaired by a biological factor such as poor frontal lobe development. This is because, as the Royal College of Psychiatrists have put it:

Biological factors such as the functioning of the frontal lobes of the brain play an important role in the development of self-control and of other abilities. The frontal lobes are involved in an individual's ability to manage the large amount of information entering consciousness from many sources, in changing behaviour, in using acquired information, in planning actions and in controlling impulsivity. Generally the frontal lobes are felt to mature at approximately 14 years of age.

5.133   As this final sentence implies, however, in an individual case involving a child under 14 years of age, it would be open to the prosecution to seek to rebut evidence of poor frontal lobe development by arguing that this particular D had matured to a sufficient degree to be fairly convicted of first degree murder. The jury should be trusted to reject implausible claims, as they are with other defences based on expert evidence.

5.134   So far as social and environmental influences on young killers are concerned, two studies have shown how these influences may, in extremely rare circumstances, lead children or young persons to kill. One study has shown that seriously disturbed children who murder have home backgrounds in which there was commonly paternal psychopathy, alcohol abuse, absence from the home, and a history of violent behaviour by fathers. Another study has shown depressive illnesses in the mothers of juvenile murderers, and histories of serious sexual and physical abuse of juvenile murderers.

5.135   Such evidence might be employed by D to suggest that he or she was developmentally immature to the extent of having substantially impaired judgement, control, or understanding. It would be open to the prosecution to seek to rebut such evidence, on the facts of an individual case. Again, the jury should be trusted to reject implausible claims. . .

In the Consultation Paper, *Murder, Manslaughter and Infanticide: Proposals for Reform of the Law* (CP19/08), the Government expressed their agreement with the Law Commission's proposals in respect of the defence of diminished responsibility with the exception of those relating to "developmental immaturity". Following the consultation, the Government reaffirmed its view.

MURDER, MANSLAUGHTER AND INFANTICIDE: PROPOSALS FOR REFORM OF THE LAW SUMMARY OF RESPONSES AND GOVERNMENT POSITION

Response to Consultation (CP(R)19/08)

DEVELOPMENTAL IMMATURITY

97. A number of respondents agreed with the Government's view that this proposal of the Law Commission should not be included. Victim Support took the view that there is a risk that this would make the defence too easy to run if it was unrelated to a medical condition. If it was included as part of the partial defence of diminished responsibility, there was a risk that it would be run routinely in cases involving young defendants in homicide cases. As impairments such as learning difficulties and autistic spectrum disorders are included under 'recognised medical condition', another legal practitioner organisation doubted whether there is a need for such a clause. The Law Reform Committee and Criminal Bar Association of the General Council of the Bar previously supported the Law Commission on this but had changed their minds and now support the Government proposal.

98. Others (including the Senior Law Lord, the Royal College of Paediatrics and Child Health, Justice, Justice for Women, a specialist in adolescent forensic psychiatry from Greater Manchester and a number of academic lawyers and, in Northern Ireland, the Law Society of Northern Ireland and Women's Aid Federation Northern Ireland) backed the Law Commission recommendation that developmental immaturity should exist as a limb within the diminished responsibility partial defence. They made the following points:

- Under 18s mature at different rates; their ability to decide to engage in criminal activity in the clear knowledge of the full implications and consequences of this must be subject to the developmental level of the young person.

- As doli incapax is no longer available, any child over the age of 10 would be held to understand the significance of their actions unless they are suffering from a 'recognised medical condition'. This is not realistic. Any reform of the partial defence of diminished responsibility needs to taken account of the abolition of doli incapax.

- Since knowing the difference between right and wrong, what is legal and illegal, is not intrinsic to the child and needs to be learned, in some cases, e.g. where a child is neglected, such learning opportunities are absent throughout childhood. It would be inappropriate to label such children as culpable criminals. A small group of vulnerable and abused young people would be at risk of being sentenced to a punishment rather than a treatment regime.

- The proposal may be in contravention of Article 40 of the UN Convention on the Rights of the Child—the right of every child alleged as, or accused of, or recognised as having infringed the penal law to be treated in a manner consistent with the promotion of the child's sense of dignity and worth, taking into account the child's age; to have the matter determined without delay by a competent, independent and impartial authority or judicial body in a fair hearing according to law, taking into account his or her age.

- An adult of 40 years with the emotional maturity of a 10 year old can claim diminished responsibility as they may be diagnosed as having a 'recognised medical condition', yet a 'normal' 10 year old cannot succeed with the plea as their development has not been arrested. In this way, more is expected of children than adults. The fact that children develop consequential reasoning as they grow older is disregarded (unless they have a 'recognised medical condition').

GOVERNMENT RESPONSE

99. The Government is not persuaded that it would be appropriate to extend the partial defence of diminished responsibility to include a developmental immaturity limb.

100. The age of criminal responsibility is set at 10 years of age. A child who has reached this age is deemed to be criminally responsible for his actions. We believe that it should remain the case that a partial defence should only be available if a child meets the proposed conditions for a diminished responsibility defence (namely, that he or she is substantially less able to understand the nature of their conduct, form a rational judgment or exercise self-control as the result of an abnormality of mental functioning arising from a 'recognised medical condition').

101. We did not receive any evidence in the consultation that the absence of a developmental immaturity provision in the existing law is causing any significant difficulties in practice, and so we remain unconvinced that it is needed.

102. We also remain of the view that including the provision would open up the defence too widely and catch inappropriate cases. We also consider that opening the door for young people to plead developmental immaturity would unnecessarily complicate the trial in many cases where a defence of diminished responsibility should not be available as the defendant is clearly in possession of all their faculties.

103. We are confident that obviously deserving cases, e.g. where the defendant is a child who has been diagnosed with autistic spectrum disorder and this has significantly impaired his ability to understand the nature of his conduct, form a rational judgment or exercise self-control (or any combination of the three), would fall within the diminished responsibility as proposed.

(b) The new defence of diminished responsibility

Note

The Government's proposals were enacted as s.52 of the Coroners and Justice Act 2009 on 12 November 2009. This section came into force on 4 October 2010 and applies to all murders committed on or after that day.

CORONERS AND JUSTICE ACT 2009

Partial defence to murder: diminished responsibility

52 Persons suffering from diminished responsibility (England and Wales)

(1) In section 2 of the Homicide Act 1957 (c. 11) (persons suffering from diminished responsibility), for subsection (1) substitute—

'(1) A person ("D") who kills or is a party to the killing of another is not to be convicted of murder if D was suffering from an abnormality of mental functioning which—
   (a) arose from a recognised medical condition,
   (b) substantially impaired D's ability to do one or more of the things mentioned in subsection (1A), and
   (c) provides an explanation for D's acts and omissions in doing or being a party to the killing.
(1A) Those things are—
   (a) to understand the nature of D's conduct;

      (b)   to form a rational judgment;

      (c)   to exercise self-control.

(1B) For the purposes of subsection (1)(c), an abnormality of mental functioning provides an explanation for D's conduct if it causes, or is a significant contributory factor in causing, D to carry out that conduct.'

(2) In section 6 of the Criminal Procedure (Insanity) Act 1964 (c. 84) (evidence by prosecution of insanity or diminished responsibility), in paragraph (b) for 'mind' substitute 'mental functioning'.

Questions

1. Will the requirement to establish a causal link between the abnormality of mental functioning and D's conduct make it more difficult for D to prove diminished responsibility than under the original s.2?

2. Will the failure to enact the Law Commission's proposal relating to developmental immaturity result in unfairness to very young offenders? For example, an adult with serious learning difficulties, and a mental age of 10, will be able to rely on abnormality of mental functioning to seek to establish impaired ability under subs.(1A) whereas a child of 10, with no intellectual impairment, learning disability or autistic spectrum disorder, but whose home environment involves alcoholism, domestic violence and an absence of appropriate parenting and discipline such that he has not been properly socialised, will not.

Notes

1. The abnormality of mental functioning has to arise from "a recognised medical condition"—a term which is wider than the three specified causes in the old s.2. It includes physical medical conditions as well as psychological and psychiatric conditions. Thus conditions such as alcohol dependency syndrome, diabetes, and epilepsy which are not mental disorders but which may affect a person's ability to do the things specified in s.2(1A), are covered. Depressive illnesses will be covered so the defence will remain potentially available to victims of prolonged domestic violence or sexual abuse. It is open to question whether some of the more generous examples of accepted pleas under the old law involving mercy killings will fall within the new law; there would have to be clear evidence of a depressive illness having the necessary impact on D's ability to do the specified things in s.2(1A).

2. But the practice of accepting guilty pleas to manslaughter by reason of diminished responsibility is one that should continue where the evidence supports this conclusion as it is in the public interest that unnecessary trials do not take place. This practice was endorsed by the Privy Council in *Robinson v The State (Trinidad and Tobago)* [2015] UKPC 34 where Lord Hughes stated (at para.29):

> "Since 1962 it has been the plainly accepted practice in England and Wales to accept pleas of guilty to manslaughter by reason of diminished responsibility where, on careful analysis, it is plain to the Crown that that is the right outcome. When in 2004 the Law Commission reviewed the law of diminished responsibility, research undertaken for it by Professor Mackay demonstrated that in a four-year sample period something like 90% of diminished responsibility outcomes were the result of acceptance of a plea, with no jury trial: Partial defences to murder Law Com No 290, Appendix B. It remains of great importance that pleas are accepted only

in cases where it is proper to do so. Generally that means cases where there is no significant material dispute either of underlying fact or of medical analysis, and moreover it is clear that the defendant's mental responsibility for the killing can properly be described as substantially impaired. There may still be the very occasional case which is of such public profile or concern that it has to be the subject of full trial. In England and Wales these decisions are facilitated by the usually ready availability of full medical reports from experienced forensic psychiatrists. It is an important contribution to this process that every person charged with murder is routinely assessed by such a psychiatrist instructed by the prosecution, and early after arrest, either in prison or, in the relatively few cases in which s/he is on bail, as a condition of bail. So long as this careful consideration is given to each case, it is plainly of public benefit for pleas of guilty of manslaughter to be accepted. This avoids trials on non-issues which will be both expensive to the public and distressing to many of those involved, whether as witnesses, or relatives of the deceased, or as defendants and their families."

3. Psychiatrists and psychologists use one of the two internationally accepted classificatory systems when diagnosing mental conditions: either the World Health Organisation: International Classification of Diseases (ICD-10); or the American Psychiatric Association: Diagnostic and Statistical Manual of Mental Disorders (DSM-IV). It is the hope of the legislators that the new terminology will lead to claims of diminished responsibility being grounded in valid medical diagnoses under these classificatory systems. While conditions not yet recognised in either classificatory system are not expressly excluded, it will be difficult to raise a defence based on a condition psychiatrists are just beginning to recognise until such condition is included in one of the classificatory systems. But suffering from a recognised medical condition is not, of itself, sufficient to ensure that D's reliance on the defence of diminished responsibility is successful, as the following case demonstrates.

R V DOWDS

[2012] EWCA Crim 281

D and his partner P were heavy drinkers with a history of violence to each other when drunk. D, having consumed a large quantity of vodka with P had an argument with her in the course of which he stabbed her about 60 times. At his trial for murder he sought to raise the defence of diminished responsibility claiming that he could not remember what happened as he was intoxicated and that intoxication was a recognised medical condition. He made no claim to being an alcoholic or to being clinically dependent on drink; rather he was electively drunk, his drinking being voluntary. At the outset of the trial, His Honour Judge Wait was invited to rule whether or not simple voluntary and temporary drunkenness was capable of founding the partial defence of diminished responsibility. He ruled that as a matter of law it could not. D proceeded to contest the trial on the basis that he lacked the intent for murder and had lost control owing to a violent attack on him by P. D was convicted of murder and appealed.

LORD JUSTICE HUGHES:

1. The issue in this appeal is whether acute voluntary intoxication is now capable of giving rise to the partial defence of diminished responsibility on an indictment for murder. It is common ground that it could not have done so prior to the amendments to section 2 Homicide Act 1957 which were made by the Coroners and Justice Act

2009 (s 52). The appellant contends that those amendments mean that voluntary and temporary drunkenness may now give rise to diminished responsibility and thus reduce murder to manslaughter. That is because, it is said, acute intoxication is a 'recognised medical condition' within section 2(1)(a) of the Homicide Act as amended.
    . . .
    5. It was not contended that the appellant was alcoholic or clinically dependent on drink. He was a heavy but elective drinker. On his own account he did not drink heavily except when he chose to do so, chiefly at weekends. He held down a responsible job which required him to be alert and clear thinking. His drinking was appropriately described by one of the reporting psychiatrists as 'binge drinking'. The appellant himself told the other reporting psychiatrist:

> 'I do not have a problem with drink. I have a problem when I drink, I just don't know when to stop. I just seem to be able to carry on drinking and I don't have any ill effect in the morning. I get a head on me and want to keep on drinking.'

    6. At the outset of the trial His Honour Judge Wait was invited to rule whether or not simple voluntary and temporary drunkenness was capable of founding the partial defence of diminished responsibility. He ruled that as a matter of law it could not. In consequence, diminished responsibility was not raised before the jury. This appeal challenges that ruling. Whilst the present offence concerns intoxication with alcohol, our conclusion must apply equally to defendants under the influence of other voluntarily-taken drugs.
    [His Lordship examined the law relating to intoxication and diminished responsibility as it existed prior to the amendments made to s.2 of the 1957 Act by the Coroners and Justice Act 2009 coming into force. He also examined the general law relating to intoxication and criminal liability (see Ch.4 above p.175).]

Amending section 2 Homicide Act 1957
    24. The initial source of the amendments to section 2 lay in a request made in June 2003 by the Home Secretary of the Law Commission to undertake a general review of the partial defences to murder. The result was the Law Commission's report Law Com No 290 in August 2004. The Commission concluded that the partial defences (provocation and diminished responsibility) ought best to be considered in the context of a wholesale review of the law of homicide generally. It did however make recommendations for changes to the law of provocation, whilst suggesting that any legislation await such general homicide review. So far as diminished responsibility was concerned, it concluded that the existing law was causing no difficulty and stood in no immediate need of amendment. It specifically advised in paragraph 5.85 that the law relating to voluntary intoxication was 'clear and satisfactory.
    25. The next step was the Commission's review of homicide generally: *Murder, Manslaughter and Infanticide* Law Com No 304 (November 2006). The Commission favoured a wholesale reform of homicide involving the creation of two degrees of murder in addition to manslaughter. Under such a proposal, the role of the partial defences would have been to apply only to first degree murder and to reduce it to second degree murder. As is well known, that radical reform did not commend itself to Parliament.
    26. The report contains no further discussion at all of the law relating to voluntary intoxication. We infer that that was because nothing had changed since 2004 when the existing law had been so clearly commended; there had so far as we are aware been no significant discussion about it in any public quarter. The Commission did slightly amend its formulation of diminished responsibility into what was substantially the form adopted by the Coroners and Justice Act 2009. (There was a suggested addition of developmental immaturity which was not adopted by Parliament but that is irrelevant to the present issue.) For present purposes the significant change in formulation was to move from 'an abnormality of mental functioning arising from an underlying condition' (2004) to 'an abnormality of mental functioning *arising* from a recognised medical condition' (2006) (our emphasis).
    27. The Commission explained the reasons for this slightly altered formulation in paragraphs 5.114–5.120. They were:

i)   the law ought no longer to be constrained by a fixed set of causes of mental malfunction but should be responsive to developments in medicine and psychiatry; and

ii)   the altered formulation would help to make clearer the relationship between the role of the medical expert and the role of the jury.

    28. As to the first of those, the Commission quoted at length from, and endorsed, evidence given to it by the Royal College of Psychiatrists. The College was concerned to establish that the partial defence should be

grounded in valid medical diagnosis, rather than in imaginative or idiosyncratic fringe opinion. In that context the College had said this:

'It would also encourage reference within expert evidence to diagnosis in terms of one or two of the accepted internationally classificatory systems of mental conditions (WHO ICD-10 and AMA DSM) without explicitly writing those systems into the legislation. . . Such an approach would also avoid individual doctors offering idiosyncratic "diagnoses". . .'

It is apparent from this, and from the total silence in the 2006 report on the subject of voluntary intoxication, that the altered formulation owed nothing whatever to any intention in any quarter to alter the law on that topic.

ICD-10 and DSM-IV

29. The World Health Organisation ('WHO') has for many years sponsored the publication of an International Statistical Classification of Diseases and Related Health Problems ('ICD') of which the current edition is ICD-10. As its full title suggests, it is a general classification of the whole range of medical conditions and health problems; it is in no sense limited to diseases or conditions of the mind. . .

30. The American Medical Association has for many years sponsored a similar classification under the title 'Diagnostic and Statistical Manual' ('DSM'). That part of it which relates to conditions of the mind is now known as DSM-IV, published under the auspices of the American Psychiatric Association. It is a very substantial volume. Like ICD-10, and as its title makes clear, it is a tool for clinical diagnosis and for statistical analysis. Its introduction begins with a statement of its priority aim 'to provide a helpful guide to clinical practice', and refers also to the goal of improving communications between clinicians and researchers and to its usefulness in the collection of clinical information. Its introductory pages contain also a specific caution about forensic use:

'When DSM-IV categories, criteria and textual descriptions are employed for forensic purposes there are significant risks that diagnostic information will be misused or misunderstood. These dangers arise because of the imperfect fit between the questions of ultimate concern to the law and the information contained in a clinical diagnosis. In most situations, the clinical diagnosis of a DSM-IV mental disorder is not sufficient to establish the existence for legal purposes of a "mental disorder", "mental disability", "mental disease" or "mental defect".'

The particular 'imperfect fit' there under consideration is the divergence between the *level* of impairment which may bring a patient within a DSM-IV classification and the level necessary to have legal impact. But exactly the same considerations apply when the question is whether the doctors' classification system addresses the legal issue in any particular case. There will inevitably be considerations of legal policy which are irrelevant to the business of medical description, classification, and statistical analysis.

31. The 'imperfect fit' to which the authors of DSM-IV refer is nowhere more clearly demonstrated than in the breadth and kind of conditions which are included in both ICD-10 and DSM-IV. ICD-10 includes, for example, 'unhappiness' (R45.2), 'irritability and anger' (R45.4) 'suspiciousness and marked evasiveness' (R46.5), 'pyromania' (F63.1), 'paedophilia' (F65.4), 'sado-masochism' (F65.5) and 'kleptomania' (F63.2). DSM-IV includes similar conditions and also such as 'exhibitionism' (569) 'sexual sadism' (573) and 'intermittent explosive disorder' (663/667). The last of these is defined as 'discrete episodes of failure to resist aggressive impulses that result in serious assaultive acts or destruction of property, where the degree of aggression is grossly out of proportion to any precipitating psychosocial stressors'. Not all of these are treated by the classification systems as mental disorders, but all are, doubtless, 'recognised medical conditions' in the sense that they are perfectly sensibly included in guides for description of patients by doctors. It follows that a great many conditions thus included for medical purposes raise important additional legal questions when one is seeking to invoke them in a forensic context. 'Intermittent explosive disorder', for example, may well be a medically useful description of something which underlies the vast majority of violent offending, but any suggestion that it could give rise to a defence, whether because it amounted to an impairment of mental functioning or otherwise, would, to say the least, demand extremely careful attention. In other words, the medical classification begs the question whether the condition is simply a description of (often criminal) behaviour, or is capable of forming a defence to an allegation of such.

32. The Supreme Court of Canada addressed a similar point in *R. v. Bouchard-Lebrun* 2011 SCC 58, in ruling that a defendant who was severely intoxicated by voluntarily taken drugs could not rely on the defence of insanity under the Criminal Code. Giving the judgment of the court, Lebel J observed at [61–62] that:

'For the purposes of the Criminal Code, "disease of the mind" is a legal concept with a medical dimension . . . the trial judge is not bound by the medical evidence, since medical experts generally take no account of the policy component of the analysis required by s. 16 Cr. C'.

The appellant's argument

33. The appellants case was put with disarming simplicity by Miss O'Neill QC and runs as follows:

i) the Act commands attention to whether there is an abnormality of mental functioning attributable to a 'recognised medical condition';

ii) ICD-10 contains, at F.10.0, the condition of 'Acute Intoxication'; it is distinguished from 'harmful use' (F10.1) and 'dependence syndrome' (F10.2); it is defined simply as 'a condition that follows the administration of a psychoactive substance resulting in disturbances in level of consciousness, cognition, perception, affect or behaviour, or other physiological functions or responses'; (we note that DSM-IV lists a similar condition of 'alcohol intoxication');

iii) that is therefore a 'recognised medical condition';

iv) that is the condition in which the defendant was when he killed his partner, whether or not he was so drunk that he could not form an intent and whether or not he is telling the truth when he asserts loss of memory;

v) intoxication involves an impairment of mental functioning and it might well, depending on the facts, affect one or more of the three functions listed in subsection (1A);

vi) therefore diminished responsibility ought to have been left to the jury.

Conclusions

34. We are here concerned only with intoxication which is (a) voluntary and (b) uncomplicated by any alcoholism or dependence. Whilst we are concerned with alcohol, our conclusions must be the same in relation to the effects of the voluntary ingestion of other drugs or substances.

35. The deceptively simple argument for the appellant by-passes the very clear general law against the background of which this new amendment to section 2 of the Homicide Act was enacted. For the reasons which we have explained, the exception which prevents a defendant from relying on his voluntary intoxication, save upon the limited question of whether a 'specific intent' has been formed, is well entrenched and formed the unspoken backdrop for the new statutory formula. There had been no hint of any dissatisfaction with that rule of law. If Parliament had meant to alter it, or to depart from it, it would undoubtedly have made its intention explicit. Such an intention cannot be inferred from the adoption in the new formulation of the expression 'recognised medical condition' because the origins of that were clearly explained by the Law Commission. They explicitly did *not* include writing the terms of ICD-10 and/or DSM-IV into the legislation, for which purpose those terms are demonstrably unsuited. See [27–28] and [30] above.

36. Having sought the assistance of counsel on the topic, we have also given consideration to whether Miss O'Neill's reading of the statute is required by the canon of statutory construction usually labelled the principle against doubtful criminality or doubtful penalisation. This is generally stated to mean that, in the words of Lord Reid in *Sweet v Parsley* [1970] AC 132:

'it is a universal principle that if a penal provision is reasonably capable of two interpretations that which is most favourable to the accused must be adopted.'

The rationale of that principle has often been stated. It is justified by the requirement to give fair warning to citizens of which conduct may attract punishment. Individuals ought not to be left to guess at what they can or cannot do without infringing the criminal law and subjecting themselves to punishment: see for example *Sweet v Parsley* per Lord Diplock at 163C, where he referred to it being contrary to principle to assume that Parliament intended to penalise one who has performed his duty as a citizen to ascertain what acts are prohibited by law and has taken all proper care to inform himself of any facts which would make his conduct unlawful. The same basis for decision was relied upon in the context of Article 7 ECHR in *Kokkinakas v Greece* (1994) 17 EHRR 397.

37. Miss O'Neill conceded that strict construction of a criminal statute may give way to other principles of interpretation, especially to the clear mischief which the Act was designed to remedy, and indeed is a canon of 'last resort'.

38. There is no occasion in this case for a definitive analysis of the circumstances in which the principle of strict

construction of penal statutes, which is alive and well even if it may often give way to other canons of construction, will or will not be applied. It is quite clear that there is no occasion for it to be applied in the present case. There is simply no occasion which can be envisaged in which any citizen might order his affairs on the basis of a misunderstanding of the extent of the partial defence of diminished responsibility. The act of killing, with intent either to kill or to do grievous bodily harm and without justification (for example that of self defence), must have taken place before there can be any question of the partial defence arising. That act is a most serious criminal offence, and there is no risk of its legal character being misunderstood. The partial defence provides no more than a mitigation, judged *ex post facto* by the court with the assistance of expert evidence.

39. In the present case, Judge Wait relied in refusing to leave diminished responsibility to the jury on the additional factor that the condition of the defendant was a transitory or temporary one. That, he was disposed to hold, was not capable of amounting to a 'recognised medical condition' for the purposes of the new section 2 of the Homicide Act. We prefer not to rest our conclusion on this consideration, although it is clearly a relevant factor. We do not think that we should rule out the possibility that there may be genuine mental conditions, in no sense the fault of the defendant and well recognised by doctors, which although temporary may indeed be within the ambit of the Act. Whether concussion, for example, is such a condition is a question which does not arise for decision in this case.

40. Nor do we attempt to resolve the many questions which may arise as to other conditions listed in either ICD-10 or DSM-IV. It is enough to say that it is quite clear that the re-formulation of the statutory conditions for diminished responsibility was not intended to reverse the well established rule that voluntary acute intoxication is not capable of being relied upon to found diminished responsibility. That remains the law. The presence of a 'recognised medical condition' is a necessary, but not always a sufficient, condition to raise the issue of diminished responsibility.

41. . .. Voluntary acute intoxication, whether from alcohol or other substance, is not capable of founding diminished responsibility.

It follows that this appeal must be dismissed.

Notes

1. If D suffers from an abnormality of mental functioning, arising from a recognised medical condition, this may support his claim of diminished responsibility if it substantially impaired his ability to do one or more of the three things listed in s.2(1A). This contrasts with the previous law which required that D's mental responsibility for acting as s/he did was substantially impaired. This test involved a moral question of degree for the jury to determine. The new law contains no reference to "responsibility" leaving the jury with a factual question rather than a moral one to resolve.

2. As with the previous law, the impairment need not be total but it must be more than minimal. In *Brown* [2011] EWCA Crim 2796, which was an appeal against sentence, the issue of the meaning of "substantially impaired" arose. In 2010, D and his wife, V, were going through a divorce which was acrimonious, the proceedings having commenced in 2007 following upon several years of marital disharmony. At October half-term, D had had his two children for the weekend and returned them as planned to V. Previously D had prepared a grave in a remote area of Great Windsor Park. He had also placed a hammer in his daughter's schoolbag. At V's house the children were sent to another room; D retrieved the hammer and killed V with multiple blows. He wrapped the body and placed it in the boot of his car. He removed the CCTV recorder from the house which recorded the feed from the security camera at the front of the house which would have recorded him placing the body in the boot of his car. He then retrieved the children (they having heard the attack and seen him putting V's body in the car boot) and drove them to his girlfriend's house while he went to Windsor Great Park and buried the body and then disposed of his blood-stained clothing, the hammer and the CCTV recorder. At his trial for murder (D's guilty plea to manslaughter not being accepted) D raised the defence of diminished responsibility presenting medical evidence to the effect that he had developed an "adjustment disorder" as a reac-

tion to the stress of the preceding years and the divorce proceedings resulting in an abnormality of mental functioning which substantially impaired his ability to exercise self-control. The jury convicted of manslaughter on the basis of diminished responsibility. The trial judge, Cooke J, took the view that an adjustment disorder was a mild disorder which rarely led to violence. This was consistent with the evidence he had heard. He also noted that in this particular case, the disorder appeared to have disappeared almost immediately after the killing. He was satisfied that, on the basis of the jury's verdict, although the appellant's culpability was diminished, it remained substantial. Cooke J, giving credit for D's guilty plea, sentenced him to 24 years' imprisonment. Cooke J explained that he considered that the verdict of the jury did not lead to the conclusion that the appellant's mental responsibility for his actions was extinguished. There remained a substantial level of culpability even at the moment when the killing itself took place, and, moreover, in the context of the post-killing aggravating features, there was nothing to suggest that the appellant's culpability was diminished by any loss of control as, at that stage, every action was carefully considered and designed to avoid discovery. Dismissing the appeal and upholding the sentence, Lord Judge CJ stated (at [23]):

"We were asked to consider whether the words 'substantially impaired' in section 52(1)(b) provided a different test to that which was applied to the term 'substantial impairment' in the 1957 Act. We do not think that it does. When Parliament enacted the 2009 Act it was perfectly well aware of the way in which the court had interpreted the phrase 'substantial impairment' for very many years, (see *R v Ramchurn* (2010) 2 Cr App R.3). Cooke J had directed the jury that the reference to 'substantially impaired' required the jury to conclude that the impairment was more than minimal. No further embellishment was suggested, and this direction formed the basis for the jury's verdict. Accordingly, in our judgment, Cooke J was entitled to reach the conclusion that the appellant's responsibility for the death of his wife, although diminished, remained substantial and that although his ability to exercise self-control was, in accordance with the jury's verdict, to be treated as substantially impaired, he 'retained real culpability' for what he had done. That was consistent with the verdict of the jury."

Thus while D's impairment of mental functioning was "substantial" in the sense of being more than minimal or trivial, and was enough to tip the scales in his favour as regards establishing the defence of diminished responsibility, his overall responsibility for the killing which involved a significant degree of planning, premeditation and preparation, and therefore his overall culpability, was not significantly reduced but remained substantial in the sense of being significant. This outcome highlights the fact that the defence of diminished responsibility simply serves to provide an escape from the automatic life sentence which follows from a conviction for murder, but does not exonerate a defendant or provide him with a means of escaping punishment commensurate with his level of responsibility and culpability.

3. In *Golds* [2014] EWCA Crim 748, however, the Court of Appeal eschewed limiting the meaning of "substantial" to "more than trivial". D suffered from schizophrenia, depression and had auditory hallucinations and paranoid delusions. He stopped taking his medication which controlled his symptoms and following an argument with his partner, V, stabbed her 22 times as he believed she was a demon. D was charged with murder and the three medical experts (two for the defence and one for the Crown) were agreed that he was suffering from a significant level of mental illness and that the criteria in s.2 were satisfied. The plea of guilty to manslaughter, however, was not accepted and the issue went to the jury who convicted D of murder. Counsel for D had contended

that the trial judge should direct the jury that his impairment must be treated as "substantial" if the effect of the abnormality of mental functioning on his ability to do the things specified in s.2(1A) was "more than trivial". The trial judge refused leaving the jury to determine for themselves the meaning of "substantial". D appealed. The essence of the appeal was that "substantial" was capable of having two different meanings either the meaning counsel had argued for at trial or a more stringent meaning to the effect that the abnormality of mental functioning only substantially impairs where, whilst not totally impairing a defendant's ability to do the specified things, it *significantly* or *appreciably* impairs that ability. The Court of Appeal dismissed the appeal accepting jurisprudence from the old defence of diminished responsibility to the effect that judges, if requested by the jury for further explanation of the meaning of "substantial" should either refuse to give it as "substantial" is an ordinary word for the jury to apply using their common sense, or if further direction was considered necessary a direction adapting one given in *Simcox* [1964] Crim. L.R. 402 should be used. As adapted this might say:

> "Do we think, looking at it broadly as common-sense people, there was a substantial impairment of his [ability to do one or more of the things listed in s. 2(1A)]? If the answer is 'no', there may be some impairment, but we do not think it was substantial, we do not think it was something that really made any great difference, although it may have made it harder [for him to do one or more of those things], then you would find him guilty."

There is a clear danger that juries will have varying understandings of the meaning of "substantially" and that they might set the standard for impairment at a particularly high level. It is difficult to see how a jury could have concluded in this case that D's ability to form a rational judgement was not substantially impaired without doing so. If "substantial" is understood in this more stringent way, does this not raise a possibility of real confusion if a jury are faced both with an issue of causation to determine (see Ch.2 above p.45) as well as the issue of diminished responsibility? It is also arguable, in light of the next case, that the ground on which the appeal was pursued was misconceived and that an appeal focusing on the un-contradicted nature of the medical evidence might have stood a greater chance of success.

4.   In *Brennan* [2014] EWCA Crim 2387 there was clear, un-contradicted evidence from all the medical experts that D met the criteria for diminished responsibility. The trial judge refused to withdraw the case from the jury and directed the jury that they "did not have to buy into the experts opinions". The jury duly convicted of murder. On appeal the Court of Appeal quashed the murder conviction and substituted a conviction of manslaughter. The Court noted that the changes in the legislation related almost entirely to psychiatric matters. This being so it would not be inappropriate for the medical experts to express an opinion on the ultimate issue of whether they considered that the criteria in s.2 were satisfied. Further, where there is no rational or proper basis for departing from uncontradicted and unchallenged expert evidence, juries may not do so. Furthermore, the Court expressed the view (at para.66) that "[a] charge of murder should not be left to the jury if the trial judge's considered view is that on the evidence taken as a whole no properly directed jury could properly convict of murder." Had *Brennan* been decided before Golds was prosecuted, it is doubtful whether a murder conviction would have been returned, or if returned upheld on appeal. This is further supported by the following observations by the Court of Appeal in *Brennan* (at paras 67–68):

> "Each case, ultimately, must be decided on its own facts and circumstances. We add, however, that in the light of the new provisions of s. 2 as amended, with its significantly different structure

and effect, pursuit by the prosecution of a charge of murder in the face of a defence of diminished responsibility which is unequivocally supported by reputable expert evidence but which is not contradicted by any prosecution expert evidence should, we venture to suggest, become relatively uncommon. There may, of course, be cases where the defence expert evidence is tentative or qualified. Possibly too there may be cases where substantial inroads can be made into the defence expert psychiatric evidence by cross-examination, even in the absence of expert evidence adduced by the Crown. Otherwise, if there is reason to think that the opinion of the defence psychiatric expert(s) supporting a defence of diminished responsibility is or may be wrong in its conclusions or wrongly premised or inadequately reasoned or inadequately related to the facts or otherwise suspect then it is surely not unreasonable (at all events in most of such cases) to expect the Crown to adduce its own expert evidence in order properly to make such points for the jury's evaluation. . .

We also add that if in any particular case there are other facts or circumstances which might cast a different light on otherwise un-contradicted defence expert medical evidence on diminished responsibility and the matter is to be left to the jury, one would expect those facts and circumstances to be highlighted by prosecuting counsel in discussion with the judge prior to closing speeches and in due course specifically identified to the jury by the judge in the summing-up: as capable of providing a rational basis on which the jury could decline to accept the expert evidence called by the defence if that evidence has not otherwise been contradicted or doubted by any expert evidence called by the Crown. "

In light of these comments it would not be surprising if little reference is made in future to *Golds*. If the expert evidence is uncontradicted, how could a jury, basing its verdict on the evidence, come to any contrary conclusion?

5.   The thing that must be impaired is D's ability to do any, or a combination, of the things listed in s.2(1A), medical evidence detailing the nature and extent of any such impairment will be quite crucial in enabling the jury to make their assessment of whether or not that impairment is substantial. The three things listed in s.2(1A) are considered below.

(i) Ability to understand the nature of D's conduct

This limb may overlap with the first limb of the M'Naghten Rules where the issue is whether D did not know the nature and quality of the act he was doing (see Ch.5 above, p.231). In the M'Naghten test the effect of the defect of reason is to rule out mens rea. The diminished responsibility defence operates where D has mens rea but his understanding is, in some way, impaired. Thus, if D is in a delusional state and stabs V believing V is a three-headed monster, D would not understand the nature and quality of his act such that he would not have the intent to kill another person. His appropriate defence, provided his defect of reason arose from a disease of the mind, would be insanity and not diminished responsibility. By contrast, however, if D suffers from a recognised medical condition which does not leave him delusional but as a result of which he does not fully understand cause and effect, and believing real life is like video games he stabs V in a fit of temper when V attempts to take a game from him, not understanding that real people cannot be revived like the characters in the video game, V's appropriate defence would be diminished responsibility. He has intended serious injury and thus has the mens rea for murder. The issue for the jury would be whether there was a more than minimal impairment of his ability to understand the nature of his conduct.

(ii) Ability to form a rational judgement

Where D's perception of reality is to some extent impaired as a result of his medical condition, this will impact on his ability to form a rational judgement. For example, a battered spouse after years of abuse develops a severe depressive illness which distorts her perception of reality such that she believes that the only way to escape her hopeless situation is to kill V, her abusive husband. The issue for the jury would be whether her illness had, in a more than minimal way, impaired her ability to form a rational judgement. While outside observers might have been able to identify alternative strategies for D, medical evidence as to the effects of the abuse on her psychology and her reasoning abilities will be quite crucial in providing a basis for the jury's determination. To an extent, this limb will overlap with the first limb as if D does not fully understand the nature of her own conduct, she will have difficulty in making rational judgements on her own actions. It may be that this limb will provide the basis for future pleas of diminished responsibility in the context of mercy killings if the medical evidence can establish that D suffers from a medical condition (perhaps some form of depression) arising from the demands of continually caring for V in distressing circumstances, such that eventually D's perception of reality becomes distorted and D gives way to V's pleas and kills V.

(iii) Ability to exercise self-control

Many medical conditions may have effects upon individuals' abilities to control their tempers and to exercise self-restraint. This limb may operate in circumstances where the separate defence of loss of control would not succeed because D's loss of self-control is not linked to one of the required qualifying triggers. For example, D, an adult with severe learning difficulties, suffers continual teasing from youths in the neighbourhood. D eventually snaps, losing his self-control and hits one of the youths with a brick, killing him. The teasing, while unkind, does not come close to constituting "circumstances of an extremely grave character" or providing D with "a justifiable sense of being seriously wronged" such as would be required to raise the defence of loss of control. Medical evidence is presented, however, that D's ability to exercise self-control is not that of a normal adult and the effects of the teasing over a period of time have led to the onset of depression which had a further impairing impact on his ability to exercise self-control. The issue for the jury would be whether or not the impairment of his ability to exercise self-control is more than minimal.

6. The third requirement of the abnormality of mental functioning if the defence is to succeed, is that it provides an explanation for D's conduct in killing (or being a party to the killing) (s.2(1)(c)). Section 2(1B) stipulates that such an explanation is provided where the abnormality of mental functioning "causes, or is a significant contributory factor in causing, D to carry out that conduct". Thus there must be a connection between D's abnormality and the killing; it is not enough that D has killed and that he does suffer from an abnormality of mental functioning. The abnormality need not be the sole cause—so other causes, such as provocative words or conduct, may be at work—but it has to be at least a significant contributory factor such that, without that abnormality, the other cause(s) would not have operated on their own to bring about the killing. Thus, if the abnormality of mental functioning, in the circumstances, made no difference to D's behaviour (i.e. he would have killed as and when he did regardless of his abnormality), the defence will fail.

For example, D suffers from an abnormality of mental functioning arising from a recognised medical condition (for example, a brain injury in childhood seriously impairing his mental development) which substantially impairs his ability to exercise self-control such that if annoyed he suffers severe fits of temper in which he becomes violent. If D kills in such a temper fit, he could potentially satisfy the conditions for diminished responsibility if charged with murder. However, if the actual killing committed by D is carried out in a cold and calculated way where D planned it and executed it with his emotions under control, his abnormality of mental functioning would not have caused or been a significant contributory factor in causing him to kill and his plea of diminished responsibility will fail. Under the previous law D may have succeeded if the jury concluded that morally he should not be held responsible for the killing as no causal connection between the abnormality of mind and the killing was required. This is, perhaps, an extreme example, but others may arise, particularly where D is not the principal but is a participant in a joint enterprise where his abnormality of mental functioning may not play any contributory part in the killing by the principal.

----

4. INVOLUNTARY MANSLAUGHTER

Notes

1. Manslaughter which has been reduced from murder because of provocation or diminished responsibility (often called "voluntary" manslaughter) has been dealt with in the preceding section. "Involuntary" manslaughter, with which this section is concerned, is a generic term comprising those homicides which occupy "the shifting sands between the uncertain . . . definition of murder and the unsettled boundaries of excusable or accidental death" (Hogan, "The Killing Ground: 1964–73" [1974] Crim. L.R. 387, 391).

2. "Involuntary" manslaughter can be divided into manslaughter by unlawful act and gross negligence manslaughter. The same case will often give rise to a consideration of both: see *R. v Goodfellow*, below p.508. In *R. v Larkin* (1944) 29 Cr. App. R. 18, a case where the jury's verdict of manslaughter could have been based on a finding of provocation or of unlawful act, the Court of Criminal Appeal deprecated the practice of asking the foreman to explain the basis of the jury's verdict. Humphreys J, for the court, at 27:

    "As we in this country think, trial by jury is the best method yet devised for dealing with serious criminal cases, and the jury is the best possible tribunal to decide whether a man is guilty and, if he is guilty, of what he is guilty, subject to the direction in law of the judge; but no one has ever suggested that a jury is composed of persons who are likely to be able to give at a moment's notice a logical explanation of how and why they arrive at their verdict. That was what Oliver, J., was inviting the jury to do in this case, and, as has been already observed, inviting the foreman to do so, and accepting from the foreman something with which, perhaps, the other eleven did not agree. The unhappy result was that the foreman, no doubt thoroughly confused, gave two totally inconsistent answers. That incident cannot, in our opinion, be of any importance whatever from the point of view of this appeal against conviction. It was something which happened after the trial was over, so far as the jury were concerned, and if it has any effect at all, it must be an effect upon the sentence. But it must be understood that this court deprecates questions being put to a jury upon the meaning of the verdict which they have returned. If the verdict appears to be inconsistent, proper questions may be put by a judge to invite the jury to explain what they mean, but where a verdict has been returned which is perfectly plain and unambiguous, it is most undesirable that the jury should be asked any further questions about it at all."

----

i. Unlawful Act Manslaughter

(a) The act causing death must be unlawful

R. V FRANKLIN

(1883) 15 Cox 163

The defendant was indicted with manslaughter. He took a box from another man's stall on West Pier, Brighton, and threw it into the sea. The box hit and killed a man who was swimming. The prosecution argued that the question of the defendant's negligence was immaterial, since it was manslaughter where death ensued in consequence of any wrongful act.

FIELD J

I am of opinion that the case must go to the jury upon the broad ground of negligence and not upon the narrow ground proposed by the learned counsel, because it seems to me—and I may say that in this view my brother Mathew agrees—that the mere fact of a civil wrong committed by one person against another ought not to be used as an incident which is a necessary step in a criminal case. I have a great abhorrence of constructive crime . . .

Verdict. Guilty

Note

Counsel in this case had relied upon *R. v Fenton* (1830) 1 Lew. 179, in which Tindal CJ had formulated this proposition:

> "If death ensues as the consequence of a wrongful act, an act which the party who commits it can neither justify nor excuse, it is not accidental death, but manslaughter. If the wrongful act was done under circumstances which show an attempt to kill, or do any serious injury in the particular case, or any general malice, the offence becomes that of murder. In the present instance the act was one of mere wantonness and sport, but still the act was wrongful, it was a trespass. The only question therefore is whether the death of the party is to be fairly and reasonably considered as a consequence of such wrongful act; if it followed from such wrongful act as an effect from a cause, the offence is manslaughter; if it is altogether unconnected with it, it is an accidental death."

Field J rejected this harsh rule that a civil wrong could constitute the unlawful act for the purposes of manslaughter. This left undecided what constituted such an unlawful act.

R. V CHURCH

[1966] 1 Q.B. 59

The appellant was mocked by a woman and fought with her knocking her unconscious. He failed to revive her and in a panic, thinking she was dead, threw her into the river where she drowned. The appellant was acquitted of murder but convicted of manslaughter. He appealed on the ground of a misdirection as to manslaughter.

EDMUND-DAVIES J

Two passages in the summing-up are here material [to manslaughter by an unlawful act causing death]. They are these: (1) 'If by an unlawful act of violence done deliberately to the person of another, that other is killed, the killing is manslaughter even though the accused never intended either death or grievous bodily harm to result. If this woman was alive, as she was, when he threw her into the river, what he did was the deliberate act of throwing a living body into the river. That is an unlawful killing and it does not matter whether he believed she was dead or not, and that is my direction to you', and (2) 'I would suggest to you, though it is of course for you to approach your task as you think fit, that a convenient way of approaching it would be to say: What do we think about this defence that he honestly believed the woman to be dead? If you think that is true, why then, as I have told you, your proper verdict would be one of manslaughter, not murder.'

Such a direction is not lacking in authority: see, for example, *Shoukatallie v The Queen* [1962] A.C. 81 and Dr Glanville Williams' *Criminal Law* (2nd edn, 1961), p.173. Nevertheless, in the judgment of this court it was a misdirection. It amounted to telling the jury that, whenever any unlawful act is committed in relation to a human being which resulted in death there must be, at least, a conviction for manslaughter. This might at one time have been regarded as good law. . . But it appears to this court that the passage of years has achieved a transformation in this branch of the law and, even in relation to manslaughter, a degree of *mens rea* has become recognised as essential. To define it is a difficult task, and in *Andrews v D.P.P.* [1937] A.C. 576, Lord Atkin spoke of the 'element of "unlawfulness" which is the elusive factor'. Stressing that we are here leaving entirely out of account those ingredients of homicide which might justify a verdict of manslaughter on the grounds of (a) criminal negligence, or (b) provocation, or (c) diminished responsibility, the conclusion of this court is that an unlawful act causing the death of another cannot, simply because it is an unlawful act, render a manslaughter verdict inevitable. For such a verdict inexorably to follow, the unlawful act must be such as all sober and reasonable people would inevitably recognise must subject the other person to, at least, the risk of some harm resulting therefrom, albeit not serious harm. See, for example, *R. v Franklin*, [above, p.495]; *R. v Senior* [1899] 1 Q.B. 283; *R. v Larkin* [1943] 1 K.B. 174 in the judgment of the court delivered by Humphrey J.; *R. v Buck & Buck* (1960) 44 Cr.App.R. 213, and *R. v Hall* (1961) 45 Cr.App.R. 366.

If such be the test, as we adjudge it to be, then it follows that in our view it was a misdirection to tell the jury *simpliciter* that it mattered nothing for manslaughter whether or not the appellant believed Mrs Nott to be dead when he threw her in the river. But, quite apart from our decision that the direction on criminal negligence was an adequate one in the circumstances, such a misdirection does not, in our judgment, involve that the conviction for manslaughter must or should be quashed.

Appeal dismissed

Notes

1.   In *Andrews v DPP* [1937] A.C. 576, Lord Atkin stated:

"There is an obvious difference in the law of manslaughter between doing an unlawful act and doing a lawful act with a degree of carelessness which the legislature makes criminal. If it were otherwise a man who killed another while driving without due care and attention would *ex necessitate* commit manslaughter."

Thus a manslaughter verdict cannot be based on an act which is unlawful simply because it has been performed negligently; it must be unlawful for some other reason, namely that the defendant had the mens rea required for the offence which constituted the unlawful act.

2.   The following case makes it clear that mens rea for the unlawful act must be established subjectively.

R. V LAMB

[1967] 2 Q.B. 981

The appellant, in fun, pointed a revolver at a friend. He knew that there were two bullets in the chambers, but neither was opposite the barrel. He pulled the trigger and because of the action of the cylinder, which rotated before firing, a bullet was fired and the friend killed. He did not appreciate that the cylinder rotated automatically. The appellant was convicted of manslaughter and appealed against this.

SACHS J

. . . [I]n the course of his summing-up, the trial judge no doubt founded himself on the part of the judgment of Edmund-Davies J. in *R. v Church* when he says: 'The unlawful act must be such as all sober and reasonable people would inevitably recognise must subject the other person to, at least, the risk of some harm resulting therefrom, albeit not serious harm.'

Unfortunately, however, he fell into error as to the meaning of the word 'unlawful' in that passage and pressed upon the jury a definition with which experienced counsel for the Crown had disagreed during the trial and which he found himself unable to support on the appeal. The trial judge took the view that the pointing of the revolver and the pulling of the trigger was something which could of itself be unlawful even if there was no attempt to alarm or intent to injure. This view is exemplified in a passage in his judgment which will be cited later.

It was no doubt on that basis that he had before commencing his summing-up stated that he was not going 'to involve the jury in any consideration of the niceties of the question whether or not the action of the accused did constitute or did not constitute an assault'; and thus he did not refer to the defence of accident or the need for the prosecution to disprove accident before coming to a conclusion that the act was unlawful.

Mr Mathew [for the Crown], however, had at all times put forward the correct view that for the act to be unlawful it must constitute at least what he then termed 'a technical assault'. In this court moreover he rightly conceded that there was no evidence to go to the jury of any assault of any kind. Nor did he feel able to submit that the acts of the defendant were on any other ground unlawful in the criminal sense of that word. Indeed no such submission could in law be made: if, for instance, the pulling of the trigger had had no effect because the striking mechanism or the ammunition had been defective no offence would have been committed by the defendant.

Another way of putting it is that *mens rea*, being now an essential ingredient in manslaughter (compare *Andrews v D.P.P.* and *R. v Church*), that could not in the present case be established in relation to the first ground except by proving that element of intent without which there can be no assault.

It is perhaps as well to mention that when using the phrase 'unlawful in the criminal sense of that word' the court has in mind that it is long settled that it is not in point to consider whether an act is unlawful merely from the angle of civil liabilities. That was first made in the 'Brighton Pier' case (*R. v Franklin*) . . .

Appeal allowed

Note

A problem decision in this area, however, is that of *Cato* [1976] 1 W.L.R. 110 (above, p.47) where the Court of Appeal suggested that the unlawful act need not itself be a crime. Lord Widgery stated, at 118:

"Strangely enough, . . . although the possession or supply of heroin is an offence, it is not an offence to take it, and although supplying it is an offence, it is not an offence to administer it . . .

Of course if the conviction on count 2 remains (that is the charge under section 23 of the Offences Against the Person Act 1861 of administering a noxious thing), then that in itself would be an unlawful act . . . .

But . . . had it not been possible to rely on [that] charge, . . . we think there would have been an unlawful act there, and we think the unlawful act would be described as injecting the deceased Farmer with a mixture of heroin and water which at the time of the injection and for the purposes of the injection the accused had unlawfully taken into his possession."

The suggestion that D could be convicted even if the s.23 count was excised from the indictment is obiter and appears to be wrong. Possession of heroin is an offence but D's possession of it did not cause the victim's death. This view is confirmed by the fact that in *Dalby* (1982) 74 Cr. App. R. 348, the Court of Appeal expressed the opinion that even the act of supplying a controlled drug to the victim was not an act which *caused* direct harm. The Court affirmed the view that the unlawful act itself must be one which subjects the victim to the risk of some harm; in the instant case it was the victim's own use of the drug in a form and quantity which was dangerous which caused the harm.

The Court of Appeal elaborated further on the error in *Cato* in *Kennedy* [1999] Crim. L.R. 65, where D supplied a syringe filled with heroin to V who injected it and died. The Court of Appeal upheld D's conviction for manslaughter on the basis either that D was guilty of the s.23 offence or that the self-injection by V was unlawful and D had assisted and wilfully encouraged this. But D could not be a secondary party to manslaughter, as V's self-injection could not amount to an unlawful act. This was recognised by the Court of Appeal in *Dias* [2001] EWCA Crim 2986 which doubted whether *Kennedy* could have been decided correctly on this point as it conflicted with *Dalby*. They concluded that there was no offence of self-injection and thus V was not a principal, with the consequence that D could not be a secondary party. When the Criminal Cases Review Commission referred the case of *Kennedy* back to the Court of Appeal on the basis that there was a real possibility that the Court of Appeal would find the conviction unsafe in light of the doubts expressed in *Dias*, the Court of Appeal upheld the conviction on the basis that D had acted in concert with V to commit the s.23 offence which amounted to the unlawful act (*Kennedy* [2005] EWCA Crim 685). While D's act of supplying the heroin-filled syringe could not satisfy the requirement of dangerousness (nor the requirement of causation) as the syringe harboured no risk in itself (it was only when a further act was performed to the syringe, that of injection, that harm could ensue), the Court of Appeal ignored this issue satisfying itself that the whole enterprise of acting in concert to administer a noxious thing is dangerous. This was not the last word on the issue, however, as the case went to the House of Lords.

R. V KENNEDY (NO.2)

[2007] UKHL 38

LORD BINGHAM OF CORNHILL

1. This is the considered opinion of the committee.

2. The question certified by the Court of Appeal Criminal Division for the opinion of the House neatly encapsulates the question raised by this appeal:

'When is it appropriate to find someone guilty of manslaughter where that person has been involved in the supply of a class A controlled drug, which is then freely and voluntarily self-administered by the person to whom it was supplied, and the administration of the drug then causes his death?'

Manslaughter

. . .

7. To establish the crime of unlawful act manslaughter it must be shown, among other things not relevant to this appeal,

(1) that the defendant committed an unlawful act;

(2) that such unlawful act was a crime (*R v Franklin* (1883) 15 Cox CC 163; *R v Lamb* [1967] 2 QB 981, 988; *R v Dias* [2001] EWCA Crim 2986, [2002] 2 Cr App R 96, para 9); and

(3) that the defendant's unlawful act was a significant cause of the death of the deceased (*R v Cato* [1976] 1 WLR 110, 116–117).

There is now, as already noted, no doubt but that the appellant committed an unlawful (and criminal) act by supplying the heroin to the deceased. But the act of supplying, without more, could not harm the deceased in any physical way, let alone cause his death. As the Court of Appeal observed in *R v Dalby* [1982] 1 WLR 425, 429, 'the supply of drugs would itself have caused no harm unless the deceased had subsequently used the drugs in a form and quantity which was dangerous'. So, as the parties agree, the charge of unlawful act manslaughter cannot be founded on the act of supplying the heroin alone.

8. The parties are further agreed that an unlawful act of the appellant on the present facts must be found, if at all, in a breach of section 23 of the Offences against the Person Act 1861. Although the death of the deceased was the tragic outcome of the injection on 10 September 1996 the death is legally irrelevant to the criminality of the appellant's conduct under the section: he either was or was not guilty of an offence under section 23 irrespective of the death.

9. As it now effectively reads, section 23 of the 1861 Act provides:

'Maliciously administering poison, etc, so as to endanger life or inflict grievous bodily harm Whosoever shall unlawfully and maliciously administer to or cause to be administered to or taken by any other person any poison or other destructive or noxious thing, so as thereby to endanger the life of such person, or so as thereby to inflict upon such person any grievous bodily harm, shall be guilty of [an offence] and being convicted thereof shall be liable . . . to [imprisonment] for any term not exceeding ten years . . .'.

The opening and closing words of the section raise no question relevant to this appeal. The substance of the section creates three distinct offences: (1) administering a noxious thing to any other person; (2) causing a noxious thing to be administered to any other person; and (3) causing a noxious thing to be taken by any other person. It is not in doubt that heroin is a noxious thing, and the contrary was not contended.

10. The factual situations covered by (1), (2) and (3) are clear. Offence (1) is committed where D administers the noxious thing directly to V, as by injecting V with the noxious thing, holding a glass containing the noxious thing to V's lips, or (as in *R v Gillard* (1988) 87 Cr App R 189) spraying the noxious thing in V's face.

11. Offence (2) is typically committed where D does not directly administer the noxious thing to V but causes an innocent third party TP to administer it to V. If D, knowing a syringe to be filled with poison instructs TP to inject V, TP believing the syringe to contain a legitimate therapeutic substance, D would commit this offence.

12. Offence (3) covers the situation where the noxious thing is not administered to V but taken by him, provided D causes the noxious thing to be taken by V and V does not make a voluntary and informed decision to take it. If D puts a noxious thing in food which V is about to eat and V, ignorant of the presence of the noxious thing, eats it, D commits offence (3).

13. In the course of his accurate and well-judged submissions on behalf of the crown, Mr David Perry QC accepted that if he could not show that the appellant had committed offence (1) as the unlawful act necessary to found the count of manslaughter he could not hope to show the commission of offences (2) or (3). This concession was rightly made, but the committee heard considerable argument addressed to the concept of causation, which has been misapplied in some of the authorities, and it is desirable that it should be clear why the concession is rightly made.

14. The criminal law generally assumes the existence of free will. The law recognises certain exceptions, in the

case of the young, those who for any reason are not fully responsible for their actions, and the vulnerable, and it acknowledges situations of duress and necessity, as also of deception and mistake. But, generally speaking, informed adults of sound mind are treated as autonomous beings able to make their own decisions how they will act, and none of the exceptions is relied on as possibly applicable in this case. Thus D is not to be treated as causing V to act in a certain way if V makes a voluntary and informed decision to act in that way rather than another. There are many classic statements to this effect. In his article *'Finis for Novus Actus?'* (1989) 48(3) CLJ 391, 392, Professor Glanville Williams wrote:

'I may suggest reasons to you for doing something; I may urge you to do it, tell you it will pay you to do it, tell you it is your duty to do it. My efforts may perhaps make it very much more likely that you will do it. But they do not cause you to do it, in the sense in which one causes a kettle of water to boil by putting it on the stove. Your volitional act is regarded (within the doctrine of responsibility) as setting a new 'chain of causation' going, irrespective of what has happened before.'

In chapter XII of *Causation in the Law*, 2nd ed (1985), p 326, Hart and Honoré wrote:

'The free, deliberate, and informed intervention of a second person, who intends to exploit the situation created by the first, but is not acting in concert with him, is normally held to relieve the first actor of criminal responsibility.'

This statement was cited by the House with approval in *R v Latif* [1996] 1 WLR 104, 115. The principle is fundamental and not controversial.

15. Questions of causation frequently arise in many areas of the law, but causation is not a single, unvarying concept to be mechanically applied without regard to the context in which the question arises. That was the point which Lord Hoffmann, with the express concurrence of three other members of the House, was at pains to make in *Environment Agency (formerly National Rivers Authority) v Empress Car Co (Abertillery) Ltd* [1999] 2 AC 22. The House was not in that decision purporting to lay down general rules governing causation in criminal law. It was construing, with reference to the facts of the case before it, a statutory provision imposing strict criminal liability on those who cause pollution of controlled waters. Lord Hoffmann made clear that (p 29E-F) common sense answers to questions of causation will differ according to the purpose for which the question is asked; that (p 31E) one cannot give a common sense answer to a question of causation for the purpose of attributing responsibility under some rule without knowing the purpose and scope of the rule; that (p 32B) strict liability was imposed in the interests of protecting controlled waters; and that (p 36A) in the situation under consideration the act of the defendant could properly be held to have caused the pollution even though an ordinary act of a third party was the immediate cause of the diesel oil flowing into the river. It is worth underlining that the relevant question was the cause of the pollution, not the cause of the third party's act.

16. The committee would not wish to throw any doubt on the correctness of *Empress Car*. But the reasoning in that case cannot be applied to the wholly different context of causing a noxious thing to be administered to or taken by another person contrary to section 23 of the 1861 Act. In *R v Finlay* [2003] EWCA Crim 3868 (8 December 2003) V was injected with heroin and died. D was tried on two counts of manslaughter, one on the basis that he had himself injected V, the second on the basis that he had prepared a syringe and handed it to V who had injected herself. The jury could not agree on the first count but convicted on the second. When rejecting an application to remove the second count from the indictment, the trial judge ruled, relying on *Empress Car*, that D had produced a situation in which V could inject herself, in which her self-injection was entirely foreseeable and in which self-injection could not be regarded as something extraordinary. He directed the jury along those lines. The Court of Appeal upheld the judge's analysis and dismissed the appeal. It was wrong to do so. Its decision conflicted with the rules on personal autonomy and informed voluntary choice to which reference has been made above. In the decision under appeal the Court of Appeal did not follow *R v Finlay* in seeking to apply *Empress Car*, and it was right not to do so.

17. In his article already cited Professor Glanville Williams pointed out (at p 398) that the doctrine of secondary liability was developed precisely because an informed voluntary choice was ordinarily regarded as a *novus actus interveniens* breaking the chain of causation:

'Principals cause, accomplices encourage (or otherwise influence) or help. If the instigator were regarded as causing the result he would be a principal, and the conceptual division between principals (or, as I prefer to call them, perpetrators) and accessories would vanish. Indeed, it was because the instigator was not regarded as causing the crime that the notion of accessories had to be developed. This is the irrefragable argument for recognising the *novus actus* principle as one of the bases of our criminal law. The final act is done by the perpetrator, and his guilt pushes the accessories, conceptually speaking, into the background. Accessorial liability is, in the traditional theory, 'derivative' from that of the perpetrator.'

18. This is a matter of some significance since, contrary to the view of the Court of Appeal when dismissing the appellant's first appeal, the deceased committed no offence when injecting himself with the fatal dose of heroin. It was so held by the Court of Appeal in *R v Dias* [2002] 2 Cr App R 96, paras 21–24, and in *R v Rogers* [2003] EWCA Crim 945, [2003] 1 WLR 1374 and is now accepted. If the conduct of the deceased was not criminal he was not a principal offender, and it of course follows that the appellant cannot be liable as a secondary party. It also follows that there is no meaningful legal sense in which the appellant can be said to have been a principal jointly with the deceased, or to have been acting in concert. The finding that the deceased freely and voluntarily administered the injection to himself, knowing what it was, is fatal to any contention that the appellant caused the heroin to be administered to the deceased or taken by him.

19. The sole argument open to the crown was, therefore, that the appellant administered the injection to the deceased. It was argued that the term 'administer' should not be narrowly interpreted. Reliance was placed on the steps taken by the appellant to facilitate the injection and on the trial judge's direction to the jury that they had to be satisfied that the appellant handed the syringe to the deceased 'for immediate injection'. But section 23 draws a very clear contrast between a noxious thing administered to another person and a noxious thing taken by another person. It cannot ordinarily be both. In this case the heroin is described as 'freely and voluntarily self-administered' by the deceased. This, on the facts, is an inevitable finding. The appellant supplied the heroin and prepared the syringe. But the deceased had a choice whether to inject himself or not. He chose to do so, knowing what he was doing. It was his act.

20. In resisting this conclusion Mr Perry relied on *R v Rogers* [2003] 1 WLR 1374. In that case the defendant pleaded guilty, following a legal ruling, to a count of administering poison contrary to section 23 of the 1861 Act and a count of manslaughter. The relevant finding was that the defendant physically assisted the deceased by holding his belt round the deceased's arm as a tourniquet, so as to raise a vein in which the deceased could insert a syringe, while the deceased injected himself. It was argued in support of his appeal to the Court of Appeal that the defendant had committed no unlawful act for purposes of either count. This contention was rejected. The court held (para 7) that it was unreal and artificial to separate the tourniquet from the injection. By applying and holding the tourniquet the defendant had played a part in the mechanics of the injection which had caused the death. There is, clearly, a difficult borderline between contributory acts which may properly be regarded as administering a noxious thing and acts which may not. But the crucial question is not whether the defendant facilitated or contributed to administration of the noxious thing but whether he went further and administered it. What matters, in a case such as *R v Rogers* and the present, is whether the injection itself was the result of a voluntary and informed decision by the person injecting himself. In *R v Rogers*, as in the present case, it was. That case was, therefore, wrongly decided.

21. It is unnecessary to review the case law on this subject in any detail. In *R v Cato* [1976] 1 WLR 110 the defendant had injected the deceased with heroin and the present problem did not arise. In *R v Dalby* [1982] 1 WLR 425 the deceased had died following the consumption of drugs which the defendant had supplied but the deceased had injected. There was apparently no discussion of section 23, but it was held that the supply could not support a conviction of manslaughter. At the trial of the present appellant there was no consideration of section 23 and the trial judge effectively stopped defence counsel submitting to the jury that the appellant had not caused the death of the deceased. In dismissing his first appeal the Court of Appeal said:

'We can see no reason why, on the facts alleged by the Crown, the appellant in the instant case might not have been guilty of an offence under section 23 of the Offences against the Person Act 1861. Perhaps more relevantly, the injection of the heroin into himself by Bosque was itself an unlawful act, and if the appellant assisted in and wilfully encouraged that unlawful conduct, he would himself be acting unlawfully.'

But the court gave no detailed consideration to the terms of section 23, and it is now accepted that the deceased's injection of himself was not an unlawful act.

22. In *R v Dias* [2002] 2 Cr App R 96 the defendant had been convicted of manslaughter. He had prepared a syringe charged with heroin which he had handed to the deceased, who had injected himself. The court recognised that the chain of causation had probably been broken by the free and informed decision of the deceased,

and noted the error in the decision on the appellant's first appeal as to the unlawfulness of the deceased's injection of himself.

23. In rejecting the appellant's second appeal in the decision now challenged, the Court of Appeal reviewed the history of the case and the authorities in some detail. The court expressed its conclusion [that the appellant's liability rested on the principle of joint responsibility as he and the deceased were acting in concert in administering the heroin]. . . Thus the essential ratio of the decision is that the administration of the injection was a joint activity of the appellant and the deceased acting together.

24. It is possible to imagine factual scenarios in which two people could properly be regarded as acting together to administer an injection. But nothing of the kind was the case here. As in *R v Dalby* and *R v Dias* the appellant supplied the drug to the deceased, who then had a choice, knowing the facts, whether to inject himself or not. The heroin was, as the certified question correctly recognises, self-administered, not jointly administered. The appellant did not administer the drug. Nor, for reasons already given, did the appellant cause the drug to be administered to or taken by the deceased.

25. The answer to the certified question is: 'In the case of a fully-informed and responsible adult, never'. The appeal must be allowed and the appellant's conviction for manslaughter quashed. The appellant must have his costs, here and below, out of central funds.

26. Much of the difficulty and doubt which have dogged the present question has flowed from a failure, at the outset, to identify the unlawful act on which the manslaughter count is founded. It matters little whether the act is identified by a separate count or counts under section 23, or by particularisation of the manslaughter count itself. But it would focus attention on the correct question, and promote accurate analysis of the real issues, if those who formulate, defend and rule on serious charges of this kind were obliged to consider how exactly, in law, the accusation is put.

Notes

1.   The history of *Kennedy* before the Court of Appeal is sad testament to the cavalier attitude of that Court on occasions to the importance of understanding and applying fundamental principles of criminal liability in every case no matter how unattractive the appellant might be. The Court managed, in one case and on two occasions, to misunderstand and misapply three important principles of criminal liability: (a) the principle of novus actus interveniens in causation; (b) the doctrine of joint principalship; and (c) the requirement for proof of an unlawful act as the foundation for a conviction of unlawful and dangerous act manslaughter. Such errors of analysis would be considered wholly unacceptable on the part of a university undergraduate the worst effect of whose misunderstanding of such principles might be embarrassment in a seminar or a poor mark in an examination. The commission, and repetition, of such error on the part of various Lord Justices of Appeal in several cases over almost a decade resulted in the appellants before them spending many additional years in prison for convictions which were unsound while also providing encouragement to the Crown Prosecution Service to continue to pursue prosecutions in similar cases (cf. Lord Bingham CJ's judgment in *R. v Edwards (William Steffan)* Case No.9707744 Z5, 18/04/98 available on Casetrack).

2.   In *Burgess* [2008] EWCA Crim 516; and *Keen* [2008] EWCA Crim 1000, manslaughter convictions arising from the supply of drugs in circumstances similar to those in *Kennedy* were quashed. The Criminal Cases Review Commission referred the case of *Finlay* (referred to by the House of Lords in their judgment) back to the Court of Appeal. In *Finlay (Paul Anthony)* [2009] EWCA Crim 1493, the Court of Appeal quashed his conviction for manslaughter.

3.   While prosecutions for unlawful act manslaughter will no longer be pursued in drug supply cases, the Crown Prosecution Service has started to resort to prosecutions for gross negligence manslaughter (see *Evans*, p.515 below).

(b) The unlawful act must be dangerous

Church made it clear that there must be an unlawful act and that it must be dangerous. Issues left unresolved included (i) whether "harm" was limited to physical harm; (ii) whether D had to be aware that his act was dangerous; (iii) if not, what information was relevant when considering the issue of dangerousness; and (iv) whether the actual form of harm which ensued from D's act must have been foreseeable by the sober and reasonable person?

In *Dawson* (1985) 81 Cr. App. R. 150, the Court of Appeal resolved the first issue declaring that there must be a risk of physical harm, rather than emotional disturbance, arising from the unlawful act. Watkins LJ went on to state (at 157) that the requirement of proving harm could be satisfied where "the unlawful act so shocks the victim as to cause him physical injury", for example, a heart attack.

The second issue was addressed in *DPP v Newbury* (directly below), the third in *Dawson* and *Watson* and the fourth in *JM and SM*.

DPP V NEWBURY

[1977] A.C. 500 HL

The appellants, two 15-year-old boys, pushed into the path of an oncoming train a piece of paving stone which some workmen had left on the parapet of a railway bridge. The stone killed the guard of the train. They were convicted of manslaughter and their appeal was dismissed by the Court of Appeal which nevertheless certified the following point of law: "Can a defendant be properly convicted of manslaughter, when his mind is not affected by drink or drugs, if he did not foresee that his act might cause harm to another?"

LORD SALMON, LORDS DIPLOCK, SIMON OF GLAISDALE AND KILBRANDON AGREEING

. . . The learned trial judge did not direct the jury that they should acquit the appellants unless they were satisfied beyond a reasonable doubt that the appellants had foreseen that they might cause harm to someone by pushing the piece of paving stone off the parapet into the path of the approaching train. In my view the learned trial judge was quite right not to give such a direction to the jury. The direction which he gave is completely in accordance with established law, which, possibly with one exception to which I shall presently refer, has never been challenged. In *R. v Larkin* (1944) 29 Cr.App.R. 18, Humphreys J. said, at p.23:

'Where the act which a person is engaged in performing is unlawful, then if at the same time it is a dangerous act, that is, an act which is likely to injure another person, and quite inadvertently the doer of the act causes death of that other person by that act then he is guilty of manslaughter.'

I agree entirely with Lawton L.J. that that is an admirably clear statement of the law which has been applied many times. It makes it plain (a) that an accused is guilty of manslaughter if it is proved that he intentionally did an act which was unlawful and dangerous and that that act inadvertently caused death and (b) that it is unnecessary to prove that the accused knew that the act was unlawful or dangerous. This is one of the reasons why cases of manslaughter vary so infinitely in their gravity. They may amount to little more than pure inadvertence and sometimes to little less than murder.

I am sure that in *R. v Church* [above, p.496] Edmund-Davies J. in giving the judgment of the court, did not intend to differ from or qualify anything which had been said in *R. v Larkin*. Indeed he was restating the principle laid down in that case by illustrating the sense in which the word 'dangerous' should be understood. Edmund-Davies J. said at p.70:

'For such a verdict' (guilty of manslaughter) 'inexorably to follow, the unlawful act must be such as all sober and reasonable people would inevitably recognise must subject the other person to, at least, the risk of some harm resulting therefrom, albeit not serious harm.'

The test is still the objective test. In judging whether the act was dangerous the test is not did the accused recognise that it was dangerous but would all sober and reasonable people recognise its danger.

Mr Esyr Lewis in his very able argument did not and indeed could not contend that the appellants' act which I have described was lawful but he did maintain that the law stated in *Larkin*'s case had undergone a change as a result of a passage in the judgment of Lord Denning M.R. in *Gray v Barr* [1971] 2 Q.B. 554, 568 which reads as follows:

'In manslaughter of every kind there must be a guilty mind. Without it, the accused must be acquitted [see *R. v Lamb, supra*]. In the category of manslaughter relating to an unlawful act, the accused must do a dangerous act with the intention of frightening or harming someone, or with the realisation that it is likely to frighten or harm someone, and nevertheless he goes on and does it, regardless of the consequences. If his act does thereafter, in unbroken sequence, cause the death of another, he is guilty of manslaughter.'

I do not think that Lord Denning M.R was attempting to revolutionise the law relating to manslaughter if his judgment is read in the context of the tragic circumstances of the case . . .

R. v Lamb was referred to by Lord Denning M.R. for the proposition that in manslaughter there must always be a guilty mind. This is true of every crime except those of absolute liability. The guilty mind usually depends on the intention of the accused. Some crimes require what is sometimes called a specific intention, for example murder, which is killing with intent to inflict grievous bodily harm. Other crimes need only what is called a basic intention, which is an intention to do the acts which constitute the crime. Manslaughter is such a crime: see *R. v Larkin* and *R. v Church*. *R. v Lamb* is certainly no authority to the contrary . . .

Lawton L.J. had observed that in manslaughter cases, some judges are now directing juries not in accordance with the law as correctly laid down in *R. v Larkin* and *R. v Church* but in accordance with the observations of Lord Denning M.R. in *Gray v Barr* taken in their literal sense. For the reasons I have already given they should cease to do so.

My Lords, I dismiss the appeal.

R. V DAWSON

(1985) 81 Cr.App.R. 150 CA

D and E robbed V's filling station wearing masks and armed with a pickaxe handle and replica gun. Shortly afterwards V, who had a serious heart condition, died of a heart attack. D and E were convicted of manslaughter and appealed.

WATKINS LJ

We look finally at the direction, 'That is to say all reasonable people who knew the facts that you know.' What the jury knew included, of course, the undisputed fact that the deceased had a very bad heart which at any moment could have ceased to function. It may be the judge did not intend that this fact should be included in the phrase 'the facts that you know'. If that was so, it is regrettable that he did not make it clear. By saying as he did, it is argued 'including the fact that the gun was a replica' and so on, the jury must have taken him to be telling them that all facts known to them, including the heart condition, should be taken into account in performing what is undoubtedly an objective test. We think there was a grave danger of that.

This test can only be undertaken upon the basis of the knowledge gained by a sober and reasonable man as though he were present at the scene of and watched the unlawful act being performed and who knows that, as in the present case, an unloaded replica gun was in use, but that the victim may have thought it was a loaded gun in working order. In other words, he has the same knowledge as the man attempting to rob and no more. It was never suggested that any of these appellants knew that their victim had a bad heart. They knew nothing about him.

A jury must be informed by the judge when trying the offence of manslaughter what facts they may and those which they may not use for the purpose of performing the test in the second element of this offence. The judge's direction here, unlike the bulk of an admirable summing-up, lacked that necessary precision and in the form it was given may, in our view, have given the jury an erroneous impression of what knowledge they could ascribe to the sober and reasonable man.

For these reasons we see no alternative to quashing the convictions for manslaughter as unsafe and unsatis-factory. The appeal against the convictions for manslaughter is therefore allowed.

R. V WATSON

[1989] 1 W.L.R. 684 CA

D and E broke a window and entered the house of Mr Moyler who, unknown to D and E, was aged 87, lived alone and suffered from a serious heart condition. D and E were disturbed by Mr Moyler and abused him verbally and left without stealing anything. Mr Moyler died 90 minutes later. D and E were convicted of manslaughter and appealed contending, inter alia, that the sober and reasonable bystander should only be ascribed the knowledge which they had at the moment they entered the house.

LORD LANE CJ

The first point taken on behalf of the appellant is this. When one is deciding whether the sober and reasonable person (the bystander) would realise the risk of some harm resulting to the victim, how much knowledge of the circumstances does one attribute to the bystander? The appellant contends that the unlawful act here was the burglary as charged in the indictment.

The charge was laid under section 9(1)(a) of the Theft Act 1968, the allegation being that the appellant had entered the building as a trespasser with intent to commit theft. Since that offence is committed at the first moment of entry, the bystander's knowledge is confined to that of the defendant at that moment. In the instant case there was no evidence that the appellant, at the moment of entry, knew the age or physical condition of Mr Moyler or even that he lived there alone.

The judge clearly took the view that the jury were entitled to ascribe to the bystander the knowledge which the appellant gained during the whole of his stay in the house and so directed them. Was this a misdirec-tion? In our judgment it was not. The unlawful act in the present circumstances comprised the whole of the burglarious intrusion and did not come to an end upon the appellant's foot crossing the threshold or windowsill. That being so, the appellant (and therefore the bystander) during the course of the unlawful act must have become aware of Mr Moyler's frailty and approximate age, and the judge's directions were accordingly correct. We are supported in this view by the fact that no one at the trial seems to have thought otherwise.

R V JM AND SM

[2012] EWCA Crim 2293

JM and SM were ejected from a nightclub by the doormen. They returned and began to assault the doormen. In the course of this affray Mr Jopling, an experienced and apparently healthy doorman, went to the assistance of his colleagues. Shortly after the affray had been subdued, Mr Jopling collapsed and died. A post-mortem established that Mr Jopling had been suffering from a renal artery aneurysm; he died from blood loss arising from a rupture to the renal artery. This was highly unlikely to have occurred spontaneously but would have been consequent on shock and a sudden surge in blood pressure due to the release of adrenalin into the circulation during the attack by the defendants and the rupture occurred either while the affray was in progress or in its immediate aftermath. The trial judge ruled that, on this evidence, it would not be open to the jury to convict of manslaughter as they could not be sure that a sober and reasonable person would inevitably recognise the risk that the deceased would die in the way he did as this was a completely different form of harm from the harm recognisable in an affray, such as the danger of being hit or suffering injuries in a fall in the course of dealing with the defendants. The prosecution appealed with leave of the trial judge.

LORD JUDGE CJ

11. The judge gave leave on the following basis:

'The critical question was whether I was right to determine that it was a requirement of establishing manslaughter that the victim died as a result of the sort of physical harm that any reasonable and sober person would inevitably realise the unlawful act in question risked causing; and whether I was right to conclude that that was what the case of *Carey* itself mandated.'

12. The defendants were charged with what is normally described as involuntary manslaughter on the basis that they did not intend Mr Jopling's death or serious injury. However his death resulted from a joint unlawful and dangerous act or acts by the defendants. Unless it is appreciated that the level of danger required for the offence is not high, the reference to 'dangerous' as part of the definition of involuntary manslaughter is liable to mislead. The risk of harm to be recognised is not dangerous in the sense that it must be potentially lethal or even serious harm: it is dangerous for this purpose because of the risk of 'some harm'. The principle, now long established, is explained in *Church* [1966] 1 QB 59:

'. . . the unlawful act must be such as all sober and reasonable people would inevitably recognise must subject the other person to, at least, the risk of some harm resulting therefrom, albeit not serious harm'.

13. In *DPP v Newbury* [1977] AC 500 the House of Lords considered a certified question in the following terms:

'Can a defendant be properly convicted of manslaughter, when his mind is not affected by drink or drugs, if he did not foresee harm to another?'

The answer was that he could be convicted of manslaughter whether he foresaw harm or not. In short, provided the defendant's actions were unlawful, and all sober and reasonable people would inevitably recognise the risk that some harm would result from his unlawful actions, he is not entitled to be acquitted merely because he himself did not foresee harm.

14. For the purposes of involuntary manslaughter an affray can constitute an unlawful and dangerous act, whether it takes the form of fear created in or direct violence suffered during the course of the affray. (See, for example, *Carey and others*).

15. The problems faced by the judge arose in the context of the clear understanding that the harm envisaged in *Church* did not extend to general stress and anxiety, but was confined to physical harm, of which shock is one manifestation. His attention was drawn to *Dawson* . . .[and] *Watson* . . ..

16. These decisions were analysed in *Carey and others*. The young victim of a minor affray ran some 109 yards up a slight incline away from the scene where she suffered a heart attack and collapsed. Later that evening she died. She had been suffering from a serious, but unknown, congenital heart condition. The defendants were convicted of manslaughter after the case was left to the jury on the basis of what we can conveniently describe as aggregation. That approach was flawed, and the conviction was quashed. However the judge's view that the manslaughter charge should not be left to the jury on the basis that the affray had caused the victim to suffer shock which led to her heart attack was endorsed. 'The affray lacked the quality of dangerousness in the relevant sense. This is because it would not have been recognised by a sober and reasonable bystander that an apparently healthy 15 year old (or indeed anyone else present) was at risk of suffering shock as a result of this affray'.

17. It was submitted by Mr Graham Reeds QC that the decision in *Carey* should be approached with considerable care. It did not alter the well-established principles identified in *Church* and applied consistently ever since. Quite apart from what he described as 'important factual differences' between *Carey* and the present case, including the minor nature of the affray in *Carey* rather than the serious incident which occurred here, *Carey* was decided on the basis of the flawed 'aggregation' misdirection. The Crown did not pursue the case on the basis of a direct physical assault on the victim. It was accepted that the victim's death was not caused by injuries which were a foreseeable result of the assault 'in the sense that the risk of such injuries would have been recognised by a sober or reasonable person having the knowledge the appellants had', or that the death was caused by the victim running away because of fear of being attacked or threatened with violence and so, making her escape. In short, in *Carey* there was no evidence of dangerousness in the sense required by *Church*.

18. Without contradiction from Mr Christopher Knox, Mr Robert Smith QC (who did not appear in the court below) accepted that the judge misdirected himself when he required the Crown to establish the fourth ingredient, that is, that the reasonable and sober person envisaged in *Church* must realise that that was a risk that the unlawful act would cause the sort of physical harm as a result of which the victim died. We agree that such a requirement provided a gloss on the ingredients of this offence which is not justified by the authorities and does not follow from the reasoning in *Dawson* and *Carey*. Indeed, the observations at the end of the judgment appear to elevate the requisite risk from an appreciation that some harm will inevitably occur into foresight of the type of harm which actually ensued and indeed the mechanism by which death occurred. Of course, unless the Crown can prove that death resulted from the defendant's unlawful and dangerous act, the case of manslaughter would fail on causation grounds. However a requirement that the bystander must appreciate the 'sort' of injury which might occur undermines the 'some' harm principle explained in *Church*, and on close analysis, is not supported or suggested by Dawson or Carey.

19. It is indeed striking that in *Carey* the court plainly accepted that if 'the facts had arguably supported' the case that the affray had caused the victim to suffer shock from which she died, the manslaughter issue should properly have been left to the jury. The heart of the judgment on this question is that the affray lacked the necessary quality of dangerousness. Although reference is made to the risk of 'suffering shock' as a result of the affray, that has to be seen in context as a reference to the fact that no one would have recognised any risk of this 15 year old suffering any harm or injury as a result of the particular affray.

20. In our judgment, certainly since *Church* and *Newbury*, it has never been a requirement that the defendant personally should foresee any specific harm at all, or that the reasonable bystander should recognise the precise form or 'sort' of harm which did ensue. What matters is whether reasonable and sober people would recognise that the unlawful activities of the defendant inevitably subjected the deceased to the risk of some harm resulting from them.

21. As we emphasise, in the present case we are concerned with and confine our decision to the circumstances of an affray in which the deceased was personally involved in the fighting which constituted the affray, rather than an individual who happened to be walking down the street and came to the scene of the fight without getting involved in it. The question whether the reasonable sober person would inevitably recognise the risk of harm going beyond concern and fear and distress to physical harm in the form of shock would have to be resolved as a question of fact rather than law.

22. In our judgment there is evidence from which a jury properly directed could conclude that sober and reasonable people observing events on 12 December 2012 would readily have recognised that all the doormen involved in the effort to control the defendants were at the risk of some harm, and that the fatal injury occurred while it was in progress or in its immediate aftermath while Mr Jopling was still subject to its effects.

23. Accordingly this appeal will be allowed.

Note

The sober and reasonable bystander will also be aware of the background to the unlawful act (which includes preparatory acts done by the accused) as this sets the act in context for the purpose of determining its objective dangerousness. In *Ball* [1989] Crim. L.R. 730, D loaded a shotgun with two cartridges taken from his pocket which contained both live and blank cartridges. He fired the gun at V killing her. Appealing against his conviction of manslaughter, D argued that the objective assessment of the danger of his act should be based on his mistaken belief that he was firing a blank cartridge and not on the actual fact that he was firing a live cartridge. Dismissing the appeal Lord Lane CJ stated:

> "[Once it is] established . . . that the act was both unlawful and that he intended to commit the assaults, the question whether the act is a dangerous one is to be judged not by the appellant's appreciation but by that of the sober and reasonable man, and it is impossible to impute into his appreciation the mistaken belief of the appellant that what he was doing was not dangerous because he thought he had a blank cartridge in the chamber. At that stage the appellant's intention, foresight or knowledge is irrelevant."

Question

Consider D's liability for manslaughter where he fires a blank cartridge and V dies: (i) as a result of diving for cover and fracturing her skull on a rock; (ii) as a result of a heart attack, V having no history of heart disease; and (iii) as a result of a cut sustained in diving for cover, V (unknown to D) being a haemophiliac.

(c) Must the unlawful act be "directed at" the victim?

R. V GOODFELLOW

(1986) 83 Cr. App. R. 23 CA

The appellant, who lived in a council house, wished to be rehoused. He set fire to his house while his wife, three children and another woman were in the house. The appellant, using a ladder, rescued two of his children, but the other child, his wife and the other woman all died as the fire spread more rapidly than had been anticipated. The appellant was convicted of manslaughter and appealed.

LORD LANE CJ

Lord Salmon in *D.P.P. v Newbury* (above, p.503) approved a dictum of Humphreys J. in *Larkin* [1943] 1 All E.R. 217, 219: 'Where the act which a person is engaged in performing is unlawful, then if at the same time it is a dangerous act, that is, an act which is likely to injure another person, and quite inadvertently he causes the death of that other person by that act, then he is guilty of manslaughter.' Their Lordships in that case (*Newbury*) expressly disapproved of a passage in the judgment of Lord Denning M.R. in the civil case of *Gray v Barr* [1971] 2 All E.R. 949, 956, in which he asserted that the unlawful act must be done by the defendant with the intention of frightening or harming someone or with the realisation that it is likely to frighten or harm someone. That decision of the House of Lords is, of course, binding upon us.

It is submitted by Mr Stewart on behalf of the appellant that this was not a case of 'unlawful act' manslaughter, because the actions of the appellant were not directed at the victim. The authority for that proposition is said to be *Dalby* (1982) 74 Cr.App.R. 348.

In that case the appellant, a drug addict, supplied a class A drug which he had unlawfully obtained to a friend, also an addict. Each injected himself intravenously. After the appellant had left, the friend administered to himself two further injections, the nature of which was unknown. When the appellant returned he was unable to wake up his friend. When medical help eventually arrived, the friend was found to be dead. The appellant was convicted of manslaughter either on the unlawful and dangerous act basis, or alternatively on the basis that he was grossly negligent in not calling an ambulance at an earlier stage.

It was held that since the act of supplying the scheduled drug was not an act which caused direct harm and since the unlawful act of supply of the dangerous drug by Dalby *per se* did not constitute the *actus reus* of the offence of manslaughter, the conviction had to be quashed. Waller L.J., at p.352, said: '. . . where the charge of manslaughter is based on an unlawful and dangerous act, it must be an act directed at the victim and likely to cause immediate injury, however slight.'

However we do not think that he was suggesting that there must be an intention on the part of the defendant to harm or frighten or a realisation that his acts were likely to harm or frighten. Indeed it would have been contrary to the dicta of Lord Salmon in *D.P.P. v Newbury (supra)* if he was. What he was, we believe, intending to say was that there must be no fresh intervening cause between the act and the death. Indeed at p.351 he said this: '. . . the supply of drugs would itself have caused no harm unless the deceased had subsequently used the drugs in a form and quantity which was dangerous' . . .

The questions which the jury have to decide on the charge of manslaughter of this nature are: (1) Was the act intentional? (2) Was it unlawful? (3) Was it an act which any reasonable person would realise was bound to subject some other human being to the risk of physical harm, albeit not necessarily serious harm? (4) Was that act the cause of death?

Whatever indications the judge may have given earlier as to his intentions, he did in fact direct the jury on this type of manslaughter in the passage which we have already quoted. It is true that he went further and added observations which were more appropriate to the *Lawrence* type of manslaughter. If anything, those passages resulted in a direction which was more favourable to the appellant than if they had been omitted.

Appeal dismissed

Note

The correctness of the decision in *Goodfellow* was confirmed by the decision of the House of Lords in *Attorney General's Reference (No.3 of 1994)* [1998] A.C. 245 (above, p.441). Not only is there no requirement for the unlawful act to be directed at the victim, but also there is no requirement that the danger or risk of harm be perceived in respect of the actual victim—a risk of harm to someone else arising from the unlawful act will suffice. Lord Hope of Craighead cited with approval the decision in *Mitchell* [1983] Q.B. 741 where D hit E who was standing in a queue in a post office. E fell against V, an elderly lady, who fell breaking her leg and died thereafter as a result of a pulmonary embolism linked to her fall. The Court of Appeal affirmed D's conviction of manslaughter. Lord Hope also cited with approval *Larkin* and *Newbury* before concluding that the accused in the instant case should have been convicted of manslaughter where he had stabbed M, a pregnant woman, which resulted in the premature birth of her child who in turn died some time later due to problems linked to her premature birth. Lord Hope was satisfied that the stabbing of the mother was an unlawful and dangerous act. Lord Hope stated (at 274):

> "There can be no doubt that all sober and reasonable people would regard that act, within the appropriate meaning of this term, as dangerous. It is plain that it was unlawful as it was done with the intention of causing her injury. As [the accused] intended to commit that act, all the ingredients necessary for *mens rea* in regard to the crime of manslaughter were established, irrespective of who was the ultimate victim of it. The fact that the child whom the mother was carrying at the time was born alive and then died as a result of the stabbing is all that was needed for the offence of manslaughter when *actus reus* for that crime was completed by the child's death. The question, once all the other elements are satisfied, is simply one of causation. The defendant must accept all the consequences of his act, so long as the jury are satisfied that he did what he did intentionally, that what he did was unlawful and that, applying the correct test, it was also dangerous . . . In my opinion that is sufficient for the offence of manslaughter."

---

ii. Gross Negligence Manslaughter

Note

The second basis upon which a person may be found guilty of involuntary manslaughter is that of gross negligence. The classic statement of this offence is that of Lord Hewart CJ in *Bateman* (1925) Cr. App. R. 8 approved by the House of Lords in *Andrews v DPP* [1937] A.C. 576. The test required there to be a duty of care owed by D to the victim, breach of which caused the victim's death and left it to the jury to determine whether the negligence of D was so gross that it demanded punishment as a crime rather than merely the imposition of civil liability and the payment of compensation. It is a very high degree of negligence which has to be established before criminal liability should ensue and for many years following these decisions the courts used the terms "recklessness" and "gross negligence" interchangeably. In *Seymour* [1983] 2 A.C. 493, a case of manslaughter arising from the reckless driving of a vehicle, the House of Lords declared that no longer would it be appropriate to refer to negligence and that the test for manslaughter was the same as for the statutory offence of causing death by reckless driving contrary to s.1(1) of the Road Traffic Act 1972. This involved the *Caldwell/Lawrence* test of recklessness: a person would be guilty of manslaughter where he did an act which created an obvious and serious risk of causing physical injury to another person and either he was conscious of the risk or he gave no thought to it. In the case which follows the House of Lords reverted to the test of gross negligence.

R. V ADOMAKO

[1995] 1 A.C. 171 HL

A, an anaesthetist, took over from another anaesthetist during the course of an operation. While he was in charge the endotracheal tube which supplied oxygen to the patient became disconnected. A first became aware that something was amiss when an alarm on the blood pressure monitor sounded some four and a half minutes after the disconnection. A carried out various checks of the equipment and administered atropine to raise the patient's pulse. Approximately nine minutes after the disconnection the patient suffered a cardiac arrest from which he died. It was only at this point that A discovered the disconnection. The prosecution alleged that A was guilty of gross negligence. A was convicted of manslaughter and appealed. The Court of Appeal dismissed his appeal certifying a point of law of general public importance:

"in cases of manslaughter by criminal negligence not involving driving but involving a breach of duty is it a sufficient direction to the jury to adopt the gross negligence test set out by the Court of Appeal in the present case following *R. v Bateman* (1925) 19 Cr.App.R. 8 and *Andrews v Director of Public Prosecutions* [1937] A.C. 576, without reference to the test of recklessness as defined in *R. v Lawrence (Stephen)* [1982] A.C. 510 or as adapted to the circumstances of the case?"

LORD MACKAY OF CLASHFERN

For the prosecution it was alleged that the appellant was guilty of gross negligence in failing to notice or respond appropriately to obvious signs that a disconnection had occurred and that the patient had ceased to breathe. . .

Two expert witnesses gave evidence for the prosecution. Professor Payne described the standard of care as 'abysmal' while Professor Adams stated that in his view a competent anaesthetist should have recognised the signs of disconnection within 15 seconds and that the appellant's conduct amounted to 'a gross dereliction of care'.

On behalf of the appellant it was conceded at his trial that he had been negligent. The issue was therefore whether his conduct was criminal.

The expert witness called on behalf of the appellant at his trial was Dr Monks. His evidence conceded that the appellant ought to have noticed the disconnection. But in his view there were factors which mitigated this failure. He considered that another independent problem either occurred or could have occurred before or at the same time as the disconnection which distracted the appellant's attention and activities. This problem would in his view have caused the patient's blood pressure to drop and may either have been a reaction to the drug being used to paralyse the patient or alternatively may have been caused by an ocular cardiac reflex.

The appellant himself said in evidence that when the alarm sounded on the Dinamap machine his first thought was that the machine itself was not working properly. Having carried out checks on the machine he then thought that the patient had suffered an ocular cardiac reflex for which he administered atropine in two successive doses. Further attempts to administer atropine by intravenous drip and to check the patient's blood pressure followed until the cardiac arrest occurred. It had never occurred to him that a disconnection had taken place. He stated in evidence that 'after things went wrong I think I did panic a bit'.

In relation to the appellant's actions during this period, Professor Payne had conceded during cross-examination that 'given that Dr Adomako misled himself the efforts he made were not unreasonable'. The period to which this evidence referred was obviously the period after the alarm had sounded on the Dinamap machine which was, as I have said, apparently some 40 minutes after the disconnection occurred . . .

In opening his very cogent argument for the appellant before your Lordships, counsel submitted that the law in this area should have the characteristics of clarity, certainty, intellectual coherence and general applicability and acceptability. For these reasons he said the law applying to involuntary manslaughter generally should involve a universal test and that test should be the test already applied in this House to motor manslaughter. He criticised the concept of gross negligence which was the basis of the judgment of the Court of Appeal submitting that its formulation involved circularity, the jury being told in effect to convict of a crime if they thought a crime had been committed and that accordingly using gross negligence as the conceptual basis for the crime of involuntary manslaughter was unsatisfactory and the court should apply the law laid down in *Seymour* [1983] 2 A.C. 493 generally to all cases of involuntary manslaughter or at least use this as the basis for providing general applicability and acceptability.

Like the Court of Appeal your Lordships were treated to a considerable review of authority. I begin with *R. v Bateman*, 19 Cr.App.R. 8 and the opinion of Lord Hewart C.J., where he said, at pp.10–11:

'In expounding the law to juries on the trial of indictments for manslaughter by negligence, judges have often referred to the distinction between civil and criminal liability for death by negligence. The law of criminal liability for negligence is conveniently explained in that way. If A has caused the death of B by alleged negligence, then, in order to establish civil liability, the plaintiff must prove (in addition to pecuniary loss caused by the death) that A owed a duty to B to take care, that that duty was not discharged, and that the default caused the death of B. To convict A of manslaughter, the prosecution must prove the three things above mentioned and must satisfy the jury, in addition, that A's negligence amounted to a crime. In the civil action, if it is proved that A fell short of the standard of reasonable care required by law, it matters not how far he fell short of that standard. The extent of his liability depends not on the degree of negligence but on the amount of damage done. In a criminal court, on the contrary, the amount and degree of negligence are the determining question. There must be *mens rea*.'

Later he said, at pp.11–12:

'In explaining to juries the test which they should apply to determine whether the negligence, in the particular case, amounted or did not amount to a crime, judges have used many epithets, such as 'culpable', 'criminal', 'gross', 'wicked', 'clear', 'complete'. But, whatever epithet be used and whether an epithet be used or not, in order to establish criminal liability the facts must be such that, in the opinion of the jury, the negligence of the accused went beyond a mere matter of compensation between subjects and showed such disregard for the life and safety of others as to amount to a crime against the state and conduct deserving punishment.'

Next I turn to *Andrews v Director of Public Prosecutions* [1937] A.C. 576 which was a case of manslaughter through the dangerous driving of a motor car. In a speech with which all the other members of this House who sat agreed, Lord Atkin said, at pp.581–583:

'of all crimes manslaughter appears to afford most difficulties of definition, for it concerns homicide in so many and so varying conditions. From the early days when any homicide involved penalty the law has gradually evolved 'through successive differentiations and integrations' until it recognises murder on the one hand, based mainly, though not exclusively, on an intention to kill, and manslaughter on the other hand, based mainly, though not exclusively, on the absence of intention to kill but with the presence of an element of 'unlawfulness' which is the elusive factor. In the present case it is only necessary to consider manslaughter from the point of view of an unintentional killing caused by negligence, that is, the omission of a duty to take care . . .

The principle to be observed is that cases of manslaughter in driving motor cars are but instances of a general rule applicable to all charges of homicide by negligence. Simple lack of care such as will constitute civil liability is not enough: for purposes of the criminal law there are degrees of negligence: and a very high degree of negligence is required to be proved before the felony is established. Probably of all the epithets that can be applied 'reckless' most nearly covers the case. It is difficult to visualise a case of death caused by reckless driving in the connotation of that term in ordinary speech which would not justify a conviction for manslaughter: but it is probably not all-embracing, for "reckless" suggests an indifference to risk whereas the accused may have appreciated the risk and intended to avoid it and yet shown such a high degree of negligence in the means adopted to avoid the risk as would justify a conviction. If the principle of *Batemans* case, 19 Cr.App.R. 8 is observed it will appear that the law of manslaughter has not changed by the introduction of motor vehicles on the road. Death caused by their negligent driving, though unhappily much more frequent, is to be treated in law as death caused by any other form of negligence: and juries should be directed accordingly.'

In my opinion the law as stated in these two authorities is satisfactory as providing a proper basis for describing the crime of involuntary manslaughter. Since the decision in *Andrews* was a decision of your Lordships' House, it remains the most authoritative statement of the present law which I have been able to find and although its relationship to *R. v Seymour* [1983] 2 A.C. 493 is a matter to which I shall have to return, it is a decision which has not been departed from. On this basis in my opinion the ordinary principles of the law of negligence apply to ascertain whether or not the defendant has been in breach of a duty of care towards the victim who has died. If such breach of duty is established the next question is whether that breach of duty caused the death of the victim. If so, the jury must go on to consider whether that breach of duty should be characterised as gross negligence and therefore as a crime. This will depend on the seriousness of the breach of duty committed by the defendant in all the circumstances in which the defendant was placed when it occurred. The jury will have to consider whether the extent to which the defendant's conduct departed from the proper standard of care incumbent upon him, involving as it must have done a risk of death to the patient, was such that it should be judged criminal.

It is true that to a certain extent this involves an element of circularity, but in this branch of the law I do not believe that is fatal to its being correct as a test of how far conduct must depart from accepted standards to be characterised as criminal. This is necessarily a question of degree and an attempt to specify that degree more closely is I think likely to achieve only a spurious precision. The essence of the matter which is supremely a jury question is whether having regard to the risk of death involved, the conduct of the defendant was so bad in all the circumstances as to amount in their judgment to a criminal act or omission.

My Lords, the view which I have stated of the correct basis in law for the crime of involuntary manslaughter accords I consider with the criteria stated by counsel although I have not reached the degree of precision in definition which he required, but in my opinion it has been reached so far as practicable and with a result which leaves the matter properly stated for a jury's determination.

My Lords, in my view the law as stated in *R. v Seymour* [1983] 2 A.C. 493 should no longer apply since the underlying statutory provisions on which it rested have now been repealed by the Road Traffic Act 1991. It may be that cases of involuntary motor manslaughter will as a result become rare but I consider it unsatisfactory that there should be any exception to the generality of the statement which I have made, since such exception, in my view, gives rise to unnecessary complexity . . .

I consider it perfectly appropriate that the word 'reckless' should be used in cases of involuntary manslaughter, but as Lord Atkin put it, 'in the ordinary connotation of that word'. Examples in which this was done, to my mind, with complete accuracy are *R. v Stone* [1977] Q.B. 354 and *R. v West London Coroner, Ex parte Gray* [1988] Q.B. 467.

In my opinion it is quite unnecessary in the context of gross negligence to give the detailed directions with regard to the meaning of the word 'reckless' associated with *R. v Lawrence* [1982] A.C. 510. The decision of the Court of Appeal (Criminal Division) in the other cases with which they were concerned at the same time as they heard the appeal in this case indicates that the circumstances in which involuntary manslaughter has to be considered may make the somewhat elaborate and rather rigid directions inappropriate. I entirely agree with the view that the circumstances to which a charge of involuntary manslaughter may apply are so various that it is unwise to attempt to categorise or detail specimen directions. For my part I would not wish to go beyond the description of the basis in law which I have already given.

In my view the summing up of the judge in the present case was a model of clarity in analysis of the facts and in setting out the law in a manner which was readily comprehensible by the jury. The summing up was criticised in respect of the inclusion of the following passage:

'Of course you will understand it is not for every humble man of the profession to have all that great skill of the great men in Harley Street but, on the other hand, they are not allowed to practise medicine in this country unless they have acquired a certain amount of skill. They are bound to show a reasonable amount of skill according to the circumstances of the case, and you have to judge them on the basis that they are skilled men, but not necessarily so skilled as more skilful men in the profession, and you can only convict them criminally if, in your judgment, they fall below the standard of skill which is the least qualification which any doctor should have. You should only convict a doctor of causing a death by negligence if you think he did something which no reasonably skilled doctor should have done.'

The criticism was particularly of the latter part of this quotation in that it was open to the meaning that if the defendant did what no reasonably skilled doctor should have done it was open to the jury to convict him of causing death by negligence. Strictly speaking this passage is concerned with the statement of a necessary condition for a conviction by preventing a conviction unless that condition is satisfied. It is incorrect to treat it as stating a sufficient condition for conviction. In any event I consider that this passage in the context was making the point forcefully that the defendant in this case was not to be judged by the standard of more skilled doctors but by the standard of a reasonably competent doctor. There were many other passages in the summing up which emphasised the need for a high degree of negligence if the jury were to convict and read in that context I consider that the summing up cannot be faulted.

For these reasons I am of the opinion that this appeal should be dismissed and that the certified question should be answered by saying:

'In cases of manslaughter by criminal negligence involving a breach of duty, it is a sufficient direction to the jury to adopt the gross negligence test set out by the Court of Appeal in the present case following *R. v Bateman*, 19 Cr.App.R. 8 and *Andrews v Director of Public Prosecutions* [1937] A.C. 576 and that it is not necessary to refer to the definition of recklessness in *R. v Lawrence* [1982] A.C. 510, although it is perfectly open to the trial judge to use the word "reckless" in its ordinary meaning as part of his exposition of the law if he deems it appropriate in the circumstances of the particular case.'

. . . I have reached the same conclusion on the basic law to be applied in this case as did the Court of Appeal. Personally I would not wish to state the law more elaborately than I have done. In particular I think it is difficult to take expressions used in particular cases out of the context of the cases in which they were used and enunciate them as if applying generally. This can I think lead to ambiguity and perhaps unnecessary complexity. The task of trial judges in setting out for the jury the issues of fact and the relevant law in cases of this class is a difficult and demanding one. I believe that the supreme test that should be satisfied in such directions is that they are comprehensible to an ordinary member of the public who is called to sit on a jury and who has no particular prior acquaintance with the law. To make it obligatory on trial judges to give directions in law which are so elaborate that the ordinary member of the jury will have great difficulty in following them, and even greater difficulty in retaining them in his memory for the purpose of application in the jury room, is no service to the cause of justice. The experienced counsel who assisted your Lordships in this appeal indicated that as a practical matter there was a danger in over elaboration of definition of the word 'reckless.' While therefore I have said in my view it is perfectly open to a trial judge to use the word 'reckless' if it appears appropriate in the circumstances of a particular case as indicating the extent to which a defendant's conduct must deviate from that of a proper standard of care, I do not think it right to require that this should be done and certainly not right that it should incorporate the full detail required in *Lawrence*.

[Lords Keith of Kinkel, Goff of Chieveley, Browne-Wilkinson and Woolf agreed with the Lord Chancellor's speech.]

Appeal dismissed

Questions

1.   Had the patient in *Adomako* survived but in a persistent vegetative state, would Dr Adomako have been liable to conviction of any other offence?

2.   Professor J.C. Smith in his "Commentary to *Adomako*" [1994] Crim. L.R. 757, 758, states, "This welcome decision by the House of Lords removes much unnecessary complication and injustice from the law of involuntary manslaughter." Do you agree?

3.   Will the threat of conviction for manslaughter and imprisonment cause similarly positioned anaesthetists not to make mistakes in future?

4.   If expert evidence discloses that a properly connected endotracheal tube should not become dis-
     connected, would a prosecution for manslaughter of the original anaesthetist who was in charge
     when the operation commenced be likely to succeed? What would be the issues a jury would have
     to consider?

Notes

1.   In *Singh (Gurphal)* [1999] Crim. L.R. 582, the Court of Appeal held that whether D owed a duty of
     care was a question of law for the judge to determine and approved the trial judge's direction that
     on a charge of gross negligence manslaughter "the circumstances must be such that a reason-
     ably prudent person would have foreseen a serious and obvious risk not merely of injury or even
     serious injury but of death." Professor J.C. Smith in his commentary to this case at p.583 states:

     "It seems that the deliberate taking of a high degree of risk of causing serious bodily harm which
     results in death (formerly murder under *Hyam* [1975] A.C. 55) must now be manslaughter by
     recklessness. But gross negligence is objective and it is accordingly appropriate that it should
     be more limited."

     This decision clarifies one of the problems with the speech of Lord Mackay in *Adomako* by requir-
     ing a risk in respect of which D was negligent to have been one of death rather than any lesser
     degree of harm.

2.   The Court of Appeal in *Misra; Srivastava* [2004] EWCA Crim 2375, while holding that the offence
     of gross negligence manslaughter did not offend the requirement of legal certainty under art.7 of
     the European Convention on Human Rights, confirmed, however, that only a risk of death will be
     sufficient to establish the offence; a risk of bodily injury or injury to health was not sufficient.

3.   In *Adomako* Lord Mackay stated that "the ordinary principles of the law of negligence apply to
     ascertain whether or not the defendant has been in breach of a duty of care towards the victim
     who has died". In *Wacker* [2002] EWCA Crim 1944, the defendant sought to place reliance on
     the principle ex turpi causa non oritur actio to argue that as he had been involved in a criminal
     enterprise with those who died, there was no duty of care in negligence and thus there could not
     be any liability for gross negligence manslaughter. In a civil action for negligence ex turpi causa
     would provide a defence to a claim. The issue for the Court of Appeal was whether this principle
     applied in respect of criminal proceedings. In the instant case the defendant drove his refriger-
     ated lorry, loaded with 60 illegal Chinese immigrants hidden behind a cargo of tomatoes, on to a
     channel ferry which disembarked at Dover. Customs and Excise officers, doing a spot check on his
     vehicle, discovered the immigrants, 58 of whom had died of suffocation on the crossing due to an
     air vent having been sealed by the defendant to reduce the risk of discovery. The Court of Appeal
     rejected the argument based on ex turpi causa on the basis that the civil law and criminal law
     served different functions. The criminal law's function was to protect individuals and might step
     in at the very point where the civil law is powerless to assist. Furthermore, the criminal law will
     act to prevent serious injury or death even where those subject to the risk of such had consented
     to it. On this basis there was no justification in public policy for concluding that the criminal law
     would not apply where the person responsible for the death and the deceased were involved
     in some joint criminal venture which involved an element of acceptance of a degree of risk in
     order to further that venture. It was clear that a claim that keeping the vent shut increased the

chances of evading detection was an argument which the Court, unsurprisingly, found singularly unattractive.

4. In *Willoughby* [2004] EWCA Crim 3365, the Court of Appeal adopted a different approach to that in *Singh* above, note 1, on the issue whether it was for the trial judge or jury to determine whether a duty of care existed. The Court expressed the view that ordinarily the trial judge should determine whether there was evidence capable of establishing a duty of care, and leave it to the jury to determine whether such a duty did exist. The Court took the view, however, that there might be exceptional circumstances where a duty of care obviously existed, such as that arising between doctor and patient or where Parliament had imposed a particular type of statutory duty, and in such cases a judge could direct the jury that a duty existed. This was in *Evans*, see below, note 6.

5. In determining whether the conduct of a defendant was so bad in all the circumstances as to amount to a criminal act or omission, the jury have a broad discretion. Factors which would be relevant to the consideration of this issue are, for example, the extent to which D's conduct fell short of that to be expected of the reasonable person, whether or not D had foreseen the risk of death, and any explanation D might offer for his behaviour.

6. In *Evans* [2009] EWCA Crim 650, the Court of Appeal upheld a conviction for gross negligence manslaughter on the basis that G had supplied heroin to her sister, C, and, on becoming aware that she had overdosed, failed to obtain medical attention for her (although she and her mother did seek to monitor and assist C). Her mother had also been convicted of manslaughter on the basis of her failure to obtain medical assistance arising from her parental duty of care. The Court based its decision in respect of G on the principle in *Miller* (p.37, above), that is a duty arising from the creation of a dangerous situation, Lord Judge CJ stating:

> "20. The question in this appeal is not whether the appellant may be guilty of manslaughter for having been concerned in the supply of the heroin which caused the deceased's death. It is whether, notwithstanding that their relationship lacked the features of familial duty or responsibility which marked her mother's relationship with the deceased, she was under a duty to take reasonable steps for the safety of the deceased once she appreciated that the heroin she procured for her was having a potentially fatal impact on her health.
>
> 21. When omission or failure to act are in issue two aspects of manslaughter are engaged."
>
> Both are governed by decisions of the House of Lords. The first is manslaughter arising from the defendant's gross negligence (*R. v Adomako* [1995] 1 A.C. 171). The second arises when the defendant has created a dangerous situation and when, notwithstanding his appreciation of the consequent risks, he fails to take any reasonable preventative steps (*R. v Miller* [1983] 2 A.C. 161).
> . . .
> 23. The decision of the House of Lords was expressed in the single opinion of Lord Diplock . . . [who] observed that he could see:
>
>> ". . . no rational ground for excluding from conduct capable of giving rise to criminal liability, conduct which consists of failing to take measures that lie within one's power to counteract a danger that one has oneself created, if at the time of such conduct one's state of mind is such as constitutes a necessary ingredient of the offence . . . I cannot see any good reason why, so far as liability under criminal law is concerned, it should matter at what point of time before the resultant damage is complete a person becomes aware that he has done a physical act which, whether or not he appreciated that it would at the time when he did it, does in fact create a risk that property of another will be damaged:

provided that at the moment of awareness, it lies within his power to take steps, either himself or by calling for the assistance of the fire brigade if this be necessary, to prevent or minimise the damage to the property at risk."

24. The mens rea necessary for arson was, and thereafter the analysis focussed on, recklessness. But the reasoning in the decision does not exclude liability where a different mens rea is required. And if, for example, the result of the fire in *Miller* had included the death of a fellow squatter, it appears to us that Miller would properly have been convicted of manslaughter by gross negligence as well as arson. (*R. v Willoughby*) . . .

31. . . . The duty necessary to found gross negligence manslaughter is plainly not confined to cases of a familial or professional relationship between the defendant and the deceased. In our judgment, consistently with *Adomako* and the link between civil and criminal liability for negligence, for the purposes of gross negligence manslaughter, when a person has created or contributed to the creation of a state of affairs which he knows, or ought reasonably to know, has become life threatening, a consequent duty on him to act by taking reasonable steps to save the other's life will normally arise.

The problem with this decision is that it appears to ignore principles of causation which played such a crucial part in the decision of *Kennedy* (above, p.498). The *Miller* principle arose where D, on becoming aware of the danger he had created, failed to act to minimise or avert that danger. The danger flowed directly from his inadvertent act. The House of Lords emphasised that the failure was "to take measures that lie within one's power to counteract a danger that one has oneself created". In *Evans*, however, the act of supply does not directly lead to any danger; it is only when G took the drug in overdose that a danger arose. Following *Kennedy*, that act was free, deliberate and informed and broke the chain of causation between the act of supply and the ensuing death. Whatever moral obloquy might be visited upon G for failing to seek medical attention (her reasons were fear of getting into trouble herself and fear that C, who had been released on licence from a detention and training order, would get into trouble), this omission could not, in the absence of a duty, give rise to liability. If G's act was not the cause of the danger (C's act being an intervening one), no duty arose. The Court of Appeal, however, eschewed any such refined analysis relying on broad brush strokes. While impressionism is attractive in art, legal judgments merit greater attention to detail if uncertainty and even injustice is not to result.

Questions

1. Did the Court of Appeal need to rely on the *Miller* principle or could liability for manslaughter on the part of G have been established on the basis of *Stone and Dobinson* and *Ruffel*?

2. Lord Judge CJ spoke of creating contributing to "the creation of a state of affairs which he knows, or ought reasonably to know, has become life threatening" which upon becoming aware of the situation would give rise to a duty to act. Consider D's liability where he is the original seller of the heroin and upon C overdosing, G telephones him and says "C has overdosed. You sort it".

3. Consider D's liability where he lends P his cigarette lighter, P lights his cigarette and several minutes later D sees P inadvertently drop his cigarette on combustible material and (a) this subsequently catches fire and burns down a building; (b) in the fire a fireman dies.

----

iii. Reform of the Law of Involuntary Manslaughter

LAW COMMISSION, *LEGISLATING THE CRIMINAL CODE: INVOLUNTARY MANSLAUGHTER* (TSO, 1996), LAW COM. NO.237

PART III: WHAT IS WRONG WITH THE PRESENT LAW?

INTRODUCTION

3.1 . . . The two major problems relate to the very wide range of conduct falling within the scope of involuntary manslaughter . . . The offence encompasses, first, cases involving conduct that falls only just short of murder, where the accused was *aware* of a risk of causing death or serious injury, although he did not *intend* to cause either; second, cases where the accused is a professional person who makes a very serious mistake that results in death; and third, cases where a relatively minor assault ends in death. This leads to problems in sentencing and labelling, including the fundamental problem that many cases currently amounting to unlawful act manslaughter involve only minor fault on the part of the perpetrator, and therefore ought not, perhaps, to be described as manslaughter at all. There are also a number of more specific problems which we consider below.

THE BREADTH OF THE OFFENCE

3.2 . . . The width of the present offence can cause problems to judges on sentencing. As Lord Lane C.J. remarked [*Walker* (1992) 13 Cr.App.R. (S) 474, 476]:

'It is a truism to say that of all the crimes in the calendar, the crime of manslaughter faces the sentencing judge with the greatest problem, because manslaughter ranges in its gravity from the borders of murder right down to those of accidental death. It is never easy to strike exactly the right point at which to pitch the sentence.'

3.3 There is a strong argument in favour of defining criminal offences in terms of narrow bands of conduct, so that the judge can have the guidance of the jury on important factual questions, such as intention or awareness of risk. We agree with the notion that

'Questions of intention . . . involve the application of a test capable of precise definition (even though the task of drawing inferences from the evidence may be difficult). Gradations of culpability based on varying degrees of intention should, therefore, be incorporated into the definition of the offences, so that the issues can be contested with all that that implies in terms of the rules of procedure, evidence and quantum of proof.' [D.A. Thomas, 'Form and Function in Criminal Law' in P. Glazebrook (ed), *Reshaping the Criminal Law* (1978), p.28.]

The same could be said of awareness of risk.

3.4 Another argument in favour of separate offences follows on from this point about sentencing. It is inappropriate that types of conduct that vary so widely in terms of fault should all carry the same descriptive label. The accused who sets fire to his house so that the council will rehouse him, knowing that his wife and children are asleep inside and that they will almost certainly be killed or seriously injured, is blameworthy in a very different way from the electrician who causes death by miswiring an electrical appliance with a high degree of carelessness. It is arguable that the label 'manslaughter' is devalued, and the more serious forms of wrongdoing that it describes might come to be regarded as less serious, because it is also used to describe less heinous crimes. By the same token, juries might be reluctant to convict, for example, a highly incompetent doctor of manslaughter because of the perceived gravity of the offence.

UNLAWFUL ACT MANSLAUGHTER

3.5 The next problem with the present law also relates to the breadth of conduct falling within involuntary manslaughter . . . [I]f a person commits a criminal act that carries a risk of causing *some* harm to another, and by chance he causes death, he will be guilty of unlawful act manslaughter. In some of these cases, the defendant would only have been guilty of a relatively trivial offence if death had not chanced to occur. For example, if D pushes V in a fight, and V staggers but does not fall, D will at most be guilty of causing actual bodily harm under section 47 of the Offences against the Person Act 1861, which carries a maximum sentence of five years' imprisonment. If, however, V loses his balance and falls to the floor, knocking his head on the pavement and thereby sustaining fatal brain injuries, D will be guilty of manslaughter.

3.6 . . . [We] consider that it is wrong in principle for the law to hold a person responsible for causing a result that he did not intend or foresee, and which would not even have been *foreseeable* by a reasonable person observing his conduct. Unlawful act manslaughter is therefore, we believe, unprincipled because it requires only that a foreseeable risk of causing *some* harm should have been inherent in the accused's conduct, whereas he is convicted of actually causing death, and also to some extent punished for doing so.

GROSS NEGLIGENCE MANSLAUGHTER AFTER *ADOMAKO*

3.9 The first problem with [the test in *Adomako*] is that it is circular: the jury must be directed to convict the defendant of a crime if they think his conduct was 'criminal'. In effect, this leaves a question of law to the jury, and, because juries do not give reasons for their decisions, it is impossible to tell what criteria will be applied in an individual case. This must lead to uncertainty in the law. The CPS has told us that prosecutors find it difficult to judge when to bring a prosecution, defendants have difficulty in deciding how to plead, and there is a danger that juries may bring in inconsistent verdicts on broadly similar evidence.

3.10 Other problems arise out of the Lord Chancellor's use of the terminology of 'duty of care' and 'negligence', and his linkage of the civil and criminal law in his speech. The meanings of these words are not entirely clear in a criminal law context, nor is it clear to what extent they mean the same things in tort and in criminal law.

3.11 As we explained in Consultation Paper No. 135, 'negligence' in the context of the crime of manslaughter probably means nothing more than 'carelessness': it does not carry the technical meaning that it has in the law of tort, where it depends on the existence of a duty of care owed and a breach of that duty. The Lord Chancellor said in *Adomako* that 'the ordinary principles of the law of negligence apply to ascertain whether or not the defendant has been in breach of a duty of care towards the victim who has died'. This equation of the civil and criminal law concepts of negligence causes no problems where, as in *Adomako* itself, a death is caused by a badly performed positive act of the accused, because it is virtually certain that both tort and criminal law would hold that a duty was owed to the deceased not to injure him by a *positive act*.

3.12 It is possible, however, that the courts in future cases of *omission* might feel obliged to apply the decision in *Adomako*. If so, they would run into difficulties, because it is by no means certain that the scope of liability for negligent omissions is the same in criminal law as it is in tort. For example, in criminal law it would seem that once someone has voluntarily taken some steps to care for another, he may be liable if his care is not adequate and the other person dies. In tort, however, there is probably no liability if the defendant abandons an effort to care for someone and that person dies, unless he causes harm through his own incompetence.

3.13 It is possible, therefore, that the decision in *Adomako* may have changed the criminal law in relation to liability for omissions, by equating it with the civil law of tort. This may have *restricted* the scope of the duty to act in criminal law, by implicitly overruling *Stone and Dobinson*; on the other hand, there *may* be cases where the law of tort imposes a more stringent duty to act than the criminal law had hitherto. The law on this subject is so unclear that it is difficult to tell whether the effect of Lord Mackay's speech was indeed to change the law, and, if so, what the implications of this change might be. It is, however, clear that the terminology of 'negligence' and 'duty of care' is best avoided within the criminal law, because of the uncertainty and confusion that surround it.

Note

The Law Commission recommended the creation of two new offences of unintentional killing, one based on recklessness and the other on gross carelessness (para.5.3). They also recommended the abolition of unlawful act manslaughter in its present form (para.5.16) although aspects of this offence appear in the offence of killing by gross carelessness (see cl.2(1)(c)(ii)). The offence retains liability for inadvertent killing but limits this to circumstances where the inadvertence is culpable.

LAW COMMISSION, *DRAFT INVOLUNTARY HOMICIDE BILL* (TSO, 1996), REPORT NO.237

Reckless killing

1.—(1) A person who by his conduct causes the death of another is guilty of reckless killing if—

(a) he is aware of a risk that his conduct will cause death or serious injury; and

(b) it is unreasonable for him to take that risk having regard to the circumstances as he knows or believes them to be.

(2) A person guilty of reckless killing is liable on conviction on indictment to imprisonment for life.

Killing by gross carelessness

2.—(1) A person who by his conduct causes the death of another is guilty of killing by gross carelessness if—

(a) a risk that his conduct will cause death or serious injury would be obvious to a reasonable person in his position;

(b) he is capable of appreciating that risk at the material time; and

(c) either—
   (i) his conduct falls far below what can reasonably be expected of him in the circumstances; or
   (ii) he intends by his conduct to cause some injury or is aware of, and unreasonably takes, the risk that it may do so.

(2) There shall be attributed to the person referred to in subsection (1)(a) above—

(a) knowledge of any relevant facts which the accused is shown to have at the material time; and

(b) any skill or experience professed by him.

(3) In determining for the purposes of subsection (1)(c)(i) above what can reasonably be expected of the accused regard shall be had to the circumstances of which he can be expected to be aware, to any circum stances shown to be within his knowledge and to any other matter relev ant for assessing his conduct at the material time.

(4) Subsection (1)(c)(ii) above applies only if the conduct causing, or intended to cause, the injury constitutes an offence.

(5) A person guilty of killing by gross carelessness is liable on conviction on indictment to imprisonment for a term not exceeding [ ] years.

3.—A person is not guilty of an offence under sections 1 or 2 above by reason of an omission unless the omission is in breach of a duty at common law.

Note

In May 2000, the Home Office published a Consultation Paper, *Reforming the Law on Involuntary Manslaughter: The Government's Proposals* based on the Law Commission Report No.237 which the Government largely accepted. The Home Office endorsed the Law Commission's recommendations of an offence of reckless killing, the abolition of unlawful act manslaughter and its replacement by an offence of killing by gross carelessness but also sought views on whether an additional homicide offence should be created to cover the situation where a death which was unforeseeable occurs and the following requirements apply (para.2.11):

- a person by his or her conduct causes the death of another;

- he or she intended to [cause some injury] or was reckless as to whether some injury was caused; and

- the conduct causing, or intended to cause, the injury constitutes an offence.

This offence would be slightly narrower than unlawful act manslaughter as at least subjective recklessness as to the risk of some injury is required but liability would still be derived from the consequence of death ensuing. A case such as *Mitchell* [1983] Q.B. 741 (above, p.509) could still arise. The Home Office provided no justification for basing liability on an accidental outcome rather than intention or foresight.

In its Consultation Paper No.177, *A New Homicide Act for England and Wales?*, the Law Commission revisited its proposals for manslaughter and modified them in light of its recommendation for the creation of two degrees of murder (see above, p.449). In their final Report *Murder, Manslaughter and Infanticide*, the Law Commission recommended an offence of manslaughter that could be committed in three ways;

(1) killing another person through gross negligence ("gross negligence manslaughter"); or

(2) killing another person:
  (a) through the commission of a criminal act intended by the defendant to cause injury, or
  (b) through the commission of a criminal act that the defendant was aware involved a serious risk of causing some injury ("criminal act manslaughter").

The recommendation for gross negligence simply reflects the current position. The recommendation regarding criminal act manslaughter is almost identical to the proposal put forward by the Government for replacing "unlawful and dangerous act" manslaughter in its Consultation Paper of 2000. In their Consultation Paper, *A New Homicide Act for England and Wales?*, the Law Commission recommended that the offence of reckless killing, with some modification, be incorporated into the provisional recommendation for "second degree murder". In their final Report, *Murder, Manslaughter and Infanticide*, the Law Commission confirmed this recommendation expressing the view that any separate offence of reckless manslaughter to cover foresight of a lesser degree of harm than that required for second degree murder would be very narrow, overlapping with gross negligence manslaughter and would make the law unduly complicated. With regard to gross negligence manslaughter, the Law Commission recommended that the prosecution be required to prove that there was gross negligence as to the risk of causing death, not merely as to causing serious injury. Consequently their recommendations on gross negligence manslaughter are a restatement of the current law. The Law Commission indicated that this reflects the views of the vast majority of consultees. They gave their reasons for this recommendation as being (para.3.59):

"Gross negligence manslaughter can be committed even when D was unaware that his or her conduct might cause death, or even injury. This is because negligence, however gross, does not necessarily involve any actual realisation that one is posing a risk of harm: it is a question of how glaringly obvious the risk would have been to a reasonable person. If liability for an offence as serious as manslaughter is to be justified in the absence of an awareness that one is posing a risk, D's negligence must relate to the risk of bringing about the very harm he or she has caused: the risk of causing death. Otherwise, the crime of manslaughter becomes unduly wide and a misleading label for what the offender has done."

The definition they gave for this offence is as follows (para.3.60):

"(1) a person by his or her conduct causes the death of another;

(2) a risk that his or her conduct will cause death would be obvious to a reasonable person in his or her position;

(3) he or she is capable of appreciating that risk at the material time; and

(4) his or her conduct falls far below what can reasonably be expected of him or her in the circumstances."

Whether anything will come of any of these proposals is open to question. The Government rejected the proposals for reframing homicide by creating two degrees of murder and moved to legislation in the Coroners and Justice Act 2009 dealing with problems relating to voluntary manslaughter, infanticide and complicity in suicide. Involuntary manslaughter remains a common law offence of both extreme breadth and perennial uncertainty as much in need of reform in 2009 as it was in 1996 when the Law Commission published the *Draft Involuntary Homicide Bill*.

----

5. OTHER UNLAWFUL HOMICIDES

i. Infanticide

INFANTICIDE ACT 1938 S.1

(1) Where a woman by any wilful act or omission causes the death of her child being a child under the age of twelve months, but at the time of the act or omission the balance of her mind was disturbed by reason of her not having fully recovered from the effect of giving birth to the child or by reason of the effect of lactation consequent upon the birth of the child, then, notwithstanding that the circumstances were such that but for this Act the offence would have amounted to murder, she shall be guilty of felony, to wit of infanticide, and may for such offence be dealt with and punished as if she had been guilty of the offence of manslaughter of the child.

(2) Where upon the trial of a woman for the murder of her child, being a child under the age of twelve months, the jury are of opinion that she by any wilful act or omission caused its death, but that at the time of the act or omission the balance of her mind was disturbed by reason of her not having fully recovered from the effect of giving birth to the child or by reason of the effect of lactation consequent upon the birth of the child, then the jury may, notwithstanding that the circumstances were such that but for the provisions of this Act they might have returned a verdict of murder, return in lieu thereof a verdict of infanticide.

Note

This offence, and defence, appeared to apply only in circumstances that might otherwise have amounted to murder as the rationale for the infanticide defence was that were there not such a defence mothers who killed their infant children would face the gallows on conviction for murder. Providing for an offence allowed the prosecution, in appropriate circumstances, to charge this at the outset rather than charging murder and leaving it for the defendant to raise the defence.

In *Kai-Whitewind* [2005] EWCA Crim 1092, the Court of Appeal added its voice to the calls for reform of the law of infanticide which had been made over several decades. It identified two particular concerns: first, the fact that the current definition does not cover circumstances subsequent to the birth, which are connected with it but not consequent upon it, for example, the stresses imposed on a mother by the absence of natural bonding with her child; and, secondly, the problem of mothers who have killed their children but who are unable to admit to it thereby rendering it difficult, or impossible, to obtain the psychiatric evidence necessary to demonstrate the disturbance to the balance of her mind.

In their Consultation Paper, *A New Homicide Act for England and Wales?*, the Law Commission provisionally proposed raising the age of the child to two years which would catch most instances of child-killing where post-natal depression plays a part. In addition, the Law Commission recommended the removal of the reference to lactation as the theory that lactation is linked to post-natal depression is erroneous. In their final Report, *Murder, Manslaughter and Infanticide*, the Law Commission recommended the retention of the defence having received further scientific research following their consultation which led them to conclude that while:

> "no psychiatric disorders (perhaps, bar one) are specific to childbirth, the incidence of certain disorders is higher following childbirth. This temporal connection indicates that some women are more vulnerable to psychiatric disorder in the postpartum period."

With regard to the lactation theory the Law Commission received further research which suggested that lactation may increase dopamine sensitivity in some women, which may trigger psychosis. This led the Law Commission to recommend the retention of the reference to lactation in the statute. The Law Commission made one recommendation of a procedural nature to deal with the second problem raised in *Kai-Whitewind*. They recommend that:

> "in circumstances where infanticide is not raised as an issue at trial and the defendant (biological mother of a child aged 12 months or less) is convicted by the jury of murder [first degree murder or second degree murder], the trial judge should have the power to order a medical examination of the defendant with a view to establishing whether or not there is evidence that at the time of the killing the requisite elements of a charge of infanticide were present. If such evidence is produced and the defendant wishes to appeal, the judge should be able to refer the application to the Court of Appeal and to postpone sentence pending the determination of the application."

Before any reform of the offence could occur, however, the Court of Appeal in *Gore* [2007] EWCA Crim 2789 delivered a judgment which tore to shreds most of the previous understanding of this offence:

> "G gave birth to a child at home unattended. Several hours later the body of the child was found in sand dunes near G's home. Pathology experts suggested the child may have died from neonatal anoxia due to blocked airways which may have arisen from lack of attention following delivery. The time of death was put at between five minutes after delivery and several hours. G was charged with infanticide on the basis that she had caused the death of the child by wilfully omitting to attend to the child or to seek medical attention following birth. G pleaded guilty albeit there was psychiatric evidence that she suffered from a hysterical dissociative state that might have founded a defence based on her mental state. The case was referred to the Criminal Cases Review Commission by the Attorney General's Interdepartmental Group set up following the decision of this court in *R. v Cannings* [2004] EWCA Crim 01 to consider homicide convictions where the victim was less than two years old. Concerns were expressed over whether the child had been born alive, as to what caused the blockage of its airways, and that there was no evidence that G wilfully omitted to care for the child. The case was referred by the Commission to the Court of Appeal on the basis that (1) it was unlikely in light of new

psychiatric evidence that G appreciated the nature of the charge; (2) G was prejudiced by the drafting of the indictment which made no mention of an intent to kill or cause GBH with consequential impact on the legal advice she received; (3) there was no evidence of an intent to kill; and (4) there were serious doubts over whether the omissions caused the death of the child. The appeal largely focused on the mental element in infanticide. The Court of Appeal held that the offence of infanticide was not confined to killings that would otherwise be murder and the mens rea of the offence was not intent to kill or cause GBH but simply that the act or omission which caused the death was wilful. Parliament had intended to create a new offence which covered situations much wider than those which would otherwise be murder. This being so, there was no defect in the indictment, G was not prejudiced and it was clear that she had wished to plead guilty."

This is a surprising decision. When the Court of Appeal had expressed concerns over infanticide in *Kai-Whitewind* the contention was that the offence should be expanded to embrace a wider range of mental/psychiatric conditions. In *Gore* the Court expanded the offence to embrace a wider range of offences, or even circumstances in which an infant might die. Despite the suggestion by Hallett LJ that infanticide carries less moral opprobrium than homicide, infanticide is a homicide offence. It had been understood to be one which arose in very limited circumstances which would otherwise amount to murder. All the debates at the time the original 1922 Act and the 1938 Act suggested that the mischief which the offence/defence was designed to address was that of women being convicted of murder, sentenced to death and experiencing that trauma only for the sentence subsequently to be commuted. The death penalty only applied to murder; a conviction of manslaughter always left the sentence at large. The Court of Appeal's construction of the statute ignores this mischief. It ignores also the fact that when originally enacted in 1922, the mens rea for murder was far from clear and, indeed, the general understanding of mens rea was still developing. The new interpretation means that all that is necessary for conviction is proof of a wilful act or omission which causes death even though the mother who acted or omitted had no intent in respect of, or foresight of, the consequences of her act or omission. In G's case it was enough that in the immediate aftermath of childbirth (with all that goes with that emotionally and physically) she failed to seek medical attention for the child such that, on one reading of the pathology evidence, the child died within five minutes of birth. That wilful omission—which means no more than voluntary—was, however, sufficient for proof of an offence of homicide. In the Court's view this is more humane than the alternative—the alternative being no homicide charge at all! It is doubtful whether a prosecution for gross negligence manslaughter based on a mother's failure to obtain medical assistance for her newborn child in the minutes immediately following its unattended birth could get off the ground.

Following the decision in *Gore* the Government in its Consultation Paper, *Murder, Manslaughter and Infanticide: Proposals for Reform of the Law* has proposed amendments to the Infanticide Act, the purpose of those amendments being "to make clear that infanticide cannot be charged in cases that would not currently be homicide at all". The Government recognised that the *Gore* interpretation of "wilful act or omission" could include negligence below the level of gross negligence. However, the proposals also accepted the widening of the offence beyond murder to include manslaughter. This aspect of the Court of Appeal's decision in *Gore* could have been remedied by any new legislation to restore matters to what they were believed to be before that decision was made. However, in the Coroners and Justice Act 2009 amendments were enacted, coming into force on 4 October 2010, expanding infanticide to cover homicides which would otherwise be manslaughter.

CORONERS AND JUSTICE ACT 2009

57   Infanticide (England and Wales)

(1)   Section 1 of the Infanticide Act 1938 (c. 36) (offence of infanticide) is amended as follows.

(2)   In subsection (1)—

(a)   for 'notwithstanding that' substitute 'if', and
(b)   after 'murder' insert 'or manslaughter'.

(3)   In subsection (2)—

(a)   for 'notwithstanding that' substitute 'if', and
(b)   after 'murder' insert 'or manslaughter'.

Questions

1.   What now is the rationale for the infanticide offence/defence?

2.   Do the changes made by s.57 address either of the concerns raised by the Court of Appeal in *Kai-Whitewind*?

3.   In *Gore*, where G gave birth alone in a flat without a telephone and the baby died possibly within five minutes of birth, what actions could G have taken in those five minutes to avoid conviction on the basis of wilful omission to care for the child?

4.   The Court of Appeal considered that a conviction of Ms Gore for infanticide was more humane than the alternative. What was "the alternative"?

----

ii. Suicide

SUICIDE ACT 1961

1 Suicide to cease to be a crime

The rule of law whereby it is a crime for a person to commit suicide is hereby abrogated.

2 Criminal liability for complicity in another's suicide

(1) A person ("D") commits an offence if—

(a)   D does an act capable of encouraging or assisting the suicide or attempted suicide of another person, and
(b)   D's act was intended to encourage or assist suicide or an attempt at suicide.

(1A) The person referred to in subsection (1)(a) need not be a specific person (or class of persons) known to, or identified by, D.

(1B) D may commit an offence under this section whether or not a suicide, or an attempt at suicide, occurs.

(1C) An offence under this section is triable on indictment and a person convicted of such an offence is liable to imprisonment for a term not exceeding 14 years.

(2) If on the trial of an indictment for murder or manslaughter of a person it is proved that the deceased person committed suicide, and the accused committed an offence under subsection (1) in relation to that suicide, the jury may find the accused guilty of the offence under subsection (1).

. . .

(4) No proceedings shall be instituted for an offence under this section except by or with the consent of the Director of Public Prosecutions.

2A Acts capable of encouraging or assisting

(1) If D arranges for a person ("D2") to do an act that is capable of encouraging or assisting the suicide or attempted suicide of another person and D2 does that act, D is also to be treated for the purposes of this Act as having done it.

(2) Where the facts are such that an act is not capable of encouraging or assisting suicide or attempted suicide, for the purposes of this Act it is to be treated as so capable if the act would have been so capable had the facts been as D believed them to be at the time of the act or had subsequent events happened in the manner D believed they would happen (or both).

(3) A reference in this Act to a person ("P") doing an act that is capable of encouraging the suicide or attempted suicide of another person includes a reference to P doing so by threatening another person or otherwise putting pressure on another person to commit or attempt suicide

2B Course of conduct

A reference in this Act to an act includes a reference to a course of conduct, and a reference to doing an act is to be read accordingly.

HOMICIDE ACT 1957 S.4

(1) It shall be manslaughter, and shall not be murder, for a person acting in pursuance of a suicide pact between him and another to kill the other or be a party to the other killing himself or being killed by a third person . . .

(3) For the purposes of this section 'suicide pact' means a common agreement between two or more persons having for its object the death of all of them, whether or not each is to take his own life, but nothing done by a person who enters into a suicide pact shall be treated as done by him in pursuance of the pact unless it is done while he has the settled intention of dying in pursuance of the pact.

Notes and Questions

1. As far as encouraging or assisting suicide is concerned the decision to prosecute rests solely with the Director of Public Prosecutions whose consent is required for any proceedings (s.2(4) of the Suicide Act 1961).

2. Would it be an offence under s.2 to publish a guide detailing methods for committing suicide? In the early 1980s, "Exit", a society campaigning for voluntary euthanasia to be legalised, published a booklet detailing methods for committing suicide. In *Attorney General v Able* [1984] 1 Q.B. 795, the Attorney General sought a declaration that "in specified circumstances" distribution of the guide was an offence under s.2(1) of the Suicide Act 1961. In response the Society sought a declaration that supply of the booklet was lawful. Wolf J refused to grant either declaration. He held that supply could be an offence where done with the necessary intent but without proof of the necessary intent it could not be said in advance that any particular supply would be an offence.

3. In 2001, Mrs Diane Pretty, who was terminally ill and who wished her husband to assist her suicide when she reached the point of life becoming intolerable, sought an undertaking from the DPP that he would not prosecute her husband in such circumstances. The DPP refused to give such an undertaking. Mrs Pretty sought to challenge the decision of the DPP as being an interference of her right to choose how and when to die which was protected by the ECHR. In *R. (on the application of Pretty) v DPP* [2002] 1 A.C. 800, the House of Lords ruled that the DPP could not be required, nor does he have the power, to give such an undertaking regardless of the compassionate factors of any particular case. Their Lordships ruled that the s.2(1) offence did not

contravene the ECHR. In *Pretty v UK* (2002) 35 E.H.R.R. 1, the European Court of Human Rights confirmed this ruling holding that the state was entitled to prohibit assisted suicide in order to protect vulnerable people who might be "helped on their way" without giving true consent.

4.   In *Purdy v DPP* [2009] UKHL 45, P suffered from a severe form of multiple sclerosis and wished to have the assurance that when life became unbearable, she would be able to travel to a country which permitted assisted suicide so that she could end her life. In order to do so, however, she would need help to travel to such a place. P's husband was willing to provide that help but there was the risk that if ever he did so, he might face prosecution under s.2(1). P sought to challenge the failure of the DPP to provide information clarifying the policy ground on which he makes decisions whether or not to consent to prosecutions for the s.2(1) offence. P argued that (i) the prohibition in s.2(1) amounted to an interference with her right to respect for her private life under art.8(1) of the ECHR; and (ii) that such interference was "not in accordance with law" under art.8(2) in the absence of an offence-specific policy. The House of Lords unanimously allowed her appeal and, departing from the decision in *Pretty*, held that art.8(1) was engaged. This required that the law should be accessible and foreseeable; and for these purposes the law included The Code for Crown Prosecutors which at the time was of little value to persons such as P as it offered no guidance at all. While their Lordships could not agree on whether the s.2(1) offence would cover someone who provided assistance where the suicide occurred abroad, as opposed to in England and Wales, they did not feel it necessary to finally determine this issue and required the DPP "to promulgate an offence-specific policy identifying the facts and circumstances which he will take into account in deciding, in a case such as . . . [P's], whether or not to consent to a prosecution under s.2(1)". On September 23, 2009 the DPP issued for consultation an *Interim Policy for Prosecutors in respect of cases of assisted suicide*. Following that consultation the final policy was issued in February 2010 (and updated in October 2014). In this document the factors for and against prosecution are listed as follows:

POLICY FOR PROSECUTORS IN RESPECT OF CASES OF ENCOURAGING OR ASSISTING SUICIDE

Public interest factors tending in favour of prosecution

43. A prosecution is more likely to be required if:

1.   the victim was under 18 years of age;

2.   the victim did not have the capacity (as defined by the Mental Capacity Act 2005) to reach an informed decision to commit suicide;

3.   the victim had not reached a voluntary, clear, settled and informed decision to commit suicide;

4.   the victim had not clearly and unequivocally communicated his or her decision to commit suicide to the suspect;

5.   the victim did not seek the encouragement or assistance of the suspect personally or on his or her own initiative;

6.   the suspect was not wholly motivated by compassion; for example, the suspect was motivated by the prospect that he or she or a person closely connected to him or her stood to gain in some way from the death of the victim;

7.   the suspect pressured the victim to commit suicide;

8.   the suspect did not take reasonable steps to ensure that any other person had not pressured the victim to commit suicide;

9. the suspect had a history of violence or abuse against the victim;

10. the victim was physically able to undertake the act that constituted the assistance him or herself;

11. the suspect was unknown to the victim and encouraged or assisted the victim to commit or attempt to commit suicide by providing specific information via, for example, a website or publication;

12. the suspect gave encouragement or assistance to more than one victim who were not known to each other;

13. the suspect was paid by the victim or those close to the victim for his or her encouragement or assistance;

14. the suspect was acting in his or her capacity as a medical doctor, nurse, other healthcare professional, a professional carer (whether for payment or not), or as a person in authority, such as a prison officer, and the victim was in his or her care;

15. the suspect was aware that the victim intended to commit suicide in a public place where it was reasonable to think that members of the public may be present;

16. the suspect was acting in his or her capacity as a person involved in the management or as an employee (whether for payment or not) of an organisation or group, a purpose of which is to provide a physical environment (whether for payment or not) in which to allow another to commit suicide.

44. On the question of whether a person stood to gain, (paragraph 43(6) see above), the police and the reviewing prosecutor should adopt a common sense approach. It is possible that the suspect may gain some benefit—financial or otherwise—from the resultant suicide of the victim after his or her act of encouragement or assistance. The critical element is the motive behind the suspect's act. If it is shown that compassion was the only driving force behind his or her actions, the fact that the suspect may have gained some benefit will not usually be treated as a factor tending in favour of prosecution. However, each case must be considered on its own merits and on its own facts.

Public interest factors tending against prosecution

45. A prosecution is less likely to be required if:

1. the victim had reached a voluntary, clear, settled and informed decision to commit suicide;

2. the suspect was wholly motivated by compassion;

3. the actions of the suspect, although sufficient to come within the definition of the offence, were of only minor encouragement or assistance;

4. the suspect had sought to dissuade the victim from taking the course of action which resulted in his or her suicide;

5. the actions of the suspect may be characterised as reluctant encouragement or assistance in the face of a determined wish on the part of the victim to commit suicide;

6. the suspect reported the victim's suicide to the police and fully assisted them in their enquiries into the circumstances of the suicide or the attempt and his or her part in providing encouragement or assistance.

46. The evidence to support these factors must be sufficiently close in time to the encouragement or assistance to allow the prosecutor reasonably to infer that the factors remained operative at that time. This is particularly important at the start of the specific chain of events that immediately led to the suicide or the attempt.

47. These lists of public interest factors are not exhaustive and each case must be considered on its own facts and on its own merits.

48. If the course of conduct goes beyond encouraging or assisting suicide, for example, because the suspect goes on to take or attempt to take the life of the victim, the public interest factors tending in favour of or against prosecution may have to be evaluated differently in the light of the overall criminal conduct.

iii. Causing or allowing the death of a child or vulnerable adult

Where a child or vulnerable adult dies in circumstances where it is clear that the death was non-accidental and caused by a parent or someone else who had care of him, it was often difficult to prove that the death was caused by one or other (or both) parents or carers. The death may have occurred while one of the parents or carers was absent. Alternatively, while it may have been possible to prove which parent was responsible for the act which was the immediate cause of death, it may have been difficult or impossible to prove whether the other parent was an accomplice in that offence. The Domestic Violence, Crime and Victims Act 2004 seeks to address this problem by creating in s.5 an offence punishable with a maximum of fourteen years' imprisonment. (The Domestic Violence, Crime and Victims (Amendment) Act 2012 extends the reach of s.5 to cover non-fatal cases where a child or vulnerable adult has suffered serious physical harm, the maximum penalty for this offence being 10 years' imprisonment.) The offence is essentially one of negligence. Section 5 (as amended) provides:

(1) A person ('D') is guilty of an offence if—
    (a)   a child or vulnerable adult ('V') dies or suffers serious physical harm as a result of the unlawful act of a person who—
        (i)   was a member of the same household as V, and
        (ii) had frequent contact with him,
    (b)   D was such a person at the time of that act;
    (c)   at that time there was a significant risk of serious physical harm being caused to V by the unlawful act of such a person; and
    (d)   either D was the person whose act caused V's death or serious physical harm or—
        (i)   D was, or ought to have been, aware of the risk mentioned in paragraph (c),
        (ii) D failed to take such steps as he could reasonably have been expected to take to protect V from the risk, and
        (iii) the act occurred in circumstances of the kind that D foresaw or ought to have foreseen.

The prosecution does not have to prove which of the three alternatives in s.5(1)(d) applies (s.5(2)). A person is to be regarded as a "member of the same household" even if he does not live at the address provided he visits it so often and for such periods of time that it is reasonable to regard him as a member of it. This could cover, for example, a grandparent who looks after a child during the day but does not sleep at the premises. "Unlawful act" is an act that constitutes an offence (s.5(5)(a)). For these purposes "act" includes a course of conduct or an omission (s.5(6)), for example, failure to feed, or clothe or seek medical attention for a child. Where D is not the person who performs the unlawful act, he will not escape liability by reason of the fact that the person who did perform it was under 10 or insane (see s.5(5)(b)). Thus, for example, a parent (D) will be liable where a sibling under the age of ten does the act which causes V's death and D failed to protect V from the risk being aware of it. Where D is not the mother or father of V, D may not be charged with this offence if he was under 16 at the time of the act that caused V's death (s.5(3)(a)). In addition, where the death is the result of a course of conduct and D has failed to take reasonable steps to protect V from the risk arising therefrom, his failure will only count against him from the point he attains the age of 16 (s.5(3)(b)).

The only circumstances where it would appear to be appropriate to charge D under this section where D is responsible for the unlawful act that causes V's death, is where D1 and D2 are the parents/carers of V and both are charged under the section it being unclear which of the two is responsible for the unlawful act. In such circumstances D1 and D2 will either each have perpetrated the act or aided and abetted the other to do so or failed to protect V. Where the prosecution can prove that one or other did the unlawful act and that the other failed to take reasonable steps to protect V in circumstances where he either was aware of the risk or ought to have been aware of it, then both should be convicted.

In *Khan* [2009] EWCA Crim 2, the Court of Appeal was faced with having to determine the meaning of "vulnerable adult". V came to England from a rural part of Kashmir to marry her cousin, H. V spoke no English and had no friends here. V and H lived with their extended family in one house which included H's mother, his sisters D and E and D's husband, F. V suffered at least three incidents of serious violence at the hands of H, the last of which caused her death. H was convicted of murder. The prosecution case against D, E and F was that during the three weeks before the final attack on her by H, it must have been apparent to D, E and F that V had been, and was being, subjected to serious physical violence at the hands of H. The prosecution contended that following the first attack on her three weeks before her death, V thereby became a vulnerable adult. D, E and F were all convicted of the s.5(1) offence and appealed their convictions. The Court of Appeal dismissed the appeals, Lord Judge CJ stating:

25. Children under the age of 16 expressly fall within the protective provisions of the Act. Adults, or near adults who are over the age of 16, are vulnerable if their ability to protect themselves from 'violence, abuse or neglect' is significantly impaired. There was some discussion whether the words 'or otherwise' found in section 5(6) extended to an individual like this unfortunate deceased, lonely and friendless in this, to her, utterly strange country, and consequently, totally dependent on her husband and his family.

26. The Act is not embarking on the impossible task of dissipating misery and unhappiness. Its objective is to protect those whose ability to protect themselves is impaired. In agreement with the judge, however, we do not rule out the possibility that an adult who is utterly dependent on others, even if physically young and apparently fit, may fall within the protective ambit of the Act. The case here proceeded on the basis that the protective provisions of the Act did not arise for consideration before the major attack on the deceased some three weeks before her death. The issue whether she was indeed vulnerable after that attack was rightly left to the jury, but if the facts had been different, we should not have ruled out the possibility that the jury might have inferred that she was already a vulnerable adult for the purposes of the Act before she sustained the violent injuries inflicted on her in the first violent attack three weeks before her death. However, in this particular case the prosecution would, on the evidence, have faced difficulty in establishing that the deceased was exposed to a significant risk of serious physical harm before that attack, and in demonstrating that any one of these appellants fell within the ambit of awareness and foresight prescribed by section 5(1)(d). The case was exclusively concerned with direct physical violence sustained by the deceased. In another case, the question whether the victim could protect himself or herself from 'abuse or neglect' might well arise in relation to an individual in [V's] situation.

27. We should add that in any event the state of vulnerability envisaged by the Act does not need to be long-standing. It may be short, or temporary. A fit adult may become vulnerable as a result of accident, or injury, or illness. The anticipation of a full recovery may not diminish the individual's temporary vulnerability.

While the legislation may originally have been passed with the view to protecting the ill, infirm and elderly, the Court was satisfied that someone in V's position—isolated and friendless in a strange country totally dependent upon her new family for all her needs—could be considered a "vulnerable adult" even though not ill or infirm.

iv. Causing death by driving

ROAD TRAFFIC ACT 1988

1. Causing death by dangerous driving.
A person who causes death of another person by driving a mechanically propelled vehicle dangerously on a road or other public place is guilty of an offence.

2. Dangerous driving.
A person who drives a mechanically propelled vehicle dangerously on a road or other public place is guilty of an offence.
2A. Meaning of dangerous driving.

(1) For the purposes of sections 1 and 2 above a person is to be regarded as driving dangerously if (and, subject to subsection (2) below, only if)—
    (a)   the way he drives falls far below what would be expected of a com petent and careful driver, and
    (b)   it would be obvious to a competent and careful driver that driving in that way would be dangerous.

(2) A person is also to be regarded as driving dangerously for the pur poses of sections 1 and 2 above if it would be obvious to a competent and careful driver that driving the vehicle in its current state would be dangerous.

(3) In subsections (1) and (2) above 'dangerous' refers to danger either of injury to any person or of serious damage to property; and in determining for the purposes of those subsections what would be expected of, or obvious to, a competent and careful driver in a particular case, regard shall be had not only to the circumstances of which he could be expected to be aware but also to any circumstances shown to have been within the knowledge of the accused.

(4) In determining for the purposes of subsection (2) above the state of a vehicle, regard may be had to any-thing attached to or carried on or in it and to the manner in which it is attached or carried.

2B. Causing death by careless, or inconsiderate, driving

A person who causes the death of another person by driving a mechanically propelled vehicle on a road or other public place without due care and attention, or without reasonable consideration for other persons using the road or place, is guilty of an offence.

3ZA. Meaning of careless, or inconsiderate, driving

(1) This section has effect for the purposes of sections 2B . . . and section 3A below.

(2) A person is to be regarded as driving without due care and attention if (and only if) the way he drives falls below what would be expected of a competent and careful driver.

(3) In determining for the purposes of subsection (2) above what would be expected of a careful and com-petent driver in a particular case, regard shall be had not only to the circumstances of which he could be expected to be aware but also to any circumstances shown to have been within the knowledge of the accused.

(4) A person is to be regarded as driving without reasonable consideration for other persons only if those persons are inconvenienced by his driving.

3ZB. Causing death by driving: unlicensed, disqualified or uninsured drivers

A person is guilty of an offence under this section if he causes the death of another person by driving a motor vehicle on a road and, at the time when he is driving, the circumstances are such that he is committing an offence under—

(a)   section 87(1) of this Act (driving otherwise than in accordance with a licence),

(b)   section 103(l)(b) of this Act (driving while disqualified), or

(c)   section 143 of this Act (using motor vehicle while uninsured or unsecured against third party risks).

3A. Causing death by careless driving when under influence of drink or drugs.

(1) If a person causes the death of another person by driving a mechanically propelled vehicle on a road or other public place without due care and attention, or without reasonable consideration for other persons using the road or place, and—
    (a)   he is, at the time when he is driving, unfit to drive through drink or drugs, or
    (b)   he has consumed so much alcohol that the proportion of it in his breath, blood or urine at that time exceeds the prescribed limit, or
    (c)   he is, within 18 hours after that time, required to provide a specimen in pursuance of section 7 of this Act, but without reasonable excuse fails to provide it, or

(d)   he is required by a constable to give his permission for a laboratory test of a specimen of blood taken from him under section 7 A of this Act, but without reasonable excuse fails to do so.

he is guilty of an offence.

(2) For the purposes of this section a person shall be taken to be unfit to drive at any time when his ability to drive properly is impaired.

(3) Subsection (1)(b), (c) and (d) above shall not apply in relation to a person driving a mechanically propelled vehicle other than a motor vehicle.

9 NON-FATAL OFFENCES AGAINST THE PERSON

In this chapter the principal offences which involve violence against the person will be examined. The first part of the chapter deals with numerous non-sexual offences of violence. These are considerable in number, ranging from a simple common assault to the serious offence of wounding or causing grievous bodily harm with intent. Also included in this part is the issue of consent and the extent to which the courts have permitted a defendant to escape liability based on the victim's consent to the activity which results in the injury.

The second part of the chapter examines sexual offences. The law on sexual offences has recently undergone extensive revision following the enactment of the Sexual Offences Act 2003. The Act is intended to strengthen, clarify and modernise the law in this difficult and sometimes controversial area. Although the Act deals with a very wide range of offences, the discussion here will be confined to rape, assault involving penetration and sexual assaults.

1. ASSAULT AND BATTERY

Criminal Justice Act 1988 s.39

Common assault and battery shall be summary offences and a person guilty of either of them shall be liable to a fine not exceeding level 5 on the standard scale, to imprisonment for a term not exceeding six months, or to both.

Notes

1. Section 40 of the same Act nevertheless provides that an indictment may include a count for common assault or battery if it is founded on the same facts or evidence as a count charging an indictable offence or is part of a series of offences of the same or similar character as an indictable offence which is also charged.

   If such a count is not included, there can be no conviction of common assault or battery: *R. v Mearns* [1991] 1 Q.B. 82 CA.

2. Assault and battery are separate statutory crimes: *R. v Taylor, R. v Little* [1992] 1 All E.R. 708. An indictment charging assault and battery is bad for duplicity, i.e. as charging more than one crime.

3. Although there are many statutory crimes, in the Offences Against the Person Act 1861 and elsewhere, which are based on the concepts of assault and battery, there is no statutory definition of those concepts, the meaning of which must be sought in case law, including civil cases, since

both assault and battery are also torts. In the past there has been a practice, in statutes and in judgments, to use the term "assault" as comprehending also a battery (see *Fagan v MPC*, directly below). Now that it is clear that they are two separate crimes which must not be rolled up in one charge, the need for a new terminology is urgent.

----

i. Actus Reus

FAGAN V METROPOLITAN POLICE COMMISSIONER

[1969] 1 Q.B. 439

Fagan was told by a police officer to park his car at a particular spot. He drove his car on to the policeman's foot. He refused for some time to reverse off. Fagan was convicted by the magistrates of assaulting a police officer in the execution of his duty. On appeal he maintained that the initial driving on the foot was not an assault, because unintentional; nor was the refusal to drive off because this was not an act.

JAMES J

(with whom Lord Parker CJ agreed, Bridge J dissenting)
In our judgment the question arising, which has been argued on general principles, falls to be decided on the facts of the particular case. An assault is any act which intentionally—or possibly recklessly—causes another person to apprehend immediate and unlawful personal violence. Although 'assault' is an independent crime and is to be treated as such, for practical purposes today 'assault' is generally synonymous with the term 'battery' and is a term used to mean the actual intended use of unlawful force to another person without his consent. On the facts of the present case the 'assault' alleged involved a 'battery'. Where an assault involves a battery, it matters not, in our judgment, whether the battery is inflicted directly by the body of the offender or through the medium of some weapon or instrument controlled by the action of the offender. An assault may be committed by the laying of a hand upon another, and the action does not cease to be an assault if it is a stick held in the hand and not the hand itself which is laid on the person of the victim. So for our part we see no difference in principle between the action of stepping on to a person's toe and maintaining that position and the action of driving a car on to a person's foot and sitting in the car whilst its position on the foot is maintained.

To constitute the offence of assault some intentional act must have been performed: a mere omission to act cannot amount to an assault. Without going into the question whether words alone can constitute an assault, it is clear that the words spoken by the appellant could not alone amount to an assault: they can only shed a light on the appellant's action. For our part we think the crucial question is whether in this case the act of the appellant can be said to be complete and spent at the moment of time when the car wheel came to rest on the foot or whether his act is to be regarded as a continuing act operating until the wheel was removed. In our judgment a distinction is to be drawn between acts which are complete—though results may continue to flow—and those acts which are continuing. Once the act is complete it cannot thereafter be said to be a threat to inflict unlawful force upon the victim. If the act, as distinct from the results thereof, is a continuing act there is a continuing threat to inflict unlawful force. If the assault involves a battery and that battery continues there is a continuing act of assault.

For an assault to be committed both the elements of *actus reus* and *mens rea* must be present at the same time. The '*actus reus*' is the action causing the effect on the victim's mind (see the observations of Parke B. in *R. v St George*, (1840) 9 C.P. 483). The '*mens rea*' is the intention to cause that effect. It is not necessary that *mens rea* should be present at the inception of the *actus reus*; it can be superimposed upon an existing act. On the other hand the subsequent inception of *mens* rea cannot convert an act which has been completed without *mens rea* into an assault.

In our judgment the Willesden magistrates and quarter sessions were right in law. On the facts found the action of the appellant may have been initially unintentional, but the time came when knowing that the wheel was on the officer's foot the appellant (1) remained seated in the car so that his body through the medium of the car was in contact with the officer, (2) switched off the ignition of the car, (3) maintained the wheel of the car on the foot and (4) used words indicating the intention of keeping the wheel in that position. For our part we cannot regard such conduct as mere omission or inactivity.

There was an act constituting battery which at its inception was not criminal because there was no element of intention but which became criminal from the moment the intention was formed to produce the apprehension which was flowing from the continuing act. The fallacy of the appellant's argument is that it seeks to equate the facts of this case with such a case as where a motorist has accidentally run over a person and, that action having been completed, fails to assist the victim with the intent that the victim should suffer.

We would dismiss this appeal.

Appeal dismissed

Question

Would the reasoning in *R. v Miller*, above p.37, provide a more satisfactory way of upholding Fagan's conviction? And see also *DPP v Santana-Bermodez* [2003] EWCH Admin 2908, above, p.40.

Notes

1. The courts have recognised that ordinary everyday life forms of contact should not be regarded as unlawful and not, therefore, constitute a battery. A police officer may tap a person on the shoulder to attract attention but he may not restrain the person (*Collins v Wilcock* [1984] 3 All E.R. 374). In *McMillan v CPS* [2008] EWHC 1457 (Admin). A, who was drunk and shouting abuse, was seen by a police officer. The officer took her by the arm to steady her and led her down some steps to the street in order to speak to her. The court held that as the officer had acted within the bounds of what were "generally acceptable standards of conduct" no assault had been committed.

2. The crucial requirement in assault is that the victim apprehended immediate unlawful violence. For some time the law was unclear whether words alone causing such an apprehension could constitute an assault. This issue has been resolved by the case which follows.

R. V IRELAND; R. V BURSTOW

[1997] A.C. 147 HL

The appellant, Ireland, had pleaded guilty to three counts charging him with assault occasioning actual bodily harm contrary to s.47 of the Offences Against the Person Act 1861. The charges arose from the appellant making a large number of unwanted silent telephone calls over a period of several months to three women. As a result of the calls the women suffered significant psychological symptoms, inter alia, palpitations, difficulty in breathing, anxiety, inability to sleep, tearfulness and stress. The Court of Appeal dismissed his appeal certifying the following point of law of general public importance for consideration by the House of Lords, namely: "Whether the making of a series of silent telephone calls can amount in law to an assault."

LORD STEYN

. . . It is to assault in the form of an act causing the victim to fear an immediate application of force to her that I must turn. Counsel argued that as a matter of law an assault can never be committed by words alone and therefore it cannot be committed by silence. The premise depends on the slenderest authority, namely, an observation by Holroyd J. to a jury that 'no words or singing are equivalent to an assault:' *Rex v Meade and Belt* (1823) 1 Lew. 184. The proposition that a gesture may amount to an assault, but that words can never suffice, is unrealistic and indefensible. A thing said is also a thing done. There is no reason why something said should be incapable of causing an apprehension of immediate personal violence, e.g. a man accosting a woman in a dark alley saying, 'Come with me or I will stab you.' I would, therefore, reject the proposition that an assault can never be committed by words.

That brings me to the critical question whether a silent caller may be guilty of an assault. The answer to this question seems to me to be 'Yes, depending on the facts.' It involves questions of fact within the province of the jury. After all, there is no reason why a telephone caller who says to a woman in a menacing way 'I will be at your door in a minute or two' may not be guilty of an assault if he causes his victim to apprehend immediate personal violence. Take now the case of the silent caller. He intends by his silence to cause fear and he is so understood. The victim is assailed by uncertainty about his intentions. Fear may dominate her emotions, and it may be the fear that the caller's arrival at her door may be imminent. She may fear the possibility of immediate personal violence. As a matter of law the caller may be guilty of an assault: whether he is or not will depend on the circumstance and in particular on the impact of the caller's potentially menacing call or calls on the victim. Such a prosecution case under s.47 may be fit to leave to the jury. And a trial judge may, depending on the circumstances, put a common sense consideration before the jury, namely what, if not the possibility of imminent personal violence, was the victim terrified about? I conclude that an assault may be committed in the particular factual circumstances which I have envisaged. For this reason I reject the submission that as a matter of law a silent telephone caller cannot ever be guilty of an offence under s.47.

LORD HOPE OF CRAIGHEAD

. . . The important question therefore is whether the making of a series of silent telephone calls can amount in law to an assault.

There is no clear guidance on this point either in the statute or in the authorities. On the one hand in *Rex v Meade and Belt* (1823) 1 Lew. 184 Holroyd J. said that no words or singing can amount to an assault. On the other hand in *Reg. v Wilson* [1955] 1 W.L.R. 493, 494 Lord Goddard C.J. said that the appellant's words, 'Get the knives' would itself be an assault. The word 'assault' as used in s.47 of the Act of 1861 is not defined anywhere in that Act. The legislation appears to have been framed on the basis that the words which it used were words which everyone would understand without further explanation. In this regard the fact that the statute was enacted in the middle of the last century is of no significance. The public interest, for whose benefit it was enacted, would not be served by construing the words in a narrow or technical way. The words used are ordinary English words, which can be given their ordinary meaning in the usage of the present day. They can take account of changing circumstances both as regards medical knowledge and the means by which one person can cause bodily harm to another.

The fact is that the means by which a person of evil disposition may intentionally or recklessly cause another to apprehend immediate and unlawful violence will vary according to the circumstances. Just as it is not true to say that every blow which is struck is an assault some blows, which would otherwise amount to battery, may be struck by accident or in jest or may otherwise be entirely justified so also it is not true to say that mere words or gestures can never constitute an assault. It all depends on the circumstances. If the words or gestures are accompanied in their turn by gestures or by words which threaten immediate and unlawful violence, that will be sufficient for an assault. The words or gestures must be seen in their whole context.

In this case the means which the appellant used to communicate with his victims was the telephone. While he remained silent, there can be no doubt that he was intentionally communicating with them as directly as if he was present with them in the same room. But whereas for him merely to remain silent with them in the same room, where they could see him and assess his demeanour, would have been unlikely to give rise to any feelings of apprehension on their part, his silence when using the telephone in calls made to them repeatedly was an act of an entirely different character. He was using his silence as a means of conveying a message to his victims. This was that he knew who and where they were, and that his purpose in making contact with them was as malicious as it was deliberate. In my opinion silent telephone calls of this nature are just as capable as words or gestures, said or made in the presence of the victim, of causing an apprehension of immediate and unlawful violence.

Whether this requirement, and in particular that of immediacy, is in fact satisfied will depend on the circumstances. This will need in each case, if it is disputed, to be explored in evidence. But that step was not necessary in this case as the appellant was prepared to plead guilty to having committed the offence. I would therefore answer the certified question in the affirmative and dismiss this appeal also.

Appeal dismissed

Note and Question

As Ireland had pleaded guilty to assault the issue whether the women had actually apprehended unlawful personal violence never had to be considered by a jury. Lord Steyn states that "a trial judge may, depending on the circumstances, put a common sense consideration before the jury, namely what, if not the possibility of imminent personal violence, was the victim terrified about?" If there is no evidence that the victim feared immediate unlawful personal violence, should such a question ever be left to the jury bearing in mind the burden of proof on the prosecution? It should be noted that the prosecution in *Ireland* was brought before the Protection from Harassment Act 1997 was enacted. Under this statute it is an offence punishable with up to six months' imprisonment to pursue a course of conduct which amounts to harassment of another (see ss.1(1) and 2(1)). A more serious offence punishable with up to five years' imprisonment may be committed where the "course of conduct causes another to fear, on at least two occasions, that violence will be used against him" (s.4(1)). There is no requirement under this offence that the fear be of "immediate" violence. The existence of this offence, however, will not preclude the need to rely on the offence of assault or assault occasioning actual bodily harm in some cases. In particular, s.4(1) requires fear to be caused on at least two occasions. This would not cover a case where D telephones V on one occasion with a specific threat of immediate unlawful violence. This could constitute an assault. If, however, D threatens the violence in the future this would not fall under either assault or s.4(1). In addition s.4(1) requires on the part of the victim a fear that violence *will* be used against him. Lord Steyn doubted that the Act would offer protection to the victim of a silent caller where she feared merely that violence *may* be used against her.

Section 43 of the Telecommunications Act 1984 creates the offence of improper use of a public telecommunication system. This offence may be committed, inter alia, by a person who: (a) makes calls of a "grossly offensive or of an indecent, obscene or menacing character"; or, who (b) makes persistent calls "for the purpose of causing annoyance, inconvenience or needless anxiety to another". This is a summary offence but there is no requirement of proof of purpose where (a) applies. Ireland's activities came within (a) and probably also within (b) but the prosecution clearly were not satisfied with a summary offence even though Parliament had increased the penalty to a maximum fine at level 5 and/or imprisonment for a maximum term of six months.

----

ii. Mens Rea

R. V VENNA

[1975] 3 All E.R. 788

D was involved in a struggle with police officers who were attempting to arrest him. He fell to the ground and then proceeded to lash out wildly with his legs. In so doing he kicked the hand of one of the police officers, fracturing a bone. His story was that he was kicking out in an attempt to get up off the ground. D was convicted of assault occasioning actual bodily harm, after the judge had directed the jury that they could find D guilty if they found that he had lashed out with his feet "reckless as to who was there, not caring one iota as to whether he kicked anybody." He appealed.

JAMES LJ

(reading the judgment of the court):
. . . In *Fagan v M.P.C.* (above), it was said: 'An assault is any act which intentionally or possibly recklessly causes another person to apprehend immediate and unlawful personal violence.' In *Fagan* it was not necessary to decide

the question whether proof of recklessness is sufficient to establish the *mens rea* ingredient of assault. That question falls for decision in the present case . . .

In our view the element of *mens rea* in the offence of battery is satisfied by proof that the defendant intentionally or recklessly applied force to the person of another. If it were otherwise, the strange consequence would be that an offence of unlawful wounding contrary to s.20 of the Offences Against the Person Act 1861 could be established by proof that the defendant wounded the victim either intentionally or recklessly, but if the victim's skin was not broken and the offence was therefore laid as an assault occasioning actual bodily harm contrary to s.47 of the 1861 Act, it would be necessary to prove that the physical force was intentionally applied.

We see no reason in logic or in law why a person who recklessly applies physical force to the person of another should be outside the criminal law of assault. In many cases the dividing line between intention and recklessness is barely distinguishable. This is such a case. In our judgment the direction was right in law; this ground of appeal fails . . .

Appeal dismissed

iii. Justifications

Note

There are particular justifications for the application of force or threats of force, e.g. cases of self-defence, prevention of crime, which were dealt with above. Physical contact which is generally acceptable in the ordinary conduct of social life (e.g. jostlings in crowds) may also be justified: see *Collins v Wilcock*, referred to in *Re F*, directly below. Necessity to preserve the life or health or well-being of the person to whom the force is applied may be a justification: see the next case. Consent may *sometimes* justify:

(a) Necessity

RE F (MENTAL PATIENT: STERILISATION)

[1990] 2 A.C. 1 HL

F, a 36-year-old mentally handicapped woman with a mental age of a small child, resided as a voluntary patient in a mental hospital. She formed a sexual relationship with a male patient. The hospital staff considered that F would be unable to cope with the effects of pregnancy and giving birth. Since other forms of contraception were unsuitable, and it was thought undesirable to curtail F's freedom of movement in order to prevent sexual activity, it was felt to be in F's best interests for her to be sterilised. F's mother concurred and sought a declaration that sterilisation would not be an unlawful act by reason only of the absence of F's consent. The declaration was granted, and upheld by the Court of Appeal. On further appeal by the Official Solicitor:

LORD BRANDON OF OAKBROOK

Part IV of the Mental Health Act 1983 contains provisions, which it is not necessary to detail, imposing restrictions or conditions on the giving to mentally disorded persons of certain kinds of treatment for their mental disorder. The Act, however, does not contain any provisions relating to the giving of treatment to patients for any conditions other than their mental disorder. The result is that the lawfulness of giving any treatment of the latter kind depends not on statute but the common law.

At common law a doctor cannot lawfully operate on adult patients of sound mind, or give them any other treatment involving the application of physical force however small ('other treatment'), without their consent. If a doctor were to operate on such patients, or give them other treatment, without their consent, he would commit the actionable tort of trespass to the person. There are, however, cases where adult patients cannot give or refuse their consent to an operation or other treatment. One case is where, as a result of an accident or otherwise, an adult patient is unconscious and an operation or other treatment cannot be safely delayed until he or she recovers consciousness. Another case is where a patient, though adult, cannot by reason of mental disability understand the nature or purpose of an operation or other treatment. The common law would be seriously defective if it failed to provide a solution to the problem created by such inability to consent. In my opinion, however, the common law does not so fail. In my opinion, the solution to the problem which the common law provides is that a doctor can lawfully operate on, or give other treatment to, adult patients who are incapable, for one reason or another, of consenting to his doing so, provided that the operation or other treatment concerned is in the best interests of such patients. The operation or other treatment will be in their best interests if, but only if, it is carried out in order either to save their lives, or to ensure improvement or prevent deterioration in their physical or mental health.

Different views have been put forward with regard to the principle which makes it lawful for a doctor to operate on or give other treatment to adult patients without their consent in the two cases to which I have referred above. The Court of Appeal in the present case regarded the matter as depending on the public interest. I would not disagree with that as a broad proposition, but I think that it is helpful to consider the principle in accordance with which the public interest leads to this result. In my opinion, the principle is that, when persons lack the capacity, for whatever reason, to take decisions about the performance of operations on them, or the giving of other medical treatment to them, it is necessary that some other person or persons, with appropriate qualifications, should take such decisions for them. Otherwise they would be deprived of medical care which they need and to which they are entitled.

In many cases, however, it will not only be lawful for doctors, on the ground of necessity, to operate on or give other medical treatment to adult patients disabled from giving their consent; it will also be their common law duty to do so.

In the case of adult patients made unconscious by an accident or otherwise, they will normally be received into the casualty department of a hospital, which thereby undertakes the care of them. It will then be the duty of the doctors at that hospital to use their best endeavours to do, by way of either an operation or other treatment, that which is in the best interests of such patients.

In the case of adult patients suffering from mental disability, they will normally, in accordance with the scheme of the Mental Health Act 1983, be either in the care of guardians, who will refer them to doctors for medical treatment, or of doctors at mental hospitals in which the patients either reside voluntarily or are detained compulsorily. It will then again be the duty of the doctors concerned to use their best endeavours to do, by way of either an operation or other treatment, that which is in the best interests of such patients.

The application of the principle which I have described means that the lawfulness of a doctor operating on, or giving other treatment to, an adult patient disabled from giving consent, will depend not on any approval or sanction of a court, but on the question whether the operation or other treatment is in the best interests of the patient concerned. That is, from a practical point of view, just as well, for, if every operation to be performed, or other treatment to be given, required the approval or sanction of the court, the whole process of medical care for such patients would grind to a halt . . .

LORD GOFF OF CHIEVELEY

My Lords, the question in this case is concerned with the lawfulness of a proposed operation of sterilisation upon the plaintiff F . . . .

I start with the fundamental principle, now long established, that every person's body is inviolate. As to this, I do not wish to depart from what I myself said in the judgment of the Divisional Court in *Collins v Wilcock* [1984] 1 W.L.R. 1172, and in particular from the statement, at p.1177, that the effect of this principle is that everybody is protected not only against physical injury but against any form of physical molestation.

Of course, as a general rule physical interference with another person's body is lawful if he consents to it; though in certain limited circumstances the public interest may require that his consent is not capable of rendering the act lawful. There are also specific cases where physical interference without consent may not be unlawful—chastisement of children, lawful arrest, self-defence, the prevention of crime, and so on. As I pointed out in *Collins v Wilcock*, a broader exception has been created to allow for the exigencies of everyday life—jostling in a street or some other crowded place, social contact at parties, and such like. This exception has been said to be founded on implied consent, since those who go about in public places, or go to parties, may be taken to have impliedly consented to bodily contact of this kind. Today this rationalisation can be regarded as artificial; and in particular, it is difficult to impute consent to those who, by reason of their youth or mental disorder, are unable to give their consent. For this reason, I consider it more appropriate to regard such cases as falling within a general exception embracing all physical contact which is generally acceptable in the ordinary conduct of everyday life.

In the old days it used to be said, for a touching of another's person to amount to a battery, it had to be a touching 'in anger' (see *Cole v Turner* (1794) 6 Mod. 149, *per* Holt C.J.); and it has recently been said that the touching must be 'hostile' to have that effect (see *Wilson v Pringle* [1987] Q.B. 237, 253). I respectfully doubt whether that is correct. A prank that gets out of hand; an over-friendly slap on the back; surgical treatment by a surgeon who mistakenly thinks that the patient has consented to it—all these things may transcend the bounds of lawfulness, without being characterised as hostile. Indeed the suggested qualification is difficult to reconcile with the principle that any touching of another's body is, in the absence of lawful excuse, capable of amounting to a battery and a trespass. Furthermore, in the case of medical treatment, we have to bear well in mind the libertarian principle of self-determination which, to adopt the words of Cardozo J. (in *Schloendorff v Society of New York Hospital* (1914) 105 N.E. 92, 93) recognises that:

'Every human being of adult years and sound mind has a right to determine what shall be done with his own body; and a surgeon who performs an operation without his patient's consent commits an assault . . .'

This principle has been reiterated in more recent years by Lord Reid in *S. v McC. (orse. S.) and M. (D.S. intervened; W. v W.* [1972] A.C. 24, 43.

It is against this background that I turn to consider the question whether, and if so when, medical treatment or care of a mentally disordered person who is, by reason of his incapacity, incapable of giving his consent, can be regarded as lawful. As is recognised in Cardozo J.'s statement of principle, and elsewhere (see e.g. *Sidaway v Board of Governors of the Bethlem Royal Hospital and the Maudsley Hospital* [1985] A.C. 871, 882, *per* Lord Scarman), some relaxation of the law is required to accommodate persons of unsound mind. In *Wilson v Pringle*, the Court of Appeal considered that treatment or care of such persons may be regarded as lawful, as falling within the exception relating to physical contact which is generally acceptable in the ordinary conduct of everyday life. Again, I am with respect unable to agree. That exception is concerned with the ordinary events of everyday life—jostling in public places and such like—and affects all persons, whether or not they are capable of giving their consent. Medical treatment—even treatment for minor ailments—does not fall within that category of events. The general rule is that consent is necessary to render such treatment lawful. If such treatment administered without consent is not to be unlawful, it has to be justified on some other principle.

Upon what principle can medical treatment be justified when given without consent? We are searching for a principle upon which, in limited circumstances, recognition may be given to a need, in the interests of the patient, that treatment should be given to him in circumstances where he is (temporarily or permanently) disabled from consenting to it. It is this criterion of a need which points to the principle of necessity as providing justification.

[After surveying the principle of necessity.]

On this statement of principle, I wish to observe that officious intervention cannot be justified by the principle of necessity. So intervention cannot be justified when another more appropriate person is available and willing to act: nor can it be justified when it is contrary to the known wishes of the assisted person, to the extent that he is capable of rationally forming such a wish. As a general rule, if the above criteria are fulfilled, interference with the assisted person's person or property (as the case may be) will not be unlawful. Take the example of a railway accident, in which injured passengers are trapped in the wreckage. It is this principle which may render lawful the actions of other citizens—railway staff, passengers or outsiders—who rush to give aid and comfort to the victims: the surgeon who amputates the limb of an unconscious passenger to free him from the wreckage; the ambulance man who conveys him to hospital; the doctors and nurses who treat him and care for him while he is still unconscious. Take the example of an elderly person who suffers a stroke which renders him incapable of speech or movement. It is by virtue of this principle that the doctor who treats him, the nurse who cares for him, even the relative or friend or neighbour who comes in to look after him, will commit no wrong when he or she touches his body.

The two examples I have given illustrate, in the one case, an emergency, and in the other, a permanent or semi-permanent state of affairs. Another example of the latter kind is that of a mentally disordered person who is disabled from giving consent. I can see no good reason why the principle of necessity should not be applicable in his case as it is in the case of the victim of a stroke. Furthermore, in the case of a mentally disordered person, as in the case of a stroke victim, the permanent state of affairs calls for a wider range of care than may be requisite in an emergency which arises from accidental injury. When the state of affairs is permanent, or semi-permanent, action properly taken to preserve the life, health or well-being of the assisted person may well transcend such measures as surgical operation or substantial medical treatment and may extend to include such humdrum matters as routine medical or dental treatment, even simple care such as dressing and undressing and putting to bed.

The distinction I have drawn between cases of emergency, and cases where the state of affairs is (more or less) permanent, is relevant in another respect. We are here concerned with medical treatment, and I limit myself to cases of that kind. Where, for example, a surgeon performs an operation without his consent on a patient temporarily rendered unconscious in an accident, he should do no more than is reasonably required, in the best interests of the patient, before he recovers consciousness. I can see no practical difficulty arising from this requirement, which derives from the fact that the patient is expected before long to regain consciousness and can then be consulted about longer term measures. The point has however arisen in a more acute form where a surgeon, in the course of an operation, discovers some other condition which, in his opinion, requires operative treatment for which he has not received the patient's consent. In what circumstances he should operate forthwith, and in what circumstances he should postpone the further treatment until he has received the patient's consent, is a difficult matter which has troubled the Canadian Courts (see *Marshall v Curry* (1933) 3 D.L.R. 260, and *Murray v McMurchy* (1949) 2 D.L.R. 442), but which it is not necessary for your Lordships to consider in the present case.

But where the state of affairs is permanent or semi-permanent, as may be so in the case of a mentally disordered person, there is no point in waiting to obtain the patient's consent. The need to care for him is obvious: and the doctor must then act in the best interests of his patient, just as if he had received his patient's consent so to do. Were this not so, much useful treatment and care could, in theory at least, be denied to the unfortunate. It follows that, on this point, I am unable to accept the view expressed by Neill L.J. in the Court of Appeal, that the treatment must be shown to have been necessary. Moreover, in such a case, as my noble and learned friend Lord Brandon of Oakbrook has pointed out, a doctor who has assumed responsibility for the care of a patient may not only be treated as having the patient's consent to act, but may also be under a duty so to act . . .

In these circumstances, it is natural to treat the deemed authority and the duty as interrelated. But I feel bound to express my opinion that, in principle, the lawfulness of the doctor's action is, at least in its origin, to be found in the principle of necessity. This can perhaps be seen most clearly in cases where there is no continuing relationship between doctor and patient. The 'doctor in the house' who volunteers to assist a lady in the audience who, overcome by the drama or by the heat in the theatre, has fainted away, is impelled to act by no greater duty than that imposed by his own Hippocratic oath. Furthermore, intervention can be justified in the case of a non-professional, as well as a professional, man or woman who has no pre-existing relationship with the assisted persons—as in the case of a stranger who rushes to assist an injured man after an accident. In my opinion, it is the necessity itself which provides the justification for the intervention.

I have said that the doctor has to act in the best interests of the assisted person. In the case of routine treatment of mentally disordered persons, there should be little difficulty in applying this principle. In the case of more serious treatment, I recognise that its application may create problems for the medical profession; however, in making decisions about treatment, the doctor must act in accordance with a responsible and competent body of relevant professional opinion, on the principles set down in *Bolam v Friern Hospital Management Committee* [1957] 1 W.L.R. 582 . . ..

[Lords Bridge of Harwich, Griffiths and Jauncey of Tullichettle agreed with Lords Brandon and Goff.]

Appeal dismissed

Note

The application of force or threats of force may sometimes be justified by the consent of the victim. Where it is so justified, neither common assault nor any statutory crime which involves assault is committed. However, sometimes the statute expressly provides that consent is no defence. Moreover, the common law does not recognise consent as a defence to some assaults, on the footing that "no one can license a crime". This doctrine, and the question of what is consent, need separate treatment.

(b) When consent may justify

R. V BROWN

[1994] 1 A.C. 212 HL

The appellants belonged to a group of sado-masochistic homosexuals who over a 10-year period from 1978 willingly participated in the commission of acts of violence against each other, including genital torture, for the sexual pleasure which it engendered in the giving and receiving of pain. The passive partner or victim in each case consented to the acts being committed and suffered no permanent injury. The activities took place in private at a number of different locations, including rooms equipped as torture chambers at the homes of three of the appellants. Video cameras were used to record the activities and the resulting tapes were then copied and distributed amongst members of the group. The tapes were not sold or used other than for the delectation of members of the group. The appellants were charged with assault occasioning actual bodily harm, contrary to s.47 of the Offences Against the Person Act 1861, and unlawful wounding, contrary to s.20 of that Act. The prosecution case was based very largely on the contents of the video tapes. At their trial, following a ruling by the trial judge that it was unnecessary for the prosecution to prove that the victim did not consent to the infliction of bodily harm or wounding upon him, the appellants pleaded guilty. Their appeal against conviction was dismissed by the Court of Appeal, which certified the following point of law of general public importance: "Where A wounds or assaults B occasioning him actual bodily harm in the course of a sado-masochistic encounter, does the prosecution have to prove lack of consent on the part of B before they can establish A's guilt under s.20 and s.47 of the 1861 Offences Against the Person Act?" On further appeal:

LORD TEMPLEMAN

. . . In the present case each of the appellants intentionally inflicted violence upon another (to whom I refer as 'the victim') with the consent of the victim and thereby occasioned actual bodily harm or in some cases wounding or grievous bodily harm. Each appellant was therefore guilty of an offence under s.47 or s.20 of the Act of 1861 unless the consent of the victim was effective to prevent the commission of the offence or effective to constitute a defence to the charge.

In some circumstances violence is not punishable under the criminal law. When no actual bodily harm is caused, the consent of the person affected precludes him from complaining. There can be no conviction for the summary offence of common assault if the victim has consented to the assault. Even when violence is intentionally inflicted and results in actual bodily harm, wounding or serious bodily harm the accused is entitled to be acquitted if the injury was a foreseeable incident of a lawful activity in which the person injured was participating. Surgery involves intentional violence resulting in actual or sometimes serious bodily harm but surgery is a lawful activity. Other activities carried on with consent by or on behalf of the injured person have been accepted as lawful notwithstanding that they involve actual bodily harm or may cause serious bodily harm. Ritual circumcision, tattooing, ear-piercing and violent sports including boxing are lawful activities.

In earlier days some other forms of violence were lawful and when they ceased to be lawful they were tolerated until well into the 19th century. Duelling and fighting were at first lawful and then tolerated provided the protagonists were voluntary participants. But where the result of these activities was the maiming of one of the participants, the defence of consent never availed the aggressor; see *Hawkins Pleas of the Crown* (1824), 8th ed., Chapter 15. A maim was bodily harm whereby a man was deprived of the use of any member of his body which he needed to use in order to fight but a bodily injury was not a maim merely because it was a disfigurement. The act of maim was unlawful because the King was deprived of the services of an able-bodied citizen for the defence of the realm. Violence which maimed was unlawful despite consent to the activity which produced the maiming. In these days there is no difference between maiming on the one hand and wounding or causing grievous bodily harm on the other hand except with regard to sentence.

When duelling became unlawful, juries remained unwilling to convict but the judges insisted that persons guilty of causing death or bodily injury should be convicted despite the consent of the victim.

Similarly, in the old days, fighting was lawful provided the protagonists consented because it was thought that fighting inculcated bravery and skill and physical fitness. The brutality of knuckle fighting however caused the courts to declare that such fights were unlawful even if the protagonists consented. Rightly or wrongly the courts accepted that boxing is a lawful activity.

In *R. v Coney* (1882) 8 Q.B.D. 534, the court held that a prize-fight in public was unlawful . . .

[A] prize-fight being unlawful, actual bodily harm or serious bodily harm inflicted in the course of a prize-fight is unlawful notwithstanding the consent of the protagonists.

In *R. v Donovan* [1934] 2 K.B. 498 the appellant in private beat a girl of seventeen for purposes of sexual gratification, it was said with her consent. Swift J. said, at p.507 that:

'It is an unlawful act to beat another person with such a degree of violence that the infliction of bodily harm is a probable consequence, and when such an act is proved, consent is immaterial.'

In *Attorney-General's Reference (No.6 of 1980)* [1981] Q.B. 715 where two men quarrelled and fought with bare fists Lord Lane, C J., delivering the judgment of the Court of Appeal said, at p.719:

'. . . It is not in the public interest that people should try to cause, or should cause, each other bodily harm for no good reason. Minor struggles are another matter. So, in our judgment, it is immaterial whether the act occurs in private or in public; it is an assault if actual bodily harm is intended and/or caused. This means that most fights will be unlawful regardless of consent. Nothing which we have said is intended to cast doubt upon the accepted legality of properly conducted games and sports, lawful chastisement or correction, reasonable surgical interference, dangerous exhibitions, etc. These apparent exceptions can be justified as involving the exercise of a legal right, in the case of chastisement or correction, or as needed in the public interest, in the other cases.'

Duelling and fighting are both unlawful and the consent of the protagonists affords no defence to charges of causing actual bodily harm, wounding or grievous bodily harm in the course of an unlawful activity.

The appellants and their victims in the present case were engaged in consensual homosexual activities. The attitude of the public towards homosexual practices changed in the second half of this century. Change in public attitudes led to a change in the law.

The Wolfenden Report (Report of the Committee on Homosexual Offences and Prostitution (1957) (Cmnd. 247)) declared that the function of the criminal law in relation to homosexual behaviour 'is to preserve public order and decency, to protect the citizen from what is offensive or injurious, and to provide sufficient safeguards against exploitation and corruption of others, particularly those who are especially vulnerable because they are young, weak in body or mind, inexperienced, or in a state of special, physical, official or economic dependence'; paragraph 13 of chapter 2.

In response to the Wolfenden Report and consistently with its recommendations, Parliament enacted s.1 of the Sexual Offences Act 1967 which provided, *inter alia*, as follows:

'(1) Notwithstanding any statutory or common law provision, . . . a homosexual act in private shall not be an offence provided that the parties consent thereto and have attained the age of 21 years.' . . .

By the Act of 1967, Parliament recognised and accepted the practice of homosexuality. Subject to exceptions not here relevant, sexual activities conducted in private between not more than two consenting adults of the same sex or different sexes are now lawful. Homosexual activities performed in circumstances which do not fall within s.1 (1) of the Act of 1967 remain unlawful. Subject to the respect for private life embodied in the Act of 1967. Parliament has retained criminal sanctions against the practice, dissemination and encouragement of homosexual activities.

My Lords, the authorities dealing with the intentional infliction of bodily harm do not establish that consent is a defence to a charge under the Act of 1861. They establish that the courts have accepted that consent is a defence to the infliction of bodily harm in the course of some lawful activities. The question is whether the defence should be extended to the infliction of bodily harm in the course of sado-masochistic encounters. The Wolfenden Committee did not make any recommendations about sado-masochism and Parliament did not deal with violence in 1967. The Act of 1967 is of no assistance for present purposes because the present problem was not under consideration.

The question whether the defence of consent should be extended to the consequences of sado-masochistic encounters can only be decided by consideration of policy and public interest. Parliament can call on the advice of doctors, psychiatrists, criminologists, sociologists and other experts and can also sound and take into account public opinion. But the question must at this stage be decided by this House in its judicial capacity in order to determine whether the convictions of the appellants should be upheld or quashed.

Counsel for some of the appellants argued that the defence of consent should be extended to the offence of occasioning actual bodily harm under s.47 of the Act of 1861 but should not be available to charges of serious wounding and the infliction of serious bodily harm under s.20. I do not consider that this solution is practicable. Sado-masochistic participants have no way of foretelling the degree of bodily harm which will result from their encounters. The differences between actual bodily harm and serious bodily harm cannot be satisfactorily applied by a jury in order to determine acquittal or conviction.

Counsel for the appellants argued that consent should provide a defence to charges under both s.20 and 47 because, it was said, every person has a right to deal with his body as he pleases. I do not consider that this slogan provides a sufficient guide to the policy decision which must now be made. It is an offence for a person to abuse his own body and mind by taking drugs. Although the law is often broken, the criminal law restrains a practice which is regarded as dangerous and injurious to individuals and which if allowed and extended is harmful to society generally. In any event the appellants in this case did not mutilate their own bodies. They inflicted bodily harm on willing victims. Suicide is no longer an offence but a person who assists another to commit suicide is guilty of murder or manslaughter.

The assertion was made on behalf of the appellants that the sexual appetites of sadists and masochists can only be satisfied by the infliction of bodily harm and that the law should not punish the consensual achievement of sexual satisfaction. There was no evidence to support the assertion that sado-masochist activities are essential to the happiness of the appellants or any other participants but the argument would be acceptable if sado-masochism were only concerned with sex, as the appellants contend. In my opinion sado-masochism is not only concerned with sex. Sado-masochism is also concerned with violence. The evidence discloses that the practices of the appellants were unpredictably dangerous and degrading to body and mind and were developed with increasing barbarity and taught to persons whose consents were dubious or worthless.

. . . The dangers involved in administering violence must have been appreciated by the appellants because, so it was said by their counsel, each victim was given a code word which he could pronounce when excessive harm or pain was caused. The efficiency of this precaution, when taken, depends on the circumstances and on the personalities involved. No one can feel the pain of another. The charges against the appellants were based on genital torture and violence to the buttocks, anus, penis, testicles and nipples. The victims were degraded and humiliated, sometimes beaten, sometimes wounded with instruments and sometimes branded. Bloodletting and the smearing of human blood produced excitement. There were obvious dangers of serious personal injury and blood infection. Prosecuting counsel informed the trial judge against the protests of defence counsel, that although the appellants had not contracted AIDS, two members of the group had died from AIDS and one other had contracted an HIV infection although not necessarily from the practices of the group. Some activities involved excrement. The assertion that the instruments employed by the sadists were clean and sterilized could not have removed the danger of infection, and the assertion that care was taken demonstrates the possibility of infection. Cruelty to human beings was on occasions supplemented by cruelty to animals in the form of bestiality. It is fortunate that there were no permanent injuries to a victim though no one knows the extent of harm inflicted in other cases. It is not surprising that a victim does not complain to the police when the complaint would involve him in giving details of acts in which he participated. Doctors of course are subject to a code of confidentiality.

In principle there is a difference between violence which is incidental and violence which is inflicted for the indulgence of cruelty. The violence of sado-masochistic encounters involves the indulgence of cruelty by sadists and the degradation of victims. Such violence is injurious to the participants and unpredictably dangerous. I am not prepared to invent a defence of consent for sado-masochistic encounters which breed and glorify cruelty and result in offences under ss.47 and 20 of the Act of 1861.

. . . Society is entitled and bound to protect itself against a cult of violence. Pleasure derived from the infliction of pain is an evil thing. Cruelty is uncivilised. I would answer the certified question in the negative and dismiss the appeals of the appellants against conviction.

LORD JAUNCEY OF TULLICHETTLE

The basic argument propounded by all the appellants was that the receivers having in every case consented to what was inflicted upon them no offence had been committed against ss.20 or 47 of the Offences Against the Person Act 1861. All the appellants recognised however that so broad a proposition could not stand up and that there must be some limitation upon the harm which an individual could consent to receive at the hand of another. The line between injuries to the infliction of which an individual could consent and injuries to whose infliction he could not consent must be drawn it was argued where the public interest required . . .

[His Lordship quoted extensively from *Coney*, *Donovan* and *Attorney General's Reference (No.6 of 1980)*.] Although the reasoning in these [last] two cases differs somewhat, the conclusion from each of them is clear, namely, that the infliction of bodily harm without good reason is unlawful and that the consent of the victim is irrelevant. In the unreported case of *R. v Boyea* (January 28, 1992) (see [1992] Crim.L.R. 23), in which the appellant was convicted of indecent assault on a woman, Glidewell L.J. giving the judgment of the Court of Appeal (Criminal Division) said:

'The central proposition in *Donovan* is in our view consistent with the decision of the court in the *Attorney-General's Reference (No.6 of 1980)*. That proposition can be expressed as follows: an assault intended or which is likely to cause bodily harm, accompanied by indecency, is an offence irrespective of consent, provided that the injury is not 'transient or trifling'.

Glidewell L.J. went on to point out that having regard to the change in social attitude towards sexual relations 'transient and trivial' must be understood in the light of conditions prevailing in 1992 rather than in 1934.

Before considering whether the above four cases were correctly decided and if so what relevance they have to these appeals, I must say a word about hostility. It was urged upon your Lordships that hostility on the part of the inflicter was an essential ingredient of assault and that this ingredient was necessarily lacking when injury was inflicted with the consent of the receiver. It followed that none of the activities in question constituted assault. The answer to this submission is to be found in the judgment of the Court of Appeal in *Wilson v Pringle* [1987] Q.B. 237 where it was said, at p.253 that hostility could not be equated with ill will or malevolence. The judgment went on to state:

'Take the example of the police officer in *Collins v Wilcock* [1984] 1 W.L.R. 1172. She touched the woman deliberately, but without an intention to do more than restrain her temporarily. Nevertheless, she was acting unlawfully and in that way was acting with hostility.'

If the appellant's activities in relation to the receivers were unlawful they were also hostile and a necessary ingredient of assault was present.

It was accepted by all the appellants that a line had to be drawn somewhere between those injuries to which a person could consent to infliction upon himself and those which were so serious that consent was immaterial. They all agreed that assaults occasioning actual bodily harm should be below the line but there was disagreement as to whether all offences against s.20 of the Act of 1861 should be above the line or only those resulting in grievous bodily harm. The four English cases to which I have referred were not concerned with the distinction between the various types of assault and did not therefore have to address the problem raised in these appeals . . .

I prefer the reasoning of Cave J. in *Coney* and of the Court of Appeal in the later three English cases which I consider to have been correctly decided. In my view the line properly falls to be drawn between assault at common law and the offence of assault occasioning actual bodily harm created by s.47 of the Offences Against the Person Act 1861, with the result that consent of the victim is no answer to anyone charged with the latter offence or with a contravention of s.20 unless the circumstances fall within one of the well known exceptions such as organised sporting contests and games, parental chastisement or reasonable surgery. There is nothing in ss.20 and 47 of the Act of 1861 to suggest that consent is either an essential ingredient of the offences or a defence thereto . . .

I would therefore dispose of these appeals on the basis that the infliction of actual or more serious bodily harm is an unlawful activity to which consent is no answer . . . Notwithstanding the views which I have come to, I think it right to say something about the submissions that consent to the activity of the appellants would not be injurious to the public interest.

Considerable emphasis was placed by the appellants on the well-ordered and secret manner in which their activities were conducted and upon the fact that these activities had resulted in no injuries which required medical attention. There was, it was said, no question of proselytising by the appellants . . .

Be that as it may, in considering the public interest it would be wrong to look only at the activities of the appellants alone, there being no suggestion that they and their associates are the only practitioners of homosexual sado-masochism in England and Wales. This House must therefore consider the possibility that these activities are practised by others and by others who are not so controlled or responsible as the appellants are claimed to be. Without going into details of all the rather curious activities in which the appellants engaged it would appear to be good luck rather than good judgment which has prevented serious injury from occurring. Wounds can easily become septic if not properly treated, the free flow of blood from a person who is H.I.V. positive or who has AIDS can infect another and an inflicter who is carried away by sexual excitement or by drink or drugs could very easily inflict pain and injury beyond the level to which the receiver had consented. Your Lordships have no information as to whether such situations have occurred in relation to other sado-masochistic practitioners. It was no doubt these dangers which caused Lady Mallalieu to restrict her propositions in relation to public interest to the actual rather than the potential result of the activity. In my view such a restriction is quite unjustified. When considering the public interest potential for harm is just as relevant as actual harm. As Mathew J. said in *Coney* at p.547:

'There is however abundant authority for saying that no consent can render that innocent which is in fact dangerous.'

Furthermore, the possibility of proselytisation and corruption of young men is a real danger even in the case of these appellants and the taking of video recordings of such activities suggest that secrecy may not be as strict as the appellants claimed to your Lordships. If the only purpose of the activity is the sexual gratification of one or both of the participants what then is the need of a video recording?

My Lords I have no doubt that it would not be in the public interest that deliberate infliction of actual bodily harm during the course of homosexual sado-masochistic activities should be held to be lawful. In reaching this conclusion I have regard to the information available in these appeals and [to] such inferences as may be drawn therefrom. I appreciate that there may be a great deal of information relevant to these activities which is not available to your Lordships. When Parliament passed the Sexual Offences Act 1967 which made buggery and acts of gross indecency between consenting males lawful it had available the Wolfenden Report (1957) (Cmnd. 247) which was the product of an exhaustive research into the problem. If it is to be decided that such activities as the nailing by A of B's foreskin or scrotum to a board or the insertion of hot wax into C's urethra followed by the burning of his penis with a candle or the incising of D's scrotum with a scalpel to the effusion of blood are injurious neither to B, C and D nor to the public interest then it is for Parliament with its accumulated wisdom and sources of information to declare them to be lawful.

Two further matters only require to be mentioned. There was argument as to whether consent, where available, was a necessary ingredient of the offence of assault or merely a defence. There are conflicting dicta as to its effect. In *Coney* Stephen J. referred to consent as 'being no defence', whereas in *Attorney-General's Reference (No. 6 of 1980)* Lord Lane C.J. referred to the onus being on the prosecution to negative consent. In *Collins v Wilcock* Goff L.J. referred to consent being a defence to a battery. If it were necessary, which it is not, in this appeal to decide which argument was correct I would hold that consent was a defence to but not a necessary ingredient in assault . . .

My Lords, I would answer the certified question in the negative and dismiss the appeals.

LORD LOWRY

. . . [After considering *Coney, Donovan, Attorney General's Reference*, and the judgment of the Court of Appeal in the instant case, and noting that the Court considered that the question of consent was immaterial:] If, as I, too, consider, the question of consent is immaterial, there are prima facie offences against ss.20 and 47 and the next question is whether there is good reason to add sado-masochistic acts to the list of exceptions contemplated in *Attorney-General's Reference*. In my opinion, the answer to that question is 'No'.

In adopting this conclusion I follow closely my noble and learned friends Lord Templeman and Lord Jauncey. What the appellants are obliged to propose is that the deliberate and painful infliction of physical injury should be exempted from the operation of statutory provisions the object of which is to prevent or punish that very thing, the reason for the proposed exemption being that both those who will inflict and those who will suffer the injury wish to satisfy a perverted and depraved sexual desire. Sado-masochistic homosexual activity cannot be regarded as conductive to the enhancement or enjoyment of family life or conducive to the welfare of society. A relaxation of the prohibitions in ss.20 and 47 can only encourage the practice of homosexual sado-masochism and the physical cruelty that it must involve (which can scarcely be regarded as a 'manly diversion') by withdrawing the legal penalty and giving the activity a judicial imprimatur. As well as all this, one cannot overlook the physical danger to those who may indulge in sado-masochism. In this connection, and also generally, it is idle for the appellants to claim that they are educated exponents of 'civilised cruelty'. A proposed general exemption is to be tested by considering the likely *general* effect. This must include the probability that some sado-masochistic activity, under the powerful influence of the sexual instinct, will get out of hand and result in serious physical damage to the participants and that some activity will involve a danger of infection such as these particular exponents do not contemplate for themselves. When considering the danger of infection, with its inevitable threat of AIDS, I am not impressed by the argument that this threat can be discounted on the ground that, as long ago as 1967, Parliament, subject to conditions, legalised buggery, now a well-known vehicle for the transmission of AIDS.

So far as I can see, the only counter-argument is that to place a restriction on sado-masochism is an unwarranted interference with the private life and activities of persons who are indulging in a lawful pursuit and are doing no harm to anyone except, possibly, themselves. This approach, which has characterised every submission put forward on behalf of the appellants, is derived from the fallacy that what is involved here is the restraint of a lawful activity as opposed [to] the refusal to relax existing prohibitions in the 1861 Act. If in the course of buggery, as authorised by the 1967 Act, one participant, either with the other participant's consent or not, deliberately causes actual bodily harm to that other, an offence against s.47 has been committed. The 1967 Act provides no shield. The position is as simple as that, and there is *no legal right to cause actual bodily harm* in the course of sado-masochistic activity . . ..

For all these reasons I would answer 'No' to the certified question and would dismiss the appeals.

LORD MUSTILL

This is a case about the criminal law of violence. In my opinion it should be a case about the criminal law of private sexual relations, if about anything at all. Right or wrong, the point is easily made . . . If the criminality of sexual deviation is the true ground of these proceedings, one would have expected that these above all would have been the subject of attack. Yet the picture is quite different.

The conduct of the appellants and of other co-accused was treated by the prosecuting authorities in three ways. First, there were those acts which fell squarely within the legislation governing sexual offences. These are easily overlooked, because attention has properly been concentrated on the charges which remain in dispute, but for a proper understanding of the case it is essential to keep them in view. Thus, four of the men pleaded guilty either as principals or as aiders and abettors to the charges of keeping a disorderly house . . .

Laskey also pleaded guilty to two counts of publishing an obscene article. The articles in question were video-tapes of the activities which formed the subject of some of the counts laid under the Act of 1861.

The pleas of guilty to these counts, which might be regarded as dealing quite comprehensively with those aspects of Laskey's sexual conduct which impinged directly on public order attracted sentences of four years reduced on appeal to eighteen months imprisonment and three months imprisonment respectively. Other persons, not before the House, were dealt with in a similar way.

The two remaining categories of conduct comprised private acts. Some were prosecuted and are now before the House. Others, which I have mentioned, were not. If repugnance to general public sentiments of morality and propriety were the test, one would have expected proceedings in respect of the most disgusting conduct to be prosecuted with the greater vigour. Yet the opposite is the case. Why is this so? Obviously because the prosecuting authorities could find no statutory prohibition apt to cover this conduct. Whereas the sexual conduct which underlies the present appeals, although less extreme, could at least arguably be brought within ss.20 and 47 of the 1861 Act because it involved the breaking of skin and the infliction of more than trifling hurt.

I must confess that this distribution of the charges against the appellants at once sounds a note of warning. It suggests that the involvement of the Act of 1861 was adventitious. This impression is reinforced when one considers the title of the statute under which the appellants are charged, 'Offences *Against* the Person'. Conduct infringing ss.18, 20 and 47 of the Act of 1861 comes before the Crown Courts every day. Typically it involves brutality, aggression and violence, of a kind far removed from the appellants' behaviour which, however worthy of censure, involved no animosity, no aggression, no personal rancour on the part of the person inflicting the hurt towards the recipient and no protest by the recipient. In fact, quite the reverse. Of course we must give effect to the statute if its words capture what the appellants have done, but in deciding whether this is really so it is in my opinion legitimate to assume that the choice of the Offences Against the Person Act as the basis for the relevant counts in the indictment was made only because no other statute was found which could conceivably be brought to bear upon them.

In these circumstances I find it easy to share the opinion expressed by Wills J. in *R. v Clarence*, a case where the accused had consensual intercourse with his wife, he knowing and she ignorant that he suffered from gonorrhoea, with the result that she was infected. The case is of general importance, since the Court for Crown Cases Reserved held that there was no offence under ss.47 and 20, since both sections required an assault, of which the wound or grievous bodily harm was the result, and that no assault was disclosed on the facts. For present purposes, however, I need only quote from the report, at p.30:

'. . . such considerations lead one to pause on the threshold, and enquire whether the enactment under consideration could really have been intended to apply to circumstances so completely removed from those which are usually understood when an assault is spoken of, or to deal with matters of any kind involving the sexual relation or act.'

I too am led to pause on the threshold. Asking myself the same question, I cannot but give a negative answer. I therefore approach the appeal on the basis that the convictions on charges which seem to me so inapposite cannot be upheld unless the language of the statute or the logic of the decided cases positively so demand. Unfortunately, as the able arguments which we have heard so clearly demonstrate, the language of the statute is opaque, and the cases few and unhelpful. To these I now turn . . .

[After considering the law on Death, Maiming, Prizefighting, "Contact" Sports, Surgery, Lawful Correction, Dangerous Pastimes, Rough Horseplay, Prostitution, and Fighting, and concluding that he would not accept that the infliction of bodily harm, and especially the private infliction of it, is invariably criminal, absent some special factor which decrees otherwise:] For these reasons, I consider that the House is free, as the Court of Appeal in the present case was not . . . free, to consider entirely afresh whether the public interest demands the interpretation of the Act of 1861 in such a way as to render criminal under s.47 the acts done by the appellants.

[After holding that the general tenor of the decisions of the European Court on the European Convention on Human Rights clearly favoured the right of the appellants to conduct their private lives undisturbed by the criminal law:] The purpose of this long discussion has been to suggest that the decks are clear for the House to tackle completely anew the question whether the public interest requires s.47 of the 1861 Act to be interpreted as penalising an infliction of harm which is at the level of actual bodily harm, but not grievous bodily harm; which is inflicted in private (by which I mean that it is exposed to the view only of those who have chosen to view it); which takes place not only with the consent of the recipient but with his willing and glad co-operation; which is inflicted for the gratification of sexual desire, and not in a spirit of animosity or rage; and which is not engaged in for profit.

My Lords, I have stated the issue in these terms to stress two considerations of cardinal importance. Lawyers will need no reminding of the first, but since this prosecution has been widely noticed it must be emphasised that the issue before the House is not whether the appellants' conduct is morally right, but whether it is properly charged under the Act of 1861. When proposing that the conduct is not rightly so charged I do not invite your Lordships' House to endorse it as morally acceptable. Nor do I pronounce in favour of a libertarian doctrine specifically related to sexual matters. Nor in the least do I suggest that ethical pronouncements are meaningless, that there is no difference between right and wrong, that sadism is praiseworthy, or that new opinions on sexual morality are necessarily superior to the old, or anything else of the same kind. What I do say is that these are questions of private morality; that the standards by which they fall to be judged are not those of the criminal law; and that if these standards are to be upheld the individual must enforce them upon himself according to his own moral standards, or have them enforced against him by moral pressures exerted by whatever religious or other community to whose ethical ideals he responds. The point from which I invite your Lordships to depart is simply this, that the state should interfere with the rights of an individual to live his or her life as he or she may choose no more than is necessary to ensure a proper balance between the special interests of the individual and the general interests of the individuals who together comprise the populace at large. Thus, whilst acknowledging that very many people, if asked whether the appellants' conduct was wrong, would reply 'Yes, repulsively wrong', I would at the same time assert that this does not in itself mean that the prosecution of the appellants under ss.20 and 47 of the Offences Against the Person Act 1861 is well founded.

This point leads directly to the second. As I have ventured to formulate the crucial question, it asks whether there is good reason to impress upon s.47 an interpretation which penalises the relevant level of harm irrespective of consent: i.e. to recognise sado-masochistic activities as falling into a special category of acts, such as duelling and prize-fighting, which 'the law says shall not be done.' This is very important, for if the question were differently stated it might well yield a different answer. In particular, if it were to be held that as a matter of law all infliction of bodily harm above the level of common assault is incapable of being legitimated by consent, except in special circumstances, then we would have to consider whether the public interest required the recognition of private sexual activities as being in a specially exempt category. This would be an altogether more difficult question and one which I would not be prepared to answer in favour of the appellants, not because I do not have my own opinions upon it but because I regard the task as one which the courts are not suited to perform, and which should be carried out, if at all, by Parliament after a thorough review of all the medical, social, moral and political issues, such as was performed by the Wolfenden Committee. Thus, if I had begun from the same point of departure as my noble and learned friend Lord Jauncey of Tullichettle I would have arrived at a similar conclusion; but differing from him on the present state of the law, I venture to differ.

Let it be assumed however that we should embark upon this question. I ask myself, not whether as a result of the decision in this appeal, activities such as those of the appellants should *cease* to be criminal, but rather whether the Act of 1861 (a statute which I venture to repeat once again was clearly intended to penalise conduct of a quite different nature) should in this new situation be interpreted so as to *make* it criminal. Why should this step be taken? Leaving aside repugnance and moral objection, both of which are entirely natural but neither of which are in my opinion grounds upon which the court could properly create a new crime, I can visualise only the following reasons:

1. Some of the practices obviously created a risk of genito-urinary infection, and others of septicaemia. These might indeed have been grave in former times, but the risk of serious harm must surely have been greatly reduced by modern medical science.

2. The possibility that matters might get out of hand, with grave results. It has been acknowledged throughout the present proceedings that the appellants' activities were performed as a pre-arranged ritual, which at the same time enhanced their excitement and minimised the risk that the infliction of injury would go too far. Of course things might go wrong and really serious injury or death might ensue. If this happened, those responsible would be punished according to the ordinary law, in the same way as those who kill or injure in the course of more ordinary sexual activities are regularly punished. But to penalise the appellants' conduct even if the extreme consequences do not ensue, just because they might have done so would require an assessment of the degree of risk, and the balancing of this risk against the interests of individual freedom. Such a balancing is in my opinion for Parliament, not the courts; and even if your Lordships' House were to embark upon it the attempt must in my opinion fail at the outset for there is no evidence at all of the seriousness of the hazards to which sado-masochistic conduct of this kind gives rise. This is not surprising, since the impressive argument of Mr Purnell Q.C. for the respondents did not seek to persuade your Lordships' to bring the matter within the Act of 1861 on the ground of special risks, but rather to establish that the appellants are liable *under the general law* because the level of harm exceeded the critical level marking off criminal from non-criminal consensual violence which he invited your Lordships to endorse.

3. I would give the same answer to the suggestion that these activities involved a risk of accelerating the spread of auto-immune deficiency syndrome, and that they should be brought within the Act of 1861 in the interests of public health. The consequence would be strange, since what is currently the principal cause for the transmission of this scourge, namely consenting buggery between males, is now legal. Nevertheless, I would have been compelled to give this proposition the most anxious consideration if there had been any evidence to support it. But there is none, since the case for the respondent was advanced on an entirely different ground.

4. There remains an argument to which I have given much greater weight. As the evidence in the present case has shown, there is a risk that strangers (and especially young strangers) may be drawn into these activities at an early age and will then become established in them for life. This is indeed a disturbing prospect, but I have come to the conclusion that it is not a sufficient ground for declaring these activities to be criminal under the Act of 1861. The element of the corruption of youth is already catered for by the existing legislation; and if there is a gap in it which needs to be filled the remedy surely lies in the hands of Parliament, not in the application of a statute which is aimed at other forms of wrong doing. As regards proselytisation for adult sado-masochism the argument appears to me circular. For if the activity is not itself so much against the public interest that it ought to be declared criminal under the Act of 1861 then the risk that others will be induced to join in cannot be a ground for making it criminal.

Leaving aside the logic of this answer, which seems to me impregnable, plain humanity demands that a court addressing the criminality of conduct such as that of the present should recognise and respond to the profound dismay which all members of the community share about the apparent increase of cruel and senseless crimes against the defenceless. Whilst doing so I must repeat for the last time that in the answer which I propose I do not advocate the de-criminalisation of conduct which has hitherto been a crime; nor do I rebut a submission that a new crime should be created, penalising this conduct, for Mr. Purnell has rightly not invited the House to take this course. The only question is whether these consensual private acts are offences against the existing law of violence. To this question I return a negative response.

Accordingly I would allow these appeals and quash such of the convictions as are now before the House.

LORD SLYNN OF HADLEY

Three propositions seem to me to be clear.

It is '. . . inherent in the conception of assault and battery that the victim does not consent' (Glanville Williams [1962] Crim.L.R. 74, 75). Secondly, consent must be full and free and must be as to the actual level of force used or pain inflicted. Thirdly, there exist areas where the law disregards the victim's consent even where that consent is freely and fully given. These areas may relate to the person (e.g. a child); they may relate to the place (e.g. in public); they may relate to the nature of the harm done. It is the latter which is in issue in the present case.

I accept that consent cannot be said simply to be a defence to any act which one person does to another. A line has to be drawn as to what can and as to what cannot be the subject of consent . . .

I do not think a line can simply be drawn between 'maiming' and death on the one hand and everything else on the other hand. The rationale for negating consent when maiming occurred has gone. It is, however, possible to draw the line, and the line should be drawn, between really serious injury on the one hand and less serious injuries on the other. I do not accept that it is right to take common assault as the sole category of assaults to which consent can be a defence and to deny that defence in respect of all other injuries. In the first place the range of injuries which can fall within 'actual bodily harm' is wide—the description of two beatings in the present case show that one is much more substantial than the other. Further, the same is true of wounding where the test is whether the skin is broken and where it can be more or less serious. I can see no significant reason for refusing consent as a defence for the lesser of these cases of actual bodily harm and wounding.

If a line has to be drawn, as I think it must, to be workable, it cannot be allowed to fluctuate within particular charges and in the interests of legal certainty it has to be accepted that consent can be given to acts which are said to constitute actual bodily harm and wounding. Grievous bodily harm I accept to be different by analogy with and as an extension of the old cases on maiming. Accordingly, I accept that other than for cases of grievous bodily harm or death, consent can be a defence. This in no way means that the acts done are approved of or encouraged. It means no more than that the acts do not constitute as assault within the meaning of these two specific sections of the Offences Against the Person Act 1861.

None of the convictions in the present cases have been on the basis that grievous bodily harm was caused. Whether some of the acts done in these cases might have fallen within that category does not seem to me to be relevant for present purposes . . .

In the present cases there is no doubt that there was consent; indeed there was more than mere consent. Astonishing though it may seem, the persons involved positively wanted, asked for, the acts to be done to them, acts which it seems from the evidence some of them also did to themselves. All the accused were old enough to know what they were doing. The acts were done in private. Neither the applicants nor anyone else complained as to what was done. The matter came to the attention of the police 'coincidentally'; the police were previously unaware that the accused were involved in these practices though some of them had been involved for many years. The acts did not result in any permanent or serious injury or disability or any infection and no medical assistance was required even though there may have been some risk of infection, even injury.

There has been much argument as to whether lack of consent is a constituent of the offence which must be proved by the prosecution or whether consent is simply raised by way of defence . . .

My conclusion is thus that as the law stands, adults can consent to acts done in private which do not result in serious bodily harm, so that such acts do not constitute criminal assaults for the purposes of the Act of 1861.

. . . I agree that in the end it is a matter of policy. It is a matter of policy in an area where social and moral factors are extremely important and where attitudes can change. In my opinion it is a matter of policy for the legislature to decide. If society takes the view that this kind of behaviour, even though sought after and done in private, is either so new or so extensive or so undesirable that it should be brought now for the first time within the criminal law, then it is for the legislature to decide. It is not for the courts in the interests of 'paternalism', as referred to in the passage I have quoted, or in order to protect people from themselves, to introduce, into existing statutory crimes relating to offences *against* the person, concepts which do not properly fit there. If Parliament considers that the behaviour revealed here should be made specifically criminal, then the Offences Against the Person Act 1861 can be amended specifically to define it. Alternatively, if it is intended that this sort of conduct should be lawful as between two persons but not between more than two persons as falling within the offence of gross indecency, then the limitation period for prosecution can be extended and the penalties increased where sado-masochistic acts are involved. That is obviously a possible course; whether it is a desirable way of changing the law is a different question.

Accordingly I consider that these appeals should be allowed and the conviction set aside.

Appeals dismissed

Questions

1. Was the case decided at first instance on the basis that the consents of the "Victims" were dubious or worthless as Lord Templeman contends?

2. If, as is alleged, juveniles were corrupted, is this relevant to the issue before the court? Of what relevance is the spectre of AIDS, the use of excrement or the suggestion of bestiality to the issue whether an offence contrary to s.47 had been committed? Is the risk of HIV infection confined to homosexual sado-masochists?

3. If society is entitled to protect itself against a cult of violence, were any unwilling members of society liable to be the victims of the sado-masochists' cult of violence, thereby demanding protection from the law? Are the "Victims" calling for protection? Are they any more protected following *Brown* than they were before if, as the Law Commission indicate in *Consent in the Criminal Law* (TSO, 1995), Consultation Paper No.139, Part X, sado-masochism is being driven further underground, education and advice on safe SM techniques is being hampered and people are afraid to seek medical assistance if they have problems?

4. It was argued that the line between what was lawful and unlawful should be drawn between actual bodily harm and grievous bodily harm. The House of Lords rejected this as it would cause problems for juries dealing with grievous bodily harm under s.20 of the Offences Against the Person Act 1861. Are all such problems removed by drawing the line between simple assault occasioning actual bodily harm contrary to s.47?

5. As all three of their Lordships in the majority focused on the homosexual aspect of these sado-masochistic encounters, is the ratio of *Brown* confined to homosexual sado-masochism?

6. In *Attorney General's Reference (No.6 of 1980)* [1981] 1 Q.B. 715 Lord Lane CJ stated (at p.719): ". . . it is not in the public interest that people should try to cause or should cause each other bodily harm for no good reason . . . [I]t is an assault if actual bodily harm is intended and/or caused." This statement was quoted with approval by all three of their Lordships in the majority in *Brown*. A and B are engaging in consensual heterosexual activity. A does something to B to which she consents, which is not intended to but which does cause an injury which is more than transient or trifling. Is A guilty of assault occasioning actual bodily harm or even indecent assault? See *R. v Boyea* [1992] Crim. L.R. 574; cf. *R. v Simon Slingsby* [1995] Crim. L.R. 570 and *R. v Savage* [1992] 1 A.C. 699 (below, p.553).

Note

Following the decision of the House of Lords, three of the appellants complained to the European Commission of Human Rights that their convictions violated their right to respect for private life guaranteed by art.8 of the Convention. In *Laskey, Jaggard and Brown v United Kingdom* (Case No.109/1995/615/703–705) the European Court of Human Rights held that while the prosecution of the applicants interfered in their private lives, this was "necessary in a democratic society" in pursuance of a legitimate aim, namely that of the "protection of health."

R. V WILSON

[1996] 3 W.L.R. 125 CA

At his wife's instigation, W branded his initials on his wife's buttocks with a hot knife. He was convicted of assault occasioning actual bodily harm contrary to s.47 of the Offences Against the Person Act 1861 and appealed.

RUSSELL LJ

. . . We are abundantly satisfied that there is no factual comparison to be made between the instant case and the facts of either *R. v Donovan* [1934] 2 K.B. 498 or *R. v Brown* [1994] 1 A.C. 212: Mrs. Wilson not only consented to that which the appellant did, she instigated it. There was no aggressive intent on the part of the appellant. On the contrary, far from wishing to cause injury to his wife, the appellant's desire was to assist her in what she regarded as the acquisition of a desirable piece of personal adornment, perhaps in this day and age no less understandable than the piercing of nostrils or even tongues for the purposes of inserting decorative jewellery.

In our judgment *R. v Brown* is not authority for the proposition that consent is no defence to a charge under s.47 of the Act of 1861, in all circumstances where actual bodily harm is deliberately inflicted. It is to be observed that the question certified for their Lordships in *R. v Brown* related only to a 'sado-masochistic encounter'. However, their Lordships recognised in the course of their speeches, that it is necessary that there must be exceptions to what is no more than a general proposition. The speeches of Lord Templeman, at p.231, Lord Jauncey of Tullichettle, at p.245, and the dissenting speech of Lord Slynn of Hadley, at p.277, all refer to tattooing as being an activity which, if carried out with the consent of an adult, does not involve an offence under s.47, albeit that actual bodily harm is deliberately inflicted.

For our part, we cannot detect any logical difference between what the appellant did and what he might have done in the way of tattooing. The latter activity apparently requires no state authorisation, and the appellant was as free to engage in it as anyone else. We do not think that we are entitled to assume that the method adopted by the appellant and his wife was any more dangerous or painful than tattooing. There was simply no evidence to assist the court on this aspect of the matter.

Does public policy or the public interest demand that the appellant's activity should be visited by the sanctions of the criminal law? The majority in *R. v Brown* clearly took the view that such considerations were relevant. If that is so, then we are firmly of the opinion that it is not in the public interest that activities such as the appellant's in this appeal should amount to criminal behaviour. Consensual activity between husband and wife, in the privacy of the matrimonial home, is not, in our judgment, normally a proper matter for criminal investigation, let alone criminal prosecution. Accordingly we take the view that the judge failed to have full regard to the facts of this case and misdirected himself in saying that *R. v Donovan* [1934] 2 K.B. 498 and *R. v Brown* [1994] 1 A.C. 212 constrained him to rule that consent was no defence.

In this field, in our judgment, the law should develop upon a case by case basis rather than upon general propositions to which, in the changing times in which we live, exceptions may arise from time to time not expressly covered by authority.

We shall allow the appeal and quash the conviction. We conclude this judgment by commenting that we share the judge's disquiet that the prosecuting authority thought it fit to bring these proceedings. In our view they serve no useful purpose at considerable public expense.

Appeal allowed with costs

Conviction quashed

Questions

1.   In what way is there an "aggressive intent" where one partner in a sexual relationship causes pain to the other at the request of the other?

2.   In light of the fact that branding was one of the activities carried out by the appellants in *Brown*,

would the Court of Appeal have arrived at the same conclusion if: (i) Mrs Wilson had requested the branding not for motives of personal adornment but because she found pain enhanced her sexual fulfilment; or (ii) Mr Wilson had confessed that he found it sexually arousing to brand his wife?

3. Russell LJ stated, "Does public policy or the public interest demand that the appellant's activity should be visited by the sanctions of the criminal law?" How does this approach compare with those of the majority and the minority in *Brown*?

4. Is this decision confined to "consensual activity between husband and wife, in the privacy of the matrimonial home" or would it apply to: (i) an unmarried couple, or (ii) a gay or lesbian couple?

5. In *Brown* Lord Mustill included religious mortification in the list of activities to which consent to actual bodily harm is a defence. In the Scottish case *William Fraser* (1847) Ark 280 at 302, Lord MacKenzie stated, "In some circumstances, a beating may be consented to, as . . . in a case of a father confessor ordering flagellation; but this is not violence or assault, because there is consent". A and B are priests living together in a homosexual relationship. A requests B to flagellate him for purposes of religious mortification. B whips A's back and buttocks causing cuts and weals which amount to actual bodily harm. Subsequently B requests A to flagellate him as he finds this sexually stimulating. A whips B's back and buttocks causing cuts and weals which amount to actual bodily harm. Do either or both instances of flagellation constitute an offence? If the answer differs what are the public policy issues which support this difference of result? Would the outcome in the second case differ if B had kept his purpose of sexual gratification secret from A and A had whipped him with equal vigour believing it was for the purpose of religious mortification?

Notes

1. In *Emmett The Times* 15 October 1999, D was convicted of two counts of assault occasioning actual bodily harm arising from consensual sexual activity with his fiancée (involving asphyxiation on the first occasion and the use of lighter fluid on the second) as a result of which she suffered "subconjunctival haemorrhages in both eyes and some petechial bruising around her neck" and "a burn, measuring some 6cm x 4cm" on her breast. The trial judge ruled that consent was not available as a defence where the parties foresaw the risk of injury arising from their consensual sexual activities. The Court of Appeal saw no reason in principle "to draw any distinction between sadomasochistic activity on a heterosexual basis and that which is conducted in a homosexual context". The Court of Appeal stated that the "actual or potential damage to which the appellant's partner was exposed in this case, plainly went far beyond that which was established by the evidence in *Wilson*".

2. The approach in *R. v Slingsby* [1995] Crim. L.R. 570 that vigorous consensual sexual activity which resulted in injury that was neither foreseen nor intended was not criminal, was endorsed in *R. v Meachen* [2006] EWCA Crim 2414. In the latter case, the defendant's convictions of inflicting grievous bodily harm and indecent assault were quashed. Thomas LJ stated:

    "It is sufficient to make clear that if the touching was with consent, then the fact that in the course of the consensual activity some bodily injury, even serious bodily injury, resulted accidentally and unintentionally, then as a matter or principle no criminality can attach."

It should be noted that now the relevant sexual offence is sexual assault contrary to s.3 of the Sexual Offences Act 2003 (see below, p.592) which differs from indecent assault as the issue of consent is relevant in every case; if V consented to D's touching in sexual circumstances, that consent will negate liability even if harm resulted. It would be strange in such circumstances if a prosecutor chose to prosecute for assault occasioning actual bodily harm.

3.   In *R. v Barnes* [2004] EWCA Crim 3246, the Court of Appeal considered the defence of consent in relation to contact sports. The view was expressed that prosecutions should be reserved for the most serious cases where the conduct complained of could properly be categorised as criminal. Players can be taken to consent to conduct that can reasonably be expected to occur as a result of taking part in the sport concerned, but not to conduct which exceeds this. Whether the conduct complained of exceeds this depends on the all circumstances including the type of sport, the level at which it is played, the nature of the act, the degree offeree used, the extent of the risk of injury and the defendant's state of mind. In a highly competitive sport played at high level, conduct outside the rules might be expected to occur in the heat of the moment. It might be that an "offender" is penalised or even sent off the field of play but this, by itself, does not necessarily indicate that the high threshold required for criminal proceedings has been reached.

It follows that a properly directed jury will need to consider whether the conduct that causes the injury (e.g. a late tackle in a football match) was not an instinctive reaction, error or misjudgement in the heat of the moment and was so obviously violent that it can be properly labelled criminal conduct.

(c) Consent and the transmission of disease

Note

In *R. v Clarence* (1888) 22 O.B.D. 23, the defendant, knowing he had a venereal disease, had sexual intercourse with his wife, causing her to contract the disease. It was argued that by concealing his condition he had practised a fraud which vitiated consent, thereby rendering the bodily contact an assault. It was held that because there was no deception as to the nature of the act, sexual intercourse, there could be no assault, and if no assault, there could be no offence of inflicting grievous bodily harm. The matter has now been revisited in the cases that follow.

R. V DICA

[2004] Q.B. 1257

The defendant, knowing that he was HIV positive, had unprotected consensual sexual intercourse with two women, who were both subsequently diagnosed as HIV positive. The defendant was charged with two counts of inflicting grievous bodily harm, contrary to s.20 of the Offences Against the Person Act 1861, on the basis that he had recklessly transmitted the disease to the women when they did not know of, and did not consent to, the risk of infection. At the end of the prosecution case, the judge ruled that it was open to the jury to convict the defendant of the offences alleged and that whether the women knew of the defendant's condition was irrelevant since, following *Brown*, they did not have the legal capacity to consent to such serious harm. Following that ruling, the defendant, who would have contended that the women had known about his condition but, nevertheless, had been willing to have sexual intercourse with him, did not give evidence. He was convicted on both counts.

JUDGE LJ

It was not in dispute that at least on the majority of occasions, and with both complainants, sexual intercourse was unprotected. Recklessness, as such, was not in issue. If protective measures had been taken by the defendant that would have provided material relevant to the jury's decision whether, in all the circumstances, recklessness was proved.

Although both women were willing to have sexual intercourse with the defendant, the prosecution's case was that their agreement would never have been given if they had known of the defendant's condition. The defendant would have contended that he told both women of his condition, and that they were nonetheless willing to have sexual intercourse with him, a case which in the light of the judge's ruling, he did not support in evidence. The suggestion would have been strongly disputed by them both. At the end of the prosecution case, Judge Philpot made two critical but distinct rulings. First, he concluded that notwithstanding the well-known decision by the Crown Cases Reserved in *R v Clarence* (1888) 22 QBD 23, it was open to the jury to convict the defendant of the offences alleged in the indictment, on the basis that its standing as 'an important precedent has been thoroughly undermined, and provides no guidance to a (first) instance judge'. His second conclusion, which in a sense was more far reaching, was that whether or not the complainants knew of the defendant's condition, their consent, if any, was irrelevant and provided no defence. Accepting the Crown's argument as advanced to him, the judge believed that the decision in the House of Lords in *R v Brown* [1994] 1 A.C. 212 (above) deprived the complainants 'of the legal capacity to consent to such serious harm'.

Following that ruling the defendant elected not to give evidence, and the issue whether the complainants consented to have sexual intercourse with him knowing of his condition was not left to the jury. Mr Carter-Manning, arguing the case on behalf of the defendant before this court, contends that both these rulings were wrong in law [His Lordship then reviewed the authorities including *R v Chan-Fook* [1994] 1 W.L.R. 689; and *R v Ireland* 1998] A.C. 147 (see below, p.567) and, in light of these authorities, continued:] . . . In our judgment, the reasoning which led the majority in *Clarence* to decide that the conviction under s.20 should be quashed has no continuing application. If that case were decided today, the conviction under s.20 would be upheld. Clarence knew, but his wife did not know, and he knew that she did not know that he was suffering from gonorrhoea. Nevertheless he had sexual intercourse with her, not intending deliberately to infect her, but reckless whether she might become infected, and thus suffer grievous bodily harm. Accordingly we agree with Judge Philpot's first ruling that, not-withstanding the decision in *Clarence*, it was open to the jury to convict the defendant of the offences alleged in the indictment . . .

[His Lordship then went on to consider the second issue, the issue of consent.]

. . . The present case is concerned with and confined to s.20 offences alone, without the burdensome fiction of deemed consent to sexual intercourse. The question for decision is whether the victims' consent to sexual intercourse, which as a result of his alleged concealment was given in ignorance of the facts of the defendant's condition, necessarily amounted to consent to the risk of being infected by him. If that question must be answered 'Yes', the concept of consent in relation to s.20 is devoid of real meaning.

The position here is analogous to that considered in *R. v Tabassum* [2000] 2 Cr.App.R. 328. The appellant was convicted of indecently assaulting women who allowed him to examine their breasts in the mistaken belief that he was medically qualified. Rose L.J. considered *Clarence*, and pointed out that in relation to the infection suffered by the wife, this was an additional, unexpected, consequence of sexual intercourse, which was irrelevant to her consent to sexual intercourse with her husband. Rejecting the argument that an 'undoubted consent' could only be negatived if the victim had been deceived or mistaken about the nature and quality of the act, and that consent was not negatived 'merely because the victim would not have agreed to the act if he or she had known all the facts', Rose L.J. observed, in forthright terms, at p 337, 'there was no true consent' . . .

. . . In our view, on the assumed fact now being considered, the answer is entirely straightforward. These victims consented to sexual intercourse. Accordingly, the defendant was not guilty of rape. Given the long-term nature of the relationships, if the defendant concealed the truth about his condition from them, and therefore kept them in ignorance of it, there was no reason for them to think that they were running any risk of infection, and they were not consenting to it. On this basis, there would be no consent sufficient in law to provide the defendant with a defence to the charge under s.20.

We must now address the consequences if, contrary to their own assertions, the complainants knew of the state of the defendant's health, and notwithstanding the risks to their own, consented to sexual intercourse.

Following Judge Philpot's second ruling, this issue was not considered by the jury. In effect the judge ruled that in law such consent (if any) was irrelevant. Having listened to the exchanges on this topic between Mr Carter-Manning, for the defendant, and the court, and on further reflection, Mr Gadsden for the Crown accepted that this issue should not have been withdrawn from the jury. Although we can take the issue relatively briefly, we must explain why this concession was right. As a general rule, unless the activity is lawful, the consent of the victim to the deliberate infliction of serious bodily injury on him or her does not provide the perpetrator with any defence. Different categories of activity are regarded as lawful. Thus no one doubts that necessary major surgery with the patient's consent, even if likely to result in severe disability (e.g. an amputation) would be lawful. However the categories of activity regarded as lawful are not closed, and equally, they are not immutable. Thus, prize fighting and street fighting by consenting participants are unlawful: although some would have it banned, boxing for sport is not . . . [His Lordship then reviewed the authorities, including *R v Brown* [1994] 1 A.C. 212; and *R v Emmett*, *The Times*, 15 October 1999 and then continued . . .]

. . . These authorities demonstrate that violent conduct involving the deliberate and intentional infliction of bodily harm is and remains unlawful notwithstanding that its purpose is the sexual gratification of one or both participants. Notwithstanding their sexual overtones, these cases were concerned with violent crime, and the sexual overtones did not alter the fact that both parties were consenting to the deliberate infliction of serious harm or bodily injury on one participant by the other. To date, as a matter of public policy, it has not been thought appropriate for such violent conduct to be excused merely because there is a private consensual sexual element to it. The same public policy reason would prohibit the deliberate spreading of disease, including sexual disease.

In our judgment the impact of the authorities dealing with sexual gratification can too readily be misunderstood. It does not follow from them, and they do not suggest, that consensual acts of sexual intercourse are unlawful merely because there may be a known risk to the health of one or other participant. These participants are not intent on spreading or becoming infected with disease through sexual intercourse. They are not indulging in serious violence for the purposes of sexual gratification. They are simply prepared, knowingly, to run the risk—not the certainty—of infection, as well as all the other risks inherent in and possible consequences of sexual intercourse, such as, and despite the most careful precautions, an unintended pregnancy. At one extreme there is casual sex between complete strangers, sometimes protected, sometimes not, when the attendant risks are known to be higher, and at the other, there is sexual intercourse between couples in a long-term and loving, and trusting relationship, which may from time to time also carry risks.

The first of these categories is self-explanatory and needs no amplification. By way of illustration we shall provide two examples of cases which would fall within the second.

In the first, one of a couple suffers from HIV. It may be the man: it may be the woman. The circumstances in which HIV was contracted are irrelevant. They could result from a contaminated blood transfusion or an earlier relationship with a previous sexual partner, who unknown to the sufferer with whom we are concerned, was himself or herself infected with HIV. The parties are Roman Catholics. They are conscientiously unable to use artificial contraception. They both know of the risk that the healthy partner may become infected with HIV. Our second example is that of a young couple, desperate for a family, who are advised that if the wife were to become pregnant and give birth, her long-term health, indeed her life itself, would be at risk. Together the couple decide to run that risk, and she becomes pregnant. She may be advised that the foetus should be aborted, on the grounds of her health, yet, nevertheless, decide to bring her baby to term. If she does, and suffers ill health, is the male partner to be criminally liable for having sexual intercourse with her, notwithstanding that he knew of the risk to her health? If he is liable to be prosecuted, was she not a party to whatever crime was committed? And should the law interfere with the Roman Catholic couple, and require them, at the peril of criminal sanctions, to choose between bringing their sexual relationship to an end or violating their consciences by using contraception?

These, and similar risks, have always been taken by adults consenting to sexual intercourse. Different situations, no less potentially fraught, have to be addressed by them. Modern society has not thought to criminalise those who have willingly accepted the risks, and we know of no cases where one or other of the consenting adults has been prosecuted, let alone convicted, for the consequences of doing so. The problems of criminalising the consensual taking of risks like these include the sheer impracticability of enforcement and the haphazard nature of its impact. The process would undermine the general understanding of the community that sexual relationships are pre-eminently private and essentially personal to the individuals involved in them. And if adults were to be liable to prosecution for the consequences of taking known risks with their health, it would seem odd that this should be confined to risks taken in the context of sexual intercourse, while they are nevertheless permitted to take the risks inherent in so many other aspects of everyday life, including, again for example, the mother or father of a child suffering a serious contagious illness, who holds the child's hand, and comforts or kisses him or her goodnight. In our judgment, interference of this kind with personal autonomy, and its level and extent, may only be made by Parliament.

This, and similar questions, have already been canvassed in a number of different papers. These include the efforts made by the Law Commission to modernise the 1861 Act altogether, and replace it with up to date legislation. In relation to sexually transmitted disease, much of the discussion initially focussed on the decision in *Clarence* 22 QBD 23, and its perceived consequences, which as we have now concluded is entirely bereft of any authority in relation to s.20 of the 1861 Act. In its report Criminal Law; Legislating the Criminal Code: Offences against the Person and General Principles (1993) (Law Com No.218) (Cm 2370), the Law Commission expressed the view that intentional or reckless transmission of disease should be capable of constituting an offence against the person: para.15.1–15.17. A second publication, Consent in the Criminal Law (1995) (Law Commission Consultation Paper No.139) made a provisional proposal that precluded a defence of consent for the proposed offence of recklessly causing seriously disabling injury: para.4.46–4.51. In 1998, in response to the activities of the Law Commission, the Home Office issued a consultation paper entitled Violence: Reforming the Offences against the Person Act 1861. In this paper, the Home Office indicated that the Government had not accepted the recommendation that there should be offences to enable the intentional or reckless transmission of disease to be prosecuted. It pointed out that the issue had ramifications going beyond the criminal law into wider considerations of social and public health policy. It stated, at para.3.16. that the Government 'is particularly concerned that the law should not seem to discriminate against those who are HIV positive, have AIDS or viral hepatitis or who carry any kind of disease'. It then went on to say that there is a strong case for arguing that society should have criminal sanctions available for use to deal with evil acts, and that it was hard to argue that the law should not be able to deal with the person who gives the disease causing serious illness to others with intent to do them such harm. It then proposed that the criminal law should apply only to those whom it can be proved beyond reasonable doubt had deliberately transmitted a disease, intending to cause serious injury. It added, at para.3.18, 'This aims to strike a sensible balance between allowing very serious intentional acts to be punished whilst not rendering individuals liable for prosecution for unintentional or reckless acts, or for the transmission of minor disease.' On this approach it would seem that the policy at that stage would have been to criminalise conduct of the nature we are considering when it fell within s.18 of the 1861 Act, but not when it falls within s.20. In the Law Commission's report in 2000, Consent in Sex Offences, no view was expressed on this topic, but it was assumed that any forthcoming legislation would not impose criminal liability for recklessly communicating HIV or other disease . . .

. . . In Judge Philpot's second ruling, he accepted the Crown's argument that the possible consent of the victims was irrelevant. For the reasons we have now given, the ruling was wrong in law.

Conclusion

We repeat that the Crown did not allege, and we therefore are not considering the deliberate infection, or spreading of HIV with intent to cause grievous bodily harm. In such circumstances, the application of what we may describe as the principle in *Brown* [1994] 1 AC 212 means that the agreement of the participants would provide no defence to a charge under s.18 of the 1861 Act.

The effect of this judgment in relation to s.20 is to remove some of the outdated restrictions against the successful prosecution of those who, knowing that they are suffering HIV or some other serious sexual disease, recklessly transmit it through consensual sexual intercourse, and inflict grievous bodily harm on a person from whom the risk is concealed and who is not consenting to it. In this context, *Clarence* 22 QBD 23 has no continuing relevance. Moreover, to the extent that *Clarence* suggested that consensual sexual intercourse of itself was to be regarded as consent to the risk of consequent disease, again, it is no longer authoritative. If however, the victim consents to the risk, this continues to provide a defence under s.20. Although the two are inevitably linked, the ultimate question is not knowledge, but consent. We shall confine ourselves to reflecting that unless you are prepared to take whatever risk of sexually transmitted infection there may be, it is unlikely that you would consent to a risk of major consequent illness if you were ignorant of it. That said, in every case where these issues arise, the question whether the defendant was or was not reckless, and whether the victim did or did not consent to the risk of a sexually transmitted disease is one of fact, and case specific.

In view of our conclusion that the trial judge should not have withdrawn the issue of consent from the jury, the appeal is allowed.

Appeal allowed

Retrial ordered

Questions

1. Is it right that a distinction is drawn between those who engage in sexual intercourse knowing there might be a risk and those who are intent on spreading the disease?

2. Is it necessary for D to have actual knowledge of his infection or is it sufficient that he realises he might be infected? Imagine that D and V are in a short-term casual relationship and D suspects he may be infected with HIV but has not undergone any testing. V, aware of the risks of casual unprotected sex, asks D whether he is HIV+. D says, "Not to my knowledge" and relying on this, V consents to unprotected sexual intercourse. If V becomes infected, has D committed the offence under s.20?

3. Do those who engage in casual unprotected sex impliedly consent to the risk of infection and if so, if D recklessly infects such a person does D commit the s.20 offence? (See *R. v Konzani* directly below.)

R. V KONZANI

[2005] 2 Cr. App. R. 14 CA

The appellant, who knew he was HIV positive, repeatedly had unprotected sexual intercourse with the three complainants without informing them of his HIV status. In consequence of having sexual inter-course with the appellant each contracted the HIV virus. The appellant was charged with inflicting grievous bodily harm contrary to s.20 of the Offences Against the Person Act 1861. At trial the appel-lant submitted that as infection with the HIV virus might be one possible consequence of unprotected sexual intercourse, the complainants had consented to the risk of contracting the HIV virus from him. The judge directed the jury that before the consent of the complainants could provide the appellant with a defence it had to be an informed and willing consent to the risk of contracting HIV. The appel-lant was convicted.

JUDGE LJ

. . . for the purposes of s.20 of the 1861 Act, the required mental ingredient of the offence is established if the defendant was reckless in the sense formulated in *R. v Cunningham* (1951) 41 Cr.App.R. 155. [1957] 2 Q.B. 396, as approved in *R. v Savage* (1992) 94 Cr.App.R. 193, [1992] 1 A.C. 699. In short, if he knew or foresaw that the complainant might suffer bodily harm and chose to take the risk that she would, recklessness sufficient for the purposes of the mens rea for s.20 was established. In the result, as we have recorded, recklessness was admitted.

To examine Mr Roberts' submissions, and his criticisms of the directions to the jury, we must turn to *R. v Dica* [2004] EWCA Crim 1103, [2004] 2 Cr.App.R. 467, where the issue of consent was addressed (a) in the context of the longstanding decision in *R. v Clarence* (1888) 22 Q.B.D. 23 that the consent of a wife to sexual intercourse carried with it consent to the risks inherent in sexual intercourse, including the risk of sexually transmitted disease, and (b) the trial judge's ruling that the consent of the complainants to sexual intercourse with an indi-vidual who was known to them to be suffering from the HIV virus could provide no defence. In *R. v Barnes* [2004] EWCA Crim 3246, [2005] 1 Cr.App.R. 507, [2005] 1 W.L.R. 910, Lord Woolf C.J. summarised the effect of the decision in Dica in this way at para.10. An HIV positive male defendant who infected a sexual partner with the HIV virus would be guilty of an offence 'contrary to s 20 of the 1861 Act if, being aware of his condition, he had sexual intercourse . . . without disclosing his condition'. On the other hand, he would have a defence if he had made the partner aware of his condition, who 'with that knowledge consented to sexual intercourse with him because [she was] still prepared to accept the risks involved.'

Dica represented what Lord Mustill in Brown described as a 'new challenge', and confirmed that in specific circumstances the ambit of the criminal law extended to consensual sexual intercourse between adults which involved a risk of the most extreme kind to the physical health of one participant. In the context of direct physical injury, he pointed out that cases involving the '. . . consensual infliction of violence are special. They have been in the past, and will continue to be in the future, the subject of special treatment by the law'. In his subsequent detailed examination of the 'situations in which the recipient consents or is deemed to consent to the infliction of violence upon him', activity of the kind currently under consideration did not remotely fall within any of the ten categories which he was able to identify. Brown itself emphatically established the clear principle that the consent of the injured person does not form a kind of all purpose species of defence to an offence of violence contrary to s.20 of the 1861 Act.

We are concerned with the risk of and the actual transmission of a potentially fatal disease through or in the course of consensual sexual relations which did not in themselves involve unlawful violence of the kind prohibited in Brown. The prosecution did not seek to prove that the disease was deliberately transmitted, with the intention required by s.18 of the 1861 Act. The allegation was that the appellant behaved recklessly on the basis that knowing that he was suffering from the HIV virus, and its consequences, and knowing the risks of its transmission to a sexual partner, he concealed his condition from the complainants, leaving them ignorant of it. When sexual intercourse occurred these complainants were ignorant of his condition. So although they consented to sexual intercourse, they did not consent to the transmission of the HIV virus . . . There is a critical distinction between taking a risk of the various, potentially adverse and possibly problematic consequences of sexual intercourse, and giving an informed consent to the risk of infection with a fatal disease. For the complainant's consent to the risks of contracting the HIV virus to provide a defence, it is at least implicit from the reasoning in Dica, and the observations of Lord Woolf C. J. in Barnes confirm, that her consent must be an informed consent. If that proposition is in doubt, we take this opportunity to emphasise it. We must therefore examine its implications for this appeal.

The recognition in Dica of informed consent as a defence was based on but limited by potentially conflicting public policy considerations. In the public interest, so far as possible, the spread of catastrophic illness must be avoided or prevented. On the other hand, the public interest also requires that the principle of personal autonomy in the context of adult non-violent sexual relationships should be maintained. If an individual who knows that he is suffering from the HIV virus conceals this stark fact from his sexual partner, the principle of her personal autonomy is not enhanced if he is exculpated when he recklessly transmits the HIV virus to her through consensual sexual intercourse. On any view, the concealment of this fact from her almost inevitably means that she is deceived. Her consent is not properly informed, and she cannot give an informed consent to something of which she is ignorant. Equally, her personal autonomy is not normally protected by allowing a defendant who knows that he is suffering from the HIV virus which he deliberately conceals, to assert an honest belief in his partner's informed consent to the risk of the transmission of the HIV virus. Silence in these circumstances is incongruous with honesty, or with a genuine belief that there is an informed consent. Accordingly, in such circumstances the issue either of informed consent or honest belief in it will only rarely arise: in reality, in most cases, the contention would be wholly artificial.

This is not unduly burdensome. The defendant is not to be convicted of this offence unless it is proved that he was reckless. If so, the necessary mens rea will be established. Recklessness is a question of fact, to be proved by the prosecution. Equally the defendant is not to be convicted if there was, or may have been an informed consent by his sexual partner to the risk that he would transfer the HIV virus to her. In many cases, as in Dica itself, provided recklessness is established, the critical factual area of dispute will address what, if anything, was said between the two individuals involved, one of whom knows, and the other of whom does not know, that one of them is suffering the HIV virus. In the final analysis, the question of consent, like the issue of recklessness is fact-specific.

[W]e accept that there may be circumstances in which it would be open to the jury to infer that, notwithstanding that the defendant was reckless and concealed his condition from the complainant, she may nevertheless have given an informed consent to the risk of contracting the HIV virus. By way of example, an individual with HIV may develop a sexual relationship with someone who knew him while he was in hospital, receiving treatment for the condition. If so, her informed consent, if it were indeed informed, would remain a defence, to be disproved by the prosecution, even if the defendant had not personally informed her of his condition. Even if she did not in fact consent, this example would illustrate the basis for an argument that he honestly believed in her informed consent. Alternatively, he may honestly believe that his new sexual partner was told of his condition by someone known to them both. Cases like these, not too remote to be fanciful, may arise. If they do, no doubt they will be explored with the complainant in cross-examination. Her answers may demonstrate an informed consent. Nothing remotely like that was suggested here. In a different case, perhaps supported by the defendant's own evidence, material like this may provide a basis for suggesting that he honestly believed that she was giving an informed consent. He may provide an account of the incident, or the affair, which leads the jury to conclude that even if she did not give an informed consent, he may honestly have believed that she did. Acknowledging these possibilities in different cases does not, we believe, conflict with the public policy considerations identified in Dica. That said, they did not arise in the present case . . .

. . . We recognise that where consent does provide a defence to an offence against the person, it is generally speaking correct that the defendant's honest belief in the alleged victim's consent would also provide a defence. However for this purpose, the defendant's honest belief must be concomitant with the consent which provides a defence. Unless the consent would provide a defence, an honest belief in it would not assist the defendant. This follows logically from *Brown*. For it to do so here, what was required was some evidence of an honest belief that the complainants, or any one of them, were consenting to the risk that they might be infected with the HIV virus by him. There is not the slightest evidence, direct or indirect, from which a jury could begin to infer that the appellant honestly believed that any complainant consented to that specific risk. As there was no such evidence, the judge's ruling about 'honest belief' was correct. In fact, the honest truth was that the appellant deceived them. In our judgment, the judge's directions to the jury sufficiently explained the proper implications to the case of the consensual participation by each of the complainants to sexual intercourse with the appellant. The jury concluded, in the case of each complainant, that she did not willingly or consciously consent to the risk of suffering the HIV virus. Accordingly the appeal against conviction will be dismissed.

Appeal dismissed

Note

The decision in *Konzani* appears to acknowledge that V is able to give informed consent despite the fact that D has deliberately concealed his condition. This appears to be at odds with the post-*Dica* decision in *R. v Barnes* [2004] EWCA Crim 3246, which was of the view that *Dica* required D to reveal his condition to the victim or the consent defence would fail.

Questions

1. Is it relevant to focus on whether or not D deliberately failed to inform V of his condition or is the relevant question whether or not V was aware of D's condition (howsoever that awareness may have been acquired) and thus able to give informed consent?

2. If the correct answer to the above question is the latter, then how can this be reconciled with D's moral culpability?

(d) Capacity to consent

Notes

1. There is no age or degree of mental affliction which as a matter of law precludes a person from consenting to the application of force to his body. (For capacity and sexual offences, see below, p.577.) Ability to consent is a matter of fact, depending on the capacity of the individual. In *R. v D* [1984] A.C. 778 at 806, a case of kidnapping, an ingredient of which is absence of consent on the part of the person taken or carried away, Lord Brandon said:

    "I see no good reason why, in relation to the kidnapping of a child, it should not in all cases be the absence of the child's consent which is material, whatever its age may be. In the case of a very young child, it would not have the understanding or the intelligence to give its consent, so that absence of consent would be a necessary inference from its age. In the case of an older child, however, it must, I think, be a question of fact for a jury whether the child concerned has sufficient understanding and intelligence to give its consent; if, but only if, the jury considers that a child has these qualities, it must then go on to consider whether it has been proved that the child did not give its consent. While the matter will always be for the jury alone to decide, I should not expect a jury to find at all frequently that a child under 14 had sufficient understanding and intelligence to give its consent."

2. As to consent to medical treatment of minors, see *Gillick v West Norfolk & Wisbech AHA* [1986] A.C. 112, where Lord Scarman quoted with approval of Addy J in the Ontario High Court in *Johnston v Wellesley Hospital* (1980) 17 D.L.R. (3d) 139 at 144:

    "But, regardless of modern trend, I can find nothing in any of the old reported cases, except where infants of tender age or young children were involved, where the Courts have found that a person under 21 years of age was legally incapable of consenting to medical treatment. If a person under 21 years were unable to consent to medical treatment, he would also be incapable of consenting to other types of bodily interference. A proposition purporting to establish that any bodily interference acquiesced in by a youth of 20 years would nevertheless constitute an assault would be absurd."

3. Capacity to consent, in the case of a fully competent adult, involves a right *not* to consent to treatment, however necessary: see *Re T* [1992] 4 All E.R. 649; and *St Georges Healthcare NHS Trust v S* [1998] 3 All E.R. 673 (in the latter case the right of a pregnant woman to refuse a caesarean operation was upheld even though the operation was necessary to preserve both the mother's life and the life of the unborn child); but no minor, of any age below 18, has power by refusing consent to treatment to override a consent by someone with parental responsibility for the minor and a fortiori a consent by the court: *Re J* [1992] 4 All E.R. 614, per Donaldson MR.

    sIn *Attorney General's Reference (No.6 of 1980)* [1981] Q.B. 715, Lord Lane CJ included "lawful chastisement or correction" in his list of lawful exceptions to the principle that a person should not cause or try to cause bodily harm to another. There is a fairly clear line of cases establishing that it was lawful for a parent or other person in loco parentis to use reasonable force to discipline their children or charges (see *Cleary v Booth* [1893] 1 Q.B. 465; *Mackie* (1973) 57 Cr. App. R. 453) provided the child is old enough to understand its purpose (*Griffin* (1869) 11 Cox. C.C. 402). But corporal punishment administered out of spite or anger or for gratification, or where the degree of force used is unreasonable, is unlawful (see *Hopley* (1860) 2 F.&F. 202; *Taylor*, *The Times*, 28 December 1983). In *A v UK* (1999) 27 E.H.R.R. 611, the European Court of Human Rights held that the UK was in breach of its obligations under art.3 of the European Convention on Human Rights in failing to provide adequate protection to children and other vulnerable individuals against treatment or punishment which could constitute "inhuman or degrading treatment". In the instant case the stepfather of the applicant had been prosecuted for assault occasioning actual bodily harm arising out of his chastisement of A using a cane which was applied with considerable force resulting in a number of severe bruises. In his defence he pleaded "reasonable chastisement" and was acquitted by the jury. The finding by the European Court of Human Rights thus placed serious doubts over the limits of the defence of reasonable chastisement.

    The Children Act 2004 s.58, now provides:

> "(1) In relation to any offence specified in subsection (2), battery of a child cannot be justified on the ground that it constituted reasonable punishment.
>
> (2) The offences referred to in subsection (1) are—
>
>   (a) an offence under s.18 or 20 of the Offences Against the Person Act 1861;
>
>   (b) an offence under s.47 of that Act;
>
>   (c) an offence under s.1 of the Children and Young Persons Act 1933 (cruelty to a person under 16)."

Any physical punishment of a child is an offence if it causes actual bodily harm or greater level of injury. Even "non-cruel" physical punishment that does not cause physical injury may still constitute an offence if the punishment is not judged to be reasonable.

Note

In *Consent in the Criminal Law*, the Law Commission make the following provisional proposals.

The need for the same principles to be adopted in relation to consent in other criminal offences in which consent is an issue

1. We provisionally propose that the proposals contained in paragraphs 12–30 below should apply not only to offences against the person and sexual offences but also to every other criminal offence in which the consent of a person other than the defendant is or may be a defence to criminal liability.

(Paragraphs 1.24–1.27)

Intentional causing of seriously disabling injury

2. We provisionally propose that the intentional causing of seriously disabling injury (as defined at paragraph 7 below) to another person should continue to be criminal, even if the person injured consents to such injury or to the risk of such injury.

(Paragraphs 4.3–4.6 and 4.47)

Reckless causing of seriously disabling injury

3. We provisionally propose that—

(1) the reckless causing of seriously disabling injury (as defined at paragraph 7 below) should continue to be criminal, even if the injured person consents to such injury or to the risk of such injury; but

(2) a person causing seriously disabling injury to another person should not be regarded as having caused it recklessly unless—

   (a) he or she was, at the time of the act or omission causing it, aware of a risk that such injury would result, and

   (b) it was at that time contrary to the best interests of the other person, having regard to the circumstances known to the person causing the injury (including, if known to him or her, the fact that the other person consented to such injury or to the risk of it), to take that risk.

(Paragraphs 4.7–4.28 and 4.48)

Secondary liability for consenting to seriously disabling injury

4. We provisionally propose that, where a person causes seriously disabling injury to another person who consented to injury or to the risk of injury of the type caused, and the person causing the injury is guilty of an offence under the proposals in paragraphs 2 and 3 above, the ordinary principles of secondary liability should apply for the purpose of determining whether the person injured is a party to that offence.

(Paragraphs 1.20–1.23)

Intentional causing of other injuries

5. We provisionally propose that the intentional causing of any injury to another person other than seriously disabling injury as defined at paragraph 7 below (whether or not amounting to 'grievous bodily harm' within the meaning of the Offences Against the Person Act 1861 or to 'serious injury' within the meaning of the Criminal Law Bill below, p.664) should not be criminal if, at the time of the act or omission causing the injury, the other person consented to injury of the type caused.

(Paragraphs 4.29 and 4.49)

Reckless causing of other injuries

6. We provisionally propose that the reckless causing of any injury to another person other than seriously disabling injury as defined at paragraph 7 below (whether or not amounting to 'grievous bodily harm' within the meaning of the Offences Against the Person Act 1861 or to 'serious injury' within the meaning of the Criminal Law Bill) should not be criminal if, at the time of the act or omission causing the injury, the other person consented to injury of the type caused, to the risk of such injury or to the act or omission causing the injury.

(Paragraphs 4.29 and 4.50)

Definition of seriously disabling injury

7. We provisionally propose that for the purpose of paragraphs 2–6 above 'seriously disabling injury' should be taken to refer to an injury or injuries which—

(1) cause serious distress, and

(2) involve the loss of a bodily member or organ or permanent bodily injury or permanent functional impairment, or serious or permanent disfigurement, or severe and prolonged pain, or serious impairment of mental health, or prolonged unconsciousness;

and, in determining whether an effect is permanent, no account should be taken of the fact that it may be remediable by surgery.

(Paragraphs 4.29–4.40 and 4.51)

Meaning of consent

8. We provisionally propose that for the purposes of the above proposals—

(1) 'consent' should mean a valid subsisting consent to an injury or to the risk of an injury of the type caused, and consent may be express or implied;

(2) a person should be regarded as consenting to an injury of the type caused if he or she consents to an act or omission which he or she knows or believes to be intended to cause injury to him or her of the type caused; and

(3) a person should be regarded as consenting to the risk of an injury of the type caused if he or she consents to an act or omission which he or she knows or believes to involve a risk of injury to him or her of the type caused.

(Paragraphs 4.3–4.28 and 4.52)

Mistaken belief in consent: offences against the person

9. We ask—

(1) whether it should in itself be a defence to an offence of causing injury to another person that—

(a) at the time of the act or omission causing the injury, the defendant believed that the other person consented to injury or to the risk of injury of the type caused, or to that act or omission, and

(b)   he or she would have had a defence under our proposals in paragraphs 5 and 6 above if the facts had been as he or she then believed them to be; or

(2)   whether such a belief should be a defence *only* if, in addition, *either*—

(a)   it would not have been obvious to a reasonable person in his or her position that the other person did not so consent, or

(b)   he or she was not capable of appreciating that that person did not so consent.

(Paragraphs 7.1–7.28 and 7.31)

Mistaken belief in consent: sexual offences

10. We provisionally propose that, if (but only if) the defence of mistaken belief in consent to injury, or to the risk of injury, or to an act or omission causing injury, were to be available in relation to offences against the person only where one of the conditions set out in paragraph 9(2) is satisfied, it should similarly be no defence to a charge of rape or indecent assault that the defendant mistakenly believed that the other person consented to sexual intercourse or to the alleged assault unless one of those conditions is satisfied.

(Paragraphs 7.29 and 7.32)

----

2. ASSAULT OCCASIONING ACTUAL BODILY HARM

Offences Against the Person Act 1861 s.47

Whosoever shall be convicted upon an indictment of any assault occasioning actual bodily harm shall be liable to . . . [imprisonment for five years].

Note

This section creates a separate statutory offence which ought to be charged as "contrary to s.47": *R. v Harrow Justices* [1985] 3 All E.R. 185 QBD.

R. V CHAN-FOOK

[1994] 1 W.L.R. 689 CA

The appellant was convicted of assault occasioning actual bodily harm following the judge's direction to the jury which stated:

"What is meant by 'actual bodily harm'? It does not have to be permanent. It does not have to be serious. It is some actual harm which interferes with the comfort of the individual for the time being, described as any hurt or injury calculated to interfere with the health or comfort of [the victim]. An assault that causes an hysterical or nervous condition is capable of being an assault causing actual bodily harm"

HOBHOUSE LJ

[The words 'actual bodily harm'] are three words of the English language which require no elaboration and in the ordinary course should not receive any. The word 'harm' is a synonym for injury. The word 'actual' indicates that the injury (although there is no need for it to be permanent) should not be so trivial as to be wholly insignificant. The purpose of the definition in s.47 is to define an element of aggravation in the assault. It must be an assault which besides being an assault (or assault and battery) causes to the victim some injury.

The danger of any elaboration of the words of the statute is that it may have the effect . . . of altering, or at the least distracting the jury from, the ordinary meaning of the words . . .

The first question on the present appeal is whether the inclusion of the word 'bodily' in the phrase 'actual bodily harm' limits harm to harm to the skin, flesh and bones of the victim. Lynskey J. [in *R. v Miller* [1954] 2 Q.B. 282] rejected this submission. In our judgment he was right to do so. The body of the victim includes all parts of his body, including his organs, his nervous system and his brain. Bodily injury therefore may include injury to any of those parts of his body responsible for his mental and other faculties. The matter was well summarised by Lord Wilberforce in *McLoughlin v O'Brian* [1983] 1 A.C. 410, 418:

'Whatever is unknown about the mind-body relationship (and the area of ignorance seems to expand with that of knowledge), it is now accepted by medical science that recognisable and severe physical damage to the human body and system may be caused by the impact, through the senses, of external events on the mind. There may thus be produced what is as identifiable an illness as any that may be caused by direct physical impact.'

As is pointed out by Lord Wilberforce earlier in his speech the conventional phrase 'nervous shock' is now inaccurate and inappropriate. Observations to the like effect are to be found in *Attia v British Gas Plc* [1988] Q.B. 304 and *Alcock v Chief Constable of South Yorkshire Police* [1992] 1 A.C. 310. In *Attia v British Gas Plc* the Court of Appeal discussed where the borderline should be drawn between on the one hand the emotions of distress and grief and on the other hand some actual psychiatric illness such as anxiety neurosis or a reactive depression. The authorities recognised that there is a line to be drawn and whether any given case falls on one side or the other is a matter for expert evidence. The civil cases are also concerned with a broader question of the boundaries of the law of negligence and the duty of care, which do not concern us.

Accordingly the phrase 'actual bodily harm' is capable of including psychiatric injury. But it does not include mere emotions such as fear or distress nor panic nor does it include, as such, states of mind that are not themselves evidence of some identifiable clinical condition. The phrase 'state of mind' is not a scientific one and should be avoided in considering whether or not a psychiatric injury has been caused; its use is likely to create in the minds of the jury the impression that something which is not more than a strong emotion, such as extreme fear or panic, can amount to actual bodily harm. It cannot. Similarly juries should not be directed that an assault which causes an hysterical and nervous condition is an assault occasioning actual bodily harm. Where there is evidence that the assault has caused some psychiatric injury, the jury should be directed that that injury is capable of amounting to actual bodily harm; otherwise there should be no reference to the mental state of the victim following the assault unless it be relevant to some other aspect of the case, as it was in *R. v Roberts*, 56 Cr.App.R. 95. It is also relevant to have in mind the relationship between the offence of aggravated assault comprised in s.47 and simple assault. The latter can include conduct which causes the victim to apprehend immediate and unlawful violence: *Fagan v Metropolitan Police Commissioner* [1969] 1 Q.B. 439. To treat the victim's fear of such unlawful violence, without more, as amounting to actual bodily harm would be to risk rendering the definition of the aggravated offence academic in many cases.

In any case where psychiatric injury is relied upon as the basis for an allegation of bodily harm, and the matter has not been admitted by the defence, expert evidence should be called by the prosecution. It should not be left to be inferred by the jury from the general facts of the case. In the absence of appropriate expert evidence a question whether or not the assault occasioned psychiatric injury should not be left to the jury . . .

Appeal allowed

Conviction quashed

Note

The decision in *Chan-Fook* was confirmed by the House of Lords in *Ireland and Burstow* [1998] A.C. 147. What is required is proof of a psychiatric condition supported by expert evidence. In *Morris* [1998] 1 Cr. App. R. 386 evidence from V's general practitioner that she suffered anxiety, fear, tearfulness, sleeplessness and physical tenseness was held to be insufficient to establish actual bodily harm.

For the mens rea required for this offence, see *R. v Savage, R. v Parmenter*, below, p.569.

---

3. MALICIOUS WOUNDING AND WOUNDING WITH INTENT

i. Malicious Wounding

OFFENCES AGAINST THE PERSON ACT 1861 S.20

Whosoever shall unlawfully and maliciously wound or inflict any grievous bodily harm upon any other person, either with or without any weapon or instrument, shall be guilty of [an offence and liable to a maximum penalty of five years' imprisonment].

Notes

Unlawfully: see Justifications.

Wound: In *C v Eisenhower* [1984] Q.B. 331, the victim was shot and an airgun pellet hit him near the eye. He sustained a bruise just below the eyebrow and fluid filling the front part of the eye for a time contained red blood cells. *Held*, a wound is a break in the continuity of the whole skin, and an internal rupturing of the blood vessels is not a wound.

Grievous bodily harm: The Court of Criminal Appeal in *R. v Metharam* [1961] 3 All E.R. 200 adopted the dictum of Viscount Kilmuir in *DPP v Smith*, that "bodily harm" needs no explanation and "grievous" means no more and no less than "really serious."

In *R. v Birmingham* [2002] EWCA Crim 2608, D inflicted 11 knife wounds on V together with bruising to the chest. None of the wounds were individually serious. The Court of Appeal held that that the jury were entitled to view the totality of the wounds as constituting really serious injury and thus amounting to grievous bodily harm.

Inflict: does "inflict" in s.20 have a narrower meaning than "cause" in s.18? In *Wilson* [1984] A.C. 242, the issue arose whether, on a trial on indictment for a charge under s.20, a jury, which was not satisfied that the victim had sustained a wound or that the injury inflicted amounted to GBH, could convict the accused of the s.47 offence if satisfied that the harm amounted to actual bodily harm. Section 6(3) of the Criminal Law Act 1967 permitted a jury to convict of another offence where "the allegations in the indictment amount to or include (expressly or by implication) an allegation of another offence". The House of Lords held that an accused could inflict GBH without necessarily committing a technical assault or battery. Thus if the allegation in the indictment for a s.20 offence did not "amount to or include" an assault, a conviction of the s.47 offence as an alternative at that trial was not possible. The option of convicting of the s.47 offence should only be presented where the prosecution had presented evidence which pointed to an assault. *Wilson* established, accordingly, that "inflict" has a wider meaning than "assault" but did not resolve the issue whether it had as wide a meaning as "cause" in s.18. Their Lordships were content to cite with approval the Australian case of *Salisbury* [1976] V.R. 452, 461 where it was stated that:

> "Grievous bodily harm may be inflicted . . . either where the accused has directly and violently inflicted' it by doing something, intentionally, which, though it is not itself a direct application of force to the body of the victim, does directly result in force being applied violently to the body of the victim, so that he suffers grievous bodily harm."

It was left to the following case to resolve the issue.

R. V IRELAND; R. V BURSTOW

[1997] A.C. 147 HL

The appellant, Burstow, was obsessed with S and stalked her over a period of several years. B had appeared before the courts on numerous occasions as a result of his behaviour towards S and had served three prison sentences. Between February and July 1995, B had, inter alia, sent S menacing letters and photographs, repeatedly telephoned her and visited her home. As a result of his actions S suffered from severe depression which was described as "grievous harm of a psychiatric nature". B was charged with inflicting grievous bodily harm contrary to s.20 of the 1861 Act. The defence argued that the House of Lords decision in *Wilson* dictated that a charge under s.20 was inappropriate there being neither an assault nor any force being applied violently to the body of the victim. The prosecution argued that "inflict upon" meant "impose upon" and that the court was not bound by *Wilson* to follow *Salisbury*. The trial judge ruled that *Salisbury* did not correctly define English law and that a charge under s.20 was appropriate. B pleaded guilty and appealed. His appeal was dismissed by the Court of Appeal which certified the following point of law of general public importance for the consideration of the House of Lords, namely: "Whether an offence of inflicting grievous bodily harm under s.20 of the Offences Against the Person Act 1861 can be committed where no physical violence is applied directly or indirectly to the body of the victim."

LORD STEYN

Reg. v Burstow: the meaning of 'inflict' in s.20

   The decision in *Reg. v Chan-Fook* opened up the possibility of applying ss.18, 20 and 47 in new circumstances. The appeal of Burstow lies in respect of his conviction under s.20. It was conceded that in principle the wording of s.18, and in particular the words 'cause any grievous bodily harm to any person' do not preclude a prosecution in cases where the actus reus is the causing of psychiatric injury. But counsel laid stress on the difference between 'causing' grievous bodily harm in s.18 and 'inflicting' grievous bodily harm in s.20. Counsel argued that the difference in wording reveals a difference in legislative intent: inflict is a narrower concept than cause. This argument loses sight of the genesis of ss.18 and 20. [As the different sections in the 1861 Act were derived from different Acts passed at different times and in differing circumstances] the difference in language is therefore not a significant factor.

   Counsel for Burstow then advanced a sustained argument that an assault is an ingredient of an offence under s.20. He referred your Lordships to cases which in my judgment simply do not yield what he sought to extract from them. In any event, the tour of the cases revealed conflicting dicta, no authority binding on the House of Lords, and no settled practice holding expressly that assault was an ingredient of s.20. And, needless to say, none of the cases focused on the infliction of psychiatric injury . . .. Counsel's argument can only prevail if one may supplement the section by reading it as providing 'inflict by assault any grievous bodily harm.' Such an implication is, however, not necessary. On the contrary, s.20, like s.18, works perfectly satisfactorily without such an implication. I would reject this part of counsel's argument.

   But counsel had a stronger argument when he submitted that it is inherent in the word 'inflict' that there must be a direct or indirect application of force to the body. Counsel cited the speech of Lord Roskill in *Reg. v Wilson (Clarence)* [1984] A.C. 242, 259e–260h, in which Lord Roskill quoted with approval from the judgment of the full court of the Supreme Court of Victoria in *Reg. v Salisbury* [1976] V.R. 452. There are passages that give assistance to counsel's argument. But Lord Roskill expressly stated, at p.260h, that he was

   'content to accept, as did the [court in *Salisbury*] that there can be the infliction of grievous bodily harm contrary to s.20 without an assault being committed.'

   In the result the effect of the decisions in *Reg. v Wilson* and *Reg. v Salisbury* is neutral in respect of the issue as to the meaning of 'inflict.' Moreover, in *Reg. v Burstow* [1997] 1 Cr.App.R. 144, 149, Lord Bingham of Cornhill C.J. pointed out that in *Reg. v Mandair* [1995] 1 A.C. 208, 215, Lord Mackay of Clashfern L.C. observed with the agreement of the majority of the House of Lords: 'In my opinion . . . the word "cause" is wider or at least not narrower than the word "inflict"' Like Lord Bingham C.J. I regard this observation as making clear that in the context of the Act of 1861 there is no radical divergence between the meaning of the two words.

That leaves the troublesome authority of the Court for Crown Cases Reserved in *Reg. v Clarence* (1888) 22 Q.B.D. 23 . . . The case was complicated by an issue of consent. But it must be accepted that in a case where there was direct physical contact the majority ruled that the requirement of infliction was not satisfied. This decision has never been overruled. It assists counsel's argument. But it seems to me that what detracts from the weight to be given to the dicta in *Reg. v Clarence* is that none of the judges in that case had before them the possibility of the inflicting, or causing, of psychiatric injury. The criminal law has moved on in the light of a developing under-standing of the link between the body and psychiatric injury. In my judgment *Reg. v Clarence* no longer assists.

The problem is one of construction. The question is whether as a matter of current usage the contextual inter-pretation of 'inflict' can embrace the idea of one person inflicting psychiatric injury on another. One can without straining the language in any way answer that question in the affirmative. I am not saying that the words 'cause' and 'inflict' are exactly synonymous. They are not. What I am saying is that in the context of the Act of 1861 one can nowadays quite naturally speak of inflicting psychiatric injury. Moreover, there is internal contextual support in the statute for this view. It would be absurd to differentiate between ss.18 and 20 in the way argued on behalf of Burstow. As Lord Bingham C.J. observed in *Reg. v Burstow* [1997] 1 Cr.App.R. 144, 149f, this should be a very practical area of the law. The interpretation and approach should, so far as possible be adopted which treats the ladder of offences as a coherent body of law. Once the decision in *Reg. v Chan-Fook* [1994] 1 W.L.R. 689 is accepted the realistic possibility is opened up of prosecuting under s.20 in cases of the type which I described in the introduction to this judgment.

For the reasons I have given I would answer the certified question in *Reg. v Burstow* in the affirmative.

LORD HOPE OF CRAIGHEAD

Reg. v Burstow: 'inflict'

In this case the appellant changed his plea to guilty after a ruling by the trial judge that the offence of unlaw-fully and maliciously inflicting grievous bodily harm contrary to s.20 of the Act of 1861 may be committed where no physical violence has been applied directly or indirectly to the body of the victim. Counsel for the appellant accepted that if *Reg. v Chan-Fook* [1994] 1 W.L.R. 689 was correctly decided, with the result that 'actual bodily harm' in s.47 is capable of including psychiatric injury, the victim in this case had suffered grievous bodily harm within the meaning of s.20. But he submitted that no offence against s.20 had been committed in this case because, although the appellant might be said to have 'caused' the victim to sustain grievous bodily harm, he had not 'inflicted' that harm on her because he had not used any personal violence against her.

Counsel based his submission on the decision in *Reg. v Clarence*, 22 Q.B.D. 23 . . . It seems to me however that there are three reasons for regarding that case as an uncertain guide to the question which arises where the bodily harm which has resulted from the defendant's conduct consists of psychiatric injury.

The first is that the judges in *Reg. v Clarence* were concerned with a case of physical, not psychiatric, injury. They did not have to consider the problem which arises where the grievous bodily harm is of a kind which may result without any form of physical contact. The second is that the intercourse had taken place with consent, as the defendant's wife was ignorant of his venereal disease. So there was no question in that case of an assault having been committed, if there was no element of violence or battery. Also, as Lord Roskill pointed out in *Reg. v Wilson (Clarence)* [1984] A.C. 242, 260c the judgments of the judges who formed the majority are not wholly consistent with each other. This casts some doubt on the weight which should be attached to the judgment when the facts are entirely different, as they are in the present case.

In *Reg. v Wilson*, Lord Roskill referred, at pp.259e–260b, with approval to the judgment of the Supreme Court of Victoria in *Reg. v Salisbury* [1976] V.R. 452, in which the following passage appears, at p.461:

'although the word "inflicts" . . . does not have as wide a meaning as the word "causes" . . . the word "inflicts" does have a wider meaning than it would have if it were construed so that inflicting grievous bodily harm always involved assaulting the victim.'

Lord Roskill said [1984] A.C. 242, 260h that he was content to accept, as was the full court in *Reg. v Salisbury*, that there can be an infliction of grievous bodily harm contrary to s.20 without an assault being committed. But these observations do not wholly resolve the issue which arises in this case, in the context of grievous bodily harm which consists only of psychiatric injury.

The question is whether there is any difference in meaning, in this context, between the word 'cause' and the word 'inflict.' The fact that the word 'caused' is used in s.18, whereas the word used in s.20 is 'inflict,' might be taken at first sight to indicate that there is a difference. But for all practical purposes there is, in my opinion, no difference between these two words. In *Reg. v Mandair* [1995] 1 A.C. 208, 215b Lord Mackay of Clashfern L.C. said that the word 'cause' is wider or at least not narrower than the word 'inflict.' I respectfully agree with that observation. But I would add that there is this difference, that the word 'inflict' implies that the consequence of the act is something which the victim is likely to find unpleasant or harmful. The relationship between cause and effect, when the word 'cause' is used, is neutral. It may embrace pleasure as well as pain. The relationship when the word 'inflict' is used is more precise, because it invariably implies detriment to the victim of some kind.

In the context of a criminal act therefore the words 'cause' and 'inflict' may be taken to be interchangeable. As the Supreme Court of Victoria held in *Reg. v Salisbury* [1976] V.R. 452, it is not a necessary ingredient of the word 'inflict' that whatever causes the harm must be applied directly to the victim. It may be applied indirectly, so long as the result is that the harm is caused by what has been done. In my opinion it is entirely consistent with the ordinary use of the word 'inflict' in the English language to say that the appellant's actions 'inflicted' the psychiatric harm from which the victim has admittedly suffered in this case. The issues which remain are issues of fact and, as the appellant pled guilty to the offence, I would dismiss his appeal.

Appeal dismissed

Questions

1. Their Lordships considered that *Clarence* was not relevant because it was concerned with physical rather than psychiatric injury. But the certified question covered bodily harm generally. Where does this leave *Clarence*?

2. If, in Lord Steyn's words, the words "cause" and "inflict" are not synonymous, in what way do they differ? Lord Hope's answer was that the word "inflict implies something which the victim is likely to find unpleasant or harmful". Does this mean that *Brown* needs reconsideration as the "victims" of sado-masochism find pain and injury pleasurable?

R. V SAVAGE; R. V PARMENTER

[1992] A.C. 699 HL

Savage intentionally threw beer at Beal, the pint glass left her hand, broke and cut Beal. She was convicted of unlawful wounding, the jury having been directed that if they were sure she deliberately threw the beer but unintentionally let go of the glass, so that Beal was wounded, they could convict of unlawful wounding. On appeal, the Court of Appeal quashed the conviction under s.20 of the Offences Against the Person Act 1861 but substituted a conviction under s.47. She appealed to the House of Lords.

Parmenter was convicted of inflicting grievous bodily harm, contrary to s.20, on his baby son. His rough handling caused the breaking of the child's arm and leg bones. His case was that he did not realise that his handling of the child would cause injury. The jury were directed that they could convict if they were sure that Parmenter should have foreseen some physical harm, albeit minor, not necessarily grievous bodily harm. On appeal, the Court of Appeal allowed his appeal, but declined to substitute a conviction under s.47. The Crown appealed to the House of Lords. Both appeals were heard together.

LORD ACKNER

After outlining the facts and the certified questions:—My Lords, I will now seek to deal with the issues raised in these appeals seriatim.

. . .

II. *Can a verdict of assault occasioning actual bodily harm be returned upon proof of an assault together with proof of the fact that actual bodily harm was occasioned by the assault, or must the prosecution also prove that the defendant intended to cause some actual bodily harm or was reckless as to whether such harm would be caused?*

Your Lordships are concerned with the mental element of a particular kind of assault, an assault 'occasioning actual bodily harm'. It is common ground that the mental element of assault is an intention to cause the victim to apprehend immediate and unlawful violence or recklessness whether such apprehension be caused (see *R. v Venna* above p.619). It is of course common ground that Mrs Savage committed an assault upon Miss Beal when she threw the contents of Tier glass of beer over her. It is also common ground that however the glass came to be broken and Miss Beal's wrist thereby cut, it was, on the finding of the jury, Mrs Savage's handling of the glass which caused Miss Beal 'actual bodily harm'. Was the offence thus established or is there a further mental state that has to be established in relation to the bodily harm element of the offence? Clearly the section, by its terms, expressly imposes no such a requirement. Does it do so by necessary implication? It uses neither the word 'intentionally' nor the word 'maliciously'. The words 'occasioning actual bodily harm' are descriptive of the word 'assault', by reference to a particular kind of consequence.

In neither *R. v Savage* nor *R. v Spratt* [1991] 2 All E.R. 210 nor in *R. v Parmenter* was the court's attention invited to the decision of the Court of Appeal in *R. v Roberts* (1972) 56 Cr.App.R. 95. This is perhaps explicable on the basis that this case is not referred to in the index to *Archbold's Criminal Pleading, Evidence and Practice* (43rd edn, 1988). The relevant text states (para.20–117): 'The mens rea required [for actual bodily harm] is that required for common assault', without any authority being provided for this proposition.

It is in fact *R. v Roberts* which provides authority for this proposition. Roberts was tried on an indictment which alleged that he indecently assaulted a young woman. He was acquitted on that charge, but convicted of assault occasioning actual bodily harm to her. The girl's complaint was that while travelling in the defendant's car he sought to make advances towards her and then tried to take her coat off. This was the last straw and, although the car was travelling at some speed, she jumped out and sustained injuries. The defendant denied he had touched the girl. He had had an argument with her and in the course of that argument she suddenly opened the door and jumped out. In his direction to the jury the chairman of quarter sessions stated: 'If you are satisfied that he tried to pull off her coat and as a result she jumped out of the moving car then your verdict is guilty.'

It was contended on behalf of the appellant that this direction was wrong since the chairman had failed to tell the jury that they must be satisfied that the appellant foresaw that she might jump out of the car as a result of his touching her before they could convict. The court rejected that submission. The test was, said the court (at 102):

'Was it [the action of the victim which resulted in actual bodily harm] the natural result of what the alleged assailant said and did, in the sense that it was something that could reasonably have been foreseen as the consequence of what he was saying or doing? As it was put in one of the old cases, it had got to be shown to be his act, and if of course the victim does something so "daft", in the words of the appellant in this case, or so unexpected, not that this particular assailant did not actually foresee it but that no reasonable man could be expected to foresee it, then it is only in a very remote and unreal sense a consequence of his assault, it is really occasioned by a voluntary act on the part of the victim which could not reasonably be foreseen and which breaks the chain of causation between the assault and the harm or injury.'

Accordingly, no fault was found in the following direction of the chairman to the jury (at 103):

'If you accept the evidence of the girl in preference to that of the man, that means that there was an assault occasioning actual bodily harm, that means that she did jump out as a direct result of what he was threatening her with, and what he was doing to her, holding her coat, telling her that he had beaten up girls who had refused his advances, and that means that through his acts he was in law and in fact responsible for the injuries which were caused to her by her decision, if it can be called that, to get away from his violence, his threats, by jumping out of the car.'

Thus, once the assault was established, the only remaining question was whether the victim's conduct was the natural consequence of that assault. The words 'occasioning' raised solely a question of causation, an objective question which does not involve inquiring into the accused's state of mind.

In *R. v Spratt* [1991] 2 All E.R. 210 at 219, McCowan L.J. said:

'However, the history of the interpretation of the 1861 Act shows that, whether or not the word "maliciously" appears in the section in question, the courts have consistently held that the mens rea of every type of offence against the person covers both actual intent and recklessness, in the sense of taking the risk of harm ensuing with foresight that it might happen.'

McCowan L.J. then quoted a number of authorities for that proposition. The first is *R. v Ward* (1871) L.R. 1 C.C.R. 356, but that was a case where the prisoner was charged with wounding with intent (s.18) and convicted of malicious wounding (s.20); next, *R. v Bradshaw* (1878) 14 Cox C.C. 83, but that was a case where the accused was charged with manslaughter, which has nothing to do with a s.47 case. Then *R. v Cunningham* [1957] 2 Q.B. 396 is quoted, a case under s.23 of the Act concerned with unlawfully and maliciously administering etc. a noxious thing which endangers life. And, finally *R. v Venna*, above, p.623 in which there was no issue as to whether in a s.47 case, recklessness had to extend to actual bodily harm. Thus none of the cases cited was concerned with the mental element required in s.47 cases. Nevertheless, the Court of Appeal in *R. v Parmenter* [1991] 2 All E.R. 225 at 232, preferred the decision in *R. v Spratt* to that of *R. v Savage* because the former was 'founded on a line of authority leading directly to the conclusion there expressed'.

My Lords, in my respectful view, the Court of Appeal in *R. v Parmenter* was wrong in preferring the decision in R. v Spratt. The decision in *R. v Roberts* was correct. The verdict of assault occasioning actual bodily harm may be returned upon proof of an assault together with proof of the fact that actual bodily harm was occasioned by the assault. The prosecution are not obliged to prove that the defendant intended to cause some actual bodily harm or was reckless as to whether such harm would be caused.

III. *In order to establish an offence under s.20 of the 1861 Act, must the prosecution prove that the defendant actually foresaw that his act would cause harm, or is it sufficient to prove that he ought so to have foreseen?*

[His Lordship concluded that the answer is that the prosecution must prove that the defendant actually foresaw that his act would cause harm.]

IV. *In order to establish an offence under s.20 is it sufficient to prove that the defendant intended or foresaw the risk of some physical harm or must he intend or foresee either wounding or grievous bodily harm?*

It is convenient to set out once again the relevant part of the judgment of Diplock L.J. in *R. v Mowatt* [1968] 1 Q.B. 421 at 426. Having considered Professor Kenny's statement, which I have quoted above, he then said:

> In the offence under s.20 . . . for . . . which [no] specific intent is required—the word 'maliciously' does import . . . an awareness that his act may have the consequence of causing some physical harm to some other person. That is what is meant by the 'particular kind of harm' in the citation from Professor Kenny's Outlines of Criminal Law (18th edn, 1962, para.158a, p.202). It is quite unnecessary that the accused should have foreseen that his unlawful act might cause physical harm of the gravity described in the section, i.e. a wound or serious physical injury. '*It is enough that he should have foreseen that some physical harm to some person, albeit of a minor character, might result.*' (My emphasis.)

Mr Sedley submits that this statement of the law is wrong. He contends that, properly construed, the section requires foresight of a wounding or grievous bodily harm. He drew your Lordships' attention to criticisms of *R. v Mowatt* made by Professor Glanville Williams and by Professor J. C. Smith in their textbooks and in articles or commentaries. They argue that a person should not be criminally liable for consequences of his conduct unless he foresaw a consequence falling into the same legal category as that set out in the indictment.

Such a general principle runs contrary to the decision in *R. v Roberts*, which I have already stated to be, in my opinion, correct. The contention is apparently based on the proposition that, as the actus reus of a s.20 offence is the wounding or the infliction of grievous bodily harm, the mens rea must consist of foreseeing such wounding or grievous bodily harm. But there is no such hard and fast principle. To take but two examples, the actus reus of murder is the killing of the victim, but foresight of grievous bodily harm is sufficient and, indeed, such bodily harm need not be such as to be dangerous to life. Again, in the case of manslaughter death is frequently the unforeseen consequence of the violence used.

The argument that, as ss.20 and 47 have both the same penalty, this somehow supports the proposition that the foreseen consequences must coincide with the harm actually done, overlooks the oft-repeated statement that this is the irrational result of this piecemeal legislation. The Act 'is a rag-bag of offences brought together from a wide variety of sources with no attempt, as the draftsman frankly acknowledged, to introduce consistency as to substance or as to form' (see Professor J. C. Smith in his commentary on *R. v Parmenter* ([1991] Crim.L.R. 43)).

If s.20 was to be limited to cases where the accused does not desire but does foresee wounding or grievous bodily harm, it would have a very limited scope. The mens rea in a s.20 crime is comprised in the word 'maliciously'. As was pointed out by Lord Lane C.J., giving the judgment of the Court of Appeal in *R. v Sullivan* [1981] Crim.L.R. 46, the 'particular kind of harm' in the citation from Professor Kenny was directed to 'harm to the person' as opposed to 'harm to property'. Thus it was not concerned with the degree of the harm foreseen. It is accordingly in my judgment wrong to look upon the decision in *R. v Mowatt* as being in any way inconsistent with the decision in *R. v Cunningham*.

My Lords, I am satisfied that the decision in *R. v Mowatt* was correct and that it is quite unnecessary that the accused should either have intended or have foreseen that his unlawful act might cause physical harm of the gravity described in s.20, i.e. a wound or serious physical injury. It is enough that he should have foreseen that some physical harm to some person, albeit of a minor character, might result.

In the result I would dismiss the appeal in *Savage*'s case but allow the appeal in *Parmenter*'s case, but only to the extent of substituting, in accordance with the provisions of s.3(2) of the Criminal Appeal Act 1968, verdicts of guilty of assault occasioning actual bodily harm contrary to s.47 of the 1861 Act for the four s.20 offences of which he was convicted.

[Lords Keith of Kinkel, Brandon of Oakbrook, Jauncey of Tullichettle and Lowry agreed.]

Appeal of Savage dismissed; appeal of Parmenter allowed in part and conviction of assault occasioning actual bodily harm substituted

ii. Wounding with Intent

OFFENCES AGAINST THE PERSON ACT 1861 S.18

Whosoever shall unlawfully and maliciously by any means whatever wound, or cause any grievous bodily harm to any person, with intent to do some grievous bodily harm to any person, or with intent to resist or prevent the lawful apprehension or detainer of any person, shall be guilty of [an offence and shall be liable to imprisonment for life].

Notes

1. The chief difference between the offences in s.18 and s.20 are: (1) in s.20 the mens rea resides in the word "maliciously", whereas in s.18, that word "adds nothing" to the definition, since the mens rea is defined expressly: *R. v Mowatt* [1968] 1 Q.B. 421 at 426; (2) in s.18 the wound or grievous bodily harm may be caused to "any person" whereas s.20 refers to "any other person" which gives rise to the interesting possibility that D could be prosecuted for the s.18 offence where he causes GBH or a wound to himself, for example, to gain discharge from military service.

2. In *R. v Bryson* [1985] Crim. L.R. 669, a case in which D's car drove into a group of people, allegedly as a deliberate act by D, a conviction under s.18 followed a direction "that (if he was driving) foresight of probable serious harm, whether he wished it or not, amounted to an intention to cause grievous bodily harm". This was held to be wrong, although in view of the overwhelming evidence of intention, the proviso was applied to uphold the conviction.

Questions

1. What lines should the direction have taken?

2. Is it a defence to a charge under s.18 that D did not have the appropriate intention by reason of voluntary intoxication?

3. Is intentional infection by disease capable of being an offence under s.18?

R. V BENTLEY

(1850) 4 Cox 406

V, a PC in plain clothes, but accompanied by others in uniform, informed D that he was arresting him for suspicion of highway robbery. V had no warrant, but reasonably believed that D was guilty. D refused to be arrested unless told why and by what authority he was being apprehended, and resisted, injuring V. At D's trial for wounding with intent to resist lawful apprehension, it was objected on his behalf that it was not shown that he knew the arrest was unlawful.

TALFORD J

If the apprehension is in point of fact lawful, we are not permitted to consider the question, whether or not he believed it to be so, because that would lead to infinite niceties of discrimination. The rule is not, that a man is always presumed to know the law, but that no man shall be excused for an unlawful act from his ignorance of the law. It was the prisoner's duty, whatever might be his consciousness of innocence, to go to the station house and hear the precise accusations against him. He is not to erect a tribunal in his own mind to decide whether he was legally arrested or not. He was taken into custody by an officer of the law, and it was his duty to obey the law.

Verdict: Guilty

Questions

What is D's position with respect to a charge under s.18 in the following cases?

1. V, seeking lawfully to arrest D, laid hands on him. D, believing that V was a person attempting to rob him, punched V on the jaw, breaking it. D admits that his belief was unreasonable, and that the force he used was more than was reasonably necessary to defend himself, but claims he did not intend or expect to break V's jaw. See Ch.5, above; and *Blackburn v Bowering* [1995] Crim. L.R. 38.

2. D pushes over V in order to resist what they both think is a lawful arrest by V. In the fall, V suffers a broken skull. In fact the arrest is unlawful. See Ch.3, above.

----

iii. Proposals for Reform

The Law Commission has recently published a scoping paper (LCCP 217) in which views on the the case for reform are assessed and whether the draft Bill (below) should constitute the basis for change.

DRAFT OFFENCES AGAINST THE PERSON BILL

1.—(1) A person is guilty of an offence if he intentionally causes serious injury to another.
(2) A person is guilty of an offence if he omits to do an act which he has a duty to do at common law, the omission results in serious injury to another, and he intends the omission to have that result.
. . .
2.—(1) A person is guilty of an offence if he recklessly causes serious injury to another.
. . .
3.—(1) A person is guilty of an offence if he intentionally or recklessly causes injury to another.
. . .
4.—(1) A person is guilty of an offence if—

   (a) he intentionally or recklessly applies force to or causes an impact on the body of another, or

(b)   he intentionally or recklessly causes the other to believe that any such force or impact is imminent.

(2) No such offence is committed if the force or impact, not being intended or likely to cause injury, is in the circumstances such as is generally acceptable in the ordinary conduct of daily life and the defendant does not know or believe that it is in fact unacceptable to the other person.

. . .

6.—(1) A person is guilty of an offence under this section if he causes serious injury to another intending to resist, prevent or terminate the lawful arrest or detention of himself or a third person.

(2) The question whether the defendant believes the arrest or detention is lawful must be determined according to the circumstances as he believes them to be.

. . .

7.—(1) A person is guilty of an offence if he assaults another intending to resist, prevent or terminate the lawful arrest or detention of himself or a third person.

(2) The question whether the defendant believes the arrest or detention is lawful must be determined according to the circumstances as he believes them to be.

(3) For the purposes of this section a person assaults if he commits the offence under s.4.

. . .

8.—(1) A person is guilty of an offence if he acts as mentioned in subsection (2) and—

(a)   he intends to cause serious injury, or
(b)   he is reckless whether serious injury is caused.

(2) A person acts as mentioned in this subsection if he—

(a)   causes an explosive substance to explode,
(b)   places a dangerous substance in any place,
(c)   delivers or sends a dangerous substance to a person,
(d)   throws a dangerous substance at or near a person, or
(e)   applies a dangerous substance to a person.

(3) For the purposes of subsection (2) a dangerous substance is an explosive substance or any other dangerous substance.

(4) In this section 'explosive substance' has the same meaning as in the Explosive Substances Act 1883.

. . .

9.—(1) A person is guilty of an offence if he acts as mentioned in s.8(2) and—

(a)   he intends to cause injury, or risk injury, or
(b)   he is reckless whether injury is caused.

. . .

10.—(1) A person is guilty of an offence if he makes to another a threat to cause the death of, or serious injury to, that other or a third person, intending that other to believe that it will be carried out.

. . .

11.—(1) A person is guilty of an offence if—

(a)   he administers a substance to another or causes it to be taken by him and (in either case) he does so intentionally or recklessly,
(b)   he knows the substance is capable of causing injury to the other, and
(c)   it is unreasonable to administer the substance or cause it to be taken having regard to the circumstances as he knows or believes them to be.

. . .

12.—(1) A person is guilty of an offence if he intentionally inflicts severe pain or suffering on another and he does the act—

(a)   in the performance or purported performance of his of official duties as a public official, or
(b)   at the instigation or with the consent or acquiescence of a public official who is performing or purporting to perform his official duties.

(2) A person is guilty of an offence if—

    (a)   he omits to do an act which he has a duty to do at common law,
    (b)   he makes the omission as mentioned in subsection (1)(a) or (b),
    (c)   the omission results in the infliction of severe pain or suffering on another, and
    (d)   he intends the omission to have that result.

(3) The following are immaterial—

    (a)   the nationality of the persons concerned;
    (b)   whether anything occurs in the United Kingdom or elsewhere;
    (c)   whether the pain or suffering is physical or mental.

. . .

Meaning of fault terms and of injury
14.—(1) A person acts intentionally with respect to a result if—

    (a)   it is his purpose to cause it, or
    (b)   although it is not his purpose to cause it, he knows that it would occur in the ordinary course of events if he were to succeed in his purpose of causing some other result.

(2) A person acts recklessly with respect to a result if he is aware of a risk that it will occur and it is unreasonable to take that risk having regard to the circumstances as he knows or believes them to be.
(3) A person intends an omission to have a result if—

    (a)   it is his purpose that the result will occur, or
    (b)   although it is not his purpose that the result will occur, he knows that it would occur in the ordinary course of events if he were to succeed in his purpose that some other result will occur.

(4) A person is reckless whether an omission will have a result if he is aware of a risk that the result will occur and it is unreasonable to take that risk having regard to the circumstances as he knows or believes them to be.
(5) Related expressions must be construed accordingly.
(6) This section has effect for the purposes of this Act.
15.—(1) In this Act 'injury' means—

    (a)   physical injury, or
    (b)   mental injury.

(2) Physical injury does not include anything caused by disease but (subject to that) it includes pain, unconsciousness and any other impairment of a person's physical condition.
(3) Mental injury does not include anything caused by disease but (subject to that) it includes any impairment of a person's mental health.
(4) In its application to s.1 this section applies without the exceptions relating to things caused by disease.

4. SEXUAL OFFENCES

In the White Paper, *Protecting the Public* (Home Office 2002), Cm.5668, the law relating to sexual offences (mainly contained in the Sexual Offences Act 1956) was described as "archaic, incoherent and discriminatory". The current law can now be found in the Sexual Offences Act 2003 (SOA 2003). The Act (which came into force on 1 May 2004) aims to modernise and strengthen the law with the intention that it be both clearer and more coherent. The SOA 2003 introduces many new offences as well as redefining many of the offences that could be found in the old legislation.

In this part of the chapter the main focus will be on the offences of rape and sexual assault, with other selected offences referred to in outline only. The case law decided under the 1956 Act will still be relevant as a guide to how the new legislation will be interpreted but we await decisions on those parts of the new Act that remain uncertain.

i. Rape

Note

There were many calls for the offence of rape to be reformed. Many (but not all) criticisms centered on the mental element, especially the perceived ease with which the defendant could achieve an acquittal on the basis of a mere honest belief in the victim's consent. Initial reform occurred following the decision of the House of Lords in *R. v R.* [1991] 1 A.C. 599 where it was held that a husband could be convicted of the rape of his wife. Section 142 of the Criminal Justice and Public Order Act 1994 placed this decision on a statutory footing and expanded the definition of rape to include anal intercourse as well as vaginal intercourse with a person who did not consent to it, the defendant either knowing that the victim did not consent or being reckless thereto. The SOA 2003 extends the definition of rape to include oral penile penetration, a type of behaviour that many would regard as just as offensive and degrading as vaginal or anal penetration.

SEXUAL OFFENCES ACT 2003

1. Rape

(1) A person (A) commits an offence if—

(a) he intentionally penetrates the vagina, anus or mouth of another person (B) with his penis,

(b) B does not consent to the penetration, and

(c) A does not reasonably believe that B consents.

(2) Whether a belief is reasonable is to be determined having regard to all the circumstances, including any steps A has taken to ascertain whether B consents.
(3) Sections 75 and 76 apply to an offence under this section.
(4) A person guilty of an offence under this section is liable, on conviction on indictment, to imprisonment for life.

79. Part I: general interpretation

(1) The following apply for the purposes of this Part.
(2) Penetration is a continuing act from entry to withdrawal.
(3) References to a part of the body include references to a part surgically constructed (in particular, through gender reassignment surgery) . . .
(9) 'Vagina' includes vulva.

Actus Reus

Notes

1.   Section 79 (2) puts the decisions in *R. v Kaitamaki* [1985] A.C. 147; and *R. v Cooper & Schaub* [1994] Crim. L.R. 531 on a statutory footing. It follows that if (using the terminology of the Act) A penetrates B with consent but B later retracts that consent, then A should withdraw. If A continues to penetrate in such circumstances this would amount to the actus reus of rape. The Act is silent as to what constitutes penetration and so it is assumed that the common law rule that the slightest degree of penetration is sufficient holds good. Certainly, as far as vaginal rape is concerned, this is supported by s.79(9) which defines "vagina" to include vulva.

2.   It remains the case that rape can only be committed by a male, at least as the principal offender,

although s.79(3) makes it clear that rape can be committed by a post-operative female to male transsexual, just as a male to female transsexual may be the victim of vaginal rape (s.79(3)). A female may aid, abet, counsel or procure the offence of rape although in many circumstances it may be more appropriate to consider the offence of causing a person to engage in sexual activity without consent (SOA 2003 s.4).

Consent—Agreement, Freedom, Capacity

74. 'Consent'

For the purposes of this part, a person consents if he agrees by choice, and has the freedom and capacity to make that choice.

Notes

1. By s.74, it seems that the draftsman intended to indicate that a lack of protest or resistance from the victim does not indicate the presence of consent. The previous law had established that it was not necessary to prove that B communicated positive dissent, it being sufficient to prove that B actually did not consent (see *R. v McAllister* [1997] Crim. L.R. 233). In appropriate cases, juries should be reminded that merely because B did not say or do anything that might indicate a lack of consent, it cannot be assumed that B did consent. Passivity on B's part, perhaps because of sheer terror, rightly cannot be taken as an indication that B has freely agreed by choice to engage in sexual conduct with A. Inclusion of the word "choice" suggests that B must be aware of the activity as well as A's identity and accordingly, freely agree to partake. It is also important to read s.74 in conjunction with the presumptions contained in ss.75 and 76 (see below, p.582). In the final analysis, the state of B's mind and whether or not real "choice" has been exercised is one for the jury to decide upon. It may be that numerous factors have to be considered in reaching this decision. Factors such as whether or not A and B were in a relationship might well have some relevance in shedding light on the issue of "choice", including the background and history of previous encounters. For example, B may know from past experience that a refusal to submit to A's demands for sexual intercourse will be met with violence even though on this occasion none is actually threatened. If B does submit on this occasion is she freely exercising choice and consenting?

2. It would seem clear that freedom of choice would be negated by violence or the threat of violence, at least where the violence or threat thereof is explicit. It is not impossible, however, to imagine more difficult cases where B claims that there was no actual freedom of choice. Consider, for example, question 3 below.

3. The meaning of capacity in s.74 of the Act is not defined but would, in this context, appear to refer to mental capacity. Elsewhere in the SOA 2003, s.30(1) creates an offence of sexual activity with a person with a mental disorder impeding choice. Section 30(2) provides that:

   B is unable to refuse if—
   (a) he lacks the capacity to choose whether to agree . . . (whether because he lacks sufficient understanding of the nature or reasonably foreseeable consequences of what is being done, or for any other reason), or
   (b) he is unable to communicate such a choice to A.

   Section 30(2)(a) clearly extends to matters such as whether B has sufficient comprehension of the sexual act and what its consequences may be. It would also appear to extend to those persons who lack capacity to choose, not because of any inherent mental disorder but because of some particular circumstance such as where, for example, B is acting as an automaton in a state of impaired consciousness.

Questions

1. Linda, an aspiring film actress, has sexual intercourse with Simon, a leading film director. Linda finds this distasteful and she would not have considered such an act had she not been hoping to be given a part in Simon's new film. Has Linda agreed by choice or is this non-consensual? Would it make any difference if Simon tells Linda that he will ensure she never works as an actress again unless she agrees to have sexual intercourse with him? If so, why is this different?

2. Linda suffers a traumatic marital breakdown and consults Simon, a divorce counsellor. Simon recognises that Linda is emotionally vulnerable and in desperate need of affection. He repeatedly tells her that having a sexual relationship with him would help her recovery. After several weeks of persuasion she submits to sexual intercourse. Several months later, Linda complains that Simon exploited her vulnerability and took advantage of her emotional state. Has Linda's freedom to make a choice been negated?

3. Linda is heavily drunk following an evening out with friends. In her drunken state she engages in sexual intercourse with Simon. The following day Linda, now sober, claims her judgement was so impaired she lacked capacity to make a choice. Do you agree that Linda lacked capacity? (See *R. v Bree*, directly below).

4. Are all persons who are unable to communicate because of mental disorder denied the opportunity of having a legally consensual sexual relationship?

R. V BREE

[2007] EWCA Crim 804

D and M had been drinking very heavily together. At one point, M was physically sick. Both D and M returned to M's student flat. M accepted that she had a "very patchy" recollection of the events. It was accepted that she did not say "no" to intercourse. D said he was "absolutely positive" that M was awake and conscious throughout the brief intercourse that took place. He testified that she had removed her own lower clothing and responded positively to foreplay prior to the intercourse. D was convicted of rape.

PRESIDENT OF THE QUEEN'S BENCH DIVISION, SIR IGOR JUDGE

Section 74 of the 2003 Act defines consent:

'. . . a person consents if he agrees by choice, and has the freedom and capacity to make that choice'.

One of the objectives of the Sexual Offences Act 2003, was to bring coherence and clarity to the meaning of consent. The provisions relating to consent represented the result of substantial discussion and Parliamentary debate about the principles which should apply to the acutely sensitive and intensely personal area of sexual relationships, whether they arise in the context of a long established marriage, or partnership, or a casual sexual encounter between total strangers. Arguments about consent abound just because consent to sexual intercourse extends from passionate enthusiasm to reluctant or bored acquiescence, and its absence includes quiet submission or surrender as well as determined physical resistance against an attacker which might expose the victim to injury, and sometimes death. The declared objective of the White Paper, Protecting the Public (Cm. 5668, 2002) was to produce statutory provisions relating to consent which would be 'clear and unambiguous'. As enacted, the legislation on this topic has not commanded totally uncritical enthusiasm. For some it goes too far, and for others not far enough. The law in the area, and our decision, must be governed by the definition of consent in section 74.

Neither 'freedom', nor 'capacity', are further defined or explained within section 74 itself, nor indeed in sections 75 and 76, which create evidential presumptions relating to consent. We note the analysis in the illuminating article, The Sexual Offences Act 2003, Rape, Sexual Assault and the Problems of Consent, (2004) CLR 328 by Professor Temkin and Professor Ashworth, that 'it might be thought that "freedom" and "choice" are ideas which raise philosophical issues of such complexity as to be ill-suited to the needs of criminal justice—clearly those words do not refer to total freedom or choice, so all the questions about how much liberty of action satisfies the "definition" remains at large'. Notwithstanding these philosophical difficulties, it is clear that for the purposes of the 2003 Act 'capacity' is integral to the concept of 'choice', and therefore to 'consent'.

Section 75 and section 76 of the 2003 Act address the issue of consent in practical situations which arise from time to time in cases of alleged sexual offences including rape. They are not, however, exhaustive. The presumptions in section 75 are evidential and rebuttable, whereas those in section 76 are irrebuttable and conclusive. In this appeal we are not concerned with either of the conclusive presumptions relating to consent specified in section 76. The common characteristic of the particular situations covered by the evidential presumptions in section 75 is that they are concerned with situations in which the complainant is involuntarily at a disadvantage. Section 75 (2) (f) is plainly adequate to deal with the situation when a drink is 'spiked', but unless productive of a state of near unconsciousness, or incapacity, this paragraph does not address seductive blandishments to have 'just one more' drink. Section 75 (2)(d) repeats well established common law principles, and acknowledges plain good sense, that, if the complainant is unconscious as a result of her voluntary consumption of alcohol, the starting point is to presume that she is not consenting to intercourse. Beyond that, the Act is silent about the impact of excessive but voluntary alcohol consumption on the ability to give consent to intercourse, or indeed to consent generally.

It is perhaps helpful to identify a number of features of the law relating to consent which although obvious are sometimes overlooked. On any view, both parties to the act of sexual intercourse with which this case is concerned were the worse for drink. Both were adults. Neither acted unlawfully in drinking to excess. They were both free to choose how much to drink, and with whom. Both were free, if they wished, to have intercourse with each other. There is nothing abnormal, surprising, or even unusual about men and women having consensual intercourse when one, or other, or both have voluntarily consumed a great deal of alcohol. Provided intercourse is indeed consensual, it is not rape.

In cases which are said to arise after voluntary consumption of alcohol the question is not whether the alcohol made either or both less inhibited than they would have been if sober, nor whether either or both might afterwards have regretted what had happened, and indeed wished that it had not. If the complainant consents, her consent cannot be revoked. Moreover it is not a question whether either or both may have had very poor recollection of precisely what had happened. That may be relevant the reliability of their evidence. Finally, and certainly, it is not a question whether either or both was behaving irresponsibly. As they were both autonomous adults, the essential question for decision is, as it always is, whether the evidence proved that the appellant had sexual intercourse with the complainant without her consent.

Before the 2003 Act, it was not difficult to identify the relevant legal principles, and for a judge to explain the law relating to the voluntary consumption of alcohol (or drugs) by a complainant. Thus, for example, in *R. v Malone* [1998] 2 CAR 447 the Court of Appeal upheld the direction:

'She does not claim to have physically resisted nor to have verbally protested. She says the drink has disabled her from doing either . . . she has told you she did not consent . . . you must be sure that the act of sexual intercourse occurred without (her) consent. Submitting to an act of sexual intercourse, because through drink she was unable physically to resist though she wished to, is not consent. If she submits to intercourse because of the drink she cannot physically resist, that, of course, is not consent. No right thinking person would say that in those circumstances she was genuinely consenting to what occurred. What occurred . . . not wishing to have intercourse but being physically unable to do anything about it . . . would plainly, as a matter of common sense be against her will. It would be without her consent'.

We record this direction as illustrative of what was regarded as an appropriate direction in the circumstances of an individual case to a particular jury, rather than a learned disquisition of the law of consent as applied to rape.

We should however highlight *R. v Lang* [1976] 62 CAR 50 which summarised the relevant principle. The jury sought guidance from the judge on the question of whether the complainant's alcohol consumption may have vitiated her consent to sexual intercourse. The court observed

'. . . there is no special rule applicable to drink and rape. If the issue be, as here, did the woman consent? the critical question is not how she came to take the drink, but whether she understood her situation and was capable of making up her mind. In *Howard* [1965] 50 CAR 56 the Court of Criminal Appeal had to consider the case of a girl under 16. Lord Parker C.J. . . . said: . . . "in the case of a girl under 16 the prosecution must prove either that she physically resisted, or, if she did not, that her understanding and knowledge was such that she was not in a position to decide whether to consent or resist". In our view these words are of general application whenever there is present some factor, be it permanent or transient, suggesting the absence of such understanding or knowledge . . .. None of this was explained to the jury. Their attention was focussed by the judge upon how she came to take drink, not upon the state of her understanding and her capacity to exercise judgment in the circumstances.'

In the context of the statutory provision in section 74, it is noteworthy that *Lang* decided thirty years or so ago, directly focussed on the 'capacity' of the complainant to decide whether to consent to intercourse or not. These are the concepts with which the 2003 Act itself is concerned.

We are not aware of any reported decisions which deal with this aspect of the new legislation. We should however refer to the much publicised case of *R. v Dougal*, heard in Swansea Crown Court, in November 2005. Having heard the evidence of the complainant, the Crown decided to offer no further evidence. Before the jury counsel for the Crown explained:

'the prosecution are conscious of the fact that a drunken consent is still a consent and that in the answer, in cross-examination, she said, in terms, that she could not remember giving her consent and that is fatal to the prosecution's case. In those circumstances the prosecution will have no further evidence on the issue of consent. This is a case of the word of the defendant against that of the complainant on that feature It is fatal to the prosecution's case. . ..'

The judge (Roderick Evans J.) directed the jury that as the prosecution was no longer seeking a guilty verdict, there was only one verdict which could be returned, and that was an acquittal. He added that he agreed with the course the prosecution had taken.

Without knowing all the details of the case, and focusing exclusively on the observations of counsel for the Crown in *Dougal*, it would be open to question whether the inability of the complainant to remember whether she gave her consent or not might on further reflection be approached rather differently. Prosecuting counsel may wish he had expressed himself more felicitously. That said, one of the most familiar directions of law provided to juries who are being asked to conclude that the voluntary consumption of alcohol by a defendant should lead to the conclusion that he was too drunk to form the intention required for proof of the crime alleged against him, is that a drunken intent is still an intent. (*R. v Sheehan and Moore* [1975] 60 CAR 308 at 312). So it is, and that we suspect is the source of the phrase that a 'drunken consent is still consent'. In the context of consent to intercourse, the phrase lacks delicacy, but, properly understood, it provides a useful shorthand accurately encapsulating the legal position. We note in passing that it also acts as a reminder that a drunken man who intends to commit rape, and does so, is not excused by the fact that his intention is a drunken intention.

Some of the hugely critical discussion arising after *Dougal* missed the essential point. Neither counsel for the Crown, nor for that matter the judge, was saying or coming anywhere near saying, either that a complainant who through drink is incapable of consenting to intercourse must nevertheless be deemed to have consented to it, or that a man is at liberty to have sexual intercourse with a woman who happens to be drunk, on the basis that her drunkenness deprives her of her right to choose whether to have intercourse or not. Such ideas are wrong in law, and indeed, offensive. All that was being said in *Dougal* was that when someone who has had a lot to drink is in fact consenting to intercourse, then that is what she is doing, consenting: equally, if after taking drink, she is not consenting, then by definition intercourse is taking place without her consent. This is unexceptionable.

In our judgment, the proper construction of section 74 of the 2003 Act, as applied to the problem now under discussion, leads to clear conclusions. If, through drink (or for any other reason) the complainant has temporarily lost her capacity to choose whether to have intercourse on the relevant occasion, she is not consenting, and subject to questions about the defendant's state of mind, if intercourse takes place, this would be rape. However, where the complainant has voluntarily consumed even substantial quantities of alcohol, but nevertheless remains capable of choosing whether or not to have intercourse, and in drink agrees to do so, this would not be rape. We should perhaps underline that, as a matter of practical reality, capacity to consent may evaporate well before a complainant becomes unconscious. Whether this is so or not, however, is fact specific, or more accurately, depends on the actual state of mind of the individuals involved on the particular occasion.

Considerations like these underline the fact that it would be unrealistic to endeavour to create some kind of grid system which would enable the answer to these questions to be related to some prescribed level of alcohol consumption. Experience shows that different individuals have a greater or lesser capacity to cope with alcohol than others, and indeed the ability of a single individual to do so may vary from day to day. The practical reality is that there are some areas of human behaviour which are inapt for detailed legislative structures. In this context, provisions intended to protect women from sexual assaults might very well be conflated into a system which would provide patronising interference with the right of autonomous adults to make personal decisions for themselves.

For these reasons, notwithstanding criticisms of the statutory provisions, in our view the 2003 Act provides a clear definition of 'consent' for the purposes of the law of rape, and by defining it with reference to 'capacity to make that choice', sufficiently addresses the issue of consent in the context of voluntary consumption of alcohol by the complainant. The problems do not arise from the legal principles. They lie with infinite circumstances of human behaviour, usually taking place in private without independent evidence, and the consequent difficulties of proving this very serious offence.

The striking feature of the summing-up, which is criticised in a number of different ways, is that it does not directly address either the general problems to which this kind of case may give rise, nor their specific application to the present case.

The jury were rightly directed that an essential requirement before the appellant could be convicted was that M did not consent to intercourse. They were told that 'a person consents if he agrees by choice and has the freedom and capacity to make that choice'. The statutory definition having been read, no further elucidation was given. Our attention was drawn to R v Olugboga [1981] 73 CAR 344, decided after the enactment of the Sexual Offences (Amendment) Act 1976. As Professor Temkin and Professor Ashworth explain, the report Setting the Boundaries: Reforming the Law on Sexual Offences(2000) which echoed a much earlier report by an advisory group chaired by Heilbron J. in November 1975, suggested that the broad approach to consent and submission adopted in Olugboga should be abandoned. In our view, even if these criticisms are justified, the judgment contains passages of continuing value. The court rejected the submission on behalf of the Crown that a trial judge was required 'merely to leave the issue of consent to a jury in a similar way to that in which the issue of dishonesty is left in trials for offences under the Theft Act'. Because of the myriad circumstances in which the issue of consent may arise, the judgment continued, 'We do not think that the issue of consent should be left to a jury without some further direction. What this should be will depend on the circumstances of each case.'

In this case the jury should have been given some assistance with the meaning of 'capacity' in circumstances where the complainant was affected by her own voluntarily induced intoxication, and also whether, and to what extent they could take that into account in deciding whether she had consented. Moreover, the judge did not address the changed way in which the prosecution put its case against the appellant. There is a significant difference between an allegation that the complainant was unconscious and for that reason not consenting to intercourse, and an allegation that, although she was capable of giving consent, despite her state, she was not in fact consenting to intercourse and was giving clear indications that she was rejecting the appellant. The potential for confusion was compounded by the fact that the complainant herself asserted, more than once, that she was unconscious at different stages of the encounter. At the same time the Crown conceded that what she believed to be and said were periods of unconsciousness should for the purposes of the trial be treated as moments of memory deficit caused by drink. Of course if the Crown was not contending that she was unconscious, that at least was consistent with the appellant's case that she was indeed conscious throughout . . . .

The questions whether she might have behaved differently drunk than she would have done sober, and whether, although and perhaps because drunk, she might have behaved as the appellant contended, and the way in which the jury should consider these important issues, were not mentioned at all . . . .

In a trial in which the issues of consent and voluntary intoxication were fundamental to the outcome, the jury were given no or no sufficient directions to enable the verdict which they reached to be regarded as safe. Accordingly the conviction was quashed.

Appeal allowed

Consent—Presumptions

75. Evidential presumptions about consent

(1) If in proceedings for an offence to which this section applies it is proved—

    (a)   that the defendant did the relevant act,

    (b)   that any of the circumstances specified in subsection (2) existed, and

    (c)   that the defendant knew that those circumstances existed,

the complainant is to be taken not to have consented to the relevant act unless sufficient evidence is adduced to raise an issue as to whether he consented, and the defendant is to be taken not to have reasonably believed that the complainant consented unless sufficient evidence is adduced to raise an issue as to whether he reasonably believed it.

(2) The circumstances are that—

    (a)   any person was, at the time of the relevant act or immediately Before it began, using violence against the complainant or causing the complainant to fear that immediate violence would be used against him;

    (b)   any person was, at the time of the relevant act or immediately Before it began, causing the complainant to fear that violence was being used, or that immediate violence would be used, against another person;

    (c)   the complainant was, and the defendant was not, unlawfully detained at the time of the relevant act;

    (d)   the complainant was asleep or otherwise unconscious at the time of the relevant act;

    (e)   because of the complainant's physical disability, the complainant would not have been able at the time of the relevant act to communicate to the defendant whether the complainant consented;

    (f)   any person had administered to or caused to be taken by the complainant, without the complainant's consent, a substance which, having regard to when it was administered or taken, was capable of causing or enabling the complainant to be stupefied or overpowered at the time of the relevant act.

(3) In subsection (2)(a) and (b), the reference to the time immediately before the relevant act began is, in the case of an act which is one of a continuous series of sexual activities, a reference to the time immediately before the first sexual activity began.

76. Conclusive presumptions about consent

(1) If in proceedings for an offence to which this section applies it is proved u that the defendant did the relevant act and that any of the circumstances specified in subsection (2) existed, it is to be conclusively presumed—

    (a)   that the complainant did not consent to the relevant act, and

    (b)   that the defendant did not believe that the complainant consented to the relevant act.

(2) The circumstances are that—

    (a)   the defendant intentionally deceived the complainant as to the nature or purpose of the relevant act;

    (b)   the defendant intentionally induced the complainant to consent to the relevant act by impersonating a person known personally to the complainant.

Notes

1.   Sections 75 and 76 set out two types of presumption. If A is proved to have committed the "relevant act", namely penetration of B's vagina, anus or mouth with his penis then, if he knows one of the circumstances set out in ss.75 or 76 exists, lack of consent may be presumed, either conclusively or rebuttably.

2.   If A is proved to have committed the "relevant act", namely penetration of B's vagina, anus or mouth with his penis then, if he knows one of the circumstances set out in s.75 exists, B will be taken not to have consented and A taken not to have had a reasonable belief in B's consent

unless A can introduce sufficient evidence to raise an issue about the truth of the facts. If one of the circumstances in s.75 is proved to exist and A does not introduce sufficient evidence (whether this is concerned with either consent or A's belief in consent) and there is no other defence available, the jury will be bound to conclude that A is guilty. If A does introduce sufficient evidence, then it will be the task of the prosecution to prove the issue to the normal criminal standard. In *Ciccarelli* [2011] EWCA Crim 2665, A touched B sexually while she was drunk and asleep. He did not know her well having only met her a couple of times before and there had never previously been any sexual activity between them. He nevertheless tried to argue that he had believed she would consent. On appeal from his conviction, Lord Judge CJ explained the operation of s.75:

> "It was suggested that section 75 of the 2003 Act reverses the ordinary principles relating to the burden of proof in criminal cases. We do not agree. Section 75 is an evidential provision. It relates to matters of evidence, and in particular evidential presumptions about consent in circumstances where, as we have already indicated, as a matter of reality and common sense, the strong likelihood is that the complainant will not, in fact, be consenting. If, however, in those circumstances there is sufficient evidence for the jury to consider, then the burden of disproving them remains on the prosecution. Therefore, before the question of the appellant's reasonable belief in the complainant's consent could be left to the jury, *some evidence beyond the fanciful or speculative had to be adduced to support the reasonableness of his belief in her consent*." (emphasis added)

While A had given evidence to the effect that he did believe she would consent, the trial judge's view was that there was nothing that might even begin to suggest a reasonable basis for such a belief. The Court of Appeal agreed; there was accordingly no evidence capable of rebutting the evidential presumption. Simply asserting a belief (if, indeed, A ever had such a belief) is a long way from providing evidence to support the reasonableness of that belief.

3. Conclusive presumptions apply if A intentionally deceives B as to the nature or purpose of the act or he intentionally impersonates a person known personally to B. When a conclusive presumption operates, A will not be able to displace the presumption no matter how much evidence he wishes to introduce. Although under the old law it was established that deceiving the victim as to the nature and quality of the act negated consent (see *R. v Williams* [1923] 1 K.B. 340) by referring to the nature or purpose of the act, it is suggested that the new law may have been extended in a way that was not foreseen. In *R. v Linekar* [1995] 2 Cr. App. R. 49, the complainant was a prostitute who agreed to intercourse for £25. The defendant never intended to pay. It was held this was not rape because the prostitute was not deceived as to the nature or quality of the act, namely sexual intercourse. Under the new law, it could be argued that she has been deceived as to the nature and purpose of the act. For the prostitute, the purpose of the act is principally one concerned with money and so a defendant who intentionally deceives about payment runs the risk that the conclusive presumption in s.76 would operate to negate consent.

Question

If A impersonates someone B knows he is not permitted to introduce any evidence that might demonstrate that B consented. If A uses violence or administers a stupefying drug to overcome B's resistance he is permitted to introduce evidence to demonstrate that B may have consented. Why?

R. V JHEETA

[2007] EWCA Crim 1699

D created a "bizarre and fictitious fantasy" relating to V's safety and his own suicidal intentions designed to encourage her to have sexual intercourse with him more frequently. There was no deception as to the nature or purpose of the act but as to the situation in which she found herself with the result that s.76(2)(a) had no application. D's deceptions, however, would be relevant evidence for a jury in considering whether there was consent under s.74.

PRESIDENT OF THE QUEEN'S BENCH DIVISION, SIR IGOR JUDGE

[After reviewing the facts His Lordship continued:] Our particular concern is with section 76(2)(a), the 'nature and purpose' of the 'relevant act'. For the purposes of sections 75 and 76, relevant act is defined by section 77. In the context of rape the relevant act is 'the defendant intentionally penetrating, with his penis . . . another person ("the complainant")'. The provisions relating to consent are not confined to rape, but do not at present require further examination. Perhaps more important, the offence of procuring a woman to have sexual intercourse by false pretences ceased to exist when the 2003 Act came into force. Hence the difference between counts one and two, and then three to six of the present indictment, and the absence of any concern about the appellant's conviction on counts one and two.

This consideration provided part of the foundation for the submission by Mr Wall that a statute which brought together all the offences of a sexual nature cannot have been intended to decriminalise deliberate conduct designed to deceive a woman into having sexual intercourse. Here, the appellant's purpose was to deceive the complainant into having sexual intercourse with him in order to alleviate or remove the problems which she, having been deceived by him, believed she faced. The result was that she submitted to intercourse because of those extraneous pressures. These submissions broadened from the narrow consideration of section 76(2)(a) of the Act into the wider question of consent as defined in section 74. The appellant's actions deprived the complainant of her freedom to choose whether or not to have intercourse with him. He pleaded guilty on the basis that at least on some occasions her freedom to choose was constrained by his actions. For the moment we shall confine our attention to the irrebuttable presumption in section 76(2)(a).

Miss Marsh submitted that the Act incorporated the common law on these issues into statute, and created the irrebuttable evidential presumptions. The fact that the presumptions in section 76 are conclusive reinforced the need for circumspection about an extended interpretation of the 'nature or purpose' of the relevant act. The deception, within the limits described in the basis of plea, is conceded, but it was not a deception about the nature or purpose of the relevant act. The complainant was sexually experienced. She was aware of the nature and purpose of intercourse, and the identity of the applicant. The advice given to the appellant was incorrect in law. There was no deception operating on the mind of the complainant about the nature or purpose of the Act. The conclusive presumptions could not be established. The plea was tendered after legal advice which did not accurately reflect the statutory provisions. Therefore the convictions are unsafe.

Our approach is to address the ambit of section 76 in the context of the creation of an irrebuttable evidential presumption, with wide application to effectively every incident of sexual touching. Professor Temkin and Professor Ashworth explained one possible consequences of a wide interpretation of 76 in their valuable article, The Sexual Offences Act 2003 (1) Rape Sexual Assault and the Problems of Consent (2004)CLR 328 at 338.

'Those who are uncomfortable with the full implications of sexual autonomy may not share the view that a conclusive presumption of absence of consent should apply where D has sex with C who is asleep at the time. The provisions of the Act on consent apply not only to rape and assault by penetration but also to touching which falls within sexual assault or causing sexual activity. A conclusive presumption of absence of consent and absence of reasonable belief in consent, if applied to all situations where C was asleep at the time, would render D liable for sexual assault if he sexually touched his partner C while C was asleep even though D was in the habit of doing so and C had not objected to this in the past'.

The writers point out that a complaint, and subsequent prosecution, would be unlikely. However it would seem pretty surprising to couples sharing a bed to be told that the law prohibited either of them from intimately touching the other while asleep, and that they would be potentially liable to prosecution and punishment, for a sexual touch of the sleeping partner as a preliminary to possible sexual activity which the sleeping partner, on awakening, might welcome. The article also addresses 'the problem' of the repeal of the offence of procuring sexual intercourse by false representations. It explains that convictions for this offence were rare, adding that 'in the unusual case where this issue occurs, the vague terms of section 74 now assume a heightened importance'.

The starting point in our analysis is to acknowledge that in most cases, the absence of consent, and the appropriate state of the defendant's mind, will be proved without reference to evidential or conclusive presumptions. When they do apply, section 75 and section 76 are directed to the process of proving the absence of consent to whichever sexual act is alleged. They are concerned with presumptions about rather than the definition of consent The evidential presumptions in section 75 continue to require the prosecution to disprove consent if, in the circumstances defined in the section, there is sufficient evidence to raise the issue. These presumptions are not conclusive, merely evidential. However section 76 raises presumptions conclusive of the issue of consent, and thus where intercourse is proved, conclusive of guilt. They therefore require the most stringent scrutiny.

In our judgment the ambit of section 76 is limited to the 'act' to which it is said to apply. In rape cases the 'act' is vaginal, anal or oral intercourse. Provided this consideration is constantly borne in mind, it will be seen that section 76 (2)(a) is relevant only to the comparatively rare cases where the defendant deliberately deceives the complainant about the *nature or purpose* of one or other form of intercourse. No conclusive presumptions arise merely because the complainant was deceived in some way or other by disingenuous blandishments of or common or garden lies by the defendant. These may well be deceptive and persuasive, but they will rarely go to the nature or purpose of intercourse. Beyond this limited type of case, and assuming that, as here, section 75 has no application, the issue of consent must be addressed in the context of section 74.

It may be helpful to reinforce these observations by reference to a number of cases at common law which provide examples of deceptions as to the nature or purpose of the act of intercourse. As to the nature of the relevant act, in *R v Flattery* [1877] 2QBD 410 the Court of Crown Cases Reserved upheld a conviction for rape where intercourse took place after the complainant, a girl of 19, was persuaded that the defendant was performing a surgical operation which would break 'nature's string' and provide a remedy for the fits to which she was subject. In *R v Williams* [1923] 1 KB 340 the conviction for rape was upheld where the defendant deceived a girl of 16 into having sexual intercourse with him to cure a problem with her breathing which prevented her from singing properly. The judge summed up the legal principles in terms approved by the Court of Criminal Appeal:

'The law has laid it down that where a girl's consent is procured by the means which the girl says this prisoner adopted, that is to say, where she is persuaded that what was being done to her is not the ordinary act of sexual intercourse but is some medical or surgical operation in order to give her relief from some disability from which she is suffering, then that is rape although the actual thing that was done was with her consent, because she never consented to the act of sexual intercourse. She was persuaded to consent to what he did because she thought it was not sexual intercourse and because she thought it was a surgical operation'.

Deception as to purpose is sometimes said to be exemplified in *R v Tabassum* [2000] 2 CAR 328, a decision described by the late Professor Sir John Smith as a 'doubtful case'. A number of women agreed to participate in a breast cancer research programme at the behest of the appellant when, as a result of what he said or did, or both, they wrongly believed that he was medically qualified or trained. They consented to a medical examination, not to sexual touching by a stranger. 'There was consent to the nature of the act, but not to its quality'. However section 76 (2)(a) does not address the 'quality' of the act, but confines itself to its 'purpose'. In the latest edition of Smith and Hogan Criminal Law, (11th edition) Professor David Ormerod identifies a better example, *R v Green* [2002] EWCA Crim 1501. Bogus medical examinations of young men were carried out by a qualified doctor, in the course of which they were wired up to monitors while they masturbated. The purported object was to assess their potential for impotence. Although the experiment did not involve any form of intercourse, it illustrates the practice of a deception as to the 'purpose' of the physical act.

These examples demonstrate the likely rarity of occasions when the conclusive presumption in section 76 (2)(a) will apply. For example, *R v Linekar* [1995] 2 CAR 49 would not fall within its ambit. The appellant promised to pay a prostitute £25 if she had intercourse with him. It was a promise he never intended to keep. On this aspect of the case, that is, that the defendant tricked the prostitute into having intercourse with him, the judge left it to the jury to consider whether his fraud vitiated her consent which was given on the basis that he would pay. The conviction was quashed. The consent given by the complainant was a real consent, which was not destroyed by the appellant's false pretence. He undoubtedly lied to her. However she was undeceived about either the nature or the purpose of the act, that is intercourse. Accordingly the conclusive presumptions in section 76 would have no application.

With these considerations in mind, we must return to the present case. On the written basis of plea the appellant undoubtedly deceived the complainant. He created a bizarre and fictitious fantasy which, because it was real enough to her, pressurised her to have intercourse with him more frequently than she otherwise would have done. She was not deceived as to the nature or purpose of intercourse, but deceived as to the situation in which she found herself. In our judgment the conclusive presumption in section 76 (2)(a) had no application, and counsel for the appellant below were wrong to advise on the basis that it did. . .

Appeal dismissed

Questions and Notes

1.   If A is infected with the HIV virus and does not reveal this to B when asked, does B agree to sexual intercourse by choice? (See *R. v Dica* [2004] EWCA Crim 1103; and *R. v Konzani* [2005] EWCA Crim 706, above pp.554 & 558).

   The law prior to the enactment of the SOA 2003 did not regard this as a matter which vitiated consent. In *B* [2006] EWCA 2945, the Court of Appeal held that the fact that A had not disclosed the fact that he was suffering from a serious sexually transmitted disease is not relevant to the issue of whether a person with whom he engaged in sexual intercourse had consented to it within the meaning of s.74 and no issues arose under the presumptions in relation to consent under ss.75 and 76. In particular, s.76 made reference only to two specific deceptions which could vitiate consent.

2.   If, however, B expressly asks A about his HIV status before agreeing to sexual intercourse and A lies, can B be said to be "agreeing by choice" where she has been deceived in respect of a consideration central to her decision?

   In *B* the Court expressed the obiter opinion that express misrepresentations were no different to implied misrepresentations. If this is correct it would have the strange result that in such a situation, if B does not contract HIV, A would not be liable to conviction of the s.20 offence and there would be no deterrent to him continuing his dangerous activities.

3.   The deficiencies in the reasoning in *B* have, at least, been recognised by the Divisional Court in *Assange v Swedish Prosecution Authority* [2011] EWHC 2489 (Admin) in the context of an appeal against extradition under a European Arrest Warrant (EAW), where the issue was whether conduct alleged to amount to the Swedish offence of sexual molestation was an offence under the law of England and Wales. The crucial issue was whether A would have been guilty of raping B if B had consented only to protected sex, but A, without B's knowledge, did not use a condom, or removed the condom he had initially worn. The Court concluded that the case raised no issue as to the presumptions in s.76 because, if there was any deception, it was not a deception as to the "nature or purpose of the relevant act". Sir John Thomas P stated (at paras [90]–[91]):

   "If the conduct of the defendant is not within s.76, that does not preclude reliance on s.74. *B* goes no further than deciding that failure to disclose HIV infection is not of itself relevant to consent under s.74. *B* does not permit A to contend that, if he deceived [B] as to whether he was using a condom or one that he had not damaged, that was irrelevant to the issue of [B's] consent to sexual intercourse as a matter of the law of England and Wales or his belief in her consent. On each of those issues, it is clear that it is the prosecution case she did not consent and he had no or no reasonable belief in that consent. Those are issues to which s.74 and not s.76 is relevant; there is nothing in *R v B* which compels any other conclusion. . . Thus, if the question is whether what is set out in the EAW is an offence under the law of England and Wales, then it is in our view clear that it was; the requirement of dual criminality is satisfied."

The Divisional Court was satisfied, quite rightly, that the fact that conduct does not fall within s.76 does not preclude reliance upon s.74. Sir John Thomas P stated (at [88]):

"It would, in our view have been extraordinary if Parliament had legislated in terms that, if conduct that was not deceptive could be taken into account for the purposes of s. 74, conduct that was deceptive could not be."

4.   If the defendant deceives the complainant about their gender does this negate consent? In *McNally* [2013] EWCA Crim 1051, the victim and defendant conducted an online relationship in which the defendant claimed to be a male when, in fact, she was female. The relationship developed over a period of several years with the defendant dressing as a male on each occasion they met. The relationship became sexual with the defendant engaging in digital penetration of the victim. The victim reported the circumstances to the police when she discovered the defendant was,in fact, a female. The court held that the defendant's deception as to gender negated the victims consent.

TEMKIN AND ASHWORTH, "THE SEXUAL OFFENCES ACT 2003: RAPE, SEXUAL ASSAULTS AND THE PROBLEMS OF CONSENT" [2004] CRIM. L.R. 328

The Act provides a general definition of consent in s.74: 'A person consents if he agrees by choice, and has the freedom and capacity to make that choice.' Where the facts of a case do not fall squarely within any of the irrebuttable or rebuttable presumptions, the arguments will focus on the application of this definition. It might be thought that 'freedom' and 'choice' are ideas which raise philosophical issues of such complexity as to be ill-suited to the needs of criminal justice—clearly those words do not refer to total freedom or choice, so all the questions about how much liberty of action satisfies the 'definition' remain at large. What the philosopher J.L. Austin said of the term 'freedom' applies equally to 'choice':

'While it has been the tradition to present this as the 'positive' term requiring elucidation, there is little doubt that to say we acted "freely" . . . is to say only that we acted not un-freely, in one or another of the heterogeneous ways of so acting (under duress, or what not). Like 'real', 'free' is only used to rule out the suggestion of some or all of its recognized antitheses.'

Perhaps in anticipation of these difficulties, the Report recommended that there should be a standard direction on the meaning of consent: depending on the circumstances of the case, juries should be told not to assume that C did freely agree just because C did not say or do anything, protest or resist or was not physically injured. Since juries will have their own basic understanding of 'freedom' and 'choice', the value of a direction along these lines would be to challenge stereotypical thinking. The government rejected the option of embodying such a direction in legislation, and so it will be for the Judicial Studies Board (and then the Court of Appeal) to develop a standard direction on consent which can be suitably tailored to the circumstances of each case. It seems unpromising that a pivotal element of the reform strategy—a new autonomy-based approach to determining consent—will effectively be left in the hands of the Judicial Studies Board.

(a) Some criticisms of the new scheme

By introducing a three-track approach to matters of consent and belief in consent-irrebuttable presumptions, rebuttable presumptions, and a general definition of consent—the Act raises a number of questions. Are the three categories intended to reflect some kind of moral hierarchy, so that the most serious cases of non-consent give rise to irrebuttable presumptions and the next most serious to rebuttable presumptions, with the remainder falling within the general definition? Or is the organising principle one of clarity and certainty, so that it is the clearest cases (not necessarily the worst) that give rise to irrebuttable presumptions and the next clearest to rebuttable presumptions, with the remainder falling within the general definition? Or is it a mixture of the two, with an added element of common law history? One would have thought that consideration ought to be given to marking out the worst cases of non-consent by means of irrebuttable presumptions, but that appears not to have happened. Various criticisms may be advanced.

(i) Are the types of fraud that give rise to the conclusive presumptions in s.76 (2) the worst cases of non-consent?
A preliminary question here is whether the types of fraud singled out by s.76(2) are necessarily the worst types of deception, compared with deception as to intentions, powers and other matters. A more pressing question, however, is whether obtaining compliance by fraud or deception is worse than other ways of avoiding true consent, such as using threats or violence, administering drugs, or taking advantage of a sleeping or unconscious person. Obtaining compliance by using violence or . . . threats of immediate violence seems no less heinous than doing so by deception, and yet the Act . . . creates a conclusive presumption in the latter case and only a rebuttable presumption in the former.

There is also a case to be made for a conclusive presumption in the situation set out in s.75(2)(f), where it is proved beyond doubt that C had a substance administered to her without her consent which was capable of stupefying or overpowering her at the time of the relevant act and D knew this. Of course D must have, as he does under this provision, the opportunity to argue that the presumption does not apply because the substance administered was incapable of causing C to be stupefied or overpowered. But if the stupefying effect is established, it is questionable whether D should be able to argue that C nevertheless consented to the subsequent sexual act and that the drug or alcohol did not in fact prevent her from consenting. Can freedom and capacity to make a choice really exist in any meaningful sense in this situation? The present terms of s.75(2)(f) leave it open to the defence to enter into an impossible area of speculation about the precise effect of the substance on C, a matter which can only confuse the jury and cannot satisfactorily be resolved.

Is there any good reason why it should be the case that, if D deceives C by means of impersonation or as to the nature of the act, non-consent is conclusively proved under s.76, but if D has sex with C when C is asleep or unconscious this supports only a rebuttable presumption? The common law drew no such distinction between these situations. The Home Office Minister, Beverley Hughes, asserted that 'one of the principles behind the proposal [in respect of the presumptions] is that we should take steps to clarify existing case law and incorporate it into statute.' However, it has always been the law that consent must be present at the time of the sexual act. This means that consent is necessarily regarded as absent once it is proved beyond doubt that C was asleep or unconscious at the time sexual intercourse took place. If absence of consent is not conclusively presumed in these situations, as it was at common law, then the law is being taken backwards rather than forwards. This new departure reflects the more far reaching and entirely unfortunate proposal of the Law Commission that consent should be defined as a subsisting, free and genuine agreement, which would have invited the defence to argue that a consent given previously had not been withdrawn.

Those who are uncomfortable with the full implications of sexual autonomy may not share the view that a conclusive presumption of absence of consent should apply where D has sex with C who is asleep at the time. The provisions of the Act on consent apply not only to rape and assault by penetration but also to touching which falls within sexual assault or causing sexual activity. A conclusive presumption of absence of consent and absence of reasonable belief in consent, if applied to all situations where C was asleep at the time, would render D liable for sexual assault if he sexually touched his partner C while C was asleep even though D was in the habit of doing so and C had not objected to this in the past. Even though complaints are unlikely to be made in such cases, this may be regarded as casting the law's net too wide. However, there was another solution, recommended by the Report: that the list of non-consent situations should apply only to rape and assault by penetration, with other cases being left to the general definition of consent. Whilst the interests of consistency and coherence argue in favour of the list of rebuttable presumptions applying to all four offences, it might have been preferable to follow the common law in cases where C was asleep at the time and to enact an irrebuttable presumption of absence of consent applying only to penetrative acts.

(ii) Should the list of circumstances in s.75 be more extensive and non-exhaustive?
In Canada and the Australian jurisdictions which have a statutory list of non-consent situations, the list is non-exhaustive. The exhaustive list in s.75 leaves no scope for further situations to be added through the common law. Only Parliament will be able to make additions to the list. The Report, on the other hand, considered that the list simply reflected obvious situations where consent was likely to be absent, including those already recognised at common law. It was just a starting point from which 'the courts will continue to develop the common

law as they consider cases where different circumstances apply.' The Minister's justification for the list was that there was 'real value in making a statement in the legislation about circumstances in which sexual activity is not acceptable.' Elsewhere the Government has claimed that 'it will provide juries with a clear framework within which to make fair and just decisions. It should also serve as a clear statement to the public more widely.' If those are among its primary purposes, the brevity of the list might be thought to be troubling, as might its potential to undermine the definition of consent in s.74. For example, it omits threats other than of immediate violence, no matter how serious such threats might be. In both the Report and Protecting the Public the list included threats or fear of serious harm or serious detriment to the complainant or to others. The Government rejected amendments that would have added other serious threats to the list, arguing that terms such as serious harm and serious detriment were too imprecise and would give rise to too much uncertainty. This gesture towards the principle of maximum certainty is laudable but unconvincing. The definition of consent itself positively sprouts uncertainties. Moreover, by restricting the fear of violence in the presumption to fear of immediate violence, the Act imposes a limitation which is not present in existing law and not required in defences such as duress and self-defence.

During the passage of the Bill through Parliament, one presumption was added to the list in s.75 (administering a stupefying substance) but another disappeared entirely. In the Report and in Protecting the Public, cases where the complainant's willingness to engage in sexual activity with the defendant was indicated only by a third party were included in the list of circumstances. The Report expressed the matter cogently as follows: 'Free agreement is an issue between sexual partners and cannot be given by others, whether husbands, partners or those in authority over the complainant'. In Canada the law provides that 'no consent is obtained where the agreement is expressed by the words or conduct of a person other than the complainant'. The Government was so persuaded by the force of these arguments that the original Bill provided that, where absence of consent was proved, belief in consent based only on evidence of anything said or done by a third party should lead to a conclusive presumption of absence of reasonable belief in consent However, this provision was opposed on two main grounds. Some argued that it tipped the scales too far against defendants, in cases where it was simply one person's word against another's: the cogency of this argument depends on whether people have been put on notice that they should never accept a third party's word in matters of sexual autonomy. The other objection was that people with a learning disability or mental disorder could not be expected to know that they were being deceived: insofar as this has substance, it is an argument against almost all objective tests in the criminal law, and might best be dealt with by way of exception or defence. In the end these two objections led the government to abandon the presumption, not only as a conclusive presumption but also as a rebuttable presumption. Cases of this kind now fall to be dealt with on general principles.

The Report further recommended that the list should include the situation where C was 'too affected by alcohol or drugs to give free agreement'. This proposal was not adopted in Protecting the Public and s.75(2)(f) is considerably narrower, since it relates only to situations where Cs intoxication is patently blameless. Whilst contributory negligence has no place in the criminal law, it is apparent that such ideas had an influence on the Government's thinking. Those who take alcohol or drugs voluntarily are placed in a different moral category from those who have had alcohol or drugs 'administered' to them by the defendant. Thus, the list of presumptions, which the Government has invested with great moral symbolism, is there to protect those who can be constructed as the 'innocent' victims of sexual assault. The many women who get raped when they are drunk and whose inebriation is more or less voluntary will have to take their chances in the legal process without the benefit of evidential presumptions. Where the intoxicant had the effect of rendering C unconscious, the presumption under s.75(2)(d) will apply.

Mens Rea

See DPP v Morgan [1976] A.C. 182, above, p.123.

Notes

The mens rea element relating to consent in rape comprises two elements: (i) A does not reasonably believe B consents; and (ii) whether a belief is reasonable is to be determined having regard to all the circumstances, including any steps A has taken to ascertain whether B consents. It must also be proved that there was an intentional penetration of the relevant orifice.

TEMKIN AND ASHWORTH, "THE SEXUAL OFFENCES ACT 2003: RAPE, SEXUAL ASSAULTS AND THE PROBLEMS OF CONSENT" [2004] CRIM. L.R. 328

[U]nder the new Act the mens rea of rape and the accompanying sexual assault offences has radically changed. The requirement of knowledge or reckless knowledge of the absence of consent, supported by the 'couldn't care less' test, has been replaced by the need to prove that 'A does not reasonably believe that B consents' (s.1(1)(c)). Should this be seen as an improvement in the law? To answer this, we need to consider several other questions.

Why was the Morgan approach thought unsatisfactory? This landmark decision was widely applauded by subjectivists for its general effects on the criminal law, since it emphasised that people ought to be judged on the facts as they believed them to be, and not on facts to which they had not given thought. If an offence requires proof of intention or recklessness in respect of a consequence or circumstance, then it is a matter of 'inexorable logic' that a mistaken belief in that respect should negative liability. Whatever the justifications for this as a general approach in the criminal law, it seemed to many that those justifications were outweighed in the case of sexual offences, where the two parties are necessarily in close proximity and where intercourse without consent would be a fundamental violation of the victim. Surely, out of respect for the autonomy and sexual choice of B, A should take the opportunity to be clear that B does consent. In most situations this is an easy thing to do and there is a strong reason for doing it This is not to suggest strict liability as to the absence of consent: it is to suggest a requirement that A acted as a reasonable person should have done in the situation in respect of ascertaining consent.

Why was the Bill changed during its parliamentary progress? The Government departed from Setting the Boundaries by opting for a reasonableness standard rather than the 'couldn't care less' test, but the clause as originally drafted was unduly complex. Moreover, its formulation turned on whether the defendant had acted as a reasonable person would, and this was attacked on the ground that a defendant with, for example, a learning disability would be judged by standards he could not attain The Bill was then amended, so that s.1(2) now states:

> 'Whether a belief is reasonable is to be determined having regard to all the circumstances, including any steps A has taken to ascertain whether B consents.'

This wording discards the 'reasonable person' in favour of a general test of what is reasonable in the circumstances. The Home Affairs Committee applauded the change as avoiding the 'potential injustice' of a test that would operate regardless of individual characteristics: 'by focussing on the individual defendant's belief, the new test will allow the jury to look at characteristics—such as learning disability or mental disorder—and take them into account.' A different approach would have been to retain the reasonable person standard but to add a defence for those mentally incapable of attaining it. The difficulty with s.1(2) is that it could empty the reasonableness test of most of its content, and justify the kind of direction laid down in the self-defence case of *United States v King*:

> 'In determining whether it is founded on reasonable grounds, the jury are not to conceive of some ideally reasonable person, but they are to put themselves in the position of the assailed person, with his physical and mental equipment, surrounded with the circumstances and exposed to the influences with which he was surrounded and to which he was exposed at the time.'

Has Parliament replaced the 'couldn't care less' test with one that is more demanding on the prosecution and more favourable to the defence? Much depends on how the phrase 'all the circumstances' comes to be interpreted. The Government's view was that 'it is for the jury to decide whether any of the attributes of the defendant are relevant to their deliberations, subject to directions from the judge where necessary.' Beverley Hughes expressed the matter slightly differently, stating that it would be for the judge 'to decide whether it is necessary to introduce consideration of a defendant's characteristics and which characteristics are relevant . . . The judge or jury can take into account all or any characteristics and circumstances that they wish to, and it is best that we leave that decision to the judge and jury for each case.' By what standards is it to be decided which characteristics are 'relevant'? Much will depend on the Specimen Directions and the approach of the Court of Appeal. But, as L'Heureux-Dube J. famously stated in Seaboyer: 'The content of any relevancy decision will be filled by the particular judge's experience, common sense and/or logic . . . This area of the law has been particularly prone to the utilisation of stereotype in the determination of relevance.'

In Protecting the Public the Government expressed its concern that the Morgan test 'leads many victims who feel that the system will not give them justice, not to report incidents or press for them to be brought to trial.'

Accordingly, it decided to alter the test 'to include one of reasonableness under the law'. But the present formulation is unlikely to provide the incentive to report or pursue the case that the Government is seeking. The broad reference to 'all the circumstances' is an invitation to the jury to scrutinise the complainant's behaviour to determine whether there was anything about it which could have induced a reasonable belief in consent. In this respect the Act contains no real challenge to society's norms and stereotypes about either the relationship between men and women or other sexual situations, and leaves open the possibility that those stereotypes will determine assessments of reasonableness. Is B's sexual history to be taken to be a relevant part of the circumstances? In answer to a question raised in Committee, the Minister agreed that the section 'should focus the court's attention on what is happening at the time of the offence' and 'should make the previous sexual history of the complainant far less relevant.' But this does not seem to reflect the natural meaning of the words 'all the circumstances,' which contain no limitation to circumstances existing at the time of the event in question. Further, it is true that s.1(2) requires consideration of 'any steps A has taken to ascertain whether B consents,' however, if A enquires about consent; B says no, but A concludes that B's 'no' is tantamount to 'yes,' is his culturally engendered belief to be regarded as reasonable or not? In deciding what it is 'relevant' to consider, what is to prevent the influence of stereotypes about B's dress, B's frequenting of a particular place, an invitation to have a drink, and so forth?

It therefore seems possible that the new element of absence of reasonable belief in consent, which forms part of the four major offences in the Act, may not impose greater duties on defendants than does the [former] law. Of course, the prosecution may take advantage of the various presumptions in ss.76 (conclusive) and 75 (rebuttable), but there will be many cases that fall outside that list of circumstances. The Act requires the prosecution to establish beyond reasonable doubt that A did not reasonably believe that B consented. Was the Government right to abandon its proposal for placing the onus of proof on the defence, once the basis for one of the rebuttable presumptions has been established?

Question

A knows that his partner B finds anal intercourse abhorrent. B consents to vaginal sexual intercourse with A entering from behind. A is in a state of voluntary intoxication and mistakenly penetrates B's anus but on hearing B's protests and realising his error, immediately withdraws. Has A the mens rea for rape?

----

ii. Assault by Penetration

SEXUAL OFFENCES ACT 2003

2. Assault by penetration

(1) A person (A) commits an offence if—

   (a) he intentionally penetrates the vagina or anus of another person (B) with a part of his body or anything else,
   (b) the penetration is sexual,
   (c) B does not consent to the penetration, and
   (d) A does not reasonably believe that B consents.

Notes

1. This is a new offence intended, in part, to replace the former offence of indecent assault. The old law was criticised for failing to adequately reflect the gravity of serious assaults involving penetration with objects or parts of the body other than the penis. It follows that the offence may be committed by a person of either sex on a person of either sex.

2.   Penetration is discussed above in the context of rape and the only difference for this offence is that the penetrated orifice is limited to vagina or anus; it does not extend to penetration of the mouth.

3.   The presumptions in ss.75 and 76 apply to this offence.

4.   Penetration must be "sexual". In s.78, an act is defined as sexual if a reasonable person would consider that: (a) whatever its circumstances or any person's purpose in relation to it, it is because of its nature sexual; or (b) because of its nature it may be sexual and because of its circumstances or the purpose of any person in relation to it (or both) it is sexual.

The Act supposes that there are two categories of "sexual" act. The first in (a) is inherently sexual and any purpose that A may have is regarded as superfluous. The second in (b) asks the jury to consider whether the circumstances and/or A's purpose turn what might, on some occasions, be interpreted as non-sexual behaviour into sexual behaviour. For example imagine that A, a customs investigation officer, asks B to remove his clothes for the apparent purpose of searching for concealed drugs. If A's purpose is not to search for drugs but to obtain sexual pleasure from seeing B's naked body what might, in other circumstances, be a non-sexual act may, should the jury so conclude, be a sexual act. If A's purpose was not sexual pleasure, nor to search for drugs, but simply to humiliate B, then it would not appear to be "sexual". The significance of the word "sexual" would seem to be much more apparent in relation to the offences under ss.3 and 4 (see below) than it does in relation to the offence under s.2 (see the question which follows).

Question

Is the requirement that an assault by penetration of the anus or vagina be *sexual* in nature really necessary? If A, a doctor, conducts an intimate internal examination of his female patient B, not because of any medical need but merely for his own sexual pleasure, would not his deception as to purpose serve to negate consent under s.76 anyway?

----

iii. Sexual assault

SEXUAL OFFENCES ACT 2003

3. Sexual assault

(1) A person (A) commits an offence if—

(a) he intentionally touches another person (B),
(b) the touching is sexual,
(c) B does not consent to the touching, and
(d) A does not reasonably believe that B consents.

Notes

1.   Many other forms of sexual misconduct formerly covered by the offence of indecent assault will fall under the ambit of this new offence. The offence requires a "touching" which is "sexual". The meaning of "sexual" is considered above.

2. Touching is defined inclusively by s.78(8) as touching (a) with any part of the body; (b) with anything else; (c) through anything, and in particular includes touching amounting to penetration. It therefore includes touching a person with an object or through their clothing.

3. The presumptions in ss.75 and 76 apply to this offence.

4. It is not necessary to show that A intended to touch B sexually, simply that A intentionally touched B. The touching must, of course, be sexual in nature and A's purpose may be important in determining whether or not the touching was sexual.

R. V H

[2005] EWCA Crim 732 (Lord Woolf CJ, Davis and Field JJ)

A approached B at 22.00 one evening as she walked across a field and said to her "Do you fancy a shag?" B ignored him whereon A grabbed B's tracksuit bottoms by the fabric, attempted to pull her towards him and, attempted unsuccessfully to put his hand over her mouth. B escaped. A was convicted of sexual assault, contrary to s.3 of the Sexual Offences Act 2003. Two issues had arisen at trial:

(i)   whether the touching of the B's tracksuit bottoms alone amounted to the "touching" of another person within the meaning of s.79(8) of the 2003 Act; and

(ii) whether anything which had occurred amounted to what a reasonable person might regard as being "sexual" within the meaning of s.78 of the Act, which provides:

Penetration, touching or any other activity is sexual if a reasonable person would consider that—
(a) whatever its circumstances or any person's purpose in relation to it, it is because of its nature sexual, or
(b) because of its nature it may be sexual and because of its circumstances or the purpose of any person in relation to it (or both) it is sexual.

THE LORD CHIEF JUSTICE

[His lordship referred to Temkin and Ashworth [2004] Crim L.R. 328 and to the relevant statutory provisions:]

8. In this case we are concerned with s.78(b). Miss Egerton who appears on behalf of the Crown accepts that (a) has no application. The nature of the touching with which we are concerned was not inevitably sexual. It is important to note that there are two requirements in s.78(b). First, there is the requirement that the touching because of its nature *may* be sexual; and secondly, there is the requirement that the touching because of its circumstances or the purpose of any person in relation to it (or both) *is* sexual.

9. Miss Egerton agreed with the view of the court expressed in argument that if there were not two requirements in (b), the opening words 'because of its nature it may be sexual' would be surplus. If it was not intended by the legislature that effect should be given to those opening words, it would be sufficient to create an offence by looking at the touching and deciding whether because of its circumstances it was sexual. In other words, there is not one comprehensive test. It is necessary for both halves of s.78(b) to be complied with.

10. It is no doubt because of this aspect of s.78(b) and the article in the Criminal Law Review that Mr West who appears on behalf of the appellant referred to *R v Court*. That case dealt with an alleged indecent assault. An assistant in a shop struck a 12 year old girl visitor twelve times for no apparent reason, outside her shorts on her buttocks. The assistant was convicted. Both this court and the House of Lords dismissed the assistant's appeal. At pages 42B–43E of his speech Lord Ackner set out his general approach. On reading that passage it is understandable why the article should have made the comment to which we referred. It is quite clear to the court that the stages approach which we have observed in s.78 is reflected in Lord Ackner's speech. The only difficulty that we have with applying Lord Ackner's approach is that he referred to *R v George* [1956] Crim.L.R. 52. In that case the prosecution relied on the fact that on a number of occasions the defendant had removed a shoe from a girl's

foot. He had done so, as he admitted, because it gave him a perverted sexual gratification. Streatfeild J. ruled that an assault became indecent only if it was accompanied by circumstances of indecency towards the person alleged to have been assaulted and that none of the assaults in that case (namely the removal or attempted removal of the shoes) could possibly amount to an indecent assault.

11. We would express reservations as to whether or not it would be possible for the removal of shoes in that way, because of the nature of the act that took place, to be sexual as sexual is defined now in s.78. That in our judgment may well be a question that it would be necessary for a jury to determine.

12. The fact that in s.78(b) there are two different questions which we have sought to identify complicates the task of the judge and that of the jury. If there is a submission of 'no case' the judge may have to ask himself whether there is a case to be left to the jury. He will answer that question by determining whether it would be appropriate for a reasonable person to consider that the touching because of its nature may be sexual. Equally, the judge will have to consider whether it would be possible for a reasonable person to conclude, because of the circumstances of the touching or the purpose of any person in relation to the touching (or both), that it is sexual. If he comes to the conclusion that a reasonable person could possibly answer those questions adversely to the defendant, then the matter would have to be left to the jury.

13. We would suggest that in that situation the judge would regard it as desirable to identify two distinct questions for the jury. First, would they, as twelve reasonable people (as the section requires), consider that because of its nature the touching that took place in the particular case before them could be sexual? If the answer to that question was 'No', the jury would find the defendant not guilty. If 'Yes', they would have to go on to ask themselves (again as twelve reasonable people) whether in view of the circumstances and/or the purpose of any person in relation to the touching (or both), the touching was in fact sexual. If they were satisfied that it was, then they would find the defendant guilty. If they were not satisfied, they would find the defendant not guilty.

14. In that suggested approach the reference to the nature of the touching in the first half refers to the actual touching that took place in that case. In answering the first question, the jury would not be concerned with the circumstances before or after the touching took place, or any evidence as to the purpose of any person in relation to the touching.

[His Lordship referred to s.62 "Committing an offence with intent to commit a sexual offence" and outlined the facts revealed by the evidence in the present case.]

24 . . .. Where a person is wearing clothing we consider that touching of the clothing constitutes touching for the purpose of the s.3 offence.

25. As against that approach Mr West relied on s.79(8) (set out above). He submits that under s.79(8)(c) touching through anything (through clothing), if pressure in some form is not brought against the body of the person concerned, there cannot be touching; there has to be some form of touching of the body of the individual who is alleged to have been assaulted, even if it be through clothing. Mr West submits that, having regard to the complainant's evidence in this case, there was no such touching.

26. It is important to note that the opening words of s.79(8) are 'touching includes touching' and in particular 'through anything'. Subsection (8) is not a definition section. We have no doubt that it was not Parliament's intention by the use of that language to make it impossible to regard as a sexual assault touching which took place by touching what the victim was wearing at the time.

27. The second unsuccessful submission made by Mr West for the case to be withdrawn from the airy was as to whether anything occurred which a reasonable person could regard as sexual within the meaning of the Act The judge's view was that there were here clearly circumstances in which the offence was alleged to have occurred, including the words alleged to have been spoken beforehand, which could make the actions which took place properly to be regarded as being sexual. In his approach at that time, and indeed in his summing-up, the judge did not take a two stage approach to s.78(b). He looked at the matter as a whole. The problem about that approach is that in a borderline case a person's intention or other circumstances may appear to show that what happened was sexual, although their nature might not have been sexual. For the reasons we have already given that approach is not one which we regard as appropriate, although we recognise that in the great majority of cases the answer will be the same whether the two stage approach is adopted or the position is looked at as a whole.

[His Lordship dealt with other grounds of appeal.]

Appeal dismissed

Question

In *R. v George* [1956] Crim. L.R. 52, A attempted to remove B's shoes finding this act to be sexually gratifying. The House of Lords held this did not constitute an indecent assault as there were no circumstances of indecency. If the same facts were to occur today would A's act be viewed as a sexual touching?

----

iv. Causing a person to engage in sexual activity without consent

SEXUAL OFFENCES ACT 2003

4. Causing a person to engage in sexual activity without consent

(1) A person (A) commits an offence if—

(a) he intentionally causes another person (B) to engage in an activity,
(b) the activity is sexual,
(c) B does not consent to engaging in the activity, and
(d) A does not reasonably believe that B consents.

Notes

1.   This offence is similar to sexual assault but does not require any form of touching. It is intended to cover, inter alia, cases where A compels others to perform sexual acts together, forced sexual acts with animals, females forcing males to engage in sexual acts and forcing B to perform a sexual act on himself. A must intentionally *cause* B to engage in the activity. It would be perfectly possible to commit the offence by words alone but there must be some form of sexual activity for the offence to be complete. The meaning of "sexual" is considered above.

2.   The presumptions in ss.75 and 76 apply to this offence.

----

v. Sexual offences against children under 13

SEXUAL OFFENCES ACT 2003

5. Rape of a child under 13

(1) A person commits an offence if—

(a) he intentionally penetrates the vagina, anus or mouth of another person with his penis, and
(b) the other person is under 13.

6. Assault of a child under 13 by penetration

(1) A person commits an offence if—

(a) he intentionally penetrates the vagina or anus of another person with a part of his body or anything else, and
(b) the other person is under 13.

7. Sexual assault of a child under 13

(1)   A person commits an offence if—

    (a)   he intentionally touches another person,
    (b)   the touching is sexual, and
    (c)   the other person is under 13.

8. Causing or inciting a child under 13 to engage in sexual activity

(1)   A person commits an offence if—

    (a)   he intentionally causes or incites another person (B) to engage in an activity,
    (b)   the activity is sexual, and
    (c)   B is under 13.

Notes

1.   The offences in ss.5–8 are, broadly speaking, equivalent to the adult version of the offences in ss.1–4. There are however, two very significant differences between the adult offences and the offences in respect of a child under 13. First, the only mens rea requirement is an intention to penetrate (ss.5 and 6), touch (s.7), or cause or incite the activity (s.8). It does not appear to be a necessary ingredient of the offence that the defendant is aware that the child is under 13.

2.   Absence of consent is irrelevant. The defendant cannot argue consent or belief in consent. In *R. v G* [2009] UKHL 13, G, aged 15, had sexual intercourse with B, aged 12. He was charged with the s.5 offence and pleaded guilty on the basis that he believed B was 15 as she had told him she was, and that she was a willing participant. The prosecution accepted that the intercourse was consensual. G appealed his conviction on the basis that if s.5 could not be read down by inclusion of a defence of reasonable belief that B was over 13, it was incompatible with art.6(2) of the European Convention. Further that the conviction and sentence constituted a disproportionate interference with respect for private life under art.8 of the Convention. He drew attention to the contrast (in terms of sentencing and of being labelled "child rapist") between a conviction for the s.5 offence as compared to a conviction of the s.9 offence (see vi below) or one of the other lesser offences in the Act. G contended it was inappropriate to prosecute a child for the s.5 offence where the intercourse had been entirely consensual. The House of Lords refused to read down s.5 finding that the presumption of mens rea was negatived by necessary implication arising from the express references in other sections of the Act to reasonable belief. As for art.8, while prosecution could produce consequences that interfered with a child's rights, factually less serious cases could be taken account of in sentencing to ensure that there was no interference that could not be justified under art.8(2). A trial judge was not, however, under a duty to substitute a lesser charge if the prosecution did not seek such substitution. An attempt to apply to the European Court of Human Rights alleging breaches of arts 6 and 8 was ruled inadmissible (see *G v UK* [2011] ECHR 1308).

Questions

1.   If the prosecution accept, as they did in *G*, that the intercourse was consensual, is it proportionate and proper to convict a child defendant of "child rape"?

2.   It was suggested that factually less serious cases prosecuted under s.5 can be treated more

leniently at sentencing stage. G had his original sentence of detention reduced to a conditional discharge. Is this an appropriate way of dealing with two children who have consensual sexual intercourse?

Question

If Simon and Linda, two precocious 12-year-olds, briefly engage in consensual mutual oral sex, is Simon a rapist? Does Linda commit the offence of sexual assault under s.7? If so, what purpose does criminalising this activity serve?

Would Simon and Linda both commit an offence under s.7 merely by kissing each other consensually?

----

vi. Sexual offences against children aged 13–16

SEXUAL OFFENCES ACT 2003

9. Sexual activity with a child

(1) A person aged 18 or over (A) commits an offence if—

(a) he intentionally touches another person (B),
(b) the touching is sexual, and
(c) either—
    (i) B is under 16 and A does not reasonably believe that B is 16 or over, or
    (ii) B is under 13.

Notes

1. This offence will extend to all intentional touching that is sexual and which is committed by a person aged 18 years or over where the child is aged between 13 and 16 years. If the child is under 13 then as regards A's knowledge of B's age, liability would appear strict. Where B is 13 or over but under 16, the prosecution have to prove either that A did not believe that B was over 16 or, if he did, that such belief was not reasonable.

2. Where A is under 18 then an offence may still be committed under s.13.

Question

If Simon, aged 18, and his girlfriend Linda, aged 15, engage in consensual petting and kissing does Simon commit an offence?

----

vii. Other offences

A full discussion of the numerous remaining offences in the 2003 Act is not possible in a work of this type. A brief statement of the principal offences follows and a specialist work should be consulted where necessary.

1. Causing or inciting a child to engage in sexual activity (s.10).

2. Engaging in sexual activity in the presence of a child (s.11).

3. Causing a child to watch a sexual act (s.12).

4. Child sex offences committed by a child or young person (s.13).

5. Arranging or facilitating commission of a child sex offence (s.14).

6. Meeting a child following sexual grooming (s.15).

7. Abuse of position of trust: sexual activity with a child (s.16).

8. Abuse of position of trust: causing or inciting a child to engage in sexual activity (s.17).

9. Abuse of position of trust: causing a child to watch a sexual act (s.19).

10. Sexual activity with a family member (s.25).

11. Inciting a child family member to engage in sexual activity (s.26).

In addition, the Act creates offences that are designed to protect children from prostitution and pornography and to protect persons who have a mental disorder. There are further provisions that deal with prostitution generally, incest, trespass with intent to commit a sexual offence, exposure, voyeurism, bestiality, necrophilia and sexual acts in a public lavatory.

10 THEFT, ROBBERY AND BURGLARY

1. THEFT

Before 1969, the law about dishonest acquisition of the property of another was contained in the Larceny Act 1916, which was a codification of a number of common law rules with certain piecemeal statutory amendments mostly occurring in the Victorian era. The principal offence was larceny, but it was a highly technical crime, too narrowly defined to cover certain quite common cases of dishonesty. The crime was tinkered with both by statute and by judicial innovation, but the basis of the crime was such that no amount of tinkering would enable it to cover the whole range of dishonest conduct involving the property of another. The basis of the offence was that the accused should take and carry away property in the possession of another; it therefore failed to cover an accused person who dishonestly misappropriated that of which he already had lawful possession, and the offences of embezzlement and fraudulent conversion had to be invented to fill some of this gap. Moreover, the law's insistence that the crime was a wrong against possession, not against ownership, meant that the law was complicated by the need to reflect the intricacies of the English law of possession. The offence of fraudulent conversion, which, in its modern form, was first created by statute in 1901, was tied neither to taking and carrying away by the accused, nor to possession as the invaded interest of the victim. It consisted essentially of the accused fraudulently converting to his own use or benefit or to the use or benefit of any other person the property of the victim. When it was decided to replace larceny, embezzlement and fraudulent conversion by a single new offence of theft, the offence of fraudulent conversion was the model taken for the new definition in s.1.

What might be called "swindling", i.e. obtaining by false pretences and certain other offences of fraud, was not swept into the new definition, and was treated separately by the Act, which contains a range of new offences of swindling, which have since been supplemented by additional offences in Theft Act 1978. See the next chapter, which deals with offences of fraud. Various other offences against property—blackmail, handling, burglary—are also contained in the Theft Act 1968, but the Act does not deal with offences of damaging property (see Ch.14).

So far as concerns theft and the other offences contained in the Theft Acts, the Acts are comprehensive and in one sense conclusive. There is nothing left of the old offences, which were all completely swept away. However, this does not mean that cases on the earlier law, and on other branches of the law such as property or contract, can be entirely ignored. Occasionally the Court of Appeal concludes that the draftsman must have had a particular decision in mind in choosing the words used in the Act. Moreover, protecting as it does property interests, theft law cannot easily avoid using the technical terms found in and given meanings by the civil law, e.g. "proprietary right or interest", "obligation".

But in general the Courts, taking the view that the object of the Theft Act was to simplify the law, resist the introduction of the complexities of the civil law into a trial for theft, and are loath to give the statutory words any technical meaning. The rules of property and contract have sometimes been disregarded in a cavalier fashion, and there has been an increasing tendency to categorise the words in the Act as "ordinary" words and to leave juries to say what they mean. The result is that the law of theft, which because of its subject matter could never be simple, has become more complicated than it need be and indeed, in some places, unprincipled and capricious.

Most of the offences in the Theft Acts appear in the Draft Criminal Code Bill. However, although the Law Commission, *A Criminal Code for England and Wales* (HMSO 1989), Law Com.177, Commentary 16.4, recognised the existence of criticisms of the Acts and the case law on them, they contented themselves with reproducing the Acts, without any changes of substance. An exception will be found on the subject of burglary with intent under s.9(1)(b) of the Theft Act 1968.

THEFT ACT 1968 S.1

(1) A person is guilty of theft if he dishonestly appropriates property belonging to another, with the intention of permanently depriving the other of it; and 'thief' and 'steal' shall be construed accordingly.

(2) It is immaterial whether the appropriation is made with a view to gain, or is made for the thief's own benefit.

(3) The five following sections of this Act shall have effect as regards the interpretation and operation of this section (and, except as otherwise provided by this Act, shall apply only for purposes of this section).

Note

The actus reus of theft is: (i) appropriating; (ii) property; (iii) belonging to another. The mens rea is found in the expressions (iv) with the intention of depriving the other of it; and (v) dishonestly. All five elements are given extended definitions by ss.2–6.

----

i. Appropriation

THEFT ACT 1968 S.3

(1) Any assumption by a person of the rights of an owner amounts to an appropriation, and this includes, where he has come by the property (innocently or not) without stealing it, any later assumption of a right to it by keeping or dealing with it as owner.

(2) Where property or a right or interest in property is or purports to be transferred for value to a person acting in good faith, no later assumption by him of rights which he believed himself to be acquiring shall, by reason of any defect in the transferor's title, amount to theft of the property.

GLANVILLE WILLIAMS, *TEXTBOOK OF CRIMINAL LAW*, 1ST EDN (LONDON: STEVENS & SONS, 1978), P.726

The phrase 'any assumption of the rights of an owner' [in s.3(1), see above] is a remarkable juristic invention. Except in special situations that the framers of the Act were probably not thinking of, it is impossible for anyone to 'assume the rights of an owner' by way of theft, in the sense of actually acquiring rights of ownership. Thieves do not normally acquire rights against the owner. One may steal a watch, but one cannot generally steal rights of ownership in the watch. The thief may act in a way that would be lawful *if* he had the rights of an owner, or *if* he were acting by authority of the owner; but he does not by stealing give himself those rights. Obviously the word 'assumption' in this context means, generally, a *usurpation* of rights. (The word 'usurpation' is given as one of the meanings of 'assumption' in the OED). What appears to be intended by this cloudy definition is that an appropriation is (or includes) anything done in relation to property by a non-owner that only the owner could lawfully do or authorise.

Notes

1. As Williams points out, it is never necessary that the owner shall lose his rights to the property as a result of D's act (and in most cases he does not). In many cases, the owner loses *possession* to D by the latter's act of appropriation, but even that is not necessary. Nothing is said about "possession" in s.3(1). It seems that if D does something in relation to property which only the owner can do, e.g. offer it for sale, it is an appropriation even if the owner's rights are not affected in any way, or even put at risk. Thus if D draws an unauthorised cheque on V's bank account, that is an appropriation of V's rights against the bank (see *R. v Kohn*, below p.623), even though in law any debit entry on V's account which the bank might make on honouring the cheque is a complete nullity, so that V's rights against the bank remain exactly as before: *Chan Man-sin v Attorney General of Hong Kong* [1988] 1 All E.R. 1. Even if the cheque is never presented, the mere fact of drawing it (a thing which only the owner of the account can do) is an assumption of the rights of the owner and therefore "amounts to an appropriation": *Re Osman* [1989] 3 All E.R. 701. In truth, as Lord Oliver pointed out in *Chan Man-sin*, (at 3) the definition of appropriation in s.3(1) is a completely artificial one.

    It does not follow that where there is an appropriation there is a complete theft, because there must in addition be an intent to deprive the owner permanently. However, this concept also has an artificial meaning (see below, p.643), and it can exist even if there is no intention that V should be deprived of the property itself.

2. Glanville Williams' choice of the word "usurpation" as being what "appropriation" means in s.3(1) is no longer entirely appropriate. This is because it contains within it the idea of acting in a way not authorised by the owner. However, although what a thief does is usually unauthorised, it need not be so: see next case, which settled a long-standing conflict of authority.

R. V GOMEZ

[1993] 1 All E.R. 1 HL

D was assistant manager of an electrical goods shop. He was approached by B, who asked to be supplied with goods in exchange for two stolen building society cheques. D agreed and asked the shop manager G to authorise the transaction, without telling him the cheques were worthless. In response to G's enquiries on the point, D falsely told him the cheques "were as good as cash". G then authorised the handing over of the goods to B in exchange for the cheques, which were dishonoured. D was convicted of theft of the goods and appealed. His appeal was allowed and the prosecution appealed to the House of Lords.

LORD KEITH OF KINKEL

My Lords, this appeal raises the question of whether two decisions of your Lordships' House upon the proper construction of certain provisions of the Theft Act 1968 are capable of being reconciled with each other and, if so, in what manner. The two decisions are *Lawrence v Metropolitan Police Commissioner* [1972] A.C. 626 and *R. v Morris* [1984] A.C. 320. The question has given rise to much debate in subsequent cases and in academic writings.

[After reciting the facts] The respondent appealed to the Court of Appeal (Criminal Division) which on April 22, 1991 (Lord Lane CJ., Hutchison and Mantell JJ.) quashed the convictions: ([1991] 1 W.L.R. 1344). Lord Lane C.J., delivering the judgment of the court, after considering *Lawrence and Morris*, said at p.1338:

'What in fact happened was that the owner was induced by deceit to agree to the goods being transferred to Ballay. If that is the case, and if in these circumstances the appellant is guilty of theft, it must follow that anyone who obtains goods in return for a cheque which he knows will be dishonoured on presentation, or indeed by way of any other similar pretence, would be guilty of theft. That does not seem to be the law. *Morris* decides that when a person by dishonest deception induces the owner to transfer his entire proprietary interests that is not theft. There is no appropriation at the moment when he takes possession of the goods because he was entitled to do so under the terms of the contract of sale, a contract which is, it is true, voidable, but has not been avoided at the time the goods are handed over.'

And later, at p.1339:

'We therefore conclude that there was de facto, albeit voidable, contract between the owners and Ballay; that it was by virtue of that contract that Ballay took possession of the goods; that accordingly the transfer of the goods to him was with the consent and express authority of the owner and that accordingly there was no lack of authorisation and no appropriation.'

The court later granted a certificate under s.1(2) of the Administration of Justice Act 1960 that a point of law of general public importance was involved in the decision, namely

'When theft is alleged and that which is alleged to be stolen passes to the defendant with the consent of the owner, but that has been obtained by a false representation, has (a) an appropriation within the meaning of s.1(1) of the Theft Act 1968 taken place, or (b) must such a passing of property necessarily involve an element of adverse interference with or usurpation of some right of the owner?'

The Crown now appeals, with leave granted here, to your Lordships' House.
    [After quoting ss.1(3), 3(1), 4(1), 7 and 15(1) Theft Act 1968]: It is to be observed that by s.26 of the Criminal Justice Act 1991 the maximum sentence for theft was reduced from 10 to 7 years. The s.15(1) penalty was left unchanged.
    The facts in *Lawrence*, as set out in the speech of Viscount Dilhorne, were these:

'The appellant was convicted on December 2, 1969, of theft contrary to s.1(1) of the Theft Act 1968. On September 1, 1969, a Mr Occhi, an Italian who spoke little English, arrived at Victoria Station on his first visit to this country. He went up to a taxi driver, the appellant, and showed him a piece of paper on which an address in Ladbroke Grove was written. The appellant said that it was very far and very expensive. Mr Occhi got into the taxi, took £1 out of his wallet and gave it to the appellant who then, the wallet being still open, took a further £6 out of it. He then drove Mr Occhi to Ladbroke Grove. The correct lawful fare for the journey was in the region of 10s. 6d. The appellant was charged with and convicted of the theft of the £6.'

The conviction was upheld by the Court of Appeal (Criminal Division) which in granting leave to appeal to your Lordships' House certified the following questions as involving a point of law of general public importance:

'(1) Whether s.1(1) of the Theft Act 1968 is to be construed as though it contained the words 'without the consent of the owner' or words to that effect and (2) Whether the provisions of s.15(1) and of s.1(1) of the Theft Act 1968 are mutually exclusive in the sense that if the facts proved would justify a conviction under s.15(1) there cannot lawfully be a conviction under s.1(1) on those facts.'

Viscount Dilhorne, whose speech was concurred in by Lord Donovan, Lord Pearce, Lord Diplock and Lord Cross of Chelsea, after stating the facts, and expressing some doubts as to what Mr Occhi had meant when he said that he 'permitted' the taxi driver to take £6, continued, at p.631:

'The main contention of the appellant in this House and in the Court of Appeal was that Mr Occhi had consented to the taking of the £6 and that, consequently, his conviction could not stand. In my opinion, the facts of this case to which I have referred fall far short of establishing that Mr Occhi had so consented.

Prior to the passage of the Theft Act 1968, which made radical changes in and greatly simplified the law relating to theft and some other offences, it was necessary to prove that the property alleged to have been stolen was taken "without the consent of the owner" (Larceny Act 1916, s.1(1)).

These words are not included in s.1(1) of the Theft Act, but the appellant contended that the subsection should be construed as if they were, as if they appeared after the word "appropriates". Section 1(1) reads as follows: "A person is guilty of theft if he dishonestly appropriates property belonging to another with the intention of permanently depriving the other of it; and 'thief' and 'steal' shall be construed accordingly."

I see no ground for concluding that the omission of the words "without the consent of the owner" was inadvertent and not deliberate, and to read the subsection as if they were included is, in my opinion, wholly unwarranted. Parliament by the omission of these words has relieved the prosecution of the burden of establishing that the taking was without the owner's consent. That is no longer an ingredient of the offence.'

Megaw L.J., delivering the judgment of the Court of Appeal, said [1971] 1 Q.B. 373, 376 that the offence created by s.1(1) involved four elements; '(i) a dishonest (ii) appropriation (iii) of property belonging to another (iv) with the intention of permanently depriving the owner of it.'

I agree. That there was appropriation in this case is clear. Section 3(1) states that any assumption by a person of the rights of an owner amounts to an appropriation. Here there was clearly such an assumption. That an appropriation was dishonest may be proved in a number of ways. In this case it was not contended that the appellant had not acted dishonestly. Section 2(1) provides, inter alia, that a person's appropriation of property belonging to another is not to be regarded as dishonest if he appropriates the property in the belief that he would have the other's consent if the other knew of the appropriation and the circumstances of it. A fortiori, a person is not to be regarded as acting dishonestly if he appropriates another's property believing that with full knowledge of the circumstances that other person has in fact agreed to the appropriation. The appellant, if he believed that Mr Occhi, knowing that £7 was far in excess of the legal fare, had nevertheless agreed to pay him that sum, could not be said to have acted dishonestly in taking it. When Megaw L.J. said that if there was true consent, the essential element of dishonesty was not established, I understand him to have meant this. Belief or the absence of belief that the owner had with such knowledge consented to the appropriation is relevant to the issue of dishonesty, not to the question whether or not there has been an appropriation. That may occur even though the owner had permitted or consented to the property being taken. So proof that Mr Occhi had consented to the appropriation of £6 from his wallet without agreeing to paying a sum in excess of the legal fare does not suffice to show that there was not dishonesty in this case. There was ample evidence that there was.

'I now turn to the third element "property belonging to another". Mr Back Q.C., for the appellant, contended that if Mr Occhi consented to the appellant taking the £6, he consented to the property in the money passing from him to the appellant and that the appellant had not, therefore, appropriated property belonging to another. He argued that the old distinction between the offence of false pretences and larceny had been preserved. I am unable to agree with this. The new offence of obtaining property by deception created by s.15(1) of the Theft Act also contains the words 'belonging to another. A person who by any deception dishonestly obtains property belonging to another, with the intention of permanently depriving the other of it commits that offence. "Belonging to another" in s.1(1) and in s.15(1) in my view signifies no more than that, at the time of the appropriation or the obtaining, the property belonging to another, with the words "belonging to another" having the extended meaning given by s.5. The short answer to this contention on behalf of the appellant is that the money in the wallet which he appropriated belonged to another, to Mr Occhi.

There was no dispute about the appellant's intention being permanently to deprive Mr Oochi of the money.

The four elements of the offence of theft as defined in the Theft Act were thus clearly established and, in my view, the Court of Appeal was right to dismiss the appeal.'

In the result, each of the certified questions was answered in the negative.

It will be seen that Viscount Dilhorne's speech contains two clear pronouncements, first that it is no longer an ingredient of the offence of theft that the taking should be without the owner's consent and second, that an appropriation may occur even though the owner has permitted or consented to the property being taken. The answer given to the first certified question was in line with those pronouncements, so even though Viscount Dilhorne was of opinion that the evidence fell short of establishing that Mr Occhi had consented to the taking of the £6 it was a matter of decision that it made no difference whether or not he had so consented.

Morris involved two cases of price label switching in a supermarket. In the first case the defendant had removed the price label from a joint of meat and replaced it with a label showing a lesser price which he had removed from another joint. He was detected at the check-out point before he had paid for the joint and later convicted of theft contrary to s.1(1) of the Theft Act. In the second case the defendant had in similar manner switched price labels on goods in a supermarket but was not arrested until after he had passed the check-out point and paid the lesser prices for the goods. He was charged with two counts of theft contrary to s.1(1) and one count of obtaining property by deception contrary to s.15(1). The jury convicted him on the counts of theft, but by directions of the recorder returned no verdict on the s.15(1) count. Appeals against conviction by both defendants were dismissed by the Court of Appeal (Criminal Division) and by this House. Lord Roskill, in the course of a speech concurred in by Lords Fraser of Tullybelton, Edmund-Davies, Brandon of Oakbrook and Brightman, at p.331 referred to the *Lawrence* case with apparent approval as having set out the four elements involved in the offence of theft and as having rejected the argument that there could not be theft within s.1(1) if the owner of the property had consented to the defendant's acts. He observed that in *Lawrence* the House did not have to consider the precise meaning of 'appropriation' in s.3(1) and continued:

'Mr Denison submitted that the phrase in s.3(1) "any assumption by a person of the rights" (my emphasis) "of an owner amounts to an appropriation" must mean any assumption of "all the rights of an owner". Since neither defendant had at the time of the removal of the goods from the shelves and of the label switching assumed all the rights of the owner, there was no appropriation and therefore no theft. Mr Jeffreys for the prosecution, on the other hand, contended that *the* rights in this context only meant *any* of the rights. An owner of goods has many rights—they have been described as "a bundle or package of rights." Mr Jeffreys contended that on a fair reading of the subsection it cannot have been the intention that every one of an owner's rights had to be assumed by the alleged thief before an appropriation was proved and that essential ingredient of the offence of theft established.

My Lords, if one reads the words "the rights" at the opening of s.3(1) literally and in isolation from the rest of the section, Mr Deni-son's submission undoubtedly has force. But the later words "any later assumption of a right" seem to me to militate strongly against the correctness of the submission. Moreover the provisions of s.2(l)(a) also seem to point in the same direction. It follows therefore that it is enough for the prosecution if they have proved in these cases the assumption by the [defendants] of any of the rights of the owner of the goods in question, that is to say, the supermarket concerned, it being common ground in these cases that the other three of the four elements mentioned in Viscount Dilhorne's speech in *Lawrence* had been fully established.

My Lords, Mr Jeffreys sought to argue that any removal from the shelves of the supermarket, even if unaccompanied by label switching, was without more an appropriation. In one passage in his judgment in *Morris*'s case the learned Lord Chief Justice appears to have accepted the submission, for he said [1983] Q.B. 587, 596: "it seems to us that in taking the article from the shelf the customer is indeed assuming one of the rights of the owner—the right to move the article from its position on the shelf to carry it to the check-out."

With the utmost respect, I cannot accept this statement as correct. If one postulates an honest customer taking goods from a shelf to put in his or her trolley to take to the checkpoint there to pay the proper price, I am unable to see that any of these actions involves any assumption by the shopper of the rights of the supermarket. In the context of s.3(1), the concept of appropriation in my view involves not an act expressly or impliedly authorised by the owner but an act by way of adverse interference with or usurpation of those rights. When the honest shopper acts as I have just described, he or she is acting with the implied authority of the owner of the supermarket to take the goods from the shelf, put them in the trolley, take them to the checkpoint and there pay the correct price, at which moment the property in the goods will pass to the shopper for the first time. It is with the consent of the owners of the supermarket, be that consent express or implied, that the shopper does these acts and thus obtains at least control if not actual possession of the goods preparatory, at a later stage, to obtaining the property in them upon payment of the proper amount at the checkpoint. I do not think that s.3(1) envisages any such act as an 'appropriation', whatever may be the meaning of that word in other fields such as contract or sale of goods law.

If, as I understand all your Lordships to agree, the concept of appropriation in s.3(1) involves an element of adverse interference with or usurpation of some right of the owner, it is necessary next to consider whether that requirement is satisfied in either of these cases. As I have already said, in my view mere removal from the shelves without more is not an appropriation. Further, if a shopper with some perverted sense of humour, intending only to create confusion and nothing more both for the supermarket and for other shoppers, switches labels, I do not think that that act of label switching alone is without more an appropriation, though it is not difficult to envisage some cases of dishonest label switching which could be. In cases such as the present, it is in truth a combination of these actions, the removal from the shelf and the switching of the labels, which evidences adverse interference with or usurpation of the right of the owner. Those acts, therefore, amount to an appropriation and if they are accompanied by proof of the other three elements to which I have referred, the offence of theft is established. Further, if they are accompanied by other acts such as putting the goods so removed and relabelled into a receptacle, whether a trolley or the shopper's own bag or basket, proof of appropriation within s.3(1) becomes overwhelming. It is the doing of one or more acts which individually or collectively amount to such adverse interference with or usurpation of the owner's rights which constitute appropriation under s.3(1) and I do not think it matters where there is more than one such act in which order the successive acts take place, or whether there is any interval of time between them. To suggest that it matters whether the mislabelling precedes or succeeds removal from the shelves is to reduce this branch of the law to an absurdity.'

The answer given to the question certified by the Court of Appeal was this:

'There is a dishonest appropriation for the purposes of the Theft Act 1968 where by the substitution of a price label showing a lesser price on goods for one showing a greater price, a defendant either by that act alone or by that act in conjunction with another act or other acts (whether done before or after the substitution of the labels) adversely interferes with or usurps the right of the owner to ensure that the goods concerned are sold and paid for at that greater price.'

In my opinion Lord Roskill was undoubtedly right when he said in the course of the passage quoted that the assumption by the defendant of any of the rights of an owner could amount to an appropriation within the meaning of s.3(1), and that the removal of an article from the shelf and the changing of the price label on it constituted the assumption of one of the rights of the owner and hence an appropriation within the meaning of the subsection. But there are observations in the passage which, with the greatest possible respect to my noble and learned friend Lord Roskill, I must regard as unnecessary for the decision of the case and as being incorrect. In the first place, it seems to me that the switching of price labels on the article is in itself an assumption of one of the rights of the owner, whether or not it is accompanied by some other act such as removing the article from the shelf and placing it in a basket or trolley. No one but the owner has the right to remove a price label from an article or to place a price label upon it. If anyone else does so, he does an act, as Lord Roskill puts it, by way of adverse interference with or usurpation of that right. This is no less so in the case of the practical joker figured by Lord Roskill than in the case of one who makes the switch with dishonest intent. The practical joker, of course, is not guilty of theft because he has not acted dishonestly and does not intend to deprive the owner permanently of the article. So the label switching in itself constitutes an appropriation and so to have held would have been sufficient for the dismissal of both appeals. On the facts of the two cases it was unnecessary to decide whether, as argued by Mr Jeffreys, the mere taking of the article from the shelf and putting it in a trolley or other receptacle amounted to the assumption of one of the rights of the owner, and hence an appropriation. There was much to be said in favour of the view that it did, in respect that doing so gave the shopper control of the article and the capacity to exclude any other shopper from taking it. However, Lord Roskill expressed the opinion that it did not, on the ground that the concept of appropriation in the context of s.3(1) 'involves not an act expressly or impliedly authorised by the owner but an act by way of adverse interference with or usurpation of those rights'. While it is correct to say that appropriation for purposes of s.3(1) includes the latter sort of act, it does not necessarily follow that no other act can amount to an appropriation and in particular that no act expressly or impliedly authorised by the owner can in any circumstances do so. Indeed, *Lawrence* is a clear decision to the contrary since it laid down unequivocally that an act may be an appropriation notwithstanding that it is done with the consent of the owner. It does not appear to me that any sensible distinction can be made in this context between consent and authorisation.

In the civil case of *Dobson v General Accident Fire and Life Assurance Corporation pic* [1990] 1 Q.B. 274 a Court of Appeal consisting of Parker and Bingham LJJ. considered the apparent conflict between *Lawrence* and *Morris* and applied the former decision. The facts were that the plaintiff had insured property with the defendant company against inter alia 'loss or damage caused by theft.' He advertised for sale a watch and ring at the total price of £5,950. A rogue telephoned expressing an interest in buying the articles and the plaintiff provisionally agreed with him that the payment would be by a building society cheque in the plaintiff's favour. The rogue called on the plaintiff next day and the watch and the ring were handed over to him in exchange for a building society cheque for the agreed amount. The plaintiff paid the cheque into his bank, which informed him that it was stolen and worthless. The defendant company denied liability under its policy of insurance on the ground that the loss of the watch and ring was not caused by theft within the meaning of the Act of 1968. The plaintiff succeeded in the county court in an action to recover the amount of his loss, and the decision was affirmed by the Court of Appeal.

One of the arguments for the defendants was that there had been no theft because the plaintiff had agreed to the transaction with the rogue and reliance was placed on Lord Roskill's statement in *Morris* at p.332 that appropriation

> 'involves not an act expressly or impliedly authorised by the owner but an act by way of adverse interference with or usurpation of those rights.'

In dealing with this argument Parker L.J. said, at p.281:

> 'The difficulties caused by the apparent conflict between the decisions in *Lawrence* and *Morris* have provided, not surprisingly, a basis for much discussion by textbook writers and contributors of articles to law journals. It is, however, clear that their Lordships in *Morris* did not regard anything said in that case as conflicting with *Lawrence* for it was specifically referred to in Lord Roskill's speech, with which the other members of the Judicial Committee all agreed, without disapproval or qualification. The only comment made was that, in *Lawrence*, the House did not have to consider the precise meaning of "appropriation" in s.3(1) of the Act of 1968. With respect, I find this comment hard to follow in the light of the first of the questions asked in *Lawrence* and the answer to it, the passages from Viscount Dilhorne's speech already cited, the fact that it was specifically argued "appropriates is meant in a pejorative, rather than a neutral, sense in that the appropriation is against the will of the owner' and finally that dishonesty was common ground. I would have supposed that the question in *Lawrence* was whether appropriation necessarily involved an absence of consent."'

[After quoting other criticisms by Parker L.J. of Lord Roskill's speech in *Morris*, and noting Bingham L.J.'s suggestion that Viscount Dilhorne's ruling might be reconciled with the reasoning in *Morris* on the ground that in *Lawrence* the victim might not in fact have consented to the taxi-driver taking anything in excess of the correct fare:]

It was argued for the respondent in the present appeal that the case of *Dobson* was wrongly decided. I disagree, and on the contrary find myself in full agreement with those parts of the judgment of Parker L.J. to which I have referred. As regards the attempted reconciliation by Bingham L.J. of the reasoning in *Morris* with the ruling in *Lawrence* it appears to me that the suggested basis of reconciliation, which is essentially speculative, is unsound. The actual decision in *Morris* was correct, but it was erroneous, in addition to being unnecessary for the decision, to indicate that an act expressly or impliedly authorised by the owner could never amount to an appropriation. There is no material distinction between the facts in *Dobson* and those in the present case. In each case the owner of the goods was induced by fraud to part with them to the rogue. *Lawrence* makes it clear that consent to or authorisation by the owner of the taking by the rogue is irrelevant. The taking amounted to an appropriation within the meaning of s.1(1) of the Theft Act. *Lawrence* also makes it clear that it is no less irrelevant that what happened may also have constituted the offence of obtaining property by deception under s.15(1) of the Act.

In my opinion it serves no useful purpose at the present time to seek to construe the relevant provisions of the Theft Act by reference to the Report which preceded it, namely the Eighth Report of the Criminal Law Revision Committee (1966) Cmnd. 2977. The decision in *Lawrence* was a clear decision of this House upon the construction of the word 'appropriate' in s.1(1) of the Act, which had stood for twelve years when doubt was thrown upon it by obiter dicta in *Morris*. *Lawrence* must be regarded as authoritative and correct, and there is no question of it now being right to depart from it

My Lords, for the reasons which I have given I would answer branch (a) of the certified question in the affirmative and branch (b) in the negative, and allow the appeal.

[Lords Browne-Wilkinson, Jauncey of Tullichettle and Slynn of Hadley agreed that the appeal should be allowed for the reasons given by Lord Keith of Kinkel. Lord Lowry dissented.]

Appeal allowed. Conviction restored

Questions

Is there a theft, and if so when does it occur, in the following situations:

(a) P lends D his bicycle to go on a two week cycling holiday to France. In fact D intends from the outset to go on from France to live in Spain. After two weeks in France he crosses the border into Spain with the bike.

(b) D, on holiday in France, hires a bicycle. At the end of the hire period D keeps the bicycle and returns to England with it. D offers the bicycle for sale and sells it to V for £100. (See *Atakpu* [1993] 4 All E.R. 215.)

(c) P tells her son D to take from her purse the cost of some groceries he has purchased at her request. P takes £5 but the groceries cost £4—he does this in front of his mother who appears to consent to him pocketing the five pounds. Would it make any difference if P knew the actual cost of the groceries and did not dissent when she saw D take the £5?

(d) D removes items from a supermarket shelf into a wire basket intending to take them to a quiet corner in the store out of sight of the checkout assistant and conceal them in his overcoat. He goes to the corner of the store as planned only to find an assistant restocking shelves. He sets down his basket and leaves.

(e) D buys a car from X believing him to be the lawful owner but in fact it belonged to P. D subsequently discovers that P is the rightful owner of the car but refuses to restore it to P. D sells the car to V for £1,000. (See *Adams* [1993] Crim. L.R. 72.)

Note

In *Gomez*, Lord Lowry gave a very strong dissenting judgment in which he argued that D should not be guilty of theft where V has transferred ownership of goods to him even though D's title to the goods is voidable due to his deception. Lord Lowry referred in detail to the 8th Report of the Criminal Law Revision Committee, *Theft and Related Offences*, (1966), Cmnd.2977 upon which the Theft Act was based. His argument was that such a case should be dealt with under the s.15(1) offence of obtaining property by deception. Had the prosecutor charged this in the first place the case before their Lordships would never have arisen. (NB: The s.15(1) offence has been replaced by fraud by false representation contrary to ss.1 and 2 of the Fraud Act 2006, see below, p.685.)

In *Gomez* the title D obtained to the property he took from the shop was voidable due to the deception. If P, having capacity, makes a gift of property to D, could D by receiving that property be guilty of theft? By gifting property a donor transfers ownership of the property to the donee. However, if there is coercion, undue influence or fraud, the transaction is voidable, that is, it may be avoided by the donor. Could a donee be considered dishonest in accepting a gift, even though there was no coercion, undue influence or fraud on the donee's part, where, for example, the donee is manipulative and takes advantage of a gullible or vulnerable donor? Clearly it would be undesirable for the criminal law to find a donee guilty of theft where the civil law would find that a valid gift had been made and that the allegedly stolen property belonged to the alleged thief. Of course, if the donor lacks the capacity necessary to make a valid gift, the transaction would be void and the property would remain that of the donor.

In *Mazo* [1996] Crim. L.R. 435, D, a maid to Lady S, was convicted of theft having cashed cheques totalling £37,000 made payable to her by Lady S. There was evidence to the effect that Lady S was elderly and suffered from confusion at times and short-term memory lapses. D's convictions were quashed as the trial judge had not given an adequate direction to the jury to consider whether Lady S had capacity to make valid gifts. The Court of Appeal accepted that it was common ground that if the gifts were valid there could not be a theft, Pill LJ quoting from the speech of Viscount Dilhorne in *Lawrence* [1972] A.C. 626, which was referred to in *Gomez* where he stated at 632:

> "a person is not to be regarded as acting dishonestly if he appropriates another's property believing that, with full knowledge of the circumstances, that other person has in fact agreed to the appropriation."

Adopting a narrow reading of *Gomez*, the Court of Appeal took it to have decided that a transaction which was done with the owner's consent could found a charge of theft if there had been deception.

In *Kendrick and Hopkins* [1997] 2 Cr. App. R. 524, the appellants' convictions for conspiracy to steal were upheld where they had drawn a large number of cheques on the victim's account. The victim, aged 99 and virtually blind, was a resident in a small residential home for the elderly run by the appellants. The Court of Appeal stated that they found it unnecessary to consider whether or not the gloss on *Gomez* adopted in *Mazo* was well-founded, being satisfied in the instant case that the jury had received an adequate direction on the question of the capacity of the victim to make valid gifts.

Mazo and *Kendrick and Hopkins* were not in conflict; a legitimate reading of them would be that liability for theft would not arise where there was a valid inter vivos gift. This position has been thrown into disarray by the case which follows.

R. V HINKS

[2000] 4 All ER 833 HL

D was convicted of theft of a television set and sums amounting to £60,000 which had been given to her by P, a 53-year-old man of limited intelligence whom she had befriended. The prosecution case had been presented on the basis that she had coerced or unduly influenced P to make the gifts. The prosecution also alleged that P lacked the mental capacity to make gifts. The judge directed the jury that they could convict of theft where D received a valid gift if they were satisfied that her conduct fell short of the standards of ordinary decent people and she realised this. The Court of Appeal upheld her conviction holding that the issue was not whether or not a gift was valid but simply whether there had been an appropriation; a gift might be clear evidence of an appropriation which could occur even though the owner consented to the property being taken. D appealed to the House of Lords.

LORD STEYN

I . . .. The certified question before the House is as follows: Whether the acquisition of an indefeasible title to property is capable of amounting to an appropriation of property belonging to another for the purposes of s.1(1) of the Theft Act 1968.

In other words, the question is whether a person can 'appropriate' property belonging to another where the other person makes him an indefeasible gift of property, retaining no proprietary interest or any right to resume or recover any proprietary interest in the property.

. . .

III. The appellant appealed to the Court of Appeal. The Court of Appeal (Rose L.J., Vice President, Douglas Brown and Dyson JJ.) dismissed the appeal: *Reg. v Hinks* [2000] 1 Cr.App.R. 1 . . . After an accurate review of the case law, and in particular the decisions of the House in *Lawrence* [1992] A.C. 626 and *Gomez* [1993] A.C. 442 Rose L.J. concluded, at p.9:

> 'In our judgment, in relation to theft, one of the ingredients for a jury to consider is not whether there has been a gift, valid or otherwise, but whether there has been appropriation. A gift may be clear evidence of appropriation. But a jury should not, in our view, be asked to consider whether a gift has been validly made because, first, that is not what s.1 of the Theft Act requires; secondly, such an approach is inconsistent with *Lawrence* and *Gomez*, and thirdly, the state of mind of a donor is irrelevant to appropriation: see, in particular, the speech of Lord Browne-Wilkinson, with which Lord Jauncey agreed, in *Gomez* at 396 and 495H . . .: The authorities, as it seems to us, make clear the importance of maintaining a distinction in relation to theft between the two quite separate ingredients of appropriation and dishonesty. Belief or lack of belief that the owner consented to the appropriation is relevant to dishonesty. But appropriation may occur even though the owner has consented to the property being taken. In the present case, the jury were so directed.'

This was the view of a strong Court of Appeal, experienced in this class of criminal work . . ..

V. The starting point must be the words of the statute as interpreted by the House in its previous decisions. The first case in the trilogy is *Reg. v Lawrence* 1971 [1972] A.C. 626 . . . [His Lordship quoted at length from the speech of Viscount Dilhorne.]

Lord Dilhorne expressly added that belief that the passenger gave informed consent (i.e. knowing that he was paying in excess of the fare) 'is relevant to the issue of dishonesty, not to the question whether or not there has been an appropriation': at p.632D. The appeal was dismissed. The ratio decidendi of *Lawrence*, namely that in a prosecution for theft it is unnecessary to prove that the taking was without the owner's consent, goes to the heart of the certified question in the present case.

The second decision of the House was *Reg. v Morris* in 1983 [1984] A.C. 320 Lord Roskill made an observation, which was in conflict with the ratio of Lawrence and had to be corrected in *Gomez*. Lord Roskill said, at p.332D:

'If one postulates an honest customer taking goods from a shelf to put in his or her trolley to take to the checkpoint there to pay the proper price, I am unable to see that any of these actions involves any assumption by the shopper of the rights of the supermarket. In the context of s.3(1), the concept of appropriation in my view involves not an act expressly or impliedly authorised by the owner but an act by way of adverse interference with or usurpation of those rights.'

It will be observed that this observation was not necessary for the decision of the case: absent this observation the House would still have held that there had been an appropriation. Lord Roskill took the view that he was following the decision in *Lawrence*. It is clear, however, that his observation (as opposed to the decision in Morris) cannot stand with the ratio of *Lawrence*. And as his observation, cast in terms of 'the honest customer', shows Lord Roskill conflated the ingredients of appropriation and dishonesty contrary to the holding in *Lawrence*.

The third decision of the House was in *Reg. v Gomez* in 1992 [1993] A.C. 442 . . . In crystalline terms Lord Keith of Kinkel speaking for all the numbers of the majority ruled at p.464 C-D: (1) The meaning of the relevant provisions must be determined by construing the statutory language without reference to the report which preceded it, namely the Eighth Report of the Criminal Law Revision Committee on Theft and Related Offences (1966) (Cmnd. 2977). (2) The observations of Lord Roskill in *Morris* [1984] A.C. 320 were unnecessary for the decision of that case; that they were in clear conflict with the ratio of *Lawrence* [1972] A.C. 626; and that they were wrong. (3) *Lawrence* must be accepted as authoritative and correct, and 'there is no question of it now being right to depart from it.' At the same time Lord Keith, at p.463 H, endorsed the judgment of Parker L.J. in the civil case of *Dobson v General Accident Fire and Life Assurance Corporation Plc*. [1990] 1 Q.B. 274 where Parker L.J. highlighted the conflict between *Lawrence* [1972] A.C. 626 and *Morris* [1984] A.C. 320 and chose to follow *Lawrence*. (4) Any act may be an appropriation notwithstanding that it was done with the consent or authorisation of the owner. In *Gomez* [1993] A.C. 442 the House was expressly invited to hold that 'there is no appropriation where the entire proprietary interest passes': at 448B. That submission was rejected. The leading judgment in Gomez was therefore in terms which unambiguously rule out the submission that s.3(1) does not apply to a case of a gift duly carried out because in such a case the entire proprietary interest will have passed. In a separate judgment (with which Lord Jauncey of Tullichettle expressed agreement) Lord Browne-Wilkinson observed, at pp.495H–196A:

'. . . I regard the word 'appropriation' in isolation as being an objective description of the act done irrespective of the mental state of either the owner or the accused. It is impossible to reconcile the decision in *Lawrence* (that the question of consent is irrelevant in considering whether there has been an appropriation) with the views expressed in *Morris*, which latter views in my judgment were incorrect.'

In other words it is immaterial whether the act was done with the owner's consent or authority. It is true of course that the certified question in *Gomez* referred to the situation where consent had been obtained by fraud. But the majority judgments do not differentiate between cases of consent induced by fraud and consent given in any other circumstances. The ratio involves a proposition of general application. *Gomez* therefore gives effect to s.3(1) of the Act by treating 'appropriation' as a neutral word comprehending 'any assumption by a person of the rights of an owner.' If the law is as held in *Gomez*, it destroys the argument advanced on the present appeal, namely that an indefeasible gift of property cannot amount to an appropriation.

VI. Counsel for the appellant submitted in the first place that the law as expounded in *Gomez* and *Lawrence* must be qualified to say that there can be no appropriation unless the other party (the owner) retains some proprietary interest, or the right to resume or recover some proprietary interest, in the property. Alternatively, counsel argued that 'appropriates' should be interpreted as if the word 'unlawfully' preceded it. Counsel said that the effect of the decisions in *Lawrence* and *Gomez* is to reduce the actus reus of theft to 'vanishing point'. He argued that the result is to bring the criminal law 'into conflict' with the civil law. Moreover, he argued that the decisions in *Lawrence* and *Gomez* may produce absurd and grotesque results. He argued that the mental requirements of dishonesty and intention of permanently depriving the owner of property are insufficient to filter out some cases of conduct which should not sensibly be regarded as theft. He did not suggest that the appellant's dishonest and repellent conduct came within such a category . . ..

At the extremity of the application of legal rules there are sometimes results which may seem strange. A matter of judgment is then involved. The rule may have to be recast. Sir John Smith has eloquently argued that the rule in question ought to be recast. I am unpersuaded. If the law is restated by adopting a narrower definition of appropriation, the outcome is likely to place beyond the reach of the criminal law dishonest persons who should be found guilty of theft. The suggested revisions would unwarrantably restrict the scope of the law of theft and complicate the fair and effective prosecution of theft. In my view the law as settled in *Lawrence* and *Gomez* does not demand the suggested revision. Those decisions can be applied by judges and juries in a way which, absent human error, does not result in injustice.

Counsel for the appellant further pointed out that the law as stated in *Lawrence* and *Gomez* creates a tension between the civil and the criminal law. In other words, conduct which is not wrongful in a civil law sense may constitute the crime of theft. Undoubtedly, this is so. The question whether the civil claim to title by a convicted thief, who committed no civil wrong, may be defeated by the principle that nobody may benefit from his own civil or criminal wrong does not arise for decision. Nevertheless there is a more general point, namely that the interaction between criminal law and civil law can cause problems: compare Beatson and Simester, 'Stealing One's Own Property' (1999) 115 L.Q.R. 372. The purposes of the civil law and the criminal law are somewhat different. In theory the two systems should be in perfect harmony. In a practical world there will sometimes be some disharmony between the two systems. In any event, it would be wrong to assume on a priori grounds that the criminal law rather than the civil law is defective. Given the jury's conclusions, one is entitled to observe that the appellant's conduct *should* constitute theft, the only available charge. The tension between the civil and the criminal law is therefore not in my view a factor which justifies a departure from the law as stated in *Lawrence* and *Gomez*. Moreover, these decisions of the House have a marked beneficial consequence. While in some contexts of the law of theft a judge cannot avoid explaining civil law concepts to a jury (e.g. in respect of s.2(1)(a)), the decisions of the House of Lords eliminate the need for such explanations in respect of appropriation. That is a great advantage in an overly complex corner of the law.

VII. My Lords, if it had been demonstrated that in practice *Lawrence* and *Gomez* were calculated to produce injustice that would have been a compelling reason to revisit the merits of the holdings in those decisions. That is however, not the case. In practice the mental requirements of theft are an adequate protection against injustice. In these circumstances I would not be willing to depart from the clear decisions of the House in *Lawrence* and *Gomez*. This brings me back to counsels' principal submission, namely that a person does not appropriate property unless the other (the owner) retains, beyond the instant of the alleged theft, some proprietary interest or the right to resume or recover some proprietary interest. This submission is directly contrary to the holdings in *Lawrence* and *Gomez*. It must be rejected. The alternative submission is that the word 'appropriates' should be interpreted as if the word 'unlawfully' preceded it so that only an act which is unlawful under the general law can be an appropriation. This submission is an invitation to interpolate a word in the carefully crafted language of the Act of 1968. It runs counter to the decisions in *Lawrence* and *Gomez* and must also be rejected. It follows that the certified question must be answered in the affirmative . . ..

My Lords, I would dismiss the appeal to the House.

LORD HOBHOUSE OF WOODBOROUGH

The trial judge, rightly, rejected a submission of no case to answer but when he came to sum up he seems to have discarded the way in which the prosecution had founded their case and directed the jury that they could convict the appellant of theft on the simple basis that she had been the recipient of a valid gift provided that the jury were satisfied that the conduct of the appellant fell short of the standards of ordinary and decent people and the appellant realised this. [In the Court of Appeal] . . . Rose LJ said [2000] 1 Cr.App.R. 1 at 9:

> 'In our judgment, in relation to theft, one of the ingredients for a jury to consider is not whether there has been a gift, valid or otherwise, but whether there has been an appropriation. *A gift may be clear evidence of appropriation*. But a jury should not, in our view, be asked to consider whether a gift has been validly made . . .'
> (emphasis supplied)

The dismissiveness of this reasoning is in itself remarkable but the proposition which needs particularly to be examined is that which I have emphasised bearing in mind that the Court of Appeal draws no distinction between a fully effective gift and one which is vitiated by incapacity, fraud or some other feature which would lead both the man in the street and the law to say that the transfer was not a true gift resulting from an actual intention of the donor to give. Another aspect of the Court of Appeal's reasoning which also has to be examined is the relationship of that proposition to the concept of dishonesty. It is explicit in the Court of Appeal judgment that the relevant definition of the crime of theft is to be found in the element of dishonesty and *R. v Ghosh* [1982] Q.B. 1053 and that this is to receive no greater definition than consciously falling below the standards of an ordinary and decent person and may include anything which such a person would think was morally reprehensible. It may be no more than a moral judgment.

The reasoning of the Court of Appeal therefore depends upon the disturbing acceptance that a criminal conviction and the imposition of custodial sanctions may be based upon conduct which involves no inherent illegality and may only be capable of being criticised on grounds of lack of morality. This approach itself raises fundamental questions. An essential function of the criminal law is to define the boundary between what conduct is criminal and what merely immoral. Both are the subject of the disapprobation of ordinary right-thinking citizens and the distinction is liable to be arbitrary or at least strongly influenced by considerations subjective to the individual members of the tribunal. To treat otherwise lawful conduct as criminal merely because it is open to such disapprobation would be contrary to principle and open to the objection that it fails to achieve the objective and transparent certainty required of the criminal law by the principles basic to human rights.

I stress once more that it is not my view that the resort to such reasoning was necessary for the decision of the present case. I would be reluctant to think that those of your Lordships who favour dismissing this appeal have fallen into the trap of believing that, without adopting the reasoning of the Court of Appeal in this case, otherwise guilty defendants will escape justice. The facts of the present case do not justify such a conclusion nor do the facts of any other case which has been cited on this appeal.

The Act
. . . [The] structure of ss.1 to 6 has had an unfortunate by-product. It has led to a practice (started by Megaw LJ in the Court of Appeal in *Lawrence*) of construing each of the words or phrases in s.1(l) as if they were independent and not part of a single complex definition. The words and phrases have an inter-relation, the one affecting the meaning of another and of the whole. Lord Browne-Wilkinson warned against this in his speech in *R. v Gomez* [1993] A.C. 442 at 495:

'But it should not be overlooked that elements (i) and (ii) . . . are interlinked: element (i) (dishonest) is an adjectival description of element (ii) (appropriation). Parliament has used a composite phrase 'dishonest appropriation'. Thus it is not every appropriation which falls within the section but only an act which answers the composite description. The fact that Parliament used that composite phrase—"dishonest appropriation"— in my judgment casts light on what is meant by the word "appropriation".'

Another point which has arisen from the general intention of the Act and its drafting is the assumption that all questions arising in connection with the law of theft should now be capable of answer without involving any concept or rule derived from the civil law or using any technical legal terminology. Whilst there can be no doubt about the general intention of the Act, to proceed from such a general intention to that assumption is simplistic and erroneous. It is, of course, part of the duty and function of the judge at the criminal trial to separate the questions of law from the questions of fact and only direct the jury on matters of law so far as the issues in the case make it necessary for them to know the law in order to decide the issues of fact and determine the defendant's guilt or innocence; but, when there are relevant questions of law, they must be recognised and the jury directed accordingly.

The truth is that theft is a crime which relates to civil property and, inevitably, property concepts from the civil law have to be used and questions answered by reference to that law. Lord Roskill (expressing sentiments similar to those voiced by others before and since) was no doubt right in *R v Morris* [1984] A.C. 320 at 334 to warn in general terms against introducing into the criminal law questions whether particular contracts were void or voidable on the ground of mistake or fraud or whether any mistake was sufficiently fundamental to vitiate a contract. But the Act at times expressly requires civil law concepts to be applied. Section 1(1) uses the expression 'belonging to another'. Thus, in some criminal cases, it may be necessary to determine whether the relevant property belonged to the alleged victim or to the defendant. In *R v Walker* [1984] Crim.L.R. 112 the case turned upon whether the article in question had been rejected by the buyer so as to revest the title to it in the seller, the defendant. (See also per Bingham LJ in *Dobson v General Accident, Fire and Life Assurance Corporation Plc* [1990] 1 Q.B. 274) This was an issue which had to be answered by reference to the civil law and about which the criminal law had nothing to say except to pose the question. (Another case which illustrated the same need to recognise and give effect to the civil law is *R v Preddy* [1996] A.C. 815 and the consequence of having failed to do so was that the Court of Appeal had then to reconsider a considerable number of wrongly based convictions.)

Section 5: 'Belonging to Another':
[His Lordship quoted s.5, see below.]

Section 5 qualifies and defines the expression 'belonging to another' and specifically makes use of a number of civil law concepts. Under subsection (1) the jury may have to decide who had the possession of the article or whether someone other than the defendant had a 'proprietary right or interest' including an equitable interest (subject to the stated exception) and receive the requisite direction as to the civil law. Subsections (2) and (3) necessitate the consideration of the law of trusts and the rights of beneficiaries and the law of bailment and agency. Subsection (4) makes provision for the situation 'where a person gets property by another's mistake'. The criterion which the subsection then applies is whether or not the recipient came under an obligation to make restoration of the property (or its value or proceeds). This is a sophisticated criterion wholly dependant upon distinctions to be drawn from the civil law. Unless the criterion is satisfied this constituent of the crime of theft has not been proved.

It is relevant to look at this example further because it is an example of a person who has acquired a defeasible title. Where the transferor has made a mistake, the mistake can be so fundamental that the transferee acquires no rights at all in respect of the chattel transferred as against the transferor. But there may be cases where the mistake does not have so absolute an effect and the transferor may only have equitable rights (*cf* subsection (1)) or restitutionary rights against the transferee. If, however, the transferee has already had validly transferred to him the legal title to and possession of the chattel without any obligation to make restoration, a later retention of or dealing with the chattel by the transferee, whether or not 'dishonest' and whether or not it would otherwise amount to an appropriation, cannot amount to theft. However much the jury may consider that his conduct in not returning the chattel falls below the standards of ordinary and decent people, he has not committed the crime of theft. The property did not belong to another.

Section 5 and, particularly, s.5(4) demonstrate that the Theft Act has been drafted so as to take account of and require reference to the civil law of property, contract and restitution. The same applies to many other sections of the Act. For example, s.6 is drafted by reference to the phrase 'regardless of the other's rights'—that is to say rights under the civil law. Section 28, dealing with the restoration of stolen goods, clearly can only work if the law of theft recognises and respects transfers of property valid under the civil law, otherwise it would be giving the criminal courts the power to deprive citizens of their property otherwise than in accordance with the law.

Section 5 shows that the state of mind of the transferor at the time of transfer may be relevant and critical. Similarly, the degree of the transferee's knowledge will be relevant to the s.5 question quite independently of any question under s.2. For instance, where there has been a mistake on the part of the transferor, the position under s.5(4) can be different depending on whether or not the transferee was aware of the mistake.

Further, it will be appreciated that the situations to which s.5 is relevant can embrace gifts as well as other transactions such as transfers for value. The prosecution must be able to prove that, at the time of the alleged appropriation, the relevant property belonged to another within the meaning given to that phrase by s.5. Where the defendant has been validly given the property he can no longer appropriate property belonging to another. The Court of Appeal does not seem to have had their attention directed to s.5. The question certified on the grant of leave to appeal is self-contradictory. The direction of the trial judge approved by the Court of Appeal is inadequate. There is no law against appropriating your own property as defined by s.5.

Section 2: 'Dishonestly':
[His Lordship quoted s.2, see below.]

Although s.2 is headed 'Dishonestly', this quotation shows that it is as much involved with the application of the concepts 'appropriation' and 'property belonging to another', (a) contemplates that the defendant believes that he has the right to appropriate the property and (b) his belief that he would have the consent of the person to whom the property belongs to appropriate it. If belief in such a right or such consent can prevent the defendant's conduct from amounting to theft (whatever the jury may think of it), how can it be said that his knowledge that he has such a right or the actual consent of the person to whom the property belongs is irrelevant? How can it be said that the right of the defendant to accept a gift is irrelevant—or the fact that the transferor has actually and validly consented to the defendant having the relevant property? Yet it is precisely these things which the judgment of the Court of Appeal would wholly exclude.

Section 2(1) is cutting down the classes of conduct which the jury are at liberty to treat as dishonest. They qualify the *Ghosh* approach and show that in any given case the court must consider whether it is adequate to give an unqualified *Ghosh* direction as the Court of Appeal held to be sufficient in the present case.

Gifts:

The discussion in the present case has been marked by a failure to consider the law of gift. Perhaps most remarkable is the statement of the Court of Appeal that 'a gift may be clear evidence of appropriation'. The making of a gift is the act of the donor. It involves the donor in forming the intention to give and then acting on that intention by doing whatever it is necessary for him to do to transfer the relevant property to the donee. Where the gift is the gift of a chattel, the act required to complete the gift will normally be either delivery to the donee or to a person who is to hold the chattel as the bailee of the donee; money can be transferred by having it credited to the donee's bank account—and so on. Unless the gift was conditional, in which case the condition must be satisfied before the gift can take effect, the making of the gift is complete once the donor has carried out this step. The gift has become the property of the donee. It is not necessary for the donee to know of the gift. The donee, on becoming aware of the gift, has the right to refuse (or reject) the gift in which case it revests in the donor with resolutive effect. (See *Halsbury's Laws*: Gifts, vol. 20, paras 48–49 and the cases cited.)

What consequences does this have for the law of theft? Once the donor has done his part in transferring the property to the defendant, the property, subject to the special situations identified in the subsections of s.5, ceases to be 'property belonging to another'. However wide a meaning one were to give to 'appropriates', there cannot be a theft. For it to be possible for there to be a theft there will have to be something more, like an absence of a capacity to give or a mistake satisfying s.5(4). Similarly, where the donee himself performs the act necessary to transfer the property to himself, as he would if he himself took the chattel out of the possession of the donor or, himself, gave the instructions to the donor's bank, s.5(1) would apply and mean that that constituent of the crime of theft would at that time have been satisfied.

If one treats the 'acceptance' of the gift as an appropriation, and this was the approach of the judge and is implicit in the judgment of the Court of Appeal (despite their choice of words), there are immediate difficulties with s.2(1)(a). The defendant did have the right to deprive the donor of the property. The donor did consent to the appropriation; indeed, he intended it. There are also difficulties with s.6 as she was not acting regardless of the donor's rights; the donor has already surrendered his rights. The only way that these conclusions can be displaced is by showing that the gift was not valid. There are even difficulties with s.3 itself. The donee is not 'assuming the rights of an owner': she has them already.

Section 3: 'Appropriates':

This is the shortest of the explanatory sections. Its purpose is undoubtedly to get away from some of the technicalities of the law of larceny which arose from the need for the defendant to have *taken* the property. It uses a different concept which does not require an acquisition of possession. The concept is any assumption of the rights of an owner (which has been held to mean 'the assumption of *any* of the rights of an owner': *R. v Morris*). The second part of subsection (1) clearly has to be read with s.5.

Subsection (2) deals with the purchase for value of a defective title and provides a further illustration of two of the points I have already made. It is drafted by reference to the position under civil law. It cross-refers to factors which are primarily relevant to honesty—'good faith' and what the defendant 'believed' he had acquired—so demonstrating again the intimate inter-relationship of the drafting of one section with another and with the definition in s.1(1) as a whole.

Section 3 does not use any qualitative expression such as '*mis*appropriates' nor does it repeat the Larceny Act expression 'without the consent of the owner'. It has thus been read by some as if 'appropriates' was a wholly colourless expression. This reading declines to draw any guidance from the context in which the word is used in the definition in s.1(1) and the scheme of ss.2 to 6. It also declines to attach any significance to the use of the word 'assumption'. This led some curious submissions being made to your Lordships.

It was for example suggested that the garage repair mechanic employed to change the oil of a car would have appropriated the car. The reasoning is that only the owner has the right to do this or tell someone to do it therefore to do it is to assume the rights of the owner. This is an absurdity even when one takes into account that some of the absurd results can be avoided by other parts of the definition of theft. The mechanic is not assuming any right he is merely carrying out the instructions of the owner. The person who accepts a valid gift is simply conforming to the wishes of the owner. The words 'appropriate' [property belonging to another] and 'assume' [the rights of that other] have a useful breadth of meaning but each of them in its natural meaning includes an element of doing something which displaces the rights of that other person. The rights of that other [the owner] include the right to authorise another [the defendant] to do things which would otherwise be an infringement of the rights of the owner.

For the sake of completeness, I should mention that it is not necessary for the present appeal to consider the questions of timing that may arise in relation to appropriation. A carrier may receive goods of which he intends to deprive the owner at a convenient moment. (*R. v Skipp* [1975] Crim.L.R. 114, *R. v Fritschy* [1985] Crim.L.R. 745.) If goods are entrusted to the defendant for one purpose and he takes possession of them for another, it may well be that he has then and there appropriated them since he is thereby assuming the rights of an owner not those of a bailee. This also helps with understanding the supermarket cases. Putting back an article which has been lifted off the shelf in order to read the label or packet does not without more assume any right of ownership. Nor does taking the article to the check-out in order to offer to buy it; that is merely to comply with an implicit request by the owner (the supermarket). On the other hand to interfere with the price label or to take the article with the purpose of smuggling it out of the shop without paying is an assumption of the rights of an owner. (*R. v Morris*)

The considerations which I have discussed now at some length all lead to the conclusion that ss.1 to 6 of the Theft Act should be read as a cohesive whole and that to attempt to isolate and compartmentalise each element only leads to contradictions. This vice is particularly clear where alleged gifts are involved. In such a situation greater care in the analysis is required under ss.2, 3 and 5 and it will normally be necessary to direct the jury in fuller terms and not merely ask them if they think that the defendant fell below the standards of an ordinary and decent person and realised that such persons would so regard his conduct.

The Authorities:
The House of Lords:

The appellant has submitted that your Lordships should, if needs be, over-rule *JR v Lawrence* [1972] A.C. 626 and *R. v Gomez* [1993] A.C. 442. I do not consider that either case should be over-ruled nor is it necessary for the decision of the present case. Neither is inconsistent with my analysis of the law. What appears to have happened is that some of the language used in the three successive House of Lords decisions (*Lawrence, Morris, Gomez*) has been misread without sufficient regard to the context in which the language in each case was used and without a constructive consideration of the intent of ss.1 to 6 as a whole . . ..

[In] *Lawrence* . . . Viscount Dilhorne with whom the other members of the House agreed said, at p.632:

'That there was an appropriation in this case is clear. Section 3(1) states that any assumption by a person of the rights of an owner amounts to an appropriation. Here there clearly was such an assumption. That an appropriation was dishonest may be proved in a number of ways. In this case it was not contended that the appellant had not acted dishonestly. Section 2(1) provides, inter alia, that a person's appropriation of property belonging to another is not to be regarded as dishonest if he appropriates the property in the belief that he would have the other's consent if the other knew of the appropriation and the circumstances of it. *A fortiori, a person is not to be regarded as acting dishonestly if he appropriates another's property believing that with full knowledge of the circumstances that other person has in fact agreed to the appropriation*' (emphasis supplied)

This passage, including the important (but sometimes overlooked) sentence which I have emphasised, supports what I have said above in relation to s.2(l)(b). He added:

'Belief or the absence of belief that the owner had with such knowledge [i.e. knowledge that £7 was far in excess of the legal fare] consented to the appropriation is relevant to the issue of dishonesty, not to the question whether or not there has been an appropriation.'

If one asks the question 'was there a dishonest appropriation?' the need to make the distinction disappears. The perceived difficulty only arises because the definition is fragmented. As I have pointed out in relation to s.5(1), where the defendant himself removes the property from the owner, he will be taking property belonging to another. The situation in *Lawrence* is not problematical. The whole transaction was driven and coloured by the taxi-driver's fraud. It does not strain the language to describe what happened as an appropriation of property belonging to another. It was never a case of consent except possibly in a technical Larceny Act sense. The damaging legacy of the *Lawrence* judgment has been the adoption of the fragmented approach and the separation of the statement that consent was not relevant to appropriation from its context and from the accompanying statement that knowledge of actual consent is incompatible with dishonesty . . ..

[In] *Morris* [1984] A.C. 320 . . . Lord Roskill . . . held that an assumption of any of the rights of an owner would suffice and answered the certified question by saying that such conduct did amount to a dishonest appropriation where it 'adversely interferes with or usurps the right of the owner to ensure that the goods concerned are sold and paid for' at the full price. Lord Roskill clearly treated the phrase 'dishonestly appropriates' as a composite one (a view which seems to have led him to distinguish the example of the practical joker: p.332).

In the Court of Appeal in *Morris* Lord Lane, C.J. [1983] Q.B. 587, 596 had expressed the opinion that merely taking the goods to the check-out in order there to pay the proper price was an appropriation. Lord Roskill disagreed [1984] A.C. 320, 332. It was not an assumption by the shopper of the rights of the supermarket.

'In the context of s.3(l), the concept of appropriation in my view involves not an act expressly or impliedly authorised by the owner but an act by way of adverse interference with or usurpation of those rights. When the honest shopper acts as I have just described, he or she is acting with the implied authority of the owner of the supermarket to take the goods from the shelf, put them in the trolley, take them to the checkpoint and there pay the correct price at which moment the property in the goods will pass to the shopper for the first time. It is with the consent of the owners of the supermarket, be that consent express or implied, that the shopper does these acts . . .'

Applying the same reasoning to the case of the dishonest shopper who removes goods from the shelf and hides them in her shopping bag intending from the very beginning to steal them, he approved the decision in *R. v McPherson* [1973] Crim.L.R. 191 that in that situation there was an appropriation.

The contentious part of this decision was (or should have been) the treatment of the assumption of *any* right of an owner as sufficient for s.3. But, given their decision on that point, the decision is wholly consistent with the decision in *Lawrence* and is free from the influence of the language of Visct. Dilhorne which I have criticised. On the same basis, the decision and the speech of Lord Roskill correctly understood the intent of ss.1 to 6 of the Theft Act: this was clearly the view of the remainder of the House and is a view I respectfully share.

However, some of the language used by Lord Roskill itself gave rise to difficulty. It was believed that he had been saying that any consent to the act of the defendant necessarily negatived appropriation and that he was contradicting *Lawrence*: fraudulently induced consent would be as conclusive as any other form of consent or authorisation. This belief was only plausible if the reader of his speech was adopting the mind-set of the Larceny Act. It is clear that Lord Roskill was not intending to contradict the decision in *Lawrence*.

It was in these circumstances that the matter of consent and fraud was brought back before your Lordships' House nine years later in *Gomez* [1993] A.C. 442 . . .

The certified question asked whether there has been an appropriation where 'that which is alleged to be stolen passes to the defendant with the consent of the owner, but that has been obtained by a false representation'. It therefore starts from the premise that there has been overt and directly relevant dishonesty and that the acquisition comes squarely within s.5(4) and (1). The significance of the argument would again seem to be to whether s.1 or s.15 was the relevant section, a point which had already been disposed of by Lawrence. The question also asked, puzzlingly in view of the premise, but obviously directed at Lord Roskill's choice of words: 'Must such a passing of property necessarily involve an element of adverse [interference] with or usurpation of some right of the owner?'. It might be thought that to obtain possession of another's goods by fraudulently causing him to allow you to do so would be a clear case of an adverse interference with his rights.

It was in this connection that Lord Keith of Kinkel said, at p.460:

'While it is correct to say that appropriation for purposes of s.3(l) includes [an unauthorised interference], it does not necessarily follow that no other act can amount to an appropriation and in particular that no act expressly or impliedly authorised by the owner can *in any circumstances* do so. Indeed *R v Lawrence* is a clear decision to the contrary since it laid down unequivocally that an act may be an appropriation notwithstanding that it is done with the consent of the owner. It does not appear to me that any sensible distinction can be made *in this context* between consent and authorisation.' (emphasis supplied)

The context is consent or authorisation induced by fraud. That was the subject matter of the primary question asked. That this is the context to which Lord Keith is referring is confirmed by his reference to *Lawrence*. Lord Keith is emphatically not saying that consent or authorisation not induced by fraud cannot be relevant to the question of appropriation for the purposes of the definition of theft.

This reading is further confirmed by quotations from the judgment of Parker L.J. in *Dobson v General Accident Fire and Life Insurance Corporation Plc* [1990] 1 Q.B. 274 which Lord Keith agreed with and adopted at p.463H:

> 'Moreover, on general principles, it would in my judgment be a plain interference or usurpation of an owner's rights by the customer if he were to remove a label which the [supermarket] owner had placed on goods or put another label on. It would be a trespass to goods and it would be usurping the owner's rights, for only he would have any right to do such an act and no one could contend that there was any implied consent or authority to a customer to do any such thing. There would thus be an appropriation.' (p.461–2)
>
> 'I have reached the conclusion that whatever *R v Morris* did decide it cannot be regarded as having over-ruled the very plain decision in R v Lawrence that appropriation can occur even if the owner consents and that *R v Morris* itself makes it plain that it is no defence to say that the property passed under a voidable contract.' (p.463)

What Parker L.J., and through him Lord Keith, is doing is rejecting the misreading of Lord Roskil's speech. Neither is saying that consent and authorisation are irrelevant to appropriation but, rather, that they do not necessarily exclude the possibility of appropriation. The consent or authority may be limited in its scope and not cover the acts done by the defendant because the defendant has an unauthorised purpose (Parker L.J.; and *Morris*) or the consent or authorisation may have been obtained by fraud (*Lawrence*; and *Gomez*). The fundamental argument which all these authorities are having to battle with is the resurrection of the former possession-based rule that consent negatived larceny, distinguishing between larceny by a trick and obtaining by false pretences. It is clear that the Theft Act declined to adopt that rule and defined theft in terms which were not dependant on it.

Lord Keith's speech includes language which is capable of giving rise to the same difficulties as that upon which I have commented in the speech of Visct. Dilhorne in *Lawrence* and it contains criticisms of the speech of Lord Roskill in *Morris* which for my part I do not consider to have been justified. But its main thrust is that consent or authorisation can be relevant to the question of appropriation though not in circumstances such as those in *Lawrence* and *Gomez*. It does not justify the decision of the Court of Appeal in the present case where *ex hypothesi* there is no fraud.

The speech of Lord Browne-Wilkinson is differently reasoned. He recognises that the Theft Act uses the composite phrase 'dishonestly appropriates'. But he then proceeds (it may be thought, inconsistently and with a lack of logic) from this to the adoption of a meaning of appropriate 'in isolation' which is devoid of any content dependant upon the mental state of the owner or the accused. He goes further than Lord Keith. But he does not refer to any of the difficulties discussed earlier which would arise from that view nor does he consider the elaboration of the criterion 'dishonestly' which is necessary in order to preserve the contextual meaning of the composite phrase. If the criterion 'appropriates' is to become less discriminating, the criterion 'dishonestly' has to become more discriminating in order to retain the meaning of the composite phrase in its context in ss.1 to 6 of the Act.

The dissent of Lord Lowry is based upon the need in his view to preserve the same type of distinction between ss.1 and 15 of the Theft Act as formerly existed between ss.1 and 32 of the Larceny Act. If anything, that disagreement lends force to my reading of the speech of Lord Keith

The Later Authorities
[His Lordship considered *Mazo*, above, p.607.] The Court of Appeal allowed her appeal. Pill LJ. giving the judgment of the Court said, at p.521:

> 'It is clear that a transaction may be a theft for the purpose of s.1(l) notwithstanding that it was done with the owner's consent if it was induced by fraud, deception or a false representation: see *Gomez*. It is also common ground that the receiver of a valid gift, *inter vivos*, could not be the subject of a conviction for theft. In *Gomez* reference was made to the speech of Visct. Dilhorne in *Lawrence*. In the course of his speech with which the other members of the House agreed Lord Dilhorne stated [p.632]: "A fortiori, a person is not to be regarded as acting dishonestly if he appropriates another's property believing that, with full knowledge of the circumstances, that other person has in fact agreed to the appropriation." It is implicit in that statement that if in all the circumstances, there is held to be a valid gift there can be no theft.'

Later in the judgment Pill L.J. referred to the criteria for deciding whether such a gift was valid as explained in *In re. Beaney* [1978] 1 W.L.R. 770, having regard to lack of comprehension and mental incapacity. He concluded, at p.523 with the timely warning that the summing-up created 'a danger that the jury would take a view that the appellant's conduct was not of a moral quality of which they could approve and convict her on that ground rather than on the true basis of the law of theft'.

In my judgment, my Lords, the explanation of the law in the judgment in *Mazo* is correct and accurately reflects the scheme and purpose of ss.1 to 6 of the Theft Act and demonstrates a correct understanding of the speech of Lord Keith in *Gomez*.

Mazo was distinguished and not followed in *R. v Kendrick and Hopkins* . . .. On the basis of *Mazo*, the summing-up was criticised as not going sufficiently deeply into the question of validity. These criticisms were rightly rejected; the summing-up was not deficient. The appeal was dismissed.

However, the Court of Appeal also criticised the judgment in *Mazo* as not reflecting what was said in *Gomez* particularly by Lord Browne-Wilkinson: the concept of appropriation was distinct from the concept of dishonesty; appropriation could be looked at 'in isolation'; other factors, including the incapacity of the donor and fraud only came in in relation to dishonesty; a simple *Ghosh* direction sufficed.

The Court of Appeal in the present case preferred to follow the judgment in *Kendrick and Hopkins* rather than that in *Mazo*. There was probably no conflict between the actual decisions in the two cases. The Court of Appeal in *Kendrick and Hopkins* were justified in dismissing the appeal and, on an overall assessment, rejecting the criticisms of the summing up in that case and upholding the safety of the convictions. They were in error in their adoption of Lord Browne-Wilkinson's view that appropriation should be looked at in isolation.

The Present Case—Conclusions:
The question certified demonstrates the further step which your Lordships are being asked to take beyond that involved in answering the question in *Gomez*. Does the primary question in *Gomez* receive the same answer if one deletes the words 'obtained by false representation'? The Court of Appeal in the present case held that it should. Two strands of reasoning led them to this conclusion. The first was that s.3(l) should be construed in isolation from the remainder of ss.1 to 6. In this they followed the lead given by Lord Browne-Wilkinson and the Court of Appeal judgment in *Kendrick and Hopkins*. I have already explained why I consider that this is wrong.

The second was the view that Lord Keith and Parker L.J. had ruled that consent of the owner is always wholly irrelevant to what acts amount to appropriation. They achieved this position only by standing on its head what Lord Keith and Parker L.J. had said. What Lord Keith and Parker L.J. confirmed was that 'consent' (in the Larceny Act sense) will not necessarily negative appropriation. What Rose L.J. has derived from this is that consent can never negative appropriation. (The incomplete quotation by Rose L.J. at [2000] 1 Cr.App.R.l, 8 from Parker L.J. is revealing.) This leads Rose L.J. directly to the position that a valid gift is fully consistent with theft, a proposition which is seriously inconsistent with the scheme of ss.1 to 6 and with other parts of the Act and which is not a proposition to be derived from any of the House of Lords decisions (with the possible exception of the speech of Lord Browne-Wilkinson in *Gomez*).

To say, as does Rose L.J. at p.10, that 'civil unlawfulness is not a constituent of the offence of theft' is of course true. That expression does not occur in s.1(l) and it is anyway not clear what it encompasses. But to proceed from there to the proposition that the civil law of property is irrelevant is, as I have explained earlier in this speech, a far greater error.

My Lords, if, contrary to my view, your Lordships are to travel down the route adopted by the Court of Appeal, your Lordships are faced with a choice between two options neither of which are consistent with dismissing this appeal. One option is to accept the 'Browne-Wilkinson' approach and adopt a sanitised concept of appropriation isolated from any context of or interdependence with the other parts of the definition and ss.1 to 6 (particularly ss.2 and 5) *and* then make the necessary qualifications of the concept of dishonesty when the factual issues raised by an individual case require it. The other is to revert to the law as stated by the majority in *Gomez* and by Visct. Dilhorne and, so far as still relevant, by your Lordships' House in *Morris*, and correctly understood by the Court of Appeal in *Mazo*. It is not an option to do neither as happened in the present case. The unqualified *Ghosh* approach cannot survive in conjunction with the 'Browne-Wilkinson' approach.

In my judgment the correct answer is that adopted by Pill L.J. but if your Lordships are of a different opinion the least that should be done is to draw attention to and confirm the provisions of ss.2 and 5 and their implications for cases where the issue raised is whether the property alleged to have been stolen was transferred to the defendant as a gift. What must be erroneous is to treat as belonging to another property which at the time of the alleged appropriation belongs to the defendant in accordance with s.5(4). Similarly it must be wrong to treat as a dishonest 'appropriation of property belonging to another' under s.2(1) an appropriation for which the defendant correctly knows (as opposed to mistakenly believes) he actually had (as opposed to would have had) the other's consent, the other knowing of the appropriation and the circumstances of it (as opposed to the other person only hypothetically having that knowledge).

My Lords, the relevant law is contained in ss.1 to 6 of the Act. They should be construed as a whole and applied in a manner which presents a consistent scheme both internally and with the remainder of the Act. The phrase 'dishonestly appropriates' should be construed as a composite phrase. It does not include acts done in relation to the relevant property which are done in accordance with the actual wishes or actual authority of the person to whom the property belongs. This is because such acts do not involve any assumption of the rights of that person within s.3(1) or because, by necessary implication from s.2(1), they are not to be regarded as dishonest appropriations of property belonging to another.

Actual authority, wishes, consent (or similar words) mean, both as a matter of language and on the authority of the three House of Lords cases, authorisation not obtained by fraud or misrepresentation. The definition of theft therefore embraces cases where the property has come to the defendant by the mistake of the person to whom it belongs and there would be an obligation to restore it—s.5(4)—or property in which the other still has an equitable proprietary interest—s.5(l). This would also embrace property obtained by undue influence or other cases coming within the classes of invalid transfer recognised in *In re Beaney*.

In cases of alleged gift, the criteria to be applied are the same. But additional care may need to be taken to see that the transaction is properly explained to the jury. It is unlikely that a charge of theft will be brought where there is not clear evidence of at least some conduct of the defendant which includes an element of fraud or overt dishonesty or some undue influence or knowledge of the deficient capacity of the alleged donor. This was the basis upon which the prosecution of the appellant was originally brought in the present case. On this basis there is no difficulty in explaining to the jury the relevant parts of s.5 and s.2(l) and the effect of the phrase 'assumption of the rights of an owner'. Where the basis is less specific and the possibility is that there may have been a valid gift of the relevant article or money to the defendant, the analysis of the prosecution case will break down under ss.2 and 5 as well as s.3 and it will not suffice simply to invite the jury to convict on the basis of their disapprobation of the defendant's conduct and their attribution to him of the knowledge that he must have known that they and other ordinary and decent persons would think it dishonest. Theft is a crime of dishonesty but dishonesty is not the only element in the commission of the crime.

I would answer the certified question in the negative. But, in any event, I would allow the appeal and quash the conviction because the summing-up failed to direct the jury adequately upon the other essential elements of theft, not just appropriation.

[Lords Slynn of Hadley and Jauncey of Tullichettle concurred in the speech of Lord Steyn. Lord Hutton delivered a speech in favour of allowing the appeal.]

Appeal dismissed

Questions

1. According to Lord Steyn whether or not there is an appropriation may be determined in isolation from the other elements of the offence of theft. If a valid gift is made by P to D, when D takes possession of the relevant property and does to it anything that might constitute an appropriation, whose property is it?

2. As the context in which the three previous cases before their Lordships had arisen involved deception, was Lord Steyn right to construe from these decisions a broader general principle that an appropriation may occur notwithstanding a valid consent to the property being taken?

3. D, a young, attractive escort goes to live with P, an elderly, ill but very rich man, as his maid. P is lonely and appreciates the care and attention D provides him. He knows D is only interested in his money but he considers that as he will soon die D may as well benefit from his wealth. Over a period of several months P makes gifts to D of several hundred thousand pounds, a car and expensive jewellery. He also has conveyed to her full legal and equitable title to his holiday home in the Lake District. P is of sound mind and D has not deceived him, coerced him or exercised undue

influence over him. She has, however, taken advantage of P's situation and illness to enrich herself and she realises many people might regard her actions as reprehensible. Could D be convicted of theft of the money, jewellery and car? Could she be convicted of theft of the holiday home? (see s.4, below). Section 148 of the Powers of Criminal Courts (Sentencing) Act 2000 provides that a court on convicting someone of theft may make an order that the stolen goods be restored to any person entitled to recover them from the thief. If D's title is indefeasible, to whom should the goods be restored? If D had given some of the money and jewellery to her sister, E, who was aware of the circumstances in which D had acquired them, could E be convicted of handling stolen goods?

4. Lord Hobhouse stated that the words "appropriate" and "assume" include "an element of doing something which displaces the rights of" the owner. In what way could D above be displacing the rights of P? Does Lord Steyn provide an answer to this conundrum?

5. P, a wealthy resident in a home for the elderly, makes a gift of a cheque for £10,000 to D her nurse. D believes P is not of sound mental capacity but takes the cheque and cashes it. Consider D's liability for theft on the basis that (a) P is not of sound mental capacity; and (b) P is of sound mental capacity.

6. Is it possible to reconcile the decision of the majority with the provisions in s.2(1)(a) and (b) relating to the circumstances in which an appropriation is not to be regarded as dishonest? Lord Hutton stated:

> "My Lords, it appears contrary to common sense that a person who receives money or property as a gift could be said to act dishonestly, no matter how much ordinary and decent people would think it morally reprehensible for that person to accept the gift. Section 2(1)(b) of the Act recognises the common sense view . . . It follows, a fortiori, that a person's appropriation of property belonging to another should not be regarded as dishonest if the other person actually gives the property to him."

7. Does it make for certainty in the law if the civil law relating to ownership of property and the criminal law of theft are inconsistent?

8. In *R. v Briggs* [2004] 1 Cr. App. R. 34, D deceived elderly relatives into giving her a signed authority authorising the conveyancers to transfer the proceeds to an account which D subsequently used to purchase another property in D's name. The jury were directed, in accordance with *Gomez*, that it was open to them to conclude there had been an appropriation of the credit balance notwithstanding that it had been transferred with consent. The Court of Appeal, apparently in ignorance of *Gomez* or *Hinks*, quashed the conviction on the basis there could be no appropriation where the victim consents to the transfer to the property, even though the defendant has practiced a deception. This case, which is contrary to the House of Lords decisions in *Gomez* and *Hinks*, may have to be regarded as an aberration. (See further M. Allen, *Textbook of Criminal Law*, 10th edn (Oxford: Oxford University Press, 2009)).

----

ii. "Property"

THEFT ACT 1968 S.4

(1) 'Property' includes money and all other property, real or personal, including things in action and other intangible property.

(2) A person cannot steal land, or things forming part of land and severed from it by him or by his directions, except in the following cases, that is to say—

    (a)   when he is a trustee or personal representative, or is authorised by power of attorney, or as liquidator of a company, or otherwise, to sell or dispose of land belonging to another, and he appropriates the land or anything forming part of it by dealing with it in breach of the confidence reposed in him; or

    (b)   when he is not in possession of the land and appropriates anything forming part of the land by severing it or causing to be severed, or after it has been severed; or

    (c)   when, being in possession of the land under a tenancy, he appropriates the whole or part of any fixture or structure let to be used with the land.

For purposes of this subsection land does not include incorporeal hereditaments; 'tenancy' means a tenancy for years or any less period and includes an agreement for such a tenancy, but a person who after the end of a tenancy remains in possession as statutory tenant or otherwise is to be treated as having possession under the tenancy, and 'let' shall be construed accordingly.

(3) A person who picks mushrooms growing wild on any land, or who picks flowers, fruit or foliage from a plant growing wild on any land, does not (although not in possession of the land) steal what he picks, unless he does it for reward or for sale or other commercial purpose.

For purposes of this subsection 'mushroom' includes any fungus, and 'plant' includes any shrub or tree.

(4) Wild creatures, tamed or untamed, shall be regarded as property; but a person cannot steal a wild creature not tamed nor ordinarily kept in captivity, or the carcase of any such creature, unless either it has been reduced into possession by or on behalf of another person and possession of it has not since been lost or abandoned, or another person is in course of reducing it into possession.

Notes

Section 4 replaced the common law definition of things capable of being stolen, which in general included only tangible moveable objects. It does not matter that the person from whom the property is appropriated is unlawfully in possession of the property (see *Smith* [2011] EWCA Crim 66 where drugs were stolen from a drug dealer and it was unsuccessfully argued on appeal that items unlawfully possessed could not constitute property). There are, however, still some things which are not or not completely within the concept of stealable things.

----

1. Corpses and body parts

At common law neither a corpse, nor parts of a corpse, could be stolen as there was no property in a corpse (see *Sharpe* (1857) Dears & B. 160). In *Kelly and Lindsay* [1998] 3 All E.R. 741, the Court of Appeal recognised an exception to this principle in affirming the convictions of the appellants for theft of 35 to 40 body parts which L had removed, at K's request, from the Royal College of Surgeons so that K, a sculptor, could make casts of them. K had retained some of the parts and disposed of others. Rose LJ stated (at 749) that "parts of a corpse are capable of being property . . . if they have acquired different attributes by virtue of the application of skill, such as dissection or preservation techniques, for exhibition or teaching purposes." Rose LJ went on to state (at 750):

"Furthermore, the common law does not stand still. It may be that if, on some future occasion, the question arises, the courts will hold that human body parts are capable of being property for the purposes of s.4, even without the acquisition of different attributes, if they have a use or significance beyond their mere existence. This may be so if, for example, they are intended for use in an organ transplant operation, for the extraction of DNA or, for that matter, as an exhibit in a trial."

2. Land

Land, and things attached to or growing on land could not in general be stolen, and although the Criminal Law Revision Committee were pressed to equate land with other property exactly, in the end they decided that the position should remain broadly as it was previously: *Theft and Related Offences*, paras 44, 47.

Questions

1. Is theft involved in any of the following cases?

    A moves the fence between his own land and that of his neighbour B, so as to take in a strip of B's land.
    C, a licensee of D's land, strips off some antique wooden panelling and sells it as firewood.
    E, an outgoing tenant of F, purports to sell some antique panelling in the house to G, the incoming tenant.
    H, tenant of J, cuts down a wood on the land and sells it as firewood.
    K enters L's land and uproots a Christmas tree growing wild, with intention of taking it home to decorate his own home.
    M is given £1 by N to collect enough wild mushrooms from L's land to make a breakfast for N.

2. Is a charge of criminal damage available in any of these cases? Compare s.10(1) of the Criminal Damage Act 1971, below p.737.

3. *Wild animals*, while alive and free, were not the subject of larceny

    Dead animals were larcenable but not, ordinarily, by the person who killed them; in other words, poaching was not larceny. The Committee, on the grounds that poaching was not popularly regarded as stealing and that to make it theft would increase the maximum penalty too greatly, decided against equating wild animals with other things.

    Various provisions making summary offences of taking deer and fish were contained in the Larceny Act 1861, which the Theft Act repeals entirely. In order to preserve these offences pending a comprehensive reform of the law of poaching, they were re-enacted substantially unchanged in Sch.1 to the Theft Act. The provisions relating to deer were superseded by the Deer Act 1980. There are also other poaching statutes, e.g. the Salmon and Freshwater Fisheries Act 1975. Moreover, legislation not concerned with protecting anyone's property in the creatures involved protects wild birds, their nests and eggs (Protection of Birds Act 1954) and endangered species (Conservation of Wild Creatures and Wild Plants Act 1975). And see Wildlife and Countryside Act 1981 s.13.

Question

A rounds up wild ponies from the moorland where they are born and reared, in order to sell them at auction. B, who disapproves of this, releases them from the auction pen and one escapes. C captures it and refuses to return it to A or to pay for it. Can the actions of A or B or C amount to theft?

4. Things in action and other intangible property

Before the Theft Act, to be stealable, property had to be tangible. Other things of value, such as a legal right, could not be stolen, and a prosecutor was driven to such shifts as charging the stealing of the piece of paper which evidenced such a right. There is now no need to do that in many cases, as a result of the wide definition of property in s.4(1); but if a piece of paper is involved and changes hands, it may still be convenient to charge the theft of the paper, because the attempt in s.4(1) to widen the concept of stealable property is not without its difficulties.

5. Things in action

A thing in action (or chose in action) is property which does not exist in a physical state, and cannot be enjoyed physically (looked at, listened to, eaten, worn, ridden, etc.), but can only be claimed by legal action. Examples are a debt, shares in a company, a copyright (see *Mensahhartey and Revlevy* [1996] Cr. App. R. 143), a trade mark, insurance cover. These things can be stolen by one who appropriates them with intent to deprive the owner permanently, e.g. a trustee or personal representative, the legal owner of shares beneficially owned by X, dishonestly assigning them to Y. A bank account is also a chose in action. The property rights involved in a bank account are often misunderstood.

Lord Goddard CJ in *R. v Davenport* [1954] 1 All E.R. 602 at 603:

> "Although we talk of people having money in a bank, the only person who has money in a bank is the banker. If I pay money into my bank, either by paying cash or a cheque, the money at once becomes the money of the banker. The relationship between banker and customer is that of debtor and creditor. He does not hold my money as an agent or trustee . . . When the banker is paying out, whether in cash or over the counter or whether by crediting the bank account of someone else, he is paying out his own money, not my money, but he is debiting me in my account with him. I have a chose in action, that is to say I have a right to expect that the banker will honour my cheque, but he does it out of his own money."

If a customer A has a credit of £500 in bank B, the only property is the chose in action, the right to call on B to honour cheques up to that amount. There is no particular sum in the bank vaults over which this right operates. The consequences are: (1) there is no question of a dishonest A stealing this thing in action from B, because by its nature it never could belong to B. Normally it belongs to A himself [but it may "belong to" someone else if another joint account holder is involved, or if it were obtained subject to an obligation to deal with it in a certain way, or by mistake with an obligation to restore: see s.5(3)(4) and *Attorney General's Reference (No.1 of 1983)* [1984] 3 All E.R. 369.] If A obtained the right to overdraw up to £500 by fraud, it is not theft by A, because this right (to call on B to honour cheques up to £500) never did or could belong to B: but see Fraud by false representation, below, p.685. (2) If A by fraud gets B to honour his cheque by paying £500 to P, it is not theft. The £500 given to P may be property, but A does not appropriate it by his fraud, since he does not assume the rights of ownership over any identifiable property; he merely causes B to assume a duty to pay P £500 out of B's general assets: *R. v Navvabi* [1986] 3 All E.R. 102.

But A's right to call on bank B may be stolen by *someone else*, as where, e.g. D is A's cashier with power to draw cheques on A's account, and draws one dishonestly in favour of his own creditor Q. When this cheque is presented and met, A will have lost part of his debt against his banker B. See next case. And even if the cheque is not met, the act of presenting it for payment is an appropriation of one of the rights of the owner, A: *Chan Man-Sin v Attorney General for Hong Kong* [1988] 1 All E.R. 1; *Re Osman* [1989] 3 All E.R. 701.

See also Griew, "Stealing and Obtaining Bank Credits" [1986] Crim. L.R. 356.

R. V KOHN

(1979) 69 Cr. App. R. 395 CA

K was a director of Panelservice Ltd, with authority to make payments on its behalf by drawing cheques against its bank account. He drew cheques against the account for his own purposes. He was charged in respect of each occasion on which he had written a cheque for his own purposes with two counts of theft, the first alleging theft of a thing in action, viz. the debt owed by the bank to Panelservice, and the second alleging theft of the cheque itself. The counts related to various dates during which the state of the bank account varied from being in credit, being in overdraft but within the limits of the overdraft facility, and being in overdraft but beyond the limits of the overdraft facility. K was convicted of theft of the things in action which the cheques represented, and of the cheques themselves. He appealed.

GEOFFREY LANE LJ

So far as the first situation is concerned, when the account is in credit, the prosecution say that, where an account is in credit the relationship of debtor and creditor exists between the bank and the customer, The customer is the creditor, the bank is the debtor. The debt is owing by the bank to the customer. That debt is something which cannot be physically handled, it is not a thing or chose in possession; it is a thing in action, namely something which can only be secured by action and, goes the argument, this is a case of a thing in action par excellence, and if it be proved that the defendant has stolen, in other words appropriated that thing in action, then the offence is made out. [After considering reported decisions on the meaning of 'chose in action':] So the prosecution start off with the advantage of the fact that that expression is plainly one which covers a multitude of matters and over the history of English law has spread really far beyond its original concept. So at first blush it would seem that the appellant's contentions on this point are a little difficult to sustain.

But what Mr Tyrrell submits is this—since we are not sure we have followed the argument, we quote what he says verbatim: 'The very act done which is relied on as interfering with the owner's rights destroys the subject matter of the theft and so there has been no appropriation. Nothing has ever come into the possession of the appellant.' What he says, we think, is that the thing in action has been destroyed before any appropriation and therefore there has been no theft.

It seems to us that the argument is quite untenable. First of all, is there a thing in action, and the answer is undoubtedly yes. Secondly, has the appellant appropriated it? The answer is yes. Was the intention permanently to deprive the owner, and again there was ample evidence upon which the jury properly directed could come to the conclusion that it was. Was it dishonest? Again there was ample evidence on which the jury could come to that conclusion.

A submission was made at the close of the prosecution case similar to that made to us, which the judge rejected. We think that he was right to reject it.

Mr Tyrrell has frankly said that his researches have brought to light no authorities which give any support to his proposition. In so far as there is authority it is against his contentions. It is contained in the writings of two eminent academic lawyers: first of all Professor Griew in his book *The Theft Acts 1968 and 1978* (3rd ed, 1978), paras 2–11, where one finds this:

'The case of an employee (D.) who has authority to draw on his employer's (P.'s) bank account and who dishonestly draws on it for unauthorised purposes seem also to be theft (assuming the account to be in credit), D. has in some manner appropriated the debt owed by the bank to P. Although nothing in the transaction operates as an assignment of that debt to D it would seem that D. has appropriated the debt or part of it by causing P's credit balance to be diminished, or at the very least taking the risk of such diminution. The case is analogous to the theft of a chattel by destruction.'

The whole of that passage, and particularly the last sentence, if it is correct, as we think it is, sounds the death knell to this particular submission on behalf of the appellant . . .

We now turn to the counts which cover the situation where the account was overdrawn, but the amount of the cheque was within the agreed limits of the overdraft. So far as this aspect of the matter is concerned, Mr. Tyrrell submits that the grant of facilities for an overdraft does not create a debt. [After considering authorities holding that specific performance is not possible on a contract to lend money, and holding that to that extent the contract does not constitute a debt] [But] if the account is in credit . . . there is an obligation to honour the cheque. If the account is within the agreed limits of the overdraft facilities, there is an obligation to meet the cheque. In either case it is an obligation which can only be enforced by action and therefore potentially a subject of theft under the provisions of the 1968 Act. The cheque is the means by which the theft of this property is achieved. The completion of the theft does not take place until the transaction has gone through to completion. . . .

[In] *William Rouse v Bradford Banking Co. Ltd.* [1894] A.C. 586, 596, Lord Herschell L.C. said:

'. . . It may be that an overdraft does not prevent the bank who have agreed to give it from at any time giving notice that it is no longer to continue, and that they must be paid their money. This I think at least it does; if they have agreed to give an overdraft they cannot refuse to honour cheques or drafts, within the limit of that overdraft, which have been drawn and put in circulation before any notice to the person to whom they have agreed to give the overdraft that the limit is to be withdrawn . . ..'

Finally the passage of Sir John Donaldson P. in *Eckman v Midland Bank Ltd* [1973] Q.B. 519, 529 a decision of the National Industrial Relations Court, Sir John Donaldson sitting as President with two other lay members:

'If, however, a bank has contracted with the contemnor in terms which the sequestrators are entitled to have transferred to them and which they can operate by authority of the writ of sequestration.'

It seems to us, in the light of those authorities and in the light of the wording of the Theft Act 1968, that in this situation, when the order to the bank is within the agreed limits of the overdraft, a thing in action certainly exists and accordingly the judge was right in rejecting the submission. The appeal so far as those particular counts are concerned must fail.

That leads us to the third situation, which affects only count 7, that being, it will be remembered, the count which dealt with the cheque presented to the bank at the time when the account was over the agreed overdraft limit which had been imposed by the bank.

The situation here is that there is no relationship of debtor and creditor, even notionally. The bank has no duty to the customer to meet the cheque. It can simply mark the cheque 'Refer to drawer.' It can decline to honour the cheque. The reasons for that are obvious. If then a bank declines to honour a cheque, there is no right of action in the customer. If they do as a matter of grace—that is all it can be—honour the cheque then that is a course which does not retrospectively create any personal right of property in the customer and does not create any duty retrospectively in the bank. It seems, therefore, on that bald statement of principle, that this count which alleged a theft of a thing in action when the account was over the agreed limit must be quashed, unless some external reason can be found for saving it . . .

We turn now to the next matter [theft of the cheques] . . . The case for the appellant is that it was not possible in law for him to steal the cheques as alleged in that: (a) he himself wrote and drew the cheques; (b) there was no possibility of Panelservice Ltd. being permanently deprived of the cheques in their character as pieces of paper since they had that character both before and after the appellant drew them; (c) there was no possibility of Panelservice Ltd. being permanently deprived of the cheques in their character as things in action since they did not acquire that character until the appellant wrote and drew them. . .

The matter seems to us to become reasonably clear . . ., if one looks at p.21 of the first volume of the transcript. Here the learned judge said to the jury: 'What is represented by the cheque is, of course, the right of the person named in it, the payee, to receive the payment represented by that cheque. So far as that cheque itself is concerned, true it is a piece of paper but it is a piece of paper which changes its character completely once it is paid because then it receives a rubber stamp or, in this case, the perforated stamp saying that it has been paid and it then also ceases to be a thing in action. That is a bill of exchange which is a thing in action as I have told you. The cheque is the same tiling. It ceases to be that or, at any rate, it ceases to be in its substance the same thing as it was before. That is an instrument on which payment falls to be made.' It seems tolerably clear from that that the judge, counsel and the jury were not considering the cheque in its capacity as a piece of paper *simpliciter*, even if one can view a cheque properly in that light. They were looking at it as a negotiable instrument in the way that the judge described.

Even if that was the way the matter was being considered, said Mr Rose, the drawing of a cheque in favour of a third party does not amount to treating oneself as an owner and therefore there is no appropriation sufficient to satisfy the requirements of s.1.

We do not consider that those submissions can be supported. The way in which the matter should be approached, we think is as Miss Goddard submitted to us, which was this. A cheque is not a piece of paper and no more. In no circumstances, in this type of situation, can it be so considered. It is a piece of paper with certain special characteristics.

The sequence of events in this case can be brought down to a simple series of facts. The defendant starts with a cheque book in his possession. It is the cheque book of the company and he is plainly in lawful possession of that book with cheques inside it. He apparently had the habit, as we have already indicated, at least occasionally, of removing blank cheques from the book, tearing out the cheque leaving the counterfoil in position, putting the cheque in his pocket and filling it in at a later stage. Still nothing wrong at all in that. He is still acting lawfully, although it may be somewhat unusual. He then makes up his mind to fill in a cheque with the amount, then the payee and the date and so on. The third party in whose favour the cheques were being made were *ex hypothesi* not entitled to those sums. The appellant was therefore using the company's cheques and the company's bank account for his own purposes. Miss Goddard suggests that there was a gradual appropriation as the events moved on in this way.

The next stage is this. He says to himself, 'I am now going to make the cheque payable to E.P. or Happy Pets or whoever it may be.' That action is unknown to Mr Aust. It is *ex hypothesi* once again contrary to the interests of the company. It is contrary to the will of the company and it is dishonest. This is dealing with the cheque not as the agent of the company duly authorised, but is dealing with the cheque as if it were his own. That seems to us is sufficient to amount to an appropriation under the Act.

So when the writing gets on to the cheque, it becomes a bill of exchange and becomes a necessary demand upon the bank to honour the bank's obligations to the customer, which is the company. But that is being done for the defendant's own purposes, and when he sends it on to the company, to Happy Pets or to E.P., it has come to the point where he has made the cheque his own. For the purposes of the Theft Act he has appropriated the cheque, and given that the other elements of the crime are present, which one must assume for purposes of this argument, the offence is complete. Be it noted it is not a matter of what happens to the document thereafter.

Consequently for purposes of these counts, that is to say the even numbered counts, the 'cheque' counts rather than the 'thing in action' counts, it does not matter whether the account of the company is in credit, it does not matter whether it is within its overdraft limits, it does not matter whether it is outside the overdraft limits, the offence is nevertheless complete.

Now to deal with the further question of whether there is an intent permanently to deprive the owner? [Here we would wish to do what the judge did, simply to cite the passage from Megaw L.J.'s judgment in *Duru and Asghar* [[1974] 1 W.L.R. 2:] 'In the view of this Court there can be no doubt that the intention of both of these appellants, as would necessarily have been found by the jury if the matter had been left to the jury on a proper direction of law (a direction which would no doubt have been given if the pleas of guilty had not been entered), was permanently to deprive the Greater London Council of that thing in action, that cheque; that piece of paper, in the sense of a piece of paper carrying with it the right to receive payment of the sum of £6,002.50 which is the amount concerned in count 3. So far as the cheque itself is concerned, true it is a piece of paper. But it is a piece of paper which changes its character completely once it is paid, because then it receives a rubber stamp on it saying it has been paid and it ceases to be a thing in action, or at any rate it ceases to be, in its substance, the same thing as it was before: that is, an instrument on which payment falls to be made. It was the intention of the appellants, dishonestly and by deception, not only that the cheques should be made out and handed over, but also that they should be presented and paid, thereby permanently depriving the Greater London Council of the cheques in substance as their things in action. The fact that the mortgagors were under an obligation to repay the mortgage loans does not affect the appellant's intention permanently to deprive the council of these cheques.'

Consequently so far as the counts involved in these supplementary grounds of appeal are concerned, particulars of which have already been detailed, the appeal must fail. The appellant was assuming the rights of the owner, that is to say the rights of the creditor vis-È-vis the bank, that is the rights of the company to demand that the bank should hand over the money. He is assuming the right to do what he likes with that part of the company's debt with which he is dealing.

The learned Lord Justice then dealt with the further grounds of appeal, discussed them and concluded: For the reasons which we have indicated it seems to us, apart from the conviction on count 7 which must be quashed, this appeal must be dismissed.

Conviction on count 7 quashed. Appeal dismissed on other counts

Notes

1. Although Geoffrey Lane LJ said that "the completion of the theft does not take place until the transaction has gone through to completion", this was held to be obiter in *Chan Man-Sin v Attorney General for Hong Kong* [1988] 1 All E.R. 1; and *Re Osman* [1989] 3 All E.R. 701; the giving of instructions to the bank to debit V's account is a usurpation of one of the rights of the owner of the account (V).

2. The Court of Appeal holds that Kohn stole not only the right which Panelservice had against the bank to have their cheques met, but also the cheques themselves (the even-numbered counts). It is held that a cheque is not only a piece of paper but also a chose in action, a right in the drawee (Happy Pets) to be paid the amount of the cheque by Panelservice. Converting a blank cheque into a valid cheque is an appropriation of Panelservice's piece of paper, and so is sending it to Happy Pets; if done with intent to deprive, it is theft. The only question is, how does Kohn permanently deprive Panelservice of the appropriated property, i.e. the cheque which will eventually find its way back to Panelservice? One answer is to say that Panelservice has to "buy" it back, by meeting the cheque, by paying Happy Pets the amount specified in the cheque. It is clear that the owner of property is permanently deprived if he is only to get it back by buying it back (see below). However the Court adopts another view (formulated in *R. v Duru*), that what the owner, Panelservice, gets back is something entirely different from what was taken from it. What was taken was a thing in action, "a piece of paper carrying with it the right to receive payment of a sum of money," and what was returned was a mere piece of paper (a cancelled cheque). The inference is that it has been stripped of all or most of its value to Panelservice. It is not at first sight clear what has been removed from the cheque which is of value to Panelservice, since its obvious value is a duty in Panelservice to pay a sum of money to the payee. Removal of this "value" does not prejudice Panelservice. The answer appears to be that while it was a cheque, Panelservice could exchange it for goods or other value. Now it has only a worthless piece of paper. However it does not seem accurate to say that Panelservice is deprived of a thing in action, because that thing in action, being a right to sue Panelservice for money, could never have been owned by Panelservice. The better view is that the cheque is a valuable security, which is a tangible thing of value, and it ceases to be such when it is paid.

    The exact status of this part of the Court of Appeals' judgment is in doubt following the House of Lords decision in *Preddy* [1996] 3 All E.R. 481. Lord Goff of Chieveley, speaking obiter, considered that an intention to permanently deprive the owner of a cheque could not be established where the cheque was obtained by deception. On this basis he considered *Duru* and *Mitchell* [1993] Crim. L.R. 788, which had applied it, were wrongly decided. This does not establish, however, whether in a situation such as that which pertained in *Kohn*, a charge of theft cannot be supported. In the deception case the cheque which returns to the drawer has on it the writing which he put there. In the *Kohn* situation, however, the cheques which returned to Panelservice had writing on them which Kohn, not they, put there. It is arguable, therefore, that the cheques, as pieces of paper, had been stolen as D's writing on them manifests his intention to, using the words of s.6(1), "treat the thing as his own to dispose of regardless of the other's rights".

3. Where a cheque is drawn by P in favour of D, the thing in action which the cheque represents, namely a right in the payee to sue the drawer for £x, belongs to D and thus cannot be stolen by D. However, if D presents the cheque for payment, the effect of this is to diminish by £x (or destroy) P's credit balance in his bank account. Could D be guilty of stealing this? In *Williams*, 13 October 2000 (Case No.1986/99) D ran a building business and targeted vulnerable elderly householders.

D's practice was to charge a modest sum for an initial piece of work to gain the customer's trust and then to charge exorbitant sums for subsequent work. D was charged with sample counts of theft of the customers' credit balances by causing cheques to be drawn in his favour and then presenting them for payment. The trial judge directed the jury that the prosecution had to prove that D had appropriated the credit balances of the customers stating, "If you get a householder to draw a cheque on a bank or building society and cause the cheque to be presented, you cause the householder's credit balance to be diminished, and accordingly take that credit balance for your own use." In upholding D's convictions the Court of Appeal referred to *Kohn* and *Graham, Ali* [1997] 1 Cr. App. R. 302, where the Court had sought to make clear that nothing it said should cast doubt on *Kohn* and "the principle that theft of a chose in action may be committed when a chose in action belonging to another is destroyed by the defendant's act of appropriation".

----

6. Other intangible property

Some intangible things can be valuable, without being a recognised thing in action. Examples are a patent, which is declared by statute to be personal property but not a thing in action: Patents Act 1977 s.30(1); and a trader's assignable export quota was held to be stolen by the person in the trader's organisation who was in charge of buying and selling such quotas when it was sold by him at a gross undervalue to a competitor: *Attorney General for Hong Kong v Nai Keung* [1987] 1 W.L.R. 1339. Other examples are kinds of information: an idea, news, "know-how", a secret, especially a trade secret. Industrial espionage is rife nowadays, and such valuables are often "stolen," in popular parlance at least. However, it seems that information is not anyway comprehended in the statutory phrase "other intangible property".

OXFORD V MOSS

(1979) 68 Cr. App. R. 183

The facts appear in the judgment of Smith J.

SMITH J

This is a prosecutor's Appeal by way of Case Stated.

On May 5, 1976, an information was preferred by the prosecutor against the defendant alleging that the defendant stole certain intangible property, namely, confidential information being examination questions for a Civil Engineering Examination to be held in the month of June 1976 at Liverpool University, the information being the property of the Senate of the University, and the allegation being that the Respondent intended permanently to deprive the said Senate of the said property.

The facts can be stated very shortly indeed. They were agreed facts. They are set out in the case and they are as follows. In May 1976 the defendant was a student at Liverpool University. He was studying engineering. Somehow (and this Court is not concerned precisely how) he was able to acquire the proof of an examination paper for an examination in Civil Engineering to be held in the University during the following month, that is to say June 1976. Without doubt the proof, that is to say the piece of paper, was the property of the University. It was an agreed fact, as set out in the case, that the respondent at no time intended to steal what is described as 'any tangible element' belonging to the paper; that is to say it is conceded that he never intended to steal the paper itself.

In truth and in fact, and in all common sense, what he was about was this. He was borrowing a piece of paper hoping to be able to return it and not be detected in order that he should acquire advance knowledge of the questions to be set in the examination and thereby, I suppose, he would be enabled to have an unfair advantage as against other students who did not possess the knowledge that he did.

By any standards, it was conduct which is to be condemned, and to the layman it would readily be described as cheating. The question raised is whether it is conduct which falls within the scope of the criminal law.

The learned stipendiary magistrate at Liverpool was of the opinion that, on the facts of the case, confidential information is not a form of intangible property as opposed to the property in the proof examination paper itself, that is the paper and the words printed thereon. He was of the opinion, further, that confidence consisted in the right to control the publication of the proof paper and was a right over property other than a form of intangible property.

Finally, he was of the opinion that by his conduct the respondent had gravely interfered with the owner's right over the paper. He had not permanently deprived the owner of any intangible property. Accordingly, the learned stipendiary magistrate dismissed the charge.

The prosecutor appeals. The question for this Court, shortly put, is whether confidential information can amount to property within the meaning of the Theft Act 1968. By s.1(1) of the statute: 'A person is guilty of theft if he dishonestly appropriates property belonging to another with the intention of permanently depriving the other of it . . . .';

By s.4(1): '"property" includes money and all other property, real or personal, including things in action and other intangible property.'

The question for this Court is whether confidential information of this sort falls within the definition contained in s.4(1). We have been referred to a number of authorities emanating from the area of trade secrets and matrimonial secrets. In particular, we were referred to *Peter Manufacturing Corporation v Corsets Silhouette Ltd* [1963] 3 All E.R. 402, to *Seager v Copydex Ltd* [1967] 2 All E.R. 415, to the case of *Argyll v Argyll* [1965] 2 W.L.R. 790, and *Fraser v Evans* 3 W.L.R. 1172.

Those are cases concerned with what is described as the duty to be of good faith. They are clear illustrations of the proposition that, if a person obtains information which is given to him in confidence and then sets out to take an unfair advantage of it, the courts will restrain him by way of an order of injunction or will condemn him in damages if an injunction is found to be inappropriate. It seems to me, speaking for my part, that they are of little assistance in the present situation in which we have to consider whether there is property in the information which is capable of being the subject of a charge of theft. In my judgment, it is clear that the answer to that question must be no. Accordingly, I would dismiss the Appeal. [Lord Widgery CJ and Wien J agreed.]

Appeal dismissed

Questions

1. It was conceded that Moss never intended to steal the paper itself. On the agreed facts need this concession have been made? See s.6(1), below, and J.R. Spencer, "The Metamorphosis of s.6 of the Theft Act" [1977] Crim. L.R. 653 see below.

2. It is not said how Moss obtained the proof. If he had used a collaborator in the University Registry, what would have been his offence?

Notes

The Court held that civil cases on protection of confidential information are of little assistance. Even if a right over something is protected by the law in some ways (e.g. by injunction, or by damages for its misuse) it does not follow that the right is intangible property, still less that it is intangible property for all purposes, i.e. that it ought to be protected by the criminal law, or by the law of theft specifically. In some areas theft is a blunt instrument where a discriminating tool is required.

----

7. Electricity

This was not stealable at common law. It is not included in the definition of property in s.4 because the dishonest use or wasting or diverting of it is made a special offence in s.13. See *Low v Blease* [1975] Crim. L.R. 513.

8. Unspecific Property

If A is charged with stealing a watch, he cannot be convicted of stealing an umbrella (see Cockburn CJ in *R. v McPherson* (1858) D.&B. 197 at 200). He must be shown to have stolen the specific property he is charged with stealing, although not necessarily the whole of it.

Machent v Quinn [1970] 2 All E.R. 255. Q was charged with stealing 35 shirts, nine pairs of trousers, four sweaters, two beach sets and two cardigans, to the total value of £199. It was proved that he stole four sweaters only, valued at £25. *Held*, he could be convicted as charged (but his sentence was to relate to the four sweaters only).

It would be different if all that could be shown was that Q had stolen some articles from the list, but not which articles. However if the articles are identical (or undifferentiated in the indictment, i.e. described as "goods"), it is no objection that the stolen ones cannot be identified.

R. v Tideswell [1905] 2 K.B. 273. T had permission to help himself to ashes in P's yard, paying for the weight taken. In collusion with P's servant, he took 32 tons 13cwts, knowing that the servant had recorded the sale as of 31 tons 3cwts only. *Held*, T could be convicted on an indictment charging him with larceny of 1 ton 10cwts.

And if it is impossible to show which particular articles A stole and when, but only that goods or money to a certain total value was appropriated in a certain period (e.g. between two stock-takings), he may be charged with, and convicted of, stealing the general deficiency, *R. v Tomlin* [1954] 2 Q.B. 274.

In charges of attempted theft, or burglary with intent to commit theft, it is not necessary to charge or prove that the accused had any particular property in mind: *Re Attorney General's References (Nos 1 and 2 of 1979)* [1980] Q.B. 180 CA.

iii. "Belonging to Another"

THEFT ACT 1968 S.5

(1) Property shall be regarded as belonging to any person having possession or control of it, or having in it any proprietary right or interest (not being an equitable interest arising only from an agreement to transfer or grant an interest).

(2) Where property is subject to a trust, the persons to whom it belongs shall be regarded as including any person having a right to enforce the trust, and an intention to defeat the trust shall be regarded accordingly as an intention to deprive of the property any person having that right.

(3) Where a person receives property from or on account of another, and is under an obligation to the other to retain and deal with that property or its proceeds in a particular way, the property or proceeds shall be regarded (as against him) as belonging to the other.

(4) Where a person gets property by another's mistake, and is under an obligation to make restoration (in whole or in part) of the property or its proceeds or of the value thereof, then to the extent of that obligation the property or proceeds shall be regarded (as against him) as belonging to the person entitled to restoration, and an intention not to make restoration shall be regarded accordingly as an intention to deprive that person of the property or proceeds.

(5) Property of a corporation sole shall be regarded as belonging to the corporation notwithstanding a vacancy in the corporation.

Notes

1. A person can only steal what belongs to another. "Belonging to another" is given an extended meaning, and covers persons who have only minor interests in the property (possession, control, any proprietary right or interest). If B has such a minor interest in property, that property can be

stolen from him by A, and it matters not whether A is also entitled to a minor (or indeed major) interest in the same property. Moreover, even if A is the entire owner, and B has no interest which the civil law will recognise, it may still be possible for A to steal the property if A got the property under an obligation.

2. Moreover a company is another person vis-à-vis its shareholders. Even if A owns all the shares in P Ltd, the property is not his, but belongs to another," viz., P Ltd, and A can steal that property: *Attorney General's Reference No.2 of 1982* [1984] 2 Q.B. 624; *R. v Philippou* (1989) 89 Cr. App. R. 290. The fact that the defendant is in complete control of the company, and so able to secure its compliance with what he does, affords him no defence. His will is not that of the company when he is engaged in a crime against the company, and anyway the consent of the owner is irrelevant in theft, according to *R. v Gomez*: see Lord Browne-Wilkinson.

3. The "belonging to another" factor, extended as it is, must exist at the time when the accused did the act which is said to be theft. If *before* he dishonestly does an act with regard to the property, it has ceased to belong to another and belongs to the accused, that act cannot be theft. See *Edwards v Ddin*, directly below. But if the dishonest act *results* in the property belonging to the accused, because the victim consents to him becoming its owner, that act is nevertheless an appropriation of property belonging to another, and can be theft; it is sufficient if the property belonged to another at the time of the dishonest act: see *R. v Gomez*, above and particularly Viscount Dilhorne in *Lawrence*.

EDWARDS V DDIN

[1976] 1 W.L.R. 942

The facts appear in the judgment of Croom-Johnson J.

CROOM-JOHNSON J

This is an appeal by way of case stated from the magistrates' court sitting at Amersham in which the defendant had an information preferred against him that he stole three gallons of petrol and two pints of oil together of the value of £1.77, the property of Mamos Garage, Amersham, contrary to s.1 of the Theft Act 1968.

On the facts as found by the justices the following things happened. The defendant arrived with a motor car and he asked for some petrol and oil to be placed in his car. Petrol and oil to the value as stated £1.77, was placed into the car at his request by the garage attendant. When he ordered the petrol and oil the defendant impliedly made to the attendant the ordinary representation of an ordinary customer that he had the means and the intention of paying for it before he left. He was not in fact asked to pay and he did not in fact pay, but the moment when the garage attendant was doing something else he simply drove away. The justices also found, as one would think was perfectly obvious, that whilst the petrol and oil had been placed in the car, either in the tank or in the sump, it could not reasonably be recovered by the garage in default of payment.

The questions therefore which have to be resolved in order to satisfy s.1 of the Act were two in number. First of all, was the defendant dishonest? It appears that the justices must have considered that that was so. Secondly, had he appropriated property belonging to another with the intention of permanently depriving the other of it? Upon that point the defence submitted successfully that at the time when the car was driven away the petrol and oil which had got into the tank or sump were in fact not the property of the garage any more but were the property of the defendant. On that basis the justices said that that particular essential ingredient of theft under s.1 of the Act had not been fulfilled and dismissed the information.

The whole question therefore was: whose petrol and oil was it when the defendant drove away? Property passes under a contract of sale when it is intended to pass. In such transactions as the sale of petrol at a garage forecourt ordinary common sense would say that the garage and the motorist intended the property in the petrol to pass when it is poured into the tank and irretrievably mixed with the other petrol that is in it, and I think that is what the justices decided.

But the prosecutor has appealed and has based his appeal on a consideration of the Sale of Goods Act 1893 and the provisions of that Act, and seeks a ruling that transfer of the petrol was conditional only and that therefore until payment the petrol remained the property of the garage.

But if one considers the provisions of the Sale of Goods Act 1893 one comes out at the same answer as common sense would dictate.

The prosecution argument went this way, that when the motorist arrives at the garage and says 'will you fill me up, please?' or 'will you give me two gallons?' then there is a contract for the sale of unascertained goods by description. In such circumstances when does the property in the petrol pass? Nothing will have been said between the motorist and the pump attendant about that, so one is thrown back on s.18 of the Sale of Goods Act 1893 and rules made under it in order to ascertain the intention of the parties.

By pouring the petrol into the tank the goods have been appropriated to the contract with the assent of both parties. If that is done unconditionally, then the property in the petrol passes to the motorist: rule 5(1). The prosecution argument then goes on that, however, there is a condition which is waiting to be fulfilled, namely, payment, and says that under s.19 of the Sale of Goods Act 1893 the garage reserves the right of disposal of the petrol until the payment has been made and that therefore the property has not passed under rule 5(1).

It is at this point that the argument breaks down. The garage owner does not reserve the right to dispose of the petrol once it is in the tank, nor is it possible to see how effect could be given to any such condition wherever petrol has been put in and is all mixed up with what other petrol is already there. Consequently one passes back to rule 5(2) of s.18, which says that where a seller delivers the goods to the buyer and does not reserve the right to dispose of them, he is deemed to have unconditionally appropriated the goods to the contract and in those circumstances the property has passed to the buyer in accordance with rule 5(1).

Reference was also made by the prosecutor to s.5 of the Theft Act 1968 which deals with one of the subsidiary definitions arising under s.1, which is the initial section dealing with theft. Section 5, which deals with but is not definitive of the expression 'belonging to another', is concerned with all manner of interests in property. It was urged upon us that the motorist is under an implied obligation to retain his car with the petrol in its tank on the garage premises and not to take it away until such time as he has paid for it, and that until that has been done the garage owner retains some proprietary interest in the petrol in the tank.

The relevant part of s.5, which is in subsection (3), reads:

'Where a person receives property from or on account of another, and is under an obligation to the other to retain and deal with that property or its proceeds in a particular way, the property or proceeds shall be regarded (as against him) as belonging to the other.'

That section in my view is not apt to cover a case such as the present where there has been an outright sale of the goods and the property in the goods has passed and the seller is only waiting to be paid. Therefore the provisions of s.5 do not affect the conclusion in the present case.

I do not enter into any discussion for the purposes of this judgment of what might have been the position if the charge had been brought under some other section of the Theft Act 1968, or if the appropriation for the purposes of s.1 had been said to have arisen at an earlier stage of events which took place. On the facts as found and on the case as it was presented to the magistrates, in my view the magistrates reached a correct conclusion in law and I would dismiss the appeal.

Appeal dismissed

Questions

1. The Court leaves open the position if the appropriation had been said to have arisen at an earlier stage of the events. *Could* the appropriation have been said to have arisen earlier than the act of driving the car away? If yes, what difference should it have made to the result?

2. Would it have made any difference if the garage had *expressly* reserved the right of disposal pending payment? Consider the effect of the following condition of sale: "The seller supplies

petrol on the understanding that from the moment of delivery until the amount supplied has been paid for, the whole of the petrol in the customer's tank shall be the property of the seller."

3.   Of what offence could Ddin have been convicted if the facts had occurred in 1979?

Notes

1.   In *Davies v Leighton* (1978) 68 Cr. App. R. 4, Lord Widgery CJ regarded the law as well settled that in a supermarket sale the property in goods does not pass to the customer until he has paid for them, and he applied this rule to a case where the goods were not picked off the shelf by the customer but, being fruit, were weighed, bagged, priced and handed over by an assistant. See J.C. Smith's commentary on this case at [1978] Crim. L.R. 576 for discussion of many of the different problems which can arise out of shop sales.

2.   The introduction of civil law contractual questions into trials for theft has been deprecated, e.g. by Lord Roskill in *R. v Morris* [1984] A.C. 320. However, if the issue is whether the property the subject of an apparent sale "belongs to another" at the time of the alleged theft by D, such questions are inevitable.

   R. v Walker [1984] Crim. L.R. 112. V bought a video recorder from D, which turned out to be defective. V returned it to D for repair and then, not getting any satisfaction, sued D in the County Court for the return of money paid for defective goods. Two days after he was served with the County Court summons, D sold the recorder to P. On D's trial for theft, the judge left it to the jury to decide on the evidence if the recorder belonged to V at the time D sold it to P. *Held*, this was not enough. "The relevant law, which was contained in the Sale of Goods Act 1979 was complicated but the judge had made no attempt to explain it. For centuries juries had decided civil actions on points arising under the law of sale of goods. There was no reason why this jury should not have had the relevant law explained to them and in the absence of such an explanation it was impossible for them to do justice in the case." *Appeal allowed*. [The relevant law is that recission of a contract of sale returns the property in the goods to the vendor, and the service of a summons for the return of the purchase price could have amounted to such a recission.]

Questions

1.   A in a pub approaches B, who works at a local garage, and says he will make it worth B's while if he "forgets" to ask for any money when he fills his vehicle with petrol. B consults his employer, who instructs B to pretend to play A's game and arranges for the police to be present. Next day, A asks B to fill his tank and when that has been done starts to drive off without paying, but is apprehended. Is this theft by A? See *R. v Gomez*, above, p.607.

2.   (i) A sees an old car parked on the hard shoulder of a motorway. It is the same model as A's car, for which he has found difficulty in obtaining spares. A removes a part from the parked car, which A thinks has merely broken down but which in fact has been abandoned there by B. Is this theft by A?

   (ii) Is it attempted theft by A?

   (iii) Would it make any difference if the car had been abandoned in Q's barn? See the next case.

R. V WOODMAN

[1974] Q.B. 754 CA

A was the owner of a disused factory. He sold all the scrap metal in the place to B. B entered the factory and removed all the scrap metal which he could easily reach, but left some which was in such an inaccessible position as to be not worth the trouble of getting. A, who thought that all the metal had been removed by B, then put a barbed wire fence around the factory to exclude trespassers. W entered the factory and removed the remaining metal. He was convicted of theft, and appealed on the ground that no-one had possession or control of the metal.

LORD WIDGERY CJ

The recorder took the view that the contract of sale between English China Clays and the Bird group had divested English China Clays of any proprietary right to any scrap on the site. It is unnecessary to express a firm view on that point, but the court are not disposed to disagree with that conclusion that the proprietary interest in the scrap had passed. The recorder also took the view on the relevant facts that it was not possible to say that English China Clays were in possession of the residue of the scrap. It is not quite clear why he took that view. It may have been because he took the view that difficulties arose by reason of the fact that English China Clays had no knowledge of the existence of this particular scrap at any particular time. But the recorder did take the view that so far as control was concerned there was a case to go to the jury on whether or not this scrap was in the control of English China Clays, because if it was, then it was to be regarded as their property for the purposes of a larceny charge even if they were not entitled to any proprietary interest.

The contention before us today is that the recorder was wrong in law in allowing this issue to go to the jury. Put another way, it is said that as a matter of law English China Clays could not on these facts have been said to be in control of the scrap.

We have formed the view without difficulty that the recorder was perfectly entitled to do what he did, that there was ample evidence that English China Clays were in control of the site and had taken considerable steps to exclude trespassers as demonstrating the fact that they were in control of the site, and we think that in ordinary and straightforward cases if it is once established that a particular person is in control of a site such as this, then prima facie he is in control of articles which are on that site.

. . . The fact that it could not be shown that they were conscious of the existence of this or any particular scrap iron does not destroy the general principle that control of a site by excluding others from it is prima facie control of articles on the site as well.

There has been some mention in argument of what would happen if in a case like the present, a third party had come and placed some article within the barbed-wire fence and thus on the site. The article might be an article of some serious criminal consequence such as explosives or drugs. It may well be that in that type of case the fact that the article has been introduced at a late stage in circumstances in which the occupier of the site had no means of knowledge would produce a different result from that which arises under the general presumption to which we have referred, but in the present case there was, in our view, ample evidence to go to the jury on the question of whether English China Clays were in control of the relevant time. Accordingly, the recorder's decision to allow the case to go to the jury cannot be faulted and the appeal must be dismissed.

Appeal dismissed

Questions

1. "In my judgment, it is quite clear that a person cannot be said to be in possession of some article which she does not realise is, or may be, in her handbag, in her room, or in some other place over which she had control", per Lord Parker CJ, in *Lockyer v Gibb* [1967] 2 Q.B. 243, a prosecution for the offence of being in possession of a controlled drug. Is this dictum inconsistent with the decision in *R. v Woodman*?

2.   Suppose W, when stripping the factory of metal, had discovered and taken away a cache of controlled drugs abandoned there by X. If, consistent with Lord Parker's dictum English China Clays were held not to have possession of the drugs, could W be convicted of stealing them?

Subsection (1): Possession, control or any proprietary right or interest

R. V BONNER

[1970] 1 W.L.R. 838 CA

B took metal from the house of W, with whom he was in partnership as demolition contractors. B said the metal was partnership property and he took it in order not to deprive W of it permanently but hold it as security for what was due to him from W out of the partnership profits. B was convicted of theft but his appeal was allowed on the ground that the verdict was in all the circumstances unsafe and unsatisfactory. However the Court of Appeal thought it right to deal with the legal point certified by the trial judge, viz. whether the jury was misdirected on the law relating to the theft by a partner of partnership property. The direction in question is quoted in the judgment of Edmund-Davies LJ below.

EDMUND DAVIES LJ

Mr Inglis-Jones has . . . submitted that the circumstances of this case a mere taking away of partnership property, even with the intention of keeping the other partner permanently out of possession of it would not per se suffice to amount to theft; there would have to be something like destruction of the metal or its sale in market overt, which would have the effect (provided there was innocence in the buyer) of transferring a good title to him and so defeating the title of the deprived partner. Defending counsel summarised the matter by submitting that for there to be an 'appropriation' within the Theft Act 1968, there must be a 'conversion' of the property by one or other of the foregoing methods, neither of which was resorted to here. Therefore, so it is submitted, there was no theft.
    Rejecting that submission, Judge Ranking directed the jury in these terms:

    '. . . even if you are satisfied that there was a full partnership between Webb and Bonner, a partner has no right to take any partnership property with the intention of permanently depriving the other of his share. Therefore, even if Bonner was a partner of Webb, if he took that lead, which was partnership property, intending to deprive Webb permanently of his share and when he did it, he knew perfectly well that he had no legal right to take it, then he is guilty of theft; he is guilty of the theft of the whole property and not just guilty of the theft of Webb's share, because the whole of it was partnership property and it had not been divided . . . and if one partner takes it he is guilty of stealing the whole of it.'

    Was this a misdirection? This court is clearly of the opinion that it was not. Sections 1, 3 and 5 of the Theft Act 1968, are here relevant . . .
    Mr Inglis-Jones has boldly submitted that, since the basic requirement of theft is the appropriation of property belonging to another, there can be no such appropriation by one co-owner of property which is the subject matter of the co-ownership or partnership; and that there can be no 'assumption . . . of the rights of an owner' in a case like the present, where one is dealing with (as Bonner claims) property belonging to a partnership.
    The whole object of the Theft Act 1968, was to get away from the technicalities and subtleties of the old law . . . ..
    The view of this court is that in relation to partnership property the provisions in the Theft Act 1968, have the following result: provided there is the basic ingredient of dishonesty, provided there be no question of there being a claim of right made in good faith, provided there be an intent permanently to deprive, one partner can commit theft of the property of another to whom he is a complete stranger.
    Early though these days are, this matter has not gone without comment by learned writers. Professor Smith in his valuable work on the Theft Act 1968, expresses his own view quite clearly in paragraph 80 under the heading 'Co-owners and partners' in this way:

'D. and P. are co-owners of a car. D. sells the car without P's consent. Since P. has a proprietary right in the car, it belongs to him under s.5(1). The position is precisely the same where a partner appropriates the partnership property.'

. . . We thus have no doubt that there may be an 'appropriation' by a partner within the meaning of the Act, and that in a proper case there is nothing in law to prevent his being convicted of the theft of partnership property. But this *excursus* is of an academic kind in the present case for we have already indicated our view regarding the unsatisfactory and unsafe nature of the verdicts returned against each of these accused. In these circumstances, all four appeals are allowed.

Appeals allowed

[Three other men who had helped Bonner had been charged with him.]

R. V TURNER (NO.2)

[1971] 1 W.L.R. 901 CA

T took his car to a garage to have it repaired. Those repairs having been practically completed, the car was left in the road outside the garage. T called at the garage and told the proprietor that he would return the following day, pay him, and take the car; instead he took the car, using his spare key, without paying for the repairs. Later he lied about the matter to the police. He was convicted of theft of the car.

LORD PARKER CJ

The words 'belonging to another' are specifically defined in s.5 of the Act, subsection (1) of which provides: 'Property shall be regarded as belonging to any person having possession or control of it, or having in it any proprietary right or interest.' The sole question was whether Mr Brown [the garage proprietor] had possession or control.

This court is quite satisfied that there is no ground whatever for qualifying the words 'possession or control' in any way. It is sufficient if it is found that the person from whom the property is taken, or to use the words of the Act, appropriated, was at the time in fact in possession or control. At the trial there was a long argument as to whether that possession or control must be lawful, it being said that by reason of the fact that this car was subject to a hire-purchase agreement, Mr Brown could never even as against the defendant obtain lawful possession or control. As I have said, this court is quite satisfied that the judge was quite correct in telling the jury they need not bother about lien, and that they need not bother about hire purchase agreements. The only question was whether Mr Brown was in fact in possession or control.

The second point that is taken relates to the necessity for proving dishonesty. Section 2(1) provides that: 'A person's appropriation of property belonging to another is not to be regarded as dishonest (a) if he appropriates the property in the belief that he has in law the right to deprive the other of it, on behalf of himself or of a third person';

The judge said in his summing up: 'Fourth and last, they must prove that the defendant did what he did dishonestly and this may be the issue which lies very close to the heart of the case.' He then went on to give them a classic direction in regard to claim of right, emphasising that it is immaterial that there exists no basis in law for such belief. He reminded the jury that the defendant had said categorically in evidence: 'I believe that I was entitled in law to do what I did.' At the same time he directed the jury to look at the surrounding circumstances. He said this: 'The prosecution say that the whole thing reeks of dishonesty, and if you believe Mr Brown that the defendant drove the car away from Carlyle Road, using a duplicate key, and having told Mr Brown that he would come back tomorrow and pay, you may think the prosecution are right.' On this point Mr Herbert says that if in fact you disregard lien entirely, as the jury were told to do, then Mr Brown was a bailee at will and this car could have been taken back by the defendant perfectly lawfully at any time whether any money was due in regard to repairs or whether it was not. He says, as the court understands it, first that if there was that right, then there cannot be theft at all, and secondly that if and in so far as the mental element is relevant, namely belief, the jury should have been told that he had this right and be left to judge, in the light of the existence of that right, whether they thought he may have believed, as he said, that he did have a right.

The court, however, is quite satisfied that there is nothing in this point whatever. The whole test of dishonesty is the mental element of belief. No doubt, though the defendant may for certain purposes be presumed to know the law, he would not at the time have the vaguest idea whether he had in law a right to take the car back again, and accordingly when one looks at his mental state, one looks at it in the light of what he believed. The jury were properly told that if he believed he had a right, albeit there was none, he would nevertheless fall to be acquitted. This court, having heard all that Mr Herbert has said, is quite satisfied that there is no manner in which this summing-up can be criticised, and that accordingly the appeal against conviction should be dismissed.

Appeal dismissed

Note

Part of the argument by the defence was that the words "possession or control" should be qualified by the word "lawful". In *Kelly and Lindsay* [1998] 3 All E.R. 741, the Court of Appeal confirmed that the word "lawful" is not to be read into s.5(1). Thus, property may be stolen from a person who is not in lawful possession of it; for example, a thief may steal property which has been stolen and remains in the possession of another thief. Or a drug user may steal drugs from his dealer, the dealer being in sufficient possession thereof to satisfy the requirements of the Theft Act even though his possession of proscribed drugs is unlawful (see *Smith* [2011] EWCA Crim 66). In *Smith* the Court of Appeal were sensitive to the havoc that might be caused were they to construe the Theft Act in such a way as to permit drug-users to steal from dealers with impunity, Lord Judge CJ stating (at [10]) that "the criminal law is concerned with keeping the Queen's peace, not vindicating individual property rights".

Questions

1. A's car was taken by some person unknown. A few days later, A saw it standing locked on the drive of B's house. Using his spare key, he drove it away. Was this theft by A? Would it make any difference if he thought that the law gave him no right to repossess himself of the car but required him to report the matter to the police and leave them to take steps to get the car back?

2. Is the following case distinguishable from *R. v Turner (No.2)*?

    In *R. v Meredith* [1973] Crim. L.R. 253, M's car was impounded by the police while he was at a football match and removed to the police station yard, where it was left locked. When M went to the police station, he found it crowded and so, rather than wait, he took his car away from the yard without contacting any policeman. He was charged with stealing the car. Under the Disposal and Removal of Vehicles Regulations 1968, the owner was liable to pay the statutory charge of £4 if his car had been causing an obstruction. On going to the police he could: (i) admit obstruction and pay £4; or (ii) refuse to pay and face prosecution for obstruction; or (iii) agree to pay and receive a bill for £4. In any event he would be allowed to take the car away for the regulations gave the police no power to retain it as against him. It was held by a Crown Court judge that M had no case to answer.

Trust Property

Notes

1. A beneficiary under a trust clearly has a proprietary right or interest in the trust property, and a defaulting trustee may be guilty of stealing that property from him. The object of the special

provision in s.5(2) is to cover cases such as a charitable trust where there is no defined beneficiary, but the trust is enforceable by someone, e.g. the Attorney General. The trust property "belongs to" that person for the purposes of theft.

2.   As to constructive trusts, it was thought that the expression "proprietary interest" covered the interest of one entitled under such a trust (with the single stated exception of an equitable interest arising from an agreement to transfer or grant an interest). However there are divergent decisions of the Court of Appeal on whether to recognise interests under constructive trusts as proprietary interests within the meaning of subs.(1). In *Attorney General's Reference (No.1 of 1985)* (below, p.638), a profit obtained by A from the unauthorised use of his employer's premises and facilities was held not to make A a constructive trustee of the profit; but the Court also held that, even if he was a constructive trustee, the trust did not give rise to a proprietary interest of the kind mentioned in subs.(1), because to convict a dishonest servant of stealing if he kept the profit would be far removed from ordinary notions of stealing.

Subsection (3): An obligation to retain and deal with the property or its proceeds in a particular way

R. V HALL

[1973] 1 Q.B. 126 CA

H, a travel agent, received money from certain clients as deposits and payments for air trips to America. He paid the money so received into his firm's general account. None of the projected flights materialised and none of the money was refunded. He was convicted of theft. He appealed on the ground that he had not, within the meaning of s.5(3), been placed under an obligation to retain and deal with in a particular way the sums paid to him.

EDMUND DAVIES LJ

Two points were presented and persuasively developed by the appellant's counsel: (1) that, while the appellant has testified that all moneys received had been used for business purposes, even had he been completely profligate in its expenditure he could not in any of the seven cases be convicted of 'theft' as defined by the Theft Act 1968; there being no allegation in any of the cases of his having *obtained* any payments by deception, counsel for the appellant submitted that, having received from a client, say, £500 in respect of a projected flight, as far as the criminal law is concerned he would be quite free to go off immediately and expend the entire sum at the races and forget all about his client . . .
    Point (1) turns on the application of s.5(3) of the Theft Act 1968 . . .
    Counsel for the appellant submitted that in the circumstances arising in these seven cases there arose no such 'obligation' on the appellant. He referred us to a passage in the Eighth Report of the Criminal Law Revision Committee which reads as follows: '*Subsection* (3) provides for the special case where property is transferred to a person to retain and deal with for a particular purpose and he misapplies it or its proceeds. An example would be the treasurer of a holiday fund. The person in question is in law the owner of the property; but the subsection treats the property, as against him, as belonging to the persons to whom he owes the duty to retain and deal with the property as agreed. He will therefore be guilty of stealing from them if he misapplies the property or its proceeds.'
    Counsel for the appellant . . . submits that the position of a treasurer of a holiday fund is quite different from that of a person like the appellant, who was in general (and genuine) business as a travel agent, and to whom people pay money in order to achieve a certain object—in the present cases to obtain charter flights to America. It is true, he concedes, that thereby the travel agent undertakes a contractual obligation in relation to arranging flights and at the proper time paying the airline and any other expenses. Indeed, the appellant throughout acknowledged that this was so, although contending that in some of the seven cases it was the other party who . . . was in breach. But what counsel for the appellant resists is that in such circumstances the travel agent

'is under an obligation' to the client 'to retain and deal with . . . in a particular way' sums paid to him in such circumstances.

What cannot of itself be decisive of the matter is the fact that the appellant paid the money into the firm's general trading account. As Widgery J. said in *R. v Yule* [1964] 1 Q.B. 5, 10, decided under s.20(1)(iv) of the Larceny Act 1916: 'The fact that a particular sum is paid into a particular banking account . . . does not affect the right of persons interested in that sum or any duty of the solicitor either towards his client or towards third parties with regard to disposal of that sum.' Nevertheless, when a client goes to a firm carrying on the business of travel agents and pays them money, he expects that in return he will, in due course, receive the tickets and other documents necessary for him to accomplish the trip for which he is paying, and the firm are 'under an obligation' to perform their part to fulfil his expectation and are liable to pay him damages if they do not. But, in our judgment, what was not here established was that these clients expected them 'to retain and deal with that property or its proceeds in a particular way,' and that an 'obligation' to do so was undertaken by the appellant. We must make clear, however, that each case turns on its own facts. Cases could, we suppose, conceivably arise where by some special arrangement (preferably evidenced by documents), the client could impose on the travel agent an 'obligation' falling within s.5(3). But no such special arrangement was made in any of the seven cases here being considered. It is true that in some of them documents were signed by the parties; thus, in respect of counts one and three incidents there was a clause to the effect that the People to People organisation did not guarantee to refund deposits if withdrawals were made later than a certain date; and in respect of counts six, seven and eight the appellant wrote promising 'a full refund' after the flights paid for failed to materialise. But neither in those nor in the remaining two cases (in relation to which there was no documentary evidence of any kind) was there, in our judgment, such a special arrangement as would give rise to an obligation within s.5(3). It follows from this that, despite what on any view must be condemned as scandalous conduct by the appellant, in our judgment on this ground alone this appeal must be allowed and the convictions quashed.

Conviction quashed

Note

In *Klineberg and Marsden* [1999] 1 Cr. App. R. 427, the appellants sold timeshare apartments. The purchasers paid the purchase price on the understanding that the money would be held by an independent trust company until the apartments were ready for occupation. Only £233 of a total of £500,000 paid was deposited with the trust company. The appellants' convictions of theft were upheld as there was a legal obligation imposed on them to deal with the purchasers' money in a particular way which had been breached. (See also *Re Kumar* [2000] Crim. L.R. 504. cf. *Floyd v DPP* [2000] Crim. L.R. 411 and commentary thereon.)

ATTORNEY GENERAL'S REFERENCE (NO.1 OF 1985)

[1986] 2 All E.R. 219 CA

D, the manager of a tied public house, was obliged by his contract of employment with P Brewery to obtain all liquor from them and pay all takings into their bank account. D secretly bought beer elsewhere and sold this keeping the profits. Three questions arose on the reference: (1) whether the moneys paid by customers in respect of the beer he had secretly obtained from elsewhere were received on account of his employer within the meaning of s.5(3); (2) whether the secret profit he had made using his employer's premises, was subject to a constructive trust in favour of the employer; and (3) if so, whether that constructive trust gave the employer a proprietary right or interest in the secret profit within the ambit of s.5(1)?

LORD LANE CJ

. . . Counsel for the Attorney-General bases his submission on two of the subsections to s.5 of the 1968 Act. First of all s.5(3) . . .

Although, goes the argument, at first sight the money which A receives from selling the beer which he bought seems to belong to him, the effect of this subsection is to make the profit element in the money notionally belong to the employers. Thus when A appropriates the profit, he is guilty of theft, assuming that he is acting dishonestly.

Whether that argument is correct or not depends on whether A can properly be said to have received property (i.e. the payment over the counter for the beer he has sold to the customer) 'on account of the employers'. We do not think he can. He received the money on his own account as a result of his private venture. No doubt he is in breach of his contract with the employers; no doubt he is under an obligation to account to the employers at least for the profit he has made out of his venture, but that is a different matter. The fact that A may have to account to B for money he has received from X does not mean necessarily that he received the money on account of B.

[His Lordship referred to s.17 of the Larceny Act 1916 which was the predecessor of s.5(3).]

Section 17 of the 1916 Act was in almost identical terms to s.68 of the Larceny Act 1861. There is a decision on the meaning of that latter section which is in point, *R. v Cullum* (1873) L.R. 2 C.C.R. 28. That was a case in which the defendant was the captain of a barge and in the exclusive service of its owner. His remuneration was half the earnings of the barge, and he had no authority to take any other cargoes except those appointed for him. It was his duty to account to his master for the proceeds of each voyage which he undertook. On one occasion, although he had been ordered to bring the barge back empty from a certain place, and forbidden to take a particular cargo, he nevertheless loaded such cargo in the barge and returned therewith, being paid by the freight owners for that service. He told his master that the barge had come back empty and he never accounted for the money which he had received. The question was whether the defendant was properly convicted of embezzlement. The Court for Crown Cases Reserved held that on those facts the defendant was not guilty. Bovill C.J. in the course of his judgment said (at 31):

'The facts before us would seem more consistent with the notion that the prisoner was misusing his master's property, and so earning money for himself, and not for his master. Under those circumstances, the money would not be received 'for' or 'in the name of, or 'on account of, his master, but for himself, in his own name and for his own account. His act, therefore, does not come within the terms of the statute, and the conviction must be quashed.'

Blackburn J. said (at 33);

'Now, in the present case, I cannot see how this was the master's property, or that the servant had authority to carry anything in this barge but the cargo he was directed to convey. He was actually forbidden to load this barge on the return voyage; he did load it, and very improperly earned money by the use of it; but in what sense he can be said to have received this sum for the use of his master I cannot understand. The test of the matter would really be this—if the person to whom the manure belonged had not paid for the carriage, could the master have said, "There was a contract with you, which you have broken, and I sue you on it?" There would have been no such contract, for the servant never assumed to act for his master, and on that ground his act does not come within the statute. I think that in no case could he have been properly convicted under the Act unless the money became that of the master.'

The other three judges comprising the court agreed with those observations. Counsel for the Attorney-General seeks to distinguish that decision on the grounds that the freight owners would imagine that the man with whom they were dealing, namely the defendant himself, was entitled to the money they paid, because they did not know of the existence of the master, whereas in the instant case the customers, he suggests, would think they were handing over their money to the employers. We doubt whether the customers would pause to consider the destination of their money or whether it would make any difference to the legal situation if they did. Alternatively it is submitted *R. v Cullum* was wrongly decided. We disagree. The argument based on s.5(3) of the 1968 Act was a late addition to the reference. We think it is misconceived.

The reference as originally drawn relied solely on arguments based on s.5(1).

The argument of the Crown is that A. was a 'constructive trustee' of the profit element in the money paid by customers over the bar for the 'bought in' beer and that accordingly the money belonged not, as might seem at first, to A. but to the beneficiary of the trust, namely the employers. The result of that, it is said, is that when A. paid the money into his bank account or otherwise appropriated it, he was guilty of theft (assuming dishonesty).

(After referring to various authorities.) We find it impossible to reconcile much of the language used in these decisions. Two matters however do emerge. The first is that if the contentions of the Crown are well-founded, and if in each case of secret profit a trust arises which falls within s.5, then a host of activities which no layman would think were stealing will be brought within the 1968 Act. As this court pointed out in *Dip Kaur v Chief Constable for Hampshire* [1981] 2 All E.R. 430 at 433, [1981] 1 W.L.R. 578 at 583:

> '. . . the court should not be astute to find that a theft has taken place where it would be straining the language so to hold, or where the ordinary person would not regard the defendant's acts, though possibly morally reprehensible, as theft.'

The second matter is this. There is a clear and important difference between on the one hand a person misappropriating specific property with which he has been entrusted, and on the other hand a person in a fiduciary position who uses that position to make a secret profit for which he will be held accountable. Whether the former is within s.5, we do not have to decide. As to the latter we are firmly of the view that he is not, because he is not a trustee . . . .

Lord Wilberforce in *Tarling (No. 1) v Government of the Republic of Singapore* (1978) 70 Cr.App.R. 77 at 110, said:

> '[The transactions] . . . would appear, prima facie, to amount to a case of persons in a fiduciary capacity making a secret profit at the expense of their companies—conduct for which there exists classical remedies in equity Breach of fiduciary duty, exorbitant profit making, secrecy, failure to comply with the law as to company accounts . . . are one thing: theft and fraud are others.'

Next there is the judgment of a powerful Court of Appeal in *Lister & Co. v Stubbs* (1890) 45 Ch.D. 1. In that case Stubbs was employed by the plaintiffs who were silk spinners, as a foreman to buy for them certain materials which they used in their business. Stubbs corruptly took from one of the firms with whom he was so dealing (Messrs Varley) large sums by way of commission, which he then invested in the purchase of land and other investments. Some of it was retained in the shape of cash. The plaintiff company sought to follow such money into the investments and moved for an injunction to restrain Stubbs from dealing with the investments, alternatively for an order directing him to bring the moneys and the investments into court. Cotton L.J. said (at. p.12):

> '. . . in my opinion this is not the money of the Plaintiffs, so as to make the Defendant a trustee of it for them, but is money acquired in such a way that, according to all rules applicable to such a case, the Plaintiffs, when they bring the action to a hearing, can get an order against the Defendant for the payment of that money to them. That is to say, there is a debt due from the Defendant to the Plaintiffs in consequence of the corrupt bargain which he entered into; but the money which he has received under that bargain cannot, in the view which I take, be treated as being money of the Plaintiffs, which was handed by them to the Defendant to be paid to Messrs Varley in discharge of a debt due from the Plaintiffs to Messrs Varley on the contract between them.'

Lindley L.J. gave judgment in similar terms (at p.15):

> 'Then comes the question, as between Lister & Co. and Stubbs, whether Stubbs can keep the money he has received without accounting for it? Obviously not. I apprehend that he is liable to account for it the moment that he gets it. It is an obligation to pay and account to Messrs Lister & Co., with or without interest, as that of debtor and creditor; it is not of trustee and *cestui que trust*. We are asked to hold that it is—which would involve consequences which, I confess, startle me . . . If by logical reasoning from the premises conclusions are arrived at which are opposed to good sense, it is necessary to go back and look again at the premises and see if they are sound. I am satisfied that they are not sound—the unsoundness consisting in confounding ownership with obligation.'

Bowen L.J. concurred with those judgments.

It seems to us that the draftsmen of the 1968 Act must have had that decision in mind when considering the wording of s.5. Had they intended to bring within the ambit of the 1968 Act a whole new area of behaviour which had previously not been considered to be criminal, they would, in our judgment, have used much more explicit words than those which are to be found in s.5. Nor do we think it permissible to distinguish that decision by saying that bribes are in a different category from such transactions as those in the instant case. There is, in our view, no distinction in principle between the two . . .

Assuming that, contrary to our views, s.5(l) does import the constructive trust into the 1968 Act, on the facts of the case the employers still obtain no proprietary interest. A trustee is not permitted to make a profit from his trust. Therefore if he uses trust property to make a profit from the trust, he is accountable for that profit. If and when such profit is identified as a separate piece of property, he may be a constructive trustee of it. However, until the profit is identifiable as a separate piece of property, it is not trust property and his obligation is to account only.

A used the employers' property and his own money to make a private profit in breach of contract. He received from customers sums of money which represented in part the cost of the beer he had bought and in part possible profit for which he was accountable to the employers. This profit element, assuming it existed, never became a separate piece of property of which A could be trustee. It remained part of a mixed fund. Therefore there never was a moment at which A was trustee of a definite fund. It follows that there never was a moment when the employers had any proprietary interest in any of the money. The money did not belong to another. There was therefore no theft.

No less difficulty would arise in the proof of dishonesty and guilty intent. A might very well say, and say truthfully, that he knew that he was breaking the terms of his contract, but the idea that he might be stealing from his employers the profit element in this transaction had never occurred to him. There are topics of conversation more popular in public houses than the finer points of the equitable doctrine of the constructive trust.

It is said in answer to that obligation that the employers could, by giving in advance the necessary warnings, instruct their servants what the true meaning of the 1968 Act is. That seems to us to be a good illustration of the objectionability of the proposition. If something is so abstruse and so far from the understanding of ordinary people as to what constitutes stealing, it should not amount to stealing.

For these reasons we think that the submissions based on s.5(l) likewise fail.

The answers to the questions posed in the reference are therefore these: (1) no; (2) if, which we do not believe, it is properly described as a trust, it is not such a trust as falls within the ambit of s.5(l) of the Theft Act 1968; (3) no.

Opinion accordingly

Notes

1. At the time *Attorney General's Reference (No.1 of 1985)* was decided the position at civil law was that an employee who took a bribe or made a secret profit by misusing his employer's property or his own position was bound to account to his employer for the profit on the basis of being a debtor. Lord Lane CJ purported to follow *Lister v Stubbs* (1890) 45 Ch D 1. In *Attorney General for Hong Kong v Reid* [1994] 1 A.C. 324, the Privy Council disapproved of *Lister v Stubbs* finding that it was inconsistent with pre-existing authorities. The Privy Council was of the view that a person in a fiduciary position who receives a bribe becomes not only a debtor for the amount of the bribe but also holds the bribe (and its proceeds) on constructive trust. If the English courts follow this highly persuasive authority such property, being under s.5(l) "any proprietary . . . interest", could be the subject of theft. This, of course, would involve overruling *Attorney General's Reference (No.1 of 1985)* but it would remove the artificial distinction the Court of Appeal has created between constructive trusts and other trusts.

2. This subsection is to a large extent redundant, because in the vast majority of cases where there is an obligation to retain and deal with the property in a certain way, the person to whom the obligation is owed will have a proprietary right or interest in the property. Thus with a bailment, the property "belongs to" the bailor, and with a trust, the property "belongs to" the beneficiary, under subs.(1), and in the case of misappropriation by the bailee or trustee there is no need of subs.(3) to secure a conviction. There are so many difficulties involved in subs.(3) that it is unwise of a prosecutor to rely on it unless it is absolutely necessary to do so, which is rarely if ever the case.

3.   It is said that the obligation must be a legal one, not a merely moral one (see *R. v Gilks* [1971] 1 W.L.R. 1341: "In a criminal statute, where a person's criminal liability is made dependent on his having an obligation, it would be quite wrong to construe that word so as to cover a moral or social obligation as distinct from a legal one"). However, an obligation arising under a domestic arrangement of a sort which the civil law would say was not enforceable by action has been held to be enough (*R. v Cullen* Unreported 1974: Smith ½ 2.76). Even if the accused is under an obligation at the moment of appropriation, he is not within the words of subs.(3) unless he received the property from or on account of the person to whom he now owes the obligation.

4.   The obligation must be to retain and deal with *that property or its proceeds* in a particular way. This excludes an obligation to perform some service or do some act in return for being given the property, e.g. as in *R. v Hall*, where B paid A money in return for A's promise to supply air tickets. A was not obliged to do anything *with* the money; his obligation was merely to perform his part of the bargain. It is the same, in most cases, if B lends A money. The only obligation in the borrower A is to repay the loan to B, not to do anything with the money lent. A owes B the amount of the loan, but a simple debtor-creditor relationship is not enough. A debtor who dishonestly puts himself in a position in which he is unable to pay his creditor does not commit theft.

The sort of situation which is within subs.3 is illustrated by *Davidge v Bunnett* [1984] Crim. L.R. 297. D shared a flat with A, B & C, the expenses being shared. A gas bill having become due, A, B & C gave D cheques for their shares, payable to D's employer, because she herself had no bank account. D cashed the cheques, paid some of the bill, but spent most of the money on Christmas presents. *Held*, D was under an obligation to apply the proceeds of the cheques towards paying the bill and was guilty of theft of the money spent on Christmas presents. A, B & C were not the owners of the money received from cashing the cheques. On the other hand, in no sense could it be said that D merely owed the money to them; what she owed them was a duty to use the fund to pay the gas bill.

In *Wain* [1995] 2 Cr. App. R. 660, the Court of Appeal, disapproving of *Lewis v Lethbridge* [1987] Crim. L.R. 59, followed *Davidge v Bunnett*. D had taken part in fundraising for a Telethon held for the charity The Telethon Trust. Events he had organised raised £2,800 which he paid into a separate bank account. Subsequently he transferred this money into his own bank account. D's conviction of theft was affirmed on the basis that he had been under an obligation to retain, if not the actual notes and coins, at least their proceeds for the benefit of the Trust.

5.   "Whether or not an obligation arises is a matter of law, because the obligation must be a legal obligation": *R. v Mainwaring* (1981) 74 Cr. App. R. 99 at 107. Nevertheless, it was said at various places (including *R. v Hall*) that although a judge could rule that any approved situation did *not* amount to a relevant obligation and direct an acquittal, he could not rule that it *did* amount to such, but must leave it to the jury to say whether the facts did amount to the sort of obligation covered by subsection 3. See also *R. v Hayes* (1976) 63 Cr. App. R. 292. But in *R. v Mainwaring*, the Court of Appeal, without reference to the previous cases, said that the judge should direct "If you find such and such, then I direct you as a matter of law that a legal obligation arose to which s.4(3) applies" (see also *Dubar* [1995] 1 Cr. App. R. 280). This is preferable in confining the jury to finding the facts, which indeed will be difficult enough in many cases. Except where a written document specifies the accused's obligation (which is a matter of construction for the judge), the jury must ask, did the payers *expect* the accused to retain and deal with the property in a particular way: see Edmund Davies LJ in *R. v Hall*). In

many cases, such as *R. v Hall* itself where the payers were the multitudinous clients of a travel agency, it will be impossible to discover any general expectation, and any proved particular expectation by an individual client might be unreasonable and unassented to by the accused. The normal practice of traders in the accused's line of business would appear to be a better guide; but even if such were proved and was to the effect that clients' money was usually kept separate, it does not follow that the clients knew of the practice and expected the accused to follow it.

Subsection (4): Property got by another's mistake

Note

This subsection was passed in order to deal with a point highlighted in one particular case—*Moynes v Cooper* [1956] 1 Q.B. 439. It was thought that if property was obtained by A from B by mistake in circumstances where B meant A to become the owner of it then, although A might be under a quasi-contractual obligation to restore the property or its value to B, in most cases B did not have any proprietary interest in the property, which belonged solely to A. The subsection provides that even if A is the only person with an interest in the property, the existence of the obligation to restore makes it theft if A dishonestly resolves not to restore. However, in 1979, it was held, apparently for the first time, in the case of *Chase Manhattan Bank v Israel-London Bank* [1981] Ch. 105 (Goulding J.), that B has not merely a quasi-contractual right to sue A for the value, but an equitable interest in the property under a constructive trust. This principle was used in *R. v Shadrokh-Cigari* to convict A of theft when he dishonestly appropriated money given to him by mistake. The property belonged to B under subs. (1), and there was no need to have recourse to subs.(4). There is never a need to have recourse to that subsection. It is not every kind of mistake which gives rise to an obligation to restore, but if a mistake does have that effect, it gives rise to a proprietary interest in the person to whom the obligation is owed. There is one case where A is under an obligation to restore within the meaning of subs.(4) although B has no proprietary interest under subs.(1); that is when the property has become lost or consumed or otherwise untraceable under equity's rules. But in such a case, A's dishonest refusal to make good to B can never be theft, because there is no identifiable property for him to appropriate. He is no more than a defaulting debtor.

Although subs.(4) is not needed, it has been used to convict people who have got property by mistake: see *Attorney General's Reference (No.1 of 1983)* 3 All E.R. 369.

----

iv. "With the Intention of Depriving Permanently"

Note

The definition of theft in s.1 requires that the appropriation should be with the *intention of permanently depriving the owner of it*.

The intention to deprive must be a settled one at the time of the appropriation. As to an intention to deprive if and only if the goods on examination turn out to be what the taker wants, see next case.

R. V EASOM

[1971] 2 Q.B. 315

E took a handbag, searched through it, found nothing to interest him, and left it with contents intact near the owner, who repossessed it. E was convicted of theft of the bag and its detailed contents.

EDMUND DAVIES LJ

In every case of theft the appropriation must be accompanied by the intention of permanently depriving the owner of his property. What may be loosely described as a 'conditional' appropriation will not do. If the appropriator has it in mind merely to deprive the owner of such of his property as, on examination, proves worth taking and then, finding that the booty is valueless to the appropriator, leaves it ready to hand to be repossessed by the owner, the appropriator has not stolen. If a dishonest postal sorter picks up a pile of letters intending to steal any which are registered, but on finding that none of them are, replaces them, he has stolen nothing, and this is so notwithstanding the provisions of s.6(1) of the Theft Act 1968. In the present case the jury were never invited to consider the possibility that such was the appellant's state of mind or the legal consequences flowing therefrom. Yet the facts are strongly indicative that this was exactly how his mind was working, for he left the handbag and its contents entirely intact and to hand, once he had carried out his exploration. For this reason we hold that the conviction of the full offence of theft cannot stand . . .

So once more, one is driven back to consider with what intention the appellant embarked upon the act of taking. This court, in *R. v Stark* (unreported), October 4, 1967, quashed the conviction for larceny of a man caught in the act of lifting a tool-kit from the boot of a car, the judge having misdirected the jury by telling them: 'Was Stark intending, if he could get away with it, and if it was worthwhile, to take the tool-kit when he lifted it out? If he picked up something, saying "I am sticking to this—if it is worthwhile," then he would be guilty.' But does it follow from all this that the appellant (as to whose identity and physical acts the verdict establishes that the jury entertained no doubt) has to go scot-free? Can he not, as the Crown originally submitted, be convicted at least of attempted theft? Even though the contents of the handbag, when examined, held no allure for him, why was he not as guilty of attempted theft as would be the pickpocket who finds his victim's pocket empty (see *R. v Ring* (1892) 61 LJ.M.C. 116). Does a conditional intention to steal count for nothing? In his *Criminal Law (The General Part)*, 2nd ed. (1961), p.52, para.23, Professor Glanville Williams says: 'A conditional intention is capable of ranking as intention for legal purposes. Thus it is no defence to an apparent burglar that his intention was merely to steal a certain paper if it should happen to be there.' He then cites the American Model Penal Code, s.2.02(6) (T.D. No. 4 pp.14, 129), which states that: 'When a particular purpose is an element of an offence, the element is established although such purpose is conditional, unless the condition negatives the harm or evil sought to be prevented by the law defining the offence.'

But as to this, all, or, at least, much, depends upon the manner in which the charge is framed. Thus, 'if you indict a man for stealing your watch, you cannot convict him of attempting to steal your umbrella' (*per* Cockburn C.J. in *R. v M'Pherson* (1857) D. & B. 197, 200)—unless, of course, the court of trial has duly exercised the wide powers of amendment conferred by s.5 of the Indictment Act 1915. In our judgment, this remains the law and it is unaffected by the provisions of s.6 of the Criminal Law Act 1967. No amendment was sought or effected in the present case, which accordingly has to be considered in relation to the articles enumerated in the theft charge and nothing else. Furthermore, it is implicit in the concept of an attempt that the person acting intends to do the act attempted, so that the *mens rea* of an attempt is essentially that of the complete crime (see *Smith and Hogan, 'Criminal Law'*, 2nd ed. (1969), p.163). That being so, there could be no valid conviction of the appellant of attempted theft on the present indictment unless it were established that he was animated by the same intention permanently to deprive Sergeant Crooks of the goods enumerated in the particulars of the charge as would be necessary to establish the full offence. We hope that we have already made sufficiently clear why we consider that, in the light of the evidence and of the direction given, it is impossible to uphold the verdict on the basis that such intention was established in this case.

For these reasons, we are compelled to allow the appeal and quash the conviction.

Appeal allowed

Notes

1. "What may be loosely described as a conditional appropriation will not do. If the appropriator has it in mind merely to deprive the owner of such of his property as, on examination, proves worth taking and then, finding that the booty is valueless to the appropriator, leaves it ready to hand to be repossessed by the owner, the appropriator has not stolen." For the subsequent history of this dictum of Edmund-Davies LJ, which caused difficulties in burglary with intent to steal, see *Attorney General's References (Nos 1 and 2 of 1979)*, below.

2. Usually, the crime of attempt is available to deal with cases of this kind. In *Attorney General's References (Nos 1 and 2 of 1979)*, Roskill LJ said of *Easom* "It seems clear from the latter part of Edmund Davies L.J's judgment that if he had been charged with an attempt to steal some or all of the contents of that handbag, he could properly have been convicted." In a case exactly like *Easom—R. v Smith & Smith* [1986] Crim. L.R. 166—just such a charge was preferred and the conviction was upheld on appeal. But since Easom was held not to intend to steal any of the listed contents of the bag, it seems odd to hold that he intended to steal "some or air of the (unlisted) contents". Listed in the indictment or not, they were all rejected by him. What he intended to steal was something which was not there, i.e. something which he would have thought worth stealing. The fact that his attempt to steal something valuable was impossible is now no bar to his being convicted of attempting to steal; and he is better dealt with by a charge of "attempted theft from a handbag", without any mention of the contents.

3. Edmund-Davies LJ says that his hypothetical dishonest postal sorter was not guilty of theft "notwithstanding the provisions of s.6(1) of the Theft Act 1968". Nevertheless, that section does apparently make theft of *some* cases of conditional intent to deprive permanently.

THEFT ACT 1968 S.6

(1) A person appropriating property belonging to another without meaning the other to lose the thing itself is nevertheless to be regarded as having the intention of permanently depriving the other of it if his intention is to treat the thing as his own to dispose of regardless of the other's rights; and a borrowing or lending of it may amount to so treating it it, but only if, the borrowing or lending is for a period and in circumstances making it equivalent to an outright taking or disposal.

(2) Without prejudice to the generality of subsection (1) above, where a person, having possession or control (lawfully or not) of property belonging to another, parts with the property under a condition as to its return which he may not be able to perform, this (if done for purposes of his own and without the other's authority) amounts to treating the property as his own to dispose of regardless of the other's rights.

J.R. SPENCER, "THE METAMORPHOSIS OF SECTION 6 OF THE THEFT ACT" [1977] CRIM. L.R. 653

An 'intention to deprive' was, of course an element of the crime of larceny. Over the course of many years, the concept had been interpreted in numerous cases. Generally, an *intention* to deprive, rather than mere recklessness, was necessary. Thus abandoning another person's property knowing there was a risk that he would never get it back was not larceny, unless the person who did so actually desired the owner to lose it, or (presumably) foresaw the virtual certainty that he would do so. However, there were three judge-made extensions of 'intention permanently to deprive' where mere recklessness, or something like it, was sufficient, (a) There was the 'ransom principle,' whereby it counted as an intention permanently to deprive if the idea was to return the property to the owner only if he was prepared to pay for it. (b) There was the 'essential quality principle,' whereby it counted as an intention permanently to deprive if the idea was to return the property only after it had undergone some fundamental change of character: a live horse taken but a dead horse returned, a valid ticket taken but a cancelled ticket returned. And (c) there was the 'pawning principle,' where it counted as an intention permanently to deprive if a person pawned another's property without his consent, hoping to be able to redeem the pledge, but knowing he might be unable to do so. The Criminal Law Revision Committee heartily approved of 'intention permanently to deprive' as so elaborated by the courts, and it was the one element of larceny which the Committee thought could be transplanted into the new crime of theft without any alteration. The Committee assumed that the old case-law would automatically be applied if the phrase were enacted in the definition of theft without any attempt at further elaboration. It therefore opposed putting a section into the Theft Act elaborating 'intention of permanently depriving,' and carefully omitted any such clause from the Draft Theft Bill which it appended to its Eighth Report. However, somebody who had the ear of the Government thought otherwise . . . [after tracing the tangled Parliamentary history of the new clause]; Not surprisingly, the courts have so far failed to spot Parliament's real intention through the obscure verbiage in which Parliament has dressed it up. To date, they have been quite mystified by the section . . .

A fair summary of the Court of Appeal's interpretation of s.6 in [R. v Warner] would be the following.

'The section was enacted to extend "intention permanently to deprive" beyond its previous interpretation; however, it was only meant to do so to some infinitesimal degree, and we are not prepared to say in which direction; any judge who drags s.6 into his summing-up can expect to be reversed on appeal.'

It has certainly not crossed anybody's mind that s.6 was designed to *preserve* the existing case law. In *Duru* [1974] 1 W.L.R. 2, the Court of Appeal applied the 'essential quality' principle, but did so without reference to s.6. And in *Easom* Edmund Davies L.J. indicated that a conditional intention to deprive was insufficient for theft, notwithstanding s.6; whereas the 'pawning principle' and the 'ransom principle', which s.6 was intended to preserve, are obvious instances of conditional intention.

Thus, as a result of s.6, the present meaning of 'intention of permanently depriving' in theft is doubly in doubt. The expression is thought to be extended beyond its literal meaning by s.6, but we do not know how far or in what direction. And we do not know, how far, if at all, the pre-1968 case law on 'intention permanently to deprive' can be relied on.

R. V LLOYD

[1985] Q.B. 829 CA

The appellant L was the chief projectionist at a cinema. He removed films from the cinema and passed them to the appellants A and B who made copies of them. All the films were returned to the cinema in a matter of hours. The pirated copies of the films were sold to the detriment of the film distributors. The appellants were convicted of conspiracy to steal and appealed. The issue on appeal was whether there could be an intention permanently to deprive in the circumstances.

LORD LANE CJ

What then was the basis of the prosecution case and the basis of the judge's direction to the jury? It is said that s.6(1) of the Theft Act 1968 brings such actions as the appellants performed here within the provisions of s.1. The judge left the matter to the jury on the basis that they had to decide whether the words of s.6(1) were satisfied by the prosecution or not. [His Lordship read s.6(1)] . . .

That section has been described by J.R. Spencer in his article (p.666), as a section which 'sprouts obscurities at every phrase' and we are inclined to agree with him. It is abstruse. But it must mean, if nothing else, that there are circumstances in which a defendant may be deemed to have the intention permanently to deprive, even though he may intend the owner eventually to get back the object which has been taken

In general we take the same view as Professor Griew in *The Theft Act 1968 and 1978*, 4th ed. (1982), p.47 para.2–73, namely, that s.6 should be referred to in exceptional cases only. In the vast majority of cases it need not be referred to or considered at all.

Deriving assistance from another distinguished academic writer, namely, Professor Glanville Williams, we would like to cite with approval the following passage from his *Textbook of Criminal Law*, 2nd ed. (1983), p.719:

'In view of the grave difficulties of interpretation presented by s.6, a trial judge would be well advised not to introduce it to the jury unless he reaches the conclusion that it will assist them, and even then (it may be suggested) the question he leaves to the jury should not be worded in terms of the generalities of the subsection but should reflect those generalities as applied to the alleged facts. For example, the question might be: "Did the defendant take the article, intending that the owner should have it back only on making a payment? If so, you would be justified as a matter of law in finding that he intended to deprive the owner permanently of his article, because the taking of the article with that intention is equivalent to an outright taking."'

Bearing in mind the observations of Edmund Davies L.J. in *R. v Warner*, [(1970) 55 Cr. App. R. 93] we would try to interpret the section in such a way as to ensure that nothing is construed as an intention permanently to deprive which would not prior to the Act of 1968 have been so construed. Thus, the first part of s.6(1) seems to us to be aimed at the sort of case where a defendant takes things and then offers them back to the owner for the owner to buy if he wishes. If the taker intends to return them to the owner only upon such payment, then, on the wording of s.6(1), that is deemed to amount to the necessary intention permanently to deprive: see, for instance, *R. v Hall* (1848) 1 Den. 381, where the defendant took fat from a candlemaker and then offered it for sale to the owner. His conviction for larceny was affirmed. There are other cases of similar intent: for instance, 'I have taken your valuable painting. You can have it back on payment to me of £X,000. If you are not prepared to make that payment, then you are not going to get your painting back.'

It seems to us that in this case we are concerned with the second part of s.6(1), namely, the words after the semi-colon:

'and a borrowing or lending of it may amount to so treating it if, but only if, the borrowing or lending is for a period and in circumstances making it equivalent to an outright taking or disposal.'

These films, it could be said, were borrowed by Lloyd from his employers in order to enable him and the others to carry out their 'piracy' exercise.

Borrowing is *ex hypothesi* not something which is done with an intention permanently to deprive. This half of the subsection, we believe, is intended to make it clear that a mere borrowing is never enough to constitute the necessary guilty mind unless the intention is to return the 'thing' in such a changed state that it can truly be said that all its goodness or virtue has gone: for example *R. v Beecham* (1851) 5 Cox C.C. 181, where the defendant stole railway tickets intending that they should be returned to the railway company in the usual way only after the journeys had been completed. He was convicted of larceny. The judge in the present case gave another example, namely, the taking of a torch battery with the intention of returning it only when its power is exhausted.

That being the case, we turn to inquire whether the feature films in this case can fall within that category. Our view is that they cannot. The goodness, the virtue, the practical value of the films to the owners has not gone out of the article. The film could still be projected to paying audiences, and, had everything gone according to the conspirators' plans, would have been projected in the ordinary way to audiences at the Odeon Cinema, Barking, who would have paid for their seats. Our view is that those particular films which were the subject of this alleged conspiracy had not themselves diminished in value at all. What had happened was that the borrowed film had been used or was going to be used to perpetrate a copyright swindle on the owners whereby their commercial interests were grossly and adversely affected in the way that we have endeavoured to describe at the outset of this judgment. That borrowing, it seems to us, was not for a period, or in such circumstances, as made it equivalent to an outright taking or disposal. There was still virtue in the film.

For those reasons we think that the submissions of Mr Du Cann on this aspect of the case are well founded. Accordingly the way in which the judge directed the jury was mistaken, and accordingly, this conviction of conspiracy to steal must be quashed.

Appeals allowed

Notes

1.   Lord Lane CJ said that it might be that the only offence of which Lloyd and his collaborators could be convicted would be conspiracy to commit a breach of the Copyright Act. However, now s.12 of the Criminal Justice Act 1987, will allow a charge of conspiracy to defraud.

2. Lord Lane's suggestion that a court should "try to interpret the section in such a way as to ensure that nothing is construed as an intention permanently to deprive which would not prior to the Act of 1968 have been so construed" appears to confirm Spencer's fear that s.6 extends the law only minimally and obscurely, at least where a borrowing or a lending is involved. Nevertheless, since the decision in *Lloyd*, other cases have taken a less restricted view of the section's ambit; and the Court of Appeal in *R. v Wille* (1988) 86 Cr. App. R. 296; and the Privy Council in *Chan Man-sin v Attorney General for Hong Kong* [1988] 1 All E.R. 1 read the section quite literally, and had no difficulty in holding that where D knew that V's bank account would not be diminished in any way by his drawing an unauthorised cheque on it, he was "nevertheless to be regarded as having the intention of permanently depriving" V, because he intended "to treat the thing (the bank account) as his own to dispose of regardless of the other's rights."

    In *Fernandes* [1996] 1 Cr. App. R. 175, Auld LJ reading the judgment of the Court of Appeal stated (at 188):

    > "In our view, s.6(1), which is expressed in general terms, is not limited in its application to the illustrations given by Lord Lane CJ in *Lloyd*. Nor, in saying that in most cases it would be unnecessary to refer to the provision, did Lord Lane suggest that it should be so limited. The critical notion, stated expressly in the first limb and incorporated by reference in the second, is whether a defendant intended 'to treat the thing as his own to dispose of regardless of the other's rights'. The second limb of subsection (1), and also subsection (2), are merely specific illustrations of the application of that notion. We consider that s.6 may apply to a person in possession or control of another's property who, dishonestly and for his own purpose, deals with that property in such a manner that he knows he is risking its loss."

3. In *Marshall* [1998] 2 Cr. App. R. 282, the Court of Appeal applied *Fernandes*. The appellants obtained used, but unexpired, tickets from passengers leaving London Underground stations and sold them on to other travellers thereby depriving London Underground of revenue. The appellants were convicted of theft of the tickets and appealed contending that tickets are analogous to cheques in that they represent a chose in action which belongs to the customer, not London Underground and, in so far as the tickets are pieces of paper, these would be returned to the possession of London Underground in due course. The Court of Appeal dismissed their appeals holding that the tickets, as pieces of paper, belonged at all times to London Underground and that the appellants by acquiring and re-selling them had the intention to treat them as their own to dispose of regardless of London Underground's rights, it being irrelevant that the tickets would find their way back into the possession of London Underground. This ruling does not fall within the ransom principle, essential quality principle or the pawning principle. The case has been subjected to criticism by Professor Smith, "Stealing Tickets" [1998] Crim. L.R. 723, who argues that the decision will not necessarily apply to all tickets as the question whether the original vendor of the ticket retains property in the ticket will depend on the terms of the contract. Professor Smith states (at 724):

    > "But a person is not bound by a condition printed on a ticket unless reasonable steps have been taken to bring it to his attention. If such steps have not been taken, the condition does not form part of the contract and it cannot be relied on to show that the ownership in the ticket did not pass. Where a ticket is obtained from a machine, the supplier must give reasonable notice to the purchaser before he inserts his money. A term printed on the ticket issued by the machine is too late; the contract is already made."

4.   In *Cahill* [1993] Crim. L.R. 142 the Court of Appeal approved the following passage in J.C. Smith, *The Law of Theft*, 6th edn (Butterworths, 1989), p.73:

> "It is submitted, however, that an intention to use the thing as one's own is not enough and that 'dispose of' is not used in the sense in which a general might 'dispose of' his forces but rather in the meaning given by the *Shorter Oxford Dictionary*: 'To deal with definitely: to get rid of; to get done with, finish. To make over by way of sale or bargain, sell.'"

In *DPP v Lavender* [1994] Crim. L.R. 297, the Divisional Court, without referring to *Cahill*, ruled that the dictionary definition of "dispose of" was too narrow and a disposal could include "dealing with" property. L had been charged with theft of two doors from the council. He had taken the doors from a council property undergoing repair and used them to replace damaged doors in his girlfriend's council flat. The justices had dismissed the information. The Divisional Court allowed the prosecution's appeal and remitted the case to the justices with a direction to convict. If "dispose of" means "deal with", it is difficult to see what purpose the words "to treat the thing as his own" serve; they appear to be superfluous. *Cahill* should be followed.

Question

1.   D, an attendant at the National Gallery, offers to sell to P, a gullible tourist, a Constable painting. If appropriation is an artificial concept and intention permanently to deprive is likewise an artificial concept, could D be convicted of theft of the painting?

R. V MITCHELL

[2008] EWCA Crim 850

V was sitting in her car when she was attacked and thrown out of the vehicle by a group of men who were being pursued by the police. The vehicle was driven away and later found abandoned a few miles away. One of the men, M, was convicted of robbery. The central issue in the case was whether M had intended permanent deprivation of V's vehicle.

RIX LJ

[11] It goes without saying that robbery involves, and we are not giving the statutory definition at this point, the use of violence in the course of and for the purpose of a theft (see s.8(1) of the Theft Act 1968: 'if he steals, and immediately before or at the time of doing so, and in order to do so') Theft involves—see s.1 of the Theft Act 1968—an intention permanently to deprive the owner of the property concerned. The question in this case was whether the facts laid by the prosecution established a case to go before the jury of violence in the pursuit of theft. Had there been an intention permanently to deprive Mr or Mrs Davis of ownership of the BMW?

[12] There is a further section in the Theft Act upon which the prosecution relied for these purposes and that is s.6(1) which provides as follows:

'A person appropriating property belonging to another without meaning the other permanently to lose the thing itself is nevertheless to be regarded as having the intention of permanently depriving the other of it if his intention is to treat the thing as his own to dispose of regardless of the other's rights; and a borrowing or lending of it may amount to so treating it if, but only if, the borrowing or lending is for a period and in circumstances making it equivalent to an outright taking or disposal.'

We are concerned essentially in this case with the section down to the semicolon. We will also, however, read s.6(2) because its provisions are also discussed in the jurisprudence of s.6 to which we will have to make mention. Section 6(2) provides:

'Without prejudice to the generality of sub-section (1) above, where a person, having possession or control (lawfully or not) of property belonging to another, parts with the property under a condition as to its return which he may not be able to perform, this (if done for purposes of his own and without the other's authority) amounts to treating the property as his own to dispose of regardless of the other's rights.'

[13] There has been some discussion in cases, as will be seen, as to whether s.6 waters down or extends or only exemplifies the underlying requirement for theft of an intention permanently to deprive. Taking the wording of s.6(1) by itself without regard to authority it would seem that there is the possibility of a s.6 intention, that is to say an intention to treat the thing as his own to dispose of regardless of the other's rights, as somewhat extending the intention permanently to deprive, because the section begins with the hypothesis that property belonging to another has been taken 'without meaning the other permanently to lose the thing itself'. Although those words carefully avoid the word 'intention', since the word 'meaning' is used instead, or the word 'deprived' since the word 'lose' is used instead, nevertheless it would appear that the purpose of the section is to render a Defendant to be regarded or deemed as having the necessary s.1 intention of permanently depriving the owner of his property if the s.6(1) intention is established. Having said that, we observe that the jurisprudence discusses the extent to which s.6 goes beyond the essential underlying intention of permanently depriving the owner of his property.

[14] A number of relevant authorities have been helpfully cited to us. We begin with *R v Warner* (1970) 135 JP 199, 55 Cr App Rep 93, [1971] Crim LR 114. That was a case in which one worker had been seen making off with the tools of a colleague which were very shortly thereafter found hidden under some scarves. It was only at trial that his real defence emerged; there had been a dispute between that Defendant and his colleague about a right of way affecting their properties which had got into the hands of solicitors and the Defendant was reacting to that dispute by removing his colleague's tools for what he insisted was only intended to be a short time, but the police had almost immediately become involved and he had lost his nerve about owning up.

[15] The Crown had invoked s.6(1) of the Theft Act and the Defendant had been convicted. His appeal was allowed. Edmund Davies L.J. referred to the Theft Act as 'aspiring to remove legal subtleties devoid of merit'. He referred to s 1 declaring that the intention of permanently depriving another of his property was an essential ingredient and said that nothing was to be found elsewhere in the Act which justified a conviction for theft in its absence. Turning then to s 6, which he considered had unfortunately confused the trial, Edmund Davies L.J. said this (at 97):

'Its object is, in no way wise to cut down the definition of "theft" contained in section 1. It is always dangerous to paraphrase a statutory enactment, but its apparent aim is to prevent specious pleas of a kind which have succeeded in the past by providing in effect, that it is no excuse for an accused person to plead absence of the necessary intention if it is clear that he appropriated another's property intending to treat it as his own, regardless of the owner's rights. Section 6 thus gives illustrations, as it were, of what can amount to the dishonest intention demanded by section 1(1). But it is a misconception to interpret it as watering down section 1.'

[16] The matter was revisited in *R v Lloyd and others* [1985] QB 829, [1985] 2 All ER 661, 149 JP 634. That case involved a conspiracy to defraud the owners of the copyright of films by removing the film reels being shown in a cinema for as short a period as made it possible to have them copied onto a video master tape before having them returned surreptitiously back to the cinema from which they had been taken. The Defendants were charged with conspiracy to steal. Section 6 was relied on to make good the intention necessary to theft in circumstances where it had been plain that the whole point of the exercise was to get the film reels back to the cinema as soon as could be done. That was another case where use of s.6 had led to a conviction but where this court had to allow an appeal.

[17] In a wide-ranging judgment, Lord Lane, CJ, considered the background of s.6 both in the common law and since the enactment of the Theft Act. He cited JR Spencer in an article in [1977] Criminal Law Review 653 for describing s.6 as a provision which 'sprouts obscurities at every phrase' and observed: 'We are inclined to agree with him'—see 834B. He then referred to the passage in Warner (which we have cited). Next he referred to *R v Duru* [1973] 3 All ER 715, [1974] 1 WLR 2, 58 Cr App Rep 151, a case involving cheques which had been stolen, paid out to the thieves and then returned in the normal course of processing to their owners. It was submitted that the return of the cheques, albeit devoid of value to their owners once they had been paid, indicated the lack of

the necessary intention under the Theft Act. But Megaw L.J. at p 8 explained that although as a piece of paper the cheque remained, subject to a rubber stamp on it, the same as before, it had entirely ceased to be a thing in action, as it had been before it had been paid, had ceased to be in substance the same thing as it was before and had become worthless. In those circumstances if it had been necessary to look to s.6, said Megaw L.J., that could have been applied since it was plain 'that the Defendants each had the intention of causing the cheque to be treated as the property of the person by whom it was to be obtained, to dispose of, regardless of the rights of the true owner'.

[18] Lord Lane then referred to further academic scholarship, that of Professor Griew, to the effect that s.6 should be referred to in exceptional cases only, since in the vast majority of cases it need not be referred to or considered at all—see 835H. A third distinguished academic, Professor Glanville Williams, was then cited with approval at 836B for this observation:

'. . . a trial judge would be well advised not to introduce it to the jury unless he reaches the conclusion that it will assist them, and even then (it may be suggested) the question he leaves to the jury should not be worded in terms of the generalities of the subsection but should reflect those generalities as applied to the alleged facts.'

[19] Lord Lane then referred to the law as it had been before the Theft Act. He said this (at 836C) '. . . we would try to interpret the section in such a way as to ensure that nothing is construed as an intention permanently to deprive which would not prior to the 1968 Act have been so construed.' In that connection he said that the section seemed to be aimed at the sort of case where a Defendant takes things and then offers them back to the owner for the owner to buy if he wishes. He referred to the 19th century case of *R v Hall* (1849) 13 JP 55, 2 Car & Kir 947n, 1 Den 381. He also referred to the early case of *R v Beecham* (1851) 5 Cox CC 181, where railway tickets had been stolen with the intention that they should be returned to the railway company in the usual way only after the journeys had been completed. Another example given was the taking of a torch battery with the intention of returning it only when its power was exhausted.

[20] Turning in the light of those examples to the case of the films, Lord Lane concluded thus (836H—837B):

'That being the case, we turn to inquire whether the feature films in this case can fall within that category. Our view is that they cannot. The goodness, the virtue, the practical value of the films to the owners has not gone out of the article. The film could still be projected to paying audiences, and, had everything gone according to the conspirators' plans, would have been projected in the ordinary way to audiences at the Odeon Cinema, Barking, who had paid for their seats. Our view is that those particular films which were the subject of this alleged conspiracy had not themselves diminished in value at all. What had happened was that the borrowed film had been used or was going to be used to perpetrate a copyright swindle on the owners whereby their commercial interests were grossly and adversely affected in the way that we have endeavoured to describe at the outset of this judgment. That borrowing, it seems to us, was not for a period, or in such circumstances, as made it equivalent to an outright taking or disposal. There was still virtue in the film.'

[21] The next case is *R v Coffey* [1987] Crim LR 498. That concerned the obtaining of machinery by a worthless cheque. The Defendant had obtained the machinery in order to put pressure upon someone with whom he had a dispute. The appeal was again allowed because the summing-up was defective but in the course of this court's judgment it was observed that this was one of those rare cases where s.6(1) could usefully be deployed before the jury, but the jury should have been invited to consider whether the taking of the machinery in the circumstances obtaining in that case was equivalent to an outright taking or disposal.

[22] In *R v Cahill* [1993] Crim LR 141 a package of newspapers had been taken by the Defendant and, he said, put outside the front door of a friend of his as a joke. Section 6(1) had been brought into play at the trial but in summing up the matter to the jury the recorder in that case had dropped from his directions the statutory words in their place 'to dispose of'. That was held to be a misdirection because this court approved what Professor Smith had said of those words in his book on The Law of Theft as follows:

'The attribution of an ordinary meaning to the language of section 6 presents some difficulties. It is submitted, however, that an intention merely to use the thing as one's own is not enough and that "dispose of" is not used in the sense in which a general might "dispose of" his forces but rather in the meaning given by the Shorter Oxford dictionary: To deal with definitely; to get rid of; to get done with, finish. To make over by way of sale or bargain, sell.'

So that appeal was allowed as well. A note by Professor Smith followed the extract of that report by way of commentary. Professor Smith pointed out that that case could have been dealt with without mentioning s.6 at all since the question was 'Did the Defendant intend the package of newspapers to be lost to the newsagent forever?'—as might well have been the case where that package had disappeared to some strange doorstep. If, however, s.6 was to be invoked at all, the question would be whether the virtue had gone out of the thing, even if the Defendant had believed that the newsagent would get his papers back the following day, but at a time when they would be quite useless to him. So upon that basis s.6 might have been correctly deployed.

[23] Finally, in *R v Fernandes* [1996] 1 Cr App Rep 175 this jurisprudence was revisited in the context of a case where a solicitor had invested client's money at his disposal in his colleague's back street money-lending business where it was lost. It was argued that s.6 should not have been deployed in that case. But in his judgment Auld L.J. accepted that this was a case of proper use of it, saying at 188E:

'We consider that section 6 may apply to a person in possession or control of another's property who, dishonestly and for his own purpose, deals with that property in such a manner that he knows he is risking its loss.

In the circumstances alleged here, an alleged dishonest disposal of someone else's money on an obviously insecure investment, we consider that the judge was justified in referring to section 6. His direction, looked at as a whole, did not water down the requirement that the jury should be sure of an intention permanently to deprive as illustrated by that provision.'

[24] It is in the light of that jurisprudence that we have to consider the ruling of the judge on the application of no case to answer. What was said to the judge was that in the circumstances of this case there was no intention permanently to deprive Mr or Mrs Davis of their BMW, nor was there an intention within s.6, which the prosecution also relied upon, to treat the thing as the Defendant's own to dispose of regardless of the owner's rights. The car had only been driven for a few miles before being abandoned. The fact of abandonment showed that there was no intention permanently to deprive the owners of it or to dispose of it irrespective of the owner's rights. The judge, however, considered that there was either in the taking or in the use or in the abandonment of the vehicle evidence capable of amounting to a disposal under s.6(1). Of those three matters—the taking, the use and the abandonment—the judge in particular had emphasised the abandonment where he said 'It appears to me that abandonment in those circumstances might amount to a disposal. That is a matter which in my judgment should be decided by a jury.'

[25] In our judgment the judge erred in these considerations. So far as the abandonment itself of the car was concerned, a matter which on this appeal Mr Jackson on behalf of the Crown has not relied upon, that of course operated as a factor in favour of the defence. Moreover, the fact that its hazard lights were left on emphasized that there was no intention to avoid drawing attention to the car. So far as the use of the vehicle is concerned, again a matter not relied upon on this appeal by Mr Jackson, its use amounted to being driven just a few miles before its abandonment. So far as the taking is concerned, that was the one matter which Mr Jackson stressed in his submissions to the court. Those submissions proceeded in this way. When he was asked whether the red Fiesta, which was the car into which Mrs Davis' assailants had decamped from the BMW later that night, had been stolen Mr Jackson answered that question with the answer 'No'. He was then asked to state what the difference was between the taking of the Fiesta and the taking of the BMW. His first response was to say that the difference was the removal of Mrs Davis by force from the BMW and also the breaking of its windows. Subsequently in his submissions he abandoned the breaking of the windows as being a critical difference. Ultimately he took his stand upon the removal of Mrs Davis by force. This for him was the critical and distinguishing feature. This was the feature which showed that her assailants intended to treat the car as their own to dispose of regardless of the other's rights.

[26] At some point during his submissions Mr Jackson, before being reminded of the words 'to dispose of', which Professor Smith had emphasised in his Law of Theft (see above) and which this court similarly picked up in *Cahill*, omitted those words and emphasised, as we can well understand him saying, that the treatment of Mrs Davis showed an intention to treat the BMW as the Defendant's own regardless of the other's rights (but omitting the words 'to dispose of'). Of course, everything about the taking and use of the BMW, like any car taken away without the owner's authority, indicates an intention to treat such a car regardless of the owner's rights. That is the test of conversion in the civil law. But not every conversion is a theft. Theft requires the additional intention of permanently depriving the owner or the substituted intention under s.6(1). The fact that the taking becomes more violent, thereby setting up a case of robbery, if there is an underlying case of theft, does not in itself turn what would be a robbery, if there was a theft, into a case of robbery without theft. The theft has to be there without the violence which would turn the theft into robbery.

[27] Turning to the Vauxhall Cavalier which was destroyed at the end of the day because it was set on fire, Mr Jackson accepted that even there was nothing about the circumstances of that case which would entitle the case of theft of the Cavalier to be left to a jury. We are not so sure of that. If it were the case that a car was taken for the purposes of destroying it, that would be a case of theft, and where another's car has been set on fire that may be some evidence on which an intention permanently to deprive or a s.6(1) intention may be inferred. It seems to us, however, that in considering that the cases of both the Fiesta and the Cavalier could not support, and indeed, as he told us, would not be prosecuted, as a case of theft, Mr Jackson was going far to demonstrate that the case of the taking of the BMW cannot be regarded as a case of theft (or therefore robbery) either. In effect, subject to Mr Jackson's necessary concession regarding the Fiesta, Mr Jackson's submissions would run the danger of turning every case of taking and driving away without authority under s.12 of the Theft Act into a case of theft, whereas of course the whole point of s.12 is to get round the problem that a car which is taken and driven away for a ride, only to be abandoned, is not easily found to be a case of theft.

[28] In our judgment the facts of this case simply do not support a case to go before a jury of theft and therefore robbery of the BMW. The BMW was plainly taken for the purposes of a getaway. There was nothing about its use or subsequent abandonment to suggest otherwise. Indeed, its brief use and subsequent abandonment show very clearly what was the obvious *prima facie* inference to be drawn from its taking which was that the occupants of the Subaru needed another conveyance that evening. We therefore consider that the judge erred in being beguiled by s.6 into leaving this count of robbery to the jury.

[29] In those circumstances, we need spend little time on ground 2 of this appeal, which was a complaint about the circumstances in which the ingredients of robbery were summed up in the judge's directions to the jury. We think that the factors for the jury to consider were put before the jury but of course the recorder never directed them, for the purposes of s.6(1) and the jurisprudence which we have considered, to ask themselves whether those factors amounted to such an outright taking or disposal or an intention within the words of s.6(1) as to amount to the equivalence of an intention permanently to deprive. We consider that the authorities which we have reviewed in this judgment show that the purpose of s.6 is not greatly to widen the requirement of s.1's intention permanently to deprive. A slightly broader definition of that intention is there provided in order to deal with a small number of difficult cases which had either arisen in the past under the common law or might arise in the future where, although it might be hard to put the matter strictly in terms of an intention permanently to deprive, in the sense of meaning the owner permanently to lose the thing itself, nevertheless something equivalent to that could be obtained through the intention to treat the thing as his own to dispose of, regardless of the other's rights, remembering Professor Smith's Oxford English dictionary use of the words 'to dispose of'. Thus, the newspaper taken but only returned on the next day when it is out of date, or a ticket which had been used, or a cheque which is paid, or something which has been substantially used up or destroyed, or something which would only be returned to its owner subject to a condition, all these are the sorts of examples to be found in the jurisprudence which discusses s.6. All of these cases are of ready equivalence to an intention permanently to deprive. None of them go any way towards extending the scope of s.6 to a case, however violent, of the taking of a car for the purposes of its brief use before being abandoned with its lights on. It must be remembered of course that a car with its licence plates on, left on the road, is utterly unlike a bundle of newspapers which have disappeared from a newsagents shop to a place where they would not be found.

Appeal allowed

v. "Temporary Deprivation"

THEFT ACT 1968 S.11

(1) Subject to subsections (2) and (3) below, where the public have access to a building in order to view the building or part of it, or a collection or part of a collection housed in it, any person who without lawful authority removes from the building or its grounds the whole or part of any article displayed or kept for display to the public in the building or that part of it or in its grounds shall be guilty of an offence.

For this purpose 'collection' includes a collection got together for a temporary purpose, but references in this section to a collection do not apply to a collection made or exhibited for the purpose of effecting sales or other commercial dealings.

(2) It is immaterial for purposes of subsection (1) above, that the public's access to a building is limited to

a particular period or particular occasion; but where anything removed from a building or its grounds is there otherwise than as forming part of, or being on loan for exhibition with, a collection intended for permanent exhibition to the public, the person removing it does not thereby commit an offence under this section unless he removes it on a day when the public have access to the building as mentioned in subsection (1) above.

(3) A person does not commit an offence under this section if he believes that he has lawful authority for the removal of the thing in question or that he would have it if the person entitled to give it knew of the removal and the circumstances of it.

(4) A person guilty of an offence under this section shall, on conviction on indictment, be liable to imprisonment for a term not exceeding five years.

(b) Taking Conveyances

Note

If A took goods from B and later abandoned them in a position whence it would naturally be expected that B would eventually recover them, it was difficult to prove that the taking was with intent to deprive B. The fact that abandoned motorcars are invariably returned, through the system of universal registration of motor vehicles, to their registered owners, made it difficult to convict a "joyrider" of larceny of the motor car. The legislature therefore invented a crime for motor vehicles (see s.217 of the Road Traffic Act 1960) which could be described as larceny without intention permanently to deprive. Boats were covered by the Vessels Protection Act 1967, and the offence was widened still further by s.12 of the Theft Act, under which aircraft are covered for the first time.

THEFT ACT 1968 S.12

(1) Subject to subsections (5) and (6) below, a person shall be guilty of an offence if, without having the consent of the owner or other lawful authority, he takes any conveyance for his own or another's use, or, knowing that any conveyance has been taken without such authority, drives it or allows himself to be carried in or on it.

(2) A person guilty of an offence under subsection (1) above shall be liable on summary conviction to a fine not exceeding level 5 on the standard scale to imprisonment for a term not exceeding six months, or to both.

(3) Offences under subsection (1) above and attempts to commit them shall be deemed for all purposes to be arrestable offences within the meaning of s.2 of the Criminal Law Act 1967.

(4) If on the trial of an indictment for theft the jury are not satisfied that the accused committed theft, but it is proved that the accused committed an offence under subsection (1) above, the jury may find him guilty of the offence under subsection (1).

(5) Subsection (1) above shall not apply in relation to pedal cycles; but, subject to subsection (6) below, a person who, without having the consent of the owner or other lawful authority, takes a pedal cycle for his own or another's use, or rides a pedal cycle knowing it to have been taken with out such authority, shall on summary conviction be liable to a fine not exceeding fifty pounds.

(6) A person does not commit an offence under this section by anything done in the belief that he has lawful authority to do it or that he would have the owner's consent if the owner knew of his doing it and the circumstances of it.

(7) For purposes of this section—

(a) 'conveyance' means any conveyance constructed or adapted for the carriage of a person or persons whether by land, water or air, except that it does not include a conveyance constructed or adapted for use only under the control of a person not carried in or on it, and 'drive' shall be construed accordingly; and

(b) 'owner' in relation to a conveyance which is the subject of a hiring agreement or hire-purchase agreement, means the person in possession of the conveyance under that agreement.

(c) Criticism

GLANVILLE WILLIAMS, "TEMPORARY APPROPRIATION SHOULD BE THEFT" [1981] CRIM. L.R. 129

That the law of theft, taken by itself, would be inadequate is recognised not only by the survival of conspiracy to defraud but by the creation of special statutory offences. It is an offence under the Post Office Act 1953, s.53, unlawfully to take a postal packet in course of transmission by post, without any necessity for an intent to deprive the owner permanently. The same is true for the taking and concealment of judicial documents. It is an offence to take fish even though the angler throws them back immediately upon catching them. Blackmail for the purpose of making a temporary acquisition of property can be punished as blackmail (see below) but a robbery for the same purpose is not robbery in law, this offence being dependent on the definition of theft. Better-known exceptions are those created by ss.11 and 12 of the Theft Act 1968 (the former inserted in response to the public indignation at the outcome of the *Goya* case). But the exceptions are rather arbitrary. Why should it be an offence to make off temporarily with a cart but not with a horse, or with a statuette from a public museum but not from an auction sale-room when the public have been invited to view the articles or from a private collection that specific people have been invited to view? Why should the statutory offence be committed by going off with a valuable duck from the grounds of a zoo if the zoo houses some of its exhibits in a building open to the public (e.g. a parrot-house) but not if the public are left entirely in the open air? Is a church a building 'where the public have access in order to view the building or part of it, or a collection or part of a collection housed in it/ or is it exclusively a place of worship? In *Ban* [1978] Crim.L.R. 244 it was ruled in the Crown Court that public access is given for devotional purposes only, and not 'in order to view'. If that is correct for the ordinary church, what about Westminster Abbey? It may be remembered that during the early hours of Christmas morning, 1950, some Glasgow students took the Stone of Scone from the Abbey, subsequently leaving it at Arbroath Abbey; so the point may not be wholly without practical importance.

The special offences do not mesh with other offences involving the concept of theft. For example, it is not burglary to break into a public museum to remove an exhibit for temporary enjoyment, or to break into a garage and take off a car for a temporary criminal purpose . . .

Suppose that a person removes a small piece of sculpture from a private exhibition or a valuable book from a University library, and returns it after a year. During that time it has of course been lost to its owner; and both the owner and the police have been put to trouble. (If the owner has made a claim upon an insurer or bailee, and been compensated on the basis of total loss, he may even find that the insurer or bailee claims the right to sell the article when it is recovered, so that the owner loses it). The taker of the article may use it in such a way as to put it at risk, or he may make a profit from it, or he may return it in an impaired condition; and if he is a person of no substance the owner's civil remedy against him will be an insufficient penalty . . .

As in the case of the missing Goya, the temporary removal of a thing may be done with the intention of causing loss to the owner, or with an intention that necessarily involves such loss. Another example of this relates to copyright and industrial espionage. It is not theft or any other offence to remove a paper that is due to be set in an examination in order to read it and then return it (See *Oxford v Moss*) even though the result is that the examining body has to go to the expense of setting another paper. Nor is it an offence to remove a film unlawfully in order to make pirated copies, or to remove a secret document in order to copy it and sell the copy to a trade rival. A conspiracy to do these things may be punished as a conspiracy to defraud, but is it right that the criminal law should take no notice of this behaviour by individuals?

Yet it is not only a question of the risk of *losing* the article. When an article is unlawfully taken, even if only for a temporary purpose and without substantial risk of permanent loss of the article, the owner suffers an immediate loss, namely in respect of the use of it . . .

One of the principal arguments for changing the law is that the value of articles lies in their use. More and more things are used by way of hiring, for longer or shorter periods, instead of by ownership. Many articles of use have comparatively short useful 'lives'. In a few years they wear out or become unfashionable or technically obsolete. Therefore, to deprive the owner of the article even for a short period is to deprive him of an appreciable part of its utility. Besides, the owner is in the dilemma of either being without the article for that time or putting himself to the expense of buying another—an expense that may turn out to have been unnecessary if the article is returned. The loss of the article will be particularly annoying if the owner has relied upon having the article for a particular purpose, which becomes frustrated . . .

Particular trouble is caused to the police and others when dangerous articles are taken, as when in 1966 a Cobalt 60 isotope was taken from a factory by someone who broke in and then dumped it in a barrel of water in the factory area; shortly afterwards the same isotope was taken again. The fact that such a dangerous article is returned reduces but by no means eliminates the danger to the public and the nuisance of those responsible for the article when it is unlawfully carried off . . .

Only two arguments against making the proposed extension of the Theft Act are worth consideration. The first, that it would be contrary to tradition, or that people would not recognise temporary appropriations as theft, can perhaps be answered by pointing to the legal systems that have this concept already. Many of the illustrations given in this article would, I think, readily be regarded as theft by many people. For example, it would, I am sure, generally be regarded as theft for a person to take a bicycle, use it for several weeks, and then abandon it on the street, even if the owner eventually recovers it. In the debate on the Theft Bill in the House of Lords, Viscount Dilhorne made the interesting point that none of the definitions of the word 'steal' in the *Oxford English Dictionary* required an intent to deprive the owner permanently; they spoke only of the dishonest taking or appropriating of the property of another. In one respect the definition of theft has always gone far beyond popular usage; the slightest moving of the article with the necessary intent is traditionally theft, though the ordinary man would not regard the theft as complete at that stage. Under the Theft Act it seems to be sufficient merely to touch the article, since touching is one of 'the rights of an owner' within s.3(1). It is strange to swallow this camel while straining at the gnat of saying that it is theft to decamp with someone's valuable article and to conceal it from him dishonestly for what may be a considerable period of time.

It may be that the reader, while accepting some of the arguments in this article, has throughout been afflicted by one other doubt. Is it seriously suggested that trivial cases of dishonestly using the property of another should be subject to prosecution as theft?

The argument about trivial cases is frequently used to oppose extensions of the law, but it is never conclusive in itself, because practically every offence covers *some* trivial matters. If an offence is needed to deal with serious misconduct, that is sufficient to justify it. Even the present law could be abused by prosecuting for trivial thefts, but in practice a sensible discretion is generally exercised. The Canadian experience bears out the view that a law of *furtum usus* is unlikely to be used oppressively . . . The question has generally arisen in Canada in connection with people who walk off with articles of furniture from beer parlours or hotels; and I see no injustice or oppression in convicting them of theft, even though they aver, after being found out, that they were about to come back with the article . . .

My main legislative proposal is that the word 'permanently' should be repealed in s.1(1) of the Theft Act 1968. It should also be repealed in s.15(1), since it was put there only out of supposed logical necessity after being put in s.1(1). There is no reason of policy why a cheat who obtains the hire of a car by deception should not be guilty of obtaining property by deception. The fact that this conduct can now be brought, somewhat awkwardly, within the offence of obtaining services under the Theft Act 1978, s.1 is no argument for not making this change in the Act of 1968 . . .

vi. "Dishonestly"

THEFT ACT 1968 S.2

(1) A person's appropriation of property belonging to another is not to be regarded as dishonest—

    (a) if he appropriates the property in the belief that he has in law the right to deprive the other of it, on behalf of himself or of a third person; or

    (b) if he appropriates the property in the belief that he would have the other's consent if the other knew of the appropriation and the circumstances of it; or

    (c) (except where the property came to him as trustee or personal representative) if he appropriates the property in the belief that the person to whom the property belongs cannot be discovered by taking reasonable steps.

(2) A person's appropriation of property belonging to another may be dishonest notwithstanding that he is willing to pay for the property.

Note

Paragraph (b) of s.2(1) clarified what was not clear before, namely, that it is not an offence where the accused knows that he has no consent to what he is doing but believes that he would have been given consent if the owner had been asked.

Question

In *R. v Thurborn* (1849) 1 Den. 387, T found in the street a banknote with no means of identification on it. As soon as he picked it up, he resolved to appropriate it to his own use, but before he could spend it, he was told who the owner was. He nevertheless disposed of the note and was held not guilty of larceny, because he did not, at the time he found the note, know how the owner could be found. In view of ss.2(1)(c) and 3(1) would T today be guilty of theft? At what stage did he assume the rights of an owner?

Note

The definition in s.2 is not a complete one. The section instances three cases where the defendant's belief means that his appropriation is not to be regarded as dishonest, but is silent or inconclusive on other cases. One situation not covered is the case of a person who takes property (e.g. money) without any colour of right, knowing that the owner does not and would not consent, but intending to restore the equivalent (e.g. other coins to the value of the money taken). Section 2(2) covers the case but not conclusively, saying that such an appropriation *may* be dishonest. See next case.

R. V FEELY

[1973] Q.B. 530

F was the manager of a bookmaker's betting shop. His employers wrote to all their managers stating that the practice of borrowing from tills was to stop. He nevertheless took £30 for his own purposes. He claimed that he always meant to return the money. He was convicted of stealing the money and appealed.

LAWTON LJ

The appeal raises an important point of law, namely, can it be a defence *in law* for a man charged with theft and proved to have taken money to say that when he took the money he intended to repay it and had reasonable grounds for believing and did believe that he would be able to do so? The trial judge, Judge Edward Jones, adjudged that such a defence is not available . . .

In s.1(1) of the Act of 1968, the word 'dishonestly' can only relate to the state of mind of the person who does the act which amounts to appropriation. Whether an accused person has a particular state of mind is a question of fact which has to be decided by the jury when there is a trial on indictment, and by the magistrates when there are summary proceedings. The Crown did not dispute this proposition, but it was submitted that in some cases (and this, it was said, was such a one) it was necessary for the trial judge to define 'dishonestly' and when the facts fell within the definition he had a duty to tell the jury that if there had been appropriation it must have been dishonestly done.

We do not agree that judges should define what 'dishonestly' means. This word is in common use whereas the word 'fraudulently' which was used in s.1(1) of the Larceny Act 1916, had acquired as a result of case law a special meaning. Jurors, when deciding whether an appropriation was dishonest can be reasonably expected to, and should, apply the current standards of ordinary decent people. In their own lives they have to decide what is and what is not dishonest. We can see no reason why, when in a jury box, they should require the help of a judge to tell them what amounts to dishonesty. We are fortified in this opinion by a passage in the speech of Lord Reid in *Cozens v Brutus* [1973] A.C. 854, a case in which the words 'insulting behaviour' in s.5 of the Public Order Act 1936, had to be construed. The Divisional Court had adjudged that the meaning of the word 'insulting' in this statutory context was a matter of law. Lord Reid's comment was as follows, at p.861: 'In my judgment that is not right. The meaning of an ordinary word of the English language is not a question of law. The proper construction of a statute is a question of law. If the context shows that a word is used in an unusual sense the court will determine in other words what that unusual sense is. But here there is in my opinion no question of the word "insulting" being used in any unusual sense . . . It is for the tribunal which decides the case to consider, not as law but as fact, whether in the whole circumstances the words of the statute do or do not as a matter of ordinary usage of the English language cover or apply to the facts which have been proved.'

When this trenchant statement of principle is applied to the word 'dishonestly' in s.1(1) of the Theft Act 1968, and to the facts of this case, it is clear in our judgment that the jury should have been left to decide whether the defendant's alleged taking of the money had been dishonest. They were not, with the result that a verdict of guilty was returned without their having given thought to what was probably the most important issue in the case . . .

Appeal allowed

Note

This case was thought by some to lay down a purely objective test of dishonesty, i.e. whatever the jury thought it was, without reference to what the defendant thought. That was felt to be too hard on the defendant, and inconsistent with the three specific cases of honesty in s.2(1), all of which are made to depend on the defendant's belief. On the other hand, making the test purely subjective (what view the defendant took of his own conduct) would be a charter of immunity for those with low or idiosyncratic moral viewpoints, e.g. Robin Hood seeing no wrong in robbing the rich to feed the poor. There followed discordant decisions, under which the meaning of dishonesty was held to be different depending upon which crime was involved or, in the case of obtaining by deception, which part of the crime was involved. See the next case, which achieves a significant degree of reconciliation, but does not remove all problems.

R. V GHOSH

[1982] Q.B. 2053

G, a consultant surgeon, obtained money by falsely pretending that it was owing as an anaesthetist's fee. He was convicted of dishonestly obtaining the money by deception, contrary to s.15 of the Theft Act 1968 and appealed.

LORD LANE CJ

The grounds of appeal are simply that the judge misdirected the jury as to the meaning of dishonesty. What the judge had to say on that topic was as follows:

'Now, finally dishonesty. There are, sad to say, infinite categories of dishonesty. It is for you. Jurors in the past and, whilst we have criminal law in the future, jurors in the future have to set the standards of honesty. Now it is your turn today, having heard what you have, to consider contemporary standards of honesty and dishonesty in the context of all that you have heard. I cannot really expand on this too much, but probably it is something rather like getting something for nothing, sharp practice, manipulating systems and many other matters which come to your mind.'

. . . *R. v Feely* . . . is often treated as having laid down an objective test of dishonesty for the purpose of s.1 of the Theft Act 1968. But what it actually decided was (i) that it is for the jury to determine whether the defendant acted dishonestly and not for the judge, (ii) that the word 'dishonestly' can only relate to the defendant's own state of mind, and (iii) that it is unnecessary and undesirable for judges to define what is meant by 'dishonestly'.

It is true that the court said, at pp.537–538:

'Jurors, when deciding whether an appropriation was dishonest, can be reasonably expected to, and should, apply the current standards of ordinary decent people.'

It is that sentence which is usually taken as laying down the objective test. But the passage goes on:

'In their own lives they have to decide what is and what is not dishonest. We can see no reason why, when in a jury box, they should require the help of a judge to tell them what amounts to dishonesty.'

The sentence requiring the jury to apply current standards leads up to the prohibition on judges from applying *their* standards. That is the context in which the sentence appears. It seems to be reading too much into that sentence to treat it as authority for the view that 'dishonesty can be established independently of the knowledge or belief of the defendant'. If it could, then any reference to the state of mind of the defendant would be beside the point.

This brings us to the heart of the problem. Is 'dishonestly' in s.1 of the Theft Act 1968 intended to characterise a course of conduct? Or is it intended to describe a state of mind? If the former, then we can well understand that it could be established independently of the knowledge or belief of the accused. But if, as we think, it is the latter, then the knowledge and belief of the accused are at the root of the problem.

Take for example a man who comes from a country where public transport is free. On his first day here he travels on a bus. He gets off without paying. He never had any intention of paying. His mind is clearly honest; but his conduct, judged objectively by what he has done, is dishonest. It seems to us that in using the word 'dishonestly' in the Theft Act 1968, Parliament cannot have intended to catch dishonest conduct in that sense, that is to say conduct to which no moral obloquy could possibly attach. This is sufficiently established by the partial definition in s.2 of the Theft Act itself. All the matters covered by s.2(1) relate to the belief of the accused. Section 2(2) relates to his willingness to pay. A man's belief and his willingness to pay are things which can only be established subjectively. It is difficult to see how a partially subjective definition can be made to work in harness with the test which in all other respects is wholly objective.

If we are right that dishonesty is something in the mind of the accused (what Professor Glanville Williams calls 'a special mental state'), then if the mind of the accused is honest, it cannot be deemed dishonest merely because members of the jury would have regarded it as dishonest to embark on that course of conduct.

So we would reject the simple uncomplicated approach that the test is purely objective, however attractive from the practical point of view that solution may be.

There remains the objection that to adopt a subjective test is to abandon all standards but that of the accused himself, and to bring about a state of affairs in which 'Robin Hood would be no robber': *R. v Greenstein*. This objection misunderstands the nature of the subjective test. It is no defence for a man to say 'I knew what I was doing is generally regarded as dishonest; but I do not regard it as dishonest myself. Therefore I am not guilty.' What he is however entitled to say is 'I did not know that anybody would regard what I was doing as dishonest.' He may not be believed; just as he may not be believed if he sets up 'a claim of right' under s.2(1) of the Theft Act 1968, or asserts that he believed in the truth of a misrepresentation under s.15 of the Act of 1968. But if he is believed, or raises a real doubt about the matter, the jury cannot be sure that he was dishonest.

In determining whether the prosecution has proved that the defendant was acting dishonestly, a jury must first of all decide whether according to the ordinary standards of reasonable and honest people what was done was dishonest. If it was not dishonest by those standards, that is the end of the matter and the prosecution fails.

If it was dishonest by those standards, then the jury must consider whether the defendant himself must have realised that what he was doing was by those standards dishonest. In most cases, where the actions are obviously dishonest by ordinary standards, there will be no doubt about it. It will be obvious that the defendant himself knew that he was acting dishonestly. It is dishonest for a defendant to act in a way which he knows ordinary people consider to be dishonest, even if he asserts or genuinely believes that he is morally justified in acting as he did. For example, Robin Hood or those ardent anti-vivisectionists who remove animals from vivisection laboratories are acting dishonestly, even though they may consider themselves to be morally justified in doing what they do, because they know that ordinary people would consider these actions to be dishonest.

Cases which might be described as borderline, such as *Boggeln v Williams* [1978] 1 W.L.R. 873, will depend upon the view taken by the jury as to whether the defendant may have believed what he was doing was in accordance with the ordinary man's idea of honesty. A jury might have come to the conclusion that the defendant in that case was disobedient or impudent, but not dishonest in what he did.

So far as the present case is concerned, it seems to us that once the jury had rejected the defendant's account in respect of each count in the indictment (as they plainly did), the finding of dishonesty was inevitable, whichever of the tests of dishonesty was applied. If the judge had asked the jury to determine whether the defendant might have believed that what he did was in accordance with the ordinary man's idea of honesty, there could have only been one answer—and that is no, once the jury had rejected the defendant's explanation of what happened.

In so far as there was a misdirection on the meaning of dishonesty, it is plainly a case for the application of the proviso to s.2(1) of the Criminal Appeal Act 1968.

Appeal dismissed

Questions

1. Does this case dispose of the "Robin Hood defence", as Lord Lane suggests? D, accused of stealing from his bookmaker, says in evidence "Bookmakers are a race apart; it would be dishonest if your grocer gave you too much change and you kept it, knowing that he had made a mistake. But it is not dishonest in the case of a bookmaker." (See *Gilks* [1971] 1 W.L.R. 1341.) Must he not be acquitted if: (i) the jury think it is not dishonest to diddle bookmakers; or (ii) the jury do not think so but think that D may have thought that reasonable people may have thought so?

2. "Dishonesty is something which laymen can easily recognise when they see it". Does this mean that 12 jurors will always agree in describing some transaction as honest or dishonest and that successive juries dealing with similar transactions will agree in the same way? If so, do you agree? Is it possible to forecast the view of a jury on the honesty of, e.g. a taking of experimental animals in order to save them from vivisection? If juries did usually hold that such a taking was not theft, how could this be reconciled with the law which allows properly licensed vivisection?

3. Is (a) good motive; or (b) necessity, generally a defence to crime? See Chs 3 and 5.

4. The judge needs to direct the jury to apply the double test of dishonesty laid down by Lord Lane (was D's conduct dishonesty by ordinary standards, and if so did he realise it was so?) only where dishonesty is a live issue, i.e. only where D is in effect saying that he thought what he was doing was not dishonest. In other cases it is potentially misleading to direct on these matters: *R. v Price* (1989) 80 Cr. App. R. 409.

5. In Victoria, under a statute in all material respects identical to the Theft Act, the Supreme Court, rejecting the reasoning in *Feely*, has held that the meaning of "dishonestly" is a matter of law for the judge, and that meaning is "with disposition to withhold from a person what is his right": *R. v Salvo* [1980] V.R. 401, 432; *R. v Brow* [1981] V.R. 738; *R. v Bonollo* [1981] V.R. 633.

R. V ROSTRON AND COLLINSON

[2003] EWCA Crim 2206

The defendants were found at night wearing diving gear on a golf course. They were collecting and removing golf balls from water hazards on the course. They were charged with theft of the golf balls.

LORD JUSTICE MANTELL

. . .we ought to say that it appears that there is a considerable trade in golf balls recovered in this way, and that they are, so it seems from the evidence given in the case, known generally as 'lake balls'. No doubt in many instances that trade is carried on quite legitimately. Indeed we are told there are companies with very considerable turnovers who deal in what are termed lake balls and one can imagine all sorts of ways in which such property could come on to the market without any prior offence having been committed. Be that as it may and returning to the present case . . . [after considering and dismissing one ground of appeal His Lordship continued:] . . . The second ground of appeal is that the learned judge failed to give what is sometimes termed a *Ghosh*, (1982) 75 Cr.App.R. 154, direction. A *Ghosh* direction is such as may be necessary where it is said on behalf of an defendant accused of theft, or indeed of any other form of dishonesty, that he believed he was entitled to do what he did. Then the question may arise whether or not he truly held that belief and whether he would have considered that other reasonable persons in the same position might have been of the same mind.

Here the learned judge chose to give a simple, straightforward, clear and fair direction; indeed, on one view, a direction which was more favourable than it needed to be to each of these appellants. He told the jury in terms that the prosecution had to prove that the defendant whose case was being considered knew that he was not entitled to go on to the golf course and remove golf balls. If that was established, then the necessary element of dishonesty had been proved, and, of course, if that were the case it would matter not what other people might think, because he could not in such circumstances have had an honest belief that he was entitled to do what he did. So the second ground of appeal also fails in our judgment.

Appeal dismissed

Questions

1. If the defendant's knew that they were not entitled to go on to the golf course and remove golf balls does it necessarily follow that this is dishonesty?

2. Who decided the issue of dishonesty in *Rostron*? Was it the jury or was it the judge? If the latter, is this not contrary to *Ghosh*?

----

2. ROBBERY

THEFT ACT 1968 S.8

(1) A person is guilty of robbery if he steals, and immediately before or at the time of doing so, and in order to do so, he uses force on any person or puts or seeks to put any person in fear of being then and there subjected to force.

(2) A person guilty of robbery, or of an assault with intent to rob, shall on conviction on indictment be liable to imprisonment for life.

Notes

1. *Theft.* Without a theft (or attempted theft in the case of assault with intent to rob) there is no robbery. Theft is complete as soon as there is an appropriation with intent to steal. See Appropriation, p.600 above, and *Corcoran v Anderton* (1980) 71 Cr. App. R. 104, where it was held that wrestling with the owner for possession of an article is an assumption of the rights of the owner and therefore theft and, if accompanied by force, robbery. But if D does not have the intent permanently to deprive at the time force is used in order to take V's property, even though he may form that intent subsequently and his actions then may amount to appropriation and the completed offence of theft, he has not committed robbery (see *Vinall* [2011] EWCA Crim 2652).

    In *R. v Robinson* [1977] Crim. L.R. 173, it was held that the law as laid down in *R. v Skivington* [1968] 1 Q.B. 166 had not been altered by the Theft Act. In *R. v Skivington*, S threatened with a knife his wife's employer in order to collect wages due to her which he had her authority to collect. The judge directed the jury that before S could maintain a defence to a charge of robbery, they must be satisfied that he had an honest belief that he was entitled to take the money in the way in which he did take it.

LORD GODDARD CJ

'In the opinion of this court the matter is plain, namely that a claim of right is a defence to robbery . . . and that it is unnecessary to show that the defendant must have had an honest belief also that he was entitled to take the money in the way that he did.'

Conviction quashed

Question

Is robbery involved in the following cases?

A is lent a lawnmower by his neighbour B. When B asks for its return, A drives him away with blows, saying he is going to keep it.

C, needing the use of a car to escape pursuit by the police, takes D's car from him at gunpoint.

E, needing the use of a car for a smash and grab raid on a shop, takes F's car from him at gunpoint. See below.

----

2. Force immediately before or at the time of the theft

ANDREWS, "ROBBERY" [1966] CRIM. L.R. 524, 525

Another advantage of the new definition is that the crime of robbery is not restricted to stealing from the person or in the presence of the person against whom force is used or threatened . . . However a problem does arise even under the new definition. Let us take the case of a defendant who assaults and binds someone and then proceeds to his victim's property some distance away where minutes or even hours later he steals. Is he guilty of robbery? The fact that the theft is away from the presence of the victim would no longer be a problem, but the new definition does restrict the scope of robbery to circumstances where the defendant 'immediately before or at the time of [stealing] wilfully uses force on any person or wilfully puts or seeks to put any person in fear of being then and there subjected to force'. Has the force been used 'immediately before' in our example? Does immediate mean seconds, minutes or hours? Presumably it is not intended to cover the situation where the violence precedes the stealing by a matter of days. Nor can one argue that the force or fear is a continuing factor if the victim remains under continuing fear or restraint, because what must be immediate is the wilful use of force not the continuing effect of it, or alternatively the putting of the person in fear or seeking to put him in fear must be immediate, not merely the continuing fear. The matter might be better put if the words 'immediately before or at the time of doing so' were left out of the definition. The crime of robbery would still be limited to where the person uses force or fear 'in order to [steal].' To further restrict it in terms of temporal proximity of force and theft is to make a defence of the criminal's divorcing in time the violence and the stealing and there seems no great reason in that. The real issue should surely be whether the force or threat of force was used *in order to steal*.

R. V HALE

(1978) 68 Cr. App. R. 415 CA

H and M entered the house of Mrs C wearing stocking masks. H put his hand over her mouth to stop her screaming. M went upstairs and came back with her jewellery box. They then tied up Mrs C and threatened harm to her child if she told the police within five minutes of their leaving. H was convicted of robbery and appealed.

EVELEIGH LJ

On behalf of the appellant it is submitted that the learned judge misdirected the jury in that the passages quoted above could indicate to them that if an accused used force in order to effect his escape with the stolen goods that would be sufficient to constitute the crime of robbery. In so far as the facts of the present case are concerned, counsel submitted that the theft was completed when the jewellery box was first seized and any force thereafter could not have been 'immediately before or at the time of stealing' and certainly not 'in order to steal'. The essence of the submission was that the theft was completed as soon as the jewellery box was seized . . .

Section 8 of the Theft Act 1968 begins: 'A person is guilty of robbery if he steals . . .' He steals when he acts in accordance with the basic definition of theft in s.1 of the Theft Act; that is to say when he dishonestly appropriates property belonging to another with the intention of permanently depriving the other of it. It thus becomes necessary to consider what is 'appropriation' or, according to s.3, 'any assumption by a person of the rights of an owner'. An assumption of the rights of an owner describes the conduct of a person towards a particular article. It is conduct which usurps the rights of the owner. To say that the conduct is over and done with as soon as he lays hands upon the property, or when he first manifests an intention to deal with it as his, is contrary to common-sense and to the natural meaning of words. A thief who steals a motor car first opens the door. Is it to be said that the act of starting up the motor is no more a part of the theft?

In the present case there can be little doubt that if the appellant had been interrupted after the seizure of the jewellery box the jury would have been entitled to find that the appellant and his accomplice were assuming the rights of an owner at the time when the jewellery box was seized. However, the act of appropriation does not suddenly cease. It is a continuous act and it is a matter for the jury to decide whether or not the act of appropriation has finished. Moreover, it is quite clear that the intention to deprive the owner permanently, which accompanied the assumption of the owner's rights, was a continuing one at all material times. This Court therefore rejects the contention that the theft had ceased by the time the lady was tied up. As a matter of common-sense the appellant was in the course of committing theft; he was stealing.

There remains the question whether there was robbery. Quite clearly the jury were at liberty to find the appellant guilty of robbery relying upon the force used when he put his hand over Mrs Carrett's mouth to restrain her from calling for help. We also think that they were also entitled to rely upon the act of tying her up provided they were satisfied (and it is difficult to see how they could not be satisfied) that the force so used was to enable them to steal. If they were still engaged in the act of stealing the force was clearly used to enable them to continue to assume the rights of the owner and permanently to deprive Mrs Carrett of her box, which is what they began to do when they first seized it . . .

Appeal dismissed

See also *Gregory* (1981) 77 Cr. App. R. 41; and *Lockley* [1995] Crim. L.R. 656.

3. Force on any person

R. V DAWSON

(1976) 64 Cr.App.R. 170 CA

D and two others came alongside a sailor, and nudged him from side to side. While he was trying to keep his balance, one of the three was enabled to take his wallet. They were convicted of robbery and appealed.

LAWTON LJ

Mr Locke had submitted at the end of the prosecution's case that what had happened could not in law amount to the use of force. He called the learned judge's attention to some old authorities and to a passage in *Archbold* . . . based on the old authorities, and submitted that because of those old authorities there was not enough evidence to go to the jury. He sought before this Court to refer to the old authorities. He was discouraged from doing so because this Court is of the opinion that in these cases what judges should now direct their attention to is the words of the statute. This had been said in a number of cases since the Theft Act 1968.

The object of that Act was to get rid of all the old technicalities of the law of larceny and to put the law into simple language which juries would understand and which they themselves would use. That is what has happened in s.8 which defines 'robbery'. That section is in these terms: 'A person is guilty of robbery if he steals and immediately before or at the time of doing so, and in order to do so, he uses force on any person or puts or seeks to put any person in fear of being then and there subjected to force.'

The choice of the word 'force' is not without interest because under the Larceny Act 1916 the word 'violence' had been used, but Parliament deliberately on the advice of the Criminal Law Revision Committee changed that word to 'force'. Whether there is any difference between 'violence' or 'force' is not relevant for the purposes of this case; but the word is 'force'. It is a word in ordinary use. It is a word which juries understand. The learned judge left it to the jury to say whether jostling a man in the way which the victim described to such an extent that he had difficulty in keeping his balance could be said to be the use of force. The learned judge, because of the argument put forward by Mr Locke, went out of his way to explain to the jury that force in these sort of circumstances must be substantial to justify a verdict.

Whether it was right for him to put that adjective before the word 'force' when Parliament had not done so we will not discuss for the purposes of this case. It was a matter for the jury. They were there to use their common sense and knowledge of the world. We cannot say that their decision as to whether force was used was wrong. They were entitled to the view that force was used.

Other points were discussed in the case as to whether the force had been used for the purpose of distracting the victim's attention or whether it was for the purpose of overcoming resistance. Those sort of refinements may have been relevant under the old law, but so far as the new law is concerned the sole question is whether the accused used force on any person in order to steal. That issue in this case was left to the jury. They found in favour of the Crown.

We cannot say that this verdict was either unsafe or unsatisfactory. Accordingly the appeal is dismissed.

Appeal dismissed

Note

R. v Clouden [1987] Crim. L.R. 56: C was seen to follow a woman who was carrying a shopping basket in her left hand. He approached her from behind and wrenched the basket down and out of her grasp with both hands and ran off with it. He was charged in two counts with robbery and theft respectively and convicted on the first count of robbery. He appealed on the grounds: (i) that there was insufficient evidence of resistance to the snatching of the bag to constitute force on the person under s.8 of the Theft Act 1968; and (ii) that the learned judge's direction to the jury on the requirement of force on the person was inadequate and confused.

Held, dismissing the appeal, the old cases distinguished between force on the actual person and force on the property which in fact causes force on the person but, following *Dawson*, the court should direct attention to the words of the statute without referring to the old authorities. The old distinctions have gone. Whether the defendant used force on any person in order to steal is an issue that should be left to the jury. The judge's direction to the jury was adequate. He told the jury quite clearly at the outset what the statutory definition was, though thereafter he merely used the word "force" and did not use the expression "on the person".

Questions

1. What exactly did *Dawson* purport to decide on the question of "force?" What did the Court in *Clouden* treat it as deciding?
2. If a pickpocket "lifts" a wallet, for it to be "force on a person" need the victim feel the movement? Need the pickpocket realise that the victim might feel the movement?

3. Is it justifiable to treat a "non-violent" removal of a bag from the victim's presence so much more seriously than simple theft if the victim is actually holding it at the time?

4. In view of the other offences necessarily involved in a robbery situation, do we need a separate crime of robbery at all?

----

3. MAKING OFF WITHOUT PAYMENT

THEFT ACT 1978 S.3

(1) Subject to subsection (3) below, a person who, knowing that payment on the spot for any goods supplied or service done is required or expected from him, dishonestly makes off without having paid as required or expected and with intent to avoid payment of the amount due shall be guilty of an offence.

(2) For the purposes of this section 'payment on the spot' includes payment at the time of collecting goods on which work has been done or in respect of which service has been provided.

(3) Subsection (1) above shall not apply where the supply of the goods or the doing of the service is contrary to law, or where the service done is such that payment is not legally enforceable.

(4) Any person may arrest without warrant anyone who is, or whom he, with reasonable cause, suspects to be, committing or attempting to commit an offence under this section.

Note

No deception is needed; only dishonesty. Nor is it material whether ownership of goods has been transferred to the defendant, nor whether he was dishonest before or after any goods were supplied or service done. Many difficulties in the way of a prosecution for theft or obtaining property by deception are thus avoided, but the wording of the present offence is not without its own difficulties, e.g. as to "on the spot", "goods supplied", "makes off" "without having paid".

Questions

1. A travels on a train without first buying a ticket, as the regulations require. When challenged at the exit barrier at his destination, he runs away. Is he still "on the spot" when he makes off? Yes, according to *Moberly v Alsop*, *The Times*, 13 December 1991 (DC).

2. A, in a self-service store, picks up an article, puts it in his pocket and dishonestly departs without paying for it. Can the article be described as "goods supplied"?

3. A, having eaten a meal at B's restaurant, persuades B to let him go without paying by falsely promising to return next day with the money. Is this "making off" by A? See *R. v Brooks & Brooks*, below.

4. A, having consumed a meal, absent-mindedly leaves without paying. On being followed out into the street by the waiter, he realises his omission, but decides not to pay and runs away. Has A dishonestly made off? See *R. v Brooks & Brooks*, below.

5. A, having consumed a meal, discovers he has no money. To avoid a fuss, he slips out of the restaurant, intending to return next day with the money. Has A made off "with intent to avoid payment of the amount due"? See *R. v Allen*, below.

In *R. v Brooks & Brooks* (1983) 76 Cr. App. R. 66 at 68, the meaning of "makes off" was considered:

"We have been referred to a fuller examination of the definition of the offence which has been made in the academic field, notably by Professor Smith in *The Law of Theft* (4th ed. 1979) paragraph 242 and Mr J. R. Spencer in an article entitled 'The Theft Act 1978', [1979] Crim. L.R. 24, in particular at p.37 thereof. Thus Professor Smith comments that the words 'makes off' should be construed in a pejorative sense and includes both a sudden and secret departure but excludes departure consented to by means of a deception. Mr Spencer relies upon one meaning given to the term "makes off" in the *Shorter Oxford Dictionary*, namely 'to depart suddenly, often with a disparaging implication, to hasten away; to decamp'.

Pausing there, it is plain that the learned compilers do not suggest that the words must always be construed in the pejorative sense. In any case it is an unnecessary construction, for the words do not stand alone. The making off must be dishonest.

Mr Spencer is of the opinion that the term suggests a sudden and unexpected departure. In so doing he fails to consider one of the alternatives given in the dictionary, namely to 'decamp,' which may be an exercise accompanied by the sound of trumpets or a silent stealing away after the folding of tents. Obviously, the term covers a wide variety of modes of departure. Nevertheless, we strongly deprecate the involvement of a jury in any philosophic study, however interesting it may be to lawyers and academics. Nor do we adopt the attitude feared by Mr Spencer of simply saying it is 'all a question of fact for the jury'.

In our opinion, the words 'dishonestly makes off' are words easily understandable by any jury which, in the majority of cases, require no elaboration in a summing-up. The jury should be told to apply the words in their ordinary natural meaning and to relate them to the facts of the case. We agree with the decision in *R. v McDavitt* [1981] Crim. L.R. 843 that 'making off' involves a departure from the spot where payment is required."

R. V ALLEN

[1985] A.C. 1029 HL

A, who had incurred a bill of £1286 at a hotel, left without paying. Two days later, he rang to explain that he was in financial difficulties, he expected to be able to pay soon, and offered to return and deposit his passport as security. When he did return he was arrested and charged with making off without payment. In answer to a question from the jury, the judge directed them that the intent to avoid payment in s.3(1) did not have to be permanent but need only apply to the date on which A had avoided the payment on the spot that had been required or expected from him by the hotel. His conviction having been quashed by the Court of Appeal, the prosecution appealed to the House of Lords.

LORD HAILSHAM OF ST. MARYLEBONE

Despite some (though not unanimous) text book opinions in an opposite sense . . . I consider [the judge's] answer to be clearly erroneous. [His Lordship read s.3(1).]

The appellant's contention was that the effect of this section is to catch not only those who intend permanently to avoid payment of the amount due, but also those whose intention is to avoid payment on the spot, which, after all, is the time at which, *ex hypothesi*, payment has been 'expected or required', and the time, therefore, when the 'amount' became 'due'.

The judgment of the Court of Appeal, with which I agree, was delivered by Boreham J. He said [1985] 1 W.L.R. 50, 57:

'To secure a conviction under s.3 the following must be proved: (1) that the defendant in fact made off without making payment on the spot (2) the following mental elements—(a) knowledge that payment on the spot was required or expected of him; and (b) dishonesty; and (c) intent to avoid payment [sc. "of the amount due"].'

I agree with this analysis. To it the judge adds the following comment:

'If (c) means, or is taken to include, no more than an intention to delay or defer payment of the amount due it is difficult to see what it adds to the other elements. Anyone who knows that payment on the spot is expected or required of him and who then dishonestly makes off without paying as required or expected must have at least the intention to delay or defer payment. It follows, therefore, that the conjoined phrase 'and with intent to avoid payment of the amount due' adds a further ingredient—an intention to do more than delay or defer—an intention to evade payment altogether.'

My own view, for what it is worth, is that the section thus analysed is capable only of this meaning. But counsel for the appellant very properly conceded that, even if it were equivocal and capable of either meaning, in a penal section of this kind any ambiguity must be resolved in favour of the subject and against the Crown. Accordingly the appeal falls to be dismissed either if on its true construction it means unambiguously that the intention must be permanently to avoid payment, or if the clause is ambiguous and capable of either meaning. Even on the assumption that, in the context, the word 'avoid' without the addition of the word 'permanently' is capable of either meaning, which Boreham J. was inclined to concede, I find myself convinced by his final paragraph, which reads:

'Finally, we can see no reason why, if the intention of Parliament was to provide, in effect, that an intention to delay or defer payment might suffice, Parliament should not have said so in explicit terms. This *might* have been achieved by the insertion of the word "such" before payment in the phrase in question. It *would* have been achieved by a grammatical reconstruction of the material part of s.3(1) thus, "dishonestly makes off without having paid and with intent to avoid payment of the amount due as required or expected". To accede to the Crown's submission would be to read the section as if it were constructed in that way. That we cannot do. Had it been intended to relate the intention to avoid "payment" to "payment as required or expected" it would have been easy to say so. The section does not say so. At the very least it contains an equivocation which should be resolved in favour of the appellant.'

There is really no escape from this argument . . . In order to give the section now under consideration the effect required the section would have to be remodelled in the way suggested by Boreham J. in the passage quoted above, or the word 'and' in the ultimate phrase would have to be read as if it meant 'that is to say' so that the required intent would be equated with 'dishonestly' in the early part of the subsection.

Apart from a minor matter not relevant to the judgment there is nothing really to be added to the judgment delivered by Boreham J.

The minor matter to which I have just referred was the disinclination of the Court of Appeal to consider the 13th Report of the Criminal Law Revision Committee, Section 16 of the Theft Act 1968 (1977) (Cmnd. 6733), which led to the passing of the Act of 1978. In accordance with present practice, this, for the purpose of defining the mischief of the Act but not to construe it, their Lordships in fact have done. The 'mischief' is covered by paras 18 to 21 of the report and it is significant that the report was accompanied by a draft Bill, s.3 of which is in terms identical with s.3 of the Act, save that the proposed penalty was three years instead of two. Though we did not use it as an aid to construction, for the purpose of defining the mischief to be dealt with by the section, I consider it to be relevant. The discussion had originated from the decision in *D.P.P. v Ray*, and the committee defined the mischief in the following terms (para.18):

'there was general support for our suggestion that where the customer knows that he is expected to pay on the spot for goods supplied to him or services done for him it should be an offence for him dishonestly to go away without having paid *and intending never to pay*.' (Emphasis mine.)

From this it is plain beyond doubt that the mischief aimed at by the authors of the report was precisely that which the Court of Appeal, construing the section without reference to the report, attributed to the section by the mere force of grammatical construction.
[Lords Scarman, Diplock, Bridge and Brightman agreed.]

Prosecutions appeal dismissed

4. BURGLARY

The popular image of a burglar is someone who, at the dead of night, breaks into a house for the purpose of stealing property. This sort of conduct would, of course, constitute burglary, but in reality, the offence may be committed in a much broader range of circumstances. Burglary, contrary to popular belief, is not restricted to breaking into house in order to commit theft. In fact, burglary can be committed in a variety of different ways, some of which involve no element of theft at all.

THEFT ACT 1968 S.9.

(1) A person is guilty of burglary if—

    (a) he enters any building or part of a building as a trespasser and with intent to commit any such offence as is mentioned in subsection (2) below; or

    (b) having entered any building or part of a building as a trespasser he steals or attempts to steal anything in the building or that part of it or inflicts or attempts to inflict on any person therein any grievous bodily harm.

(2) The offences referred to in subsection (l)(a) above are offences of stealing anything in the building or part of a building in question, of inflicting on any person therein any grievous bodily harm and of doing unlawful damage to the building or any thing therein.

(3) A person guilty of burglary shall on conviction on indictment be liable to imprisonment for a term not exceeding—

    (a) where the offence was committed in respect of a building or part of a building which is a dwelling, fourteen years;

    (b) in any other case, ten years.

(4) References in subsections (1) and (2) above to a building, and the reference in subsection (3) above to a building which is a dwelling, shall apply also to an inhabited vehicle or vessel, and shall apply to any such vehicle or vessel at times when the person having a habitation in it is not there as well as at times when he is.

Note

The range of conduct prohibited by this section was before the Theft Act distributed between the offences of burglary, housebreaking and sacrilege, and the law was found in ss.25, 26 and 27 of the Larceny Act 1916. There were many intricate and confusing differences between the different offences; burglary proper needed a dwelling-house, a breaking and entering, and an intention to commit a felony, and it had to be committed in the night. The present offence may take place at any time of day. Any kind of building is now covered, and vehicles and vessels are also covered provided they are inhabited. Burglary in such a vehicle or vessel, or in a dwelt-in building, attracts a higher maximum penalty.

----

i. Entry

Note

Breaking, round which a great number of technicalities clustered, is no longer necessary, but entry is still required. This, too, was a highly technical concept, and as entry is not defined in the Act, it remains a question to that extent the pre-existing meaning is still operative. In that meaning, the law made a distinction between entry by the defendant's body and entry by an instrument wielded by him.

R. V HUGHES

(1785) 1 Leach 406

H with intent to steal property from a house, inserted a centre bit into a door near the bolt. The end of the bit penetrated the door but no part of the prisoner's body entered the house. He was indicted for burglary. On the question of whether there was an entry:

COUNSEL FOR THE PRISONER

It has been held that the smallest degree of entry whatever is sufficient to satisfy the law. Putting a hand, or a foot, or a pistol over the threshold of the door, or a hook or other instrument through the broken pane of a window . . . have been decided to be burglarious entries; but the principle of all these new determinations is, that there has been such a previous breaking of the castle of the proprietor, as to render his property insecure . . . And in those cases where an instrument has formed any part of the question, it has always been taken to mean, not the instrument by which the breaking was made, but the instrument, as a hook, a fork or other thing by which the property was capable of being removed, introduced subsequent to the act of breaking . . . In the present case, the introduction of the instrument is part of the act of breaking, but it is impossible to conceive that it was introduced for the purpose of purloining property, for it is incapable of performing such an office.

The prisoner was acquitted

Note

But the insertion of any part of the body was an entry, whether the purpose of the insertion was to commit the ulterior felony or merely to effect entry: see *R. v Bailey* (1818) R. & R. 341.

However a remark in *R. v Collins*, by Edmund Davies LJ that the defendant had to have made "an effective and substantial entry" has proved problematic. In *R. v Brown* [1985] Crim. L.R. 212, it was held that whether there has been an entry is a question of fact for the jury. In this case D leaned through a broken shop window and stole goods. The Court of Appeal did not think that the word "substantial" was of any assistance. This left the problem, however, that entry of part of the body could be effective for one ulterior offence, as in this case for stealing, but not for another such as rape. While a charge of attempted burglary would be available for cases where partial entry would not be "effective" to commit the ulterior offence, this is not really a satisfactory solution.

In *R. v Ryan* [1996] Crim. L.R. 320, D was found by an elderly householder trapped with his head and arm inside a window. He was convicted of burglary but appealed contending that his actions could not constitute an "entry" as he could not have stolen anything as he was firmly stuck. The Court of Appeal held, following *Brown*, that entry of part of his body could constitute an entry and it was irrelevant whether or not he was capable of stealing anything. The Court did not go so far as to declare that the insertion of any part of D's body is sufficient to constitute an entry preferring to leave the matter to juries to decide. It is likely that the question of "effectiveness" is now no longer relevant but a firmer declaration of the law by the Court of Appeal would have resolved the matter once and for all. Furthermore, by leaving the issue to the jury to decide, rather than expressly affirming the common law rule, similar cases may end up being decided differently by different juries.

Question

Suppose D puts a child under 10 through a window, not to steal but to open a door and admit D who will himself steal. Is that entry by D?

----

ii. As a Trespasser

Note

In the case that follows, *R. v Collins*, the defendant was convicted of burglary with intent to rape, contrary to s.9(1)(a) of the Theft Act 1968. The offence of rape was, at the time, one of the prohibited offences listed in s.9(2). The Sexual Offences Act 2003 repealed the offence of rape from s.9(2) and created a new and distinct offence of "trespassing with intent to commit a sexual offence" (see above Ch.9). However, on the two central issues of "entry" and "trespass", *Collins* remains a leading authority.

R. V COLLINS

[1973] 1 Q.B. 100

C was convicted of burglary with intent to commit rape in the circumstances outlined in the judgment below.

EDMUND-DAVIES LJ

. . . Let me relate the facts. Were they put into a novel or portrayed on the stage, they would be regarded as being so improbable as to be unworthy of serious consideration and as verging at times on farce. At about 2 o'clock in the early morning of Saturday, July 24, 1971, a young lady of 18 went to bed at her mother's home in Colchester. She had spent the evening with her boyfriend. She had taken a certain amount of drink, and it may be that this fact affords some explanation of her inability to answer satisfactorily certain crucial questions put to her at the trial.

She has the habit of sleeping without wearing night apparel in a bed which is very near the lattice-type window of her room. At one stage in her evidence she seemed to be saying that the bed was close up against the window which, in accordance with her practice, was wide open. In the photographs which we have before us, however, there appears to be a gap of some sort between the two, but the bed was clearly quite near the window.

At about 3.30 or 4 o'clock she awoke and she then saw in the moonlight a vague form crouched in the open window. She was unable to remember, and this is important, whether the form was on the outside of the window sill or on that part of the sill which was inside the room, and for reasons which will later become clear, that seemingly narrow point is of crucial importance.

The young lady then realised several things: first of all that the form in the window was that of a male; secondly, that he was a naked male; and thirdly, that he was a naked male with an erect penis. She also saw in the moonlight that his hair was blond. She thereupon leapt to the conclusion that her boyfriend, with whom for some time she had been on terms of regular and frequent sexual intimacy, was paying her an ardent nocturnal visit. She promptly sat up in bed, and the man descended from the sill and joined her in bed and they had full sexual intercourse. But there was something about him which made her think that things were not as they usually were between her and her boyfriend. The length of his hair, his voice as they exchanged what was described as 'love talk', and other features led her to the conclusion that somehow there was something different. So she turned on the bed-side light, saw that her companion was not her boyfriend and slapped the face of the intruder, who was none other than the defendant. He said to her, 'Give me a good time tonight', and got hold of her arm, but she bit him and told him to go. She then went into the bathroom and he promptly vanished.

The complainant said that she would not have agreed to intercourse if she had known that the person entering her room was not her boyfriend. But there was no suggestion of any force having been used upon her, and the intercourse which took place was undoubtedly effected with no resistance on her part.

The defendant was seen by the police at about 10.30 later that same morning. According to the police, the conversation which took place then elicited these points: He was very lustful the previous night. He had taken a lot of drink . . . He went on to say that he knew the complainant because he had worked around her house. On this occasion, during sexual intercourse—and according to the police evidence he added that he was determined to have a girl, by force if necessary, although that part of the police evidence he challenged—he went on to say that he walked around the house, saw a light in an upstairs bedroom, and he knew that this was the girl's bedroom. He found a step ladder, leaned it against the wall and climbed up and looked into the bedroom. He could see through the wide-open window a girl who was naked and asleep. So he descended the ladder and stripped off all his clothes, with the exception of his socks, because apparently he took the view that if the girl's mother entered the bedroom it would be easier to effect a rapid escape if he had his socks on than if he was in his bare feet. That is a matter about which we are not called upon to express any view, and would in any event find ourselves unable to express one.

Having undressed, he then climbed the ladder and pulled himself up on to the window sill. His version of the matter is that he was pulling himself in when she awoke. She then got up and knelt on the bed, she put her arms around his neck and body, and she seemed to pull him into the bed. He went on: 'I was rather dazed because I didn't think she would want to know me. We kissed and cuddled for about 10 or 15 minutes and than I had it away with her but found it hard because I had had so much to drink.'

The police officer said to the defendant: 'It appears that it was your intention to have intercourse with this girl by force if necessary, and it was only pure coincidence that this girl was under the impression that you were her boyfriend and apparently that is why she consented to allowing you to have sexual intercourse with her.' It was alleged that he then said, 'Yes, I feel awful about this. It is the worst day of my life, but I know it could have been worse.' Thereupon the officer said to him—and he challenges this: 'What do you mean, you know it could have been worse?,' to which he is alleged to have replied: 'Well, my trouble is drink and I got very frustrated. As I've told you, I only wanted to have it away with a girl and I'm only glad I haven't really hurt her.'

Then he made a statement under caution, in the course of which he said: 'When I stripped off and got up the ladder I made my mind up that I was going to try and have it away with this girl. I feel terrible about this now, but I had too much to drink. I am sorry for what I have done.'

In the course of his testimony, the defendant said that he would not have gone into the room if the girl had not knelt on the bed and beckoned him into the room. He said that if she had objected immediately to his being there or his having intercourse he would not have persisted. While he was keen on having sexual intercourse that night, it was only if he could find someone who was willing. He strongly denied having told the police that he would if necessary, have pushed over some girl for the purpose of having intercourse . . .

Now, one feature of the case which remained at the conclusion of the evidence in great obscurity is where exactly Collins was at the moment when, according to him, the girl manifested that she was welcoming him. Was he kneeling on the sill outside the window or was he already inside the room, having climbed through the window frame, and kneeling upon the inner sill? It was a crucial matter, for there were certainly three ingredients that it was incumbent upon the Crown to establish. Under section 9 of the Theft Act, 1968, which renders a person guilty of burglary if he enters any building or part of a building as a trespasser and with the intention of committing rape, the entry of the accused into the building must first be proved. Well, there is no doubt about that, for it is common ground that he did enter this girl's bedroom. Secondly, it must be proved that he entered as a trespasser. We will develop that point a little later. Thirdly, it must be proved that he entered as a trespasser with intent at the time of entry to commit rape therein.

The second ingredient of the offence—the entry must be as a trespasser—is one which has not, to the best of our knowledge, been previously canvassed in the courts . . .

What does that involve? According to the editors of Archbold Criminal Pleading Evidence & Practice, 37th ed. (1969), para.1505: 'Any intentional, reckless or negligent entry into a building will, it would appear, constitute a trespass if the building is in the possession of another person who does not consent to the entry. Nor will it make any difference that the entry was the result of a reasonable mistake on the part of the defendant, so far as trespass is concerned.' If that be right, then it would be no defence for this man to say (and even were he believed in saying), 'Well, I honestly thought that this girl was welcoming me into the room and I therefore entered, fully believing that I had her consent to go in.' If Archbold is right, he would nevertheless be a trespasser, since the apparent consent of the girl was unreal, she being mistaken as to who was at her window. We disagree. We hold that, for the purposes of section 9 of the Theft Act, a person entering a building is not guilty of trespass if he enters without knowledge that he is trespassing or at least without acting recklessly as to whether or not he is unlawfully entering.

A view contrary to that of the editors of *Archbold* was expressed in Professor Smith's book on *The Law of Theft*, 1st ed. (1968), where, having given an illustration of an entry into premises, the author comments, at paragraph 462: 'It is submitted that D . . . should be acquitted on the ground of lack of *metis rea*. Though, under the civil law, he entered as a trespasser, it is submitted that he cannot be convicted of the criminal offence unless he knew of the facts which caused him to be a trespasser or, at least, was reckless.'

The matter has also been dealt with by Professor Griew, who in paragraph 4–05 of his work *The Theft Act 1968* has this passage: 'What if D. wrongly believes that he is not trespassing? His belief may rest on facts which, if true, would mean that he was not trespassing: for instance, he may enter a building by mistake, thinking that it is the one he has been invited to enter. Or his belief may be based on a false view of the legal effect of the known facts: for instance, he may misunderstand the effect of a contract granting him a right of passage through a building. Neither kind of mistake will protect him from tort liability for trespass. In either case, then, D. satisfies the literal terms of section 9(1): he "enters . . . as a trespasser." But for the purposes of criminal liability a man should be judged on the basis of the facts as he believed them to be, and this should include making allowances for a mistake as to rights under the civil law. This is another way of saying that a serious offence like burglary should be held to require *mens rea* in the fullest sense of the phrase: D. should be liable for burglary if he knowingly trespasses or is reckless as to whether he trespasses or not. Unhappily it is common for Parliament to omit to make clear whether *mens rea* is intended to be an element in a statutory offence. It is also, though not equally, common for the courts to supply the mental element by construction of the statute.'

We prefer the view expressed by Professor Smith and Professor Griew to that of the editors of *Archbold*. In the judgment of this court there cannot be a conviction for entering premises 'as a trespasser' within the meaning of s.9 of the Theft Act unless the person entering does so knowing that he is a trespasser and nevertheless deliberately enters, or, at the very least, is reckless as to whether or not he is entering the premises of another without the other party's consent.

Having so held, the pivotal point of this appeal is whether the Crown established that this defendant at the moment that he entered the bedroom knew perfectly well that he was not welcome there or, being reckless as to whether he was not welcome or not, was nevertheless determined to enter. That in turn involves consideration as to where he was at the time that the complainant indicated that she was welcoming him into her bedroom. If, to take an example that was put in the course of argument, her bed had not been near the window but was on the other side of the bedroom, and he (being determined to have her sexually even against her will) climbed through the window and crossed the bedroom to reach her bed, then the offence charged would have been established. But in this case, as we have related, the layout of the room was different, and it became a point of nicety which had to be conclusively established by the Crown as to where he was when the girl made welcoming signs, as she unquestionably at some stage did.

How did the judge deal with this matter? We have to say regretfully that there was a flaw in his treatment of it. Referring to section 9, he said 'There are three ingredients. First is the question of entry. Did he enter into that house? Did he enter as a trespasser? That is to say, was the entry, if you are satisfied that there was an entry, intentional or reckless? And, finally, and you may think this is the crux of the case as opened to you by Mr. Irwin, if you are satisfied that he entered as a trespasser, did he have the intention to rape this girl?'

The judge then went on to deal in turn with each of these three ingredients. He first explained what was involved in 'entry' into a building. He then dealt with the second ingredient. But here he unfortunately repeated his earlier observation that the question of entry as a trespasser depended on 'was the entry intentional or reckless?' We have to say that this was putting the matter inaccurately. This mistake may have been derived from a passage in the speech of counsel for the Crown when replying to the submission of 'no case'. Mr. Irwin at one stage said: 'Therefore, the first thing that the Crown have got to prove, my Lord, is that there has been a trespass which may be an intentional trespass, or it may be a reckless trespass.' Unfortunately the judge regarded the matter as though the second ingredient in the burglary charged was whether there had been an intentional or reckless entry, and when he came to develop this topic in his summing up that error was unfortunately perpetuated. The judge told the jury: 'He had no right to be in that house, as you know, certainly from the point of view of the girl's parent. But if you are satisfied about entry, did he enter intentionally or recklessly? What the prosecution say about that is, you do not really have to consider recklessness because when you consider his own evidence he intended to enter that house, and if you accept the evidence I have just pointed out to you, he in fact did so. So, at least, you may think, it was intentional. At the least, you may think it was reckless because as he told you he did not know whether the girl would accept him.'

We are compelled to say that we do not think the judge by these observations made sufficiently clear to the jury the nature of the second test about which they had to be satisfied before this young man could be convicted of the offence charged. There was no doubt that his entry into the bedroom was 'intentional'. But what the accused had said was, 'She knelt on the bed, she put her arms around me and then I went in.' If the jury thought he might be truthful in that assertion, they would need to consider whether or not, although entirely surprised by such a reception being accorded to him, this young man might not have been entitled reasonably to regard her action as amounting to an invitation to him to enter. If she in fact appeared to be welcoming him, the Crown do not suggest that he should have realised or even suspected that she was so behaving because, despite the moonlight, she thought he was someone else. Unless the jury were entirely satisfied that the defendant made an effective and substantial entry into the bedroom without the complainant doing or saying anything to cause him to believe that she was consenting to his entering it, he ought not to be convicted of the offence charged. The point is a narrow one, as narrow maybe as the window sill which is crucial to this case. But this is a criminal charge of gravity and, even though one may suspect that his intention was to commit the offence charged, unless the facts show with clarity that he in fact committed it he ought not to remain convicted.

Some question arose as to whether or not the defendant can be regarded as a trespasser *ab initio*. But we are entirely in agreement with the view expressed in *Archbold*, again in paragraph 1505, that the common law doctrine of trespass *ab initio* has no application to burglary under the Theft Act, 1968. One further matter that was canvassed ought perhaps to be mentioned. The point was raised that, the complainant not being the tenant or occupier of the dwelling house and her mother being apparently in occupation, this girl herself could not in any event have extended an effective invitation to enter, so that even if she had expressly and with full knowledge of all material facts invited the defendant in, he would nevertheless be a trespasser. Whatever be the position in the law of tort, to regard such a proposition as acceptable in the criminal law would be unthinkable.

We have to say that this appeal must be allowed on the basis that the jury were never invited to consider the vital question whether this young man did enter the premises as a trespasser, that is to say knowing perfectly well that he had no invitation to enter or reckless of whether or not his entry was with permission . . .

Appeal allowed

R. V JONES AND SMITH

[1976] 3 All E.R. 54

J and S were convicted of burglary contrary to s.9(1)(b) of the Theft Act 1968. They had entered the house of S's father and stolen two television sets. S's father had reported the theft to the police at the time, but at the trial, he gave evidence to the effect that he had given S unreserved permission to enter the house, stating that S "would not be a trespasser in the house at any time". J and S appealed.

JAMES LJ

The next ground of appeal relied on by Counsel for the appellants in his argument is that which is put forward in the first of each of the defendants' grounds. It is the point upon which Counsel had laid the greatest stress in the course of his argument. The argument is based upon the wording of the Theft Act 1968, section 9(1)(b) . . .

The important words from the point of view of the arguments in this appeal are 'having entered any building . . . as a trespasser.' This is a section of an Act of Parliament which introduced a novel concept. Entry as a trespasser was new in 1968 in relation to criminal offences of burglary. It was introduced in substitution for, as an improvement upon, the old law which required considerations of breaking and entering and involved distinctions of nicety which had bedevilled the law for some time.

Counsel for the appellants argued that a person who had a general permission to enter premises of another person cannot be a trespasser. His submission is as short and as simple as that. Related to this case he says that a son to whom a father has given permission generally to enter the father's house cannot be a trespasser if he enters it even though he had decided in his mind before making the entry to commit a criminal offence of theft against the father once he had got into the house and had entered that house solely for the purpose of committing that theft. It is a bold submission. Counsel frankly accepts that there has been no decision of the court since this Act was passed which governs particularly this point. He has reminded us of the decision in *Byrne v Kinematograph Renters Society Ltd* [1958] 1 W.L.R. 762, which he prays in aid of his argument. In that case persons had entered a cinema by producing tickets not for the purpose of seeing the show, but for an ulterior purpose.

It was held in the action, which sought to show that they entered as trespassers pursuant to a conspiracy to trespass, that in fact they were not trespassers. The important words in the judgment are (at p.776): 'They did nothing that they were not invited to do . . .' That provides a distinction between that case and what we consider the position to be in this case.

Counsel has also referred us to one of the trickery cases, *R. v Boyle*, [1954] 2 Q.B. 292, and in particular to a passage in the judgment of that case (at p.295). He accepts that the trickery cases can be distinguished from such a case as the present because in the trickery cases it can be said that that which would otherwise have been consent to enter was negatived by the fact that consent was obtained by a trick. We do not gain any help in the particular case from that decision.

We were also referred to *R. v Collins*, and in particular to the long passage of Edmund Davies L.J., where he commenced the consideration of what is involved by the words 'the entry must be "as a trespasser"'. Again it is unnecessary to cite that long passage in full; suffice it to say that this court on that occasion expressly approved the view expressed in Professor Smith's book on the Law of Theft, and also the view of Professor Griew in his publication on the Theft Act 1968 on this aspect of what is involved in being a trespasser.

In our view the passage there referred to is consonant with the passage in the well known case of *Hillen and Pettigrezu v I.C.I. (Alkali) Ltd* [1936] A.C. 65 where, in the speech of Lord Atkin, these words appear:

'My Lords, in my opinion this duty to an invitee only extends so long as and so far as the invitee is making what can reasonably be contemplated as an ordinary and reasonable use of the premises by the invitee for the purposes for which he has been invited. He is not invited to use any part of the premises for purposes which he knows are wrongfully dangerous and constitute an improper use. As Scrutton L.J. has pointedly said (*The Carlgarth, the Ontarama* [1927] P. 93 at 110) "When you invite a person into your house to use the stair case you do not invite him to slide down the banisters."'

The decision in *R. v Collins* in this court, a decision on the criminal law, added to the concept of trespass as a civil wrong only the mental element of *mens rea*, which is essential to the criminal offence. Taking the law as expressed in *Hillen and Pettigrezu v I.C.I. (Alkali) Ltd* and *R. v Collins*, it is our view that a person is a trespasser for the purpose of section 9(1)(b) of the Theft Act 1968 if he enters premises of another knowing that he is entering in excess of the permission that has been given to him to enter, providing the facts are known to the accused which enable him to realise that he is acting in excess of the permission given or that he is acting recklessly as to whether he exceeds that permission, then that is sufficient for the jury to decide that he is in fact a trespasser.

In this particular case it was a matter for the jury to consider whether, on all the facts, it was shown by the prosecution that the appellants entered with the knowledge that entry was being effected against the consent or in excess of the consent that had been given by Mr Alfred Smith to his son Christopher. The jury were, by their verdict, satisfied of that. It was a novel argument that we heard, interesting but one without, in our view, any foundation

Finally, before parting with the matter, we would refer to a passage of the summing-up to the jury which I think one must read in full. In the course of that the recorder said:

'I have read out the conversation they had with Detective Sergeant Tarrant and in essence Smith said, "My father gave me leave to take these sets and Jones was invited along to help. If that account may be true, that is an end of the case, but if you are convinced that that night they went to the house and entered as trespassers and had no leave or licence to go there for that purpose, and they intended to steal these sets and keep them permanently themselves, acting dishonestly, then you will convict them. Learned counsel for the prosecution did mention the possibility that you might come to the conclusion that they had gone into the house with leave or licence of the father and it would be possible for you to bring in a verdict simply of theft but, members of the jury, of course it is open to you do to that if you felt that the entry to the house was a consequence of the father's leave or licence, but what counts of course for the crime of burglary to be made out is the frame of mind of each person when they go into the property. If you go in intending to steal, then your entry is burglarious, it is to trespass because no one gave you permission to go in and steal in the house."'

Then the recorder gave an illustration of the example of a person who is invited to go into a house to make a cup of tea and that person goes in and steals the silver and he went on:

'I hope that illustrates the matter sensibly. Therefore you may find it difficult not to say, if they went in there they must have gone in order to steal because they took elaborate precautions, going there at dead of night, you really cannot say that under any circumstances their entry to the house could have been other than trespass.'

In that passage that I have just read the recorder put the matter properly to the jury in relation to the aspect of trespass and on this ground of appeal as on the others we find that the case is not made out, that there was no misdirection, as I have already indicated early in the judgment, and in those circumstances the appeal will be dismissed in the case of each of the appellants.

Appeals dismissed

Questions

1. Smith was not residing with his father at the time of the theft. Would it have made any difference if he had been so residing?

2. A knocks on the door of his neighbour, Miss B. Miss B, recognising him and thinking his call is purely social, invites him in, and he goes in. In fact A's intention is steal from Miss B. On the question of whether A is guilty of burglary, do the cases of *Collins*, and *Jones and Smith* give different answers?

3. Does it follow from *Jones and Smith* that an intending shoplifter necessarily commits burglary as soon as he walks through the door of the shop? Consider the following from Dawson J in *Barker v R.* (1983) 57 A.L.J.R. 426 at 440 High Court of Australia:

    "It is essential to recognise that the offence consists both of an intentional entry as a trespasser and an intent to steal at the time of entry. The distinction must be maintained because a person accused of burglary may enter premises with an intention to steal but nevertheless in the belief that he is entitled to enter. A person who enters premises with apparent consent but with intent to steal, such as an ordinary shoplifter, is likely to believe at the time he enters the premises that he has the same right of entry as other persons notwithstanding the criminal purpose for which he enters. If interrupted before attempting to steal anything, no doubt he would say that he had done nothing wrong and was entitled to be on the premises. And if he believed that to be so, as he very well might, the mental element required to prove entry as a trespasser would be lacking, notwithstanding evidence of that other aspect of intent required for burglary, an intent to steal at the time of entry. Before there can be a burglary there must be an entry as a trespasser with intent to enter as a trespasser as well as with intent to steal."

4. If A, while in a shop, forms the intent to steal, that is no offence. If he attempts to steal or actually steals, he is liable to seven years imprisonment. But whether or not he steals or attempts to steal, if he formed the intent to steal before entering the shop, he is (subject to Dawson J's remarks) liable to 10 years imprisonment. What policy of the law can be thought to demand this extra punishment?

----

iii. Buildings or Parts of Buildings

Notes

1. The word "building" in statute law has had many different meanings given to it. Under the Malicious Damage Act 1861, the word was held to cover a house which was unfinished but substantially complete and with a roof on; *R. v Manning* (1871) L.R. 1 C.C.R. 338. In *Stevens v Gourlay* (1859) 7 C.B. (N.S.) 99, the CCCR held that both the ordinary meaning and the presumed intention

of the legislature must be looked at. Thus a wooden structure intended as a shop was held to be a building for the purposes of the Metropolitan Building Act 1855, the court holding that an object of the Act was to prevent the metropolis from being covered by combustible structures. The ordinary meaning was held to require a structure of considerable size and intended to be permanent or at least to endure for a considerable time. Vehicles are not buildings unless they are inhabited, thus a houseboat treated as a dwelling is a building: *Coleman* [2013] EWCA Crim 544). It seems to be agreed that tents are not buildings and that portability alone does not prevent a structure from being a building. Apart from that, little can be said with confidence, and puzzles such as a band-stand, or telephone kiosk, will have to be elucidated as and when cases arise.

2.   Entry as a trespasser into a "part" of a building, *either* with intent to commit a relevant crime in that part, or followed by the commission of a relevant crime in that part is also burglary, even if there is no trespassory entry of the building as a whole. Most "parts" of buildings, e.g. rooms, cause no difficulty, but doubt might be caused by less differentiated areas, e.g. separate counters in a department store. It seems that there must be at least some physical demarcation for an area to be a "part" for the purposes of the law of burglary.

R. v Walkington (1979) 1 W.L.R. 1169 at 1175: W was convicted of burglary by entering a part consisting of a movable three-sided enclosure round a till in a department store. On appeal: Geoffrey Lane LJ. One really gets two extremes, as it seems to us. First of all you have the part of the building which is shut off by a door so far as the general public is concerned, with a notice saying "Staff Only" or "No admittance to customers." At the other end of the scale you have for example a single table in the middle of the store, which it would be difficult for any jury to find properly was a part of the building, into which the licensor prohibited customers from moving.

Here, it seems to us, there was a physical demarcation. Whether there was sufficient to amount to an area from which the public were plainly excluded was a matter for the jury. It seems to us that there was ample evidence on which they could come to the conclusion: (a) that the management had impliedly prohibited customers entering that area, and (b) that this particular defendant knew of that prohibition.

----

iv. Intent to Commit an Offence in the Building

ATTORNEY GENERAL'S REFERENCES (NOS 1 AND 2 OF 1979)

[1980] Q.B. 180

The references arose out of two cases in each of which the judge directed an acquittal.

In Case 1, A was discovered ascending the stairs to the private rooms above a grocer's shop, where he had no right to be. He said he was looking for money to steal. He was charged with burglary with intent to steal.

In Case 2, B at 03.15 was discovered by a householder trying to force the french windows of her house. He said he wasn't going to damage anything, only to see if there was anything lying around. He was charged with attempting to enter the house with intent to steal therein.

ROSKILL LJ

The matters arising for determination are of wide general importance for the administration of justice both in the Crown Court and in magistrates' courts. There appears from what we have been told by counsel and from an admirable memorandum prepared by the Law Commission for the assistance of the court on these references, to be a question of law which is causing and has caused considerable confusion, and has led to what would appear to be unjustified acquittals as a result of circuit judges or their deputies in the Crown Court and also magistrates' courts acceding to submissions that there was no case to answer, the submissions being based on a single sentence in the judgment of this court in *R. v Husseyn* (Note) (1977) 67 Cr.App.R. 131, decided on December 8, 1977, the court consisting of Viscount Dilhorne, Lord Scarman and the late Cusack J. The Attorney-General has referred two such cases decided in the Crown Court to this court in order that a decision may be obtained whether the acquittals with which we are immediately concerned, and also certain other acquittals of which we have been told, were in fact justified.

The question referred to in Reference No. 1 is:

'Whether a man who has entered a house as a trespasser with the intention of stealing money therein is entitled to be acquitted of an offence against section 9(1)(a) of the Theft Act 1968 on the grounds that his intention to steal is conditional upon his finding money in the house.'

The answer of this court to this question is 'No'. In the second reference the question is:

'Whether a man who is attempting to enter a house as a trespasser with the intention of stealing anything of value which he may find therein is entitled to be acquitted of the offence of attempted burglary on the ground that at the time of the attempt his said intention was insufficient to amount to 'the intention of stealing anything' necessary for conviction under section 9 of the Theft Act 1968.'

The answer of this court to this question is also 'No.' . . .

[In *R. v Husseyn* Viscount Dilhorne expressed strong disapproval of the use of 'conditional intention. In their memorandum the Law Commission stated that' conditional intention 'means that the accused does not know what he is going to steal but intends that he will steal whatever he finds of value or worthwhile stealing.']

We respectfully agree with Viscount Dilhorne's stated strong disapproval of the phrase, but if it is to be used, it should only be used for that limited purpose set out in the last sentence which I have read. In paragraph 13 the [Law Commission memorandum] goes on:

'The doctrine finds its first expression in the statement of Lord Scarman in *R. v Husseyn*, that "it cannot be said that one who has it in mind to steal only if what he finds is worth stealing has a present intention to steal." *R. v Husseyn* was a case of attempted theft and, taken literally, the statement means that a conditional intent to steal in the sense of an intention to steal whatever the accused may find worth stealing or of value is insufficient to ground a charge of attempted theft. It follows from this that a charge or indictment for attempted theft must necessarily be quashed as bad in law if it specifies the mental element as "intending, at that time, to steal whatever he might find worth stealing (or of value) therein". Thus, wherever the prosecution has to establish an intention to steal as one of the constituents of a theft-related offence, it must prove a fixed and settled intention, contemporaneous with the act forming the other (actus reus) element of the offence, on the part of the accused permanently to deprive someone of a specified identifiable object which either exists or is believed by the accused to exist in or near the scene of his operations (or "the target", as the references aptly describe it). This is self-evident in cases of completed theft or "successful" burglary or robbery where, *ex hypothesi*, the accused is charged with having appropriated a specific identifiable object. The importance of the doctrine lies in the field of attempted theft or other cases where, although an intention to steal is required, the relevant *actus reus* does not postulate that anything should necessarily have been appropriated. These offences include burglary, attempted burglary, assault with intent to rob, or, as a suspected person, loitering with intent to steal or rob.'

Thus the so called doctrine of 'conditional intention' is described.

It will be useful to go through some of the cases to show how this so called doctrine has developed and to explain, as each member of this court is satisfied is the position, that the whole problem arises from a misunderstanding of a crucial sentence in Lord Scarman's judgment, which must be read in the context in which it was uttered, namely an indictment which charged an attempt to steal a specific object.

[His Lordship then considered *R. v Stark* Unreported 5 October 1967; *R. v Easom*; *R. v Husseyn*, and continued:] Lord Scarman [in *R. v Husseyn*] dealt with the law relating to attempts at p.132 and said that in that respect there was no misdirection by the judge. But his Lordship then went on:

'Very different considerations apply when one comes to consider the way the learned judge summed up the issue of intention. The learned judge said that the jury could infer that what the young men were about was to look into the holdall and, if its contents were valuable, to steal it. In the view of this court that was a misdirection. What has to be established is an intention to steal at the time when the step is taken, which constitutes or which is alleged to constitute, the attempt. Edmund Davies L.J. put the point in *R. v Easom*. In every case of theft the appropriation must be accompanied by the intention of permanently depriving the owner of his property. What may be *loosely* described as a "conditional" appropriation will not do. If the appropriator has it in mind merely to deprive the owner of such of his property as, on examination, proves worth taking and then, finding that the booty is valueless to the appropriator, leaves it ready to hand to be repossessed by the owner, the appropriator has not stolen.' The direction of the learned judge in this case is exactly the contrary. It must be wrong, for it cannot be said that one who has it in mind to steal only if what he finds is worth stealing has a present intention to steal.'

We were asked to say that either that last sentence was wrong or that it was *obiter*. We are not prepared to do either. If we may say so with the utmost deference to any statement of law by Lord Scarman, if this sentence be open to criticism, it is because in the context it is a little elliptical. If one rewrites that sentence, so that it reads: 'It must be wrong, for it cannot be said that one who has it in mind to steal only if what he finds is worth stealing has a present intention to steal *the specific item charged*,' (our emphasis added), then the difficulties disappear, because, as already stated, what was charged was attempted theft of a specific object just as what had been charged in *R. v Easom* had been the theft of a number of specific objects.

[His Lordship then considered *R. v Hector* (1978) 67 Cr. App. R. 224, and continued]. So we have these four cases: *Stark*, *Easom*, *Husseyn* and *Hector*. In each the charge related to specific objects and in each the conviction was quashed because there had been a misdirection or because the Crown was not in a position to prove that there was on the part of the accused person or persons at the relevant time an intent to steal or to attempt to steal the specific objects which were the subject of the charges or for both those reasons. None of those cases is authority for the proposition that if a charge is brought under section 9(1) of entering any building or part of a building as a trespasser with intent to steal, the accused is entitled to acquittal unless it can be shown that at the time he entered he had the intention of stealing specific objects.

The last case to which it is necessary to refer is *R. v Walkington* [1979] 1 W.L.R. 1169. Mr Tudor Price for the Attorney-General and Mr. Simon Brown, who has appeared as *amicus curiae*, both agree that if *R. v Walkington* is right, as they submitted and as we think it clearly is, that decision is conclusive as to the answer in Reference No. 1, for the reasons given by Geoffrey Lane L.J. in giving the judgment of the court . . .

In *R. v Walkington* the indictment was for burglary. At the beginning of his judgment Geoffrey Lane L.J. set out the indictment, at p.1171:

'Statement of offence: Burglary, contrary to section 9(1)(a) of the Theft Act 1968. Particulars of offence: Terence Walkington on January 15th, 1977, entered as a trespasser part of a building known as Debenhams Store with intent to steal therein'

Be it noted there was no averment in those particulars of any intention to steal any specific or identified objects. Geoffrey Lane L.J., after dealing with the first point which is presently irrelevant, dealt with the second and relevant point, at p.1176:

. . . 'These submissions are based upon the decision of this court in *R. v Husseyn*: if we may say so respectfully, a most powerful court, because it consisted of Viscount Dilhorne, Lord Scarman and Cusak J.'

The Lord Justice then read the headnote and the passage—in Lord Scarman's judgment upon which we have already commented. Geoffrey Lane L.J. said, at pp.1177–1178:

'What Mr Osborne suggests to us is that that last passage—the last two sentences—meets the situation in this case and that if the facts were that the defendant in this case had it in mind only to steal if what he found was worth stealing, then he had no intention to steal. That is the way he put it. First of all we would like to say that the particulars of offence in *R. v Husseyn* were that the two men . . . "attempted to steal a quantity of sub-aqua equipment". Plainly what considerations have to be applied to a charge of attempting to steal a specific article are different considerations from those which have to be applied when one is considering what a person's intent or intention may be under section 9 of the Theft Act 1968. That, we feel, is sufficient to distinguish our case from *R. v Husseyn*.'

Then the Lord Justice read what Lord Scarman himself had said about *R. v Husseyn* in *D.P.P. v Nock* [1978] A.C. 979. I will return to this shortly—and said, at p.1178:

'In this case there is no doubt that the defendant was not on the evidence in two minds as to whether to steal or not. He was intending to steal when he went to that till and it would be totally unreal to ask oneself, or for the jury to ask themselves, the question, what sort of intent did he have? Was it a conditional intent to steal if there was money in the till or a conditional intention to steal only if what he found there was worth stealing? In this case it was a cash till and what plainly he was intending to steal was the contents of the till, which was cash. The mere fact that the till happened to be empty does not destroy his undoubted intention at the moment when he crossed the boundary between the legitimate part of the store and the illegitimate part of the store. The judge's direction which we have cited already covered that point, and the matter was accurately left to the jury.

It has again been pointed out to us, and it is right that we should make reference to it, that that decision in *R. v Husseyn* has apparently been causing some difficulty to judges of the Crown Court.'

The Lord Justice then referred to two cases reported in the Criminal Law Review and said that the brief report in the latter case would suffice to demonstrate the difficulties which had arisen. After reading that report Geoffrey Lane L.J. went on, at p.1179:

'A reading of that would make the layman wonder if the law had taken leave of its senses, because, if that is the proper interpretation to be applied to section 9(1)(a), there will seldom, if ever, be a case in which section 9(1)(a) will bite. It seems to this court that in the end one simply has to go back to the words of the Act itself which we have already cited, and if the jury are satisfied, so as to feel sure, that the defendant has entered any building or part of a building as a trespasser, and are satisfied that at the moment of entering he intended to steal anything in the building or that part of it, the fact that there was nothing in the building worth his while to steal seems to us to be immaterial. He nevertheless had the intent to steal. As we see it, to hold otherwise would be to make nonsense of this part of the Act and cannot have been the intention of the legislature at the one when the Theft Act 1968 was passed. Nearly every prospective burglar could no doubt truthfully say that he only intended to steal if he found something in the building worth stealing.

So, whilst acknowledging that these recent decisions do provide difficulties which have been pointed out to us clearly by Mr. Osborne, it seems to us in the end that one must have regard to the wording of the Act. If that is done, the meaning, in our view, is clear.'

I come back to what Lord Scarman himself said in *D.P.P. v Nock* [1978] A.C. 979. The relevant passage is at pp.999 to 1000. His Lordship, after referring to the decision of the House of Lords in *Haughton v Smith* said at p.1000:

'We were invited by the Crown to express an opinion as to the correctness or otherwise of three decisions of the Court of Appeal, *R. v Easom, Partington v Williams* (1975) 62 Cr.App.R. 220 and *R. v Husseyn*. Easom and Husseym (to which I was a party) were, I think, correctly decided: but each, like every other criminal appeal, turned on its particular facts and on the way in which the trial judge directed the jury on the law. In *Easom* Edmund Davies L.J. emphasised that in a case of theft the appropriation must be accompanied by the intention of permanently depriving the owner of his property. This, of course, follows from the definition of theft in section 1(1) of the Theft Act 1968. All that *Husseyn* decided was that the same intention must be proved when the charge is one of attempted theft unfortunately in *Husseyn* the issue of intention was summed up in such a way as to suggest that theft, or attempted theft, could be committed by a person who had not yet formed the intention which the statute defines as a necessary part of the offence. An intention to steal can exist even though, unknown to the accused, there is nothing to steal: but, if a man be in two minds as to whether to steal or not, the intention required by the statute is not proved.'

We venture to draw particular attention to the opening part of that last sentence: 'An intention to steal can exist even though, unknown to the accused, there is nothing to steal . . .'

We had an interesting discussion, with the help of Mr Tudor Price and Mr Simon Brown, how, in these cases of burglary or theft or attempted burglary or theft, it is in future desirable to frame indictments. Plainly it may be undesirable in some cases to frame indictments by reference to the theft or attempted theft of specific objects. Obviously draftsmen of indictments require the maximum latitude to adapt the particulars charged to the facts of the particular case, but we see no reason in principle why what was described in argument as a more imprecise method of criminal pleading should not be adopted, if the justice of the case requires it, as for example, attempting to steal some or all of the contents of a car or some or all of the contents of a handbag. The indictment in *R. v Walkington* is in no way open to objection. There is no purpose in multiplying further examples. It may be that in some cases further particulars might be asked for and if so the prosecution could in a proper case no doubt give them without difficulty. The important point is that the indictment should correctly reflect that which it is alleged that the accused did, and that the accused should know with adequate detail what he is alleged to have done.

Taking as an example the facts in *R. v Easom*, plainly what the accused intended was to steal some or all of the contents of the handbag if and when he got them into his possession. It seems clear from the latter part of Edmund Davies L.J's judgment that if he had been charged with an attempt to steal some or all of the contents of that handbag, he could properly have been convicted, subject of course to a proper direction to the jury.

It follows that this court respectfully and whole-heartedly adopts Geoffrey Lane L.J's judgment on the second question in *R. v Walkington* which, as I have already said, is conclusive of the answer in the first reference.

So far as the answer in the second reference is concerned, it would, as Mr Simon Brown very properly agreed, be very strange if a different answer had to be given in the second reference, which is concerned with attempted burglary, from that given in the first reference. In our view, notwithstanding the argument that Mr Shepherd attempted to advance in the first of the two Divisional Court cases, it is impossible to justify giving different answers according to whether the charge is burglary or attempted burglary, theft or attempted theft or loitering with intent to commit an arrestable offence, which in most cases will be theft. In our view both principle and logic require the same answers in all these cases.

For those reasons the answers in the two references will be, as I have already indicated, 'no' in the first and 'no' in the second.

Opinions accordingly

Note

On conditional intent in theft, see above.

----

v. The Ulterior Offence

Notes

1. It will be noted that the list of possible ulterior offences is different according to whether the charge is entering with intent under s.9(1)(a) or entering and committing under s.9(1)(b). Thus if A enters B's house as a trespasser with the intention of quarrelling with B, and in the course of the quarrel he deliberately breaks B's priceless Ming vase, A is not guilty of burglary, but he is guilty of burglary if he punches B and breaks his nose. And he is guilty of burglary if, when he entered, he intended to do either of these two things.

2. The wording of s.9(1)(b) does not require that, after trespassory entry, D should commit the *offence* of inflicting grievous bodily harm on any person in the building, only that he should inflict grievous bodily harm. It is thus possible on the wording for D to be guilty of burglary if he enters as a trespasser and *accidently*, even *lawfully*, inflicts grievous bodily harm. This was not intended, and the Draft Criminal Code Bill cl.147(b) puts right the mistake by requiring D to commit an offence of theft, attempted theft, or causing or attempting to cause serious bodily harm.

3.   The only dishonest offence in either list is theft: fraudulent abstraction of electricity under s.13 of the Theft Act is not covered: *Low v Blease* [1975] Crim. L.R. 513.

----

5. AGGRAVATED BURGLARY

THEFT ACT 1968 S.10

(1) A person is guilty of aggravated burglary if he commits any burglary and at the time has with him any firearm or imitation firearm, any weapon of offence, or any explosive; and for this purpose—

   (a) 'firearm' includes an airgun or air pistol, and 'imitation firearm' means anything which has the appearance of being a firearm, whether capable of being discharged or not; and
   (b) 'weapon of offence' means any article made or adapted for use for causing injury to or incapacitating a person, or intended by the person having it with him for such use; and
   (c) 'explosive' means any article manufactured for the purpose of producing a practical effect by explosion, or intended by the person having it with him for that purpose.

(2) A person guilty of aggravated burglary shall on conviction on indictment be liable to imprisonment for life.

Note

1.   *"At the time."* The time is the time of the burglary charged. In the case of entry with intent under s.9(1)(a), it is the time of entry as a trespasser. In the case of an ulterior offence after trespassory entry under s.9(1)(b), it is the time of the ulterior offence. In *R. v Francis* [1982] Crim. L.R. 363 CA, A and B banged on V's door with sticks, and then entered as trespassers. They discarded their sticks, but later stole articles in the house. The judge directed that the prosecution had to prove that they were armed when they entered. *Held*, if a person entered a building as a trespasser and stole under s.9(1)(b), he committed burglary at the moment he stole and he committed aggravated burglary only if he had with him a weapon of offence at the time when he stole.

Question

When D enters as a trespasser with intent to steal, he is not armed with a weapon of offence. Once inside the house, he picks up a golf club in case he is disturbed by the occupier. Being disturbed by the occupier, he threatens him with the club and then steals a valuable clock. Is D guilty of aggravated burglary? See *R. v O'Leary* (1986) 82 Cr. App. R. 341; and *R. v Kelly* (1992) 97 Cr. App. R. 245.

2.   *"Has with him"*: This means "knowingly" has with him: *R. v Cugullere* [1961] 1 W.L.R. 858; and one who has forgotten that he has the article with him is not "knowing" for this purpose: *R. v Russell* (1984) 81 Cr. App. R. 315. It is an open question whether it must be shown that D, who knowingly has an article, also knows that it is a weapon of offence: see *R. v Warner* [1969] 2 A.C. 256; *R. v Pierre* [1963] Crim. L.R. 513, decided under different statutes, which suggest the answer "No." The words "has with him" do not require that D should be actually carrying the weapon of offence at the time of the offence: *R. v Kelt* (1977) 3 All E.R. 1099 at 1102; an accomplice may be carrying it.

Where the firearm or weapon of offence is being carried by an accomplice, however, the offence of aggravated burglary will only be committed where the accomplice enters the building (see *Klass* [1998] 1 Cr. App. R. 453; and *Wiggins* [2012] EWCA Crim 885) as the gravamen of the offence is entry into a building with a weapon; if the accomplice carrying the weapon remains outside the burglary would not be an aggravated one.

3. *"Made or adapted for use for causing injury or incapacitation"*: If D at the relevant time has with him such an article, it is immaterial whether he intends it for such use. As to whether an article is so made or adapted, if it is one about which a realistic question can arise, it is for the jury to decide: *R. v Williamson* (1977) 67 Cr. App. R. 35, e.g. a sheath knife, where it would depend on the sort of knife in the sheath. But with a flick knife, the jury must take judicial notice that it is so made: *R. v Simpson* [1983] 3 All E.R. 789.

4. *"Intended by the person having it with him for such use."* If an article is not made or adapted for use for causing injury to or incapacitating a person, it is nevertheless a weapon of offence if "intended by the person having it with him for such use." The intended use need not be with respect to the particular burglary D is engaged in: *R. v Stones* (1989) 89 Cr. App. R. 26 CA. If A has with him a coil of rope with which he intends to tie up a watchman on the premises, the rope is a weapon of offence and if burglary is involved it will be aggravated burglary. But suppose A has with him an article, not otherwise a weapon of offence, which he does not intend to use on this or any other occasion, for injuring or incapacitating, but which, perhaps on the spur of the moment, he does in fact use for such purposes. A has a rope which he intends to use to lower stolen goods out of a window, but on being surprised by a watchman B, uses the rope to tie B up. Does A have with him an article intended for such use? In *R. v Kelly* (1992) 97 Cr. App. R. 245, it was held that it was sufficient that he had it with him at the time when he used it (distinguishing cases on similar wording in the Prevention of Crime Act 1953 s.1).

11   FRAUD

Note

The Theft Acts 1968 and 1978 and the Theft (Amendment) Act 1996 created a range of offences which contained the common element that the proscribed consequence was brought about as a result of the accused's dishonest deception. These offences covered obtaining property, services, a money transfer or a pecuniary advantage by deception and evading liability by deception.

The need to prove that someone had been deceived resulting in the relevant obtaining by D both created problems and left lacunae in the law. While it might be acceptable to conclude that a representation could be implied from D's words or conduct as well as express in order to amount to a deception (see *DPP v Ray* [1974] A.C. 370) it did stretch matters somewhat to suggest that an obtaining was the result of a deception where V was completely indifferent to the truth or otherwise of the implied representation D made when purchasing goods using a cheque supported by a cheque guarantee card (*Metropolitan Police Commissioner v Charles* [1977] A.C. 177) or by using a credit card to make the purchase (*Lambie* [1982] A.C. 449). In *Charles*, V was assured of payment because of the guarantee card being used even though D's bank account was overdrawn and he was no longer authorised to use the card; the false representation their Lordships construed from the facts was that D had authority to use the card—a representation he impliedly made in presenting it to support his cheques. The decision was only explicable if deception did not require a positive belief in the truth of the representation which was, in fact, false, it being sufficient that V was ignorant of the truth and acted in reliance upon the representation of authority. In *Lambie* where D purchased goods using a credit card when her authority to do so had been rescinded, the House of Lords held that the only inference to be drawn from the evidence of her use of the credit card was that V, the shop assistant, relied upon D's implicit representation that she had authority to use the card and that had V known the truth she would not have concluded the sale. V's evidence, however, was to the effect that the only thing she was concerned about was that the store be paid which would be assured if the conditions for credit card transactions (e.g. checking the signature) were observed. However, no amount of stretching the meaning of words could bring D's act within the definition of the deception offences where no human agent was deceived by D; if D used a false coin to obtain items from a machine, no person was deceived so no conviction could ensue. With the increasing use of electronic transactions involving no human agents (e.g. internet shopping and internet banking), this lacuna was a particular cause of concern. Similarly the deception offences could not be stretched to cover D's activities where D abused his own position of trust to enrich himself as, again, this did not involve anyone being deceived. The new offence of fraud seeks to provide for these situations while also covering situations such as those in *Charles* and *Lambie* without resorting to strained definitions of key elements of the offence.

In their Report on *Fraud* (TSO, 2002), Law Com. No.276, Cm.5560, the Law Commission came to the conclusion that a general offence of fraud would improve the criminal law stating (at para.1.6):

"(1) It should make the law more comprehensible to juries, especially in serious fraud trials. The charges which are currently employed in such trials are numerous, and none of them adequately describe or encapsulate the meaning of 'fraud'. The statutory offences are too specific to offer general description of fraud. Thus, at present, juries are not given a straightforward definition of fraud. If they were, and if that were the key to the indictment, it should enable them to focus more closely on whether the facts of the case fit the crimes as charged.

(2) A general offence of fraud would be a useful tool in effective prosecutions. Specific offences are sometimes wrongly charged, in circumstances when another offence would have been more suitable. This can result in unjustified acquittals and costly appeals. . . A generalised crime which nonetheless provides a clear definition of fraudulent behaviour may assist prosecutors to weigh up whether they have a realistic chance of securing a conviction.

(3) Introducing a single crime of fraud would dramatically simplify the law of fraud. Clear, simple law is fairer than complicated, inaccessible law. If a citizen is contemplating activities which could amount to a crime, a clear, simple law gives better guidance on whether the conduct is criminal, and fairer warning of what could happen if it is. Furthermore, when a defendant is charged with a clear, simple law, they will be better able to understand their options when pleading to the charge; and, if pleading not guilty, they will be better able to conduct their defence.

(4) A general offence of fraud would be aimed at encompassing fraud in all its forms. It would not focus on particular ways or means of committing frauds. Thus it should be better able to keep pace with developing technology."

In 2004, the Government, while broadly accepting the Law Commission's proposals, issued a Consultation Paper, *Fraud Law Reform: Consultation on Proposals for Legislation* (Home Office, 2004), followed by its response to the consultation in *Fraud Law Reform: Government Response to Consultations* (Home Office Criminal Policy Unit, 2005). In 2005, the Government introduced the Fraud Bill which largely adopted the Law Commission's recommendations with the exception that it did not provide for the abolition of the common law offence of conspiracy to defraud because of concerns expressed in the consultation as to limitations on the scope of statutory conspiracy which meant that certain types of secondary participation in fraud might only be caught by the common law offence.

In November 2006, the Fraud Act 2006 was enacted, coming into force on 15 January 2007. The Act repealed the deception offences in ss.15, 15A, 16, and 20(2) of the Theft Act 1968 and ss.1 and 2 of the Theft Act 1978. The Fraud Act created one offence of fraud in s.1 which could be committed in three different ways—by false representation (s.2(1)), by failing to disclose information (s.3) and by abuse of position (s.4). The Act also creates the offences of possession of articles for use in frauds (s.6), making or supplying articles for use in frauds (s.7), participating in fraudulent business carried on by sole trader (s.9), participating in fraudulent business carried on by company (s.10), and obtaining services dishonestly (s.11).

The major difference is that the old deception offences were *result* crimes as the deception had to lead to either the obtaining of property, services, a money transfer or a pecuniary advantage, or the evasion of a liability, whereas the new offence of fraud is a *conduct* crime there being no need to prove that any result ensued. The Fraud Act 2006 also creates a new offence of obtaining services dishonestly; this is a result crime like the offence of obtaining services by deception which it replaced but it is not limited by the concept of a deception. The 2006 Act further creates the offences of possession of any article for use in a fraud (s.6), and making or supplying any article for use in a fraud (s.7). It is testament to the drafting of the Fraud Act that there have been no appeals to the Court of Appeal in respect of its meaning or ambit in the first 34 months of its operation.

----

1. FRAUD

1 Fraud

(1) A person is guilty of fraud if he is in breach of any of the sections listed in subsection (2) (which provide for different ways of committing the offence).

(2) The sections are—

    (a) section 2 (fraud by false representation),
    (b) section 3 (fraud by failing to disclose information), and
    (c) section 4 (fraud by abuse of position).

Note

Section 1(1) of the Fraud Act 2006 creates the general offence of fraud which is committed where a person breaches ss.2, 3, or 4 which provide for different ways of committing the offence. On summary conviction the maximum sentence is 12 months' imprisonment or a fine up to the maximum or both. Following conviction on indictment the maximum sentence is 10 years' imprisonment or a fine or both.

    In the text which follows reference will be made to cases under the Theft Acts as these are still relevant when construing some of the terminology and considering some of the concepts in the Fraud Act 2006.

----

i. Fraud by false representation

2 Fraud by false representation

(1) A person is in breach of this section if he—

    (a) dishonestly makes a false representation, and
    (b) intends, by making the representation—
        (i) to make a gain for himself or another, or
        (ii) to cause loss to another or to expose another to a risk of loss.

(2) A representation is false if—

    (a) it is untrue or misleading, and
    (b) the person making it knows that it is, or might be, untrue or misleading.

(3) 'Representation' means any representation as to fact or law, including a representation as to the state of mind of—

    (a) the person making the representation, or
    (b) any other person.

(4) A representation may be express or implied.

(5) For the purposes of this section a representation may be regarded as made if it (or anything implying it) is submitted in any form to any system or device designed to receive, convey or respond to communications (with or without human intervention).

Notes

1. This is a conduct crime which means that there is no need to prove that any particular result ensued. The actus reus consists of the making of a false representation. There is no requirement that anyone should actually believe or act upon the representation. The offence is complete upon a false representation being made with the requisite mens rea. There is also no requirement that D actually obtain anything as a result of the false representation although this will generally be D's purpose. The mens rea for the offence requires proof of dishonesty, an intent to make a gain whether for himself or another, or to cause a loss to another or expose another to the risk of loss, and knowledge that the representation is, or might be, untrue or misleading. In relation to dishonesty, the test in *Ghosh* applies, that is first whether D's conduct would be regarded as dishonest by the ordinary standards of reasonable and honest people, and secondly whether D was aware that his conduct would be so regarded (see p.656 above noting that the qualifications in s.2 of the Theft Act 1968 do not apply to the offence of fraud). "Gain" and "loss" for the purposes of ss.2–4 are defined in s.5 (below) consistently with the definition in s.34(2)(a) of the Theft Act 1968 (see below, p.712).

2. In an era where inflated claims within, and omissions from, CVs and job application forms has become almost *de rigueur*, *Razoq* [2012] EWCA Crim 674, is a timely reminder that such actions may amount to crimes. D, who was a doctor suspended from practice by the hospital where he worked, applied for, and obtained, several locum positions (earning from them £100,000) having failed to disclose his suspension, and falsely claiming qualifications and experience he did not have. He was convicted of seven offences involving breaches of ss.2 and 3. In relation to the s.2 offences, the issue for the jury was whether his lies as regards his experience and his qualifications were told with a view to gaining the positions for which he applied.

----

5 'Gain' and 'loss'

(1) The references to gain and loss in sections 2 to 4 are to be read in accordance with this section.

(2) 'Gain' and 'loss'—

    (a) extend only to gain or loss in money or other property;
    (b) include any such gain or loss whether temporary or permanent;

    and 'property' means any property whether real or personal (including things in action and other intangible property).

(3) 'Gain' includes a gain by keeping what one has, as well as a gain by getting what one does not have.

(4) 'Loss' includes a loss by not getting what one might get, as well as a loss by parting with what one has.

The Government gave their analysis of the offence of fraud in their response to the 2004 consultation.

HOME OFFICE CRIMINAL POLICY UNIT, *FRAUD LAW REFORM: GOVERNMENT RESPONSE TO CONSULTATIONS* (2005)

(footnotes omitted)

Fraud by false representation (Question 1)

13. Most respondents welcomed this first limb of the general offence. They felt it had advantages over the existing law—in removing the difficulty of proving that the representation operated on the mind of the victim, and in addressing the following:

- cases where the victim is indifferent as to whether the representation is false or not;

- the activity of 'phishing' (i.e. the practice of sending requests which falsely claim to originate from banks, asking customers to re-register or 're-activate' their accounts at a replica bank website, with the aim of using the information provided to transfer money out of these accounts);

- 'application fraud' (the giving of false information in applying for eg a mortgage);

- dishonest doorstep trading.

14. The main controversy concerned the proposal that this offence will be committed not only when the defendant knows that his representation is false or misleading, but when he is 'aware that it might be'. The phrase is precedented, for example in section 6 of the Public Order Act 1986, where one of the conditions for several offences (eg riot and violent disorder) is that the person is 'aware that his conduct may be' harmful in one way or another (eg violent). However some respondents thought the phrase is too vague and potentially too wide.

15. One respondent suggested it should be replaced by the criterion that the offender had 'no reasonable grounds for believing it to be true'. We considered this and a similar alternative formulation: that the offender 'knows or ought to have known' that his representation was, or might be, false or misleading. The problem with objective tests like these is that any crime of dishonesty by its very nature requires a subjective fault and a case that failed a subjective test would be likely also to fail the *Ghosh* dishonesty test. Thus while such tests may be welcome to some, because they set a lower threshold for the offence than the 'aware that it might be' formulation, there may be objections to them in principle, for little practical gain.

16. We therefore concentrated on the suggestions for replacement which were based on a subjective test. There were 2 main proposals:

- *Cunningham* recklessness

- 'Knowing' (that it might be)

Several respondents were specifically opposed to the use of 'reckless' in view of the problems this term has posed in the past. Those who favoured it said it is well precedented (eg in section 15 of the Theft Act 1968) and argued that its meaning is now clearer, following the House of Lords decision in *R. v. G and another* [see p.108 above]. However many law enforcers think that an offender could make a false representation without being 'reckless' at any point. In practice subjective (*Cunningham*) recklessness is akin to awareness, but it was pointed out to us that there is a difference in that the former includes not only awareness of the risk, but the additional test that it was unreasonable of the offender to take the risk in all the circumstances known to him. It is therefore a slightly tighter and more complex test.

17. 'Knowing' was proposed as the most straightforward alternative to 'aware'. 'Know' is one of the dictionary meanings of 'aware' and vice versa. There is therefore little if any difference between the two, but 'know' is better precedented and less likely to give rise to technical arguments. We therefore decided to replace 'is aware that it might be' with 'knows that it might be'. The essential point is that an offence should be committed not only where the offender knows that he is making a representation that **is** false or misleading, but where he knows that it **might be** false or misleading.

18. There was a view from a few respondents that it would be going too far to provide that an offence is committed when the defendant knows his representation 'might be' misleading. An example was given of a seller of a Renoir painting which turns out to be incorrectly attributed. It was argued that, given the inevitable uncertainties in such areas, the seller would only be able to protect himself from a fraud charge if he had said 'I honestly believe

this to be a Renoir' rather than 'This is a painting by Renoir'. We do not agree as the 'dishonesty' requirement will assist in drawing the line in marginal cases. But if the consequence were that sellers became more cautious in their statements this does not seem an undesirable result.

19. The question of the meaning of 'misleading' was raised. It was suggested that it means less than wholly true and capable of an interpretation to the detriment of the victim. We would agree with that.

20. Cases of negligent misrepresentation were also raised: one example was where a person hires a car for a fixed period but fails to return it at the end of that time. It was argued that although this may be technically an offence, prosecutors are likely to advise at present that this is a matter for the parties to resolve in the civil courts. We think that the Bill does not change this practical position.

. . .

Definitions (Question 4)

30. Most respondents agreed that the definitions of 'gain', 'loss' and 'property' should be aligned with those used in the law of theft and accepted that the current definitions were tried and tested and had not given rise to problems. One pointed out that the same definitions also occur in the Trade Marks Act 1994.

31. Several respondents suggested that the definition of property should be expanded to include confidential financial data. We do not think any such change is appropriate or necessary, as simply by accessing confidential information, the offender will usually 'intend to make a gain'—albeit an economic gain from wrongful exploitation of the material, rather than a gain of the material itself. As long as that is his intention he is caught by the new offence. If he does not have that intention then fraud is arguably not the appropriate concept anyway. The Bill covers cases where, for example, an employee makes a gain by obtaining information by fraudulent means—for example, by abusing his position of trust. The new offence of being equipped to commit fraud also helps in this context: it will ensure that the possession of confidential financial information with the intent of committing fraud is a crime. In our view that strikes at the mischief, in a more practical way.

32. It was suggested that, as in the Theft Act, the term 'property' should be defined as including intangible property. We agree. That will ensure that intangible things that can be property—notably intellectual property—are covered. However an essential problem will remain in that it is unusual for intellectual property to be 'gained' or 'lost' when someone misuses it. Normally the mischief lies in unauthorised duplication or use. But if a person abuses his position or makes a false representation in order to interfere (in some way) with intellectual property, or to access confidential information, a person will usually be aiming at an economic gain and so will be caught by the general fraud offence anyway.

Note

The gain or loss must be in money or other property. In *Gilbert* [2012] EWCA Crim 2392, D used a false representation in order to open a bank account. D's conviction was quashed, however, as the bank account itself was not money or other property. While D might have used the account in the future to transact business and make a financial gain from such activity, the link between any such gain and the false representation was too tenuous and could not support a conviction for fraud.

Questions

Can D be liable for fraud in the following cases:

(a) D writes a letter to V, his elderly aunt, falsely stating that he is penniless and asking her for a loan to pay his university fees. The letter is lost in the post and never delivered to V.

(b) D attends a car boot sale. While P, stall-holder in the vehicle next to D, is distracted by a customer, D moves behind P's stall and offers to sell an antique vase on the stall to V who is showing an interest in it. D intends to pocket the money.

(c) Returning to his own stall a customer V enquires about a figurine on D's stall. D states, "I believe it is early 19th century Dresden". Such a figurine would be highly valuable. D, however, does not know anything about the figure's origins simply saying what he thinks might persuade V to purchase it. Would it make any difference if it turned out that the figurine actually was an example of early 19th century Dresden? (cf. *Deller* (1952) 36 Cr. App. R. 184.)

(d) D, knowing the PIN for his father's credit card, uses it without his authority to purchase some clothes from Next. The transaction goes through and his father's account is debited. What is the representation D has made in completing the transaction? Would it make any difference if, having entered his PIN on the terminal at the till, a fault in the telephone line prevented the transaction from being authorised?

(e) D, knowing the PIN for his father's debit card, uses it at a cash machine (ATM), without his father's authority, to withdraw cash.

(f) D advertises his car for sale stating in the advertisement "in good running order, very reliable, low running costs". Subsequently the car develops an intermittent fault which causes the engine to cut out. D discovers it will be very costly to repair. Two weeks after the initial advertisement, V responds and arranges to view the vehicle. V also takes a short test drive during which the engine does not cut out. D makes no oral representations to V as to the state of the vehicle. Does it make any difference to D's liability whether V buys the vehicle or not? (cf. *DPP v Ray* [1974] A.C. 370; *Rai* [2000] 1 Cr. App. R. 242.)

(g) D holds a garage sale with a large banner stating "Garage Sale to support Children in Need". D raises £500. Consider D's liability where: (a) he gives £10 to Children in Need but keeps the remainder; or (b) where he gives £250 to each of his children who need it to pay for the school history trip to Belgium which D cannot afford since losing his job.

(h) D has a grudge against V whom he wishes to impoverish. D inveigles his way into V's trust and then represents to him that he has inside information about a horse which is certain to win a race and he encourages V to bet £1000 on it. It is D's belief that the horse is certain to lose. Would it make any difference to D's liability if, on the race being run, the horse won?

----

ii. Fraud by failing to disclose information

3 Fraud by failing to disclose information

A person is in breach of this section if he—

(a) dishonestly fails to disclose to another person information which he is under a legal duty to disclose, and

(b) intends, by failing to disclose the information—

    (i)   to make a gain for himself or another, or
    (ii) to cause loss to another or to expose another to a risk of loss.

Note

The Law Commission recommended in the Law Commission's Report, *Fraud* (paras 7.22–7.34), a wider offence which would have incorporated situations falling short of a legal duty of disclosure where there was a moral duty to do so because V trusted D to make disclosure of information and it was reasonable to expect him to do so. The Law Commission provided the following example (at para.7.33):

> "For example, a dealer buying an antique is guilty of fraudulent nondisclosure if she knows that the seller is trusting her to disclose any marked discrepancy between the price offered and the true value of the item, *and* it is reasonable to expect her to do so. This is a question of degree. If the dealer knows that she can resell the item for £10,000, but does not disclose this and offers only £2,000, it would be open to a jury to conclude that her failure to disclose the true value was unreasonable. It would be otherwise if she did not expect to be able to resell the item for more than, say, £4,000, because it is not reasonable to expect a dealer to disclose the full extent of the reasonable profit she hopes to make, and such a mark-up would be within the bands of what is reasonable. In such a case we would expect the court to direct an acquittal, on the basis that no reasonable jury could be sure that it was reasonable to expect the defendant to disclose the information in question."

There would be a large number of imponderables in the above situation which a jury would be left to determine before convicting the antique dealer. The Law Commission identified these (para.7.34):

> "Whether the defendant is trusted to make disclosure, and if so whether a failure to disclose the information in question is unreasonable, will depend on a variety of factors—for example, whether the defendant is believed by the other to have special expertise, and if so whether the defendant has induced the other to believe this; whether the other has such expertise; the value of the transaction, from the other's point of view; whether the other is in receipt of legal, financial or other advice; and so on. A trial judge would of course remind a jury of any such factor that may have particular relevance to the facts of the case."

The Government in its response to the consultation concluded that the above proposal would create an undesirably wide offence with the potential for conflict between the civil law and criminal law.

HOME OFFICE CRIMINAL POLICY UNIT, *FRAUD LAW REFORM: GOVERNMENT RESPONSE TO CONSULTATIONS* (2005)

(footnotes omitted)

Fraud by failing to disclose information (Question 2)

21. This second limb of the general offence was generally welcomed, subject to the point discussed below. There was a suggestion that failure to disclose could in some cases amount to a false representation, and that therefore such cases were already covered by the first limb. However it was recognised that it might be helpful, particularly for juries, to have the point made clear on the face of the law.

22. The point of controversy was the proposal that this offence should extend to situations where a person dishonestly fails to disclose information which he is under no legal duty to disclose, but which the other person trusts him to disclose. There was substantial opposition to this proposal. One of the main arguments was that this would intrude on the caveat emptor principle, and create a conflict between civil and criminal law, in that it would become criminal not to provide information which you are entitled to withhold under civil law. *Arlidge and Parry on Fraud* says that this result would be 'bizarre'. The Law Commission argued that this situation already exists in relation to the law of theft, following the House of Lords decision in *Hinks* [see above, p.608]. In that case Lord Steyn said that in a practical world there will always be some disharmony between the systems.

23. The other main objection was the lack of certainty: while the requirement of 'dishonesty', which underlies all 3 limbs of the new fraud offence, provides a measure of protection, it will be necessary to make a judgement in each cases as to whether the 'victim' is trusting the defendant to disclose the information. The example of a person selling a car who does not reveal that he has successfully camouflaged some damage to the bodywork with filler is one example presented to us of a situation where it is arguable that the purchaser trusts a disclosure to be made, but consensus is lacking and it will be hard to say where the line should be drawn. It was pointed out that this is a problem not only for juries but for police in deciding what to investigate. It was argued that the conduct covered by Clause 3 (4) may be dishonest and morally reprehensible, but that does not mean it should be criminal.

24. Others argued against this that if the offence is restricted to situations where there is already a legal duty to provide information then it adds little to the existing law, as the failure to meet the legal obligation will carry its own sanction. Also criminal prosecutions may then hinge on civil arguments about whether the duty exists. They argued that it was desirable to cover cases such as the Law Commission's example of a vulnerable person being exploited by an antiques dealer, but some said that it was difficult to cover such cases without creating an undesirably wide offence.

25. Having carefully considered the arguments on both sides we were persuaded that failure to disclose information should not be fraud unless (inter alia) a legal duty is breached. In particular, we share the concerns over extending the criminal law into areas where something may be morally dubious, but not clearly seen as criminal. We believe even if we limit the offence to legal duties it will add to the existing law, as the existing sanctions for such failure may be of a civil nature and be both difficult to pursue and unlikely to lead to a sufficient sanction.

Note

The actus reus comprises a failure to disclose to another information which D is under a legal duty to disclose. The mischief which is targeted is that of V acting, or omitting to act, to his economic detriment in reliance upon his trusting D to disclose to him information relevant to his decision and D failing to make such disclosure. The mens rea for this offence is (1) an intention to make a gain or cause a loss (or expose to the risk of loss) as for fraud by false representation; and (2) dishonesty. There is no requirement that D should know that he is under, or might be under, a legal duty to disclose information. D's ignorance of such a legal duty, however, will be highly relevant to the question whether or not he was dishonest.

The Law Commission provided the following explanation for the offence which is reproduced in the Explanatory Notes to the Fraud Act 2006 (para.18):

> ".28 . . . Such a duty may derive from statute (such as the provisions governing company prospectuses), from the fact that the transaction in question is one of the utmost good faith (such as a contract of insurance), from the express or implied terms of a contract, from the custom of a particular trade or market, or from the existence of a fiduciary relationship between the parties (such as that of agent and principal).
>
> 7.29 For this purpose there is a legal duty to disclose information not only if the defendant's failure to disclose it gives the victim a cause of action for damages, but also if the law gives the victim a right to set aside any change in his or her legal position to which he or she may consent as a result of the non-disclosure. For example, a person in a fiduciary position has a duty to disclose material information when entering into a contract with his or her beneficiary, in the sense that a failure to make such disclosure will entitle the beneficiary to rescind the contract and to reclaim any property transferred under it."

The Explanatory Notes give the following examples (at para.19):

"For example, the failure of a solicitor to share vital information with a client within the context of their work relationship, in order to perpetrate a fraud upon that client, would be covered by this section. Similarly, an offence could be committed under this section if a person intentionally failed to disclose information relating to his heart condition when making an application for life insurance."

In *Razoq* (above, p.686) as regards the s.3 offences, the contractual documents relating to each position required disclosure, his failure to disclose his suspension breached an express legal duty arising under contract. Even if the contracts had not contained such express terms, it would have been open to the jury to convict if satisfied that the legal duty arose: (1) as an implied term of the contract and the conditions under which the doctor was registered with the GMC; or (2) because the contracts into which he entered were contracts of utmost good faith.

Question

Can D be liable for fraud in the following cases:

(a) D continues making payments to his insurance company for life insurance without disclosing that he recently suffered a heart attack. The life insurance policy requires him to disclose any changes to his general health.

(b) D, a consultant, refers a private patient to an NHS trust hospital for treatment omitting to declare that he is a private patient thereby avoiding any charges to himself or the patient for use of the NHS facilities. (cf. *Firth* (1990) 91 Cr. App. R. 217.)

----

iii. Fraud by abuse of position

4 Fraud by abuse of position

(1) A person is in breach of this section if he—

    (a) occupies a position in which he is expected to safeguard, or not to act against, the financial interests of another person,

    (b) dishonestly abuses that position, and

    (c) intends, by means of the abuse of that position—

        (i) to make a gain for himself or another, or

        (ii) to cause loss to another or to expose another to a risk of loss.

(2) A person may be regarded as having abused his position even though his conduct consisted of an omission rather than an act.

Note

This provision aims to deal with the mischief where V has voluntarily placed D in a privileged position and D, by virtue of that position is expected to act to safeguard V's financial interests or not act against those interests. D may have direct access to, or control over, V's property or simply because of his position may be able to act in relation to V's property in a way which impacts upon V's financial position. The Law Commission explained the offence they proposed as follows.

LAW COMMISSION, *FRAUD* (TSO, 2002), LAW COM. NO.276

Secret abuse of position

7.35 The kind of conduct we have described as 'non-disclosure' is broadly analogous to, though in our view distinct from, that of positive misrepresentation which brings about a transfer of property or some other economic consequence. It is in the nature of the situation that the person who trusts the defendant to disclose the information in question will act, or omit to act, in reliance on the defendant's failure to do so.

7.36 In addition to this case, however, we believe that some kinds of conduct can properly be described as fraudulent on the ground that they amount to an abuse of an existing position of trust, even if there is no question of the victim's thereby being induced to act or omit to act. The difference between this case and that of non-disclosure is that in this case the defendant does not need to enlist the victim's co-operation in order to secure the desired result. An example would be the employee who, without the knowledge of his employer, misuses his or her position to make a personal profit at the employer's expense.

7.37 The essence of the kind of relationship which in our view should be a prerequisite of this form of the offence is that the victim has voluntarily put the defendant in a privileged position, by virtue of which the defendant is expected to safeguard the victim's financial interests or given power to damage those interests. Such an expectation to safeguard or power to damage may arise, for example, because the defendant is given authority to exercise a discretion on the victim's behalf, or is given access to the victim's assets, premises, equipment or customers. In these cases the defendant does not need to enlist the victim's *further* co-operation in order to secure the desired result, because the necessary co-operation has been given in advance.

7.38 The necessary relationship will be present between trustee and beneficiary, director and company, professional person and client, agent and principal, employee and employer, or between partners. It may arise otherwise, for example within a family, or in the context of voluntary work, or in any context where the parties are not at arm's length. In nearly all cases where it arises, it will be recognised by the civil law as importing fiduciary duties, and any relationship that is so recognised will suffice. We see no reason, however, why the existence of such duties should be essential. This does not of course mean that it would be entirely a matter for the fact-finders whether the necessary relationship exists. The question whether the particular facts alleged can properly be described as giving rise to that relationship will be an issue capable of being ruled upon by the judge and, if the case goes to the jury, of being the subject of directions.

7.39 The abuse of position may be an omission as well as a positive act—for example, where an employee omits to take up a chance of a crucial contract, intending to enable an associate to pick up the contract instead.

7.40 We do not think, however, that dishonest abuse of position per se should be enough to constitute fraudulent conduct. In accordance with Stephen's view that fraud involves either deceit or secrecy, we believe that, in order to qualify as fraud, an abuse of position (in the absence of misrepresentation) should be not only dishonest but also *secret*—that is, undisclosed to the victim. If the defendant lets the victim know what is happening, in our view the defendant's conduct cannot properly be described as fraud.

7.41 Arguably it follows that there should be *no* liability if, although the victim has no knowledge of the abuse at the time when it occurs, the defendant intends to disclose it in due course. Such an intention could not, however, be a complete defence in all circumstances. No-one would say, for example, that a particular abuse was not fraudulent because the culprit intended to make disclosure many years later, in his memoirs or on his deathbed. We have tried to identify the circumstances in which an intention to disclose ought to be a defence, but have been unable to formulate principled criteria which would not yield arbitrary results. It should be remembered, in any event, that the offence always requires proof of dishonesty. If the defendant is unable to make disclosure (for example, because the victim is uncontactable), but intends to do so at the first opportunity, it is unlikely that dishonesty could be proved. We have therefore decided to recommend simply that, with one exception, the abuse of position must occur without the victim's knowledge, or that of a person acting on the victim's behalf.

7.42 The exception relates to the situation where the defendant *thinks* that the victim is unaware of the defendant's conduct, but is mistaken.

Note

The Government disagreed with the Law Commission on the issue of secrecy.

HOME OFFICE CRIMINAL POLICY UNIT, *FRAUD LAW REFORM: GOVERNMENT RESPONSE TO CONSULTATIONS* (2005)

Fraud by abuse of position (Question 3)

26. There was general support for this 3rd limb of the general offence, which recognised that this type of behaviour is not well addressed by the existing law, as there may be cases where no deception is involved, or is at least difficult to prove. Examples were given of frauds by local and central government officials, internal banking frauds, the financial abuse of the elderly and Probate fraud, some of which was committed via Enduring Powers of Attorney. (It is however worth noting that in most cases where public officials are concerned the common law crime of misconduct in a public office should be available).

27. A minority opposed it on the grounds that it was too wide, with insufficient definition of crucial points—notably the relationships covered and the meaning of 'abuse'—and that it would bring to the police many complaints which are currently dealt with under civil law, for example by suing for breach of contract or by dismissal for gross misconduct. One respondent said they were strongly opposed to criminalising people simply as a result of the breakdown of everyday commercial and fiduciary relationships. We think however that while 'simple' breakdown of relationships could lead to allegations of 'abuse' of position, the offence will only be committed if the defendant is dishonest and seeks to make a gain or cause a loss. That is something more than a breakdown of relationships.

28. There was wide support for 'secrecy' as an ingredient of the offence—secrecy is a 'hallmark' of fraud, as one of our respondents put it. It was accepted that an open abuse is no less reprehensible than a secret abuse, but while an open abuse might be rightly subject to sanction, the argument was that it should not fall under the criminal law of fraud. A secrecy requirement helps separate fraud from other offences (eg blackmail) and matters better dealt with under civil law. However some were concerned that, while secrecy would almost invariably be part of the offending behaviour in practice, it was difficult to define and represented an unnecessary complication, which could lead to technical arguments in court. There could be arguments about whether there had been an intention to disclose in the future, and about whether the employer knew what was going on, if a surveillance operation was in place. It was argued that the mischief lay in the dishonest abuse and that the value-laden concepts of 'dishonesty' and 'abuse' were sufficient in themselves to set the parameters for the offence.

29. We accept these arguments and in the light of this concern we decided to delete the secrecy requirement proposed by the Law Commission.

Note

The offence may be committed both by act or omission. The question whether or not D is in the necessary position in relation to V and his financial interests is initially one for the judge who will determine whether the relationship is capable of falling within the section, and then it is for the jury to determine whether or not it does. The Explanatory Notes to the Fraud Act 2006 provide the following examples (at paras 22 and 23):

> "An employee of a software company who uses his position to clone software products with the intention of selling the products on would commit an offence under this section.
>
>   Another example covered by this section is where a person who is employed to care for an elderly or disabled person has access to that person's bank account and abuses his position by transferring funds to invest in a high-risk business venture of his own."

In the first example, if D went ahead with his scheme he would hold the profits on constructive trust for his employer, but there is some doubt whether or not he could be convicted of theft of those profits (see *Attorney General's Reference (No.1 of 1985)* [1986] Q.B. 491 at p.638 above). The care assistant, however, could be convicted of theft of V's credit balance (cf. *Williams (Roy)* [2001] 1 Cr. App. R. 362). The advantage of the fraud offence, of course, is that it may be charged when D first acts to abuse his position before any loss might be suffered by V. In *Doukas* [1978] 1 W.L.R. 372, D, a waiter at a hotel, was found in possession of bottles of wine which he intended to substitute for his employer's bottles when a customer ordered wine. He would then make out a separate bill and pocket the money paid by the customer. D would now be guilty of fraud by abuse of position.

The Explanatory Notes provide the following example of a commission of this offence arising from an omission (at para.21):

> "an employee who fails to take up the chance of a crucial contract in order that an associate or rival company can take it up instead at the expense of the employer, commits an offence under this section."

The mens rea for this offence is: (1) an intention to make a gain or cause a loss (or expose to the risk of loss) as for fraud by false representation; and (2) dishonesty. There is no requirement that D should know that he is in a position of trust in relation to V, although it is difficult to believe a judge would leave to a jury such a relationship if there was no evidence of knowledge on D's part. In any event, D's ignorance of the position of trust, however, will be highly relevant to the question whether or not he was dishonest.

Question

Can D be liable for fraud in the following cases:

(a) D is a film projectionist at a cinema. D copies films to DVDs and provides these DVD's to X who, unknown to D makes further copies and sells these at car boot sales.

(b) D is an employee of a mobile phone company. D, aggrieved that he was overlooked for promotion, copies the company's customer account database and passes this on to a rival company which uses the information to contact customers offering them new contracts before their existing contracts expire.

(c) V who is elderly and in declining health grants a power of attorney to D, her son, giving him power to conduct her financial affairs. D's business has cash flow problems because some customers are late paying their bills. D transfers £10,000 from V's account to his own business account to tide him over until late paying customers make their payments. Six months later, when all his customers have paid their accounts, D transfers £10,000 plus interest to V's account.

----

2. OBTAINING SERVICES DISHONESTLY

11 Obtaining services dishonestly

(1) A person is guilty of an offence under this section if he obtains services for himself or another—

    (a) by a dishonest act, and
    (b) in breach of subsection (2).

(2) A person obtains services in breach of this subsection if—

    (a) they are made available on the basis that payment has been, is being or will be made for or in respect of them,

    (b)   he obtains them without any payment having been made for or in respect of them or without payment having been made in full, and

    (c)   when he obtains them, he knows—

         (i)   that they are being made available on the basis described in paragraph (a), or

        (ii)   that they might be,

but intends that payment will not be made, or will not be made in full.

Note

Section 11 of the Fraud Act 2006 creates the offence of obtaining services dishonestly to replace the offence of obtaining services by deception contrary to s.1 of the Theft Act 1978. The maximum penalty on summary conviction is the same as for fraud but on conviction on indictment the maximum penalty is five years' imprisonment (s.11(3) of the Fraud Act 2006). Unlike the offence of fraud, this is a result crime as it must be proved that the services have actually been obtained. Unlike the offence of obtaining services by deception, this offence does not require there to be any deception and thus there is no need to prove that the provider of the service has been deceived. The Law Commission explained the deficiencies in the s.1 obtaining services by deception offence as follows.

LAW COMMISSION, *FRAUD* (TSO, 2002), LAW COM. NO.276

8.1 Because it requires proof of deception, the offence under section 1 of the 1978 Act fails to catch a person who succeeds in obtaining a service dishonestly but without deceiving anyone. This may happen in various ways. (1) The service may be obtained by the defendant's failure to disclose a material fact, rather than by a positive deception.

(2) The service may not be provided for the defendant personally, but for anyone who is there to receive it. For example, the defendant climbs over the fence of a football ground and watches the match without paying the admission charge.

(3) The service may not be provided directly by people at all, but through a machine. For example, the defendant downloads, via the internet, software or data for which a charge is made, or which is available only to those within a certain category of person who have paid to be included within that category, by giving false credit card or identification details; or receives satellite television transmissions by using an unauthorised validation card in a decoder.

(4) Some cases are a hybrid of types (2) and (3). For example, the defendant gives false credit card details to an automated booking system, or tenders a forged or stolen credit card to an electronic vending machine, and thus obtains a ticket for a journey or entertainment. There is no deception of the booking system (because it is not a person), nor of the staff who check the tickets of the passengers or audience (because the staff are only interested in whether each person has a ticket, not how they got it).

Note

The Government provided its view of the new offence and its ambit.

HOME OFFICE CRIMINAL POLICY UNIT, *FRAUD LAW REFORM: GOVERNMENT RESPONSE TO CONSULTATIONS* (2005)

New offence of obtaining services dishonestly (Question 5)

35. Very nearly all respondents welcomed this offence to combat problems with the 'deception' of automated service provision. The Law Commission noted in their report that arguably the new focus on 'misrepresentation'

will ensure this type of case is covered, but the problem is not confined to the deception of machines and the new offence deals with the obtaining of services dishonestly by whatever means.

36. Examples of services which respondents thought should be covered include the opening of a bank account, the setting up of a company, downloading software or music from the internet. We believe these are all covered within the normal meaning of the term 'services'.

37. An example mentioned by the Law Commission that is **not** covered by the new offence is where parents, who have every intention of paying all relevant fees, lie about a child's religious upbringing in order to obtain a place at a fee paying school. This case is in principle covered by the existing offence in section 1 of the 1978 Act, as it is not necessary under that provision to show that the defendant intended to avoid payment. One respondent thought that this type of case should be covered by the criminal law as there is loss to the school in that they have accepted a pupil they would not otherwise have taken and a loss to another family whose child has not obtained a place. We however agree with the Law Commission that this type of gain and loss should not be a matter for the criminal law of fraud and that the new offence should apply only where there is an intention not to pay.

38. A few respondents believed that the requirement that the defendant only be 'aware that the services **might be** chargeable' was too low and that it would assist unscrupulous service providers (of whom they say there is an increasing number, on the net). However the majority felt the overall dishonesty requirement provides sufficient protection for the innocent client.

Note

The Explanatory Notes to the Fraud Act 2006 give the example of D climbing over a wall to watch a football match without paying the entrance fee. D does not deceive anyone in order to gain admission to the ground, but he does obtain a service which is provided on the basis that people pay for it. The absence of requirement that anyone be deceived also catches the situation where D engages in a transaction resulting in the obtaining of a service without any human agent determining that the service should be provided to D. The Explanatory Notes give the example of D using false credit card details to obtain data or software via an automated process over the internet where that data or software is made available only to those who have paid for access rights to that service. A further example given is that of D attaching a decoder to her television to enable viewing access to cable/satellite television channels for which she has no intention of paying.

The offence requires that there be a dishonest act resulting in D or another obtaining services, so an omission will not suffice. In the example above of the football match, the act would be climbing into the ground. If the relevant act is a false representation, for example, D says to the turnstile operator at the football ground that the person behind is paying for him, D could also be liable to conviction for fraud by false representation. It must be proved that as a result of D's dishonest act he obtained a service to which the section applies. If D is stopped immediately after he climbs into the ground and before he has an opportunity to view the football match, he would not have obtained any service at that point. If, for example, owing to someone else's mistake, D is given access to satellite television channels which are only available to customers who have paid in advance for them, D's use of the channels would not amount to an offence as he has not performed any act which led to the obtaining of them. His omission to inform the provider of their mistake cannot amount to a dishonest act. Of course, a convoluted argument could be constructed that each time D switches to the relevant channel there is a separate obtaining of the service. Everything would then hinge on whether or not a jury would be satisfied that tuning into that channel was a dishonest act and that it was done with the requisite knowledge and intent.

The offence only applies to services which are made available on the basis that "payment has been, is being or will be made for or in respect of them". If the services are obtained on the understanding that no payment will be made for them, D cannot be guilty of this offence. For example, if D approaches a taxi and falsely represents to the taxi driver that she has been robbed and is unable to pay for the fare and he agrees to drive her to her destination for no charge, she has not obtained "services" under s.11 as the service was not made available on the basis that it would be paid for. D could be liable to conviction of fraud by false representation. By contrast, if D orders a taxi intending not to pay the fare and, when it arrives at her address, she gets into it and is driven to her destination where she then runs off without paying the taxi driver, D will have obtained services dishonestly. She would also be liable to conviction for fraud by false representation as by getting into the taxi she impliedly represents she is an honest customer who will pay for the fare. In addition, she could be convicted of making off without payment.

"Services" are not defined in the Act which leaves room for argument over what constitutes a service. Where a credit card is obtained or bank account opened as a result of a false representation, the card or account does not, itself, amount to a service but rather provides access to a range of facilities which underlie the card or account (see *Sofroniou* [2004] 1 Cr. App. R. 35). This participation in the banking system is a service (*Sofroniou*) and could support a conviction for the s.11 offence provided there is some charge for the service whether through an annual fee or other bank charges. It is arguable that the low interest rate on a current account or the higher interest rate on a credit card (and the commission fee levied on shops and businesses) means that these services are made available on the basis that payment has been or will be made for them. Thus inducing a bank to open an account with the intention of running up an overdraft on it and not repaying it, or to issue a credit card with the intent of spending up to the credit limit and not paying off the debt thereby incurred or interest charges on that debt, could constitute obtaining services dishonestly provided D had the necessary knowledge and intent.

The services which may be the subject of the s.11 offence must be services made available on the basis that payment has been, is being or will be made for or in respect of them. D must obtain the relevant service either without paying for it or without paying in full for it. If D obtains a service by means of a false representation but pays for it in full, he would not appear to commit this offence. For example, D, aged 14, gains access to a cinema to watch an 18-plus film by convincing the sales assistant that he is 18. D pays for his ticket and watches the film. D does not commit the offence of fraud by false representation as he does not make a gain in terms of property or cause any loss to the cinema operator. D would have committed an offence under s.1 of the 1978 Act.

There are three elements to the mens rea for this offence. The first is dishonesty. In determining whether D's act was dishonest, the *Ghosh* test applies (see above, p.658). Secondly, D must know either that the services are being made available on the basis that payment has been, is being or will be made for or in respect of them or that they might be being made available on that basis. Thirdly, D must intend either not to pay for the service or not to pay in full for it. This intention must exist at the point that D obtains the service. It would appear, however, that the intent should also exist when D does the relevant act which leads to the obtaining if that act is to be considered dishonest. If D has the intent on doing the dishonest act but changes his mind before the obtaining occurs, he will not be liable for the s.11 offence although, of course, he may be liable for attempt.

It is not clear whether the intent not to pay means an intent never to pay as opposed to an intent not to pay at the time when payment is due. By analogy with making off without payment, it is assumed that an intent never to pay is what is required (see *Allen* [1985] A.C. 1029.

----

3. POSSESSION OF ARTICLES FOR USE IN FRAUD

Note

Section 25 of the Theft Act 1968 created the offence of going equipped for any burglary, theft or cheat (which covered deception offences). The Law Commission proposed amending the offence to replace "cheat" with "fraud". The Home Office proposed a much wider reform.

HOME OFFICE CRIMINAL POLICY UNIT, *FRAUD LAW REFORM: CONSULTATION ON PROPOSALS FOR LEGISLATION* (2004)

Possessing equipment to commit frauds

39. Section 25 of the 1968 Act (going equipped for stealing etc.) makes it an offence for a person to have with him, when not at his place of abode, any article for use in the course of or in connection with any burglary, theft or cheat. 'Cheat' is currently defined in section 25(5) to mean an offence under section 15 of the 1968 Act (obtaining property by deception). The person's intent to commit a specific crime does not have to be proved, and what needs to be established by the prosecution depends on the article in question and/or the circumstances.

40. We believe that section 25 merits reconsideration because the offence is outdated in relation to its application to fraud offences. Its restriction to possession of relevant articles outside of the defendant's 'place of abode' is unhelpful in relation to modern frauds which can easily take place from home computers. We consider that we should add to the Bill a new offence, replacing Section 25 (so far as it applies to 'cheats'), and covering possession of equipment to commit frauds whether at home or elsewhere. (As regards 'going equipped' to commit burglary and theft, section 25 would stand as it is). The difficult question is how should this new offence be constructed?

41. We suggest that the new offence might, like section 25, criminalise the possession of articles (defined so as to include computer software) 'for use in the course of or in connection with' the commission or facilitation of a fraud. This could criminalise mere possession of articles which can have an entirely innocent purpose (for example, devices for reading credit cards can have legitimate uses in clubs). We suggest therefore that it would be a defence to show that there was 'lawful authority or reasonable excuse'. This formulation seems appropriate to deal with the circumstances of e.g. credit card readers.

42. Like section 25, the new provision might also contain a special provision in relation to articles which are specifically 'made or adapted' for committing frauds. Examples cited by police are the computer programme 'creditmaster IV' which generates (genuine) credit card numbers on request; computer templates for producing blank utility bills; and draft letters in connection with 'advance fee' frauds. Such items have no known legitimate use, so in their case it is reasonable to provide that mere possession of such articles is evidence that they were intended 'for use in the course of or in connection with' fraud.

Note

The consultation received a generally favourable response.

HOME OFFICE CRIMINAL POLICY UNIT, *FRAUD LAW REFORM: GOVERNMENT RESPONSE TO CONSULTATIONS* (2005)

New offence of possessing equipment to commit fraud (Question 7)

46. The proposal for this new offence was welcomed by almost everybody. It represents an addition to the Law Commission proposals, and replaces the 'going equipped to commit a cheat' offence in section 25 of the Theft Act 1968. Those respondents who had doubts were mainly concerned that proof of intent should be required. We accept the arguments against criminalisation of the simple possession of any article which could be used in a

fraud, given that many have legitimate uses and that we are capturing articles kept at home. We believe that the prosecution should have to prove a general intention that the article be used by the possessor (or someone else) for a fraudulent purpose, though they should not have to prove intended use in a particular fraud. The caselaw on section 25 establishes that the offence requires an intention that the article be used for some future fraud, although the intention may be general rather than specific and the intended use may be by someone else. We intend to use similar wording in order to attract that case law.

6 Possession etc. of articles for use in frauds

(1)   A person is guilty of an offence if he has in his possession or under his control any article for use in the course of or in connection with any fraud.

(2)   A person guilty of an offence under this section is liable—

(a)   on summary conviction, to imprisonment for a term not exceeding 12 months or to a fine not exceeding the statutory maximum (or to both);

(b)   on conviction on indictment, to imprisonment for a term not exceeding 5 years or to a fine (or to both).

Note

This is potentially a very wide offence and could cover possession of pen and paper to write a letter containing a false representation, or possession of something as sophisticated as a cloning machine to clone credit cards. Mr Doukas, on his way to work in possession of the bottles of wine he intends to use to sell to customers in the restaurant, would now commit this offence. There is no need to prove that D possessed the relevant article to be used in the course of or in connection with a specific fraud, it being sufficient to prove that he had a general intention (see *Ellames* 60 Cr. App. R. 7. This will be easier to do, however, where the relevant article has no legitimate purpose, for example, the credit card cloning machine.

Section 8 defines "article" to include "any program or data held in electronic form" thereby avoiding esoteric arguments about whether or not an "article" has to be tangible.

----

4. MAKING OR SUPPLYING ARTICLES FOR USE IN FRAUD

7 Making or supplying articles for use in frauds

(1)   A person is guilty of an offence if he makes, adapts, supplies or offers to supply any article—

(a)   knowing that it is designed or adapted for use in the course of or in connection with fraud, or
(b)   intending it to be used to commit, or assist in the commission of, fraud.

(2)   A person guilty of an offence under this section is liable—

(a)   on summary conviction, to imprisonment for a term not exceeding 12 months or to a fine not exceeding the statutory maximum (or to both);
(b)   on conviction on indictment, to imprisonment for a term not exceeding 10 years or to a fine (or to both).

Note

This is a companion offence to the s.6 offence seeking to provide for any remaining activities that facilitate or support the commission of fraud offences. For example D would commit this offence if, knowing E intends to seek to defraud customers in his pub, he makes E a fake charity collection box to place on his counter E intending to keep the proceeds himself. Similarly the person supplying Mr Doukas with bottles of wine would commit this offence if he knew Mr Doukas intended to sell them to customers in the restaurant where he worked. Likewise D would commit this offence where he supplies a credit card cloning machine to E. The Explanatory Notes to the Fraud Act 2006 give as an example, a person who makes devices to attach to electricity meters to cause them to malfunction and not record the electricity used.

12 BLACKMAIL

The essence of the offence of blackmail lies in the blackmailer's use of threats to gain property, either for himself or another. Alternatively, the blackmailer may threaten with the intention of causing some form of loss to the victim without necessarily making a tangible gain for himself. The offence is quite widely drafted and there has been much discussion about the apparent oddity that blackmail may be committed by performing two separate acts which, taken individually, may be morally and legally right, yet combine to make a moral and legal wrong (see MacKenna *"Blackmail: a Criticism"* and Lindgren *"Unravelling the Paradox of Blackmail"*, below p.709).

THEFT ACT 1968 S.21

(1) A person is guilty of blackmail if, with a view to gain for himself or another or with intent to cause loss to another, he makes any unwarranted demand with menaces; and for this purpose a demand with menaces is unwarranted unless the person making it does so in the belief—

   (a) that he has reasonable grounds for making the demand; and
   (b) that the use of the menaces is a proper means of reinforcing the demand.

(2) The nature of the act or omission demanded is immaterial, and it is also immaterial whether the menaces relate to action to be taken by the person making the demand.

(3) A person guilty of blackmail shall on conviction on indictment be liable to imprisonment for a term not exceeding fourteen years.

i. Demand with Menaces

Notes

Neither "demand" nor "menaces" is defined by the Act. "Menaces", where it was used in the statutory predecessor of the present section (i.e. s.29(1) of the Larceny Act 1916) had acquired a definite meaning, being exactly synonymous with threat.

Thorne v Motor Trade Association [1937] A.C. 797 per Lord Atkin (at 806):

> "If the matter came to us for decision for the first time I think there would be something to be said for a construction of 'menace' which connotes threats of violence and injury to person or property, and a contrast which might be made between 'menaces' and 'threats,' as used in other sections of the various statutes. But in several cases it has been decided that 'menace' in this subsection and its predecessors is simply equivalent to threat."

Lord Wright (at 817):

"I think the word 'menace' is to be liberally construed and not as limited to threats of violence but as including threats of any action detrimental to or unpleasant to the person addressed. It may also include a warning that in certain events such action is intended."

But "threat" was regarded as too wide by the draftsmen of the Theft Act 1978.

The Law Commission, *Theft and Related Offences*, § 123: "We have chosen the word 'menaces' instead of 'threats' because notwithstanding the wide meaning given to 'menaces' in *Thorne's* case . . . we regard that word as stronger than 'threats' and the consequent slight restriction of the scope of the offence seems to us right."

R. V LAWRENCE AND POMROY

(1971) 57 Cr. App. R. 64 CA

L and P were convicted of blackmail in that on January 20, with a view to gain for themselves they made an unwarranted demand of £70 from T with menaces. P had done some work for T. T, not being satisfied with the work, had paid part only of the contract price and had indicated that the balance of £70 would be paid when the work was completed to his satisfaction. On 16 January, P had asked T for the £70 and, on being refused, said that unless T paid up, he had better look over his shoulder whenever he went out. On 20 January, P again visited T, this time in company with L, a big man. The conversation on that occasion is set out in the judgment of Cairns LJ, below. L and P appealed on the grounds that the judge failed to give: (a) a definition of menaces; and (b) a direction on proviso (b) of s.21(1).

CAIRNS LJ

Detective Constable Walters said that in company with other officers he was concealed behind the door of Thorn's house when the appellants arrived on January 20. He heard a conversation about the £70 which ended with Lawrence saying: 'Now listen, I've got an interest in the £70, see,' and then after a pause: 'Come out of the house and we'll sort this lot out now.' Thorn said: 'No' and Lawrence said: 'Come on mate, come outside.' The police officers then revealed themselves and Walters said that he saw the appellants outside the door. He said to Lawrence: 'What is your name?' and Lawrence said: 'Leave off, what do you want to know for?' Pomroy said: 'Yes it's all right, we only want my money.' Lawrence said: 'Leave me out, I've only come to help my mate,' and when asked gave his name to the police. The appellants were told that they were being arrested for demanding money from Thorn. After caution Lawrence said: 'That's nice, we've been well set up.' Pomroy said: 'But he does owe me money . . .'

The first point we deal with is the contention that the judge gave the jury no definition of what constitutes a menace. It is said that they should have been directed in accordance with *R. v Clear* [1968] 1 Q.B. 670, that they must consider what the effect would be in the mind of a reasonable man of the words and actions of the two defendants. The word 'menaces' is an ordinary English word which any jury can be expected to understand. In exceptional cases where because of special knowledge in special circumstances what would be a menace to an ordinary person is not a menace to the person to whom it is addressed, or where the converse may be true, it is no doubt necessary to spell out the meaning of the word. But, in our view, there was no such necessity here. The judge made it abundantly clear that the issue for the jury was whether the two men had gone to Thorne's house merely to ask reasonably for payment, on Pomroy's part to ask reasonably for payment and on Lawrence's part merely as a companion, or whether they had gone to threaten and frighten him into paying. That was quite a sufficient explanation of what is meant by menaces.

Next, should the judge have directed the jury on the proviso to s.21(1)(b) of the Theft Act: that is to say, as to whether the accused believed that what they did was a proper way of enforcing the debt? Neither of them suggested at the trial that, if menaces were used by them, it was a proper means of enforcement. It is true that the police evidence was that when Pomroy's statement was read to him, Lawrence said: That's about it, what's wrong with that?' but he repudiated that in his evidence and said that his reaction had been 'It's a lot of nonsense.'

Where on the face of it the means adopted to obtain payment of a debt is not the proper way of enforcing it and where the accused does not at his trial set up the case that he believed it to be, there is no need for any direction to be given on the proviso . . .

Appeals dismissed

Note

As to the exceptional cases mentioned by Cairns LJ where it is necessary to spell out the meaning of "menaces", the Court of Appeal in *R. v Garwood* [1987] said:

> "It seems to us that there are two possible occasions on which a further directive on the meaning of the word menaces may be required. The first is where the threats might have affected the mind of an ordinary person of normal stability but did not affect the person actually addressed. In such circumstances that would amount to a sufficient menace: see *R. v Clear* [1968] 1 Q.B. 670. The second situation is where the threats in fact affected the mind of the victim, although they would not have affected the mind of a person of normal stability. In that case, in our judgment, the existence of the menaces is proved providing that the accused man was aware of the likely effect of his actions on the victims."

R. v Harry [1972] Crim. L.R. 32 (Crown Ct.): H sent letters to 115 local shopkeepers asking them to buy immunity posters by contributing to a Student Rag Appeal in aid of charity. The purpose of the poster was to "protect you from any Rag Activity which could in any way cause you inconvenience". The poster read "These premises are immune from Rag 73 activities whatever they may be." In directing an acquittal of blackmail, Judge Petre said "Menaces is a strong word. You may think that menaces must be of a fairly stern nature to fall within the definition."

TREACY V DIRECTOR OF PUBLIC PROSECUTIONS

[1971] A.C. 537 HL

T wrote and posted in England a letter addressed to a woman in Germany, which letter contained a demand. T argued that he was not triable in England, not having made the demand in England.

LORD DIPLOCK

. . . Arguments as to the meaning of ordinary everyday phrases are not susceptible of much elaboration. The Theft Act, 1968, makes a welcome departure from the former style of drafting in criminal statutes. It is expressed in simple language as used and understood by ordinary literate men and women. It avoids so far as possible those terms of art which have acquired a special meaning understood only by lawyers in which many of the penal enactments which it supersedes were couched. So the question which has to be answered is: Would a man say in ordinary conversation: 'I have made a demand' when he had written a letter containing a demand and posted it to the person to whom the demand was addressed? Or would he not use those words until the letter had been received and read by the addressee?

My answer to that question is that it would be natural for him to say 'I have made a demand' as soon as he had posted the letter, for he would have done all that was in his power to make the demand. He might add, if it were the fact: 'but it has not reached X yet', or: 'I made a demand but it got lost in the post.' What, at any rate, he would not say is: 'I shall make a demand when X receives my letter,' unless he contemplated making some further demand after the letter had been received.

I see nothing in the context or in the purpose of the section to indicate that the words bear any other meaning than that which I have suggested they would bear in ordinary conversation . . .

As respects the purpose of the section, I see no reason for supposing that Parliament did not intend to punish conduct which is anti-social or wicked—if that word is still in current use—unless the person guilty of the conduct achieves his intended object of gain to himself or loss caused to another. The fact that what a reasonable man would regard as an unwarranted demand with menaces after being posted by its author goes astray and never reaches the addressee, or reaches him but is not understood by him, or because of his unusual fortitude fails to disturb his equanimity, as was the case in *R. v Clear* [1968] 1 Q.B. 670, may be a relevant factor in considering what punishment is appropriate but does not make the conduct of the author himself any less wicked or anti-social or less meet to be deterred.

My Lords, all that has to be decided upon this aspect of the instant appeal is whether the appellant 'made a demand' when he posted his letter to the addressee. In the course of the argument many other and ingenious ways in which a blackmailer may choose to send his demand to his victim have been canvassed, and many possible, even though unlikely, events which might intervene between the sending of the demand by the blackmailer and its receipt and comprehension by the victim have been discussed. These cases which so far are only imaginary may fall to be decided if they ever should occur in real life. But unless the purpose of the new style of drafting used in the Theft Act, 1968, is to be defeated they, too, should be decided by answering the question: 'Are the circumstances of this case such as would prompt a man in ordinary conversation to say: "I have made a demand"?'

For both the reasons which I have given I would dismiss this appeal.

Appeal dismissed

Notes

1. A possible danger in "the new style of drafting used in the Theft Act, 1968", is illustrated by the fact that of the five Law Lords concerned in *Treacy's* case, three thought that posting a letter containing a demand was making a demand, but two thought that no demand was made until the letter reached the addressee. A technical term at least has the merit that its meaning is precise and can be the subject of a precise direction to the jury.

2. Both demand and menaces may be implicit, rather than explicit. See the next case.

R. V COLLISTER AND WARHURST

(1955) 39 Cr. App. R. 100

C and W, who were police officers, were charged with demanding money with menaces, under s.30 of the Larceny Act 1916. C told W, in the presence of P, that P had been importuning him. The prosecutor protested, but W said to him, "This is going to look very bad for you." They arranged to meet him on the next day, W telling C in P's hearing to type out a report on the matter but to hold it up and use it only if P failed to keep the appointment. When they met next day, W asked P whether he had brought anything with him, and P handed over five one pound notes.

PILCHER J DIRECTED THE JURY

What you have got to be satisfied with in this case is that these two men, working in concert, intended to convey, and did in fact convey, to Mr Jeffries in the first place that they, being police officers, intended to take him to the West Central Police Station on a charge of importuning, or to put in a report about him, unless Jeffries then or later paid them money. That, I think, is putting it as simply as I can put it. You need not be satisfied that there was an express demand for money in words. You need not be satisfied that any express threats were made, but if the evidence satisfies you that, although there was no such express demand or threat, the demeanour of the accused and the circumstances of the case were such that an ordinary reasonable man would understand that a demand for money was being made upon him and that that demand was accompanied by menaces—not perhaps direct, but veiled menaces—so that his ordinary balance of mind was upset, then you would be justified in coming to the conclusion that a demand with menaces had been made . . .

They were convicted and on appeal this direction
was held to be perfectly proper

R V LAMBERT

[2009] EWCA Crim 2860

LORD JUSTICE MOSES: . . .

[This appeal] raises the question as to whether the alleged blackmailer is guilty of the offence within the meaning of section 21 of the Theft Act 1968, when he poses as a victim as opposed to the one who is going to be the aggressor or who will arrange for aggression to occur. . .

The prosecution case was that this [appellant] . . . was owed money by the grandson and had [telephoned the grandmother] in order to impose the pressure of menaces . . .. He was alleged to have said . . .: 'Nana, this is Aaron [the name of the grandson]. They've got me tied up. They want £5,000, Nana.' To the grandmother's ears the person sounded distressed, as though he was crying. Fortunately she was of a robust disposition and said to the caller: 'You've got a cheek to ask for £5,000. I don't have £5 let alone £5,000.' 'Well [said the caller] they want £5,000' and still appeared to be crying. 'I bloody haven't got it' she said. So the caller hung up. She believed it was her grandson and she was scared. The person made a second call and asked for money again. She responded that the best thing for him was to call his mother. . . . The grandmother sensibly got in touch with her son, the father of the apparent caller and the police were called. . .

Mr Parish, on behalf of this [appellant], took the point at the close of the prosecution case that no offence had been committed within the scope of section 21. . .

Mr Parish submitted that the demand was not unwarranted and furthermore that, since the caller was not pretending either to carry out action against the man, Aaron, nor had it in his power to do so, he could not be guilty of blackmail. Blackmail required, so he submitted, either that the person attempting the blackmail was proposing to carry out the menace identified with the demand, or had it in his power to carry out that which was menaced.

We do not agree. We think it makes absolutely no difference whether the person pretending that someone has been tied up and will be hurt if money is not handed over is pretending to be the victim, or pretending to be the aggressor or pretending that he has it within his power to see that harm comes to the fictitious victim.

The essence of the offence which the prosecution must prove is, first of all, that there was an unwarranted demand. Mr Parish submits that there was no unwarranted demand in this case. But it is by now well established that the demand does not have to be made in terms of a demand or requirement or obligation. It can be couched in terms which are by no means aggressive or forceful. Indeed, the more suave and gentle the request, the more sinister in the circumstances it might be. If one needs authority for so obvious a proposition, one can find it in the decision of this court in *R v Collister* [1955] 39 Cr App R 100 . . ..

In our view, there was clearly a demand in this case and it was unwarranted. No justification was offered for imposing pressure upon the grandmother to hand over money to her grandson so that this defendant could be paid what the grandson owed him.

The next question is whether it was accompanied by menaces. Mr Parish again submits that it was not, since what was threatened by the caller was not that he would do something or allow others to do something but rather that he would suffer violence from others. That, as we have already indicated, is wholly irrelevant. What the caller was seeking to do was to impose upon the grandmother the pressure that were she not to hand over the money, her grandson would suffer violence. It is the essence of the offence that the offender intends and does impose . . . 'menacing pressures.' That case has an extraordinary series of facts which it is not necessary to summarise in this case. The court dismissed an application to argue that the [appellant] was not guilty of blackmail because he had merely pretended that others required security fees on the false basis that his victim was under threat. But the matter was clearly not argued in full. It did not need it to be. In those circumstances, we agree with Mr Parish that it is not authority which disposes of his argument.

But what does dispose of his argument is the very language of the statutory offence under section 21. There was, in this case, an unwarranted demand with menaces. It avails Mr Parish nothing to draw attention to cases where a hostage himself or herself reports the threat under which she suffers. In such a case there clearly is no unwarranted demand and the statutory requirements of section 21(1) are not fulfilled. An innocent agent, who merely reports that someone else is under threat cannot be guilty of an offence of blackmail because that innocent agent in making that report is not himself or herself making any unwarranted demand.

For those reasons we do not think that there is anything in the argument advanced by Mr Parish and the judge, His Honour Judge Boggis, was correct in declining to withdraw the case from the jury. In his ruling he said:

'. . . there is no basis in law for Mr Parish's submission that the demander must be instrumental in authorising the action to be taken. That is contrary to the very heart of the offence, an unwarranted demand accompanied by menaces. It being irrelevant whether the menaces relate to action taken by the demander or somebody else, and it also being irrelevant whether the demander is in any position to effect menace. It is how the demand and menace affects the victim that matters.'

We agree.

Appeal dismissed

ii. Unwarranted

CRIMINAL LAW REVISION COMMITTEE'S 8TH REPORT, *THEFT AND RELATED OFFENCES* (TSO, 1966), CMND.2977

§ 118 As to the illegality of making the demand we are decidedly of the opinion that the test should be subjective, namely whether the person in question honestly believes that he has the right to make the demand. This means in effect adopting the test of whether there is a claim of right, as in 1916, s.30, and not the test whether there is in fact a reasonable cause for making the demand, as in 1916, s.29(1)(i). Since blackmail is in its nature an offence of dishonesty, it seems wrong that a person should be guilty of the offence by making a demand which he honestly believes to be justified. Moreover to adopt the objective test seems to involve almost insuperable difficulty. It would be necessary either to set out the various kinds of demand which it was considered should be justified or to find an expression which would describe exactly these kinds but not others. The former course might in theory be possible; but the provision would have to be very elaborate, and it would involve the risk which attends any attempt to list different kinds of conduct for the purpose of a criminal offence—that of including too much or too little. Moreover there is much room for disagreement as to what kinds of demand should or should not be treated as justified. The latter course seems impossible having regard to the results which have followed from making liability depend on the absence of a 'reasonable and probable cause.' Any general provision would probably have to use some such uninformative expression, and it would be almost bound to cause similar difficulty and uncertainty.

§ 119 It is in relation to the question when it is permissible to employ threats in support of a demand that differences of opinion become most acute. Several situations are possible. A. may be owed £100 by B. and be unable to get payment. Perhaps A. needs the money badly and B. is in a position to pay; or perhaps A. can easily afford to wait and B. is in difficulty. Should it be blackmail for A. to threaten B. that, if he does not pay, A. will assault him—or slash the tyres of his car—or tell people that B. is a homosexual, which he is (or which he is not)—or tell people about the debt and anything discreditable about the way in which it was incurred? On one view none of these threats should be enough to make the demand amount to blackmail. For it is no offence merely to utter the threats without making the demand (unless for some particular reason such as breach of the peace or defamation); nor would the threat become criminal merely because it was uttered to reinforce a demand of a kind quite different from those associated with blackmail. Why then should it be blackmail merely because it is uttered to reinforce a demand for money which is owed? On this view no demand with menaces would amount to blackmail, however harsh the action threatened unless there was dishonesty. This is a tenable view, though an extreme one. In our opinion it goes too far and there are some threats which should make the demand amount to blackmail even if there is a valid claim to the thing demanded. For example, we believe that most people would say that it should be blackmail to threaten to denounce a person, however truly, as a homosexual unless he paid a debt. It does not seem to follow from the existence of a debt that the creditor should be entitled to resort to any method, otherwise non-criminal, to obtain payment. There are limits to the methods permissible for the purpose of enforcing payment of a debt without recourse to the courts. For example, a creditor cannot seize the debtor's goods; and in *Parker* (1910) 74 J.P. 208, it was held . . . that a creditor who forged a letter from the Admiralty to a sailor warning him to pay a debt was guilty of forgery notwithstanding the existence of the debt.

§ 120 If it is agreed that some threats should make a demand amount to blackmail, the difficulty is to draw the line between different kinds of threats in a way which would be generally accepted. It may be thought that a threat to cause physical injury or damage to property should always be sufficient, even though one does not ordinarily think of such threats in connection with blackmail. A threat to injure a person in relation to his business, for example by cutting off supplies to a retailer if he will not pay a debt or persists in breaking an agreement, would probably not be regarded as rightly included in blackmail. Some might think that any threat to disclose a matter not connected with the circumstances giving rise to the debt should be included; but opinion may differ widely about threats to disclose some discreditable conduct which resulted in the debt being incurred. Probably most people would say that the offence should not extend to a threat to disclose the existence of a debt. For example, it is not blackmail to threaten to post the name of a betting defaulter at Tattersalls (see *Russell on Crime*, 12th ed., pp.881–882). As in the case of demands, the possible courses seem to be to lay down a subjective test, depending on whether the person who utters the threat believes in his right to do so, or an objective test, whether by specifying the kinds of threats which should or should not be permissible or by means of a general provision to cover the latter. For reasons similar to those given in paragraph 118 concerning the demand we think that the only satisfactory course would be to adopt a subjective test and to make criminal liability depend on whether the person who utters the threat believes in the propriety of doing so.

§ 122 At first we proposed to include a requirement that a person's belief that he has reasonable grounds for making the demand or that the use of the menaces is proper should be reasonable belief. There would be a case for this in policy; for it may be thought that a person who puts pressure on another by menaces of a kind which any reasonable person would think ought to be blackmail should not escape liability merely because his moral standard is too low, or his intelligence too limited, to enable him to appreciate the wrongness of his conduct. The requirement might also make the decision easier for the jury; for if they found that the demand was unwarranted or that the menaces were improper, they would not have to consider whether the accused believed otherwise. But we decided finally not to include the requirement. To require that an honest belief, in order to be a defence, should be reasonable would have the result that the offence of blackmail could be committed by mere negligence (for example, in not consulting a lawyer or, as did Bernhard, in consulting the wrong kind of lawyer). [See *R. v Bernhard* [1938] 2 K.B. 264.]

SIR BRIAN MACKENNA, "BLACKMAIL: A CRITICISM" [1966] CRIM. L.R. 466

5. A man's belief that he has reasonable grounds for making a demand depends on two matters:

(a) his belief that the facts of the case are such-and-such; and

(b) his opinion upon these facts that it would be reasonable to make the demand.

In a particular case one man's belief that there are reasonable grounds for making a demand may differ from another's because of a difference in their beliefs about the facts (one believing the facts to be X., the other to be Y.), or because of a difference in their opinions upon the same facts (one opinion that those facts give a reasonable ground for making the demand, the other that they do not).

6. 'Reasonable grounds' in [section 21(l)(a)] cannot be limited to such as are believed to give a legally enforceable claim. To many it would seem reasonable to demand satisfaction of a claim recognised by the law as valid though unenforceable by legal action for some technical reason, such as the want of a writing or the expiration of the period of limitation. To some it would seem equally reasonable to demand payment of a claim incapable in any circumstances of being enforced by action, such as the claim to be paid a winning bet. There may be many other cases in which a moral, as distinct from a legal, right would seem to some at least a reasonable ground for making a demand. On these questions there could be differences of opinion, particularly as to whether on the facts of the case the person demanding had a moral right to the thing demanded. There could be similar 'moral' differences about the propriety of using threats.

7. The Committee intend that the test shall be subjective in both the respects indicated in 5 above: (i) the facts shall be taken to be those which the defendant believed to exist, and (ii) his opinion as to whether those facts gave him a reasonable ground for making a demand (or made it proper for him to use threats) will be the only relevant

one. His own moral standards are to determine the Tightness or wrongness of his conduct. This appears from a sentence in paragraph 122 where the Committee discuss (and dismiss) the possible objection to [s.21(l)(a)] that 'it may be thought that a person who puts pressure on another by menaces of a kind which any reasonable person would think ought to be blackmail should not escape liability merely because his moral standard is too low, or his intelligence too limited, to enable him to appreciate the wrongness of his conduct.'

8. That a sane man's guilt or innocence should depend in this way on his own opinion as to whether he is acting rightly or wrongly is, I think, an innovation in our criminal law.

9. The claim of right which excuses a taking that might otherwise be theft under section 1 of the Larceny Act 1916, may of course be a mistaken claim, and the mistake may be one of law or of fact. A man's mistaken belief that the rules of the civil law make him the owner of a certain thing is as good an excuse as his mistaken belief that the thing is X. when it is in fact Y. But [s.21(1)] goes further than this, and gives efficacy to the defendant's moral judgments whatever they may be. That is surely something different. It is one thing to hold that the defendant is excused if he believes the civil law to be X. when it is Y. It is another to excuse him in any case where he thinks that what he is doing is morally right, though according to ordinary moral notions he may be doing something very wrong.

R. V HARVEY

(1980) 72 Cr. App. R. 139 CA

H and others paid £20,000 to S for what was thought to be a consignment of cannabis, but in fact was a load of rubbish. They kidnapped S's wife and small child and told S they would maim and kill his family unless he gave them their money back. They were convicted of blackmail and appealed.

BINGHAM J

The learned judge in his direction to the jury quoted the terms of the subsection and then continued as follows: 'Now where the defence raise this issue, in other words, where they say that the demand is warranted and where they say they believe they had reasonable cause for making the demand and that the use of the menaces was a proper way of reinforcing the demand, it is for the prosecution to negative that allegation. It is not for the defendants to prove it once they have raised it. It is for the prosecution to prove that they had no such belief. Now is that clear? It is not easy and I do not want to lose you on the way. It has been raised in this case so you have got to ask yourself this. Has the prosecution disproved that these defendants or those who have raised the matter believed that they had *reasonable* grounds for making the demand? Certainly you may say to yourselves that they have been ripped off to the tune of £20,000. They had been swindled . . . As I say, on this question of reasonable ground for making a demand, you may say to yourselves: "Well, they did have reasonable ground for making the demand in this sense, that they had put money into this deal, they had been swindled by Scott, and it was reasonable to demand the return of their money." So you may say: "Well, the prosecution have not negatived that but what about the second leg of the proviso, the belief that the use of menaces is a proper method of reinforcing the demand?" Now it is for you to decide what, if any, menaces were made, because that is a question of evidence. If you decide that the threats or menaces made by these accused, or any of them, were to kill or to maim or to rape, or any of the other matters that have been mentioned in evidence—I mention about three that come into my mind—then those menaces or threats are threats to commit a criminal act, a threat to murder, a threat to rape, or a threat to blow your legs or kneecaps off, those are threats to commit a criminal offence and surely everybody in this country, including the defendants, knows those are criminal offences. The point is that this is a matter of law. It cannot be a proper means of reinforcing the demand to make threats to commit serious criminal offences. So I say to you that if you look at these two counts of blackmail and you decide that these defendants, or any of them, used menaces, dependent upon the menaces you decide were used, the threats that were used, but if you decide that these threats were made by these men to commit criminal offences against Scott, they cannot be heard to say on this blackmail charge that they had reasonable belief that the use of those threats was a proper method of reinforcing their demand.'

Later, when prosecuting counsel drew attention to the learned judge's erroneous reference to 'reasonable' belief, he added the following: 'I do not think it affects the point I was seeking to make, that where the demand or the threat is to commit a criminal offence, and a serious criminal offence like murder and maiming and rape, or whatever it may be, it seems hard for anybody to say that the defendants had a belief that was a proper way of reinforcing their demand. That is the point.'

For the appellants it was submitted that the learned judge's direction, and in particular the earlier of the passages quoted, was incorrect in law because it took away from the jury a question properly falling within their province of decision, namely, what the accused in fact believed. He was wrong to rule as a matter of law that a threat to perform a serious criminal act could never be thought by the person making it to be a proper means. While free to comment on the unlikelihood of a defendant believing threats such as were made in this case to be a proper means, the judge should nonetheless (it was submitted) have left the question to the jury. For the Crown it was submitted that a threat to perform a criminal act can never as a matter of law be a proper means within the subsection, and that the learned judge's direction was accordingly correct. Support for both these approaches is to be found in academic works helpfully brought to the attention of the Court.

The answer to this problem must be found in the language of the subsection, from which in our judgment two points emerge with clarity: (1) the subsection is concerned with the belief of the individual defendant in the particular case: '. . . a demand with menaces is unwarranted unless *the person making it* does so in the belief . . .' (added emphasis). It matters not what the reasonable man, or any man other than the defendant, would believe save in so far as that may throw light on what the defendant in fact believed. Thus the factual question of the defendant's belief should be left to the jury. To that extent the subsection is subjective in approach, as is generally desirable in a criminal statute. (2) In order to exonerate a defendant from liability his belief must be that the use of the menaces is a 'proper' means of reinforcing the demand. 'Proper' is an unusual expression to find in a criminal statute. It is not defined in the Act, and no definition need be attempted here. It is, however, plainly a word of wide meaning, certainly wider than (for example) 'lawful.' But the greater includes the less and no act which was not believed to be lawful could be believed to be proper within the meaning of the subsection. Thus no assistance is given to any defendant, even a fanatic or a deranged idealist, who knows or suspects that his threat, or the act threatened, is criminal, but believes it to be justified by his end or his peculiar circumstances. The test is not what he regards as justified, but what he believes to be proper. And where, as here, the threats were to do acts which any sane man knows to be against the laws of every civilised country no jury would hesitate long before dismissing the contention that the defendant genuinely believed the threats to be a proper means of reinforcing even a legitimate demand.

It is accordingly our conclusion that the direction of the learned judge was not strictly correct. If it was necessary to give a direction on this aspect of the case at all (and in the absence of any evidence by the defendants as to their belief we cannot think that there was in reality any live issue concerning it) the jury should have been directed that the demand with menaces was not to be regarded as unwarranted unless the Crown satisfied them in respect of each defendant that the defendant did not make the demand with menaces in the genuine belief both—(a) that he had had reasonable grounds for making the demand; and (b) that the use of the menaces was in the circumstances a proper (meaning for present purposes a lawful, and not a criminal) means of reinforcing the demand.

The learned judge could, of course, make appropriate comment on the unlikelihood of the defendants believing murder and rape or threats to commit those acts to be lawful or other than criminal.

On the facts of this case we are quite satisfied that the misdirection to which we have drawn attention could have caused no possible prejudice to any of the appellants. Accordingly, in our judgment, it is appropriate to apply the proviso to s.2(1) of the Criminal Appeal Act 1968, and the appeals are dismissed.

Appeals against conviction dismissed

Questions

1. On the Criminal Law Revision Committee's proposal for a subjective test of propriety, Sir Brian MacKenna comments: "That a sane man's guilt or innocence should depend this way on his own opinion as to whether he is acting rightly or wrongly is, I think, an innovation in our criminal law". Has not the law reached this position with regard to theft? See *Ghosh*, above, p.658.

2. "No act which was not believed to be lawful could be believed to be proper within the meaning of the subsection . . . The test is not what he regards as justified, but what he believes to be

proper"—Bingham J, above. Is this consistent with the subjective test of propriety proposed by the Criminal Law Revision Committee, § 120?

3.   Can mistake of law be relevant in this connection?

4.   In the following cases, D, on trial for blackmail, contends that his request and threat were perfectly justified. How ought the judge to deal with the issue in his directions to the jury?

   (a)   D, with his entourage, arrives in England from a country where it is common for thieves to have their right hands cut off. D discovers that a member of his entourage, P, has been stealing money from him. He warns P that unless he returns the money, D will cut off his right hand.

   (b)   D, who uses his car daily to get to work, discovers that his road fund licence has expired. Not having the money to renew it, he asks P, his mother, for the money. When P refuses D says; "Driving an unlicensed car is a crime. Unless you give me the money, I will certainly commit this crime every day. You wouldn't want that on your conscience, would you?"

Note

G. Williams, *Textbook of Criminal Law*, 2nd edn (1983), p.837: "A factor of prime importance in a blackmail case will frequently be the secrecy or the openness of the transaction. A man who thinks he is acting properly in making a threat will not try to conceal his identity, and demand that money should be left in used pound notes at a telephone kiosk. Again, it is in practice impossible for a defendant both to argue that he did not utter the menaces and that if he did they were justified. So, if he chooses merely to deny the menaces, and the jury find against him and the menaces are prima facie improper, the judge need not direct the jury on the unscrupulous mental element".

----

iii.   With a View to Gain, etc.

THEFT ACT 1968 S.34

. . . (2) For the purposes of this Act—

   (a)   'gain' and 'loss' are to be construed as extending only to gain or loss in money or other property, but as extending to any such gain or loss whether temporary or permanent; and

      (i)   'gain' includes a gain by keeping what one has, as well as a gain by getting what one has not; and
      (ii)   'loss' includes a loss by not getting what one might get, as well as a loss by parting with what one has.

Note

R. v Parkes [1973] Crim. L.R. 358. D was charged with blackmail (inter alia). The evidence adduced by the prosecution showed that in one instance the money demanded was undoubtedly money owed to D by the complainant and, indeed, long overdue. In the other instance there was some issue as to whether or not the money demanded was a debt but the submission was made and ruled upon the basis that it was a debt owing by the complainant to D.

It was submitted that to demand what is lawfully owing to you was not a demand "with a view to gain" within the meaning of s.21(1) of the Theft Act 1968, as interpreted by s.32(2)(a) of that Act. Judge

Dean QC ruled that by demanding money lawfully owing to him D did have a view to "gain." Section 34(2)(a)(i) defines gain as including "getting what one has not"; by intending to obtain hard cash as opposed to a mere right of action in respect of the debt D *was* getting more than he already had and accordingly the submission failed.

R. v Bevans [1988] Crim. L.R. 236: D, suffering from osteoarthritis, went to a doctor's surgery, produced a gun and threatened to shoot the doctor if he did not give him an injection of a pain-killing drug. *Held*, upholding his conviction of blackmail, the drug was property; the demand involved gain for D; the fact that his ulterior motive was relief from pain rather than economic gain was immaterial.

Note

If the immediate object is to get property, the motive for making an unwarrantable demand with menaces is irrelevant. But if D's immediate object is to get a service rather than property or money, it may still be blackmail if his *motive* is financial. The words *"with a view* to gain" are capable of comprehending an ulterior motive of gain, e.g. D demands that V vote for him in an election for a company directorship, *so that* D will gain director's fees. See next case which concerned a different crime but one which also requires a view to gain or intent to cause loss.

R. V GOLECHHA AND CHORARIA

(1990) 90 Cr. App. R. 241 CA

G and C were convicted of falsification of accounts, contrary to s.17(1) of the Theft Act 1968, in that they dishonestly and with a view to gain for themselves or with intent to cause loss to another falsified certain bills of exchange. Their object was alleged to be to obtain a bank's forbearance to enforce against them certain other bills which had matured. On appeal:

LORD LANE CJ FOR THE COURT

'. . . When he came to sum up, the learned judge . . . directed the jury as follows:

> 'Going back to count one, you will see that after the word "dishonestly" we get "and with a view to gain for themselves." Now you may not have thought that this required a great deal of your consideration, but there are certain things that have to be proved. The dishonest falsification, if you find that there was such a thing, must be with a view to gain for the person or persons who are doing the falsifying. As a matter of law I will tell you that the mere fact that Johnson Matthey credited the dollar current account of Berg [a company owned and run by Golechha] with a sum which represented the discounted value of the bill does not amount to gain if you stop there. All that has happened is that there has been a paper plus put on the account and that does not amount to gain if you stop there. But if you decide that what the defendant Golechha and the defendant Choraria or either of them had in view—there is the word "with a view to gain"—went further than just getting a credit, a paper plus on Berg's account, but that what they were after was that Golechha should be able to turn that credit to practical use by drawing on it, converting it to cash in order to raise hard finance to buy goods, confirm deals and so forth, if you come to that view or that decision I should say, and you decide that that was the view that these people or either of them had in mind, members of the jury, that would amount to gain. That is a matter of fact for you.'

. . . Mr Blair Q.C. for the Crown submitted, rightly in our view, that in the passage we have cited from the summing up the learned judge was . . . directing the jury [that] the mere crediting of the account . . . was not in law a gain; but if they concluded that the object of the defendants was to turn that paper credit, by drawing on it, to cash for the purposes of trade, that would amount to gain. Mr Blair submits that the judge's interpretation of the section was perfectly reasonable and indeed correct. Parliament deliberately chose the words 'with a view to gain'—a phrase plainly admitting of some flexibility—precisely in order to cover cases such as the present.

As to the distinct argument to the effect that a mere forbearance to sue cannot in any event constitute a gain, Mr Blair contended that here too the judge was correct to regard his interpretation as affording an answer to it. He argued that even if all that was sought to be achieved by means of putting in place the last three bills was a forbearance on the part of the bank from suing on the earlier bills, the appellants were by that means trying to keep what they had in the sense that they were seeking to preserve a facility upon which they could in practice draw, whether or not it was enforceable in law.

In his reply to these submissions Mr Marshall-Andrews for Golechha . . . concentrated on two submissions only: first, that the judge's interpretation of section 17 is incorrect, and second that, even if it be correct, it does not meet the forbearance to sue point.

Mr Marshall-Andrews developed the first point in this way. He argued that the words 'with a view to gain' must refer to the gain sought to be obtained by the falsification. They were included so as to incorporate temporary gain and keeping what you have, but there was in truth no distinction between the expressions 'with a view to gain' and the expression 'with intent to obtain property.' It was not legitimate to look at the property into which that which was obtained might be converted . . .

We see the attractions, from a practical common sense point of view, of the judge's interpretation of the section, while at the same time appreciating the force of Mr Marshall-Andrews' argument against it. However we find it unnecessary in the present case further to examine or to seek to resolve this matter, because we have reached the clear conclusion that Mr Marshall-Andrews' . . . second answer to Mr Blair's submissions is conclusive in favour of the appellants.

Put in its simplest form, the prosecution's argument on forbearance to sue amounts to this: that even if all that the appellants sought to achieve was forbearance on the part of the bank to enforce their rights under an earlier bill, they were seeking by that means to preserve the facility. This argument is superficially attractive, but fallacious. Even if it be assumed in favour of the Crown that the first two bills reflected genuine trade transactions—as to which there was no evidence one way or the other—all that had been brought into existence was a debt owed by Berg to the bank: a debt which existed at all times. To speak of 'preserving the facility' by means of the placing of the falsified bills is to attribute to the facility characteristics which it does not possess. A debtor is not possessed of any proprietary rights: he does not have money, and the chose in action represented by the debt is owned by the creditor. Accordingly, while it may well be that the three falsified bills were falsified with a view to securing the bank's forbearance from enforcing their rights on the earlier bills, this did not and could not constitute falsification with a view to gain (that is gain by keeping money or other property). It was designed simply to postpone the enforcement of an obligation.

If it be accepted for present purposes that the learned judge's construction of the words 'with a view to gain' was correct, and that it is therefore legitimate to see how funds sought to be obtained on the strength of a falsified bill would be used by the defendant, that cannot avail the prosecution in a case where all that the defendant had in view was the forbearance to enforce an existing indebtedness. If the desired forbearance is obtained, this neither gives to the defendant nor allows him to retain anything on which he can draw or which he can convert into cash or goods. Such a case is quite distinct from one in which the object in view is to obtain an advance.

If, which we do not, we had any doubts as to the correctness of this analysis, they would be dispelled by the reflection that section 16 of the 1968 Act or s.2 of the 1978 Act are entirely apt to found charges based on the sort of conduct we have been considering.

It follows that, since it was at the very least a distinct possibility that the appellants' object in falsifying the bills in question was merely to obtain the bank's forbearance, the judge's failure to invite the jury to consider whether that was the position and to direct them that if it was the defendants were not guilty of the offence charged was a misdirection.

Accordingly these appeals must on that ground be allowed.

Convictions quashed

Note

Blackmail is a sort of inchoate offence in that the making of the unwarranted demand with menaces is the full crime, even if the demand is not acceded to and no property is got as a result. If property is got as a result, then theft and robbery may also be committed. But blackmail is also a "fall-back" offence, in that if property is got but claim of right prevents a conviction of theft or robbery it will be blackmail if the jury think D knew the menaces used were improper. The fact that D is or thinks he is entitled to what he gets does not mean that he does not act "with a view to gain." Similarly if the menaces used do not amount to the use of force on a person or the putting or seeking to put a person in fear of imminent force, it cannot be robbery but can be blackmail.

The extracts which follow highlight a problem with the offence of blackmail in terms of its breadth.

JAMES LINDGREN, "UNRAVELLING THE PARADOX OF BLACKMAIL" (1984) 84 COL. L.R. 670

In blackmail, the heart of the problem is that two separate acts, each of which is a moral and legal right, can combine to make a moral and legal wrong. For example, if I threaten to expose a criminal act unless I am paid money, I have committed blackmail. Or if I threaten to expose a sexual affair unless I am given a job, once again I have committed blackmail. I have a legal right to expose or threaten to expose the crime or affair, and I have a legal right to seek a job or money, but if I combine these rights it is blackmail. If both a person's ends—seeking a job or money—and his means—threatening to expose—are otherwise legal, why is it illegal to combine them? Therein lies what has been called the 'paradox of blackmail.' . . .

Not surprisingly, drawing the line between legitimate and illegitimate threats has proved impossible without an accepted theory . . .

One group of theories examines different parts of the blackmail transaction, postulating that the wrongfulness of blackmail consists in what the blackmailer threatens to do if not paid, in what he offers to do if paid, in what he is seeking or in what he is selling. These theories fail chiefly because no single part of the blackmail transaction, taken separately, is necessarily wrong. Since the conduct these theories identify may be wrong in blackmail but legitimate elsewhere, they fail to adequately distinguish legitimate from illegitimate behavior. A second group of theories centers on the purpose served by a law of blackmail—either to discourage invasions of privacy or to prevent the waste of economic resources. These theories fail because they do not explain either why blackmail is forbidden where these harms are absent or why we do not prohibit many other activities that create the same harms . . .

III. A NEW THEORY OF BLACKMAIL

A. Distinguishing Legitimate from Illegitimate Threats
We now turn to the main problem—distinguishing blackmail from legitimate bargaining. Merely identifying the element of threat will not solve the problem. Even highly coercive threats are present in many types of legitimate economic bargaining. For example, an injured potential plaintiff may threaten to sue unless a settlement is reached. A seller may threaten to sell to someone else unless the buyer agrees to pay the price demanded. Or a bank may threaten to foreclose on a loan that will destroy a business as well as someone's way of life. The problem is to distinguish legitimate threats from illegitimate ones; we must explain why the same threat when made by one person can be permissible, but when made by another person in different circumstances can be blackmail.

Let us first examine informational blackmail. Here the blackmailer threatens to tell others damaging information about the blackmail victim unless the victim heeds the blackmailer's request, usually a request for money. The blackmailer obtains what he wants by using extra leverage. But that leverage belongs more to a third person than to the blackmailer. The blackmail victim pays the blackmailer to avoid involving third parties; he pays to avoid being harmed by *persons other than the blackmailer*. When the reputation of a person is damaged, he is punished by all those who change their opinion of him. They may 'punish' him by treating him differently or he may be punished merely by the knowledge that others no longer respect him.

Thus when a blackmailer threatens to turn in a criminal unless paid money, the blackmailer is bargaining with the state's chip. The blackmail victim pays to avoid the harm that the state would inflict; he pays because he believes that he can thereby suppress the state's potential criminal claim. Of course, this does not effect a legally binding settlement, but the leverage is effective precisely to the extent that the victim believes that he has reached an effective settlement. Likewise, when a blackmailer threatens to expose damaging but noncriminal behavior unless paid money, he is also turning third-party leverage to his own benefit. What makes his conduct blackmail is that he interposes himself parasitically in an actual or potential dispute in which he lacks a sufficiently direct interest. What right has he to make money by settling other people's claims?

At the heart of blackmail, then, is the triangular nature of the transaction, and particularly this disjunction between the blackmailer's personal benefit and the interests of the third parties whose leverage he uses. In effect, the blackmailer attempts to gain an advantage in return for suppressing someone else's actual or potential interest. The blackmailer is negotiating for his own gain with someone else's leverage or bargaining chips.

This misuse of another's leverage is perhaps seen most clearly in noninformational blackmail, in situations where a formal agency relationship exists—for instance, where a labor union leader threatens to cause a strike unless he is given a personal payoff. There the labor leader is turning group power and a group dispute to personal benefit. The pressure on the blackmail victim would be the same if the blackmailer's agency relationship were merely informal—for instance, where an influential businessman threatens to cause a strike unless he is given a personal payoff. Notice that the victim of blackmail probably does not care whether the threatener is a labor leader or an influential businessman, an authorized agent or an unauthorized one. What the victim fears is a strike. Whoever seeks a personal payoff by credibly wielding the power of a third party to harm the victim is a blackmailer . . .

What emerges from these examples is the observation that blackmail is the misuse of an informal (or formal) power of agency or representation. Under my theory, blackmail is the seeking of an advantage by threatening to press an actual or potential dispute that is primarily between the blackmail victim and someone else. The blackmailer threatens to bring others into the dispute but typically asks for something for himself; he turns someone else's power, usually group power, to personal benefit. The bargaining is unfair in that the threatener uses leverage that is less his than someone else's.

Thus in a general sense, the law of blackmail promotes principled negotiations by outlawing a particular kind of unfair bargaining. A blackmailer uses a type of extra leverage to exact unearned payments, convert causes of action to cash, or resolve disputes other than on their merits. The law of blackmail tries to compel people to resolve their disputes by means the legal system provides or prefers, such as civil suits. It also discourages the settlement of disputes by persons who are neither parties to those disputes nor agents for those parties. Thus blackmail law is a manifestation of a core principle of our legal system, the assignment of enforcement rights to the victim: an individual enforces a private wrong and the state enforces a public wrong. This enforcement principle is extremely broad. It applies in civil law and criminal law, in public law and private law. It has been justified by economic analysis and doctrines of individual liberty, by natural law and constitutional law. It is fundamental to the organization of our courts and to our system of procedure.

But the exclusive assignment principle is not monolithic—quite the contrary. It takes different forms in tort, contract and criminal law, and its configurations have changed over time. For example, in torts and contracts different people are assigned enforcement rights today than were assigned such rights before the decline of privity doctrines. Criminal claims are assigned to the state. Tort and contract claims are assigned to the victim of those kinds of wrongdoing. And claims that would be nonredressable in court, such as the right to change one's opinion of someone, are assigned to the person who would change his mind . . .

Conclusion

Thus blackmail differs from ordinary bargaining and threats because the leverage used belongs less to the threatener than to a third party. It becomes clear why, in the paradoxical case, otherwise legitimate conduct becomes illegitimate in blackmail. The problem is not with anything intrinsic to the threat, or any other aspect of the conduct, which may remain legitimate when taken in isolation. Rather, the problem essentially is that the wrong person is making the threat; the blackmailer's own interest is not sufficient to justify his using that leverage. Thus the leverage being used, while legitimate in the hands of another, is illegitimate in the hands of the blackmailer.

13   HANDLING

The offence of handling is concerned with convicting those who assist thieves in the "disposal" of goods which have been stolen. Handling "will punish not only receivers, but also those who knowingly convey stolen goods to any place after the theft, those who take charge of them and keep them on their premises or hide them on the approach of the police, those who negotiate for the sale of the goods and the like." (Criminal Law Revision Committee, *Theft and Related Offences* § 128). If, as is often the case, what is done amounts to a dishonest appropriation of the property with intent permanently to deprive the owner, it will also constitute the offence of theft.

When looking at the definition of the offence, despite appearances to the contrary, it should be remembered that only one offence is created, although there are a myriad of ways in which it can be committed.

The most frequently cited justification for the offence, and the fact that it carries a higher maximum penalty than theft, is that if there were no receivers or handlers for stolen goods then there would not be so many thieves (see *R. v Battams* (1979) 1 Cr. App. R. 15).

THEFT ACT 1968 S.22

(1) A person handles stolen goods if (otherwise than in the course of stealing) knowing or believing them to be stolen goods he dishonestly receives the goods, or dishonestly undertakes or assists in their retention, removal, disposal or realisation by or for the benefit of another person, or if he arranges to do so.

(2) A person guilty of handling stolen goods shall on conviction on indictment be liable to imprisonment for a term not exceeding fourteen years.

i. Stolen Goods

THEFT ACT 1968 S.24

(1) The provisions of this Act relating to goods which have been stolen shall apply whether the stealing occurred in England or Wales or elsewhere, and whether it occurred before or after the commencement of this Act, provided that the stealing (if not an offence under this Act) amounted to an offence where and at the time when the goods were stolen; and references to stolen goods shall be construed accordingly.

(2) For purposes of those provisions references to stolen goods shall include, in addition to the goods originally stolen and parts of them (whether in their original state or not)—

(a) any other goods which directly or indirectly represent or have at any time represented the stolen goods in the hands of the thief as being the proceeds of any disposal or realisation of the whole or part of the goods stolen or of goods so representing the stolen goods; and

(b) any other goods which directly or indirectly represent or have at any time represented the stolen goods in the hands of a handler of the stolen goods or any part of them as being the proceeds of any disposal or realisation of the whole or part of the stolen goods handled by him or of goods so representing them.

(3) But no goods shall be regarded as having continued to be stolen goods after they have been restored to the person from whom they were stolen or to other lawful possession or custody, or after that person and any other person claiming through him have otherwise ceased as regards those goods to have any right to restitution in respect of the theft.

(4) For the purposes of the provisions of this Act relating to goods which have been stolen (including subsection (1) to (3) above) goods obtained in England or Wales or elsewhere either by blackmail or in the circumstances described in section 15(1) of this Act shall be regarded as stolen; and 'steal/ 'theft' and 'thief shall be construed accordingly.

THEFT ACT 1968 S.34

(2) For the purposes of this Act—

(b) 'goods,' except in so far as the context otherwise requires, includes money and every other description of property except land, and includes things severed from the land by stealing.

Notes

1. It has to be shown that "goods" within the meaning of s.34(2)(b), were stolen (or obtained by blackmail or deception: s.24(4)) by someone (who may be the present defendant: see below); that the property the subject of the charge is either those goods or represents them (s.24(2)); and that, at the time of the alleged handling, the goods were still stolen goods (s.24(3)).

2. Section 24(2) was explained by the Criminal Law Revision Committe, § 138 as follows, "It may seem technical; but the effect will be that the goods which the accused is charged with handling must, at the time of the handling or at some previous time, (i) have been in the hands of the thief or of a handler, and (ii) have represented the original stolen goods in the sense of being the proceeds direct or indirect, of a sale or other realisation of the original goods."

3. As to the definition of "goods", compare "property" in s.4(1).

ATTORNEY GENERAL'S REFERENCE (NO.1 OF 1974)

[1974] Q.B. 744

The facts appear in the Court's opinion.

LORD WIDGERY CJ

The facts of the present case, which I take from the terms of the reference itself, are these:

> 'A police constable found an unlocked, unattended car containing packages of new clothing which he suspected, and which in fact subsequently proved to be stolen. The officer removed the rotor arm from the vehicle to immobilise it, and kept observation. After about ten minutes, the accused appeared, got into the van and attempted to start the engine. When questioned by the officer, he gave an implausible explanation, and was arrested.'

Upon those facts two charges were brought against the respondent: one of stealing the woollen goods, the new clothing, which were in the back of the car in question and secondly and alternatively of receiving those goods knowing them to be stolen. The trial judge quite properly ruled there was no evidence to support the first charge, and that he would not leave that to the jury, but an argument developed as to whether the second count should be left to the jury or not. Counsel for the respondent in the court below had submitted at the close of the prosecution case that there was no case to answer, relying on section 24(3) of the Theft Act 1968. That provides as follows:

'. . . no goods shall be regarded as having continued to be stolen goods after they have been restored to the person from whom they were stolen or to other lawful possession or custody . . .'

The rest of the subsection is not relevant and I do not read it. It was therefore contended in the court below on the facts to which I have already referred that by virtue of section 24(3) the goods had been restored to other lawful possession or custody, namely the custody or possession of the police officer before the respondent appeared on the scene and sought to drive the car away. If that argument was sound of course it would follow that there was no case for the respondent to answer, because if in fact the police constable had restored the stolen goods to his own lawful possession or custody before the act relied upon as an act of receiving occurred, it would follow that they would not be stolen goods at the material time.

After hearing argument, the judge accepted the submission of the respondent and directed the jury that they should acquit on the receiving count. That has resulted in the Attorney-General referring the following point of law to us for an opinion. He expresses the point in this way:

'Whether stolen goods are restored to lawful custody within the meaning of section 24(3) of the Theft Act 1968 when a police officer, suspecting them to be stolen, examines and keeps observation on them with a view to tracing the thief or a handler.'

One could put the question perhaps in a somewhat different way by asking whether upon the facts set out in the reference the conclusion as a matter of law was clear to the effect that the goods had ceased to be stolen goods. In other words, the question which is really in issue in this reference is whether the trial judge acted correctly in law in saying that those facts disclosed a defence within section 24(3).

Subsection (3) is not perhaps entirely happily worded. It has been pointed out in the course of argument that in the sentence which I have read there is only one relevant verb, and that is 'restore.' The section contemplates that the stolen goods should be restored to the person from whom they were stolen or to other lawful possession or custody. It is pointed out that the word 'restore' although it is entirely appropriate when applied to restoration of the goods to the true owner, is not really an appropriate verb to employ if one is talking about a police officer stumbling upon stolen goods and taking them into his own lawful custody or possession.

We are satisfied that despite the absence of another and perhaps more appropriate verb, the effect of section 24(3) is to enable a defendant to plead that the goods had ceased to be stolen goods if the facts are that they were taken by a police officer in the course of his duty and reduced into possession by him.

Whether or not section 24(3) is intended to be a codification of the common law or not, it certainly deals with a topic upon which the common law provides a large number of authorities. I shall refer to some of them in a moment, although perhaps not all and it will be observed that from the earliest times it has been recognised that if the owner of stolen goods resumed possession of them, reduced them into his possession again, that they thereupon ceased to be stolen goods for present purposes and could certainly not be the subject of a later charge of receiving based on events after they had been reduced into possession. It is to be observed that at common law nothing short of a reduction into possession, either by the true owner or by a police officer acting in the execution of his duty, was regarded as sufficient to change the character of the goods from stolen goods into goods which were no longer to be so regarded.

I make that assertion true by a brief reference from the cases to which we have been referred. The first is *R. v Dolan* (1855) 6 Cox C.C. 449. The facts there were that stolen goods were found in the pocket of a thief by the owner. The owner sent for a policeman, and the evidence given at the subsequent trial showed that after the policeman had taken the goods from the thief, the thief, the policeman and the owner went towards the shop owned and occupied by the prisoner at which the thief had asserted that he was hoping to sell the stolen goods. When they got near the shop the policeman gave the goods to the thief, who then went on ahead into the shop with a view to selling the goods, closely followed by the owner and the policeman, who proceeded to arrest the shop keeper. It was held there

'that the prisoner was not guilty of feloniously receiving stolen goods; inasmuch as they were delivered to him under the authority of the owner by a person to whom the owner had bailed them for that purpose.'

Put another way, one can explain that decision on the broad principle to which I have already referred: the goods had already been returned to the possession of the owner before they were then released by him into the hands of the thief in order that the thief might approach the receiver with a view to the receiver being arrested. The principle thus enunciated is one which, as I have already said, is to be found in the other authorities to which we have been referred.

The next one which is similar is *R. v Schmidt* (1866) L.R. 1 C.C.R. 15. The reference in the headnote suffices:

'Four thieves stole goods from the custody of a railway company, and afterwards sent them in a parcel by the same company's line addressed to the prisoner. During the transit the theft was discovered; and, on the arrival of the parcel at the station for its delivery, a policeman in the employ of the company opened it, and then returned it to the porter whose duty it was to deliver it, with instructions to keep it until further orders. On the following day the policeman directed the porter to take the parcel to its address, when it was received by the prisoner, who was afterwards convicted of receiving the goods knowing them to be stolen, . . .'

And it was held by the Court for Crown Cases Reserved 'that the goods had got back into the possession of the owner, so as to be no longer stolen goods and that the conviction was wrong.' Again unquestionably they had been reduced into the possession of the owner by the hand of the police officer acting on his behalf. They had not been allowed to continue their course unaffected. They had been taken out of circulation by the police officer, reduced into the possession of the owner or of the officer, and it matters not which, and thus had ceased to be stolen goods for present purposes . . .

Then there is a helpful case, *R. v Villensky* [1892] 2 Q.B. 597. Again it is a case of a parcel in the hands of carriers. This parcel was handed to the carriers in question for conveyance to the consignees, and whilst in the carriers' depot it was stolen by a servant of the carriers who removed the parcel to a different part of the premises and placed upon it a label addressed to the prisoners by a name by which they were known and a house where they resided. The superintendent of the carriers on receipt of information as to this and after the inspection of the parcel, directed it to be placed in the place from which the thief had removed it and to be sent with a special delivery receipt in a van accompanied by two detectives to the address shown on the label. At that address it was received by the prisoners under circumstances which clearly showed knowledge on their part that it had been stolen. The property in the parcel was laid in the indictment in the carriers and an offer to amend the indictment by substituting the names of the consignees was declined. The carriers' servant pleaded guilty to a count for larceny in the same indictment. It was there held by the Court for Crown Cases Reserved

'that as the person in which the property was laid'—that is the carriers—'had resumed possession of the stolen property before its receipt by the prisoners, it had then ceased to be stolen property, and the prisoners could not be convicted of receiving it knowing it to have been stolen.'

On p.599 there is a brief and valuable judgment by Pollock B. in these terms:

'The decisions in *Dolan*, and *Schmidt*, are, in my judgment, founded on law and on solid good sense, and they should not be frittered away. It is, of course, frequently the case that when it is found that a person has stolen property he is watched; but the owner of the property, if he wishes to catch the receiver, does not resume possession of the stolen goods; here the owners have done so, and the result is that the conviction must be quashed.'

We refer to that brief judgment because it illustrates in a few clear words what is really the issue in the present case. When the police officer discovered these goods and acted as he did, was the situation that he had taken possession of the goods, in which event, of course, they ceased to be stolen goods? or was it merely that he was watching the goods with a view to the possibility of catching the receiver at a later stage? I will turn later to a consideration of those two alternatives.

Two other cases should, I think, be mentioned at this stage. The next one is *R. v King* [1938] 2 All E.R. 662. We are now getting to far more recent times. The appellant here was convicted with another man of receiving stolen goods knowing them to have been stolen. A fur coat had been stolen and shortly afterwards the police went to a flat where they found the man Burns and told him they were enquiring about some stolen property. He at first denied that there was anything there but finally admitted the theft and produced a parcel from a wardrobe. While a policeman was in the act of examining the contents of the parcel, the telephone bell rang. Burns answered it and the police heard him say: 'Come along as arranged.' The police then suspended operations and about 20 minutes later the appellant arrived, and, being admitted by Burns, said 'I have come for the coat. Harry sent me.'

This was heard by the police, who were hiding at the time. The coat was handed to the appellant by Burns, so that he was actually in possession of it. It was contended that the possession by the police amounted to possession by the owner of the coat, and that, therefore, the coat was not stolen property at the time the appellant received it. Held by the Court of Appeal: that the coat had not been in the possession of the police and it was therefore still stolen when the appellant received it . . .

The most recent case on the present topic, but of little value in the present problems is *Haughton v Smith*, in the House of Lords. The case being of little value to us in our present problems, I will deal with it quite briefly. It is a case where a lorry load of stolen meat was intercepted by police, somewhere in the North of England, who discovered that the lorry was in fact full of stolen goods. After a brief conference they decided to take the lorry on to its destination with a view to catching the receivers at the London end of the affair. So the lorry set off for London with detectives both in the passenger seat and in the back of the vehicle, and in due course was met by the defendant at its destination in London. In that case before this court it was conceded, as it had been conceded below, that the goods had been reduced into the possession of the police when they took possession of the lorry in the North of England, so no dispute in this court or later in the House of Lords was raised on that issue. It is, however, to be noted that three of their Lordships, when the matter got to the House of Lords, expressed some hesitation as to the propriety of the prosecution conceding in that case that the goods had been reduced to the possession of the police when the lorry was first intercepted. Since we cannot discover on what ground those doubts were expressed either from the report of the speeches or from the report of the argument, we cannot take advantage of that case in the present problem.

Now we return to the present problem again with those authorities in the background: did the conduct of the police officer, as already briefly recounted, amount to a taking of possession of the woollen goods in the back seat of the motor car? What he did, to repeat the essential facts, was: that seeing these goods in the car and being suspicious of them because they were brand new goods and in an unlikely position, he removed the rotor arm and stood by in cover to interrogate any driver of the car who might subsequently appear. Did that amount to a taking possession of the goods in the back of the car? In our judgment it depended primarily on the intentions of the police officer. If the police officer seeing these goods in the back of the car had made up his mind that he would take them into custody, that he would reduce them into his possession or control, take charge of them so that they could not be removed and so that he would have the disposal of them, then it would be a perfectly proper conclusion to say that he had taken possession of the goods. On the other hand, if the truth of the matter is that he was of an entirely open mind at that stage as to whether the goods were to be seized or not and was of an entirely open mind as to whether he should take possession of them or not, but merely stood by so that when the driver of the car appeared he could ask certain questions of that driver as to the nature of the goods and why they were there, then there is no reason whatever to suggest that he had taken the goods into his possession or control. It may be, of course, that he had both objects in mind. It is possible in a case like this that the police officer may have intended by removing the rotor arm both to prevent the car from being driven away and to enable him to assert control over the woollen goods as such. But if the jury came to the conclusion that the proper explanation of what had happened was that the police officer had not intended at that stage to reduce the goods into his possession or to assume the control of them, and at that stage was merely concerned to ensure that the driver, if he appeared, could not get away without answering questions, then in that case the proper conclusion of the jury would have been to the effect that the goods had not been reduced into the possession of the police and therefore a defence under section 24(3) of the Theft Act 1968 would not be of use to this particular defendant.

In the light of those considerations it has become quite obvious that the trial judge was wrong in withdrawing the issue from the jury. As a matter of law he was not entitled to conclude from the facts which I have set out more than once that these goods were reduced into the possession of the police officer. What he should have done in our opinion would have been to have left that issue to the jury for decision, directing the jury that they should find that the prosecution case was without substance if they thought that the police officer had assumed control of the goods as such and reduced them into his possession. Whereas on the other hand, they should have found the case proved, assuming that they were satisfied about its other elements, if they were of the opinion that the police officer in removing the rotor arm and standing by and watching was doing no more than ensure that the driver should not get away without interrogation and was not at that stage seeking to assume possession of the goods as such at all. That is our opinion.

Opinion accordingly

It is not always a question of fact whether the owner or police have reduced the goods into possession. In *MPC v Streeter* (1980) 71 Cr. App. R. 113, the owner's security officer initialled the goods and alerted the police, who kept watch and followed the defendant when he picked up the goods. It was held by the Divisional Court that the magistrates were wrong to conclude that this was a reduction into the possession of the owner, and the case was sent back with a direction to convict.

----

ii. Otherwise than in the Course of Stealing

R. V PITHAM & HEHL

(1986) 65 Cr. App. R. 45 CA

P and H were charged with burglary along with M. M was convicted of burglary but P and H were acquitted, when it appeared that M had invited them into the victim's house and offered them the victim's furniture. They paid him for it and took it away. P and H were also charged with handling stolen goods and were convicted of this. They appealed on the ground that the handling was not "otherwise than in the course of stealing."

LAWTON LJ

. . . What was the appropriation in this case? The jury found that the two appellants had handled the property *after* Millman has stolen it. That is clear from their acquittal of these two appellants on count 3 of the indictment which had charged them jointly with Millman. What had Millman done? He had assumed the rights of the owner. He had done that when he took the two appellants to 20 Party Road, showed them the property and invited them to buy what they wanted. He was then acting as the owner. He was then, in the words of the statute, 'assuming the rights of the owner.' The moment he did that he appropriated McGregor's goods to himself. The appropriation was complete. After this appropriation had been completed there was no question of these two appellants taking part, in the words of section 22, in dealing with the goods 'in the course of the stealing.'

It follows that no problem arises in this case. It may well be that some of the situations which the two learned professors envisage and discuss in their books may have to be dealt with at some future date, but not in this case. The facts are too clear.

Mr Murray suggested the learned judge should have directed the jury in some detail about the possibility that the appropriation had not been an instantaneous appropriation, but had been one which had gone on for some time. He submitted that it might have gone on until such time as the furniture was loaded into the appellants' van. For reasons we have already given that was not a real possibility in this case. It is no part of a judge's duty to give the jury the kind of lecture on the law which may be appropriate for a professor to give to a class of undergraduates. We commend the judge for not having involved himself in a detailed academic analysis of the law relating to this case when on the facts it was as clear as anything could be that either these appellants had helped Millman to steal the goods, or Millman had stolen them and got rid of them by sale to these two appellants. We can see nothing wrong in the learned judge's approach to this case and on that particular ground we affirm what he did and said . . .

Appeal dismissed

1.   Does it follow that Millman, the thief, was also guilty of handling? See forms of handling below.

2.   If he was guilty, is that a satisfactory result? See below.

CRIMINAL LAW REVISION COMMITTEE'S 8TH REPORT, *THEFT AND RELATED OFFENCES* (TSO, 1966), CMND.2977

§ 131 [Justifying the phrase 'otherwise than in the course of the stealing'] Under the definition a thief may be liable for handling if, after the theft is complete, he does some of the things mentioned in the definition for someone else, for example if he helps a receiver to dispose of the goods. Since it might be thought too severe to make a thief guilty of handling in such a case, we thought of providing that a thief should not be guilty of handling by reason of doing any of the things mentioned in the definition in respect of goods which he has himself stolen. But we decided not to include the provision. If after the theft is complete the thief takes part in a separate transaction for the disposal of the goods, it seems right that he should be guilty of handling like anybody else involved in the transaction.

Notes

1. This compromise by the Criminal Law Revision Committee is not without its awkwardness in practice. The offences of theft and handling are not entirely mutually exclusive, in that D can be guilty of both if, after the theft is complete, he takes part in a separate transaction for the disposal of the goods. But apart from the difficult question of what is a separate transaction, as to which see *R. v Pitham & Hehl*, above, in practice in many cases where D is inferentially guilty of handling, by being in possession of goods which have recently been stolen by someone, there will be nothing to suggest one way or the other whether he was the thief and his possession arose out of the stealing. Although separate counts for theft and handling may be included in one indictment, the difficulty remains that the jury may well be sure that D is guilty of either theft *or* handling, but are not sure which. In such a case, they may not convict of either. Their duty is to consider the theft which made the goods stolen goods, and if they are satisfied that D committed it, to convict him of theft. If they are not so satisfied, they must acquit him of theft and go on to consider whether he handled the goods with guilty knowledge. They are not entitled to say, "We are satisfied he committed one or the other", and then go on to convict of the offence which seems more probable: see *Attorney General for Hong Kong v Yip Kai-Foon* [1988] 1 All E.R. 153.

2. Of course many (though not all) acts of handling are themselves appropriations of property belonging to another with intent to deprive the owner permanently. Any handler who deals with the goods himself (as opposed to merely "arranging", or "assisting" someone else), commits theft when he does so, and if the alternative count for theft is drafted sufficiently widely to cover both the original taking and the subsequent dealing with the goods, then even if there is doubt about whether the original theft was by him and his act of handling was in the course of that theft, he may still, on a suitably careful direction, be convicted of theft in respect of the appropriation in the act of handling. See *Stapylton v O'Callaghan* [1973] 2 All E.R. 782.

Question

Were Pitham and Hehl rightly acquitted of burglary? (See, below, Ch.14.) When they took the goods from Millman, did not they dishonestly appropriate property belonging to the victim? Did they not enter the victim's house as trespassers with the intent to commit that theft? See next case.

    R. v Gregory (1981) 77 Cr. App. R. 41 CA. The jury were allowed to convict D of burglary if they thought that he had gone to V's house at the invitation of A and B with the intention of buying V's goods which they had stolen. D appealed on the ground that since, according to *R. v Pitham & Hehl*, the theft of the goods by A & B would have been complete by the time D dealt with them, his offence was handling, not burglary. In upholding the conviction, the Court of Appeal distinguished *R. v Pitham & Hehl* as being a case of "what might be called instantaneous appropriation. But not every appropriation need be or indeed is instantaneous."

[After quoting Eveleigh LJ in *R. v Hale*.]

"Nor do we think that in a given criminal enterprise involving theft there can necessarily be only one 'appropriation' within section 3(1) of the Theft Act 1968. It seems to us that the question of whether, when and by whom there has been an appropriation of property has always to be determined by the jury having regard to the circumstances of the case. The length of time involved, the manner in which it came about and the number of people who can properly be said to have taken part in an appropriation will vary according to those circumstances. In a case of burglary of a dwelling-house and before any property is removed from it, it may consist of a continuing process and involve either a single appropriation by one or more persons or a number of appropriations of the property in the house by several persons at different times during the same incident. If this were not a correct exposition of the law of appropriation, startling and disturbing consequences could arise out of the presence of two or more trespassers in a dwelling-house. Thus a person who may have more the appearance of a handler than the thief can nevertheless still be convicted of theft, and thus of burglary, if the jury are satisfied that with the requisite dishonest intent, he appropriated, or took part in the appropriation, of another person's goods."

Question

To uphold the conviction, was it necessary to distinguish *R. v Pitham & Hehl*?

----

iii. Forms of Handling

Notes

1. The offence is not confined to "receiving", as before 1968. It can be committed either by receiving or by undertaking or assisting in the goods' retention, removal, disposal or realisation by or for the benefit of another person", or "arranging" to do any of these things.

2. If the goods are not in fact stolen goods when any of these forms of handling is done, it is not the full offence (see *Haughton v Smith*), although it may be an attempt to handle (see *R. v Shivpuri*). An arrangement to receive or to undertake or assist in the goods' retention etc. entered into before they are stolen, may well be conspiracy to handle, but it is not the full offence (see *R. v Park* (1988) 87 Cr. App. R. 164 CA), unless, presumably, the arrangement is ratified or confirmed in some way after the theft has taken place.

3. Receiving, or arranging to receive, may be entirely on the accused's own account; but if the form of handling alleged is one of the other matters mentioned in s.22(1), it must be "by or for the benefit of another person". On the meaning of this expression, see *R. v Bloxham*, below.

R. V PITCHLEY

(1972) 57 Cr. App. R. 30 CA

P's son handed P £150 in order that P should look after it for him. According to P, he paid it into his post office savings account, and then later became aware that the £150 was stolen. Because he did not wish to give his son away, P did nothing about the money in the account until he was interviewed some days later by the police. He was convicted of dishonestly handling goods, namely the sum of £150 . . . knowing or believing the same to be stolen goods. He appealed.

CAIRNS LJ

The indictment . . . simply charged handling stolen goods without specifying whether it was under the first limb or under the second limb, and if the latter, under which part of the second limb of section 22(1) of the Theft Act; but the case that was presented by the prosecution at the trial was clearly presented in the alternative, that it was either under the first limb of receiving, or under the second limb for assisting in the retention of stolen goods . . .

The main point that has been taken by Mr Kalisher, who is appearing for the appellant in this court, is that, assuming that the jury were not satisfied that the appellant received the money knowing it to have been stolen, and that is an assumption which clearly is right to make, then there was no evidence after that, that from the time when the money was put into the savings bank, that the appellant had done any act in relation to it. His evidence was, and there is no reason to suppose that the jury did not believe it, that at the time when he put the money into the savings bank he still did not know or believe that the money had been stolen—it was only at a later stage that he did. That was on the Saturday according to his evidence, and the position was that the money had simply remained in the savings bank from the Saturday, to the Wednesday when the police approached the appellant. It is fair to say that from the moment when he was approached he displayed the utmost frankness to the extent of correcting them when they said it was £100 to £150 and telling them where the post office savings book was so that the money could be got out again and restored to its rightful owner.

But the question is: Did the conduct of the appellant between the Saturday and the Wednesday amount to an assisting in the retention of this money for the benefit of his son Brian? The court has been referred to the case of *Brown* (1969) 53 CrApp.R. 527 which was a case where stolen property had been put into a wardrobe at the appellant's house and when the police came to inquire about it the appellant said to them: 'Get lost'. The direction to the jury had been on the basis that it was for them to consider whether in saying: 'Get lost', instead of helping the police constable, he was dishonestly assisting in the retention of stolen goods. This court held that that was a misdirection but there are passages in the judgment in the case of *Brown* which, in the view of this court, are of great assistance in determining what is meant by 'retention' in this section. I read first of all from p.528 setting out the main facts a little more fully: 'A witness named Holden was called by the prosecution. He gave evidence that he and others had broken into the cafe and had stolen the goods, and that he had brought them to the appellant's flat, where, incidentally, other people were sleeping, and had hidden them there; and he described how he had taken the cigarettes out of the packets, put them in the plastic bag and hidden them in the wardrobe. Holden went on to say that later and before the police arrived he told the appellant where the cigarettes were; in other words, he said that the appellant well knew that the cigarettes were there and they had been stolen.' There was no evidence that the appellant had done anything active in relation to the cigarettes up to the time when the police arrived. The Lord Chief Justice, Lord Parker, in the course of his judgment at p.530 said this: 'It is urged here that the mere failure to reveal the presence of the cigarettes, with or without the addition of the spoken words 'Get lost', was incapable itself of amounting to an assisting in the retention of the goods within the meaning of the subsection. The court has come to the conclusion that that is right. It does not seem to this court that the mere failure to tell the police, coupled if you like with the words 'Get lost', amounts in itself to an assisting in their retention. On the other hand, those matters did afford strong evidence of what was the real basis of the charge here, namely, that knowing that they had been stolen, he permitted them to remain there or, as it has been put, provided accommodation for these stolen goods in order to assist Holden to retain them.' Having said that the direction was incomplete the Lord Chief Justice went on to say: 'The Chairman should have gone on to say: But the fact that he did not tell the constable that they were there and said 'Get lost' is evidence from which you can infer, if you think right, that this man was permitting the goods to remain in his flat, and to that extent assisting in their retention by Holden.'" In this present case there was no question on the evidence of the appellant himself, that he was permitting the money to remain under his control in the savings bank book, and it is clear that this court in the case of *Brown* regarded such permitting as sufficient to constitute retention within the meaning of retention. That is clear from the passage I have already read, emphasised in the next paragraph, the final paragraph of the judgment, where the Lord Chief Justice said (at p.531): 'It is a plain case in which the proviso should be applied. It seems to this court that the only possible inference in these circumstances, once Holden was believed is that this man was assisting in their retention by housing the goods and providing accommodation for them, by permitting them to remain there.' It is important to realise that that language was in relation to a situation where there was no evidence that anything active had been done by the appellant in relation to the goods.

In the course of the argument, Nield J. cited the dictionary meaning of the word 'retain'—keep possession of, not lose, continue to have. In the view of this court, that is the meaning of the word 'retain' in this section. It was submitted by Mr Kalisher that, at any rate, it was ultimately for the jury to decide whether there was retention or not and that even assuming that what the appellant did was of such a character that it could constitute retention, the jury ought to have been directed that it was for them to determine as a matter of fact, whether that was so or not. The court cannot agree with that submission. The meaning of the word 'retention' in the section is a matter of law in so far as the construction of the word is necessary. It is hardly a difficult question of construction because it is an ordinary English word and in the view of this court, it was no more necessary for the Deputy Chairman to leave the jury the question of whether or not what was done amounted to retention than it would be necessary for a judge in a case where goods had been handed to a person who knew that they had been stolen for him to direct the jury it was for them to decide whether or not that constituted receiving.

We are satisfied that no complaint of the summing-up which was made can be sustained and that there is no ground on which this verdict could be said to be unsafe or unsatisfactory. The appeal is therefore dismissed.

Appeal dismissed

R. V KANWAR

[1982] 2 All E.R. 528

K's husband brought home stolen goods. K, knowing they were stolen, used them to furnish the house. Later she told lies to police officers about the goods in order to persuade them that they were not stolen. She was convicted of handling stolen goods by dishonestly assisting in their retention, and appealed.

CANTLEY J

In *R. v Thornhill*, decided in this court on May 15, 1981 (unreported), and in *R. v Sanders*, it was held that merely using stolen goods in the possession of another does not constitute the offence of assisting in their retention. To constitute the offence, something must be done by the offender, and done intentionally and dishonestly, for the purpose of enabling the goods to be retained. Examples of such conduct are concealing or helping to conceal the goods, or doing something to make them more difficult to find or to identify. Such conduct must be done knowing or believing the goods to be stolen and done dishonestly and for the benefit of another.

We see no reason why the requisite assistance should be restricted to physical acts. Verbal representations, whether oral or in writing, for the purpose of concealing the identity of stolen goods may, if made dishonestly and for the benefit of another, amount to handling stolen goods by assisting in their retention within the meaning of section 22 of the Theft Act 1968.

The requisite assistance need not be successful in its object. It would be absurd if a person dishonestly concealing stolen goods for the benefit of a receiver could establish a defence by showing that he was caught in the act. In the present case, if, while the police were in one part of the house, the appellant, in order to conceal the painting had put it under a mattress in the bedroom, it would not alter the nature of her conduct that the police subsequently looked under the mattress and found the picture because they expected to find it there or that they caught her in the act of putting it there.

The appellant told these lies to the police to persuade them that the picture and the mirror were not the stolen property which they had come to take away but were her lawful property which she had bought. If that was true, the articles should be left in the house. She was, of course, telling these lies to protect her husband, who had dishonestly brought the articles there but, in our view, she was nonetheless, at the time, dishonestly assisting in the retention of the stolen articles.

In his summing up, the judge directed the jury as follows:

'It would be quite wrong for you to convict this lady if all she did was to watch her husband bring goods into the house, even if she knew or believed that they were stolen goods because, no doubt, you would say to yourselves, What would she be expected to do about it? Well, what the Crown say is that she knew or believed them to be stolen and that she was a knowing and willing party to their being kept in that house in those circumstances. The reason the Crown say that, and we shall be coming to the evidence, is that when questioned about a certain number of items, [the appellant] gave answers which the Crown say were not true and that she could not possibly have believed to be true and that she knew perfectly well were untruthful. So, say the prosecution, she was not just an acquiescent wife who could not do much about it, she was, by her conduct in trying to put the police officers as best she could off the scent, demonstrating that she was a willing and knowing party to those things being there and that she was trying to account for them. Well, it will be for you to say, but you must be satisfied before you can convict her on either of these counts, not only that she knew or believed the goods to be stolen, but that she actively assisted her husband in keeping them there; not by just passive acquiescence in the sense of saying, What can I do about it? but in the sense of saying, How nice to have these things in our home, although they are stolen goods.'

In so far as this direction suggests that the appellant would be guilty of the offence if she was merely willing for the goods to be kept and used in the house and was thinking that it was nice to have them there, although they were stolen goods, it is a misdirection. We have considered whether on that account the conviction ought to be quashed. However, the offence was established by the uncontradicted evidence of the police officer which, looked at in full, clearly shows that in order to mislead the officer who had come to take away stolen goods, she misrepresented the identity of the goods which she knew or believed to be stolen. We are satisfied that no miscarriage of justice has occurred and the appeal is accordingly dismissed.

Appeal dismissed

R. v Sanders (1982) 75 Cr. App. R. 84 CA: A, who owned a garage, stole some equipment. It was found in the garage being used by D, the son of A, who was employed there. He admitted he knew it was stolen. *Held*, mere use of goods knowing them to be stolen was not enough to found a conviction of assisting in the retention of them; he must have concealed, disguised, or held the goods pending disposal.

R. v Coleman [1986] 56: D and his wife purchased a flat in their joint names with money the wife had stolen, as D well knew. *Held*, the actus reus was assisting in the disposal of the money, not getting the benefit, and the fact that D had benefited from what his wife did was no proof that he had assisted her. There had to be evidence of helping or encouraging. On a proper direction, the jury could properly have inferred that D told his wife to use the stolen money or agreed that she should do so; but they were not so directed, and it was impossible to say whether they would have done so; they might have inferred that the wife acted without assistance.

Questions

1. A, after stealing a gold watch, deposits it in the potting shed of his friend B. Later B and C, another friend, notice the watch, recognise it as stolen, and guess that A will return and remove it when he has the opportunity. Because they do not wish to shop A, both B and C reply Get lost when asked by a policeman if they have seen the watch. On this evidence, can either of them be convicted of handling?

2. A gives a fur coat to his wife B. He later tells her that he had stolen it in a burglary, but she continues to wear it. Is B guilty of handling?

3. A gives a fur coat to his wife B. When he later tells B that he bought the coat with the proceeds

of a burglary he had committed, B sells the coat to a friend. Does B undertake the disposal or realisation of the coat for the benefit of another? See the next case.

R. V BLOXHAM

[1982] 1 All E.R. 582 HL

B agreed to buy a car which, unknown to him, had been stolen. Several months later, he became convinced that it had been stolen, because his vendor failed to produce the registration documents. B therefore sold the car to a man he did not know who was prepared to buy it without the documents. B was charged with handling stolen goods contrary to s.22 of the Theft Act 1968. After a ruling by the trial judge that the sale was a dishonest realisation of the car for the benefit of another person, B pleaded guilty. He appealed on the ground that the judge's ruling was wrong in law.

LORD BRIDGE OF HARWICH

The critical words to be construed are 'undertakes . . . their . . . disposal or realization . . . for the benefit of another person.' Considering these words first in isolation, it seems to me that, if A sells his own goods to B, it is a somewhat strained use of language to describe this as a disposal or realisation of the goods for the benefit of B. True it is that B obtains a benefit from the transaction, but it is surely more natural to say that the disposal or realisation is for A's benefit than for B's. It is the purchase, not the sale, that is for the benefit of B. It is only when A is selling as agent for a third party C that it would be entirely natural to describe the sale as a disposal or realisation for the benefit of another person.

But the words cannot, of course, be construed in isolation. They must be construed in their context . . . The . . . words contemplate four activities (retention, removal, disposal, realisation). The offence can be committed in relation to any one of these activities in one or other of two ways. First, the offender may himself undertake the activity *for the benefit* of another person. Second, the activity may be undertaken *by* another person and the offender may assist him . . . If the analysis holds good it must follow, I think, that the category of other persons contemplated by the subsection is subject to the same limitations in whichever way the offence is committed. Accordingly, a purchaser, as such, of stolen goods cannot, in my opinion, be 'another person' within the subsection, since his act of purchase could not sensibly be described as a disposal or realisation of the stolen goods by him. Equally, therefore, even if the sale to him could be described as a disposal or realisation for his benefit, the transaction is not, in my view, within the ambit of the subsection . . .

Appeal allowed: Conviction quashed

Question

What offence was committed by Bloxham if (i) the purchaser from him knew or believed that the car was stolen. (ii) the purchaser did not know or believe that?

Note

Where A and B are jointly charged in one count on an indictment with handling by or for the benefit of another person, the other person must be someone other than the co-accused. In *Gingell* [2000] 1 Cr. App. R. 88, Gingell was convicted of handling and the particulars of the offence were as follows:

Andrew Camper and Stewart Matthew Albert Gingell on a day between the 20th day of April 1997 and the 30th day of April 1997 dishonestly undertook or assisted in the retention removal disposal or realisation of stolen goods namely a Vauxhall L22 RPU belonging to Stephen Bate by or for the benefit of another or dishonestly arranged so to do knowing or believing the same to be stolen goods.

In respect of Gingell the other person was alleged to be Andrew Camper, his co-accused. In quashing Gingell's conviction Waller LJ stated:

> As a matter of plain language this count charged Camper and Gingell with undertaking or assisting 'for the benefit of another'. As a matter of plain language that must be someone other than Camper or Gingell. That being so, as it seems to us, in this case the appellant Gingell was in fact convicted of an offence which was not the offence proved by the Crown and that being so his appeal against conviction must be allowed.

----

iv. Knowing or Believing them to be Stolen Goods

Notes

1. *R. v McCullum* (1973) 57 Cr. App. R. 645: M was charged with handling by assisting in the retention of stolen guns and ammunition. The guns and ammunition were in a suitcase in her possession. Part of her case was that she did not know what was in the suitcase. A direction by the trial judge that knowledge or belief that the suitcase contained stolen goods without knowledge of the nature of the goods was sufficient, was upheld by the Court of Appeal, even though the indictment had specified the goods as guns and ammunition.

2. *R. v Hulbert* (1979) 69 Cr. App. R. 243 CA: H was charged with handling stolen clothes. H admitted to the police that she bought them at low prices in public houses from persons who told her they were stolen. *Held*, the information from the sellers was evidence that she knew they were stolen, but not evidence that they were stolen (being hearsay). However, her appeal was dismissed because the *circumstances*, admitted by her, (namely purchases in public houses at low prices) were prima facie evidence that the goods were stolen.

3. The previous law required the accused to receive knowing that the goods were stolen. The Criminal Law Revision Committee, *Theft and Related Offences* § 134, justified the addition of the alternative "or believing" as follows:

    > It is a serious defect of the present law that actual knowledge that the property was stolen must be proved. Often the prosecution cannot prove this. In many cases indeed guilty knowledge does not exist, although the circumstances of the transaction are such that the receiver ought to be guilty of an offence. The man who buys goods at a ridiculously low price from an unknown seller whom he meets in a public house may not *know* that the goods were stolen, and he may take the precaution of asking no questions. Yet it may be clear on the evidence that he *believes* that the goods were stolen. In such cases the prosecution may fail (rightly, as the law now stands) for want of proof of guilty knowledge. We consider that a person who handles stolen goods ought to be guilty if he believes them to be stolen. A purchaser who is merely careless, in that he does not make sufficient inquiry, will not be guilty of the offence under the new law any more than under the old.

4.   The prosecution must prove that the requisite knowledge or belief existed at the time the actus

reus was performed (*Williams* [1994] 934). Where handling by receiving is charged the relevant point in time is when D receives or acquires the goods; if he only acquires this knowledge or forms this belief some time later, this will not suffice (*Brook* [1993] 455). But note that dishonest retention may constitute theft or an offence contrary to s.93B of the Criminal Justice Act 1988.

5. *R. v White* (1859) 1 F. & F. 665: W was charged with receiving lead, he well knowing it to have been stolen. Bramwell B (to the jury): "The knowledge charged in this indictment need not be such knowledge as would be acquired if the prisoner had actually seen the lead stolen; it is sufficient if you think the circumstances were such, accompanying the transaction, as to make the prisoner believe that it had been stolen." Since a receiver or handler can only rarely "know" about the history of the goods, this direction may be thought to be only common sense. The question is, what is added by the inclusion of the words "or believing" in s.22?

6. *Haughton v Smith* [1975] A.C. 485 HL: Viscount Dilhorne, at 503: "It is, in my opinion, clear that section 22(1) of the Theft Act 1968 does not make the handling of goods which are not stolen goods an offence if a person believes them to have been stolen. The offence created by that section is in relation to goods which are stolen and it is an ingredient of the offence that the accused must know or believe them to have been stolen. The word 'believing' was, I think, inserted to avoid the possibility of an accused being acquitted when there was ample evidence that he believed the goods stolen, but no proof that he knew they were."

R. V FORSYTH

[1997] 2 Cr. App. R. 299 CA

D was convicted of handling £400,000 knowing or believing that it had been stolen from Polly Peck International by its chairman and chief executive, Asil Nadir. D appealed on the ground, inter alia, that the judge had misdirected the jury as to knowledge or belief by directing them that the shutting of eyes to the obvious was equivalent to belief.

BELDAM LJ

6. *The judge's direction on 'knowing or believing' that the money was stolen.*
   The judge based his direction on the case of Hall (1985) 81 Cr.App.R. 260 at 264. The judge said:

   Knowing or believing are words of ordinary usage in the English language. A person may be said to know the money is stolen when she is told by someone with first hand knowledge, such as the thief, that such is the case. Belief of course is something short of knowledge. It may be said to be the state of mind of a person who says to himself I cannot say I know for certain that this money is stolen, but there can be no other reasonable conclusion in the light of all the circumstances, in the light of all that I have heard and seen.
      Either of these two states of mind is enough to establish guilt. It is sufficient to constitute belief even if the defendant says to herself: 'Despite all that I have heard I refuse to believe what my brain tells me is obvious'. You cannot shut your eyes to the obvious. But what is not enough to establish guilt is mere suspicion, i.e.: 'I suspect that this money may be stolen but it may be on the other hand that it is not.' This state of mind does not fall within the words 'knowing or believing'.

The judge had this direction typed out and given to each member of the jury. The appellant objected and urged that the jury should simply be directed in the words of the section without further elaboration and particularly without the gloss suggested.

The appellant criticised this direction. The prosecution had to prove that the appellant actually knew or actually believed that the money she handled in Geneva was stolen. The words 'knowing' or 'believing' cover the state of mind of those who are subjectively sure of the unlawful provenance of the goods. Whilst an accused's belief that goods are stolen may be inferred by the jury from all the circumstances of the transaction, the word 'belief' does not import an objective test nor is belief the same as 'shutting one's eyes to the obvious'. The judge's direction blurred the distinction between actual belief and evidence from which it may be inferred by indicating that it could be constituted:

(a) By unreasonable uncertainty and

(b) By a refusal to believe the obvious.

Further, by contrasting these states with 'mere' suspicion, the direction suggested that real or weighty suspicion may be enough to constitute belief. Belief is not to be equated with suspicion or even great suspicion and the jury may have been left with the impression that it was. That impression could have been reinforced when, towards the end of the summing-up, the judge returned to the subject after reminding the jury that the appellant had said in evidence that she did not know the money was stolen or believe it to be, nor did she suspect it was stolen. Commenting on these answers the judge said:

'What the prosecution have to prove on this aspect is at the time she handled the money or the chose in action the defendant either knew or believed that it was stolen but mere suspicion would not be enough.'

It is beyond question that even great suspicion is not to be equated with belief. Ever since the judgment of Lord Widgery C.J. in *Atwal v Massey* (1971) 56 Cr.App.R. 6, references to suspicion in exegesis of the word 'believing' in sec. 22 of the Theft Act have given rise to difficulty. In that case Lord Widgery emphasised that the question was a subjective one and he posed it in these terms:

'. . . was the appellant aware of the theft or did he believe the goods to be stolen or did he, suspecting the goods to be stolen, deliberately shut his eyes to the consequences?'

But as James L.J. said in *Griffiths* (1974) 60 Cr.App.R. 14:

'There is a danger in the adoption of the passage cited from the judgment in *Atwal v Massey* as the direction to the jury unless great care is taken to avoid confusion between the mental element of knowledge or belief and the approach by which a jury may arrive at the conclusion as to knowledge or belief. To direct the jury that the offence is committed if the defendant, suspecting the goods were stolen, deliberately shut his eyes to the circumstances as an alternative to knowing or believing the goods were stolen is a misdirection. To direct the jury that, in common sense and in law, they may find that the defendant knew or believed the goods to be stolen because he deliberately closed his eyes to the circumstances is a perfectly proper direction.'

James L.J. thus stressed the difference between evidence from which a jury might infer belief and their being directed that shutting the eyes to circumstances of suspicion is equivalent to belief. In *Moys* (1984) 79 Cr.App.R.72, 74 this Court had to consider a direction which included the passage:

'Thirdly, the prosecution has to satisfy you so that you are sure that at the time the horse came into his possession the defendant knew or believed that it was stolen. Believed in that sense means that he suspected very strongly that it was stolen and shut his eyes to that possibility altogether . . .'

The Court held this to be a misdirection. The judge had told the jury that suspicion coupled with a deliberate shutting of eyes was not merely an alternative but was equivalent to belief. That was incorrect and a material misdirection. Lord Lane C.J., after reviewing the cases referred to in *Griffiths* and the case of *Grainge* (1973) 59 Cr.App.R. 3, said at p.6 that mistakes in this branch of the law were frequent and suggested a direction in these terms:

'The question is a subjective one and it must be proved that the defendant was aware of the theft or that he believed the goods to be stolen. Suspicion that they were stolen, even coupled with the fact that he shut his eyes to the circumstances, is not enough, although these matters may be taken into account by the jury when deciding whether or not the necessary knowledge or belief existed.'

Old concepts, however, tend to recur. In *Hall* (1985) 81 Cr.App.R. 260, Boreham J. giving the judgment of the Court over which Lord Lane presided said at p.264 after dealing with knowledge:

'Belief, of course, is something short of knowledge. It may be said to be the state of mind of a person who says to himself: I cannot say I know for certain that these goods are stolen, but there can be no other reasonable conclusion in the light of all the circumstances, in the light of all that I have heard and seen. Either of those two states of mind is enough to satisfy the words of the statute. The second is enough (that is, belief) even if the defendant says to himself: Despite all that I have seen and all that I have heard, I refuse to believe what my brain tells me is obvious. What is not enough, of course, is mere suspicion. I suspect that these goods may be stolen, but it may be on the other hand that they are not. That state of mind, of course, does not fall within the words "knowing or believing"'.

In subsequent cases (*Harris (Martin)* (1987) 84 Cr.App.R. 75 and *Toor* (1987) 85 Cr.App.R. 116) the appellant complained of a failure by the judge to follow the judgment in *Hall* but as Lawton L.J. said at p.79 in *Harris*:

'It may well be that in many cases, depending on how the case for the Crown is conducted, it is necessary to give the kind of direction to which Boreham J. referred in *Hall*; but we doubt whether it is necessary is every case.'

It is a trite observation that every summing-up should be tailored to the circumstances of the particular case the jury have to decide. It seems to us it was incumbent on the judge to do so in this case. The judge devoted a long passage in his summing-up to the many questions put to the appellant when she was interviewed asking her why she had not enquired where the £400,000 had come from and what she imagined was the purpose of the transaction in which she had taken part. These questions were clearly aimed at highlighting circumstances of suspicion which should have put her on enquiry. In essence the appellant's defence was that she completely trusted Mr Nadir and having regard to his immense wealth and enormous income it did not occur to her to question this particular transaction. She had on one previous occasion been asked to handle a sum of £200,000 though not in these circumstances. Colloquially it might be said that her state of mind was 'I could not believe that somebody like Mr Asil Nadir would need to steal money or would involve me in a dishonest transaction'. We think that in such a case it was a mistake to embark on an attempt to give examples of particular states of mind which might be regarded as equivalent to belief. The ordinary meaning of belief is the mental acceptance of a fact as true or existing. In the context of this case it meant that the appellant had in fact accepted that the money she was asked to handle had been stolen. We doubt whether a jury unversed in legal dialectics would be likely to subject the direction they were given to the careful analysis required to differentiate the concepts of 'not knowing for certain', 'there being no other reasonable conclusion' and 'refusing to believe what my brain tells me is obvious'. This last concept appears to contain the paradox that it refers to a person whose mind does not in fact believe but whose brain sends him the message that it does. Whilst it is true that the direction as a whole is couched in subjective terms, we think it is open to misinterpretation. The appellant had said that she could not believe the money was stolen in spite of all the circumstances of suspicion suggested to her. Although it might have been obvious to others, it was not to her because of her trust and confidence in the integrity of Mr Nadir. We think the form of the directions may have left the jury with the impression that the appellant was guilty even though in her mind she could not accept that the goods were stolen. Thus the jury may have concluded that the appellant was guilty if they were satisfied that there were circumstances of great suspicion from which the only conclusion which could reasonably be drawn was that the goods were stolen but which the appellant because of her knowledge of and faith in Mr Nadir could not bring herself to believe so that her eyes had been closed to what was obvious. We doubt whether on a charge of handling it is necessary or helpful to attempt an exposition of the meaning of the word 'belief' by equating it with different and less easily understood states of mind. Between suspicion and actual belief there may be a range of awareness. In the present case, to say that mere suspicion is not enough could have been taken by the jury to imply that great suspicion, coupled with an inability to believe that the money was stolen, was equivalent to belief which it plainly is not. If the judge thought that the jury might find difficulty with the concept of 'belief', it seems to us that he ought to have made it clear to them that they had to be satisfied that the appellant actually believed that the money was stolen. In our view the judge ought to have followed the guidance given in Moys which is clear and more readily understandable by a jury and avoids the potential for confusion inherent in a *Hall* direction.

On this crucial issue the judge's direction could have led the jury to find the appellant guilty without finding that she actually believed the money was stolen. Accordingly we think he misdirected them.

Appeal allowed
Conviction quashed

v. Dishonesty

Notes

1. Dishonesty must exist at the time of the act alleged to constitute handling. On Dishonesty in Theft.

2. In a case at York Assizes in 1971, it was held by Shaw J that a person who, on instructions from the owner, arranged with the thieves for the return of the goods, was not guilty of *dishonestly* assisting in the goods' disposal. See Harvey, "What Does Dishonesty Mean?" [1972] 213. In *R. v Roberts* (1985) 84 Cr. App. R. 117, a case on dishonesty generally, one ground of appeal was that dishonest in s.22 meant dishonest in relation to the loser of the goods and not dishonest in a more general way. The Court of Appeal held that the York case was no authority for this, but as Roberts was not acting for the owner, the question of whether dishonesty must be vis-à-vis the owner did not really arise. But in the York case, D was acting throughout for the owner, who had recruited him for the purpose of recovering the goods. Smith comments, [1986] 123:

> "It is very difficult to see how the sole owner of the stolen property could be said to be dishonest for the purposes of handling; and, as the defendant was identified with her, it seems to follow that he could not be held to be dishonest either. The same act may frequently constitute [both theft and handling]. The House of Lords held in *Morris* that theft 'involves not an act expressly or impliedly authorised by the owner but an act by way of adverse interference with or usurpation of the owner's rights.' Probably a similar principle ought to apply to handling. This suggests that the true test of dishonesty is whether there is dishonesty *vis-à-vis* the owner (or one of the owners, if there is more than one). Who else is there in respect of whom the act specified in s.22 could be dishonest? Since they are all acts of dealing with property, it seems that they could only be dishonest with respect to someone with a proprietary interest. Perhaps the court has the public in mind but it is noteworthy that in the 1972 case Shaw J did not find considerations of public policy to be of assistance. The public interest in matters of this kind is defended by the offences of perverting the course of justice and those contained in ss.4 and 5 of the Criminal Law Act 1967 as well as section 23 of the Theft Act 1968 (Advertising rewards for return of goods stolen or lost)."

Questions

1. In *R. v Matthews* [1950] 1 All E.R. 137, M received what he well knew were stolen goods, intending to hand them over to the police. Later, he changed his mind and did not hand them over. It was held that this did not amount to receiving stolen goods. If a similar case arose today, would M be guilty of handling? See forms of handling, above.

2. B owed A £10. Being short of cash, A broke into B's desk and helped himself to £10. He later admitted to the police that he knew he had no right to do this. A shared the money with C. C knew how A got the money, but thought that since B owed A £10, A was entitled to help himself. A was convicted of theft. Ought C to be convicted of handling?

----

vi. Dishonestly retaining a wrongful credit

The decision of the House of Lords in *Preddy* [1996] 3 W.L.R. 255 (above) had further ramifications for the law of handling. These were identified by the Law Commission.

LAW COMMISSION, *OFFENCES OF DISHONESTY: MONEY TRANSFERS* (TSO, 1996), LAW COM. NO.243

6.2 Section 24(4) provides that goods are 'stolen' if they are obtained, in England or Wales or elsewhere, by blackmail or in the circumstances described in section 15(1). Before *Preddy* it would have been generally assumed that a credit balance resulting from an inter-account transfer procured by deception was stolen goods, because it was obtained in the circumstances described in section 15(1). On this assumption, the offence of handling would be committed if, knowing or believing the funds to be stolen goods, a person dishonestly receives them or deals with them in any of the other ways set out in section 22(1). According to *Preddy*, however, the funds are not obtained in the circumstances described in section 15(1); therefore they are probably not stolen goods, and subsequent dealings with them fall outside section 22(1).

6.3 Moreover, even if the funds in question *were* stolen goods, there would be a further difficulty in applying section 22(1) to them where they are transferred to another account. Before *Preddy* it had been held by the Court of Appeal in *Attorney-General's Reference (No 4 of 1979)* [1981] 1 W.L.R. 667 that a person who dishonestly accepts a transfer of stolen funds from another's account into his or her own account is 'receiving' stolen goods within the meaning of section 22(1). But it is hard to see how this reasoning can survive *Preddy*. It assumes that the funds received by the transferee are the *same* funds as those that, before the transfer, were in the transferor's account; and according to *Preddy* this is not so.

6.4 It might be argued that the funds received are '. . . stolen' by virtue of section 24(2) of the 1968 Act [above]

6.5 But this rule applies only to goods which represent (or have represented) the stolen goods *in the hands of the thief or of a handler*; and in the case of stolen funds which are transferred to another account, this requirement is not satisfied. According to *Preddy*, the funds obtained by the transferee have never been in the hands of the thief at all; and the transferee, in whose hands they are, cannot be regarded as a handler until it has first been determined that the funds received are stolen goods. It would obviously be circular to argue (a) that those funds are stolen goods, (b) that the transferee is therefore a handler of stolen goods, (c) that the requirements of s.24(2) (b) are therefore satisfied, and (d) that the funds received are therefore stolen goods.

6.6 Moreover, even if the funds obtained by the transferee could somehow be brought within the terms of section 24(2), so that they were stolen goods once the transferee had received them, it would still be hard to see how the transferee could be said to have *received stolen goods*: that expression would seem to mean that the goods received must have been stolen goods *before* the transferee received them, not that it is sufficient if they *became* stolen goods once the transferee had received them.

6.7 It is true that this problem existed even before *Preddy*: it appears to extend to any case where stolen goods in the hands of the thief are converted into other goods in the hands of another, for example where the thief pays stolen cash into another's bank account. However, before *Preddy* it appeared not to extend to the case where a stolen credit balance is moved from one account to another, because the *Attorney-General's Reference* assumed the property to be the same property throughout. If this is not the case, as *Preddy* makes clear it is not, the lacuna is now a great deal more serious than was previously thought.

The Law Commission recommended the creation of a new offence which Parliament enacted in s.2 of the Theft (Amendment) Act 1996 which inserted a new s.24A into the Theft Act 1968.

THEFT ACT 1968 S.24A

Dishonestly retaining a wrongful credit

(1) A person is guilty of an offence if—

   (a) a wrongful credit has been made to an account kept by him or in respect of which he has any right or interest;

   (b) he knows or believes that the credit is wrongful; and

   (c) he dishonestly fails to take such steps as are reasonable in the circumstances to secure that the credit is cancelled.

(2) References to a credit are to a credit of an amount of money.

(2A) A credit to an account is wrongful to the extent that it derives from—

   (a) theft;

   (b) blackmail;

   (c) fraud (contrary to section 1 of the Fraud Act 2006); or

   (d) stolen goods.

Note

In *Offences of Dishonesty: Money Transfers*, para.6.20, the Law Commission provide the following examples of how the new offence will operate:

(1) A, by deception, dishonestly obtains a transfer of funds from V's account into his own. A is guilty of obtaining a money transfer by deception, and also (unless he has an immediate change of heart and returns the money) of retaining a credit from a dishonest source—though we doubt that any sensible prosecutor would charge the latter, because it would be harder to prove and would confuse a jury.

(2) A steals funds from V's account by transferring them into his own. (He may, for example, be authorised to draw on V's account.) A is guilty of theft and also (unless he returns the money) of retaining a credit from a dishonest source.

(3) A blackmails V into transferring funds from V's account into his own. A is guilty of blackmail and also (unless he returns the money) of retaining a credit from a dishonest source.

(4) A, by deception, theft or blackmail, obtains a transfer of funds from V's account into B's. A is guilty of obtaining a money transfer by deception or of theft or blackmail (as the case may be). The credit to B's account is therefore wrongful. B is guilty of retaining a credit from a dishonest source if, knowing or believing the credit to be wrongful, she dishonestly fails to take reasonable steps to cancel it.

(5) A, by deception, theft or blackmail, obtains a transfer of funds from V's account into his own, and transfers the proceeds to B's. B's position is the same as in example (4). If B transfers the proceeds to C's account, the same rules apply in respect of C's liability; and so on, ad infinitum.

(6) A steals banknotes (or obtains them by deception or blackmail) and pays them into B's account. B, if she knows the circumstances but does not take steps to cancel the credit, is guilty of retaining a credit from a dishonest source.

(7) A obtains a money transfer by deception, theft or blackmail, withdraws the proceeds from his account and hands the cash to B. The cash is stolen goods. If B knows or believes this, she is guilty of handling.

(8) A obtains a money transfer by deception, theft or blackmail and transfers the proceeds to B's account. B dishonestly withdraws the proceeds and hands the cash to C. The cash is stolen goods, and C is guilty of handling if he knows or believes this. If he pays the cash into D's account, the credit is wrongful, and D is guilty of retaining a credit from a dishonest source if she knows or believes this but takes no steps to cancel it.

14   CRIMINAL DAMAGE

The principal offences concerned with damage to property are contained in the Criminal Damage Act 1971. The aim of the Act is to protect property from harmful interference and it does so by creating a small number of wide, general, offences. The primary offence, contained in s.1, is simple criminal damage, punishable with a maximum sentence of ten years' imprisonment. A further offence is created that deals with damage that intentionally or recklessly endangers life. Where the damage is caused by fire (whether simple damage or "dangerous" damage), the Act provides that the offence shall be charged as one of arson. The maximum sentence for damage that intentionally or recklessly endangers life, or where the damage is by fire, is one of life imprisonment. The Draft Criminal Code proposes no substantial changes, except as to "Lawful Excuses" see below.

1. DESTROYING OR DAMAGING PROPERTY

CRIMINAL DAMAGE ACT 1971 SS.1 AND 4

Section 1: (1) A person who without lawful excuse destroys or damages any property belonging to another intending to destroy or damage any such property or being reckless as to whether any such property would be destroyed or damaged shall be guilty of an offence.

(2) A person who without lawful excuse destroys or damages any property, whether belonging to himself or another:

(a) intending to destroy or damage any property or being reckless as to whether any property would be destroyed or damaged; and

(b) intending by the destruction or damage to endanger the life of another or being reckless as to whether the life of another would be thereby endangered;

shall be guilty of an offence.

(3) An offence committed under this section by destroying or damaging property by fire shall be charged as arson.

Section 4: (1) A person guilty of arson under s.1 above or of an offence under s.1(2) above (whether arson or not) shall on conviction on indictment be liable to imprisonment for life.

(2) A person guilty of any other offence under this Act shall on conviction on indictment be liable to imprisonment for a term not exceeding ten years.

Notes

1.   If the damage or destruction is by fire, the offence must be charged as arson. Moreover, since a heavier penalty is provided, it is a different offence from criminal damage, and if arson is charged,

there can be no conviction on that indictment of criminal damage in either of its forms: see *R. v Cooper & Cooper* [1991] Crim. L.R. 524.

2. As to criminal damage, there are two offences in s.1, a simple offence and an aggravated one. The differences between them are connected with the expressions "belonging to another" and "without lawful excuse" (see p.741), and with the additional mens rea required for the aggravated offence. The common features are the destroying or damaging of any property. "Property" is defined in s.10, below, but neither "destroy" nor "damage" is defined. Destroy may be surplusage, since it is hardly possible to destroy property without damaging it.

CRIMINAL DAMAGE ACT 1971 S.10

(1) In this Act 'property' means property of a tangible nature, whether real or personal, including money and:

(a) including wild creatures which have been tamed or are ordinarily kept in captivity, and any other wild creatures or their carcasses if, but only if, they have been reduced into possession which has not been lost or abandoned or are in the course of being reduced into possession; but

(b) not including mushrooms growing wild on any land or flowers, fruit or foliage of a plant growing wild on any land.

For the purpose of this subsection, 'mushroom' includes any fungus and 'plant' includes any shrub or tree. [Compare the definition of property in s.4 of the Theft Act 1968].

R. V WHITELEY

(1991) 93 Cr. App. R. 25 CA

D was a computer hacker, who gained unauthorised access to a computer network and altered data contained on discs in the system. Charged under s.1(1) of the Criminal Damage Act 1971, he was convicted on counts in which the crown case was that he caused damage to the discs by way of alteration of the state of the magnetic particles on them so as to delete and add files. The discs themselves were not physically damaged, but the jury were directed that once the particles were written on the disc, they formed part of it and were therefore capable of sustaining damage. On appeal:

LORD LANE CJ for the Court

The evidence before the jury was that the discs are so constructed as to contain upon them thousands, if not millions, of magnetic particles. By issuing commands to the computer, impulses are produced which magnetise or demagnetise those particles in a particular way. By that means it is possible to write data or information on the discs and to program them to fulfil a variety of functions. By the same method it is possible to delete or alter data, information or instructions which have previously been written on to the disc. The argument advanced on behalf of the appellant, when reduced to its essence, seems to us to be this. That since the state of the magnetic particles on the disc is not perceptible by the unaided human senses, for instance of sight or touch, therefore the appellant's admitted activities only affected the 'intangible information contained' on the disc itself. Even if the absence of such a perceptible change is not fatal to the prosecution, goes on the submission, interference with the particles cannot amount to damage in law.

 It seems to us that that contention contains a basic fallacy. What the Act requires to be proved is that tangible property has been damaged, not necessarily that the damage itself should be tangible. There can be no doubt that the magnetic particles upon the metal discs were a part of the discs and if the appellant was proved to have intentionally and without lawful excuse altered the particles in such a way as to cause an impairment of the value or usefulness of the disc to the owner, there would be damage within the meaning of s.1. The fact that the alteration could only be perceived by operating the computer did not make the alterations any the less real, or the damage, if the alteration amounted to damage, any the less within the ambit of the Act.

We have been referred to a number of authorities which to a greater or lesser extent bear upon this problem. *Fisher* (1865) L.R. 1 C.C.R. 7: Here the defendant was convicted of damaging a steam engine. He had plugged up the feed-pipe and displaced other parts so as to render it temporarily useless and potentially explosive. There was no removal of any part, no cutting, no breaking and no lesion (as it was put). The conviction was upheld by the Court of Crown Cases Reserved. Pollock C.B. put the matter as follows at p.9:

'It is like the case of spiking a gun, where there is no actual damage to the gun, although it is rendered useless . . . Surely the displacement of the parts was a damage . . . if done with intent to render the machine useless.'

It should however be noted that the charge was brought under the Malicious Damage Act 1861 which provided by s.14 as follows:

'Whosoever shall unlawfully and maliciously cut, break, or destroy, or damage with intent to destroy or to render useless, . . . any machine or engine . . .'

In *Tacey* (1821) Russ. and Ry. 452, the allegation was that the defendant had mischievously damaged a frame used for stocking—making, by unscrewing and taking away a part of the machine, so rendering the whole useless. The judge reserved the point of whether mere removal of a part in these circumstances could amount to 'damag-ing.' It was held that it could. These two cases seem to demonstrate that no actual lesion to the tangible object is necessary. In *Henderson and Batley* (unreported, November 29, 1984), this Court had to consider the meaning of 'damage' in s.1(1) of the 1971 Act. The property allegedly damaged was a development land site upon which the defendants had dumped 30 lorry loads of rubble, which the owners had to remove at a cost of some £2,000. The argument advanced by the defendants was that what they had done could not be said to have damaged the land. The trial judge ruled against them and his decision was upheld on appeal, on the grounds that damage can be of various kinds and that the definition found in the *Concise Oxford Dictionary*, (6th ed., p.256) namely 'injury impairing value or usefulness,' was appropriate to cover the facts of the case. It was a question for the jury to decide whether damage had been proved.

That decision was cited by Stephen Brown L.J. in the Divisional Court decision of *Cox v Riley* (1986) 83 Cr.App.R. 54, where the facts were not altogether dissimilar from those in the instant case. A disgruntled employee had erased from the printed circuit card a computer program which controlled a computerised saw belonging to his employers. The saw was thereby put out of action. He was charged with damaging the circuit card. It was contended on behalf of the prosecutor that by removing the information stored upon the card, the defendant had damaged the card within the meaning of s.1(1). On behalf of the defendant it was argued that the program in question did not exist in a tangible form and therefore was not property within the meaning of s.10(1), and secondly, that erasing a program from the printed circuit card did not amount to damage. 'Damage', it was con-tended, should be given its 'original meaning'. This argument was amplified by counsel on the basis that because the program could not be seen or touched in the ordinary physical sense, the removal of the program could not amount to causing damage.

Stephen Brown L.J. in rejecting that argument in the course of his judgment at pp.56, 57, 58, said this:

'It has to be observed that the property referred to in the charge was the plastic circuit card, which undoubt-edly . . . is property of a tangible nature . . . the only possible argument which [counsel] could put forward is that there was no damage within the meaning of the Act . . . The defendant . . . wished to put out of action, albeit temporarily, the computerised saw, and he was able to do that by operating the computer blanking mechanism in order to erase from the printed circuit card the relevant programs. That made it necessary for time and labour and money to be expended in order to replace the relevant programs on the printed circuit card . . . It seems to me to be quite untenable to argue that . . . this . . . did not amount to causing damage to property.'

We respectfully agree with those conclusions. *Morphitis v Salmon* [1990] Crim.L.R. 48 was another decision of the Divisional Court. The facts of the case are immaterial, but in the course of delivering his judgment, with which Lloyd L.J. agreed, Auld J., in the transcript of the judgment, having cited the decision in *Cox v Riley*, said this:

'The authorities show that the term "damage" for the purpose of this provision, should be widely interpreted so as to include not only permanent or temporary physical harm, but also permanent or temporary impairment of value or usefulness.'

The effect of those various decisions, in our judgment, is as follows: Any alteration to the physical nature of the property concerned may amount to damage within the meaning of the section. Whether it does so or not will depend upon the effect that the alteration has had upon the legitimate operator (who for convenience may be referred to as the owner). If the hacker's actions do not go beyond, for example, mere tinkering with an otherwise 'empty' disc, no damage would be established. Where, on the other hand, the interference with the disc amounts to an impairment of the value or usefulness of the disc to the owner, then the necessary damage is established . . .

Appeal dismissed

Note

The effect of this decision in so far as it relates to computers was reversed by s.3(6) to the Computer Misuse Act 1990 which itself has now been repealed by the Police and Justice Act 2006. The Police and Justice Act 2006 has inserted a new subs.(5) into s.10 of the 1971 Act which provides:

"(5) For the purposes of this Act a modification of the contents of a computer shall not be regarded as damaging any computer or computer storage medium unless its effect on that computer or computer storage medium impacts its physical condition."

The accused in *Whiteley* would now be guilty of an offence under s.3 of "Unauthorised acts with intent to impair, or with recklessness as to impairing, operation of a computer, etc.". The decision in *Whiteley* remains good authority in so far as it is appropriate to other situations where information is stored in magnetic form (e.g. audio and video tapes).

See Wasik, "The Computer Misuse Act 1990" [1990] Crim. L.R. 767; and N. MacEwan, "The Computer Misuse Act 1990: Lessons from its Past and Predictions for its Future" [2008] Crim. L.R. 955.

Roe v Kingerlee [1986] Crim. L.R. 735. D smeared the walls of a police cell with mud, which cost £7 to clean off. The Magistrates held that there was nothing amounting to damage, but on appeal by the prosecutor, *Held*: What constitutes criminal damage is a matter of fact and degree and it is for the justices, applying their common sense, to decide whether what occurred was damage or not. It is not necessary that the damage should be permanent before an act can constitute criminal damage . . .. In the circumstances of the present case, what occurred so far as the walls of the cell were concerned could amount to criminal damage. The justices were wrong to take the view that as a matter of law it could not . . . The application of graffiti to a structure will not necessarily amount to causing criminal damage. That must be a question of fact and degree for the tribunal of fact.

In *R. v Faik* [2005] EWCA Crim 2381, the accused blocked a toilet in a police cell and flushed it repeatedly causing his own cell and adjoining cells to flood. The blanket used to block the toilet could not be used until it had been cleaned and dried and all the cells had to be cleaned by contractors before they were again usable. The conviction for criminal damage was upheld.

A. The Simple Offence: Without Danger to Life

i. Belonging to Another

CRIMINAL DAMAGE ACT 1971 S.10

(2) Property shall be treated for the purposes of this Act as belonging to any person:

(a) having the custody or control of it;

(b) having in it any proprietary right or interest (not being an equitable interest arising only from an agreement to transfer or grant an interest); or

(c) having a charge on it.

(3) Where property is subject to a trust, the persons to whom it belongs shall be so treated as including any person having a right to enforce the trust.

(4) Property of a corporation sole shall be so treated as belonging to the corporation notwithstanding a vacancy in the corporation.

Note

An owner may be guilty of criminal damage to his own property if it also belongs to another within the meaning of s.10. But if D mistakenly believes property is his when it is not, he may be liable for criminal damage if he also believes someone else has a proprietary interest in it (see *Seray-Wurie v DPP* [2012] EWHC 208 (Admin)).

----

ii. Without Lawful Excuse

CRIMINAL DAMAGE ACT 1971 S.5

(1) This section applies to any offence under s.1(1) above and any offence under s.2 or 3 above other than one involving a threat by the person charged to destroy or damage property in a way which he knows is likely to endanger the life of another or involving an intent by the person charged to use or cause or permit the use of something in his custody or under his control so to destroy or damage property.

(2) A person charged with an offence to which this section applies shall, whether or not he would be treated for the purpose of this Act as having a lawful excuse apart from this subsection, be treated for those purposes as having a lawful excuse:

(a) if at the time of the act or acts alleged to constitute the offence he believed that the person or persons whom he believed to be entitled to consent to the destruction or damage to the property in question had so consented, or would have so consented to it if he or they had known of the destruction or damage and its circumstances; or

(b) if he destroyed or damaged or threatened to destroy or damage the property in question or, in the case of a charge of an offence under s.3 above, intended to use or cause or permit the use of something to destroy or damage it, in order to protect property belonging to himself or another or a right or interest in property which was or which he believed to be vested in himself or another, and at the time of the act or acts alleged to constitute the offence he believed:

(i)   that the property, right or interest was in immediate need of protection; and

(ii) that the means of protection adopted or proposed to be adopted were or would be reasonable having regard to all the circumstances.

(3) For the purpose of this section it is immaterial whether a belief is justified or not if it is honestly held.

(4) For the purpose of subsection (2) above a right or interest in property includes any right or privilege in or over land, whether created by grant, licence or otherwise.

(5) This section shall not be construed as casting doubt on any defence recognised by law as a defence to criminal charges.

Notes

1. All the offences in the Act must be committed "without lawful excuse". But as to the simple offence (not the aggravated offence) s.5 gives particular cases of beliefs which count as lawful excuse. None of the beliefs need be reasonable, provided they are generally held. But see *R. v Hill* directly below.

2. The definition of lawful excuse is not exhaustive: see s.5(5). Thus any other defence to the use of force will avail, e.g. duress, prevention of crime, arrest of offenders, self-defence. However these, defences are only effective if the measures taken by D are objectively reasonable: see above. The test under s.5(2) is subjective. In *Chamberlain v Lindon* [1998] 1 W.L.R. 1252 the Divisional Court upheld the decision of the Nuneaton Justices to acquit D of criminal damage where he had demolished a wall built by D on C's land as D honestly believed such action was reasonably necessary in the circumstances to protect his right of vehicular access across C's land and that delay would prejudice his rights. The court also held that s.5(2) did not contain any requirement that the defendant had to exhaust any alternative remedies, for example, in the civil courts, before self-redress was permitted as the longer the wall remained, the more urgent was the need to remove it to avoid any suggestion of acquiescence in the obstruction; this supported D's belief that his property (i.e. the right of way) was in immediate need of protection.

3. In *Merrick* [1996] 1 Cr. App. R. 130 counts of simple criminal damage were dismissed on the basis of lawful excuse but the trial proceeded for the counts under s.1(2) where, according to the Court of Appeal, "the defence of lawful excuse did not apply". There was no investigation of who actually owned the cabling and the trial proceeded on the basis that the householder did and could consent to its removal. If this was so, D was not placing reliance on s.5(2)(a) but rather on the fact of consent which is an "excuse apart from this subsection".

4. The fact that subs.(2) and (3) deal specifically with mistaken belief in the consent of the owner and mistaken belief in a right to be protected has been held to mean that such mistakes can ground a defence even though they arise as a result of self-induced intoxication: see *Jaggard v Dickinson* [1980] 3 All E.R. 716.

Question

D, whose trousered leg is being attacked by P's small dog, strikes the dog with his walking stick. If D is prosecuted under the Act for killing the dog, what difference might it make whether D acted to prevent injury to his leg or to prevent damage to his trousers?

R. V HILL

(1988) 89 Cr. App. R. 74 CA

Hill was apprehended outside a US Naval Base in Dyfed in possession of a hacksaw blade. She admitted that she intended to use it to cut the perimeter fence of the base. She was convicted of having the blade with intent without lawful excuse to use it to damage property belonging to another, contrary to s.3 of the Criminal Damage Act 1971 (see below). She said that she feared that the presence of the base would at some future time attract a nuclear strike by Soviet missiles, which would damage her property in the vicinity. The object of her proposed activity was to make the US authorities close the base. She claimed that she was acting with lawful excuse in that her property was in immediate need of protection and that the means of protection proposed would be reasonable having regard to all the circumstances. The judge in effect directed the jury to convict. [Another woman was also convicted on the same charge in precisely similar circumstances]. On appeal:

LORD LANE CJ for the Court

The learned judge . . . directed the jury to convict on two bases. The first basis was this, that what the applicant did or proposed to do could not, viewed objectively, be said to have been done to protect her own or anyone else's property under s.5(2)(b) which I have just read. It is simply, he concluded, part of a political campaign aimed at drawing attention to the base and to the risks as she described them raised by the presence of the base in Pembrokeshire. It aimed further at having the base removed. He came to the conclusion that the causative relationship between the acts which she intended to perform and the alleged protection was so tenuous, so nebulous, that the acts could not be said to be done to protect viewed objectively.

The second ground was with reference to the provision that the lawful excuse must be based upon an immediate need for protection. In each case the judge came to the same conclusion that on the applicant's own evidence the applicant could not be said to have believed under the provisions of s.5(2)(b)(i) that the property was in immediate need of protection . . .

The judge in each case relied upon a decision of this Court in *Hunt* (1978) 66 Cr.App.R. 105. We have the advantage also of having that report in transcript. We also have before us a more recent decision of this Court in *Ashford and Smith* (unreported) decided on May 26, 1988, in which very similar considerations were raised to those which exist in the present case. It also has the advantage of having set out the material findings of the Court in *Hunt* which were delivered by Roskill L.J. I am referring to p.4 of the transcript in *Ashford and Smith*, and it will help to set out the basis of the decision not only in *Ashford and Smith* but also in *Hunt* if I read the passage. It runs as follows:

'The judge relied very largely upon the decision of this Court in *Hunt* (1978) 66 Cr.App.R. 105. That was a case in which the appellant set fire to a guest room in an old people's home. He did so, he said, to draw attention to the defective fire alarm system. "He was charged with arson, contrary to s.1(1) of the Criminal Damage Act 1971. He sought to set up the statutory defence under s.5(2) by claiming to have had a lawful excuse in doing what he did and that he was not reckless whether any such property would be destroyed. The trial judge withdrew the defence of lawful excuse from the jury and left the issue of recklessness for them to determine. The jury by a majority verdict convicted the appellant. On appeal." "Held, that, applying the objective test, the trial judge had ruled correctly because what the appellant had done was not an act which in itself did protect or was capable of protecting property; but in order to draw attention to what in his view was an immediate need for protection by repairing the alarm system; thus the statutory defence under s.5(2) of the Act was not open to him; accordingly, the appeal would be dismissed."'

'Giving the judgment of the Court Roskill L.J. said, at p.108: "Mr Marshall-Andrews" submission can be put thus: if this man honestly believed that that which he did was necessary in order to protect this property from the risk of fire and damage to the old people's home by reason of the absence of a working fire alarm, he was entitled to set fire to that bed and so to claim the statutory defence accorded by s.5(2). I have said we will assume in his favour that he possessed the requisite honest belief. But in our view the question whether he was entitled to the benefit of the defence turns upon the meaning of the words In order to protect property belonging to another.' It was argued that those words were subjective in concept, just like the words in the latter part of s.5(2)(b) which are subjective. 'We do not think that is right. The question whether or not a particular act of destruction or damage or threat of destruction or damage was done or made in order to protect property belonging to another must be, on the true construction of the statute, an objective test. Therefore we have to ask ourselves whether, whatever the state of this man's mind and assuming an honest belief, that which he admittedly did was done in order to protect this particular property, namely the old people's home in Hertfordshire?' 'If one formulates the question in that way, in the view of each member of this Court, for the reason Slynn J. gave during the argument, it admits of only one answer: this was not done in order to protect property; it was done in order to draw attention to the defective state of the fire alarm. It was not an act which in itself did protect or was capable of protecting property.'

Then the judgment in *Ashford and Smith*, delivered by Glidewell L.J. continued as follows: 'In our view that reasoning applies exactly in the present case. *Hunt* is, of course, binding upon us. But even if it were not, we agree with the reasoning contained in it.'

Now it is submitted by Mr Bowyer to us that the decision in *Hunt* and the decision in *Ashford and Smith* were wrong and that the test is a subjective test. In other words the submission is that it was a question of what the applicant believed, and accordingly it should have been left to the jury as a matter of fact to decide what it was the applicant did believe.

We are bound by the decision in *Hunt* just as the Court in *Ashford and Smith* were bound, unless that case can be demonstrated to have been wrongly decided in the light of previous authority. Mr Bowyer endeavoured to persuade us that the decision which I have read of Roskill L.J. flew in the face of the decision of the House of Lords in *Chandler v Director of Public Prosecutions* [1964] A.C. 763. [After rejecting this submission]

That leaves us with the fact that we are bound by the decision in *Hunt*. But we add that we think that *Hunt* was correctly decided, for this reason. There are two aspects to this type of question. The first aspect is to decide what it was that the applicant, in this case Valerie Hill, in her own mind thought. The learned judge assumed, and so do we, for the purposes of this decision, that everything she said about her reasoning was true . . . Up to that point the test was subjective. In other words one is examining what is going on in the applicant's mind.

Having done that, the judges in the present cases—and the judge particularly in the case of Valerie Hill—turned to the second aspect of the case, and that is this. He had to decide as a matter of law, which means objectively, whether it could be said that on those facts as believed by the applicant, snipping the strand of the wire, which she intended to do, could amount to something done to protect either the applicant's own home or the homes of her adjacent friends in Pembrokeshire.

He decided, again quite rightly in our view, that that proposed act on her part was far too remote from the eventual aim at which she was targeting her actions to satisfy the test.

It follows therefore, in our view, that the judges in the present two cases were absolutely right to come to the conclusion that they did so far as this aspect of the case is concerned, and to come to that conclusion as a matter of law, having decided the subjective test as the applicants wished them to be decided.

The second half of the question was that of the immediacy of the danger. Here the wording of the Act, one reminds oneself, is as follows: She believed that 'the property . . . was in immediate need of protection'.

Once again the judge had to determine whether, on the facts as stated by the applicant, there was any evidence on which it could be said that she believed there was an immediate need of protection from immediate damage. In our view that must mean evidence that she believed that immediate action had to be taken to do something which would otherwise be a crime in order to prevent the immediate risk of something worse happening The evidence given by this woman (and the evidence given by the other applicant was very similar) drives this Court to the conclusion, as they drove the respective judges to the conclusion, that there was no evidence on which it could be said that there was that belief . . .

Appeal dismissed

Questions

1.   The words "in order to protect property" are suggestive of the purpose behind the acts of destruction or damage. Can a purpose exist "objectively" or is it something which, to use Professor J.C. Smith's words, can "only exist in someone's mind—and, in this context, that must be the mind of the defendant"? If that is so of what relevance should be evidence as to the remoteness of the damage from the achievement of protection or the inefficacy of the damage to effect protection?

(cf. Lord Lane CJ's dictum in *R. v Williams (Gladstone)*, on the evidential relevance of the reasonableness or unreasonableness of D's beliefs.)

2. Who decides generally whether a defendant's state of mind amounts to "Intention" and is this a question of fact or of law? How does this compare to the Courts' decisions regarding "purpose" under this provision? Is the fact that "purpose" arises in the context of a defence a plausible explanation of any difference of approach? (cf. duress and see *Valderrama-Vega*.)

Note

The provisions on lawful excuse are sorted out and extended to defence of person by cll.184, 185 of the Draft Criminal Code Bill, which apply to the "simple" offences and not to the "aggravated" offences. The definition of "lawful excuse" is still not to be exhaustive; common law defences preserved by cl.45(c) may apply.

DRAFT CRIMINAL CODE BILL

184. A person does not commit an offence to which this section applies if—

(a) he knows or believes that the person whom he believes to be entitled to consent to the destruction or damage has so consented; or

(b) he believes that that person would so consent if he knew of the destruction or damage and its circumstances.

185.—(1) A person does not commit an offence to which this section applies by doing an act which, in the circumstances which exist or which he believes to exist, is immediately necessary and reasonable—

(a) to protect himself or another from unlawful force or injury; or

(b) to prevent or terminate the unlawful detention of himself or another; or

(c) to protect property (whether belonging to himself or another) from unlawful appropriation, destruction or damage.

(2) Section 44(3) (meaning of 'unlawful') applies for the purposes of this section.

iii. Intending to Destroy or Damage any such Property

R. V SMITH

[1974] Q.B. 354

S, a tenant of a flat, installed some stereo equipment and, with the consent of the landlord, put in certain roofing, wall panels and flooring to mask the electric wiring. These fixtures thereupon belonged to the landlord by law, but S did not know this. When he was given notice to quit he damaged the fixtures in order to remove the wiring. He said he thought he was damaging his own property. He was convicted of an offence under s.1(1) of the Criminal Damage Act 1971, and appealed.

JAMES LJ

The appellant's defence was that he honestly believed that the damage he did was to his own property, that he believed that he was entitled to damage his own property and therefore he had lawful excuse for his actions causing the damage. In the course of his summing up the deputy judge directed the jury in these terms:

'Now, in order to make the offence complete, the person who is charged with it must destroy, or damage that property belonging to another, "without lawful excuse," and that is something that one has got to look at a little more, members of the jury, because you have heard here that, so far as each defendant was concerned, it never occurred to them, and you may think, quite naturally never occurred to either of them, that these various additions to the house were anything but their own property . . . But members of the jury, the Act is quite specific, and so far as the defendant David Smith is concerned lawful excuse is the only defence which has been raised. It is said that he had a lawful excuse by reason of his belief, his honest and genuinely held belief that he was destroying property which he had a right to destroy if he wanted to. But, members of the jury, I must direct you as a matter of law, and you must, therefore, accept it from me, that belief by the defendant David Smith that he had the right to do what he did is not lawful excuse within the meaning of the Act. Members of the jury, it is an excuse, it may even be a reasonable excuse, but it is not, members of the jury a lawful excuse, because, in law, he had no right to do what he did. Members of the jury, as a matter of law, the evidence, in fact, discloses, so far as David Smith is concerned, no lawful excuse at all, because, as I say, the only defence which he has raised is the defence that he thought he had the right to do what he did. I have directed you that that is not a lawful excuse, and, members of the jury, it follows from that that so far as David Smith is concerned, I am bound to direct you as a matter of law that you must find him guilty of this offence with which he is charged.'

It is contended for the appellant that that is a misdirection in law, and that, as a result of the misdirection, the entire defence of the appellant was wrongly withdrawn from the jury . . .

The offence created [by s.10] includes the elements of intention or recklessness and the absence of lawful excuse. There is in s.5 of the Act a partial 'definition' of lawful excuse . . ..

[After reading s.5(2), (3), (5), his Lordship continued:]

It is argued for the appellant that an honest, albeit erroneous, belief that the act causing damage or destruction was done to his own property provides a defence to a charge brought under s.1(1). The argument is put in three ways. First, that the offence charged includes the act causing the damage or destruction and the element of *mens rea*. The element of *mens rea* relates to all the circumstances of the criminal act. The criminal act in the offence is causing damage to or destruction of 'property belonging to another' and the element of *mens rea*, therefore, must relate to 'property belonging to another', Honest belief, whether justifiable or not, that the property is the defendant's own negatives the element of *mens rea*. . .

It is conceded by Mr Gerber [for the Crown] that there is force in the argument that the element of *mens rea* extends to 'property belonging to another'. But it is argued, the section creates a new statutory offence and that it is open to the construction that the mental element in the offence relates only to causing damage to or destroying property. That if in fact the property damaged or destroyed is shown to be another's property the offence is committed although the defendant did not intend or foresee damage to another person's property.

We are informed that so far as research has revealed this is the first occasion on which this court has had to consider the question which arises in this appeal.

It is not without interest to observe that, under the law in force before the passing of the Criminal Damage Act 1971, it was clear that no offence was committed by a person who destroyed or damaged property belonging to another in the honest but mistaken belief that the property was his own or that he had a legal right to do the damage. In *R. v Twose* (1879) 14 Cox C. C. 327 the prisoner was indicted for setting fire to furze on a common. Persons living near the common had occasionally burned the furze in order to improve the growth of grass but without the right to do so. The prisoner denied setting fire to the furze and it was submitted that even if it were proved that she did she could not be found guilty if she *bona fide* believed she had a right to do so whether the right were a good one or not. Lopes J. ruled that if she set fire to the furze thinking she had a right to do so that would not be a criminal offence.

Upon the facts of the present appeal the charge, if brought before the Act of 1971 came into force, would have been laid under s.13 of the Malicious Damage Act 1861, alleging damage by a tenant to a building. It was a defence to a charge under that section that the tenant acted under a claim of right to do the damage.

If the direction given by the deputy judge in the present case is correct, then the offence created by s.1(1) of the Act of 1971 involves a considerable extension of the law in a surprising direction. Whether or not this is so depends upon the construction of the section. Construing the language of s.1(1) we have no doubt that the *actus reus* is 'destroying or damaging any property belonging to another.' It is not possible to exclude the words 'belonging to another' which describes the 'property.' Applying the ordinary principles of *mens rea*, the intention and recklessness and the absence of lawful excuse required to constitute the offence have reference to property belonging to another. It follows that in our judgment no offence is committed under this section if a person destroys or causes damage to property belonging to another if he does so in the honest though mistaken belief that the property is his own, and provided that the belief is honestly held it is irrelevant to consider whether or not it is a justifiable belief.

In our judgment, the direction given to the jury was a fundamental misdirection in law. The consequence was that the jury were precluded from considering facts capable of being a defence to the charge and were directed to convict . . .

Appeal allowed

Notes

1. In this case, D's mistake was one of law; it would make no difference if the mistake was one of fact. For example, after his exams D burns a textbook believing it is his when, in fact, it is his flatmate P's textbook which he has picked up by mistake.

2. It is also not necessary to prove that D knows or realises that what he is doing to the property of another constitutes "damage" in law. In *Seray-Wurie*, D wrote with a black marker pen on a parking notice which the management company of the residential premises where he lived had placed in the car park for the information of residents. This amounted in law to damage even though he may not have believed it did. D agreed he wrote on the notice, intending to do so; his motives for doing so (his disagreement with the management company) could not alter the fact that his action amounted to damage and his action was intentional.

Question

In *Jaggard v Dickinson*, the accused, because she was drunk, thought that the owner of the property had consented to her damaging it. It was held that since the case came under s.5(2)(a), she was entitled to be acquitted notwithstanding that her mistake was due to self-induced intoxication. But in *R. v Smith*, the Court rejected the argument that his case came under s.5. Does this mean that if Miss Jaggard thought it was her *own* window she was breaking, her drunken mistake would not have saved her?

----

iv. Being Reckless as to Whether any such Property would be Destroyed or Damaged

Note

In the context of criminal damage, recklessness was originally defined by the House of Lords in *Caldwell* to include inadvertence to an obvious risk of damage to property. The decision in *Caldwell* has now been reversed by *G* [2003] UKHL 50. The House provided the following subjective definition for recklessness:

'A person acts recklessly within the meaning of s.1 of the Criminal Damage Act 1971 with respect to—

(i)   a circumstance when he is aware of a risk that it exists or will exist;

(ii) a result when he is aware of a risk that it will occur;

and it is, in the circumstances known to him, unreasonable to take the risks.'

The test is not whether the risk was obvious but rather whether D was aware of the risk and unreasonably took it.

Is the simple offence involved in the following cases?

(a)   D intends to damage P's property and unexpectedly damages Q's property.

(b)   D is reckless as to harm to P and unexpectedly damages P's property.

B. The Aggravated Offence: With Danger to Life

Note

Since the gravamen of the offence is danger to life, the property damaged need not belong to the accused. The extended meaning of "without lawful excuse" in s.5 does not apply, and in addition to the mens rea required for the simple offence he must intend to endanger the life of another or be reckless as to whether another's life is endangered.

R. V STEER

[1988] A.C. 111 HL

S fired a shot through a window pane behind which Mr & Mrs G were standing. The pane was broken by the shot, but they were not hurt. It was accepted that S did not intend to endanger their lives. He was charged, inter alia, with damaging property being reckless whether the life of another would be endangered. On the judge's ruling against his submission that the endangering must by the damage to the window, not by the act which caused damage to the window, he pleaded guilty to the charge. His appeal against the ruling was allowed by the Court of Appeal. The prosecution further appealed.

LORD BRIDGE OF HARWICH

We must, of course, approach the matter on the footing, implicit in the outcome of the trial, that the respondent, in firing at the bedroom window, had no intent to endanger life, but accepts that he was reckless whether life would be endangered.

Under both limbs of s.1 of the 1971 Act it is the essence of the offence which the section creates that the defendant has destroyed or damaged property. For the purpose of analysis it may be convenient to omit reference to destruction and to concentrate on the references to damage, which was all that was here involved. To be guilty under subsection (1) the defendant must have intended or been reckless as to the damage to property which he caused. To be guilty under subsection (2) he must additionally have intended to endanger life or been reckless whether life would be endangered 'by the damage' to property which he caused. This is the context in which the words must be construed and it seems to me impossible to read the words 'by the damage' as meaning 'by the danger or by the act which caused the damage'. Moreover, if the language of the statute has the meaning for which the Crown contends, the words 'by the destruction or damage' and 'thereby' in subsection 2(b) are mere surplusage. If the Crown's submission is right, the only additional element necessary to convert a subsection (1) offence into a subsection (2) offence is an intent to endanger life or recklessness whether life would be endangered simpliciter.

It would suffice as a ground for dismissing this appeal if the statute were ambiguous, since any such ambiguity in a criminal statute should be resolved in favour of the defence. But I can find no ambiguity. It seems to me that the meaning for which the respondent contends is the only meaning which the language can bear.

The contrary construction leads to anomalies which Parliament cannot have intended. If A. and B. both discharge firearms in a public place, being reckless whether life would be endangered, it would be absurd that A., who incidentally causes some trifling damage to the property, should be guilty of an offence punishable with life imprisonment, but that B., who causes no damage, should be guilty of no offence. In the same circumstances, if A. is merely reckless but B. actually intends to endanger life, it is scarcely less absurd that A should be guilty of the graver offence under s.1(2) of the 1971 Act, B. of the lesser offence under s.16 of the Firearms Act 1968.

Counsel for the Crown did not shrink from arguing that s.1(2) of the 1971 Act had created, in effect, a general offence of endangering life with intent or recklessly, however, the danger was caused, but had incidentally included as a necessary, albeit insignificant, ingredient of the offence that some damage to property should also be caused. In certain fields of legislation it is sometimes difficult to appreciate the rationale of particular provisions, but in a criminal statute it would need the clearest language to persuade me that the legislature had acted so irrationally, indeed perversely, as acceptance of this argument would imply.

It was further argued that to affirm the construction of s.1(2)(b) adopted by the Court of Appeal would give rise to problems in other cases in which it might be difficult or even impossible to distinguish between the act causing damage to property and the ensuing damage caused as the source of danger to life. In particular, it was suggested that in arson cases the jury would have to be directed that they could only convict if the danger to life arose from falling beams or similar damage caused by the fire, not if the danger arose from the heat, flames or smoke generated by the fire itself. Arson is, of course, the prime example of a form of criminal damage to property which, in the case of an occupied building, necessarily involves serious danger to life and where the gravity of the consequence which may result as well from recklessness as from a specific intent fully justifies the severity of the penalty which the 1971 Act provides for the offence. But the argument in this case is misconceived. It is not the match and the inflammable materials, the flaming firebrand or any other inflammatory agent which the arsonist uses to start the fire which causes danger to life, it is the ensuing conflagration which occurs as the property which has been set on fire is damaged or destroyed. When the victim in the bedroom is overcome by the smoke or incinerated by the flames as the building burns, it would be absurd to say that this does not result from the damage to the building.

Counsel for the Crown put forward other examples of cases which he suggested ought to be liable to prosecution under s.1(2) of the 1971 Act, including that of the angry mob of striking miners who throw a hail of bricks through the window of the cottage occupied by the working miner and that of people who drop missiles from motorway bridges on passing vehicles. I believe that the criminal law provides adequate sanctions for these cases without the need to resort to s.1(2) of the 1971 Act. But, if my belief is mistaken, this would still be no reason to distort the plain meaning of that subsection . . .

[Lords Griffiths, Ackner, Oliver and Goff agreed]

Appeal dismissed

Note

The fact that lives are not endangered is irrelevant if it was D's intention by the damage to endanger life (see *Dudley* [1989] Crim. L.R. 57) or he was reckless thereto (*Sangha* [1988] 2 All E.R. 385). In *Dudley*, D had set fire to P's house in pursuit of a grievance. D threw a fire bomb at the house but P and his family quickly extinguished the fire and only trivial damage was caused. D's conviction of arson being reckless whether life would be endangered was affirmed by the Court of Appeal. The relevant time was when D did the act which caused the damage; if at that time he was aware of a risk of danger to life or if he intended to endanger life, he had the requisite mens rea.

R. V ASQUITH, WEBSTER AND SEAMANS

[1995] 1 Cr. App. R. 492 CA

The appellants pushed a coping-stone from the parapet of a railway bridge on to a pas-senger train passing below. The stone landed on the bulkhead of a carriage, showering the passengers with glass fibre and polystyrene from the roof, but did not fall into the compart-ment. No one was injured. The appellants were convicted of criminal damage intending to endan-ger life.

LORD TAYLOR CJ

As to the dropping of stones from bridges, the effect of the statute may be thought strange. If the defendant's intention is that the stone itself should crash through the roof of a train or motor vehicle and thereby directly injure a passenger or if he was reckless only as to that outcome, the section would not bite. That would follow from the ratio in *Steer* and is no doubt why Lord Bridge made the comment he did about missiles from motorway bridges. If, however, the defendant intended or was reckless that the stone would smash the roof of the train or vehicle so that metal or wood struts from the roof would descend upon a passenger, endangering life, he would surely be guilty. This may seem to many a dismal distinction.

Unfortunately, the learned judge was not referred to *R. v Steer*. In his summing-up, he directed the jury as follows at p.52E–G:

'If a man pushed, deliberately pushed, a coping-stone weighting about 2 cwt over a railway bridge, timing it to fall so as to strike the roof of a passing train, the very pushing, the weight, the depth of the fall, the timing, entitle you to presume that there was an intention on the part of the pusher to do the damage to the roof of the train for a start, and having regard to what a dangerous act you may think it was, you could judge an inten-tion in the mind of the pusher to endanger the life of any passenger upon whom such a heavy object, having penetrated the roof, might well fall.'

Clearly, having regard to the decision in *Steer*, the last few words of that passage amounted to a misdirection. If the intention was that the stone itself should endanger the life of the passengers, then the 'pusher' would not be guilty of this offence. Had the learned judge, instead of the last few words he used, said; 'You could judge an intention in the mind of the pusher to endanger the life of any passengers by causing the roof to descend on such passengers following the impact of the falling stone', he would properly have left an issue to the jury to consider.

Note

In *Wenton* [2010] EWCA Crim 2361, D's conviction for damaging property being reckless whether life was endangered, was quashed. D had first broken a window using a brick; he then threw a container of petrol into the house with a lighted piece of paper but the petrol did not ignite. The Court of Appeal considered *Asquith* and *Warwick*, and pointed out, somewhat exasperatedly, that the act which caused the damage was throwing the brick whereas the act which caused the endangerment was throwing the petrol container and lighted paper into the house, the two acts being unrelated. Had the petrol ignited and damage had been caused by the fire, D could have been convicted of arson being reckless whether life was endangered. Had the prosecutor analysed the circumstances properly, D could have been successfully prosecuted for attempted arson being reckless as to whether that intended damage by fire would endanger life.

Questions

1. D is on top of a cliff and drops a large stone on to a tent below which he believes to be unoccupied. The stone penetrates the canvass and seriously injures V. Has D committed the s.1(2) offence or any other offence against the person?

2. D fills up a lemonade bottle with a clear liquid weed-killer which is poisonous to humans and leaves it in a cupboard in his kitchen realising that there is a risk that someone might drink it in mistake for lemonade but not caring whether or not they do. Has D committed any offence at this point? If there had been 50mls of lemonade in the bottle when D added the weed-killer would your answer differ? Is the danger any different in the latter situation? Is D's behaviour any more or less culpable in the latter situation?

3. Should there be an offence of intentionally or recklessly endangering life regardless of how the endangerment may be intended or foreseen to arise?

----

2. OTHER OFFENCES

CRIMINAL DAMAGE ACT 1971 SS.2 AND 3

2. A person who without lawful excuse makes to another a threat, intending that that other would fear it would be carried out—

(a) to destroy or damage any property belonging to that other or a third person; or

(b) to destroy or damage his own property in a way which he knows is likely to endanger the life of that other or a third person;

shall be guilty of an offence.

3. A person who has anything in his custody or under his control intending without lawful excuse to use it or cause or permit another to use it—

(a) to destroy or damage any property belonging to some other person; or

(b) to destroy or damage his own or the user's property in a way which he knows is likely to endanger the life of some other person;

shall be guilty of an offence.

Notes

1. As with s.1, both of these sections have a pair of offences, a simple offence and an aggravated offence, i.e. one referring to danger to life (although the maximum penalties—10 years' imprisonment—are the same). With the offences in ss.2(a) and 3(a), but not with the offences in ss.2(b) and 3(b), the lawful excuse provisions in s.5 apply, and the threatened property must belong to someone else.

2. There need be no intention to carry out the threat in s.2, merely an intention that the person to whom it is made would fear that it would be carried out. If there is such an intention, it makes no difference that such a fear is not aroused in that person.

3. For the offence in s.3, "in his possession" was rejected by the Law Commission on account of the

difficulties centred round the question of when a person can be said to be in possession of something without knowing: see *Warner v Commissioner of Police* [1969] A.C. 256.

CRIME AND DISORDER ACT 1998

28.—(1) An offence is racially or religiously aggravated for the purposes of section [30] below if—

(a)   at the time of committing the offence, or immediately before or after doing so, the offender demonstrates towards the victim of the offence hostility based on the victim's membership (or presumed membership) of a racial or religious group; or

(b)   the offence is motivated (wholly or partly) by hostility towards members of a 'racial or religious group based on their membership of that group.

(2) In subsection (1)(a) above—
'membership', in relation to a racial or religious group, includes association with members of that group;
'presumed' means presumed by the offender.
(3) It is immaterial for the purposes of paragraph (a) or (b) of subsection (1) above whether or not the offender's hostility is also based, to any extent, on any other factor not mentioned in that paragraph
(4) In this section 'racial group' means a group of persons defined by reference to race, colour, nationality (including citizenship) or ethnic or national origins.
(5) In this section 'religious group' means a group of persons defined by reference to religious belief or lack of religious belief.
30.—(1) A person is guilty of an offence under this section if he commits an offence under s.1(1) of the Criminal Damage Act 1971 (destroying or damaging belonging to another) which is racially or religiously aggravated for the purposes of this section.
(2) A person guilty of an offence under this section shall be liable—

(a)   on summary conviction, to imprisonment for a term not exceeding six months or to a fine not exceeding the statutory maximum, or to both;

(b)   on conviction on indictment, to imprisonment for a term not exceeding fourteen years or to a fine, or to both.

Note

The increased penalties for racially or religiously motivated criminal damage reflect society's particular concern and distaste for offences committed with cultural hatred. There are two distinct components to the aggravated offence. First, the defendant must commit the offence under s.1(1) of the 1971 Act. Secondly, the offence must be "racially" or "religiously" aggravated as defined in s.28 of the 1998 Act. In *DPP v Green* [2004] EWHC 1225 (Admin) the court stated that an offence may be considered racially or religiously aggravated if accompanied by any racial or religious abuse even if the defendant is not acting from a religious or racial motive. That the courts seem willing to adopt a liberal approach to interpreting "race" or "hostility" is evident from the decision in *DPP v M* [2004] EWHC 1453 (Admin). D became involved in an altercation inside a Turkish kebab shop. In the course of the argument a window was broken and D, at some point during the fracas, uttered the words "bloody foreigners". The court upheld D's conviction for the racially aggravated offence stating that the words "foreigners" was capable of describing a racial group by reference to nationality and the word "bloody" indicated hostility.

INDEX